Cyprinid Fishes

Cyprinid Fishes

Systematics, biology and exploitation

Edited by

Ian J. Winfield

Institute of Freshwater Ecology
Windermere Laboratory
Ambleside
Cumbria
UK

and

Joseph S. Nelson

Department of Zoology
University of Alberta
Edmonton
Alberta
Canada

CHAPMAN & HALL
London · New York · Tokyo · Melbourne · Madras

UK	Chapman and Hall, 2–6 Boundary Row, London SE1 8HN
USA	Van Nostrand Reinhold, 115 5th Avenue, New York NY10003
JAPAN	Chapman and Hall Japan, Thomson Publishing Japan, Hirakawacho Nemoto Building, 7F, 1–7–11 Hirakawa-cho, Chiyoda-ku, Tokyo 102
AUSTRALIA	Chapman and Hall Australia, Thomas Nelson Australia, 102 Dodds St, South Melbourne, Victoria 3205
INDIA	Chapman and Hall India, R. Seshadri, 32 Second Main Road, CIT East, Madras 600 035

First edtition 1991

© 1991 Ian J. Winfield and Joseph S. Nelson

Typeset in 10/12 Photina
by Thomson Press (India) Ltd, New Delhi
Printed in Great Britain
by St. Edmundsbury Press, Bury St Edmunds, Suffolk

ISBN 0 412 34920 5 (HB) 0 442 31231 8 (USA)

British Library Cataloguing in Publication Data
Cyprinid Fishes: Systematics, biology and exploitation
    1. Cyprinoidei
    I. Winfield, Ian J. II. Nelson, Joseph S. (Joseph
Schieser), 1937–
597.52

    ISBN 0-412-34920-5

Library of Congress Cataloging-in-Publication Data
Cyprinid fishes: systematics, biology, and exploitation/editied by
    Ian J. Winfield and Joseph S. Nelson.
        p.   cm.—(Fish and fisheries series; 3)
    Includes bibliographical references and index.
    1. Cyprinidae. 2. Fisheries. I. Winfield, Ian J., 1959–
    II. Nelson, Joseph S., 1937– . III. Series.
    QL638.C94C96 1991
    597′.52—dc20   90–20440
                                                              CIP

Dedicated to the work and ideals of the United Nations

May people live in peace

Contents

Contributors   xiv
Series forword *T. J. Pitcher*   xviii
Preface *I. J. Winfield and J. S. Nelson*   xxi

1   Systematics and biogeography: an overview   1
    G. J. Howes

    1.1   Introduction   1
    1.2   Hybrids and cyprinid taxonomy   8
    1.3   Classification and systematics of the Cyprinidae   8
    1.4   Phylogenetic relationships of the subfamilies   17
    1.5   Biogeography   19
    Acknowledgements   28
    References   28

2   The fossil record of the Cyprinidae   34
    T. M. Cavender

    2.1   Introduction   34
    2.2   The cyprinid fossil record by geographic area   37
    2.3   Discussion   45
    2.4   Summary and conclusions   48
    Acknowledgements   49
    References   49

3   Morphometric investigations in cyprinid biology   55
    S. A. Schaefer

    3.1   Introduction   55
    3.2   Overview of morphometrics   56
    3.3   Analyses and applications   65

3.4   Applications in the study of the Cyprinidae   71
3.5   Conclusion   78
Acknowledgements   79
References   79

4   Molecular and cytological investigations   83
    D. G. Buth, T. E. Dowling and J. R. Gold

    4.1   Introduction   83
    4.2   Allozymes and isozymes   83
    4.3   Chromosomes   95
    4.4   Mitochondrial and nuclear DNA   104
    4.5   Summary   113
    Acknowledgements   114
    References   114

5   Cyprinids of Eurasia   127
    P. Bǎnǎrescu and B. W. Coad

    5.1   Description of Eurasia   127
    5.2   Diversity   129
    5.3   Zoogeography   138
    5.4   Biology   141
    5.5   Further research   149
    Acknowledgements   150
    References   150

6   Cyprinids of South East Asia   156
    W. J. Rainboth

    6.1   Introduction   156
    6.2   Drainage basins   158
    6.3   Systematics and diversity   169
    6.4   Historical and ecological biogeography   178
    6.5   General biology   185
    6.6   Postscript   192
    Acknowledgements   192
    Generic distribution list   193
    References   202

7   Cyprinids of Africa   211
    P. H. Skelton, D. Tweddle and P. B. N. Jackson

    7.1   Introduction   211
    7.2   Taxonomic diversity and relationships   214
    7.3   Biogeography   221

7.4	General biology	223
7.5	Fisheries	228
7.6	Conservation	230
7.7	Future research	232
	References	233

8 Cyprinids of the New World   240
   R. L. Mayden

8.1	Introduction	240
8.2	Major river drainages and cyprinid diversity	241
8.3	Diversity and taxonomy	242
8.4	Ecological and historical biogeography	246
8.5	Life histories	250
8.6	Human use	255
8.7	Introduced species	256
8.8	Future research	257
	Acknowledgements	257
	Species list	257
	References	261

9 Cyprinids of Australasia   264
   A. R. Brumley

9.1	Species introduced into Australia	264
9.2	Species introduced into New Zealand	268
9.3	Undesirable introductions	270
9.4	Useful introductions	278
9.5	Prevention of further releases	279
	Acknowledgements	280
	References	281

10 Brain and sensory systems   284
    K. Kotrschal, R. Brandstätter, A. Gomahr, H. Junger,
    M. Palzenberger and M. Zaunreiter

10.1	Introduction	284
10.2	Brain	285
10.3	Vision	294
10.4	Chemosenses	303
10.5	Lateral line	317
10.6	Conclusions: the diversified sensory world of cyprinids, a result of adaptation, constraints and growth shifts	319
	Acknowledgements	322
	Abbreviations	322
	References	323

11 Acoustico-lateralis system   332
    M. Chardon and P. Vandewalle

    11.1 Introduction   332
    11.2 Auditory apparatus   334
    11.3 Equilibration function of the labyrinths   343
    11.4 Lateral line system   344
    11.5 Concluding remarks   346
    Acknowledgements   347
    Abbreviations   347
    References   348

12 Diets and feeding behaviour   353
    E. H. R. R. Lammens and W. Hoogenboezem

    12.1 Introduction   353
    12.2 Diets   354
    12.3 Pelagic feeding behaviour   355
    12.4 Benthic feeding behaviour   363
    12.5 Switching between pelagic and benthic feeding   368
    12.6 Concluding remarks and implications for non-
          European cyprinids   371
    Acknowledgements   372
    References   372

13 Food capture and oral processing   377
    F. A. Sibbing

    13.1 Introduction   377
    13.2 General plan of the cyprinid feeding apparatus   378
    13.3 Food capture   380
    13.4 Internal selection of food   389
    13.5 Food transport towards the chewing cavity   398
    13.6 Mastication and deglutition   398
    13.7 Adjusting food handling to the type of food   404
    13.8 Versatility in food handling and feeding guilds   405
    13.9 Feeding and the success of cyprinid fish   407
    References   408

14 Digestion   413
    R. Hofer

    14.1 Introduction   413
    14.2 Chemical processing of proteins   413
    14.3 Processing of plant diets   415

14.4   Digestive processes in cyprinid larvae   420
Acknowledgements   421
References   421

15   Physiological energetics and ecophysiology   426
     W. Wieser

     15.1   Physiological energetics   426
     15.2   Ecophysiology i: Life under conditions of oxygen
            deficiency   432
     15.3   Ecophysiology ii: Temperature relationships   435
     15.4   Ecophysiology iii: Periodicity   445
     15.5   Ion regulation and water balance   448
     15.6   Concluding remarks   450
     Acknowledgements   450
     References   450

16   Growth and production   456
     R. H. K. Mann

     16.1   Introduction   456
     16.2   Growth   458
     16.3   Production   474
     Acknowledgements   477
     References   477

17   Reproduction and life history   483
     C. A. Mills

     17.1   Introduction   483
     17.2   Physiology of reproduction   483
     17.3   Spawning   485
     17.4   Egg and larval development   489
     17.5   Ecology of eggs   492
     17.6   Ecology of larvae   494
     17.7   Reproductive strategies   497
     References   504

18   Social behaviour, homing and migration   509
     R. J. F. Smith

     18.1   The sensory basis of social communication   509
     18.2   The formation of social groups   511
     18.3   Social aspects of predator–prey interactions   513
     18.4   Social aspects of foraging and feeding   516

	18.5	Reproduction and parental care	519
	18.6	Migration and homing	521
	18.7	Conclusions	524
	References		524

19 Interspecific interactions 530
L. Persson

	19.1	Introduction	530
	19.2	A general description of lake fish community structure and succession	530
	19.3	Mechanistic bases of species interactions involving cyprinids	532
	19.4	The influence of ontogenetic niche shifts on species interactions involving cyprinids	537
	19.5	The roles of competition and predation in species interactions involving cyprinids	538
	19.6	Species interactions and the size structure of cyprinid populations	545
	19.7	Concluding remarks and implications for non-European cyprinids	546
	Acknowledgements		547
	References		547

20 The role of cyprinids in ecosystems 552
I. J. Winfield and C. R. Townsend

	20.1	Introduction	552
	20.2	Interactions with plants	552
	20.3	Interactions with invertebrates	556
	20.4	Interactions with vertebrates	560
	20.5	Indirect interactions	563
	20.6	Closing remarks	566
	References		567

21 Fisheries 572
M. Bnińska

	21.1	Introduction	572
	21.2	Economic, ecological and social significance of cyprinids	575
	21.3	Basic principles of cyprinid fisheries and management	578
	21.4	Current status and prospects of cyprinid fisheries and management	587
	References		588

22 Aquaculture   590
    H. R. Lin and R. E. Peter

    22.1 Introduction   590
    22.2 Culture systems   591
    22.3 Nutrition and growth   598
    22.4 Inducing breeding   601
    22.5 Rearing larvae   608
    22.6 Selection and genetics   611
    22.7 Concluding remarks   616
    Acknowledgements   617
    References   617

Author index   623

Taxonomic index   648

Subject index   660

Contributors

Petru M. Bănărescu
Institute of Biology, Laboratory of Evolutionary Biology, Str. Frumoasa 31, Corp B, 78116 Bucureşti, Romania

Maria Bnińska
Inland Fisheries Institute, blok 5, 10-957 Olsztyn–Kortowo, Poland

Roland Brandstätter
Department of Zoology, The University of Salzburg, Hellbrunnerstrasse 34, A-5020 Salzburg, Austria

Andrea R. Brumley
Kaiela Fisheries Research Station, Department of Conservation, Forests and Lands, P.O. Box 1226, Shepparton, Victoria 3630, Australia

Donald G. Buth
Department of Biology, University of California (UCLA), Los Angeles, California 90024-1606, USA

Ted M. Cavender
Museum of Zoology, The Ohio State University, Columbus, Ohio 43210, USA

Michel Chardon
Laboratory of Functional Morphology, Institute of Zoology, University of Liege, Belgium

Brian W. Coad
Ichthyology Section, National Museum of Natural Sciences, P.O. Box 3443, Stn D, Ottawa, Ontario KIP 6P4, Canada

Thomas E. Dowling
Department of Zoology, Arizona State University, Tempe, Arizona 85287-1501, USA

John R. Gold
Department of Wildlife and Fisheries, Texas A & M University, College Station, Texas 77843-2258, USA

Andreas Gomahr
Department of Zoology, The University of Salzburg, Hellbrunnerstrasse 34, A-5020 Salzburg, Austria

Rudolf Hofer
Zoologisches Institut der Universitat Innsbruck, Technikerstrasse 25, A-6020 Innsbruck, Austria

Wim Hoogenboezem
Department of Experimental Animal Morphology and Cell Biology, Agricultural University Wageningen, Marijkeweg 40, 6709 PG Wageningen, The Netherlands

Gordon J. Howes
Department of Zoology, British Museum (Natural History), Cromwell Road, London SW7 5BD, England

Peter B. N. Jackson
J. L. B. Smith Institute of Ichthyology, Private Bag 1015, Grahamstown 6140, South Africa

Heidi Junger
Department of Zoology, The University of Salzburg, Hellbrunnerstrasse 34, A-5020 Salzburg, Austria

Kurt Kotrschal
Department of Zoology, The University of Salzburg, Hellbrunnerstrasse 34, A-5020 Salzburg, Austria

Eddy H. R. R. Lammens
Limnological Institute, De Akkers 47, 8536 VD Oosterzee, The Netherlands

Hao-ren Lin
Department of Biology, Zhongshan University, Guangzhou, P. R. China

Richard H. K. Mann
Institute of Freshwater Ecology, Eastern Rivers Group, c/o The Institute of
Terrestrial Ecology, Monks Wood Experimental Station, Abbots Ripton,
Huntingdon PE17 2LS, UK

Richard L. Mayden
Department of Biology, the University of Alabama, Box 870344, Tuscaloosa,
Alabama 35487-0344, USA

Chris A. Mils (deceased)
Institute of Freshwater Ecology, Windermere Laboratory, Ambleside, Cumbria
LA22 OLP, UK

Joseph S. Nelson
Department of Zoology, University of Alberta, Edmonton, Alberta T6G 2E9,
Canada

Margit Palzenberger
Department of Zoology, The University of Salzburg, Hellbrunnerstrasse 34, A-
5020 Salzburg, Austria

Lennart Persson
Department of Animal Ecology, University of Umea, S-901 87 Umea, Sweden

Richard E. Peter
Department of Zoology, University of Alberta, Edmonton, Alberta T6G 2E9,
Canada

Walter J. Rainboth
Department of Biology, University of California (UCLA), Los Angeles, California
90024-1606, USA

Scott A. Schaefer
Department of Ichthyology, Academy of Natural Sciences, 19th and the
Parkway, Philadelphia, Pennsylvania, USA

Ferdinand A. Sibbing
Department of Experimental Animal Morphology and Cell Biology, Agricul-
tural University Wageningen, Marijkeweg 40, 6709 PG Wageningen, The
Netherlands

Paul H. Skelton
J. L. B. Smith Institute of Ichthyology, Private Bag 1015, Grahamstown 6140,
South Africa

R. Jan F. Smith
Biology Department, University of Saskatchewan, Saskatoon, Saskatchewan
S7N OWO, Canada

Colin R. Townsend
Department of Zoology, University of Otago, P.O. Box 56, Dunedin, New
Zealand

Denis Tweddle
Fisheries Department, P.O. Box 27, Monkey Bay, Malawi

Pierre Vandewalle
Research Associate, F. N. R. S., Belgium

Wolfgang Wieser
Zoologisches Institute der Universitat Innsbruck, Technikerstrasse 25, A-
6020 Innsbruck, Austria

Ian J. Winfield
Institute of Freshwater Ecology, Windermere Laboratory, Ambleside, Cumbria
LA 22 OLP, UK

Monika Zaunreiter
Department of Zoology, The University of Salzburg, Hellbrunnerstrasse 34,
A-5020 Salzburg, Austria

Series foreword

Among the fishes, a remarkably wide range of biological adaptations to diverse habitats has evolved. As well as living in the conventional habitats of lakes, ponds, rivers, rock pools and the open sea, fish have solved the problems of life in deserts, in the deep sea, in the cold Antarctic, and in warm waters of high alkalinity or of low oxygen. Along with these adaptations, we find the most impressive specializations of morphology, physiology and behaviour. For example we can marvel at the high-speed swimming of the marlins, sailfish and warm-blooded tunas, air breathing in catfish and lungfish, parental care in the mouth-brooding cichlids and viviparity in many sharks and toothcarps.

Moreover, fish are of considerable importance of the survival of the human species in the form of nutritious and delicious food of numerous kinds. Rational exploitation and management of our global stocks of fishes must rely upon a detailed and precise insight of their biology.

The Chapman and Hall *Fish and Fisheries Series* aims to present timely volumes reviewing important aspects of fish biology. Most volumes will be of interest to research workers in biology, zoology, ecology and physiology, but an additional aim is for the books to be accessible to a wide spectrum of non-specialist readers ranging from undergraduates and postgraduates to those with an interest in industrial and commercial aspects of fish and fisheries.

This volume, the third in the *Fish and Fisheries Series*, presents a synoptic biology of the Cyprinidae, one of the most successful groups of teleosts in temperate and subtropical fresh waters. This diverse family includes the streamlined carps, deep-bodied bottom-living breams, benthic rheophobic river fishes, silvery lacustrine shoaling fishes, colourful barbs, small short-lived dace and minnows. Although not generally considered amongst the most progressive teleosts, cyprinids have independently evolved some intriguing features. For example, they possess advanced protrusible jaws for feeding by pipette action, amazingly precise hearing, and an alarm substance which presents an enigma for evolutionary biology.

Ian Winfield (IFE) and Joseph Nelson (Alberta) have welded together 22 review chapters from 36 internationally respected cyprinid biologists. The theme of the book progresses from fossil, morphological and biochemical taxonomy, through zoogeography, nervous, sensory and energetic physiology, reproduction, behaviour, ecology and community dynamics, and concludes with applied essays on fisheries and aquaculture. For fish biologists, this book should become the major source of information about this ubiquitous family of freshwater fishes.

Dr Tony J. Pitcher
Editor, Chapman and Hall Fish and Fisheries Series
Reader in Biology, Bangor

CHAPMAN & HALL FISH AND FISHERIES SERIES

1. Ecology of Teleost Fishes
   R. J. Wootton
2. Cichlid Fishes: Behavior, ecology and evolution
   Edited by M. H. A. Keenleyside
3. Cyprinid Fishes: Systematics, biology and exploitation
   Edited by I. J. Winfield and J. S. Nelson
4. Early Life History of Fish: An energetics approach
   E. Kamler
5. Fisheries Acoustics
   D. N. MacLennan and E. J. Simmonds

Forthcoming titles

Fish Chemoreception
Edited by T. Hara

Behaviour of Teleost Fishes, 2nd edn
Edited by T. J. Pitcher

Fish Swimming
J. Videler

Sea Bass
G. Pickett and M. Pawson

Fisheries Ecology, 2nd edn
Edited by T. J. Pitcher and P. Hart

Preface

The Cyprinidae is one of the two largest families of vertebrates in the world; the only family that might contain more species is also a group of fishes, the mainly marine Gobiidae. Cyprinids are also widely distributed around the world, are abundant in a variety of habitats, and consequently have considerable applied importance to mankind. They are important as prey for other animals and are widely known in the aquarium trade and in research laboratories. In addition, their desirable attributes for fisheries and aquaculture have been long appreciated, although more recent studies have shown that they can also have significant undesirable characteristics. As a result, the biology of cyprinids is a subject of relevance to a wider audience than just the world's ichthyologists.

The cyprinids are currently one of the most widely studied groups of fishes as they have interested biologists from many disciplines, who often share little in common apart from their subject of research. Studies on these fishes, and fish biology in general, have developed enormously in recent years and have seen great advances in equipment, techniques, and theory. As such, we feel that this is an opportune time to produce an extensive review of our knowledge of cyprinid biology, which we have attempted to do employing the unifying theme of the success of cyprinids in aquatic communities. The result is a text which although concise is unavoidably large, reflecting the attention given to this group of fishes.

A major aim of this book is to encourage communication among specialists studying different areas of related but perhaps mutually unfamiliar research. In short, we provide a series of reviews that in addition to introducing their subject, also offer a signposted path into a vast literature. We hope that this book will be of use to senior undergraduate and graduate students, and particularly to researchers of fundamental and applied cyprinid biology. We are confident that at least parts of it will appeal to other biologists sharing similar systems and concepts, if not a primary interest in this taxonomic group.

The book comprises three broadly recognizable sections. The first part discusses what cyprinids are and where they are to be found through a series of chapters on evolution, diversity and distribution. The biology of individuals is then considered in terms of their basic life processes, and then finally, reviews are given of cyprinid populations and communities and the ways in which they interact with the rest of the freshwater ecosystem, including Man.

There is a great deal of heterogeneity in studies using cyprinids. While some workers may be studying goldfish to elucidate general problems in vertebrate biology, such as understanding how the pituitary gland functions, others may be studying some unique aspect of the biology of a particular species. We have assembled some of the world's leading researchers of cyprinid biology. Although authors have been free to use their own style of writing, we hope we have succeeded in producing a book consisting of an interconnected series of works on an exciting group of vertebrates, rather than merely a linear series of discrete chapters.

Many people and organizations have been of direct or indirect assistance during the production of this book. We should like to thank in particular the following people for their invaluable help as special referees: Gunnar Andersson, Colin Bean, Don Buth, Simon Guthrie, Lars Johansson, Richard Mayden, Tony Pitcher, Walter Rainboth, Curt Strobeck, Walter Verraes, Mark V. H. Wilson, Brian Wood, and Bob Wootton. We are also indebted to Tony Pitcher for his help as Series Editor, and to Nigel Balmforth, Jo Asser, Bob Carling and Tim Hardwick for their help at the publishers' end of things. Chuck Hollingworth's copy-editing was precise, comprehensive and, above all, respectful of the mental and physical well-being of the authors. I. J. W. is also grateful to many former colleagues at the University of Ulster Freshwater Laboratory, and particularly to its Director Brian Wood, for their help and encouragement given during the major part of this book's gestation period. Finally, we thank Denise Winfield and Claudine Nelson for their continuous support and understanding.

While this book was going to press we were greatly saddened to hear of the death of Chris Mills at the tragically early age of 36 years following a short illness. The loss of Chris is a tremendous blow to fish ecology and he will be sorely missed by many colleagues and friends.

Ian J. Winfield
Joseph S. Nelson
March, 1990

Chapter one

Systematics and biogeography: an overview

G. J. Howes

1.1 INTRODUCTION

Cyprinids are a diverse family, rich in problems of evolutionary interest. Their use in aquaculture and as tools for genetic and physiological investigations make their identification very important. Unfortunately, their taxonomy and classification is unsatisfactory; the historical reasons are discussed here and a revised classification is presented. First, a brief overview of cyprinid anatomy, diversity and ecology is given.

Cyprinids are known to the angler, aquarist and fishery biologist under the common names of carps, barbs, minnows, roaches, rudds, daces, bitterlings, rasboras, danios and gudgeons. Their chief characteristics, the lack of jaw teeth and the possession of a (usually) protrusile upper jaw and pharyngeal (throat) teeth, are discussed in more detail below. In all, there are some 1700 valid species in at least 220 genera, making the family the most speciose of all freshwater teleost fishes. The family has a wide geographical distribution and occurs in much of mainland Eurasia, Japan, most of the East Indian islands, Africa and North America. Although primarily fresh water, some species can tolerate and even breed in saline water.

Anatomical characteristics

Cyprinids are characterized by the following features: a protrusile mouth actuated by a median bone (the kinethmoid); toothless jaws; toothless palate; enlarged, tooth-bearing pharyngeal bones (modified last gill arches); basioccipital with an enlarged ventroposterior process enclosing the dorsal aorta and bearing a keratinized pad against which the pharyngeal teeth exert grinding force; highly developed fifth levator muscle which originates from an exceptionally deep subtemporal fossa; anterior (rostral) and posterior barbels often present. None of these characters is unique to the Cyprinidae, and all are shared with other cypriniform families. Therefore, the features cited indicate that as presently recognized, the Cyprinidae is either a primitive (plesiomorphic) lineage with respect to the other families or it is non-monophyletic.

Taxonomic position

The order Cypriniformes comprises of six families: Cyprinidae, Catostomidae, Cobitidae, Gyrinocheilidae, Psilorhynchidae and Homalopteridae (including the Gastromyzonidae; p. 19). The combined total numbers of genera and species contained in the five last families are *c.* 25 and 300, respectively.

The Cypriniformes is one of four orders constituting the series Otophysi, an entirely freshwater group (apart from some catfishes), which together with the Anotophysi (Gonorhynciformes) forms the superorder Ostariophysi. The three co-orders are the Characiformes, Siluriformes and Gymnotiformes. In the latest review of ostariophysan phylogenetic relationships, Fink and Fink (1981) regard the Siluriformes as containing two suborders, the Siluroidei (Catfishes) and the Gymnotoidei (electric eels and knifefishes). Most classifications have recognized the Cyprinoidei as a suborder, and it has been common taxonomic usage to refer to 'cyprinoids' as the group containing cyprinids and related families. Since no other suborders of cypriniform fishes are recognized, it is best to use 'cypriniforms' when referring to the entire assembly.

Morphological and trophic diversity

There is a general opinion amongst ichthyologists that cyprinids are a taxonomically difficult group, an opinion which appears to stem from another, namely that they all look the same (Lowe-McConnell, 1975, comments on the supposed uniformity of body shape). However, cyprinids have considerable morphological diversity (Fig. 1.1), equal to that of characiforms.

The standard minnow morphotype may be represented by the Eurasian *Phoxinus* or the Nearctic *Notropis* (Fig. 1.1(a) and (b)), although it must not

---

Fig. 1.1 Morphological diversity of cyprinid fishes illustrated by outline drawings of representatives of the subfamilies recognized herein (A, Alburninae; Ac, Acheilognathinae; C, Cyprininae; Cu, Cultrinae; G, Gobioinae; L, Leuciscinae; R, Rasborinae; ?, subfamily assignment uncertain). A, *Phoxinus* (L); B, *Notropis* (L); C, *Cyprinus* (C); D, *Opsariichthys* (R); E. *Hypophthalmichthys* (L); F. *Tinca* (?); G. *Barbus s. str.* (C); H. *Ochetobius* (L); I. *Diptychus* (C. shizothoracine lineage: note tile scales along the anal fin base – the total amount of squamation is shown in this species, *D. maculatus*); J. *Chalcalburnus* (A); K. *Labeo* (C); L. *Garra* (C); M. *Semiplotus* (C); N. *Puntius* (C); O. *Chela* (R); P. *Rhodeus* (Ac, female with extended ovipositor); Q. *Thrissocypris* (?); R. *Caecopyris* (?); S. *Gila cypha* (L); T. *Pelecus* (?A); U. *Rhinogobio* (G); V. *Erythroculter* (Cu); W. *Osteobrama* (?; note serrated dorsal spine); X. *Coreius* (?). Scale bars, 2 cm.

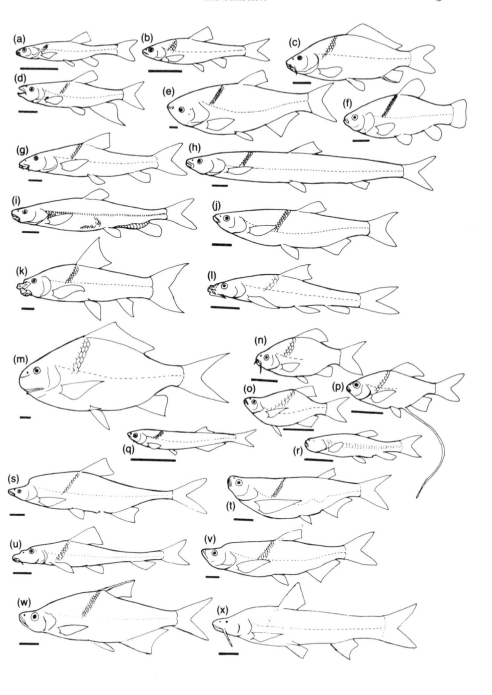

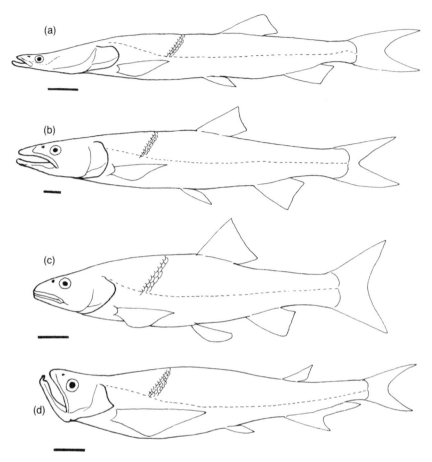

Fig. 1.2 Predatory, mainly piscivorous, cyprinids. (a), *Luciobrama*; (b), *Elopichthys*; (c), *Ptychocheilus* ((a)–(c) all Leuciscinae); (d), *Macrochirichthys* (Rasborinae). Scale bars, 5 cm.

necessarily be implied that these taxa represent a generalized or plesiomorphic type. The carp, *Cyprinus* (Fig. 1.1 (c)), is often thought of as a typical cyprinid and the barbs are the most widespread tropical forms, but they are also highly variable in head shape, body depth and scale size. Many cyprinids have highly modified lip structures, often referred to as sucker mouths. *Labeo* and *Garra*, for example (Fig. 1.1 (k) and (l)), both possess complex frills and pelmets of outer and inner labial tissue and buccal furrows and protruberances (Fig. 1.3 (b) and Reid, 1982). The bodies of these taxa are often depressed and their heads bear elaborate horny tubercles of complex geometrical shapes that may provide hydrodynamic stability in fast-flowing water (Reid, 1978). Labeins and garrins are aufwuchs feeders, some *Labeo* even feeding from the surface mulch covering the backs of *Hippopotamus* (Root and Root, 1971).

Most barbs lack elaborate lip structures but may have a horny (keratinized) lower lip. This mouth form is known as a sector mouth and for the most part is common to epilithic grazers such as *Cyprinion, Semiplotus, Capoeta* and *Varicorhinus* (Fig. 1.3(a)). These fishes usually have broad, often massive heads bearing specific patterns of tubercles; their bodies are deep with anteriorly shortened and strengthened vertebral columns. The North American *Acrocheilus*, commonly known as chiselmouth, has a lower lip, developed similarly to that of *Capoeta*, which it uses to collect filamentous algae, although it digests the diatoms contained within the algal filaments (Moodie, 1966).

Phytophagous cyprinids are also represented by silver and bighead carps (*Hypophthalmichthys* (Fig. 1.1(e)), which eat phytoplankton filtered through modified gill rakers and a coiled, branchial organ, Microscopic diatoms also form much of the diet of some schizothoracins, along with detritus (Subla and Sunder, 1982). Macrophytes are eaten by such carps as *Ctenopharyngodon* and *Squaliobarbus*. Carps eat a variety of food; Sibbing *et al.* (1986) have shown

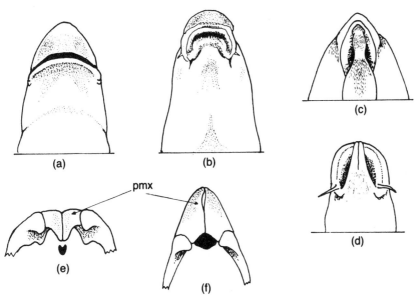

Fig. 1.3 (a) to (d) Mouth types. (a), *Semiplotus* (sector mouth with keratinized lower lip, ventral view); (b), *Labeo* (sucking mouth, ventral view); similar scoop mouth types in (c), *Scaphognathops* and (d), *Mandibularca* (both ventral views). (e) and (f) Upper jaws and kinethmoid position (solid black) in (e), *Barilius*; (f), *Elopichthys* pmx, premaxilla. ((a) based on Howes, 1982; (b) after Reid, 1982; (c) after Taki, 1974; (d) drawn from California Academy specimen SU41915; (e) and (f) reproduced with permission from Howes, 1978.)

that although the carp jaw and pharyngeal mechanism can utilize a broad spectrum of foods, they are best in selecting and manipulating medium-sized items, and material harder than vegetable and fleshy material.

The small *Rasbora, Danio* and barilin (Fig. 1.1(d)) species populating rivers of India, South East Asia and Africa are for the most part predatory, feeding on insects and their larvae. Most species exhibit a subsurface-feeding morphotype in which the dorsum of the body is straight and the superior mouth is obliquely aligned; many of these species also have a body pattern of vertical bars.

Only two genera of cyprinids, *Elopichthys* (Fig. 1.2(b)) and *Ptychocheilus* (Fig. 1.2(c)), both of which include the biggest members of the family, are entirely piscivorous. *Elopichthys bambusa* (2 m in length) lives in the Amur and larger rivers of China. Its upper jaw has become modified, having the kinethmoid expanded between the premaxillaries, which limits its jaw protrusion (Fig. 1.3(f); Howes, 1978). In North America, its counterpart as a piscivore, the Colorado squawfish, *Ptychocheilus lucius* of the Colorado River, formerly grew to 1.8 m and over 45 kg but now reaches only half that size and inhabits quiet tributaries.

The Colorado River tributaries are also a refuge for the woundfin, *Plagiopterus*, in which the caudal fin skeleton is strengthened by hypertrophy of the principal rays, and bony tail chubs of the genus *Gila*. One species (*G. cypha*) exhibits a 'rapids morphology': the body is humped, with a streamlined profile and extremely narrow caudal peduncle (Fig. 1.1(s)).

The assorted group of cyprinids known as cultrins (taxonomic discussion p. 14), all share a similar morphology of compressed body with a keel-like belly, dorsal fin set well back, and narrow head with obliquely set mouth. The most extreme cultrin-like morphology is that of *Macrochirichthys* (Fig. 1.2(d)), an inhabitant of the Mekong River, which has an especially large gape and a specialized vertebral column with a muscular system providing a neck-bending mechanism (Howes, 1979). Such a facility is also found in the small-bodied South East Asian genus *Chela* (Fig. 1.1(o)). In *Macrochirichthys* the sharp head-raising movement is a means of obtaining prey at the surface, but in *Chela* it appears to provide an escape mechanism whereby the rapid backward thrust of the head propels the fish towards and across the surface (Lindsey, 1978).

Another predatory cyprinid having a specialized head morphology is the aspinin, *Luciobrama* (Fig. 1.2(a)). Its head is elongated, not rostrally (as is usual among teleosts) but postorbitally, its entire buccal–branchial cavity being extended and forming a narrow tube which maximizes suction feeding (Howes, 1978).

Other examples of cyprinid morphological and trophic diversity are the small *Anaecypris* from Portugal (Collares-Perreira, 1983) and *Pectinocypris* from Thailand, in which the gill rakers number over 100 (Kottelat, 1982). The insectivorous *Thryssocypris* (Fig. 1.1(q)) from the Kapuas River, Borneo, is the morphological counterpart of a freshwater anchovy (Roberts and Kottelat,

1984); it has a non-protrusile upper jaw and an extensive maxilla included in the gape.

The omuls, *Oreoleuciscus*, of Mongolian lakes and rivers, pose particular problems of identification with regard to their polymorphism, showing marked sexual dimorphism in head shape and ecophenotypic variability in body shape and size (Travers, 1989). Polymorphism in head and mouth shape is also present in a group of cyprinids of the genus *Barbodes* endemic to Lake Lanao on the Philippine island of Mindanao. Another Lake Lanao genus, described by Herre (1924) as *Mandibularca*, was thought by Myers (1960) to exhibit a unique jaw morphology and exemplify a 'supralimital specialization'. Myers had apparently overlooked Smith's (1945) description of *Scaphognathops stejnegeri* from the Mekong River, in which the lower jaw is of a similar scoop type to that of *Mandibularca* (Fig. 1.3(c) and (d)). Taki (1974) has described another species from the Mekong in which the jaw is less modified.

The schizothoracins, commonly and confusingly known as snow-trouts, occur in the Himalayan region. They too have a varied body and mouth morphology, one of their characteristic features being the presence of tile-like scales along the base of the anal fin (Fig. 1.1(i)).

Gobioinines (gudgeons; Fig. 1.1(u)) are bottom-dwelling cyprinids represented widely in Eurasia by the genus *Gobio*; they are absent from North America, and most taxa occur in eastern China, Korea and Japan. Several genera are characterized by a bony encapsulation of the swim bladder, similar to that in some catfishes.

Habitats

Cyprinids occur in almost every kind of freshwater habitat – large and small rivers, torrential streams, still pools, lakes, estuaries and underground watercourses. They can withstand a temperature range of 0–40 °C, although the period of adjustment varies considerably. For example, *Carassius auratus* can regulate from 20 to 28 °C in 24 h whereas *Pimephales promelas* requires 14 d to adjust from 24 to 16 °C (Fry, 1971). *Gila boraxobius*, endemic to the south-western Oregon thermal Borax Lake, can withstand a temperature range of 16–30 °C. Many cyprinids are highly tolerant of saline conditions. Populations of *Abramis* and *Rutilus* inhabit the low-salinity Black, Caspian and Aral seas (Berg, 1949), and *Rutilus* inhabits the coastal waters of Gotland, Sweden (A. C. Wheeler, pers. comm.); *Pelecus* (Fig. 1.1(t)) forages at sea on crustaceans and anchovies and the Nearctic *Mylocheilus* inhabits estuaries and has been taken in seawater off British Columbia (Carl *et al.*, 1967). Likewise, *Tribolodon* lives part of its life at sea (Okada, 1960).

Cave-dwelling cyprinids occur in Africa, Arabia and the Middle East; they are represented by three monotypic genera of barbin affinity (*Caecobarbus, Barbopsis* and *Phreatichthys*), three garrin taxa (*Typhlogarra, Iranocypris* and *Garra barriemae*), and one, *Caecocypris* from Iraq (Fig. 1.1(r)), of unknown affinities (Banister and Bunni, 1980). *Barbopsis* and the *Garra* species are microphthalmic, but in the other taxa the eyes are redundant, and all have reduced or no body pigmentation.

1.2   HYBRIDS AND CYPRINID TAXONOMY

More naturally occurring intergeneric hybrids have been reported for cyprinids, and particularly leuciscines, than for any other group of teleosts (Schwartz, 1972, 1981). Formerly (Howes, 1981) I expressed the opinion that in many cases intergeneric hybridization was a taxonomic artefact resulting from imprecise generic diagnosis, and that in those cases the parental genera were synonyms; e.g. *'Scardinius'* × *Rutilus*; *'Aristichthys'* × *Hypophthalmichthys*. Many authors still attempt to recognize cyprinid genera on the basis of degree of difference; in other words, on 'generic' characters (e.g. Shutov, 1969; Hensel, 1978; Bogutskaya, 1986b).

My earlier remarks (Howes, 1981) that all records of European intergeneric hybrids were ones involving new ecological situations have been upheld by two recently reported examples, *Leuciscus* × *Chalcalburnus* from Lake Volvi, Greece (Economidis and Sinis, 1988) and *Capoeta* × *Barbus* from the Jordan River drainage (Mir *et al.*, 1988). In both cases the otherwise temporally separated breeding seasons of the parental genera have been amalgamated, in the former owing to disrupted migration routes, and in the latter to changed climatic conditions.

1.3   CLASSIFICATION AND SYSTEMATICS OF THE CYPRINIDAE

The history of cypriniform (or cyprinoid) classification has been well documented by Hensel (1970). Since Cuvier (1817) established the Cy-prinidae, workers such as Bonaparte (1846), Bleeker (1863) and Günther (1868) recognized subgroups of cyprinids, many of which remain in current classifications as subfamilies. The original diagnoses of these categories were based largely on the nature of pharyngeal dentition and the presence or absence and number of barbels. The early acceptance of pharyngeal teeth as being the principal taxonomic character led ultimately to the classifications of Tchang (1930) and Chu (1935), who between them recognized 11 groups or subfamilies. These workers dealt principally with Asian (Chinese) cyprinids. For North American taxa, Fowler (1924) acknowledged six subfamilies, one of which, the Abramidinae, also occurs in Eurasia. Wu's (1964) classification of Chinese cyprinids recognized ten subfamilies, while Jayaram (1981) acknow-ledge six in India. The most radical departure from these classifications has been that of Gosline (1978), who proposed only five subfamilies. The latest analysis of subfamily classification (Arai, 1982) recognizes 12, based partly on karyotypes.

Earlier classifications are the products of traditional taxonomy. Workers sought characters to differentiate subfamilies, but generally ignored their interrelationships. On the contrary, a good deal of speculation has been given to the search for ancestors of modern cyprinids. Regan (1911, 1922), Gregory (1933) and Nikolsky (1954) considered *Opsariichthys* and *Barilius* to represent the ancestral or primary type of cyprinid. On the other hand, Kryzanovskii (1947) argued that *Barbus* was the most primitive. Gosline (1978) relied on zoogeographic evidence in nominating a "cyprinine rather than a leuciscine-like" ancestor.

As with many groups, we do not have good evidence that cyprinid subgroups are monophyletic, and if so, how they are related to one another. The off-quoted dictum concerning cyprinid groups, that they are arbitrary (e.g. Bănărescu, 1967), implies that such groupings may not represent phylogenetic lineages. The acceptance of subfamilies as phylogenetic realities can lead to misleading analyses of cyprinid biogeography.

The only testable hypothesis of cyprinid subgroup interrelationships published in the form of a cladogram is that by Chen *et al.* (1984). They recognized, as did Bonaparte (1846) and Nikolsky (1954), that there are two major lineages, which they named the Leuciscini and Barbini. These two series are subdivided, respectively, into sister tribes: Danionines and Leuciscines; Barbines and Tincanes. Further subdivisions of these lineages produce ten subfamilies. Regrettably, Chen *et al.* have not obeyed the strictures of cladistic methodology. Each sister lineage is apparently recognized by an autapomorphy, but no synapomorphy is given for each sister pair. For example, the lineages indicated as tribes Danionines and Leuciscines are related as sister taxa by a set of opposing characters; e.g. "Danionines; circumorbital series well-developed; trigeminal facialis foramen within the prootic; Leuciscines: circumorbital series is not developed; trigeminal facialis foramen between prootic and pterosphenoid or on parasphenoid." Furthermore, such characters as these seem to occur mosaically throughout cyprinids and are unreliable indicators of monophyly, at least at this level (Howes, 1980). Chen *et al.* (1984) unwisely accepted traditionally recognized subfamilial groupings as monophyletic and incorporated them into their cladogram.

It seems a taxonomic anomaly that there should be only six or seven cypriniform families, one of which, the Cyprinidae, contains *c.* 80% of all species, whereas the Characiformes and Siluriformes have over 20 families apiece, but fewer species. This skewed classification reflects our approach to cyprinid taxonomy more than any supposed lack of morphological diversity. Few comparative anatomical studies of cyprinids have been made, and most classifications have relied on external features or on the morphology and arrangement of pharyngeal teeth. There has been a traditional acceptance of cyprinid monophyly, and in this regard, few workers have subjected the cyprinids to any rigorous taxonomic analysis, i.e. cladistics. My own work since about 1980 has been directed toward such analyses, and it is on the basis of my hypotheses of phylogenetic relationships that the following classification is based.

Subfamily classification

Cyprinids are regarded as taxonomically difficult and Regan (1911) stated that they defied sub-categorization. The recognition of two principal lineages was made by Bonaparte (1846) for European cyprinids and by Nikolsky (1954) for cyprinids as a whole. I believe this division to be valid (Howes, 1987, enumerates characters for each subfamily). The dichotomy between leuciscines and cyprinines has been recognized principally on the presence or absence of barbels.

Raffin-Peyloz (1955) observed that barbel structure of *Cyprinus* and *Barbus* is more complex than that of *Tinca* and *Gobio*. In the first two genera the barbels have a discrete histological zonation, with the maxillary barbel lacking tastebuds but having a double nerve supply and muscular bundles; *Gobio* and *Tinca* possess only posterior barbels.

In addition to these barbel types, I find another in 'rasborine' taxa (e.g. *Esomus, Nematabramis, Rasbora*), in which the basal part of the maxillary barbel is in the form of a cartilaginous nodule adhering to the palatine. In *Luciosoma* (Fig. 1.4(a)), the distal tip of the nodule extends into the barbel forming a core, and in *Nematabramis* that core is stiffened (Fig. 1.4(b)). The epidermis of the barbel appears to be an extension of the lip tissue, lacking papillae and surrounding in collar-like fashion the basal nodule. A single branch of the trigeminal maxillaris nerve runs over the maxilla and innervates the barbel. The posterior barbel is a simple extension of the lip tissue and is innervated by a nerve branch emanating from the same root as that supplying the maxillary barbel. Even in those rasborines which lack barbels, the fascia of the tissue connecting the maxillary dermis with the palatine is highly fibrous and forms a thickened area below the lateral border of the palatine. A branch of the palatine nerve runs medially into this area.

Correlated with the type of barbel is the pattern of innervation. Howes (1981) pointed to the presence in some cyprinids of a maxillary foramen through which the maxillaris branch of the trigeminal nerve enters the rostral barbel. This condition was taken to be synapomorphic for those taxa, which were thus grouped as the subfamily Cyprininae (but see Psilorynchidae).

Among some other cypriniforms the innervation patterns are as follows. Cobitidae, Catostomidae, Leuciscinae and *Ellopostoma*: maxillaris nerve runs anteriorly to exit from beneath the anteroventral border of the maxilla, to pass between it and the ascending process of the premaxilla to innervate the labial tissue, or in the case of cobitids, the anterior barbel. Gobioninae: maxillary

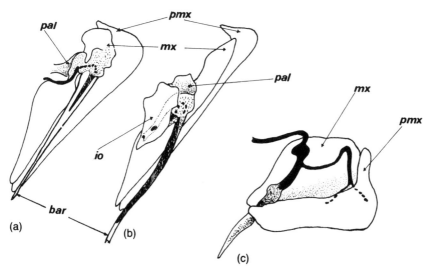

Fig. 1.4 Barbels and innervation. (a), *Luciosoma setigerum* (lateral view); (b), *Nematabramis alestes* (lateral view); (c), *Gobio gobio* (medial view). The nerve is shown as solid black and its course through the proximal nodule as a dashed line; the stiffened barbel core is hatched. Abbreviations: bar, barbel; io, first infraorbital; mx, maxilla; pal, palatine; pmx, premaxilla.

nerve runs medial to the maxilla then bifurcates, the main branch running ventrally and entering the single, posterior barbel; the smaller nerve branch continues forward, curves dorsally, then descends to exit from beneath the anteroventral margin of the maxilla and innervate the labial tissue (Fig. 1.4(c)). Gyrinocheilidae: maxillary nerve runs laterally to pass over and course along the outer surface of the maxilla, then to branch and innervate the labial tissue. Psilorynchidae: maxillary nerve passes through a maxillary foramen to innervate the thick fatty tissue surrounding the upper jaw and snout. Since this is the same condition as described under Cyprinidae, there seems, at least on this character, no reason to recognize a separate family.

Gilbert and Bailey (1972) considered barbels to have evolved several times in the Cyprinidae, an opinion also expressed by Fink and Fink (1981: 346). The different barbel morphotypes and their innervation patterns support these views. Arai (1982) suggested that barbelled cyprinids are more primitive than those lacking barbels, the higher number of barbels representing the more plesiomorph condition. I disagree, partly on grounds of commonality (more cyprinid taxa lack barbels than possess them) and partly because those that do have barbels also possess modifications to the nerve course and maxilla which are derived with respect to those taxa lacking barbels. Further evidence to support the derived nature of barbels is that during ontogeny of cyprinins, the ventral border of the maxilla is sometimes notched, the circumference of the notch later being closed by the growth of bone and surrounding the maxillaris nerve. I have also found adult specimens where notched and foraminate conditions occur on either side. Secondary loss of barbels is also evident in squaliobarbin cyprinids (Howes, 1981: 39–40) and *Barbus* (Banister and Bunni, 1980). *Carassius* appears to represent another example of barbel loss as it usually lacks anterior and posterior barbels; posterior barbels are found in some populations and often develop on one side only (Nikolyukin, 1948), as in *Carassius* × *Cyprinus* hybrids.

On the basis of barbel distribution, morphotype and innervation, three categories of cyprinids can be recognized: Cyprininae, Gobioninae and Rasborinae. Of those that lack or sporadically possess barbels, I recognize the Leuciscinae, Acheilognathinae, Cultrinae and Alburninae. The following is a synopsis of those subfamilies with their diagnostic characters.

Subfamily Cyprininae

Cyprinini Bonaparte, 1846; Barbinae Bleeker, 1859; *auct.*; Schizothoracinae Berg, 1912; *auct.*; Garrinae Fowler, 1924; *auct.*; Labeonini Bleeker, 1859; Labeoninae *auct.*; Oreininae Fowler, 1924.

Characterized by a medial rostral process of the supraethmoid; elongate lachrymal; anterior and posterior barbels; maxillary foramen for maxillaris nerve innervating anterior barbel; sometimes, serrated enlarged dorsal fin ray and anal ray.

This is by far the largest subgroup of cyprinids, having its distribution throughout Africa, India, South East Asia, the Levant and Middle East, part of China, Western Europe and the Caspio–Pontic region.

Barbin lineage (= Barbini, Barbinae (part) auct.) Characterized by foraminated dilatator fossa; lateral ethmoid articular facet. Comprises: *Barbus s. str.*, and *Aulopyge*; other 'barbins', e.g. *Varicorhinus, Capoeta, Cyprinus. Carassius, Probarbus.*

Labein linage (= Labeini, Labeoinae, Garrine auct.) Characterized by vomero-palatine organ, double-foraminated dilatator fossa and hypertrophied supraneural bones, the anterior usually contacting the cranium. Includes: *Labeo, Garra, Typhlogarra, Osteocheilus, Cirrhinus, Labeobarbus, Tylognathus s.str.*, and possibly also *Catla* and *Barbichthys* (Reid, 1982).

Squaliobarbin lineage (Howes, 1981) Characterized by several derived cranial osteological and myological features, e.g. enlarged subtemporal fossa; palatine articulating with lateral border of supraethmoid; enlarged intercalar; divided levator posterior muscle. Comprises: *Squaliobarbus, Ctenopharyngodon* and *Mylopharyngodon.*

Schizothoracin lineage (= Schizothoracinae, Schizothoracini, Oreininae) Characterized by possession of a medial parasphenoid strut, absence of uroneurals, tile-like anal scales. Contains 11 genera including *Schizothorax, Diptychus, Gymnocypris, Schizocypris,* and *Chuanchia* (Wu, 1984; Howes, 1987).

Cyprinion–Onychostoma lineage (Chen, 1989). Characterized by an interdigitating symphysial dentary joint and several derived jaw and cranial osteological and myological features. Contains *Cyprinion, Onychostoma, Semiplotus,* and *Scaphiodonichthys* (Howes, 1982; Chen, 1989).

Other taxa, including *Barbus sensu lato, Puntius, Tor, Oreodaimon, Pseudobarbus* and *Gibelion* constitute the remainder of the Cyprininae. (*Mystacoleucus,* although possessing both anterior and posterior barbels, lacks a maxillary foramen, the nerve innervating the maxillary barbel passing beneath that bone.)

Subfamily Gobioninae

Gobioninae Jordan and Fowler, 1903; *auct.* (part).

Recognized as monophyletic by Hosoya (1986) on the basis of derived, sensory canal patterns; supraoccipital and frontal morphology; modification of the anterior vertebrae which in some taxa contribute to an ossified swimbladder capsule. Hosoya includes the following genera: *Hemibarbus, Squalidus, Gobio, Mesogobio, Acanthogobius, Gobiobotia, Pseudogobio, Abbottina, Saurogobio, Rhinogobio, Microphysogobio* and *Biwia.*

Although he excludes genera formerly placed in the subfamily (Ramaswami, 1955), Hosoya does not indicate to which cyprinid lineages they should be assigned, or indeed whether they form a monophyletic group. Thus, the following taxa remain *incertae sedis: Gnathopogon, Sarcocheilichthys, Pungtungia, Pseudopungtungia, Coreoleuciscus, Ladislavia* and *Coreius* (Fig. 1.1(x)).

Subfamily Acheilognathinae

Acheilognathini Bleeker, 1863; Rhodeina Günther, 1868; *auct.*

Recognized as monophyletic on the basis of the following synapomorphies: ovipositor in females; males with tubercle-bearing 'plates'; absence of uroneurals; coracoid foramen reduced or absent (Hosoya, 1986: 498). Included taxa: *Acheilognathus* (incl. *Paracheilognathus, Acanthorhodeus* and *Pseudoperilampus*), *Rhodeus* (Fig. 1.1(p)) and *Tanakia* (generic revision, Arai and Akai, 1988).

Subfamily Leuciscinae

Leuciscini Bonaparte, 1846; Abramiformes Dybowski, 1862; Chondostomini Bleeker, 1863; Hypophthalmichthina Günther 1868, Xenocypridinae Günther, 1868; Pogonichthi Girard, 1859; Elopichthyini Berg, 1912; Abramidini, Abramidinae *auct.*

Characterized by absence of a maxillary (rostral) barbel and maxillary foramen; connective tissue connection between lateral ethmoid and entopterygoid; 1st supraneural articulating with or narrowly separated from the neural complex; modally high number of vertebrae.

As characterized here, it is doubtful whether the Leuciscinae can be recognized as a monophyletic assemblage. However, within that assemblage, the following monophyletic lineages have been identified:

Abramin lineage (Howes, 1981). Includes Abramini, Abraminae (part, *auct.*); characterized by derived basicranial, gill-arch and suspensorial muscle morphology. Includes *Abramis, Rutilus, Chondrostoma, Xenocypris, Plagiognathops, Distoechodon* and *Hypophthalmichthys* (= *Aristichthys*), Howes, 1981; possibly also includes the North American *Orthodon*.

Aspinin lineage (Howes, 1984b). Characterized by cranial elongation, high vertebral number, and derived gill raker morphology. Includes *Aspius, Elopichthys, Luciobrama, Pseudaspius, Genghis, Aspiolucius, Oreoleuciscus, Aspiopsis, Pogonichthys* and *Tribolodon*; possibly also includes *Luciocyprinus* (Kottelat, 1983), but according to Lin Renduan (pers. comm., Jan. 1986), this genus possesses cyprinine synapomorphies.

Phoxinin lineage (Howes, 1985). Characterized by comb-like thoracic scales. Comprises *Phoxinus* (Fig. 1.1(a)) and *Couesius*. Monophyly is not supported by osteological characters.

The remaining taxa include the majority of North American cyprinids. As yet no suite of synapomorphies has been identified that would indicate that the North American leuciscines constitute a monophyletic lineage. One suspects that Nearctic genera have their sister groups amongst those Eurasian lineages already identified or with the 'Leuciscus' assemblage. Nearly all the Eurasian leuciscine taxa are accommodated by the three monophyletic groups so far proposed; the exceptions are *Leuciscus* itself and several Mediterranean and Levantine taxa, namely *Phoxinellus, Tropidophoxinellus, Paraphoxinus, Pararhodeus, Anaecypris, Leucaspius, Spinophoxinellus, Acanthorutilus, Rhyncocypris, Lagowskiella, Eupsallasella* and *Ochetobius* (Fig. 1.1(h)).

Subfamily *Cultrinae*

Cultrinae Nikolsky, 1954 (part); Cultrinae Bănărescu, 1967 (part); Cultrine group Howes, 1979 (part).

In a previous discussion of the Cultrinae (Howes, 1979), both Nikolsky's and Bănărescu's concepts of the subfamily were criticized as being non-monophyletic. Bănărescu (1967) had recognized 21 genera constituting the subfamily. I had accepted six as constituting a cultrin monophyletic lineage, but did not indicate those synapomorphies which allied the six genera; these are as follows: vomer extending anterior to the ethmoid and forming a floor to the kinethmoid cavity; ethmoid bloc elongated and depressed; extensive posterocranial platform involving parietals, supraoccipital and epioccipitals, the major contribution being from the parietals, on the surface of which the sensory canal is produced as a prominent ridge; lateral ethmoid wall with ventral spine-like projection; dilatator fossa extending onto the surface of the frontal; extensive area of contact between the pterosphenoid and parasphenoid; parasphenoid flared anteriorly with a deep ventral groove; exoccipitals with a posterior depression and prominent posterior process; enlarged, well-ossified 3rd dorsal ray; expanded 1st anal radial; pelvic bone expanded and vertically orientated; pelvic axial lobes are present in some taxa.

Included taxa: *Culter, Erythroculter* (Fig. 1.1(v)), *Ischikauia, Chanodichthys, Megalobrama, Parabramis, Sinibrama, Ancherythroculter, ?Longiculter.*

Osteobrama (Fig. 1.1(w)) and *Rhotee* should probably be included in this Subfamily; they share with *Parabramis* an enlarged dorsal ray, and radial, 3rd and 4th supraneurals and basioccipital process. The genus *Rhotee*, as it stands, is non-monophyletic: *R. cotio* appears to be more closely related to '*Puntius*' *proctozysron* than to other *Rhotee* species; both have a deeply indented ethmoid notch, shallow dentary, serrated anal fin spine and a thin, bow-shaped 4th epibranchial.

Subfamily Alburninae

Alburni Girard, 1859; Alburniformes Dybowski, 1862; Leuciscinae (part) *auct.*; Abramidinae (part) *auct.*; Cultrinae (part) Bănărescu, 1967; Cheline group (part) Howes, 1979.

The taxa assigned to this subfamily have formerly been placed amongst leuciscines and cultrins, but they can immediately be distinguished as a monophyletic group by the following suite of synapomorphies: an elongate basicranial foramen (between the parasphenoid and basioccipital); expansion of neural spine of PU2 (pre-ural centrum); lateral ethmoid with truncated wings, sometimes with spinous ventral extension; laterally compressed parasphenoid with outwardly curved ascending processes; extensive carotid foramina separated in the midline by only a narrow portion of the parasphenoid; frontals transversely convex; supraorbital reduced; posterior wall of epioccipital depressed; ventral border of coracoid serrated or fretted; 3rd neural process sloped caudad; cranially originating intermuscular bones; pelvic bone expanded and orientated vertically; pectoral axial lobes in some taxa.

Howes (1979) recognized a lineage named as the cheline group, since one of the included genera was *Chela*. It is now apparent, however, that *Chela* is more closely related to rasborine taxa (p. 16). Those other genera included in the cheline assemblage are, on the basis of the synapomorphies listed above, allied more closely with *Alburnus*.

Included taxa: *Alburnus, Chalcalburnus, Pseudolaubuca, Paralaubuca, Hemiculter, Hemiculterella, Alburnoides, ?Leucalburnus* (*Acanthalburnus* is probably synonymous with *Alburnus*, distinguished only by its thickened dorsal ray, which appears to be a morphoclinal feature within *Alburnus*).

The genus *Pelecus* (Fig. 1.1(t)) is characterized by many autapomorphies, and it shares with some rasborins (*Macrochirichthys, Oxygaster*) a head-elevating mechanism, extensive and fretted coracoid and concave frontals. However, it shares with the alburnines most of the features listed above, and with *Hemiculterella* a posteriorly directed sphenotic process, medial ramification of the supraorbital sensory canal above the sphenotic, and an erratic lateral line course. It is the sister group to other alburnines.

'Subfamily' Rasborinae

Rasborinae Weber and de Beaufort, 1916; Barilinae Regan, 1922; Danioinae

Bănărescu, 1968; cheline group (part) Howes, 1979; bariliine group Howes, 1980, 1983.

This large assemblage contains most taxa not accommodated by the other subfamilies. It is characterized by a barbel morphotype which appears to have been derived independently from that of cyprinines and other barbelled groups (p. 11). Not all included taxa, however, possess barbels, and their inclusion is based principally on resemblances of jaw and ethmo-palatine morphology. As the polarity of these features has still to be assessed, the monophyly of the group is suspect. That said, one lineage, the rasborin, can be identified on the basis of the following synapomorphies.

Rasborin lineage. Characterized by shallow ethmoid bloc, mesethmoid extending to form a shelf and flooring the ethmoid notch; kinethmoid lamellate, perforated, or in the form of a diamond, triangle or crescent; supraethmoid sometimes with a bowl-shaped depression; vomer anteriorly upturned; palatine often expanded with a strong lateral process overlapping the maxilla and (in some taxa) bearing the cartilaginous nodular base of the rostral barbel; dentary with an anteroventral indentation in some taxa; branchiostegal rays reduced to three in some genera.

Included taxa: *Esomus, Luciosoma, Parluciosoma, Rasbora* (*sensu stricto* and *lato*), *Nematabramis, Chela, Inlecypris, Danio, Brachydanio, Bengala, Pseudorasbora, ?Thryssocypris* (the upturned vomer and thin, compressed kinethmoid indicate its inclusion).

Howes (1980) recognized a bariliin group on the basis of a posttemporal–subtemporal fossa connection, but this feature occurs in other cyprinid groups and cannot be considered as synapomorphic. Several taxa included in the bariliin group have now been reassigned to the rasborin lineage, but for the others there is no single shared derived feature that unites them. Within this heterogeneous complex, however, two or three characters suggest relationships with taxa previously assigned to the cheline group (Howes, 1979): they are the straight, forwardly directed arms of the mesethmoid and expanded (often modified) lateral processes of the 1st vertebra, and are shared by *Barilius* (part), *Salmostoma, Oxygaster, Macrochirichthys, Parachela, Securicula, Aspidoparia* and *Raiamas*.

Allied to this assemblage (or part of it) are the neobolin genera, considered as a monophyletic group (Howes, 1984a), namely *Engraulicypris, Leptocypris, Neobola, Mesobola, Rastrineobola* and *Chelaethiops*. A further group of taxa with parallel rows of dentary tubercles, body striping, and (sometimes) well-marked sexual dimorphism in colour pattern and anal fin shape is represented by *Opsariichthys, Zacco, Opsaridium* and '*Barilius*' (South East Asian species).

The taxonomic position of *Tinca*

The inclusion of the monotypic Eurasian genus *Tinca* in any one of the above subfamilies is a taxonomic problem. Kryzanovskii (1947) recognized a separate category, the Tincinae, to contain this genus, on the grounds that *Tinca* rarely hybridizes with either cyprinines or leuciscines. Berg (1949) also considered its taxonomic position doubtful but retained *Tinca* in the Leuciscinae. Dumitrescu and Bănărescu (1979) concluded from their biochemical studies that *Tinca* was more closely allied to *Carassius* than to *Phoxinus* or *Rutilus* and so referred it to the Cyprininae. On the basis of its karyotype ($2n = 48$) and ratio of branched dorsal/anal fin rays, Arai (1982) suggested the removal of *Tinca* from the Leuciscinae but was uncertain of its correct taxonomic position. Chen *et al.* (1984) regarded *Tinca* as the plesiomorphic sister group to the Barbinae, its single derived feature being the separation between the infraorbital and supraorbital sensory canals. This, however, is a feature also possessed by leuciscines and alburnines (Gosline, 1978). Bogutskaya (1986a) summarized osteological, karyological and hybridization data and concluded that *Tinca* "stands apart from other groups of cyprinid genera". Howes (1987) regarded *Tinca* as a leuciscine, but noted that it shared one synapomorphy with cyprinines, namely an articulation between the lateral ethmoid and entopterygoid. Of those characters listed as shared with leuciscines, all but two (forked neural complex and 1st free supraneural articulating with neural complex) are plesiomorphic. Chen (1987) rejected Chen *et al.*'s (1984) opinion on the uniqueness of *Tinca* and regarded it as a member of the Leuciscinae.

Until a complete anatomical comparison is made between *Tinca* and other cyprinids to establish its phylogenetic position, it is regarded as *incertae sedis*.

1.4 PHYLOGENETIC RELATIONSHIPS OF THE SUBFAMILIES

As it stands, the 'Cyprinidae' is a 'non-group': no synapomorphies have yet been identified that demonstrate its monophyly. However, monophyly for some constituent groups (i.e. subfamilies) can be recognized and it is the relationships of these groups, one with another, that will establish a revised concept of 'cyprinids'. The establishment of such relationships will entail the recognition of those clades as families.

Although earlier in this account I have been at pains to emphasize the necessity for recognizing only monophyletic lineages of cypriniforms, I have been guilty of acknowledging three paraphyletic assemblages, the 'Cyprininae', 'Leuciscinae' and 'Rasborinae'. Since, however, I cannot satisfactorily relate those clades within these groups to one another, I am using them merely as categories of taxonomic convenience. I have no evidence to suggest that the 'cyprinines' are more closely related to 'leuciscines', 'rasborines' or alburnines than to gobionines, or, for that matter, to any of the other cypriniform families such as Catostomidae or Cobitidae.

Of the three identified leuciscine clades, the abramin lineage does not appear to be closely related to the aspinin or phoxinin; however, the last two are probably sister groups (Howes, 1984b). In turn, their relationships lie with an as yet unidentified assemblage of the *Leuciscus* complex or with some group of North American taxa. According to Bogutskaya (1986b), the abramine group *sensu* Howes (1981) is non-monophyletic since the basicranial synapomorphies are possessed by a wider group of taxa. However, this simply means that the extent of the clade is widened and relationships with other 'leuciscines' can be established.

There is no recognized synapomorphy to indicate that North American cyprinids form a monophyletic group (p. 14). The phoxinin lineage contains a single genus, *Phoxinus*, which occurs in both Eurasia and North America. This distribution is unique amongst cyprinids and therefore invites a reappraisal of the generic status of other American taxa in the light of any synapomorphies with Eurasian ones (e.g. are *Notemegonius* and *Alburnus* synonymous?).

The Alburninae and Cultrinae both share several synapomorphies: an expanded and vertically orientated pelvic bone, depressed epioccipital wall, reduced postcleithra and pectoral axial lobes. The Alburninae also shares certain derived features of the vertebral column with some 'rasborin' taxa, e.g. *Oxygaster* and *Macrochirichthys*. Features uniting the Alburninae, Cultrinae, Rasborinae and Leuciscinae are tenuous; all share a forked neural complex with a grooved dorsal surface; all but the Rasborinae lack rostral barbels, most included taxa possess many anal fin rays (more than seven) and have the first unbranched dorsal ray placed posteriorly to the centre of the body, and the Rasborinae lack a strong ligamentous connection between the entopterygoid and lateral ethmoid. According to Chen *et al.* (1984), a synapomorphy for the Leuciscini (which corresponds to the assemblage of groups under discussion) is that the hyoid artery does not link to the supraorbital artery. I have not investigated this character.

Interrelationships of 'cyprinine' lineages are obscure. There are some indications that the barbin lineage (i.e. *Barbus s.str.*) may be more closely related to the schizothoracin than to any of the others so far identified. There is, however, no evidence to indicate a close relationship between the South East Asian barbins, generally lumped under *Puntius*, and the so-called African *Barbus*. Concerning the latter, Skelton (1980, 1988) has shown that they are a polyphyletic assemblage.

Arai (1982) relates the Barbinae (included here in the Cyprininae) to the Gobioninae on the basis of their possessing five or six branched anal fin rays, two or four barbels, and both having some species with $2n = 98–100$ chromosomes. A low number of anal fin rays appears to be plesiomorphic for ostariophysans, and the majority of cyprinines and gobionines have a diploid chromosome number of 50; barbels are apomorphic, but are of different morphotypes and have different innervation patterns in the two groups. Therefore Arai's contention of close relationship cannot be supported on those characters.

A final point concerns hierarchical levels in classifying cyprinids. Using cladistics, Sawada (1982) made several changes to the classification of cobitids whereby he recognized them as a superfamily (Cobitoidea), its constituents being the families Cobitidae and Homalopteridae containing, respectively, the subfamilies Botiinae and Cobitiinae, and Nemacheilinae and Homalopterinae (also containing the Gastromyzontidae *sensu* Hora, 1950). Sawada merely noted the other cypriniform groups as the Catostomidae and 'other cyprinids'. His classification is thus ambiguous with regard to the status of the other cypriniform families. If the cobitids are to be elevated to superfamily rank, they must stand as co-ordinate with other cypriniforms. As such, the Catostomidae, Gyrinocheilidae, Psilorhynchidae and Cyprinidae would have superfamily status. The Cyprinidae would so be regarded as the superfamily Cyprinoidea, with its subfamilies (as recognized in this chapter) being elevated to family level.

1.5 BIOGEOGRAPHY

The documentation of cyprinid distribution is encapsulated in the following statement of Croizat (1958: 131): "It is of course well known that the time-honoured pastime of rigging up even better 'zoogeographic' provinces or the like has no end because, . . . life perversely tends to interdigitate all over, thus voiding man's clever schemes!"

Distribution of subgroups

The distribution of the Cyprinidae has mostly been documented as part of regional ichthyofaunal compilations. Mori (1936), Berg (1949) and Bănărescu (1975) have, however, paid particular attention to broader aspects of cyprinid distribution, and Bănărescu has documented the ranges of three subfamilies, namely Leuciscinae, Barbinae (= Cyprininae) and Gobioninae. We can only appreciate the true nature of cyprinid distribution by understanding the pattern of its constituent monophyletic elements; any distributional pattern shared between these taxa may have a common explanation.

Since the subgroups of the Cyprinidae recognized here are constituted somewhat differently from those recognized by previous authors, different geographical areas are encompassed.

Leuciscinae
Distribution throughout mainland Eurasia (excluding Arabia, India and South East Asia), Japan and North America. In Eurasia, leuciscines extend from the Iberian Peninsula eastward into central Italy, then through the Balkans and Anatolia into the Levant. Few taxa extend across Siberian Asia through the Arctic basin drainage and none inhabit the Kamchatka Peninsula. The

southerly extent of leuciscines in Asia is marked by the Syr and Amu-Dar'ya systems and eastward by the Volga–Urbal rivers. A few taxa occur in Mongolian lakes and rivers but none on the Tibetan Plateau. In East Asia, leuciscines extend from the north of Sakhalin through the Amur basin and Korea to embrace the major river systems of China (Huang Ho and Yangtze) southward to Yunnan where the Nan Shan complex forms its south-eastern limit. Further east, the subfamily extends into Japan (apart from western Sakhalin). No leuciscine extends further south than Hanoi, or enters the Mekong system. In North America, leuciscines are the only representatives of the Cyprinidae, and extend across the continent from Labrador to the Mackerzie and Yukon basins of the northwest and have a north–south range from the Hudson Bay drainage to Mexico.

The distributions of the leuciscine lineages so far recognized are as follows:

Aspinin lineage. (Fig. 1.5(a)) One genus, *Aspius*, occurs in central and eastern Europe, the Black, Caspian and Aral sea basins and the Tigris–Euphrates basin; it is joined by *Aspiolucius* in the Amu-Dar'ya. The central Asian endemic genera *Aspiopsis* and *Oreoleuciscus* occur respectively in Sinkiang and Mongolia; Berg (1949) considered *Oreoleuciscus* as part of the Arctic basin fauna since it occurs in the Ob drainage. Of the other six genera, five have a north–south range through China, Korea and Japan, whilst the sixth, *Pogonichthys*, lies in western North America (Howes, 1984b).

Abramin lineage. (Fig. 1.5(a)) Of the eight (nine including *Pseudobrama*) genera, four (*Abramis, Rutilus, Chondrostoma* and *Acanthobrama*) occur in western and eastern Europe, through the Caspian–Pontic and Mediterranean regions (*sensu* Berg, 1949) to the Urals and into the Levant and Tigris–Euphrates basin; they do not extend into central Asia. Of the other four genera, *Xenocypris, Plagiognathops* and *Distoechodon* (Xenocypridinae of other authors) are confined to China. Li (1986) has shown that these three genera have a nested distribution, whereby the assumed (and widespread) genus *Xenocypris* includes within its range the successively derived *Plagiognathops* and *Distoechodon.* (Li also incorrectly includes *Acanthobrama*, but the species he names, *A. simonis*, should be referred to *Pseudobrama.*) The fourth genus, *Hypophthalmichthys*, which is regarded as the sister group to the others, is naturally restricted to the Amur (it is widespread throughout India and South East Asia owing to its introduction; Howes, 1981). *Rutilus* has the widest distribution, extending through Europe from east of the Pyrenees and north of the Alps (the '*Rutilus*' species of the Iberian Peninsula and Italy are of doubtful generic status) to embrace the Black and Caspian sea basins as far east as Lake Chany in central Siberia. One species is endemic to Lake Baikal and the Lena. The distribution of *Chondrostoma* coincides for the most part with that of *Rutilus* (Elvira, 1987), except that it penetrates the Iberian Peninsula.

Phoxinin lineage. (Fig. 1.6) *Phoxinus* has a disrupted distribution through Eurasia, being absent in the east from Kamchatka and Japan and in the west from most of Italy, part of the Balkan peninsula and Anatolia; in the north it

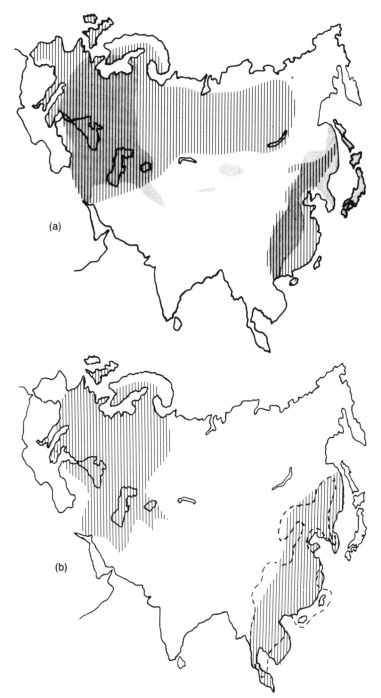

Fig. 1.5 The dichotomous distribution of cyprinid subfamilies in Eurasia. (a), Aspinin (shaded) and abramin (vertical hatching) lineages of Leuciscinae; (b), Alburninae (vertical hatching) and Cultrinae (broken line). Maps drawn on Zenithal equal-area projection.

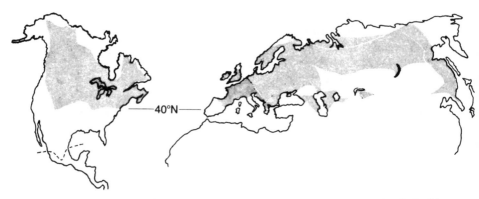

Fig. 1.6 Distribution of the phoxinin lineage (*Phoxinus* + *Couesius*). The dashed line across Central America indicates the southerly limit of cyprinids in America. Map drawn on Oxford equal-area projection.

enters the Arctic basin and extends from Murmansk to Kolyma, and south to the Amur and the river systems of Siberia (including Lake Baikal), China, Korea and the Ob drainage of Mongolia. In North America, most species are concentrated in the central and eastern United States but *P. neogaeus* reaches as far north-west as the Mackenzie River in the North-west territories of Canada. Similarly, *Couesius*, the probable sister group of *Phoxinus* (Howes, 1985), has an equally broad distribution and, like *Phoxinus*, possibly once had an equally large longitudinal one (see also p. 27).

Cultrinae (Fig. 1.5 (b))
As recognized here, this subfamily embraces China (including Formosa and Hainan), Korea and the Amur basin. Some taxa occurring in Thailand, previously thought to be cultrines, have been referred to alburnines (*Culter* and *Cultrops* species; Bănărescu, 1971).

Alburninae (Fig. 1.5 (b))
Alburnines exhibit a dichotomous east–west distribution in Eurasia. In the west the representative genera are *Alburnus*, *Alburnoides* and *Chalcalburnus*. *Alburnus* is the most widespread, extending from the eastern part of Scandinavia to the Urals, south-west to the Pyrenees, through the Alps, the Danube drainage, Black, Caspian and Aral sea basins and the Tigris–Euphrates. The group is absent from central Asia but occurs again in an area from the Amur to northern Vietnam, represented by *Hemiculter*, *Hemiculterella* and *Pseudolaubuca*. The last ranges across China south to Yunnan, from which point *Paralaubuca* extends into the Menam and Mekong drainage. Bănărescu (1971) notes that *Paralaubuca* is one of the few genera to occur in the central part of the Malaysian Peninsula yet remain absent from the Indonesian archipelago.

Acheilognathinae

This is an entirely Eurasian (Holarctic) assemblage with only one genus, *Rhodeus*, embracing the entire range of the group, extending from France across central Europe, the Black, Caspian and Aegean sea basins. The group is absent from central Asia but occurs in the Amur basin, China, Korea and Japan. Acheilognathines are naturally absent from the Arctic basin, including Scandinavia, and from England (introduced), Italy and the Iberian Peninsula. Berg (1949, vol. 3: 342) has drawn attention to the disrupted east–west distribution of *Rhodeus*.

Cyprininae (Fig. 1.7)

Few cyprinine taxa occur in northern Eurasia; those that do are concentrated in Europe and eastern Asia. Most cyprinines inhabit Africa, India and South East Asia, including most of Indonesia. The distribution of the recognized monophyletic lineages is as follows:

Barbin lineage. Barbus *s. str.* occurs throughout Europe, including the Iberian Peninsula and Mediterranean region, the Black, Caspian and Aral sea basins, where it coexists with *Capoeta*, into the Levant and the

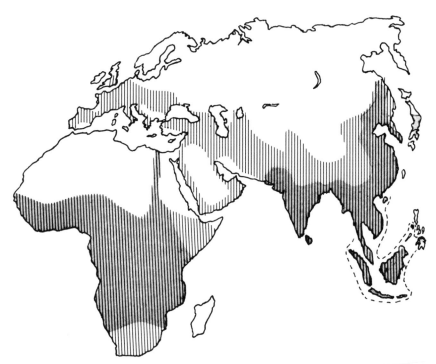

Fig. 1.7 Distribution of Cyprininae (vertical hatching) and Rasborinae (shaded). (Broken line indicates limit of distribution.)

Tigris–Euphrates basin. The eastern limit of these taxa is marked by the Urals and the southern by the Tien Shan. The carps, *Carassius* and *Cyprinus*, are native both to China and to the Danube basin and probably had a more widespread distribution (Balon, 1974); both are now widely introduced in the tropics and temperate regions. *Aulopyge* has a restricted distribution in Yugoslavia (Howes, 1987).

Cyprinion–Onychostoma lineage. This lineage extends from the Arabian Peninsula, through the Tigris–Euphrates basin, Iran, Afghanistan and Pakistan (Fig. 1.8). Two genera, *Semiplotus* and *Schaphiodonichthys*, range south of the Himalayas into Burma and the Shan States while *Onychostoma* lies in Laos, Vietnam and Yunnan extending north–east to the Yangtze. Chen (1989) recognizes three subgroups of *Onychostoma*, each with a restricted distribution.

Schizothoracin lineage. This group is clustered on the Tibetan Plateau and has a semicircular range around the Takla Makan (Sinkiang) encompassing the Tien Shan, Hindu Kush and Himalaya. Taxa occur on both faces of these ranges, the more plesiomorphic members of each lineage seemingly having the widest distribution (Wu, 1984).

Labein lineage. This is the most widespread of the cyprinin lineages but is

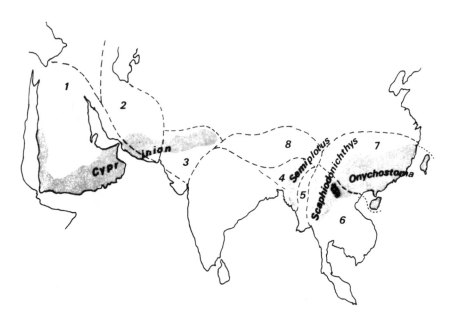

Fig. 1.8 Distribution of the *Cyprinion–Onychostoma* lineage in relation to the disposition of Asian lithographic plates (1, Arabian; 2, Iranian; 3, Afghanistanian; 4, Shillong; 5, Western Burmese; 6, South East Asian; 7, Yangtze; 8, Qinhai–Tibet). (Compiled in part from Taki, 1974; Mitchell, 1981; Leith, 1982.) Map drawn on Zenithal equal-area projection.

predominantly South East Asian (of the 12 recognized labein taxa, nine occur in South East Asia, five of which are shared with India, namely *Cirrhina*, *Osteocheilus*, *Crossocheilus*, *Labeo* and *Garra*). The last two also occur in Africa, lower China (records of *Labeo* from Formosa are based on introductions) and the Tigris–Euphrates, Helmund and Indus drainages; *Garra* also occurs in Arabia.

Squaliobarbin lineage. The three genera of this lineage, *Squaliobarbus*, *Mylopharyngodon* and *Ctenopharyngodon*, are entirely East Asiatic, occurring in Amur, China (including Formosa) and Korea. There is a dubious record for Hanoi (Howes, 1981: 41). All three taxa have been widely introduced, both in the tropics and in temperate countries.

Gobioninae

Of the eleven genera constituting this subfamily (Hosoya, 1986), only *Gobio* has a wide distribution involving Europe. It is, however, absent from the Iberian Peninsula, central and southern Italy, Greece, Anatolia, Norway, northern Sweden, Finland and Scotland. In Asia, *Gobio* occurs in the Ob, Yenisey and Irtysh but is absent from the Balkhash basin; further east it occurs in the Amur and north-east Korea and as far north as the Taz mouth (Gyda Peninsula), but is absent from Kamchatka. The other gobionine genera are restricted to China, Korea and Japan.

Rasborinae (Fig. 1.7)

These are distributed throughout Africa, India, South East Asia and Indonesia. Some taxa occur in China, the Amur basin, Korea and Japan (*Zacco*, *Opsariichthys*, *Pseudorasbora*). Only one taxon, *Barilius mesopotamicus*, extends into south-western Eurasia, where it is endemic to the Tigris–Euphrates system and Iran (Coad and Krupp, 1983). Rasborins occupy all of the islands of Indonesia and part of the Philippines.

Regional distributions

Eurasia has 155 genera (containing *c*. 1060 species) within which China has 70, sharing seven with both South East Asia and India, two exclusively with the former *Balantocheilus* and *Onychostoma*), and one exclusively with India (*Oreinus*). South East Asia has 42 genera, 31 of which are endemic and four shared exclusively with India. No species are shared exclusively between South East Asia and Africa. The distribution of those species in Europe and northern and eastern Asia (the Holarctic) has received most extensive comment from Mori (1936), Berg (1949) and Bănărescu (1975). These authors have recognized various ichthyofaunal provinces based on the presence or absence of certain taxa. Although there is an overlapping distribution of some widespread forms throughout these provinces, there are recognizable areas of endemism (i.e., West Balkanian and Pontic–Caspian

Provinces of Berg, 1949) and common demarcation zones (see Patterns, below).

Although large bodies of data exist in the form of distributional records for South East Asian and Indonesian cyprinids (e.g. Weber and de Beaufort, 1916; Smith, 1945), these have not been used in providing distributional analyses of the regions. Cranbrook (1981) has mapped the ranges of some rasborines amongst Indonesian islands, thus providing a useful base-line for further research on distributional patterns in this region.

The cyprinids of North America have rarely been recognized as belonging to more than a single subfamily, be it termed the Leuciscinae or the Abramidinae. There has not been a history of ichthyogeographical partitioning. Instead, workers have been concerned more with the recognition of specific drainage faunas than with relationships of those taxa. Of the 39 genera (based on Lee *et al.*, 1980), 14 have an entirely western distribution, two are endemic to Mexico and three occur in central and eastern drainages. The present-day distributions are generally believed to have been derived in the wake of Pleistocene glacial retreat, the fishes having dispersed northward from southern (mostly Mississippian) refugia. This approach is exemplified in Hocutt and Wiley (1986).

Africa has 23 genera (containing *c.a.* 476 species, 13 of which are lake endemics); of these, 14 are cyprinine, 8 rasborine and one (the North African '*Phoxinellus*') is leuciscine. Only three genera are shared with Eurasia, namely *Garra, Labeo* and *Barbus* (the last is paraphyletic), and one (*Raiamas*) with India. There has been no broad treatment of African cyprinid distribution. Roberts (1975) recognized several ichthyofaunal provinces on the basis of endemism, but apart from the Cape and Maghreb regions, none involve specific groups of cyprinids. The proposed phylogenetic relationships of pan-African rasborins (Howes, 1980, 1985) are too broad in scope to provide a picture of area relationships, although a study of West African rasborins (Howes and Teugels, 1989) has revealed a trichotomy among Upper and Lower Guinean Provinces and Zaire, one already predicted by Roberts (1975). The Cape Province contains elements that suggest its relationships lie closer to areas outside Africa (Reid, 1978, 1982; Howes, 1985, 1987).

Patterns and processes

From the distributional data of the various subfamilies presented above, the following principal features emerge:

1. Leuciscinae occur only in Europe and north-eastern Asia (Holarctic) and North America;
2. Cyprininae occur in Europe and western Asia, but principally in Africa, India and South East Asia, including Indonesia;
3. Rasborinae occur in Africa, India and South East Asia, and marginally in western and eastern Asia;

4. Gobioninae and Acheilognathinae occur only in Holarctic Asia;
5. Cultrinae occur only in East Asia;
6. Alburninae occur in Europe, western and eastern Asia, and the upper part of South East Asia.

The most striking distributional pattern in northern Eurasia is an east–west dichotomy separated by central Asia (Fig. 1.5). This pattern is exhibited by alburnines, leuciscines, acheilognathines, gobionines and cyprinines, and was recognized by Berg (1949), who gives examples of other biota that display a similar disrupted pattern.

There is a general north–south dichotomy between the Rasborinae and all other groups (apart from the Cyprininae), although the subfamily is represented in parts of China and Japan, but west of India it occurs only in the Tigris–Euphrates basin (Fig. 1.7).

There is as yet only one known trans-Pacific link, involving aspinin leuciscines: the Californian *Pogonichthys* is regarded as the sister taxon to the remainder of the lineage, centred in China. According to Hopkirk (1973), "*Pogonichthys* is probably the most primitive cyprinid genus in North America." The distribution of *Phoxinus* in both Eurasia and North America suggests a possible trans-Atlantic link. One suspects, in the absence of proof of monophyly for nearctic cyprinids, many other trans-Atlantic connections between genera, as amongst percid fishes (Patterson, 1981).

Explanations for the above-noted distributional patterns depend largely on one's biogeographical philosophy. Dispersalists conclude (Hora, 1937; Briggs, 1979, 1984; Bănărescu, 1975) that cyprinids originated in South East Asia or China and spread westward, invading India and Africa. Vicariographers recognize repeated dichotomies and trichotomies of subfamilies and genera as indicative of perhaps tectonic events involving the disruption of a previously widespread biota. Panbiogeographers see tracks marking the distributional boundaries of cyprinid groups as indicative of past large-scale, 'form-making' processes.

In considering the distribution of cyprinid subgroups, perhaps it is more revealing to note their areas of absence rather than presence. Why, for example, are there no cyprinines in North America? Is this because they evolved after North America drifted from Eurasia? Or perhaps the North American Catostomidae are cyprinines, i.e. the sister group to one or other of the cyprinine lineages, or even the gobionines. Why are leuciscines absent from all regions south of the Equator? Is it merely environmental, or more a reflection of their original range and the disposition of Gondwanaland?

It is surely not a meaningless coincidence that the boundaries of accreted Eurasian lithospheric plates should match the limits of those dichotomized subfamilies (Howes, 1984b) and certain genera (Fig. 1.8), and that patterns of alburnine distribution in the Pontic–Caspian region should coincide with the presumed boundaries of the Pliocene Aralo–Caspian Sea (Adams, 1981). The distribution of cyprinines and rasborines is almost entirely Gondwanic

(Fig. 1.7), and their northern limits, on various parts of the Eurasian plates, may indicate subsequent dispersal after the Indian–Asian amalgamation. The Yunnan region of China presents clear examples of vicariance amongst cyprinoid and other groups (Chu, 1986; Chen, 1989) whose distributions coincide with the boundaries of the Shillong and Western Burma plates (Mitchell, 1981).

Clearly, cyprinid subgroups have been differentiated since possibly the Eocene (Chang and Chow, 1986) and certainly since the Oligocene (Gaudant, 1984) and Miocene (e.g. Uyeno, 1969; Liu, 1985). The fact that North America and Eurasia share only leuciscines suggests that this group was already established and widespread throughout Laurasia before the continents parted in the Palaeogene (unless there was a subsequent, trans-Pacific dispersal from Eurasia). If cyprinids were so subdivided at this early stage, why is not one group represented in South America? Ecological explanations may be advocated, such as competitive exclusion by characiforms or adverse environmental conditions. Perhaps a more likely explanation is that the West African part of Gondwanaland was not inhabited by cypriniforms during the time of continental rifting. Certainly, during what would probably have been the formative period of cyprinid evolution, the drainage patterns in Africa excluded to a greater degree that part of the future continent still attached to South America (McCauley *et al.*, 1986).

Another possibility is that cypriniforms do occur in South America, and that contrary to the notions of Fink and Fink (1981), gymnotiforms are the sister group of cypriniforms rather than of siluroids. What are purported to be cypriniform pharyngeal bones and teeth have been reported by Gayet (1982) from the Cretaceous of Bolivia. If these are indeed cypriniform remains, then the present-day absence of this group is even more puzzling.

ACKNOWLEDGEMENTS

This chapter has benefited greatly from the criticisms of the editors and my colleagues, Ian Harrison, Gordon Reid and Alwyne Wheeler.

REFERENCES

Adams, C. G. (1981) An outline of Tertiary palaeogeography, in *The Evolving Earth* (ed. L. A. M. Cocks), British Museum (Natural History) and Cambridge University Press, London, pp. 221–35.

Arai, R. (1982) A chromosome study on two cyprinid fishes *Acrossocheilus labiatus* and *Pseudorasbora pumila pumila*, with notes on Eurasian cyprinids and their karyotypes. *Bull. natn Sci. Mus., Tokyo, Ser. A* (*Zool.*), **8** (3) 131–52.

Arai, R. and Akai, Y. (1988) *Acheilognathus melanogaster*, a senior synonym of *A. moriokae*, with a revision of the genera of the subfamily Acheilognathinae

(Cypriniformes, Cyprinidae). *Bull. natn Sci. Mus. Tokyo, Ser. A. (Zool.)* **14** (4), 199–213.

Balon, E. K. (1974) Domestication of the carp *Cyprinus carpio* L. *Misc. Publs. Life Sci. Div. R. Ont. Mus.*, 27 pp.

Bănărescu, P. (1967) Studies on the systematics of Cultrinae (Pisces, Cyprinidae) with description of a new genus. *Revue roum. Biol. Zool.*, **9** (2), 75–86.

Bănărescu, P. (1968) Remarks on the genus *Chela* Hamilton–Buchanan (Pisces, Cyprinidae) with description of a new subgenus. *Anuali Mus. civ. Stor. nat. Giacomo Doria*, **78**, 53–63.

Bănărescu, P. (1971) Revision of the genus *Paralaubuca* Bleeker (Pisces, Cyprinidae). *Trav. Mus. Hist. nat. 'Grigore Antipa'*, **11**, 348–55.

Bănărescu, P. (1975) *Principles and problems of Zoogeography* (English translation by R. Georgescu, and N. Brzezovschii, US Dept of Commerce and National Science Foundation, Washington), 214 pp.

Banister, K. E. and Bunni, M. K. (1980) A new blind cyprinid fish from Iraq. *Bull. Br. Mus. nat. Hist. (Zool.)*, **38** (3) 151–8.

Berg, L. S. (1912) *Faune de la Russie*, Pisces **3**. Imperial Academy of Sciences, St Petersburg, 846 pp.

Berg, L. S. (1949) *Freshwater Fishes of the U.S.S.R. and Adjacent Countries*. vol. 2 (English translation of 4th edn, 1964), I.P.S.T., Jerusalem, 496 pp.

Bleeker, P. (1859) Conspectus systematis Cyprinorum. *Natuurk. Tijdschr. Ned.-Indië*, **20**, 421–41.

Bleeker, P. (1863) *Atlas ichthyologique des Indes Orientales Needlandaises*. Cyprins **3**. Amsterdam, pp. 1–150.

Bogutskaya, N. G. (1986a) To the position of the tench *Tinca tinca* (L.) in the system of cyprinid fishes (Cyprinidae). *Proc. zool. Inst. Leningrad*, **154**, 49–65.

Bogutskaya, N. G. (1986b) A contribution to the question of taxonomic relations of species from the genera *Abramis, Blicca* and *Vimba* (Cyprinidae). *Vop. Ikhtiol.*, **26**, 576–84.

Bonaparte, C. L. (1846) Catalogo metodico dei pesci Europei. *Atti Soc. ital. Sci. nat.*, 1–95.

Briggs, J. C. (1979) Ostariophysan zoogeography: an alternative hypothesis. *Copeia* 1979, 111–18.

Briggs, J. C. (1984) Centers of origin in biogeography. *Biogeographical Monogr.*, no. 1, 95 pp.

Carl, G. C., Clemens, W. A. and Lindsey, C. C. (1967) The fresh-water fishes of British Columbia. *BC Prov. Mus. Hand.*, **5**, 192 pp.

Chang, M.-M. and Chow, C.-C. (1986) Stratigraphic and geographic distributions of the Late Mesozoic and Cenozoic fishes of China, in *Indo-Pacific Fish Biology* (Proc. Second Int. Conf. Indo-Pac Fishes) (eds T. Uyeno, R. Arai, T. Taniuchi *et al.*), pp. 529–39.

Chen, X.-L., Yue, P.-Q. and Lin, R.-D. (1984) Major groups within the family Cyprinidae and their phylogenetic relationships. *Acta Zootaxonomica Sinica*, **9**, 424–40.

Chen, X.-Y. (1987) Studies on the phylogenetic relationships of Chinese leuciscine fishes (Pisces: Cypriniformes). *Acta Zootaxonomica Sinica*, **12**, 427–39.

Chen, Y. (1989) Anatomy and phylogeny of the cyprinid fish genus *Onychostoma* Günther, 1896. *Bull. Br. Mus. nat. Hist. (Zool.)*, **55** (1), 109–21.

Chu, X.-L. (1986) Ichthyofauna and its geographical subdivision in Yunnan, China, in *Indo-Pacific Fish Biology*. (Proc. Second Int. Conf. Indo-Pac Fishes) (eds T. Uyeno, R. Arai, R. Taniuchi, *et al.*) pp. 471–6.

Chu, Y. T. (1935) Comparative studies on the scales and on the pharyngeals and their teeth in Chinese cyprinids, with particular reference to anatomy and evolution. *Biol. Bull. St John's Univ., Shanghai*, **2**, 1–225.

Coad, B. W. and Krupp, F. (1983) Redescription of *Barilius mesopotamicus* Berg 1932, a poorly known cyprinid fish from the Tigris–Euphrates basin. *Cybium*, **7**, 47–56.

Collares-Perreira, M.J. (1983) Les phoxinelles circum-Méditerranéens (avec la description d *Anaecypris* n. gen.) (Poissons, Cyprinidae). *Cybium*, **7** (3), 1–7.

Cranbrook, The Earl of (1981) The vertebrate faunas, in *Wallace's Line and Plate Tectonics* (Oxford monographs on biogeography (ed. T. C. Whitmore), Oxford University Press, Oxford, pp. 54–61.

Croizat, L. (1985) *Panbiogeography*, **2a**. Publ. by author, Caracas, 771 pp.

Cuvier, G. (1817) *Le Règne Animal*, **2**, Fortin, Masson et C. Librasis, Paris, 532 pp.

Dumitrescu, M. and Bănărescu, P. (1979) A biochemical contribution to the taxonomical position of the genus *Tinca* (Pisces, Cyprinidae). *Trav. Mus. Hist. nat. 'Grigore Antipa'*, **20**, 362–6.

Dybowski, B. (1862) *Versuch einer Monographie der Cyprinoides Livlands nebst einer synoptischen Aufzahlung der europaischen Arten dieser Familie*, Laakmann, Dorpet, 215 pp.

Economides, P. S. and Sinis, A. I. (1988) A natural hybrid of *Leuciscus cephalus macedonicus* × *Chalcalburnus chalcoides macedonicus* (Pisces, Cyprinidae) from Lake Volvi (Macedonia, Greece). *J. Fish Biol.*, **32**, 592–605.

Elvira, B. (1987) Taxonomic revision of the genus *Chondrostoma* Agassiz, 1835 (Pisces, Cyprinidae). *Cybium*, **11** (2), 111–40.

Fink, S. V. and Fink, W. L. (1981) Interrelationships of the ostariophysan fishes (Teleostei). *Zool. J. Linn. Soc.*, **72** (4), 297–353.

Fowler, H. W. (1924) Notes on North American cyprinoid fishes. *Proc. Acad. nat. Sci. Philad.*, **76**, 389–416.

Fry, F. E. J. (1971) The effect of environmental factors on the physiology of fish, in *Fish Physiology*, vol. 6 (eds W. S. Hoar and D. J. Randall), Academic Press, London, pp. 1–98.

Gaudant, J. (1984) Nouvelles recherches sur les Cyprinidae (Poissons téléostéens) Oligocenes des Limagnes. *Geobios, Lyon*, **17**, 659–66.

Gayet, M. (1982) Cypriniformes Crétacés en Amerique du Sud. *C.r. hebd. Séanc. Acad. Sci., Paris*, **295**, 1037–40.

Gilbert, C. R. and Bailey, R. M. (1972) Systematics and zoogeography of the American cyprinid fish *Notropis* (*Opsopoedus*) *emiliae*. *Occ. Pap. Mus. Zool. Univ. Mich.*, **664**, 1–35.

Girard, C. (1859) Fishes, in General Report upon the Zoology of the Second Pacific Railroad Routes: *US Pac. RR Surv.*, **10** (4), 1–400.

Gosline, W. A. (1978) Unbranched dorsal-fin rays and subfamily classification in the fish family Cyprinidae. *Occ. Pap. Mus. Zool. Univ. Mich.*, **684**, 1–21.

Gregory, W. K. (1933) Fish skulls: a study of the evolution of natural mechanisms. *Trans. Am. phil. Soc.*, **2**, i–vii, 75–481.

Günther, A. (1868) *Catalogue of Fishes in the British Museum*, Vol. 7, British Museum, London, 512 pp.

Hensel, K. (1970) Review of the classification and the opinions on the evolution of Cyprinoidei (Eventognathi) with an annotated list of genera and subgenera described since 1921. *Annot. Zool. Bot.* **57**, 1–45.

Hensel, K. (1978) Morphology of lateral-line canal system of the genera *Abramis*, *Blicca* and *Vimba* with regard to their ecology and systematic position. *Acta Univ. Carol. (Biol.)*,1975–76, **12**, 105–49.

Herre, A. W. C. T. (1924) Distribution of the true fresh-water fishes in the Philippines. *Philipp. J. Sci.*, **24**, 249–307.

Hocutt, C. H. and Wiley, E. D. (eds) (1986) *The Zoogeography of North American Freshwater Fishes*, Wiley-Interscience, New York, 866 pp.

Hopkirk, J. D. (1973) Endemism in fishes of the Clear Lake region of central California. *Univ. Calif. Publs. Zool.*, **96**, 1–135.

Hora, S. L. (1937) Comparison of the fish-faunas of the northern and southern faces of the great Himalayan range. *Rec. Indian Mus.*, **39**, 241–50.

Hora, S. L. (1950) Notes on homalopterid fishes in the collections of certain American museums. *Rec. Indian Mus.*, **68**, 45–57.

Hosoya, K. (1986) Interrelationships of the Gobioninae (Cyprinidae), in *Indo-Pacific Fish Biology* (Proc. Second Int. Conf. Indo-Pac. Fishes (eds T. Uyeno, R. Arai, T. Taniuchi, *et al.*), pp. 484–501.

Howes, G. J. (1978) The anatomy and relationships of the cyprinid fish *Luciobrama macrocephalus* (Lacépède). *Bull. Br. Mus. nat. Hist. (Zool.)*, **34** (1), 1–64.

Howes, G. J. (1979) Notes on the anatomy of the cyprinid fish *Macrochirichthys macrochirus* (Valenciennes), 1844, with comments on the Cultrinae (Pisces, Cyprinidae). *Bull. Br. Mus. nat. Hist. (Zool.)*, **36** (3), 147–200.

Howes, G. J. (1980) The anatomy and classification of bariliine cyprinid fishes. *Bull. Br. Mus. nat. Hist. (Zool.)*, **37** (3), 129–98.

Howes, G. J. (1981) Anatomy and relationships of the Chinese major carps *Ctenopharyngodon* Steind., 1866 and *Hypophthalmichthys* Blkr, 1860. *Bull. Br. Mus. nat. Hist. (Zool.)*, **41** (1), 1–52.

Howes, G. J. (1982) Anatomy and evolution of the jaws in the semiplotine carps with a review of the genus *Cyprinion* Heckel, 1843 (Teleostei: Cyprinidae). *Bull. Br. Mus. nat. Hist. (Zool.)*, **42** (4), 299–335.

Howes, G. J. (1983) Additional notes on bariliine cyprinid fishes. *Bull. Br. Mus. nat. Hist. (Zool.)*, **45**, 95–101.

Howes, G. J. (1984a) A review of the anatomy, taxonomy, phylogeny and biogeography of the African neoboline cyprinid fishes. *Bull. Br. Mus. nat. Hist. (Zool.)*, **47** (3), 151–85.

Howes, G. J. (1984b) Phyletics and biogeography of the aspinine cyprinid fishes. *Bull. Br. Mus. nat. Hist. (Zool.)*, **47** (5), 283–303.

Howes, G. J. (1985) A revised synonymy of the minnow genus *Phoxinus* Rafinesque, 1820 (Teleostei: Cyprinidae) with comments on its relationships and distribution. *Bull. Br. Mus. nat. Hist. (Zool.)* **48** (1), 57–74.

Howes, G. J. (1987) The phylogenetic position of the Yugoslavian cyprinid fish genus *Aulopyge* Heckel, 1841, with an appraisal of the genus *Barbus* Cuvier & Cloquet, 1816 and the subfamily Cyprininae. *Bull. Br. Mus. nat. Hist. (Zool.)*, **52**, 165–96.

Howes, G. J. and Teugels, G. G. (1989) New bariliine cyprinid fishes from West Africa, with a consideration of their biogeography. *J. nat. Hist.*, **23**, 873–902.

Jayaram, K. C. (1981) *The Freshwater Fishes of India, Pakistan, Bangladesh, Burma and Sri Lanka*: A Handbook, Zool. Surv. of India, Calcutta, 475 pp.

Jordan, D. S. and Fowler, H. W. (1903) A review of the cyprinoid fishes of Japan. *Proc. U.S. natn. Mus.*, **26**, (1334), 811–62.

Kottelat, M. (1982) A small collection of fresh-water fishes from Kalimantan, Borneo, with descriptions of one new genus and three new species of Cyprinidae. *Revue suisse Zool.*, **89**, 419–37.

Kottelat, M. (1983) Status of *Luciocyprinus* and *Fustis* (Osteichthyes: Cyprinidae). *Zool. Res.*, **4**, 383–8.

Kryzanovskii, S. G. (1947) Sistema semeistva karpovych ryb (Cyprinidae). *Zool. Zh.*, **26**, 53–64.

Lee, D. S., Gilbert, C. R., Hocutt, C. H. *et al.* (eds) (1980) *Atlas of North American Freshwater Fishes*, North Carolina St. Mus. Nat. Hist., Raleigh, NC, 854 pp.

Leith, W. (1982) Rock assemblages in central Asia and the evolution of the southern Asian margin. *Tectonics*, **1**, 303–18.

Li, S. (1986) Discussion on the geographical distribution of the Xenocypridinae in China. in *Indo-Pacific Fish Biology* (Proc. Second Int. Conf. Indo-Pac. Fishes) (eds T. Uyeno, R. Arai, T. Taniuchi, *et al.*) pp. 480–83.

Lindsey, C. C. (1978) Form, function and locomotory habits in fish, in *Fish Physiology*, Vol. 7 (eds W. S. Hoar and D. J. Randall), Academic Press, London, pp. 1–100.

Liu, X. (1985) Fish fossils from the hominoid bearing locality at Shihuiba, Lufeng, Yunnan. *Acta Anthropologica Sinica*, **4** (2), 109–12.

Lowe–McConnell, R. H. (1975) *Fish Communities in Tropical Freshwaters*, Longman, London, 337 pp.

McCauley, J. F., Breed, C. S., Schaber, G. G., *et al.* (1986) Paleodrainages of the eastern Sahara – the radar rivers revisited (SIR-A/B implications for a mid-Tertiary trans-African drainage system). *IEEE Trans. Geosci. Remote Sens.*, GE-24 (4), 624–47.

Mir, S., Al–Absy, A. and Krupp, F. (1988) A new natural intergeneric hybrid from the Jordan river drainage, with a key to the large barbine cyprinids of the southern Levant. *J. Fish Biol.*, **32**, 931–6.

Mitchell, A. H. G. (1981) Phanerozoic plate boundaries in mainland SE Asia, the Himalayas and Tibet. *J. geol. Soc., Lond.*, **138**, 109–22.

Moodie, G. E. E. (1966) Some factors affecting the distribution and abundance of the chiselmouth (*Acrocheilus alutaceus*), MSc thesis, University of British Columbia. (53 pp.)

Mori, T. (1936) *Studies on the Geographical Distribution of Freshwater Fishes in Eastern Asia*, Chosen, 88 pp.

Myers, G. S. (1960) The endemic fish fauna of Lake Lanao, and the evolution of higher taxonomic categories. *Evolution*, **14**, 323–33.

Nikolsky, G. V. (1954) *Special Ichthyology*, 2nd edn, Moscow, 458 pp.

Nikolyukin, N. I. (1948) Interspecific hybrids of bony fishes, their morphology and taxonomic value. *Zool. Zh.*, **4**, 343–53.

Okada, Y. (1960) Studies on the freshwater fishes of Japan II. Special Part. *J. Fac. Fish. pref. Univ. Mie–Tsu*, **4** (2), 267–588.

Patterson, C. (1981) The development of the North American fish fauna – a problem of historical biogeography, in *The Evolving Biosphere* (eds P. H. Greenwood and P. L. Forey), British Museum (Natural History) and Cambridge Univ. Press, London, pp. 265–81.

Raffin–Peyloz, R. (1955) Étude histologique des barbillons de quelques poissons d'eau douce. *Trav. Lab. Hydrobiol. Piscic. Univ. Grenoble*, **47**, 73–97.

Ramaswami, L. S. (1955) The skull and Weberian apparatus in the subfamily Gobioninae (Cyprinidae). *Acta Zool., Stockh.*, **36**, 127–58.

Regan, C. T. (1911) The classification of the teleostean fishes of the order Ostariophysi 1. Cyprinoidei. *Ann. Mag. nat. Hist.*, **8**, 13–32.

Regan, C. T. (1922) The distribution of the fishes of the order Ostariophysii. *Bijdr. Dierk.*, **22**, 203–7.

Reid, G. M. (1978) A systematic study of labeine cyprinid fishes with particular reference to the comparative morphology, functional morphology and mor-phometrics of African *Labeo* species, PhD thesis, University of London. (770 pp.)

Reid, G. M. (1982) The form, function and phylogenetic significance of the vomero-palatine organ in cyprinid fishes. *J. nat. Hist.*, **16**, 497–510.

Roberts, T. R. (1975) Geographical distribution of African freshwater fishes. *Zool. J. Linn. Soc.*, **57**, 249–319.

Roberts, T. R. and Kottelat, M. (1984) Description and osteology of *Thrissocypris*, a new genus of anchovy-like cyprinid fishes based on two new species from southeast Asia. *Proc. Calif. Acad. Sci.*, **43** (11), 141–58.

Root, J. and Root, A. (1971) Mzima, Kenya's spring of life. *Natn. geogr. Mag.*, **140**, 350–73.

Sawada, Y. (1982) Phylogeny and zoogeography of the superfamily Cobitoidea (Cyprinoidei, Cypriniformes). *Mem. Fac. Fish. Hokkaido Univ.*, **28** (2), 65–223.

Schwartz, F. J. (1972) World literature to fish hybrids with an analysis by family, species and hybrid. *Publs. Gulf Coast Res. Lab. Mub.*, no. 3, 328 pp.

Schwartz, F. J. (1981) World literature to fish hybrids with an analysis by family, species and hybrid. *NOAA tech. Rep.* NMFS SSRF, no. 750, Supp. 1, 507 pp.

Shutov, V. A. (1969) Revision of the genus *Blicca* and some data concerning phyletic relationships between representatives of the genus *Abramis* (Pisces, Cyprinidae). *Zool. Zh.* **48**, 1105–7.

Sibbing, F. A., Osse, J. W. and Terlouw, A. (1986) Food handling in the carp (*Cyprinus carpio*): its movement patterns, mechanisms and limitations, *J. Zool., Lond.*, **210**, 161–203.

Skelton, P. H. (1980) Systematics and biogeography of the redfin *Barbus* species (Pisces, Cyprinidae) from southern Africa, PhD thesis, Rhodes University. (417 pp.)

Skelton, P. H. (1988) A taxonomic revision of the redfin minnows (Pisces, Cyprinidae) from southern Africa. *Ann. Cape Prov. Mus. (nat. Hist.)*, **16** (10), 201–307.

Smith, H. M. (1945) The freshwater fishes of Siam, or Thailand. *Bull. U.S. natn. Mus.*, **188**, 1–622.

Subla, B. A. and Sunder, S. (1982) Biology of an indigenous carp *Schizothorax curvifrons* Heckel from a stretch of R. Jhelum with certain hydrobiological parameters. *Second scientific report (1982)*, Centre of Research and Development, University of Kashmir, 24 pp.

Taki, Y. (1974) New species of the genus *Scaphognathops* Cyprinidae, from the Lao Mekong river system. *Jap. J. Ichthyol.*, **21** (3), 129–36.

Tchang, T. L. (1930) Contribution à l'étude morphologique, biologique et taxonomique des Cyprinides du bassin du Yangtze. *Thèses Fac. Sci. Univ. Paris, Ser A*, **209**. (171 pp.)

Travers, R. A. (1989) Systematic account of collection of fishes from the Mongolian People's Republic: with a review of the hydrobiology of the major Mongolian drainage basins. *Bull. Br. Mus. nat. Hist. (Zool.)*, **55** (2), 173–207.

Uyeno, T. (1969) Miocene cyprinid fishes from Mae Sot Basin, northwestern Thailand. *Geol. Palaeontol. Southeast Asia*, **7**, 93–6.

Weber, M. and de Beaufort, L. F. (1916) *The Fishes of the Indo–Pacific Archipelago*, Vol. 3, Brill, Leiden, 455 pp.

Wu, X. (1964) *The Cyprinoid Fishes of China*, Vol. 1, People's Press, Shanghai, 228 pp.

Wu, Y. (1984) Systematic studies on the cyprinid fishes of the subfamily Schizothoracinae from China. *Acta Biologica Plateau Sinica*, **12** (3), 119–33.

Chapter two

The fossil record of the Cyprinidae

T. M. Cavender

2.1 INTRODUCTION

Because of the importance of cyprinid fishes in freshwater communities throughout much of the world, the fossil history of the family greatly interests many people. Fossils can indicate the latest possible date of origin of a phyletic line, and may reveal geographic distribution and the environment occupied. Sometimes well-preserved fossils can increase knowledge concerning the primitive or derived morphology of osteological characters used in systematics. One of the most striking features of the cyprinid fossil history is the paucity of museum specimens and published records, especially for the early and middle parts of the Cenozoic Era. In most major land areas where cyprinids live today, evidence of their existence before the Miocene and Pliocene epochs is sparse or unknown. Since cyprinids dominate today's freshwater fish communities, it is difficult to believe that they have done so for only the last 10–20 million years (m. y) in areas such as western North America, Europe, Africa and India. The Asian–Oriental region may differ, although many more fossils are needed.

When the cyprinid fossil record is first examined, the thoroughness of recovery and identification is usually questioned. Because fossil cyprinids are usually small, they could easily be overlooked or, if found, not recognized as Cyprinidae. However, it is not difficult to recognize cyprinid fossils because their toothless jaws and pharyngeal teeth are usually evident. There are probably few discoveries of cyprinid fossils to be made among catalogued museum collections world-wide. Pharyngeal arches, and even single teeth, also form excellent material for the study of fossil Cyprinidae. Probably no other elements are more important in working out the taxonomy and relationships of a fossil cyprinid than the pharyngeal arch and teeth (Rutte, 1962; Smith, 1975; Uyeno, 1961).

The discovery of isolated pharyngeal teeth has greatly increased our knowledge of cyprinid history, especially in Africa where the record is meagre. Screening for small amphibian, reptile, and mammal teeth has often produced a bonus in the form of cyprinid pharyngeal teeth. Thus, palaeontologists have probably not overlooked many cyprinid fossils in their recovery work.

Here I summarize and discuss the cyprinid fossil record according to six major geographic areas (Europe, North America, Siberia, Africa, India, and the Asian-Oriental region (including Japan, Thailand and Indonesia)). The space devoted to each section reflects not only the number of known fossil cyprinids but also the availability to me of literature. Most papers on fossil cyprinids are not published in English. I regret any errors of translation.

In reference to the geologic time scale of the Cenozoic, see Romer (1966, Table 4) for information on the European, Asian, and North American stage names of the Cenozoic epochs. In reference to the radio-isotope dates for the stage boundaries (which are continually being modified and corrected), see Pomerol (1982), Berggren *et al.* (1985), Berggren (1986) and Prothero (1989). Figure 2.1 illustrates the geologic time scale of the Cenozoic era, with subdivisions, European age names and radiometric dates.

For higher-level taxonomic characters, I have referred to Fink and Fink (1981). In discussing different phyletic lines within the family Cyprinidae, I use the clade names employed by Cavender and Coburn (in press); the cladogram therein is modified from that of Chen *et al.* (1984). Similar to Howes (1987), Cavender and Coburn suggest that cyprinids evolved along two main branches, the subfamilies Cyprininae and Leuciscinae. Skeletal characters that support these two phyletic lines reflect different adaptations to feeding. Leuciscines have a distinctive mechanism associated with the lifting of the head when the mouth is opened and tend to prey upon aquatic and terrestrial insects of all types. They often feed with rapid swimming movements. Cyprinines tend to have a stiff anterior trunk and keep the head mostly rigid during feeding. They may employ a better-developed suction method of feeding and appear to have slower swimming movements when feeding. Both lines evolved herbivorous scrapers, grazers and filter feeders. Within the Leuciscinae are a number of secondary branches with clade names such as Barilini, Rasborini, Cultrini, Acheilognathini, Leuciscini and Phoxinini. Within the Cyprininae are such clades as the Barbini, Labeonini, Cyprinini and Schizothoracini. The controversial Tincini is placed in the Leuciscinae, and the Gobionini in the Leuciscinae. American cyprinids are all considered as members of the clade Phoxinini except *Notemigonus* which is a leuciscin. Phoxinins in part have a northern distribution in North American and Eurasia. Their adaptation to higher-latitude freshwater habitats may help explain their successful invasion of North America during the Tertiary in contrast to most other groups.

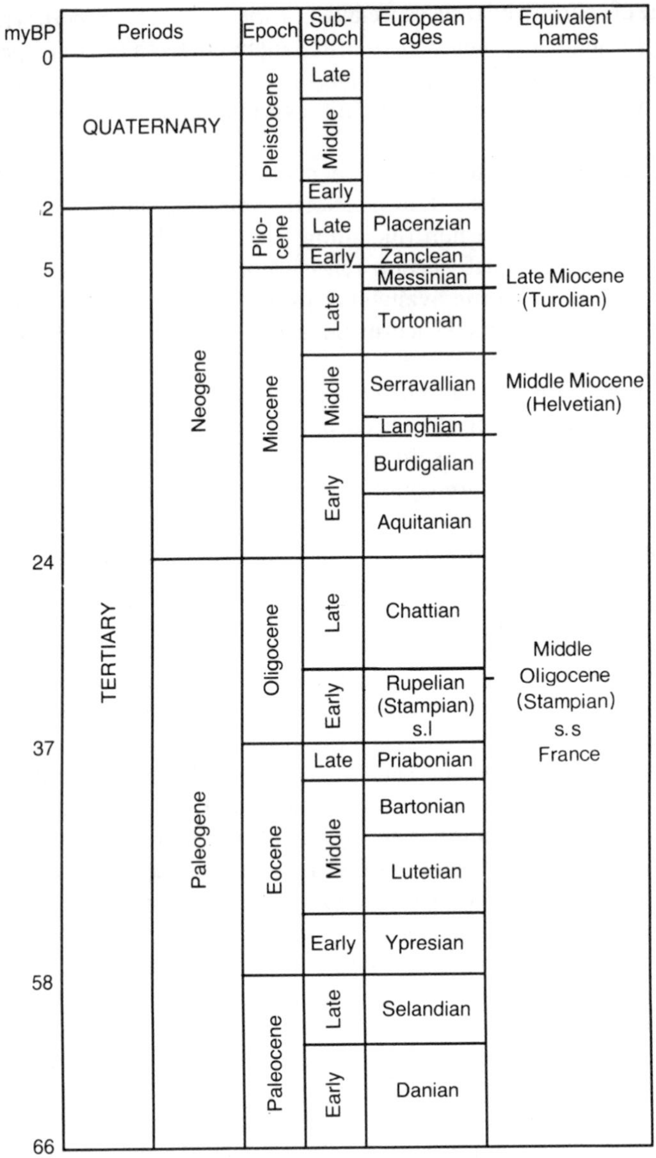

myBP	Periods	Epoch	Sub-epoch	European ages	Equivalent names
0		Pleistocene	Late		
	QUATERNARY		Middle		
			Early		
2		Plio-cene	Late	Placenzian	
5			Early	Zanclean	
		Miocene	Late	Messinian	Late Miocene (Turolian)
	Neogene			Tortonian	
			Middle	Serravallian	Middle Miocene (Helvetian)
				Langhian	
			Early	Burdigalian	
				Aquitanian	
24		Oligocene	Late	Chattian	
	TERTIARY		Early	Rupelian (Stampian) s.l	Middle Oligocene (Stampian) s.s France
37		Eocene	Late	Priabonian	
			Middle	Bartonian	
	Paleogene			Lutetian	
			Early	Ypresian	
58		Paleocene	Late	Selandian	
			Early	Danian	
66					

Fig. 2.1 Geologic time scale of the Cenozoic era including subdivisions, European age names and radiometric dates (adapted from Ingersoll and Ernst, 1987).

2.2   THE CYPRINID FOSSIL RECORD BY GEOGRAPHIC AREA

Europe

The earliest fossil cyprinid cited in the literature that is based on skeletal remains (omitting scales and otoliths) is the early Eocene '*Blicca*' *croydonensis* from the Woolwich Beds of the London Basin. This fossil consists of a fragmentary head and anterior trunk of a fish that might have reached 250 mm in total length. It was described by White (1931), who compared it to the white bream, *Blicca bjoerkna*, a leuciscine cyprinid of the *Abramis* group. From White's description and figures, I greatly doubt that this fossil belongs to the genus *Blicca*; it may not even be a member of the family Cyprinidae.

In comparison to a leuciscine cyprinid the fossil disagrees in the following ways: (1) The postorbital process of the frontal is weakly developed. (2) The parietals are exceedingly narrow in relation to the length of the frontal. (3) The supraoccipital is exposed in the skull roof, apparently dividing the parietals posteriorly, and White's figure seems to show the supraoccipital commissure crossing the back margin of the supraoccipital (these are unusual characters for a primitive cyprinid but are not unknown in the family). (4) The dilator fossa is not developed on the frontal; such development is a feature found in most leuciscines. (5) The scales are very large for a leuciscine and have numerous radii (20–30) in the posterior field. Basal radii are also described as being present; this is not typical for members of the *Abramis* group of leuciscines.

In lateral view the shape of the cleithrum suggests that the fossil is a cyprinid or cyprinoid, but the form of the opercle and the preopercle does not. The most critical element, the opercular arm, is missing in the fossil. If the opercular canal, which is unique for the Cyprinidae, were present, there would be no question as to the family assignment. As it stands, it is difficult to assign this fossil without question to the family Cyprinidae. Andrews *et al.* (1967) cited this specimen as the earliest record for the family. Pomerol (1982) placed the Woolwich Beds near the Palaeocene–Eocene boundary. Some of the features of '*Blicca*' *croydonensis*, such as its large scales and skull roof, suggest that a comparison with the primitive cypriniphysan *Chanoides* (Patterson, 1984a) might be helpful in determining its systematic position.

In continental Europe cyprinids are not known from the Palaeocene or Eocene. None of the well-known Eocene freshwater faunas such as from the middle Eocene oil shales of Germany show signs of cyprinids. The earliest undoubted cyprinids from continental Europe are mid-Oligocene (Stampian), (Gaudant, 1977a, 1979a; Gaudant and Rousset, 1979). The mid-Oligocene cyprinid from southern France was referred to the genus *Varhostichthys* (Gaudant and Rousset, 1979).

Two genera are known from the upper Stampian beds of Limagnes, France: *Varhostichthys* and '*Leuciscus*' (Gaudant, 1984a). They occur in lacustrine sediments which have been dated by the associated ostracod fauna. The 'Leuciscus' species was placed in the subgenus *Palaeoleuciscus* and is very similar to *Leuciscus (Palaeoleuciscus) primigenius* from the mid-Oligocene beds near Oberdorf (Gaudant, 1977a). Both forms have an upturned mouth, about 39 total vertebrae and nine principal rays in the anal and dorsal fins. The anal fin position is forward as in extant European leusciscines. *L. primigenius* was probably a small species of less than 50 mm standard length. It was found in association with a primitive percoid, *Dapalis*. Another Oligocene record of *Palaeoleuciscus* comes from the District of Jura, Switzerland (Gaudant, 1979a) and is found in association with *Esox*, *Umbra* and the frog, *Palaeobatrachus*. The fossil-bearing beds in Jura are calcareous, lacustrine sediments formed in the middle or upper Stampian. The Swiss *Palaeoleuciscus* is also small (< 50 mm standard length).

It is interesting that fishes thought to be cool-water forms, based on comparison with living taxa, appeared in the Oligocene of Europe with *Esox primaevus* (Gaudant, 1978) from the middle Stampian of the Apt basin (France) and with the smelt, *Enoplophthalamus* (Gaudant and Burkhardt, 1984) from the early Oligocene of Altkirch (Haut-Rhin, France) as well as from the middle and upper Oligocene of France and Germany (Gaudant, 1985).

Other Palaeogene European cyprinids are known from the lacustrine, upper Oligocene sediments of Rott (near Bonn, Germany) which have yielded two forms: *Palaeorutilus papyraceus* and *Tarsichthys macrurus* (Gaudant, 1988). These cyprinids were found in association with an esocoid (*Esox papyraceus*) and an osmerid. Weiler (1933, 1934, 1960, 1963, 1965, 1966) has published extensively on late-Oligocene, Miocene, Pliocene, and Pleistocene cyprinid fossils from Germany. In north-eastern Spain a late Oligocene–early Miocene lacustrine locality has produced a cyprinid known only from isolated pharyngeal teeth and named *Rutilus antiquus* by Cabrera and Gaudant (1985). This species is similar to species of the Spanish Miocene, *Rutilus pachecoi* and 'Leuciscus' antunesi (Cabrera and Gaudant, 1985).

In Czechoslovakia, late Oligocene–early Miocene freshwater sediments have yielded *Leuciscus (Palaeoleuciscus) socoloriensis* and *Varhostichthys brevis* (Obrhelová, 1969). Of somewhat younger age (Aquitanian–Burdigalian) is *Palaeotinca egerians* (Obrhelová, 1969). This species is also known from Burdigalian (early middle Miocene) to late middle Miocene (Burdigalian–Tortonian) beds in Czechoslovakia.

Obrhelová (1969, 1970a, b, c, 1971) has documented the expansion of cyprinid fishes during the Miocene epoch in Czechoslovakia. In the Aquitanian (lower Miocene), a few extinct genera were present which were similar to, or the same as, those from the late Oligocene. By middle Miocene (Helvetian) times, new species had appeared such as *Palaeotinca obtruncata*. During the Tortonian (late Miocene) to Pliocene the cyprinid fauna expanded into one of modern aspect, with mostly extant genera present. Weiler (1933, 1934) and Rutte (1962) described the late Oligocene and Miocene cyprinid fishes of

Germany, which show the same trends as in Czechoslovakia. By late Miocene times, the following cyprinid genera had appeared in Europe: *Aspius, Gobio, Leuciscus, Tinca, Barbus, Alburnus, Carassius, Rhodeus, Cyprinus,* and *Scardinius.*

In the early or middle Miocene near Ankara, Turkey, two types of cyprinids are known. Paicheler *et al.* (1978) reported a leuciscine, *Leuciscus (Palaeoleuciscus) etilus,* and a cyprinine, *Barbus* sp. The vertebrate fauna associated with the fishes suggests a warm subtropical climate. Shallow lacustrine conditions prevailed in this region where the cyprinids were preserved.

Gaudant (1980b) revised the famous Miocene fish fauna of Öhningen, Germany and listed ten species from there, three of which are cyprinids: *Leuciscus (Palaeoleuciscus) oeningensis, Tinca furcata* and *'Lebias' furcatus,* which Gaudant recognized as an undescribed genus with a low number of vertebrae (35 or 36) and relatively long-based dorsal and anal fins with 13 or 14 principal rays. Rutte (1962) identified seven genera and described one new cyprinid genus (*Serrodens*) based on a study of the pharyngeal teeth recovered from Öhningen.

From eastern Europe, Gaudant (1977b, 1984b) described middle to late Miocene cyprinids belonging to the extant genera *Leuciscus* and *Rutilus.* The middle Miocene (Helvetian) cyprinids from Povea de Santeram (Gaudant, 1977b) are of two types (both undescribed) and known only from their pharyngeal teeth. The late Miocene (Turolian) locality from Ternal, Spain (Gaudant, 1984b) yielded a well-preserved cyprinid described as *'Rutilus' pachecri.* It appears to be a leuciscine, based on its forward anal fin suspension, but differs from the extant *Rutilus* in its short-based anal with seven principal rays.

Of special interest is the late Miocene (Messinian) cyprinid referred to *Leuciscus oeningensis* Agassiz by Cavallo and Gaudant (1987). This cyprinid was found in brackish lagoonal deposits of Cherasco, (Piedmont, Italy) and may have been able to disperse in salt water similar to *Tribolodon hakonensis* of Japanese waters. The Cherasco cyprinid was found in association with marine or brackish-water species of the families Gobiidae, Mugilidae and Cyprinodontidae. Additionally, a salmonid assigned to the genus *Salvelinus* occurred at the locality and was taken as an indicator of cool climatic conditions at that latitude in the late Miocene.

Members of the family Cobitidae first appeared in Europe with cyprinids in the Miocene and Pliocene deposits. From the Czechoslovakian oil shales, Laube (1901) described *'Noemachilus' tenes.* The generic assignment was questioned by Obrhelová (1970c). From the Pliocene lignitic shales of France Gaudant (1976) referred a fossil cobitid to the extant species *Cobitis taenia.*

A note on characoid fishes from Europe. Characoids have been known from Eocene lake deposits of central France for many years (review, Weitzman, 1962). These specimens were described under the two genera *Prohydrocyon* and *Procharacinus.* Gaudant (1980a) described complete specimens of a lower

Eocene characoid from western France which he named *Eurocharax tourainei*. They were found in brackish-water sediments deposited along the margin of a shallow marine embayment. Gaudant (1980a) discussed in detail the evidence for saltwater tolerance of these early characiform fishes and their palaeoecologic significance. Somewhat younger characiform teeth are now known from the early Oligocene of France (Gaudant, 1979b). Patterson (1975) listed an Eocene characoid fossil from England and later commented on the characoid fossil record in general (Patterson, 1984a). He mentioned a Palaeocene record from North Africa and possible late Cretaceous characiform teeth from Bolivia, described by Gayet (1982).

Summary of the European fossil Cyprinidae

The earliest fossil cyprinid reported in the literature is '*Blicca*' *croydonensis* from the early Eocene beds of the London Basin. The incomplete, single specimen does not fit well with any extant cyprinid genus and it may be incorrectly assigned to the Cyprinidae. However, it might belong to a primitive cypriniform or cypriniphysan stem group and should be restudied to learn its systematic position. In continental Europe, cyprinids first appear in the mid-Oligocene of Germany and France. By the late Oligocene to early Miocene, cyprinids are known from France, Germany, Spain and Czechoslovakia. Some of the earliest European cyprinids (*Palaeoleuciscus*) belong to the subfamily Leuciscinae (clade Leuciscini) based on their anal fin suspension and median fin characters. Others (*Varhostichthys*) may be leuciscines of the tribe Tincini (Obrhelová, 1970a). Few forms are known in the European cyprinid fauna until Miocene times. By the late Miocene the Cyprinidae had diversified into many of the extant genera characteristic of today's European fauna. Members of the genus *Palaeotinca* appeared in the early to middle Miocene of south central Europe. Undoubted members of the subfamily Cyprininae with serrated spines (*Barbus*) are first known from the middle Miocene of Czechoslovakia. *Palaeocarassius*, a cyprinine very similar to the extent *Carassius*, was present in the late Miocene of Czechoslovakia. Cobitids apparently arrived in Europe during the early Miocene.

Of particular interest is the fact that at least 20 m.y before the cyprinids appeared in Europe, the characoid *Eurocharax* was living in brackish water along the coastal margin of western France and other characiforms were in Eocene freshwater habitats of France. The early Eocene date for *Eurocharax* also makes it slightly younger than the oldest known characoid fossil from Africa (Palaeocene).

North America

The oldest cyprinids from North America are Oligocene in age. Three forms are under study at the Ohio State University Museum of Zoology. All three come from plant-bearing lacustrine shales at three different sites in the Pacific North-west of the United States and represent extinct genera. Their pharyngeal teeth show that cyprinids were well differentiated into a variety of feeding types by the middle to late Oligocene time in North America. The two forms closest to the Pacific margin belong to the western clade of North American cyprinids (Coburn and Cavender, in press). The cyprinids are dated as Oligocene (probably middle to late Oligocene) by their associated floras. The cyprinid from northern California was preserved in sediments laid down in a cypress (*Taxodium*) swamp probably similar to that now occurring in the Mississippi and Arkansas River bottom lands. The cyprinid from farther north (southern Washington) on the Pacific slope is associated with an extinct salmonid, *Eosalmo*. It has a stout pharyngeal arch similar to that of the extant *Mylocheilus*. The third Oligocene fossil cyprinid comes from the John Day Basin of Oregon and is associated with leaves of the famous Bridge Creek Flora of the lower John Day Formation. The flora in the basal part of the John Day Formation was dated radiometrically as 31.1 m.y BP (Evernden and James, 1964). The date comes close to that of the mid-Oligocene cool maximum (30–31 m.y BP, Prothero, 1989). The lower John Day Formation has also yielded a fossil mudminnow, *Novumbra oregonensis* (Cavender, 1969), and an extinct catostomid referable to the genus *Amyzon*.

Early Miocene cyprinids are known from several Arikareean sites in western Montana. These sites are just east of the present Continental Divide. Cyprinid pharyngeals that come from the fish bearing lenses in the Cabbage Patch Beds are associated with centrarchid and amiid remains. Other early to mid-Miocene sedimentary basins in southwestern Montana such as Flint Creek and Gold Creek (Rasmussen, 1973) have also yielded cyprinid pharyngeals.

Eastman (1917) illustrated a small cyprinid he incorrectly assigned to *Osmerus* from the middle Miocene 'Cement Plant Beds' of the Madison River Valley. This cyprinid occurs in lacustrine shales and represents an undescribed form; I have recently collected additional material of this species. One of the rarest Miocene cyprinids comes from the lake shales preserved on top of Sentinel Butte in western North Dakota. The associated centrarchid remains indicate that the age of these shales is probably middle Miocene. The pharyngeal arch of the Sentinel Butte species shares characters with that of the eastern cyprinid genus *Semotilus*.

Unlike the Oligocene and early Miocene, by late Miocene times cyprinids were widely distributed in western North America. Late Miocene to Pliocene cyprinid sites are known from western Oregon, Idaho, Nevada, Arizona, California, Texas, Kansas, and Nebraska. Uyeno (1960), Smith (1981) and Cross *et al.* (1986) review the late Cenozoic records of fossil cyprinids. More than 12 extant genera are represented in the late Cenozoic of North America. In Mexico, cyprinids are not known until the Pliocene (Miller and Smith, 1986; Smith *et al.*, 1975).

The best-known late Cenozoic cyprinid fauna is from the Fossil Lake Idaho–Snake River basin where both lacustrine and fluviatile sediments accumulated from the late Miocene to well into the Pleistocene (Smith, 1975). The Miocene cyprinids came from the western part of the lake basin in south-east Oregon and are found at sites in the Deer Creek Formation. The Pliocene records came from the Glenns Ferry Formation of Idaho (Smith, 1975), and Pleistocene records came from floodplain sediments that overlie it.

The Pliocene Lake Idaho cyprinid fauna has been studied in detail by Smith (1975), who has clearly demonstrated the relationships of the Lake Idaho cyprinids to extant taxa. Ten species belonging to eight genera (one of which is extinct) have been described. The Miocene–Pliocene fossils found in the fluviatile and lacustrine sediments of the Lake Idaho–Snake River Basin demonstrate the extent of the adaptive radiation and trophic specialization achieved by North American Cyprinidae before the end of the Cenozoic.

I have examined nearly all the major museum fossil collections for cyprinid material of Oligocene or older age (Cavender, 1986). Other workers also have examined the collections, and no cyprinids have been found older than mid-Oligocene. Well-known fossil sites (e.g. Florissant, radiometrically dated to 34–38 m. y BP, Epis, 1969), have yielded many thousands of fossil specimens of plants and insects along with a modest number of fishes, but no Cyprinidae. The Green River Formation has produced enormous numbers of fossil fishes, especially at the middle Eocene Fossil Butte and Farson localities (Grande, 1980). In British Columbia, Wilson (1977) did not find cyprinids at any of the middle Eocene localities that produced so many other fishes. Many other early Oligocene, Eocene and Palaeocene fish-producing sites from North America have failed to yield cyprinid fossils. Therefore, it appears that cyprinids arrived during the mid-Oligocene at middle latitudes in North America, appearing first in the Pacific North-west near the continental margin.

Summary of the North American cyprinid record
Although the North American fossil fish record is filled with stratigraphic gaps and is biased towards the western half of the continent, the fossil history of cyprinids is better known here than in any geographic area but Europe. A few cyprinid localities are present from the Oligocene and indicate that the Cyprinidae first appeared in North America about 31 m. y BP, in mid-Oligocene times. The fossil sites lie between 40° and 44° N latitude and are associated with fossil *Taxodium* floras, indicating climatic cooling since the middle Eocene. The appearance of cyprinids at 40° N may have coincided with a world-wide cooling maximum and a pronounced lowering of sea level. These facts support the idea that cyprinids moved south from higher latitudes in response to climatic changes, both in Europe and North America. Cyprinids may also have reached North America from Asia across the Bering Land Bridge when the sea level was lowered during the mid-Oligocene. Initially, cyprinids belonging to the subfamily Leuciscinae first migrated into both Europe and North America. Most cyprinids now living at northern latitudes are leuciscines or derivatives of this group, and in North America all are phoxinins except a single leuciscin genus, *Notemigonus*.

Siberia

Many taxa have been reported from Neogene localities in western Siberia (Sytchevskaya, 1980). The fossil cyprinid fauna is very similar to that described for the Neogene of Europe. Soviet authors such as V. V. Bogachev and B. A. Schtylko (papers cited in Danil'chenko, 1967 and Sytchevskaya, 1980) gave a long list of genera. Lebedev (1959) worked on the Neogene fauna of western Siberia, and Yakovlev (1960, 1961) commented on the fauna and discussed its zoogeographic significance. Bănărescu (1960) also stressed the importance and close relationship of the Siberian fauna to that of Europe and mentioned the fossil taxa. Bănărescu (1973) developed the thesis that much of the European freshwater fish fauna originated in Siberia. Sytchevskaya (1980) listed the following nominal cyprinid genera as occurring in the Neogene of western Siberia: *Abramis*, *Alburnoides*, *Alburnus*, *Aspiurnus*, *Aspius*, *Blicca*, *Carassius*, *Chondrostoma*, *Gobio*, *Hemibarbus*, *Leuciscus*, *Rutilus*, *Scardinius* and *Tinca*. All but *Carassius* are members of the Leuciscinae. Nearly all are represented today in the European fauna. Danil'chenko (1967) listed *Cyprinus* from the Palaeogene of Siberia. In the western Soviet Union, Yakovlev (1959) described a cyprinine, *Barbus orientalis*, from the Upper Miocene of the Caucasus.

Africa

Greenwood (1974) and Van Couvering (1977) have reviewed the Cenozoic freshwater fish records in Africa. The fossil record for cyprinids in Africa is poorer than those of North America and Europe. All reported occurrences are either *Barbus*-like or *Labeo*-like forms. The earliest records for African Cyprinidae are from several localities in the late early Miocene of Kenya (Van Couvering, 1977). Other cyprinid localities in Kenya are dated somewhat later in the Miocene, and there are middle Miocene cyprinid remains from the Beglia Formation of Tunisia (Greenwood, 1973). In Pliocene deposits, Greenwood (1972) reported *Labeo* and *Barbus* from a site at Fish Hill, Wadi Natrun, Egypt. In the western Rift Valley region, which has been intensively searched for vertebrate fossils, the earliest records are middle Pleistocene at Katunda, Tanzania (Greenwood and Howes, 1975). Miocene records are in northern and eastern Africa. Only Pleistocene records are known from central Africa (Zaire) and large areas of the western and southern parts of the continent are without a cyprinid fossil record. The African cyprinid fauna consists mostly of three clades: a large labeonin clade as defined by Reid (1985), a barbin clade (Howes, 1987) and a barilin clade including the African neobolin group (Howes 1980, 1984). These three clades share a distributional pattern which includes Africa and South East Asia. Van Couvering (1977) and Greenwood (1973) interpreted the fossil record in Africa to indicate that cyprinids must have migrated from South East Asia through the Near East and entered Africa in late early Miocene times about 18 m. y BP. This coincides with the

African–Eurasian land-mammal exchange made possible by the continental drift of the African plate into the Eurasian continent. Van Couvering (1977) and Menon (1964) suggested that other freshwater fishes (e.g. clariids and members of the genus *Garra*) also entered Africa from Asia by this Middle Eastern route.

India

The Indian subcontinent has the poorest record for cyprinid fossils of any region reviewed, despite considerable palaeontological work in the Neogene Siwalik Hills. Menon (1959) compiled an extremely useful bibliography for the fossil fishes of India. The oldest published cyprinid record (Hora, 1938) is for 'cyprinid' scales from the lower Palaeogene (Palaeocene?) Intertrappean beds of the Central Provinces. However, scales are poor diagnostic fossils for the Cyprinidae because scale characters overlap between Cyprinidae, Catostomidae and Characoidea.

Asian–Oriental Region

Sytchevskaya (1986) investigated Palaeogene cyprinids from the USSR and Mongolia, described several new genera, and listed taxa for several localities. The oldest cyprinid fossils such as *Parabarbus* are from the middle Eocene of Kazakhstan. The fossils identified included pharyngeal teeth. Sytchevskaya showed that by lower- to mid-Oligocene times cyprinids became more numerous in North Asia. Palaeogene records included *Rutilus* , *Palaeotinca* and *Tribolodon* of the Leuciscinae, and *Parabarbus, Eodiptychus* and *Schizothorax* of the Cyprininae. The North Asian Palaeogene (Oligocene) fauna was dominated by cyprinoids (catostomids and cyprinids). Sytchevskaya (1986) believed that the Eurosiberian cyprinid fauna surviving today and represented by the many Neogene fossils reviewed above (p. 43) was derived from the older North Asian one.

Some Neogene cyprinid localities are known from Japan. The oldest is Miocene in age. Uyeno *et al.* (1975) referred specimens from a late Cenozoic locality of Oita Prefecture to three extant Japanese species: *Hemibarbus barbus, Zacco temminkii* and *Acheilognathus lanceolata*. Inoue and Uyeno (1968) discussed an unnamed cypriniform fossil from the Eocene Horokabetsu Formation of Central Hokkaido; this specimen lacked the head and tail necessary for accurate determination to family. Uyeno (1978) reported the first fossil record of *Cyprinus carpio* from Taiwan but its age was not precisely determined (Miocene–Pleistocene). Nakajima (1986) reported Pliocene cyprinid pharyngeal teeth from Japan and reviewed the Neogene cyprinid records.

From the Miocene of Thailand, Uyeno (1969) reported *Puntius* and an undescribed cyprinid similar to the genus *Hypophthalmichthys*.

In the Palaeogene of Hunan Province, China (Hsiawangu Formation), Cheng (1962) described an extinct species of *Osteochilus* and assigned another to the Recent species *O. linliensis*. This taxonomic determination indicates that the locality may be younger than suggested by Cheng (late Tertiary instead of early Tertiary). Liu and Su (1962) described a Pliocene fauna from the Yushe basin, Shanxi, China. Danil'chenko (1967) listed four genera: *Leuciscus, Carassius, Pseudorasbora,* and *Ctenopharyngodon* from the Pliocene of China. The genus *Cyprinus* was also listed from the Palaeogene of China; Young and Chow (1956) reviewed some of the discoveries. Liu (1957) described a new cyprinid fish from Guangdon (Kwangtung), China and Chang and Chow (1978) and Zhang and Zhou (1986) published additional records for taxa included in the leuciscin, xenocyprinin and cyprinin groups.

Sumatra in Indonesia produced an important series of cyprinid fossils (Günther, 1876; Sanders, 1934). The fauna may be as old as Eocene which would make it one of the few Palaeogene localities in South East Asia, but most species have been assigned to extent genera, indicating a possible Miocene or younger age. Seven cyprinid species were described: *Rasbora antiqua, Rasbora mohri, Thynnichthys amblyostoma, Osteochilus fossilis, Puntius bussyi, Barbus megacephalus* and *Eocypris sumatranus*. Only the last (*Eocypris*) is extinct. The Leuciscinae is represented by *Rasbora* and the Cyprininae by *Osteochilus, Thynnichthys, Puntius, Barbus,* and *Eocyprinus*. Reid (1985) considered *Osteochilus* a member of his subfamily Labeoninae.

Summary of the Asian–Oriental Region
What little is known of the fossil record of cyprinids in eastern Asia suggests that they had a long history there. Some fossils are as old as middle Eocene and indicate that a diversified cyprinid fauna may have existed in the Paleogene. Many zoogeographers (Darlington, 1957; Briggs, 1979; Bănărescu, 1972) locate the centre of the origin for the Cyprinidae in the Oriental region, where almost all the major groups and subgroups of cyprinids now live. From this evolutionary centre, cyprinids have dispersed to other geographic regions. The fossil record does not refute this hypothesis, because fewer groups of cyprinids are present further from the Asian–Oriental region (i.e. in Europe, Africa, and North America).

2.3   DISCUSSION

Fossil record

Patterson (1975, 1984a, b) has commented on the fossil record for the ostariophysans and otophysans (*sensu* Rosen and Greenwood, 1970), pointing out that these are ancient groups which were widespread in the late Mesozoic. Patterson (1984a) described in detail a marine otophysan, *Chanoides*, from the Eocene of Monte Bolca, Italy which he concluded was the sister group to all

Recent otophysans (cypriniforms, characiforms, siluriforms). Most new knowledge gained from the fossil *Chanoides* underscored Patterson's remarks on how little is known about ostariophysan phylogeny and fossil history.

Judging from the few jaw teeth discovered, characiforms are at least as old as late Cretaceous or Palaeocene and, although no undoubted fossils exist, it is reasonable to assume that cypriniforms may be just as old. At least two cypriniform families, the Catostomidae and Cyprinidae, were in evidence by the middle Eocene and it is likewise reasonable to assume that the Cobitidae were established by the middle Eocene. If the cladistic arrangement of cypriniform families (Siebert, 1987) is used, the fossil record for one group can shed light on the other (as far as minimum age and place of origin).

Catostomids have a much better Eocene fossil record than do cyprinids. The oldest North American suckers are *Amyzon gosiutensis* from the middle Eocene Green River Formation (Grande *et al.*, 1982) and *A. aggregatum* from the middle Eocene lacustrine shales of British Columbia (Wilson, 1977). These species are very similar to each other and are obviously closely related. The report of suckers from the Palaeocene Paskapoo Formation of Canada (as cited in Cavender, 1986) has proven to be an incorrect interpretation of Wilson's (1980) work. Wilson identified the fossils in question as cyprinoids that could be catostomids.

Fossil suckers were widespread in western North America during the Palaeogene (review, Cavender, 1986). In Asia, a diverse assemblage of fossil suckers are known from the late Eocene of Mongolia and the Eocene–Oligocene of Kazakhstan and Siberia (Hussakof, 1932; Sytchevskaya, 1986). Interestingly, they probably belong to different genera well removed from the extant Chinese sucker *Myxocyprinus*. From what is known, catostomids were widespread in western North America and eastern Asia by late Eocene times; however, cyprinids also living in Asia at similar latitudes during the Palaeogene apparently did not reach North America (or at least south to the latitude $40°$ N) until 20 m. y later.

Correlation of climatic change with the first appearance of the Cyprinidae

The Cyprinidae is the largest freshwater family of fishes. Where cyprinids exist today in the lakes and streams of North America and Europe, for example, they tend to dominate in the numbers of species and individuals. This probably was not always so, because the fossil record indicates that cyprinids had a slow beginning in the late Palaeogene and did not begin their extensive radiation at temperate latitudes until the Miocene in both Europe and North America.

The Eocene freshwater deposits in these two continents are strikingly similar in certain aspects of their fish faunas. During middle Eocene times about 50 m. y BP, the climate was much warmer than today at the same latitude (Wolfe, 1978, 1981). Fossils from the Green River Formation of Wyoming indicate rich subtropical forest vegetation along with heat-loving animals like crocodiles and freshwater sting-rays. The fish fauna of the Green River Formation consisted of archaic elements such as bowfins, gars, a gonorhynchid ostariophysan, osteoglossiforms, and various types of primitive, freshwater percoids ('percichthyids'). The middle Eocene faunas of Europe, such as in the Lutetian Messel oil shale of Germany, possessed most of these groups of fishes. North American Eocene faunas differed in one major aspect, the presence of two groups of otophysan fishes: the suckers (Catostomidae) and freshwater catfishes (Hypsidoridae and Ictaluridae).

At the close of the Eocene a major extinction event eliminated many aquatic and terrestrial forms, including some freshwater fishes. This event is now correlated with a world-wide change in climate as temperatures dropped significantly below those of the middle Eocene. Prothero (1989) has pointed out that the extinctions which make up the 'Terminal Eocene Event' are actually a complex series of stepwise events spanning over 10 m. y rather than a simple, abrupt occurrence. Prothero also discussed the rapid and continuing changes in interpretation of the Palaeogene time scale which up to now have been most confusing. Improved radiometric methods place the Eocene–Oligocene boundary between 33.5 and 34 m. y BP, considerably later than the value (36.5) used by Berggren *et al.* (1985). Two late Eocene extinction events occurred at about 40 and 38 m. y BP, and the mid-Oligocene event at about 30.5 m. y BP. Prothero (1989) showed that four extinction events spaced about 2 m. y apart took place near the end of the Eocene, beginning about 40 m. y BP. He looked for a cause that would induce climatic stress over a 10 m. y interval when a 10 °C cooling in global temperatures took place. These postulated climatic changes centre on the alterations in ocean currents resulting from the separation of Australia from Antarctica, and the possible occurrence of Antarctic glaciation and formation of Antarctic sea ice. Furthermore, the opening of the Greenland–Norway passage, allowing exchange between Arctic and Atlantic waters, may have occurred near the Eocene–Oligocene boundary.

The mid-Oligocene event with the most severe cooling was marked by one of the biggest sea-level drops in Tertiary history. Sea level was thought to have dropped significantly more than the maximum fluctuation during the Pleistocene (Vail *et al.*, 1977; Vail and Hardenbol, 1979).

In general, climatic cooling as shown in fossil assemblages of North America and Europe resulted in the replacement of the mid-Eocene tropical forests by cypress (*Taxodium*) swamps and reed marshes in the late Eocene (Prothero, 1989). European forests tended to be replaced by open semi-humid vegetation, and forest-dwelling mammals were replaced by ground-dwelling, grazing herbivores adapted to open country. The replacement of tropical biomes by temperate ones in the areas mentioned could also be interpreted as a southward shift of the biomes in response to the change in climate.

Fishes associated with cool water (e.g. Tertiary osmerids and esocids) began to appear in the early Oligocene faunas of Europe. During the mid-Oligocene a few cyprinid genera appeared in both North America and Europe. The Oligocene cyprinids of Europe are represented by the subfamily Leuciscinae.

Pharyngeal teeth of the Oligocene cyprinids suggest an insectivorous diet similar to that of many cyprinids living today. There may be a correlation between the first record of cyprinids at temperate latitudes in North America and Europe and the Oligocene radiation of insects; the number of insect families in North America increased greatly in the Oligocene epoch (Wilson, 1978a, b). Some important food sources for freshwater fishes first appeared in the Oligocene, and in some insect groups such as the Diptera the number of families has increased since the Oligocene.

2.4 SUMMARY AND CONCLUSIONS

The earliest cyprinid fossils are of Eocene age in Eurasia and Oligocene age in North America. Some identifications or age determinations are uncertain. The early Eocene '*Blicca' croydonensis* is based on incomplete material and is only questionably referred to the Cyprinidae. The Eocene cyprinid fauna from Sumatra with six genera does not have a well-established age based on radio-isotope dating, and may be younger than Eocene. Early Tertiary deposits from northern and central Asia contain both cyprinids and catostomids. The oldest Asian cyprinids belong to a middle Eocene fauna from Kazakhstan and have been assigned to the extinct genus *Parabarbus*. By early Oligocene times, representatives of the two major cyprinid phyletic groups (Leuciscinae and Cyprininae) were in evidence. Cyprinids probably dominated freshwater ichthyofaunas as early as the Oligocene in parts of Asia, but apparently not until the Miocene in Siberia, Europe and North America. The European and Siberian Miocene cyprinid faunas are very similar in composition and are most likely of a common Asiatic origin. Several phyletic groups are represented in these assemblages, including the cyprinins, barbins, gobionins, tincins, acheilognathins, leuciscins and phoxins. The North American Miocene cyprinid fauna belongs to one phyletic group, the Phoxinini, that may have crossed the Bering land-bridge during earrly Tertiary times. The leuciscins also may have made the crossing, but left only one descendant in *Notemigonus*. No known fossil cyprinid genera are shared between North America and Eurasia, but Europe and Siberia share an impressive number of taxa, including *Abramis, Alburnus, Aspius, Blicca, Carassius* or *Palaeocarassius, Chondrostoma, Gobio, Leuciscus, Rutilus, Scardinius, Tinca* and *Palaeotinca*. Excluding South America and Australia, Africa was the last major land area to be invaded by the Cyprinidae. This occurred in the Miocene, about 18 m.y BP. Barilins, labeonins and barbins had successful radiations in Africa following their immigration.

Radiation of cyprinids into many specialized feeding types had occurred by the late Miocene in the Euro–Siberian region and also about the same time in western North America. In East and North Asia, the fossil record indicates a somewhat earlier cyprinid radiation at the end of the Palaeogene. The correlation of cyprinid radiation with global climatic change and the first appearance of many insect families presents an interesting problem for further research.

ACKNOWLEDGEMENTS

I would like to thank J. S. Nelson and M. V. H. Wilson, of the University of Alberta, for their critical comments on the manuscript. R. LeHew, of the Ohio State University, provided considerable assistance in word processing of the manuscript and bibliography. L. Grande of the Field Museum of Natural History provided bibliographic assistance.

REFERENCES

Andrews, S. M., Gardiner, B. G., Miles, R. S. and Patterson, C. (1967) Pisces, in *The Fossil Record: A Symposium With Documentation*, Geological Society of London, pp. 637–83.

Bănărescu, P. (1960) Einige fragen zur Herkunft und Verbreitung der Süsswasserfisch-fauna der Europaisch–Mediterranen unterregion. *Arch. Hydrobiol.*, **57** (1/2), 16–134.

Bănărescu, P. (1972) The zoogeographical position of the East Asian fresh-water fish fauna. *Revue roum. Biol. Zool.* **17**, 315–23.

Bănărescu, P. (1973) Some reconsiderations on the zoogeography of the Euro-Mediterranean fresh-water fish fauna. *Revue roum. Biol. Zool.* **18**, 257–64.

Berggren, W. A. (1986) Geochronology of the Eocene–Oligocene, in *Terminal Eocene Events* (eds C. Pomerol and I. Premoli-Silva), Elsevier, Amsterdam, pp. 349–56.

Berggren, W. A., Kent, D. V. and Flynn, J. J. (1985) Paleogene geochronology and chronostratigraphy, in *The Chronology of the Geological Record* (ed. N. J. Snelling), *Mem. geol. Soc. Lond.* **10**, pp. 141–95.

Briggs, J. C. (1979) Ostariophysan zoogeography: an alternative hypothesis. *Copeia*, **1979**, 111–18.

Cabrera, Ll. and Gaudant, J. (1985) Los Ciprínidos (Pisces) del sistema lacustre Oligocénico–Miocénico de los Monegros (sector SE de la Cuenca del Ebro, provincias de Lleida, Tarragona, Huesca y Zaragoza). *Acta geòl. Hisp.* **20** (3/4), 219–26.

Cavallo, O. and Gaudant, J. (1987) Observations complémentaires sur l'ichthyofauna des Marnes Messiniennes de Cherasco (Piémont): implications géodynamiques. *Boll. Soc. paleont. ital.* **26** (1–2), 177–98.

Cavender, T. M. (1969) An Oligocene mudminnow (family Umbridae) from Oregon with remarks on relationships within the Esocoidei. *Occ. Pap. Mus. Zool. Univ. Mich.*, **660**, 1–33.

Cavender, T. M. (1986) Review of the fossil history of North American freshwater fishes, in *The Zoogeography of North American Freshwater Fishes* (eds. C. H. Hocutt and E. O. Wiley), John Wiley & Sons, NY, pp. 699–724.

Cavender, T. M. and Coburn, M. M. (in press). Phylogenetic relationships of North American Cyprinidae, in, *Systematics, Historical Ecology, and North American*

Freshwater Fishes. (ed. R. L. Mayden), Stanford Univ. Press, Palo Alto, Calif.

Chang, Mee-mann [= Zhang Miman] and Chia-chien Chow (1978) On the fossil fishes in Mesozoic and Cenozoic oil-bearing strata from East China and their sedimentary environment. *Vertebrata Palasiatica*, **16**, 229–37.

Chen, X., Yue, P. and Lin, R. (1984) Major groups within the family Cyprinidae and their phylogenetic relationships. *Acta Zootaxon. Sinica*, **9**, 424–40.

Cheng, C. C. (1962) Fossil fishes from the early Tertiary of Hsiang-Hsiang, Hunan, with a discussion of the age of the Hsiawanpu Formation. *Vertebr. palasiat.* **6**, 342–3.

Coburn, M. M. and Cavender, T. M. (in press) Interrelationships of North American cyprinid fishes, in *Systematics, Historical Ecology, and North American Freshwater Fishes* (ed. R. L. Mayden), Stanford Univ. Press, Palo Alto, Calif.

Cross, F. B., Mayden, R. L. and Stewart, J. D. (1986) Fishes in the western Mississippi basin (Missouri, Arkansas and Red Rivers), in *The Zoogeography of North American Freshwater Fishes* (eds C. H. Hocutt and E. O. Wiley), John Wiley & Sons, NY, pp. 363–412.

Danil'chenko, P. G. (1967) Superorder Teleostei, in *Fundamentals of Paleontology*, **11**, Israel Program for Scientific Translations, Jerusalem, pp. 603–712.

Darlington, P. J. jun. (1957) *Zoogeography: The Geographical Distribution of Animals*, John Wiley, NY.

Eastman, C. R. (1917) Fossil fishes in the collection of the United States National Museum. *Proc. U.S. natu. Mus.*, **52**, 235–304.

Epis, R. C. (1969) Proposed Florissant Fossil Beds National Monument. *Mines Mag.*, **59**(5), 10–13.

Evernden, J. F. and James, G. T. (1964) Potassium–argon dates and the Tertiary floras of North America. *Am. J. Sci.*, **262**, 945–74.

Fink, S. V. and Fink, W. L. (1981) Interrelationships of the ostariophysan fishes (Teleostei). *Zool. J. Linn. Soc.*, **72**, 297–353.

Gaudant, J. (1975) Présence du genre *Tinca* Cuv. (Poisson Téléostéen, Cypriniforme) dans le Villafranchien de Senèze (Haute-Loire). *Geobios, Lyon*, **8**, 353–4.

Gaudant, J. (1976) Découverte d'un Cobitidae (Poisson Téléostéen, Cypriniforme) dans le Pliocene continental des environs de Rochefort-Montagne (Puy-De-Dome). *Geobios, Lyon*, **9**, 673–9.

Gaudant, J. (1977a) Nouvelles observations sur l'ichthyofaune stampienne d'Oberdorf (Canton de Soleure). *Eclog. geol. Helv.*, **70**, 789–809.

Gaudant, J. (1977b) Contributions à la paléontologie du Miocène moyen. Continental du basin du tage II. Observations sur les dents pharyngiennes de poissons cyprinidés Póvoa de Santarém. *Ciênc. Terra*, **3**, 129–41.

Gaudant, J. (1978) Découverte du plus ancien representant connu du genre *Esox* L. (Poisson Téléostéen, Esocoidei) dan le Stampien moyen du bassin d'Apt (Vaucluse). *Géol. Méd.*, **5**, 257–68.

Gaudant, J. (1979a) Contribution a l'étude des vertébrés Oligocénes de Soluce (Canton du Jura). *Eclog. geol. Helv.*, **72**, 871–95.

Gaudant, J. (1979b) Sur la présence de dents de Characidae (Poissons Téléostéens, Ostariophysi) dans les 'Calcaires a Bythinies' et les 'Sables Bleutes' du Var. *Geobios, Lyon*, **12**, 451–7.

Gaudant, J. (1980a) *Eurocharax tourainei* (Poisson Téléostéen, Ostariophysi): nouveau Characidae fossile des 'Calcaires a Bythinies' du Var. *Geobios, Lyon*, **13**, 683–703.

Gaudant, J. (1980b) Mise au point sur l'ichthyofaune miocéne d'Öhningen (Baden, Allemagne). *C.r. hebd. Séanc. Acad. Sci. Paris*, **291D**, 1033–6.

Gaudant, J. (1984a) Nouvelles recherches sur les Cyprinidae (Poissons Téléostéens) Oligocènes des limagnes. *Geobios, Lyon*, **17**, 659–66.

Gaudant, J. (1984b) Sur les poissons fossiles (Téléostéens, Cyprinidae) des gypses

Turoliens du Fosse de Teruel: essai d'approche paleoécologique. *Estudios geol. Inst. Invest. geol. Lucas Mallada*, **40**, 463–72.

Gaudant, J. (1985) Mise en évidence d'Osmeridae (Poissons Téléostéens, Salmoniformes) dans l'Oligocène lacustre d'Europe occidentale. *C.r. hebd. Séanc. Acad. Sci. Paris*, Ser. II, **300** (2), 79–82.

Gaudant, J. (1988) Mise au point sur l'ichthyofaune oligocène de Rott, Stösschen et Orsberg (Allemagne), *C.r. hebd. Séanc. Acad. Sci. Paris*, Ser. II, **306**, 831–4.

Gaudant, J. and Burkhardt, T. (1984) Sur la découverte de poissons fossiles dans les marnes grises rayées de la zone fossilifère (Oligocène basal) d'Altkirch (Haut-Rhin). *Sci. geol. Bull.*, **37** (2), 153–71.

Gaudant, J. and Rousset, C. (1979) Découverte de restes de Cyprinidae (Poissons Téléostéens) dans l'Oligocene moyen de Marseille (Bouches-du-Rhone). *Geobios,Lyon*, **12**, 331–7.

Gayet, M. (1982) Découverte dans le Crétacé supérieur de Bolivie des plus anciens Characiformes connus, *C. hebd. Séanc. Acad. Sci. Paris*, **294D**, 1037–40.

Grande, L. (1980) Paleontology of the Green River Formation, with a review of the fish fauna. *Bull. geol. Surv. Wyo.*, **63**, 1–333.

Grande, L., Eastman, J. T. and Cavender, T. M. (1982) *Amyzon gosiutensis*, a new catostomid fish from the Green River Formation. *Copeia*, **1982**, 523–32.

Greenwood, P. H. (1972) New fish fossils from the Pliocene of Wadi Natrun, Egypt. *J. Zool., Lond.*, **168**, 503–19.

Greenwood, P. H. (1973) Fish fossils of the Late Miocene of Tunisia. *Notes Serv. Géol. Tunisie*, **37**, 41–72.

Greenwood, P. H. (1974) Review of Cenozoic fish faunas in Africa. *Ann. Geol. Surv. Egypt*, **4**, 211–32.

Greenwood, P. H. and Howes, G. J. (1975) Neogene fossil fishes from the Lake Albert–Lake Edward Rift (Zaire). *Bull. Br. Mus. nat. Hist., Geol.*, **26** (3), 66–127.

Günther, A. (1876) Contributions to our knowledge of the fish-fauna of the Tertiary deposits of the Highlands of Padang, Sumatra. *Geol. Mag.*, **2** (3), 433–40.

Hora, S. L. (1938) On fossil fish scales from the Intertrappean beds at Deothan and Kheri, Central Provinces, *Rec. geol. Surv. India*, **73**, 267–94.

Howes, G. J. (1980) The anatomy, phylogeny and classification of the bariliine cyprinid fishes. *Bull. Br. Mus. nat. Hist., Zool.*, **37**, 129–98.

Howes, G. J. (1984) A review of the anatomy, taxonomy, phylogeny and biogeography of the African neoboline cyprinid fishes. *Bull. Br. Mus. nat. Hist., Zool.*, **47** (3), 151–85.

Howes, G. J. (1987) The phylogenetic position of the Yugoslavian cyprinid fish genus *Aulopyge* Heckel, 1841, with an appraisal of the genus *Barbus* Cuvier & Cloquet, 1861 and the subfamily Cyprinidae. *Bull. Br. Mus. nat. Hist., Zool.*, **52** (5), 165–96.

Hussakof, L. (1932). The fossil fishes collected by the Central Asiatic Expeditions, *Am. Mus. Novit.*, **553**, 1–19.

Ingersoll, R. V. and Ernst, W. G. (eds) (1987) *Cenozoic Basin Development of Coastal California*, Prentice–Hall, Englewood Cliffs, NJ.

Inoue, M. and Uyeno, T. (1968) Occurrence of two Paleogene fish fossils at Oyubari coal mine in central Hokkaido, Japan. *Bull. natu. Sci. Mus., Tokyo*, **11** (3), 319–26.

Laube, G. (1901) Synopsis der Wirbeltierefauna der böhmischen Braunkohlen Formation. *Abh. Lotos*, **2**, 107–86.

Lebedev, V. D. (1959) Neogene fauna of freshwater fishes in the Zaisan depression and the west Siberian lowland. *Vop. Ikhtiol.*, **12**, 28–69 (in Russian).

Liu, H. T. (1957) A new fossil cyprinid fish from Maoming, Kwangtung. *Vertebr. palasiat.*, **1** (1), 151–3.

Liu, H. T. and Su, T. (1962) Pliocene fishes from the Yushe basin, Shansi, *Vertebr. palasiat.*, **6** (1), 20.

Menon, A. G. K. (1959) Catalogue and bibliography of fossil fishes of India. *J. palaeont. Soc. India*, **4**, 51–60.

Menon, A. G. K. (1964) Monograph of the cyprinid fishes of the genus *Garra* Hamilton. *Mem. Indian Mus.* **14**(4), 173–260.

Miller, R. R. and Smith, M. L. (1986) Origin and geography of the fishes of central Mexico, in *The Zoogeography of North American Freshwater Fishes* (eds C. H. Hocutt and E. O. Wiley), John Wiley & Sons, NY, pp. 487–517.

Nakajima, T. (1986) Pliocene cyprinid pharyngeal teeth from Japan and East Asia: Neogene cyprinid zoogeography, in *Indo–Pacific Fish Biology: Proceedings of the Second International Conference on Indo–Pacific Fishes, Ichthyological Society of Japan, Tokyo* (eds. T. Uyeno, R. Arai, T. Taniuchi and K. Matsuura), pp. 502–13.

Obrhelová, N. (1969) Die Karpfenfische im tschechoslowakischen Süsswassertertiär. *Čas. Miner. Geol.*, **14**, 39–52.

Obrhelová, N. (1970a) Die osteologie der Vorläufer von *Tinca tinca* (Pisces) aus dem Süsswassertertiar der ČSSR. *Abh. Staatl. Mus. Mineral. Geol.*, *Dresden*, **16**, 99–209.

Obrhelová, N. (1970b) Fische aus den Süsswasserablagerungen des Villafranchium im Süden der ČSSR. *Geologie*, **19**, 569–87.

Obrhelová, N. (1970c) Fische aus dem Süsswassertertiär im Süden von Čechy. *Geologie*, **19**, 967–1001.

Obrhelová, N. (1971) Vergleichende osteologie der gattung '*Leuciscus*' (Pisces) aus tertiären Schichten der nördlichen und westlichen ČSSR. *Paläont. Abhandl.*, *Berlin* (A), **4**(3), 549–660.

Paicheler, J. C., Broin, F. de, Gaudant, G., Mourer-Chauvire, C., Rage, J. C. and Vergnaud-Grazzini, C. (1978) Le Bassin Lacustre Miocène de Bes-Konak (Anatolie-Turquie): Géologie et introduction à la paléontologie des vertébrés. *Geobios. Lyon*, **11**, 43–65.

Patterson, C. (1975) The distribution of Mesozoic freshwater fishes. *Mem. Mus. natn. Hist. Paris*, Ser. A, **88**, 156–74.

Patterson, C. (1984a) *Chanoides*, a marine Eocene otophysan fish (Teleostei: Ostariophysi). *J. Vert. Paleont.*, **4**, 430–56.

Patterson, C. (1984b) Family Chanidae and other teleostean fishes as living fossils, in *Living Fissils* (eds N. Eldredge and S. M. Stanley), Springer-Verlag, New York pp. 132–9.

Pomerol, C. (1982) *The Cenozoic Era, Tertiary and Quaternary*. Ellis Horwood Ltd, Chichester, 272 pp.

Prothero, D. R. (1989) Stepwise extinction and climatic decline during the later Eocene and Oligocene, in *Mass Extinctions* (ed. S. K. Donovan), Columbia Univ. Press, NY, pp. 217–34.

Rasmussen, D. L. (1973) Extension of the middle Tertiary unconformity into western Montana. *Northwest Geol.*, **2**, 27–35.

Reid, G. M. (1985) A revision of African species of *Labeo* (Pisces: Cyprinidae) and a re-definition of the genus. *Theses Zool.*, **6**, 1–322.

Romer, A. S. (1966) *Vertebrate Paleontology*, 3rd edn, The University of Chicago Press, Chicago and London, 468 pp.

Rosen, D. E. and Greenwood, P. H. (1970) Origin of the Weberian apparatus and the relationships of the ostariophysan and gonorphynchiform fishes. *Am. Mus. Novit.*, **2428**, 1–25.

Rutte, E. (1962) Schlundzähne von Süsswasserfischen. *Palaeontographica*, Abt A, **120**(4–6), 165–212.

Sanders, M. (1934) Die fossilen fische der Alttertiaren Süsswasserablagerungen aus Mittel–Sumatra. *Verh. Geol.-mijnb. Genoot. Ned.*, **11**, 1–143.

Siebert, D. J. (1987) Interrelationships among families of the order Cypriniformes (Teleostei), PhD dissertation, The City University of New York, 354 pp.

Smith, G. R. (1975) Fish of the pliocene Glenns Ferry Formation, southwest Idaho. *Pap. Paleontol. Mus. Paleontol. Univ. Mich.*, **14**, 1–68.

Smith, G. R. (1981) Late Cenozoic freshwater fishes of North America. *A. Rev. Ecol. Syst.*, **12**, 163–93.

Smith, M. L., Cavender, T. M. and Miller, R. R. (1975) Climatic and biogeographic significance of a fish fauna from the Late Pliocene–Early Pleistocene of the Lake Chapala Basin (Jalisco, Mexico), in *Studies on Cenozoic Paleontology and Stratigraphy* (eds. G. R. Smith and N. E. Friedland), Univ. Mich. Pap. Paleont., **12**, pp. 29–38.

Sytchevskaya, E. K. (1980) Order Cypriniformes, in *Fossil Bony Fishes of the USSR* (ed. L. E. Novitskaya), *Trudy Paleont. Inst. Akad. Nauk, SSSR*, **179**, 50–61 (in Russian).

Sytchevskaya, E. K. (1986) Paleogene freshwater fish fauna of the USSR and Mongolia. *Trans. Joint Soviet–Mongolian Paleontological Expedition*, **29**, 1–157 (in Russian with English summary).

Uyeno, T. (1960) Osteology and phylogeny of American cyprinid fishes allied to the genus *Gila*, PhD dissertation, Univ. Michigan, Ann Arbor, MI.

Uyeno, T. (1961) Late Cenozoic cyprinid fishes from Idaho with notes on other fossil minnows in North America. *Pap. Mich. Acad. Sci. Arts, Lett.*, **46**, 329–44.

Uyeno, T. (1969) Miocene fishes from Mae Sot Basin, northwestern Thailand. *Geol. Palaeontol. Southeast Asia*, **7**, 93–6.

Uyeno, T. (1978) A preliminary report on fossil fishes from Ts'o-chen, Tai-nan. *Sci. Rep. Geo. & Paleo., Taiwan Mus.*, **1**, 5–17.

Uyeno, T., Kimura, S. and Hasegawa, Y. (1975) Freshwater fishes from Late Cenozoic deposits in Kusu Basin, Oita Prefecture, Japan. *Mem. natl. Sci. Mus. (Tokyo)*, **8**, 57–66.

Vail, P. R. and Hardenbol, J. (1979) Sea-level changes during the Tertiary. *Oceanus*, **22**, 71–9.

Vail, P. R., Mitchum, R. M., jun. and Thompson, S., III (1977) Seismic stratigraphy and global changes of sea levels. Part 4: Global cycles of relative changes of sea level. *Am. Assoc. Petrol. Geol. Mem.* **26**, 83–97.

Van Couvering, J. A. H. (1977) Early records of freshwater fishes in Africa. *Copeia*, **1977**, 163–6.

Weiler, W. (1933) Die fischreste aus dem Oberpliozän von Willerhausen. *Arch. Hydrobiol.*, **25**, 291–304.

Weiler, W. (1934) Die fische des Steinheimer Beckens. *Palaeontographica*, **8**, 1–20.

Weiler, W. (1960) Die fischreste aus den Ziegeleitonen von Ravolzhausen bei Hanau (Hessen). *Notizbl. hess. Landesamt. Bodenforsch Wiesbaden*, **88**, 20–8.

Weiler, W. (1963) Die fischfauna des Tertiärs im oberrheinischen Graben, des Manzer–Beckens, des unteren Maintals und der Wetterau, unter besonderer Berücksichtigung des Untermiozäns. *Abh. senckenberg. naturforsch. Ges.*, **504**, 1–75.

Weiler, W. (1965) Die fischfauna des interglazialen Beckentons von Bilhausen bei Gottingen. *Neues Jb. Geol. Palaeont., Abh.*, **123** (2), 202–19.

Weiler, W. (1966) Die fischfauna des Helvets von Ivancice (Eibenschitz) in Mahren. *Paläont. Z.*, **40**, 118–43.

Weitzman, S. H. (1962) The systematic position of Piton's presumed Characid fishes from the Eocene of central France. *Stanford ichthyol. Bull.*, **7** (4), 114–23.

White, E. I. (1931) *The Vertebrate Faunas of the English Eocene*, Vol. 1, British Museum (Natural History), London, 123 pp.

Wilson, M. V. H. (1977) Middle Eocene freshwater fishes from British Columbia. *Contr. Life Sci. Div. R. Ont. Mus.*, **113**, 1–61.

Wilson, M. V. H. (1978a) Paleogene insect faunas of western North America. *Quaest. Entomol.*, **14**, 13–34.

Wilson, M. V. H. (1978b) Evolutionary significance of North American Paleogene insect faunas. *Quaest. Entomol.*, **14**, 35–42.

Wilson, M. V. H. (1980) Oldest known *Esox* (Pisces: Esocidae), part of a new Paleocene teleost fauna from western Canada. *Can. J. Earth Sci.*, **1783**, 307–12.

Wolfe, J. A. (1978) A paleobotanical interpretation of Tertiary climates in the northern hemisphere. *Am. Scient.*, **66**, 694–703.

Wolfe, J. A. (1981) A chronological framework for Cenozoic megafossil floras of northwestern North America and its relation to marine technology. *Spec. Pap. geol. Soc. Am.*, **184**, 39–47.

Yakovlev, V. N. (1959) *Barbus orientalis*, a new barbel species from the Upper Miocene of the Caucasus. *Materialy-k osnonovoni paleontology*, ii, Moskva, **3**, 121–2 (in Russian).

Yakovlev, V. N. (1960) Taxonomic position of freshwater fishes from the West Siberia Neogene. *Paleont. Zh.*, **3**, 102–8 (in Russian).

Yakovlev, V. N. (1961) Distribution of the freshwater fishes of the holarctic Neogene and zoogeographic zoning. *Vop. Ikhtiol.*, **I**(2), 209–20 (in Russian).

Young, C. C. and Chow, M. M. (1956) Latest discoveries in vertebrate paleontology in China. *Acta Scient. Sin.*, **5**, 603–10.

Zhang, Miman and Jiajian Zhou (1985) Tertiary fish fauna from coastal region of Bohai Sea. Memoirs of the Institute of Vertebrate Palaeontology and Palaeoanthropology, *Acad. sin.*, **17**, 1–60.

Chapter three

Morphometric investigations in cyprinid biology

S. A. Schaefer

3.1 INTRODUCTION

Following the publication of *Multivariate Morphometrics* (Blackith and Reyment, 1971), the field of morphometrics has witnessed a renaissance in both theory and practice. Bookstein (1977, 1982) attributed the theoretical foundation of morphometrics to D'Arcy Thompson's *On Growth and Form* (1942), which sought to express biological form in terms of physical laws. There followed a long period of quiescence, when little or no advancement to the conceptual framework was made. Meanwhile, the foundations of multivariate statistics were being laid by T. W. Anderson, R. A. Fisher, H. Hotelling, C. R. Rao, and others.

Several obstacles prevented application of multivariate statistics to biological problems. The absence of rapid computational techniques was partly overcome by the pocket calculator and was abolished by mainframe statistical packages. The availability and moderate cost of several packages for the microcomputer places multivariate statistical techniques within reach of many users. The second obstacle was somewhat more intractable: the choice of appropriate statistical methods for a given biological problem, and the attendant difficulty of interpreting the results. The problems posed by this second obstacle were the focus of Blackith and Reyment's book. They remark that practical experience is the only way a biologist may learn to choose and interpret his multivariate analyses (1971: *v*). Case studies were presented and analysed to illustrate the statistical background required and the often subtle, intuitive nature of biological interpretation involved in, for example, factor analysis.

Since 1977 there has been a return to the conceptual foundation of D'Arcy Thompson and a closer examination of the theoretical principles behind morphometric techniques (e.g. Bookstein, 1977, 1978, 1982; Bookstein *et al.*, 1985). While morphometrics can be broadly defined as a body of techniques for describing body form (Reist, 1986), a somewhat more narrowly defined usage is currently popular. Bookstein (1982: 451) views morphometrics as the empirical fusion of geometry and biology. Bookstein *et al.* (1985: 256) define morphometrics as 'the statistical analysis of biological homology treated as geometrical deformation'. The 'new morphometrics' of the Michigan Morphometrics Study Group (Bookstein *et al.*, 1985) is not simply about quantitative description of the phenotype, but also about phenotypic change with respect to a homology function in a multivariate setting.

Bookstein (1982: 451) remarked that the morphometric literature was oriented entirely with respect to application rather than methodology. The balance of treatment has now swung heavily in the favour of method. Biologists, especially non-systematists, may easily be confused by the proliferation of terms, techniques, and theoretical arguments favouring one method over another. The publication of *Morphometrics in Evolutionary Biology* (Bookstein *et al.*, 1985) marked a milestone in the synthesis of theory and method. One criticism of this book, however, has been the lack of clear applicability due to the lack of software for performing the suggested analyses. The 'shear' algorithm, written for Statistical Analysis System (SAS) by Les Marcus and David Swofford (see appendix A.5.1.2 of Bookstein *et al.*, 1985), is one of three notable exceptions and has been widely used. Bookstein *et al.* (1985: *ix*) stated that computer programs for the techniques described therein were being assembled into an exportable statistics package; none are yet available.

In this chapter I provide a general overview of the newer morphometric techniques and review some of their applications to cyprinid biology. For reviews of Bookstein *et al.* (1985) see Reyment (1986), Schindel (1986), Smith (1987), and Felley (1988). Section 3.2 gives an overview of methodology, e.g. data format, data acquisition, and measurement error. I briefly discuss statistical analyses and types of applications in Section 3.3 and review the few case studies involving cyprinid fishes in Section 3.4. While most applications have involved problems of systematics, the methods are general and may be applied to ecological, fisheries, and evolutionary investigations.

3.2   OVERVIEW OF MORPHOMETRICS

The specific goals of a morphometric approach are paramount to the appropriate choice of method. The fundamental goal is the description of form. Most applications of the method have sought contrasts between classes of objects as a guide to discrimination, be they individual shapes (i.e. organisms or their parts), populations, species, or communities.

Data

The new morphometrics offers no universal protocol for selecting variables to be studied, except that they be numerous and sample the entire form (Strauss and Bookstein, 1982: 114). Morphometric data typically fall into four categories (and often in some combination): distances, angles, co-ordinates, and radial functions of boundary outlines. Traditional data sets from bilaterally symmetric organisms (e.g. Hubbs and Lagler (1964) for fishes; Fig. 3.1) involve distance measures chosen by convention, often because of *a priori* notions of taxonomic value. Humphries *et al.* (1981). Strauss and Bookstein (1982), and Bookstein *et al.* (1985: 45–6) have criticized the use of such data on several grounds. First, these distances generally tend to be aligned with only a few axes, thereby biasing the potential contrasts toward longitudinal directions and resulting in an uneven coverage of form. Second, the choice of long distances, as opposed to short segments, can bias the covariance structure of the data. The information contained in short segments

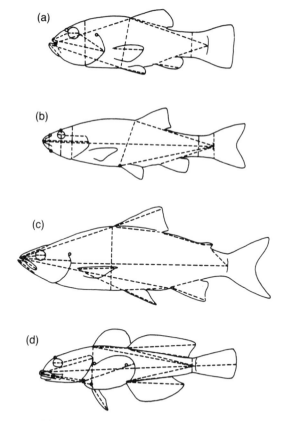

Fig. 3.1 Conventional distance measures for fish morphometrics. Dotted lines represent projections of measurements onto the midsagittal plane; small circles indicate positions of width measures. (a) *Cyprinodon*; (b) Cyprinidae; (c) ciscoes; (d) *Cottus*. (Reproduced with permission from Bookstein *et al.*, 1985.)

is more localized, with a tighter covariance among variables. Other objections stem from the omission of biological homology.

Bookstein *et al.* (1985: 144–52) present an example of the failure of traditional character sets to produce general contrasts among forms. The method of biorthogonal grids was used to model the patterns of shape change during growth by using shape data for two species of atherinid fishes. Their results indicated that the principal directions of growth were oriented at oblique angles relative to the longitudinal body axis. These directions are among those that are not sampled by traditional measures. The extent that different intraspecific growth trajectories contribute toward interspecific shape differences will dictate the degree to which such traditional data fail to describe significant shape contrasts.

Angles are rarely used as primary data (but see Tissot, 1988; Wie and Kennett, 1988). Measurement error for short distances can be propagated when extrapolated to longer distances. Some workers believe that expressing shape contrasts in terms of the angle between two points with reference to a third will remove the confounding effects of size. Departures from isometry in most circumstances violate this assumption and involve statistical problems similar to those caused by using ratios.

Landmarks and homology

The Michigan Group has argued for a different convention. They focus instead on homologous landmarks of form. Anatomical landmarks are identified by conventional rules of biological homology (spatial, ontogenetic, and phylogenetic congruence). Positions of the landmarks relative to a particular coordinate system become the raw data for analysis (Fig. 3.2). 'Extremal' variables, representing maximum or minimum distances, are strictly avoided since these rarely provide information on homology (Strauss and Bookstein, 1982: 114). Geometric location is thus wedded to biological homology. The geometric deformations indicated in the statistical analysis can thus be given an evolutionary or ontogenetic interpretation.

The insistence on homologous landmarks is an important contribution of the Michigan Group to the foundation of morphometric method. However, the procedure by which homologous landmarks are identified is not discussed (Felley, 1988) and deserves some comment. Homology in morphometrics does not adequately conform to the concept of biological homology; instead it merges geometric and phylogenetic definitions (Bookstein, 1982). Take the often-used landmark for fishes, the tip of the snout. Assuming that one can define the snout of a fish, how is the tip to be defined? Generally, this is defined as the most anterior point on the midline, projected perpendicularly with respect to the longitudinal body axis (suitably defined). But does this represent a true homologous comparison between forms? Let's say that the tip, so

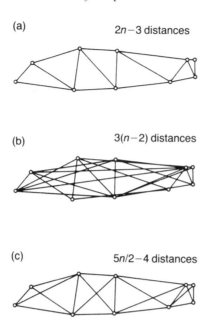

(a)   2n−3 distances

(b)   3(n−2) distances

(c)   5n/2−4 distances

Fig. 3.2 Patterns of distance measures between ten coplanar landmarks (circles, $n = 10$). (a) Triangulation; (b) 'globally redundant' design (Rohlf and Archie, 1978); (c) box truss. (Reproduced with permission from Bookstein *et al.*, 1985.)

defined, specifies some point on the premaxilla. At one level, premaxillae in a given group of fishes are homologous. The tip of the snout might not involve the premaxilla in both members of a pairwise comparison. In a group of closely related fishes that are phenetically similar, this is rather unlikely. But there is another level, that of intrinsic homology, or homology specific to the premaxilla. Does that most anterior point specify the same location on the premaxilla, relative to other homologous points on the bone, when comparing two forms? I suggest that in most cases it does not, but is determined by geometry alone. In the same way, the often-used landmark 'fin origin' may specify geometric rather than biological homology. Evolutionary loss of anterior fin elements across species produces one example where geometrical and biological landmark homologies do not correspond.

Geometric coordinates (i.e. Cartesian, polar, elliptic, etc.) are not considered to be acceptable data since they fail to incorporate homology information: e.g. Cartesian coordinates represent the distance from a point to a fixed line (the axis) which is arbitrarily defined. While the point does measure distance upon the form, the arbitrary reference axis carries no biological meaning. Bookstein *et al.* (1985: 50) point out one use of coordinates as raw data that does satisfy their criteria. The origin of the reference axis is set by the homologous landmarks themselves (e.g. origin [0.0] set at one landmark and y-axis passing through another landmark). In this way the data are co-ordinated, each point is measured with respect to two others, and all points are measured homologously from form to form.

In the absence of biological homology, such as occurs with shape outlines or arcs between homologous points, methods of orthogonal decomposition such as Fourier analysis can be applied. The Fourier method attempts to describe form in terms of a radius function: the distance from a central axis to the boundary outline as a function of angle relative to a starting reference ray, integrated over the entire outline (reviewed in Younker and Ehrlich, 1977; Rohlf and Ferson, 1983; Rohlf and Archie, 1984). Bookstein *et al.* (1982) dismiss Fourier analysis for representation of biological shape on the grounds that contrasts in shape are generally uninterpretable. The *n*th term in the Fourier series may not have biological meaning, especially with shapes having corners, requiring a large number of Fourier terms for adequate fit (Read and Lestrel, 1986). Bookstein *et al.* (1982: 92) accept Fourier analysis only in the complete absence of information on biological homology. But certain forms often lack homologous landmarks, or at least enough of them. Ehrlich *et al.* (1983) have criticized several of their objections on the grounds that they present only abstract examples where the method fails, unrelated to any real organisms. Ehrlich *et al.* (1983: 205) agree that Fourier descriptors may sometimes be difficult or impossible to interpret, but argue that this limitation can only be evaluated by empirical studies of organisms. Read and Lestrel (1986) point out that neither homologous point measures nor Fourier descriptors capture complete information about shape. The important decision, they argue, is not about which method is better, but whether it directly measures those aspects of shape likely to be biologically informative and of specific interest.

The truss network

To overcome inherent weaknesses of traditional character sets, Strauss and Bookstein (1982) proposed the truss network: a geometric protocol for character selection. The truss is a systematic pattern of measurement intermediate between simple triangulation and a globally redundant data set. The triangulation network (Fig. 3.2(a)) has advantages over the traditional character data (Fig. 3.1) in representation of diagonal measures and more even coverage of shape. The globally redundant design (Fig. 3.2(b)) attempts to account for random measurement error by averaging individual mismeasurements over many measures. Given any reference triangle, distances are measured to any three other ones (Rohlf and Archie, 1978). Note that this set is not totally redundant in that distances between all possible landmark pairs are not measured. In the truss (Fig. 3.2(c)), each quadrilateral shares one edge with the preceding quadrilateral, adding only one extra distance measure over that in the triangulation network, while still overrepresenting the form.

Apart from the advantage of including oblique and vertical distances for a more even coverage of shape, the principal advantage of the truss network includes: (1) the ability to reconstruct the form from the original data (archival), and (2) recognition and compensation for random measurement error (Strauss and Bookstein, 1982: 114). When landmarks are suitably spaced upon the outline, the quadrilaterals will approach an idealized truss. Measurement errors are indicated when the truss cells depart from coplanarity. In a coplanar truss, the sixth distance is uniquely specified by the first five and will vary from this exact value by measurement error (its own plus that present in the first five distances). Strauss and Bookstein (1982) suggest that measurement error be removed by 'flattening the truss'. An average form is computed by regression of measured distances on a composite measure of body size (i.e. the first principal component in intergroup analysis), followed by reconstruction of the form (archival) using the distances provided by the regression functions at the particular body size. Two examples of truss flattening are presented in Bookstein *et al.* (1985: 57–61). McGlade and Boulding (1986) applied the corrections in a study of pollock (*Pollachius virens*) and haddock (*Melanogrammus aeglefinus*) stocks and provided FORTRAN V programs for performing the computations. I have not seen this method of correction applied in other studies. Measurement error in general is quite often ignored in morphometric studies.

Methods of data acquisition

Given a defined set of variables, there are three basic methods of acquiring the data for morphometric analysis: (1) manual distance measurement, (2) manual digitization, and (3) automated video digitization. Several factors can influence the choice of method, but two criteria stand out. First, the method of data acquisition should yield variables that are accurate, precise in repeated measures, and unaffected by specimen orientation or change of operator (White *et al.*, 1988). Second, ease of operation and speed are desirable.

Manual distance measurement is by far the most widely used, and the method of choice in 31 of 42 empirical studies published since 1981 surveyed here. Dividers, calipers, or ocular micrometers (measuring reticles) are used to measure linear distances between landmarks. With even a few variables per specimen, this method can be quite tedious and time consuming, with fatigue reducing data quality. Digital-readout calipers interfaced with the computer can save much time. Users without access to more sophisticated methods will continue to rely on manual measurement.

Digitized data acquisition is increasingly popular. In manual digitization for landmark data, the 'object' is placed on a digitizing tablet and x, y co-ordinates are produced for each landmark. The term 'object' refers to one of several possible means of representing the specimen, usually in two dimensions, although data in the third dimension can be obtained by repositioning the specimen and digitizing again. Cheverud *et al.* (1983) discussed another method for morphometrics in three dimensions. The object can be a photograph, radiograph, perimeter tracing, or the specimen itself. For specimens without landmarks, outlines can be digitized in stream mode, yielding a series of x,y coordinates describing the form.

Video digitization offers automated data acquisition (see Fink, 1987; White *et al.*, 1988 for techniques and hardware details). The basic system consists of a video camera, high resolution video monitor, microcomputer, mouse, imaging board (frame grabber) for analogue video-to-digital signal conversion, and software. Several software packages are available and differ in hardware requirements, menu format, and flexibility. Some offer data acquisition as both co-ordinates and outlines. Images can also be stored on computer disc for reanalysis.

Comparative studies of the utility of these methods are rare (see Rohlf and Archie, 1984; Dickinson *et al.*, 1987; White *et al.*, 1988). While the advantages of rapid data collection and absence of transcription errors in automated data acquisition are easily recognized, are there other advantages? Are the methods comparable in variance due to measurement error? What are their limitations?

The problem of measurement error is rarely addressed in morphometric studies (Baumgartner *et al.*, 1988: 469; Pankakoski *et al.*, 1987 are exceptions). Fink (1987: 70) reported observing less than 2% measurement error for video digitization. As an empirical evaluation of measurement error, I next compare character variance from video digitization and manual measurement on a set of fish specimens.

Analysis of measurement error

Thirty specimens from a collection of the Asian cyprinid *Puntius binotatus* (ANSP 88038), representing this species' typically wide range in adult body size, were examined. Eight anatomical landmarks were chosen to approximate the body outline (Fig. 3.3). Data were collected as interpoint distances using the truss network for both manual measurement and video digitization techniques.

Helios needle-point dial calipers were used to take manual measurements. The data were transcribed onto paper and entered into the statistics package in two separate steps. The video imaging system consisted of a COHU 4810 solid-state CCD video camera, Nikon 28 mm f/2.8 photo lens, Electrohome monochrome high-resolution display monitor, PCVisions Plus imaging board, Acer 910 80286 PC, and MorphoSys version 1.10. Specimens were placed in the video field and the eight landmarks were digitized. Straight pins were inserted in the specimen to locate landmarks 2, 3 and 4. Fifteen interpoint

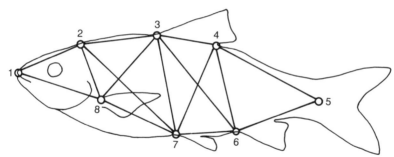

Fig. 3.3 Distance measures used to examine measurement error on *Puntius binotatus*. Numbers designate homologous landmarks of form; solid lines designate linear distance measures between landmarks.

distances were computed after appropriate scaling, and entered into the statistics package.

There are quite different potential sources of measurement error in the two methods of data acquisition. Manual measurement error may occur at three steps: (1) reading the caliper dial, (2) transcription onto paper, and (3) keypunch errors. The video system eliminates transcription error, but has other sources not present in manual mode. The accuracy and precision with which one can digitize landmarks depends on the quality and resolution of the video system. In this case, landmarks 7 and 8 were particularly difficult to locate reliably from specimen to specimen and adjustments to lens aperture and lighting direction were not consistently helpful.

In video mode, the three-dimensional object is viewed and digitized in two dimensions. The level of error introduced for a measure is a function of the magnitude of the component in the third dimension, perpendicular to the midsagittal plane. For example, consider three points (Fig. 3.3), of which two lie on the midsagittal plane (landmarks 2 and 6) and a third (landmark 8) does not. The distance between landmarks 2 and 8 computed by digitization is a projection of the z-component of point 8 onto the midsaggital plane and will under-represent the actual linear distance by a factor proportional to arcsin-(α), where α is the angle from the x, y plane to point 8 in the z direction. With compressed fish, this error is minimal. Also, a component of error is introduced whenever the midsagittal plane of the specimen is not perpendicular to the camera angle. Distortion of the video image can be significant as well (Fink, 1987). These sources of error do not apply for manual measurements on hand-held specimens. Thus, the possibility of measurement error can be qualitatively different for the two methods of data acquisition. Which method will yield the more precise data?

To compare measurement error for the two methods, three specimens were measured ten times for each variable. The coefficient of variation (CV) was computed for each variable following Haldane (1955):

$$CV = 100\,[(1 + 0.25n)\,SD/Y], \qquad (3.1)$$

where n is the sample size, SD is the standard deviation, and Y is the mean. Values of CV for each variable were computed for the grand sample ($n = 30$) and for the repeated measures on the three specimens. Standard deviations for the CVs were computed according to Sokal and Rohlf (1981: 139). The proportion of the variation present in the total data set due to measurement error was estimated for each variable as:

$$PME = 100\,(CV_e/CV_t), \qquad (3.2)$$

where CV_e is the mean of the three CVs from the repeated measures, and CV_t is the total CV computed over the entire sample.

For the 15 variables measured from 30 specimens, video digitization required a mean of 1.8 minutes per specimen, compared to 4.1 minutes per specimen by hand. Video digitization saved additional time since the software computed the interpoint distances, which were saved in ASCII format and input to the statistics package. When using calipers on hand-held specimens,

Table 3.1 Summary statistics in the analysis of measurement errors

Distance*	Caliper[†]				Video[†]			
	CV_t	SE_{cv}	CV_e	PME (%)	CV_t	SE_{cv}	CV_e	PME (%)
1–2	20.69	2.78	1.48	7.18	19.88	2.67	1.66	8.37
2–3	23.03	3.12	1.91	8.29	22.22	3.01	0.92	4.13
3–4	23.69	3.22	3.96	16.71	26.54	3.66	1.71	6.43
4–5	23.58	3.20	1.94	8.26	21.16	2.85	1.47	6.93
5–6	24.65	3.37	2.24	9.11	21.45	2.89	2.98	13.89
6–7	25.73	3.53	2.78	10.80	24.00	3.27	3.86	16.08
7–8	27.24	3.76	1.93	7.09	27.20	3.76	3.24	11.91
1–8	20.42	2.74	1.52	7.46	19.84	2.66	1.99	10.01
2–8	21.73	2.93	1.07	4.95	21.49	2.90	2.97	13.82
2–7	23.97	3.26	1.29	5.37	23.34	3.17	1.44	6.18
3–8	24.74	3.38	1.54	6.22	22.19	3.00	1.87	8.44
3–7	23.96	3.27	0.78	3.27	22.12	2.99	1.69	7.65
3–6	22.54	3.05	1.27	5.63	23.18	3.15	1.62	6.99
4–7	24.89	3.41	1.40	5.63	22.43	3.04	1.67	7.43
4–6	24.56	3.36	1.51	6.13	22.74	3.08	1.23	5.41
1–5	22.33	3.02	0.48	2.16	21.26	2.86	0.52	2.44

*Inter-landmark measures (Fig. 3.3).
[†]Statistics: CV_t, total coefficient of variation (CV) from entire data set (30 specimens); SE_{cv}, standard error of CV_t; CV_e, average CV for three specimens in ten repeated measurements; PME, proportion (%) of variation in the total data caused by measurement error.

variables generally cannot be measured sequentially. One must reposition the caliper points on the landmarks even for quadrilaterals sharing an edge.

Values of the summary statistics, CVs and estimated measurement error are given in Table 3.1. Considering the entire data set of 16 measures on 30 individuals, the caliper data were more variable overall, compared to the video data across variables. The total coefficient of variation (CV_t) and its corresponding standard error (SE_{cv}) were significantly greater for the caliper measures (Wilcoxon sign-rank test, $P < 0.02$). However, averaged over the three specimens, the digitized data were no more precise than were the caliper data. The coefficient of variation due to measurement error (CV_e) was not significantly different across variables for the two methods of measurement. For both methods, measurement error varied from about 2% to 17%. The amount of error differed across variables (Fig. 3.3). The repeated distances measured between landmarks 3 and 4 and between 6 and 7 were least precise for both caliper and digitized data.

The dependence of the error CV on the mean of the variable is presented in Fig. 3.4. The variables involving the shortest distances between landmarks were less precise than those involving longer distances. This curvilinear relationship between CV and the mean of a measure is well known, suggesting that variability of a measure sharply increases when the mean passes below a certain threshold limit (Soulé, 1982; Rohlf *et al.*, 1983; Pankakoski *et al.*, 1987). In this example, the data are limited in the absence of values between character mean of 25 to 50 (Fig. 3.4(a)); the values greater than 50 mm appear to skew the curve to the right. Figure 3.4(b) presents the relationship of measurement error to character mean after removal of these two points. The relationship is similar for the two methods and it appears that the threshold may fall between a mean of 12 and 19 mm.

In summary, for the example presented here, manual and digitized data acquisition methods do not differ significantly in precision. There may be real differences in accuracy, but that could not be evaluated here. Of the potential sources of error, image resolution may be most critical for video digitization, whereas transcription error may be most critical for caliper measurement. A four-fold decrease in time required per specimen may be achieved when using a video system for measuring many variables on many specimens. However, given the large potential for measurement error observed here for both methods (range 2–17%), caution must be exercised and users should attempt to evaluate and correct for measurement error in morphometric studies.

3.3   ANALYSES AND APPLICATIONS

Detailed comparison of the several statistical methods available to the morphometrician is beyond the scope of this chapter. My goal in this section

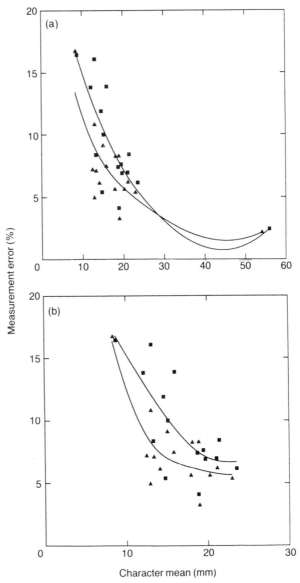

Fig. 3.4 Comparison of measurement error between caliper (▲) and video digitized (■) methods. Solid lines, distance-weighted least squares fit to points: lower curve, caliper data; upper curve, video data. (a) All data ($n = 30$); (b) two data points > 50 mm removed.

is to contrast the different methods through a brief survey of the more penetrating applications from recent publications using multivariate morphometrics.

Four multivariate methods most frequently applied to biological problems are discriminant functions (DFA), the related canonical variates (CVA), canonical correlation (CCA), and principal-components analysis (PCA). All are related in using a linear compound of the *n* variables multiplied by their respective coefficients to maximize intragroup variance.

If group structure is known, or assumed in advance, then DFA or CVA are appropriate. DFA attempts to construct the linear compound, or discriminant axis, which maximizes group separation. Specimens of unknown group membership can then be classified by the discriminant function. Except for classifying unknowns (e.g. Misra and Ni, 1983; Kenchington, 1986), DFA is seldom used alone. CVA is the correlate of PCA when groups are known or assumed. Its main use is in revealing underlying relationships among groups and variables. While in PCA the latent factors are generally orthologous, or uncorrelated with one another, in CVA this is not necessarily so. CCA is useful when one is interested in knowing if (and how) two or more sets of variables covary. If groups are not known in advance, then PCA is the most appropriate tool. The general goal in PCA is to reduce the dimensionality of the data set by representing the observed variables as functions of a smaller number of latent factors which are uncorrelated with one another and ideally can be interpreted. A modification of PCA, known as sheared principal components analysis (S-PCA), is a method for discriminating *a priori* groups (recognized by other criteria) on the basis of shape, independent of size (Humphries *et al.*, 1981).

Principal components analysis

PCA is by far the most widely used multivariate method in morphometrics. However, applications typically involve comparisons of *a priori* groups (i.e. populations, species, sexes, etc.) and thus depart from generalized PCA. Its use, instead of the more appropriate CVA, is directed toward evaluating hypotheses of *a priori* group structure.

Tissot (1988) used PCA to examine patterns of geographic variation and heterochrony in two species (two *a priori* groups) of marine Indo-Pacific molluscs. Heterochrony was suggested as a possible explanation for the observed morphological similarity between adult *Cypraea caputdraconis* and juvenile *C. caputserpentis*, two closely related species. Two sets of variables were examined: (1) measures on juvenile shells sectioned at the widest point perpendicular to the coiling axis, and (2) measures on adult shells. Five ontogenetic series were obtained from pre-adult shells (four *C. caputdraconis* and one *C. caputserpentis*) showing varying stages of shell development.

PCA on adult shells yielded three components accounting for > 70% of the

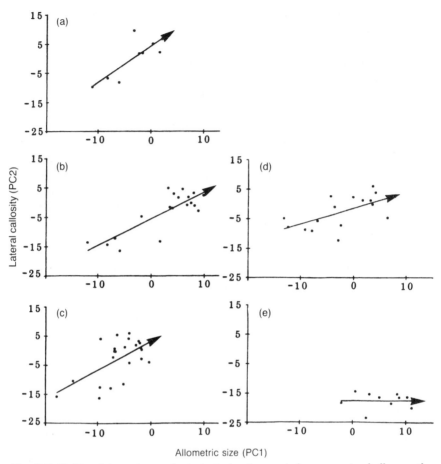

Fig. 3.5 Multivariate ontogenetic trajectories (arrows) from cowrie shell growth trajectories. Islands: (a) Ambon; (b) Cocos–Keeling; (c) Oahu; (d) Okinawa; (e) Easter. (Reproduced with permission from Tissot, 1988.)

total variation. Eigenvector loadings on PC1 were positive (all but the single angular measure) and significantly correlated with allometric loadings for each variable (slope of the regression of the variable against shell length), whereas loadings for PC2 and PC3 were not. In general, magnitude of the loading depicts the strength of the variable's association with that factor, while its sign reflects direction of allometry relative to general size. Thus, PC1 largely described variation among shell measures related to both overall size and ontogenetic size increase. Loadings on PC2 were interpreted as describing contrasts in development of the lateral shell callus, and those for PC3 described variation in tooth row length.

Ontogenetic trajectories (regressions of scores along PC1 and PC2) were linear (Fig. 3.5). Regression slopes depict rate of shape change relative to size,

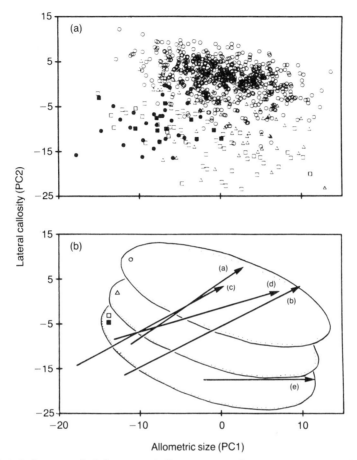

Fig. 3.6 Ordination of adult cowrie shell measures and ontogenetic trajectories from principal component scores. (a) Symbols: ○, Indo-West Pacific (IWP) *Cypraea caputserpentis* adults; ●, juvenile IWP *C. caputserpentis*; △, paedomorphic *C. caputserpentis*; □, Easter Island *C. caputdraconis*; ■, Sala y Gómez *C. caputdraconis*, (b) Ontogenetic trajectories (see Fig. 3.5) in relation to spread of component scores for adult shells. (Reproduced with permission from Tissot, 1988.)

and analysis of covariance showed significant differences among slopes and intercepts. Scatter plots of component scores (Fig. 3.6(a)) depict both onto-genetic and geographic variation, although no *a priori* groups were clearly separable. Figure 3.6(b) shows the general pattern in overlap of the *a priori* group clusters in relation to the ontogenetic trajectories from Fig. 3.5. Neoteny and post-displacement were suggested to explain interspecific differences in slope and intercept.

Sheared principal components analysis (S-PCA) has received much atten-tion; however, most applications have involved fishes (see Dickinson *et al.,*

1987; Dickinson, 1986 for two non-fish applications). Bookstein *et al.* (1985) and Rohlf and Bookstein (1987) expand the method beyond that presented in Humphries *et al.* (1981), and Bookstein *et al.* (1985: 101–24) and Chernoff (1986) provide applications. The rationale behind S-PCA follows from two problems: (1) most applications involve multi-group comparison, while PCA was originally intended for single-group analysis (Tissot, 1988); differences in size among groups can confound shape variance among PCs (Humphries *et al.*, 1981); (2) samples of organisms often incorporate several different ontogenetic stages so morphometric variation incorporates both shape and allometry (Shea, 1985). In S-PCA, the second and subsequent components are calculated so as to remove inter-group size. PC1 represents size plus shape (largely allometric), while subsequent PCs represent size-free shape factors. Non-programmers can use the SAS program provided in Bookstein *et al.* (1985: Appendix A.5.1.2) and modifications in Rohlf and Bookstein (1987: 367) for performing S-PCA. Two comments about the method have been well noted. First, S-PCA does not improve discrimination among groups, but aids in the interpretation of their contrasts, since shape separation is 'sheared' to be perpendicular to PC2 (Chernoff, 1986). Second, S-PCA is effective only when patterns of within-group size are similar among groups. Otherwise, nonsensical components can result (Tissot, 1988).

Decisions about group distinction are based on the separation of clusters in plots of component scores. Non-overlap between clusters is considered evidence supporting *n*-dimensional phenetic difference between groups. Significance tests of these hypotheses are not possible. One way to address this question is to examine the 95% (or some other level) confidence ellipsoid about the mean of the cluster of scores (Sokal and Rohlf, 1981: 594—601; Owen and Chmielewski, 1985). Departures from multivariate normality make this problematic (Morrison, 1967; but see Jolicouer, 1963). Gibson *et al.* (1984) present a jackknife procedure for PCA: the jackknife is a general technique for estimating parameters and their variance by iteratively removing a datum and recomputing the parameter of interest. Their approach provided eigenvalues and estimates of their variance. Multivariate analysis of variance (MANOVA) can then be applied to the PCs as significance tests for inter-group differentiation.

Canonical correlations

Tissot (1988) was interested in associations between shell morphology and surface seawater temperature for the cowrie species. He used CCA to determine whether the patterns of association between temperature (three variables: yearly minimum, maximum and average) and morphology were identical for the two species.

Scores on the first canonical morphological axis were plotted against those for the first environmental axis (Fig. 3.7). Scores for the *C. caputdraconis*

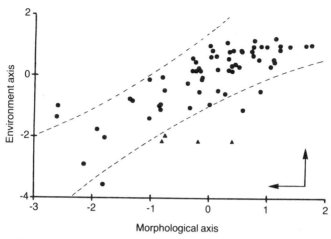

Fig. 3.7 Ordination of sample means on first environmental canonical axis versus first morphological canonical axis. Points represent canonical variates scores (●, *Cyprea caputserpentis*; ▲, *C. caputdraconis*); dashed lines designate 95% confidence limits; vertical arrow, increasing temperature; horizontal arrow, decreasing callosity. (Reproduced with permission from Tissot, 1988.)

specimens fall outside the 95% confidence interval for scores overall. This species deviates from the ecomorphological trends present in samples of *C. caputserpentis*. The morphology of small *C. caputdraconis* reflects different development of the lateral callus with respect to *C. caputserpentis* development at the same temperature (Tissot, 1988: 113).

3.4   APPLICATIONS IN THE STUDY OF THE CYPRINIDAE

The morphometric methods of Humphries *et al.* (1981) and Bookstein *et al.* (1985) have been widely applied to problems in systematic ichthyology. However, applications involving cyprinid fishes are few. On an international scale, cyprinid studies have generally applied univariate statistical approaches using ratios of variables against standard length and, less frequently, univariate regression. Univariate analysis and reliance on ratios to 'correct' for body size variation remains prevalent.

Multivariate analysis of hybrids

One of the first multivariate analyses involving cyprinids is that of Smith (1973) on hybrid intermediacy. Suspected hybrids between *Acrocheilus alutaceus* and *Richardsonius balteatus* were examined using PCA and DFA. The single suspected hybrid was intermediate between, and fell outside, the clusters of presumed parental species in the projection of scores along PC1 and PC2. The author, struck by the obvious phenetic intermediacy of the hybrid at the outset, questioned the power of, and need for, PCA in such cases. Of the 34 variables studied, 11 that contributed most heavily to the discrimination were excluded from the data and the analysis was repeated. The result, based on 23 variables, none of which would discriminate the populations alone or in pairs, showed almost the same degree of discrimination as with the inclusive data set, although the hybrid individual fell closer to *R. balteatus* in the secondary analysis. This result demonstrates the value of exploiting the patterns of covariation among characters and the power of exploratory PCA (Smith, 1973: 398).

Suspected hybrids between *Rhinichthys cataractae, R. osculus,* and *Richardsonius balteatus* posed additional problems. Plots of the component scores along PC1 and PC2 for the three species showed one individual (hybrid b) intermediate between *R. cataractae* and *R. osculus,* one individual (hybrid a) intermediate between *R. osculus* and *Richardsonius balteatus,* and two individuals (hybrids c and d) each falling within or very near the cluster of one parental species. When PCA was repeated for hybrids b, c, d and their parental species pairs, hybrids b and c were intermediate, while hybrid d again fell very near the *R. osculus* cluster. Hybrid d was interpreted as a backcross individual between a hybrid and *R. osculus.*

Two biological assumptions are required in the use of DFA in hybrid studies (e.g. Smith, 1973; Colgan *et al.,* 1976): (1) that parental species are known *a priori* and (2) that hybrids are intermediate in the absence of a known hybrid sample. Ross and Cavender (1981) presented numerous patterns of character expression in laboratory-reared hybrids of known parentage that were not intermediate (see also Miller and Behnke, 1985). Neff and Smith (1979) discussed the usefulness of, and assumptions behind, multivariate analysis of hybrid fishes, also using laboratory-reared hybrids of known parentage. If the parentage of suspected hybrids is unknown, Neff and Smith (1979: 180) point out that DFA can only yield information about the relative importance of characters as discriminators between groups and the relative positions of the centroids of those groups, two aspects outside the goal of identification of hybrids in wild-caught samples.

Bookstein *et al.* (1985: 115–22) suggest a method which permits separate analysis of the variance explained by morphometric and meristic data and enhances the discrimination between parents and their putative hybrids. The scatter of scores along PC1 and PC2 for the combined data (Fig. 3.8(a)) showed large overlap among species and their hybrids. Ordination by morphometric characters alone (Fig. 3.8(b)) showed that a portion of the variance within groups along PC1 and PC2 retained a strong size component. Sheared components (Fig. 3.8(c)) showed reasonable separation among clusters and clarified the identity of hybrids. Meristic information was restored in a plot of sheared morphometric PC2 against meristic PC1

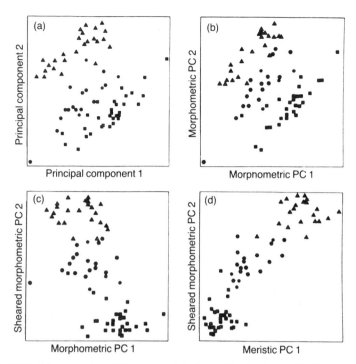

Fig. 3.8 PCA of three species of *Gila* and their hybrids: ■, *G. robusta*; filled hexagons, *G. cypha*; ▲, *G. elegans*; ●, hybrids. (a) Mixed morphometric and meristic data; (b) pre-sheared morphometric clusters; (c) sheared morphometric clusters; (d) restoration of meristic information, with increased discrimination. (Reproduced with permission from Bookstein *et al.*, 1985.)

(Fig. 3.8(d)). Discrimination was enhanced and the possibility of additional hybrid specimens was suggested.

Ecology

Felley (1984) applied multivariate morphometrics in a study of the association between morphology and habitat preferences for cyprinids from the south-central USA. He tested the widely held hypothesis that morphological differences between species can be used to predict resource use. The utility of two sets of morphological predictors was compared. The first set was chosen *a priori*, to reflect patterns of covariation between morphology and ecology, expected from knowledge of functional morphology of other fishes (e.g. Gatz, 1979). The second set was chosen *a posteriori*, based on the results of an exploratory factor analysis.

For the associations between morphology and ecology to be considered predictive, Felley (1984) required a significant result in two statistical tests: (1)

multivariate regression of the morphological variables against environmental variables, and (2) successful cross-validation in terms of significant product-moment and rank correlations between observed and predicted values on a second group of species. No characters from the *a priori* set successfully predicted resource use, although several significant associations were suggested by factor analysis. Pectoral and pelvic-fin size and swim bladder size were associated with preferred depth in the water column. Eye size, gill raker length and number, intestine length, and cerebellum size were associated with food habits. However, two sets of *a posteriori* characters did successfully predict resource use. Fin size, distance of the dorsal fin from the centre of gravity, and scale size predicted preferred depth in the water column, while intestine length, peritoneum pigmentation, and cerebellum size predicted food habits, as judged by significant regression and cross-validation results. Felley (1984) urged caution in extrapolating eco-morphological relationships across species groups.

Systematics

Applications of multivariate morphometrics to cyprinid systematics continue to involve morphological discrimination of taxa. A review of the vast literature on cyprinid systematics revealed many papers dealing with morphometrics in the most general sense: mensural characters and differences among taxa. However, fewer used a multivariate approach. Those employing some aspect of the methodology in Bookstein *et al.* (1985) were fewer still and restricted in treatment to the cyprinid fauna of North America and Mexico.

Chernoff and Miller (1981) studied the systematics and variation of *Notropis sallei* from central Mexico. They note that this species has had a confused taxonomic history, with assignment to no fewer than eight genera, seven species, and 16 nominal taxa. Its variation was said to be comparable to that found in several other highly variable American minnows, such as *Notropis atherinoides* (Bailey and Allum, 1962), *N. cornutus* (Gilbert, 1964), *Pimephales promelas* (Vandermeer, 1966), and *Campostoma anomalum* (Burr, 1976). Chernoff and Miller used PCA to judge the phenetic distance among populations as an aid to making taxonomic judgments. No distinct population clusters were discovered, suggesting a single species. The authors note that its great morphological variability may be the product of adaptations of separate populations to diverse and often isolated physical environments, despite the species' restricted geographic distribution relative to those of other highly variable American cyprinids.

Chernoff *et al.* (1982) were the first to apply S-PCA to a problem involving cyprinids. The bluntnose shiner, *Notropis simus*, a Rio Grande endemic, was thought to have been extirpated in its range by the mid-1960s (Hubbs *et al.*, 1977). The authors examined the possibility that *Notropis orca*, the phantom shiner, was a junior synonym of *N. simus* and that the potentially undescribed

'Pecos shiner' (Koster, 1957) was also conspecific with *N. simus*. They concluded that *N. orca* was distinct from *N. simus* and recognized two subspecies within *N. simus*: *N. s. simus* and *N. s. pecosensis*. The latter subspecies was more heavily pigmented than the former, having a more distinct, broader dusky lateral stripe, sometimes ending in a caudal spot in *N. s. pecosensis*. On the basis of morphometrics, the *N. orca* cluster of component scores along PC1 and sheared PC2 was distinct from that for *N. s. simus*. The similar analysis for the subspecies pair, however, did not reveal clear separation. A similar result was obtained for meristic PC1 vs. sheared morphometric PC2.

This highlights an interesting methodological aspect of PCA for exploratory systematics. The utility of PCA for discrimination is potentially greatest for pair-wise comparisons, as between *N. orca* and *N. s. simus*, and between *N. s. simus* and *N. s. pecosensis* (Chernoff *et al.*, 1982). But their study was clearly a three-taxon problem. Would the decision to accept three nominal taxa have been supported had the authors run the PCA on all three taxa simultaneously rather than pairwise?

Matthews *et al.* (1982) studied the systematics of the *Rhinichthys atratulus* complex of eastern and central North America. The complex consists of three largely allopatric taxa considered to be subspecifically distinct: *R. a. atratulus* (eastern blacknose dace), *R. a. obtusus* (southern blacknose dace), and *R. a. meleagris* (central blacknose dace). The *R. a. atratulus* form is recognizably different from the other subspecies, however the latter two subspecies are not recognizably different and none of the distinguishing features used by earlier workers was consistently useful either. The authors examined morphometric variation of fishes from a zone of syntopy between *R. a. obtusus* and *R. a. atratulus* and compared this to variation between forms in allopatry.

PCA and DFA were used to study patterns of morphological variation among populations. In PCA, characters are generally standardized to zero mean and unit variance, based on the pooled among-groups standard deviations. To obtain a more powerful maximum discrimination between *R. a. atratulus* and *R. a. obtusus*, Matthews *et al.* ran PCA on 20 meristic plus morphometric characters from specimens of known subspecies identity from allopatric reference populations, using characters standardized by the pooled within-groups standard deviations. Fishes from the zone of overlap (un-knowns) were projected onto the principal axes resulting from the PCA on the reference samples. The PCA resulted in complete separation of the reference samples along PC1 and PC2. Dace from the overlap zone showed evidence of genetic exchange between subspecies. Of these specimens, 10% clustered with reference *R. a. obtusus*, 48% with reference *R. a. atratulus*, and 42% were intermediate. When nuptial coloration was considered along with the PCA functions, all but 28% of the overlap samples were considered intermediate. Matthews *et al.* interpret this as evidence for interfertility in the overlap zone, resulting from either a hybrid zone between distinct species, or a zone of intergradation between taxa not fully differentiated at the species level. Given the small population size and relative isolation of the overlap-zone fishes, relative to populations from nearby tributaries, the authors accept the possibility that these two forms maintain their own evolutionary tendencies, and therefore recommend retaining the accepted trinomials for the two forms studied.

Schaefer and Cavender (1986) studied a similar problem concerning the subspecific taxonomic status of *Notropis spilopterus*. PCA and DFA were used to determine patterns of character variation among eastern (*N. s. spilopterus*) and western (*N. s. hypsisomatus*) subspecies. Because aspects of body shape were used to discriminate subspecies initially (Gibbs, 1957), the authors chose a truss system of measurement rather than the traditional character set. Their results suggested that subspecies not be recognized because of discordant character covariation among populations. Populations assigned to *N. s. hypsisomatus* were not phenetically uniform, nor distinct from those assigned to *N. s. spilopterus* on the basis of S-PCA. This was supported by *a posteriori* DFA which failed to classify a significant proportion of individuals to subspecies on the basis of geographic location.

Matthews (1987) performed an elegant study of the multivariate morphometrics of *Cyprinella* (formerly *Notropis*) *lutrensis* throughout its range in mid- and south-central USA. Four subspecies of *C. lutrensis* have been recognized in the literature: *C. l. lutrensis*, widespread in central USA; a slender Texas coastal plains form, *C. l. suavis*; *C. l. forbesi* from Illinois and north-east Missouri; and *C. l. blairi* known from two localities in the Big Bend Region of Texas (perhaps extinct). To characterize morphological trends across populations, Matthews (1987: 620) recognized that it is not practical to perform multivariate analyses on data sets involving many individuals (in this case $n = 1024$). Following Chernoff (1982), he reduced the data to population means for all characters, after verifying that at least some populations were distinguishable in the scatterplot of PC scores. Mantel and spatial autocorrelation analyses were used to examine the relationship between morphological divergence and geographic location. Briefly, the Mantel analysis compares the morphological 'distance' matrix with a matrix of geographic distance among localities by performing *t*-tests among all possible pairs of locations (Douglas and Endler, 1982). In contrast to the meristic data, which showed significant pattern in comparison of morphology and reciprocals of straight-line distance among localities, the morphometric data showed little or no significant pattern in relatedness of populations across geographic or stream-connectivity distances. Thus, neighbouring populations within a given region tend to be meristically similar, but neither more nor less so at greater distances. Spatial autocorrelation results were similar, with significant positive autocorrelation of meristic PC1 scores across geographic distances up to 400 km, non-significant from 500 to 700 km, and significant but negative from 800 to 1300 km. The same pattern was not observed for the morphometric data.

With respect to the systematics of the complex, the broad geographic scale of the study did not permit rigorous evaluation of subspecies validity. On the basis of conservative interpretation of the multivariate results, Matthews (1987) made the following recommendations: (1) The *lepidus* form from the Nueces–Frio drainage should be elevated to full species (= *Cyprinella lepida*). In morphology and coloration, this form was more distinct from all other *C. lutrensis* material than were any two *C. lutrensis* populations different from each other. (2) *C. l. lutrensis* from Illinois and upper Mississippi drainage and north-eastern Missouri may well represent the subspecies *C. l. forbesi* recognized by Hubbs and Ortenberger (1929). (3) *C. l. lutrensis* from Texas–Louisiana coastal lowlands are distinct from populations in central Texas and the Great Plains. For both (2) and (3), fine-scale regional studies would be required before more definitive statements about subspecies validity could be made.

Mayden (1988) examined morphometric variation between species of the *Notropis zonatus* species group of the interior highlands of North America. The ability to discriminate males of the three species (*N. zonatus*, *N. pilsbryi*, and *N. cardinalis*) did not depend upon morphometric information alone; a number of meristic, pigmentation, morphological and allozymic features, alone and in combination, did quite well. Morphometric analyses were presented to describe patterns of mensural character variation among species. Characters chosen were largely traditional, measuring distances aligned with the longitudinal axis, together with some body depth measures of questionable homology. For males, the lengths of dorsal and pectoral fins and width of the lateral stripe were most useful as characters for separating *N. cardinalis* from *N. pilsbryi* and *N. zonatus* along S-PC2. The last two species were not separable along either S-PC2 or S-PC3. No similar analysis on females for all three species was presented. Mayden (1988) did not discuss whether interpretation of the character loadings benefited from shearing the PCs.

Phylogenetics

Bookstein *et al.* (1985) discuss some perceptive applications of the methods for describing change in form among taxa and their ontogenies. Their principal interests were directed toward application of morphometrics to analysis of heterochrony, evolutionary and ecological morphology. Using general size as a proxy for biological time (Strauss, 1987), rates of shape change can be quantified and compared across taxa to describe evolutionary patterns of morphological change. While intellectually pleasing, the study of occupied and unoccupied morphological 'space' is empty at present (but see Strauss, 1988).

I see little empirical role for morphometrics in phylogeny reconstruction. The field offers procedures for quantitative description of form, but remains purely phenetic. The major obstacle to more general phylogenetic application beyond post-hoc inference involves definition of characters compared across taxa. Morphometric contrasts (when most informative) are multidimensional, making traditional concepts of 'character' and 'character-state' abstract reductions. Also, the factors underlying such contrasts are not independent – certainly not statistically, and probably not genetically either. Morphometric contrasts are seldom discrete, but generally continuous in nature. For cladistic analyses by means other than phenetic 'distance', some method of character coding is required. Despite arguments to the contrary (Archie, 1985), continuous quantitative variables are generally not appropriate for cladistic analysis, because no objective criteria exist for partitioning the variation into discrete states (Pimentel and Riggins, 1987). This makes it impossible to group organisms on the basis of what they have versus what they lack, the very nature of cladistic method.

In summary, the role of morphometrics in empirical phylogenetics has yet to be precisely defined. Bookstein *et al.* (1985) remain optimistic, but the methods are phenetic in nature, and grouping taxa on the basis of overall similarity runs contrary to phylogenetic method.

3.5   CONCLUSION

Considering that the majority of players in the Michigan Morphometrics Study Group are primarily ichthyologists, it is not surprising that North American ichthyologists were first bombarded with such new phrases as box truss, landmarks of form, and sheared second component. My review of the literature indicated that in the seven years since publication of Humphries *et al.* (1981), several North American biologists have accepted the newer methods, publishing results for various organisms. North American ichthyologists account for more than 50% of all papers published since 1981 that cite either Humphries *et al.* (1981) or Bookstein *et al.* (1985). However, non-North American biologists are either unfamiliar with these methods or have not incorporated them into their studies.

One reason for this reluctance concerns how distance measures are used in particular studies. In systematics, the distance, rather than the landmark, has been regarded as the 'character'. Many applications in systematics have been concerned with taxon discrimination, rather than the more general shape archival. The deficiencies of traditional character sets are not necessarily appreciated when morphometrics is used in this manner. The strengths of the newer morphometrics approach are therefore not used for the purposes intended.

Secondly, except for S-PCA, the computational means for the analyses of Bookstein *et al.* (1985) are not widely available. For example, the method of biorthogonal grids can only be performed on the University of Michigan MIDAS mainframe system.

Despite these limitations, the theoretical foundation of morphometrics and the synthesis of geometry and biological homology afforded by the Michigan Group will probably foster continued progress in multivariate morphometrics for years to come.

ACKNOWLEDGMENTS

For discussion and criticism I thank Darrell Siebert, William Smith–Vaniz, Richard Strauss, and Ed Theriot. George Davis kindly permitted use of his video system.

REFERENCES

Archie, J. W. (1985) Methods for coding variable morphological features for numerical taxonomic analysis. *Syst., Zool.* **34**, 326–45.
Bailey, R. M. and Allum, M. O. (1962) Fishes of South Dakota. *Misc. Publ. Mus. Zool., Univ. Mich.*, **119**, 1–131.
Baumgartner, J. V., Bell, M. A. and Weinberg, P. H. (1988) Body form differences between the Enos Lake species pair of threespine sticklebacks (*Gasterosteus aculeatus* complex). *Can. J. Zool.*, **66**, 467–74.
Blackith, R. E. and Reyment, R. A. (1971) *Multivariate Morphometrics*, Academic Press, London, 412 pp.
Bookstein, F. L. (1977) The study of shape transformation after D'Arcy Thompson. *Mathl. Biosci.*, **34**, 177–219.
Bookstein, F. L. (1978) *The Measurement of Biological Shape and Shape Change* (Lecture Notes in Biomathematics, Vol. 24), Springer-Verlag, New York, 191 pp.
Bookstein, F. L. (1982) Foundations of morphometrics. *Ann. Rev. Ecol. Syst.*, **13**, 451–70.
Bookstein, F. L., Strauss, R. E., Humphries, J. M., Chernoff, B., Elder, R. L. and Smith, G. R. (1982) A comment upon the uses of Fourier methods in systematics. *Syst. Zool.*, **31**, 85–91.
Bookstein, F. L., Chernoff, B., Elder, R., Humphries, J., Smith, G. and Strauss, R. (1985) *Morphometrics in Evolutionary Biology*. Spec. Publs. Acad. nat. Sci. Philad, **15**, 277 pp.
Burr, B. M. (1976) A review of the Mexican stoneroller, *Campostoma ornatum* Girard (Pisces: Cyprinidae). *Trans. S. Diego Soc. nat. Hist..*, **18**, 127–44.
Chernoff, B. (1982) Character variation among populations and the analysis of biogeography. *Am. Zool.*, **22**, 425–39.
Chernoff, B. (1986) Systematics of American atherinid fishes of the genus *Atherinella*. I. The subgenus *Atherinella. Proc. Acad. nat. Sci. Philad.*, **138**, 86–188.
Chernoff, B. and Miller, R. R. (1981) Systematics and variation of the aztec shiner, *Notropis sallei*, a cyprinid fish from Central Mexico. *Proc. biol. Soc. Wash.*, **94**, 18–36.
Chernoff, B., Miller, R. R. and Gilbert, C. R. (1982) *Notropis orca* and *Notropis simus*, cyprinid fishes from the American southwest, with description of a new subspecies. *Occ. Pap. Mus. Zool., Univ. Mich.*, **698**, 46 pp.
Cheverud, J. M., Lewis, J. L., Bachrach, W. and Lewis, W. D. (1983) The measurement of form and variation in form: an application of three-dimensional quantitative morphology by finite-element methods. *Am. J. phys. Anthropol.*, **62**, 151–65.
Colgan, P. W., Ballantyne, P. K. and Wilson, M. V. H. (1976) Numerical taxonomy of

hybridizing *Lepomis* (Centrarchidae) in Lake Opinicon, Ontario, *Can. J. Zool.*, **54**, 42–7.

Dickinson, T. A. (1986) Topodeme differentiation in Ontario taxa of *Crataegus* (Rosaceae: Maloideae): Leaf morphometric evidence. *Can. J. Bot.*, **64**, 2738–47.

Dickinson, T. A., Parker, W. H. and Strauss, R. E. (1987) Another approach to leaf shape comparisons. *Taxon*, **36**, 1–20.

Douglas, M. E. and Endler, J. A. (1982) Quantitative matrix comparisons in ecological and evolutionary investigations. *J. theor. Biol.*, **99**, 777–95.

Ehrlich, R., Pharr, R. B., jun. and Healy–Williams, N. (1983) Comments on the validity of Fourier descriptors in systematics: a reply to Bookstein *et al. Syst. Zool.*, **32**, 202–6.

Felley, J. D. (1984) Multivariate identification of morphological–environmental relationships within the Cyprinidae (Pisces). *Copeia*, **1984**, 442–55.

Felley, J. D. (1988) Review: Morphometrics in Evolutionary Biology, by F. L. Bookstein, B. Chernoff, R. Elder, J. Humphries, G. Smith, and R. Strauss, 1985. *Copeia*, **1988**, 1106–7.

Fink, W. L. (1987) Video digitizer: a system for systematic biologists. *Curator*, **30**, 63–72.

Gatz, A. J., jun. (1979) Community organization in fishes as indicated by morphological features. *Ecology*, **60**, 711–18.

Gibbs, R. H., jun. (1957) Cyprinid fishes of the subgenus *Cyprinella* of *Notropis* II. Distribution and variation of *Notropis spilopterus*, with the description of a new subspecies. *Lloydia*, **20**, 186–209.

Gibson, A. R., Baker, A. J. and Moeed, A. (1984) Morphometric variation in introduced populations of the common myna (*Acridotheres tristis*): an application of the jackknife to principal component analysis. *Syst. Zool.*, **33**, 408–21.

Gilbert, C. R. (1964) The American cyprinid fishes of the subgenus *Luxilus* (genus *Notropis*). *Bull. Fla. St. Mus. biol. Sci.*, **8**, 95–194.

Haldane, J. B. S. (1955) The measurement of variation. *Evolution*, **9**, 484.

Hubbs, C., Miller, R. R., Edwards, R. J., Thompson, K. W., Marsh, E., Garrett, G. P., Powell, G. L., Morris, D. J. and Zerr, R. W. (1977). Fishes inhabiting the Rio Grande, Texas and Mexico, between El Paso and the Pecos confluence. *Symposium on the Importance, Preservation, and Management of the Riparian Habitat, 9 July 1977, Tuscon, Arizona*, US Dept Agric. Forest Serv., Gen. Tech. Rep. RM-43, pp. 91–7.

Hubbs, C. L. and Lagler, K. F. (1964) *Fishes of the Great Lakes Region*, Univ. Mich. Press, Ann Arbor, Michigan, 213 pp.

Hubbs, C. L. and Ortenberger, A. I. (1929) Fishes collected in Oklahoma and Arkansas in 1927. *Publs Univ. Okla. Biol. Surv.*, **1**, 47–112.

Humphries, J. M., Bookstein, F. L., Chernoff, B., Smith, G. R., Elder, R. L. and Poss, S. G. (1981) Multivariate discrimination by shape in relation to size. *Syst. Zool.*, **34**, 381–96.

Jolicouer, P. (1963) The multivariate generalization of the allometry equation. *Biometrics*, **19**, 497–9.

Kenchington, T. J. (1986) Morphological comparison of two northwest Atlantic redfishes, *Sebastes fasciatus* and *S. mentella*, and techniques for their identification. *Can. J. Fish. Aquat. Sci.*, **43**, 781–7.

Koster, W. J. (1957) *Guide to the Fishes of New Mexico*, Univ. New Mexico Press, Albuquerque, 116 pp.

McGlade, J. M. and Boulding, E. G. (1986) The truss: A geometric and statistical approach to the analysis of form in fishes. *Can. tech. Rep. Fish. aquat. Sci.*, no. 1457, 68 pp.

Matthews, W. J. (1987) Geographic variation in *Cyprinella lutrensis* (Pisces: Cyprinidae) in the United States, with notes on *Cyprinella lepida*. *Copeia*, **1987**, 616–37.

Matthews, W. J., Jenkins, R. E. and Styron, J. T. jun. (1982) Systematics of two forms of blacknose dace, *Rhinichthys atratulus* (Pisces: Cyprinidae) in a zone of syntopy, with a review of the species group. *Copeia*, **1982**, 902–20.

Mayden, R. L. (1988) Systematics of the *Notropis zonatus* species group, with description of a new species from the interior highlands of North America. *Copeia*, **1988**, 153–73.

Miller, D. L. and Behnke, R. J. (1985) Two new intergeneric hybrids from the Bonneville Basin, Utah. *Copeia*, **1985**, 509–14.

Misra, R. K. and Ni, I.-H. (1983) Distinguishing beaked redfishes (deepwater redfish, *Sebastes mentella* and Labrador redfish, *S. fasciatus*) by discriminant analysis (with covariance) and multivariate analysis of covariance. *Can. J. Fish. aquat. Sci.*, **40**, 1507–11.

Morrison, D. F. (1967) *Multivariate Statistical Methods*, McGraw–Hill, New York, 338 pp.

Neff, N. A. and Smith, G. R. Multivariate analysis of hybrid fishes. *Syst. Zool.*, **28**, 176–96.

Owen, J. G. and Chmielewski, M. A. (1985) On canonical variates analysis and the construction of confidence ellipses in systematic studies. *Syst. Zool.*, **34**, 366–74.

Pankakoski, E., Vaisanen, R. A. and Nurmi, K. (1987) Variability of muskrat skulls: measurement error, environmental modification, and size allometry. *Syst. Zool.*, **36**, 35–51.

Pimentel, R. A. and Riggins, R. (1987) The nature of cladistic data. *Cladistics*, **3**, 201–9.

Read, D. W. and Lestrel, P. E. (1986) Comment on uses of homologous-point measures in systematics: a reply to Bookstein *et al*. *Syst. Zool.*, **35**, 241–53.

Reist, J. D. (1986) An empirical evaluation of coefficients used in residual and allometric adjustment of size covariation. *Can. J. Zool.*, **64**, 1363–8.

Reyment, R. A. (1986) Review: F. L. Bookstein, B. Chernoff, R. Elder, J. Humphries, G. Smith, and R. Strauss. 1985. Morphometrics in Evolutionary Biology. *Biometrics*, **42**, 1002–3.

Rohlf, F. J. and Archie, J. W. (1978) Least-squares mapping using interpoint distances. *Ecology*, **59**, 126–32.

Rohlf, F. J., and Archie, J. W. (1984) A comparison of Fourier methods for the description of wing shape in mosquitoes (Diptera: Culicidae). *Syst. Zool.*, **33**, 302–17.

Rohlf, F. J. and Bookstein, F. L. (1987) A comment on shearing as a method for "size correction". *Syst. Zool.*, **36**, 356–67.

Rohlf, F. J. and Ferson, S. (1983) Image analysis, *Numerical Taxonomy* (NATO ASI Ser. G, Ecol. Sci., no. 1) (ed. J. Felsenstein), Springer-Verlag, New York, pp. 583–99.

Rohlf, F. J., Gilmartin, A. J. and Hart, G. (1983) The Kluge–Kerfoot phenomenon – a statistical artifact. *Evolution*, **37**, 501–5.

Ross, M. R. and Cavender, T. M. (1981) Morphological analyses of four experimental intergeneric cyprinid hybrid crosses. *Copeia*, **1981**, 377–87.

Schaefer, S. A. and Cavender, T. M. (1986) Geographic variation and subspecific status of *Notropis spilopterus* (Pisces: Cyprinidae). *Copeia*, **1986**, 122–30.

Schindel, D. E. (1986) Essay review: morphometrics in evolutionary biology: the geometry of size and shape change, with examples from fishes. *Am. J. Sci.*, **286**, 510–12.

Shea, B. T. (1985) Bivariate and multivariate growth allometry. *J. Zool., Lond.*, **206A**, 367–90.

Smith, G. R. (1973) Analysis of several hybrid cyprinid fishes from western North America. *Copeia*, **1973**, 395–410.

Smith, M. L. (1987) Review: Morphometrics in Evolutionary Biology. F. Bookstein, B.

Chernoff, R. Elder, J. Humphries, G. Smith, and R. Strauss, 1985. *Cladistics*, **3**, 97–9.

Sokal, R. R. and Rohlf, F. J. (1981) *Biometry*, 2nd edn, W. H. Freeman, San Francisco, 857 pp.

Soulé, M. E. (1982) Allometric variation. 1. The theory and some consequences. *Am. Nat.*, **120**, 751–64.

Strauss, R. E. (1987) On allometry and relative growth in evolutionary studies. *Syst. Zool.*, **36**, 72–5.

Strauss, R. E. (1988) The importance of phylogenetic constraints in comparison of morphological structure among fish assemblages, in *Community and Evolutionary Ecology of North American Stream Fishes*, (eds. W. J. Matthews and D. C. Heins), Univ. Oklahoma Press, Norman, Okla, pp. 136–43.

Strauss, R. E. and Bookstein, F. L. (1982) The truss: body form reconstruction in morphometrics. *Syst. Zool.*, **31**, 113–35.

Thompson, D'A. W. (1942) *On Growth and Form*, abridged edn (ed. J. T. Bonner), Cambridge Univ. Press, Cambridge, UK, 346 pp.

Tissot, B. N. (1988) Geographic variation and heterochrony in two species of cowries (genus *Cypraea*). *Evolution*, **42**, 103–17.

Vandermeer, J. H. (1966) Statistical analysis of geographic variation of the fathead minnow, *Pimephales promelas*. *Copeia*, **1966**, 457–66.

White, R. J., Prentice, H. C. and Verwijst, T. (1988) Automated image acquisition and morphometric description. *Can. J. Bot.*, **66**, 450–67.

Wie, K.-Y. and Kennett, J. P. (1988) Phyletic gradualism and punctuated equilibrium in the late Neogene planktonic foraminiferal clade *Globoconella*. *Paleobiology*, **14**, 345–63.

Younker, J. L. and Ehrlich, R. (1977) Fourier biometrics: harmonic amplitudes as multivariate shape descriptors. *Syst. Zool.*, **26**, 336–42.

Chapter four

Molecular and cytological investigations

D. G. Buth, T. E. Dowling and J. R. Gold

4.1 INTRODUCTION

Molecular and cytogenetic studies of cyprinid fishes continue to contribute to our understanding of this diverse and fascinating group. Advances in technology have facilitated the resolution of characters that were formerly beyond measurement. Although some characters derived from these studies have been employed in investigations of gene evolution, genomic organization, and mechanistic aspects of organismic evolution, most applications with cyprinid fishes have addressed questions regarding historical evolution, i.e. phylogenetic relationships and, to a lesser extent, zoogeography. These techniques have also been applied at the population level, but to a lesser degree.

Studies of gene products or the genes themselves have revealed variation at several levels of organization. Highly variable characters are valuable in assessing geographic patterns of gene flow among populations, including the limits of gene pools whose uniqueness requires taxonomic recognition. Less variable characters are useful in the study of subfamilial, and inter- and intrageneric relationships. These higher taxonomic levels are attracting great interest in research on cyprinids, as well as on other fishes.

Here we present information on cyprinid allozymic, isozymic, and cytogenetic characteristics and their research applications. Some additional modern molecular methods hold considerable potential but have yet to be used widely with cyprinids. For North American species, we employ taxonomic assignments of Mayden (1989) (see also Chapter 8).

4.2 ALLOZYMES AND ISOZYMES

Allozyme electrophoresis is a precise and cost-effective method for comparing populations, species, and closely related genera (Bush and Kitto, 1978). Buth

(1984a) reviewed applications of allozyme variation in studies of cyprinid fishes, and as he predicted, allozyme data are increasingly used, especially for investigations of hybridization and introgression, population structure, biochemical identification of taxa, and phylogenetic systematics. The numerous studies published since 1984 do not result from any technological breakthrough in the generation of allozyme data, but rather reflect an increased interest in cyprinid fishes throughout the world and the spread of the basic technology making these studies possible. Allozymes provide a particulate data base that can be generated cheaply, using supplies and materials common to basic biochemistry. Allozymes are among the least expensive biochemical tools.

Isozyme characters (*sensu* Whitt, 1983, 1987; Buth, 1984b), including gene number, tissue-specific expression, and heteropolymer formation, have been applied in several studies of cypriniform fish systematics (Ferris and Whitt, 1977a, 1978; Buth, 1980; Rainboth *et al.*, 1986) but have not been widely applied to cyprinids, except in studies of development (Frankel, 1983, 1985). Isozyme characters related to gene duplication and silencing (p. 92) may prove especially useful in studies of karyotypic polyploids (p. 99). Isozyme characters may vary at a number of levels of organization (Buth, 1984b), making it difficult *a priori* to identify an optimal taxonomic level for their application. Additional investigation of isozyme characters in diploid cyprinids is necessary before their utility in comparative studies can be assessed.

Methods

As allozyme studies of cyprinids proliferate, communication and comparison of their results become very important. Voucher specimens should be deposited in museum collections for taxonomic verification by subsequent investigators (Buth, 1984a). Allozyme data should be presented in their most informative fashion, as genotype arrays instead of allele frequencies. Genotype arrays permit the direct assessment of agreement with Hardy–Weinberg equilibrium expectations, measurement of direct-count heterozygosity, and other genetic variables. Communication of allozyme results is facilitated by a stable, informative system of enzyme and locus nomenclature. Enzyme nomenclature should follow the recommendations of the International Union of Biochemistry (IUBNC, 1984) using these enzyme names and their Enzyme Commission (EC) numbers. Buth (1983) discussed locus nomenclature and proposed a system appropriate to both diploid and polyploid cyprinids.

The number of allozyme products required for a study may depend upon the problems and taxa examined. Although a single enzyme system may reveal a pattern of phyletic, geographic, or ontogenetic variation that answers a particular question, usually the most informative enzyme system is unknown (or non-existent) and many systems must be screened to identify informative patterns of variation. The number of gene products examined in current studies increases as more and more systems known in other organisms are studied in cyprinids. Buth (1984a) summarized the tissue and buffer optima for the products of 36 allozyme loci from nine cyprinid studies (c. 1974–82). Information on additional loci (Magee and Philipp, 1982; Goodfellow *et al.*, 1982, 1984; Dowling and Moore, 1985a; Minckley *et al.*, 1989) allows the allozyme list to be increased to 60 loci (Table 4.1) Not all loci reported in these studies are listed in the table: some loci of problematic or poorly known systems are excluded. For example, Goodfellow *et al.* (1982) reported three acid phosphatase loci ('ACP-A, ACP-B, ACP-C') without zymogram document-ation for several North American cyprinids. Most other studies of cyprinids reported only one or two acid phosphatase loci from several tissues (Utter and Folmar, 1978; Dowling and Moore, 1985a; Minckley *et al.*, 1989). Multiple acid phosphatases from the liver of *Cyprinus carpio* may be due to posttrans-lational modification of the enzyme (Kubicz *et al.*, 1981), so caution must be exercised when interpreting the genetic control of poorly known systems.

Variation

Our knowledge of the distribution of genetic variation within and among populations is essential for an evolutionary interpretation of interactions and for the management of endangered or commercially important taxa (Allendorf, 1983). Estimates of gene flow using *F*-statistics (Wright, 1965) and the methods of Slatkin (1981, 1985) can be calculated easily from allozyme data. However, few studies of cyprinid population structure have employed these methods.

The codominant allele interaction of allozymes allows the unambiguous identification of homozygous and heterozygous genotypes at each locus. Quantification of heterozygosity (as the mean proportion of loci heterozygous per individual) is important for the study of population structure and genomic interactions such as hybridization and introgression. Because heterozygosity levels can be influenced by several evolutionary factors, differences among species in average heterozygosity should be interpreted with caution (Avise, 1977). The most substantial comparisons of cyprinid heterozygosity have come from the studies of North American cyprinids by Avise and Ayala (1976) and Avise (1977), who examined the gene products of 14–24 loci of 60 species. Mean heterozygosity ($\pm$ SE) per cyprinid species was estimated as 0.052 ± 0.004 (Avise, 1977), a value comparable to that (0.055 ± 0.036) reported for 106 species of ten orders of fishes other than the Cypriniformes (Smith and Fujio, 1982). However, variation among cyprinid species was not distributed symmetrically about this mean value (Fig. 4.1) because many North American cyprinids exhibited relatively low heterozygosities. Avise noted a pattern of lower-than-average heterozygosity in western North American cyprinids, and in eastern North American cyprinids from genera

Table 4.1 Enzymes (and non-specifically stained proteins), loci, tissue sources and electrophoretic conditions reported for cyprinid fishes

Enzyme/Protein	Enzyme Commission number	Structure*	Locus[†]	Tissue source	Electrophoretic conditions[‡]
Acid phosphatase	3.1.3.2	D	Acp-1	Liver, brain, muscle	A, B, C
Aconitate hydratase (mitochondrial)	4.2.1.3	M	mAcoh-A	Muscle	B, D, E
Aconitate hydratase (cytosolic)	4.2.1.3	M	sAcoh-A	Liver	B, C, D
Adenosine deaminase	3.5.4.4	M	Ada-1	Muscle	E
Adenylate kinase	2.7.4.3	M	Ak-A	Muscle	C, F
Alcohol dehydrogenase	1.1.1.1	D	Adh-1	Liver	A, G, H, I
Aspartate aminotransferase (mitochondrial)	2.6.1.1	D	mAat-A	Liver, muscle	A, C, E, F
Aspartate aminotransferase (cytosolic)	2.6.1.1	D	sAat-A	Heart, liver, muscle	A, C, E, F
Calcium binding protein	Non-specific	M	Cbp-1[a]	Muscle	C
Calcium binding protein	Non-specific	M	Cbp-2[a]	Muscle	C
Catalase	1.11.1.6	T	Cat-1	Liver	I
Creatine kinase	2.7.3.2	D	Ck-A	Muscle	C, G
Creatine kinase	2.7.3.2	D	Ck-B	Brain	G
Creatine kinase	2.7.3.2	D	Ck-C	Stomach	G
Cytosol aminopeptidase	3.4.11.1	M	Pep-E[b] sAp-1	Muscle	C, D
Dihydrolipoamide dehydrogenase	1.8.1.4	?	Ddh-1	Liver	C
Dipeptidase	3.4.13.11	D	Pep-A[b]	Muscle	B, J

Enzyme	EC number		Locus	Tissue	Alleles
Dipeptidase	3.4.13.11	T?	Pep-S[b]	Muscle	B, J
Esterase	3.1.1.-	M	Est-1	Muscle	A, G, J
Esterase	3.1.1.-	M	Est-2	Brain	J
Fructose-bisphosphate aldolase	4.1.2.13	T	Fba-A	Muscle	C
Fructose-bisphosphate aldolase	4.1.2.13	T	Fba-C	Brain	B, C
Fumarate hydratase	4.2.1.2	T	Fumh-1	Brain, muscle	B, E
General protein	Non-specific	?	Gp-1[a]	Muscle	C
Glucose-6-phosphate dehydrogenase	1.1.1.49	?	G6pdh-A	Muscle	C
Glucose-6-phosphate dehydrogenase	1.1.1.49	?	G6pdh-B	Liver	C
Glucose-6-phosphate isomerase	5.3.1.9	D	Gpi-A	Brain, liver, muscle	A, F, G, H
Glucose-6-phosphate isomerase	5.3.1.9	D	Gpi-B	Heart, muscle	A, F, G, H
Glyceraldehyde-3-phosphate dehydrogenase	1.2.1.12	T	Gapdh-A	Muscle	B, C
Glyceraldehyde-3-phosphate dehydrogenase	1.2.1.12	T	Gapdh-C	Eye	C
Glycerol-3-phosphate dehydrogenase	1.1.1.8	D	G3pdh-A	Muscle	A, C, D, H
Hexokinase	2.7.1.1	M	Hk-1	Muscle	C
3-Hydroxybutarate dehydrogenase	1.1.1.30	D	3Hbdh-1	Liver	C
L-Iditol dehydrogenase	1.1.1.14	T	Iddh-A	Liver	C, I, K
Isocitrate dehydrogenase (mitochondrial)	1.1.1.42	D	mIcdh-A	Heart, liver, muscle	A, B, E, H, L

Table 4.1 (*Continued*)

Table 4.1 (*Continued*)

Enzyme/Protein	Enzyme Commission number	Structure*	Locus[†]	Tissue source	Electrophoretic conditions[‡]
Isocitrate dehydrogenase (cytosolic)	1.1.1.42	D	sIcdh-A	Liver, muscle	A, B, E
Isocitrate dehydrogenase (cytosolic)	1.1.1.42	D	sIcdh-B[c]	Liver	E
L-Lactate dehydrogenase	1.1.1.27	T	Ldh-A	Muscle	B, C, D, F, G, H, J
L-Lactate dehydrogenase	1.1.1.27	T	Ldh-B	Brain, heart, muscle	B, C, D, F, G, H, J
L-Lactate dehydrogenase	1.1.1.27	T	Ldh-C	Liver	B, D, G
Malate dehydrogenase (mitochondrial; NAD-dependent)	1.1.1.37	D	mMdh-A	Brain, liver, muscle	A, B, C, D, G, H
Malate dehydrogenase (cytosolic; NAD-dependent)	1.1.1.37	D	sMdh-A	Brain, liver, muscle	A, B, C, D, G, H
Malate dehydrogenase (cytosolic; NAD-dependent)	1.1.1.37	D	sMdh-B	Muscle	A, B, C, D, G, H
Malate dehydrogenase (mitochondrial; NADP-dependent)	1.1.1.40	T	mMdhp-A[d]	Muscle	B, D
Malate dehydrogenase (cytosolic; NADP-dependent)	1.1.1.40	T	sMdhp-A[d]	Liver, muscle	A, B

Enzyme	EC number	Structure	Locus	Tissue	Buffers
Mannose-6-phosphate isomerase	5.3.1.8	M	Mpi-1	Muscle	F
α-Mannosidase	3.2.1.24	?	αMan-1	Muscle	F
Peptidase-C	3.4.-.-	M	Pep-C[b]	Brain, eye	B
Phosphoglucomutase	5.4.2.2	M	Pgm-A	Liver, muscle	C, D, F, H, J
Phosphoglucomutase	5.4.2.2	M	Pgm-B	Brain	B, C
Phosphogluconate dehydrogenase	1.1.1.44	D	Pgdh-1	Brain, liver, muscle	B, D, H
Proline dipeptidase	3.4.13.9	D	Pep-D[b]	Muscle	B, J
Purine-nucleoside phosphorylase	2.4.2.1	Tr	Pnp-1	Brain	B
Pyruvate kinase	2.7.1.40	T	Pk-1	Muscle	C
Superoxide dismutase (cytosolic)	1.15.1.1	D	sSod-A	Brain, liver, muscle	B, C, G, F
Tripeptide aminopeptidase	3.4.11.4	M?	Pep-B[b]	Muscle	B, J
Triose-phosphate isomerase	5.3.1.1	D	Tpi-A	Brain	H
Triose-phosphate isomerase	5.3.1.1	D	Tpi-B	Muscle	H
Xanthine dehydrogenase	1.1.1.204	D	Xdh-A	Liver	D, I

*D, dimer; M, monomer; T, tetramer; Tr, trimer.

†a, Buth (1982); b, Frick (1983); c, found only in some species; d, 'malic enzyme'.

‡A, amine–citrate (Clayton and Tretiak, 1972); B, tris–citrate (Whitt, 1970); C, histidine–citrate (Brewer, 1970): D, tris–citrate II (Selander et al., 1971); E. Phosphate–citrate (Selander et al., 1971); F, 'Poulik' (Selander et al., 1971); G, EDTA–borate–tris (Wilson et al., 1973); H, tris–citrate–EDTA (Avise et al., 1975); I, borate (Sackler, 1966); J, lithium hydroxide (Selander et al., 1971); K, tris–phosphate (Op't Hof et al., 1969); L, phosphate (Wolf et al., 1970).

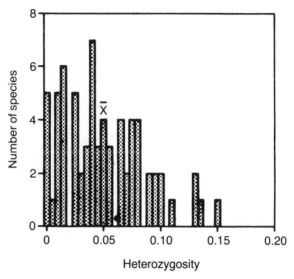

Fig. 4.1 Distribution of heterozygosity values (H) among 69 species of North American cyprinid fishes as reported by Avise (1977). $\bar{X}$, mean.

other than *Notropis sensu lato*. The significance of this observation is obscured slightly because *Notropis* is no longer considered a monophyletic assemblage (Mayden, 1989). An assessment of patterns of heterozygosity levels among subgroups of the North American cyprinid assemblage awaits a rigorous phylogenetic estimate of their relationships in order to recognize group membership. Only then can the phyletic component of variation be separated from other evolutionary factors to facilitate the study of the latter. However, as noted by Smith and Fujio (1982), virtually all large-scale surveys of heterozygosities among species are limited severely by the use of different proteins in different species. Comparisons of the heterozygosities reported for cyprinids by Avise (1977) are of limited value because of the inequality of the allozyme data base.

The use of genetic similarity/distance coefficients (e.g. Nei, 1972, 1978; Rogers, 1972) has been a popular way of quantifying allozyme differences between pairs of populations or species. Although the mean values of these coefficients increase with taxonomic rank in almost every group of organisms studied, their range between taxonomic categories overlaps so much that divergence measures cannot be used to assign taxonomic rank unequivocally. Overlap of genetic similarity coefficients calculated between cyprinids from population to genus is depicted in Fig. 4.2. Buth and Mayden (1981) argued that the taxonomic status of cyprinids should be based on their geographic patterns of variation, not on the magnitude of the variation. Distinguishing among patterns of geographic integration (intergrade zones of subspecies), introgression (partial gene transfer between species), and temporally or geographically random hybridization (yet maintaining the genomic integrity

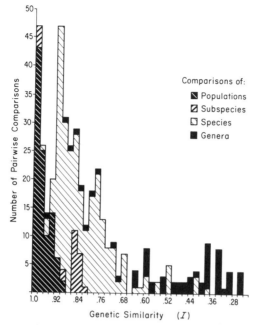

Fig. 4.2 Distribution of Nei's (1972) genetic similarity coefficients (*I*), calculated from pairwise conparisons at a variety of taxonomic levels in selected cyprinid studies. Levels compared: black, genera; thin hatching, species; thick hatching, subspecies; thin white hatching, populations. (Modified from Buth, 1984a, and reproduced with permission.)

of semispecies or species), requires rigorous geographic sampling and study, e.g. for the *zonatus* and *cornutus* species-groups of *Luxilus* (Buth and Mayden, 1981; Dowling and Moore, 1984, 1985 a, b; Dowling *et al.*, 1989) or for species of the genus *Moroco* (Min and Yang, 1986).

Allozyme variation in cyprinids has been used to test several evolutionary models dealing with speciation episodes (Avise and Ayala, 1975, 1976; Avise, 1978); problems with these models are discussed later (p. 106).

Hybridization and introgression

Hybridization among species of cyprinids is quite common. The use of allozyme methods to detect F_1 and backcross hybrids and to quantify gene flow between species has become standard. However, the taxonomic and systematic significance of hybridization is overstated. In their test of phenetic and cladistic methods using a hybridization data base, McAllister and Coad (1978) assumed that cyprinid taxa with closer taxonomic affinities are more likely to hybridize than are more distant taxa. This assumption is likely to be incorrect in some cases, especially in more recently diverged forms. For species that originate in a vicariant event, continued evolution in allopatry may result in divergence in many traits, but not necessarily in those involving reproductive isolating mechanisms. Such traits are not usually tested in allopatry, and the retention of the ability to interbreed may be a primitive trait and therefore cannot be used to infer 'close relationships' among taxa. Stated differently, the ability to interbreed has no bearing on the taxonomy of the forms involved unless the genetic interactions yield a new, genetically isolated species or result in the complete breakdown of the gene pools of the parentals.

The study of hybridization among cyprinids has revealed some interesting genetic phenomena, including alternative means of reproduction. Frankel (1983, 1985) noted developmental asynchrony in allozyme expression in hybrids of *Barbus*, presumably due to incompatibility involving paternal and maternal regulatory genes. Hybridization of divergent taxa, e.g., *Cyprinus carpio* × *Carassius auratus* or *Alburnus alburnus* × *Rutilus rubilio*, may yield an F_1 generation as shown by allozyme expression (Danzmann and Down, 1982; Berrebi *et al.*, 1989), yet rarely may involve any backcrossing. In another example, allozyme data confirmed that female *Ctenopharyngodon idella* × male *Hypophthalmichthys nobilis* yielded diploids of unknown reproductive status and sterile triploids (Beck *et al.*, 1983). Natural and artificial hybridization of *Phoxinus eos* and *P. neogaeus* yielded fertile all-female triploids whose allozyme profiles suggested that their reproductive mode may include a mixture of hybridogenesis and gynogenesis (Joswiak *et al.*, 1982; Dawley *et al.*, 1987; Stasiak *et al.*, 1988). Allozyme analysis also served to clarify the reproductive mode of intraspecific triploids of *Rutilus alburnoides* (Collares-Pereira, 1987). Allozyme expression of natural hybrids of tetraploid *Barbus* identified these as backcrosses, indicating fertility of the F_1s (P. Berrebi *et al.*, unpubl.).

If the hybridization process continues to include backcrosses to either of the parental species, genes of one species could enter the genome of the other, i.e., introgression would be possible. Allozyme evidence of introgressive hybridization between *Compostoma anomalum* and *C. oligolepis* (Rakocinski, 1980) and between *Luxilus cornutus* and *L. chrysocephalus* (Dowling and Moore, 1984) has demonstrated that the genetic integrity of these cyprinid species can be maintained despite interbreeding. Selection against hybrids of the latter species pair has been estimated at 9.2% y^{-1} (Dowling and Moore, 1985b). A selective advantage may be maintaining a gene of introgressive origin in some populations of *Cyprinella lutrensis* (Zimmerman and Richmond, 1981). Menzel (1976, 1977) suggested that *Luxilus albeolus* arose through introgressive hybridization of *Luxilus cornutus* and *L. cerasinus*. However, the data also are compatible with a sequence of divergence followed by introgression, the latter of which had nothing to do with the speciation process in this case. Additional studies are necessary to ascertain whether introgressive hybridization has any influence in cyprinid speciation.

Gene duplication and silencing

The tetraploid condition of certain cyprinids has been known for some time (Ohno *et al.*, 1967). More recent karyological investigations have identified more species as tetraploids, or even higher-level polyploids, based on their increased (double) number of chromosomes or DNA contents (p. 99) Speciation via polyploidization would be expected to·yield, initially, a form expressing all of its genes in duplicate (Ohno, 1970). However, a member of a duplicate gene pair is often silenced, resulting in 'functional diploidization' of gene expression (Ferris and Whitt, 1977a). The loss of duplicate gene expression has been correlated with morphological advancement (Ferris and Whitt, 1977a) and can be used to infer phylogenetic relationships (Ferris and Whitt, 1978; Buth, 1979b); it may hold considerable potential for application in tetraploid cyprinid lineages, e.g. certain *Barbus* (P. Berrebi *et al.*, unpubl.).

Studies of isozyme expression in selected cyprinid tetraploids have often documented retained duplicate genes (Buth, 1984a). However, these studies were limited to one or a few enzyme systems, and the role of gene silencing was not clearly understood. Wider screening of enzyme systems for isozyme expression was carried out in *Cyprinus carpio* (Ferris and Whitt, 1977b) and *Carassius auratus* (Woods and Buth, 1984). These species still express 52% and 19%, respectively, of their genes in duplicate. Therefore, in terms of gene expression, *Cyprinus carpio* is more similar to ancestral tetraploid condition than is *Carassius auratus*. None of the other polyploid cyprinids has been examined in comparable detail for gene expression. Comparisons of gene expression within lineages of polyploids will be especially interesting.

Differences in gene number may also exist among diploid cyprinids. The expression of a second supernatant/cytosolic locus in the isocitrate dehydrogenase system (= sIcdh-B) has been noted in some but not all diploid European and North American cyprinids (Dowling and Moore, 1985a; M. J. Collares-Pereira and M. M. Coelho, unpubl.; J. Joswiak, unpubl.; R. Lawson *et al.*, unpubl.). The taxonomic distribution and evolutionary significance of this and other possible gene differences have yet to be ascertained.

Systematics and biogeography

Allozymes have been used to identify cyprinid species; the procedure need involve only a few diagnostic gene products (Ferguson, 1981). This information can be communicated as a key, employing allozyme electrophoretic mobilities matched to external standards (Avise, 1974), or using internal mobility standards if the enzyme systems involved are multilocus in nature (Buth, 1980). As more is learned about gene expression in cyprinids and related families, keys may also employ heteropolymer assembly, tissue specificity, and gene duplication/silencing characters. Another way of communicating identification information is to generate a taxon × taxon matrix containing those allozyme loci exhibiting complete allelic differences between each pair of species (Crabtree and Buth, 1987). Such a 'diagnostic matrix' facilitates the choice of key enzyme systems, which allow us to distinguish interspecific hybrids from normal genic heterozygotes.

The application of allozyme data to phylogenetic inference in cyprinids has been useful at the generic and subgeneric levels. Studies at the level of tribe or subfamily may be possible if loci with limited variation are chosen. Intergeneric and intrageneric studies of cyprinid relationships have employed a wide variety of numerical analyses. Indeed, cyprinid allozyme data bases have frequently been used to test new numerical methods. One of the most widely used clustering techniques in allozyme studies is the unweighted pair group method with arithmetic averages (UPGMA; Sneath and Sokal, 1973). This method reveals levels of overall similarity, not evolutionary (genealogical) relationships, and for that and other mathematical reasons is inferior to other 'genetic distance' orientated clustering methods such as the distance Wagner procedure (Swofford, 1981). Avise and Ayala (1976) employed the latter in their study of several western North American cyprinids, as did Stein *et al.* (1985) for species in the *Lythrurus roseipinnis* complex. The latter study also employed a new method (PHYLAL) developed by Rogers (1984). The use of 'genetic distance' methods, however, has been debated (Farris, 1981, 1985, 1986; Felsenstein, 1984, 1986), and concerns about the independence of allozyme characters and their additivity must be addressed if these methods are to be considered valid. Early experiments in coding allozyme data as discrete characters for phylogenetic analysis of cyprinids included the use of compatibility analysis in *Campostoma* (Buth and Burr, 1978) and frequency-coding of allelic characters clustered using the Wagner procedure in *Luxilus* (Buth, 1979a). Both of these applications are invalid because the level of character coding (the 'allele as character' with presence or absence as states) is inappropriate (Buth, 1984b).

If treated as discrete characters and states, allozyme data could be coded qualitatively or quantitatively, using the locus as the character with the allelic composition of each locus as states (Buth, 1984b). Dimmick (1987) employed such coding in his study of relationships among selected species of North American cyprinids. The conservative nature of this coding scheme yielded few useful characters and necessitated a consensus tree approach to extract phylogenetic information from several equally parsimonious trees. Swofford and Berlocher (1987) note that character coding of allozyme data is extremely vulnerable to sampling error and recommend their recently developed method (FREQPARS), which retains the frequency information of an allozyme data set while fitting these data to a tree topology using maximum parsimony.

Allozyme applications in cyprinid biogeography are scarce because few studies employ a broad geographic sampling strategy, or have employed rigorous phylogenetic methods to ascertain the phylogeny of the group. Sampling across the range of a species may reveal its genetic structure (e.g. in *Luxilus pilsbryi*, Buth and Mayden, 1981), which may warrant the recognition of new taxa (Mayden, 1988; Yang *et al.*, unpubl.). Cyprinid biogeography is in critical need of phylogenies to provide a perspective from which the geographic pattern of divergence may be viewed.

4.3 CHROMOSOMES

Relative to other fish groups, cyprinids have been fairly well studied cytogenetically in terms of basic chromosome numbers and karyotypic configurations. Reasons for this are probably the large number of species in the family (stimulating an interest in interspecific comparisons for taxonomic or systematic purposes), the general ease of capture of many, if not most cyprinid species, and the economic importance (particularly in Asia) of many species. Although most published chromosome data on cyprinids and other fishes detail chromosome and chromosome arm numbers, several studies have adapted the chromosome banding methods commonly in use in higher vertebrates (especially mammals) to use in cyprinids (Ueda and Ojima, 1978; Takai and Ojima, 1986; Mayr *et al.*, 1986; Amemiya, 1987; Amemiya and Gold, 1988, 1990; Gold *et al.*, 1988). These banding methods increase the power and sensitivity of chromosome analysis enormously and their application to fish cytogenetics can be expected to increase dramatically in the near future.

Chromosome numbers

Chromosome numbers have been reported for approximately 435 cyprinid species, subspecies, or chromosomal races. The distribution of reported chromosome numbers by subfamily is shown in Table 4.2; full details (sources etc.) may be obtained from the third author (J.R.G.). The subfamilial assignments of various taxa used by us differ from those of Arai (1982) and Yu *et al.* (1987), and were based primarily on Rainboth (see Chapter 6). Other generic names were also changed in response either to published revisions or to the suggestions of W. J. Rainboth (pers. comm.). Polyploid forms in the genera *Carassius* and *Cyprinus* were assigned only a single chromosome number depending on ploidy level, i.e. tetraploid ($2n = 100$), hexaploid ($2n = 150$) and octaploid ($2n = 200$) in *Carassius auratus* and tetraploid ($2n = 100$) and hexaploid ($2n = 150$) in *Cyprinus carpio*.

As shown in Table 4.2, 52 of the 435 species or chromosomal forms are evidently polyploid on the basis of chromosome numbers greater than 90. This has been confirmed in many of these taxa by analysis of genome size (Zan *et al.*, 1986). The two species with $2n = 78$ chromosomes (*Opsariichthys uncirostris* and a Chinese race of *Zacco platypus*) appear to be diploids (Zan *et al.*, 1986). Among the putatively diploid cyprinids ($2n$ range = 42–78), 282 of the 383 species or chromosomal forms examined have $2n = 50$ chromosomes. The strong mode of $2n = 50$ has led several authors (e.g., Cataudella *et al.*, 1977; Arai, 1982; Yu *et al.*, 1987) to hypothesize that $2n = 50$ is the plesiomorphic chromosome number for the family. This hypothesis has been based primarily on the commonality principle as opposed to outgroup comparison (Watrous

Table 4.2 Distribution of chromosome numbers reported for Cyprinidae

Subfamily	N^*	Diploid ($2n$) chromosome number															
		42	44	46	48	50	52	54	70	78	96	98	100	102	148	150	> 200
Acheilognathinae	23	1	13	2	7												
Alburninae	13				10	3											
Cultrinae	17				17												
Cyprininae	133		2	12	12	63	2	2			5	6	23	1	10	6	1
Danioninae	24				8	13			1	2‡							
Gobioninae	53			1		52											
Leuciscinae†	167				15	147	4	1									
Unknown	5				1	4											
Total	435	1	13	5	70	282	6	3	1	2‡	5	6	23	1	10	6	1

*Number of species, subspecies, or chromosomal races.
†Includes 107 North American cyprinids: 105 have $2n = 50$, one has $2n = 48$, and one has $2n = 52$.
‡One of the reports of $2n = 78$ is Zacco platypus (Arai, 1982), which also has been reported to have $2n = 48$ (Yu et al., 1987).

and Wheeler, 1981). With regard to the latter, however, there are simply too few data for appropriate comparisons. Only two species of Gonorhynchiformes (the appropriate outgroup to the Otophysi, *sensu* Fink and Fink, 1981) have been karyotyped: one has $2n = 32$ chromosomes, whereas the other has $2n = 28$ chromosomes (Ojima, 1985). Within the Cypriniformes, species in all six families (*sensu* Lauder and Liem, 1983) have been karyotyped, although extensive work has been carried out in only three (including the Cyprinidae). One of these, the Catostomidae, is tetraploid in that all 20 or so catostomid species karyotyped have 96–100 chromosomes (Uyeno and Smith, 1972; Yu *et al.*, 1987; J. R. Gold, unpubl.). The other, the Cobitidae, contains both diploid and tetraploid species, although of the 35 putatively diploid (*2n* range = 40–52) cobitids karyotyped, 26 have $2n = 50$ chromosomes (Yu *et al.*, 1987; W. H. LeGrande, pers. comm.). Only four species in the remaining three cypriniform families have been karyotyped: *Gyrinocheilus aymonieri* (Gyrinocheilidae) has $2n = 48$ chromosomes, *Psilorhynchus balitoria* (Psilorhynchidae) has $2n = 50$ chromosomes, and both *Vanmanenia pingchowensis* and *Hemimyzon abbreviata* (Homalopteridae) have $2n = 50$ chromosomes (Hinegardner and Rosen, 1972; Khuda-Bukhsh *et al.*, 1986; Rainboth *et al.*, 1986; Yu *et al.*, 1987). From these data, one could argue that $2n = 50$ chromosomes is plesiomorphic for Cypriniformes (and for Cyprinidae), although again the hypothesis would be based almost exclusively on commonality.

The uniformity of chromosome numbers within the Cyprinidae is striking, and clearly indicates that chromosome structural changes such as fissions or fusions that precipitate (non-polyploid) changes in chromosome number have been relatively infrequent. However, there are subfamilies (cf. Table 4.2) in which none of the diploid species examined has 50 chromosomes, and even in subfamilies in which $2n = 50$ predominates, many diploid species have other than 50 chromosomes. Given the hypothesis that $2n = 50$ is plesiomorphic for the Cyprinidae, some authors (e.g. Arai, 1982; Yu *et al.*, 1987) have hypothesized that changes in diploid chromosome numbers may represent chromosomal synapomorphies. Yu *et al.* (1987), for example, united the Cultrinae, Acheilognathinae, and two subfamilies (Hypophthalmichthyinae and Xenocypridinae) now placed in the Leuciscinae (Rainboth in Chapter 6; see also Howes in Chapter 1) on the basis of a presumed synapomorphic change from $2n = 50$ to $2n = 48$ chromosomes. Similar logic might suggest that the same could also hold for species with other than $2n = 50$ chromosomes in subfamilies where $2n = 50$ is the dominant mode. In our view, this type of reasoning is fraught with peril, given the absence of evidence demonstrating the homology of the presumed fusion events. In several rodent groups, for example, G- or R-cromosome banding has unequivocally shown that taxa that have the same chromosome number, and which clearly have been derived via chromosomal fusion/fission events from some ancestral chromosome number, need not have experienced the same fusion/fission events (Capanna, 1982; Larson *et al.*, 1984; Corti *et al.*, 1986; Qumsiyeh *et al.*,

1987). Stated differently in terms of cyprinid chromosome numbers, the single (presumed) fusion event that hypothetically occurred in an ancestor to the Cultrinae might not be the same (presumed) fusion event that hypothetically occurred in an ancestor to the Acheilognathinae or any other species (or species group) with $2n = 48$ chromosomes. For this reason, we regard inferences on cyprinid phylogeny based solely on diploid chromosome numbers as premature.

Other types of chromosome structural changes (e.g. pericentric inversions, translocations, heterochromatin additions/deletions) that do not change chromosome number have been inferred in cyprinids on the basis of reported differences in fundamental chromosome arm numbers (Cataudella *et al.*, 1977; Manna and Khuda-Bukhsh, 1977; Gold *et al.*, 1979, 1981; Rishi, 1981; Zan *et al.*, 1986; Tripathi and Sharma, 1987). Direct evidence that some of these types of chromosomal change must have occurred during cyprinid evolution has been indirectly provided by studies employing NOR (see p. 101) or C-banding (Takai and Ojima, 1986; Gold and Amemiya, 1986; Gold *et al.*, 1986, 1988; Amemiya, 1987; Amemiya and Gold, 1988). In addition, in those studies where the overall quality of metaphase karyotypes examined is good (e.g. Cataudella *et al.*, 1977; Gold and Avise, 1977; Li *et al.*, 1986; Amemiya and Gold, 1987a), it is clear that the numbers of meta-, submeta-, and acrocentric chromosomes within cyprinid complements differ among species. However, cyprinid chromosomes are relatively small (the average cyprinid chromosome is roughly $4-6\ \mu m$ in length), and the quality of many of the metaphases from which arm number estimates have been generated is not particularly good. Many reports of cyprinid chromosome arm numbers should therefore be viewed sceptically, as should phylogenetic or cytogenetic inferences based on chromosome arm number differences.

Heterologous sex chromosomes based on cytological heteromorphy have been reported in only three cyprinid species: *Carassius auratus* (cited from Yu *et al.*, 1987) *Scardinius erythrophthalmus* (Chiarelli *et al.*, 1969), and *Garra lamta* (Khuda-Bukhsh *et al.*, 1986). In *G. lamta*, the authors could not rule out the possibility that the heteromorphism might have been autosomal. The same may also be true for the putative sex chromosomes in *S. erythrophthalmus* because no sex-specific chromosomal heteromorphisms were found in individuals studied by Cataudella *et al.* (1977). There also is genetic evidence of male heterogamety among cultivated stocks of *Carassius auratus* (Yamamoto and Kajishima, 1969), and Ueda and Ojima (1978) and Ojima and Takai (1979) have observed a sex-related C-band heteromorphism in *C. auratus* involving the short arm of the second largest submetacentric chromosome in the complement. On the whole, however, sex chromosomes in cyprinids, as in most fishes (Gold, 1979), appear to have remained relatively undifferentiated.

Polyploidy

There are at least 52 polyploid cyprinid taxa as adduced from chromosome numbers and, in many cases, genome sizes (Table 4.2). This estimate includes three chromosomal polyploids ($2n = 100$, 150, 200) in *C. auratus* and two ($2n = 100$, 150) in *Cyprinus carpio*. The polyploid taxa are distributed in three tribes (Cyprinini, Oreinini, Systomini) of the subfamily Cyprininae (*sensu* Rainboth in Chapter 6). All but two taxa examined from the Cyprinini have been polyploid. One exception was a Romanian population of the crucian carp, *Carassius carassius*, reported as possessing $2n = 50$ chromosomes (Raicu *et al.*, 1981). This report is problematic, and should possibly be considered anomalous, given the extensive chromosomal work on *Carassius* in which no individual with fewer than 94 chromosomes has ever been found. The other exception is a group of small 'barbs' from Africa, placed in the genus *Barbus*. None of these species is similar morphologically to the Euro-Caspian members of *Barbus* (W. J. Rainboth, pers. comm.), all of which appear to be tetraploid. All taxa examined from the Oreinini have been either tetraploid or hexaploid.

Diakinesis chromosomes have been examined in males of tetraploid *C. auratus* and *Cyprinus carpio*, and in both, the meiotic karyotypes were essentially bivalent (Ohno *et al.*, 1967). The two species might be alloploids, and were possibly derived from interspecific hybridization between two diploid species. However, as noted by Ohno *et al.* (1967), the two species could have arisen from ancestral autotetraploids in which the four original homologues have diverged into two different pairs. Without question, an interesting problem for future research is the issue of whether polyploid cyprinids are auto- or alloploids, and if the latter, exactly which species might have participated in alloploidization events.

Except for hexaploids and octaploids of *Carassius auratus*, and possibly the hexaploid *Cyprinus carpio*, most cyprinid polyploids are presumed to have 'normal' bisexual reproduction. Polyploid chromosome numbers have often been reported from individuals of both sexes (Ohno *et al.*, 1967; Ojima *et al.*, 1972; Cataudella *et al.*, 1977; Khuda-Bukhsh, 1980, 1982), and no one has yet reported an excess of females (as found in hexaploid and octaploid *C. auratus*), other than what might be expected from greater female longevity. While bisexual reproduction might be expected for the tetraploid species which could have become effectively diploidized (*sensu* Ohno *et al.*, 1969), the observation (Oellermann, 1989) that at least five of the hexaploid species in *Barbus* reproduce bisexually is somewhat surprising. It is unknown whether the hexaploids in the Oreinini reproduce bisexually.

Nearly all hexaploid and octaploid *C. auratus* reproduce by gynogenesis, in which unreduced ova are stimulated to develop by sperm of conspecific tetraploids or of other species, but where fusion of maternal and paternal nuclei does not occur (Cherfas, 1966; Kobayashi *et al.*, 1970; Ojima and

Asano, 1977; Ueda and Ojima, 1978; Penaz *et al.*, 1979; Schultz, 1980). The offspring are essentially clones of their maternal parent and all are expected to be female. The occurrence of hexaploid male *C. auratus*, however, has been confirmed by chromosome analysis (Muramoto, 1975; Zan *et al.*, 1986), and in one instance the hexaploid males were found to have normal testes and sexual behaviour (Zan *et al.*, 1986). Moreover, their sperm possessed only 50% of the DNA of somatic cells, suggesting that a 'normal' meiosis occurred. As noted by Zan *et al.* (1986), these findings indicate first, that some hexaploid *C. auratus* may be evolving into a self-maintainable gynogenetic system, and second, that if a 'normal' meiosis occurred in females, it would not be impossible for the gynogenetic system to return to a bisexual mode. A similar suggestion has also been made by Russian workers (cited from Penaz *et al.*, 1979). Tetraploid ($2n = 100$) gynogens of *C. auratus* also occur, at least in Europe (Schultz, 1980).

Chromosome numbers reported for both tetraploid and hexaploid *C. auratus* vary considerably, from 94 to 104 among the tetraploids, and from 150 to 165 among the hexaploids (Muramoto, 1975; Penaz *et al.*, 1979; Ojima, 1985). This might appear to suggest that fusion/fission or other chromosomal rearrangements that affect chromosome number have occurred more frequently than in diploid cyprinids. However, some of this variation stems from the presence of microchromosomes (Ohno *et al.*, 1967; Muramoto, 1975; Ueda and Ojima, 1978; Penaz *et al.*, 1979), and unquestionably some variation must arise from problems encountered in spreading and enumerating so many chromosomes. Moreover, given the polyploid background, some of the variation could result from true aneuploidy. The latter supposition is supported by the reports of odd chromosome numbers in many individuals (Muramoto, 1975; Penaz *et al.*, 1979).

One last topic that merits brief mention is the intriguing possibility that at least some of the cyprinid polyploidizations may represent derived, single-step transitions (apomorphies) which ostensibly could unite several species, or species groups, into putatively monophyletic lineages. Several authors (e.g. Arai, 1982; Zan *et al.*, 1986; Yu *et al.*, 1987) have proposed that the polyploid cyprinids are related phylogenetically, and have used polyploidization as part of their arguments. Additional suggestive evidence along these lines is that although chromosome numbers differ among both tetraploid and hexaploid forms, the same chromosome numbers typically occur in species belonging to the same genus or related species group. Examples include three Euro-Caspian barbs (*Barbus barbus, B. meridionalis,* and *B. plebius*) which have $2n = 100$ (Park, 1974; Cataudella *et al.*, 1977), the six tetraploid ($2n = 100$) species of *Tor* (Khuda-Bukhsh *et al.*, 1986; Zan *et al.*, 1986), the two tetraploid ($2n = 96$) species of *Pseudobarbus* (Oellermann, 1989), and the three tetraploid ($2n = 100$) species of *Spinibarbus* (Yu *et al.*, 1987). Exceptions include five hexaploid species of South African yellowfish (*Barbus*), of which two have 148 chromosomes and three have 150 (Oellermann, 1989), and the genus

Schizothorax, which contains three tetraploid ($2n = 98$) and seven hexaploid ($2n = 148$) species (Khuda-Bukhsh *et al.*, 1986; Zan *et al.*, 1986; Yu *et al.*, 1987). The two yellowfish with $2n = 148$ appear on morphological grounds to constitute a different species group from the three species with $2n = 150$ (Oellermann, 1989). With regard to *Schizothorax*, and assuming that the hexaploids are not gynogenetic, the genus may not be monophyletic. Finally, it is interesting to note that nearly all the cyprinid polyploids have chromosome numbers that represent multiples or combinations of 48 or 50 chromosomes. This suggests the notion that the tetraploid cyprinids with 96, 98, and 100 chromosomes could have arisen from hybridizations between species with 48, 48 and 50, and 50 chromosomes, respectively, and that the (presumably bisexual) hexaploid cyprinids with 148 and 150 chromosomes arose from hybridizations between diploid species with 48 or 50 chromosomes and tetraploid species with 98 or 100 chromosomes.

Chromosomal NOR banding and cytosystematics

Chromosomal banding in cyprinids is limited primarily to visualizations of the chromosomal nucleolus organizer regions (NORs). Briefly, NORs are chromosomal sites intimately related to nucleolus formation in interphase and containing the genes for the 18S and 28S ribosomal RNA genes (Howell, 1982). NORs are generally detected by a silver nitrate method (Howell, 1982), although GC base-pair-enhancing DNA fluorochromes (such as chromomycin A3) will differentiate NORs of many lower vertebrates (Schmid, 1982; Amemiya and Gold, 1986, 1987b). NOR banding patterns are known for almost 100 cyprinids (Mayr *et al.*, 1986; Takai and Ojima, 1986; Amemiya, 1987; Gold *et al.*, 1988, unpubl.). The most extensive use of cyprinid NORs as taxonomic or systematic characters has been carried out by Gold and colleagues (Gold, 1984; Gold and Amemiya, 1986; Amemiya, 1987; Amemiya and Gold, 1988, 1990; Gold *et al.*, 1988, unpubl.). These workers have assayed NOR variation within and among 69 North American cyprinids, most of which belong to a putatively monophyletic assemblage defined by an opening in the posterior myodome (Coburn, 1982; Mayden, 1989). Their findings are summarized briefly here.

First, the number of NOR-bearing chromosomes among the 69 species ranges from a single pair in 46 species, to two pairs in 20 species, to three pairs in three species. A total of 12 morphologically different NOR-bearing chromosomes (= NOR chromosome phenotypes) have been identified on the basis of the position (terminal or interstitial) of the NORs, the type of chromosome (metacentric, submetacentric, etc.) on which NORs are located, and the relative size of NOR-bearing chromosomes within complements. In all but two of the 69 species examined, the NORs have been located in terminal chromosomal positions. The 12 different NOR chromosome phenotypes (Fig. 4.3) are distributed on at least 15 different chromosomes because two

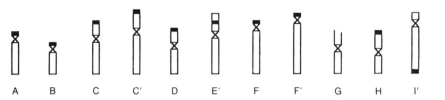

A   B   C   C'   D   E'   F   F'   G   H   I'   J

Fig. 4.3 Computer-assisted representations of standard NOR chromosome pheno-types. NORs are indicated by darkened areas. NOR chromosome phenotypes: A, NOR terminal on short arm of medium-sized acro-/subtelocentric; B, NOR terminal on short arm of small acro-subtelocentric; C, NOR terminal on short arm of large submetacen-tric; D, NOR terminal on short arm of medium to large submetacentric; E, NOR subterminal on short arm of large submetacentric; F, NOR terminal on short arm of large acro-/subtelocentric; G, NOR terminal on one arm of large metacentric; H, NOR terminal on one arm of medium metacentric; I, NOR terminal on long arm of large acro-/subtelocentric; J, NOR terminal on short arm of small submetacentric. Prime (') denotes the largest chromosome in the complement.

pairs of NOR chromosomes of the A phenotype occur in *Campostoma anomalum*, two pairs of the B phenotype occur in two species of the genus *Nocomis*, and two pairs of the D phenotype occur in *Semotilus atromaculatus* and *Phenacobius mirabilis*. Summed together, the interspecific variations in the number of NOR pairs and NOR chromosome phenotypes result in 24 discrete NOR conditions. Twelve different NOR conditions have been found among the 46 species with a single NOR pair and 12 different NOR conditions among the 23 species with more than one or multiple NOR pairs. Comparison of the interspecific NOR variation in North American cyprinids with that from 22 Asian cyprinids (Takai and Ojima, 1986) reveals several similarities. More than half the Asian cyprinids (14 of 22 species) had only a single NOR pair, and all NORs were in terminal positions. Collectively, the interspecific patterns of NOR variation in cyprinids are similar to those in other fishes (Foresti *et al.*, 1981; Galetti *et al.*, 1984, 1985; Moreira-Filho *et al.*, 1984; Phillips and Ihssen, 1985; Takai and Ojima, 1986).

Second, the degree of interspecific variations in NORs in North American cyprinids appears at odds with their apparent conservation in standard or gross karyotypes. Nearly all species examined have $2n = 50$ chromosomes, and (estimated) diploid chromosome arm numbers generally range from 92 to 100 (Gold *et al.*, 1980; Amemiya and Gold, 1987a). The 24 NOR conditions suggest that a minimum of 23 different chromosomal rearrangements or changes involving an NOR have occurred since the 69 species last shared a common ancestor. Although NOR banding itself does not provide the resolution to ascertain the nature of NOR chromosome rearrangements, Gold and Amemiya (1986), Amemiya (1987), and Amemiya and Gold (1988) have used C-banding to demonstrate that at least a few of the interspecific NOR chromosome differences stem from classical chromosomal rearrangements such

as inversions and translocations. This finding suggests that if the rearrange-
ment frequencies for all the chromosomes are similar to that for the NOR
chromosomes, the rate of chromosomal evolution within North American
Cyprinidae is considerably greater than believed.

Third, intraspecific variations (heteromorphisms) in NORs have been
detected in *c.* 10–13% of all North American cyprinids examined, regardless of
species. These heteromorphisms include enlargements (amplifications) of NOR
sites, and NOR sites which are presumed to be functionally inactive. Both types
of heteromorphisms appear common in fishes (Foresti *et al.*, 1981; Moreira-
Filho *et al.*, 1984; Takai and Ojima, 1986); Gold (1984) and Gold and
Amemiya (1986) give examples of both in cyprinids. Importantly, both types
of intraspecific heteromorphisms differ qualitatively from the types of NOR
differences found interspecifically. This reinforces the observations (below)
that interspecific NOR differences can serve as taxonomic and systematic
characters.

Finally, comparisons of the NOR conditions among the 69 North American
cyprinids assayed have revealed several similarities, which yield phenetic
relationships that are not discordant with present concepts of North American
cyprinid taxonomy. Examples include (1) three species of the genus *Pimephales*
with NORs located terminally on the short arm of a medium-to-large
submetacentric chromosome pair; (2) four species of the genus *Cyprinella*
whose NORs are located terminally on one arm of a medium metacentric pair;
(3) five other species in *Cyprinella* whose NORs are located terminally on the
short arm of a large submetacentric chromosome pair which also is the largest
chromosome pair in the complement; and (4) three species of the genus
Pteronotropis that have at least one NOR situated on the short arm of a large
acrocentric chromosome pair (Amemiya, 1987; Amemiya and Gold, 1988,
1990; Gold *et al.*, 1988, unpubl.). NORs also are often useful in differentiating
morphologically similar species that differ in NOR phenotype. A good example
may be found in Amemiya and Gold (1988). Taken together, these observations indicate that NORs can be taxonomically informative characters.

The use of NORs to infer hypotheses of phylogenetic relationships, however,
has been limited to species in which other types of bands (primarily C-bands)
have been employed to test interspecific homologies of NOR chromosomes
(Amemiya and Gold, 1988, 1990). The central difficulty in using NORs for
phylogenetic inference stems from the problem of establishing interspecific
homologies of NOR-bearing chromosomes. NOR banding alone does not
provide the resolution necessary to determine if the same NOR phenotype
found in different species actually represents the same homologous character.
As an example, nearly 20 North American cyprinid species possess a single
pair of NOR chromosomes with the NOR located terminally on the short arm of
a medium-to-large submetacentric chromosome (Amemiya, 1987; P. K. Zoch
and J. R. Gold, unpublished). These species belong to at least nine different
morphological assemblages, as defined by Coburn (1982) and Mayden (1989),

suggesting that some of the NOR chromosomes are either homoplastic or non-homologous. The interpretation of homoplastic NOR locations is not surprising, because most North American cyprinids have from six to eight pairs of medium-to-large submetacentric chromosomes in their complements. Nonetheless, the studies by Amemiya and Gold (1988, 1990) and later work (Zoch and Gold, unpubl.) indicate clearly the potential usefulness of NORs in cyprinid phylogenetics, provided that alternative types of bands can be used to assign homology among NOR chromosomes.

4.4   MITOCHONDRIAL AND NUCLEAR DNA

Advances in molecular biology (e.g. DNA cloning) have opened frontiers in evolutionary biology. In general, DNA methods have been used in two types of studies: those that examine characteristics of genomes such as genome organization, genome size, or DNA–DNA hybridization, and those that examine the sequence of specific DNA molecules through restriction endonuclease analysis or nucleotide sequencing. Most evolutionary or systematic studies that have focused upon differences at the sequence level have employed mitochondrial DNA (mtDNA). Nuclear genes such as ribosomal DNA (rDNA) or protein-coding genes have been used less frequently. DNA sequences are characterized either by using restriction endonucleases (bacterial enzymes which recognize and cleave DNA molecules at specific 4–6 base sequences), or by directly obtaining the nucleotide sequence of the molecule in question. Restriction endonuclease analysis is used more often than direct sequence analysis because it is quicker and cheaper. More information on these DNA technologies and their applications to evolutionary biology is in Maniatis *et al.* (1982), Avise and Lansman (1983), Brown (1983, 1985), Wilson *et al.* (1985), Avise *et al.* (1987), Hillis (1987), Kreitman (1987), Moritz *et al.* (1987), Quinn and White (1987a), and Sibley *et al.* (1987). The use of DNA technologies for the study of fishes has been limited primarily to mtDNA (e.g. Berg and Ferris, 1984; Graves *et al.*, 1984; Gyllensten *et al.*, 1985; Avise *et al.*, 1987; Ferris and Berg, 1987; Gyllensten and Wilson, 1987; Kornfield and Bogdanowicz, 1987; Avise and Vrijenhoek, 1987).

Applications of these methods to studies of cyprinids are rare, and only baseline data have been reported, but these studies suggest considerable potential for applying DNA technologies to studies of cyprinids on several levels of organization.

Organization of nuclear genomes

Studies of nuclear genome organization in fishes are limited to few species. The basic features or patterns of DNA sequence organization in fishes (including cyprinids), however, appear largely similar to those in other vertebrates if not most eukaryotes. Schmidtke *et al.* (1979) studied the reassociation kinetics of six cyprinid species (including two tetraploids) and found that the proportions of highly repeated, moderately repeated, and unique or single-copy DNAs in all six genomes fell within the ranges reported for other eukaryotes (Fristrom and Clegg, 1988; Hartl *et al.*, 1988). Studies in other fishes (primarily salmonids) have yielded similar results (Gharrett *et al.*, 1977; Hanham and Smith, 1980). No data on the basic interspersion pattern(s) of cyprinid DNAs have been published, but from other fishes and metazoans as a whole, it is likely that cyprinids possess primarily the short-period or '*Xenopus*' interspersion pattern (Davidson *et al.*, 1975; Hanham and Smith, 1979). Moyer *et al.* (1988) isolated, cloned, and sequenced the basic monomer repeat unit of a highly repeated, satellite DNA from the cyprinid *Cyprinella lutrensis*; this satellite DNA was typical of many, if not most, eukaryotic satellite DNAs in size, copy number, presumed tandem arrangement, internal repetition, and the presence of subfamilies of sequences.

Considerably more has been published on DNA base composition and nucleotide distribution of fish (including cyprinid) nuclear genomes. Hudson *et al.* (1980), using density gradient centrifugation, and Karel and Gold (1987) and Gold and Karel (1988), using thermal denaturation, have examined nuclear DNAs from nearly 70 fish species including 25 cyprinids. The range of %GC values among these species appears lower than that of other vertebrates (Thiery *et al.*, 1976; Guttman *et al.*, 1977; Mayfield, 1977; Olmo, 1981), but well within the extremes reported for vertebrates as a whole. Alternatively, with the exception of three cyprinid species (next paragraph), the nuclear genomes of fishes (including the other 22 cyprinids examined) display considerable uniformity in nucleotide distributions and lack DNA components that differ significantly in base-pair composition from mainband DNA. This is in sharp contrast to the nuclear genomes of species in other major vertebrate groups, where numerous, typically GC base-pair-rich DNA components occur in addition to mainband DNA (Thiery *et al.*, 1976; Guttman *et al.*, 1977; Mayfield, 1977; Olmo, 1981). The molecular reason for this difference may be the absence in 'genomically uniform' species of long (> 200 kilobase) DNA segments called isochores (Cuny *et al.*, 1981; Bernardi *et al.*, 1985) that differ from mainband DNA in GC base-pair composition. Of interest is the suggestion that the occurrence of isochores may be responsible for the G- and R- banding patterns typically observed on higher vertebrate metaphase chromosomes (Medrano *et al.*, 1988). As discussed by Hartley and Horne (1985) and others, G- and R- bands, produced respectively by trypsin or heat-denaturation, have not been produced reliably on fish chromosomes. This may result from the absence of isochore occurrence or genome compartmentalization.

The three exceptions are the cyprinids *Cyprinella lepida*, *C. lutrensis*, and *C. venusta*, all of which possess a discrete, heavy (i.e. GC base-pair-rich) melting component in their genomes (Karel and Gold, 1987). This component has nearly the same %GC value in all three species and differs considerably from the %GC values of the respective mainband DNAs. However, the displacement from the mainband DNAs and the near identity of %GC values among the three species suggest that the heavy component reflects a large, comparatively GC base-pair-rich satellite DNA family rather than the presence of isochore compartmentalization. This hypothesis is supported by the fact that the satellite DNA of *C. lutrensis* characterized by Moyer *et al.* (1988) has the same %GC content as the heavy melting component found by Karel and Gold (1987).

Genome sizes

Genome sizes (nuclear DNA contents) are known for well over 100 cyprinid species or subspecies (Ohno *et al.*, 1967; Bachmann *et al.*, 1972; Hinegardner and Rosen, 1972; Kang and Park, 1973; Zan *et al.*, 1986; Gold *et al.*, 1990). The reported range in cyprinid DNA values per cell varies from 1.6 to 7.0 pg, but includes species that by chromosomal evidence are obviously tetraploids or hexaploids. Among strictly diploid cyprinids, the reported range is from *c.* 1.6 to 4.4 pg, although some DNA values reported before about 1975 should be viewed with caution, given subsequent methodological and equipment advances. On the whole, however, both the average and range of genome sizes in diploid cyprinids are somewhat greater than those in most diploid teleost fishes (Hinegardner and Rosen, 1972; Gold, 1979). Interestingly, nearly all the diploid cyprinids examined for genome size have $2n = 48$–50 chromosomes, despite a more than twofold difference in DNA content. This differs from diploid teleosts as a whole, where a significant, positive correlation exists between chromosome number and genome size (Hinegardner and Rosen, 1972). This difference suggests that changes in genome size in cyprinids have occurred primarily through regional amplifications or losses of DNA, rather than through chromosome structural changes which increase or decrease chromosome numbers.

The most extensive work on cyprinid genome sizes has been carried out by Gold and colleagues, who have used North American cyprinids to study the dynamics and evolution of genome size itself (Gold and Price, 1985; Gold and Amemiya, 1987; Gold *et al.*, 1990). These workers have studied genome size variation within and among nearly 50 diploid cyprinid species, almost all of which belong to a putatively monophyletic assemblage defined by an opening in the posterior myodome (Coburn, 1982; Mayden, 1989). Although much of this work is still in progress, the salient findings are outlined briefly below.

First, the distribution of DNA values within populations of diploid cyprinid species is continuous and normal, suggesting that DNA quantity changes at this level are small, involve both gains and losses of DNA, and are cumulative and independent in effect. Furthermore, the distribution of genome sizes across cyprinid species, although non-normal, is essentially continuous and overlapping, suggesting that differences between species also result from the steady accumulation of relatively small changes in DNA quantity. This pattern of continuous genome size change typifies many animal groups (Bachmann *et al.*, 1972, 1985) and differs markedly from the discontinuously distributed species DNA values found in many plant groups (Narayan, 1982; Cavalier-Smith, 1985). Additional discussion on the problem of continuous versus discontinuous genome size distributions may be found in Ragland and Gold (1989).

Second, the DNA that is free to vary quantitatively within diploid cyprinid genomes appears to be 4–5% of the total DNA. This quantity is approximately the same as that theoretically needed for the entire cyprinid structural gene component if one assumes a liberal figure of 50 000 structural genes in the cyprinid genome and 1500 coding DNA base pairs per gene. In all likelihood, however, the DNAs gained or lost from cyprinid genomes are probably not coding sequences *per se* because this would be expected to interfere significantly with normal cellular processes.

Third, no associations have yet been found in diploid cyprinids between interspecific variation in genome size and differences in several life history parameters, including body size. Although limited in scope, these findings indicate that the correlations found in other organisms (Bennett, 1976; Mazin, 1980; Shuter *et al.*, 1983) between genome size and certain life history characteristics may be spurious. Additional discussion may be found in Gold and Amemiya (1987) and Ragland and Gold (1989), but the cyprinid (and other) genome size data suggest that the models of Cavalier-Smith (1980) and Szarski (1983) relating genome size variation to adaptive phenomena may be oversimplified or inapplicable to complex, higher eukaryotes.

Finally, the cyprinid genome size data have been compared to similar data (Ragland, 1986; Ragland and Gold, 1989) from the North America sunfishes (Centrarchidae) to see whether changes in genome size are concentrated in speciation episodes. Tests using theoretical models developed by Avise and Ayala (1975, 1976) and Avise (1978) indicate that considerable changes in genome size occur during, or are associated with, cyprinid speciation episodes. These findings, however, should be viewed as tentative, in part because the evidence is essentially correlative, and in part because of objections to the models (Mayden, 1986). In addition, intraspecific genome size variation in diploid cyprinids can often be as great as interspecific variation, casting some doubt on the ideas of a strong relationship between genome size change and speciation (for further discussion see Ragland, 1986; Regland and Gold, 1989; Gold *et al.*, 1990).

DNA–DNA hybridization

Hybridization of single-copy nuclear DNA (scnDNA) has been used extensively to infer taxonomic relationships among species, particularly birds (reviews Sibley and Ahlquist, 1983; Cracraft, 1987; Sibley *et al.*, 1987). The degree of scnDNA divergence in vertebrates appears too low for use in population-level studies (Coccone *et al.*, 1987). The only DNA–DNA hybridization studies performed on fishes were by Gharrett *et al.* (1977) and Hanham and Smith (1980). Work on other organismal groups (references above) suggest that DNA–DNA hybridization could be a valuable method for analysing cyprinid phylogenetic relationships, although there is extensive disagreement about the value of DNA–DNA hybridization data for systematic inference (Templeton, 1985, 1986; Fitch, 1986; Ruvolo and Smith, 1986; Saitou, 1986; Cracraft, 1987; Sibley *et al.*, 1987).

Mitochondrial DNA

Several unique properties of mtDNA make it particularly useful for molecular investigations: (1) it is a relatively small, circular molecule ranging in size from 16.2 to 19.5 kilobases (kb) in fishes, including cyprinids (Avise *et al.*, 1984; Berg and Ferris, 1984; Graves *et al.*, 1984; Beckwitt and Petruska, 1985; Birt *et al.*, 1986; Thomas *et al.*, 1986; Beckwitt and Aoyagi, 1987; T. E. Dowling, unpubl.; L. R. Richardson and J. R. Gold, unpubl.); (2) it is highly compact, with few non-coding regions, and gene content and order appear to be conserved in all vertebrates (Araya *et al.*, 1984; Moritz *et al.*, 1987); (3) it is maternally and clonally inherited without recombination (Avise and Lansman, 1983), and usually exists in only one genotype per individual, although there are exceptions (Densmore *et al.*, 1985; Bermingham *et al.*, 1986; Moritz *et al.*, 1987; Bentzen *et al.*, 1988); and (4) in vertebrates, it evolves five to ten times as rapidly as scnDNA (Brown *et al.*, 1979; Vawter and Brown, 1986; Moritz *et al.*, 1987). This combination of features permits relatively easy isolation and analysis of mtDNA, particularly for the study of maternal lineages in closely related populations and or species.

Population genetics

Because of its rapid evolution, mtDNA will usually vary among individuals within a species. This variability, coupled with haploid inher·tance, makes mtDNA a sensitive marker for analyses of population genetic structure and estimates of gene flow between populations (DeSalle *et al.*, 1 87). However, the absence of recombination and the pattern of maternal inheritance make mtDNA analagous to a single nuclear gene with many allelic states. As a result, multiple gene diversity estimates and variances, which are derived from multiple loci using nuclear genes or allozymes (Nei, 1973, 1977; Weir and Cockerham, 1984), cannot be obtained with mtDNA.

There are two approaches for the analysis of population structure with mtDNA. Phylogenetic analysis of individual haplotypes has been used to identify groups of populations, with the extent of divergence (i.e. the number of diagnostic restriction-site changes) between groups providing an indication of population structure (Avise *et al.*, 1987). This approach, however, is generally not sensitive enough to detect subdivision among recently established or nearby populations. In such cases a second approach has been employed, involving a single estimate of gene diversity and comparison of the frequency of polymorphic characters among sampled populations (DeSalle *et al.*, 1986, 1987).

Few studies have used mtDNA to evaluate cyprinid population structure. Hanzawa *et al.* (1987) analysed populations of Japanese dace, *Tribolodon hakonensis*, and differentiated all specimens collected from three geographic regions. In a preliminary analysis, Vyse (pers. comm.) compared mtDNA variation in the endangered Kendall Warm Springs dace, *Rhinichthys osculus thermalis*, to that of its putative progenitor, *R. o. yarrowi*, from the Green River in Wyoming. The mtDNA restriction-site variation in *R. o. thermalis* appears to be a subset of that found in *R. o. yarrowi*, suggesting that the population of *R. o. thermalis* was founded recently by only a few individuals. Dowling and Hoeh (unpubl.) used mtDNA to study population structure in the cyprinids *Luxilus cornutus* and *L. chrysocephalus* from Michigan and Ohio, respectively, and found evidence for differentiation of populations among river drainages.

Hybridization and introgression

The maternal inheritance of mtDNA allows its use as a marker for inferring the maternal genome in F_1 hybrids and subsequent backcross individuals, permitting tests of reciprocity of hybridization and directionality of introgression. The lack of paternal contribution of mtDNA, however, makes it necessary to analyse hybrids by using other diagnostic characters (e.g. allozymes, morphology) so that hybrids can be identified. The utility of mtDNA in hybridization studies can be demonstrated by discussing two categories of examples: (1) those in which the maternal component and clonal diversity of unisexual hybrids have been identified; and (2) those in which reciprocity, directionality, and extent of introgression across varying degrees of genetic and taxonomic divergence have been examined.

Morphological, biochemical, and tissue-graft analyses have shown that hybrids between the northern redbelly dace, *Phoxinus eos*, and the finescale dace, *P. neogaeus*, are members of a unisexual complex consisting of diploids, triploids, and diploid–triploid mosaics (Joswiak *et al.*, 1985; Dawley *et al.*, 1987; Dawley and Goddard, 1988). Restriction endonuclease analysis of mtDNAs from unisexual hybrids and both parental species from several localities demonstrated that *P. neogaeus* was always the maternal parent (Goddard *et al.*, 1989). Geographic sampling, however, revealed that the mtDNAs of unisexual hybrids varied considerably among localities, indicating that multiple hybridization events must have occurred (Goddard *et al.*, 1989).

Analyses of mtDNA have also been used to study hybridization among members of the North American genus *Luxilus*. Two of the more divergent members of the genus, *L. cerasinus* and *L. cornutus*, coexist at only a few locations in the James River drainage, Virginia, with sympatry believed to be the result of recent stream capture or introduction. Analyses of morphological and allozymic characters from specimens collected at one of these localities indicated that F_1 and backcross hybrids constitute *c.* 34% of the population; the majority of these (*c.* 90%) were F_1 hybrids (Meagher *et al.*, unpubl.). MtDNA analysis demonstrated that most F_1 hybrids had haplotypes of *L. cerasinus* (Meagher and Dowling, unpubl.). The non-random distribution of mtDNAs among the F_1 hybrids may be the result of size differences between the two species. The smaller male *L. cerasinus* might be unable to compete successfully for nest sites with larger male *L. cornutus*, or they might be unable to clasp and mate with larger female *L. cornutus*.

Meagher *et al.* (unpubl.) also provide the first evidence for sympatry of *L. cornutus* and *L. albeolus*. These two forms are usually distinguished by three scale counts, the ranges of which overlap (Gilbert, 1964). Allele frequency differences occur at several allozymic loci, although none is diagnostic (Buth, 1979a; Meagher and Dowling, unpubl.). MtDNA analysis provided the first diagnostic characters for the two forms, and also demonstrated the occurrence of introgressive hybridization between these two forms (Meagher and Dowling, unpubl.).

Finally, mtDNA analysis has been used to document and analyse extensive hybridization between *L. cornutus* and *L. chrysocephalus*. Morphological and allozymic character analyses initially revealed extensive hybridization and backcrossing (Dowling and Moore, 1984). Cohort analysis of some samples provided evidence for selection against adult hybrids (Dowling and Moore, 1985a). Examination of mtDNA haplotypes from individuals collected from several different localities where the two species are sympatric revealed differences in the extent and direction of hybridization (Dowling *et al.*, 1989). In rivers draining eastward into Lake Erie, F_1 and backcross hybrids generally had mtDNAs of *L. chrysocephalus*; whereas in rivers draining westward into Lake Michigan, F_1 and backcross hybrids tended to have mtDNAs of *L. cornutus*. Comparisons across localities indicated that introgression of nuclear genes was dependent upon the proportion of each species at a particular locality, with genes introgressing from the common into the rare species. In eastward-draining rivers, mtDNA introgression demonstrated the same frequency-dependent pattern, but in westward-draining rivers, introgression of mtDNA always proceeded from *L. cornutus* into *L. chrysocephalus*, independent of the proportions of the two species at any particular locality. MtDNA analysis thus indicated differences in mode of reproductive isolation between geographic regions.

Systematics and biogeography
Mitochondrial DNA also serves as an excellent marker for inference of hypotheses of phylogenetic relationships, at least among closely related species or species groups, so mtDNA analysis can often be a valuable tool for testing biogeographic hypotheses. Restriction sites or nucleotide sequences are usually coded as discrete characters, facilitating their analysis by cladistic or

phenetic methods. Because of the complex nature of restriction sites, the loss of any given site is much more likely than is a gain (Templeton, 1983; DeBry and Slade, 1985; Li, 1986). For example, for a restriction enzyme that recognizes a six-base-pair sequence, there are six ways to lose a site, but only one specific sequence provides that particular site. This results in increased numbers of convergent losses of sites, particularly for more divergent comparisons. Also, the apparent frequency of interspecific mtDNA transfer (reviews, Moritz *et al.*, 1987; Dowling *et al.*, 1989) and the persistence of ancestral polymorphisms (Neigel and Avise, 1985) necessitate caution when applying mtDNA characters to the inference of phylogenetic relationships. Because a small fraction of the genome is sampled, stochastic effects may produce a topology (i.e. a gene tree, *sensu* Nei, 1987) that is incompatible with the true phylogeny of the group (i.e. the species tree – Nei, 1987). The best measure of accuracy of phylogenetic hypotheses inferred from mtDNA data would be tests of congruence with other data sets (e.g. from allozymes, karyology, or morphology). Increased resolution may also be achieved by pooling different data sets from the same individuals or operational taxonomic units (OTUs) (Hillis, 1987).

As with other molecular techniques, analysis of mtDNA has an upper limit beyond which convergence of characters makes phylogenetic relationships difficult to resolve. Variation in the rate of mtDNA evolution among genes and among populations or taxa prohibits determination of specific levels of sequence divergence at which convergence impedes phylogenetic resolution. For example, Dowling and Brown (1989) failed to resolve phylogenetic relationships among four species of North American Cyprinidae, even though sequence divergence between most of the species was less than 12%. They concluded that extremely rapid rates of evolution for specific regions of the mtDNA molecule produced considerable homoplasy, possibly preventing phylogenetic resolution.

Perhaps the most important consideration in phylogenetic analysis using mtDNA is sampling strategy. Because of the rigours and expense involved in generating molecular data, single individuals are often used to represent discrete taxa. This is usually sufficient if little or no variation occurs within species, but otherwise, failure to completely sample the extant variation could seriously compromise phylogenetic inferences. P. E. Smouse *et al.* (unpubl.) analysed mtDNA restriction site variation within and between populations of four species of cyprinids with regard to the effect of sampling strategy on phylogenetic reconstruction. Most mtDNA variation in these species was distributed among populations, and the choice of any single population to represent a species greatly affected phylogenetic inference. This suggests that for phylogenetic analysis using mtDNA, sampling multiple populations (particularly for widely distributed species) will prove more important than replicative sampling at a single locality.

Variation in rates of evolution among genes should make mtDNA a useful marker for analysing phylogenetic relationships across a variety of taxonomic levels. The considerable variation in rates of evolution among many mito-chondrial genes (Brown, 1985) should allow mitochondrial genes evolving at rates appropriate for a particular problem to be used. Analysis of mitochondrial rDNA, for example, appears to be useful for distinguishing several North American cyprinid genera (T. E. Dowling, unpubl.).

Nuclear DNA

As with mtDNA, nuclear genes evolve at different rates, and so can be useful for addressing questions at a variety of hierarchical levels, from individuals within populations (Jeffreys *et al.*, 1985 a, b) to the phylogeny of 'life' (Pace *et al.*, 1986). Unlike mtDNA, most nuclear genes (with the exception of sex-linked genes) are diploid, with the degree of complexity varying from single loci (Aquadro *et al.*, 1986; Kreitman and Aguade, 1986) to multigene families (Edgell *et al.*, 1983). Members of multigene families appear to evolve in concert (Arnheim, 1983), and hence may be subject to the phenomenon of 'molecular drive' (Dover *et al.*, 1982).

Two types of nuclear gene markers have been used for population studies: (1) hypervariable sequences ('DNA fingerprints') or rapidly evolving single-copy sequences (Jeffreys *et al.* 1985 a, b; Quinn and White, 1987 a, b), and (2) the non-transcribed spacer (NTS) region of the ribosomal DNA (rDNA) gene cluster (Flavell *et al.*, 1986; Suzuki *et al.*, 1987; Williams *et al.*, 1985, 1987). These markers have seen limited use, but show promise for the analysis of paternity and maternity testing and for measuring the extent of population structuring.

Nuclear DNA markers have vast potential for the analysis of hybridization and introgression. They can act as unambiguous markers identifying parti-cular taxa and can be used like allozyme markers (p. 91) to study these phenomena. The choice of marker is not constrained by detectability by function (unlike allozymes), providing an immense number of potential markers.

A variety of nuclear DNA markers have employed restriction site maps or DNA sequences of nuclear genes to allow investigators to infer phylogenetic hypotheses at different hierarchical levels (Hillis and Davis, 1986, 1987; Koop *et al.*, 1986 a, b; Miyamoto *et al.*, 1987). Problems concerning rates of evolution, convergence, and sampling strategies discussed for mtDNA (p. 111) are also applicable to analyses of nuclear DNA. Also, as with the analysis of mtDNA, particular genes or portions of genes can be used for phylogenetic analysis at specific levels of divergence. Analyses of nuclear gene variation using recombinant DNA techniques should prove extremely useful as markers for inferring phylogenetic relationships across a wide range of hierarchical categories and organisms.

4.5 SUMMARY

Studies of molecular and cytogenetic characteristics of cyprinid fishes have greatly expanded our knowledge of this species-rich family. Appropriate methods have clarified (1) the biology of hybridization, including introgression and the maintenance of genomic integrity, (2) speciation via the genetics of triploidy and tetraploidy, (3) population structure within species, and (4) systematic and biogeographic relationships among species. These characters are valuable supplements facilitating the identification of species.

Allozyme and cytogenetic data, including basic chromosome numbers and karyotypic configurations, have been generated for many cyprinid species, which nevertheless represent only a fraction of the known extant species. Cyprinid allozymes vary at several levels of organization, making this data base ideal for population-level studies as well as for the assessment of interspecific relationships. The codominant nature of allozyme expression facilitates the identification of F_1 and backcross hybrids and allows the quantification of introgressive gene flow. Cyprinid polyploidy has been confirmed using gene expression data, chromosome numbers, and direct measures of DNA content. In terms of chromosome numbers, it is quite clear that two groups of cyprinids can be recognized: those that have $c.$ $2n = 50$ (presumed plesiomorphic diploids) and those that have $c.$ $2n = 100$ (presumed apomorphic tetraploids). Questions regarding the taxonomic and geographic distribution of these tetraploids are opening up interesting avenues for future research. Isozyme characters (e.g. numbers of duplicate loci retained or silenced and tissue specificity of gene expression) will probably become important in future studies of cyprinid polyploids.

Chromosome banding techniques are limited to visualizing the nucleolus organizer regions (NORs). The levels of NOR variability revealed in cyprinids have been higher than expected. The problem of homology now limits applications of NORs in cyprinid cytosystematics, although technical improvements should increase the information potential of chromosome characteristics.

Studies of the mitochondrial DNA (mtDNA) of cyprinids are rare. However, several unique properties of mtDNA (e.g. maternal and clonal inheritance, rapid evolution) make it an especially desirable data base for studies of hybridization (to examine reciprocity and directionality of introgression) and of population-level and interspecific relationships. The considerable variation in rates of evolution among many of the mitochondrial genes should allow the choice of genes evolving at appropriate rates to address problems at a variety of levels of organization. This area of research is especially promising and could provide much-needed answers to questions of higher-level relationships among the Cyprinidae.

Many molecular techniques, including DNA–DNA hybridization and those involving nuclear DNA, await application in cyprinid studies. The potential here is considerable. Refinement of these techniques will allow tests of hypotheses supported or questioned by some of the other data bases. Recombinant DNA techniques should prove to be extremely useful at a variety of levels.

It is satisfying to note that molecular and cytogenetic studies of cyprinids are on the increase. Technological advances have provided many new tools awaiting application, and the choice of the right tool for a particular biological question becomes important. The Cyprinidae are a diverse and fascinating group and many questions remain to be answered.

ACKNOWLEDGMENTS

This chapter was supported, in part, by the UCLA Dept of Biology Fisheries Program (to D. G. Buth), by the National Science Foundation (BSR-8717320 to T. E. Dowling and BSR-8415428 to J. R. Gold), and by Texas Agricultural Experiment Station Project H-6703 (to J. R. Gold). Anthony A. Echelle, Thomas R. Haglund, Rodney L. Honeycutt, Richard L. Mayden, Walter J. Rainboth, and Curtis Strobeck provided critical appraisals of the manuscript. We are especially indebted to Walter J. Rainboth for his assistance regarding cyprinid taxonomy.

REFERENCES

Allendorf, F. W. (1983) Isolation, gene flow, and genetic differentiation among populations, in *Genetics and Conservation: A Reference for Managing Wild Animal and Plant Populations* (eds C. M. Schonewald–Cox, S. M. Chambers, B. McBryde and W. L. Thomas), Benjamin/Cummings Publ. Co., Menlo Park, Cal., pp. 51–65.

Amemiya, C. T. (1987) Cytogenetic and cytosystematic studies on the nucleolus organizer regions of North American cyprinid fishes, unpubl. PhD dissertation, Texas A&M Univ., College Station, Texas.

Amemiya, C. T. and Gold, J. R. (1986) Chromomycin A3 stains nucleolus organizer regions of fish chromosomes. *Copeia*, **1986**, 226–31.

Amemiya, C. T. and Gold, J. R. (1987a) Karyology of 12 species of North American Cyprinidae from the southern United States. *Cytologia*, **52**, 715–19.

Amemiya, C. T. and Gold, J. R. (1987b) Chromomycin staining of vertebrate chromosomes: enhancement of banding patterns by NaOH. *Cytobios*, **49**, 147–52.

Amemiya, C. T. and Gold, J. R. (1988) Chromosomal NORs as taxonomic and systematic characters in North American cyprinid fish. *Genetica*, **76**, 81–90.

Amemiya, C. T. and Gold, J. R. (1990) Chromosomal NOR phenotypes of seven species of North American Cyprinidae, with comments on cytosystematic relationships in the *Notropis volucellus* species-group, *Opsopoedus emilae*, and the genus *Pteronotropis*. *Copeia*, **1990**, 68–78.

Aquadro, C. F., Deese, S. F., Bland, M. M., Langley, C. H. and Lauric-Ahlberg, C. C. (1986) Molecular population genetics of the alcohol dehydrogenase gene region of *Drosophila melanogaster*. *Genetics*, **114**, 1165–90.

Arai, R. (1982) A chromosome study on two cyprinid fishes, *Acrossocheilus labiatus* and *Pseudorasbora pumila pumila*, with notes on Eurasian cyprinids and their karyotypes. *Bull. natn. Sci. Mus., Tokyo,* **8A**, 131–52.

Araya, A., Amthauer, R., Leon, G. and Krauskopf, M. (1984) Cloning, physical mapping and genome organization of mitochondrial DNA from *Cyprinus carpio* oocytes. *Molec. gen. Genet.,* **196**, 43–52.

Arnheim, N. (1983) Concerted evolution of multigene families, in *Evolution of Genes and Proteins* (eds M. Nei and R. K. Koehn) Sinauer Associates, Sunderland, MA, pp. 38–61.

Avise, J. C. (1974) Systematic value of electrophoretic data. *Syst. Zool.,* **23**, 465–81.

Avise, J. C. (1977) Genic heterozygosity and rate of speciation. *Paleobiology,* **3**, 422–32.

Avise, J. C. (1978) Variance and frequency distributions of genetic distance in evolutionary phylads. *Heredity, Lond.,* **40**, 225–37.

Avise, J. C. and Ayala, F. J. (1975) Genetic change and rates of cladogenesis. *Genetics,* **81**, 757–73.

Avise, J. C. and Ayala, F. J. (1976) Genetic differentiation in speciose versus depauperate phylads: evidence from the California minnows. *Evolution,* **30**, 46–58.

Avise, J. C. and Lansman, R. A. (1983) Polymorphism of mitochondrial DNA in populations of higher animals, in *Evolution of Genes and Proteins* (eds M. Nei and R. K. Koehn), Sinauer Associates, Sunderland, MA, pp. 165–90.

Avise, J. C. and Vrijenhoek, R. (1987) Mode of inheritance and variation of mitochondrial DNA in hybridogenetic fishes of the genus *Poeciliopsis. Mol. Biol. Evol.,* **4**, 514–25.

Avise, J. C., Arnold, J., Ball, R. M., Bermingham, E., Lamb, T., Neigel, J. E., Reeb, C. A. and Saunders, N. C. (1987) Intraspecific phylogeography: the mitochondrial DNA bridge between population genetics and systematics. *A. Rev. Ecol. Syst.,* **18**, 489–522.

Avise, J. C., Bermingham, E., Kessler, L. G. and Saunders, N. C. (1984) Characterization of mitochondrial DNA variability in a hybrid swarm between subspecies of bluegill sunfish (*Lepomis macrochirus*). *Evolution,* **38**, 931–41.

Avise, J. C., Smith, J. J. and Ayala, F. J. (1957) Adaptive differentiation with little genic change between two native California minnows. *Evolution,* **29**, 411–26.

Bachman, K., Chambers, K. L. and Price, H. J. (1985) Genome size and natural selection; observation and experiments in plants, in *The Evolution of Genome Size* (ed. T. Cavalier–Smith), John Wiley & Sons, NY, pp. 267–76.

Bachman, K., Goin, O. B. and Goin, C. J. (1972) Nuclear DNA amounts in vertebrates. *Brookhaven Symp. Biol.,* **23**, 419–50.

Beck, M. L., Biggers, C. L. and Dupree, H. K. (1983) Electrophoretic analysis of protein systems of *Ctenopharyngodon idella* (Val.), *Hypophthalmichthys nobilis* (Rich.) and their F_1 triploid hybrid. *J. Fish Biol.,* **22**, 603–11.

Beckwitt, R. and Aoyagi, S. (1987) Mitochondrial DNA sequence variation in domesticated goldfish, *Carassius auratus. Copeia,* **1987**, 219–22.

Beckwitt, R. and Petruska, J. (1985) Variation in mitochondrial DNA genome size among fishes of the family Scorpaenidae. *Copeia,* **1985**, 1057–8.

Bennett, M. D. (1976) DNA amount, latitude, and crop plant distribution. *Environ. exp. Bot.,* **16**, 93–108.

Bentzen, P., Leggett, W. C. and Brown, G. G. (1988) Length and restriction site heteroplasmy in the mitochondrial DNA of American shad (*Alosa sapidissima*). *Genetics,* **118**, 509–18.

Berg, W. J. and Ferris, S. D. (1984) Restriction endonuclease analysis of salmonid mitochondrial DNA. *Can. J. Fish. aquat. Sci.,* **41**, 1041–7.

Bermingham, E., Lamb, T. and Avise, J. C. (1986) Size polymorphism and heteroplasmy in the mitochondrial DNA of lower vertebrates. *J. Hered.,* **77**, 249–52.

Bernardi, G., Olofsson, B., Filipski, J., Zerial, M., Salinas, J., Cuny, G., Meunier-Rotival, M. and Rodier, F. (1985) The mosaic genome of warm-blooded vertebrates. *Science*, **228**, 953–8.

Berrebi, P., Dupont, F., Cattaneo-Berrebi, G. and Crivelli, A. J. (1989) An isozyme study of the natural cyprinid hybrid *Alburnus alburnus* × *Rutilus rubilio* in Greece. *J. Fish Biol.*, **34**, 307–13.

Birt, T. P., Green, J. M. and Davidson, W. S. (1986) Analysis of mitochondrial DNA in allopatric anadromous and nonanadromous Atlantic salmon, *Salmo salar. Can. J. Zool.*, **64**, 118–20.

Brewer, G. J. (1970) *An Introduction to Isozyme Techniques*, Academic Press, NY.

Brown, W. M. (1983) Evolution of animal mitochondrial DNA, in *Evolution of Genes and Proteins* (eds M. Nei and R. K. Koehn), Sinauer Associates, Sunderland, MA, pp. 62–88.

Brown, W. M. (1985) The mitochondrial genome of animals, in *Molecular Evolutionary Genetics* (ed. R. MacIntyre), Plenum Press, NY, pp. 95–130.

Brown, W. M., George, M., jun. and Wilson, A. C. (1979). Rapid evolution of animal mitochondrial DNA. *Proc. natn. Acad. Sci. U.S.A.*, **76**, 1967–71.

Bush, G. L. and Kitto, G. B. (1978) Application of genetics to insect systematics and analysis of species differences, in *Biosystematics in Agriculture* (ed. J. A. Romberger), Allenheld, Osmun and Co., Montclair, NJ, pp. 89–118.

Buth, D. G. (1979a) Biochemical systematics of the cyprinid genus *Notropis* I. The subgenus *Luxilus. Biochem. Syst. Ecol.*, **7**, 69–79.

Buth, D. G. (1979b) Duplicate gene expression in tetraploid fishes of the tribe Moxostomatini (Cypriniformes, Catostomidae). *Comp. Biochem. Physiol.*, **63B**, 7–12.

Buth, D. G. (1980) Evolutionary genetics and systematic relationships in the catostomid genus *Hypentelium. Copeia*, **1980**, 280–90.

Buth, D. G. (1982) Locus assignments for general muscle proteins of darters (Etheostomatini). *Copeia*, **1982**, 217–19.

Buth, D. G. (1983) Duplicate isozyme loci in fishes: origins, distribution, phyletic consequences, and locus nomenclature, in *Isozymes: Current Topics in Biological and Medical Research*, Vol. 10: *Genetics and Evolution* (eds M. C. Rattazzi, J. G. Scandalios and G. S. Whitt), Alan R. Liss, Inc., NY, pp. 381–400.

Buth, D. G. (1984a) Allozymes of the cyprinid fishes: variation and application, in *Evolutionary Genetics of Fishes* (ed. B. J. Turner), Plenum Publ. Corp., NY, pp. 561–90.

Buth, D. G. (1984b) The application of electrophoretic data in systematic studies. *A. Rev. Ecol. Syst.*, **15**, 501–22.

Buth, D. G. and Burr, B. M. (1978) Isozyme variability in the cyprinid genus *Campostoma. Copeia*, **1978**, 298–311.

Buth, D. G. and Mayden, R. L. (1981) Taxonomic status and relationships among populations of *Notropis pilsbryi* and *N. zonatus* (Cypriniformes: Cyprinidae) as shown by the glucosephosphate isomerase, lactate dehydrogenase, and phosphoglucomutase enzyme systems. *Copeia*, **1981**, 583–90.

Caccone, A. G., Amato, D. and Powell, J. R. (1987) Intraspecific DNA divergence in *Drosophila*: a study of parthenogenetic *D. mercatorum. Mol. Biol. Evol.*, **4**, 343–50.

Capanna, E. (1982) Robertsonian numerical variation in animal speciation: *Mus musculus*, an emblematic model, in *Mechanisms of Speciation* (ed. C. Barigozzi), Alan R. Liss, Inc., NY, pp. 155–77.

Cataudella, S., Sola, L., Accame Muratori, R. and Capanna, E. (1977) The chromosomes of 11 species of Cyprinidae and one Cobitidae from Italy, with some remarks on the problem of polyploidy in the Cypriniformes. *Genetica*, **47**, 161–71.

Cavalier-Smith, T. (1980) r- and K- tactics in the evolution of protist developmental systems: cell and genome size, phenotype diversifying selection and cell cycle patterns. *Bio Systems*, **12**, 43–59.

Cavalier-Smith, T. (1985) Cell volume and the evolution of eukaryotic genome size, in *The Evolution of Genome Size* (ed. T. Cavalier-Smith). John Wiley & Sons, NY, pp. 105–84.

Cherfas, N. B. (1966) Natural triploidy in females of the unisexual forms of the goldfish (*Carassius auratus gibelio* Bloch). *Sov. Genet.*, **2**, 9–13.

Chiarelli, B., Ferrantelli, O. and Cucchi, C. (1969) The caryotype of some Teleostea fish obtained by tissue culture in vitro. *Experientia*, **25**, 426–7.

Clayton, J. W. and Tretiak, D. N. (1972) Amine-citrate buffers for pH control in starch gel electrophoresis. *J. Fish. Res. Bd Can.*, **29**, 1169–72.

Coburn, M. M. (1982) Anatomy and relationships of *Notropis atherinoides*, unpubl. PhD dissertation, Ohio State Univ., Columbus, Ohio.

Collares-Pereira, M. J. (1987) The evolutionary role of hybridization: the example of natural Iberian fish populations, in *Proceedings of a World Symposium on Selection, Hybridization, and Genetic Engineering in Aquaculture, Bordeaux 27–30 May, 1986*, Vol. 1, pp. 83–92.

Corti, M., Capanna, E. and Estabrook, G. F. (1986) Microevolutionary sequences in house mouse chromosomal speciation. *Syst. Zool.*, **35**, 163–75.

Crabtree, C. B. and Buth, D. G. (1987) Biochemical systematics of the catostomid genus *Catostomus*: assessment of *C. clarki, C. plebeius*, and *C. discobolus* including the Zuni sucker, *C. d. yarrowi. Copeia*, **1987**, 843–54.

Cracraft, J. C. (1987) DNA hybridization and avian phylogenetics. *Evol. Biol.*, **21**, 47–96.

Cuny, G., Soriano, P., Macaya, G. and Bernardi, G. (1981) The major components of the mouse and human genomes: preparation, basic properties, and compositional heterogeneity. *Eur. J. Biochem.*, **111**, 227–33.

Danzmann, R. G. and Down, N. E. (1982) Isozyme expression in F_1 hybrids between carp and goldfish. *Biochem. Genet.*, **20**, 1–15.

Davidson, E. H., Galau, G. A., Angerer, R. C. and Britten, R. J. (1975) Comparative aspects of DNA organization in Metazoa. *Chromosoma*, **51**, 253–9.

Dawley, R. M. and Goddard, K. A. (1988) Diploid–triploid mosaics among unisexual hybrids of the minnows *Phoxinus eos* and *Phoxinus neogeaus. Evolution*, **42**, 649–59.

Dawley, R. M., Schultz, R. J. and Goddard, K. A. (1987) Clonal reproduction and polyploidy in unisexual hybrids of *Phoxinus eos* and *Phoxinus neogeaus* (Pisces; Cyprinidae). *Copeia*, **1987**, 275–83.

DeBry, R. W. and Slade, N.A. (1985). Cladistic analysis of restriction endonuclease cleavage maps within a maximum likelihood framework. *Syst. Zool.*, **34**, 21–34.

Densmore, L. D., Wright, J. W. and Brown, W. M. (1985) Length variation and heteroplasmy are frequent in mitochondrial DNA from parthenogenetic and bisexual lizards (genus *Cnemidophorus*). *Genetics*, **110**, 698–707.

DeSalle, R., Giddings, L. V. and Templeton, A. R. (1986) Mitochondrial DNA variability in natural populations of Hawaiian *Drosophila*. I. Methods and levels of variability in *D. silvestris* and *D. heteroneura* populations. *Heredity, Lond.*, **56**, 75–85.

DeSalle, R., Templeton, A., Mori, I., Pletscher, S. and Johnston, J. S. (1987) Temporal and spatial heterogeneity of mtDNA polymorphisms in natural populations of *Drosophila mercatorum. Genetics*, **116**, 215–23.

Dimmick, W. W. (1987) Phylogenetic relationships of *Notropis hubbsi, N. welaka*, and *N. emilae* (Cypriniformes: Cyprinidae). *Copeia*, **1987**, 316–25.

Dover, G. A., Brown, S., Coen, E., Dallas, J., Strachan, T. and Trick, M. (1982) The dynamics of genome evolution and species differentiation, in *Genome Evolution* (eds G. A. Dover and R. B. Flavell), Academic Press, London, pp. 343–72.

Dowling, T. E. and Brown, W. M. (1989) Allozymes, mitochondrial DNA, and levels of phylogenetic resolution among four minnow species (*Notropis*: Cyprinidae). *Syst. Zool.*, **38**, 126–43.

Dowling, T. E. and Hoeh, W. R. The extent of introgression outside the contact zone between *Notropis cornutus* and *Notropis chrysocephalus* (Pisces: Cyprinidae). *Evolution*, in press.

Dowling, T. E. and Moore, W. S. (1984) Level of reproductive isolation between two cyprinid fishes, *Notropis cornutus* and *N. chrysocephalus*. *Copeia*, **1984**, 617–28.

Dowling, T. E. and Moore, W. S. (1985a) Genetic variation and divergence of the sibling pair of cyprinid fishes, *Notropis cornutus* and *N. chrysocephalus*. *Biochem. Syst. Ecol.*, **13**, 471–6.

Dowling, T. E. and Moore, W. S. (1985b) Evidence for selection against hybrids in the family Cyprinidae (genus *Notropis*). *Evolution*, **39**, 152–8.

Dowling, T. E., Smith, G. R. and Brown, W. M. (1989) Reproductive isolation and introgression between *Notropis cornutus* and *Notropis chrysocephalus* (family Cyprinidae): comparison of morphology, allozymes, and mitochondrial DNA. *Evolution*, **43**, 620–34.

Edgell, M. H., Hardies, S. C., Brown, B., Voliva, C., Hill, A., Phillips, S., Comer, M., Burton, F., Weaver, S. and Hutchinson, C. A., III (1983) Evolution of the mouse α globin complex locus, in *Evolution of Genes and Proteins* (eds M. Nei and R. K. Koehn), Sinauer Associates, Sunderland, MA, pp. 1–13.

Farris, J. S. (1981) Distance data in phylogenetic analysis, in *Advances in Cladistics: Proceedings of the First Meeting of the Willi Hennig Society* (eds V. A. Funk and D. R. Brooks), New York Botanical Garden, Bronx, NY, pp. 3–23.

Farris, J. S. (1985) Distance data revisited. *Cladistics*, **1**, 67–85.

Farris, J. S. (1986) Distances and statistics. *Cladistics*, **2**, 144–57.

Felsenstein, J. (1984) Distance methods for inferring phylogenies: a justification. *Evolution*, **38**, 16–24.

Felsenstein, J. (1986) Distance methods: a reply to Farris. *Cladistics*, **2**, 130–43.

Ferguson, M. M. (1981) Identification and species characterization of some North American minnows by electrophoresis. *Biochem. Syst. Ecol.*, **9**, 89–91.

Ferris, S. D. and Berg, W. J. (1987) The utility of mitochondrial DNA in fish genetics and fishery management, in *Population Genetics and Fisheries Management* (eds N. Ryman and F. Utter), University of Washington Press, Seattle, pp. 277–99.

Ferris, S. D. and Whitt, G. S. (1977a). Loss of duplicate gene expression after polyploidisation. *Nature, Lond.*, **265**, 258–60.

Ferris, S. D. and Whitt, G. S. (1977b) The evolution of duplicate gene expression in the carp (*Cyprinus carpio*). *Experientia*, **33**, 1299–1301.

Ferris, S. D. and Whitt, G. S. (1978) Phylogeny of tetraploid catostomid fishes based on the loss of duplicate gene expression. *Syst. Zool.*, **27**, 189–203.

Fink, S. V. and Fink, W. L. (1981) Interrelationships of the ostariophysan fishes (Teleostei). *Zool. J. Linn. Soc.*, **72**, 297–353.

Fitch, W. M. (1986) Commentary. *Mol. Biol. Evol.*, **3**, 296–8.

Flavell, R. B., O'Dell, M., Sharp, P., Nevo, E. and Beiles, A. (1986) Variation in the intergenic spacer of ribosomal DNA of wild wheat, *Triticum dicoccoides*, in Israel. *Mol. Biol. Evol.*, **3**, 547–58.

Foresti, F., Almeida Toledo, L. M. and Toledo, S. A. (1981) Polymorphic nature of nucleolus organizer regions in fishes. *Cytogenet. Cell Genet.*, **31**, 137–44.

Frankel, J. S. (1983) Allelic asynchrony during *Barbus* hybrid development. *J. Hered.*, **74**, 311–12.

Frankel, J. S. (1985) Ontogenetic patterns of enzyme locus expression in *Barbus* hybrids (Cypriniformes, Teleostei). *Comp. Biochem. Physiol.*, **82B**, 413–17.

Frick, L. (1983) An electrophoretic investigation of the cytosolic di- and tripeptidases of fish: molecular weights, substrate specificities, and tissue and phylogenetic distributions. *Biochem. Genet.*, **21**, 309–22.

Fristrom, J. W. and Clegg, M. T. (1988) *Principles of Genetics* 2nd edn. Chiron Press, NY.

Galetti, P. M., DaSilva, E. B. and Cerminaro, R. T. (1985) A multiple NOR system in the fish *Serrasalmus spilopeura* (Serrasalminae, Characidae). *Revta Brasil. Genet.*, **8**, 479–84.

Galetti, P. M., Foresti, F., Bertolo, L. A. C. and Moreira-Filho, O. (1984) Characterization of eight species of Anostomidae (Cypriniformes) fish on the basis of the nucleolar organizer region. *Caryologia*, **37**, 401–6.

Gharrett, A. J., Simon, R. C. and McIntyre, J. D. (1977) Reassociation and hybridization properties of DNAs from several species of fish. *Comp. Biochem. Physiol.*, **56B**, 81–5.

Gilbert, C. R. (1964) The American cyprinid fishes of the subgenus *Luxilus* (genus *Notropis*). *Bull. Fla St. Mus. biol. Sci.*, **8**, 95–194.

Goddard, K. A., Dawley, R. M. and Dowling, T. E. (1989) Origin and genetic relationships of diploid, triploid, and diploid–triploid mosaic biotypes in the *Phoxinus eos–neogeaus* unisexual complex, in *Biology of Unisexual Vertebrates* (eds R. M. Dawley and J. P. Bogart), New York State Museum, Albany, pp. 268–80.

Gold, J. R. (1979) Cytogenetics, in *Fish Physiology*, Vol. 8 (eds W. S. Hoar, D. J. Randall, and J. R. Brett), Academic Press, NY, pp. 353–405.

Gold, J. R. (1984) Silver-staining and heteromorphism of chromosomal nucleolus organizer regions in North American cyprinid fishes. *Copeia*, **1984**, 133–9.

Gold, J. R. and Amemiya, C. T. (1986) Cytogenetic studies in North American minnows (Cyprinidae). XII. Patterns of chromosomal NOR variation among fourteen species. *Can. J. Zool.*, **64**, 1869–77.

Gold, J. R. and Amemiya, C. T. (1987) Genome size variation in North American minnows (Cyprinidae). II. Variation among 20 species. *Genome*, **29**, 481–9.

Gold, J. R. and Avise, J. C. (1977) Cytogenetic studies in North American minnows (Cyprinidae). I. Karyology of nine California genera. *Copeia*, **1977**, 541–9.

Gold, J. R. and Karel, W. J. (1988) DNA base composition and nucleotide distribution among fifteen species of teleostean fishes. *Comp. Biochem. Physiol.*, **90B**, 715–19.

Gold, J. R. and Price, H. J. (1985) Genome size variation among North American minnows (Cyprinidae). I. Distribution of the variation in five species. *Heredity, Lond.*, **54**, 297–305.

Gold, J. R. Amemiya, C. T. and Ellison, J. R. (1986) Chromosomal heterochromatin differentiation in North American cyprinid fishes. *Cytologia*, **51**, 557–66.

Gold, J. R., Karel, W. J. and Strand, M. R. (1980) Chromosome formulae of North American fishes. *Progve. Fish Cult.*, **42**, 10–23.

Gold, J. R., Whitlock, C. W., Karel, W. J. and Barlow, J. A. (1979) Cytogenetic studies in North American minnows (Cyprinidae). VI. Karyotypes of thirteen species in the genus *Notropis*. *Cytologia*, **44**, 457–66.

Gold, J. R., Womac, W. D. Deal, F. H. and Barlow, J. A. (1981) Cytogenetic studies in North American minnows (Cyprinidae). VII. Karyotypes of thirteen species from the southern United States. *Cytologia*, **46**, 105–15.

Gold, J. R., Zoch, P. K. and Amemiya, C. T. (1988) Cytogenetic studies of North American minnows (Cyprinidae). XIV. Chromosomal NOR phenotypes of eight species from the genus *Notropis*. *Cytobios*, **54**, 137–47.

Gold, J. R., Ragland, C. J. and Schliesing, L. J. (1990) Genome size variation and evolution in North American cyprinid fishes. *Genet. Sel. Evol.*, **22**, 11–29.

Goodfellow, W. L., jun., Hocutt, C. H., Morgan, R. P. II and Stauffer, J. R., jun. (1984) Biochemical assessment of the taxonomic status of "*Rhinichthys bowersi*" (Pisces: Cyprinidae). *Copeia*, **1984**, 652–9.

Goodfellow, W. L., jun., Morgan, R. P. II, Hocutt, C. H. and Stauffer, J. R., jun. (1982) Electrophoretic analysis of *Campostoma anomalum, Rhinichthys cataractae* and their F_1 offspring. *Biochem. Syst. Ecol.*, **10**, 95–8.

Graves, J. E., Ferris, S. D. and Dizon, A. E. (1984) Close genetic similarity of Atlantic and Pacific skipjack tuna (*Katsuwonis pelamis*) demonstrated with restriction endonuclease analysis of mitochondrial DNA. *Mar. Biol.*, **79**, 315–9.

Guttman, T., Vitek, A. and Pivec, L. (1977) High resolution thermal denaturation of mammalian DNAs. *Nucl. Acids Res* **4**, 285–97.

Gyllensten, U. and Wilson, A. C. (1987) Mitochondrial DNA of salmonids: inter- and intraspecific variability detected with restriction endonucleases, in *Population Genetics and Fisheries Management* (eds N. Ryman and F. Utter), University of Washington Press, Seattle, pp. 301–17.

Gyllensten, U., Leary, R. F., Allendorf, F. W. and Wilson, A. C. (1985) Introgression between two cutthroat trout subspecies with substantial karyotypic, nuclear and mitochondrial genome divergence. *Genetics*, **111**, 905–15.

Hanham, A. and Smith, M. J. (1979) Sequence organization in the genomic DNA of the chum salmon, *Oncorhynchus keta*. *Can J. Zool*, **57**, 1878–86.

Hanham, A. and Smith, M. J. (1980) Sequence homology in the single-copy DNA of salmon. *Comp. Biochem. Physiol*, **65B**, 333–8.

Hanzawa, N., Yonekawa, H. and Numachi, K. (1987) Variability in mitochondrial DNA in Japanese dace, *Tribolodon hakonensis* (Cyprinidae). *Jap. J. Genet.*, **62**, 27–38.

Hartl, D. L., Freifelder, D. and Snyder, L. A. (1988) *Basic Genetics*, Jones and Bartlett, Boston, MA.

Hartley, S. E. and Horne M. T. (1985) Cytogenetic techniques in fish genetics. *J. Fish Biol.*, **26**, 575–82.

Hillis, D. M. (1987) Molecular versus morphological approaches to systematics. *A. Rev. Ecol. Syst.*, **18**, 23–42.

Hillis, D. M. and Davis, S. K. (1986) Evolution of ribosomal DNA: fifty million years of recorded history in the frog genus *Rana*. *Evolution*, **40**, 1275–88.

Hillis, D. M. and Davis, S. K. (1987) Evolution of the 28S ribosomal RNA gene in anuarans: Regions of variability and their phylogenetic implications. *Mol. Biol. Evol.*, **4**, 117–25.

Hinegardner, R. and Rosen, D. (1972) Cellular DNA content and the evolution of teleostean fishes. *Am. Nat.*, **106**, 621–44.

Howell, W. M. (1982) Selective staining of nucleolus organizer regions (NORs). *Cell Nucleus*, **11**, 89–142.

Hudson, A. P., Cuny, G., Cortadas, J., Haschmeyer, A. E. V. and Bernardi, G. (1980) An analysis of fish genomes by density gradient centrifugation. *Eur. J. Biochem.*, **112**, 203–10.

IUBNC [International Union of Biochemistry. Nomenclature Committee] (1984) *Enzyme Nomenclature, 1984*, Academic Press, Orlando, Florida.

Jeffreys, A. J., Wilson, V. and Thein, S. L. (1985a) Hypervariable "minisatellite" regions in human DNA. *Nature, Lond.*, **314**, 67–73.

Jeffreys, A. J., Wilson, V. and Thein, S. L. (1985b) Individual-specific "fingerprints" of human DNA. *Nature, Lond.*, **316**, 76–9.

Joswiak, G. R., Stasiak, R. H. and Koop, B. F. (1985) Diploidy and triploidy in the hybrid minnow *Phoxinus eos* × *Phoxinus neogeaus* (Pisces: Cyprinidae). *Experientia*, **41**, 505–7.

Joswiak, G. R., Stasiak, R. H. and Moore, W. S. (1982) Allozyme analysis of the hybrid *Phoxinus eos* × *Phoxinus neogaeus* (Pisces: Cyprinidae) in Nebraska. *Can. J. Zool.*, **60**, 968–73.

Kang, Y. S. and Park, F. H. (1973) Studies on the karyotypes and comparative DNA values in several Korean cyprinid fishes. *Korean J. Zool.*, **16**, 97–108.

Karel, W. J. and Gold, J. R. (1987) A thermal denaturation study of genomic DNAs from North American minnows (Cyprinidae: Teleostei). *Genetica*, **74**, 181–7.

Khuda-Bukhsh, A. R. (1980) A high number of chromosomes in the hillstream cyprinid, *Tor putitora* (Pisces). *Experientia*, **36**, 173–4.

Khuda-Bukhsh, A. R. (1982) Karyomorphology of two species of *Tor* (Pisces: Cyprinidae) with a high number of chromosomes. *Experientia*, **38**, 82–3.

Khuda-Bukhsh, A. R., Chanda, T. and Barat, A. (1986) Karyomorphology and evolution in some Indian hillstream fishes with particular reference to polyploidy in some species, in *Indo-Pacific Fish Biology: Proc. Second Int. Conf. Indo-Pac. Fishes* (eds T. Uyeno, R. Arai, T. Taniuchi and K. Matsuura), Ichthyological Society of Japan, Tokyo, pp. 886–98.

Kobayashi, H., Kawashima, Y. and Takeuchi, N. (1970) Comparative chromosome studies in the genus *Carassius* especially with the finding of polyploidy in the Ginbuna (*Carassius auratus langsdorfii*). *Jap. J. Ichthyol.*, **17**, 153–60.

Koop, B., Goodman, M., Xu, P., Chan, K. and Slightom, J. L. (1986a) Primate η-globin DNA sequences and man's place among the great apes. *Nature, Lond.*, **319**, 234–8.

Koop, B., Miyamoto, M. M., Embury, J. E., Goodman, M., Czelusniak, J. and Slightom, J. L. (1986b) Nucleotide sequence and evolution of the orangutan η-globin gene region and surrounding alu repeats. *J. Mol. Evol.*, **24**, 94–102.

Kornfield, I. and Bogdanowicz, S. D. (1987) Differentiation of mitochondrial DNA in *Clupea harengus*. *Fishery Bull. Fish Wildl. Serv. U.S.*, **85**, 561–8.

Kreitman, M. (1987) Molecular population genetics, in *Oxford Survey of Evolutionary Biology*, Vol. 4 (eds P. H. Harvey and L. Partridge), Oxford Univ. Press, NY, pp. 38–60.

Kreitman, M. and Aguade, M. (1986) Genetic uniformity in two populations of *Drosophila melanogaster* as revealed by filter hybridization of four-nucleotide-recognizing restriction enzyme digests. *Proc. natn. Acad. Sci. U.S.A.* **83**, 3562–6.

Kubicz, A., Dratewka-Kos, E. and Zygmuntowicz, R. (1981) Multiple molecular forms of the acid phosphatase from *Cyprinus carpio* liver: isolation and comparison with those of *Rana esculenta*. *Comp. Biochem. Physiol.*, **68B**, 437–43.

Larson, A., Prager, E. M. and Wilson, A. C. (1984) Chromosomal evolution, speciation and morphological change in vertebrates: the role of social behavior. *Chromosomes Today*, **8**, 212–28.

Lauder, G. V. and Liem, K. F. (1983) The evolution and interrelationships of the Actinopterygian fishes. *Bull. Mus. comp. Zool.*, **150**, 95–197.

Li, K., Li, Y., Gui, J., Xie, X. and Zhou, T. (1986) Studies on the karyotypes of Chinese cyprinid fishes. IX. Karyotypes of nine species of Abramidinae and one species of Xenocyprininae. *Acta hydrobiol. sin.*, **10**, 189–93.

Li, W.-H. (1986) Evolutionary change of restriction cleavage sites and phylogenetic inference. *Genetics*, **113**, 187–213.

McAllister, D. E. and Coad, B. W. (1978) A test between relationships based on phenetic and cladistic taxonomic methods. *Can. J. Zool.*, **56**, 2198–210.

Magee, S. M. and Philipp, D. P. (1982) Biochemical genetic analyses of the grass carp (female) × bighead carp (male) F_1 hybrid and the parental species. *Trans. Am. Fish. Soc.*, **111**, 593–602.

Maniatis, T., Fristch, E. F. and Sambrook, J. (1982) *Molecular Cloning: A Laboratory Manual*, Cold Spring Harbor Publ., NY.

Manna, G. K. and Khuda-Bukhsh, A. R. (1977) Karyomorphology of cyprinid fishes and cytological evaluation of the family. *Nucleus, (Calcutta)*, **20**, 119–27.

Mayden, R. L. (1986) Speciose and depauperate phylads and punctuated evolution: fact or artifact? *Syst. Zool.*, **35**, 591–602.

Mayden, R. L. (1988) Systematics of the *Notropis zonatus* species group, with a description of a new species from the Interior Highlands of North America. *Copeia*, **1988**, 153–73.

Mayden, R. L. (1989) Phylogenetic studies of North American minnows, with emphasis on the genus *Cyprinella* (Teleostei: Cypriniformes). *Misc. Publs. Mus. nat. Hist. Univ. Kansas*, No. 80.

Mayfield, J. E. (1977) A comparison of the differential melting profiles with the CsCl density profiles of DNA from *Escherichia coli*, cow, mouse, rat, and chicken. *Biochim. biophys. Acta*, **477**, 97–101.

Mayr, B., Rab, P. and Kalat, M. (1986) NORs and counterstain-enhanced fluorescence studies in Cyrinidae of different ploidy level. *Genetica*, **69**, 111–18.

Mazin, A. L. (1980) Amounts of nuclear DNA in anurans of the USSR. *Experientia*, **36**, 190–91.

Meagher, S. and Dowling, T. E. Hybridization between the cyprinid fishes *Luxilus albeolus*, *L. cornutus*, and *L. cerasinus*, with comments on the proposed hybrid origin of *L. albeolus*. *Copeia*, in press.

Medrano, L., Bernardi, G., Couturier, J., Dutrillaux, B. and Bernardi, G. (1988) Chromosome banding and genome compartmentalization in fishes. *Chromosoma*, **96**, 178–83.

Menzel, B. W. (1976) Biochemical systematics and evolutionary genetics of the common shiner species group. *Biochem. Syst. Ecol.*, **4**, 281–93.

Menzel, B. W. (1977) Morphological and electrophoretic identification of a hybrid cyprinid fish *Notropis cerasinus* × *Notropis c. cornutus*, with implications on the evolution of *Notropis albeolus*. *Comp. Biochem. Physiol.*, **57B**, 215–18.

Min, M. S. and Yang, S. Y. (1986) Classification, distribution and geographic variation of two species of the genus *Moroco* in Korea. *Korean J. Syst. Zool.*, **2**, 63–78.

Minckley, W. L., Buth, D. G. and Mayden, R. L. (1989) Origin of broodstock and allozyme variation in hatchery-reared bonytail, an endangered North American cyprinid fish. *Trans. Am. Fish. Soc.*, **118**, 131–7.

Miyamoto, M. M., Slightom, J. L. and Goodman, M. (1987) Phylogenetic relationships of humans and African apes as ascertained from DNA sequences (7.1 kilobase pairs) of the μ-globin region. *Science*, **238**, 369–73.

Moreira-Filho, O., Bertollo, L. A. C. and Galetti, P. M., jun. (1984) Structure and variability of nucleolar organizer regions in Parodontidae fish. *Can. J. Genet. Cytol.*, **26**, 564–8.

Moritz, C., Dowling, T. E. and Brown, W. M. (1987) Evolution of animal mitochondrial DNA: relevance for population biology and systematics. *A. Rev. Ecol. Syst.*, **18**, 269–92.

Moyer, S. P., Ma, D. P., Thomas, T. L. and Gold, J. R. (1988) Characterization of a highly repeated satellite DNA from the cyprinid fish *Notropis lutrensis*. *Comp. Biochem. Physiol.*, **91B**, 639–46.

Muramoto, J. (1975) A note on triploidy of the Funa (Cyprinidae, Pisces). *Proc. Japan Acad.*, **51**, 583–7.

Narayan, R. K. J. (1982) Discontinuous DNA variation in the evolution of plant species. The genus *Lathyrus*. *Evolution*, **36**, 877–91.

Nei, M. (1972) Genetic distance between populations. *Am. Nat.*, **106**, 283–92.

Nei, M. (1973) Analysis of gene diversity in subdivided populations. *Proc. natn. Acad. Sci. U.S.A.*, **70**, 3321–3.

Nei, M. (1977) F-statistics and analysis of gene diversity in subdivided populations. *Ann. hum. Genet.*, **41**, 225–33.

Nei, M. (1978) Estimation of average heterozygosity and genetic distance from a small number of individuals. *Genetics*, **89**, 583–90.

Nei, M. (1987) Stochastic errors in DNA evolution and molecular phylogeny, in *Evolutionary Perspectives and the New Genetics* (ed. H. Gershowitz), Alan R. Liss, Inc., NY, pp. 131–47.

Neigel, J. E. and Avise, J. C. (1985) Phylogenetic relationships of mitochondrial DNA under various demographic models of speciation, in *Evolutionary Processes and Theory* (eds E. Nevo and S. Karlin), Academic Press, NY, pp. 515–34.

Oellermann, L. K. (1989) The karyology and taxonomy of the South African yellowfish, unpubl. MS thesis, Rhodes Univ., Grahamstown, South Africa.

Ohno, S. (1970) *Evolution by Gene Duplication*, Springer-Verlag, NY.

Ohno, S., Muramoto, J., Christian, L. and Atkin, N. B. (1967) Diploid–tetraploid relationship among old-world members of the fish family Cyprinidae. *Chromosoma*, **23**, 1–9.

Ohno, S., Muramoto, J., Klein, J. and Atkin, N. B. (1969) Diploid–tetraploid relationship in clupeoid and salmonoid fish. *Chromosomes Today*, **2**, 137–47.

Ojima, Y. (1985) *The Fish Chromosome Data Retrieval List*. Dept. Biol., Fac. Sci., Kwansei Gakuin Univ., Nishiomiya, Japan.

Ojima, Y. and Asano, N. (1977) A cytological evidence for gynogenetic development of the Ginbuna (*Carassius auratus langsdorfii*). *Proc. Japan Acad.*, **53**, 138–42.

Ojima, Y. and Takai, A. (1979) Further cytogenetical studies on the origin of the goldfish. *Proc. Japan Acad.*, **55**, 346–50.

Ojima, Y., Hayashi, M. and Ueno, K. (1972) Cytogenetical studies in lower vertebrates. X. Karyotypes and DNA studies in 15 species of Japanese Cyprinidae. *Jap. J. Genet.*, **47**, 431–40.

Olmo, E. (1981) Evolution of genome size and DNA base composition in reptiles. *Genetica*, **57**, 39–50.

Op't Hof, J., Wolf, U. and Krone, W. (1969) Studies on isozymes of sorbitol dehydrogenase in some vertebrate species. *Humangenetik*, **8**, 178–82.

Pace, N. R., Olsen, G. J. and Woese, C. R. (1986) Ribosomal RNA phylogeny and the primary lines of evolutionary descent. *Cell*, **45**, 325–6.

Park, E. H. (1974) A list of the chromosome numbers of fishes. *Review, College of Liberal Arts & Sciences, Seoul Nat. Univ.*, **20**, 346–72.

Penaz, M., Rab, P. and Prokes, M. (1979) Cytological analysis, gynogenesis and early development of *Carassius auratus gibelio*. *Acta Sci. nat. Acad. Sci. Bohemoslov (Brno)*, **13**, 1–33.

Phillips, R. B. and Ihssen, P. E. (1985) Chromosome banding in salmonid fish: nucleolar organizer regions in *Salmo* and *Salvelinus*. *Can. J. Genet. Cytol.*, **27**, 433–40.

Quinn, T. W. and White, B. N. (1987a) Analysis of DNA sequence variation, in *Avian Genetics* (eds F. Cooke and P. A. Buckley), Academic Press, London, pp. 163–98.

Quinn, T. W. and White, B. N. (1987b) Identification of restriction fragment length polymorphisms in genomic DNA of the lesser snow goose. *Mol. Biol. Evol.*, **4**, 126–43.

Qumsiyeh, M. B., Hamilton, M. J. and Schlitter, D. A. (1987) Problems in using Robertsonian rearrangements in determining monophyly: examples from the genera *Tatera* and *Gerbillus*. *Cytogenet. Cell Genet.*, **44**, 198–208.

Ragland, C. J. (1986) Nuclear DNA content variation in the North American sunfish (Pisces, Centrarchidae), unpubl. MS thesis, Texas A&M Univ., College Station, TX.

Ragland, C. J. and Gold J. R. (1989) Genome size variation in the North American sunfish genus *Lepomis* (Pisces: Centrarchidae). *Genet. Res.*, **53**, 173–82.

Raicu, P., Taisescu, E. and Bănărescu, P. (1981) *Carassius carassius* and *C. auratus*, a pair of diploid and tetraploid species. *Cytologia*, **46**, 233–40.

Rainboth, W. J., Buth, D. G. and Joswiak, G. R. (1986) Electrophoretic and karyological characters of the gyrinocheilid fish, *Gyrinocheilus aymonieri*. *Biochem. Syst. Ecol.*, **14**, 531–7.

Rakocinski, C. F. (1980) Hybridization and introgression between *Campostoma oligolepis* and *C. anomalum pullum* (Cypriniformes: Cyprinidae). *Copeia*, **1980**, 584–94.

Rishi, K. K. (1981) Chromosomal studies on four cyprinid fishes. *Int. J. Acad. Ichthyol.*, **2**, 1–4.

Rogers, J. S. (1972) Measures of genetic similarity and genetic distance. *Univ. Tex. Publs.*, **7213**, 145–53.

Rogers, J. S. (1984) Deriving phylogenetic trees from allele frequencies. *Syst. Zool.*, **33**, 52–63.

Ruvolo, M. and Smith, T. F. (1986) Phylogeny and DNA–DNA hybridization. *Mol. Biol. Evol.*, **3**, 285–9.

Sackler, M. L. (1966) Xanthine oxidase from liver and duodenum of the rat: histochemical isolation and electrophoretic heterogeneity. *J. Histochem. Cytochem.*, **14**, 326–33.

Saitou, N. (1986) On the delta Q-test of Templeton. *Mol. Biol. Evol.*, **3**, 282–4.

Schmid, M. (1982) Chromosome banding in Amphibia. VII. Analysis of the structure and variability of NORs in Anura. *Chromosoma*, **87**, 327–44.

Schmidtke, J., Scmitt, E., Leipoldt, M. and Engel, W. (1979) Amount of repeated and non-repeated DNA in the genomes of closely related fish species with varying genome sizes. *Comp. Biochem. Physiol.*, **64B**, 117–20.

Schultz, R. J. (1980) Role of polyploidy in the evolution of fishes, in *Polyploidy – Biological Relevance* (ed. W. H. Lewis), Plenum Press, NY, pp. 313–40.

Selander, R. K., Smith, M. H., Yang, S. Y., Johnson, W. E. and Gentry, J. B. (1971) Biochemical polymorphism and systematics in the genus *Peromyscus*: I. Variation in the old-field mouse (*Peromyscus polionotus*), in *Studies in Genetics*, Vol. VI, *Univ. Tex. Publs*, **7103**, pp. 49–90.

Shuter, B. J., Thomas J. E., Taylor, W. D. and Zimmerman, M. (1983) Phenotypic correlates of genomic DNA contents in unicellular eukaryotes and other cells. *Am. Nat.*, **122**, 26–44.

Sibley, C. G. and Ahlquist, J. E. (1983) Phylogeny and classification of birds based on the data of DNA–DNA hybridization, in *Current Ornithology* (ed. R. F. Johnston), Plenum Press, NY, pp. 245–92.

Sibley, C. G., Ahlquist, J. E. and Sheldon, F. H. (1987) DNA hybridization and avian phylogenetics – reply to Cracraft. *Evol. Biol.*, **21**, 97–125.

Slatkin, M. (1981) Estimating levels of gene flow in natural populations. *Genetics*, **99**, 323–35.

Slatkin, M. (1985) Rare alleles as indicators of gene flow. *Evolution*, **39**, 53–65.

Smith, P. J. and Fujio, Y. (1982) Genetic variation in marine teleosts: high variability in habitat specialists and low variability in habitat generalists. *Mar. Biol.*, **69**, 7–20.

Sneath, P. H. A. and Sokal, R. R. (1973) *Numerical Taxonomy*, Freeman, San Francisco, CA.

Stasiak, R. H., Joswiak, G. R. and Berven, K. A. (1988) Laboratory development of the hybrid *Phoxinus eos* × *Phoxinus neogaeus* (Pisces: Cyprinidae). *Experientia*, **44**, 262–3.

Stein, D. W., Rogers, J. S. and Cashner, R. C. (1985) Biochemical systematics of the *Notropis roseipinnis* complex (Cyprinidae: subgenus *Lythrurus*). *Copeia*, **1985**, 154–63.

Suzuki, H., Moriwaki, K. and Nevo, E. (1987) Ribosomal DNA (rDNA) spacer polymorphism in mole rats. *Mol. Biol. Evol.*, **4**, 602–10.

Swofford, D. L. (1981) On the utility of the distance Wagner procedure, in *Advances in Cladistics: Proc. First Meeting of the Willi Hennig Society* (eds V. A. Funk and D. R. Brooks), New York Botanical Garden, Bronx, NY, pp. 25–43.

Swofford, D. L. and Berlocher, S. H. (1987) Inferring evolutionary trees from gene frequency data under the principle of maximum parsimony. *Syst. Zool.*, **36**, 293–325.

Szarski, H. (1983) Cell size and the concept of wasteful and frugal evolutionary strategies. *J. theor. Biol.*, **105**, 201–9.

Takai, A. and Ojima, Y. (1986) Some features on nucleolus organizer regions in fish chromosomes, in *Indo-Pacific Fish Biology: Proc. Second Int. Conf. Indo-Pac. Fishes* (eds T. Uyeno, R. Arai, T. Taniuchi and K. Matsuura), Ichthyological Society of Japan, Tokyo, pp. 899–909.

Templeton, A. R. (1983) Phylogenetic inference from restriction endonuclease cleavage site maps with particular reference to humans and apes. *Evolution*, 37, 221–44.

Templeton, A. R. (1985) The phylogeny of the hominoid primates: a statistical analysis of the DNA–DNA hybridization data. *Mol. Biol. Evol.*, 2, 420–33.

Templeton, A. R. (1986) Further comments on the statistical analysis of DNA–DNA hybridization data. *Mol. Biol. Evol.*, 3, 290–5.

Thiery, J. P., Macaya, G. and Bernardi, G. (1976) An analysis of eukaryotic genomes by density gradient centrifugation. *J. molec. Biol.*, 108, 219–35.

Thomas, W. K., Withler, R. E. and Beckenbach, A. T. (1986) Mitochondrial DNA analysis of Pacific salmonid evolution. *Can. J. Zool.*, 64, 1058–64.

Tripathi, N. K. and Sharma, O. P. (1987) Cytological studies on six cyprinid fishes. *Genetica*, 73, 243–6.

Ueda, T. and Ojima, Y. (1978) Differential chromosomal characteristics in the Funa subspecies (*Carassius*). *Proc. Japan Acad.*, 54B, 283–8.

Utter, F. and Folmar, L. (1978) Protein systems of grass carp: allelic variants and their application to management of introduced populations. *Trans. Am. Fish. Soc.*, 107, 129–34.

Uyeno, T. and Smith, G. R. (1972) Tetraploid origin of the karyotype of catostomid fishes. *Science*, 175, 644–6.

Vawter, L. and Brown, W. M. (1986) Nuclear and mitochondrial DNA comparisons reveal extreme rate variation in the molecular clock. *Science*, 234, 194–6.

Watrous, L. E. and Wheeler, Q. D. (1981) The out-group comparison method of character analysis. *Syst. Zool.*, 30, 1–11.

Weir, B. S. and Cockerham, C. C. (1984) Estimating F-statistics for the analysis of population structure. *Evolution*, 38, 1358–70.

Whitt, G. S. (1970) Developmental genetics of the lactate dehydrogenase isozymes of fish. *J. exp. Zool.*, 175, 1–36.

Whitt, G. S. (1983) Isozymes as probes and participants in developmental and evolutionary genetics, in *Isozymes: Current Topics in Biological and Medical Research*, Vol. 10, *Genetics and Evolution* (eds M. C. Rattazzi, J. G. Scandalios and G. S. Whitt), Alan R. Liss, Inc., NY, pp. 1–40.

Whitt, G. S. (1987) Species differences in isozyme tissue patterns: their utility for systematic and evolutionary analyses, in *Isozymes: Current Topics in Biological and Medical Research*, Vol. 15: *Genetics, Development, and Evolution* (eds M. C. Rattazzi, J. G. Scandalios and G. S. Whitt), Alan R. Liss, Inc., NY, pp. 1–26.

Williams, S. M., DeSalle, R. and Strobeck, C. (1985) Homogenization of geographical variants at the nontranscribed spacer of rDNA in *Drosophila mercatorum*. *Mol. Biol. Evol.*, 2, 338–46.

Williams, S. M., Furnier, G. R., Fuog, E. and Strobeck, C. (1987) Evolution of the ribosomal DNA spacers of *Drosophila melanogaster*: different patterns of variation of X and Y chromosomes. *Genetics*, 116, 225–32.

Wilson, A. C., Cann, R. L., Carr, S. M., George, M., jun., Gyllensten, U. B., Helm-Bychowski, K., Higuchi, R. G., Palumbi, S. R., Prager, E. M., Sage, R. D. and Stoneking, M. (1985) Mitochondrial DNA and two perspectives on evolutionary genetics. *Biol. J. Linn. Soc.*, 26, 375–400.

Wilson, F. R., Whitt, G. S. and Prosser, C. L. (1973) Lactate dehydrogenase and malate dehydrogenase isozyme patterns in tissues of temperature acclimated goldfish (*Carassius auratus*). *Comp. Biochem. Physiol.*, 46B, 105–16.

Wolf, U., Engel, W. and Faust, J. (1970) Zum mechanismus der diploidisierung in der wirbeltierevolution: koexistenz von tetrasomen und disomen genloci der isocitrat-dehydrogenasen bei der regenbogenforelle (*Salmo irideus*). *Humangenetik*, 9, 150–6.

Woods, T. D. and Buth, D. G. (1984) High levels of gene silencing in the tetraploid goldfish. *Biochem. Syst. Ecol.*, **12**, 415–21.

Wright, S. (1965) The interpretation of population structure by F-statistics with special regard to systems of mating. *Evolution*, **19**, 395–420.

Yamamoto, T. and Kajishima, T. (1969) Sex-hormonic induction of reversal of sex differentiation in the goldfish and evidence for its male heterogamety. *J. exp. Zool.*, **168**, 215–22.

Yu, X., Zhou, T., Li, K., Li, Y. and Zhou, M. (1987) On the karyosystematics of cyprinid fishes and a summary of fish chromosome studies in China. *Genetica*, **72**, 225–36.

Zan, R., Song, Z. and Liu, W. (1986) Studies on karyotypes and nuclear DNA contents of some cyprinoid fishes, and notes on fish polyploids in China, in *Indo-Pacific Fish Biology: Proc. Second Int. Conf. Indo-Pac. Fishes* (eds T. Uyeno, R. Arai, T. Taniuchi and K. Matsuura), Ichthyological Society of Japan, Tokyo, pp. 877–885.

Zimmerman, E. G. and Richmond, M. C. (1981) Increased heterozygosity at the Mdh-B locus in fish inhabiting a rapidly fluctuating thermal environment. *Trans. Am. Fish. Soc.*, **110**, 410–16.

Chapter five

Cyprinids of Eurasia

P. Bănărescu and B. W. Coad

5.1 DESCRIPTION OF EURASIA

The Eurasian landmass is the largest in the world. It encompasses 44.43 m. km² or 36.7% of land compared to 30.27 m. km² (20.4%) for Africa and 24.26 m. km² (16.3%) for North America. The highest point on the globe is found in Eurasia (Everest, 8848 m), as is the lowest (Dead Sea, − 400 m). It also has the largest lake (Caspian Sea, 371 000 km²) and the deepest (Baikal, 1620 m). The Yangtze River is the third longest after the Nile and the Amazon at 6380 km, the Ob'–Irtysh is the fifth at 5410 km, the Yellow (Huang He) is sixth at 4672 km, the Amur eighth at 4416 km, the Lena ninth at 4400 km and the Mekong eleventh at 4184 km. The geography of this area is covered in general texts, e.g. the series *Ecosystems of the World* (ed. D. W. Goodall, Elsevier, Amsterdam). Van der Leeden (1975) summarizes statistics on water resources.

Eurasia is surrounded by seas and oceans and its only land connection is a narrow one to Africa at the Sinai Peninsula. On the Pacific coast there is a series of large islands, from Japan in the north to the Philippines, Borneo, Sumatra and Java in the south. The only other large islands with cyprinids are Sri Lanka and the British Isles.

The geomorphology and climate of such a large landmass extending from north of the Arctic Circle to south of the Equator naturally show great variation from tundra to rain forest, from true desert to lush river valleys and from steppe to complex mountain chains. Cyprinids are found over all of Eurasia except the far north, the waterless deserts of Arabia and Central Asia and the highest mountains.

The rivers and lakes (excluding South East Asia – see Rainboth, Chapter 6) may be divided into various major areas based on geography, history and ichthyofaunas (Fig. 5.1). These are (a) Europe, including north-west Africa, central and northern Anatolia, Transcaucasia, the Caspian Sea basin of Iran and the lower reaches of the Aral Sea basin; (b) South-west Asia or West Asia, including southern Iran and the eastern borderlands, the Tigris–Euphrates basin, southern Anatolia, the Levant and the Arabian Peninsula; (c) Siberia, including Arctic Ocean drainages and northern Pacific Ocean drainages;

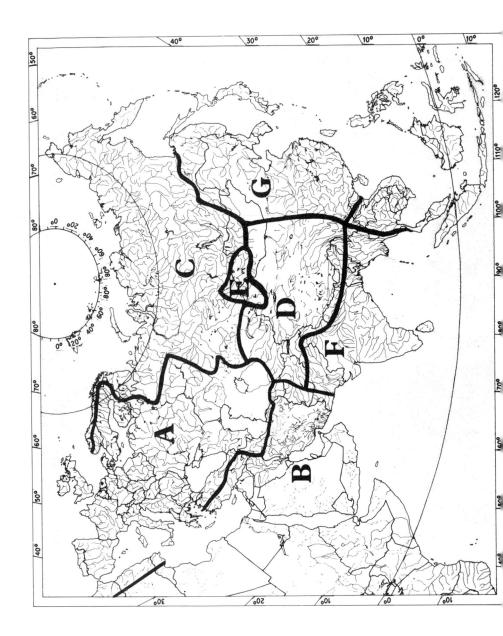

(d) Central or High Asia, including internal basins and the upper reaches of rivers draining through other areas, e.g. the Huang He and Yangtze draining east to the Pacific Ocean, the Mekong, Irrawaddy, Salween, Brahmaputra, Ganges (Ganga) and Indus draining south to the Indian Ocean, the Amu- and Syr- Dar'ya draining west to the Aral Sea and the Helmand draining west to an internal basin – the High Asian basin is the only one not corresponding to present-day hydrography; (e) Western Mongolia, comprising refugial areas south of the Sayan and Altai mountains; (f) South Asia, comprising the Indian subcontinent and Burma (basins of the Salween, Sittang and Irrawaddy and the western slope of the north Malayan Peninsula); (g) East Asia, including the Amur River basin south to the Song koi or Red River of Vietnam with Sakhalin, Japan, Taiwan and Hainan Dao.

5.2 DIVERSITY

Sources

The diversity of cyprinids in Eurasia is much greater than in sub-Saharan Africa or North America. We treat here for general counts of diversity all of Eurasia, including South East Asia which is described in Chapter 6. South-west Arabia with nine species (Krupp, 1983) is also included, although some authorities place it zoogeographically as part of sub-Saharan Africa. The cyprinids of the Mediterranean fringe of north-west Africa comprising four species are also included as their affinities are European, not sub-Saharan African (Almaça, 1979).

Counts of genera and species are based on Don E. McAllister's *Working List of the Fishes of the World* (unpublished). Many areas have been poorly studied, few taxa have received adequate revisions and conflicting views exist on specific and generic limits, so any counts of genera and species are by no means final. However, they do give a comparative picture of diversity between continents, between river basins and between areas.

Generic descriptions peak at intervals. The first major peak was in the 1850s and 1860s, when 52 new genera were described in 20 y, more than in the previous 100 y. From 1870 to 1929 the average number of descriptions per decade was about 12, yet in the 1930s this increased to 27. The period from 1940 to 1979 was another low with only four new descriptions per decade. The 1980s saw an upsurge with 15 new genera appearing, often the result of revisionary studies. These variations are attributable to the timing of expeditions to new areas and the work of comparatively few students of cyprinid systematics.

Fig. 5.1 Areas of Eurasia. A, Europe; B, South-west or West Asia, C, Siberia; D, Central or High Asia; E, Western Mongolia; F, South Asia; G, East Asia (two-point equidistant projection).

Taxa

Eurasia contains *c*. 227 genera and *c*. 1293 species of cyprinids. This may be contrasted with sub-Saharan Africa with 22 genera and 469 species, and North America with 41 genera and 263 species. Over one-third of the genera in Eurasia (37%) are monotypic, 16% have only two species, and 87% have ten or fewer species. The most diverse genera are *Puntius* (*c*. 130 species), *Schizothorax* (*c*. 57), *Rasbora* (*c*. 51), *Barbus* (*c*. 41), *Labeo* (*c*. 41) and *Garra* (*c*. 40).

The great diversity of Eurasian cyprinids at the generic level necessitates selection when discussing taxa. Recognition of subfamilies varies greatly (Howes, Chapter 1; Nelson, 1984), with as few as four or as many as 13 having been used by various authors and with varying views on included genera. However, all subfamilies are found in Eurasia. Subfamilies are mentioned in passing below and further discussion may be found elsewhere in this volume, in Gosline (1978), Arai, (1982), Chen *et al.* (1984) and works by Howes (1978, 1982, 1984a, 1985).

River basins

Table 5.1 summarizes diversity by river basin. These were selected to reflect size, geography and diversity and necessarily also reflect available knowledge. All basins drain to the sea or an internal sump and are not tributary to larger rivers which could potentially increase diversity without respect to length or latitude.

The greatest diversity is found in the east, where even a small river like the Nanliu Jiang of southern China has more species than rivers ten times its length in central and western Eurasia. The great rivers draining northern Eurasia to the Arctic Ocean have relatively few cyprinids, as do the desert rivers of Central Asia and Arabia. Rivers on the fringes of Eurasia have a low diversity, whether in the Iberian Peninsula (Guadalquivir), Ireland (Shannon), Sri Lanka (Mahaweli Ganga) or Kamchatka (which has none). Where they do occur, cyprinids are the most speciose family; in 21 of the 56 rivers in Table 5.1, more than half the ichthyofauna is cyprinids. On average they contribute 44% of the species in a river basin.

Drainage size (measured as river length) is significantly correlated with number of species ($P < 0.001$): large drainages have more species. Both latitude and longitude are significantly correlated with number of species ($P < 0.05$): northern latitudes have fewer species than southern ones, while eastern longitudes have more species than western ones.

Lakes show little diversity and usually have similar faunas to tributary rivers. The old, deep Lake Baikal, for example, has only six species of cyprinids, none endemic. Lake Er Hai of the Yunnan Plateau, however, contains six species of *Cyprinus*, five of which are endemic (Wu, 1987; Wang, 1979) and

Table 5.1 Diversity of cyprinids in Eurasian river basins*

River basin	Length (km)	Mouth		Genera	Species	% of ichthyofauna
		Lat. N	Long. E			
Yangtze (Chang and Jinsha)	6380	31	122	53	97	48
Ob'–Irtysh	5410	67	69	7	13	33
Amur	4416	54	141	37	46	46
Lena	4400	74	127	6	9	20
Volga	3685	46	48	20	27	42
Indus	3057	24	68	25	63	42
Euphrates	2928	30	49	15	24	46
Danube	2816	45	30	20	34	39
Amu–Dar'ya	2537	44	59	14	19	58
Ganges	2510	23	91	18	50	37
Kolyma	2148	70	161	3	4	15
Xi	2012	22	113	64	111	61
Don	1967	47	40	19	26	42
Pechora	1786	68	54	6	8	24
Kura	1513	39	49	19	31	54
Liao He	1448	41	122	23	30	53
Dnestr	1409	46	30	20	30	39
Helmand	1400	31	66	7	13	48
Rhine	1319	52	4	16	20	40
Tedzhen	1127	38	60	7	8	62
Chu	1126	45	67	13	17	59
Ili	1094	45	74	3	8	57
Mahanadi	901	20	87	17	49	49
Rhône	813	43	5	12	16	31

Table 5.1 (Continued)

River basin	Length (km)	Mouth		Genera	Species	% of ichthyofauna
		Lat. N	Long. E			
Sakarya	788	41	31	19	22	55
Po	652	45	13	9	13	36
Safid	647	37	50	19	25	46
Guadalquivir	644	37	6W	4	5	19
Terek	591	44	47	15	23	53
Hadramawt (al masilāh)	563	15	51	3	6	75
Ulungur He	560	47	87	4	4	57
Kamchatka	539	56	162	0	0	0†
Tumen	521	43	131	10	14	39
Mand	480	28	51	6	12	55
Mashkel	430	28	63	4	5	50
Büyük Menderes	402	37	27	8	11	26
Pishin	402	29	65	3	3	60
Zaindeh	402	32	53	4	7	88
Orontes	386	36	36	11	26	76
Thames	370	51	0	10	11	30
Çoruh	369	42	42	16	18	33
Shannon	354	53	9W	5	5	23
Adour	338	44	2W	10	11	35
Minho	338	42	9W	4	5	21
Mahaweli	332	8	81	6	11	58
Jordan	322	32	36	6	12	46
Kor	322	30	53	8	11	69
Talas	322	44	70	4	7	70

Ebinur	280	45	83	3	3	38
Nanliu	220	22	109	33	40	73
Clyde	171	56	5W	5	5	22
Litāni	145	33	35	3	3	38
Qin	120	22	109	13	15	60
Piniós	77	38	21	5	5	26
Neva	74	60	30	14	18	38
Sele	64	41	15	6	6	22

Sources: Mori (1936), Berg (1948–49), Job et al. (1955), Turdakov (1963), Ladiges and Vogt (1965), Wheeler (1969), Kuru (1971, 1980), Maitland (1972), Mirza (1975, 1980, 1982), Ichthyology Laboratory, Hupei Institute of Hydrobiology (1976), Jayaram and Singh (1977), Institute of Zoology, Academia Sinica et al. (1979), Coad (1981), Srivastava (1980), Zhen et al. (1980), Fisheries Research Institute, Guangxi Zhuang Tribe Self-Governed Territory and Institute of Zoology, Academia Sinica (1981), Delmastro (1982), Erk'akan and Kuru (1982), Krupp (1983, 1987), De Silva (1985), unpublished data of B.W.C.
† 21 non-cyprinid species.

Inlé Lake of the Shan Plateau of Burma has six endemics including *Sawbwa resplendens* (Annandale, 1918).

Areas

Europe

This area is also known as the Euro-Mediterranean and has been reviewed by Bănărescu (1960). It has a relatively poor complement of subfamilies. Three subfamilies well represented in East Asia (p. 136) are here represented by single species (Acheilognathinae, *Rhodeus sericeus amarus*; Cultrinae, *Pelecus cultratus*) or a single genus (Gobioninae, *Gobio* with seven species).

The Cyprininae are more numerous and include the closely related *Carassius* and *Cyprinus* with East Asian relatives, and the related monotypic *Tinca*, which has no obvious East Asian relatives. *Barbus*, as defined in Howes (1987), is confined to Europe and South-west Asia and has at least 20 species. It appears to be related to the East Asian *Sinocyclocheilus* and High Asian Schizothoracini. *Aulopyge* is monotypic and found only on the western Balkan slope of the Adriatic Sea (Howes, 1987). *Capoeta* is found in the east of this area and in South-west Asia.

The Leuciscinae is a polyphyletic assemblage (Howes, 1980) and is used here for convenience. *Phoxinus* is Holarctic with several species in North America; other genera are Palaearctic, found from Europe to East Asia, including *Leuciscus* and *Eupallasella*. *Rutilus* is Euro-Siberian. Other genera are exclusively European or are also found in South-west Asia. Genera with central European species include *Abramis*, *Blicca* and *Leucaspius*, although some may extend into southern Europe; genera with central European and endemic southern European/South-west Asian species include *Chondrostoma*, *Alburnus*, *Alburnoides*, *Chalcalburnus*, *Vimba*, *Scardinius*, *Aspius* and the subgenera *Squalius* and *Telestes* or *Leuciscus*; and genera with southern European or southern European/South-west Asian species include *Anaecypris* and *Iberocypris* of the Iberian Peninsula, *Pachychilon* and *Phoxinellus* in the western Balkans, *Pseudophoxinus* from Greece to Iran, *Ladigesocypris* in Rhodes and south-west Anatolia, *Leucalburnus* in western Anatolia and eastern Transcaucasia, *Acanthalburnus* in eastern Transcaucasia, *Aspiolucius* and *Capoetobrama* in the Aral Sea basin.

South-west Asia or West Asia

The fauna of this area is poor, with about 22 genera and 80 species; more than 90% of the latter are endemic. They are in two subfamilies, Leuciscinae and Cyprininae. The Leuciscinae include the endemic *Acanthobrama*, a relative of the Euro-Siberian *Rutilus*, with seven species in the Tigris–Euphrates basin, the Levant and north-western Saudi Arabia. Other leuciscines are also European in their affinities, at either the specific or generic levels, and include such genera as *Leuciscus*, *Alburnus*, *Alburnoides*, *Chalcalburnus*, *Aspius* and *Pseudophoxinus*. The cyprinines also have genera with European affinities (some *Barbus*, *Capoeta*), while others are South Asian (the endemic *Cyprinion* perhaps closest to the Himalayan *Semiplotus*) or African (some non-European '*Barbus*' – see Howes, 1987) or widely distributed across Asia through Southwest Asia to Africa (*Garra*). *Hemigrammocapoeta* and *Hemigarra* are endemic.

Barilius mesopotamicus of the Tigris–Euphrates basin and southern Iran is of uncertain relationships and generic placement, and may be a member of the South Asian and African Danioninae.

The aridity of this area limits the fauna, and most species are unspecialized, living equally well in rivers, ponds and swamps. Several species are found in underground waters in Iran, Iraq and Oman and are depigmented and eyeless (*Iranocypris*, *Typhlogarra*, *Caecocypris* and *Garra*).

Siberia

The very large rivers of Siberia are poor in species because of the unfavourable climatic conditions, and none of the ten cyprinid species are endemic. Several genera now found exclusively in Europe lived in Siberia in the late Pliocene. Disjunct distributions between Europe and East Asia were once continuous. *Gobio gobio*, *Phoxinus phoxinus* and *Eupallasella percnura* are found also in Europe and northern East Asia; *Rutilus rutilus*, *Leuciscus leuciscus*, *L. idus*, *Tinca tinca* and *Carassius carassius* are Euro-siberian, while *Lagowskiella czekanowskii* and *L. lagowskii* are shared with northern East Asia.

Central or High Asia

This area is characterized by the snow trouts, tribe Schizothoracini of Cyprininae (= Schizothoracinae) (Bǎnǎrescu, 1983). There are 11 genera with about 97 species, all endemic to this area or its immediate fringe. The base of the anal fin is covered by a sheath of enlarged scales, while the rest of the body scales are minute or absent. The mouth is usually inferior, fleshy and papillose or provided with a horny plate. Schizothoracini may be related to barbine fishes. The southern Indian *Lepidopygopsis* has been placed in this tribe but this is questionable.

The two most plesiomorphic genera, *Schizopyge* and *Schizothorax* (= *Oreinus*), are found throughout most of High Asia. The more specialized *Diptychus* and *Schizopygopsis* are widely distributed too, but occur mostly in the upper reaches of rivers. *Gymnodiptychus* is confined to the northern and eastern drainages, *Gymnocypris* to the southern and eastern ones. More restricted distributions are found in *Schizocypris* (western High Asia), *Aspiorhynchus* (Tarim River basin), *Oxygymnocypris* (upper Brahmaputra) and the highly specialized *Herzensteinia* (upper Yangtze), *Chuanchia* and *Platypharodon* (upper Huang He basin).

Western Mongolia

This small area comprises several lakes in the upper drainage of the Ob' and Manas He. There are two sister genera, *Oreoleuciscus* (= *Acanthorutilus*) with about three species and the monospecific *Aspiopsis*, belonging to the aspinine lineage of the Leuciscinae, disjunctly distributed in Europe and South-west Asia and East Asia but absent from Siberia proper. Three species of the Holarctic genus *Phoxinus* are also found here.

This fauna is a relictual and refugial one, consisting mainly of the now disjunctly distributed aspinine lineage which once was probably much richer than now.

South Asia

South Asia has as rich a fauna as East Asia, but lacks the familial diversity. It shares Cyprininae and Rasborinae with East Asia and Africa, but is more speciose than either, and it shares Cultrinae with East Asia but is less speciose. A single Acheilognathinae is present in the Mekong basin (*Acanthorhodeus diegnani*). There are no Gobioninae or Leuciscinae in South Asia.

Several genera are widely distributed throughout this area (*Poropuntius, Crossocheilus,* and *Rasbora*), others extend beyond it (*Cirrhinus* and *Puntius* also in East Asia, *Labeo* in Africa, and *Garra* in East Asia, South-west Asia and Africa), while others are endemic (*Securicula* in the Indus, Ganges–Brahmaputra and Mahanadi rivers, sister group to the Indo-Burmese *Salmostoma; Horadandia* in Sri Lanka, a relative of *Rasbora; Lepidopygopsis* of south-west India, of uncertain relationships but similar to the Schizothoracini of High Asia; *Rohtee*, possibly a relative of the Indo-Burmese *Osteobrama*, in the Krishna (Kistna) and Godavary rivers; *Catla*, probably a relative of the South East Asian *Catlocarpio*, throughout India; and *Parasilorhynchus* with two species in the Western Ghats, and no close relatives). Six other genera are shared only with Burma, namely *Aspidoparia, Salmostoma, Amblypharyngodon, Brachydanio, Semiplotus* and *Osteobrama*. *Cyprinion* is shared with South-west Asia. Other genera are widely distributed in South Asia, in East Asia, in Africa or in all three. Jayaram (1981) summarizes the fauna of India and neighbouring countries.

East Asia

East Asia shares with South East Asia the distinction of having the richest cyprinid faunas. All subfamilies are found in East Asia and two, Gobioninae and Acheilognathinae, are almost endemic (Bănărescu, 1972).

Gobioninae comprises 20 genera (Bănărescu and Nalbant, 1973), all but *Gobio* being endemic, with about 100 species. Hosoya (1986) reviewed their interrelationships and excluded eight genera, which are retained here for convenience. They are small to mid-sized fishes, most living on the bottom or in running waters, having an inferior mouth, barbels, and many papillae on the lips or chin. In East Asia, *Gobio* is restricted to the north, from the Amur to the Huang He basins, and is absent from Japan. *Biwia* is endemic to Japan, *Pungtungia* is found in Japan and Korea, *Ladislavia* in the Amur basin and Korea, and *Acanthogobio* in the Huang He basin. Three genera are endemic to Korea.

Other genera are more widely distributed in East Asia, while the three most specialized genera with reduced and encapsulated swim bladders, the rheophilic *Gobiobotia, Microphysogobio* and *Saurogobio*, are found on the mainland, Taiwan and Hainan but not Japan. *Coreius* and *Rhinogobio* are found in the central part of the mainland and are absent from the islands, the Amur and the Xi Jiang basins.

The Acheilognathinae are small, deep-bodied fishes characterized by the female's long ovipositor. There are seven genera, and about 40 species. The most speciose genera are *Acheilognathus*, which is mainly Japanese, and *Acanthorhodeus*, which is mainly Chinese with only a single species in Japan. *Tanakia* is endemic to Japan and there is an unnamed genus with three species in southern China and northern Vietnam (incorrectly placed in *Pararhodeus*). *Rhodeus* is widely distributed in East Asia and is the only genus with a European representative.

The Cultrinae, with 13 endemic genera (and about 40 species) in East Asia, are probably polyphyletic and are shared with South Asia and possibly Europe (*Pelecus*). They include (after Howes, 1979) the cultrine group with five or six East Asian genera and *Paralaubuca* of South East Asia, the hemicultrine group with three endemic East Asian genera, and the *Hemiculturella* group with two East Asian genera and possibly the European *Pelecus*. The cultrine *Parabramis* and *Megalobrama* are deep-bodied benthic feeders while the others are elongate, mid-water feeders. *Erythroculter* is a large-mouthed predator. Most Cultrinae are widely distributed in East Asia but absent from Japan except for a single species of *Ischikauia*. Those Culturinae with restricted ranges are to be found in southern China, such as *Anabarilius* which has speciated in Yunnan.

The Rasborinae (= Danioninae) have 11 endemic East Asian genera and more than 20 species. Their relationships are questionable, whether among themselves or with South Asian and African genera assigned to the same subfamily. *Zacco* and *Opsariichthys* are found from the Amur south to northern Vietnam with their sister group, *Barilius*, in southern Asia and other related genera in Africa (Howes, 1980, 1983). A second lineage includes *Aphyocypris* throughout East Asia, *Hemigrammocypris* in Japan, *Tanichthys* and two other genera in southern China and northern Vietnam. Four other rasborine genera are dissimilar and of uncertain affinities, namely the widely distributed *Ochetobius, Atrilinea* of southern China, *Xenocyprioides* of the Xi Jiang basin and *Gobiocypris* of the upper Chang Jiang. Two species of the South Asian and South East Asian genus *Rasbora* are also found in East Asia.

The Leuciscinae comprise 15 genera, including several found in northern Eurasia, namely *Phoxinus, Eupallasella, Leuciscus* and *Lagowskiella*. *Rhynchocypris* is another cold-adapted genus but is endemic to East Asia. The aspinine lineage has five East Asian genera and eight species. Howes (1981) considers that *Hypophthalmichthys, Xenocypris* and related genera form a monophyletic lineage whose sister group is the Euro-Siberian *Rutilus–Abramis–Chondrostoma* lineage. Chen *et al.* (1984) assign the former to a distinct subfamily, the Xenocyprininae, a sister group of the Cultrinae.

The very large subfamily Cyprininae has many genera and species in East Asia. The squaliobarbine group consists of three monotypic genera with a wide distribution and economic importance namely *Ctenopharyngodon, Mylopharyngodon* and *Squaliobarbus*. Howes (1981) places this group as the sister group of all other cyprinines, while Chen *et al.* (1984) place them in the Leuciscinae. The true carps (tribe Cyprinini) are predominately East Asian, and *Cyprinus* here has about 13 species and two related genera. *Carassius auratus* is also native to East Asia. The schizothoracines have some representatives which enter East Asia proper, but much more numerous are the 'barbs', a heterogenous assemblage of unrelated genera concentrated in southern China and northern Vietnam, with only a few reaching northern China (species of *Acrossocheilus* and *Onychostoma*) and being absent from Korea, Japan and the Amur basin. About 16 genera and 60 species are endemic to East Asia, about 30 species are prevalently southern Asian (*Osteocheilus, Puntius,* etc.) or more widely distributed (*Garra,* which extends to Africa). The relationships of many East Asian and South Asian genera are unclear and those of the endemics are particularly obscure. Some possible relationships are *Sinocyclocheilus* of the upper Chang Jiang with European and South-west Asian *Barbus,* the widely distributed *Onychostoma* with the South-west Asian *Capoeta, Acrossocheilus* with the South Asian *Poropuntius, Sinilabeo* with the South Asian and African *Labeo* and *Ptychido, Semilabeo* and *Rectoris* with *Crossocheilus* and *Garra*.

In summary, East Asia is the richest area in Eurasia, with all subfamilies present and two almost endemic. Many genera and species are widely distributed while many others are endemic to major river basins, the Korean Peninsula or Japan.

5.3   ZOOGEOGRAPHY

Zoogeographical studies of Eurasian cyprinids are hampered by the poor state of systematic knowledge. Polyphyletic assemblages and uncertain or conflicting interpretations of generic relationship do not lend themselves to a clear analysis. However, some points do arise from distributional data or have been advanced in the literature, and some are discussed below (for additional comments and other views see Chapters 1 and 6).

High Asia and the schizothoracines

The schizothoracines have evolved in relation to the stages of upheaval of the Qinghai–Xizang Plateau (Cao *et al.,* 1981; Wu, 1984). It is suggested that early Pliocene, primitive barbine fishes gave rise to forms analogous to the fossil

Plesioschizothorax macrocephalus. An initial rise of the plateau to an altitude of 1250–2500 m favoured forms able to adapt to the marked changes in environment; these became members of a group represented by *Schizothorax*. A subsequent rise eliminated most of the schizothoracines except those on the fringes of the uplift and those that could adapt. The latter formed a group represented by *Diptychus*, found at an altitude of 3750 m. A third rise moved *Diptychus* to the edge of the tableland, while much of the centre became occupied by the highly specialized *Gymnocypris*, *Schizopygopsis* and relatives at an altitude of 4000–4750 m.

Dispersal or vicariance?

The ichthyofauna of South Asia, including cyprinids, comprises genera overwhelmingly found to the east in South East Asia and South China or comprises genera closely related to eastern ones (Jayaram, 1974; Lowe–McConnell, 1975). East Asia is regarded as a dispersal centre because of the relative diversity of taxa (Bănărescu, 1972). Some taxa in East Asia are regarded as immigrants, such as Pleistocene *Leuciscus* and *Phoxinus*, but these are far outnumbered by autochthonous taxa.

It is generally supposed that India received its cyprinid fauna from the east, beginning in the early Eocene, and that some groups reached Africa via the Arabian Peninsula (summary, Briggs, 1987). Various evolutionary waves of taxa have been described to account for the current diversity of this area (Menon, 1964). Lowered sea levels and a more extensive drainage pattern during pluvial periods would have enabled Pleistocene movements between Asia and Africa. *Garra* is still found in a continuous arc from Africa to China while other taxa, such as the labeine group (Reid, 1985) and the bariliines (Howes, 1980), have an interrupted distribution, being absent from South-west Asia. The current fauna of South-west Asia is therefore depauperate under this hypothesis.

East Asia is said to be a dispersal centre and North America, Siberia (and West Mongolia from Siberia), Europe and South-west Asia were colonized from this centre. Certainly East Asia has been a centre of evolution for cyprinids since the early Pliocene. Nakajima (1986) describes pharyngeal tooth fossils of seven subfamilies from Japan, representing a fauna different from the extant one. This older fauna spread to the mainland in the middle to late Miocene and became extinct in Japan because shallow and large lakes disappeared during the middle to late Pleistocene and were replaced by torrential rivers.

Howes (1980) presents an alternative explanation. Instead of East Asia being an 'evolutionary centre' with 'dispersal' westwards, he advocates a Gondwanic distribution (when India was part of Africa in the early Cretaceous and before its drift northwards to contact Asia in the Palaeocene) for bariliines, barbines and labeines. Present distribution is then a vicariant event. However, this pushes the origin of cyprinids, and in particular the lineages mentioned above, too far into the past.

Chen *et al.* (1984) present a third hypothesis, which has two 'lines' of distribution, the north and south. The north line arose from Europe and extended to Siberia, East Asia and then North America; the south line came from Africa to South Asia and then East Asia. Both lines cross in East Asia, explaining its diversity of Cyprinidae.

Howes (1980, 1981) rightly points out the difficulties of elaborating dispersal hypotheses on the bases of conflicting views in the literature on palaeogeography and our poor knowledge of phylogenetic relationships.

Europe, origins and influence of the fauna

Europe was isolated from Siberia until the Eocene and had no cyprinids (J. Gaudant, pers. comm. to P.M.B.). Cyprinids from Siberia penetrated Europe beginning in the Oligocene, entering an area defined as central Europe (Bănărescu, 1960). Forty cyprinid species are extant in this area, with the Danube basin having 34 species.

The southern peninsulas of Europe, Anatolia and South-west Asia contain species of genera found in central Europe. Mountain ranges such as the Pyrenees and Alps may have been barriers to dispersal, but once they were crossed, dispersal was facilitated by the Miocene desiccation of the Mediterranean Sea: the Sarmatian Sea of South-east Europe was initially a barrier but it soon developed into a complex of freshened lakes favouring dispersal. The current diversity in rivers belonging to the Black, Caspian and Aral seas and the northern slopes of the Aegean Sea are due to this development.

Trans-Pacific or trans-Atlantic relationships?

Howes (1984b) briefly reviews earlier authors who have advocated trans-Pacific links. In addition, *Phoxinus* is found in Eurasia and eastern North America, and the monotypic genus *Notemigonus* of eastern North America shares osteological characters with the European and South-west Asian genus *Alburnoides* (unpublished data, B.W.C.).

The usual explanation for the presence of cyprinids in North America is a dispersalist one, using the Bering land bridge, which has been available at intervals since the late Cretaceous. A vicariant explanation requires agreement on plate numbers and disposition in the Pacific.

Area cladograms for other fish taxa suggest that western North America is more closely related to eastern North America and to Europe than to Asia (Patterson, 1981). North America had a temperate connection to Europe in the Eocene (and possibly into the Miocene) and perhaps a trans-Atlantic link. The Eocene may be too early; cyprinid fossils in North America date only to the Oligocene according to Cavender (1986) who, however, states that *Notemigonus* reached eastern North America from Europe at an unknown date.

The resolution of these suggested links and their vicariant or dispersalist nature will require more work on the relationships of North American and Eurasian cyprinids.

5.4 BIOLOGY

General accounts of Eurasian cyprinid biology may be found in Nikol'skii (1961), Nikolsky (1963), Breder and Rosen (1966), Aleev (1969), Grzimek (1973), Norman and Greenwood (1975), Sterba (1983), and Wheeler (1985).

Body form

Eurasian cyprinids show considerable variation in body form. Terete forms are common but some are robust (*Cyprinus carpio*) or deep-bodied (*Abramis brama*), while a few have the elongate jaws of a predator (*Elopichthys bambusa*). Body form may change under the influence of habitat or diet. *Carassius carassius, C. auratus* and others have both deep-bodied forms and an elongate form (known as morpha *humilis* in *Carassius* spp.), which are found in confined habitats or when subject to starvation.

Swimmers in fast water are rounded in cross-section, e.g. *Tor tor*, *Schizothorax* spp., *Leuciscus* spp. In slow or still waters, bodies are compressed, e.g. *Rutilus* spp., *Abramis* spp. Some residents of fast waters stay close to the bottom and rarely enter the full flow, e.g. *Garra* spp., *Gobio* spp. These are depressed or have flat bellies and an arched back, the pectoral and pelvic fins are low, lateral and muscular, and eyes are high on the head. Such bottom dwellers often have reduced swim bladders, sometimes encased in bone, which reduce buoyancy. The mouth is often modified into a sucker. In *Garra* the upper lip becomes thickened and covered by papillae, the upper jaw is not protrusible and a disc-like papillated sucker is found on the lower head surface behind the mouth.

The majority of cyprinids are small, less than 30 cm long when adult. The largest in Eurasia, *Catlocarpio siamensis* of Cambodia and Thailand, may attain 3 m, of which about one-third is the head. It is capable of towing a fisherman's boat for hours. The yellowcheek, *Elopichthys bambusa*, of the Amur River south to Vietnam may attain 2 m and 40 kg. *Tor tor* of India exceeds 1.5 m and weighs 54 kg, and the putitor or golden mahseer, *Tor putitora*, reaches 2.75 m. The 'Tigris salmon', *Barbus esocinus*, is said to reach 2.3 m and 136 kg (Mahdi, 1962). The smallest cyprinid (and smallest adult vertebrate in fresh water and smallest member of the Ostariophysi) is the recently described *Danionella translucida* from Burma, which is only 12 mm SL, with females mature at 10 mm SL. This species is also remarkable for its lack of scales and of a lateral line system, its transparency, and the separation of the anterior and posterior swim bladder chambers (Roberts, 1986).

A number of species have anatomical peculiarities, but most conform to a basic cyprinid plan without the elaborations of body parts seen in some other fish families. *Sawbwa resplendens* of the Inlé Lake, Burma lacks scales, while *Acanthobrama centisquama* of the Levant, as its name suggests, is abundantly scaled, but the scales all lack radii, a unique feature. Large *Tor* species may have only 25 scales in the lateral line but are almost 3 m long; individual scales are the size of a hand. Members of the Schizothoracinae have enlarged scales around the anus and anal fin, forming a sheath. Abramidinae and Cultrinae have a naked belly keel which in pelagic species has a camouflaging function in eliminating a ventral shadow. Barbels in some species are very long, e.g. *Esomus danrica*, in others variably present, e.g. *Barbus luteus*. The lips of *Ptychidio jordani* are elaborately fimbriated. Hypertrophied lips are not uncommon in certain *Barbus* and *Tor* species, giving them a bizarre appearance (Hora, 1943). A spine-like ray at the anterior portion of the dorsal fin is found in a variety of unrelated genera and is assumed to serve a protective function. Certainly the spiny bitterling, *Acheilognathus asmussii*, appears in only 19% of predator diets while the spineless common bitterling, *Rhodeus sericeus*, is found in 81% of diets (the two species represent 70% and 30% of catches respectively, so availability is not a confusing factor).

Eurasian cyprinids are the only ones to show tetraploidy in such diverse genera as *Cyprinus*, *Carassius*, *Barbus*, *Aulopyge* and *Acrossocheilus*, probably developed independently.

The majority of Eurasian cyprinids are silvery on the flanks with a darker, often blue-green, back and lighter belly (e.g. the bleak, *Alburnus alburnus*); this is a pelagic pattern found in fish of open waters. Some have a demersal pattern where the back and sides are dark but the belly is light, e.g. gudgeons, *Gobio* spp., while others have a schooling pattern such as a dark stripe on the flank (*Lagowskiella lagowskii*) or spots on the flank or dorsal fin, which help in orientation of schooling species. The dorsal fin spot of *Acanthorhodeus asmussii* is lost when the fish matures and becomes solitary. Other species are brightly coloured and patterned with stripes, bars and spots and so are popular in the aquarium trade, e.g. danios, rasboras, barbs, 'sharks' (i.e. *Labeo* spp.), etc. They are well illustrated in aquarium books such as Sterba (1983).

Age

The life span of *Danionella* has been estimated at less than 1 y and many small temperate species live less than 2 y. Larger species live longer, although how long is often a mixture of myth and the difficulties of aging techniques. A female koi, *Cyprinus carpio*, from Japan named Hanako was estimated to be 223 y old by growth ring examination (Wood, 1976), but 50 + y is probably a truer estimate. An English pet goldfish, *Carassius auratus*, died at the age of 41.

Habitat

Eurasian cyprinids are found from melting snow water (*Phoxinus*, *Schizothorax*) at oxygen concentrations of $5-7\,\mathrm{ml}\,\mathrm{l}^{-1}$ or more to hot springs and warm lowlands (*Barbus callensis* in Algeria at 37–8 °C, *Cyprinion watsoni* in Iran at 38 °C, carp at 36–7 °C) at oxygen levels of $0.5\,\mathrm{ml}\,\mathrm{l}^{-1}$. Temperature is often limiting, e.g. *Gobio gobio* in Europe is found between the 15 and 27 °C July isotherms, which determine its breeding or feeding success, although individuals can tolerate higher and lower temperatures. *Schizopygopsis stoliczkae* is found at over 4500 m in Tibet (Stewart, 1911) and Afghanistan (unpubl. data, B.W.C.). *Garra tibanica ghorensis* is found near the Dead Sea shore at $-400\,\mathrm{m}$ (Krupp, 1982).

Cyprinids are primary freshwater fishes, but *Tribolodon* species from eastern Asia have been found 5 km out to sea although they must return to fresh water to breed. Carp, bream (*Abramis brama*), *Barbus brachycephalus*, roach (*Rutilus rutilus*), and shemaya, *Chalcalburnus chalcoides*, enter the Caspian and Aral seas (14‰) but spawn in fresh water. Only the shemaya can spawn at 10–11‰.

Desiccation can be a problem. *Carassius carassius* can survive several weeks buried in mud. Other species also tolerate poor conditions, e.g. *Abramis brama* is favoured as a food fish because it can be carried wrapped in damp cloth and remains alive and fresh.

Many cyprinids show migratory behaviour. Residents of brackish water enter rivers to spawn. The Aral Sea barbel, *Barbus brachycephalus*, migrates over 1000 km as does *Rutilus frisii*. *Ctenopharyngodon idella* and *Hypophthalmichthys molitrix* leave lakes and concentrate in deep holes in the lower reaches of rivers. Even carp can jump low weirs on their migration. *Chalcalburnus chalcoides aralensis* and *Pelecus cultratus* feed on amphipods in the Aral Sea and follow the diurnal migrations of their prey to and from the surface.

Food

Cyprinids have a specialized feeding mechanism which involves a protrusible jaw (protrusibility sometimes lost), a branchiostegal pumping system and a pharyngeal mill. The majority eat small aquatic insects, crustaceans, worms and detritus or whatever is available. Most young cyprinids eat zooplankton. Diet is usually obvious from mouth and gut anatomy. Even when the principal food is invertebrates, cyprinids can supplement their diet with plant material, either algae (e.g. *Phoxinus phoxinus*) or higher plants (e.g. *Rutilus rutilus*). Or they may take advantage of opportunity, e.g. the bleak, *Alburnus alburnus*, feeds in schools, taking zooplankton and also insects from the surface.

Variation in diet has long been recognized in Chinese polyculture where several species are farmed together, including *Hypophthalmichthys molitrix* which eats phytoplankton (gill rakers attached to each other to form a sieve and gut 15 times body length), *Hypophthalmichthys nobilis* which eats zooplankton, *Ctenopharyngodon idella* which eats bottom plants (crushing pharyngeal mill and very elongate gut), and *Mylopharyngodon piceus* which eats snails and clams (molar or crushing pharyngeal teeth). *C. idella* has the added advantage that it will neatly clip the grass overhanging the pond!

Cyprinids that feed on macrophytes are rare, and grass carp, *C. idella*, is often touted as a weed-removal solution to overgrown waterways. The rudd, *Scardinius erythrophthalmus*, also eats large plants.

Piscivorous cyprinids are also comparatively rare, not unusually because of the lack of jaw teeth. They include the yellowcheek, *Elopichthys bambusa*, of the Amur basin, the asp, *Aspius aspius* of Europe and the Near East, the star gazer, *Erythroculter erythropterus*, from eastern Asia, and the marinka, *Schizothorax pseudaksaienesis* of Central Asia, among others.

Fish with barbels eat zoobenthos and there are numerous examples in Eurasian cyprinids. Thick rubbery lips and barbels are usually associated with sucking food from or around stones. Fish with a subterminal, often suctorial mouth, cutting edge to the lower jaw, and a long gut, scrape aufwuchs off rocks, e.g. *Capoeta, Garra, Chondrostoma, Labeo*, and *Xenocypris*. Brittan (1961) reviews feeding adaptations of cyprinids in general; see also Chapters 12 and 13.

Reproduction

The majority of cyprinids are broadcast spawners, often spawning over or between plants (adhesive eggs) or on rocks or gravel (non-adhesive) and leave their eggs unattended (Breder and Rosen, 1966; Balon, 1975). This type of spawning lends itself readily to hybrid formation where schools overlap. Some species have poisonous roe as a protective measure against predators, e.g. *Schizothorax* spp. and relatives, *Acrossocheilus* spp., *Lissocheilichthys wenchowensis, Barbus barbus*, and *Tinca tinca* (Wu *et al.*, 1978). Parental care is rare but does occur. The European moderlieschen, *Leucaspius delineatus*, which lays eggs in spirals or rings on plant stems, is aided by enlarged genital papillae. The male guards and fans the eggs and covers them with a bacteriostatic dermal mucus. *Abbottina rivularis* of the Amur River excavates saucer-shaped nests on the sandy bottom which are defended by the male. *Pseudorasbora parva* of eastern Asia spawns under stones and the male cleans the cavity with its tubercles. The most unusual form of reproduction is found in the bitterlings such as *Rhodeus sericeus* of Europe. The female deposits her eggs via a long ovipositor (up to twice body length) into the mantle cavity of a swan mussel (*Anodonta cygnea*). She conditions the mussel by repeated nudging of the valves so they do not close on the ovipositor. Milt is drawn in by the mussel's respiratory current and fertilizes the eggs. Only about 100 eggs are laid, as they are protected from predators and against desiccation by the mussel's ability to move into deeper water. In the absence of mussels, bitterlings do not even become sexually mature. Another bitterling, *Acanthorhodeus*, produces unusual worm-shaped larvae which stay in the mantle cavity until they can swim freely. The gudgeons, *Sarcocheilichthys* spp., also deposit eggs in mussels with an ovipositor but are unrelated to the bitterlings. The fry of *Salmostoma* spp. of India hang by a sticky thread from the water surface.

Spawning usually occurs in the spring in northern climes but *Tribolodon brandti* of eastern Asia spawns from June to September. *Rasbora daniconia* spawns in South India in September–October, the rainy season. Tropical species may resorb their eggs if the monsoon fails. *Puntius sophore* of India spawns in January in relatively cold water.

Many species produce 50 000 to 150 000 eggs, but counts can go as high as 2 m. (possibly 7 m.) in carp, although these are deposited in batches of about 500. The eggs of *Elopichthys bambusa* are exceptionally large, with a diameter of 6.75 mm. The eggs of *Ctenopharyngodon idella*, *Hypophthalmichthys molitrix*, *Hypophthalmichthys nobilis*, *Mylopharyngodon piceus*, *Hemiculter* spp., and *Xenocypris macrolepis* are pelagic and drift downstream; the young fish must travel upstream to regain lost ground. *Saurogobio*, *Gobiobotia*, *Microphysogobio* and *Pelecus* all produce pelagic eggs in rivers but the fry hug the bottom in their upstream journey. *Ctenopharyngodon* eggs can drift 160 km downstream and take 30–40 d to hatch.

Cyprinid sexes are not usually very distinctive outside the spawning season, but when reproducing they may develop bright nuptial colours and become covered in tubercles. *Phoxinus phoxinus* males become emerald green on the back and sides, and the mouth corner turns carmine, the throat black and the underside orange-red. Tubercles are epidermal structures which vary in development, size and extent between species and between sexes (males are more highly tuberculate than females) and therefore have systematic significance. Wiley and Collette (1970) and Collette (1977) review the occurrence of tubercles in Eurasian cyprinids. Tubercles serve to maintain contact between sexes during spawning, to stimulate females to breed, as weapons in defence of nests and territories, as sex and species indicators and possibly as aids in cleaning or excavating nest sites. In *Phoxinus* there are up to 40 large, pointed tubercles on the head, snout, and in a row over the eye, small tubercles fringing scales, and tubercles lining the pectoral fin rays following the branchings. There is a callus-like patch of up to nine rows of tuberculate scales on the belly in front of the pectoral fin, each scale having up to six tubercle points, a feature also found in the North American *Phoxinus*.

Another remarkable adaptation is the development of unculi, horny projections arising from single cells, which are morphologically related to the multicellular tubercles (Roberts, 1982). Unculi are restricted to Ostariophysan fishes and are most apparent on lips, other mouth parts, ventral discs and the anterior abdomen in Eurasian cyprinids. Unculi probably serve in protection of skin, in adhesion, in hydrodynamic effects and in rasping by increasing skin roughness. *Garra* is said to climb vertical walls of rock moistened by a waterfall, aided no doubt by unculi on the mouth, ventral disc and paired fins.

Threatened species

Habitat deterioration is threatening many species of cyprinids in Eurasia, but few have been adequately studied in this regard. The IUCN Red List (1988) gives only two species from Turkey as endangered, *Acanthorutilus handlirschi* and *Tylognathus klatti*, and only seven species from Sri Lanka as endangered, (including *Barbus srilankensis* and *Labeo fisheri*), and four other *Barbus* spp., along with *Rasbora vaterifloris*, as vulnerable. The Sri Lankan species were the subject of a special study, and evidently most countries would benefit from a detailed assessment of the status of their ichthyofauna. Lelek (1987) lists 82 species of native European cyprinids of which none are listed as endangered, nine (11%) as vulnerable, three (4%) as rare, five (6%) as intermediate and 19 (23%) as combinations of endangered, vulnerable, rare and intermediate, for a total of 36 or almost half this fauna. Surprisingly, this includes natural populations of carp, *Cyprinus carpio*, classed as vulnerable–endangered.

Some species must be considered threatened by their restricted distribution. These include cave fishes such as *Caecocypris basimi* and *Typhlogarra widdowsoni* of Iraq (Trewavas 1955; Banister and Bunni, 1980), *Iranocypris typhlops* of Iran (Bruun and Kaiser, 1944), *Garra dunsirei* and hypogean *Garra barreimiae* of Oman (Banister, 1984, 1987) and *Typhlobarbus nudiventris* from Yunnan (Chu and Chen, 1982).

Legends and history

Cyprinids have long been intimately associated with man. Sacred fish ponds are reported from Mesopotamia in 3000 BC. Fish culture in China extends back to at least 475 BC when Fan Li wrote a treatise on the subject. Carp were the primary object of culture until the Tang Dynasty came to power in AD 68. The name of the Royal Family and the Chinese word for carp, 'li', were similar, and the carp became a royal fish and could not be caught or eaten. This stimulated cultivation of grass carp and other species.

The carp became the emblem of the Japanese samurai because it "withstands opposition and swims against the current" and is the symbol of courage, energy and firmness. The mahseer of India is sacred to Hindus, and in Iran a number of cyprinid species associated with mosques and shrines are 'sacred', such as *Capoeta* spp.

Cyprinids have figured in stories and legends, some of which may have an element of truth which the reader is left to judge. *Hypophthalmichthys molitrix* is reputed to leap into boats and sink them. A hailstone the size of a hen's egg fell at Essen in 1806 and contained a frozen crucian carp. Presumably the carp had been lifted by a waterspout to a height sufficient for ice formation. The tench is reputed to be a doctor fish and other species will come up to it and rub their wounds against its copiously slimy body. The pike is supposed to forbear eating the tench as it is the principal customer of this doctor fish. Applied to humans, tench will reputedly cure fever, headache, toothache and jaundice. *Esomus danrica* has been reported to glide through the air, but this is now believed to be merely an instance of leaping.

Cyprinids also appear in literature, such as Chaucer's *Prologue* to the *Canterbury Tales* in whose day 'breme' (*Abramis brama*) were cultivated:

> "Full many a fair patriarch hadde he in mewe,
> And many a Breme and many a Luce in stewe."

The proverb 'as sound as a roach' (*Rutilus rutilus*) lacks impact to the modern ear; the word roach was once spelt 'roche' and the proverb is a pun on that French word.

Leptobarbus hoevenii of Sumatra, Borneo and Thailand is known as the 'mad fish'. It will wait under ripening chaulmoogra trees for fermented fruit to fall. Eating this fruit soon renders this fish drunk and schools can be seen floating helplessly in the water, safe only because their flesh has become inedible.

Human use

Cyprinids have long been popular food fishes in Eurasia. Wu *et al.* (1964) list 73 species of economic importance in China, and Jhingran (1975) lists 71 species for India. Brown (1983) reviews world fish farming according to the major countries and species. In 27 countries of Eurasia, cyprinids constitute 33% of the species farmed. *Chondrostoma nasus* are smoked and pickled along the Danube and the lowly gudgeon, *Gobio gobio*, at 8–14 cm is eaten in France. Even the minnow, *Phoxinus phoxinus*, named for the Latin minimus on account of its small size (8 cm), has been eaten. Isaak Walton gives a recipe for minnow-tansy (fried with egg-yolks, cowslips, primrose and tansy) and William of Wykeham gave a banquet for Richard ii in 1394 at which seven gallons (about 32 l) of minnows were served. However, the major species are the common carp, *Cyprinus carpio*, the grass carp, *Ctenopharyngodon idella*, the silver carp, *Hypophthalmichthys molitrix*, the bighead, *Hypophthalmichthys nobilis*, and the black carp, *Mylopharyngodon piceus*. These are all Asian species which have been widely introduced outside their natural range and are extensively cultivated in fish farms (see also Chapter 22). The most popular of these is the common carp, and its domestication has been traced by Balon (1974). Carp were once very important in England, where they were introduced for the observance of Fast Days: in the reign of Elizabeth i there were 145 of these! Carp are very important economically; the world catch exceeds 200 000 tons (*c.* 182 000 t).

The Food and Agriculture Organization of the United Nations publishes Fisheries Synopses of species "of present or potential economic interest". The cyprinid species dealt with are *Cyprinus carpio* (Alikunhi, 1966), for Asia and the Far East; Sarig, 1966, for the Near East and Europe), *Catla catla*, an Indian species (Jhingran, 1968), *Abramis brama* of Europe (Backiel and Zawisza, 1968), *Labeo rohita* of India (Khan and Jhingran, 1975), *Cirrhinus mrigala* of India (Jhingran and Khan, 1979), *Ctenopharyngodon idella* (Shireman and Smith, 1983) and *Aristichthys* (or *Hypophthalmichthys*) *nobilis* (Jennings, 1988). Horvath *et al.* (1985) have produced illustrated guides to the mass production of eggs, early and advanced fry, and fingerlings of the common carp. Jhingran and Pullin (1985) is a hatchery manual for the common carp, Chinese major carps (i.e. grass, silver and bighead) and Indian major carps (i.e. *Catla catla*, *Labeo rohita* and *Cirrhinus mrigala*).

Dill and Ben-Tuvia (1988) detail the inland fisheries of Israel, an example of cyprinid usage involving both native and cultivated, exotic species. Four indigenous species are fished: the long-headed barbel, *Barbus longiceps*, the large-scaled barbel, *B. canis*, the Damascus barbel, *Capoeta damascina*, and the 'Tiberias sardine' or lavnun, *Acanthobrama terraesanctae*. Cultivated fishes are primarily the common carp, introduced in 1933, and secondarily the silver carp, grass carp, bighead and black carp. None of the Chinese carps reproduces naturally. The carp accounted for 6863 t in 1984, 52% of the total inland water catch including cultured fish, and has been as high as 11 600 t, in 1973, 74% of total catch. In Lake Kinneret, the catch of lavnun reached 1313 t in 1979 so cultivated cyprinids are an important contributor to the fisheries of Israel.

Many cyprinids are important as the quarry of anglers. The large mahseers, *Tor* spp., are justly famous, as is the Indian trout, *Barilius bola*, which will take a fly or spoon and leaps when hooked. However, it is in Europe that cyprinids reach their angling apotheosis. This contrasts strongly with North America, where cyprinids are relegated to the role of bait or, as in the case of the common carp, regarded as pests. Great Britain has a 'Carp Society', complete with a magazine, *Carp Fisher*, and a newsletter, *Cyprinews*, and specially designed rods all directed at catching *Cyprinus carpio*. That this species can be worthy of time, expense and effort is outlined delightfully by Paisley (1987), who cites the English carp record (from Redmire Pool) of 23.4 kg, a fish known individually and only caught nine times in 21 y despite intensive efforts with anglers fishing continually, day and night, for a week at a time.

Great Britain has over 4 m. anglers, organized into clubs which issue licences, day, month and season tickets, sponsor competitions at various levels, fight against pollution, enter national and world championship matches and represent the angling fraternity to the Government through the National Anglers Council. There are six newspapers and magazines for freshwater anglers. The *Angling Times* appears weekly, runs to 32 pages and carries numerous colour illustrations and extensive advertising. Many of the species sought after are cyprinids. Housby (1987) in *A Specialist Angler's*

Guide to Big Fish, describes nine species, six of which are cyprinids. Bailey (1987) devotes a book to the roach, *Rutilus rutilus.* A considerable industry has developed based on the capture (and release alive!) of cyprinid fishes. Certain species are cultivated and used to restock fishing waters, e.g. *Tinca tinca* in Belgium and Luxembourg.

Another major industry involving cyprinids is the aquarium trade. Most colourful aquarium cyprinid species come from South East Asia (*c.* 115 are listed in Axelrod *et al.,* 1986) as well as the breeding and development of koi varieties, *Cyprinus carpio* (Axelrod, 1988) and goldfish varieties, *Carassius auratus.*

Cyprinids have also been put to other uses. The zebra danio, *Brachydanio rero,* the goldfish and the minnow, *Phoxinus phoxinus,* are commonly used as laboratory animals. The latter has even been used to test for melanosarcoma in humans. Blood from patients induces the red spawning coloration. Many cyprinids are used in traditional Chinese medicine. Grass carp intestines steamed with deep-fried dumplings, pepper and eggs are said to improve vision, while gall bladder extracts can be used for high blood pressure, coughs, deafness, scalds and burns (Wu *et al.,* 1978). Scales of *Alburnus alburnus, Leucaspius delineatus* and *Pelecus cultratus* have been made into artificial pearls. Guanine crystals are extracted to make 'essence d'orient' and then coated on the inside of glass beads.

5.5   FURTHER RESEARCH

The scope for further research on Eurasian cyprinids is immense. Very few genera have been adequately revised to place the systematics and nomenclature on a firm footing. Some species are still only known from the type series. New species are still being found regularly, *c.* 85 in the 1980s (cf. North America, with only 10 new species in the 1980s). The biology of all but a few commercial or common western European species is unknown. Basic data are lacking on such features as age, growth, population dynamics, spawning conditions, behaviour, larval and spawning characters, diet, parasities, use to man, conservation status and distribution.

Fish farming has been called the 'blue revolution' and cyprinids are an important food in many parts of Eurasia. Fish farming relieves pressure on natural populations, is labour intensive and is suitable for the developing world. It can be very productive, e.g. in West Bengal a fish–duck system produces up to $4000\,kg\,ha^{-1}\,y^{-1}$ and a fish–pig system up to $7000\,kg\,ha^{-1}\,y^{-1}$. Excess food from ducks and pigs and their faeces feed the fish or fertilize the pond. However, attempts to increase yields may have serious side-effects, and much theoretical and practical work needs to be done to farm cyprinids effectively and economically. For example, Scholtissek and Naylor (1988) have pointed out that pigs can act as mixing vessels for bird and human influenza viruses, which normally do not meet. Reassortment of genetic material occurs in the pigs, creating new human influenza strains and potential pandemics. Mixed agriculture and aquaculture may be a serious health hazard on a world scale, and any transfers of cyprinid species carry the danger of introduction of fish diseases and parasites, while escapees can compete for food and habitat with native species.

Cyprinids are affected by increasing human populations and industralization and the consequent demand for water management. Pollution is a widespread phenomenon (Coad, 1980). Technology now exists for large-scale water transfer projects. The Chinese plan the world's largest dam project on the Yangtze, costing $13.2 billion, which will destroy valuable fisheries (Jhaveri, 1988; Wu, 1987). India plans to build 30 large, 135 medium and 3000 minor dams on the Narmada River, costing $6 billion (Sattaur, 1989). The USSR planned major diversions of north-flowing Siberian rivers and others to irrigate the water-poor lands of the south and to raise the Caspian Sea level. A global climate change was predicted and fortunately these plans were shelved (Voropaev and Kosarev, 1982; Pearce, 1984; Perera, 1989). Such immense projects will have great effects on cyprinid habitats, fisheries and on individuals. Since so little is known of cyprinid biology, effective prediction or formulation of management plans are hindered, and there is scope for much valuable further research.

ACKNOWLEDGEMENTS

We are indebted to Dr C.-T. Shih, Canadian Museum of Nature, Ottawa, for his translation of Chinese articles.

REFERENCES

Aleev, Yu. G. (1969) *Function and Gross Morphology in Fish*, Israel Program for Scientific Translations, Jerusalem, 268 pp.

Alikunhi, K. H. (1966) Synopsis of biological data on common carp *Cyprinus carpio* (Linnaeus, 1758). (Asia and Far East). *F.A.O. Fish. Synopsis*, No. 31.1, 73 pp.

Almaça, C. (1979) Les espèces et la spéciation chez les *Pseudophoxinus* nord-africains (Pisces, Cyprinidae). *Bull. Mus. natn. Hist. nat., Paris*, **A. 1**, 279–84.

Annandale, N. (1918) Fish and fisheries of the Inle Lake. *Rec. Indian Mus.*, **14**, 33–64.

Arai, R. (1982) A chromosome study on two cyprinid fishes, *Acrossocheilus labiatus* and *Pseudorasbora pumila pumila*, with notes on Eurasian cyprinids and their karyotypes. *Bull. natn. Sci. Mus., Tokyo*, **A, 8** (3), 131—52.

Axelrod, H. R. (1988) *Koi Varieties. Japanese Coloured Carp – Nishikigoi*, Tropical Fish Hobbyist Publs, Neptune City, NJ, 144 pp.

Axelrod, H. R., Burgess, W. E., Pronek, N. and Walls, J. G. (1986) *Dr. Axelrod's Atlas of Freshwater Aquarium Fishes*, 2nd edn, Tropical Fish Hobbyist Publs, Neptune City, NJ, 782 pp.

Backiel, T. and Zawisza, J. (1968) Synopsis of biological data on the bream *Abramis brama* (Linnaeus, 1758). *F.A.O. Fish. Synopsis*, No. 36, 110 pp.

Bailey, J. (1987) *Roach. The Gentle Giants*, Crowood Press, Ramsbury, Marlborough, Wiltshire, 160 pp.

Balon, E. K. (1974) Domestication of the carp *Cyprinus carpio* L. *Misc. Publs Life Sci. Div. R. Ont. Mus.*, 37 pp.

Balon, E. K. (1975) Reproductive guilds of fishes: a proposal and definition *Can. J. Zool.*, **32**, 821–64.

Bǎnǎrescu, P. (1960) Einige Fragen zur Herkunft und Verbreitung der Süsswasserfisch-fauna der europäisch-mediterranen Unterregion. *Arch. Hydrobiol.*, **57**, 16–134.

Bǎnǎrescu, P. (1972) The zoogeographical position of the East Asian fresh-water fish fauna. *Revue roum. Biol. (Zool.)*, **17**, 315–23.

Bǎnǎrescu, P. (1983) On the affinities and derivation of the aquatic fauna of High Asia. *Revue roum. Biol. (Biol. anim.)*, **28** (2), 97–101.

Bǎnǎrescu, P. and Nalbant, T. T. (1973) Pisces, Teleostei Cyprinidae (Gobioninae). *Tierreich*, **93**, 1–304.

Banister, K. E. (1984) A subterranean population of *Garra barreimiae* (Teleostei: Cyprinidae) from Oman, with comments on the concept of regressive evolution. *J. nat. Hist.*, **18**, 927–38.

Banister, K. E. (1987) Two new species of *Garra* (Teleostei–Cyprinidae) from the Arabian Peninsula. *Bull. Br. Mus. nat. Hist. (Zool.)*, **52** (1), 59–70.

Banister, K. E. and Bunni, M. K. (1980) A new blind cyprinid fish from Iraq. *Bull. Br. Mus. nat. Hist. (Zool)*, **38** (3), 151–8.

Berg, L. S. (1948–49) *Freshwater Fishes of the U.S.S.R. and Adjacent Countries*, 4th edn. Israel Programme for Scientific Translations, Jerusalem (1962–65).

Breder, C. M. and Rosen, D. E. (1966) *Modes of Reproduction in Fishes*, Tropical Fish Hobbyist Publs, Neptune City, NJ, 941 pp.

Briggs, J. C. (1987) *Biogeography and Plate Tectonics (Developments in Palaeontology and Stratigraphy*, vol. 10), Elsevier, Amsterdam, 204 pp.

Brittan, M. R. (1961) Adaptive radiation in Asiatic cyprinid fishes, and their comparison with forms from other areas. *Proc. Ninth Pac. Sci. Congr.*, **10**, 18–31.

Brown, E. E. (1983) *World Fish Farming: Cultivation and Economics*, 2nd edn, AVI Publ. Co., Westport, Conn., 516 pp.

Bruun, A. F. and Kaiser, E. W. (1944) *Iranocypris typhlops* n.g., n.sp., the first true cave fish from Asia. *Dan. Scient. Invest. Iran*, **4**, 1–8.

Cao, W.-X., Chen, Y.-Y., Wu, Y.-F. and Zhu, S.-Q. (1981) Origin and evolution of schizothoracine fishes in relation to the upheaval of Qinghai-Xizang Plateau. *Proc. Symp. Qinghai-Xizang (Tibet) Plateau, Geol. Ecol. Stud.*, vol. 2, Science Press, Beijing, pp. 1053–60.

Cavender, T. M. (1986) Review of the fossil history of North American freshwater fishes, in *The Zoogeography of North American Freshwater Fishes* (eds C. H. Hocutt and E. O. Wiley), Wiley, NY, pp. 699–724.

Chen, X.-L., Yue, P.-Q. and Lin, R.-D. (1984) Major groups within the family Cyprinidae and their phylogenetic relationships. *Acta Zootaxonomica Sinica*, **9**, 424–40.

Chu, X. and Chen, Y. (1982) A new genus and species of blind cyprinid fish from China with special reference to its relationships. *Acta zool. sin.*, **28**, 383–8.

Coad, B. W. (1980) Environmental change and its impact on the freshwater fishes of Iran. *Biol. Conserv.*, **19**, 51–80.

Coad, B. W. (1981) Fishes of Afghanistan, an annotated checklist. *Natl Mus. nat. Sci. (Ottawa) Publs Zoology*, **14**, 26 pp.

Collette, B. B. (1977) Epidermal breeding tubercles and bony contact organs in fishes. *Symp. zool. Soc. Lond.*, **39**, 225–68.

Delmastro, G. B. (1982) Guida ai pesci del bacino del Po – e delle acque dolci d'Italia –, CLESAV, Milano, 190 pp.

De Silva, S. S. (1985) The Mahaweli Basin (Sri Lanka), in Inland fisheries in multiple-purpose river basin planning and development in tropical Asian countries: three case studies (ed. T. Petr), *F.A.O. Fish. Biol. tech. Pap.* no. 265, 91–166.

Dill, W. A. and Ben-Tuvia, A. (1988) The inland fisheries of Israel. *Bamidgeh*, **40** (3), 75–104.

Erk'akan, F. and Kuru, M. (1982) Systematical researches on the Sakarya basin fishes (Pisces). *Hacettepe Bull. nat. Sci. Eng.*, Ankara, **11**, 15–24.

Fisheries Research Institute, Guangxi Zhuang Tribe Self-Governed Territory and Institute of Zoology, Academia Sinica (eds) (1981) *Freshwater Fishes of Guangxi*, Guangxi Renmin Press, Nanning, Guangxi, 257 pp.

Gosline, W. A. (1978) Unbranched dorsal-fin rays and subfamily classification in the fish family Cyprinidae. *Occ. Pap. Mus. Zool. Univ. Mich.*, **684**, 1–21.

Grzimek, B. (1973) *Fishes*, I (*Grzimek's Animal life Encyclopedia*, Vol. 4), Van Nostrand Reinhold, NY, 531, pp.

Hora, S. L. (1943) The game fishes of India. XVI. – The mahseers or the large-scaled barbels of India. 9. Further observations on mahseers from the Deccan. *J. Bombay nat. Hist. Soc.*, **44** (1), 1–8.

Horvath, L., Tamas, G. and Coche, A. G. (1985) Common Carp. Parts. 1 and 2: 1. Mass production of eggs and early fry. *F.A.O. Training Series*, No. 8, 87 pp.; 2. Mass production of advanced fry and fingerlings in ponds. *F.A.O. Training Series*, No. 9, 85 pp.

Hosoya, K. (1986) Interrelationships of the Gobioninae (Cyprinidae), in *Indo-Pacific Fish Biology: Proc. Second Int. Conf. Indo-Pac. Fishes* (eds. T. Uyeno, R. Arai, T. Taniuchi and K. Matsuura), Ichthyological Society of Japan, Tokyo, pp. 484–501.

Housby, T. (ed.) (1987) *Specimen Hunter's Handbook. A Specialist Anglers Guide to Big Fish*, Blandford Press, Poole, Dorset, 144 pp.

Howes, G. J. (1978) The anatomy and relationships of the cyprinid fish *Luciobrama macrocephalus* (Lacepède). *Bull. Br. Mus. nat. Hist. (Zool.)*, **34** (1), 1–64.

Howes, G. J. (1979) Notes on the anatomy of *Macrochirichthys macrochirus* (Valenciennes), 1844, with comments on the Cultrinae (Pisces, Cyprinidae). *Bull. Br. Mus. nat. Hist (Zool.)*, **36** (3), 147–200.

Howes, G. J. (1980) The anatomy, phylogeny and classification of bariliine cyprinid fishes. *Bull. Br. Mus. nat. Hist. (Zool.)*, **37** (3), 129–98.

Howes, G. J. (1981) Anatomy and phylogeny of the Chinese Major Carps *Ctenopharyngodon* Steind., 1866 and *Hypophthalmichthys* Blkr., 1860. *Bull. Br. Mus. nat. Hist. (Zool.)*, **41** (1), 1–52.

Howes, G. J. (1982) Anatomy and evolution of the jaws in the semiplotine carps with a review of the genus *Cyprinion* Heckel, 1843 (Teleostei: Cyprinidae). *Bull. Br. Mus. nat. Hist. (Zool.)*, **42** (4), 299–335.

Howes, G. (1983) Additional notes on bariliine cyprinid fishes. *Bull. Br. Mus. nat. Hist. (Zool.)*, **45** (2), 95–101.

Howes, G. J. (1984a) A review of the anatomy, taxonomy, phylogeny and biogeography of the African neoboline cyprinid fishes. *Bull. Br. Mus. nat. Hist. (Zool.)*, 47(3), 151–85.

Howes, G. (1984b) Phyletics and biogeography of the aspinine cyprinid fishes. *Bull. Br. Mus. nat. Hist. (Zool.)*, **47** (5), 283–303.

Howes, G. J. (1985) A revised synonymy of the minnow genus *Phoxinus* Rafinesque, 1820 (Teleostei: Cyprinidae) with comments on its relationships and distribution. *Bull. Br. Mus. nat. Hist. (Zool)*, **48** (1), 57–74.

Howes, G. J. (1987) The phylogenetic position of the Yugoslavian cyprinid fish genus *Aulopyge* Heckel, 1841, with an appraisal of the genus *Barbus* Cuvier & Cloquet, 1816 and the subfamily Cyprininae. *Bull. Br. Mus. nat. Hist. (Zool.)*, **52** (5), 165–96.

Ichthyology Laboratory, Hupei Institute of Hydrobiology (1976) *Fishes of the Yangtze River*, Science Press, Peking, 278 pp.

Institute of Zoology, Academia Sinica, Xinjiang Institute of Biology, Soil and Desert, Academia Sinica and Fishery Bureau of the Uighur Autonomous Region (1979) *Fishes of Xinjiang*, Xinjiang People's Press, Xinjiang, 71 pp.

IUCN (1988) *1988 IUCN Red List of Threatened Animals*, International Union for Conservation of Nature and Natural Resources, Switzerland and UK, Gland and Cambridge, 154 pp.

Jayaram, K. C. (1974) Ecology and distribution of fresh-water fishes, amphibians and reptiles, in *Ecology and Biogeography in India* (ed. M. S. Mani), *Monographiae biol.*, **23**, 517–84.

Jayaram, K. C. (1981) *The Freshwater Fishes of India, Pakistan, Bangladesh, Burma and Sri Lanka – A Handbook*, Zoological Survey of India, Calcutta, 475 pp.

Jayaram, K. C. and Singh, K. P. (1977) On a collection of fish from North Bengal. *Rec. Zool. Surv. India.* **72**, 243–75.

Jennings, D. P. (1988) Bighead carp (*Hypophthalmichthys nobilis*): Biological Synopsis. FAO Synopsis NMFS/5/151, Biological Report, 88 (29), Fish and Wildlife Service, Washington, DC, 47 pp.

Jhaveri, N. (1988) The Three Gorges Debacle. *Ecologist*, **18** (2/3), 56–63.

Jhingran, V. G. (1968) Synopsis of biological data on catla *Catla catla* (Hamilton, 1822). *F.A.O. Fish. Synopsis*, No. 32, Rev. 1, 78 pp.

Jhingran, V. G. (1975) *Fish and Fisheries of India*, Hindustan Publ. Corp. (India), Delhi, 954 pp.

Jhingran, V. G. and Khan, H. A. (1979) Synopsis of biological data on the mrigal *Cirrhinus mrigala* (Hamilton, 1822). F.A.O. Fish Synopsis, No. 120, 78 pp.

Jhingran, V. G. and Pullin, R. S. V. (1985) *A hatchery manual for the Common, Chinese and Indian Major Carps (ICLARM Studies and Reviews.* Vol. 11), Asian Development Bank, International Center for Living Aquatic Resources Management, Manila, 191 pp.

Job, T. J., David, A. and Das, N. K. (1955) Fish and fisheries of the Mahanadi in relation to the Hirakud Dam. *Indian J. Fish.*, **2**, 1–36.

Khan, H. A. and Jhingran, V. G. (1975) Synopsis of biological data on rohu *Labeo rohita* (Hamilton, 1822). *F.A.O. Fish. Synopsis*, No. 111, 100 pp.

Krupp, F. (1982) *Garra tibanica ghorensis* subsp. nov. (Pisces: Cyprinidae), an African element in the cyprinid fauna of the Levant. *Hydrobiologia*, **88**, 319–24.

Krupp, F. (1983) Freshwater Fishes of Saudi Arabia and Adjacent Regions of the Arabian Peninsula. *Fauna of Saudi Arabia*, **5**, 568–636.

Krupp, F. (1987) Freshwater ichthyogeography of the Levant. Proceedings of the Symposium on the Fauna and Zoogeography of the Middle East, Mainz, 1985. *Beih. Tübinger Atlas Vorderen Orients*, **A** (*Naturwiss.*), **28**, 229–37.

Kuru, M. (1971) The fresh-water fish fauna of Eastern Anatolia. *Istanb. Üniv. Fen Fak. Mecm.* **B**, **36** (3–4), 137–47.

Kuru, M. (1980) Türkiye Tatlisu Baliklari Katalogu. Hacettepe üniversitesi Fen Fakültesi Yayinlari Yardimci Kitapler Dizisi 1, 73 pp.

Ladiges, W. and Vogt, D. (1965) *Die Süsswasserfische Europas bis zum Ural und Kaspischen Meer*, Verlag Paul Parey, Hamburg and Berlin, 250 pp.

Lelek, A. (1987) *The Freshwater Fishes of Europe*. Volume 9. *Threatened Fishes of Europe*. AULA Verlag, Wiesbaden, 343 pp.

Lowe-McConnell, R. H. (1975) *Fish Communities in Tropical Freshwaters. Their distribution, ecology and evolution*, Longman, London and NY, 337 pp.

Mahdi, N. (1962) *Fishes of Iraq*, Ministry of Education, Baghdad, 82 pp.

Maitland, P. S. (1972) A key to the freshwater fishes of the British Isles with notes on their distribution and ecology. *Scient. Publs. Freshwat. biol. Ass.*, No. 27, 1–139.

Menon, A. G. K. (1964) Monograph of the cyprinid fishes of the genus *Garra*. *Mem. Indian Mus.*, **14** (4), 173–260.

Mirza, M. R. (1975) Freshwater fishes and zoogeography of Pakistan. *Bijdr. Dierk.*, **45** (2), 143–80.

Mirza, M. R. (1980) The systematics and zoogeography of the freshwater fishes of Pakistan and Azad Kashmir. *Proc. First Pakistan Congr. Zool.*, Quaid-i-Azam University, Islamabad, pp. 1–41.

Mirza, M. R. (1982) *A Contribution to the Fishes of Lahore*, Polymer Publs, Lahore, 48 pp.

Mori, T. (1936) *Studies on the Geographical Distribution of Freshwater fishes in Eastern Asia*, Keijo, 88 pp.

Nakajima, T. (1986) Pliocene cyprinid pharyngeal teeth from Japan and East Asia Neogene cyprinid zoogeography, in *Indo-Pacific Fish Biology: Proc. Second Int. Conf. Indo-Pac. Fishes* (eds. T. Uyeno, R. Arai, T. Taniuchi and K. Matsuura), Ichthyological Society of Japan, Tokyo, pp. 502–13.

Nelson, J. S. (1984) *Fishes of the World*, 2nd edn, Wiley, NY, 523 pp.

Nikol'skii, G. V. (1961) *Special Ichthyology*, Israel Program for Scientific Translations, Jerusalem, 538 pp.

Nikolsky, G. V. (1963) *The Ecology of Fishes*, Academic Press, London and NY, 352 pp.

Norman, J. R. and Greenwood, P. H. (1975) *A History of Fishes*, Ernest Benn, London, 467 pp.

Paisley, T. (1987) Confessions of a carp fisher. *Fisheries*, **12** (3), inside front cover, 19–21.

Patterson, C. (1981) The development of the North American fish fauna – a problem of historical biogeography, in *The Evolving Biosphere* (ed. P. L. Forey), British Museum (Natural History), London, pp. 265–81.

Pearce, F. (1984) Fall and rise of the Caspian Sea. *New Scient.*, **104** (1433), 10–11.

Perera, J. (1989) Abandoned canal scheme saves the Caspian Sea. *New Scient.*, **121** (1655), 30.

Reid, G. McG. (1985) *A Revision of African Species of Labeo (Pisces: Cyprinidae) and a Re-definition of the Genus*, Verlag von J. Cramer, Braunschweig, 322 pp.

Roberts, T. R. (1982) Unculi (horny projections arising from single cells), an adaptive feature of the epidermis of Ostariophysan fishes. *Zool. Scr.*, **11** (1), 55–76.

Roberts, T. R. (1986) *Danionella translucida*, a new genus and species of cyprinid fish from Burma, one of the smallest living vertebrates, *Env. Biol. Fishes*, **16** (4), 231–41.

Sarig, S. (1966) Synopsis of biological data on common carp *Cyprinus carpio* (Linnaeus; 1758). (Near East and Europe). *F.A.O. Fish. Synopsis*, No. 31.2, 35 pp.

Sattaur, O. (1989) Dam unleashes India's reservoirs of anger. *New Scient.*, **121** (1655), 32–3.

Scholtissek, C. and Naylor, E. (1988) Fish farming and influenza pandemics. *Nature, Lond.*, **331** (6153), 215.

Shireman, J. V. and Smith, C. R. (1983) Synopsis of biological data on the grass carp, *Ctenopharyngodon idella* (Cuvier and Valenciennes, 1844). *F.A.O. Fish. Synopsis*, No. 135, 86 pp.

Srivastava, G. J. (1980) *Fishes of U. P. and Bihar*, Vishwavidyalalaya Prakashan, Varanasi, 207 pp.

Sterba, G. (1983) *The Aquarium Encyclopedia*, MIT Press, Cambridge, Mass., 607 pp.

Stewart, F. H. (1911) Notes on Cyprinidae from Tibet and the Chumbi Valley, with a description of a new species of *Gymnocypris*. *Rec. Indian Mus.*, **6**, 73–92.

Trewavas, E. (1955) A blind fish from Iraq, related to *Garra*. *Ann. Mag. nat. Hist.*, Ser. 12, **8**, 551–5.

Turdakov, F. A. (1963) *Fishes of Kirgizii*, 2nd edn, Izdatel' Stro Akademii Nauk Kirgizskoy, SSR, Frunze, 283 pp.

van der Leeden, F. (1975) *Water Resources of the World. Selected Statistics*, Water Information Center, Port Washington, NY, 568 pp.

Voropaev, G. and Kosarev, A. (1982) The fall and rise of the Caspian Sea. *New Scient.*, **94** (1300), 78–80.

Wang, Y. (1979) On the classification, distribution, origin and evolution of the fishes referred to the subfamily Cyprininae of China, with description of a new species. *Acta hydrobiol. sin.*, **6**, 419–38.

Wheeler, A. (1969) *The Fishes of the British Isles and North-West Europe*, Macmillan, London, 613 pp.

Wheeler, A. (1985) *The World Encyclopedia of Fishes*, Macdonald, London, 368 pp.

Wiley, M. L. and Collette, B. B. (1970) Breeding tubercles and contact organs in fishes: their occurrence, structure and significance. *Bull. Am. Mus. nat. Hist.*, **143** (3), 143–216.

Wood, G. L. (1976) *The Guinness Book of Animal Facts and Feats*, 2nd edn. Guinness Superlatives Ltd, Enfield, 255 pp.

Wu, Hanling, Jin, X. and Ni, Y. (1978) *The Ichthyotoxic and Medicinal Fishes of China*, Science and Technology Press, Shanghai 301 pp.

Wu, Hsien-Wen, Yang, G.-R., Yue, P.-Q. and Huang, H.-J. (eds) (1964) *The Economic Animals of China. Freshwater Fishes*, Science Press, Peking, 159 pp.

Wu, Huisheng (1987) Possible effects of the proposed eastern route diversion of Changjiang (Yangtze) River water to the northern provinces with emphasis on the hydrobiological environment of the main water bodies along the transfer route, in *Regulated Streams. Advances in Ecology* (eds. J. F. Craig and J. B. Kemper), Plenum Press, NY, 431 pp.

Wu, Y. (1984) Systematic studies on the cyprinid fishes of the subfamily Schizothoracinae from China. *Acta Biological Plateau Sinica*, **3** (3), 119–40.

Zhen. P.-S., Huang, H.-M., Chang, Y.-L. and Dai, D.-Y. (1980) *Fishes of the Tumen River*, Jilin Renmin Press, Changchun, Jilin, 111 pp.

Chapter six

Cyprinids of South East Asia

W. J. Rainboth

6.1 INTRODUCTION

Regional scope

South East Asia includes all of the Asian continent south-east of the Tibetan Plateau. Within this region are Burma, the Indo-Chinese and Malay peninsulas, the Philippine and Indo-Malayan archipelagos. The river systems of South-East Asia begin with the Tonkin Gulf drainages at the north-east and encompass all basins further south and continental islands of the Sunda shelf (Fig. 6.1). The region extends westward across the southern part of the continent to the Irrawaddy River of Burma. For purposes of zoogeographic comparison, the faunas of the three areas surrounding and adjoining South East Asia will be included also. Directly west of South East Asia is the Indian subcontinent, and to the north-west is the Tibetan Plateau. North of South East Asia is Central East Asia. Comparisons with neighbouring faunas to the north and west will include all basins from the Yangtze River, the Tibetan Plateau and the Tarim basin north of Tibet, southward to Baluchistan. This chapter provides an overview of the Cyprinidae in an area where cyprinid diversity reaches its zenith. The geography and the geological history of South East Asia will be summarized first, then the faunal changes that occur from the South East Asian zoogeographic region through to adjoining parts of Asia will be examined. Finally, interesting aspects of the biology and ecology of South East Asian cyprinids will be presented.

Diversity – endemism

Cyprinid diversity in South East Asia is staggering in comparison to that in other parts of the family range. Within Asia, south of the Soviet Union and east of Afghanistan and Iran, there are 1260+ species of some 205 recognized genera. Thus, in an area 72% of the size of North America, there are five times

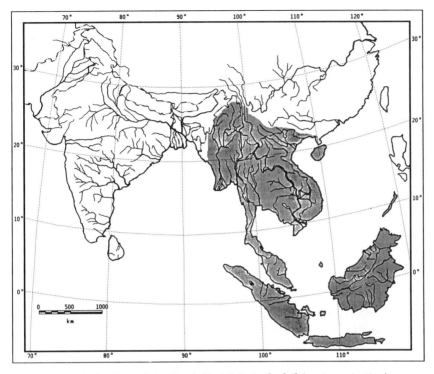

Fig. 6.1 Southern Asia; South East Asia is shaded (conic projection).

as many cyprinid species and five times as many genera. Although the African tropics may ultimately be shown to have comparable numbers of fish species, the African cyprinid fauna is not as diverse at the generic and subfamilial levels.

At the family-group level (including subfamilies, tribes and subtribes), only China has greater diversity than South East Asia, owing to a rich East Asian fauna as well as a light representation of lineages which are more typical of South Asia. Scattered representatives of more-northern lineages occur in South East Asia (e.g. Acheilognathinae, Alburninae, Oreinini), particularly in the rivers with headwaters in Yunnan Province of China, or in Tibet. Some subfamilies, such as the Danioninae and Cyprininae, are shared with the great tropical freshwater fauna of Africa.

Approximately 70 genera of cyprinids are endemic to South East Asia, and many other genera found there have a few representatives living outside the region. By comparison, *c.* 95 genera are endemic to the East Asian region, and 15 are endemic to High Asia (the Tibetan Plateau). Components of different faunas may be present in rivers which traverse different faunal regions. A striking example is the Lancang Jiang (upper Mekong), which has a High

Asian fauna in its head waters on the Tibetan Plateau, components of the East Asian fauna as it passes through Yunnan Province, and a South East Asian fauna throughout its middle and downstream reaches.

Faunal composition

The dominant group of cyprinids throughout South East Asia is the subfamily Cyprininae. There are more than three times as many species of cyprinines as there are species in any other subfamily, and cyprinine species in South East Asia represent 60% of the total number of cyprinid species in South East Asia. Members of other subfamilies may reside in greater numbers elsewhere, but other groups do not abound in the broad variety of habitats used by cyprinines. The second most diverse subfamily in South East Asia is the Danioninae. The five remaining subfamilies in South East Asia or adjacent waters are the Acheilognathinae, Alburninae, Cultrinae, Gobioninae, and Leuciscinae.

Although the cyprinines dominate tropical Asian faunas, the temperate latitudes have greater representation by other subfamilies, particularly the Gobioninae. The gobionines increase in diversity through the northern margin of the cyprinine range, eventually replacing them completely north of the Yangtze and Yellow River (Huang He) basins. Other subfamilies which become diverse at the northern boundary of the range of the Cyprininae are the Acheilognathinae, Alburninae, Cultrinae, and Leuciscinae. The Leuciscinae have a Palaeartic distribution, whereas the Acheilognathinae reach maximum diversity just as the Cyprininae decrease, and then decrease markedly themselves through north-eastern China.

6.2   DRAINAGE BASINS

Physiographic features

South East Asia and adjacent regions are home to many of the world's great rivers (Table 6.1). To the north are the Yangtze (Chang Jiang) and the Pearl (Xi Jiang) (Fig. 6.2). The Yangtze is the third largest river in the world, based on mean annual discharge, after the Amazon and Zaire rivers. Immediately following the Yangtze in ranking by discharge are the Brahmaputra and Ganges, with the great rivers of South East Asia proper, the Irrawaddy and the Mekong, ranked twelfth and fourteenth (Welcomme, 1985).

In describing the physiographic features of South East Asia, we will begin with the continental islands of the Sunda shelf and proceed westward across South East Asia. The three major islands in Sundaland are Borneo, Sumatra, and Java. Each island has mountain ranges which separate the head waters of their river systems. The climate is generally perhumid (moist year-round) on Borneo and Sumatra, with some seasonality at the northern tips of each island (Whitmore, 1985). Java has a monsoon climate. The original vegetation over

Table 6.1 Size of rivers in and immediately adjacent to basins of South East Asia and the Indian subcontinent

Basin*	Length (km)	Drainage area[†] (1000 km²)	Mean discharge[†] (1000 m³ s⁻¹)
Yangtze (China) (1)	5980	1920	21.8
Mekong (SE Asia) (8)	4193	811	12.0
Brahmaputra (India) (31)	2903	935	19.2
Indus (Pakistan)	2900	1178	3.6
Salween (Burma) (27)	2820	324	2.5
Tarim (China)	2750	907	,0.2
Ganges (India) (31)	2650	1059	18.7
Irrawaddy (Burma) (29)	2100	424	13.5
Xi Jiang (Pearl) (China) (4)	1935	448	12.6
Godavari (India)	1451	313	3.6
Krishna (India)	1290	259	2.0
Narmada (India)	1290	98	1.2
Hong (Vietnam)	1150	120	3.9
Kapuas (Kalimantan) (20)	1010	102	–
Chao Phraya (Thailand) (9)	995	110	0.7
Tapti (India)	910	64	0.6
Mahanadi (India) (32)	903	132	1.9
Barito (Kalimantan) (19)	887	–	–
Hari (Sumatra) (16)	800	40	–
Cauvery (India)	766	80	0.9
Mahakam (Kalimantan) (24)	720	–	–
Rajang (Sarawak) (21)	565	–	–
Musi (Sumatra) (17)	524	56	–
Dong Nai (Vietnam) (7)	484	22	–
Pahang (Malaysia) (12)	459	27	–
Sittang (Burma) (28)	419	–	–
Perak (Malaysia) (13)	406	17	–
Baram (Sarawak) (22)	403	–	–
Mae Khlong (Thailand) (10)	400	27	0.4
Kajan (Kalimantan) (23)	400	–	–
Tenasserim (Burma) (26)	400	–	–
Inderagiri (Sumatra)	400	–	–
Kahayan (Kalimantan)	363	–	–
Solo (Java) (18)	350	16	0.1
Kampar (Sumatra) (15)	323	–	–
Mindanao (Philippines) (25)	320	5	–
Rokan (Sumatra) (14)	282	–	–
Kelantan (Malaysia) (11)	242	5	–

*Numbers in parentheses denote labels on Fig. 6.2.
[†]–, Uncertain.

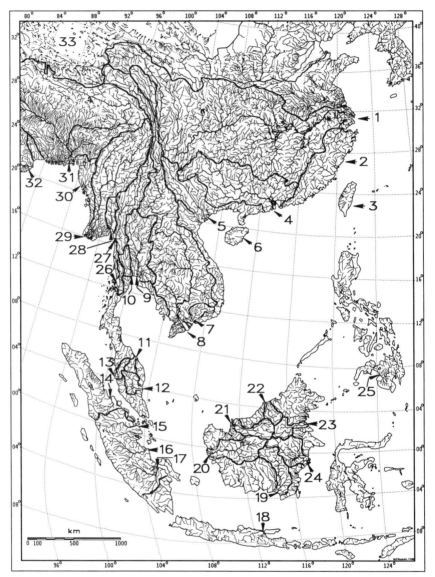

Fig. 6.2 The major rivers of South East Asia and adjacent areas; drainages are outlined; in Sumatra, lines separate North, Central, and South Sumatra. Rivers (italicized) and areas: 1, *Yangtze*; 2, Zhejiang–Fujian; 3, Taiwan; 4, *Xi Jiang (Pearl)*; 5, Hong; 6, Hainan; 7, *Dong Nai*, 8, *Mekong*; 9, *Chao Phraya*; 10, *Mae Khlong*; 11, *Kelantan*; 12, *Pahang*; 13, *Perak*; 14, *Rokan*; 15, *Kampar*; 16, *Hari*; 17, *Musi*; 18, *Solo*; 19, *Barito*; 20, *Kapuas*; 21, *Rajang*; 22, *Baram*; 23, *Kajan*; 24, *Mahakam*; 25, *Mindanao*; 26, *Tenasserim*; 27, *Salween*; 28, *Sittang*; 29, *Irrawaddy*; 30, Arakan coast; 31, *Meghna* (*Ganges–Brahmaputra*); 32, *Mahanadi*; 33, central Tibet. (Miller oblated stereographic projection.)

much of the Sundaland was tropical rain forest, with swamp forest in coastal lowlands, much of which remains on Borneo, less on Sumatra. The original monsoon (seasonal) forests of Java have largely disappeared through human activities. Many of the rivers of Borneo are pristine in comparison to other river systems of Asia. There are several large lakes scattered through the mountains of Sumatra and some have endemic species of cyprinids. The largest of these volcanic lakes, Lake Toba, lies in a huge caldera with 1300 km^2 surface area and depth 400–500 m. Rivers draining the lakes or plateaus of Sumatra pass through stretches of high gradient (305 m in 11 km) on the way to the coastal plain.

North of the Sunda shelf is the Philippine Archipelago of which some of the southern and central islands are inhabited by native cyprinids: Mindanao, Basilan, Palawan, Mindoro, and Panay. About half of Mindanao is perhumid and the other islands are seasonal to slightly seasonal. The best-known cyprinid fauna in the Philippines is that of Lake Lanao on the island of Mindanao.

The present-day Asian mainland begins at the tip of the Malay Peninsula. Peninsular Malaysia has a perhumid climate and much of its central mountain range is covered by rain forest. The narrowest part of the Malay Peninsula is the Isthmus of Kra, which is also a point of climatic demarcation. South of the isthmus, the climate is slightly seasonal, and north of it are pronounced seasons. This change at the isthmus is represented biologically by the transition from evergreen rain forest to monsoon forest. Monsoon forest is the principal vegetation type of the Indo-Chinese Peninsula, Thailand, Burma, India, and Sri Lanka. The Mergui Range runs down the centre of the upper part of the peninsula and forms the boundary between the wetter Burmese side on the west and the dry Thai side to the east. Just to the east of the peninsula is the mouth of the Chao Phraya, a large river which is the central drainage of Thailand, between the Malay and Indo-Chinese peninsulas. Just to the west are the Tenasserim and Salween rivers, which drain the continuous highland of the Shan Plateau and the Mergui Range.

The principal river of the Indo-Chinese Peninsula is the Mekong, which passes through six countries and is one of the great rivers of the world. The waters of the Mekong pass through regions displaying an array of environmental conditions, many shared with the Salween. The sources of the Salween and Mekong are on the Tibetan Plateau in Qinghai Province of China, at an elevation of over 5000 m, where the climate is extreme. The long, harsh winters and chilly summers (0–10 °C mean July temperature), coupled with low precipitation (annual rainfall 250–500 mm), produce vegetation of upland pasture or semi-tundra. The Mekong and Salween pass through Tibet where their paths come near other great drainages of southern and eastern Asia in a hydrographic feature important to our understanding of regional zoogeography. In south-eastern Tibet, a circle of 60 km radius would include land drained by the Yangtze (China), Mekong (South East Asia), Salween

(Burma), Irrawaddy (Burma), and Brahmaputra (India), rivers which have vastly different faunas downstream. The steep, forested, parallel river gorges of the Salween, Mekong, and Yangtze have valley floors at elevations of 1000–1500 m and are separated by mountain ranges of over 5000 m. These compressed basins, particularly the Mekong and Salween, receive no major tributary streams for great distances (380 km for the Mekong and 480 km for the Salween). The area has a much more moderate climate than at the rivers' sources. As the Mekong (Lancang Jiang) and Salween (Nu Jiang) pass through Yunnan Province, the climate becomes much warmer and wetter with 1700+ mm annual rainfall coming between the months of May and October in southern Yunnan. The winters in southern Yunnan and throughout the rest of the Mekong and Salween rivers are nearly frost-free. Interestingly, southern Yunnan has tropical lowland evergreen rain forest similar to that in Malaysia, even though the rainfall is decidedly seasonal (Whitmore, 1985). There are also scattered patches of tropical evergreen rain forest among the predominant monsoon (seasonal) forests southward in the Indo-Chinese Peninsula. The Shan Plateau has mostly subtropical hardwood forest with some scrub forest and grassland, becoming tropical evergreen forest to the south on the Mergui Range. A rainfall pattern similar to that found in southern China predominates throughout the Mekong and Salween basins, causing great cyclical changes in flow. Unlike many smaller rivers of the perhumid tropics, which change depending on unpredictable local rainfall patterns, the Mekong and Salween experience a predictable annual onset of flood regime. With the beginning of flood season, water clarity decreases as particulate material remains suspended owing to increased current speed. The depth increases by 20–30 m and the current becomes treacherous. The powerful flow has cut several long underwater canyons > 100 m in depth on the Khorat Plateau, yet the entire river course on the Khorat Plateau has a youthful appearance. This contrasts strongly with that of the Salween on the Shan Plateau. The river passes through Yunnan and the Shan Plateau in the most extensive system of canyons and gorges (often 1000 m deep) of any river system in the world (Bender, 1983), a testament to the erosional power of seasonal rivers. Prolonged erosion has cut the main channel well below the tributary channel levels. In dry season, the tributaries flow into the main stem by cascade or cataract, which is likely to enhance fish endemism. In the western part of the Salween basin on the Shan Plateau is Inle Lake, which has several species of endemic fishes, including cyprinids.

As the Mekong passes into the great Cambodian plain, it assumes characteristics which are largely absent from the lower Salween, one of the few major tropical rivers which lacks an extensive floodplain. In south central Kampuchea, the Mekong joins with the Tonle Sap. The Tonle Sap is the outlet of the Great Lake at the upper end of the huge floodplain (70 000 km^2) of the lower Mekong. During the dry season, the lake has a maximum depth of about 3 m and during the flood season it expands from

2600 to 25 000 km². During the early part of the flood season, the Tonle Sap reverses direction and the lake fills with water from the Mekong. Later, the direction changes and the combined Mekong and Tonle Sap flow out to the South China Sea through the four river mouths in Vietnam. The entire region is floodplain and produces a major part of the Mekong fishery harvest estimated to be a minimum of $500\,000\,\mathrm{t}\,\mathrm{y}^{-1}$, much of which consists of cyprinids (Lagler, 1976).

Another major river of South East Asia, the Irrawaddy, drains the western slope of the Shan Plateau and the eastern slope of the Arakan Yoma. The source of the Irrawaddy is at the south-eastern corner of Tibet, where the conditions are extreme. The northernmost part of the Irrawaddy basin has elevations above 4200 m and mean temperatures during the warmest months of 0 °C. In contrast to the arid upper reaches of the Mekong and Salween, the uppermost reaches receive $> 4\,\mathrm{m}\,\mathrm{y}^{-1}$ precipitation. The delta is also a wet region with evergreen rain forest, receiving nearly $3\,\mathrm{m}\,\mathrm{y}^{-1}$, in contrast to the lowland savannah and thorn forest in the centre of the basin. The central area receives $0.5\,\mathrm{m}\,\mathrm{y}^{-1}$ due to the presence of a rain shadow from the Arakan Yoma range to the west.

History

The history of the river systems in South East Asia is fascinating and complex. Indeed, river configurations have changed considerably during the Quaternary alone. Stream captures of various magnitudes have changed river alignments as a result of local tectonic or hydrologic processes. Such events have been very important in South East Asia, which has been an area of high tectonic activity throughout the Cenozoic. Another type of process which changes river configurations is the development of extended Pleistocene river basins during periods of sea-level retreat. Extended Pleistocene basins have been a major source of faunal exchange in only a few places around the world. Although a similar phenomenon occurred on the North Sea Shelf of Europe, it is probably fair to state that the Sundaland is the classic example of continental shelf dispersal during sea-level retreat.

The presence of a vast submarine bank encompassing three of the greater islands in the Malay Archipelago was remarked on by Wallace (1869, 1880), who compared their biota and concluded that the islands must have been connected to each other and to the Asian mainland in recent times. Although the mechanism Wallace proposed for subsidence of these shallow seas was erroneous, the conclusions about connections were correct. Later, Molengraaff and Weber (1921) noted that the entire shelf might have become exposed during Pleistocene glacial periods. The extent of continental surface exposure has varied greatly during the Pleistocene, and the shallow sea floor which connects the islands is actually a system of drowned river valleys. Sea levels are within 6 or 7 m of their highest since the Miocene. The most recent sea-level rise amounted to *c.* 120 m, before which nearly all the continental shelf would have been exposed. The recent cycle of regression and transgression was only one of several, the magnitudes of which have summarized in detail (Batchelor, 1979). If varying sea levels were the only variable in the shape of the exposed landmasses, then attempted reconstructions of past drainage configuration would be fairly simple. Interpretation of bottom topography can be difficult. Various river configurations have been inferred (Beaufort, 1951; Tjia, 1980). Differences in reconstruction have resulted from various interpretations of the history of the actively changing margin of the Sunda arc, or different conclusions about the effects of tidal scour in channels between islands. Continuous geological change makes inferences about the exposed surface of Sundaland progressively more difficult for increasing lengths of time.

The drowned river paths of the most recent sea regression indicate that formerly continuous basins covering large areas of Sundaland have become fragmented, with parts of former rivers found on multiple islands or on the mainland. The southern side of Borneo, the northern side of Java, and the southern tip of Sumatra were all drained by the East Sunda River during the late Pleistocene according to Beaufort (1951). However, the reconstruction of the rivers of this area has recently been revised by Tjia (1980), who concluded that the rivers draining the southern coast of Sumatra and part of the northern coast of Java flowed through the Sunda Strait (Fig. 6.3). The rivers from the western side of Borneo, central Sumatra, and the western tip of the Malay Peninsula formed the North Sunda River. In the northern Straits of Malacca, rivers of northern Sumatra and western Malaya took a north-westerly path to debouch into the Indian Ocean. East of the Malay Peninsula, a great river flowed in the present Gulf of Thailand and South China Sea. This great northern river would have drained both the Malay and Indo-Chinese peninsulas. Further to the north, shallow seas inside the boundary of the continental shelf allowed a single river to drain Hainan Island and all the Tonkin Gulf rivers. Similarly, the Salween and Sittang rivers shared a common course in the present-day Gulf of Martaban.

The confluence of extended Pleistocene river basins is one way in which river systems of South East Asia have changed since the Quaternary and late Tertiary. Other changes, in the form of stream captures, have occurred on land which is currently above sea level. High tectonic activity in Cenozoic South East Asia, producing elevation and gradient changes, has altered the hydrography in important ways. Stream captures of various magnitudes have occurred throughout the current mainland during the Cenozoic and several important captures have happened in the Pelistocene.

In South East Asia an important sequence of stream captures has resulted in the modern configuration of the Mekong, which was not a major river before the Pleistocene (Workman, 1977). In the middle to upper Pleistocene, the Chao Phraya lost its head waters to the growing Mekong, and other stream

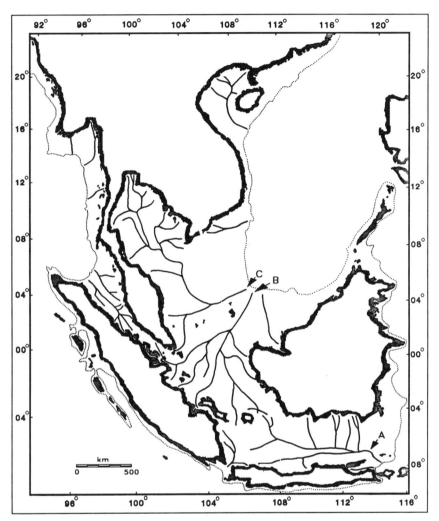

Fig. 6.3 Extended Pleistocene rivers of South East Asia, drawn to 160 m isobath (not shown; dotted line follows 200 m isobath). A, East Sunda River; B, West Sunda River; C, North Sunda River. (Miller oblated stereographic projection.)

captures occurred near Xieng Khouang and Vapi. Deeply incised valleys covered by recent sediments on the Khorat Plateau indicate that the generally flat appearance of the plateau is a recent feature in an area which had pronounced relief before and during the early Pleistocene. Although valleys can be cut well below the current sea level during sea regressions, obstructions such as the lava flows near the mouth of the Mun or Khone Falls would prevent such cutting today.

On the Cambodian plain, downstream from the Khorat Plateau, many changes in river configurations have occurred during and since the Pleistocene, a period of high tectonic activity. A series of lava flows across south-eastern Cambodia indicates the location of a hinge joint, which has allowed the southern part of Cambodia and Vietnam to subside. The most recent subsidence in the lower Mekong caused the formation of the Great Lake in a former river channel *c.* 5200 y ago (Carbonnel, 1963), but this minor event was not accompanied by any lava flows. Among known drainage alterations was a change in the large river which flowed down the present channel of the Stung Sen: it may have looped around through the channel of the present day Tonle Sap (river of the great lake) and exited the land through the upper Gulf of Thailand (Carbonnel, 1972). The Mekong is also known to have exited Cambodia directly into the Gulf of Thailand at Kampot (Fontaine and Workman, 1978), and this path may have been the immediate predecessor to the present course through Vietnam.

The rivers of Burma have also been reconfigured, but not on the same scale as the Mekong. The major Burmese rivers flow through two regions having completely different origins. The Salween leaves the Tibetan Plateau and flows through the Shan Plateau, which is composed of Palaeozoic and Mesozoic formations, and ultimately extends southward through the Malay Peninsula. The Irrawaddy and Sittang flow along parallel courses through broad plains that formed in the Cenozoic and become younger progressively southwards. At least one major stream capture has occurred in which the Irrawaddy–Chindwin took the head waters of the Sittang near the modern city of Mandalay. The uppermost reaches of Burmese rivers on the Tibetan Plateau have changed drastically since the Pliocene, when the average elevation was 2500 m instead of > 5000 m today, and the deciduous mixed forests have given way to alpine steppes (Xu, 1981). The rivers of eastern Tibet have also experienced faunal changes resulting from the development of an extreme environment. Whether or not the rivers have changed in configuration is another matter, and the subject of diverse opinions. There has been repeated discussion of the possible piracy of the Irrawaddy head waters by rivers now part of the Brahmaputra system; however, there is no strong evidence for such an event.

Cyprinid faunas

Major studies of cyprinid faunas in South East Asia have occasionally been confined to single drainage basins, but have more often followed national boundaries. Therefore, studying the fauna of a large river often requires the use of references limited by political subdivisions. Included in this brief literature review are major faunistic references for river systems, countries or even general regions within and surrounding South East Asia. The most useful of all works have been taxonomic revisions of cyprinid subfamily groups, which were not limited by national boundaries (Bănărescu and Nalbant,

1973). Generic revisions are much more common, but listing the most recent revisions in an area having some 200 genera would not be practical. The references mentioned here are only a small fraction of those on distributions summarized later, but can introduce the literature on fish faunas of South East Asia published since 1960 or of seminal importance.

Eastern Asia

General works on the cyprinids of this region are those by Tchang (1933) and Wu *et al.* (1964, 1977). Bănărescu and Nalbant (1973) revised the primarily East Asian cyprinid subfamily Gobioninae. Li (1981) discussed the zoogeography of Chinese fishes. The cyprinids of Japan were discussed in detail by Okada (1960) and the Korean cyprinids by Chyung (1961). For northern China, Berg (1909, 1964) treated the fishes of the Amur (Heilong Jiang). The fishes of the Yellow Sea affluents, the Liao He and the Yalu Jiang, were listed by Xie (1981, 1986). Chen *et al.* (1986) provided species listings of rivers in the Qin Ling mountain range which separates the middle Huang He (Yellow) from the Chang Jiang (Yangtze). The Yangtze fishes and their distributions have been published in Anon. (1976), Tan (1980) and Wu *et al.* (1979). Chu (1984, 1985) studied the fishes of Fujian Province. Cheng *et al.* (1981) discussed the fishes of the southermost major drainage of China, the Xi Jiang (Pearl). The highly endemic faunas of lakes in Yunnan Province have been compared by Li (1982).

High Asia

The cyprinids of high Asia have had less written about them than those of lower altitudes. High Asia consists primarily of Xizang Zizhigu and Qinghai provinces of China, and the cyprinid fauna appears to be central Asian rather than East Asian. Important early publications were by Day (1876, 1878), Kessler (1876, 1879), Herzenstein (1888), Zugmayer (1910, 1913), Stewart (1911), Lohberger (1929), and Chang (1944). More recently, studies on the Schizothoracinae, the dominant group of cyprinids of high Asia, have been published by Fang (1936), Vasnetzov (1950), Nikolsky (1954), Tsao and Wu (1962), and Cao *et al.* (1981). Recent faunal studies include Li *et al.* (1966). Wu and Chen (1979), and Wu and Wu (1984, 1988).

Indian subcontinent

There is voluminous literature on the fishes of the Indian subcontinent, including some of the earliest publications on Asian fishes. Hamilton's (1822) initial treatise on the Gangetic fauna was followed by M'Clelland's (1839) monograph on the cyprinids of the Ganges and Brahmaputra rivers. Day's first major work (1865) dealt with fishes of Malabar, but he is better known for his monumental treatise on Indian fishes (1875–78), a remarkable accomplishment in its time and still an important source of information. During the first half of the 20th century, the dominant figure in Indian ichthylogy was Sunder

Lal Hora. Jayaram (1976) compiled in index to Hora's 400+ publications. Another extensive bibliographic listing was by Mirza (1978) for Pakistan. Jayaram's (1981) general work on the freshwater fishes includes keys to, and distribution of, all of the recognized species. Of the cyprinid faunas on the Indian subcontinent, probably the best known is the fauna of the Indo–Gangetic plains and southern face of the Himalayas. Besides the articles mentioned earlier, faunistic studies and distributional lists have been published by Datta and Majumdar (1970), De Witt (1960), Menon (1962, 1974), Mirza (1975), Pillai and Yazdani (1977), Rahman (1975), Sen (1985), Shrestha (1981), and Srivastava (1968). South of the Gangetic basin, the fish fauna of the Mahanadi has been studied by Job *et al.* (1955), the Coromandel Coast fauna was summarized by Menon (1966), the Cauvery by Jayaram *et al.* (1982), Goa by Tilak (1969), and Sri Lanka by Deraniyagala (1952).

South East Asia
Different geographical areas within South East Asia have different fish literature origins. The fish literature of Sundaland in the 19th century can be traced largely to the efforts of Pieter Bleeker, one of the most prolific writers in ichthyology. Among his 520 ichthyological papers were several important papers (1859, 1860a, 1863 a, b) on cyprinid classification in South East Asia, and he first described many genera recognized today. His work on cyprinids was summarized by Weber and de Beaufort (1916). Faunistic and distributional studies in Sundaland have been made by Vaillant (1893, 1902), Popta (1906), Fowler (1905), Inger and Chin (1962), Imaki *et al.* (1978), and Roberts (1989) on the island of Borneo. Bleeker wrote several major faunal studies (1858, 1860 a, b) on fishes of Sumatra. These were followed by Volz (1907), who catalogued the fauna. Alfred (1966) reviewed the freshwater fishes of Singapore. The freshwater fishes of peninsular Malaya were characterized by Mohsin and Ambak (1983). On the Indo-Chinese Peninsula the freshwater fishes have been studied by Sauvage (1881), Fily and d'Aubenton (1966), Taki (1974, 1975, 1978), Rainboth *et al.* (1976), Kottelat (1985), and Mai and Nguyen (1988). The freshwater fish fauna of the Tonkin Gulf drainages has been studied by Chevey and Lemasson (1937) and summarized by Mai (1978, 1985). Smith (1945) reviewed the freshwater fishes of Thailand, and the fishes of the Mae Khlong (Meklong) were studied by Johnsen (1963–64). Suvatti (1981) has provided an annotated listing with synonymies of fishes from Thailand. Much of the study of Burmese fish faunas was by British and later by Indian researchers. One of the earliest publications was by Blyth (1860) on the fishes of the Sittang River. Day (1875–78) included information on distribution of Burmese fishes; Vinciguerra (1890) published a monograph on them. Annandale (1918) wrote about the fishes of Inle Lake, which has endemic species of cyprinids. Other writers, most notably Mukerji (1932, 1933, 1934), Hora and Mukerji (1934 a, b), and Prashad and Mukerji (1929), have described collections from various parts of Burma. More recent publications on Burmese fishes were by Tint Hlaing (1967) and Win (1971).

6.3   SYSTEMATICS AND DIVERSITY

Ichthyological systematists have made many attempts to discover cyprinid generic relationships. However, the problem is difficult, and most efforts have met with only partial success. The diversity alone is overwhelming, and single subfamilies may be found on more than one continent. To determine the relationships of the members of a fauna, it may be necessary to study specimens which originate on another continent.

The distributions of the genera of South East Asian cyprinids are presented and discussed later (p. 179). A subfamilial classification scheme of all 200 cyprinid genera of South East Asia is presented (see also Chapter 1). Groupings at various taxonomic ranks came from numerous and varied sources. Among the genera of cyprinids in South East Asia are many whose relationships are poorly known. Consequently, this classification, like others before it, will have unnatural groupings.

Systematics

Any study directed at solving relationships within or between cyprinid subfamilies has meaning for eastern Asia, where they all occur. There have been various attempts to solve some of the difficult evolutionary problems posed by the cyprinids. Some authors have tried to take a single character or character suite and examine a wide array of Asian cyprinid genera, often including several subfamilies. These characters may be osteological (Chu, 1935; Gosline, 1975, 1978), morphological (Gosline, 1974; Kafuku, 1958, 1975, 1986; Matthes, 1963; Reid, 1982; Roberts, 1982), or chromosomal (Arai, 1982). Other authors have looked at multiple characters of various types while using numerous taxa (Bǎnǎrescu and Nalbant, 1973; Hosoya, 1986; Howes, 1978 through 1987; Meng, 1985; Ramaswami, 1955 a, b; Reid, 1985). In recent years the trend has been to erect classifications based on phylogenetic systematics. However, few recent studies have provided readers with data in character-state matrices so that overall reliability can be determined for characters which have been postulated as synapomorphies; Chen did provide a matrix of coded character-states (1987b), and complete data matrices in non-coded form (1987a). The many revisions of genera in the literature of this region are cited in recent faunistic works (p. 167).

Just as the groupings of genera came from various sources, the names for the subfamilies, tribes, and subtribes have several origins. Most of the names used here have been used previously (Table 6.2). Many names may be found that apply to some of these groups, but these are likely to be the oldest. Bleeker's (1859, 1863a) classifications of the Cyprinidae have supplied most family-group names used here. Ultimately, other names might be used depending on the final assessment of relationships between the genera. The problematic genus *Rohtee* (Sykes, 1838) was split by Bleeker (1863a) and its members were type species of the type genera for two family-group names, the Osteobramae

Table 6.2 Names of higher taxonomic categories in this chapter. Group names lacking author citation are used here for the first time

	Present	Original		
Category	Name	Name	Author	Date
Family	Cyprinidae	Cyprinia	Rafinesque	1815
Subfamily	Cyprininae	"	"	"
Tribe	Cyprinini	"	"	"
Subtribe	Cyprini	"	"	"
Subtribe	Tores	Torini	Karaman	1971
Tribe	Squaliobarbini	Squaliobarbinae	Howes	1981
Tribe	Systomini	Systomi	Bleeker	1863a
Subtribe	Systomi	"	"	"
Subtribe	Osteobramae	Osteobramae		
Subtribe	Poropuntii	Previously unused		
Tribe	Semiplotini	Semiploti	Bleeker	1863a
Tribe	Oreinini	Oreini	"	"
Tribe	Labeonini	Labeonini	"	1859
Subtribe	Labeones	"	"	"
Subtribe	Garrae	Garrae	"	1863a
Subfamily	Acheilognathinae	Acheilognathini	"	"
Subfamily	Gobioninae	Gobiones	"	"
Tribe	Gobionini	"	"	"
Tribe	Sarcocheilichthyini	Sarcochilichthyna	Kryzanowsky	1947
Subfamily	Leuciscinae	Leuciscini	Bonaparte	1845
Tribe	Leuciscini	"	"	"
Tribe	Chondrostomini	Chondrostomi	Agassiz	1855
Tribe	Aspiini	Aspii	Bleeker	1863a
Subfamily	Alburninae	Alburni	Girard	1858
Subfamily	Cultrinae	Cultrinae	Nikolsky	1954
Subfamily	Danioninae	Daniones	Bleeker	1863a
Tribe	Danionini	"	"	"
Tribe	Oxygastrini	Oxygastri	"	1859

and the Smiliogastrini. The latter name has priority over the name of Cultrinae, where some of the species currently placed in *Rohtee* probably belong (see Chapter 1). If *R. belangeri* is placed in the Cultrinae, then the name Smiliogastrinae will become available for that group. The name Osteobramae has been adapted for a subtribe of Cyprininae here. Application of family-group names as specified in the International Code of Zoological Nomen-clature (Anonymous, 1985) will be a time-consuming process, due to the vast literature and often erratic use of generic names by early authors.

For the Gobioninae, I have used the taxonomy of Bănărescu and Nalbant (1973) at the generic and specific levels. The family has been revised by Hosoya (1986), who restricted the definition to those genera which I have included in the tribe Gobionini. Hosoya did not find synapomorphies uniting the remaining genera. Therefore, the Sarcocheilichthyini may represent an unnatural group. However, until further information becomes available, they will be maintained as a single group based on Bănărescu and Nalbant (1973). Another result of Hosoya's (1986) phylogenetic study is that certain synapomorphies of the Gobionini are shared with the Homalopteridae and Psilorhynchidae. Those groups have not been included in this chapter. Roberts (1987) estimated that there are 58 species in 12 genera of the Homalopterinae and 52 species in 15 genera of the Gastromyzontinae.

The use of the remaining subfamilies generally follows Howes (Chapter 1), but with some exceptions. For instance, *Ochetobius* has been placed in the Aspiini, as indicated by Chen (1987b). There is also a difference in the Semiplotini from Howes's (1982) concept. In it I have included the 'Scaphiodon-like' genera from peninsular India. These bear little resemblance to *Osteochilus*, but I am not certain whether they are related more closely to *Scaphognathops* or to *Cyprinion*. Also included in the Semiplotini is *Schizocypris*, although this genus (and *S. ladigesi*, in particular) may be related instead to *Capoeta trutta*. Further, I am not convinced that Howes' concept of the Semiplotini represents a monophyletic group. The tree produced had a great deal of homoplasy, possibly associated with the mouthparts, which are known to be quite labile within certain populations of various *Cyprinion* species. Furthermore, the pharyngeal teeth of *Cyprinion* are spoon-shaped with truncate tips, just as they are in *Capoeta trutta* and *Schizocypris ladigesi*, whereas the teeth of *Scaphiodonichthys* are round and slender with recurved tips, as in the Poropuntii of South East Asia. I think it more likely that *Scaphiodonichthys* is related to *Onychostoma*, and *Cyprinion* is related to *Schizocypris* and other groups from western Asia. However, I am keeping the Semiplotini as a group here, because it is the best that has been published.

In this classification, *Luciocyprinus* has been included in the Oreinini. Although *Luciocyprinus* has been placed in the 'Barbinae' by various Chinese authors, some of the characters listed as synapomorphies, e.g. the five branched rays in the anal fin, triserial pharyngeal teeth, and compressed pharyngeal process, could apply equally well to the Oreinini. The two species of

Luciocyprinus lack the enlarged scales that typically surround the vent and base of the anal fin in the Oreinini. The genus *Sinocyclocheilus* has also been included in the Oreinini, and it also lacks the large scales at the vent and base of the anal fin.

The Chondrostomatini have been expanded here to include the genera formerly comprising the Xenocypridinae of author. *Amblypharyngodon*, *Catlocarpio*, and *Thynnichthys* may be related to each other and to *Hypophthalmichthys* (Howes, 1981). Whether such similarities are superficial or not needs thorough study, as does their relationship with *Gibelion* (*Catla* of authors), which is possibly a labeonine (Reid, 1982). *Amblypharyngodon*, *Catlocarpio*, and *Thynnichthys*, along with *Gibelion*, may represent a sister group to the Labeonini, but in the absence of conclusive information I have abstained from erecting a new group for them. Although these four genera fit uncomfortably with any other group listed here, I have classified them in the traditional manner. If they form a monophyletic group including *Gibelion*, then they would derive their name from Bleeker (1863a), who used the term Catlae.

The squaliobarbines of Howes (1981) may be a sister group of the Cyprininae. The group has been extended here to include *Atrilinea*. Another difference with most classifications is the inclusion of *Leptobarbus* with the Danionini. Although all species of *Leptobarbus* grow much larger than the other members of the tribe, in many ways they (particularly *L. hoeveni*) appear to be large, barbelled rasboras. The resemblance is so striking that Fowler (1937) named a new genus and species, *Filirasbora rubripinna*, using juvenile *Leptobarbus hoeveni*. Interestingly, Bleeker (1863b: 116) created a group called the Leptobarbi which included the Indo-Malayan species of the genera *Leptobarbus*, *Gnathopogon*, *Rasbora*, *Rasborichthys*, and *Thynnichthys*. *Gnathopogon javanicus* was actually a barb-like cyprinid which Günther (1868) renamed *Barbus aphya* because *javanicus* was preoccupied in *Barbus*. Actually, Bleeker's specimen, used later by Günther, is a juvenile *Leptobarbus hoeveni*.

As more is learned about the genera of South East Asian cyprinids, several large genera will be broken into smaller genera, which I hope will be monophyletic. The genus *Rasbora* Bleeker has had one group of species removed from it and placed in a new genus, *Parluciosoma* Howes. Although the new genus does not seem to belong in *Rasbora*, I am not yet certain how to distinguish the two genera on external characteristics and cannot classify species into one of the two genera without extraordinary effort. So, for the purposes of this chapter, both remain in *Rasbora*. Another problematic genus, *Puntius*, consists of several lineages. Although I have removed a number of genera which are not particularly closely related to *Puntius* and put them in another subtribe (the Poropuntii), the remaining species in *Puntius* still constitute several genera. The number of species recorded in the distribution table (p. 193) is the number of species that I have seen and examined in detail. with the addition of some species from descriptions which represented fishes that were different from anything I have seen.

Certain generic epithets for the South East Asian genera may be unfamiliar or applied in ways slightly different from common usage. The genus *Barilius* has been split into two groups following Howes' (1983) information on the differences between the lineages that formerly made up the genus. Most species in the genus, including all the South East Asian species, take the oldest applicable generic name, *Opsarius* (M'Clelland, 1838). Another generic name which is not commonly used is *Bangana* (Hamilton, 1822, type: *Cyprinus dero*) which replaces *Tylognathus* of Heckel. Other generic names used include *Chanodichthys* (Bleeker, 1859) replacing *Erythroculter* (Berg, 1909), and *Gibelion* (Heckel, 1843) replacing *Catla* (Valenciennes, 1844).

Diversity

The freshwater fish faunas of East and South East Asia are dominated by cyprinids. Using the freshwater fishes of Thailand as an example (Smith, 1945), the total of 549 species was composed of 214 cyprinids (39%), 99 siluroids (18%), 80 gobioids (15%), 48 cobitids and homalopterids (9%), 18 anabantoids (3%), 14 clupeids and engrulids (3%), 57 species of other primarily marine families (10%), and 19 assorted species from freshwater families (3%). The cyprinoid fishes accounted for 48% of the species. Taki (1978) found that the cyprinoids made up 49% of the Mekong fauna and siluroids another 20% (both proportions quite similar to Smith's figures), and that the percentage of cyprinoids increased progressively upstream, reaching 60% in the upper middle Mekong at Luang Prabang, Laos. This increase in cyprinid dominance upstream occurs simultaneously with a general decrease in overall upstream diversity. The domination, in total numbers of species, of freshwater fish faunas by cyprinids, and the longitudinal zonation of these cyprinid species, is repeated throughout South East Asia (Vaas, 1952; Inger and Chin, 1962; Johnson, 1967; Bishop, 1973; Mohsin and Ambak, 1983; Roberts, 1989).

Another type of comparative diversity is the relative diversity of higher-level taxa in parts of a drainage basin. Any measure of this type of diversity relies on the higher-level classification being used. The total numbers of species in various family groups of cyprinids have been summed for the eastern half of Asia, south of the border of the Soviet Union. For the large basins which have been subdivided, parallel trends are apparent during the progression from downstream to upstream areas. In the Yellow River (Table 6.3, nos 6–8), the numbers of acheilognathines and gobionines decrease upstream, whereas the number of oreinines increases. For the Yangtze (nos 9–11), the same pattern occurs even more markedly with the same fish groups. In the Yangtze, the Poropuntii appear in fair numbers. The poropuntiins inhabit upland (but not alpine) areas, reaching their greatest diversity in the middle Yangtze in Sichuan and Guizhou provinces. In the Mekong (nos 22–4), all groups that appear in the lower Mekong have equal or larger numbers in the middle

Table 6.3 Numbers of species-level taxa in 63 river basins of eastern and south-eastern Asia. Great rivers, such as the Yellow, Yangtze, Mekong, Irrawaddy, Ganges and Indus have been subdivided into major components

Taxon*†‡

Basin	Ache.	Sar.	Gob.	Cho.	Leu.	Asp.	Albu.	Cult.	Oxy.	Dan.	Squ.	Cy.	To.	Os.	Sys.	Po.	Sy.	Ore.	Sem.	La.	Ga.
Subfamily	Ache.	Gobi.	Gobi.	Gobi.	Leuc.	Leuc.	Albu.	Cult.	Oxy.	Dani.	Squ.	Cypr.	Cypr.	Cypr.	Cypr.	Cypr.	Cypr.	Cypr.	Cypr.	Lab.	Lab.
Tribe										Dan.		Cypr.	Cypr.	Cypr.	Sys.	Sys.	Sys.	Ore.	Sem.	Lab.	Lab.
Subtribe		Sar.	Gob.	Cho.	Leu.	Asp.						Cy.	To.	Os.	Sys.	Po.	Sy.			La.	Ga.
1. Heilong Jiang (Amur)	5	7	12	3	8	4	4	10	3	–	3	3	–	–	–	–	–	–	–	–	–
2. Liao He	7	5	20	3	3	1	3	9	2	1	3	2	–	–	–	–	–	–	–	–	–
3. Yalu Jiang	7	6	16	2	6	–	1	2	2	1	2	2	–	–	–	–	–	–	–	–	–
4. Korea	6	9	18	–	2	3	1	–	3	–	–	2	–	–	–	–	–	–	–	–	–
5. Japan	13	9	8	–	2	6	–	1	3	2	–	2	–	–	–	–	–	–	–	–	–
6. L. Huang He	10	11	31	4	3	1	4	8	2	1	3	2	–	–	2	–	–	4	–	–	–
7. Wei He	5	5	12	2	2	–	1	1	1	–	1	2	–	–	1	–	–	4	–	–	–
8. U. Huang He	–	4	10	1	1	–	–	1	–	–	1	2	–	–	1	–	–	17	–	–	–
9. L. Chang Jiang	17	15	43	10	2	3	6	12	3	1	4	2	2	–	11	–	–	1	–	2	3
10. U. Chang Jiang	10	9	22	10	1	3	8	14	6	1	3	4	3	–	16	–	–	25	–	2	7
11. Jinsha Jiang	3	5	11	2	–	–	8	1	1	1	1	5	2	–	6	–	–	38	–	–	3
12. Qaidam Pendi	–	–	–	–	–	–	–	–	–	–	–	–	–	–	–	–	–	16	–	–	1
13. Tarim–Yarkant	–	–	–	–	–	–	–	–	–	–	–	2	–	–	–	–	–	14	–	–	–
14. Ili He	–	–	–	1	3	–	–	–	–	–	–	1	–	–	–	–	–	5	–	–	–
15. N. Tien Shan	–	–	2	3	6	1	–	–	–	–	–	4	–	–	–	–	–	5	–	–	–
16. Central Tibet	–	–	–	–	–	–	–	–	–	–	–	–	–	–	–	–	–	6	–	–	–
17. Zhejiang–Fujian	10	7	14	3	1	–	7	8	5	2	2	4	1	–	9	1	–	–	–	2	1
18. Taiwan	3	1	6	2	–	–	3	4	3	2	–	2	3	–	5	2	–	–	–	1	–
19. Xi Jiang	8	6	13	3	–	2	16	13	4	5	1	15	4	–	21	1	–	11	–	7	13
20. Song Hong	8	2	11	4	–	3	4	9	6	3	2	7	5	–	22	3	–	1	2	13	16
21. Hainan	2	1	7	2	–	–	4	5	4	4	–	4	2	–	5	1	–	–	–	3	2
22. L. Mekong	2	1	–	–	–	–	2	–	4	12	–	2	2	14	6	6	–	1	–	15	1

23. M. Mekong	1	5	11	15	2	5	16	15	9	–	1	19	8
24. Lancang Jiang	–	2	5	2	8	3	7	12	1	10	1	12	5
25. C. Thailand	1	4	12	17	2	5	14	18	10	–	1	25	10
26. E. Malay Pen.	–	2	8	26	1	5	8	6	9	–	–	19	4
27. Perak	–	–	4	10	1	4	5	4	5	–	–	7	1
28. N. Sumatra	–	–	1	12	–	3	3	2	9	–	–	3	1
29. C. Sumatra	–	–	7	26	2	3	15	4	9	–	–	25	5
30. S. Sumatra	–	–	1	3	–	4	2	1	3	–	–	6	1
31. Java	–	–	4	7	–	2	7	2	6	–	–	13	2
32. South Borneo	–	–	3	9	–	2	6	1	5	–	–	10	2
33. East Borneo	–	–	3	9	1	2	5	2	5	–	–	14	4
34. North Borneo	–	–	3	9	–	–	2	4	4	–	–	6	4
35. S. Philippines	–	–	–	2	–	–	–	–	22	–	–	–	–
36. C. Philippines	–	–	–	4	–	2	–	–	7	–	–	–	–
37. Sarawak	–	–	6	13	–	3	3	2	5	–	–	7	3
38. Kapuas	–	–	7	8	2	4	16	4	13	–	–	20	5
39. Salween–Tenasserim	1	–	4	41	1	2	5	14	7	6	1	9	7
40. Sittang	–	–	2	10	–	2	3	1	5	–	–	7	2
41. L. Irrawaddy	–	–	2	9	–	4	4	2	5	8	–	8	1
42. U. Irrawaddy	1	–	5	12	–	6	5	6	5	–	1	11	10
43. Arakan coastal	2	–	9	15	–	2	1	2	13	–	2	9	–
44. Meghna	1	–	12	13	–	2	1	2	13	–	1	11	1

Table 6.3 (Continued)

Table 6.3 (*Continued*)

Basin	Ache.	Gobi.		Leuc.			Albu.	Cult.	Dani.		Squ.	Cypr.								
Subfamily / Tribe	Ache.	Sar.	Gob.	Cho.	Leu.	Asp.	Albu.	Cult.	Oxy.	Dan.	Squ.	Cyp.		Sys.			Ore.	Sem.	Lab.	
Subtribe												Cy.	To.	Os.	Po.	Sy.			La.	Ga.
45. Suma	–	–	–	–	–	–	–	–	12	14	–	–	4	1	2	13	3	1	15	7
46. Brahmaputra	–	–	–	–	–	–	–	–	13	13	–	–	5	1	2	13	9	1	14	9
47. Yarlung Zangbo Jiang	–	–	–	–	–	–	–	–	–	–	–	–	1	1	1	–	19	–	2	1
48. Eastern Ganges	–	–	–	–	–	–	–	–	17	12	–	–	5	1	1	12	8	1	14	5
49. Western Ganges	–	–	–	–	–	–	–	–	13	6	–	–	4	1	–	8	7	–	9	4
50. Mahanadi	–	–	–	–	–	–	–	–	11	7	–	–	2	3	–	13	–	–	10	1
51. Godavari	–	–	–	–	–	–	–	–	9	11	–	1	2	4	1	10	–	1	18	3
52. Krishna	–	–	–	–	–	–	–	–	9	8	–	1	2	4	3	7	–	1	14	4
53. Cauvery	–	–	–	–	–	–	–	–	13	12	–	–	2	3	10	22	–	3	17	5
54. Sri Lanka	–	–	–	–	–	–	–	–	–	9	–	–	2	–	–	13	–	–	5	2
55. Kerala	–	–	–	–	–	–	–	–	8	6	–	–	2	1	4	12	1	1	6	2
56. Mid. west coast	–	–	–	–	–	–	–	–	5	2	–	–	2	–	5	10	–	1	4	2
57. Tapti–Narmada	–	–	–	–	–	–	–	–	2	5	–	–	1	1	–	11	–	–	2	3
58. Kutch	–	–	–	–	–	–	–	–	1	2	–	–	1	2	–	5	–	–	3	–
59. Lower Indus	–	–	–	–	–	–	–	–	8	7	–	–	2	2	–	10	2	2	15	2
60. Punjab–Him. Prad.	–	–	–	–	–	–	–	–	9	6	–	–	3	1	–	11	2	2	10	2
61. Kashmir	–	–	–	–	–	–	–	–	7	4	–	–	1	1	–	7	19	1	6	2
62. Kabul	–	–	–	–	–	–	–	–	6	4	–	–	1	1	–	7	8	1	6	2
63. Baluchistan	–	–	–	–	–	–	–	–	3	2	–	–	2	–	–	5	4	5	10	3

*Subfamilies: Ache., Acheilognathinae; Gobi., Gobioninae; Leuc., Leuciscinae; Albu., Alburninae; Cult., Cultrinae; Dani., Danioninae; Cypr., Cyprininae.
†Tribes: Sar., Sarcocheilichthyini; Gob., Gobionini; Cho., Chondrostomini; Leu., Leuciscini; Asp., Aspiini; Oxy., Oxygastrini; Dan., Danionini; Squ., Squaliobarbini; Cyp., Cyprinini; Sys., Systomini; Ore., Oreinini; Sem., Semiplotini; Lab., Labeonini.
‡Subtribes: Cy., Cyprinii; To., Tores; Os., Osteobramae; Po., Poropuntii; Sy., Systomi; La., Labeones; Ga., Garrae.

Mekong. In the upper Mekong (Lancang Jiang), many of the groups found downstream still occur, but in reduced numbers. Much of the Lancang Jiang in Yunnan Province is still subtropical and retains tropical faunal elements. Parts of the river above the long gorge in northern Yunnan are distinctly alpine and have the oreinine fauna. Of three sections of the greater Brahmaputra (nos. 44, 46, and 47), the middle Brahmaputra is the most diverse, particularly in the numbers of labeonines. The faunal differences between the middle Brahmaputra and the Yarlung Zangbo Jiang (Tsangpo) are profound, with nearly everything found in the downstream reaches disappearing in the face of overwhelming domination by the oreinines. The same trend toward domination by the oreinines at high altitudes also occurs in the Indus. This trend continues within the Oreinini at the uppermost reaches of the rivers, with 85% of the species of *Schizothorax* occurring at altitudes of 1250 to 2500 m, but being replaced by *Diptychus* at 2750–3750 m, which are replaced by species of *Schizocypris* and *Gymnocypris* at 3750–4750 m (Cao *et al.*, 1981).

An ecological aspect of diversity is illustrated by the array of species at single localities. It has long been recognized that a single locality will produce a much more limited array of species than an entire basin. Several studies made in various parts of South East Asia (Borneo, Sumatra, and Malaya) were summarized by Lowe–McConnell (1975). Geisler *et al.* (1979) examined the diversity of fishes in three small streams and found that two streams in peninsular Thailand had fewer cyprinids and more anabantoids than expected, whereas a stream on the Khorat Plateau was dominated by cyprinoids. However, the water in the two peninsular streams was soft and acidic, whereas that of the plateau stream was hard, well buffered, and alkaline. Johnson (1967) documented a blackwater fauna, which includes several cyprinids, and air-breathing anabantoids. However, most of the cyprinid species of the blackwater fauna do not inhabit streams as far north as the streams sampled by Geisler *et al.* Heckman (1979) studied rice-field ecology and found a high ratio of anabantoids to cyprinoids. However, one can certainly expect that, as the stream size increases, the pattern of cyprinid predominance will be repeated.

Fossil record

More palaeontological information on cyprinid fishes is available from areas bordering on South East Asia than from South East Asia itself. A considerable body of literature exists for eastern Asia, particularly for Japan (Nakajima, 1986, and references therein). Throughout central Asia and Mongolia, many studies have been reported by Soviet researchers; for example, Sytchevskaya (1986) produced a major study on the Palaeogene fish fauna of the region, including the description of four new cyprinid genera (*Eodiptychus, Palaeotinca, Parabarbus,* and *Zaissanotinca*) from various parts of Oligocene. Researchers on the Indian subcontinent have also been actively studying fossil fishes, including cypriniforms from Kashmir (Gaur and Kotlia, 1987; Sahni *et al.*, 1984).

Cyprinids were reported from the Eocene of central Sumatra by Günther (1876) and in a monograph by Sanders (1934). The cyprinid genera and species known from the locality include *Rasbora antiqua*, *R. mohri*, *Thynnichthys amblyostoma*, *Osteochilus fossilis*, *Puntius bussyi*, *Barbus megacephalus*, and *Eocyprinus sumatranus*. From Thailand, in the present-day Salween drainage, Uyeno (1969) reported finding an unidentified cyprinid and an unnamed species of *Puntius*. The lacustrine deposits of the Mae Moh basin in central Thailand have produced cypriniform fishes of Miocene age (Chaodumrong *et al.*, 1983, and references therein). However, compared to other parts of Asia, very little has been done with fossil fishes of any group, including the cyprinids, in the last half-century (Uyeno, 1984).

6.4   HISTORICAL AND ECOLOGICAL BIOGEOGRAPHY

For more than a hundred years South East Asia has been a focus of zoogeographical interest. The great naturalist Alfred Russell Wallace was so impressed with the striking patterns of animal distribution in this area that he considered the process of evolution in his search for an explanation. The region contains the classic zoogeographic boundary known to this day as Wallace's line. The original line of Wallace was based on zoogeographical as well as geographical information and was drawn along the easternmost margin of the Sunda shelf (George, 1981). Later studies by Wallace moved the line eastward to include the Celebes (Wallace, 1910). However, Wallace's first line (Wallace, 1863) is the boundary with the greatest utility for defining the distribution of primary freshwater fishes in general, and the Cyprinidae in particular.

The first zoogeographic study to examine freshwater fish faunas in relation to the submerged rivers of Sundaland demonstrated the faunal similarity of rivers belonging to the same Pleistocene basins (Weber, in Molengraaff and Weber, 1921). Weber also commented on the faunal differences between the Mahakam River of the east coast of Borneo, and the Kapuas of the west coast, noting the similarity of the fish faunas of the Kapuas and the Musi River of Sumatra. Others, such as Krempf and Chevey (1934), examined the distributions of fishes from the Indo-Chinese Peninsula, and compared them to the fish distributions of Sundaland. An important discussion of fish distribution in Sundaland was given by Beaufort (1951) in a book which reached a broad audience and provided many students with their first exposure to the drowned river basins of South East Asia. Inger and Chin (1962) discussed the zoogeography of the freshwater fishes of North Borneo and of Borneo in general. Bănărescu (1972) pointed out the pronounced differences between the East Asian fauna and the South East Asian fauna, and mentioned that the fish fauna of the small coastal drainages of Annam cordillera (Vietnam) resembled the fish fauna of East Asia rather than that of South East Asia.

Taki's (1975, 1978) studies on the zoogeography of the Mekong fishes produced some interesting generalizations about the fish faunas of the middle and lower Mekong, the Chao Phraya, and the Greater Sunda Islands. Taki found that the non-ostariophysan fauna of the Mekong was composed of widespread species of South East Asia, and that almost all genera were shared among all four areas. The siluroids and cyprinoids demonstrated two different patterns of distribution, an upland and a lowland pattern, which were attributed to habitat preferences. The lowland species were found in large rivers and were distributed in the lower Chao Phraya and often in the Greater Sunda Islands. The upland species of the middle Mekong were found in smaller streams and their congeners were more likely to be found in the small streams of the upper Chao Phraya than in the large streams of the lower Mekong. Thus, an adjacent river system had greater faunistic similarity to both the lower and middle Mekong than these sections had to each other.

Mohsin and Ambak (1983) made a comparative listing of species found on the islands and mainland surrounding peninsular Malaysia. They used the same number of fish distribution zones, but divided peninsular Malaysia into faunal regions different from those proposed by Johnson (1967). Chu (1986) summarized the zoogeography of Yunnan, which probably has the greatest fish diversity of any province in China. Chu's diagram of river system relationships among the six major drainages of Yunnan was based on numbers of shared genera. The dendrogram indicated that there were two major units, each composed of three drainages. One unit was formed by the upper reaches of the Xi Jiang (Nampan Jiang), which was most similar to the upper Hong (Yuan Jiang). This pair of drainages associated most closely with the upper Yangtze (Jinsha Jiang). The second group comprised the upper Irrawaddy and upper Salween (Nu Jiang) pair, which paired next with the upper Mekong (Lancang Jiang).

Distribution patterns

The pattern of change in cyprinid faunas of the eastern half of central and southern Asia was obvious from the sums of species by basin for the different family-group taxa (Table 6.3). However, that method of data summary causes some information about the distribution of genera and species to be lost, and relies on the family-group classification being used. The best way to display information about species distributions would be as a single matrix (species by drainage) of presence–absence coded data. With over 1250 species-level taxa, such a listing is not possible here, so the list was condensed to include only the generic distributions over a reduced southern region.

This generic distribution list (p. 193) accomplishes multiple aims, classifying each genus, giving its distribution and the total number of species in the genus for the region. Many genera that have ranges outside the tallied region have additional species excluded from the total given here. More than 400 references were used to develop this list. Much literature remains to be incorporated, but it would probably not change the known ranges of the genera (although it might for some of the species). Therefore, this list will provide a reasonable assessment of the ranges of these genera. The main difficulty to be overcome is a lack of knowledge about the fish faunas of some regions. Field surveys with intensive collecting over the range of physical characteristics found in the fresh waters of South East Asia are almost non-existent. With few exceptions, reliable and complete distribution lists still remain to be compiled. The best available sources for South East Asia have already been cited (p. 168).

There are many questions about faunal relationships which might be asked regarding various subsections of South East Asia. To take a quantitative first look at the faunal relationships of the rivers using the distributions of the genera provided here, I used unweighted pair-group (UPGMA) clustering of the geometric mean of matching presences and absences divided by their marginal totals. The coefficient is a metric and a logical extension of Ochiai's (1957) zoogeographic coefficient to include matching absences (Legendre and Legendre, 1983: 177; Sokal and Sneath, 1963: 130). Although it is possible to treat these data by methods used in phylogenetic systematics, the complexities of reporting such analyses would rapidly overwhelm this chapter, and the entire subject will be dealt with in detail elsewhere (Rainboth, in prep.). The dendrogram resulting from this analysis (Fig. 6.4) yields one possible view of the similarities of these faunas, and provides the first quantitative result towards the resolution of several faunistic questions.

The main dichotomy in the dendrogram (between branches A and B) separates the faunas of central Asia from the faunas of southern Asia. For central Asia, there are important differences between the faunas of eastern central Asia (East Asia; C) and high Asia (D). For southern Asia, the most distinct fauna is the relict fauna of the Philippines (E), which lacks most of the faunal elements found in the other parts of the region (F). The next major dichotomy is between the faunas of South Asia or the Indian subcontinent (G) and South East Asia (H). The South Asian region has the faunas of the Indian peninsula (I), of the Indo–Gangetic plains and tributary streams (J), and of central Burma (K). Smaller faunas affiliated with these are the Sri Lankan fauna and the depauperate cyprinid fauna of the Kutch, a coastal lowland surrounded by a vast salt marsh, in the Indian state of Gujarat.

South East Asia

The South East Asian faunal resemblances merit detailed discussion. First, consider the Pleistocene basin reconstruction for drainages of Java, southern Borneo, and south-eastern Sumatra, all of which debouch into the Java Sea.

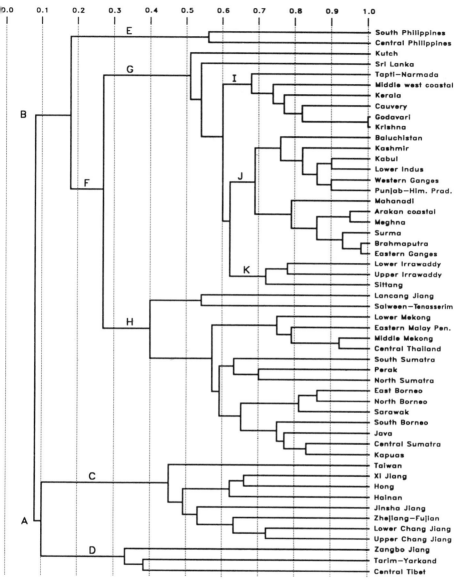

Fig. 6.4 Dendrogram of cyprinid faunal similarity, based on UPGMA clustering of Sokal and Sneath's (1963) similarity coefficient. Major branch labels: A, southern Asia; B, central Asia; C, East Asia; D, high Asia; E, Philippines; F, non-Philippine southern Asia; G, Indian subcontinent; H, South East Asia; I, peninsular India; J, Indo–Gangetic plains; K, central Burma.

There have been inferences that the drainages of south-east Sumatra connected to those of western Java and passed through the Sunda Strait, or even exited the shelf through the Sunda Strait without joining any Javanese drainages (Tjia, 1980). Other interpretations indicated that the drainages of south-eastern Sumatra connected to those of southern Borneo, with their combined systems attaching later to the Javanese drainage (Beaufort, 1951). Any or all of these patterns may have existed at one time or another; possibly Tjia's (1980) pattern was the most recent. This analysis indicates that Javanese and South Bornean faunas of the East Sunda drainage most closely resemble the central Sumatra rivers and the Kapuas River of the North Sunda drainage. The similarity of the basins of the North Sunda River was one of the first zoogeographical observations in this region (Weber, in Molengraaff and Weber, 1921). The fauna of South-east Sumatra pairs more closely with the fauna of North Sumatra and the Perak River of the Straits of Malacca, perhaps because the faunas of South-east Sumatra and South Borneo are still rather poorly known.

The similarity of the faunas of the Perak and North Sumatra is not surprising given the configuration of the extended Pleistocene rivers, but may be surprising in light of the faunal divisions reported in Mohsin and Ambak (1983). Their faunal divisions put the Perak and the Pahang of the eastern side of the Malay Peninsula in the same faunal zone. Here, however, the eastern side of the peninsula pairs first with the middle Mekong–central Thailand pair, with the three joining the lower Mekong next (Fig. 6.4). Thus, the Pahang tends to share more genera with the Indo-Chinese Peninsula than with the Perak, which resembles North Sumatra. The resemblance of the Chao Phraya–Mae Khlong (central Thailand) fauna to those of the subsections of the Mekong agrees completely with Taki's (1975, 1978) assessments.

For the upper Mekong (Lancang Jiang) and the Salween, this analysis indicates that their faunal similarity with the Irrawaddy and Sittang is fairly remote, mainly owing to the strong resemblance of the Irrawaddy fauna to that of the great Indo–Gangetic system. This is interesting because of the extended Pleistocene river shared by both the Salween and the Sittang. Yet the Sittang, a former main channel of the Irrawaddy, with a fauna primarily of the lowland floodplains, would not be expected to contribute greatly to the fauna of a fast, upland river like the Salween, which has almost no floodplain at all. Thus, the faunas of the Salween and the Lancang Jiang are primarily faunas of the Shan Plateau. This does not resolve any questions about the possible beheading of the Irrawaddy or Chindwin by tributaries of the Brahmaputra, but it is certainly thought-provoking. After all, the Irrawaddy and Sittang drain the western slope of the Shan Plateau just as the Irrawaddy and Chindwin drain the eastern slope of the Patkai–Naga Hills. This interesting problem deserves further study.

Although the relationships of the Irrawaddy fauna to the Indo–Gangetic fauna and the Salween to the Lancang Jiang conflict with Chu's (1986) expectations, the faunas of the rest of the rivers draining Yunnan Province agree completely with his results. The dendrogram (Fig. 6.4) portrays the similarity of the Hong River to the Xi Jiang and the resemblance of this pair to the upper Yangtze (Jinsha Jiang). These faunas of the East Asian rivers support Bănărescu's (1972) contention that the Hong River of the Tonkin gulf is more closely affiliated with the East Asian fauna than with the South East Asian fauna. The distinctive East Asian fauna differs strongly from the South–South East Asian fauna, with which it clusters last.

Some comments on the zoogeography of this region are in order here. The poorly known faunas of South-east Sumatra and South Borneo will be used as an example. The problem of drainage configuration should be studied in more detail if collections can be obtained from southern Sumatra and South Borneo. This has importance for our ability to do proper descriptions of the Indonesian fauna. With much of the original freshwater habitat being so highly modified in Java, many species which were described from there may no longer exist, and are now known only from scant type material. For instance, in the genus *Tor*, some species which may now be extinct were described from Java and seem not to occur elsewhere. Their names are misapplied to a variety of species throughout South East Asia, confounding any biological studies in which the identification of these species has importance. However, it may be possible to find conspecifics in the upper reaches of the South Bornean or South Sumatran drainages. This is only a single example of what is possible here, but the study and solution of these zoogeographical problems can aid both biological and conservation research.

Areas of high endemism

In South East Asia, as in other parts of the world, endemic faunas of cyprinids have developed in lakes and often in small river basins which have not had water exchange with other systems for a long period of time. In South East Asia, several lakes have supported endemic species and sometimes entire endemic faunas. South East Asian lakes with endemic faunas are Lake Lanao on the Mindanao Plateau of the Philippines, Inle Lake on the Shan Plateau of Burma, the lakes of the lake district of Yunnan Province of China and Danau (Lake) Tawar and others along the mountain range of Sumatra.

Lake Lanao
The best-known South East Asian endemic cyprinid fauna is that of Lake Lanao. This fauna has received great attention as an example of explosive speciation in the last 10 000 y (Myers, 1960). This notion has recently been called into question for a variety of reasons (Reid, 1980): there can be no question that the fauna is endemic, but the age of the lake, the actual size of the fauna, the exact distributions of its members, and the length of isolation are certainly suspect. Of the 23 cyprinid species known from Mindanao Island, 15

are reported from Lake Lanao. Nineteen species known from Mindanao are endemic, whether they are found in Lake Lanao or not. Endemic species are known from several rivers of Mindanao, which would have an endemic fauna even if Lake Lanao did not exist. Little is known about the original habitats of many of the species, because they were acquired by purchase in fish markets and have not been collected since: it is still not known which of these species 'collected at Dansalan' might be expected from the lake or from the tributary or outlet streams, and whether this changes during the course of the year. Although over-description of the fauna may be a problem, any such possibility will require detailed examination and analysis of as much of the original material as is still available. Myers (1960) was convinced that "most if not all of the species described by Herre are distinct", but he did not trust Fowler's (1941) identifications.

Ecophenotypic plasticity in *Barbus intermedius* of East Africa, mentioned by Reid (1980) as a justification for 'judicious pruning' of the Lanao flock, has little relevance for Asian '*Puntius*', which are not particularly closely related to the African large barbs. Asian '*Puntius*' usually demonstrate little morphological variation within populations and species, and the expected lack of variation is the cause of taxonomic difficulties with '*Puntius*' *binotatus*. The systematics of the '*Puntius*' *binotatus* complex is one of the most difficult population–species problems of the continent. By usual description, '*Puntius*' *binotatus* would seem to be a complex of vagile colonizers which seem to inhabit every body of fresh water in even the smallest islands of Sundaland. However, another view might perceive them as a very old and established group of head-water species that tenaciously hold their habitat during periods of sea regression and invasion by any other head-water species that might occasionally venture into the lower courses of the great rivers which drained Sundaland. '*Puntius*' *binotatus* expresses morphological variation if all populations resembling a general *binotatus* morphotype are treated as a single species. However, they probably do not form a single species, and determining the morphology and geographical range of each species now synonymized with *binotatus* would be a formidable task. Ancestry of the Lanao fauna has been attributed to '*Puntius*' *binotatus*, although only some of the species bear resemblance to this presumed ancestor, which does not occur there now notwithstanding citations to the contrary. Some of the Philippine species may be related to *binotatus*, although the Mindanao species flock probably pre-dates greatly the appearance of *binotatus*.

Discussions of allopatric versus sympatric speciation and the problems of crossing land bridges have accomplished little. Until we are certain of the identity of Herre's species and can relate such information to large modern collections (at Hamburg University, in particular), we are wasting our efforts. For '*Puntius*' to reach the island several times would have been no problem, and extraordinary means of dispersal are unnecessary. With a '*Puntius*' known from the North Sunda River in the Eocene, a Miocene origin of Mindanao could mean that these fishes were there from the very beginning. Given that Miocene sea level may have regressed to 1000 m below the present levels (Batchelor, 1979, and references therein), a modern deep section 270 m below present sea level in the south Sulu corridor would not have been a major obstacle through the Miocene or most of the Pliocene and during at least one regression episode early in the Pleistocene. The entire fauna could have been established on the island long before the lake's mid-Pliocene origin (Lewis, 1978). I believe that the '*Puntius*' fauna on Mindanao represents (or represented if extinct) a relict fauna of forms reminiscent of early Sundaland '*Puntius*'.

Other endemic faunas

Much space has been given to the Lanao fauna, mainly because of its fame and influence on concepts of 'theoretical evolution'. However, there are lesser-known endemic cyprinid faunas restricted to lakes in South East Asia.

Inle Lake on the southern Shan Plateau may represent one of the few remaining lakes in a large limestone karst region which was sprinkled with lakes that have now disappeared. Inle Lake has an endemic cyprinid fauna consisting of two species of the genus *Microrasbora* and one species in each of two endemic genera, *Sawbwa* and *Inlecypris*. Another endemic cyprinid is a strange, highly compressed barb which I am currently identifying as *Percocypris compressiformis*, although it may require a genus of its own. Another endemic barb, of the genus *Poropuntius*, is the only totally herbi-vorous member of a normally insectivorous–omnivorous genus: this species subsists entirely on a diet of aquatic macrophytes.

Further north, the continuation of the upland Shan Plateau in Yunnan Province of China has another lake district which also has an extensive network of caves. The fauna of the region's lakes has been studied by Li (1982), who lists some 36 endemic species of cyprinids. However, numerous species have been described since 1982. Many species are cavernicoles which appear in surface waters seasonally, sometimes in rivers or lakes. The genera with species endemic to the region are *Mesocyprinus*, *Cyprinus*, *Hemicultrella* (*Anabarilius* of authors), *Schizothorax*, *Xenocypris*, *Spinibarbus*, *Poropuntius*, *Luciocyprinus*, *Discogobio*, *Percocypris*, *Acanthorhodeus*, and cavernicolous genera *Sinocyclocheilus* and *Typhlobarbus*, both of which have species that lack eyes. This is a fascinating and diverse fauna with endemism at several levels.

6.5 GENERAL BIOLOGY

Much of the research on the general biology of cyprinid fishes of southern Asia has a fishery orientation, and the volume of literature is strongly weighted towards applied studies of commercially important species. However, litera-ture from the realm of pure ecology is beginning to appear from South East Asia, and knowledge about the fishes and their ecology and general biology is rapidly improving. Studies on the biology and ecology of South East Asian fishes have been summarized by Lowe–McConnell (1975, 1987). South East Asian cyprinid biology is similar in many aspects to that of other tropical cyprinids, but the sheer diversity of cyprinids in South East Asia implies a greater variety of biological specializations. This section will deal only with some of the more unusual and little-known aspects of cyprinid biology in South East Asia. In some instances, this information is related anecdotally from first-hand observations.

Size

Southern Asia has some of the largest and smallest representatives of the Cyprinidae. At least two genera have species which are tiny, with a maximum adult size of < 20 mm. The smallest of these, and probably the smallest cyprinid, is the Burmese species *Danionella translucida*: the largest known specimen is 12 mm in standard length. Roberts (1986) found ripe or ripening ovaries in females of 10.3–11.3 mm. Some species of *Rasbora* have adult sizes < 20 mm, e.g. *R. maculata* and *R. urophthalma* (Brittan, 1954). Several cyprinids of southern Asia grow to be quite large, with the longest fish being *Tor putitora* (Hamilton, 1822) of the Brahmaputra. Hamilton's posthumously published report (Day and Buchanan, 1877) on the fish and fisheries of Bengal states that this species ". . . is often found nine feet in length, and six feet is the usual size. The scales are exceedingly large, being like the hand, and at Dacca are often made into the cards with which people game." *Tor putitora* is replaced in the Ganges by *T. mosal*, which attains well over 1 m in length (4–5 feet, according to Hamilton), but grows nowhere near as large as *T. putitora* is known to have grown. Both of these fishes, as well as some other species of *Tor*, are powerful swimmers, voracious predators, and have a deserved reputation as some of the most spectacular freshwater game fishes in the world. In Thailand, the largest cyprinid is *Catlocarpio siamensis*, which recently has been seen to grow to 2.5 m and has undoubtedly reached 3 m (Smith, 1945). It is a herbivore, like many other large cyprinids in South East Asia.

Migration and spawning

Spawning activities of South East Asian cyprinids are accomplished in a variety of ways, often entailing extended migrations upstream or downstream. Other species may migrate laterally, from the stream they inhabit into temporarily flooded riparian forest. The timing of spawning is usually related to the annual rainfall cycle of the seasonal tropics, with the timing becoming less precise in the perhumid tropics. When the seasonal rainfall patterns are extremely predictable, spawning may occur in a correspondingly predictable fashion. Some of the most striking seasonal breeding patterns in southern Asia are found on the Indian subcontinent. The breeding-cycle predictability of the major carps (all important as pond-culture species) is so pronounced that large 'fish seed' industries have grown in the human cultures that exploit them. The communal breeding of *Gibelion catla*, *Labeo rohita*, and *Cirrhinus mrigala* in the Halda River of Bangladesh, a freshwater tidal zone, tributary to the Karnafuli, been studied by Patra and Azadi (1985) and Tsai *et al.* (1981). These three carps breed simultaneously, although in different proportion, during either the new- or full-moon periods (but not both) of the first two months of the rainy season. These new- and full-moon periods (usually in May and June) coincide with the heaviest thunderstorms of the coming rainy season, and the first period to have a major thunderstorm sets the pattern (of new-moon or full-moon spawning) for the year. Spawning occurs along a straight stretch in the river, just above a U-shaped bend, timed to the slowest flow during the peak of high tide, during a driving rainstrom. Precipitation seems to be very important, as major carps skip entire breeding seasons if the rains fail or are delayed (Jhingran, 1975). Perhaps the most surprising result of these studies was that the nursery ground for the major carp fry and fingerlings was the Bay of Bengal, which has a reduced salinity during rainy season (Tsai *et al.*, 1981). Adult carps occasionally venture out into the Bay of Bengal during higher salinity regimes. During the dry season immediately before Tsai *et al.*'s study, I collected a *Labeo calbasu* by otter trawl between the mouth of the Meghna (combined Ganges–Brahmaputra) and the mouth of the Karnafuli (to which the Halda is a tributary), in water that had a salinity of *c*. 20‰. Although *Labeo calbasu* is not known to spawn communally with the major carps, it is closely related and is common in the lower Karnafuli estuary. Lunar periodicity has been found in Mekong cyprinids also (Blache and Goossens, 1954; Fily and d'Aubenton, 1966), but the estuarine spawning of major carps is probably unique to the Halda River of Bangladesh.

Large species which spawn in rivers are not the only fishes to be highly reliant on the first storms of the rainy season. Small cyprinids of the Gangetic floodplains, especially *Puntius* spp., immediately begin to move out onto flooded land when the first rainstorm occurs. The first rains of the south-west monsoon are often violent storms with lightning, high winds, and driving rain. During one of these storms, I saw some small *Puntius* swimming through water shallower than the depth of their bodies on a soccer field which had been totally dry 15 minutes earlier. Going 'downstream', I found a swarm of them racing up a small rivulet which drained from the field into an artificial pond some 20 km away. When the 30 minute cloudburst stopped, the field became littered with dying *Puntius* and *Esomus* as the water percolated into the soil. A friend who was about 60 km away when the same storm hit saw fish all over the ground after the storm was over. In both places, the inhabitants thought that it had rained fishes. It is not surprising that in Bangladesh, 80% of which is annually inundated for prolonged periods during the rainy season, the members of the floodplain fauna quickly attempt to make use of new resources. If the migrants reach unexploited permanent water, they become major winners in the annual spawning sweepstakes.

In South East Asia, other interesting phenomena occur during the cycle of rainy and dry seasons. During the dry season, the water of the middle Mekong appears blue or bluish-green from a distance and is clear enough that small cyprinids at depths of up to 2 m can be seen from the surface and identified to generic level; the main course of the river supports a diverse and specialized cyprinid community in the dry season. When the rainy season commences, the water rises, flow speed increases, and water becomes brown and opaque. This is a gradual process accompanied by changes in the cyprinid fauna, in which the upland species disappear from the main stream and are replaced by several species of catfishes, clupeids, and a lowland cyprinid fauna of species common in the Great Lake (Tonle) of Cambodia. The upland cyprinids leave the main channel and congregate in flooded riparian forest or move up tributary streams of various sizes. Meanwhile, species which were already in the tributary streams move out into seasonally flooded ditches, grasslands and rice fields (pers. obs.). At the end of the rainy season, the fishes move downstream, gradually reconstituting the dry-season communities after pronounced multispecies migrations which support major artisanal fisheries (Smith, 1945). The migrations of cyprinids which occur in seasonal tropical rivers are not simply breeding migrations, but rather are migrations to new or superior living space. When put in context of the river continuum concept (Vannote *et al.*, 1980), it may be that the behaviour of cyprinid populations reflects seasonal shifts in community equilibria for other organisms as well. This may reconcile the observations of many authors that the high diversity in the tropics does not translate into high diversity at any single locality. At any one time, a locality may have few species in comparison to the diversity of the entire drainage, but the same locality may support several faunas over the course of a year, some of which differ almost totally. The standard practice of making spot maps for fish distributions has a seasonal aspect which might yield different maps for dry and rainy seasons.

The mechanics of breeding for many South East Asian cyprinids, particularly the smaller species, are well known through their popularity in the aquarium trade. Of course, studies of wild fishes in their natural habitats are preferable, but many types of group-specific behaviour may approximate the behaviour of wild individuals. Breder and Rosen (1966) summarize the breeding behaviour of several major groups of cyprinids.

Feeding

Dietary preferences of South East Asian cyprinids have been delineated in several studies of fish community trophic levels. In south-eastern Sumatra,

Vass *et al.* (1953) studied fishes of the Komering and Ogan rivers. On the island of Borneo, Vaas (1952) studied the diets of fishes of the Kapuas River. Some of the most detailed information on freshwater fish diets is known for North Borneo, where Inger (1955) and Inger and Chin (1962) studied the dietary habits and general ecology of fishes from several drainages. In Malaya, the feeding habits and ecology of the fish community of Sungai Gombak were studied by Bishop (1973), those in Tasek Bera by Mizuno and Furtado (1982), and those in all of peninsular Malaya by Mohsin and Ambak (1983). The diets of some cyprinids in several drainages of Thailand were reported by Mizuno and Mori (1970). Taki (1978) listed the dietary habits of numerous species from the Mekong. Smith (1945) also gives some scattered anecdotal diet information.

From these studies, it is possible to make a summary listing of general dietary information for the cyprinid genera (Table 6.4). There seems to be conflicting information in various reports. However, given the general inclination towards opportunistic feeding for most species, differing reports are not surprising, and may reflect local abundance of various types of food. Certain genera (e.g. *Puntius*) are listed in several categories, but this has resulted from species differences. Some *Puntius* eat primarily insects, whereas others eat plant material or some combination of both plant and animal matter.

Although not detectable in such a generic summary as Table 6.4, a trend which was noticeable during its compilation was that the herbivorous species which took animal matter were usually those that ate the large plant material. Omnivorous species that primarily ate animal matter usually ate medium-sized endogenous or exogenous animal food. The only species to contradict this trend was *Thynnichthys thynnoides*, a planktivore which subsists on microscopic plant or animal matter. Medium or large plant or animal food sustains *Leptobarbus*. Although *Probarbus* eats mostly large plant matter, it does take animal matter, primarily molluscs, which it crushes with a single row of large, molariform pharyngeal teeth on each arch. *Probarbus* has a highly protractile mouth (as is found in the Catostomidae), which can make vertical contact with the bottom while the fish maintains a nearly horizontal attitude. The tribe Labeonini generally eat microscopic plant matter, periphyton, or detritus. Larger members of the group, such as the major carps of India, are valued species for aquaculture because of their fast growth and simple dietary requirements. At least two species of *Lobocheilus* kept in aquaria will tear off and eat the scales of their tank mates (pers. obs.). Most of the Danionini are carnivorous, although several take occasional plant matter. The barbs, or Systomini, are found in each of the possible groups except one, but most will take exogenous arthropods. The only cyprinid listed as a predator of large fish is *Hampala macrolepidota*; the other, smaller species of *Hampala* eat smaller prey. Similarly, species of *Tor* and *Raiamas* of the Indian subcontinent are large fishes and consequently eat large prey.

Table 6.4 Feeding habits of South East Asian cyprinids*

Herbivores	Omnivores	Carnivores
a. Small plant matter –	a. Primarily plant matter –	a. Exogenous –
Periphyton, plankton, algae, detritus	*Barbodes*	Arthropods
	Mystacoleucus	
Amblyrhynchichthys	*Probarbus*	*Chela*
Bangana	*Puntius*	*Danio*
Catlocarpio	*Scaphognathops*	*Esomus*
Dangila		*Luciosoma*
Epalzeorhynchos	b. Primarily animal matter –	*Nematabramis*
Garra	*Balantiocheilos*	*Opsarius*
Henicorhynchus	*Cycloheilichthys*	*Parachela*
Labeo	*Esomus*	*Rasbora*
Lobocheilus	*Leptobarbus*	
Mekongina	*Nematabramis*	b. Endogenous –
Osteochilus	*Poropuntius*	Small food
Sikukia	*Puntius*	Zooplankton
Thynnichthys	*Rasbora*	*Dangila*
	Tor	*Thynnichthys*

b. Large plant matter –

Macrophytes, seeds, fruits, inundated land plants	Medium food Aquatic insects, shrimp, fish
Barbodes	*Cosmochilus*
Leptobarbus	*Cyclocheilichthys*
Probarbus	*Hampala*
Puntioplites	*Leptobarbus*
Punitius	*Macrochirichthys*
	Onychostoma
	Opsarius
	Oxygaster
	Parachela
	Paralaubuca
	Puntius
	Raiamus
	Rasbora
	Scaphiodonichthys
	Large food
	Large fish, crabs
	Hampala

*Generic names are updated. Inclusion of a genus in more than one category is due to differences in species or individuals included in various reports. Several herbivores and carnivores have omnivorous tendencies.

6.6 POSTSCRIPT

This chapter has offered an introduction to the Asian cyprinids. The glimpse has been necessarily superficial, given the generic and higher-level diversity of the cyprinids in this region. Certain aspects of their biology, such as the extreme array of body shapes, have been omitted, although the range of sizes has been briefly noted. Indeed, a thorough treatment of the Asian cyprinids would already be well beyond the stage of being just a single book. So, in this chapter, I have attempted to give the reader an introduction to the fish faunas and their faunistic literature for South East Asia and the adjoining regions.

However, the main focus has been an original quantitative study of the zoogeography of South East Asian cyprinids, so the region's general geography and Quaternary geological history have been included. No summary of drainage history is available for the Quaternary, so the most relevant primary literature has been used. Although it would have been interesting to examine multiple species distributions separately and determine the likelihood of certain river captures, that was not possible here. An important part of this chapter was the inclusion of a distribution table for the genera of South East Asia. I would be interested in published information that would help to fill in any missed parts of the ranges of these genera.

ACKNOWLEDGEMENTS

I am greatly indebted to the late Professor Karl Lagler, who gave me the opportunities to spend several years in Asia studying the fishes of the Mekong River and the delta of the Ganges. I also thank my wife Allison, who read the manuscript and made helpful comments. Work leading to this paper was supported by National Science Foundation grants BSR83-07102 and BSR85-16738 to me and to Donald G. Buth at the University of California, Los Angeles.

GENERIC DISTRIBUTION LIST

Distribution of genera by drainage basin: ×. present; .. absent (semicolons are placed between groups of ten to facilitate visual scanning). Some basins are subdivided. Basins (river names in italics): 1. lower Chang Jiang; 2. upper Chang Jiang; 3. Jinsha Jiang; 4. Tarim–Yarkant; 5. central Tibet; 6. Zhejiang–Fujian; 7. Taiwan; 8. Xi Jiang; 9. Hong; 10. Hainan; 11. lower Mekong; 12. middle Mekong; 13. Lancang Jiang; 14. Chao Phraya–Mae Khlong; 15. Malay Peninsula east; 16. Perak; 17. North Sumatra; 18. central Sumatra; 19. South Sumatra; 20. Java; 21. South Borneo; 22. East Borneo; 23. North Borneo; 24. South Philippines; 25. central Philippines; 26. Sarawak; 27. Kapuas; 28. Salween–Tenasserim; 29. Sittang; 30. lower Irrawaddy; 31. upper Irrawaddy; 32. Arakan coastal; 33. Meghna; 34. Surma; 35. Brahmaputra; 36. Yarlung Zangbo Jiang; 37. eastern Ganges; 38. western Ganges; 39. Mahanadi; 40. Godavari; 41. Krishna; 42. Cauvery; 43. Sri Lanka; 44. Kerala; 45. middle west coast; 46. Tapti–Narmada; 47. Kutch; 48. lower Indus; 49. Punjab–Himachal Pradesh; 50. Kashmir; 51. Kabul; 52. Baluchistan.

	No. taxa in area	1–10	11–20	21–30	31–40	41–50	51,52
Acheilognathinae							
Acanthorhodeus	14	× × × . . × . × × . :	× . . ×				
Acheilognathus	3	× × . . × . × .					
Paracheilognathus	3	× × . . . × × × × .					
Pararhodeus	3	× . . . . . . × .					
Pseudoperilampus	2	× . . . × . × × × ;					
Rhodeus	3	× × . . . × × × × × ;					
Gobioninae							
Sarcocheilichthyini							
Coreius	3	× × × . . . × .					
Gnathopogon	5	× × × . . . × .					
Pseudorasbora	3	× × × . . × × × × .					
Sarcocheilichthys	8	× × × . . × . × × × ;					

Generic distribution list (*Continued*)

	No. taxa in area	Drainage basin number					
		1–10	11–20	21–30	31–40	41–50	51.52
Gobionini							
Abbottina	1	x x x . . x					
Acanthogobio	1	x x					
Belligobio	2	x x x . . x					
Gobio (Gobio)	3	x x					
Gobiobotia	16	x x x . . x x x x x					
Hemibarbus	4	x x x . . x x x x x					
Microphysogobio	22	x x x . . x x x x x x					
Paracanthobrama	2	x x x . . x					
Pseudogobio	2	x . . . x . x					
Rhinogobio	4	x x x . . x . . x					
Saurogobio	7	x x x . . x . x x x					
Squalidus	9	x x . . x x x x x x					
Leuciscinae							
Chondrostomini							
Acanthobrama	1	x x					
Distoechodon	3	x x x . x x x					
Hypophthalmichthys	3	x x . . x x					
Plagiognathops	1	x x . . x					
Rutilus	1	x					
Xenocyprioides	1	 x					
Xenocypris	5	x x x . x x x					

Leuciscini		
Lagowskiella	1	× ×
Rhynchocypris	1	× . . . . ×
Aspiini		
Elopichthys	1	× × . . . × ×
Luciobrama	1	× × . . . ×
Ochetobius	1	× × . . . × ×
Alburninae		
Hemiculter	3	× × . . × × × × . × ×
Hemicultrella	22	. × × . × . × × × × . ×
Longiculter	1	. . . . . ×
Paralaubuca	4	. . . . . × × × × ×
Pseudohemiculter	4	× × × . × . × × × ×
Pseudolaubuca	4	× × . . × . × × ×
Rasborinus	2	. . × × × × × ×
Cultrinae		
Ancherythroculter	3	. × . . . ×
Chanodichthys	9	× × × . × × × × ×
Culter	1	× × . × × . ×
Hainania	1	. . × ×
Megalobrama	4	× × . × × × × ×
Parabramis	1	× × . × . × . ×
Sinibrama	5	× × . × × × ×
Toxabramis	3	× . . × . × ×

Generic distribution list (*Continued*)

	No. taxa in area	Drainage basin number					
		1–10	11–20	21–30	31–40	41–50	51.52
Danioninae							
Oxygastrini							
Aspidoparia	2				· · x x x x · · · x	· · · · x ·	x x
Barilius	7				· x x x x x x	x x x x x x	x x
Luciosoma	6		· x x x x x x	· · x ·	·	·	
Macrochirichthys	1		· · x x x x x ·	· · x ·	·	·	
Opsariichthys	1	x x · · · x x x x ·		· · x x · x		·	·
Opsarius	19		· x · x x x x	x x · · x x x x x	x x x x x	x x
Oxygaster	2		· x · x x x x x x x ·	· x ·	·	·	
Parachela	7		· · x x x x x x · x ·	· x · x x x x ·	·	·	
Parazacco	2		· x x x x ·	· ·	·	·	
Raiamas	3		· · x x x x	· x x x ·	· x x x ·	x x x ·	
Salmostoma	14			x x x · x x x · x x	x x x x x · x x	x x x x x x x	x x
Securicula	1				· x ·	· x x x x ·	x x
Zacco	8	x x x · x x x x x x ·		·	·	·	·
Danionini							
Amblypharyngodon	4				· x x x x x x x x	x x x x x x · x ·	
Aphyocypris	3	x x · · ·			· x ·	·	x
Bengala	1				· x x x x ·	·	·
Brachydanio	10		· x x x x x ·		x x x x x x ·	· · x · ·	·
Candidia	1	· · · x ·			·	·	·
Chela	7		· x · x x x ·		x x x · · x ·	· x ·	x x
Danio	16		· · x · x x x ·	x x x x x x · x	x · x x x x x x	x · x x x x x	x x

Taxon	
Danionella	1
Esomus	6
Gobiocypris	1
Horadandia	1
Inlecypris	1
Leptobarbus	4
Microrasbora	2
Nematabramis	4
Nicholsicypris	1
Pectenocypris	2
Rasbora	64
Rasborichthys	1
Tanichthys	1
Thryssocypris	2
Yaoshanicus	2
Cyprininae	
Squaliobarbini	
Atrilinea	2
Ctenopharyngodon	1
mylopharyngodon	1
Squaliobarbus	1
Cyprinini	
Cyprini	
Carassioides	1
Carassius	1
Catlocarpio	1
Cyprinus (Mesocyprinus)	5

Generic distribution list (Continued)

	No. taxa in area	Drainage basin number					
		1–10	11–20	21–30	31–40	41–50	51,52
Cyprinus (Cyprinus)	16	x x x x · x x x x x x : · x · · · · · · · x ·
Laichowcypris	1	· · · · · x ·
Procypris	2	· x x · · x x ·
Thynnichthys	4	· · · · · : x x · x x x x · · x · · · · · · · · · · · · · · · · · · x : x · · · · · · · · · · · · · · · ·
Barbus (inc. sedis)	1	· · · · · · · : · x · · · · · · · · · · · · · ·
Tores							
Naziritor	1	· ·
Neolissochilus	19	· · · x · · x x x x x x x x · x : · · x x x x x : x · x x x x · · · x x · · · x · · · · · · · · · · · · ·
Probarbus	1	· · · · · · · : x · x x ·
Spinibarbus	7	x x x · x x x x x : ·
Tor	17	· · · · · : x x x x x x x x x : x x x · · x x x x x x x x x x · x x x x x x x x x · x · x x x · · : x x
Systomini							
Osteobramae							
Albulichthys	1	· · · · · · · : x · · · · x · · · · · · x ·
Amblyrhynchichthys	1	· · · · · : x x · x x · · · · · · · x ·
Balantiocheilos	1	· · · · · : x x · x · · · · · · · · x ·
Cosmochilus	3	· · · · · : x x x x · · · x x · · · · · · · x x ·
Cyclocheilichthys	9	· · · · · : x x · x x x x x x x x x x : x x x x x x x : x ·
Mystacoleucus	6	· · · · · : x x x x x x x x x : · · · x x ·
Puntioplites	5	· · · · · : x x x x x x · x · · · · x ·
Rohtee	10	· · · · · : · · · · · · · · · · : x x x x x x x x x x x x x x x x : x x · x · x · · x · x · x x x : x ·

Rohteichthys	1
Sikukia	2
Poropuntii	
Acrossocheilus	24
Barbodes	8
Chagunius	3
Discherodontus	3
Folifer	3
Hypselobarbus	12
new genus	12
Onychostoma	20
Percocypris	3
Poropuntius	32
Scaphognathops	2
Systomi	
Cephalokompsus	1
Hampala	5
Mandibularca	1
Oreichthys	4
Ospatulus	2
Puntius	109
Sawbwa	1
Spratellicypris	1

Generic distribution list (Continued)

	No. taxa in area	Drainage basin number					
		1–10	11–20	21–30	31–40	41–50	51.52
Oreinini							
Aspiorhynchus	1	. . x	. . . .	. . . .	. . . .	. . . .	. : . .
Chuanchia	1	. x	. . . .	. . . .	. . . .	. . . .	. : . .
Diptychus (Diptychus)	1	. . . x	. . . .	. . . .	. . . .	. . . .	. : . .
D. (Gymnodiptychus)	2	. x x x	. . . .	. . . .	. . . .	. . . .	x : . .
D. (Ptychobarbus)	5	. x x	. . . . x	. . . .	. . . . . x	. . . .	x : . .
Gymnocypris (Gymnocypris)	12	. x x x x	. . x	. . . .	. x x x	. . . .	x : . .
G. (Oxygymnocypris)	1	. . . .	. . . .	. . . .	. x	. . . .	. : . .
Herzensteinia	1	. x x . x	. . . .	. . . .	. . . .	. . . .	. : . .
Lepidopygopsis	1	. . . .	. . . .	. . . .	. . . .	. . . . . . x . . .	. : . .
Luciocyprinus	2	. x . . . x x . . .	. . . . x	. . . .	. . . .	. . . .	. : . .
Oreinus	24	x x x x . . x . . .	. . . . x	. . . . . . x . x .	. x x . x x	. . . .	x x x x
Platypharodon	1	. x	. . . .	. . . .	. . . .	. . . .	. : . .
Schizopygopsis	11	. x x x x x	. . . .	. . . . . x	. . . x	. . . .	x : x x
Schizothorax	36	. x x x	. . . . x	. . . . . x	. x x x x x	. . . . . . x . . .	x : x x
Sinocyclocheilus	12	. x x	. . x x	. . . .	. . . . x	. . . .	. : . .
Tetrostichodon	1	. . . .	. . . .	. . . . . . x . . .	. . . . . x	. . . .	. : . .
Semiplotini							
Cyprinion	4	. . . .	. . . .	. . . .	. . . .	. . . .	x x x : x x
Kantaka	1	. . . .	. . . .	. . . .	. . . .	. . . . . . x . . .	. : . .
Osteochilichthys	3	. . . .	. . . .	. . . .	. . . .	x : x x . x x . . .	. : . .
Scaphiodonichthys	3	. . . . . x . x x x	. . . .	. . . . x	. . . .	. . . .	. : . .

Semiplotus	2
Labeonini	
Labeones	
Bangana	23
Barbichthys	1
Cirrhinus	10
Dangila	12
Gilbelion	1
Henicorhynchus	4
Labeo	29
Lobocheilus	11
Neorohita	1
Osteochilus	26
Ptychidio	2
Garrae	
Crossocheilus	10
Discogobio	3
Epalzeorhynchos	6
Garra	38
Mekongina	1
Paracrossocheilus	2
Parasinilabeo	1
Parapsilorhynchus	2
Placocheilus	2
Rectoris	3
Semilabeo	3
Sinocrossocheilus	2
Typhlobarbus	1

REFERENCES

Agassiz, J. L. R. (1855) Synopsis of the ichthyological faunà of the Pacific slope of North America, chiefly from the collection made by the expedition under the command of Capt. C. Wilkes, with recent additions and comparisons with eastern types. *Am. J. Sci.*, (2), **19**, 71–99.

Alfred, E. R. (1966) The fresh-water fishes of Singapore. *Zool. Verh., Leiden*, **78**, 1–68.

Annandale, N. (1918) Fish and fisheries in the Inle Lake. *Rec. Indian Mus.*, **14**, 33–64.

Anonymous (1976) *The fishes of the Yangtze River*, Science Press, Beijing, 278 pp. (in Chinese)

Anonymous (1985) *International Code of Zoological Nomenclature*, adopted by the 20th General Assembly of the International Union of Biological Sciences, International Trust for Zoological Nomenclature in association with British Museum (Natural History) London, University of California Press, Berkeley and Los Angeles, 338 pp.

Arai, R. (1982) A chromosomal study on two cyprinid fishes, *Acrossocheilus labiatus* and *Pseudorasbora pumila pumila*, with notes on Eurasian cyprinids and their karyotypes. *Bull. Natn. Sci. Mus., Tokyo*, **8A** (3), 131–52.

Bănărescu, P. (1972) The zoogeographical position of the East Asian fresh-water fish fauna. *Rev. roum. Biol. (Zool.)*, **17** (5), 315–23.

Bănărescu, P. and Nalbant, T. (1973) Pisces, Teleostei, Cyprinidae (Gobioninae). *Tierreich*, **93**, 1–304.

Batchelor, B. C. (1979) Discontinuously rising Late Cenozoic eustatic sea-levels, with special reference to Sundaland, Southeast Asia. *Geologie Mijnb.*, **58**, 1–20.

Beaufort, L. F. de (1951) *Zoogeography of the Land and Inland Waters*, Sidgwick and Jackson, London, 208 pp.

Bender, F. (1983) *Geology of Burma*. Beiträge zur regionalen Geologie der Erde, Vol. 16, Gebrüder Bonträger, Berlin, 293 pp.

Berg, L. S. (1909) Fishes of the Amur basin. *Zap. Akad. Nauk. SSSR*, **24**(9), 270 pp. (in Russian)

Berg, L. S. (1964) *Freshwater Fishes of the USSR and Adjacent Countries*. II, Israel Prog. Sci. Transl., Jerusalem, 496 pp. (English translation of the 1949 edition)

Bishop, J. E. (1973) Limnology of a small Malayan river Sungai Gombak. *Monographiae biol.*, **22**, 1–485.

Blache, J. and Goossens, J. (1954) Monographie pisicole d'une zone de pêche au Cambodge. *Cybium*, **8**, 1–49.

Bleeker, P. (1858) Zesde bijdrage tot de kennis der vischfauna van Sumatra. Visschen van Padang, Troessan, Priaman, Siboga en Palembang. *Act. Soc. Sci. Indo–Neerl.*, **3**, 1–50.

Bleeker, P. (1859–60) Conspectus systematis cyprinorum. *Natuurk. Tijdschr. Ned.–Indië*, **20**, 421–41.

Bleeker, P. (1860a) Ordo Cyprini: karpers. *Act. Soc. Sci. Indo–Neerl.*, **7**, 1–492.

Bleeker, P. (1860b) Achste bijdrage tot de kennis der vischfauna van Sumatra. Visschen van Benkoelen, Priaman, Tandjong, Palembang en Djambi. *Act. Soc. Sci. Indo–Neerl.*, **8**, 1–88.

Bleeker, P. (1863a) Systema cyprinoideorum revisum. *Neder. Tijdschr. Dierk.*, **1**, 187–218.

Bleeker, P. (1863b) *Atlas Ichthyologique des Indes Orientales Néérlandaises*, Vol. III, *Cyprins*, De Breuk and Smits, Leiden, 148 pp.

Blyth, E. (1860) Report on some fishes received from the Sitang River and its tributary streams, Tenasserim provinces. *J. Asiat. Soc. Beng.*, **29**, 138–74.

Bonaparte, C. L. (1845) Catalogo metodico dei pesci Europei. *Atti. Sci. Ital.*, **1845**, 1–95.

Breder, C. M. and Rosen, D. E. (1966) *Modes of Reproduction in Fishes*, Natural History Press, Garden City, NY, 941 pp.

Brittan, M. R. (1954) A revision of the Indo–Malayan fresh-water fish genus *Rasbora*. *Monogr. Inst. Sci. Tech. Manila*, **3**, 1–224.

Cao, W.-X., Chen, Y.-Y., Wu, Y.-F. and Zhu, S. Q. (1981) Origin and evolution of schizothoracine fishes in relation to the upheaval of Qinghai-Xizang Plateau, in *Geological and Ecological Studies of Qinghai-Xizong Plateau*, Vol. 2 (ed. D. S. Liu), Science Press, Beijing, pp. 1053–60.

Carbonnel, J. P. (1963) Vitesse d'accumulation des sédiments récents du Grand Lac du Cambodge d'après le carbone 14. Corrélation stratigraphiques et morphologiques. *C. r. hebd. Séanc. Acad. Sci., Paris*, **257**, 2514–16.

Carbonnel, J. P. (1972) Le Quarternaire cambodgien – structure et stratigraphie, *Mém. O.R.S.T.O.M.*, **60**, 1–252.

Chang, H. W. (1944) Notes on the fishes of western Szechuan and eastern Sikang. *Sinensia, Nanking*, **15**, 27–60.

Chaodumrong, P. *et al.* (1983) A review of the Tertiary sedimentary rocks of Thailand, *Proc. Workshop Stratigraphic Correlation Thailand and Malaya*, Vol. 1 (ed. P. Nutalaya), pp. 159–87.

Chen, J.-X., Xu, T.-Q., Fang, S.-M., Song, S.-L., and Wang, X.-T. (1986) Fish fauna in Qin Ling mountain area and its zoogeographical characteristics. *Trans. Chinese Ichthy. Soc.*, **5**, 65–85. (in Chinese with English abstract)

Chen, X.-L., Yue, P.-Q. and Lin, R.-D. (1984) Major groups within the family Cyprinidae and their phylogenetic relationships. *Acta Zootaxonomica Sinica*, **9**, 424–40.

Chen, X.-Y. (1987a) Studies on the skeleton of leuciscine fishes of China, with particular reference to its significance in taxonomy. *Acta Zootaxonomica Sinica*, **12**, 311–22. (in Chinese with English summary)

Chen, X.-Y. (1987b) Studies on the phylogenetic relationships of Chinese leuciscine fishes (Pisces, Cypriniformes). *Acta Zootaxonomica Sinica*, **12**, 427–39. (in Chinese with English summary)

Cheng, P.-S., *et al.* (1981) *The Freshwater Fishes of Guangxi*, People Publ., Guangxi, 251 pp. (in Chinese)

Chevey, P. and Lemasson, J. (1937) Contribution à l'étude des poissons des eaux douces tonkinoises. *Notes Inst. Océan. Indochine*, **33**, 1–183.

Chu, X.-L. (1986) Ichthyofauna and its geographical subdivision in Yunnan, China, in *Indo–Pacific Fish Biology:Proc. Second Int. Conf. Indo–Pac. Fishes, Tokyo*, (eds. T. Uyeno, R. Arai, T. Taniuchi and K. Matsuura), Ichthyological Society of Japan, Tokyo, pp. 471–6.

Chu, Y.-T. (1935) Comparative studies on the scales and on the pharyngeals and their teeth in Chinese cyprinids, with particular reference to taxonomy and evolution. *Biol. Bull. St. John's Univ., Shanghai*, **2**, 1–225.

Chu, Y.-T. (1984) *The Fishes of Fujian Province, Part I*, Fujian Science and Technology Press, Fuzhou, 528 pp. (in Chinese)

Chu, Y.-T. (1985) *The Fishes of Fujian Province. Part II*, Fujian Science and Technology Press, Fuzhou, 700 pp. (in Chinese with English summary)

Chyung, M. K. (1961) *Illustrated Encyclopedia: the Fauna of Korea (2), Fishes*, Central Book Publishing Co., Seoul, Korea, 861 pp. (in Korean with English preface and marine ecology summary)

Datta, A.K. and Majumdar, N. (1970) Fauna of Rajasthan, India. Part 7. Fishes. *Rec. Zool. Surv. India*, **62**, 63–10C.

Day, F. E. (1865) *The Fishes of Malabar*, Quaritch, London, 293 pp.

Day, F. E. (1875–78) *The Fishes of India; Being a Natural History of the Fishes Known to Inhabit the Seas and Fresh Waters of India, Burma and Ceylon*, Text and atlas in 4 parts, Taylor and Francis, London, 78 pp.

Day, F. E. (1876) On the fishes of Yarkand. *Proc. zool. Soc. Lond.*, **1876**, 781–807.

Day, F. E. (1878) *Scientific Results of the Second Yarkand Mission. Ichthyology.* Calcutta, pp. 1–25.

Day, F. E. and Buchanan (Hamilton), F. (1877) The fish and fisheries of Bengal, in *A Statistical Account of Bengal*, Vol. 20 (ed. W. W. Hunter), Trabrier, London, pp. 1–120.

Deraniyagala, P. E. P. (1952) *A Coloured Atlas of Some Vertebrates from Ceylon, 1, Fishes*, Ceylon Government Press, Colombo, 149 pp.

De Witt, H. (1960) A contribution to the ichthyology of Nepal. *Stanford ichthyol. Bull.*, **7**(4), 63–88.

Fang, P. W. (1936) On some schizothoracid fishes from western China preserved in the National Research Institute of Biology, Academia Sinica. *Sinensia, Nanking*, **7**, 421–58.

Fily, M. and D'Aubenton, F. (1966) *Cambodia, Report of Fisheries Technology in the Great Lake and the Tonle Sap, 1962–1963* [English version]. Ministry of Foreign Affairs, Republic of France, 509 pp.

Fontaine, H. and Workman, D. R. (1978) Review of the geology and mineral resources of Kampuchea, Laos and Vietnam, in *Proc. Third Regional Conf. Geology Mineral Resources Southeast Asia, Bangkok* (ed. P. Nutalaya), Asian Inst. Technology, Bangkok, pp. 541–603.

Fowler, H. W. (1905) Some fishes from Borneo. *Proc. Acad. nat. Sci. Philad.*, **57**, 455–523.

Fowler, H. W. (1937) Zoological results of the third de Schauensee Siamese Expedition. Part 8. Fishes obtained in 1936. *Proc. Acad. nat. Sci. Philad.*, **89**, 125–264.

Fowler, H. W. (1941) Contributions to the biology of the Philippine Archipelago and adjacent regions. *Bull. U.S. Natn. Mus.*, **100** (13), 1–879.

Gaur, R. and Kotlia, P. S. (1987) Palaeontology, age, palaeoenvironment and palaeoecology of the Karewa inter-montane basin of Kashmir (Jammu and Kashmir, India). *Riv. ital. Paleontol. Stratigr.* **93**, 237–50.

Geisler, R., Schmidt, G. W. and Sookvibul, S. (1979) Diversity and biomass of fishes in three streams typical of Thailand. *Int. Rev. ges Hydrobiol.*, **64**, 673–97.

George, W. (1981) Wallace and his line, in *Wallace's Line and Plate Tectonics* (ed. T. C. Whitmore) (*Oxford Monographs on Biogeography*), Clarendon Press, Oxford, pp. 3–8.

Girard, C. (1858) *Fishes of North America, Observed on a Survey for a Railroad Route from the Mississippi River ro the Pacific Ocean*, War Department, Washington, 400 pp.

Gosline, W. A. (1974) Certain lateral-line canals of the head in cyprinid fishes, with particular reference to the derivation of the North American forms. *Jap. J. Ichthyol.*, **21**(1), 9–15.

Gosline, W. A. (1975) The cyprinid dermosphenotic and the subfamily Rasborinae. *Occ. Pap. Mus. Zool. Univ. Mich.*, **673**, 1–13.

Gosline, W. A. (1978) Unbranched dorsal-fin rays and subfamily classification in the fish family Cyprinidae. *Occ. Pap. Mus. Zool. Univ. Mich.*, **684**, 1–21.

Günther, A. (1868) *Catalogue of the Fishes in the British Museum*, London, 512 pp.

Günther, A. (1876) Contributions to our knowledge of the fish-fauna of the Tertiary deposits of the highlands of Padang, Sumatra. *Geol. Mag.*, (2), **3**, 433–40.

Hamilton, F. (1822) *An Account of the Fishes Found in the River Ganges and its Branches*, Archibald Constable and Co. Edinburgh, and London, 405 pp.

Heckel, J. J. (1843) Abbildungen und Beschreibungen der Fische Syriens nebst einer neuen Classification und Characteristik sämmtlicher Gattungen der Cyprinen, in *Reisen in Europa, Asien und Africa, mit besonderer Rücksicht auf die naturwissenschaftlichen Verhältnisse der betreffenden Länder unternommen in den Jahren 1835 bit 1841*, etc., (ed. J. V. Russegger), Vol. 1, Part 2, pp. 993–1099.

Heckman, C. W. (1979) Rice field ecology in northeastern Thailand. *Monographiae biol.*, 1–216.

Herzenstein, S. M. (1888) Fische. Wissenschaftliche Resultate der von N. M. Przewalski nach Central-Asien unternommenen Reisen. *Zool. Theil.*, **3** (2), 1–262.

Hora, S. L. and Mukerji, D. D. (1934a) Notes on fishes in the Indian Museum. XXII. On a collection of fish from the S. Shan States and the Pegu Yomas, Burma. *Rec. Indian Mus.*, **36**, 123–38.

Hora, S. L. and Mukerji, D. D. (1934b) Notes on fishes in the Indian Museum. XXIII. On a collection of fish from the S. Shan States, Burma. *Rec. Indian Mus.*, **36**, 353–70.

Hosoya, K. (1986) Interrelationships of the Gobioninae, in *Indo-Pacific Fish Biology: Proc. Second Int. Conf. Indo-Pac Fishes, Tokyo*, (eds. T. Uyeno et al.), pp. 484–501.

Howes, G. J. (1978) The anatomy and relationships of the cyprinid fish *Luciobrama macrocephalus* (Lacepède). *Bull. Br. Mus. nat. Hist. (Zool.)*, **34** (1), 1–64.

Howes, G. J. (1979) Notes on the anatomy of *Macrochirichthys macrochirus* (Valenciennes), 1844, with comments on the Cultrinae (Pisces, Cyprinidae). *Bull. Br. Mus. nat. Hist. (Zool.)*, **36** (3), 147–200.

Howes, G. J. (1980) The anatomy, phylogeny and classification of the bariliine cyprinid fishes. *Bull. Br. Mus. nat. Hist. (Zool.)*, **37** (3), 129–98.

Howes, G. J. (1981) Anatomy and phylogeny of the Chinese major carps *Ctenopharyngodon* Steind., 1866 and *Hypophthalmichthys* Blkr., 1860. *Bull. Br. Mus. nat. Hist. (Zool.)*, **41** (1), 1–52.

Howes, G. J. (1982) Anatomy and evolution of the jaws in the semiplotine carps with a review of the genus *Cyprinion* Heckel, 1843 (Teleostei: Cyprinidae). *Bull. Br. Mus. nat. Hist. (Zool.)*, **42** (4), 299–335.

Howes, G. J. (1983) Additional notes on bariliine cyprinid fishes. *Bull. Br. Mus. nat. Hist. (Zool.)*, **45** (2), 95–101.

Howes, G. J. (1984) Phyletics and biogeography of the aspinine cyprinid fishes. *Bull. Br. Mus. nat. Hist. (Zool.)*, **47** (5), 283–303.

Howes, G. J. (1985) A revised synonymy of the minnow genus *Phoxinus* Rafinesque, 1820 (Teleostei: Cyprinidae) with comments on its relationships and distribution. *Bull. Br. Mus. nat. Hist. (Zool.)*, **48** (1), 57–74.

Howes, G. J. (1987) The phylogenetic position of the Yugoslavian cyprinid fish genus *Aulopyge* Heckel, 1841, with an appraisal of the genus *Barbus* Cuvier & Cloquet, 1816 and the subfamily Cyprininae. *Bull. Br. Mus. nat. Hist. (Zool.)*, **52** (5), 165–96.

Imaki, A., Kawamoto, A. and Suzuki, A. (1978) *A List of Freshwater Fishes Collected from the Kapuas River, West Kalimantan, Indonesia*, Inst. Breeding Res., Tokyo Univ. Agric., 52 pp.

Inger, R. F. (1955) Ecological notes on the fish fauna of a coastal drainage of North Borneo. *Fieldiana, Zool.*, **37**, 47–90.

Inger, R. F. and Chin, P. K. (1962) The fresh-water fishes of North Borneo. *Fieldiana, Zool*, **45**, 1–268.

Jayaram, K. C. (1976) Index Horana: An index to the scientific fish names occurring in all the publications of the late Dr. Sunder Lal Hora. *Rec. Zool. Zurv. India, Misc. Publs. Occ. Pap.*, **1**, 191 pp.

Jayaram, K. C. (1981) *The Freshwater Fishes of India, Pakistan, Bangladesh, Burma and Sri Lanka – a Handbook*, Zoological Survey of India, Calcutta, 475 pp.

Jayaram, K. C., Venkateswarlu, T. and Ragunathan, M. B. (1982) A survey of the Cauvery River system with a major account of its fauna. *Rec. Zool. Surv. India, Misc. Publs. Occ. Pap.*, **36**, 1–115.

Jhingran, V. G. (1975) *Fish and Fisheries of India*, Hindustan Publ., Delhi, 954 pp.

Job, T. J., David, A. and Das, K. N. (1955) Fish and fisheries of the Mahanadi in relation to the Hirakud Dam. *Indian J. Fish.*, **2**, 1–36.

Johnsen, P. (1963–64) Notes on fishes along the river Kwai Noi in western Thailand. *Siam Soc. nat. Hist. Bull.*, **20** (3–4), 143–54, 257–63, 265–8.

Johnson, D. S. (1967) Distributional patterns in Malayan freshwater fish. *Ecology*, **48**, 722–30.

Kafuku, T. (1958) Speciation in cyprinid fishes on the basis of intestinal differentiation, with some references to that among catostomids. *Bull. Freshwat. Fish. Res. Lab., Tokyo*, **8**, 45–78.

Kafuku, T. (1975). An ontogenetical study of intestinal coiling pattern in Indian carps. *Bull. Freshwat. Fish. Res. Lab., Tokyo*, **27**, 1–19.

Kafuku, T. (1986) Distribution and phylogeny of cyprinids in the Indo-Pacific based on intestinal coiling patterns. in *Indo-Pacific Fish Biology: Proc. Second Int. Conf. Indo-Pac. Fishes, Tokyo*, (eds. T. Uyeno *et al.*), pp. 477–9.

Karaman, M. S. (1971) Susswasserfische der Turkei, 8 Teil. Revision der Barben Europas, Vorderasiens, und Nordafrikas. *Mitt. Hamb. zool. Mus. Inst.*, **67**, 157–254.

Kessler, K. T. (1876) Descriptions of fishes collected by Col. Przewalski in Mongolia, in Przewalski, N., *Mongolia i Strana Tangutov*, Vol. 2, No. 4, pp. 1–36. (in Russian)

Kessler, K. T. (1879) Beiträge zur Ichthyologie von Central-Asien. *Bull. Acad. Sci. St Petersbourg*, **25**, 282–310.

Kottelat, M. (1985) Fresh-water fishes of Kampuchea, a provisory annotated check-list. *Hydrobiologia*, **121**, 249–79.

Krempf, A. and Chevey, P. (1934) The continental shelf of French Indo-China and the relationship which formerly existed between Indo-China and the East Indies. *Proc. Fifth Pan Pacific Sci. Cong.*, **5**, 849–52.

Kryzanowsky, S. G. (1947) Sistema semejstra karpovych ryb (Cyprinidae). *Zool. Zh.*, **26**(1), 53–64.

Lagler, K. F. (1976) *Fisheries and Integrated Mekong River Basin Development*, Univ. Michigan School of Nat. Res., Ann Arbor (executive volume), 367 pp.

Legendre, L. and Legendre, P. (1983) *Numerical Ecology*, Elsevier, NY, 419 pp.

Lewis, W. M. (1978) A compositional, phytogeographical and elementary structural analysis of the phytoplankton in a tropical lake: Lake Lanao, Philippines. *J. Ecol.*, **66**, 213–66.

Li, S.-S. (1982) The fish fauna and its differentiation in the upland lakes of Yunnan. *Acta zool. sin.*, **28** (2), 169–76. (in Chinese with English abstract)

Li, S.-Z. (1981) *Studies on Zoogeographical Divisions for Freshwater Fishes of China*, Science Press, Beijing, 292 pp. (in Chinese)

Li, S.-Z., Tai, T.-Y., Chang, S.-Y, Ma, K.-C., Ho, C.-W. and Kao, S.-T. (1966) Notes on a collection of fishes from north Sinkiang, China. *Acta zool. sin.*, **18** (1), 41–56. (in Chinese with English summary)

Lohberger, K. (1929) Weitere Fische aus dem Thian-Schan. *Sber. Akad. Wiss. Wien, Abt. 1*, **138**, 335–45.

Lowe-McConnell, R. H. (1975) *Fish Communities in Tropical Freshwaters: Their Distribution, Ecology and Evolution*, Longman, London, 337 pp.

Lowe-McConnell, R. H. (1978) *Ecological Studies in Tropical Fish Communities*, Cambridge Univ. Press, Cambridge, 382 pp.

M'Clelland, J. M. (1838) Observations on six new species of Cyprinidae, with an outline of a new classification of the family. *J. Asiat. Soc. Beng.*, **7**, 941–7.

M'Clelland, J. M. (1839) Indian Cyprinidae. *Asiatic Researches, Calcutta*, **19**, 217–468.

Mai, D. Y. (1978) *Identification of the Freshwater Fishes of the North of Vietnam*, Hanoi, 339 pp. (in Vietnamese)

Mai, D. Y. (1985) Species composition and distribution of the freshwater fish fauna of the north of Vietnam. *Hydrobiologia*, **121**, 281–6.

Mai, D. Y. and Nguyen, V. T. (1988) Species composition and distribution of the freshwater fish fauna of southern Vietnam. *Hydrobiologia*, **160**, 45–51.

Matthes, H. (1963) A comparative study on the feeding mechanism of some African Cyprinidae (Pisces, Cypriniformes). *Bijdr. Dierk.*, **33**, 3–35.

Meng, Q.-W. (1985) A comparative study of the neurocrania of Chinese cyprinid fishes. *Trans. Chinese Ichthy. Soc.*, **4**, 13–39. (in Chinese with English summary)

Menon, A. G. K. (1962) A distributional list of the fishes of the Himalayas. *J. zool. Soc. India*, **14** (1 + 2), 23–32.

Menon, A. G. K. (1966) On a collection of fish from the Coromandel coast of India including Pondicherry and Karaikkal areas. *Rec. Indian Mus.*, **59**, 369–404.

Menon, A. G. K. (1974) *A check-list of the Fishes of the Himalayan and the Indo-Gangetic Plains*, Inland Fish. Soc. India, Spec. Publ. **1**, 136 pp.

Mirza, M. R. (1975) Freshwater fishes and zoogeography of Pakistan. *Bijdr. Dierk.*, **45** (2), 143–80.

Mirza, M. R. (1978) History of ichthyology in Pakistan. *Biologia, Lahore*, **24**, 305–48.

Mizuno, T. and Furtado, J. I. (1982) Ecological notes on fishes, in *Tasek Bera: The Ecology of a Freshwater Swamp* (eds J. Furtado and S. Mori), *Monographiae biol.*, **47**, 321–54.

Mizuno, T. and Mori, S. (1970) Preliminary hydrobiological survey of some Southeast Asian inland waters. *Biol. J. Linn. Soc.*, **2**, 77–117.

Mohsin, A. K. M. and Ambak, M. A. (1983) *Freshwater Fishes of Peninsular Malaysia*, Penerbit Universiti Pertanian Malaysia, Kuala Lumpur, 284 pp.

Molengraaff, G. A. F. and Weber, M. (1921) On the relation between the Pleistocene glacial period and the origin of the Sunda Sea (Java and South China Sea) and its influence on the distribution of coral reefs and on the land and freshwater fauna. *Kon. Akad. Wet. Amsterdam*, **23**, 395–439.

Mukerji, D. D. (1932) On a collection of fish from lower Burma. *Rec. Indian Mus.*, **34**, 281–6.

Mukerji, D. D. (1933) Report on Burmese fishes collected by Lt. Col. R. W. Burton from the tributary streams of the Mali Hka river of the Myitkyina district (upper Burma). Part 1. *J. Bombay nat. Hist. Soc.*, **36**, 812–31.

Mukerji, D. D. (1934) Report on Burmese fishes collected by Lt. Col. R. W. Burton from the tributary streams of the Mali Hka river of the Myitkyina district (upper Burma). Part 2. *J. Bombay nat. Hist. Soc.*, **37**, 38–80.

Myers, G. S. (1960) The endemic fish fauna of Lake Lanao, and the evolution of higher taxonomic categories. *Evolution*, **14**, 323–33.

Nakajima, T. (1986) Pliocene cyprinid pharyngeal teeth from Japan and East Asia Neogene cyprinid zoogeography, in *Indo-Pacific Fish Biology: Proc. Second Int. Conf. Indo-Pac. Fishes, Tokyo*, (eds T. Uyeno *et al.*), pp. 502–13.

Nikolsky, G. V. (1954) *Special Ichthyology*, Sovetskaya Nauka, Moscow, 456 pp. (in Russian)

Ochiai, A. (1957) Zoogeographic studies on the soleoid fishes found in Japan and its neighboring regions. *Bull. Jap. Soc. scient. Fish.*, **22**, 526–30.

Okada, Y. (1960) Studies on the freshwater fishes of Japan. II. Special part. *J. Fac. Fish. pref. Univ. Mie-Tsu*, **4**, 267–588.

Patra, R. W. R. and Azadi, M. A. (1985) Hydrological conditions influencing the spawning of major carps in the Halda River, Chittagong, Bangladesh. *Bangladesh J. Zool.*, **13** (2), 63–72.

Pillai, R. S. and Yazdani, G. M. (1977) Fish fauna of the Garo Hills, Meghalaya (India). *Rec. Zool. Surv. India*, **72**, 1–22.

Popta, C. M. L. (1906) Résultats ichthyologiques des voyages scientifiques de Monsieur le Professeur Dr. A. W. Nieuwenhuis dans le centre de Bornéo (1898 et 1900). *Notes Leyden Mus.*, **27**, 1–304.

Prashad, B. and Mukerji, D. D. (1929) The fish of the Indawgyi Lake and streams of the Myitkyina district (upper Burma). *Rec. Indian Mus.* **31** (3), 161–223.

Rafinesque–Schmaltz, C. S. (1815) *Analyse de la Nature, ou Tableau de l'Univers et des Corps Organisés*, Palermo, 224 pp.

Rahman, A. K. A. (1975) A check list of the freshwater bony fishes of Bangladesh. *Bull. Chandpur Freshwater Fish. Sta.*, **1**, 1–18.

Rainboth, W. J., Lagler, K. F. and Sontirat, S. (1976) *Maps of Freshwater Fish Distribution in the Lower Mekong Basin*. Mekong Basinwide Fishery Studies, Univ. Michigan School of Nat. Res./Mekong Committee Working Document No. 31, Mekong Secretariat, 406 pp.

Ramaswami, L. S. (1955a) Skeleton of cyprinoid fishes in relation to phylogenetic studies: 6. The skull and Weberian apparatus of the subfamily Gobioninae (Cyprinidae). *Acta zool., Stockh.*, **36** (3), 199–242.

Ramaswami, L. S. (1955b) Skeleton of cyprinoid fishes in relation to phylogenetic studies: 7. The skull and Weberian apparatus of the subfamily Cyprininae (Cyprinidae). *Acta zool., Stockh.*, **36** (3), 199–242.

Reid, G. McG. (1980) "Explosive Speciation" of carps in Lake Lanao (Philippines) – fact or fancy? *Syst. Zool.*, **29**, 314–16.

Reid, G. McG. (1982) The form, function and phylogenetic significance of the vomero-palatine organ in cyprinid fishes. *J. nat. Hist.*, **16**, 497–510.

Reid, G. McG. (1985) A revision of the African species of *Labeo* (Pisces, Cyprinidae) and a re-definition of the genus. *Theses Zoologicae*, **6**, 1–322.

Roberts, T. R. (1982) Unculi (horny projections arising from single cells), an adaptive feature of the epidermis of ostariophysan fishes. *Zool. Scripta*, **11** (1), 55–76.

Roberts, T. R. (1986) *Danionella translucida*, a new genus and species of cyprinid fish from Burma, one of the smallest living vertebrates. *Env. Biol. Fishes*, **16**, 231–41.

Roberts, T. R. (1987) The Bornean gastromyzontine fish genera *Gastromyzon* and *Glaniopsis* (Cypriniformes, Homalopteridae), with descriptions of new species. *Proc. Calif. Acad. Sci.*, **42**, 497–524.

Roberts, T. R. (1989) The freshwater fishes of western Borneo (Kalimantan Barat, Indonesia), *California Acad. Sci.*, **14**, 1–210.

Sahni, A., Srikantia, S. V., Ganesan, T. M. and Wangdus, C. (1984) Tertiary fishes and molluscs from the Kuksho formation of the Indus group, near Nyoma, Ladakh. *J. geol. Soc. India*, **25** (II), 742–7.

Sanders, M. (1934) Die fossilen Fische der Altertiären Süsswasserablagerungen aus Mittel-Sumatra. *Verh. geol.-mijnb. Genoot. Ned. (Geol.)*, **11**, 1–144.

Sauvage, H. E. (1981) Recherches sur la faune ichthyologique de l'Asie et description d'espèces nouvelles de l'Indo-Chine. *Nouv. Archs. Mus. Hist. nat., Paris*, **4**, 123–94.

Sen, T. K. (1985) The fish fauna of Assam and the neighbouring north-eastern states of India. *Rec. Zool. Surv. India, Misc. Publ. Occ. Pap.*, **64**, 1–216.

Shrestha, J. (1981) *Fishes of Nepal*, Tribhuvan Univ., Kathmandu, 318 pp.

Smith, H. M. (1945) The freshwater fishes of Siam or Thailand. *Bull. U.S. natn. Mus.*, **188**, 1–622.

Sokal, R. R. and Sneath, P. H. A. (1963) *Principles of Numerical Taxonomy*, W. H. Freeman, San Francisco, 359 pp.

Srivastava, G. J. (1968) *Fishes of Eastern Uttar Pradesh*, Vishwavidyalaya Prakashan, Varanasi, 163 pp.

Stewart, F. H. (1911) Notes on Cyprinidae from Tibet and the Chumbi Valley, with a description of a new species of *Gymnocypris*. *Rec. Indian Mus.*, **6**, 73–92.

Suvatti, N. C. (1981) *Fishes of Thailand*, Royal Institute, Bangkok, 379 pp.

Sykes, W. H. (1839) On the fishes of the Deccan. *Proc. zool. Soc. Lond.*, **1838**, 157–65.

Sytchevskaya, E. K. (1986) Palaeogene freshwater fish fauna of the U.S.S.R and Mongolia. *Trudy Sovm. Sov.-Mongol. Paleont. Eksped.*, **29**, 1–154.

Taki, Y. (1974) *Fishes of the Lao Mekong Basin.* US Agency for International Development, Mission to Laos, 232 pp.

Taki, Y. (1975) Geographic distribution of primary freshwater fishes in four principal areas of Southeast Asia. *South East Asian Stud.* (*Kyoto Univ.*), **13** (2), 200–14.

Taki, Y. (1978) An analytical study of the fish fauna of the Mekong Basin as a biological production system in nature. *Res. Inst. Evol. Biol., Tokyo Spec. Publ.*, **1**, 77 pp.

Tan, J.-H. (1980) *The Fishes of Hunan*, Sci. Tech. Publ., Hunan, 228 pp. (in Chinese).

Tchang, T. L. (1933) The study of Chinese cyprinoid fishes. Pt 1. *Zool. Sinica*, ser. **B**, **2** (1), 1–247.

Tilak, R. (1969) A study of the freshwater and estuarine fishes of Goa. 2. Notes on fishes found within the territory of Goa. *Rec. Zool. Surv. India*, **67**, 67–120.

Tint Hlaing, U. (1967) A classified list of fishes of Burma. *Occ. Pap. Indo-Pacif. Fish. Coun.*, **67**/10, 24 pp.

Tjia, H. D. (1980) The Sunda shelf, Southeast Asia. *Z. Geomorph. N. F.* **24**, 405–27.

Tsai, C.-F., Islam, M. N., Karim, M. R., and Rahman, K. U. M. S. (1981) Spawning of major carps in the lower Halda River, Bangladesh. *Estuaries*, **4** (2), 127–38.

Tsao, W. S. and Wu, H. W. (1962) Notes on the schizothoracid fishes from western Szechuan and adjacent territory. *Acta hydrobiol. sin.*, **2**, 79–110.

Uyeno, T. (1969) Miocene cyprinid fishes from Mae Sot Basin, northwestern Thailand. *Geol. Palaeontol. Southeast Asia*, **7**, 93–6.

Uyeno, T. (1984) Summary of fossil fish records from Southeast Asia. *Geol. Palaeontol. Southeast Asia*, **25**, 305–7.

Vaas, K. F. (1952) Fisheries in the lake district along the River Kapuas in West Borneo. *Proc. Indo-Pacif. Fish. Coun.*, sec. **2**, (10), 1–10.

Vaas, K. F., Sachlan, M. and Wiraatmadja, G. (1953) On the ecology and fisheries of some inland waters along the Rivers Ogan and Komering in Southeast Sumatra. *Contr. Inland Fish. Res. Sta., Bogor* [Pember. Balai Besar Penjel. Pertau. Bogor], **3**, 1–32.

Vaillant, L. L. (1893) Contribution à l'étude de la faune ichthyologique de Bornéo. *Nouv. Archs. Mus. Hist. nat., Paris* (3), **5**, 23–114.

Vaillant, L. L. (1902) Résultats zoologiques de l'expédition scientifique Néerlandaise au Bornéo central. *Notes Leyden Mus.*, **24**, 1–166.

Valenciennes, A. (1844) in Cuvier. G. and Valenciennes, A., *Histoire Naturelle des Poissons*, Vol. 17, Paris.

Vannote, R. L., Minshall, G. W., Cummins, K. W., Sedell, J. R. and Cushing, C. E. (1980) The river continuum concept. *Can. J. Fish. aquat. Sci.*, **37**, 130–37.

Vasnetzov, V. V. (1950) Phylogenesis of the high-Asiatic cyprinid fishes (Schizothoracinae). *Trudy Inst. Morf. Zhivot.* **2**, 3–84. (in Russian)

Vinciguerra, D. (1890) Viaggio de Leonardo Fea in Birmania e regioni vicine (Pesci). *Annali Mus. civ. Stor. nat. Giacomo Doria*, **9** (2), 129–362.

Volz, W. (1907) Catalogue of the fishes of Sumatra. *Natuurk. Tijdschr. Ned.-Indië*, **66**, 35–250.

Wallace, A. R. (1863) On the physical geography of the Malay Archipelago. *J. Roy. Geog. Soc.*, **33**, 217–34.

Wallace, A. R. (1869) *The Malay Archipelago: the Land of the Orang-utan, and the Bird of Paradise. A Narrative of Travel with Studies of Man and Nature*, Macmillan, London, 2 vols., 478 and 524 pp.

Wallace, A. R. (1880) *Island Life or the Phenomena and Causes of Insular Faunas and Floras Including a Revision and Attempted Solution of the Problem of Geological Climates*, Macmillan, London, 563 pp.

Wallace, A. R. (1910) *The World of Life*, Chapman and Hall, London.

Weber, M. and de Beaufort, L. F. (1916) *The Fishes of the Indo-Australian Archipelago. 3. Ostariophysi: II. Cyprinoidea, Apodes, Synbranchi*, E. J. Brill, Leiden, 455 pp.

Welcomme, R. L. (1985) River fisheries. *F.A.O. Fish. Biol. tech. Pap.* **262**, 1–330.

Whitmore, T. C. (1985) *Tropical Rain Forests of the Far East*, 2nd edn, Oxford University Press, NY, 352 pp.

Win, K. (1971) A taxonomy of fishes of Taung Tha Man in upper Burma. *J. Life Sci., Union of Burma*, **4**, 39–63.

Workman, D. R. (1977) Geology of Laos, Cambodia, South Vietnam and the eastern part of Thailand. *Overseas Geol. Miner. Resour*, **50**, 1–33.

Wu, H. W. *et al.* (1964) *The Cyprinid Fishes of China*. Vol. I (pp. 1–228), Sci. Tech. Press, Shanghai. (in Chinese)

Wu, H. W. *et al.* (1977) *The Cyprinid Fishes of China*. Vol. II (pp. 229–598), Sci. Tech. Press, Shanghai. (in Chinese)

Wu, L. *et al.* (1979) *Catalogue of the vertebrates of Guizhou*, People Publ., Guizhou, 123 pp. (in Chinese)

Wu, Y.-F. and Chen, Y. (1979) Notes on fishes from Golog and Yushu region of Qinghai Province, China. *Acta Zootaxonomica Sinica*, **4**, 287–96. (in Chinese with English summary)

Wu, Y.-F. and Wu, C.-Z. (1984) Notes on fishes Lake Sunm Cuo of Qinghai Province, China. *Acta Zootaxonomica Sinica*, **9**, 326–9. (in Chinese with English summary)

Wu, Y.-F. and Wu, C.-Z. (1984) Notes on fishes from Lake Sunm Cuo of Qinghai Province, China. *Acta Zootaxonomica Sinica*, **9**, 326–9. (in Chinese with English summary)

Xie, Y.-H. (1981) Ichthyofauna of the Liao He. *Trans. Chinese Ichthy. Soc.*, **2**, 111–20. (in Chinese with English summary)

Xie, Y.-H. (1986) The fish fauna of the Yalu River. *Trans. Chinese Ichthy. Soc.*, **5**, 91–100. (in Chinese with English summary)

Xu, R. (1981) Vegetational changes in the past and the uplift of the Qinghai–Xizang Plateau, in *Geological and Ecological Studies of Qinghai–Xizang Plateau*, (ed. D. S. Liu), Vol. 1, Science Press, Beijing, pp. 139–44.

Zugmayer, E. (1910) Beiträge zur Ichthyologie von Zentral-Asien. *Zool. Jb., Abt. Syst.*, **29**, 275–98.

Zugmayer, E. (1913) Wissenschaftliche Ergebnisse der Reise von Prof. Dr. G. Merzbacher im zentralen und östlichen Thian-Schan 1907–8. *Abh. bayer. Akad. Wiss.*, **26B** (14), 1–13.

Chapter seven

Cyprinids of Africa

P. H. Skelton, D. Tweddle and P. B. N. Jackson

7.1 INTRODUCTION

Africa straddles the tropics and contains a wide range of biotopes from rain forests to major deserts. Temperate climates occur only in the extreme south and in restricted zones of high altitude. The western half of the continent is well watered within tropical latitudes, but rainfall is seasonal in the north, east and south. Dry desert or semi-desert conditions prevail in the north and to the south-west. On a broad scale the continental landscape comprises an elevated plateau impressed with the basins of major drainages of the Nile, Niger, Zaire, Zambezi and the Orange (Roberts, 1975; Beadle, 1981). The palaeohistorical view is that some of these basins were formerly major areas of endorheic drainage, possibly forming immense inland lakes that were later captured by encroaching coastal systems (Beadle, 1981). There are few extant large endorheic drainages in Africa, but Lake Chad and the Okavango basins are notable examples. The Great Lakes of Central and East Africa are prominent features and their faunal histories are closely interwoven with the geomorphological evolution of the East African Rift system. Drainage evolution throughout Africa is intricately associated with the distribution patterns of freshwater fishes.

About ten African ichthyofaunal provinces are recognized (Roberts, 1975) (Fig. 7.1). Although they are not strict biogeographical units (Greenwood, 1983), they are useful entities for discussing regional patterns of fish distribution. Roberts (1975) partitioned Africa into low and high sectors, high Africa lying to the south and east of a line drawn from the north of the Ethiopian highlands, down and around the rim of the Zaire basin to the Atlantic coast off Angola. The riverine fish faunas of high Africa are relatively poor and dominated by the cyprinids. Those of low Africa include the species-rich Guinean, Zairean and Nilo–Sudanic faunas and include many archaic and phyletically isolated groups such as the polypterids, notopterids, and large proportions of certain anotophysans (e.g. Kneriidae).

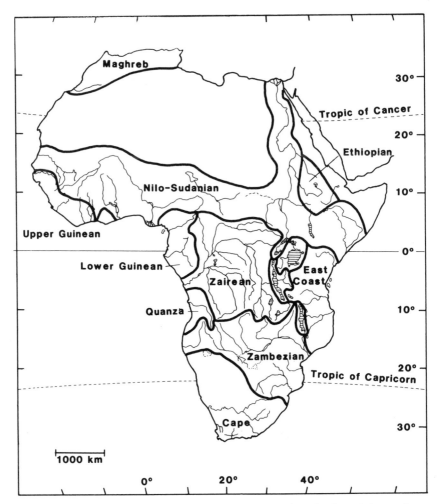

Fig. 7.1 General drainage and ichthyofaunal provinces of Africa (after Roberts, 1975). Great Lakes provinces (not labelled) are, from the north, Victoria, Tanganyika, and Malaŵi.

Africa contains virtually all the main groups of ostariophysan fishes (lacking only the gymnotiforms). The cyprinids are a major component of the total fish fauna, exceeded in number of species only by the cichlids, which dominate the African Great Lakes (Beadle, 1981; Lowe–McConnell, 1987, 1988). The Cyprinidae have a pan-African distribution and form the most widespread fish family from the Maghreb region of north-western Africa to the coastal streams of the Cape in the south.

Table 7.1 The genera and species of African cyprinids and their distribution within the ichthyofaunal provinces as shown in Fig. 7.1. Species numbers mainly from Daget *et al.* (1984); some species occur in more than one column.

Genus	Species	MG	N–S	UG	LG	ZR	QU	ZM	ET	SO	CA	EC	LT	LM	LV
Acapoeta	1	0	0	0	0	0	0	0	0	0	0	0	1	0	0
Barboides	1	0	0	0	1	0	0	0	0	0	0	0	0	0	0
Barbopsis	1	0	0	0	0	0	0	0	0	1	0	0	0	0	0
Barbus	288	4	39	30	37	79	15	33	5	1	17	27	16	7	9
Caecobarbus	1	0	0	0	0	1	0	0	0	0	0	0	0	0	0
Coptostomabarbus	2	0	0	0	0	2	0	1	0	0	0	0	0	0	0
Phraetichthys	1	0	0	0	0	0	0	0	0	1	0	0	0	0	0
Prolabeo	1	0	0	1	0	0	0	0	0	0	0	0	0	0	0
Prolabeops	1	0	0	0	1	0	0	0	0	0	0	0	0	0	0
Pseudobarbus	7	0	0	0	0	0	0	0	0	0	7	0	0	0	0
Sanagia	1	0	0	0	1	0	0	0	0	0	0	0	0	0	0
Varicorhinus	32	1	0	2	7	9	6	2	1	0	0	0	4	0	0
Xenobarbus	1	0	0	0	0	0	0	0	0	0	0	1	0	0	0
Garra	10	0	5	0	2	2	0	0	2	1	0	0	0	0	0
Labeo	78	0	13	6	5	25	1	11	0	4	4	10	3	3	2
Chelaethiops	5	0	1	0	0	3	0	0	0	0	0	0	2	0	0
Engraulicypris	1	0	0	0	0	0	0	0	0	0	0	0	0	1	0
Leptocypris	8	0	1	3	1	3	0	0	0	0	0	0	0	0	0
Mesobola	4	0	0	0	0	1	0	1	0	1	0	1	1	0	1
Neobola	3	0	2	0	0	0	0	0	0	1	0	1	0	0	0
Opsaridium	9	0	1	0	1	6	0	1	0	0	0	1	0	2	0
Raiamas	18	0	5	5	2	7	1	0	0	0	0	0	2	2	0
Rastrineobola	1	0	0	0	0	0	0	0	0	0	0	0	0	0	1
Pseudophoxinus	2	2	0	0	0	0	0	0	0	0	0	0	0	0	0
Total	477	7	67	47	57	138	23	49	8	10	28	41	29	13	13

7.2 TAXONOMIC DIVERSITY AND RELATIONSHIPS

The overall diversity of African cyprinids (Fig. 7.2) is low compared to that of the cyprinid faunas of Eurasia and North America (Briggs, 1979). There are about 477 species in 24 genera (Table 7.1) assembled from three subfamilies, the cyprinines, the bariliines, and the leuciscines. Relationships are often complex and in certain cases closest affinities are recognized with Asian lineages rather than congeneric African groups (Howes, 1980, 1983, 1984, 1987; Reid, 1978, 1985). The affinities of species from the Maghreb are with European cyprinids (Almaca, 1976).

Cyprinines

The vast majority (366 or 77%) of African species are included in only two cyprinine genera: *Barbus, sensu lato* (60.5%) and *Labeo* (16.5%) (Fig. 7.2). Although several *Barbus* subgenera are recognized (e.g. *Clypeobarbus* and *Enteromius*), relationships within this genus and its 'satellite' genera are poorly understood. It is generally acknowledged that *Barbus* (*sensu lato*) is a polyphyletic assemblage that requires taxonomic reorganization (Lévêque,1983; Howes, 1987).

Most (75–80%) of African *Barbus* species (Fig. 7.3) are of small to medium size (i.e., reaching *c.* 150 mm SL). The remainder are larger, exceeding 150 mm SL and in some cases they may reach 700–900 mm SL and weigh many kilograms. Most large species have scales with longitudinal striations, and small or medium species have scales with radiating striations. Large *Barbus* are notoriously variable in body and fin proportions, and especially in the form and shape of the mouth (e.g. Jubb, 1967; Banister, 1973), so their taxonomy is often complex and confused. The interrelationships among these species are not well known although a few 'supra-specific complexes' are recognized, e.g. the *Barbus intermedius* complex in East Africa (Banister, 1973). The larger species usually require larger rivers and water bodies and therefore have relatively circumscribed distributions within hydrologically connected basins (Banister, 1973).

The numerous *Barbus* species with radially striated scales may be grouped into three general categories based on the nature of the unbranched dorsal fin ray (Boulenger, 1907, 1911), namely bony and serrated, spinous without serrations, or slender, segmented and flexible. Species with a serrated dorsal spine occur mainly in East and southern Africa (Greenwood, 1962; Jubb, 1967) as well as in the Zaire basin (e.g. Poll, 1967) and adjacent coastal systems (e.g. Mahnert and Gery, 1982). However, these species are few in West Africa (Lévêque and Paugy, 1984). Most are medium to small species, although there are a few larger ones such as *Barbus andrewi* and *B. serra* from the south-west Cape, *B. mattozi* from the Limpopo, Zambezi and Cunene rivers, and *B. litamba* in Lake Malaŵi.

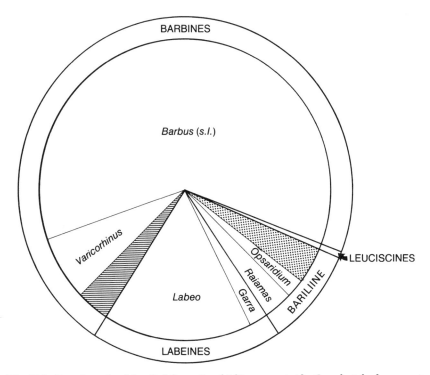

Fig. 7.2 Generic and subfamilial diversity of African cyprinids. Crosshatched segment represents small barbine genera including *Barboides*, *Barbopsis*, *Caecobarbus*, *Coptostomabarbus*, *Phraetichthys*, *Prolabeo*, *Prolabeops*, *Pseudobarbus*, *Sanagia* and *Xenobarbus*. Stippled segment represents small bariliine genera including *Chelaethiops*, *Engraulicypris*, *Leptocypris*, *Mesobola*, *Neobola* and *Rastrineobola*. The Leuciscine genus represented is *Pseudophoxinus*. Diversity determined from Daget *et al.* (1984).

The group with a strong simple spine includes only three closely related species that may even be a single polytypic species (*B. trimaculatus*, *B. poechii* and *B. jacksoni*) (Greenwood, 1962). These species are widely distributed in southern and East Africa and are common where they occur.

The largest group of barbine minnows consists of those with a slender, flexible dorsal fin ray. Several distinct lineages are included, e.g. the subgenus *Enteromius*, which is characterized by species having prominent pit-lines on the head (Greenwood, 1970), and *Clypeobarbus*, which has deep midlateral scales and characteristic tubercles on the head and mouth (Poll and Lambert, 1961). The subgenus *Enteromius* includes a single widely distributed species *Barbus radiatus* in southern and East Africa (Stewart, 1977) and a small group of species in West Africa (Hopson and Hopson, 1965; Lévêque and Paugy,

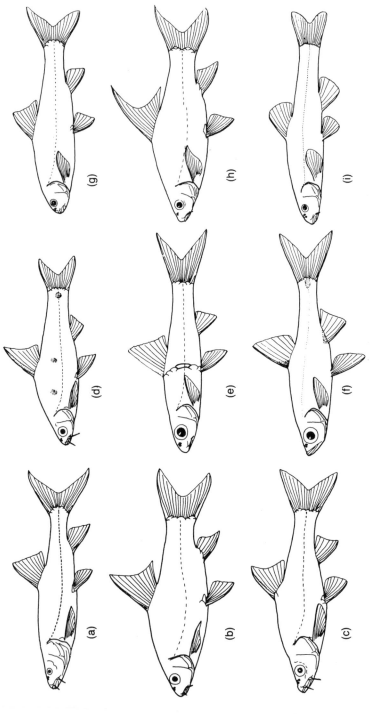

Fig. 7.3 Representative African barbine fishes. (a), *Barbus kimberleyensis*; (b), *M. Macrolepis*; (c), *B. mattozi*; (d), *B. jacksoni*; (e), *B. (Ceypeobarbus) schoutedeni*; (f), *Coptostomabarbus bellcrossi*; (g), *Varicorhinus nelspruitensis*; (h), *Sanagia velifera*; (i), *Pseudobarbus quathlambae*.

1984). Many of the small flexible-rayed species are colourful and attractive or have prominent pigment patterns such as spots, stripes or a mid-lateral band. Males are often brightly coloured, develop small tubercles, and have broader and longer fins than the females.

The genus *Varicorhinus*, with 32 species, is a polyphyletic assemblage (K. Banister, pers. comm.). The genus *Pseudobarbus* comprises a distinct lineage of seven minnow-sized species from the Cape Fold Mountains and the Lesotho Drakensberg that are characterized by a suite of unique characters including bright red fins, prominent nuptial tubercles on the head, scales and fins, distinctive pharyngeal teeth and alimentary tract, and various skeletal characters (Skelton, 1988). Two small species of *Coptostomabarbus* from the upper Zaire and Okavango–Zambezi systems are distinguished by an unusual superior mouth (Poll, 1969). Three monotypic genera of blind cave species are known, *Phraetichthys* and the naked *Barbopsis* from Somalia and *Caecobarbus* from Zaire. Other monotypic satellite genera include the miniature species (maximum SL 18 mm) *Barboides gracilis* from the lower Guinean province (Thys van den Audenaerde, 1975), *Prolabeo batesi* from Sierra Leone, and *Sanagia velifera* from Cameroon (Risch and Thys van den Audenaerde, 1985). *Prolabeops cameroonensis* has also been included in the barbine group by Reid (1982). *Xenobarbus* is a monotypic genus from Tanzania that is known only from the type specimens. It differs from other African cyprinids in having a pair of barbels on the lower jaw in addition to two pairs on the upper jaw (Norman, 1923).

Reid (1982) defined the labeine fishes in terms of several derived features including the presence of a vomero-palatine organ, the neural complex of the Weberian apparatus contacting the neurocranium, the form of the basioccipital process, and the superficial labial fold developed posterior to the lower jaw. The mouth, pharyngeal apparatus and intestine of *Labeo* species are specialized for benthic algal grazing (Matthes, 1963; Reid, 1985). Many African labeines are adapted to fast currents (e.g. Fig. 7.4 (b, e)).

Reid (1985) recognized six informal 'groups' of *Labeo* species, which may become subgenera or even genera. Three are widespread (i.e. nearly pan-African): the '*forskahlii*' group is the largest, with between 19 and 24 species; the '*niloticus*' group has seven to 11 species; and the '*coubie*' group has eight to 13 species. The remaining groups are more regionalized, as follows: the '*umbratus*' group of four species in southern Africa; the '*macrostoma*' group of four species in Zaire and the west coast; and the '*gregorii*' group of two to five species from the east coast.

Garra is the only other labeine genus in Africa, with about ten species distributed in the East Coastal, Nilo–Sudanic, Guinean and Zairean provinces (Menon, 1964). *Garra* (Fig. 7.4(e)) are generally small fishes with a sucker-like mouth and a streamlined body similar to the rheophilic labeos. One African species, *Garra tibanica*, is also distributed in Arabia and the Levant (Krupp, 1982).

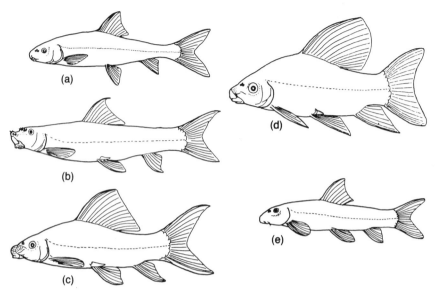

Fig. 7.4 Representative African labeine fishes. (a), *Labeo seeberi*; (b), *L. annectens*; (c), *L. coubie*; (d), *L. longipinnis*; (e), *Garra dembeensis*.

Bariliines

The bariliine lineage includes eight African and several Asiatic genera. The relationships of the African genera, as established by Howes (1980, 1983, 1984) and summarized in Fig. 7.5, indicate that the genus *Opsaridium* is more closely related to the Asiatic *Barilius* than to the other African genera. With this exception, the African genera form a lineage in which *Raiamas* (which also includes two Asiatic species) is the most primitive sister group. The 'Neoboline' genera are a distinct subgroup, and *Engraulicypris* and *Leptocypris* are derived taxa.

Bariliine cyprinids are generally streamlined, large-eyed, open-water carnivores with large mouths (Fig. 7.6). *Opsaridium* and *Raiamas* species are superficially similar, their differences being mainly osteological and anatomical (Howes, 1980). *Opsaridium* species are sexually dimorphic with mature males having an extended anal fin, well-developed pectoral axial lobes, prominent tubercles on the head, body and fins, and distinctively pigmented dorsal fins. *Opsaridium* is distributed mainly in the Zaire, Zambezi, east coastal rivers of Tanzania, and Lake Malaŵi. One species, *O. ubangense* (Fig. 7.6(a)), extends from Lake Malaŵi and the upper Zaire to the lower Guinean province (Lévêque and Bigorne, 1983). *Raiamas* (Fig. 7.6(b)) includes five West African species and nine or ten species in the Zairean and lower Guinean provinces.

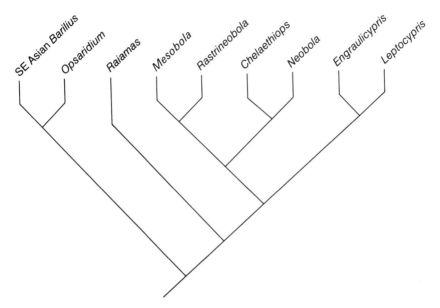

Fig. 7.5 Relationships of African bariline fishes (after Howes, 1984).

Neobolines are mostly small, open-water shoaling species. The monotypic *Rastrineobola argentea* (Fig. 7.6(d)) occurs in Lakes Victoria and Kyoga, where it is pelagic and produces planktonic eggs (Greenwood, 1966). Three of the four known species of *Mesobola* have restricted distributions (*M. bredoi* in Lake Albert, *M. moeruensis* in the Luapula–Mweru, *M. spinifer* in the Malagarasi drainage); the fourth species, *M. brevianalis* (Fig. 7.6(c)), is widespread in the Zambezian province, including an isolated population in the lower Orange River. *Chelaethiops* (Fig. 7.6(e)) is primarily a Zairean genus with species in adjacent systems, including Lake Tanganyika, Lake Rukwa, and one species in the Nilo–Sudanic province. The three species of *Neobola* (Fig. 7.6(f)) are restricted to the rivers of northern Kenya and Somalia, including Lake Turkana.

The monotypic *Engraulicypris sardella* (Fig. 7.6(g)) is endemic to the open waters of Lake Malaŵi. *Leptocypris* species (Fig. 7.6(h)) includes eight species which occur in West Africa, the Nilo–Sudan and Zaire (Lévêque and Bigorne, 1983; Howes and Teugels, 1989).

Leuciscines

This subfamily is represented by two species of *Pseudophoxinus* (Fig. 7.7) from the Maghreb region (Boulenger, 1911). The phyletic and biogeographical relationships of these species are with European leuciscines (Almaca, 1976).

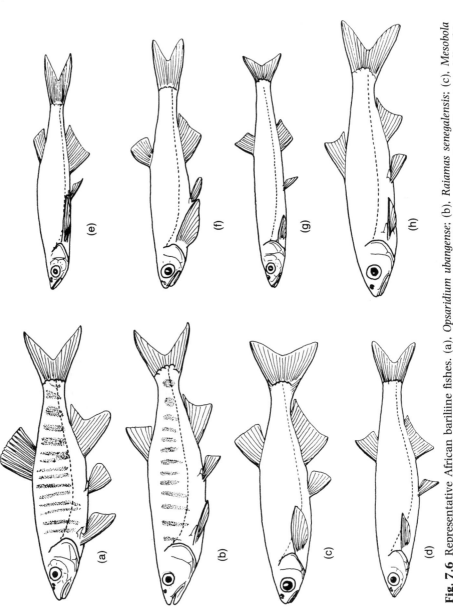

Fig. 7.6 Representative African bariline fishes. (a), *Opsaridium ubangense*; (b), *Raiamas senegalensis*; (c), *Mesobola breviamalis*; (d), *Rastrineobola argentea*; (e), *Chelaethiops elongatus* (f), *Neobola bottegoi*; (g), *Engraulicypris sardella*; (h),

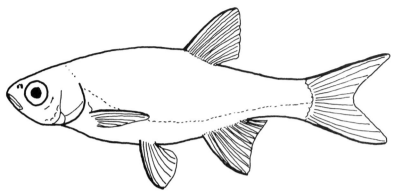

Fig. 7.7 Representative African leuciscine, *Pseudophoxinus callensis.*

Introduced species

Several cyprinids have been introduced into many African countries, mainly for aquaculture (Moreau *et al.*, 1988). Carp, *Cyprinus carpio*, were initially introduced to the Cape as ornamental fish but have been widely used since then in aquaculture and for recreational angling. This species is established in many natural waters throughout Africa. Other cyprinids introduced for aquaculture include the grass carp, *Ctenopharyngodon idella*, the silver carp, *Hypophthalmichthys molitrix*, and the tench, *Tinca tinca*. Several feral populations of goldfish, *Carassius auratus*, are also known (e.g. de Moor and Bruton, 1988).

7.3 BIOGEOGRAPHY

Lowe–McConnell (1987) summarized current perceptions of African freshwater fish distribution in five categories: (1) widely distributed remnants of archaic elements, (2) endemic families, (3) Gondwanic elements shared with South America, (4) elements shared with the Orient, some of possible Gondwanic origin, and (5) marine derivatives. Cyprinids are components of the fourth category. According to one interpretation, the cyprinids evolved in South East Asia and dispersed to Africa via connections in the north-east (Briggs, 1979). African cyprinid fossils date back only to the Miocene (van Couvering, 1977). Recent phylogenetic studies and the emergence of vicariance biogeographical theory challenge this dispersalist view. However, even higher-level ostariophysan interrelationships not universally resolved and the picture is still too complex to formulate acceptable hypotheses explaining the obvious African–Asian fish-distribution 'track'.

  Although the extant fauna of the Maghreb shows clear European affinities (Roberts, 1975; Almaca, 1976), Greenwood (1983) points out that the known

Miocene fauna of that region included only Afro-tropical elements. The Nilo–Sudanic fauna (Daget and Durand, 1981) includes several widespread species with distributions brought about through connected or previously connected systems. The fragmentation (vicariance) of populations has occurred through both hydrographic and climatic changes (Beadle, 1981). Relict populations of several cyprinids and other fish groups still exist in Saharan refugia (Du Mont, 1982). Banister (1973), Banister and Clarke (1977) and Krupp (1982) discussed African–Arabian fish distributions in the light only of dispersal between the two areas. However, the geomorphological evolution of this region involving, among other things, rifting and marine incursion (the Red Sea), provides a likely scenario in which alternative vicariance explanations can be considered.

Phyletic relationships and the distribution of the speciose Zairean–tropical West African fish fauna are not sufficiently well understood to say much about their biogeographical relationships. In these generally well-watered areas, both head-water connections and coastal communications undoubtedly have been involved in bringing about specific distributions.

The Zairean and Zambezian faunas overlap broadly (Poll, 1967; Bell–Cross, 1968; Bowmaker *et al.*, 1978; Jackson, 1986). The Zambezian fauna extends to drainages both north and south along the east coast, phasing out rapidly in the Maputaland region (Bruton and Kok, 1980). Many eastern and southern African cyprinids, especially the small *Barbus* species, have widespread distributions from South Africa through to East Africa. Examples are *Barbus paludinosus*, *B. trimaculatus* (Greenwood, 1962) and *B. radiatus* (Stewart, 1977). Such widespread eastern distributions contrast with the much more restricted extensions of Zambezian cyprinids into the Zairean–west tropical areas. This is difficult to explain given the wide-ranging west tropical distributions of several other Zambezian fish species such as the characins *Micralestes acutidens*, *Brycinus imberi* and *Hydrocynus vittatus*, the African pike *Hepsetus odoe*, the mormyrid *Mormyrus anguilloides*, and the clariid *Heterobranchus longifilis*.

One distinctive distribution pattern within the Zambezian province, involving cyprinids and other fishes, circumscribes the Okavango–upper Zambezi–Kafue–Bangweulu/Mweru and certain Lake Malaŵi drainages (Bell–Cross, 1968; Tweddle, 1982; Jackson, 1986). Although the geological and hydrographical histories of these now largely separate drainages are not fully explained, the associated fish distributions argue strongly in favour of the now interrupted but formerly contiguous drainage system (broadly described and labelled by Bell–Cross, 1968, as the WETBID or western basin of internal drainage).

The middle and lower Zambezi fish fauna is partly distinct from that of the upper Zambezi, the Kafue and the Okavango (Jubb, 1961). The history of the lower Zambezi relates closely to the development of the Malaŵian rift system and associated drainages. The Malaŵi Rift cut and captured the head waters of east coast rivers, including the Rufiji and Ruvuma, so much of Lake Malaŵi's fauna has east-coast affinities, e.g. *Barbus eurystomus* from Lake Malaŵi is related to *B. macrolepis* from the Ruaha and Rufigi rivers (Banister and Clarke, 1980). Other Lake Malaŵi cyprinids have broader geographical relationships, e.g. *B. johnstonii* with the widespread *B. marequensis*, and *B.litamba* with *B. mattozi*. Tweddle *et al.* (1979) stressed that the falls and rapids separating the lower and upper Shire have been, and still are, a complete barrier to the upward movement of fishes (except anguillid eels).

Cyprinids dominate the Cape ichthyofaunal province, increasingly so further southwards (Bowmaker *et al.*, 1978). Skelton (1986) divided the fauna according to their respective distributions into two groups, the Karoid and Cape groups. Karoid cyprinids include the yellowfishes (large *Barbus* species), the 'umbratus' group labeos, and at least two distinctive species complexes of *Barbus* minnows (the *B. anoplus* and *B. pallidus* complexes). The distribution of these fishes is centred on the Orange River basin and encroaching adjacent drainages. The outgroup relationships of the Karoid species are not clear, although Reid (1978) suggests that the *Labeo umbratus* group species are related to Asiatic labeines.

Endemic Cape fishes are mainly confined to Cape Fold Mountain drainages and include *Galaxias zebratus*, the anabantid genus *Sandelia* and at least three distinctive groups of barbine cyprinids. The cyprinids include two relatively large species, *Barbus andrewi* and *B. serra*, that, strangely, are similar to the European *Barbus* (*s. str.*) (Howes, 1987). In addition, there is a lineage of redfin minnows (*Pseudobarbus* spp.) that is distributed in a vicariant pattern consistent with the hydrographic history of the region (Skelton, 1986, 1988).

7.4   GENERAL BIOLOGY

Reproductive strategies

Barbines. Large *Barbus* species are primarily riverine forms, and although several species are lake dwellers, all are riverine spawners (Tomasson *et al.*, 1984). Sexual dimorphism is not marked in these fishes. A single annual upstream breeding migration occurs and spawning takes place over shallow instream gravel beds where a salmon-like redd is made. Fecundity is moderately high; the eggs are relatively large and take several days to hatch. The embryos are immobile until the yolk sac is absorbed. Small *Barbus* species have a variety of breeding strategies, seldom involving an upstream migration. Sexual dimorphism involving coloration and the development of minute tubercles on the head and pectoral fins of males is characteristic. Typically, spawning of small barbs involves individual pairs of fishes (e.g. *B. viviparus*, Polling, 1972). Massed upstream migration does occur, (e.g. for *B. mattozi*, Donnelly, 1980), and massed congregation of breeding fish is also characteristic for certain species (e.g. in both *B. calidus* and *B. erubescens*, males congregate in schools for breeding (Skelton, 1988)). Small barbs may be either once-a-season spawners (e.g. *B. treurensis*, Kleynhans, 1987) or multiple spawners over an extended breeding season (e.g. *B. trevelyani*, Gaigher, 1975; *B. anoplus*, Cambray and Bruton, 1984). Breeding sites may also be instream over rocky bottoms (e.g. *B. calidus* and *B. erubescens*) but most species lay eggs in vegetation in quiet pools, backwater or floodplain habitats (e.g. *B. fasciolatus* and *B. multilineatus*, Axelrod *et al.*, 1984). No nest or redd is made; the eggs are generally scattered and left unguarded.

Labeines. All labeines, including lacustrine species, undergo a mass annual upstream migration and are obligatory total spawners with relatively small eggs and high fecundity (Tomasson *et al.*, 1984). Spawning occurs in flowing water but, unlike large *Barbus* species, there is usually a lateral movement onto adjacent floodplains or flooded river banks, where the eggs are shed over temporarily inundated vegetation. Exceptionally, *Labeo* species may spawn instream on rocky-based substrata, e.g. *L. capensis* in the rock main channel of the lower Orange River (Cambray, 1985). Populations often have highly variable year-class strengths which depend on prevailing conditions (Tomasson *et al.*, 1984).

Bariliines. These fishes migrate upstream to spawn in running water, e.g. the Mpasa, *Opsaridium microlepis*, in Lake Malaŵi (Tweddle, 1983), and *O. moorii* in Lake Tanganyika (Marlier, 1953). *O. microlepis* is a fractional spawner, but there are no data for other bariliine species.

Neobolines. Although neobolines are not known to undergo spawning migrations, their breeding biology is not well studied. The eggs and larvae of certain lacustrine species are pelagic (FAO, 1982).

Feeding

Barbines. Most species of large *Barbus* are omnivores tending towards carnivory. Some species are more specialized feeders, e.g. *B. kimberleyensis* in the Orange River and *B. litamba* in Lake Malaŵi are primarily piscivores, whereas *B. eurystomus* from Lake Malaŵi is a molluscivore. In many species the form of the mouth shows wide intraspecific feeding adaptation, from large hypertrophied lips (rubber-lips) to a horny (keratinized) scraping type (the so-called *Varicorhinus* mouth form) (e.g. Crass, 1964; Jubb, 1967). The *Varicorhinus* mouth form is adapted for scraping algae and aufwuchs from submerged rocks and other substrata. Hypertrophied lips are most suited for grubbing between loose rocks and pebbles. Small *Barbus* species in Africa are usually unspecialized facultative feeders on invertebrates and organic matter, including algae (Cambray, 1983).

Labeines. Labeines are characterized by a complex ventral mouth, homodont pharyngeal teeth which are close together to form a single grinding surface, and long coiled intestines, features all suited for specialized epibenthic microphagy (Matthes, 1963; Reid, 1982, 1985). *Labeo* species conform to two general ecological groups: one favours large, frequently turbid, open water bodies where the main food items are diatoms, filamentous algae and organic detritus; the second group favours flowing waters and tends to be more microphytophagous than the first (Matthes, 1963). In Lake Malaŵi, competitive exclusion might occur because *L. mesops* grazes over fine sand or mud, whereas *L. cylindricus* is a rock scraper. *Garra* feed mainly on epibenthic aufwuchs and have raking -type pharyngeal teeth and a shorter intestine than that of *Labeo* (Matthes, 1963).

Bariliines. These fishes are all predators, with smaller species feeding on invertebrates such as insects and crustacea and larger ones on fishes (Matthes, 1963).

Neobolines. The neobolines are chiefly open-water planktivores, although riverine species such as *Mesobola brevianalis* include allochthonous items, especially insects, and vegetable matter in their diet (Matthes, 1963; Crass, 1964; Pienaar, 1978).

Habitat preferences

Barbines. Large *Barbus* and *Varicorhinus* species are essentially riverine forms, although several have adapted to lentic situations without completely dispensing with their ancestral riverine nature. There is often a preference for strong running water, such as found in rapids and pools below waterfalls. Several species, including *B. marequensis*, *B. trachypterus* and *B. altianalis*, are commonly known as gorge fish on account of their penchant for strong currents below waterfalls. Few species appear to have adapted well to man-made impoundments on rivers; the best examples are from southern temperate species like *B. aeneus* and *B. kimberleyensis* of the Orange River (Tomasson *et al.*, 1984).

In contrast, small barbines, by virtue of their small size and generalized feeding habits, are mainly found in vegetated marginal habitats of rivers and lakes. Exceptionally there are species such as *B. hospes* from the Orange River, which occupies open-water habitats. In southern Africa the widespread *B. anoplus* is a particularly versatile species, being common in a wide variety of habitats in both permanent and temporary rivers; it has successfully colonized the open waters of a large man-made impoundment (Cambray and Bruton, 1984).

Labeines. *Labeo* and *Garra* species are typically riverine forms, some strongly adapted to currents (Reid, 1985). Several *Labeo* species are lacustrine, migrating to affluent rivers to breed, e.g. *L. mesops* in Lake Malaŵi, *L. altivelis* in Lake Mweru, *L. victorianus* in Lake Victoria, *L. coubie* in Lake Albert, and *L. forskahlii* in Lake Edward. Sometimes fluviatile and even torrenticulous forms are also found along wave-washed shores of lakes, e.g. Greenwood (1966) recorded *Garra johnstonii* from the Victoria Nile and the rocky shores of Lake Victoria.

Bariliines. These are mainly shoaling species favouring flowing inshore waters of rivers. In lakes, bariliines range off shore and feed in the open waters, but migrate to affluent rivers to breed.

Neobolines. Both riverine and lacustrine species occur. The species endemic to large lakes, such as *Engraulicypris sardella* and *Rastrineobola argentea*, are pelagic shoaling species. Riverine species (e.g. *Mesobola brevianalis*) inhabit quiet water with vegetation cover as well as open-water habitats (Crass, 1964; Pienaar, 1978).

Phenotypic plasticity

An important and, until recently, little understood attribute of some smaller *Barbus* is their ability to proliferate in harsh environments that support few others fish species. Such fish can exist in more stable environments with many species present, but thrive in harsher abiotic environments from which more generalized species are absent. Phenotypic plasticity is well known in *Tilapia* (Noakes and Balon, 1982) and has also been reported for *Barbus paludinosus* in endorheic systems (Jackson, 1989). In the highly turbid and saline Lake Chilwa, Malaŵi, for example, this species rapidly recolonized the refilling lake after it had dried out in 1968. By 1972 catches of 2000 t were recorded, and by 1976 9000 t (50% of a three-species fishery) by Furse *et al.* (1979b). However, in the adjacent clear Lake Chiuta, which has a similar overall fish fauna, *B. paludinosus* is a minor component of more diverse multispecies fishery.

Lacustrine adaptations

Most lacustrine cyprinids are not readily distinguishable from conspecifics in neighbouring river systems. There are occasionally small differences between riverine and lacustrine cyprinid populations, e.g. in Lake Malaŵi *Labeo cylindricus* reaches up to 1 kg, twice the size that it does elsewhere in its extensive distribution. *Barbus johnstonii* has two distinct morphs in Lake Malaŵi, a fleshy-lipped omnivorous form and a horny-lipped, aufwuchs-scraping form which was previously recognized as a separate species of *Varicorhinus*. However, in the affluent and effluent rivers of Lake Malaŵi, a wide range of mouth forms encompassing both extremes can be found. Neither of the other endemic large *Barbus* species that occur in Lake Malaŵi, the predatory *B. litamba* and the molluscivorous *B. eurystomus*, show particular adaptations to the lacustrine environment, and both return to affluent rivers to spawn.

Other cyprinids in African Great Lakes show distinctive adaptations to the lacustrine environments, e.g. *B. profundus* in Lake Victoria (Greenwood, 1970; Stewart, 1977). Lake Malaŵi has three pelagic cyprinids: two related predatory species of *Opsaridium* ('Mpasa', *O. microlepis*, and 'Sanjika', *O. microcephalus*) and the zooplanktivorous 'Usipa', *Engraulicypris sardella*. *Opsa-*

ridium ubangense occurs in affluent rivers of the Lake only and is a medium-sized species (to 200 mm SL) adapted to fast currents. Its body shape (fusiform) and coloration (vertical bars with orange–pink tints to the fins and ventral areas) are remarkably similar to those of trout and Atlantic salmon parr. In contrast, Mpasa is, like oceanic salmon, a uniformly silver fish with only a trace of the vertical barring characteristic of the genus. The Mpasa is the largest African bariliine, attaining a total length of over 70 cm and a weight of 4 kg (Tweddle, 1987). Mpasa are rarely found in commercial catches, except in the rainy season when they congregate in river mouths before the spawning migration. Mpasa spawn in clear, well-oxygenated water over gravel beds in which the eggs hatch and develop (Tweddle, 1983). They tend to lose condition as the spawning season progresses because, being fractional spawners, they remain in the rivers for some time but meanwhile do not feed extensively. Thus the life histories of these bariliines show remarkable convergence with those of salmonids (Tweddle and Lewis, 1983).

Sanjika is intermediate in both size and coloration between Mpasa and *O. ubangense*, and appears to have less marked adaptations to open-water habitats. However, Sanjika may also breed on exposed rocky shores of the lake where wave action increases the oxygen content, in which case it appears to be more fully adapted to lacustrine habitats than Mpasa.

The natural mortality rate of Usipa, *Engraulicypris sardella*, exceeds 99.5% per year (FAO, 1982) and hence it can be regarded as an annual species. The number of Usipa vary annually by orders of magnitude (FAO, 1982; Lewis and Tweddle, 1988; Tweddle and Lewis, 1988). These fluctuations are likely to result from changes in productivity acting through a phytoplankton–larval Usipa food chain (Tweddle and Lewis, 1988). Larval Usipa occur in the pelagic zone throughout the year (FAO, 1982), ensuring that the species is able to take advantage of transient bursts of nutrients. Usipa do not undertake spawning runs up affluent streams, eggs are likely to be pelagic, and larvae are found throughout the lake. Mouthparts are protrusible and highly specialized for zooplankton feeding. Usipa, therefore, are greatly adapted to the pelagic zone.

Adaptation of riverine species to artificial impoundments

In recent decades many African rivers have been drastically modified by damming, some with big reservoirs (Davies, 1979). River regulation affects fish communities in different ways; some species adapt readily and thrive under lentic conditions, whilst others, especially the cyprinids, do not adjust easily and are often greatly reduced or eliminated from the impounded waters (Jackson *et al.*, 1988). In Lake Kariba on the Zambezi River the first species to disappear was the bariliine *Opsaridium zambezense*, and *Labeo altivelis* and *L. congoro* declined to insignificant levels in the main basins (Begg, 1974). Similar changes in the populations of these species occurred in Lake Cahora Bassa (Bernacsek and Lopes, 1984). In general, labeines have not adapted to the impounded waters of man-made lakes. In Lake Nasser (closed in 1964), for example, the catches of *Labeo niloticus* declined from 22.6% in 1964 to 12.7% of the total catches in 1970–72 (Latif, 1976). Similarly in Volta Lake, *Labeo* populations soon became greatly reduced (Evans and Vanderpuye, 1973).

In contrast to these large tropical reservoirs, in Lake Le Roux on the Orange River in South Africa, several cyprinid species including *Labeo capensis*, *L. umbratus*, *Barbus aeneus* and *B. anoplus* have become well established (Cambray, 1983; Cambray and Bruton, 1984, 1985; Tomasson *et al.*, 1984).

7.5 FISHERIES

In certain areas large-scale cyprinid fisheries exist. In Lake Malaŵi the Usipa, *Engraulicypris sardella*, fishery has catches of 50 000 + t annually (Lewis and Tweddle, 1988). There are also the highly valued Mpasa, *Opsaridium microlepis*, and Sanjika, *O. microcephalus*, fisheries in the same lake (Tweddle, 1981). In Lake Chilwa, catches of $9000\,t\,y^{-1}$ of the small *Barbus paludinosus* are recorded (Furse *et al.*, 1979b). In Lake Victoria, the interactions between Ndagaa, *Rastrineobola argentea*, and Nile perch, *Lates niloticus* are being investigated, but the status of other large cyprinids in the fishery of that lake is largely unknown.

Spawning strategies, fishery exploitation and aquaculture potential

The preference for rivers of most larger African cyprinids renders them vulnerable to overexploitation and environmental changes through catchment degradation and river regulation. Certain spawning strategies are more vulnerable than others to these varied anthropogenic factors. Several *Labeo* fisheries have declined, partly because the species are total spawners with specific ecological requirements. The Malaŵi fishery provides a good example. Here the bariliines are fractional spawners (Tweddle, 1983), so short-term unfavourable conditions do not have large-scale effects on recruitment. The breeding success of Mpasa, *Opsaridium microlepis* is related to the river water levels (Tweddle, 1987); higher levels allow more fish to withstand the fishing pressure around the river mouths, provide more suitable habitat for the larväe and juveniles, and mitigate the widespread but illegal use of fish poisons in the rivers. Spawning *Labeo mesops* tend to use smaller streams that are more vulnerable than larger rivers to environment perturbations. Consequently, the *Labeo* fishery has collapsed but the Mpasa fishery has not. The stocks of Mpasa recovered after a dry cycle in the 1970s and, provided catchment conservation receives due attention, ought to continue to yield good catches (Tweddle, 1981, 1983, 1985). Many total-spawning species (e.g. *Labeo* spp.) can be produced using artificial methods, but only restricted numbers of the fractional spawners (e.g. Mpasa) are possible. Aquacultural techniques could be used to support the stocks of an environmentally vulnerable species facing collapse.

Labeo fisheries

Several African *Labeo* fisheries such as *L. mesops* in Lake Malaŵi, *L. altivelis* in the Luapula River, Zambia, and *L. victorianus* in Lake Victoria, declined drastically in abundance in the 1950s and 1960s. These declines were attributed primarily to increased fishing pressures and the availability of nylon netting. In Lake Victoria there was increased use of small-meshed drifting gill nets in the lower reaches of rivers (Cadwalladr, 1965a). The decline of *L. altivelis* in the Luapula River was attributed (Jackson, 1961) to the development of a large-scale fishery in the late 1940s supplying the copper mines of Northern Rhodesia (Zambia) and Belgian Congo (Zaire). An additional by-product of this fishery was a 'caviar' of *Labeo* roe.

In 1960, the Fisheries Department of Nyasaland (now Malaŵi) (Anon., 1961) recorded declining catches of *L. mesops* in Lake Malaŵi in spite of increased lengths of gill nets set. Iles (1962) suggested that catches of *L. mesops* could be increased tenfold without detriment to the stocks. This prediction was based on the known high fecundity and the assumption that fishing mortality was lower than natural mortality over the first breeding period. Although heavy fishing pressure has contributed to the decline of *L. mesops*, its life cycle also contributed. Adult fishes are vulnerable to overfishing when they gather near river mouths before their breeding migration. The fish spawn on flooded banks, where the eggs develop rapidly and hatch within two days, and the larvae, are carried downstream by the floodwaters (Anon., 1964, 1965). Under favourable conditions, recruitment should be high and stock recovery rapid. However, the continued scarcity of *L. mesops* indicates that other factors, such as a deterioration in stream conditions, are involved. Deforestation is damaging river catchments throughout Malaŵi, and streams which formerly flowed for extended periods are now characterized by brief flash-flood flows in which the water is heavily laden with silt. Such conditions are unfavourable for *Labeo* spawning because the eggs are either stranded by rapidly receding floodwaters or smothered by silt, or both. The net result of these varied threats is that the *Labeo* population will remain low unless proposed artificial breeding programmes and other remedies are successful.

Rastrineobola argentea in Lake Victoria

The introduction of Nile perch, *Lates niloticus*, to Lake Victoria has been controversial because of the impact of the species on endemic cichlids (Jackson, 1960; Fryer, 1960; Barel *et al.*, 1985; Ribbink, 1986). An unexpected consequence of the Nile perch population explosion was the change from a complex cichlid-based food web to a simpler system where the perch feed on the shrimp *Caridina nilotica*, the cyprinid *Rastrineobola argentea* and juvenile Nile perch (HEST, 1988). The food chains supporting these prey species are short and direct between primary producer and predator, e.g. organic sediments → *Caridina* → Nile perch, and phytoplankton → zooplankton → *R. argentea* → Nile perch.

The populations of both *R. argentea* and *C. nilotica* have increased in spite of the growth of Nile perch stocks, but the modal length of adult *R. argentea* has decreased; Wanink (1988) attributed this decrease to either size-selective predation from Nile perch, or relative food depletion as a result of an increased population of *R. argentea* itself. Similarly, during a year of exceptionally high abundance, the Usipa, *Engraulicypris sardella*, of Lake Malaŵi grew more slowly than in other years, and Tweddle and Lewis (1988) inferred increased intraspecific competition for food.

7.6 CONSERVATION

Fourteen African cyprinid species are on the IUCN *Red List of Threatened Animals* (IUCN, 1988); the majority are from the temperate Cape fauna (Skelton, 1987). Threats to these species include introduced alien predators such as bass, *Micropterus* spp., and trout, *Oncorhynchus mykiss* and *Salmo trutta*, and habitat destruction from agricultural, industrial and domestic sources. The high endemism of the Cape fauna, together with restricted distribution ranges, sensitive life-history characteristics and narrow ecological tolerances as a result of long isolation on a geological time scale, have made this fauna particularly vulnerable to perturbation by man (Skelton, 1987).

Daget *et al.* (1988) provide a broad overview of the conservation of African freshwater fishes. Habitat destruction, particularly from large-scale environmentally damaging activities such as mining, agriculture, afforestation and deforestation, is probably the major threat to African fresh waters and their biota. Few African cyprinids are sought by the aquarium trade, but certain species like the blind cave fish, *Caecobarbus geertsi*, and other cave species are vulnerable to collecting because of their novelty appeal and restricted distribution.

Urbanization, industrialization and agricultural development are more advanced in South Africa than in many other African countries. However, large-scale change in the rurual landscape is widespread, especially where population pressures are rising and mining, industrial development, rural settlement, overgrazing, deforestation and agricultural intensification are rapidly expanding. Tweddle (1983) illustrates a typical example of rural landscape change affecting river status in Malaŵi.

Species with restricted distributions or isolated relic communities are especially vulnerable and often require special conservation attention. An example of a threatened relic community is in the Ruo River, a tributary of the lower Zambezi system in Malaŵi. The Ruo arises on the Mulanje Massif and drains to the lower Shire River (Fig. 7.8). The fish community in the upper reaches is isolated by the 60 m-high Zoa Falls and includes the cyprinids *Barbus eutaenia*, *B. choloensis*, another undescribed small *Barbus* species, and *Varicorhinus nelspruitensis*, as well as the small mountain catlet, *Amphilius natalensis*, and the mormyrid, *Hippopotamyrus ansorgii*. These species do not occur elsewhere in Malaŵi but this fauna most closely resembles those of the escarpment streams of the Limpopo and Incomati rivers in the Transvaal, Republic of South Africa (Furse *et al.*, 1979a). Several alien fish species

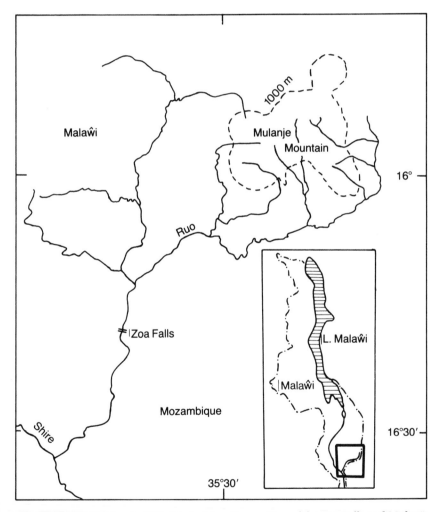

Fig. 7.8 The Ruo River in Malaŵi, showing the position of the Zoa Falls and Mulanje Mountain.

(including bass, *Micropterus salmoides*, bluegills, *Lepomis macrochira*, and carp, *Cyprinus carpio*) have been introduced to dams in the catchment of the upper Ruo and threaten the indigenous community. A fourth exotic, the South American poeciliid *Phalloceros caudimaculatus*, has colonized the river itself.

Many African rivers are regulated to some extent (Davies, 1979). Fish passways on dams and weirs in Africa are virtually non-existent, although a few experimental structures have been built on certain South African systems. Water extraction for agriculture and industry is also an increasing threat to river fishes, especially in the relatively dry or seasonally dry areas such as the Sahel, north-eastern and East Africa, and southern Africa.

Introduction and translocation of fishes is an ever-increasing threat to native African species (Moreau *et al.*, 1988). The introduction of game species such as trout, *Oncorhynchus mykiss* and *Salmo trutta*, and bass, *Micropterus* spp., was actively initiated and promoted in colonial times and continues to occur in various countries. Many such introductions resulted in damaging impacts to native species, including the elimination of local populations (e.g. Skelton, 1987; de Moor and Bruton, 1988). The emphasis has changed to introductions for aquacultural purposes, so accidental releases into natural systems are an increasing threat. In addition, interbasin transfer systems are causing the mixing of closely related but genetically distinct fish stocks (de Moor and Bruton, 1988).

Overfishing is a problem for certain African cyprinid species, especially the labeos, which are vulnerable to both heavy fishing and environmental degradation (Section 7.5).

7.7   FUTURE RESEARCH

Taxonomy

Many African cyprinid species still await discovery and description. There is also a great need for species-level revisions, especially broad revisions on a regional basis as is being done for the West African fauna by the ORSTOM organization (Office de la Recherche Scientifique et Technique d'Outre-Mer, France) (Lévêque, Paugy and Teugels, in prep.).

The phylogeny and interrelationships of African cyprinids at all taxonomic levels are poorly explored. An understanding of the evolution and biogeography of African cyprinids, especially the larger barbine and labeine genera, would benefit greatly from studies similar to those of Howes (1980, 1983, 1984) on other groups.

New approaches to systematic problems are needed. Few cytotaxonomic and electrophoretic studies on African cyprinids have been published. Recent studies on the karyology of certain southern African *Barbus* (Oellermann, 1988) indicate that a wide range of ploidy occurs in this genus as it stands.

Biology

The few available biological studies on African cyprinids usually concern the large species of economic and recreational value (e.g. Fryer and Whitehead, 1959; Cadwalladr, 1964, 1965b; Mulder, 1973a,b; Tweddle, 1983, 1987; Eccles, 1983, 1986). Some notable studies on the biology of smaller species have been made (e.g. Reynolds, 1973; Payne, 1975), especially from southern Africa (e.g. Gaigher, 1975; Donnelly, 1982; Cambray, 1983; Cambray and Bruton, 1984, 1985; Cambray and Stuart 1985). Early-life-history studies of African cyprinids are also scarce (Cambray and Teugels 1989) but can have useful conservation or management implications. Further research on these and other biological aspects can only be encouraged.

Conservation

Most African countries are Third World nations, where questions of conservation are seldom considered above issues of day-to-day survival. Wherever possible, governments and large-scale developers should ensure that due regard is paid to the conservation of the environment and natural resources. Fish conservation cannot be divorced from general environmental conservation. Rivers and lakes depend intimately on the health and wellbeing of their catchments; the destruction of the catchment will ultimately destroy the aquatic habitats and biota. Where specific actions directly affect fishes, e.g. instream constructions, fishing activities, and introduction of alien organisms, it is vital that such actions are researched, regulated and managed for minimal impact. The introduction of alien organisms should be carefully considered and investigated if problems are to be avoided (Courtenay and Robins, 1989). Greater interaction, and co-operation between governments and controlling agencies of different countries, is required when alien introductions are being considered to multinational water bodies or rivers.

REFERENCES

Almaça, C. (1976) Zoogeografia e especiacão des cyprinídeos da Península Ibérica. *Colecçao Nat. N. Ser.* **4**, 1–28.

Anon. (1961) *Annual Report of the Department of Game, Fish and Tsetse Control, for the year ended 31st December, 1960*, Zomba, Government Printer, 27 pp.

Anon. (1964) *Labeo mesops*, in *Annual Report of the Dept of Agriculture and Fisheries for the Year 1963, Fisheries Research (Part II)*, pp. 4–14.

Anon. (1965) *Labeo mesops*, in *Annual Report of the Dept of Agriculture and Fisheries for the Year 1964, Fisheries Research (Part II)*, pp. 4–9

Axelrod, H. R., Emmens, C. W., Burgess, W. E. and Pronek, N. (1984) *Exotic Tropical Fishes*, Expanded edn, TFH Publications, Neptune City, NJ.

Banister, K. E. (1973) A revision of the large *Barbus* (Pisces, Cyprinidae) of East and Central Africa. Studies on African Cyprinidae Part II. *Bull. Br. Mus. nat. Hist. (Zool.)* **26** (1), 1–148.

Banister, K. E. and Clarke, M. A. (1977) The freshwater fishes of the Arabian Peninsula. *J. Oman Stud. (Spec. Rep.)*, **1977**, 111–54.

Banister, K. E. and Clarke, M. A. (1980) A revision of the large *Barbus* (Pisces, Cyprinidae) of Lake Malawi, with a reconstruction of the history of the southern African Rift Valley lakes. *J. nat. Hist.*, **14**, 483–542.

Barel, C. D. N., Dorit, R., Greenwood, P. H., Fryer, G., Hughes, N., Jackson, P. B. N., Kawanabe, H., Lowe-McConnell, R. H., Nagoshi, M., Ribbink, A.J., Trewavas, E., Witte, F. and Yamaoka, K. (1985) Destruction of fisheries in Africa's lakes. *Nature* (Lond.), **315**, 19–20.

Beadle, L. C. (1981) *The Inland Waters of Tropical Africa. An Introduction to Tropical Limnology*, 2nd edn, Longman, London, 475 pp.

Begg, G. (1974) The distribution of fish of riverine origin in relation to the limnological characteristics of the five basins of Lake Kariba. *Hydrobiologia*, **44**, 277–85.

Bell-Cross, G. (1968). The distribution of fishes in Central Africa. *Fish. Res. Bull. Zambia*, **4**, 3–20.

Bernacsek, G. M. and Lopes, S. (1984) Cahora Bassa (Mozambique). *CIFA Tech. Pap.*, **10**, 21–42.

Boulenger, G. A. (1907). *Zoology of Egypt: The Fishes of the Nile*, Egyptian Government, 478 pp.

Boulenger, G. A. (1911) *Catalogue of the Fresh-water Fishes of Africa in the British Museum (Natural History)*. Vol. 2, Trustees of the British Museum (Natural History), London.

Bowmaker, A. P., Jackson, P. B. N. and Jubb, R. A. (1978) Freshwater Fishes, in *Biogeography and Ecology of Southern Africa* (ed. M.J.A. Werger), *Monographiae biol.*, **31**, 1181–1230.

Briggs, J. C. (1979) Ostariophysan zoogeography: an alternative hypothesis. *Copeia*, **1979** (1), 111–17.

Bruton, M. N. and Kok, H. M. (1980) The freshwater fishes of Maputaland, in *Studies on the Ecology of Maputaland* (eds M. N. Bruton and K. H. Cooper), Rhodes University, Grahamstown and the Natal Branch of the Wildlife Society, Durban, pp. 210–44.

Cadwalladr, D. A. (1964) Investigation of the biology of *Labeo victorianus* Boulenger, in relation to its fishery. *East. Afr. Freshw. Fish. Res. Org.*, *Ann. Rep.* 1962/63, Appendix H, 63–74.

Cadwalladr, D. A. (1965a) The decline in the *Labeo victorianus* Blgr. (Pisces: Cyprinidae) fishery of Lake Victoria and an associated deterioration in some indigenous fishing methods in the Nzoia River, Kenya. *East Afr. agric. For. J.*, **30**, 249–58.

Cadwalladr, D. A. (1965b) Notes on the breeding biology and ecology of *Labeo victorianus* Boulenger (Pisces: Cyprinidae) of Lake Victoria. *Revue Zool. Bot. afr.*, **72**, 109–34.

Combray, J. A. (1983) The feeding habits of minnows of the genus *Barbus* in Africa, with special reference to *Barbus anoplus* Weber. *J. Limnol. Soc. sth Afr.*, **9**, 12–22.

Cambray, J. A. (1985) Observations on the spawning of *Labeo capensis* and *Clarias gariepinus* in the regulated lower Orange River, South Africa. *S. Afr. J. Sci.*, **81**, 318–21.

Cambray, J. A. and Bruton, M. N. (1984) The reproductive strategy of a barb, *Barbus anoplus* (Pisces, Cyprinidae), colonizing a man-made lake in South Africa. *J. Zool. (Lond)*, **204**, 143–68.

Cambray, J. A. and Bruton, M. N. (1985) Age and growth of a colonizing minnow, *Barbus anoplus*, in a man-made lake in South Africa. *Env. Biol. Fishes*, **12** (2), 131–41.

Cambray, J. A. and Stuart, C. T. (1985) Aspects of the biology of a rare redfin minnow,

Barbus burchelli (Pisces, Cyprinidae) from South Africa. *S. Afr. J. Zool.*, **20**(3), 155–65.

Cambray, J. A. and Teugels, G. G. (1989) Selected annotated bibliography of early developmental studies of African freshwater fishes. *Ann. Cape prov. Mus. (nat. Hist.)*, **18**(2), 31–56.

Courtenay, W. R. and Robins, C. R., (1989) Fish introductions: good management, mismanagement, or no management? *Crit. Rev. Aquat. Sci.*, **1**(1), 159–172.

Crass, R. S. (1964) *Freshwater Fishes of Natal*, Shuter and Shooter, Pietermaritzburg, 167 pp.

Daget, J. and Durand J.-R. (1981) Poissons, in *Faune et Flore aquatiques de l'Afrique Sahelo–soudanienne* (Coll. Initiations, Documentations et Techniques, No. 45) (eds. J. R. Durand and C. Lévêque), ORSTOM, Paris, pp. 687–771.

Daget, J., Gaigher, I. G. and Ssentongo, G. W. (1988) Conservation, in *Biology and Ecology of African Freshwater Fishes* (eds. C. Lévêque, M. N. Bruton and G. W. Ssentongo), ORSTOM, Paris, pp. 481–91.

Daget, J., Gosse, J. P., and Thys van den Audenaerde, D. F. E. (1984) *Check-list of the Freshwater Fishes of Africa*, Vol. 1, ORSTOM, Paris, MRAC, Tervuren.

Davies, B. R. (1979) Stream regulation in Africa: a review, in *The Ecology of Regulated Streams* (eds. T. V. Ward and J. A. Stanford), Plenum Press, New York, pp. 133–42.

de Moor, I. J. and Bruton, M. N. (1988) Atlas of alien and translocated indigenous aquatic animals in southern Africa. *Sth Afr. Nat. Sci. Progr. Rep.* No. 144, 310 pp.

Donnelly, B. G. (1980) The energetics of a population of *Barbus mattozi* Guimaraes, 1884 (Pisces, Cyprinidae). Unpubl. PhD. thesis, University of Zimbabwe, Harare. (177 pp.).

Donnelly, B. G. (1982) The food of *Barbus mattozi* Guimaraes, 1884 (Pisces, Cyprinidae) in a Zimbabwe impoundment. *J. Limnol. Soc. sth Afr.*, **8**(1), 23–8.

Du Mont, H. J. (1982) Relict distribution patterns of aquatic animals: another tool in evaluating late Pleistocene climate changes in the Sahara and Sahel. *Palaeoecol. Afr.*, **14**, 1–24.

Eccles, D. H. (1983) Feeding biology of smallmouth yellowfish, in Limnology and Fisheries Potential of Lake Le Roux (eds B. R. Allanson and P. B. N. Jackson), *S. Afr. nat. Sci. Prog. Rep.*, No. 77, 65–76.

Eccles, D. H. (1986) Diet of the cyprinid fish *Barbus aeneus* (Burchell) in the P. K. Le Roux Dam, South Africa, with special reference to the effect of turbidity on zooplanktivory. *S. Afr. J. Zool.*, **21**, 257–63.

Evans, W. A. and Vanderpuye, J. (1973) Early development of the fish populations and fisheries in Volta Lake, in W. C. Ackermann, G. F. White and E. B. Worthington (eds), *Man-made Lakes, their Problems and Environmental Effects. Geophys. Monogr.* **17**, 114–20.

FAO (1982) Biological studies on the pelagic ecosystem of Lake Malawi. *Rome, FAO, FI:DP/MLW/75/019, Tech. Rep.* **1**, 182 pp.

Fryer, G. (1960) Concerning the proposed introduction of Nile Perch into Lake Victoria. *East Afr. agric. For. J.*, **25**, 267–70.

Fryer, G. and Whitehead, P. J. P. (1959) The breeding habits, embryology and larval development of *Labeo victorianus* Boulenger. *Revue. Zool. Bot. afr.*, **59**(1–2), 33–49.

Furse, M. T., Kirk, R. G., Morgan, P. R. and Tweddle, D. (1979a) Fishes: distribution and biology in relation to changes, in *Lake Chilwa: Studies of Change in a Tropical Ecosystem* (eds. M. Kalk, A. J. McLachlan and C. Howard-Williams), *Monographiae biol.*, **35**, 175–208.

Furse, M. T., Morgan, P. R. and Kalk, M. (1979b) The fisheries of Lake Chilwa, in *Lake Chilwa: Studies of Change in a Tropical Ecosystem* (eds. M. Kalk, A. J. McLachlan and C. Howard-Williams), *Monographiae biol.*, **35**, 209–29.

Gaigher, I. G. (1975) The ecology of a minnow, *Barbus trevelyani* (Pisces, Cyprinidae) in the Tyume River, Eastern Cape. *Ann. Cape Prov. Mus.*, **11** (1), 1–19.

Greenwood, P. H. (1962) A revision of certain *Barbus* species (Pisces, Cyprinidae) from East, Central and South Africa. *Bull. Br. Mus. nat. Hist. (Zool.)*, **8** (4), 153–208.

Greenwood, P. H. (1966) *The Fishes of Uganda*. The Uganda Society, Kampala, 131 pp.

Greenwood, P. H. (1970) A revision of the cyprinid species *Barbus (Enteromius) radiatus* Peters, 1853, with a note on the synonymy of the subgenera *Beirabarbus* and *Enteromius*. *Revue Zool. Bot. afr.*, **82** (1–2), 1–13.

Greenwood, P. H. (1983) The zoogeography of African freshwater fishes: bioaccountancy or biogeography? in *Evolution, Time and Space: The Emergence of the Biosphere (Systematics Association Special Volume* 23) (eds R. W. Sims, J. H. Price and P. E. S. Whalley), Academic Press, London and New York, pp. 179–99.

HEST (1988) *Haplochromis Ecology Survey Team: Progress Report 1987* (Reports from the *Haplochromis* Ecology Survey Team (HEST) and the Tanzanian Fisheries Research Institute (TAFIRI) operating in Lake Victoria, 48), 18 pp.

Hopson, A. J. and Hopson, J. (1965) *Barbus* (Pisces, Cyprinidae) of the Volta region. *Bull. Br. Mus. nat. Hist. (Zool.)*, **13**, 99–149.

Howes, G. J. (1980) The anatomy, phylogeny and classification of bariliine cyprinid fishes. *Bull. Br. Mus. nat. Hist. (Zool.)*, **37** (3), 129–98.

Howes, G. J. (1983) Additional notes on bariliine cyprinid fishes. *Bull. Br. Mus. nat. Hist. (Zool.)*, **45** (2), 95–101.

Howes, G. J. (1984) A review of the anatomy, taxonomy, phylogeny and biogeography of the African neoboline cyprinid fishes. *Bull. Br. Mus. nat. Hist. (Zool.)*, **47** (3), 151–85

Howes, G. J. (1987) The phylogenetic position of the Yugoslavian cyprinid fish genus *Aulopyge* Heckel, 1841, with an appraisal of the genus *Barbus* Cuvier & Cloquet, 1816 and the subfamily Cyprininae. *Bull. Br. Mus. nat. His. (Zool.)*, **53** (5), 165–96.

Howes, G. J. and Teugels, G. G. (1989) New bariliin cyrinid fishes from West Africa, with a consideration of their biogeography. *J. nat. Hist.*, **23**, 873–902.

Iles, T. D. (1962) Further notes on gill-net experiments on *Labeo mesops* (Günther). *Rep. jt Fish. Res. Org. Nth. Rhod.*, **10**, 48–55.

IUCN (1988) *Red List of Threatened Animals*, International Union for Conservation of Nature and Natural Resources, Gland, Switzerland. 154 pp.

Jackson, P. B. N. (1960) On the desirability or otherwise of introducing fishes to waters that are foreign to them. *Publs Cons. Scient. Afr. S. Sahara*, **63**, 157–64.

Jackson, P. B. N. (1961) *The Fishes of Northern Rhodesia*, Government Printer, Lusaka, 140 pp.

Jackson, P. B. N. (1986) Fish of the Zambezi system, in *The Ecology of River Systems* (eds B. R. Davies and K. F. Walker), *Monographiae biol.*, **60**, 269–88.

Jackson, P. B. N. (1989) Prediction of regulation effects on natural biological rhythms in south-central African freshwater fish. *Regul. Rivers Res. Mgt*, **3**, 205–20.

Jackson, P. B. N., Marshall, B. E. and Paugy, G. (1988) Fish communities in man-made lakes, in *Biology and Ecology of African Freshwater Fishes* (eds C. Lévêque, M. N. Bruton and G. W. Ssentongo), ORSTOM, Paris, pp. 325–50.

Jubb, R. A. (1961) *An Illustrated Guide to the Freshwater Fishes of the Zambezi River, Lake Kariba, Pungwe, Sabi, Lundi, and Limpopo Rivers*. Stuart Manning, Bulawayo, 171 pp.

Jubb, R. A. (1967) *Freshwater Fishes of Southern Africa*, A. A. Balkema, Cape Town, 247 pp.

Kleynhans, C. J. (1987) A preliminary study of aspects of the ecology of a rare minnow *Barbus treurensis* Groenewald, 1958 (Pisces, Cyprinidae) from the eastern Transvaal, South Africa. *J. Limnol. Soc. sth Afr.*, **13** (1), 7–13.

Krupp, F. (1982) *Garra tibanica ghorensis* sub sp. nov. (Pisces: Cyprinidae) an African element in the cyprinid fauna of the Levant. *Hydrobiologia*, **88**, 319–24.

Latif, A. F. A. (1976) Fish and fisheries of Lake Nasser, in *The Nile: Biology of an Ancient River* (ed. J. Rzoska), *Monographiae biol.*, **29**, 294–307.

Lévêque, C. (1983) Le genre *Barbus* (Pisces, Cyprinidae) en Côte d'Ivoire. *Cybium*, **7** (3), 61–86.

Lévêque, C. and Bigorne, R. (1983) Revision des *Leptocypris* et *Raiamias* de l'Afrique de l'Ouest. *Rev. Hydrobiol. trop.*, **16** (4), 373–93.

Lévêque, C. and Paugy, D. (1984) *Guide des Poissons d'Eau douce de la Zone du Programme de Lutte contre l'Onchocercose en Afrique de l'Ouest*, ORSTOM-OMS, Paris, 393 pp.

Lewis, D. S. C. and Tweddle, D. (1988) The yield of Usipa (*Engraulicypris sardella*) from the Nankumba Peninsula, Lake Malaŵi (1985–1986). Unpubl. Report, Malaŵi Fisheries Department.

Lowe-McConnell, R. H. (1987) *Ecological Studies in Tropical Fish Communities*, Cambridge University Press, Cambridge, 382 pp.

Lowe-McConnell, R. H. (1988) Broad characteristics of the ichthyofauna, in *Biology and Ecology of African Freshwater Fishes* (eds. C. Lévêque, M. N. Bruton and G. W. Ssentongo), ORSTOM, Paris, pp. 93–112.

Mahnert, V. and Gery, J. (1982) Poissons du bassin de l'Ivindo IX. Notes sur le genre *Barbus* (Cyprinidae). *Revue suisse Zool.*, **89**, 461–95.

Marlier, G. (1953) Étude biogéographique du bassin de la Ruzizi, basée sur la distribution des poissons. *Annls Soc. r. zool. Belg.*, **84**, 175–224.

Matthes, H. (1963) A comparative study of the feeding mechanisms of some African Cyprinidae (Pisces, Cypriniformes). *Bijdr. Dierk.*, **33**, 1–35.

Menon, A. G. K. (1964) Monograph of the cyprinid fishes of the genus *Garra* Hamilton. *Mem. Ind. Mus.*, **14** (4), 173–260.

Moreau, J., Arrignon, J. and Jubb, R. A. (1988) Les introductions d'espèces étrangeres dans les eaux continentales africaines, in *Biology and Ecology of African Freshwater Fishes* (eds C. Lévêque, M. N. Bruton and G. W. Ssentongo), ORSTOM, Paris, pp. 395–426.

Mulder, P. F. S. (1973a) Aspects on the ecology of *Barbus kimberleyensis* and *Barbus holubi* in the Vaal River. *Zool. Afr.*, **8**, 1–4.

Mulder, P. F. S. (1973b) Aspects on the ecology of *Labeo capensis* and *Labeo umbratus* in the Vaal River. *Zool. Afr.*, **8**, 15–25.

Noakes, D. L. G. and Balon, E. K. (1982) Life histories of tilapias, an evolutionary perspective, in *Biology and Culture of Tilapias* (eds R. S. V. Pullen and R. H. Lowe–McConnell), ICLARM, Manila, pp. 61–82.

Norman, J. R. (1923) A new cyprinoid fish from Tanganyika territory, and two new fishes from Angola. *Ann. Mag. nat. Hist.*, (**9**), **12** (74), 694–6.

Oellermann, L. K. (1988) The karyology and taxonomy of the southern African yellowfish (Pisces: Cyprinidae). Unpubl. MSc. thesis, Rhodes University, Grahamstown, South Africa. (123 pp.).

Payne, A. I. (1975) The reproductive cycle, condition and feeding in *Barbus liberiensis*, a tropical stream-dwelling cyprinid. *J. Zool., Lond.*, **176**, 247–69.

Pienaar, U. de V. (1978) *The Freshwater Fishes of the Kruger National Park*, Trustees of the National Parks Board, Pretoria, 91 pp.

Poll, M. (1967) Contribution à la faune ichthyologique de l'Angola. *Publ. Cult. Cia Diamantes Angola*, **75**, 381 pp.

Poll, M. (1969) Description et ostéologie d'une nouvelle espèce de Cyprinidae attribuée au genre *Coptostomabarbus* David et Poll. *Bull. Acad. r. Belg.* (**5**), **55** (3), 117–24.

Poll, M. and Lambert, J. (1961) *Barbus schoutedeni*, espèce nouvelle du sous-genre *Clypeobarbus. Revue Zool. Bot. afr.*, **64** (3–4), 265–71.

Polling, L. (1972) Spawning of *Barbus viviparus. Afr. Aquar.* August 1972, 11–13.

Reid, G. McG. (1978) A systematic study of labeine cyprinid fishes with particular reference to *Labeo* species. Unpubl. PhD. thesis, University London. (770 pp.).

Reid, G. McG. (1982) The form, function and phylogenetic significance of the vomeropalatine organ in cyprinid fishes. *J. nat. Hist.*, **16**, 497–510.

Reid, G. McG. (1985) A revision of African species of *Labeo* (Pisces: Cyprinidae) and a redefinition of the genus. *Theses Zoologicae*, **6**, 322 pp.

Reynolds, J. D. (1973) Biological notes on *Barbus* species (Pisces, Cyprinidae) in the Volta Lake, Ghana. *Revue Zool. Bot. afr.*, **87**, 815–21.

Ribbink, A. J. V. L. (1986) Perspectives in species conservation. *Annls Mus. r. Afr. cent. Sci. zool.*, **251**, 163–70.

Risch, L. and Thys van den Audenaerde, D. F. E. (1985) Note sur la présence de *Chrysichthys longidorsalis* (Pisces Bagridae) et de *Sanagia velifera* (Pisces Cyprinidae) dans le Nyong (Cameroun). *Revue Zool. afr.*, **99**, 87–96.

Roberts, T. R. (1975) Geographical distribution of African freshwater fishes. *Zool. J. Linn. Soc.*, **57** (4), 249–319.

Skelton, P. H. (1986) Distribution patterns and biogeography of non-tropical southern African freshwater fishes. *Palaeoecol. Afr.*, **17**, 211–30.

Skelton, P. H. (1987) South African Red Data Book – Fishes. *S. Afr. nat. Sci. Progr. Rep.*, No. 137, 199 pp.

Skelton, P. H. (1988) A taxonomic revision of the redfin minnows (Pisces, Cyprinidae) from southern Africa. *Ann. Cape. prov. Mus. (nat. Hist.)*, **16** (10), 201–307.

Stewart, D. J. (1977) Geographic variation of *Barbus radiatus* Peters, a widely distributed African cyprinid fish. *Env. Biol. Fishes*, **1** (2), 113–25.

Thys van den Audenaerde, D. F. E. (1975) Note on the synonymy of *Barboides* Brüning, 1929 and *Raddabarbus* Thys, 1971 (Pisces, Cyprinidae). *Revue Zool. afr.*, **90**, 197–203.

Tomasson, T., Cambray, J. A. and Jackson, P. B. N. (1984) Reproductive biology of four large riverine fishes (Cyprinidae) in a man-made lake, Orange River, South Africa. *Hydrobiologia*, **112**, 179–95.

Tweddle, D. (1981) The importance of long-term data collection on river fisheries, with particular reference to the cyprinid *Opsaridium microlepis* (Günther, 1864) fisheries of the affluent rivers of Lake Malawi, in Seminar on river basin management and development (ed. J. M. Kapetsky), *CIFA* (Comm. Inland Fish. Afr.) *Tech. Pap. / Doc. Tech. CPCA* **8**, 145–63.

Tweddle, D. (1982) The fishes of the Malaŵi Northern Region game reserves. *Nyala*, **7** (2), 99–108.

Tweddle, D. (1983) Breeding behaviour of the mpasa, *Opsaridium microlepis* (Günther) (Pisces: Cyprinidae), in Lake Malawi. *J. Limnol. Soc. sth. Afr.*, **9** (1), 23–8.

Tweddle, D. (1985) The importance of the National Parks, Game Reserves and Forest Reserves of Malawi to fish conservation and fisheries management. *Nyala*, **11** (1) 5–11.

Tweddle, D. (1987) An assessment of the growth rate of mpasa, *Opsaridium microlepis* (Günther, 1864) (Pisces: Cyprinidae) by length frequency analysis. *J. Limnol. Soc. sth Afr.*, **13** (2), 52–7.

Tweddle, D. and Lewis, D. S. C. (1983) Convergent evolution between the Lake Malawi mpasa (Cyprinidae) and the Atlantic salmon (Salmonidae). *Luso: J. Sci. Technol. Malawi*, **4** (1), 11–20.

Tweddle, D. and Lewis, D. S. C. (1988) A note on the biology of usipa in relation to the controversy over the possibility of exotic introductions into Lake Malawi. Unpubl. report, Malawi Fisheries Department.

Tweddle, D., Lewis, D. S. C. and Willoughby, N. G. (1979) The nature of the barrier separating the Lake Malawi and Zambezi fish faunas. *Ichthyol. Bull. Rhodes Univ.*, **39**, 1–9.

Van Couvering, J. A. H. (1977) Early records of freshwater fishes in Africa. *Copeia*, **1977** (1), 163–6.

Wanink, J. H. (1988) *Recent changes in the zooplanktivorous/insectivorous fish community of the Mwanza Gulf* (Reports from the *Haplochromis* Ecology Survey Team (HEST) and the Tanzanian Fisheries Research Institute (TAFIRI) operating in Lake Victoria, 45), 8 pp.

Chapter eight

Cyprinids of the New World

R. L. Mayden

8.1 INTRODUCTION

New World cyprinids occur naturally throughout North America, extending as far north as the Yukon and Mackenzie river systems and terminating in southern Mexico (Barbour and Miller, 1978). Their southern terminus is the Rio Papaloapan of the Atlantic Slope and the Rio Verde, draining part of the Pacific Slope (Miller and Smith, 1986). The family is primarily temperate, with only a few members extending into the tropics. Fossil and recent evidence indicate that this group has never occurred naturally in South America or remaining Central America.

Minnows represent by far the most speciose fish family in North America. A total of 286 Recent species in 53 genera are recognized, some of which have not yet been formally described. The second most abundant family for the continent is the Percidae, containing about 160 Recent species. Nearly all of the cyprinid genera are endemic to the continent. The genus *Phoxinus*, however, maintains a nearly Holarctic distribution with North American members related to European species; several species of western genera have phylogenetic affinities with Asian groups. Introduced species number only nine, and generally have had a negative impact on the native fauna. At least ten species are thought to be extinct, while an additional 25 species and subspecies are listed as threatened or endangered.

Cyprinids represent an important ecological and evolutionary component in most aquatic communities of North American inland waters and have been the focus of numerous evolutionary and ecological investigations. With the great diversity exhibited by this family in ecological attributes, behaviour, morphology, and distribution, they represent one of the most informative groups conducive to advancements in comparative and evolutionary biology.

8.2 MAJOR RIVER DRAINAGES AND CYPRINID DIVERSITY

The cyprinid fauna of North America inhabits diverse aquatic environments accounting for > 1 m. km^2 of the surface of the continent. These species are widespread across several discrete physiographic provinces. Most watersheds have remained intact since the Pleistocene; some, however, have experienced considerable modification in the last several million years, primarily as a result of continental glaciation, aridity, and tectonism. More recently, some watersheds have been dramatically altered by human activities, most of which have been detrimental to cyprinid species. Only general patterns can be summarized here relative to cyprinid diversity, but regional drainage histories and environments are treated in Hocutt and Wiley (1986).

For New World cyprinids, the most significant flowing waterway is the Mississippi River, its basin covering > 3 m. km^2 (one-eighth of the continent), which travels 6000 km from its Missouri River head waters. A total of 337 freshwater species inhabit this system, 119 (35%) of which are minnows. Within the Mississippi waterway, several major drainages can be identified. In the west, the Missouri drains, > 1 m. km^2, has 138 species, and 44 cyprinids (32%); the Arkansas River covers 409 000 km^2 and has 55 cyprinid species (39% of 141 in all); and the Red River encompasses 166 300 km^2, has 152 native species, and 43 minnow species (28%). Portions of the present Mississippi formerly travelled northward into the Hudson Bay and St Lawrence systems, eastward to the Atlantic Slope, or southward in the west into the Plains River. Most importantly, much of this basin was formerly part of the major pre-Pleistocene Teays River.

East of the Mississippi, two major drainages contain the richest cyprinid faunas in North America, the Cumberland and Tennessee rivers and the Mobile Basin. The great diversity of these systems results largely from minimal impact by glaciation and a prolonged period of moist climatic conditions. The Cumberland and Tennessee rivers have the highest cyprinid diversity per unit area. Together, in draining about 153 000 km^2, they have 241 fish species, of which 80 are cyprinids (33%). The Mobile Basin contains the second largest fauna per unit area (114 000 km^2), with 47 cyprinid species out of 158 species (29%).

The Hudson Bay Basin rivals the Mississippi River in size, with a watershed of 3 884 000 km^2. Its native fauna and cyprinid diversity is, however, considerably lower, with only 101 total species and 31 cyprinids (31%). This impoverished fauna has resulted largely from the impact of the Laurentian ice sheets on the drainage system. The Mackenzie River ranks as the third largest watershed on the continent and extends for > 2000 km. This northern drainage was also greatly influenced by Laurentian glacial advance, as well as the Cordilleran ice sheet, and contains only 13 cyprinids (24%) of a total of 53 native fish species. Further south, the Columbia River Basin, covering

671 000 km², has a comparable fish diversity, with only 12 cyprinids (23%) and 52 species in all.

The climatic history imposed upon south-west drainages has been quite different from those of northern and north-western watersheds. The South-west Basins and Range Province, comprising most of the area between the Sierra Nevada and Rocky Mountains and extending into Mexico, dominates a large part of the west. Here, many rivers are endorheic and have maintained a state of isolation throughout much of the Cenozoic. As many as 150 discrete drainage units can be identified in this area (Minckley *et al.*, 1986). Cyprinids here are generally adaptable and are known to inhabit head-water streams as well as lowland rivers. This region is home to some of the largest native minnows in North America.

Two major watersheds cover most of the south-west, the Colorado River and Rio Grande. They are somewhat similar in size (650 000 and 500 000 km²), but differ greatly in their native ichthyofauna: the Colorado River fauna consists of only 32 species, 16 (50%) of which are cyprinids; the Rio Grande fauna includes 121 species and 43 (36%) cyprinids. In Mexico, the southern most major river systems with cyprinids include the Rio Panuco on the Atlantic and Rio Balsas on the Pacific. The fauna is about as diverse as in typical western drainages discussed above, but the cyprinid faunas are reduced, primarily as a result of being peripheral in distribution. In the Rio Panuco, the total ichthyofauna includes only 51 species, 11 of which are cyprinids, and six of these are endemic. The extreme situation occurs in the Rio Balsas, with 20 fish species and only two cyprinids, one of which (*Hybopsis boucardi*) is endemic. The southern limit for the family is two relatively small drainages in southern Mexico. The upper Rio Papaloapan on the Atlantic Slope has one endemic species, *Hybopsis moralesi*, while the Pacific Rio Verde/Atoyac harbours the endemic *H. imeldae*. In these drainages, cyprinid species constitute 2.5% and 16% of their respective fish faunas.

8.3   DIVERSITY AND TAXONOMY

Native New World cyprinids comprise 53 genera and about 286 species (Table 8.1; species list, p. 257). The age of the fauna is traced to at least the Oligocene (Cavender, 1986). It is likely that the fauna will be discovered to be considerably older once phylogenetic relationships are advanced for New World cyprinids and other cyprinid taxa. Although considerable research is needed with regard to intrafamilial relationships, the North American fauna has traditionally been placed in the subfamily Leuciscinae (Hubbs and Lagler, 1958; Gosline, 1978). Miller (1958) and Bănărescu (1973) viewed the fauna as having a polyphyletic origin by considering *Notemigonus* to be more closely related to the genus *Abramis* or members of the subfamily Abramidinae. Howes

Table 8.1 Geographic distribution of New World cyprinid genera, expressed as number of species for each genus in each area*

Genus	Geographic areas[†]													
	A	B	C	D	E	F	G	H	I	J	K	L	M	N
Acrocheilus												1	1	
Algansea											7			
Aztecula											1			
Compostoma	1	2	1	1	3	2	2	2	1	2		1		
Clinostomus		1	2	2	1	1	2							
Couesius	1	1	1				1	1					1	1
Cyprinella	1	2	2	6	15	5	5	6	3	9	1	2		
Dionda									2	4	6	2		
Eremichthys												1		
Ericymba		1	1	1	1	1	1							
Erimonax						1								
Erimystax		1				3	2	2						
Evarra											3			
Exoglossum		2	1	1			2							
Extrarius					3	1	1	1	1	1				
Gila											7	18	3	
Hemitremia					1	1								
Hesperoleucus												1		
Hybognathus	2	2	2	1	3	2	5	5	3	1			1	1
Hybopsis	1	3	1	7	8	2	4	5	2		5	1		
Iotichthys												1		
Lavinia												1		
Lepidomeda												4		
Luxilus	1	2	1	4	3	3	4	5						
Lythrurus		1		1	7	5	3	3	2					
Macrhybopsis	1	1			1	1	3	3	1					
Margariscus	1	1	1	1			1	1						1
Meda												1		
Moapa												1		
Mylocheilus													1	1
Mylopharodon												1		
Nocomis	1	2	1	3	2	3	5	2						
Notemigonus	1	1	1	1	1	1	1	1	1					
Notropis	10	15	9	20	30	20	22	26	13	12	1			2
Opsopoeodus		1		1	1	1	1	1	1					
Oregonichthys												1	1	
Orthodon												1		
Phenacobius		1			2	3	3	1	1	1				

(Continued)

Table 8.1 (*Continued*)

Genus	Geographic areas[†]													
	A	B	C	D	E	F	G	H	I	J	K	L	M	N
Phoxinus	2	3	2	2	1	4	4	3						2
Pimephales	3	3	1	1	3	3	3	4	2	2				1
Plagopterus												1		
Platygobio	1						1	1		1				1
Pogonichthys												2		
Pteronotropis				1	4									
Ptychocheilus												4	1	1
Relictus												1		
Rhinichthys	2	2	2	2	2	2	2	2		1		7	3	1
Richardsonius												2	1	1
Semotilus	2	2	2	3	2	1	1	1	1	1				
Stypodon										1				
Yuriria											2			
Species index[‡]	1.9	2.3	2.0	3.0	4.4	3.0	3.3	3.5	2.4	3.2	3.7	2.3	1.4	1.2

*Division of geographic regions into areas, and numbers of species, are extracted from Hocutt and Wiley (1986); see also Fig. 8.1. Distributions of taxa are available from the author.
[†]Areas: A, Hudson Bay; B, Great Lakes; C, Appalachians; D, Atlantic Slope; E, Eastern Gulf, F, Tennessee–Cumberland; G, Mississippi–Ohio; H, Western Mississippi; I, Western Gulf; J, Rio Grande; K, Central Mexico; L, Southwest Basins; M, Cascadia; N, Yukon-Mackenzie.
[‡]Number of species/genus: see Fig. 8.2(a).

(1981), however, found no evidence to support a closer relationship of *Notemigonus* to Old World minnows.

Regardless of the affinities of *Notemigonus*, and the existing supraspecific relationships within the family, this fauna is not a monophyletic assemblage within the Leuciscinae. Howes (1984) evaluated aspinine cyprinids and found the western North American genus *Pogonichthys*, and possibly *Lavinia*, *Ptychocheilus*, *Mylopharodon*, and *Gila* (part), to be involved in a clade with the Asia genus *Tribolodon*. This Asian connection has been much discussed and is replicated by multiple taxa (Howes, 1984). Further support for a polyphyletic origin of the fauna arises from sister group relationships in the phoxinine group (*Phoxinus* and *Couesius*) (*sensu* Howes, 1985). *Phoxinus* has a Holarctic distribution and is monophyletic with respect to *Couesius*, necessitating an ancient and widespread Holarctic distribution for the clade (see also Section 1.3).

The systematics and taxonomy of many New World cyprinids is in a state of flux. Only recently has the fauna been under such rigorous scrutiny to determine sister group relationships (Mayden, 1989). Recent comparative studies of fauna have elucidated relationships which in some cases are inconsistent with previous, well-established taxonomies. Although taxonomic changes accompanying these revisions may be interpreted as cumbersome, they promote universal and consistent communication of genealogical descent within the fauna.

Several important investigations of cyprinid species diversity and variation exist for this fauna. However, few studies have provided hypotheses of species relationships employing a phylogenetic framework in character analysis, *sensu* Willi Hennig, but most efforts are focused instead on groupings within the unnatural genus '*Notropis*' (Mayden, 1989). Notable exceptions include the works by Barbour and Miller (1978) and Jensen and Barbour (1981) on *Algansea*, Woodman (1987) on *Rhinichthys*, Coburn (1982) on *Notropis*, Buth (1979) and Mayden (1988) on *Luxilus*.

Phylogenetics of major species groups and genera were not undertaken before 1979. Revisionary investigations were resisted chiefly because of difficulties with the exceptionally large and unnatural genus '*Notropis*' and because the classification of New World minnows had been considered stable since much of the work by Jordan (Gilbert, 1964). This apparent stability led most to suppose that the relationships of species were understood. More recently, two morphological systematic studies have focused on groupings within '*Notropis*', and have evaluated some higher relationships. Coburn (1982) focused on the subgenus *Notropis*, while Mayden (1989) examined species relationships in *Cyprinella* and several other clades. Both investigations were beneficial in outlining particular problem areas in cyprinid systematics and in warning that the existing taxonomy was inadequate and misleading. A different classification therefore exists, incorporating only information about species relationships (Table 8.1 and p. 257). Important changes include the recognition of the genera *Cyprinella*, *Luxilus*, *Lythrurus*, *Opsopoeodus*, and *Pteronotropis* from '*Notropis*', and a dismemberment of '*Hybopsis*' into *Macrhybopsis*, *Extrarius*, *Erimystax*, *Erimonax*, *Oregonichthys*, *Yuriria*, *Platygobio*, and *Hybopsis*. The real *Hybopsis* is further altered to include some species of previously recognized '*Notropis*'.

Even after revisionary changes, the largest genus remains *Notropis*, with 72 species (p. 257). However, as now conceived, this genus is probably not a natural taxon. Within *Notropis* some monophyletic groups are recognizable and are listed as species groups or subgenera, while others remain to be assigned to clades (p. 257). Other diverse genera include *Cyprinella*, *Gila*, and *Hybopsis* (p. 257). Twenty-five genera are monotypic, several of which are western and exist largely because they possess 'unique' morphologies and because we know little about their relationships. Significant studies have described the fauna and have detailed extensive variation, but species interrelationships are largely unknown. For example, considerable literature exists concerning the variation of forms in the genus *Rhinichthys*, as well as alternative hypotheses of relationships. Confusion has been compounded by the similar monotypic genera *Tiaroga* and *Agosia*, both maintained largely because of trenchant differences. Much of this confusion evaporated, however, when Woodman (1987) examined relationships of *Rhinichthys* and found that these two 'genera' were most closely related to species within *Rhinichthys*.

8.4 ECOLOGICAL AND HISTORICAL BIOGEOGRAPHY

Evolution of the fauna has culminated in several distinctive patterns of distribution. Some appear to be more amenable to historical (systematic) explanations, while others are best explained in terms of ecological processes. The most notable patterns are the basic faunal differences between drainages east and west of the Rocky Mountains (Table 8.1), and the disproportionate diversity of specific geographic regions in North America (Fig. 8.1).

Western rivers are, or were, characterized by the genera *Acrocheilus*, *Algansea*, *Aztecula*, *Eremichthys*, *Evarra*, *Gila*, *Hesperoleucas*, *Iotichthys*, *Lavinia*, *Lepidomeda*, *Meda*, *Moapa*, *Mylocheilus*, *Mylopharodon*, *Oregonichthys*, *Orthodon*, *Plagopterus*, *Pogonichthys*, *Ptychocheilus*, *Relictus*, *Richardsonius*, and *Yuriria*. A different set of genera is endemic to eastern drainages of the Mississippi System, including *Clinostomus*, *Ericymba*, *Erimonax*, *Erimystax*, *Exoglossum*, *Hemitremia*, *Luxilus*, *Lythrurus*, *Macrhybopsis*, *Nocomis*, *Notemigonus*, *Notropis*, *Opsopoeodus*, *Phenacobius*, *Pteronotropis*, and *Semotilus*. Some taxa are represented in both eastern and western drainages for various reasons. For example, western populations or representatives of the genera *Couesius*, *Hybognathus*, *Margariscus*, and *Platygobio* inhabit rivers of the Cascadia and Yukon regions and occur there because of a transfer from the Mississippi River System. Other genera have both western and eastern representatives. Included here are species of *Campostoma*, *Cyprinella*, *Dionda*, *Hybopsis*, *Phoxinus*, and *Rhinichthys*. All of these taxa are fairly widespread and have southern representatives in Pacific and Atlantic rivers.

Patterns of diversity within a genus and across major geographic regions provide further biogeographic information. For most cyprinids with eastern representatives, the greatest diversity occurs in the Eastern Gulf region (Fig. 8.1). Here, several endemic species occur, including three species of *Campostoma*, 15 *Cyprinella*, three *Extrarius*, seven *Hybopsis*, seven *Lythrurus*, 29 *Notropis*, and four *Pteronotropis*. For many western genera, species diversity reaches its maximum in the Southwest Basins or Cascadia regions, or both (Fig. 8.1). One major area of endemism is the Central Plateau of Mexico. This region is characterized by the four endemic genera *Algansea*, *Aztecula*, *Evarra*, and *Yuriria*, as well as noticeable diversity in the genera *Dionda* and *Hybopsis*.

Several major areas of endemism are evident for North American cyprinids. These include rivers of the Central Highlands (Mayden 1985, 1988), the Mobile Basin (Swift *et al.*, 1986), some mid-Atlantic rivers (Hocutt *et al.*,

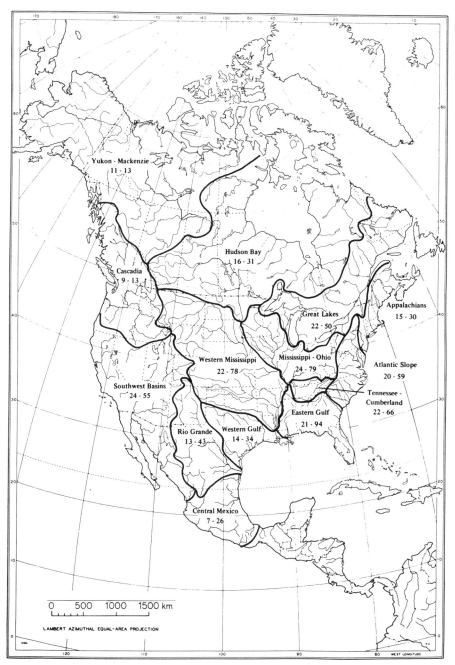

Fig. 8.1 Native cyprinid species diversity in major geographic regions in North America. For each region, the number of genera is given first, then the number of species; data are modified from Hocutt and Wiley (1986).

1986), the Rio Grande and Rio Panuco (Miller and Smith, 1986; Smith and Miller, 1986), and the Colorado River (Minckley *et al.*, 1986). In the Great Basin physiographic province, small endorheic rivers also harbour minor endemic faunas which are extremely limited in distribution. For example, species of *Eremichthys, Iothichthys, Lepidomeda, Meda, Moapa, Relictus, Rhinichthys* and some *Gila* are restricted to one or a few small drainages or springs. In eastern rivers, species with the most restricted ranges include *Notropis mekistocholas* in the Cape Fear River, *N. rupestre* in portions of the Cumberland River, *N. cahabae* in the Cahaba River *Semotilus lumbee* in the Carolina Sandhills, and *Pteronotropis euryzonus* in the middle Chattahoochee River.

Figure 8.2 shows two interpretations of the diversity patterns, and disproportionate rates of speciation, of North American cyprinids. First, the scatterplot (Fig. 8.2(b)) of a linear measure of diversity (number of species per number of genera) groups the 14 geographic areas (Fig. 8.1) into three clusters. However, points fall into a given cluster for different reasons (see below). Second, the number of species per genus also varies, and geographic areas fall into other groupings on that basis (Fig. 8.2(a) and shaded regions of Fig. 8.2(b)).

The lowermost cluster consists of Central Mexico, Yukon–Mackenzie, and Cascadia, all at the extremes in cyprinid distribution. The northern most areas, Yukon–Mackenzie and Cascadia, have nearly as many species as genera. Central Mexico has limited diversity, but has more than three times as many species as genera and is most similar to eastern areas if one compares number of species per genus (Fig. 8.2(a)).

The intermediate cluster includes western Gulf rivers and the Rio Grande, as well as the northern Hudson Bay and Appalachian rivers. This clustering basically includes areas with a moderate number of taxa, but is a composite if one examines species indices for each area: the Rio Grande rivers have as many species per genus as the diverse eastern drainages (Fig. 8.1(a)).

The third cluster includes those regions with the most cyprinid species and genera. This clustering too, is artificial if one considers the species index and geographic locations of each region. All areas share a similar high number of species, but per genus, three subgroupings are obvious. Drainages of the Great Lakes and Southwest Basins are included here, but they share a similar low number of species per genus with north-western and north-eastern regions (Fig. 8.2(a)). All other regions of this cluster, with the exception of the eastern Gulf of Mexico, have a high number of species per genus, like the Rio Grande and Central Mexico.

The above observations are best explained by, and consistent with, three different linear relationships between numbers of species and genera (Fig. 8.2(b), shaded areas and point E). The various diversity relationships may result from differing climatic and drainage histories, and inherent patterns of speciation within the groups involved. Regions with a similar low number of species per genus, but with a general increasing number of species, include the

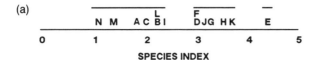

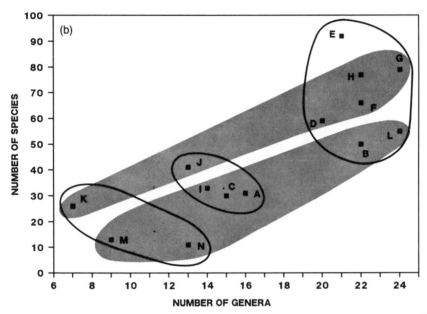

Fig. 8.2 Cyprinid species diversity in relation to number of genera. (a) Groupings (short-black bars) based upon a simple index, the numbers of species per genus (Table 8.1). (b) Relationship between number of species and number of genera. Groupings from the species index (shaded) represent distinctive bivariate relationships shared by separate geographic areas. Contours enclose clusters of areas. (See text for explanation). Areas (see Fig. 8.1): A, Hudson Bay; B, Great Lakes; C, Appolachians; D, Atlantic Slope; E, Eastern Gulf; F, Tennessee–Cumberland; G, Mississippi–Ohio; H, Western Mississippi; I, Western Gulf; J, Rio Grande; K, Central Mexico; L, Southwest Basins; M, Cascadia; N, Yukon–Mackenzie.

Cascadia, Yukon–Mackenzie, Western Gulf, Hudson Bay, Appalachians, Great Lakes, and Southwest Basins. Those with a moderate diversity include Central Mexico, Rio Grande, Atlantic Slope, Tennessee–Cumberland, Western Mississippi, and upper Mississippi–Ohio rivers. The Eastern Gulf rivers have by far the greatest cyprinid diversity and diversity per genus in North America, with about 4.4 species per genus.

The general trend of increasing numbers of species per area is associated with increasing proximity of a river to the Mississippi River System. Eastern Gulf drainages compound this with a history of extended isolation and optimal climatic conditions (Mayden, 1988). Drainages of the Southwest Basin are the exception to this trend. Although the number of species per genus is similar there to those associated with the Mississippi River, Southwest Basin drainages are characterized by a largely unique, yet depauperate fauna for its size. Furthermore, many of these western genera contain only one or a few species.

8.5 LIFE HISTORIES

New World cyprinids display an astonishing array of attributes characterizing their life cycles. For many species, however, almost nothing more is known than the body size, habitat, and associated species. Consequently, it is unlikely that we can fully appreciate the significance of the fauna without an increased interest in their biologies.

Size and life span

For most minnows the adult body size ranges from about 50 to 80 mm SL, with a maximum of nearly 100 mm. The extremes are found in western species. The Colorado squawfish, *Ptychocheilus lucius*, is the largest recorded native species, having reached 1.8 m total length and 45 kg (Jordan and Evermann, 1896). Today, no species reaches this size and very few specimens exceed 18 kg (Moyle, 1976). The Mexican *Notropis tropicus* and *N. saladonis* have the smallest maximum size for the fauna, reaching only 37 and 38 mm SL, respectively (Hubbs and Hubbs, 1958; Hubbs and Miller, 1975).

Little is known about the age distributions for many species. In general, individuals of most species live a maximum of 2–4 y, with some western and eastern ones reaching 5 or 6 y. Extremes range from a probable annual species, *Lythrurus roseipinnis* (Heins and Bresnick, 1975) to species of the genus *Ptychocheilus* which live up to 11+ y (Moyle, 1976). Individuals of *Notemigonus crysoleucas* may live for 9 y (Carlander, 1969).

Reproduction

Since Breder and Rosen's (1966) outstanding review of the diversity of reproductive modes, studies of individual species have contributed to our understanding of these fishes.

Time of spawning

The reproductive season for most species occurs in spring and summer months, largely between March and August. For many, however, the actual spawning period may last only 1–2 months, as in species of *Campostoma*, *Nocomis*, *Dionda*, *Luxilus*, *Cyprinella*, and some *Notropis*. Others, like species of *Pimephales*, *Relictus*, *Lythrurus*, and several *Notropis*, may have a prolonged spawning period, extending from early March until September. For more tropical species of *Dionda*, *Hybopsis*, *Cyprinella*, and *Campostoma*, breeding colours and spawning occur earlier in the year, from December to April. *Rhinichthys chrysogaster* spawns throughout the year (Minckley, 1980).

Most of the small eastern minnows and many western species mature in the first or second year of life. In contrast, some of the larger western species do not mature as early. *Ptychocheilus grandis* does not mature until its third or fourth summer and *P. lucius* matures between 5 and 7 y. For some species, age of maturity also depends upon the sex. In *Hybognathus*, females of some species mature at 1 y, whereas males mature at 2 y. A similar phenomenon occurs in *Lavinia*, but females mature at 2 or 3 y and males at 1–3 y (Moyle, 1976).

Fecundity

Reproductive investment by New World minnows has received considerable attention in recent years. Little synthetic work has involved fecundity for the group, but Heins and Rabito (1986), Heins and Baker (1988), and Coburn (1986), address developmental stages of oocytes, their ultimate sizes, and possible phylogenetic and ecological determinants of oocyte size.

It is difficult to estimate fecundity of these fishes. Many species if not all, are fractional spawners, depositing only portions of their mature eggs in one spawning run and spawning several times in a season. A further complication is that for all these fishes, the number of eggs produced is largely dependent upon body size: in general, larger fishes produce more eggs. Fecundity estimates range from < 60 (*Lythrurus roseipinnis*, Heins and Bresnick, 1975) to > 26 000 (*Lavinia exilicauda*, Moyle, 1976). With the correlation of body size, the larger female *Ptychocheilus lucius* probably produced the largest number of eggs. A 50 cm female develops > 17 000 mature oocytes (Moyle, 1976).

Egg size is also known to vary across taxonomic groups and associated habitats of the species (Coburn, 1986) but is conserved in many genera. Oocyte size ranges from 0.64 mm in *Notropis buchanani* to 2.0 mm in *Campostoma anomalum*. Cyprinids from montane or upland habitats typically develop larger oocytes than do those from lowland habitats or large rivers and lakes (Coburn, 1986). Between these two extremes is a group of riverine and upland species. Lowland species nearly always produce oocytes < 1 mm, whereas upland taxa have a mean mature oocyte diameter 1.36 mm. Oocyte size and degree of territoriality also proved to be significantly associated for the fauna. In general, species with a high degree of parental care and territoriality produced larger eggs than those that typically spread or spray their gametes with no continued attention. Thus, species of *Campostoma*, *Cyprinella*, *Luxilus*, *Semotilus*, and *Rhinichthys* produce some of the largest oocytes for the fauna. An exception to this obvious pattern of reproductive investment is found in the genus *Pimephales*: territoriality and nest construction is better developed than in many genera, yet *Pimephales* spp. have oocytes with diameters of only 1 mm (Coburn, 1986).

Sexual dimorphism

Some type of dimorphic trait is expressed in most species, through body size and shape, genital papillae, fin lengths, tuberculation, or coloration. In general, sexual differences are more pronounced in species that are highly territorial, have some form of parental care, or carry out their life cycles in high-gradient and clear rivers.

The most obvious traits involve breeding coloration. During the reproductive season of most eastern and many western species, males are brightly coloured with pigments on their fins and bodies. Males of some taxa are then so different from females that they may appear to represent different species. Some of the most striking examples of sexual dimorphism include species of *Clinostomus, Cyprinella, Hemitremia, Hybopsis, Luxilus, Lythrurus, Phoxinus, Pteronotropis, Richardsonius*, and some *Notropis*. In these species, male typically develop diagnostic patterns of reds, yellows, and blues, as well as spectacular iridescent patterns, rivalling colourful exotic acquarium species. Members of other genera either do not possess very striking colour patterns or have only minor colour differences, generally expressed as more intense patterns of melanophore deposition.

The second most notable dimorphic trait includes the presence or absence of breeding tubercles, or pearl organs, and their patterns of development. These keratinized organs develop primarily on the head, lateral body scales, and pectoral fins of males during the breeding season. In many species, tubercles are also present in females, but here the size and number of organs is considerably reduced. The onset of tubercle development can occur at a very early stage in some taxa. For example, in the eastern species *Notropis semperasper* some juveniles as small as 17 mm SL (age group 0) develop tubercles on the head. In the Mexican species *Notropis chihuahua*, tubercles form on the head and median fins in specimens as small as 28 mm SL.

The size of these ephemeral organs and their distribution patterns on the body are closely associated with the degree of territoriality, parental care, and nest construction: typically, species displaying a high degree of each have enlarged tubercles. Excellent examples include members of the genera *Campostoma, Couesius, Cyprinella, Dionda, Luxilus, Margariscus, Nocomis, Pimephales, Pteronotropis*, and *Semotilus*. In most of these taxa, males possess enlarged tubercles of different shapes at various locations on their heads.

Breeding habits are also associated with the types of tubercles formed. Species that breed in currents and require body contact during spawning will have greater development of tubercles. Tubercles in these species are best developed on the dorsal surface of the pectoral fins, along the flank scales, and sometimes along the caudal peduncle and venter of the head (species of *Cyprinella, Luxilus, Phenacobius, Extrarius, Gila, Erimonax, Dionda, Campostoma*, and *Rhinichthys* offer examples of this pattern). Most of these species spawn in noticeable current and the male and female are in close contact. This is executed effectively by the male placing one pectoral fin beneath the breast of the female, his head over her nape or head, and wrapping his caudal fin around her caudal peduncle. Thus, tubercles on males in these regions would improve fertilization of oocytes.

Many species also have very fine tubercles that appear to be relatively unmodified. Most of these species provide little or no parental investment to the young, breed in slow-moving water, or do not defend any territories. Examples include species of *Hybognathus, Ericymba, Extrarius, Macrhybopsis, Notemigonus, Lythrurus,* and many *Notropis.* In these fishes the minute tubercles are spread across the head, body, and fins in a simple pattern.

Considerably less noticeable than coloration or tuberculation are traits concerning fin and body shapes. In some species, the body and fins may undergo differential metamorphosis between males and females during the reproductive season. Females usually exhibit only a distention of the abdomen from carrying a complement of oocytes. Males, however, may display quite radical differences. In male *Pimephales* the nape becomes greatly swollen and is used to clean and prepare nest areas, as well as for the production of a fungicide to inhibit brood contamination. Males of several other taxa develop some body swelling during reproduction, but the extreme situation is present in species of *Nocomis.* Members of the *N. micropogon* and *N. leptocephalus* species groups (Lachner, 1952; Mayden, 1987) develop large swellings on the occipital and interorbital areas, greatly altering the males' general appearance. In *Cyprinella,* some males have elongate median fins and swollen snouts during the spawning season. Extreme fin elongation occurs in *Notropis hubbsi* and *Pteronotropis welaka*; breeding males produce greatly enlarged dorsal and anal fins.

Additional sexual dimorphic traits in some genera would include differential growth rates of the sexes (Lachner, 1952) and maximum body size attained by one sex. For many species, females exceed males in overall body size (Breder and Rosen, 1966). In species with well-developed nest-building behaviours or those with territorial tendencies (e.g. *Nocomis, Semotilus,* and *Cyprinella*), males are typically larger than females.

Spawning and nesting
Several reproductive modes have been hypothesized for New World cyprinids; many are summarized by Breder and Rosen (1966). Although the complexities of any behavioural trait are difficult to measure, the simplest mode of spawning appears to involve minimal body contact between the sexes, and spraying and abandoning eggs over the substratum. This occurs in a variety of species over sand, silt, gravel, or vegetation. Some species have adhesive eggs. Examples include species of *Hybognathus, Lavinia, Ptychocheilus, Gila, Mylocheilus,* and some *Notropis* and *Phoxinus.* This mode of spawning has been modified slightly in some species which spawn in current. Here both sexes make more contact, must stay together to ensure fertilization, and partially bury their bodies in the substratum. Species of *Phoxinus, Clinostomus, Phenacobius, Orthodon,*

Hesperoleucas, Richardsonius, Margariscus, Rhinichthys, Notemigonus, and some *Notropis* and *Dionda,* are examples.

One modification of this type of behaviour appears to be the construction of a nest for the eggs. This has occurred in at least three different ways: the species build a mound, sweep out an area, or dig a pit or trough-and-ridge. A disc is a simple nest construction performed by some *Rhinichthys.* The male clears an area by sweeping his caudal fin and guards the eggs in this hollowed disc.

Among cyprinids, mound and pit construction are unique behaviours to a small group of eastern genera *Semotilus, Campostoma, Nocomis,* and *Exoglossum.* This evolutionary innovation has evolved independently in each group: this conclusion is based upon the phylogenetic inferences derived from generic relationships (Mayden, 1989), and the varying methods of construction. The general pattern is for a male to roll stones with his head, or carry stones in his mouth, to or from the construction site. Building materials are generally taken from nearby sites or from mounds constructed by other males. Spawning occurs over the structure with one male and one female, or more than one individual of each sex. The eggs generally drop between stones and are guarded by defending males. The size of the structure varies with the species and the time of year, with larger nests occurring earlier in the season. Nests of *Nocomis* may be 1.8 m in diameter and 1 m in height.

Another mode of reproduction involves the use of nests constructed by other species. Spawning minnows of some species of *Luxilus, Lythrurus, Phoxinus,* and subgenera *Hydrophlox* and *Notropis* of the genus *Notropis,* use the mound nests described above or pit nests of species in the family Centrarchidae. Individuals deposit their eggs in these nests and leave the embryos to the protection of the host. In most cases, the host species is oblivious to their presence and defends the nest from potential predators and conspecifics. Hunter and Hasler (1965) hypothesized that in associations like these, the spawning of host species or the presence of their gametes and spawning fluids in the water are stimuli that initiate spawning of the associated species. However, the associated taxa also spawn in the absence of host nests. Generally, all associated species spawning over host nests have red breeding coloration, enlarged tubercles, and maintain close body contact during the spawning act in the substratum. Typically, more than one male spawns with a single female as she approaches the nest site, although communal spawnings occur.

One of the most specialized modes of spawning within the fauna includes the act of depositing eggs on the protected surfaces of objects, including stones, logs, and stumps. This protects the embryos and occurs in the genera *Pimephales, Cyprinella,* and *Opsopoeodus,* but is manifested in slightly different ways. Species of *Pimephales* and *Opsopoeodus* (L. M. Page, pers. comm.) clear a sheltered area beneath an object, deposit their eggs on its underside, and males remain to protect the young. During the spawning act the sexes invert to fertilize and attach the adhesive eggs to the overlying surface. Within *Cyprinella*, all species studied deposit their eggs in crevices between objects (Rabito and Heins, 1985; Mayden, 1989). Males guard a crevice area and attract females to the spawning site through visual displays and sound production. Once enticed, the female accompanies the male to the crevice and the inject several adhesive eggs and milt into the narrow, slit-like opening. Males then remain to guard the nest and may spawn with additional females. *Cyprinella lutrensis* is unique in the genus in having a life history flexible enough to spawn either in a crevice-type structure or over a variety of substrata typical of many other minnows (Minckley, 1959).

Food and feeding habits

A wide array of food habits exists for native cyprinids, but for many, feeding is so varied that any discrete classification based on food is difficult. Probably the most restricted type of feeding would include specialization on vegetation, other fishes, or plankton. *Acrocheilus* and *Campostoma* are believed to be phylogenetically distant, yet have elongate intestines and specialized feeding strategies for scraping algae and diatoms from the substratum. Several other genera are known to feed on vegetation, such as *Dionda, Pimephales, Hybognathus,* and some *Gila,* but these taxa also forage regularly on animal materials. Piscivory is generally limited to the largest species in the fauna. Representatives of this guild include larger specimens of *Ptychocheilus, Gila,* and *Eremichthys*. Species of *Lavinia* and *Orthodon* have numerous, fine gill rakers and specialize in feeding on plankton. For some species, like *Mylopharodon conocephalus*, ontogeny dictates a varied diet; this species feeds mainly upon benthic insects and plankton as juveniles, but as adults the dentition changes to accommodate more plant material (Moyle, 1976).

Other species may be considered primarily carnivores or omnivores with quite varied diets. Their food includes aquatic and terrestrial insects, molluscs, crustaceans, and to a lesser degree vegetation and vegetable matter. Dipteran, ephemeropteran, and trichopteran insects usually account for most of their diets. Feeding habits of this group, however, may vary considerably from primarily visual hunters to species with specialized taste organs on barbels, bodies, and fins. Typically, species inhabiting large turbid rivers rely heavily upon such organs and have reduced eyes. Species typical of clear streams and lakes, however, are primarily sight feeders throughout the water column and are adversely affected by reduced visibility.

8.6 HUMAN USE

The use of native cyprinids by humans has been restricted to a handful of species. Usually they have been employed as bait for fishing, or for farming and forage. A few species have been sought as aquarium pets. Generally, the more colourful species of *Notropis, Pteronotropis, Cyprinella, Luxilus,* and *Lythrurus* are used for the aquarium trade. Those most commonly used for bait include species of *Pimephales,* primarily the fathead minnow, and *Notemigonus crysoleucas.* These species are hardy, commonly reared in aquaculture, and marketed nation-wide by bait dealers. Many other minnows have been caught privately for bait, most frequently by individuals with minnow seines in local creeks. An unfortunate, yet common outcome has been the 'bait-bucket' introduction of species into non-native watersheds.

Large individuals of some species endemic to western drainages and a few eastern species are eaten occasionally. Western members include *Orthodon, Mylocheilus,* and *Ptychocheilus.* In the east, species of *Campostoma, Margariscus, Platygobio, Nocomis,* and *Semotilus* are irregularly sought by anglers for food and sport. Because cyprinids form such a major component of the North American ichthyofauna (p. 257), many species are widely used for scientific research covering an array of topics. Some species such as the hardy *Pimephales promelas* have also been used by certain agencies for environmental monitoring and water-quality testing procedures.

8.7   INTRODUCED SPECIES

At least nine exotic cyprinids have been introduced into the New World. These include *Carassius auratus* (goldfish), *Ctenopharyngodon idella* (grass carp), *Cyprinus carpio* (common carp), *Hypophthalmichthys molotrix* (silver carp), *H. nobilis* (bighead carp), *Leuciscus idus* (ide), *Rhodeus sericeus* (bitterling), *Scardinius erythrophthalmus* (rudd), and *Tinca tinca* (tench). Most are from South East Asia, but some occur naturally in Europe. The goldfish was the first documented exotic species in North America; released in the late 1600s, it was introduced primarily for aquarium use and bait. Other species have been introduced largely for aquaculture, control of unwanted vegetation, or for food and sport (Courtenay *et al.*, 1986).

The adverse impact of exotic species upon native aquatic ecosystems and fish faunas in general has not as yet been appreciated by those largely responsible for the introductions. The common carp tolerates a wide range of habitats and competes with native species (Becker, 1983), and grass carp are now reproducing naturally. The other species have not been in these waters long enough for their impacts to be assessed, but they may also outcompete natives with a lower reproductive potential as a result of significantly altered habitats. With their typically high tolerance for fluctuation of environmental variables, some species appear certain to expand their ranges. It is unfortunate that those ultimately responsible for the introductions do not appreciate, use, or consider the native fauna when given the option to import exotics.

8.8 FUTURE RESEARCH

Great species diversity, varied biogeographic patterns, and a understanding of the genealogical relationships of species form the baseline data for productive investigations in evolutionary biology and ecology. The North American cyprinids form one of the largest taxonomic groupings of fishes in the New World and offer the ingredients for informative studies in these areas. Few faunas are as diverse and as well known biologically. Recent progress with systematic relationships of native species and their ecologies therefore should not only be applauded but should be strongly encouraged. Without data of this nature for any group of organisms, our advances in evolutionary biology will only progress slowly and indirectly.

Advances in historical biogeography have also benefited recently from this diverse assemblage of species. A synthesis of information will soon be attainable for investigations into the evolution of the Cyprinidae and the origin of the New World fauna as a whole. For example, not until more detailed phylogenies exist for many species will it be possible to offer hypotheses concerning the proportion of the fauna having European and Asian affinities. Likewise, although several interesting areas of endemism occur and distinct geographic regions can be identified, biologists are largely without direct estimates of the origins of the patterns. Thus, these fishes offer nearly unlimited opportunities for biologists to test many theories currently advertised in ecological and evolutionary arenas and to deal with origins of ecological traits and associations, as well as with modes of speciation and rates of character change. Given the tremendous value of the fauna to many areas of science, it is to be hoped that it will be uniformly appreciated should individual species face questionable destiny.

ACKNOWLEDGMENTS

I thank Ian Winfield and Joseph Nelson for the opportunity to contribute to this volume and for editorial assistance. I also thank B. M. Burr, B. R. Kuhajda, M. J. Mayden, M. F. Mettee, L. M. Page and J. Reese for information or technical assistance. This research was supported by the National Science Foundation (grant BSR 8614431) and is contribution number 119 from the Aquatic Biology Program at the Department of Biology, University of Alabama.

SPECIES LIST

The following list of New World native cyprinid species includes only taxonomically described species. Taxonomy is constructed from the author's assessment of relationships within the family and is consistent with known phylogenetic relationships. (E) denotes a species thought or known to be extinct.

Acrocheilus alutaceus
Algansea aphanea
Algansea avia
Algansea barbata
Algansea lacustris
Algansea monticola
Algansea popoche
Algansea tincella
Aztecula[1] *sallei*

Campostoma anomalum
Campostoma oligolepis
Campostoma ornatum
Campostoma pauciradii
Clinostomus elongatus
Clinostomus funduloides
Couesius plumbeus
Cyprinella[1] *analostana*
Cyprinella bocagrande
Cyprinella caerulea
Cyprinella callisema
Cyprinella callistia
Cyprinella callitaenia
Cyprinella camura
Cyprinella chloristia
Cyprinella formosa
Cyprinella galactura
Cyprinella garmani
Cyprinella gibbsi
Cyprinella leedsi
Cyprinella lepida
Cyprinella lutrensis
Cyprinella nivea
Cyprinella ornata
Cyprinella panarcys
Cyprinella proserpina
Cyprinella pyrrhomelas
Cyprinella rutila
Cyprinella spiloptera
Cyprinella trichroistia
Cyprinella venusta
Cyprinella whipplei
Cyprinella xaenura
Cyprinella xanthicara

Dionda argentosa
Dionda catostomops
Dionda diaboli
Dionda dichroma
Dionda episcopa
Dionda erimyzonops
Dionda ipni
Dionda mandibularis
Dionda melanops
Dionda rasconis
Dionda serena

Eremichthys acros
Ericymba buccata
Erimonax monacha
Erimystax[1] *cahni*
Erimystax dissimilis
Erimystax harryi
Erimystax insignis
Erimystax x-punctata
Evarra bustamantei (E)
Evarra eigenmanni (E)
Evarra tlahuacensis (E)
Exoglossum laurae
Exoglossum maxillingua
Extrarius[1] *aestivalis*

Gila alvordensis
Gila atraria
Gila bicolor
Gila boraxobius
Gila coerulea
Gila conspersa
Gila copei
Gila crassicauda (E)
Gila cypha
Gila ditaenia
Gila elegans
Gila intermedia
Gila modesta
Gila nigrescens
Gila orcutti
Gila pandora
Gila pulchra

Gila purpurea
Gila robusta

Hemitremia flammea
Hesperoleucus symmetricus
Hybognathus amarus
Hybognathus argyritis
Hybognathus hankinsoni
Hybognathus hayi
Hybognathus nuchalis
Hybognathus placitus
Hybognathus regius
Hybopsis[1] *alborus*
Hybopsis amblops
Hybopsis amecae (E)
Hybopsis ammophilus
Hybopsis amnis
Hybopsis aulidion (E)
Hybopsis bifrenatus
Hybopsis boucardi
Hybopsis calientis
Hybopsis dorsalis
Hybopsis hypsinotus
Hybopsis imeldae
Hybopsis labrosus
Hybopsis lineapunctatus
Hybopsis longirostris
Hybopsis moralesi
Hybopsis rubrifrons
Hybopsis sabinae
Hybopsis winchelli
Hybopsis zanemus

Iotichthys phlegethontis

Lavinia exilicauda
Lepidomeda albivallis
Lepidomeda altivelis
Lepidomeda mollispinis
Lepidomeda vittata
Luxilus albeolus
Luxilus cardinalis
Luxilus cerasinus
Luxilus chrysocephalus
Luxilus coccogenis
Luxilus cornutus
Luxilus pilsbryi
Luxilus zonatus

Luxilus zonistius
Lythrurus[1] *ardens*
Lythrurus atrapiculus
Lythrurus bellus
Lythrurus fumeus
Lythrurus lirus
Lythrurus roseipinnis
Lythrurus snelsoni
Lythrurus umbratilis

Macrhybposis[1] *gelida*
Macrhybopsis meeki
Macrhybopsis storeriana
Margariscus margarita
Meda fulgida
Moapa coriacea
Mylocheilus caurinus
Mylopharodon conocephalus

Nocomis asper
Nocomis biguttatus
Nocomis effusus
Nocomis leptocephalus
Nocomis micropogon
Nocomis platyrhynchus
Nocomis raneyi
Notemigonus crysoleucas
Notropis[2]
  Subgenus Notropis[3]
Notropis amabilis
Notropis amoenus
Notropis ariommus
Notropis atherinoides
Notropis candidus
Notropis jemezanus
Notropis nazas
Notropis oxyrhynchus
Notropis perpallidus
Notropis photogenis
Notropis rubellus
Notropis scepticus
Notropis semperasper
Notropis shumardi
Notropis stilbius
Notropis telescopus
  Subgenus Alburnops
Notropis bairdi
Notropis blennius

Notropis buccula
Notropis edwardraneyi
Notropis girardi
Notropis orca
Notropis potteri
Notropis simus
   Subgenus *Hydrophlox*[1]
Notropis baileyi
Notropis chiliticus
Notropis chlorocephalus
Notropis chrosomus
Notropis leuciodus
Notropis lutipinnis
Notropis nubilus
Notropis rubricroceus
   N. texanus species group[1]
Notropis altipinnis
Notropis anogenus
Notropis boops
Notropis chalybaeus
Notropis heterodon
Notropis petersoni
Notropis texanus
Notropis xaenocephalus
   N. volucellus species group[1]
Notropis buchanani
Notropis cahabae
Notropis heterolepis
Notropis maculatus
Notropis ozarcanus
Notropis rupestre
Notropis spectrunculus
Notropis tropicus
Notropis volucellus
Notropis wickleffi
   Relationships unresolved
Notropis aguirrepequenoi
Notropis asperiforns
Notropis atrocaudalis
Notropis braytoni
Notropis chihuahua
Notropis cummingsae
Notropis greenei
Notropis harperi
Notropis hubbsi[4]
Notropis hudsonius
Notropis hypsilepis
Notropis ludibundus[5]

Notropis mekistocholas
Notropis ortenburgeri
Notropis procne
Notropis saladonis
Notropis scabriceps
Notropis tristis[6]
Notropis uranoscopus

Opsopoeodus emiliae
Oregonichthys[1] *crameri*
Orthodon microlepidotus

Phenacobius catostomus
Phenacobius crassilabrum
Phenacobius mirabilis
Phenacobius teretulus
Phenacobius uranops
Phoxinus cumberlandensis
Phoxinus eos
Phoxinus erythrogaster
Phoxinus neogaeus
Phoxinus oreas
Phoxinus tennesseensis
Pimephales notatus
Pimephales promelas
Pimephales tenellus
Pimephales vigilax
Plagopterus argentissimus
Platygobio[1] *gracilis*
Pogonichthys ciscoides (E)
Pogonichthys macrolepidotus
Pteronotropis[1] *euryzonus*
Pteronotropis hypselopterus
Pteronotropis signipinnis
Pteronotropis welaka
Ptychocheilus grandis
Ptychocheilus lucius
Ptychocheilus oregonensis
Ptychochelius umpquae

Relictus solitarius
Rhinichthys atratulus
Rhinichthys bowersi
Rhinichthys cataractae
Rhinichthys chyrsogaster[7]
Rhinichthys cobitus[7]
Rhinichthys deaconi (E)
Rhinichthys evermanni

Rhinichthys falcatus	*Semotilus corporalis*
Rhinichthys osculus	*Semotilus lumbee*
Richardsonius balteatus	*Semotilus theoreauianus*
Richardsonius egregius	*Stypodon signifer*
Semotilus atromaculatus	*Yuriria alta*

[1] Following Mayden (1989).
[2] Genus as used here does not denote a monophyletic group, but does contain some monophyletic assemblages.
[3] Following Coburn (1982) and Mayden (unpubl. data).
[4] Following Dimmick (1987).
[5] Previously known as *N. stramineus* (Mayden and Gilbert, 1989).
[6] Previously known as *N. topeka* (Mayden and Gilbert, 1989).
[7] following Woodman (1987).

REFERENCES

Bănărescu, P. (1973) Some reconsiderations of the zoogeography of the Euro–Mediterranean fresh-water fish fauna. *Revue roum. Biol. (Zool.)*, **18**, 257–64.

Barbour, C. D. and Miller, R. R. (1978) A revision of the Mexican cyprinid fish genus *Algansea*. *Misc. Publs. Mus. Zool. Univ. Mich.*, **155**, 72 pp.

Becker, G. C. (1983) *Fishes of Wisconsin*, Univ. Wisconsin Press, Madison, 1052 pp.

Breder, C. M., jun. and Rosen, D. E. (1966) *Modes of Reproduction in Fishes*. T.F.H. Publications, Neptune City, NJ, 941 pp.

Buth, D. G. (1979) Biochemical systematics of the cyprinid genus *Notropis* I. The subgenus *Luxilus*. *Biochem. Syst. Ecol.*, **7**, 69–79.

Carlander, K. D. (1969) *Handbook of Freshwater Fishery Biology*. Vol. 1, Iowa State Univ. Press, Ames, 752 pp.

Cavender, T. M. (1986) Review of the fossil history of North American freshwater fishes, in *The Zoogeography of North American Freshwater Fishes* (eds C. H. Hocutt and E. O. Wiley), John Wiley and Sons, New York, pp. 699–724.

Coburn, M. M. (1982) Anatomy and relationship of *Notropis atherinoides*, unpubl. PhD dissert., Ohio State Univ. (384 pp).

Coburn, M. M. (1986) Egg diameter variation in eastern North American minnows (Pisces: Cyprinidae): correlation with vertebral number, habitat, and spawning behavior. *Ohio J. Sci.*, **86**, 110–20.

Courtenay, W. R., jun., Hensley, D. A., Taylor, J. N. and McCann, J. A. (1986) Distribution of exotic fishes in North America, in *The Zoogeography of North American Freshwater Fishes* (eds. C. H. Hocutt and E. O. Wiley), John Wiley and Sons, New York, pp. 675–98.

Dimmick, W. W. (1987) Phylogenetic relationships of *Notropis hubbsi*, *N. welaka*, and *N. emiliae* (Cypriniformes: Cyprinidae). *Copeia*, **1987**, 316–25.

Gilbert, C. R. (1964) American cyprinid fishes of the subgenus *Luxilus* (Genus *Notropis*). *Bull. Fla St. Mus.*, **8** (2), 95–194.

Gosline, W. A. (1978) Unbranched dorsal-fin rays and subfamily classification of the fish family Cyprinidae. *Occ. Paps Mus. Zool. Univ. Mich.*, **684**., 1–21.

Heins, D. C. and Baker, J. A. (1988) Egg sizes in fishes: do mature ooctyes accurately demonstrate size statistics of ripe ova? *Copeia*, **1988**, 238–40.

Heins, D. C. and Bresnick, G. I. (1975) The ecological life history of the cherryfin shiner, *Notropis roseipinnis*. *Trans. Am. Fish. Soc.*, **104**, 516–23.

Heins, D. C. and Rabito, F. G., jun. (1986) Spawning performance in North American minnows: direct evidence of the occurrence of multiple clutches in the genus *Notropis*. *J. Fish Biol.*, **28**, 343–57.

Hocutt, C. H. and Wiley, E. O. (eds). (1986) *The Zoogeography of North American Freshwater Fishes*, John Wiley and Sons, New York, 866 pp.

Hocutt, C. H., Jenkins, R. E. and Stauffer, J. R., jun. (1986) Zoogeography of the fishes of the central Appalachians and central Atlantic Coastal Plain, in *The Zoogeography of North American Freshwater Fishes* (eds. C. H. Hocutt and E. O. Wiley), John Wiley and Sons, New York, pp. 161–211.

Howes, G. (1981) Anatomy and phylogeny of the Chinese major carps *Ctenopharyngodon* Steind., 1866 and *Hypophthalmichthys* Blkr., 1860. *Bull. Br. Mus. nat. Hist. (Zool.)*, **41** (1), 1–52.

Howes, G. (1984) Phyletics and biogeography of the aspinine cyprinid fishes. *Bull. Br. Mus. nat. Hist. (Zool.)*, **47** (5), 283–303.

Howes, G. (1985) A revised synonymy of the minnow genus *Phoxinus* Rafinesque, 1820 (Teleostei: Cyprinidae) with comments on its relationships and distribution. *Bull. Br. Mus. nat. Hist. (Zool.)*, **48** (1), 57–74.

Hubbs, C. L. and Hubbs, C. (1958) *Notropis saladonis*, a new cyprinid fish endemic in the Rio Salado of northeastern Mexico. *Copeia*, **1958**, 297–307.

Hubbs, C. L. and Lagler, K. F. (1958) *Fishes of the Great Lakes Region*, Univ. Michigan Press, Ann Arbor, 213 pp.

Hubbs, C. L. and Miller, R. R. (1975) *Notropis tropicus*, a new cyprinid fish from eastern Mexico. *Southwest. Nat.*, **20**, 121–31.

Hunter, J. R. and Hasler, A. D. (1965) Spawning association of the redfin shiner, *Notropis umbratilis*, and the green sunfish, *Lepomis cyanellus*. *Copeia*, **1965**, 265–81.

Jensen, R. J. and Barbour, C. D. (1981) A phylogenetic reconstruction of the Mexican cyprinid fish genus *Algansea*. *Syst. Zool.*, **30**, 41–57.

Jordan, D. S. and Evermann, B. W. (1896) Fishes of North and Middle America. *Bull. U.S. natn Mus.*, **47** (1–4), 3705 pp.

Lachner, E. A. (1952) Studies of the biology of the cyprinid fishes of the chub genus *Nocomis* of the northeastern United States. *Am. Midl. Nat.*, **48**, 433–66.

Mayden, R. L. (1985) Biogeography of Ouachita Highland fishes. *Southwest. Nat.*, **30**, 195–211.

Mayden, R. L. (1987) Historical ecology and North America Highland fishes: a research program in community ecology, in *Community and Evolutionary Ecology of North American Stream Fishes* (eds. W. J. Matthews and D. C. Heins), Univ. Oklahoma Press, Norman, pp. 210–22.

Mayden, R. L. (1988) Systematics of the *Notropis zonatus* species group, with description of a new species from the Interior Highlands of North America. *Copeia*, **1988**, 153–73.

Mayden, R. L. (1989) Phylogenetic studies of North American minnows, with emphasis on the genus *Cyprinella* (Teleostei: Cypriniformes). *Misc. Publs Mus. nat. Hist., Univ. Kansas.*, No. 80, 189 pp.

Mayden, R. L. and Gilbert, C. R. (1990) *Notropis ludibundus* (Girard) and *Notropis tristis* (Girard), replacement names for *N. stramineus* (Cope) and *N. topeka* (Gilbert) (Teleostei: Cypriniformes). *Copeia*, **1990**, 1084–9.

Miller, R. R. (1958) Origin and affinities of the freshwater fish fauna of western North America. *Publs Am. Ass. Advmt Sci.*, **51** (1958), 187–222.

Miller, R. R. and Smith, M. L. (1986) Origin and geography of the fishes of central Mexico, in *The Zoogeography of North American Freshwater Fishes* (eds. C. H. Hocutt and E. O. Wiley), John Wiley and Sons, New York, pp. 487–517.

Minckley, W. L. (1959) Fishes of the Blue River Basin, Kansas. *Univ. Kansas Publs Mus. nat. Hist.*, **11**, 401–42.

Minckley, W. L. (1980) *Agosia chrysogaster* Girard, Longfin dace, in *Atlas of North American Freshwater Fishes* (eds. D. S. Lee, C. R. Gilbert, C. H. Hocutt, R. E. Jenkins, D. E. McAllister, and J. R. Stauffer, jun.), North Carolina State Museum Nat. Hist., Raleigh, p. 141.

Minckley, W. L., Hendrickson, D. A. and Bond, C. E. (1986) Geography of western North American freshwater fishes: description and relationships to intracontinental tectonism, in *The Zoogeography of North American Freshwater Fishes* (eds. C. H. Hocutt and E. O. Wiley), John Wiley and Sons, New York, pp. 519–613.

Moyle, P. B. (1976) *Inland fishes of California*, Univ. California Press, Los Angeles, 405 pp.

Rabito, F. G., jun. and Heins, D. C. (1985) Spawning behaviour and sexual dimorphism in the North American cyprinid fish *Notropis leedsi*, the bannerfin shiner. *J. nat. Hist.*, **19**, 1155–63.

Smith, M. L. and Miller, R. R. (1986) The evolution of the Rio Grande Basin as inferred from its fish fauna, in *The Zoogeography of North American Freshwater Fishes* (eds. C. H. Hocutt and E. O. Wiley), John Wiley and Sons, New York, pp. 457–85.

Swift, C. C., Gilbert, C. R., Bortone, S. A., Burgess, G. H. and Yerger, R. W. (1986) Zoogeography of the freshwater fishes of the southeastern United States: Savannah River to Lake Pontchartrain, in *The Zoogeography of North American Freshwater Fishes* (eds. C. H. Hocutt, and E. O. Wiley), John Wiley and Sons, New York, pp 213–65.

Woodman, D. A. (1987) The evolutionary history of the genus *Rhinichthys*: hypotheses and tests, unpubl. PhD diss., Univ. Nebraska, Lincoln. (314 pp.).

Chapter nine

Cyprinids of Australasia

A. R. Brumley

There are no native cyprinids in Australia, New Zealand or New Guinea despite the great diversity in South East Asia. Cyprinids reach Borneo and Java but do not occur naturally any further east.

9.1 SPECIES INTRODUCED INTO AUSTRALIA

Major drainage basins and their fish fauna

Regular rainfall occurs only in northern and eastern coastal regions. Most of Australia is arid and has ephemeral rivers draining into salt lakes. Lake Eyre, in central Australia, is one of the largest (Fig. 9.1) but is usually dry. These areas have just a few of the 18 freshwater fish families in Australia. The total fauna, including species that enter estuarine areas, is depauperate. This is said to relate to the sparseness of reliable fresh water (McKay, 1984), the isolation of the continent for 50 m.y, and the geologic and climatic conditions throughout (Merrick and Schmida, 1984).

In Australia, the greatest diversity of freshwater fish species is in the coastal streams of the north and north-east (Merrick and Schmida, 1984). These streams, which are subject to summer tropical rains, support species of grunters (Teraponidae), rainbowfishes (Melanotaeniidae), eeltail catfishes (Plotosidae), bonytongues (Osteoglossidae) and giant perches (Centro-pomidae).

The mountains of the Great Dividing Range run close to the whole eastern and south-eastern coast and provide runoff for many short coastal drainage systems. The more temperate streams in the south have blackfish (Gadop-sidae), galaxiids (Galaxiidae), southern smelts (Retropinnidae), southern grayling (Prototroctidae) and gobies (Gobiidae). Galaxiids and gobies are also found in the few streams of the temperate south-west. There is one very large internal freshwater basin that drains the south-east inland areas into the

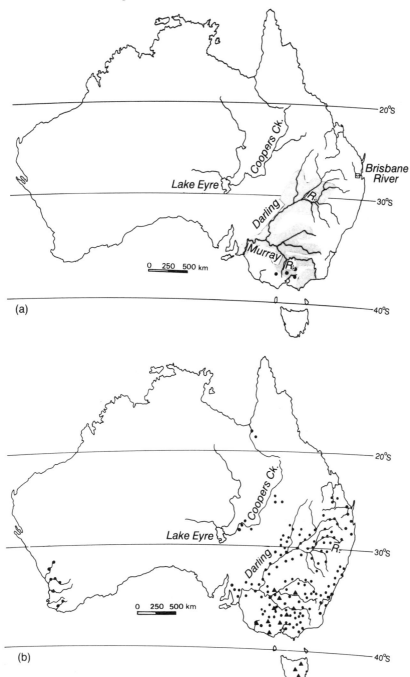

Fig. 9.1 Distribution of introduced cyprinid fishes in Australia. (a) Shading, carp; □, rosy barb; ●, roach, (b) ▲, Tench; ●, goldfish.

Murray River, which flows into the sea in South Australia, and the Darling River, a major northern tributary (Fig. 9.1). The Murray–Darling River is one of the longest rivers in the world (3700 km), comparable to large systems of some continents (Mekong – Asia, Niger – Africa, Volga – USSR., Madeira – South america) although smaller than the Mississippi–Missouri River of North America (6030 km). The Murray–Darling area, which has fewer native families and species than the coastal areas, has the percichthyids as the major family. It was the Murray–Darling and tributaries that was the setting for the introduction of European fish species.

Salmonids, percids and cyprinids were introduced into Australia for sport during the 1800s, and by the 1960s nine species were said to be established (Weatherley and Lake, 1967). Further to these imports, species of the poeciliids, cichlids and cyprinids were introduced for ornamental and aquarium uses. The total number of successful introduced species was 22 by 1984 (McKay, 1984). However, some of these speecies either did not survive or do not have self-maintaining populations, so the number of successful introductions is probably 19 (Fletcher, 1986). The history of these introductions and their impact on the native fauna are discussed by Weatherley and Lake (1967), Lake (1978), Tilzey (1980), Merrick and Schmida (1984), McKay (1984) and Fletcher (1986). Cyprinid species are a large part of any discussion of exotic fish introductions into Australia and their presence has had a notable effect on the freshwater environment and current species composition (Fletcher, 1986).

Introduced cyprinids

The history of the introduction of cyprinids into Australia began after acclimatization societies were formed in the mid-1800s to introduce familiar European species. Tench, *Tinca tinca*, roach, *Rutilus rutilus*, goldfish, *Carassius auratus*, and carp, *Cyprinus carpio*, were present by 1880 (McKay, 1984) (Table 9.1). Crucian carp, *Carassius carassius*, were reputedly introduced in 1876 (Weatherley and Lake, 1967), but crucian carp have never been confirmed in Australia, so early reports were likely misidentified goldfish (Fletcher, 1986). The initial spread of goldfish and carp may have been due to accidental releases of aquarium fish, whereas tench and roach were released into streams for anglers.

The occurrence of a strain of carp, now found in a large area of south-eastern Australia, results from an accidental release into the Murray River of fish imported for an aquaculture venture in southern Victoria in 1960 (Shearer and Mulley, 1978). This strain spread rapidly throughout the Murray–Darling river system and is now common throughout this and several coastal river systems in south-eastern Australia (Fig. 9.1(a)). In recent surveys of Victorian waters, carp and goldfish were more abundant than any native species (Brumley *et al.*, 1987). Goldfish were also accidentally released into

Table 9.1 Dates and reasons for the introduction of five cyprinid species into Australia

Species	Dates of introductions	Reason for acclimatization	Area of current major abundance	References for distribution
Tinca tinca (tench)	1876	Familiar sport	Murray–Darling basin; only locally abundant	Merrick and Schmida (1984). Cadwallader and Backhouse (1983). Cadwallader (1983)
Rutilus rutilus (roach)	1860–80	Coarse angling	Streams in southern Victoria; restricted	Cadwallader and Backhouse (1983)
Puntius conchonius (rosy barb)	1970	Accidental escape of aquarium fish	Brisbane; restricted (may not be self-maintaining)	Arthington et al. (1983)
Carassius auratus (goldfish)	1860–70, 1876	Ornamental	Murray–Darling basin; extremely widespread	Merrick and Schmida (1984), Llewellyn (1983)
Cyprinus carpio (carp)				
—'Prospect strain'	1850–60	Ornamental	Sydney; restricted	Shearer and Mulley (1978)
—'Singapore strain' (koi carp)	1876	Ornamental	Murrumbidgee basin; restricted	Shearer and Mulley (1978)
—'River strain' hybrid	1960–64	Aquaculture	Murray–Darling basin; extremely widespread	Pollard et al. (1980). Hume et al. (1983a), Brumley et al. (1987)

natural waterways. Their spread has been perpetuated by continued releases of aquarium fish, and the use by anglers of live goldfish as bait (which is illegal only in the state of Victoria, south of the Murray River). Consequently, goldfish is the most widespread of all introduced fish in Australia and is found in the Murray–Darling basin, the inland Coopers Creek, most eastern coastal streams, some streams in Western Australia and many lentic water bodies throughout southern Australia (Fig. 9.1(b)).

Roach has only a restricted range in a few streams in Victoria but may be locally abundant (Fig. 9.1(a)). Tench occur in south-eastern Australia in tributaries of the Murray River and some southern coastal streams, and in Tasmania (Fig. 9.1(b)).

During this century exotic fish from many families including several barb species in the cyprinid family have been imported for aquarists (McKay, 1984). Of these, only one cyprinid, the rosy barb, *Puntius conchonius*, has become established in the wild, probably accidentally (Arthington *et al.*, 1983).

9.2   SPECIES INTRODUCED INTO NEW ZEALAND

Fish fauna

New Zealand's temperate climate, with plentiful rainfall, ensures many permanent streams and lakes on both major islands. The largest river is the Waikato in the North Island which begins above Lake Taupo. Despite the abundance of freshwater habitat, there are only seven families, with a total 27 species, of indigenous freshwater fishes (McDowall, 1978). These are similar to the fishes found in the coastal areas of south-eastern Australia (galaxiids, southern smelts, and southern grayling). These and the remaining fish (gudgeons, anguillids, a flounder and mugiloidids) are neither very large nor greatly suitable for sport fishing, so as Europeans colonized New Zealand in the 1800s they began introducing fish.

Initially, more than 20 acclimatization societies attempted to import many species between 1864 and 1905. These included species of salmonids and cyprinids which have become the dominant members of the 18 exotic species now established. The history of these introductions and the effects on the native fauna, especially by salmonids, have been discussed by McDowall (1968, 1984, 1987). Cyprinids have been introduced at various times and have generally been more accepted in New Zealand than in Australia.

Introduced species

The first cyprinids introduced were tench, carp and probably goldfish (Table 9.2). Crucian carp have been mentioned but these were probably misidentified goldfish (McDowall, 1979). There was renewed interest by

Table 9.2 Dates and reasons for the introduction of six cyprinid species into New Zealand

Species	Dates of introductions	Reason for acclimatization	Area of current major abundance	References for distribution
Tinca tinca (tench)	1867	Recreational angling	Oamaru (South Island), Otaki, Waikato	McDowall (1979)
Carassius auratus (goldfish)	1867	Ornamental	Widespread though intermittent	McDowall (1987), Cadwallader (1983)
Cyprinus carpio (carp)	Ponds – ?1967	Ornamental	May not have survived	Pullan (pers. comm.)
Koi carp	Wild – 1983	Ornamental	Waikato	McDowall (1987)
Scardinius erythrophthalmus (rudd)	1970s (illegally)	Coarse angling	Waikato	Cadwallader (1977, 1978b)
Ctenopharyngodon idella (grass carp)	1971	Control of aquatic weeds	Parkinsons Lake, Waiuku; water storage, Waihi; lower Waikato R.	McDowall (1979)
Hypophthalmichthys molitrix (silver carp)	1969–70	Control of aquatic weeds	Lake Orakai (Tutira Lake)	McDowall (1979)

anglers in the 1940s and 1950s to reintroduce many species that had not survived earlier shipments or stockings. Cyprinid species such as barbel, *Barbus barbus*, and rudd, *Scardinius erythrophthalmus*, were proposed, as were dace, *Phoxinus* spp., (perhaps for bait), but government bodies were against further exotic introductions that might affect the native biota. However, rudd were imported illegally for farm ponds and were liberated in the North Island by at least one keen angler during the 1970s (Table 9.2).

Of the six cyprinids in New Zealand, tench and goldfish have the longest history and have become the most widespread, because since about 1970, anglers have inadvertently spread goldfish or deliberately released tench. Tench now occur in streams and small lakes on both islands (Fig. 9.2). Goldfish have become widespread (Fig. 9.2) and locally abundant in many small lakes (McDowall, 1987) and the larger reservoirs including Lakes Karapiro, Maraetai, Rotoaira and Whakamaru (Cadwallader, 1983). Rudd, which were also spread by anglers, appear to be confined to the lentic waters in the North Island (Fig. 9.3). A self-maintaining population of rudd has been found in Lake Atiamuri, a reservoir in the upper Waikato River (Cadwallader, 1978b), and has since spread throughout the lower Waikato (R. M. McDowall, pers. comm.).

In the 1970s the Fisheries Research Division decided that possible biological control of aquatic weeds could justify the import of grass carp, *Ctenopharyngodon idella*, and silver carp, *Hypophthalmichthys molitrix* (Table 9.2). They were brought in under government control and kept in hatcheries. Silver carp from a hatchery at Hawke Bay have only been released to Lake Orakai in 1978–79 (McDowall, 1987) and have not been spread elsewhere into the wild (Fig. 9.3). The distribution of grass carp is also very restricted (Fig. 9.3). They initially remained in controlled ponds at Rotorua and in Parkinsons Lake (McDowall, 1987), but are now in a few drainage channels and some ponds (R. M. McDowall, pers. comm.).

The remaining cyprinid species found in New Zealand is the koi carp, the brightly coloured strain of *Cyprinus carpio* (Table 9.2). These probably came in with shipments of goldfish but were only identified in captivity in the 1970s. Their release was certainly not desired, but nevertheless koi carp were found in the wild in 1983 (McDowall, 1987). The Waikato River system is the largest river to have koi carp (Fig. 9.3), but they also occur in the lower reaches of several streams in the North Island (Pullan, 1984).

9.3 UNDESIRABLE INTRODUCTIONS

Carp – a noxious species

Australia. Although the river strain of carp is now widespread in south-eastern Australia, attempts were made to prevent their spread. Owing to

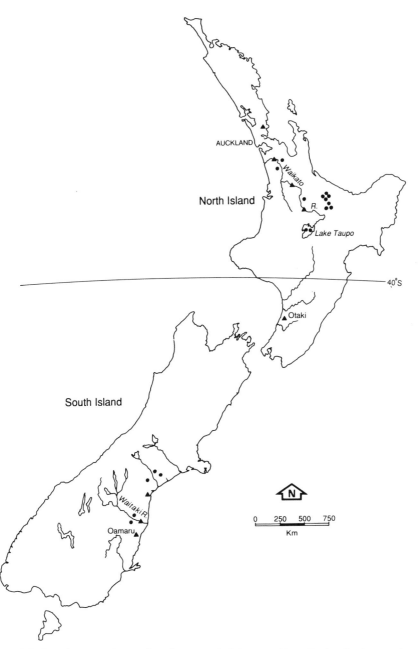

Fig. 9.2 Distribution of introduced cyprinid fishes in New Zealand. ▲, tench; ●, goldfish.

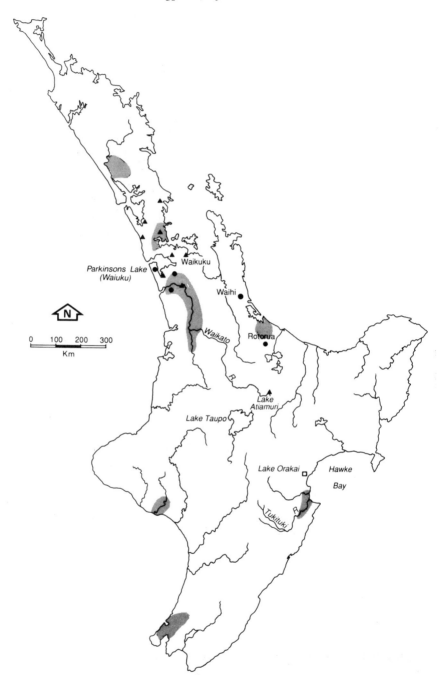

Fig. 9.3 Distribution of cyprinid fishes that occur only in the North Island of New Zealand. Shading, koi carp; □, silver carp; ●, grass carp; ▲, rudd.

adverse effects of carp in North America, a venture to culture imported mirror carp in Victoria (at Boolara) was stopped in 1961 after 12 months' operation, and sale of such carp to farm ponds was banned. In 1962 carp were declared noxious and attempts were made to eradicate them; all known ponds where carp had been released were poisoned with rotenone by the Victorian Fisheries Department.

However, in 1964 an accidental release of a few carp occurred in a lake near the Murray River, close to its confluence with the Darling River. From here, this strain began spreading with spectacular success. The river strain, which became known as Boolara strain, was probably a hybrid of the cultured mirror carp and a scaled variety of unknown origin (Hume *et al.*, 1983a). This was then reported to hybridize with the 'Yanco strain', a koi variety, known for some time in the Murrumbidgee River system (Mulley and Shearer, 1980). A broad genetic makeup was thus present in the rapidly spreading carp populations.

In victoria the attitude towards carp was conditioned by the North American viewpoint, which held carp as a pest that increases turbility, uproots plants and destroys habitat for waterfowl and native fish (Thrienen and Helm, 1954; Robel, 1961; King and Hunt, 1987; MacCrimmon, 1968). Carp populations became obvious in certain drying wetlands and below weirs.

Fig. 9.4 Congregation of carp in the Mitchell River (Victoria) behind a freshwater barrier, March 1988. Carp between 30 and 60 cm were 'thrashing' in shallow water (photo courtesy of Bairnsdale Advertiser).

Fig. 9.4 shows a congregation of carp behind a barrier to movement from waters that became highly saline in an estuarine river. Similar masses of carp caused public concern during the 1960s. As American federal and state agencies had spent millions of dollars in attempting to control carp populations during the 1950s, the government in Victoria likewise proposed to control carp (Wharton, 1977). This led to a 3 y research programme on the dynamics of the established population of carp in the wild and the possible effects on the environment (1979–82).

This study suggested that populations of carp did not increase turbidity, and there was no association between high carp densities and high turbidity (Fletcher *et al.*, 1985). The habitat is one of turbid rivers with flood plain billabongs (ox-bow lakes) that are flooded during winter and spring in wet years. A typical billabong in a floodplain forest of *Eucalyptus camaldulensis* (red gum) (Fig. 9.5) has a cycle of growth of water plants after a flood, then increasing turbidity and diminishing vegetation as the billabong dries. Carp may accentuate these changes only if very abundant (Fletcher *et al.*, 1985).

Floods certainly aided the initial spread of carp, allowing fish to enter lakes and billabongs and move up rivers above weirs and barriers that would normally be impassable to them. Flooding also allows good growth and spawning success of carp, probably by increasing food availability (Hume

Fig. 9.5 A drying billabong in floodplain forest of the Goulburn River (summer 1981) with a few aquatic plants (*Ottelia ovalifolia* and *Triglochin procera*) and, as the waters were receding, semi-aquatic species on the mud. Carp are common in such habitats and have been blamed for declining vegetation (photo A. Brumley).

et al., 1983a). Successive large floods during the early 1970s accentuated an explosion of the new strain. In the 1980s the numbers of carp declined, owing both to the sparcity of wet years and perhaps to a natural decline after a population explosion of a new species. In the Victorian study the growth rates of carp varied greatly between years and among habitats; rates ranged from the fastest to the slowest recorded for the world (0.1 mm/day at one site but up to 1.5 mm/day at another site).

A commercial fishery for carp began in several states during the 1970s either by existing fishermen whose proportion of native fish was declining (Reynolds, 1976) or by new electrofishing operators fishing solely for carp. The catch increased rapidly. In Victoria the highest catch record occurred in 1976–77, nearly 600 t (Hume *et al.*, 1983a), then both catch and the number of operators declined. Outlets closed when catches of carp declined. Now only a few fishermen exploit the occasional large concentration of fish such as in drying lakes or streams. They use simple gear (Fig. 9.6). The fishery did not control the populations of carp, but rather the decline reflected a natural occurrence. A commercial venture would be unprofitable before 'eradication of carp from the wild' would be effected (Morison, 1989).

When populations of native fish declined, carp were considered as a possible cause (Backhouse, 1982). The diet of carp is said to overlap with those of

Fig. 9.6 Commercial fishermen for carp usually alone, using boat electro-shocking equipment or fyke nets to exploit scattered large populations of carp (photo courtesy of Bairnsdale Advertiser).

native bony bream, *Nematalosa erebi*, catfish, *Tandanus tandanus*, and tench (Cadwallader, 1978a; Reynolds, 1979), but detailed analyses, especially of sympatric populations, have not been carried out. Hume *et al.* (1983a) showed that plant matter was a minor dietary component of most carp in Victoria, and that invertebrates were of greatest importance. Young carp fed mainly on microcrustaceans, which remained in the diet of larger fish; large carp consumed mid-water and bottom-dwelling insects; only very large carp ate plant matter. This shows a similarity in major food items to the diet of native silver perch, *Bidyanus bidyanus* (Cadwallader, 1979). It remains only speculation that carp could cause the decline of silver perch populations. More likely explanations for the decline of native species include altered water regimes in rivers, presence of artificial barriers, pollution, and destruction of fish habitat (Cadwallader, 1978a).

To summarize the Australian situation, carp is an established and major fish species in south-eastern rivers. Although there is no direct evidence of effects on the environment and native flora and fauna, it is still an unwanted alien. It is not being controlled by a fisheries industry, and populations are retarded only by slow growth during occasional years without flood.

New Zealand. The rapid spread and dominance of this unwanted species is of concern in New Zealand, where koi carp population explosions are a potential threat. Carp were declared noxious in New Zealand to hinder the spread of the koi hybrid, which by 1980 had appeared in fish ponds and farm ponds. Eradication from such ponds was attempted (Pullan, 1982) in much the same way as in Victoria (Australia) 20 y earlier, but a population of self-maintaining koi carp was found in the Waikato River in 1983 (McDowall, 1987) and Pullan's (1984) survey found koi carp elsewhere in the North Island. The potential for an extensive successful spread may not be as great as in Australia, because the koi hybrid may not be as vigorous in the wild and their red coloration may allow easy predation. However, they may breed with another strain of carp and produce a new successful hybrid as happened in Australia. For these reasons it would be wise at this stage to contain carp as much as possible, because control is too difficult once a species becomes successfully established. An internal report on assessing the impact of koi carp, made in February 1988, proposed a research programme (S. Hanchet, pers. comm.).

Goldfish gone wild

Goldfish, *Carassius auratus*, have been imported and kept as ornamental fish in aquaria, farm ponds and zoos and often released in lakes by enthusiasts. In Australia, anglers have spread goldfish to streams, rivers and many other lakes. As a consequence, goldfish appear in most permanent freshwater systems of Australia. They are also widespread in New Zealand but do not have the same nuisance status.

Their variable coloration and size makes them desirable as an ornamental species, but in the wild they have been confused with other species. Brightly coloured orange goldfish are known in the wild but more commonly, without selective breeding, they appear green–silver–grey. Smaller goldfish were probably misidentified as crucian carp, *Carassius carassius*, in New Zealand (McDowall, 1979), and early Australian specimens thought to be crucian carp were goldfish (Fletcher, 1986). Large goldfish can be similarly misidentified as carp, *C. carpio*, because goldfish may grow to be as large as a medium-sized carp. In the Victorian Carp Research Program, goldfish caught in steams and lakes ranged from 60 to 300 mm. (Hume *et al.*, 1983a).

Carp and goldfish hybridize in many parts of the world. In Australia, Shearer and Mulley (1978) reported hybrids of goldfish and the Yanco strain of carp, and hybrids with the Boolara strain were reported soon after the spread of this strain (Hume *et al.*, 1983b). Hybrids were found wherever both carp and goldfish occurred. Hybrids between koi carp and goldfish have also been reported in New Zealand (Pullan and Smith, 1987), and their presence may also become commonplace. These hybrids are all considered fertile, so their occurrence introduces new genetic makeup into wild populations.

Goldfish have been accepted as having nuisance value, but little work has been done into their biology or effects on the environment. While studying sympatric populations of carp and goldfish, Hume *et al.* (1983a) found goldfish to mature when quite small (female, 53 mm; male, 65 mm; $n = 750$). Successful spawning occurred at one site after rises in water level, as in carp. Growth of goldfish was slow for most seasons but increased after floods in spring or summer to maximum of 0.4 mm d^{-1}. This increase relates to the dominant food items being microcrustanceans and bottom insects which became more abundant after floods. Secondary items in the diet were algae, plant matter and detritus. Analysis of the diet of carp, goldfish and hybrids at one site showed that hybrids were intermediate in the order of major food items (Hume *et al.*, 1983b).

Small goldfish eat microcrustaceans and may affect the food available to other small fish. We can only speculate that competition might exist. Goldfish do not appear to be eaten by desirable fish. In Australia, goldfish were rarely found in stomachs of Murray cod, *Maccullochella peeli*, and golden perch, *Macquaria ambigua*, (Hume *et al.*, 1983a). In New Zealand, although goldfish were released as forage fish for brown trout, *Salmo trutta*, in lakes of the central North Island, they are not an important resource (McDowall, 1987).

Goldfish continue to be a major import into Australia and so there remains the chance of bringing in diseases. McKay (1984) reported that in one year (1978–79) 2.4–3.0×10^5 goldfish were imported into the city of Melbourne for the aquarium trade. The nationwide figures for goldfish in the 1980s must be in the millions. Fletcher (1986) suggested that a viral pancreatic necrosis that has been isolated in goldfish overseas (Adair and Ferguson, 1981) might be brought in. This could affect salmonids introduced into Australia.

As hobbyists and anglers continue to release fish with new genetic makeup, it is likely that the species will be the most genetically vigorous fish of the future. Populations with nuisance status will probably persist in all major freshwater bodies of Australia.

Rudd – a rough fish

Despite an interest by anglers in rudd as a coarse angling species, the New Zealand government decided against their introduction. To prevent illegal releases they declared rudd a noxious species in 1980. Anglers were responsible for their introduction and spread in northern waters of New Zealand that were poor for trout, *Salmo trutta* and *S. mykiss*. In other areas, trout were a preferred fish, and anglers thought that rudd would be an unnecessary addition.

When rudd were first established, Cadwallader (1977) reviewed their biology and discussed the implications in New Zealand. As rudd could do well in lakes and slow-flowing rivers, he said there was potential for further spread throughout New Zealand. He also speculated that rudd could compete with native galaxiids and retropinnids, and possibly trout. However, as trout prefer fast-flowing waters or deep lakes, they might be excluded from any major adverse effects. McDowall (1979) said that it was too early to evaluate the long-term effects of the recently spread populations of rudd. There has been no follow-up to Cadwallader's speculations.

9.4   USEFUL INTRODUCTIONS

Weed control by grass carp

During the 1950s and 1960s, eutrophication of many lakes in New Zealand resulted in excessive phytoplankton and macrophyte growth. To avoid long-term usage of herbicides, biological control by grass carp, *Ctenopharyngodon idella*, was suggested. A tightly controlled, stepwise investigation began in New Zealand in 1971, when fry were imported from Hong Kong and placed in research ponds near Rotorua (Edwards and Hine, 1974).

World-wide, grass carp are probably one of the most successful exotic fish used to control aquatic plants (Shireman, 1984), but work proceeded in New Zealand to ensure that they would be suitable for the cool waters with no adverse interactions. Edwards (1974) monitored the growth of the imported fry and found that, in summer at least, young fish would eat the major problem weeds. Two-year-old fish were then stocked in a farm drainage ditch and found to reduce the standing crop of some submerged aquatic species (Edwards and Moore, 1975). Controlled acclimatization of grass carp continued, and in 1975–76, the then 4+ to 6+ specimens were stocked in two small lakes to investigate effects in the natural environment. These investigations showed that grass carp could be useful in controlling species of aquatic weeds (Mitchell, 1980) without adverse effects on water quality (Mitchell *et al.*, 1984). Perhaps releases should be confined to channels and restricted waterways to avoid adverse effects in lakes on native smelt, *Retropinna retropinna*, and trout *Salmo mykiss* (Mitchell, 1986; Rowe, 1984). Studies continued without a final decision to allow releases to farmers or managers of water bodies (McDowall, 1984).

The situation changed in 1984 when grass carp were accidentally released into the lower Waikato River (McDowall, 1987). Natural spread is unlikely as water temperatures probably need to be 20–30 °C for spawning, but McDowall (1987) had said that reproduction was possible in the lower Waikato. A specimen captured in the Waikato River weighed 12 kg and was > 1 m long (I. Roxburgh, Dept Conserv., pers. comm).

In Australia, Mitchell (1978) proposed that grass carp might be imported to control aquatic weeds. However, this is unlikely to occur; one consequence of even a tightly controlled import is an accidental escape, as shown in New Zealand.

Silver carp

The history of silver carp, *Hypophthalmichthys molitrix*, in New Zealand has not been as complex as that of grass carp. Its use for weed control is limited as it can only control planktonic algae. Fish held in Lake Orakai have been released to one other lake and have not reproduced (McDowall, 1987).

Angling for tench and roach

Survival by tench, *Tinca tinca*, in both countries has pleased some anglers. Weatherley (1974) described the fishing potential for tench in the island state of Tasmania. Tench have been fished commercially in southern Australia; however, numbers caught declined after carp populations exploded (Reynolds, 1976), possibly due to an overlap in diet with carp (Reynolds, 1979). McDowall (1987) states that tench are being increasingly exploited in the North Island of New Zealand.

Roach, *Rutilus rutilus*, are also a coarse angling fish in Europe, but they have a restricted occurrence in Australia and are seldom fished for. Both roach and tench are useful as aquarium fish, with roach the more handsome (Cadwallader and Backhouse, 1983).

9.5 PREVENTION OF FURTHER RELEASES

Overall, most cyprinids introduced into the two countries have successfully established feral populations. These are not generally considered desirable and may even be regarded as pests. New generation of anglers born in Australia and New Zealand prefer to fish for native species or salmonids, or wish to conserve the native fauna. Therefore, the outlook is to prevent further exotic introductions, control existing feral populations, and conserve and increase numbers of native species.

A model of the establishment of these successful species in Australia has been proposed by Arthington and Mitchell (1986). They describe a propagule of individuals that establish a reproducing population due to either high fecundity or high oviparity, and also suitable environment and a good dispersal mechanism. This may be shown by the spread of carp in New Zealand. If new releases are undesirable, there is a need for tight preventive controls. The lesson is seen in New Zealand, where rudd became a successful introduction from an illegal import.

In Australia most imports will come via the aquarium trade. McKay (1984) reviews changes to approved imports. A list of species was proposed for continued importation. This list precludes any species that might fall into six categories of detrimental effects, such as causing environmental damage or harm to native animals. It can now be enforced by the *Wildlife Protection (Regulation of Export and Imports) Act 1982*, which seeks to prevent the introduction of live plants and animals that could adversely affect the Australian natural environment. A few hundred species are permitted for import and these are carefully checked on arrival. Despite tight controls on imports, new exotic fish may enter Australia. The list of approved fish includes several species of *Puntius* and *Capoeta* (= *Barbus*) as well as *Carassius auratus*, so there is still the possibility of further feral populations. After the prohibition of imports, Morison (1988) discussed two further preventive stages. Once fish become present in the country, either they may be killed or their release and sale may be immediately restricted. Secondly, species that have established feral populations in restricted areas may be declared noxious, their possession prohibited, and the fish killed.

Morison's second stage of prevention is the most difficult to enforce. Carp in Australia had reached that stage, but it was not possible to control their spread. Koi carp and rudd in New Zealand have already gone beyond the possibility of restricted control, although management of these unwanted species should continue. Prevention of introductions must lie in action at the import stage. Enforcement of regulations to restrict movement must occur to prevent releases of allowed imports such as grass carp in New Zealand and aquarium species in Australia.

ACKNOWLEDGEMENTS

My interest in cyprinids developed during the years of research on the Carp Program and I thank colleagues, Doug Hume and Sandy Morison. Thanks for critical reading of the manuscript go to Bob McDowall and Phillip Cadwallader.

REFERENCES

Adair, B. M. and Ferguson, H. W. (1981) Isolation of infectious pancreatic necrosis (IPN) virus from non-salmonid fish. *J. Fish. Dis.*, **4**, 69–76.

Arthington, A. H. and Mitchell, D. S. (1986) Aquatic and invading species, in *Ecology of Biological Invasions: an Australian Perspective* (eds R. H. Groves and J. J. Burdon), Aust. Acad. of Science, Canberra, pp. 34–53.

Arthington, A. H., Milton, D. A and McKay, R. J. (1983) Effects of urban development and habitat alterations on the distribution and abundance of native and exotic freshwater fish in the Brisbane region, Queensland. *Aust. J. Ecol.*, **8**, 87–101.

Backhouse, G. N. (1982) Introduced fishes of Victorian inland waters. *Aust. Ranger Bull.*, **2** (1), 10–12.

Brumley, A. R., Morison, A. K. and Anderson, J. R. (1987) *Revision of the conservation status of several species of warmwater native fish after surveys of selected sites in northen Victoria (1982–84)*. Tech. Rep. No. 33, Arthur Rylah Institute for environmental Research, Dept Conservation, Forests and Lands, Victoria, Australia, 93 pp.

Cadwallader, P. L. (1977) Introduction of rudd *Scardinius erythrophthalmus* into New Zealand. I. *Review of the ecology of rudd and the implications of its introduction into New Zealand*. Fisheries Tech. Rep. No. 147, Ministry of Agriculture and Fisheries, New Zealand, pp. 1–18.

Cadawallader, P. L. (1978a). Some causes of the decline in range and abundance of native fish in the Murray–Darling River system. *Proc. R. Soc. Vict.*, **90**, 211–23.

Cadwallader, P. L. (1978b) Acclimatisation of rudd *Scardinius erythrophthalmus* (Pisces: Cyprinidae), in the North Island of New Zealand (Note). *N.Z. J. mar. freshwat. Res.*, **12** (1), 81–2.

Cadwallader, P. L. (1979) Distribution of native and introduced fish in the Seven Creeks River system, Victoria. *Aust. J. Ecol.*, **4**, 361–85.

Cadwallader, P. L. (1983) A review of fish stocking in the larger reservoirs of Australia and New Zealand. *FAO Fish. Circ.*, No. 757, 38 pp.

Cadwallader, P. L. and Backhouse, G. N. (1983) *A guide to the Freshwater Fish of Victoria*, Vic. Govt Printer, Melbourne, 249 pp.

Edwards, D. J. (1974) Weed preference and growth of young grass carp in New Zealand. *N.Z. J. mar. freshwat. Res.*, **8**, 341–50.

Edwards, D. J. and Hine, P. M. (1974) Introduction, preliminary handling, and diseases of grass carp in New Zealand. *N.Z. J. mar. freshwat. Res.*, **8**, 441–54.

Edwards, D. J. and Moore, E. (1975) Control of water weeds by grass carp in a drainage ditch in New Zealand. *N. Z. J. mar. freshwat. Res.*, **9**, 283–92.

Fletcher, A. R. (1986) Effects of introduced fish in Australia, in *Limnology in Australia* (eds P. DeDeckker and W. D. Williams), CSIRO, Melbourne and Dr. W. Junk, Dordreeht, pp. 231–8.

Fletcher, A. R., Morison, A. K. and Hume, D. J. (1985) Effects of carp, *Cyprinus carpio* L., on communities of aquatic vegetation and turbidity of waterbodies in the lower Goulburn River basin. *Aust. J. Mar. Freshwat. Res.*, **36**, 311–27.

Hume, D. J., Fletcher, A. R. and Morison, A. K. (1983a) *Carp Program Final Report*, Carp Program Pub. No. 10, Arthur Rylah Institute for Environmental Research, Ministry for Conservation, Victoria, Australia, 213 pp.

Hume, D. J., Fletcher, A. R. and Morison, A. K. (1983b) Interspecific hybridization between carp (*Cyprinus carpio* L.) and goldfish (*Carassius auratus* L.) from Victorian waters. *Aust. J. Mar. Freshwat. Res.*, **34**, 915–19.

King, D. R. and Hunt, G. S. (1987) Effect of carp on vegetation in a Lake Erie marsh. *J. Wildl. Mgmt*, **31** (1), 181–8.

Lake, J. S. (1978) *Australian Freshwater Fishes: an Illustrated Field Guide*, Nelson, Melbourne, 160 pp.

Llewellyn, L. C. (1983) The distribution of fish in New South Wales. *Aust. Soc. Limnol. Spec. Publ.* No. 7, 23 pp.

MacCrimmon, H. R. (1968) Carp in Canada. *Bull. Fish. Res. Bd Can.*, No. 165, 93 pp.

McDowall, R. M. (1968) Interactions of the native and alien faunas of New Zealand and the problem of fish introductions. *Trans. Am. Fish. Soc.*, **97**, 1–11.

McDowall, R. M. (1978) *New Zealand Freshwater Fishes – a Guide and Natural History*, Heinemann Educational Books, Auckland, 230 pp.

McDowall, R. M. (1979) *Exotic fishes in New Zealand. Dangers of illegal releases*. Fish. Res. Div. Info. Leaflet No. 9, Ministry of Agriculture and Fisheries, Christchurch, 17 pp.

McDowall, R. M. (1984) Exotic fishes – the New Zealand experience, in *Distribution, Bioloogy and Management of Exotic Fishes* (eds W. R. Courtenay, jun., and J. R. Stauffer, jun.), Johns Hopkins Univ. Press, Baltimore, Maryland, pp. 200–14.

McDowall, R. M. (1987) Impacts of exotic fishes on the native fauna, in *Inland Waters of New Zealand*, (ed. A. B. Viner), DSIR Bulletin 241, Wellington, pp. 333–47.

McKay, R. J. (1984) Introduction of exotic fishes in Australia, in *Distribution, Biology and Management of Exotic Fishes*, (eds W. R. Courtenay, jun. and J. R. Stauffer, jun.), Johns Hopkins University Press, Baltimore, Maryland, pp. 177–99.

Merrick, J. R. and Schmida, G. E. (1984) *Australian Freshwater Fishes–Biology and Management*, Griffin Press Ltd, Netley, S. Australia, 409 pp.

Mitchell, C. P. (1980) Control of water weeds by grass carp in two small lakes. *N.Z. J. Mar. Freshwat. Res.*, **14**, 381–90.

Mitchell, C. P. (1986) Effects of introduced grass carp on populations of two species of small native fishes in a small lake. *N.Z. J. Mar. Freshwat. Res.*, **20**, 219–30.

Mitchell, C. P., Fish, G. R. and Burnet, A. M. R. (1984) Limnological changes in a small lake stocked with carp. *N.Z. J. Mar. Freshwat. Res.*, **18**, 103–14.

Mitchell, D. S. (1978) *Aquatic Weeds in Australian Inland Waters*, Aust. Govt Pub., 183 pp.

Morison, A. K. (1989) Management of introduced species in the Murray–Darling Basin – a discussion paper, in *Proc. Workshop for Native Fish Management*, 16 June 1988, Murray–Darling Basin Commission, Canberra, pp. 149–61.

Mulley, J. C. and Shearer, K. D. (1980) Identification of natural 'Yanco' × 'Boolara' hybrids of the carp *Cyprinus carpio* Linneaus. *Aust. J. Mar. Freshwat. Res.*, **31**, 409–11.

Pollard, D. A., Llewellyn, L. C. and Tilzey, R. D. J. (1980) Management of freshwater fish and fisheries, in *An Ecological Basis for Water Resource Management* (ed. W. D. Williams), A.N.U. Press, Canberra, pp. 227–70.

Pullan, S. (1982) Eradication of koi carp proves difficult. *Freshwater Catch*, Winter 1982, **15**, 24.

Pullan, S. (1984) *Koi in the Waikato River System (2)*. Internal Report, N.Z. Min. Agric. and Fish., 18 pp.

Pullan, S. and Smith, P. J. (1987) Identification of hybrids between koi (*Cyprinus carpio*) and goldfish (*Carassius auratus*). *N.Z. J. Mar. Freshwat. Res.*, **21**, 41–6.

Reynolds, L. F. (1976) Decline of the native fish species in the River Murray. *S.A.F.I.C.*, **8**, 19–24.

Reynolds, L. F. (1979) Problems associated with European carp. *Proc. Symp. Biol. Microbiol. Water, Canberra, 1977*, Australian Water Resources Council, Canberra, pp. 159–64.

Robel, R. J. (1961) The effects of carp populations on the production of waterfowl food plants in a western waterfowl marsh. *Trans. 26th Am. Wildl. Nat. Res. Conf.*, 147–59.

Rowe, D. K. (1984) Some effects of eutrophication and the removal of aquatic plants by grass carp (*Ctenopharyngodon idella*) on rainbow trout (*Salmo gairdnerii*) in Lake Parkinson, New Zealand, *N.Z. J. Mar. Freshwat. Res.*, **18**, 115–27.

Shearer, K. D. and Mulley, J. C. (1978) The introduction and distribution of the carp, *Cyprinus carpio* Linnaeus, in Australia. *Aust. J. Mar. Freshwat. Res.*, **29**, 551–64.

Shireman, J. V. (1984) Control of aquatic weeds with exotic fishes, in *Distribution, Biology and Management of Exotic Fishes* (eds W. R. Courtenay, jun., and J. R. Stauffer, jun.), Johns Hopkins Univ. Press, Baltimore, Maryland, pp. 302–11.

Thrienen, C. W. and Helm, W. R. (1954) Experiments and observation designed to show carp destruction of aquatic vegetation. *J. Wildl. Mgmt*, **18** (2), 247–51.

Tilzey, R. D. J. (1980) Introduced fish, in *An Ecological Basis for Water Resource Management* (ed. W. D. Williams), A.N.U. Press, Canberra, pp. 271–9.

Weatherley, A. H. (1974) Introduced freshwater fish, in *Biogeography and Ecology in Tasmania*, (ed. W. D. Williams), B. V. Publishers, The Hague, pp. 141–70.

Weatherley, A. H. and Lake, J. S. (1967) Introduced fish species in Australian inland waters, in *Australian Inland Waters and their Fauna* (ed. A. H. Weatherley), Australian National University Press, Canberra, pp. 217–39.

Wharton, J. C. F. (1977) Impact of exotic animals, expecially European carp *Cyprinus carpio*, on native fauna. *Fish. Wildl. Pap. Min. Conserv. Victoria*, No. 20, 13 pp.

Chapter ten

Brain and sensory systems

K. Kotrschal, R. Brandstätter, A. Gomahr, H. Junger,
M. Palzenberger and M. Zaunreiter

Dedicated to Professor W. Wieser on the occasion of his 65th birthday

10.1 INTRODUCTION

A single cyprinid species, the goldfish, *Carassius auratus*, is one of the most intensely studied research models in neurobiology and biology in general. In contrast our knowledge of other cyprinids is sparse and patchy.

Within the frame of this chapter it would be unsuitable just to review goldfish neurobiology. Instead, we must look for patterns of brain and sensory systems, and their possible relevance for sensory capacities, within a range of cyprinids. To investigate sensory diversification and specialization among cyprinids, the comparative method (Northcutt, 1988) is employed for pinpointing structural differences between and within species as well as between different-sized specimens of one species. Detailed knowledge of goldfish may provide a basis for the interpretation of our comparative data.

The advantages of cyprinids for investigating ecomorphological patterns of brain and sensory systems are evident. A diversity of species is available in Europe (Ladiges and Vogt, 1965; present volume) from most freshwater and even brackish habitats. Moreover, cyprinids have diversified into virtually all available niches (Schiemer, 1985, 1988; Chapter 12).

Aside from ecological diversification, a second criterion for qualifying as a faunal group well suited to ecomorphological research (Goldschmid and Kotrschal, 1989) is met, namely close relatedness. We may therefore be reasonably confident that cyprinid brains and sensory systems are assembled from the same basic neuronal elements according to the same basic pattern of circuitry although quantities and ratios of these elements may differ between different species and life history stages, depending on ecological requirements (Werner, 1984) and growth (p. 293).

So, our present contribution is a first, necessarily incomplete and superficial attempt to reflect the sensory diversification of European cyprinids. We discuss the brain, vision, chemosenses, and the lateral line system.

10.2 BRAIN

Introduction

Teleost brains reflect life styles (Ariens Kappers *et al.*, 1936; Bauchot *et al.*, 1977; Brandstätter and Kotrschal, 1990a, b; M H. Evans, 1931, 1932, 1935, 1940; H. E. Evans, 1952; Geiger, 1956a,b; Herrick, 1905; Khanna and Singh, 1966; Kotrschal and Junger, 1988; Miller and Evans, 1965; Schnitzlein, 1964; Uchihashi, 1953). Habitat requirements and food preferences can readily be associated with brain shapes because in the most variable part of the teleost brain, the brain stem (Kotrschal and Junger, 1988), both the somatosensory and viscerosensory columns (Nieuwenhuys and Pouwels, 1983) are segregated into discrete lobuli, which can be associated with distinct sensory faculties and innervation areas (Fig. 10.1) (Atema, 1971). These are the lobus facialis (vii) for external taste (and touch) and the lobus vagus (x) for oropharyngeal taste and touch sensitivity (Fig. 10.1), as well as the central acoustic area (Ariens Kappers *et al.*, 1936; Evans, 1932), the crista cerebellaris and the eminentia granularis, which are associated to a differing extent with auditory, ampullary and lateral line sensitivity (Davis and Northcutt, 1983). The lobus glossopharyngeus (ix) is the primary termination area of fibres innervating mainly taste buds surrounding the anterior, 1. gill slit. It is sandwiched between facial and vagal lobes. For the different brain connections of olfaction, taste and the common chemical sense in fish see Finger (1987, 1988). Brain connections of the brain stem acoustico-lateralis areas are reviewed by Echteler (1985) and McCormick and Braford (1988).

By comparing the external morphology of a few cyprinid brains, Evans (1952) distinguished between sight feeders, mouth tasters and skin tasters. A quantitative comparison of brain shapes in a variety of North American shiners was performed by Huber and Rylander (1991). Clear-water habitats correlated with a relatively large optic tectum, whereas species from turbid waters show enlarged facial, but not vagal, lobes. Also in blind cave fish, external taste tends to be highly developed (Parzefall, 1986). Thus brain structures covary with ecology.

Comparative, quantitative morphology of the cyprinid brain

The present comparative account is based on quantitative brain histology in 59 specimens from 27 species of cyprinids (Table 10.1). Brain areas were standardized by conversion into % of total brain volume to facilitate comparison. The 17 areas measured were chosen on grounds of functional relevance and demarcability and exceeded 80% of total brain volume

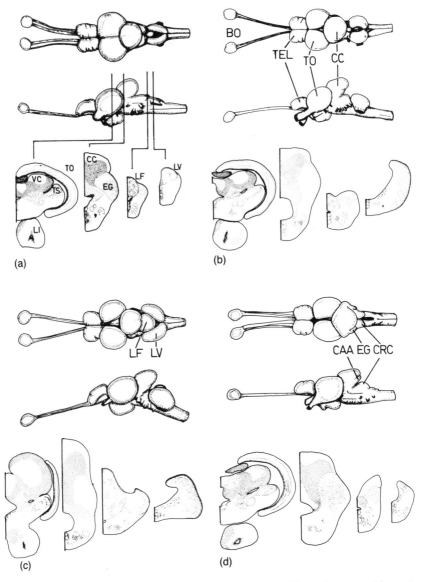

Fig. 10.1 Representative cyprinid brain types in dorsal and lateral views, with semi-diagramatic representations of cross-sections at (a) representative planes, the tectum opticum (TO), the corpus cerebelli (CC), the lobus facialis (LF) and the lobus vagus (LV). (a) The roach, *Rutilus rutilus*, brain represents the generalized type. (b) The brain of bream, *Abramis brama*, shows well-developed taste lobes, acoustico-lateralis lobes and vision. (c) Carp, *Cyprinus carpio*, represents the chemosensory brain type. (d) Sabre carp, *Pelecus cultratus*, is characterized by highly developed acoustico-lateralis lobes. Compare the appearance of carp and sabre carp brain stem lobes. For abbreviations see list, p. 288.

Table 10.1 Species considered for quantitative brain histology

Species	Common name*	Brain type[†]	n[‡]	Weight range (g)
Abramis ballerus	Blue bream	abr, ac-lat	2	92, 97
A. brama	Bream	abr, chem	3	45–462
A. sapa	Whiteye bream	abr, gen	2	85, 87
Alburnoides bipunctatus	Schneider	gen	2	14
Alburnus alburnus	Bleak	gen, c-lat	2	18, 26
Aspius aspius	Asp	gen	2	110, 155
Barbus barbus	Barbel	chem	1	570
Blicca bjoerkna	White bream	abr, gen	2	68, 113
Carassius auratus	Goldfish	chem	3	64–99
C. carassius	Crucian carp	chem	2	8, 9
Chalcalbunus chalcoides	Shemaya	gen, ac-lat	2	68, 85
Chondrostoma nasus	Nase	gen	3	175–923
Ctenopharyngodon idella	Grass carp	gen	2	49, 50
Cyprinus carpio	Carp	chem	3	51–496
Gobio gobio	Gudgeon	chem	2	21, 32
Hypophthalmichthys molitrix	Silver carp	ac-lat	2	113, 133
Leucaspius delineatus	Sun bleak	gen	2	2, 3
Leuciscus cephalus	Chub	gen	2	118, 133
L. idus	Orfe	gen	3	8–750
L. leuciscus	Dace	gen	2	15
Pelecus cultratus	Sabre carp	ac-lat	2	61, 66
Phoxinus phoxinus	Minnow	gen, chem	1	2
Rhodeus sericeus	Bitterling	gen	2	4, 5
Rutilus rutilus	Roach	gen	4	52–397
Scardinius erythrophthalmus	Rudd	gen	2	64, 140
Tinca tinca	Tench	chem	2	111, 136
Vimba vimba	Vimba	gen	2	46, 47

*Mainly according to Maitland (1981).
[†]See Figs. 10.1–10.4; abr, abramine brain; ac-lat, acoustico-lateralis brain; chem, chemosensory brain; gen, generalized brain.
[‡]Number of specimens.

(methodological details, Kotrschal and Junger, 1988, Kotrschal and Palzenberger, 1991). Information on structure and function of the areas measured is provided by Davis and Northcutt (1983). As brain morphology changes substantially during growth (Brandstätter and Kortschall, 1990a,b; p. 293), only brains of adults were chosen for quantitative comparison.

Interspecific variability of brain areas
The brain stem is the most variable part of the cyprinid brain (Fig. 10.1) (Kotrschal and Junger, 1988) and in the actinopterygian fishes in general (Evans, 1932, 1935; Nieuwenhuys and Pouwels, 1983).

Table 10.2 Brain areas measured, ranked according to decreasing coefficients of interspecific variation (VR%) calculated from 27 species and 59 specimens

Rank	Area	Abbreviation	Mean relative volume* (%)	Standard deviation	VR[†] (%)
1	Lobus facialis	LF	1.6	1.7	103.5
2	Nucleus habenularis	NH	0.1	0.1	78.3
3	Lobus vagus	LV	4.9	3.7	76.3
4	Central acoustic area	CAA	0.7	0.4	48.9
5	Crista cerebellaris	CRC	2.0	0.8	40.0
6	Eminentia granularis	EG	1.7	0.7	37.2
7	Valvula cerebelli	VC	6.9	2.6	36.7
8	Stratum marginale (TO)	SM	3.1	1.1	35.2
9	Torus longitudinalis	TL	1.0	0.3	32.2
10	Bulbus olfactorius	BO	2.4	0.8	31.5
11	Tectum opticum	TO	17.2	4.2	24.3
12	Corpus cerebelli	CC	13.2	3.1	23.6
13	Telencephalon	TEL	8.6	1.9	22.4
14	Diencephalon	DI	11.1	2.5	22.2
15	Torus semicircularis	TS	1.4	0.3	22.2
16	Mesencephalic tegmentum	MT	7.4	1.4	18.8
17	Brain stem except for sensory lobes	BS	17.9	4.0	18.3

*Mean volume as % of total brain volume.
[†]Coefficient of variation (100 × standard deviation/mean).

Table 10.2 lists the 17 brain areas in order of decreasing coefficients of variation. The highly variable chemosensory lobes for external and internal taste are followed by acoustico-lateralis areas. Visual centres are relatively low in interspecific variability. In general, primary sensory areas contribute most to interspecific variability, whilst secondary or multimodal centres are similar in relative sizes within the species considered.

Correlations between brain areas; principal components analysis

Correlations between different brain areas do not necessarily indicate causal relationships, which in terms of functional brain morphology means direct fibre connections. Yet a correlation matrix (Table 10.3) is a valuable tool for generating working hypotheses on functional connectivity, especially of multi-tasking areas like the valvula cerebelli, or may help to interpret the relationships between different sensory faculties (Jolicoeur and Baron, 1980).

The optic tectum as a whole covaries with most other brain areas, positively with vision centres and acoustico-lateralis centres, negatively with taste

Table 10.3 One-tailed significance values for the correlation matrix[†] of brain areas (ranks, abbreviations as in Table 10.2). Only significance values below 0.1 are shown

	1 LF	2 NH	3 LV	4 CAA	5 CRC	6 EG	7 VC	8 SM	9 TL	10 BO	11 TO	12 CC	13 TEL	14 DI	15 TS	16 MT	17 BS
1 LF	–																
2 NH		–															
3 LV	+***		–														
4 CAA	–**			–													
5 CRC	–***			+***	–												
6 EG	–**			+***	+***	–											
7 VC	+***		+***		–*	–*	–										
8 SM	–***		–***	+***	+***	+***	–***	–									
9 TL	–0			+**	+0	+*		+*	–								
10 BO	+0									–							
11 TO	–***		–***		+***	+**	–***	+***	+0	–*	–						
12 CC				+***	+***	+**	+***	+***		+0	–**	–					
13 TEL				–0			–**			+*		–0	–				
14 DI				–***	–***	–***	–***				+***	–***	+***	–			
15 TS	–**		–*					+*		–*	+***	+*		+*	–		
16 MT	–***		–***				–***	+*		–0	+***	–**	–***	+**	+**	–	
17 BS	–0		–**								–0	–*	–***	–*		+**	–

0a ≤ 0.1
*a ≤ 0.05
**a ≤ 0.01
***a ≤ 0.001
+ denotes positive correlation
– denotes negative correlation
[†]Pearsen's product moment correlation coeffient (sokal and Rohlf, 1981).

centres (Table 10.3). The positive correlations of the marginal stratum with both, the optic tectum and the torus longitudinalis with acoustico-lateralis areas, as well as a pronounced development of the latter in the plankton feeders (p. 291; Kotrschal and Junger, 1988), indicate substantial communication between lateral line and vision in species feeding on small organisms (Northmore, 1984).

Significantly positive correlations of the valvula cerebelli (Finger, 1983b) with brain stem taste centres, and negative ones with visual areas, indicate a role of the valvula in processing the brain stem chemosensory information in cyprinids.

Principal components analysis (PCA) extracted five significant (scree-test) (Fahrmeier and Hamele, 1984) factors (Table 10.4). The first two axes incorporate the major sensory faculties and account for c. 50% of total variability. Factor 1 represents an axis that is correlated positively with visual areas, negatively with the taste centres and the valvula cerebelli. A second axis

Table 10.4 Factor loadings on the first five factors extracted by PCA (loadings below 0.5 not shown). Factor 1 represents a chemosensory (neg.) and visual (pos.) axis, factor 2 is determined by the acoustico-lateralis areas (pos.) and factor 3 is an olfactory (pos.) and brain stem (neg.) axis.

Area*	Var.† / Cum. var.†	Factor 1 26.9 / 26.9	Factor 2 21.9 / 48.8	Factor 3 11.4 / 60.2	Factor 4 7.3 / 67.5	Factor 5 6.2 / 73.7
1 LF		−0.815				
2 NH					+0.572	+0.536
3 LV		−0.690				
4 CAA			+0.840			
5 CRC			+0.826			
6 EG			+0.739			
7 VC		−0.794				
8 SM		+0.777				
9 TL						−0.761
10 BO				+0.511	−0.549	
11 TO		+0.875				
12 CC			+0.731			
13 TEL				+0.722		
14 DI			−0.743			
15 TS		+0.523				
16 MT		+0.73				
17 BS				−0.810		

*ranks, abbreviations as in Table 10.2.
†Var., variance explained by each factor: cum. var., cumulative variance.

(factor 2, Table 10.4) is determined by the acoustico-lateralis areas together with the corpus cerebelli and correlates negatively with the diencephalon. Factor 3 is an olfactory axis.

Cyprinid brain types

All comparisons, both qualitative (Fig. 10.1) and quantitative (Tables 10.2, 10.4), point to brain stem chemosense, acoustico-lateralis and vision as causing most of the interspecific variation in cyprinid brains. Therefore the same specimens as before were plotted in morphospaces (Fig. 10.2) constructed with the original variables.

The plot of brain stem taste versus vision (Fig. 10.2(a)) shows the negative correlation between these two faculties already indicated by PCA axis 1. 'Chemosensory brains' (e.g. carp, Fig. 10.1) are relatively low in visual areas and vice versa. Abramine brains (e.g. bream, *Abramis brama*, Fig. 10.1; including the three species in the nominal genus *Abramis* plus *Vimba vimba* and *Blicca bjoerkna*) show an intermediate position in all their sensory faculties. There are no species high in both vision and taste, nor are there species low in both.

In Figure 10.2(b), relative volumes of the vagal lobe are plotted versus the facial lobe. There is no general correlation between external and internal taste. Instead, chemosensory brains show at least three different trends. A relatively moderate facial lobe representation of the external skin taste (lack of barbels) is paired with a large vagal lobe for the oropharyngeal sorting apparatus in goldfish, in crucian carp, *Carassius carassius*, but also in bream. A second group (with small lip barbels), tench, *Tinca tinca*, and common carp, *Cyprinus carpio*, shows parallel development of outer and inner taste centres (Fig. 10.2(b)). In a third group with large barbels, gudgeon, *Gobio gobio*, and barbel, *Barbus barbus*, a small vagal lobe is accompanied by a huge facial lobe. It seems that sorting and the decision on palatability of prey is divided between the taste systems at the outer skin and those in the oropharyngeal cavity: the more external discrimination is feasible, the less internal is necessary. Most species considered are low in both taste lobes, and the abramines are intermediate (Fig. 10.2(b)).

A plot of the relative volumes of the sum of acoustico-lateralis areas (EG + CRC + CAA) versus the tectum opticum (Fig. 10.2(c)) shows that species with moderately sized acoustico-lateralis brain lobes may be found over the whole range of optic tectum volumes. Species with large acoustico-lateralis areas consistently also show relatively large optic lobes, but there were no species low in optic tectum and high in acoustic-lateralis areas. Abramines are intermediate to high (Fig. 10.2(c)) in both sensory faculties.

As taste and acoustico-lateralis centres contribute most to interspecific variability in cyprinid brain morphology (Table 10.2), a plot (Fig. 10.2(d)) leads to the recognition of major brain types (Kotrschal and Junger, 1988; Kotrschal *et al.*, 1987; compare Fig. 10.1). Most species show generalized brains (e.g. roach, *Rutilus rutilus*, Fig. 10.1), which are low in taste and

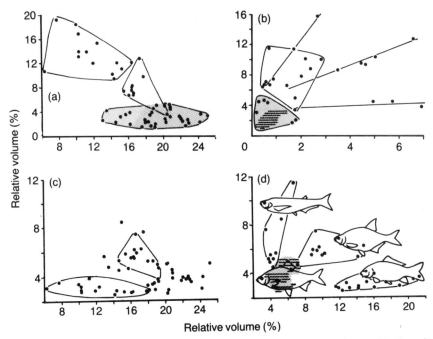

Fig. 10.2 (a) to (d): Morphospaces obtained by plotting relative volumes (% of total brain volume) of major sensory brain lobes. Data represent 59 specimens from 27 species (Table 10.1). (a) Relative volume of the tectum opticum (x-axis) versus relative volumes of brain stem taste lobes (y-axis, = lobus facialis + lobus vagus). Stippled area, generalized brain types. Minimal polygons enclose groups of generalized (lower polygon), abramine (middle polygon) and chemosensory (upper polygon) brains. (b) Relative volume of the lobus facialis (external taste, x-axis) versus relative volume of the lobus vagus (internal taste, y-axis). Stippled area within lower polygon, generalized brains; hatching, high concentration of data points, beyond resolution in the present graph. Upper polygon encloses abramine brains. Filled lines indicate different trends in the relative developments of external versus internal taste: representative species are (upper line) crucian carp, (middle line) carp, (lower line) barbel. (c) Relative volume of the tectum opticum (x-axis) versus the sum of acoustico-lateralis lobes (y-axis, eminentia granularis + crista cerebellaris + central acoustic area). Chemosensory (lower polygon) and abramine (upper polygon) brains are emphasized. (d) Plot of brain areas contributing most to interspecific variability and appearance of representative species, the brains of which are depicted in Fig. 10.1. The plot of brain stem chemosense (x-axis, lobus facialis + lobus vagus) versus sum of acoustico-lateralis lobes (y-axis, as in (c)) reveals distinct grouping into major brain types (compare Fig. 10.1). Stippled area, generalized brains (representative species, roach); hatching, highest concentration of data points which cannot be resolved in the present graph. Other polygons enclose acoustico-lateralis brains (upper; representative species, sabre carp), abramine brains (middle; bream) and chemosensory brains (lower right; carp).

acoustico-lateralis representations, but relatively high in optic tectum volumes
(Fig. 10.2(a) and (c)). A small group of species, the sabre carp, *Pelecus cultratus*
(Fig. 10.1), silver carp, *Hypophthalmichthys molitrix*, and to a lesser extent the
shemaya, *Chalcalburnus chalcalburnus*, and bleak, *Alburnus alburnus*, show an
acoustico-lateralis brain (Fig. 10.2(d)). A well-defined group of species shows
chemosensory brains (compare Figs. 10.1, 10.2(a), 10.2(d)).

Brain growth patterns

Fish generally show indeterminate growth. Despite much interest in changes
of sensory systems and behaviour during early life history (reviews, Huntingford, 1986; Noakes and Godin, 1988), the intriguing questions of possible
growth-related changes in brain morphology have not attracted much
attention (Geiger, 1956a).

In comparative investigations on postlarval brain growth from juveniles to
large adults, it was found that a variety of shifts in brain morphology patterns
occur due to allometric growth within the brain (Brandstätter and Kotrschal,
1990b). In all species studied, these shifts in relative volumes of different brain
areas are most pronounced during the juvenile period, but continue throughout life, well into the large adult stages. Two types of growh-related shifts may
be distinguished, namely those present in all species and others specific for
certain brain types.

In all species, there is a steady decrease with growth of the optic tectum and

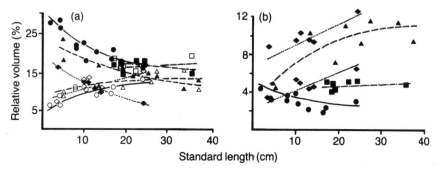

Fig. 10.3 (a) Decrease in relative volume (% of total brain volume) of the tectum
opticum (filled symbols), and increase in relative size of the corpus cerebelli (open
symbols), with increasing standard length in four representative cyprinid brains
(compare Fig. 10.1). Circles and solid curves, roach (generalized brain); triangles
and dashed curves, bream (abramine brain); diamonds and dotted curves, carp
(chemosensory brain); squares and morse curves, sabre carp (acoustico-lateralis
brain). (b) Increases or decreases with standard length in relative volumes (% of total
brain volume) of selected brain stem sensory lobes in representative cyprinid brains
(symbols as in (a); upper dotted curve, carp lobus vagus; dashed curve, bream lobus
vagus; lower dotted curve, carp lobus facialis; morse curve, sabre carp crista
cerebellaris; solid curve, roach lobus vagus). Areas which grow isometrically were
not considered.

a slight, but steady increase in size of the corpus cerebelli (Fig. 10.3(a)), suggesting a common growth pattern in all cyprinids.

However, other, mainly primary sensory areas decrease or increase in a species-specific way (Fig. 10.3(b)). Therefore, brains of cyprinids and probably of teleosts in general are not invariant during the postlarval period, but grow into their specific types, never attaining a definite final morphology.

The late larval outgrowth (Brandstäter and Kotrschal, 1990a) and permanent growth of primary sensory areas, which generate specialized brain types (chemosensory or acoustico-lateralis; Figs. 10.2 and 10.3) within the species studied, support the hypothesis that the generalized brain types (Fig. 10.2(d), e.g. roach, *Rutilus rutilus*) may be close to the mainstream of cyprinid evolution. This is also supported by the numerical dominance of generalized brain types (Table 10.1). The ontogenetic separation of the specialized brains from the generalized species pool may demonstrate how these brains have diverged during phylogenetic development.

10.3   VISION

Introduction

Cyprinids have elaborate colour vision (von Frisch, 1912; Lythgoe, 1988, Wunder, 1925). Goldfish as well as other cyprinids have three spectral maxima in a visual system that works from 360 to 750 nm, from the infrared into the ultraviolet range (Lythgoe, 1988; Neumeyer, 1988). Polarized light can probably be perceived (Kleerekoper *et al.*, 1973; Waterman, 1981). Brightness discrimination ability seems intermediate when compared with that of other marine teleosts (review, Blaxter, 1988). Unlike photopic colour vision (by cones), relatively little is known about the mechanisms of scotopic sensitivity (by rods) and the discrimination of movements (Guthrie, 1986).

The retina

Eye sizes vary considerably within the species considered (Fig. 10.4). A larger eye means more retinal area, more receptor cells per visual angle and therefore a potentially higher resolving power than a small eye (Otten, 1981; Van der Meer, 1986; Van der Meer and Anker, 1984). This is backed by ecology, as the large-eyed species are planktivores, whereas bottom feeders have small eyes (Fig. 10.4). Also, clear-water species among American shiners have larger eyes than species from turbid waters (Huber and Rylander, 1991).

The basic bauplan (the fundamental structure and organization) of the eye and of the duplex retina is conserved in the vertebrates (Schnakenbeck, 1962;

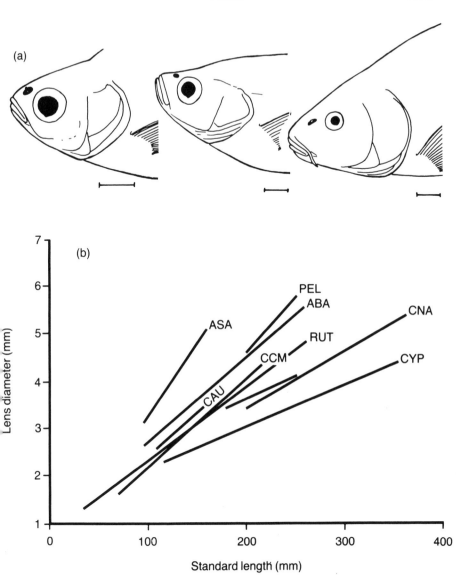

Fig. 10.4 (a) Eye sizes, from large to small, in (left) in whiteye bream, *Abramis sapa*, (centre) sabre carp, *Pelecus culratus*, and (right) tench, *Tinca tinca*. Scale bars 10 mm. (b) Log-log plot of lens diameter versus body weight in representative species, to show relative sizes of the eye. All regression lines significant, based on 5–20 measurements in each species: 1, whiteye bream; 2, sabre carp; 3, blue bream, *Abramis ballerus*; 4, shemaya, *Chalcalburnus chalcoides*; 5, roach, *Rutilus rutilus*, 6, asp, *Aspius aspius*; 7, goldfish, *Carassius auratus*; 8, nase, *Chondrostoma nasus*; 9, carp, *Cyprinus carpio*.

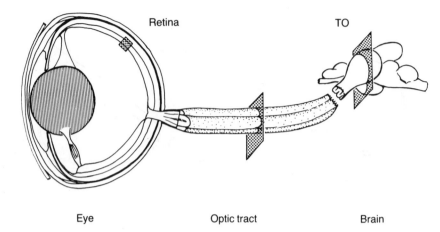

Fig. 10.5 Elements of the teleostean visual system: the eye with the retina, optic tract and optic tectum (TO), not to scale. Stippled areas show planes of histological sections depicted in later figures. (Modified with permission from Zaunreiter *et al.*, 1989.)

Walls, 1967), yet there may be considerable variation in the numbers, types and ratios of receptor cells, interneurones and retinal ganglion cells (Guthrie, 1986).

We still lack sufficient data even for the more important cyprinid species, listed in Table 10.1. However, the basic cyprinid retinal pattern (Figs 10.5 and 10.6) (Engström, 1960) seems to apply to most of the species, except for chemosensory types with a regressively modified visual system, like tench, goldfish and crucian carp, or species that are specialized in parts of the system, like the asp, *Aspius aspius*. (p. 305).

There is probably no sensory system that changes as dramatically with growth, from larva to large adults, as vision (Ali, 1964; Blaxter 1975; Blaxter and Staines, 1970; Boehlert, 1979; Easter 1985; Easter *et al.*, 1977, 1981; Fernald, 1983; 1985 a, b, 1988; Hitchcock, 1987; Kock, 1982; Kock and Reuter, 1978 a, b; Kotrschal *et al.*, 1990; Macy, 1981; Macy and Easter, 1979; Marotte, 1980; Otten, 1981; Raymond, 1985, 1988; Raymond Johns, 1981, 1982; Raymond Johns and Easter, 1977; Raymond Johns and Fernald, 1981; Sandy and Blaxter, 1980; Wagner, 1974). When comparing structural aspects of the neuronal visual system, including retina, optic tract and central visual areas (Fig. 10.5), the dynamic, lifelong, growth-related shifts of this system deserve prime attention, particularly as these shifts may help to explain ecological shifts during ontogeny (Blaxter, 1968a, b; Boehlert, 1979; Fernald, 1984; 1988; Kotrschal *et al.*, 1990; Powers and Easter, 1983; Werner, 1984).

Euteleost larvae are the smallest autonomous vertebrates. Most are visually orientated plankton feeders (Blaxter 1968b, 1969; Li *et al.*, 1985; Mark *et al.*,

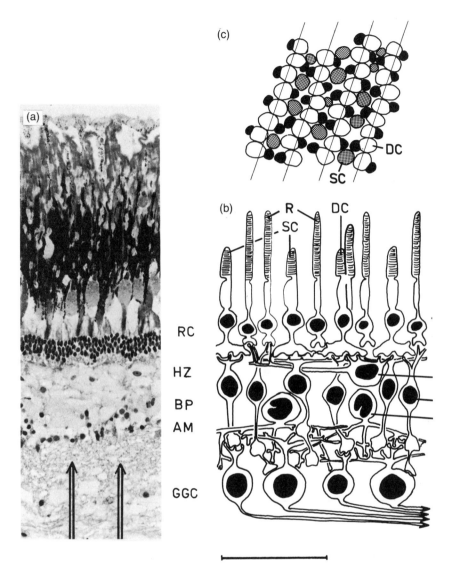

Fig. 10.6 Retinal structure and connectivity. (a) Semithin cross-section through the retina of adult roach. Arrows indicate path of light. (b) Diagram, modified after Dowling and Boycott (1966). (c) Camera-lucida drawing of a semithin tangential section through the retinal outer segment layer of roach, showing typical cyprinid cone mosaic pattern: double cones (DC) shown as black-and-white twins; single cones (SC) stippled; parallel lines follow rows of double cones. For abbreviations see list (p. 322). Scale bar, *c.* 100 μm.

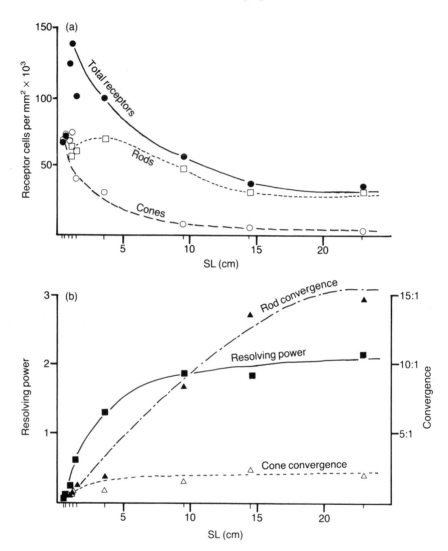

Fig. 10.7 Changes with growth in selected retinal parameters, expressed per constant area (1 mm^2) of temporal retina in a size-series of nine roach (short-tickmarks on x-axis). Data from histological historesin tangential and cross-sections (Zaunreiter, unpubl.). Left y-axis: ●, total receptor cell numbers; ○, cones; □, rods. Inner right y-axis: △, cone convergence (ratio cones:ganglion cells); ▲, rod convergence. Outer right (stippled) y-axis: ■ and broadly stippled curve, increase of photopic resolving power (cones per visual angle) with growth.

1989). To gain enough receptors per visual angle for adequate resolution of the retinal image, small cones have to be packed in high densities into the larval retinas (Fig. 10.7; present retinal data derived from quantitative histology, Zaunreiter *et al.*, 1991). Indeed, all larvae of euphotic teleosts were found to have pure-cone retinae. To maintain high resolution at the receptor level, a low convergence ratio from cones to ganglion cells is necessary in fish larvae. Therefore the numbers of ganglion cells and fibres in the optic tract are relatively high in small fish (Fig. 10.7), necessitating a relatively large optic tectum (Fig. 10.3(a)) (Brandstätter and Kotrschal, 1990a, b).

Limited space in the larval retina constrains the simultaneous optimization of both resolving power and sensitivity of the photopic cone system. With retinal stretch during growth (Ali, 1964; Müller 1952; Wagner 1974), cones increase in size (Zaunreiter *et al.*, 1989) and gain sensitivity. Despite increasing distanes between the retinal cones, their numbers per visual angle increase. Therefore, both photopic sensitivity and resolving power improve during postlarval growth (Otten, 1981; Raymond, 1988; Van der Meer and Anker, 1984).

During growth, rods are added by mitosis throughout the retina, whereas cone formation is restricted to the growth zone in the retinal marginal rim (Fernald, 1985b; Raymond, 1985; Raymond Johns, 1981; Raymond Johns and Fernald, 1981). This difference leads to a shift in the numerical ratio between the two receptor types (Fernald, 1988) (Fig. 10.7), which is accompanied by shifts in ganglion cell receptive field sizes (Hitchcock, 1987; Hitchcock and Easter, 1986) and shifts in ratios between different types of retinal ganglion cells (Fig. 10.7 and p. 305). These lifelong, qualitative and quantitative shifts in the visual systems of teleosts may change visual capacities (Raymond, 1988).

In cyprinids, as in most other teleosts, size constraints in the larval visual system may restrict larval niches (Hairston *et al.*, 1982; Kotrschal *et al.*, 1990; Li *et al.*, 1985; Mark *et al.*, 1989; Wanzenböck and Schiemer, 1989). During subsequent juvenile and adult growth, release from this constraint occurs and species shift towards their specific sensory apparatus and niches.

The optic tract

The optic tract consists mainly of afferent axons (Northcutt, 1983; Vanegas, 1983) originating from retinal ganglion cells and terminating in the contralateral optic tectum, but also in pretectal areas (Northcutt and Wullimann, 1988; Wullimann and Meyer, 1989). This tract may be fasciculated (bundled), as in a new chemosensory species like goldfish and crucian carp (Easter *et al.*, 1981), but is pleated in all remaining species (compare Northcutt and Wullimann, 1988) (Fig. 10.8). The optic tracts are

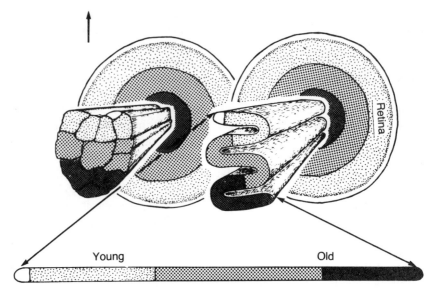

Fig. 10.8 Chronotopic and retinotopic mapping of concentric retinal areas within fasciculated (left: goldfish and crucian carp) and pleated (right: all other species) optic tracts. Small arrow points dorsally. Bar identifies growth zone (no stippliing), peripheral retina (light stippling), medial retina (moderate stippling), and central retina (heavy stippling). Fasciculated tract mapping drawn according to Bernhardt and Easter (1986).

organized retinotopically and chronotopically in a schematically clear way (Bernhardt and Easter, 1986; Bunt, 1982; Springer and Mednick, 1986; Fig. 10.8). Concentric fields in the retina translate into a linear fibre arrangement within the ribbon of the pleated optic tract. Fibres of neurones from the growth zone in the peripheral retina are added to the dorsal edge of the ribbon. Fibres from the nasal, caudal, temporal and ventral retina are appropriately mapped across the width of the band (Bernhardt and Easter, 1986). Fibre diameters in the optic tract are correlated with soma and receptive field sizes of the retinal ganglion cells (Ito and Murakami, 1984).

For all these reasons, the optic tract contains much structural information on retinal ganglion cells, making it an easily accessible window into the retina. Therefore, fibre-diameter frequency analysis was used to study retinal changes with growth and interspecific differences (Junger and Kotrschal, unpubl.). A total of 42 tracts from a size series of eight species were analyzed; in all, c. 200 000 fibres were counted and measured.

Fibre frequencies are relatively similar when compared between different sampling areas within a particular optic tract (except for the growth zone). Therefore fibre frequency distributions were pooled for each tract investigated and were standardized to the same area. Two major fibre peaks, small and large, are present, in each tract (Fig. 10.9). There is evidence from large specimens that each of these peaks may consist of two subclasses of fibre (Junger and Kotrschal, unpubl.; Hitchcock and Easter, 1986; Ito and Murakami, 1984) resulting in a total of four basic fibre classes.

Changes with growth affect fibre diameters and ratios between small and large fibres. During growth, fibre diameters increase steadily (Figs. 10.9 and 10.10), reflecting the adjustment of the dendritic field sizes of retinal ganglion cells (Hitchcock and Easter, 1986) to retinal expansion. The very similar log-normal distribution of fibre frequencies in all species examined may be explained by growth, which enlarges small initial differences in fibre calibres.

A more specific shift with growth affects ratios between small and large fibres (note peak shifts between small and large specimens, Figs 10.10 and 10.11). In all species investigated, the percentage of large fibres (and thus large retinal ganglion cells) increases steadily with growth. However, the rate of increase may differ drastically between species (Fig. 10.11). There is evidence (Wartzok and Marks, 1973) that ganglion cells with large receptive fields are predominantly movement detectors.

The hypothesis that large ganglion cells are motion detectors is supported not only by their resemblance to mammalian alpha-type ganglion cells (Peichl *et al.*, 1987), but also by a striking association between the rate of ontogenetic increase of large optic tract fibres (Fig. 10.11) and feeding style. In taste-orientated benthic feeders, like carp and crucian carp, large fibres increase only slightly and do not exceed 5% of all optic tract fibres in the adults. Roach and chub, *Leuciscus cephalus*, are versatile, generalized feeders, and large fibres exceed 5% in big specimens. Bleak, bream and sabre carp are predominantly plankton and surface feeders and may have more than 15% large fibres. The piscivorous asp seems to be specialized with respect to movement detection: large specimens may have more than 40% large fibres in their optic tracts (Fig. 10.11).

Tectum opticum and pretectal areas

The optic tectum is the major target of optic tract fibres (Northcutt, 1983; Schmidt, 1979), but afferents also terminate in pretectal nuclei (Northcutt and Wullimann, 1988), which show a characteristic pattern in cyprinids (Wullimann and Meyer, 1989). No substantial variation could be detected in the pretectal system of the cyprinids we investigated. The relatively minor variability of the optic tectum as compared to other primary sensory areas of the brain (Table 10.2) may be explained by its integrative function. Besides primary visual fibres, the tectum also receives input from the telencephalon, the contralateral tectum, the torus longitudinalis and cerebellum (Finger, 1983b).

Still, tectal size and structure correlate with the ecology of species (Kishida, 1979; Winkelmann and Winkelmann, 1968) (Figs. 10.1, 10.2 (a) and (c)). The

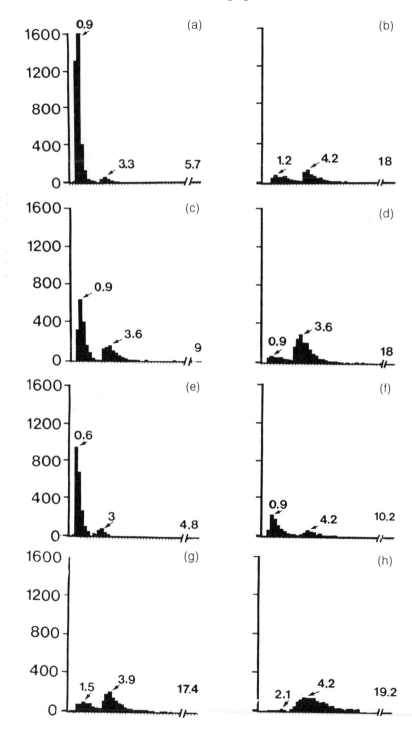

size of the optic tectum as a whole is roughly predictable from the number of incoming optic tract fibres. A rather close relationship seems to exist between the width of the stratum marginale of the tectum (Fig. 10.12) and feeding style. Benthivorous and generalized species show relatively narrow strata marginalia, whereas these are wide in planktivores. The piscivorous asp shows only an intermediate marginal stratum, indicating that it is mainly particle size that determines its width. The stratum marginale consists of parallel fibres originating from the torus longitudinalis (Vanegas, 1983). Quantitative brain morphology (Table 10.3) shows that both stratum marginale and torus longitudinalis have clear positive correlations with acoustico-lateralis areas. Conjugated eye movements and prey-search behaviour can be elicited by superficial electrical stimulation of the tectum (Northmore, 1984; reviews, Guthrie, 1986; Vanegas, 1983). Therefore the marginal stratum may be seen as an integratory neuropil, where vision receives guidance by lateral line information, probably relayed via the cerebellum, in cyprinids preying on small, planktonic items.

During growth, all species investigated show a similar decrease in the relative size of the tectum opticum (Fig. 10.3(a)) which may be explained by the decreasing number of newly formed fibres. On the contrary, the relative size of the stratum marginale increases with growth (unpublished), which indicates differentiation of this system.

10.4   CHEMOSENSES

Introduction

Water as a solvent is an excellent carrier for chemical stimuli (Atema, 1988; Atema *et al.*, 1988; Carr, 1988). This may be one reason why fish are equipped with a variety of chemosensory input channels, defined by the organ systems central connections, sensory capacities and biological roles (Bardach and Atema, 1971; Caprio, 1988; Finger, 1988; Gomahr *et al.*, 1988; Herrick, 1905, 1906). Generally, three different chemosenses are recognized: olfaction, mediated via the olfactory mucosa, taste via taste buds, and an ill-defined

---

Fig. 10.9 Diameter frequencies of optic tract fibres in small and large individuals of representative cyprinids. Class intervals (x-axis): 0.3 μm. All histograms standardized to the same area. The large fibres were sampled at 25 × the area of small fibres. Peak values for small and large fibres, and range in diameter of large fibres, are given. Total fibres numbers in the optic tracts: (a) small roach (5.2 cm SL), 131 000; (b) large roach (22 cm SL), 420 000; (c) small bream (4.9 cm SL), 104 000; (d) large bream (33 cm SL), 250 000; (e) small carp (3.4 cm SL), 54 000; (f) large carp (24 cm SL), 179 000; (g) small asp (20 cm SL), 247 000; (h) large asp (35.7 cm SL), 281 000 (species names, Table 10.1).

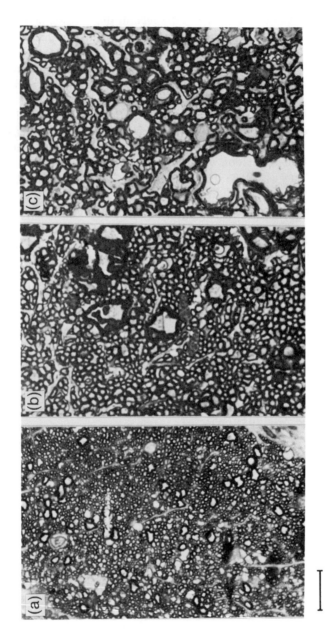

Fig. 10.10 Semithin sections of the optic tracts of (a) early juvenile (1.5 cm SL). (b) late juvenile (5.2 cm SL). and (c) adult (23 cm SL) roach. Note increasing fibre diameters. Scale bar. 10 μm.

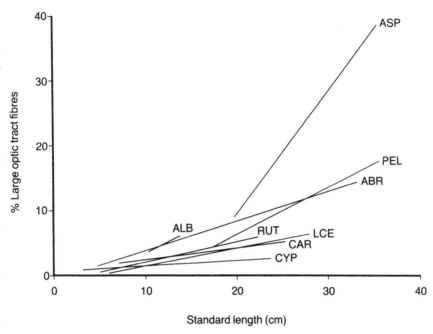

Fig. 10.11 Shifts in relative abundance (% of all fibres) of large optic tract fibres with increasing standard length in eight representative cyprinids (species names, Table 10.1). Note strong linear increases with growth in the plankton-feeding bream and sabre carp, and especially in the piscivorous asp.

"common chemical sense" (Parker, 1912, quoted from Silver, 1987). Solitary chemosensory cells (SCCs) (Whitear, 1971) are present in most teleosts (Reutter, 1986; Whitear, pers. comm.) and may mediate a chemosensation different from taste and olfaction (Finger, 1982; Kotraschal, 1991; Peters *et al.*, 1991; Silver and Finger, 1984). It is unknown whether the SCCs are the cellular substrate for the general chemosense.

Olfaction

The olfactory organ is similar in morphology within the teleosts (reviews, Caprio, 1988; Hara, 1982, 1986). A flap of skin covers the olfactory groove which contains the mucosal rosette and forms the rostral and caudal nostrils (Fig. 10.13). Water is forced through the nasal cavity either during swimming by pressure differences between the anterior and posterior nostrils, or by ciliary beat (cyclosmates and isosmates, Doving *et al.*, 1977). The nose may be able to extract spatial information from turbulent odour plumes (Atema, 1977, 1988) and is involved in learning complex tasks in connection with chemical stimuli (Zippel, 1989).

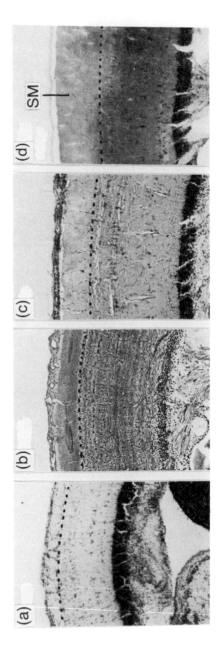

Fig. 10.12 Details of the tectum opticum in representative species (a) carp: (b) roach: (c) asp: (d) sabre carp: (species names, Table 10.1). Paraffin sections stained with bodian (carp, roach and asp), or cryostat section stained with cresyl-violet (sabre carp). Note differing relative width of the stratum marginale (SM), which is particularly wide in the plankton feeders. Dotted line marks boundary between SM and rest of the optic tectum. Scale bar, 100 μm.

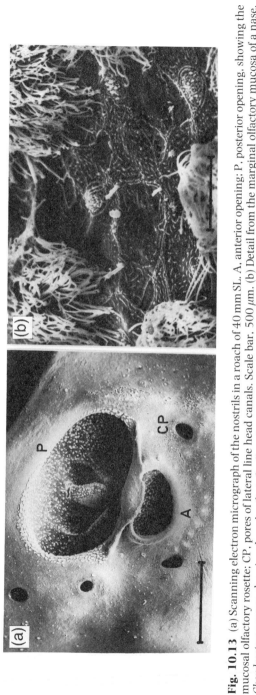

Fig. 10.13 (a) Scanning electron micrograph of the nostrils in a roach of 40 mm SL. A, anterior opening; P, posterior opening, showing the mucosal olfactory rosette; CP, pores of lateral line head canals. Scale bar, 500 μm. (b) Detail from the marginal olfactory mucosa of a nase, *Chondrostoma nasus*, showing densely ciliated cells, a few apices of solitary chemoreceptor cells protruding between squamous epidermal cells and pit openings (short brushes or microvilli) of ionocytes. Scale bar, 10 μm.

The olfactory mucosa in cyprinids contains primary sensory receptor cells, supporting cells and basal cells (Caprio, 1988; Getchell and Getchell, 1987; Hara, 1986). The sensory cells extend a dendritic protrusion into the nasal cavity and send their axons into the bulbus olfactorius (review, Scott and Harrison, 1987). The apical dendrite may be ciliated or microvillous (Caprio, 1988).

In cyprinids, the olfactory bulb is attached to the olfactory organ. The distance between the bulb and the telencephalon is bridged by the secondary olfactory tracts (Fig. 10.1). As the brain grows considerably slower than the body (Geiger, 1956a), the distance between the olfactory bulb and the telencephalon increases with size of the fish.

Gross morphology of the olfactory organs, as well as quantitative histology of the olfactory bulbs, reveal intermediate interspecific variation of the olfactory system in the cyprinids studied (Table 10.2). The olfactory bulb size is positively correlated among other areas, and also with the facial lobe (Table 10.3). This agrees with Huber and Rylander (1991) in that the olfactory bulb and the facial lobe covary and both are relatively large in species from turbid waters.

The olfactory mucosa may host two fundamentally different chemosenses. One is 'classical' olfaction. Its structural substrate is the olfactory sensory cells, which are highly sensitive to neutral L-α-amino acids (Caprio, 1988) in fish. As revealed by electrophysiology, fish may smell amino acids in dilutions as low as 10^{-9}M. Behavioural threshlds may be well below 10^{-10}M. A second mucosal chemosensory system may consist of the nervus terminalis (olfactoretinalis system) which sends terminals of supposed chemosensory function into the olfactory mucosa. Their biological role is still enigmatic; pheromone reception in context with sexual behaviour are discussed (Demski and Schwanzel-Fukuda, 1987).

Experiments by von Frisch (1941) pointed to the olfactory organ as the site of 'schreckstoff' (alarm substance) perception in cyprinids (reviews, Hara, 1986; Smith, 1982; see also Chapter 18).

Taste

The sense of taste is associated with specialized end organs, the taste-buds (TB, Fig. 10.14) (reviews, Caprio, 1988; Kinnamon, 1987). Taste-buds contain sensory and supporting cells; their formation is induced by the innervating nerves. In most fishes, except external TBs in the gadids, there is also a basal cell, resembling a merkel cell. Contrary to a prevailing view (Caprio, 1988; Kinnamon, 1987; Reutter, 1986) that synaptic specializations are found on supporting cells and also between sensory and supporting cells and basal cells, Jakubowski and Whitear (1986, 1989) and Kitoh et al. (1987) could demonstrate synapses only between nerves and sensory cells, and between nerves and basal cells.

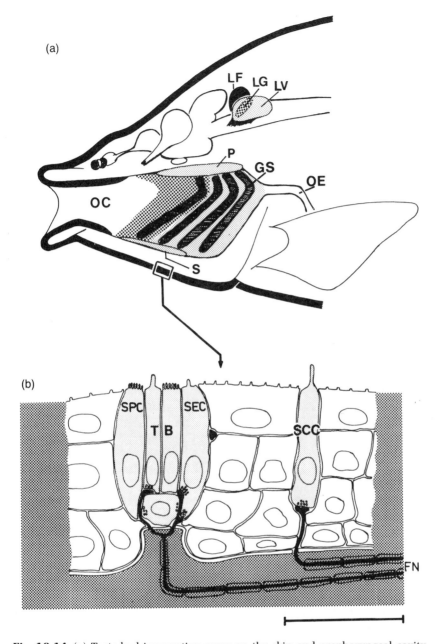

Fig. 10.14 (a) Taste-bud innervation areas on the skin and oropharyngeal cavity, as well as their primary sensory brain stem areas, in cyprinids. Black, area innervated by facialis branches (VII); dark stipple, area innervated by glossopharyngeal components (IX); light stipple, vagal (X) innervation. (b) Diagram of the two specialized arrangements of epidermal chemoreceptor cells, the taste-buds (TB, with sensory cells (SEC), supporting cells (SPC) and a basal cell) and the solitary chemoreceptor cells (SCC), innervated by afferent nerve fibres. Scale bar, *c.* 50 μm. (Modified with permission from Gomahr *et al.*, 1988.) Abbreviations, p. 322.

Primary taste centres in the brain stem show characteristic descending and ascending connections, with the secondary gustatory nucleus and with diencephalic areas (Finger 1983a, 1987, 1988; Morita and Masai, 1980; Morita and Finger, 1985b).

In most fishes, TBs are not restricted to the oral cavity, but also occur in the skin of the body (Fig. 10.14 to 10.17). These external TBs are particularly abundant in the ostariophysian fishes (Atema, 1971; Bardach and Atema, 1971; Kiyohara *et al.*, 1980).

External TBs and those in the anterior oral cavity are innervated by the branches of the facial nerve (Kiyohara *et al.*, 1985b), the orophyaryngeal TBs around the anterior gill slit are supplied from the glossopharyngeal nerve, while the remaining gill slits as well as the palatal organ are innervated from nerve fibres terminating in the lobus vagus (Atema, 1971; Luiten, 1975; Morita and Finger, 1985) (Fig. 10.14).

In all fishes investigated, TBs are amino-acid sensitive (Konishi and Zotterman, 1961; Marui, 1977), but to a different spectrum of amino acids as the olfactory organ (see also Atema, 1977, for a distinction between olfaction and taste). Thresholds of the external taste system (review, Caprio, 1988) may be as low as in olfaction, but seem to be higher in the oropharyngeal system. Taste-buds also respond to tactile stimulation (Davenport and Caprio, 1982; Kiyohara *et al.*, 1985a; Marui and Caprio, 1982; Peters *et al.*, 1987). It seems to be this peculiar combination of chemo- and tactile sensitivity that suits TBs so well to detecting food and oropharyngeal sorting (Sibbing, 1988). It was shown for the palatal organ that sensory and motor innervation are precisely and somatotopically mapped in the vagal lobe (Finger, 1989; Morita and Finger, 1985a,b, 1987).

Remarkable interspecific differences exist in numbers and arrangement of oropharyngeal TBs (Pohla *et al.*, 1986) associated with oropharyngeal sorting. These TBs are situated at the gill rakers (Fig. 10.15), and in high densities in the palatal organ, the fleshy, dorsal, tongue-like sorting pad of cyprinids (Fig. 10.14) (Sibbing 1982, 1988; Sibbing and Uribe, 1985). The largest palatal organs, together with the highest concentrations of TBs at the gill rakers, are found in benthivorous winnowers such as carp, crucian carp and bream. The most elaborate rakers are present in plankton feeders, e.g. blue bream, *Abramis ballerus* (Fig. 10.15(c)).

Densities and distribution of external TBs were compared in 11 species of cyprinids (Gomahr *et al.*, 1988; Gomahr and Kotrschal, 1991); species in which four or more individuals were examined are listed in Table 10.5. TB pores were stained with 2% silver nitrate prior to counting (Fig. 10.16; details, Gomahr *et al.*, 1988).

External TBs decrease in density from rostral to caudal and from ventral to dorsal. In the surface-orientated sun bleak, *Leucaspius delineatus*, and sabre carp, *Pelecus cultratus*, but also in the bitterling, *Rhodeus sericeus*, TB densities were approximately equal on the dorsal and ventral head surfaces

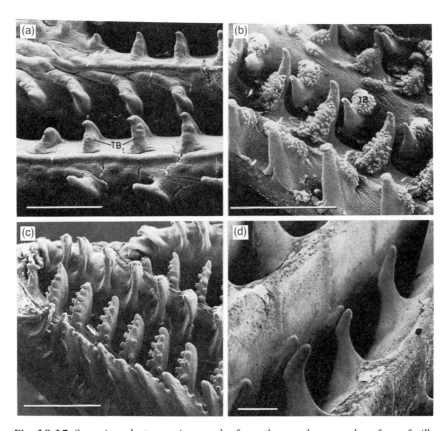

Fig. 10.15 Scanning electron micrographs from the oropharyngeal surface of gill bars, showing gill rakers and adjoining taste-buds in representative cyprinids. (a) Omnivorous roach, *Rutilus rutilus*; simple rakers bear pads of taste-buds (TB). (b) Benthivorous and planktivorous bream, *Abramis brama*; rakers bear elaborate pads of hillock-type taste-buds (TB). (c) Planktivorous blue bream, *A. ballerus*, with elaborate first-, second- and third-order rakers, but only a few taste-buds. (d) Piscivorous asp, *Aspius aspius*; simple rakers, no taste-buds. Scale bars, 1 mm. (Modified with permission from Pohla *et al.*, 1986.)

(Table 10.5). Highest TB densities occur on the gular skin. Among fins, the pectorals and pelvics were high in TBs. TB densities varied considerably between conspecifics, but were similar on the two sides of an individual's body.

Species in Table 10.5 are ranked from high to low TB densities. Owing to high intraspecific variability, differences were only significant between white bream, bream, roach and bleak ($P < 0.05$, one-way analysis of variance). The ranking in Table 10.5 is supported by its significant correlation with a ranking of species according to relative sizes of their facial lobes (p. 291; $P < 0.001$, Spearman's rank test). The order of species towards decreasing TB densities correlates roughly with an ecological rank from bottom feeding to planktivory

Table 10.5 Species in which taste-bud (TB) densities were counted in four or more individuals; species ranked according to decreasing densities of TBs. Results are only shown from sample areas where relatively complete sets of data exist. * Entries are mean number of taste-buds mm^{-2}, ± standard deviation; – signifies missing or insufficient data

Species	n†	Total‡	Head		Fins	
			Gular	Forehead	Pectoral	Pelvic
Phoxinus phoxinus (minnow)	4	142	297 ± 75	95 ± 77	138 ± 64	83 ± –
Blicca bjoercna (white bream)	17	109	291 ± 74	147 ± 59	120 ± 38	91 ± 43
Carassius carassius (crucian carp)	4	80	162 ± 24	82 ± 14	90 ± 21	92 ± –
Vimba vimba (vimba)	4	79	285 ± 71	93 ± 35	150 ± 13	–
Abramis brama (beam)	9	68	190 ± 91	82 ± 28	125 ± 81	140 ± 132
Rutilus rutilus (roach)	16	57	178 ± 57	36 ± 19	89 ± 42	65 ± 26
Alburnus alburnus (bleak)	17	51	145 ± 57	44 ± 21	64 ± 20	45 ± –
Leucaspius delineatus (sun bleak)	4	7	18 ± 3	15 ± 1	0	0
Pelecus cultratus (sabre carp)	4	6	11 ± 5	17 ± 4	0	0
Rhodeus sericeus (bitterling)	4	4	11 ± 4	10 ± 3	0	0

* Source: modified with permission from Gomahr et al. (1988).
† Number of individuals investigated.
‡ Mean number of taste-buds mm^{-2} in five different body areas sampled.

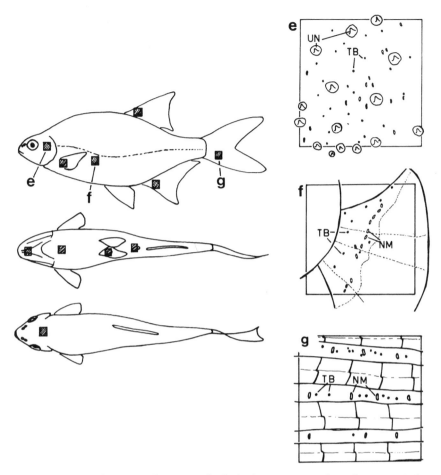

Fig. 10.16 Sample areas where taste-buds (TB) were counted, and representative distribution patterns of TBs in a few areas (e, f, g). NM, superficial neuromasts; UN, unculi (horny epidermal protrusions, nuptial dress of male cyprinids). (Modified with permission from Gomahr *et al.*, 1988.)

and surface feeding. The lack of ecological data makes it impossible to judge the influence of water turbidity in the species' habitats on the development of the taste systems (Huber, personal communication).

On different parts of the skin, typical TB distribution patterns can be found (Fig. 10.16). Along the scaleless skin of the head, patterns are irregular, yet neighbouring TBs maintain similar distances to one another. Distribution patterns are more regular on skin with underlying scales or fin rays. Taste-buds may be found mainly at the relatively deep epidermis in the corners formed by scales. On the pectoral fins, TBs occur in rows, following the fin rays, whereas on the caudal fin, TBs are arranged in rows on the fin web, alternating with neuromasts (Fig. 10.16).

During growth, TB density seems to be relatively constant (Gomahr *et al.*, 1988), although the size ranges investigated were insufficient to provide a definite answer.

Solitary chemosensory cells

As well as taste-buds, a second type of specialized epidermal chemoreceptor cells, solitary chemosensory cells (SCCs, Fig. 10.14(b)) is found in the skin of bony fishes (Lane, 1977; Lane and Whitear, 1982; Reutter, 1986; Schulte and Holl, 1972; Whitear, 1952, 1971, 1991). SCCs occur scattered in the epidermis and protrude a single apical villus between the squamous epidermal cells (Figs 10.14(b), 10.17). Their fine structure resembles TB receptor cells (Kotrschal *et al.*, 1984; Lane, 1977; Whitear, 1971; Whitear and Kotrschal, 1988), oligovillous cells from lamprey skin (Whitear and Lane, 1983) and the stiftchenzellen of frog tadpoles (Whitear, 1976).

Probably owing to the unfavourable, scattered arrangement of SCCS and uncertainties on their innervation (but see Reutter, 1974), these presumed (on fine structural grounds) chemosensory cells attracted only modest scientific attention until the modified anterior dorsal fin of some gadide fish, the rocklings, was characterized as a chemosensory organ (Kotrschal and Whitear, 1988; Kotrschal *et al.*, 1984; Peters *et al.*, 1987; Whitear and Kotrschal, 1988) containing high SCC densities and numbers. There, SCCs synapse with a peculiar fibre class of the recurrent facial nerve (Whitear and Kotrschal, 1988), which terminate somatotopically in a special dorsal area of the brain stem facial lobe (Kotrschal and Whitear, 1988). Therefore rocklings became, besides sea-robins, *Prionotus carolinus* (Finger, 1982; Silver and Finger, 1984), the most important models for structural and functional investigations in the enigmatic SCC system.

The SCCs of the anterior dorsal fin of rocklings do not overlap functionally with the TB system (Kotrschal *et al.*, 1989; Peters *et al.*, 1987, 1989, 1991). Responses from the facial components innervating the pelvic fin TBs could be obtained with amino acids and food stimuli. Responses from the anterior dorsal fin SCCs, however, could only be triggered with body mucus from other teleosts and water in which fish had been kept. No responses could be obtained with body mucus from conspecifics. At least for the rocklings, the SCC system probably works as a specialized 'fish detector', which is in agreement with results from Baatrup and Doving (1985) in brook lamprey, *Lampetra planeri*, solitary receptors. Whether this is also true for other fish remains to be shown.

An SEM survey on density and distribution of SCCs in cyprinid skin revealed their numerical importance. SCCs are very numerous in the seven species (Table 10.6), often exceeding the number of chemosensory cells organized into

Fig. 10.17 Scanning electron micrographs of cyprinid skin, showing: (a) a flat taste-bud pore dorsal to the upper lip in bleak. *Alburnus alburnus*; (b) taste-bud on a hillock lateral to the posterior nostril in nase, *Chondrostoma nasus*; (c) a field of solitary chemosensory cell apices surrounding a free neuromast in nase. Scale bars, 10 μm.

Table 10.6 Numbers of sensory apices of solitary chemosensory cells (SCCs) per 2000 μm^2 of epidermis, as revealed by SEM.* Between 73 and 134 head areas and 33–58 body areas (2000 μm^2 each) were scanned for SCC apices in each specimen. TBs were counted according to Gomahr et al. (1988)

Species	n[†]	Mean SL (mm)	SSC density[‡]		SSC no. (head)[§]		TB no. (head)[¶]	
			Head ($2000\ \mu m^{-2}$)	Body ($2000\ \mu m^{-2}$)	Total ($\times 10^3$)	%	Total ($\times 10^3$)	%
Abramis ballerus (blue bream)	3	40	2.2 ± 0.1	3.3 ± 0.7	148	73	55	27
Alburnus alburnus (bleak)	4	41	1.8 ± 0.3	1.3 ± 0.2	66	57	50	43
Chondrostoma nasus (nase)	8	47	2.3 ± 0.9	4.4 ± 2.5	104	61	68	39
Leuciscus cephalus (chub)	10	85	3.8 ± 1.1	3.3 ± 1.3	652	84	128	16
Phoxinus phoxinus (minnow)	3	100	1.9 ± 0.1	2.3 ± 0.1	954	83	200	17
Rutilus rutilus (roach)	6	45	7.9 ± 3.2	3.8 ± 1.0	246	83	51	17
Scardinius erythrophthalmus (rudd)	5	80	2.3 ± 0.8	0.9 ± 0.6	1062	88	150	12

* Kotrschal (unpubl.); table modified from Gomahr et al. (1988).
[†] Number of specimens investigated.
[‡] Means (± SD) in the areas scanned. Densities elsewhere on the head and body may differ from these values (e.g. compare total numbers for bleak and minnow, which have similar densities).
[§] Total, rough estimate of average numbers of SCCs on the head of specimens of the SL investigated. %, estimated proportion of all chemosensory cells (SSC + TB) on the head.
[¶] Total, rough estimate of average numbers of taste-bud sensory cells on the head of specimens of the SL investigated. %, as for SCCs.

taste-buds. Contrary to the polar arrangement of TBs along the body, SCCS are rather homogeneously distributed; high SCC densities occur around free neuromasts (Fig. 10.17(c)). Similar densities and distribution patterns are also found in catfish, caracinids and perciforms (Kotrschal, 1991).

The function(s) and biological role(s) of the SCC system are unknown. The presence in cyprinids of three specialized and well-developed chemosensory input channels (for prey detection and handling, olfaction, external and internal taste) decreases the probability that SCCs are just one more chemosense related to feeding. High numbers and relatively even distributions of these cells suggest that they form a low-threshold water sampler, possibly enabling the fish to recognize a stimulus gradient. Whether cyprinid SCCs are detectors of allospecific fish mucus (Baatrup and Doving, 1985; Kotrschal *et al.*, 1989; Peters *et al.*, 1987, 1989, 1991), or whether they respond to feeding-related stimuli (Silver and Finger, 1984, sea-robin pectoral fin rays) remains to be investigated.

10.5 LATERAL LINE

Introduction

Neuromasts, the receptors of the lateral line system, are groups of hair cells which either occur on the skin surface (Fig. 10.17) or are sunken into canal systems (review, Coombs *et al.*, 1988). Hair cells are secondary sensory cells, originating from placodes. Both the apex of single hair cells and their arrangement within a neuromast are polar. Hair cells are depolarized, hyperpolarized, or do not react at all, depending on the direction of stimulation. The so-called stereocilia of the hair cells are modified microvilli, which are movement-synchronized within a single neuromast by an apical mucoid cupula. At these modified villi, changes in membrane potential are induced by relatively slight mechanical stimulation (Howard *et al.*, 1988).

Neuromasts respond to displacement of their cupula by water currents and low frequencies with a general best response around 100 Hz or below (Denton and Gray, 1988). Higher frequencies are perceived by the inner ear (Chardon, and Vandewalle Chapter 11; Hawkins, 1986; Popper *et al.*, 1988, Schuijf and Hawkins, 1976; but see Kalmijn, 1988, for a critical discussion), with a best frequency range of 500–1000 Hz (review, Blaxter, 1988). The functional features of the system are influenced by efferent innervation and by peripheral filtering, the placement of neuromasts, either superficially or in various types of lateral line canals (Coombs *et al.*, 1988; Denton and Gray, 1988; Webb, 1989). Neuromasts may be used as a proprioceptive system during swimming, for communication (e.g. to facilitate shoaling, Bleckmann, 1986; Pitcher, 1986), or to detect the specific vibrations from prey organisms (Montgomery and Macdonald, 1987); they are also an efficient system to discriminate the direction and distance of struggling prey, particularly at the water surface where surface waves may be used as a source of information (Bleckmann, 1988; Wilcox, 1988).

The cyprinid lateral line system

As revealed by SEM, numbers and distribution of superficial neuromasts do not seem to deviate from the ordinary teleost pattern (Coombs *et al.*, 1988). Particularly on top of the head, these free neuromasts are arranged in rows at *c.* 45° to the body axis. In surface-dwelling cyprinids, this dorsal head surface is orientated parallel to the water surface, and so may facilitate the discrimination of surface waves (Bleckmann, 1988).

Canals were stained *in situ* (Jakubowski, 1965) with haematoxyline, followed by clearing. The principal arrangement of lateral line canals is the same in all cyprinids considered (Fig. 10.18) and is close to the common teleost pattern (Coombs *et al.*, 1988; Webb, 1989). In most species, the trunk canal is complete and consists of a single straight canal in the centre of the body leading from the head to the caudal peduncle. In sabre carp, *Pelecus cultratus*, as in other surface-dwelling fish (Webb, 1989), this trunk canal swings ventrally immediately posterior to the insertion of the pectoral fin and runs caudally, closely following the ventral keel. A reduction of the posterior trunk canal is shown by the small sun bleak, *Leucaspius delineatus*, which inhabits pools and ponds.

The head canal system varies in relative canal width and in distance of the pores to the canal lumen (Fig. 10.18). All cyprinids examined show narrow, unbranched bony canals (Coobs *et al.*, 1988). There is a clear relationship between the width of the canal and feeding style. Very narrow canals with pores opening close to the canal are present in chemosensory, benthivorous species like the tench *Tinca tinca* (Fig. 10.18(a)), or in crucian carp, *Carassius carassius*. Plankton feeders like the breams, and also the surface-feeding sabre carp, show wider canals, with relatively displaced openings, especially in the opercular canal. Generalized species, such as the roach, *Rutilus rutilus*, are

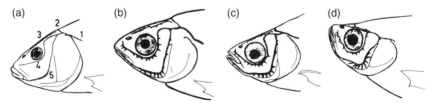

Fig. 10.18 Variation in cyprinid lateral line head canal width in representative species ((a) tench; (b) roach; (c) bream; (d) sabre carp; species names, Table 10.1). Camera lucida drawings from *in-situ* stained and cleared specimens (method, Jakubowsky, 1965). 1, Trunk canal; 2, supratemporal canal; 3, supraorbital canal; 4, suborbital canal; 5, opercular canal.

intermediate. As the piscivorous asp, *Aspius aspius*, exhibits the generalized pattern in its head canals, it seems that wide canals are associated with feeding on small particles.

In addition, large acoustico-lateralis brain areas (Figs 10.1, 10.2(c) and (d)) are associated with the wide lateral line canals. It thus seems that plankton feeders have a highly developed lateral line. Montgomery and Macdonald (1987) showed that lateral line receptors may be tuned to the movements of their planktonic prey. Brain morphology (p. 285) suggests that lateral line input provides directional guidance for vision in the plankton-feeding cyprinids (Sections 10.2 and 10.3).

10.6   CONCLUSIONS: THE DIVERSIFIED SENSORY WORLD OF CYPRINIDS, A RESULT OF ADAPTATIONS, CONSTRAINTS AND GROWTH SHIFTS

Sensory biology is a field of necessarily reductionistic research, where depth is easier to achieve than understanding of something as alien as the sensory worlds of other organisms. Still, although in many fields we lack a backup from experimental, functional and behavioural work, our present data allow some general statements on sensory differentiation in cyprinids.

Different cyprinids have different views of their aquatic environment. This may apply to life history stages, to individuals (Magurran, 1986) as well as to species. Changes in morphology, physiology and behaviour during early life history have attracted much attention (El-Fiky *et al.*, 1987 Noakes and Godin, 1988). The dramatic shift in body size from hatching to adult is in itself sufficient to explain drastic ecological shifts (Werner, 1984). Fish grow from prey into predators; their potential for resource allocation changes; the imperative of fast growth in the juveniles demands a different life style than does the primacy of reproduction in the adults.

The peripheral and central sensory as well as locomotory systems are subject to size-related shifts with growth. Larvae and juveniles of all species are primarily visually orientated. Sensory and locomotory capacities in larvae may be hampered by developmental (El-Fiky *et al.*, 1987; Mark *et al.*, 1989) or size (Kotrschal *et al.*, 1990) constraints. Juveniles grow and diversify into their adult sensory morphologies and capacities (Fig. 10.19) and into their specific habitats and food niches.

The biological roles of sensory systems may be in the wide fields of resource allocation or organismic interactions. Natural selection shaping forms and functions of sensory systems may be particularly powerful in the contexts of detecting prey and avoiding being eaten. Most senses, except probably for taste, are to a varying degree concerned with predator avoidance.

On the other hand, the feeding style of a species and its habitat (water turbidity, bottom structure etc.) specifically shape the sensory apparatus

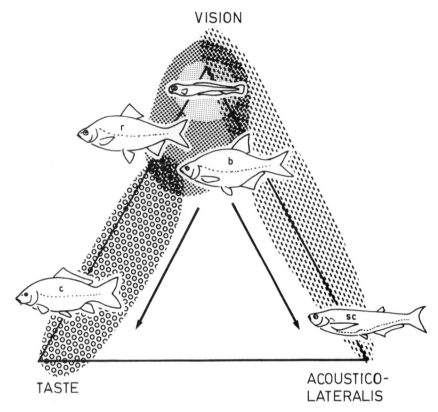

VISION

TASTE

ACOUSTICO-
LATERALIS

Fig. 10.19 Summary of changes during growth in relative importance of the major sensory faculties: vision, acoustico-lateralis and taste. The diagram illustrates the hypothesis of ontogenetic shifts into specific modes of perception. The larvae of different species have similar sensory equipment and are mainly visually orientated (light stipple). By differential allometric growth, species develop into generalized (e.g. (r) roach, *Rutilus rutilus*, dark stipple), abramine (e.g. (b) bream, *Abramis brama*, dark stipple), chemosensory (e.g. (c) carp, *Cyprinus carpio*, circles), and acoustico-lateralis–visual (e.g. (sc) sabre carp, *Pelecus cultratus*, stipple-hatching) sensory types. Arrows symbolize sensory differentiation during growth along major sensory axes.

(Peter, 1979), as shown by the present contribution. Also, the most interspecifically variable parts of the cyprinid brain are the central termination areas of external and internal taste, both of which are mainly engaged in prey detection. We may therefore point at feeding as the principal biological role with respect to sensory diversification of cyprinids.

We conclude that evolution produced several major cyprinid brain and sensory types:

1. **Generalized** species acquire a cyprinid standard of external and internal taste and acoustico-lateralis senses, but still seem to rely primarily on

vision. These species are widely distributed, but dominate in clear-water habitats. Most species are generalized feeders;

2. **Chemosensory** species show well-developed external and internal taste-bud (TB) systems and relatively large olfactory bulbs. Their visual systems seem regressively modified, as exemplified by fasciculated optic tracts, a very low proportion of large (probably motion-detecting) retinal ganglion cells, and a small optic tectum. These fish are benthic feeders, often in murky waters;

3. **Acoustico-lateralis** species have large corresponding brain centres which are intricately related to a highly developed visual system. The lateral line may have developed into a guidance system for vision in species feeding on small particles. Typically, these species are pelagic or surface dwellers and feed on plankton and items from the surface (anflug) in both clear and relatively turbid water.

This summary of sensory types emphasizes some correlations with major habitat variables, such as distance to the bottom and water transparency. Different habitats demand different feeding patterns and feeding modes, which in turn require different sensory capacities to discriminate food from non-food (Kamil, 1988). A gradient with respect to where (external to internal), and by which sensory means, this distinction is made can be seen by proceeding from piscivorous, through planktivorous towards benthivorous and omnivorous species.

The piscivorous asp, *Aspius aspius*, shows only moderately developed external and internal taste systems as well as acoustico-lateralis areas. However, the particularly abundant large retinal ganglion cells in asp suggest that this species is visually specialized for discrimination of movements. As also evidenced by the lures of successful asp fishermen, silvery, moving objects in the appropriate size range are recognized as prey, evidently necessitating neither further visual resolution of patterns and shapes, nor oropharyngeal taste evaluation (Fig. 10.15(d)).

Also the bulk of prey discrimination in planktivorous species seems mainly an external task, employing vision and the lateral line. Yet particle retention, and discrimination (probably to a differing degree), are done by the gill rakers (Sibbing, 1988) (Fig. 10.15).

Benthivorous species often use external and internal taste systems to prey on items concealed from visual detection. Detection and discrimination may mainly be accomplished by external taste, as (probably) in the barbel, *Barbus barbus*. In benthivorous winnowers, discrimination of prey may be mainly or entirely a function of the oropharyngeal cavity (Sibbing, 1988), as in carp, *Cyprinus carpio*, tench, *Tinca tinca*, crucian carp, *Carassius carassius*, and bream, *Abramis brama*. Bream have a sorting apparatus, richly equipped with taste-buds (Fig. 10.15(b)), which discriminates food from non-food.

Although small size constrains the visual system during early life history (Kotrschal *et al.*, 1990), constraints (Maynard Smith *et al.*, 1985) seem to play a minor role in limiting the evolution of cyprinid sensory diversification. Adaptation is probably more important when adult systems are concerned. It seems that the cyprinid sensory diversification patterns reflect the occupation of available peaks in the adaptive landscape (Simpson, 1944). Although this hypothesis cannot yet be tested rigorously by Bock's (1980) synthetic approach, as a second-best choice (Northcutt, 1988) the comparative method points to adaptation and thus selection as the major evolutionary mechanism.

We conclude that cyprinid sensory morphology, both peripheral and central, as well as sensory diversification is predictably and intimately related to habitat and feeding style.

ACKNOWLEDGEMENTS

We gratefully acknowledge funding of our work over the past five years by the Fonds zur Förderung der wissenschaftlichen Forschung in Österreich, Proj. no. S-35, and steady support from H. Adam, A. Goldschmid and W. Wieser. Significant help and material was provided by A. Herzig, A. Jagsch, E. Kainz, C. Kapeller, W.-D. Krautgartner, A. Lametschwandtner, the Weber family in Loimersdorf, the Forstverwaltung Eckhartsau, and others. Constructive comments by J. Atema, M. Whitear and an anonymous referee improved our contribution.

ABBREVIATIONS

AM	amacrine cells	NH	nucleus habenularis
BO	bulbus olfactorius	NM	neuromast
BP	bipolar cells	OC	orobranchial cavity
BS	brain stem except for sensory lobes	OE	oesophagus
		P	palatal organ
CAA	central acoustic area	R	rods
CC	corpus cerebelli	RC	receptor cells
CRC	crista cerebellaris	S	sublingual organ
DC	double cones	SC	single cones
DI	diencephalon	SCC	solitary chemosensory cells
EG	eminentia granularis	SEC	sensory cell
FN	facial nerve fibres	SM	stratum marginale
GGC	ganglion cells	SPC	supporting cell
GS	gill slits	TB	taste bud
HZ	horizontal cells	TEL	telencephalon
LF	lobus facialis	TL	torus longitudinalis
LG	lobus glossopharyngeus	TS	torus semicircularis
LI	lobus inferior	TO	tectum opticum
LV	lobus vagus	UN	unculi
MT	mesencephalic tegmentum	VC	valvula cerebelli

REFERENCES

Ali, A. M. (1964) Stretching of retina during growth of salmon (*Salmo salar*). *Growth*, **28**, 83–9.

Ariens Kappers, C. U., Huber, C. G. and Crosby, E. C. (1936) *The Comparative Anatomy of the Nervous System of Vertebrates, Including Man*, Macmillan, NY.

Atema, J. (1971) Structures and functions of the sense of taste in catfish (*Ictalurus natalis*). *Brain, Behav. Evolut.*, **4**, 273–94.

Atema, J. (1977) Functional separation of smell and taste in fish and crustacea. *Olfaction Taste Proc. Int. Symp.* **6**, 165–74.

Atema, J. (1988) Distribution of chemical stimuli, in *Sensory Biology of Aquatic Animals* (eds J. Atema, R. R. Fay, A. N. Ropper and W. N. Tavolga), Springer-Verlag, NY, pp. 29–56.

Atema, J., Fay, R. R., Popper, A. N. and Tavolga, W. N. (eds) (1988) *Sensory Biology of Aquatic Animals*, Springer-Verlag, NY.

Baatrup, E. and Doving, K. B. (1985) Physiological studies on solitary receptors of the oral disc papillae in the adult brook lamprey, *Lampetra planeri* (Bloch). *Chem. Sens.*, **10**, 559–66.

Bardach, J. E. and Atema, J. (1971) The sense of taste in fishes, in *Handbook of Sensory Physiology*, IV 2 (ed. L. M. Beidler), Springer, Berlin, NY pp. 293–336.

Bauchot, R., Bauchot, M. L., Platel, R. and Ridet, J. M. (1977) Brains of Hawaiian tropical fishes: brain size and evolution. *Copeia*, **1977**, 42–6.

Bernhardt, R. and Easter, S. S., Jun. (1986) Map of retinal position onto the cross section of the optic pathway of goldfish. *J. comp. Neurol.*, **254**, 493–510.

Blaxter, J. H. S. (1968a) Visual thresholds and spectral sensitivity of herring larvae. *J. exp. Biol.*, **48**, 39–53.

Blaxter, J. H. S. (1968b) Light intensity, vision and feeding in young plaice. *J. exp. mar. Biol. Ecol.*, **2**, 293–307.

Blaxter, J. H. S. (1969) Visual threshold and spectral sensitivity of flatfish larvae. *J. exp. Biol.*, 221–30.

Blaxter, J. H. S. (1975) The eyes of larval fish, in *Vision in Fishes* (ed. M. A. Ali), Plenum Press, NY, pp. 427–43.

Blaxter, J. H. S. (1988) Sensory performance, behavior and ecology of fish, in *Sensory Biology of Aquatic Animals* (eds J. Atema, R. R. Fay, A. N. Popper and W. W. Tavolga), Springer-Verlag, NY, pp. 203–32.

Blaxter, J. H. S. and Staines, M. (1970) Pure-cone retinae and retinomotor responses in larval teleosts. *J. mar. biol. Ass. U.K.*, **50**, 449–60.

Bleckmann, H. (1986) Role of the lateral line in fish behaviour, in *The Behaviour of Teleost Fishes* (ed. T. J. Pitcher), Croom Helm, London and Sydney, pp. 177–202.

Bleckmann, H. (1988) Prey identification and prey localization in surface-feeding fish and fishing spiders, in *Sensory Biology of Aquatic Animals* (eds J. Atema, R. R. Fay, A. N. Popper and W. N. Tavolga), Springer-Verlag, NY, pp. 619–41.

Bock, W. J. (1980) The definition and recognition of biological adaptation. *Am. Zool.*, **20**, 217–27.

Boehlert, G. W. (1979) Retinal development in postlarval through juvenile *Sebastes diploproa*: adaptations to a changing photic environment. *Revue. can. Biol.*, **38**, 265–80.

Brandstätter, R. and Kotrschal, K. (1990a) Life history of roach, *Rutilus rutilus* (Cyprinidae, Teleostei): a qualitative and quantitative study on the development of sensory brain areas. *Brain, Behav., Evolut.*, **34**, 35–42.

Brandstätter, R. and Kotrschal, K. (1990b) Brain growth patterns from juveniles to adults in four mid-European cyprinid fishes (Cyprinidae, Teleostei), roach (*Rutilus*

rutilus), bream (*Abramis brama*), carp (*Cyprinus carpio*) and sabre-carp (*Pelecus cultratus*). *Brain, Behav. Evolut.*)., **35**, 195–211.

Bunt, S. M. (1982) Retinotopic and temporal organization of the optic nerve and tracts in the adult goldfish. *J. comp. Neurol.*, **206**, 209–26.

Caprio, J. (1988) Peripheral filters and chemoreceptor cells in fishes, in *Sensory Biology of Aquatic Animals* (eds J. Atema, R. R. Fay, A. N. Popper and W. N. Tavolga), Springer-Verlag, NY, pp. 313–38.

Carr, W. E. S. (1988) The molecular nature of chemical stimuli in the aquatic environment, in *Sensory Biology of Aquatic Animals* (eds J. Atema, R. R. Fay, A. N. Popper and W. N. Tavolga), Springer-Verlag, NY, pp. 3–27.

Coombs, S., Janssen, J. and Webb, J. F. (1988) Diversity of lateral line systems: evolutionary and functional considerations, in *Sensory Biology of Aquatic Animals* (eds J. Atema, R. R. Fay, A. N. Popper and W. N. Tavolga), Springer-Verlag, NY, pp. 553–93.

Davenport, D. E. and Caprio, C. (1982) Taste and tactile recordings from the Ramus recurrens facialis innervating flank taste buds in the catfish. *J. comp. Physiol.*, **147**, 217–29.

Davis, R. E. and Northcutt, R. G. (eds) (1983) *Fish Neurobiology*. Vol. II. Higher brain areas and functions, Univ. Michigan Press, Ann Arbor.

Demski, L. S. and Schwanzel-Fukuda, M. (eds) (1987) *The Terminal Nerve (Nervus terminalis) Structure, Function and Evolution (Ann. N.Y. Acad. Sci.*, **519**), NY Academy of Sciences, NY.

Denton, E. J. and Gray, J. A. B. (1988) Mechanical factors in the excitation of the lateral lines of fishes, in *Sensory Biology of Aquatic Animals* (eds J. Atema, R. R. Fay, A. N. Popper and W. N. Tavolga), Springer-Verlag, NY, pp. 595–617.

Doving, K. B., Dubois-Dauphin, M., Holley, A. and Jourdan, F. (1977) Functional anatomy of the olfactory organ of fish and their ciliary mechanism of water transport. *Acta zool., Stockh.*, **58**, 245–55.

Dowling, J. E. and Boycott, B. B. (1966) Organization of the primate retina: electron microscopy. *Proc. R. Soc.*, **B**, **166**, 80–111.

Easter, S. S., jun., Raymond Johns, P. and Baumann, L. R. (1977) Growth of the adult goldfish eye – I: optics, *Vision Res.*, **17**, 469–77.

Easter, S. S., jun., Rusoff, A. C. and Kish, P. E. (1981) The growth and organization of the optic nerve and tract in juvenile and adult goldfish. *J. Neurosci.*, **1**, 793–811.

Echteler, S. (1985) Organization of central auditory pathways in a teleost fish, *Cyprinus carpio. J. comp. Physiol.* **A**, **156**, 267–80.

Engström, K. (1960) Cone types and cone arrangements in the retina of some cyprinids. *Acta Zool., Stockh.*, **41**, 277–95.

El-Fiky, N., Hinterleitner, S. and Wieser, W. (1987) Differentiation of swimming muscles and gills, and development of anaerobic power in the larvae of cyprinid fish (Pisces, Teleostei). *Zoomorphology*, **107**, 126–32.

Evans, H. E. (1952) The correlation of brain pattern and feeding habits in four species of cyprinid fishes. *J. comp. Neurol.*, **97**, 133–42.

Evans, M. H. (1931) A comparative study of the brains in British cyprinoids in relation to their habits of feeding, with special reference to the anatomy of the Medulla oblongata. *Proc. R. Soc.* **B**, **108**, 233–57.

Evans, M. H. (1932) Further observations on the Medulla oblongata of cyprinoids; and a comparative study of the Medula of clupeoids and cyprinoids with special reference to the acoustic tubercles. *Proc. R. Soc.* **B**, **111**, 247–80.

Evans, M. H. (1935) The brain of *Gadus*, with special reference to the Medulla oblongata and its variation according to feeding habits of different Gadidae – I. *Proc. R. Soc.* **B**, **117**, 56–68.

Evans, M. H. (1940) *Brain and Body of Fish*, The Technical Press Ltd, London.

Fahrmeier, L. and Hamele, A. (eds) (1984) *Multivariate Statistiche Verfahren*, De Gruyter, Berlin and New York, 603 pp.

Fernald, R. D. (1983) Aquatic adaptations in fish eyes, in *Fish Neurobiology* (eds R. E. Davis and R. G. Northcutt), Vol. I, Univ. Michigan Press, Ann Arbor, pp. 435–66.

Fernald, R. D. (1984) Vision and behavior in an African cichlid fish. *Am. Scient.*, **72**, 58–65.

Fernald, R. D. (1985a) Growth of the teleost eye: novel solutions to complex constraints. *Env. Biol. Fishes*, **13**, 113–23.

Fernald, R. D. (1985b) Growth of the visual system in the African cichlid fish, *Haplochromis burtoni*. Accommodation. *Vision Res.*, **25**, 163–70.

Fernald, R. D. (1988) Aquatic adaptations in fish eyes, in *Sensory Biology of Aquatic Animals* (eds J. Atema, R. R. Fay, A. N. Popper and W. N. Tavolga), Springer-Verlag, New York, pp. 435–66.

Finger, T. E. (1982) Somatotopy of the representation of the pectoral fin and free fin rays in the spinal cord of the sea robin, *Prionotus carolinus*. *Biol. Bull. mar. Biol. Lab.*, *Woods Hole.*, **163**, 154–61.

Finger, T. E. (1983a) The gustatory system in teleost fish, in *Fish Neurobiology* (eds R. G. Northcutt and R. E. Davis), Vol. I, Univ. Michigan Press, Ann Arbor, pp. 285–311.

Finger, T. E. (1983b) Organization of the teleost cerebellum, in *Fish Neurobiology* (eds R. G. Northcutt and R. E. Davis), Vol. I, Univ. Michigan Press, Ann Arbor, pp. 261–84.

Finger, T. E. (1987) Gustatory nuclei and pathways in the central nervous system, in *Neorobiology of Taste and Smell* (eds T. E. Finger and W. L. Silver), J. Wiley, NY, pp. 331–54.

Finger, T. E. (1988) Organization of the chemosensory systems within the brains of bony fishes, in *Sensory Biology of Aquatic Animals* (eds J. Atema, R. R. Fay, A. N. Popper and W. N. Tavolga), Springer-Verlag, NY, pp. 339–63.

Finger, T. E. (1989) Sensorimotor mapping and oropharyngeal reflexes in goldfish. *Chemorec. Abstr.*, **17**, 6.

Frisch, K. von (1912) Über die farbige Anpassung bei Fischen. *Zool. Jb., Abt. Zool. Physiol.*, **32**, 171–230.

Frisch, K. Von (1941) Über einen Schreckstoff der Fischhaut und seine biologische Bedeutung. *Z. Vergl. Physiol.*, **29**, 46–145.

Geiger, W. (1956a) Quantitative Untersuchungen über das Gehirn der Knochenfische, mit besonderer Berücksichtigung seines relativen Wachstums. *Acta anat.*, **26**, 121–63.

Geiger, W. (1956b) Quantitative Untersuchungen über das Gehirn der Knochenfische, mit besonderer Berücksichtigung seines relativen Wachstums. *Acta anat.*, **27**, 324–350.

Getchell, T. V. and Getchell, M. L. (1987) Peripheral mechanisms of olfaction: biochemistry and neurophysiology, in *Neurobiology of Taste and Smell* (eds T. E. Finger and W. L. Silver), J. Wiley, NY, pp. 91–124.

Goldschmid, A. and Kotrschal, K. (1989) Ecomorphology: development and concepts. *Fortschr. Zool.*, **36**.

Gomahr, A., Kotrschal, K. and Goldschmid, A. (1988) Die chemosensorischen Zellen in der Haut bei den heimischen Karpfenfischen (Teleostei, Cyprinidae): Geschmacksknospen und freie (Sinneszellen. *Öst. Fisch.*, **41**, 241–53.

Gomahr, A., Palzenberger, M. and Kotrschal, K. (1991) Density distribution of external taste buds in Cyprinids (Cyprinidae, Teleostei). A quantitative study. *Env. Biol. Fish.* (in press).

Guthrie, D. M. (1986) Role of vision in fish behaviour, in *The Behaviour of Teleost Fishes* (ed. T. J. Pitcher), Croom Helm, London and Sydney, pp. 75–113.

Hairston, N. G., jun., Kao, T. L. and Easter, S. S. (1982) Fish vision and the detection of planktonic prey. *Science*, **218**, 1240–42.

Hara, T. J. (ed.) (1982) *Chemoreception in Fishes*, Elsevier, Amsterdam.

Hara, T. J. (1986) Role of olfaction in fish behaviour, in *The Behaviour of Teleost Fishes* (ed. T. J. Pitcher), Croom Helm, London and Sydney, pp. 152–76.

Hawkins, A. D. (1986) Underwater sound and fish behaviour, in *The Behaviour of Teleost Fishes* (ed. T. J. Pitcher), Croom Helm, London and Sydney, pp. 114–51.

Herrick, C. J. (1905) The central gustatory paths in the brains of bony fishes. *J. comp. Neurol.*, **15**, 375–456.

Herrick, C. J. (1906) On the centers of taste and touch in the medulla oblongata of fishes. *J. comp. Neurol.*, **16**, 403–39.

Hitchcock, P. F. (1987) Constant dendritic coverage by ganglion cells with growth of the goldfish retina. *Vision Res.*, **27**, 17–22.

Hitchcock, P. F. and Easter, S. S. jun. (1986) Retinal ganglion cells in goldfish: a qualitative classification into four morphological types, and a quantitative study of the development of one of them. *J. Neurosci.*, **6**, 1037–50.

Haward, J., Roberts, W. M. and Hudspeth, A. J. (1988) Mechanoelectrical transduction by hair cells. *A. Rev. Biophys. biophys. Chem.*, **17**, 99–124.

Huber, R. and Rylander, M. K. (1991) Brain morphology is correlated with preferred turbidity in minnows of the genus *Notropis* and related genera (Cyprinidae). *Env. Biol. Fish.* (in press).

Huntingford, F. A. (1986) Development of behaviour in fishes, in *The Behaviour of Teleost Fishes* (ed. T. J. Pitcher), Croom Helm, London and Sydney, pp. 47–70.

Ito, H. and Murakami, T. (1984) Retinal ganglion cells in two teleost species, *Sebasticus marmoratus* and *Navodon modestus*. *J. comp. Neurol*, **229**, 80–96.

Jakubowski, M. (1965) Cutaneous sense organs in fishes. II. The structure of lateral line organs in the burbot (*Lota lota*) and pike (*Esox lucius*). *Acta biol. cracov.*, **8**, 87–99.

Jakubowski, M. and Whitear, M. (1986) Ultrastructure of taste buds in fishes. *Folia Histochem. Cytobiol.*, **24**, 310–311.

Jakubowski, M. and Whitear, M. (1990) Comparative morphology and cytology of taste buds in teleosts. *Z. mikrosk.-anat. Forsch.*, (in press).

Jolicoeur, P. and Baron, G. (1980) Brain center correlations among Chiroptera. *Brain Behav. Evolut.*, **17**, 419–31.

Kalmijn. Ad. J. (1988) Hydrodynamic and acoustic field detection, in *Sensory Biology of Aquatic Animals* (eds J. Atema, R. R. Fay, A. N. Popper and W. N. Tavolga), Springer-Verlag, NY, pp. 83–130.

Kamil, A. C. (1988) Behavioural ecology and sensory biology, in *Sensory Biology of Aquatic Animals* (eds J. Atema, R. R. Fay, A. N. Popper and W. N. Tavolga), Springer-Verlag, NY, pp. 189–201.

Khanna, S. S. and Singh, H. R. (1966) Morphology of the teleostean brain in relation to feeding habits. *Proc. natn. Acad. Sci. India*, **336**, 306–16.

Kinnamon, J. C. (1987) Organization and innervation of taste buds, in *Neurobiology of Taste and Smell* (eds T. E. Finger and W. L. Silver), J. Wiley, NY, pp. 277–98.

Kishida, R. (1979) Comparative study on the teleostean optic tectum. *J. Hirnforsch.*, **20**, 57–67.

Kitoh, J., Kiyohara, S. and Yamashita, S. (1987) Fine structure of taste buds in the minnow. *Nippon Suisan Gakkai-shi*, **53**, 1943–50.

Kiyohara, S., Hidaka, I., Kitoh, J. and Yamashita, S. (1985a) Mechanical sensitivity of the facial nerve fibers innervating the anterior palate of the puffer, *Fugu pardalis*, and their central projection to the primary taste center. *J. comp. Physiol. A*, **157**, 705–16.

Kiyohara, S., Shiratani, T. and Yamashita, S. (1985b) Peripheral and central distribution of major branches of the facial taste nerve in the carp. *Brain Res., Osaka*, **325**, 57–69.

Kiyohara, S., Yamashita, S. and Kitoh, J. (1980) Distribution of taste buds on the lips and inside the mouth in the minnow, *Pseudorasbora parva*. *Physiol. Behav.*, **24**, 1143–47.

Kleerekoper, H., Matis, J. H., Timms, A. M. and Gensler, P. (1973) Locomotor response of the goldfish to polarized light and its e-vector. *J. comp. Physiol.*, **86**, 27–36.

Kock, J. H. (1982) Neuronal addition and retinal expansion during growth of the crucian carp eye. *J. comp. Neurol.*, **209**, 264–74.

Kock, J. H. and Reuter, T. (1978a) Retinal ganglion cells in the crucian carp (*Carassius carassius*). I. Size and number of somata in eyes of different size. *J. comp. Neurol.*. **179**, 535–48.

Kock, J. H. and Reuter, T. (1978b) Retinal ganglion cells in crucian carp (*Carassius carassius*). II. Overlap, shape and tangential orientation of dendritic trees. *J. comp. Neurol.*, **179**, 549–68.

Konishi, J. and Zotterman, Y. (1961) Taste functions in the carp. An electrophysiological study on gustatory fibres. *Acta physiol. scand.*, **52**, 150–61.

Kotrschal, K. (1991) Quantitative scanning electron microscopy of solitary chemoreceptor cells in cyprinids and other teleosts. *Env. Biol. Fish.* (in press).

Kotrschal, K. and Junger, H. (1988) Patterns of brain morphology in mid-European Cyprinidae (Pisces, Teleostei): a quantitative histological study. *J. Hirnforsch.*, **29**, 341–52.

Kotrschal, K. and Palzenberger, M. (1991) Neuroecology of cyprinids (Cyprinidae, Teleostei): comparative, quantitative histology reveals diverse brain patterns. *Env. Biol. Fish.* (in press).

Kotrschal, K. and Whitear, M. (1988) Chemosensory anterior dorsal fin in rocklings (*Gaidropsarus* and *Ciliata*, Teleostei, Gadidae): somatotopic representation of the Ramus recurrens facialis as revealed by transganglionic transport of HRP. *J. comp. Neurol.*, **268**, 109–20.

Kotrschal, K., Adam, H. Brandstätter, R., Junger, H., Zaunreiter, M. and Goldschmid, A. (1990) Larval size constraints determine directional ontogenetic shifts in the visual system of teleosts. A mini-review. *Z. Zool. Syst. Evolut.-forsch.* **28**, 166–82.

Kotrschal, K., Atema, J. and Peters, R. (1989) A novel chemosensory system in fish: do rocklings (*Ciliata mustela*, Gadidae) use their solitary chemoreceptor cells as fish detectors? *Biol. mar. biol. Lab. Woods Hole*, **177**, 328.

Kotrschal, K., Junger, H., Palzenberger, M., Brandstätter, R., Gomahr, A. and Goldschmid, A. (1987) Die Gehirne heimischer Karpfenfische (Teleostei, Cyprinidae). *Öst. Fisch.*, **40**, 163–71.

Kotrschal, K., Whitear, M. and Adam, H. (1984) Morphology and histology of the anterior dorsal fin of *Gaidropsarus mediterraneus* (Pisces, Teleostei), a specialized sensory organ. *Zoomorphologie*, **104**, 365–72.

Ladiges, W. and Vogt, D. (1965) *Die Süßwasserfische Europas*. Paul Parey Verlag, Hamburg, Berlin.

Lane, E. B. (1977) Structural aspects of skin sensitivity in the catfish, *Ictalurus*, PhD thesis, University of London.

Lane, E. B. and Whitear, M. (1982) Sensory structures on the surface of fish skin. I. Putative chemoreceptors. *Zool. J. Linn. Soc.*, **74**, 141–51.

Li, K. T., Wetterer, J. K. and Hairston, N. G. (1985) Fish size, visual resolution and prey selectivity. *Ecology*, **66**, 1729–35.

Luiten, P. G. M. (1975) The central projections of the trigeminal, facial and anterior lateral line nerves in the carp (*Cyprinus carpio* L.). *J. comp. Neurol.*, **160**, 399–417.

Lythgoe, J. N. (1988) Light and vision in the aquatic environment, in *Sensory Biology of Aquatic Animals* (eds J. Atema, R. R. Fay, A. N. Popper and W. N. Tavolga), Springer-Verlag, NY, pp. 57–82.

McCormick, C. A. and Braford, M. R. jun. (1988) Central connections of the octavolateralis system: evolutionary considerations, in *Sensory Biology of Aquatic animals* (eds J. Atema, R. R. Fay, A. N. Popper and W. N. Tavolga), Springer-Verlag, NY, pp. 733–56.

Macy, A. (1981) Growth-related changes in the receptive field properties of retinal ganglion cells in goldfish. *Vision Res.*, **21**, 1491–6.

Magurran, A. E. (1986) Individual differences in fish behaviour, in *The Behaviour of Teleost Fishes* (ed. T. J. Pitcher), Croom Helm, London and Sydney, pp. 338–65.

Maitland, P. S. (1981) *Freshwater Fishes of Britain and Europe*. Hamlyn, London, NY, Sydney, Toronto.

Mark, W., Wieser, W. and Hohenauer, C. (1989) Interactions between developmental processes, growth, and food selection in the larvae and juveniles of *Rutilus rutilus* (L.) (Cyprinidae). *Oecologia*, **78**, 330–7.

Marotte, L. R. (1980) Goldfish retinotectal system: continuing development and synaptogenesis. *J. comp. Neurol.*, **193**, 319–34.

Marui, T. (1977) Taste responses in the facial lobe of the carp, *Cyprinus carpio*, L. *Brain Res., Amsterdam*, **177**, 479–88.

Marui, T. and Caprio, J. (1982) Electrophysiological evidence for the topographical arrangement of taste and tactile neurons in the facial lobe of the channel catfish. *Brain Res., Amsterdam*, **231**, 185–90.

Maynard Smith, J., Burian, R., Kauffman, S., Alberch, P., Campbell, J., Goodwin, B., Lande, R., Raup, D. and Wolpert, L. (1985) Developmental constraints and evolution. *Q. Rev. Biol.*, **60**, 260–87.

Miller, R. J. and Evans, H. E. (1965) External morphology of the brain and lips in catastomid fishes. *Copeia*, **1965**, 467–87.

Montgomery, J. C. and Macdonald, J. A. (1987) Sensory tuning of lateral line receptors in Antarctic fish to the movement of planktonic prey. *Science*, **235**, 195–6.

Morita, Y. and Finger, T. E. (1985a) Topography and laminar organization of the vagal gustatory system in the goldfish, *Carassius auratus*, *J. comp. Neurol.*, **238**, 187–201.

Morita, Y. and Finger, T. E. (1985b) Reflex connections of the facial and vagal gustatory systems in the brainstem of the bullhead catfish, *Ictalurus nebulosus*. *J. comp. Neurol.*, **231**, 547–58.

Morita, Y. and Finger, T. E. (1987) Topographic representation of the sensory and motor roots of the vagus nerve in the medulla of goldfish, *Carassius auratus*. *J. comp. Neurol.*, **264**, 231–49.

Morita, Y. and Masai, H. (1980) Central gustatory paths in the crucian carp, *Carassius carassius*, *J. comp. Neurol.*, **191**, 119–32.

Müller, H. (1952) Bau und Wachstum der Netzhaut des Guppy (*Leistes reticulatus*). *Zool. Jb.*, **63**, 275–324.

Neumeyer, C. (1985) An ultraviolet receptor as a fourth receptor type in goldfish color vision. *Naturwiss.*, **72**, 162–3.

Neumeyer, C. (1988) *Das Farbsehen des Goldfisches*, Thieme-Verlag, Stuttgart, NY.

Nieuwenhuys, R. and Pouwels, E. (1983) The brain stem of actinopterygian fishes, in *Fish Neurobiology* (eds R. G. Northcutt and R. E. Davis), Vol. I, Univ. Michigan Press, Ann Arbor, pp. 25–88.

Noakes, D. L. G. and Godin, J.-G. J. (1988) Ontogeny of behavior and concurrent developmental changes in sensory systems in teleost fishes, in *Fish Physiology*, Vol. XIB (eds W. S. Hoar and D. J. Randall), Academic Press, NY, pp. 345–95.

Northcutt, R. G. (1983) Evolution of the optic tectum in ray-finned fishes, in *Fish Neurobiology* (eds R. E. Davis and R. G. Northcutt), Vol. II, Univ. Michigan Press, Ann. Arbor., pp. 1–42.

Northcutt, R. G. (1988) Sensory and other neural traits and the adaptationist program:

mackerels of San Marco? in *Sensory Biology of Aquatic Animals* (eds J. Atema, R. R. Fay, A. N. Popper and W. N. Tavolga), Springer-Verlag, NY, pp. 869–83.

Northcutt, R. G. and Davis, R. S. (eds) (1983) *Fish Neurobiology*, Vol. I, Brain stem and sense organs, Univ. Michigan Press, Ann Arbor.

Northcutt, R. G. and Wullimann, M. F. (1988) The visual system in teleost fishes: morphological patterns and trends, in *Sensory Biology of Aquatic Animals* (eds J. Atema, R. R. Fay, A. N. Popper and W. N. Tavolga), Springer-Verlag, NY, pp. 515–52.

Northmore, D. P. M. (1984) Visual and saccadic activity in the goldfish torus longitudinalis. *J. comp. Physiol.*, **A**, **155**, 333–40.

Otten, E. (1981) Vision during growth of a generalized *Haplochromis* species: *H. elegans* Trewavas 1933 (Pisces, Cichlidae). *Neth. J. Zool.*, **31**, 650–700.

Parzefall, J. (1986) Behavioural ecology of cave-dwelling fishes, in *The Behaviour of Teleost Fishes* (ed. T. J. Pitcher), Croom Helm, London and Sydney, pp. 433–58.

Peichl, L., Buhl, E. H. and Boycott, B. B. (1987) Alpha ganglion cells in the rabbit retina. *J. comp. Neurol.*, **263**, 25–41.

Peter, R. E. (1979) The brain and feeding behavior, in *Fish Physiology*, Vol. VIII (eds W. S. Hoar and D. J. Randall), Academic Press, NY, pp. 121–59.

Peters, R. C., Krautgartner, W.-D. and Kotrschal, K. (1990) A novel chemosensory system in fish: electrophysiological evidence for mucus detection by solitary chemoreceptor cells in rocklings (*Ciliata mustela*, Gadidae). *Biol. Bull. mar. biol. Lab.*, *Woods Hole*.

Peters, R. C., Van Steenderen, G. W. and Kotrschal, K. (1987) A chemoreceptive function for the anterior dorsal fin in rocklings (*Gaidropsarus* and *Ciliata*: Teleostei: Gadidae): electrophysiological evidence. *J. mar Biol. Ass. U.K.*, **67**, 819–23.

Peters, R. C., Kotrschal, K. and Krautgartner, W.-D. (1991) Solitary chemoreceptor cells of *Ciliatoi muskela* (Gadidae, Teleostei) are tuned to mucoid stimuli. *Chem. Sens.* (in press).

Pitcher, T. J. (1986) Functions of shoaling behaviour in teleosts, in *The Behaviour of Teleost Fishes* (ed. T. J. Pitcher), Croom Helm, London and Sydney, pp. 294–337.

Pohla, H., Palzenberger, M. and Goldschmid, A. (1986) Der Kiemenreusenapparat europäischer Karpfenfisch-Arten (Teleostei, Cyprinidae). *Öst. Fisch.*, **39**, 94–104.

Popper, A. N. Rogers, P. H. Saidel, W. M. and Cox, M. (1988) Role of the fish ear in sound processing, in *Sensory Biology of Aquatic Animals* (eds J. Atema, R. R. Fay, A. N. Popper and W. N. Tavolga), Springer-Verlag, NY, pp. 687–710.

Powers, M. K. and Easter, S. S. (1983) Behavioral significance of retinal structure and function in fishes, in *Fish Neurobiology*, Vol. II (eds R. G. Northcutt and R. E. Davis), Univ. Michigan Press, Ann. Arbor., pp. 377–404.

Raymond, P. A. (1985) The unique origin of rod photoreceptors in the teleost retina. *TINS*, **8**, 12–17.

Raymond, P. A. (1988) Visual consequences of continued addition of rod photoreceptors during growth of teleost fish. *American Society of Ichthyologists and Herpetologists (ASHI) meeting 1988*, p. 160, Ann. Arbor., Michigan.

Raymond Johns, P. (1981) Growth of fish retinas. *Am. Zool.*, **21**, 447–58.

Raymond Johns, P. (1982) Formation of photoreceptors in larval and adult goldfish. *J. Neurosci.*, **2**, 178–98.

Raymond Johns, P. and Easter, S. S. jun., (1977) Growth of the adult goldfish eye. II. Increase in retinal cell number. *J. comp. Neurol.*, **176**, 331–42.

Raymond Johns, P. and Fernald, R. D. (1981) Genesis of rods in teleost fish retina. *Nature, Lond.*, **293**, 141–42.

Reutter K. (1974) Cholinergic innervation of scattered sensory cells in fish epidermis. *Cell. Tissue Res.*, **149**, 143–5.

Reutter, K. (1986) Chemoreceptors, in *Biology of the Integument, 2, Vertebrates* (eds J. Bereiter-Hahn, A. G. Matoltsy and K. S. Richards), Springer, Berlin etc., pp. 586–604.

Sach, L. (1982) *Statistiche Methoden*, Springer Verlag, Berlin.

Sandy, J. M. and Blaxter, J. H. S. (1980) A study of retinal development in larval herring and sole. *J. mar. Biol. Ass. U.K.*, **60**, 59–71.

Schiemer, F. (1985) Die Bedeutung der Augewässer als Schutzzonen für die Fischfauna. *Öst. Wasserw.* **37**, 239–45.

Schiemer, F. (1988) Gefährdete Cypriniden – Indikatoren für die ökologische Intaktheit von Flußsystemen. *Natur. Landsch.* **63**, 370–73.

Schmidt, J. T. (1979) The laminar organization of optic nerve fibres in the tectum of goldfish. *Proc. R. Soc.* **B, 205**, 287–306.

Schnakenbeck, W. (1962) Acrania (Cephalochordata) – Cyclostomata – Pisces, in *Handbuch der Zoologie*, Vol. 6, Half 1, Part 1 (eds J.-G. Helmcke, H. V. Lengerken and D. Starck), Walter de Gruyter and Co., Berlin, pp. 905–1115.

Schnitzlein, H. N. (1964) Correlation of habit and structure in the fish brain. *Am. Zool.*, **4**, 21–32.

Schuijf, A. and Hawkins, A. D. (eds) (1976) Sound reception in fish, *Developments in Aquaculture and Fisheries Science*, 5, Elsevier Sci. Publ. Comp. Amsterdam, Oxford, NY.

Schulte, E. and Holl, A. (1972) Feinbau der Kopftentakel und ihrer Sinnesorgane bei *Blennius tentacularis* (Pisces, Blenniiformes). *Mar. Biol.*, **12**, 67–80.

Scott, J. W. and Harrison, T. A. (1987) The olfactory bulb: anatomy and physiology, in *Neurobiology of Taste and Smell* (eds T. E. Finger and W. L. Silver), J. Wiley, NY, pp. 151–78.

Sibbing, F. A. (1982) Pharyngeal mastication and food transport in the carp *(Cyprinus carpio* L.): a cineradiographic and electromyographic study. *J. Morph.*, **177**, 223–58.

Sibbing, F. A. (1988) Specializations and limitations of utilization of food by carp, *Cyprinus carpio*: a study of oral food processing. *Env. Biol. Fishes*, **22**, 161–78.

Sibbing, F. A. and Uribe, R. (1985) Regional specializations in the oropharyngeal wall and food processing in the carp (*Cyprinus carpio* L.). *Neth. J. Zool.*, **35**, 377–422.

Silver, W. L. (1987) The common chemical sense, in *Neurobiology of Taste and Smell* (eds T. E. Finger and W. L. Silver), J. Wiley, NY, pp. 65–87.

Silver, W. L. and Finger, T. E. (1984) Electrophysiological examination of a non-olfactory, ion-gustatory chemosense in the searobin, *Prionotus carolinus*. *J. comp. Physiol. A*, **154**, 167–74.

Simpson, G. G. (1944) *Tempo and Mode in Evolution*, Columbia University Press, NY.

Smith, R. J. F. (1982) The adaptive significance of alarm substance–fright reaction system, in *Chemoreception in Fishes* (ed. T. J. Hara), Elsevier. Amsterdam, pp. 327–42.

Sokal, R. R. and Rohlf, F. J. (1981) *Biometry*, 2nd edn, W. H. Freeman, New York, 565 pp.

Springer, A. D. and Mednick, A. S. (1986) Retinotopic and chronotopic organization of goldfish retinal ganglion cell axons throughout the optic nerve. *J. comp. Neurol.*, **247**, 221–32.

Uchihashi, K. (1953) Ecological study of Japanese teleosts in relation to the brain morphology. *Bull. Japan Sea reg. Fish. Res. Lab.*, **2**, 1–166.

Van der Meer, H. J. (1986) Functional morphology of the cichlid retina. *Acta morph. neerl.-scand.*, **24**, 294.

Van der Meer, H. J. and Anker, G. Ch. (1984) Retinal resolving power and sensitivity of the photopic system in seven haplochromine species (Teleostei, Cichlidae). *Neth. J. Zool.*, **34**, 197–209.

Vanegas, H. (1983) Organization and physiology of the teleostean optic tectum, in

Fish Neurobiology Vol. II (eds R. G. Northcutt and R. E. Davis), Univ. Michigan Press, Ann Arbor, pp. 43–87.

Wagner, H.-J. (1974) Die Entwicklung der Netzhaut von *Nannacara anomala* (Regan) (Cichlidae, Teleostei) mit besonderer Berücksichtigung regionaler Differenzierungsunterschiede. *Z. Morph. Tiere*, **79**, 113–31.

Walls, G. L. (1967) *The Vertebrate Eye and its Adaptive Radiation*. Hafner Publ. Co., NY, London.

Wanzenböck, J. and Schiemer, F. (1989) Prey detection in cyprinids during early development, *Can. J. Fish. aquat. Sci.*, **46**, 995–1001.

Wartzok, D. and Marks, W. B. (1973) Directionally selective visual units recorded in optic tectum of the goldfish. *J. Neurophysiol.*, **36**, 588–604.

Webb, J. F. (1989) Gross morphology and evolution of the mechanoreceptive lateral-line system in teleost fishes. *Brain, Behav. Evolut.*, **33**, 34–53.

Werner, E. E. (1984) The mechanisms of species interactions and community organization in fishes, in *Ecological Communities. Conceptual Issues and the Evidence* (eds D. R. Strong, Jun., D. Simberloff, L. G. Abele and A. B. Thistle), Princeton Univ. Press, Princeton, NJ, pp. 360–83.

Whitear, M. (1952) The innervation of the skin of teleost fishes. *Q. J. Microsc. Sci.*, **93**, 298–305.

Whitear, M. (1971) Cell specialization and sensory function in fish epidermis. *J. Zool., Lond*, **163**, 237–64.

Whitear, M. (1976) Identification of the epidermal "Stiftchenzellen" of frog tadpoles by electron microscopy. *Cell Tissue Res.*, **175**, 391–402.

Whitear, M. (1991) Solitary chemoreceptor cells, in *Chemoreception in Fishes* (ed. T. J. Hoira (in press).

Whitear, M. and Kotrschal, K. (1988) The chemosensory anterior dorsal fin in rocklings (*Gaidropsarus* and *Ciliata*, Teleostei, Gadidae): activity, fine structure and innervation. *J. Zool., Lond.*, **216**, 339–66.

Whitear, M. and Lane, E. B. (1983) Oligovillous cells of the epidermis: sensory elements of lamprey skin. *J. Zool., Lond.*, **199**, 359–84.

Wilcox, R. S. (1988) Surface wave reception in invertebrates and vertebrates, in *Sensory Biology of Aquatic Animals* (eds J. Atema, R. R. Fay, A. N. Popper and W. N. Tavolga), Springer-Verlag, NY, pp. 643–63.

Winkelmann, E. and Winkelmann, L. (1986) Vergleichend histologische Untersuchungen zur funktionellen Morphologie des Tectum opticum verschiedener Teleostier. *J. Hirnforsch.*, **10**, 1–16.

Wullimann, M. F. and Meyer, D. L. (1989) Evolution of the putative cholinergic visual pathways to the hypothalamus in teleost fishes. *Proc. 17th Göttingen Neurobiol. Conf.* (eds N. Elsner and W. Singer), Abstract 330, Thieme Verlag, Stuttgart, NY.

Wunder, W. (1925) Physiologische und vergleichend-anatomische Untersuchungen an der Knochenfischnetzhaut. *Z. vergl. Physiol.*, **3**, 1–61.

Zaunreiter, M., Adam, H., Brandstätter, R., Goldschmid, A., Junger, H. and Kotrschal, K. (1989) Der Gesichtssinn der Karpfenfische: I. Bau des Auges, der Netzhaut (Retina), des optischen Nerven (Tractus opticus) und des primären visuellen Hirnzentrums (Tectum opticum). *Öst. Fisch.* **42**, 128–38.

Zaunreiter, M., Junger, H. and Kotrschal, K. (1991) Retinal morphology in cyprinid fishes: a quantitative histological study on ontogenetic changes and interspecific variation. *Vision Res.* (in press).

Zippel, H. P. (1989) Function and regeneration of central olfactory pathways in goldfish: post-lesion discrimination behaviour. In *Proc. 17th Göttingen Neurobiol. Conf.*, (eds N. Elsner and W. Singer), Abstract 43, Thieme Verlag, Stuttgart, NY.

Chapter eleven

Acoustico-lateralis system

M. Chardon and P. Vandewalle

11.1   INTRODUCTION

The broadly accepted unity of the acoustico-lateralis system of fishes rests on the identity of ontogenetical origins and of the structure of the neuromasts (Fig. 11.1). Identity of origins has been demonstrated in *Salmo* (Wilson and Mattocks, 1897), but not in cyprinids. In *Rutilus rutilus* observed at hatching, the system develops from one distinct placode for the otic vesicle and two contiguous placodes for the lateral line (Lekander, 1949).

The epidermal sensory hair cells of the neuromasts are innervated by branches of the eighth cranial nerve. Each hair cell has an apical bundle of hair-like processes, made up of one kinocil (true cilium) protruding at one end of an array of stereocilia (microvilli on a cuticle plate) which decrease in height with increasing distance from the kinocil (Nakajima and Wang, 1974; Platt, 1977; Platt and Popper, 1981). In a lateral line neuromast and in the ampullae of the semicircular canals (p. 344), the stereocilia are covered by and attached to a gelatinous 'cupula'. In the cavities of the labyrinth, the stereocilia of the maculae are embedded in a gelatinous otolithic (non-cellular) membrane containing the otolith (Flock, 1971; Platt and Popper, 1981) (Fig. 11.1). Liquid movements around a neuromast result in movements of the cupula or otolithic membrane and bending of the stereocilia and consequently in shearing forces and electrophysiological transduction. The angle between the direction of the shearing force and the longitudinal axes of the bundles of stereocilia determines the amplitude of the polarization modification (Van Bergeijk, 1967; Flock, 1971; Sand, 1981). Excitation of the sensory cells is in turn transduced into modifications of the impulse rate of the saccular neurones in a way that has been extensively observed in the goldfish, *Carassius auratus* (Furukawa and Ishii, 1967; Fay, 1981).

As far as is known, these structures and mechanisms are constant in teleosts, and do not present any important peculiarity in cyprinids.

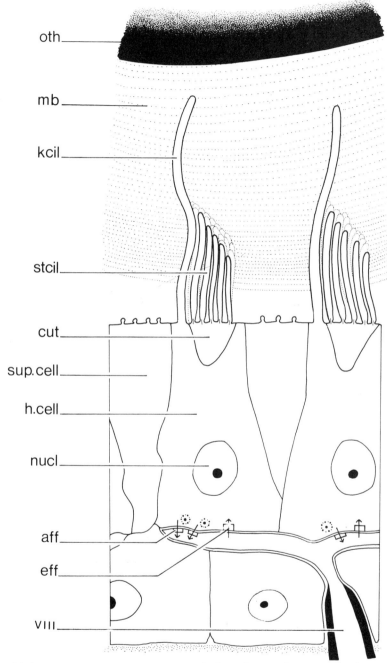

oth

mb

kcil

stcil

cut

sup. cell

h. cell

nucl

aff

eff

VIII

Fig. 11.1 Diagrammatic representation of the relations between the hair cells of a neuromast and the otolith in the saccule of *Carassius auratus* (mainly after Nakajima and Wang, 1974; Platt and Popper, 1981). Abbreviations, p. 347.

11.2 AUDITORY APPARATUS

The auditory apparatus of cyprinids is typically otophysan (*sensu* Fink and Fink, 1981) and consists of the modified labyrinths, the Weberian ossicles and the swim bladder, especially its anterior chamber (Fig. 11.6).

Cyprinids, and especially the goldfish, are the most commonly used animal material for research on hearing in fishes. About one-half of the papers on this subject involve goldfish and related species, although not all can be cited here.

Labyrinths

The membranous labyrinths are built in a classical manner: a pars superior with a utricle bearing three semicircular canals, and a pars inferior composed of a sacculus and a lagena. Each semicircular canal is dilated at one end in an ampulla. The utricle, saccule and lagena each contain an otolith, a large, crystalline, calcium carbonate concretion. These structures are well described in *Phoxinus laevis* by von Frisch and Stetter (1932), Wohlfahrt (1932), in several other species by Ramaswami (1955a,b), and in *Gobio gobio* by Vandewalle (1974) (Figs 11.2, 11.3).

The proportions and shape of the labyrinths are typical of the Otophysi, in which the pars superior is not (or almost not) modified (Grassé, 1958; Popper and Coombs, 1982). It is almost completely separated by a constriction from the pars inferior, which is greatly transformed in the Otophysi: the lagena is larger than the sacculus (Schnakenbeck, 1955) and opens into it only by a

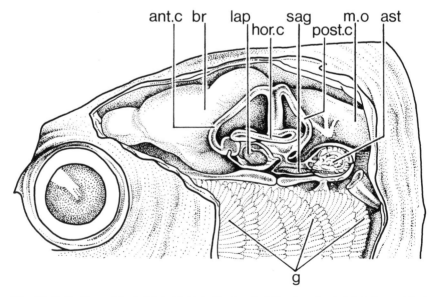

Fig. 11.2 Position of the left labyrinth in the head of *Phoxinus laevis* (slightly modified after von Frisch and Stetter, 1932). Abbreviations, p. 347.

(a)

(b)

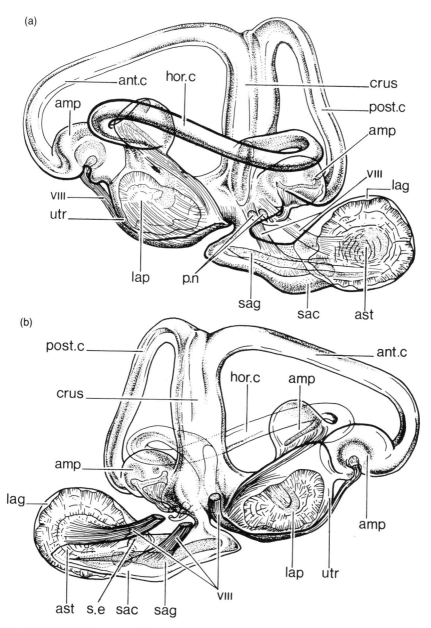

Fig. 11.3 Left labyrinth of *Phoxinus laevis*, as seen from (a) the outer side and (b) the inner side (slightly modified after Wohlfahrt, 1932). Abbreviations, p. 347.

restricted orifice. The left and right labyrinths communicate by the canalis communicans transversus, which extends backward on the mid line as the sinus endolymphaticus (Weber, 1820, cited in Grassé, 1958). The posterior end of the latter is surrounded by a lymphatic space (the sinus impar perilymphaticus) which seems not to be a part of the perilymphatic space of the labyrinths, that space being incomplete in Osteichthyes (Grassé, 1958). The sinus impar is more probably a neoformation, as shown by its development in the catfish, *Clarias gariepinus*, from two 'bubbles' in the connective tissue (Radermaker *et al.*, 1989).

The labyrinths are included in the lateroposterior parts of the neurocranium. The pars inferior is almost completely embedded in bone and cartilage, but the utricle and a part of the semicircular canals are free in the cavum cranii (Mahy, 1975; Chardon, 1968) (Figs 11.2, 11.4).

The otoliths have been described by Retzius (1881) in many cyprinids, by Wohlfahrt (1932), von Frisch and Stetter (1932) and De Burlet (1929) (relations with the macula, position of the sagitta relative to the sinus endolymphaticus), Platt (1977), Platt and Popper (1981), Popper and Coombs (1982), Popper and Platt (1983) (relations with the macula). The shape of the otoliths is species specific; at higher levels it is also characteristic of Cyprinidae and of Otophysi. The saccular otolith (sagitta) is shaped as a rod anteriorly broadened by wings; it lies in a parasagittal plane, perpendicular to the mouth of the canalis communicans; such a position seems to facilitate response to endolymph motion (De Burlet, 1929; Van Bergeijk, 1967) (Figs 11.4(d), 11.5).

The pattern of orientation of the stereocilia bundles relative to the kinocils of the hair cells of the saccule and lagena, described in *Carassius auratus* and *Labeo chrysophekadion*, is typically otophysan. The macular surface of the sacculus is divided by a horizontal line into two areas with opposite vertical orientations of the bundles of stereocilia (Fig. 11.5(e)), whereas in the lagena (Fig. 11.5(f)) a sinuous line separates two areas of various opposite orientations (Platt, 1977; Platt and Popper, 1981; Popper and Platt, 1983). These authors propose that these patterns are related to a specialization of the auditory function. The saccular otolith, which stands just in front of the aperture of the sinus endolymphaticus (De Burlet, 1934), would be efficiently brought into motion by endolymph movements (Van Bergeijk, 1967) resulting from sound pressure waves. The lagenar otolith, which is almost screened from the endolymph movements by the utriculo–saccular constriction, would work as an accelerometer registering particle displacement waves. The sacculus would register low-amplitude pressure waves and the lagena would locate sounds.

Weberian ossicles and anterior vertebrae

The auditory function of the Weberian ossicles was proposed by Weber (1820, cited in Grassé, 1958) but the true homology with vertebral elements was

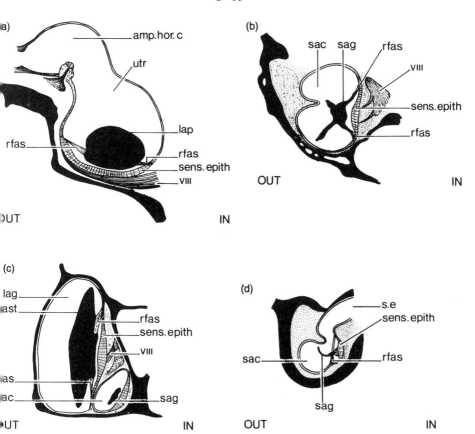

· **Fig. 11.4** (a) to (c) Diagrammatic sections through the three main cavities of the labyrinth in *Phoxinus laevis* ((a), utricle; (b), saccule; (c), lagena) (slightly modified after von Frisch and Stetter, 1932). (d) Diagrammatic vertical section through the saccule of a cyprinid fish, showing the position of a branch of the otolith facing the aperture of the canalis communicans transversus (s.e.) (slightly modified after Grassé, 1958, and De Burlet, 1934). Abbreviations, p. 347; rfas, Randfasern, sections through the more or less fibrous limit of the cupula, as seen in light microscopy. In: direction of the middle; out; direction of the skin.

established later by Geoffroy St Hilaire (cited in Grassé, 1958), while the systematic importance was first claimed by Sagemehl (1885). Chranilov's (1927) functional study on *C. auratus* was improved by Alexander (1959). The many anatomical descriptions are concordant (e.g. Ramaswami, 1955a,b; Vandewalle, 1974).

The symmetrical chains of three ossicles (from rear to front, tripus, intercalarium and scaphium) joined by interossicular ligaments link the swim bladder to the labyrinths (Fig. 11.6). Each ossicle articulates more or less

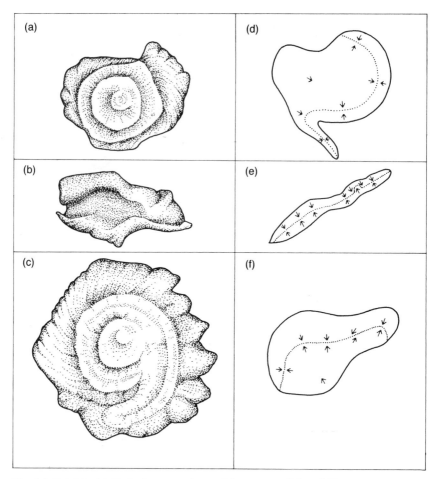

Fig. 11.5 (a) to (c) Utricular, saccular and lagenar otoliths of *Chorosomus neogaeus* (redrawn from Mahy, 1975). (d) to (f) Maculae corresponding to the utricular, saccular and lagenar otoliths of *Carassius auratus*. Dotted line is limit between hair cells, the bundles of stereocilia of which are orientated in opposite senses; arrows show orientation of the bundles (redrawn from Platt, 1977).

movably to one of the first three vertebral centra; this connection is consistent with their origin. The first two ossicles are transformed basidorsals, and the tripus is a basiventral, seemingly with its rib. Other non-vertebral analgen (primordia) seem to participate in their formation with the above-mentioned vertebral elements (Matveiev, 1929; Watson, 1939; Kulshrestha, 1977; Vandewalle *et al.*, 1989). The tripus attaches on the edge of the dorsal slit of the tunica externa (p. 341) by a sort of thin recurved hook, the transformator tripodis, which in turn attaches by a fan-shaped ligament (the fibres of which

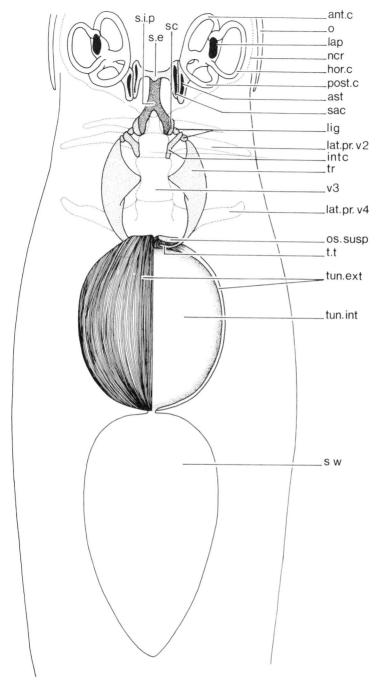

Fig. 11.6 Diagrammatic representation of the Weberian apparatus *sensu lato*; a tunica interna and a tunica externa are present in both anterior and posterior chambers (combined after Chranilov, 1927; Schnakenbeck, 1955; Vandewalle, 1974). Abbreviations, p. 347.

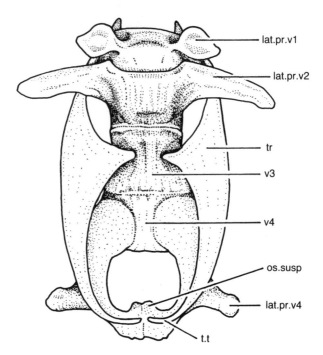

lat.pr.v1

lat.pr.v2

tr

v3

v4

os.susp

lat.pr.v4

t.t

Fig. 11.7 First four vertebrae of *Pelecus cultratus* in ventral view (redrawn from Chranilov, 1927). Abbreviations, p. 347.

are orientated like those of the tunica externa) to a fourth ossicle, the os suspensor. The os suspensor is fixed to the parapophysis of the fourth vertebra, consistently with developmental data showing its homology with a basiventral. The anterior end of the os suspensor extends lateroventrally across the tripus (Fig. 11.7).

The cyprinids' Weberian apparatus is conservative: the anterior vertebral centra are independent and movable and of roughly equal size, although the first one is shorter and the third is longer. The ossicles are large and provided with an articular process. According to Chardon (1968), the mobility of the anterior centra and the conservation of articular processes of the scaphium and intercalarium are functionally linked in fishes able to bind the anterior end of the backbone laterally. Such articulations and the weight of the ossicles probably increase the acoustic impedance, which is possibly partly balanced by the large volume of the swim bladder and the existence of fluid-filled spaces in which the chains of ossicles move freely. If the transformatores move to the midline, the scaphia pull laterally on the walls of the sinus impar (Fig. 11.6, s.i.p); as the anterior arm of the tripus (prolonged by the intercalarium and scaphium) is longer than the posterior one, the amplitude of the movement is increased. The backward movement of the ossicles is helped by the elastic recoil of a ligament running from the posteromesial edge of the tripus to the parapophysis of the fourth vertebra (Alexander, 1966).

The first four vertebral centra are modified as a consequence of the Weberian specialization (Chranilov, 1927). The first step is the reduction in length of the first two centra, either for shortening the distance between the swim bladder and the sinus impar, or for strengthening the Weberian region (Gayet and Chardon, 1987); good examples are *Opsariichthys tau* (Regan, 1911; Fink and Fink, 1981), *Leuciscus cephalus* and *Alburnus chalcoides* (Chranilov, 1927), *Barbus barbus* (Vandewalle, 1974), and *Macrochirichthys macrochirus* (Howes, 1979). The second vertebra is much reduced in *Leuciscus idus* and *Abramis brama*; the fusion is more or less complete in *Tinca tinca*, *Abramis brama* (Chranilov, 1927), the Gobioninae in general (Ramaswami, 1955a), *Schizothorax richardsonii* (Dixit and Bisht, 1972), and many others.

Swim bladder

The swim bladder is divided into two chambers joined by a median canal. It is usually large, but is reduced in the genera *Discognathus* and *Gyrinochilus* (Ramaswami, 1955a,b). The anterior chamber (camera aerea Weberiana) works as a transducer transforming sound pressure waves into periodical movements (Enger, 1969; Popper, 1974; Fay and Popper, 1974; Astafeva and Vaitulevich, 1974; Altman *et al.*, 1984). A role in hydrostatic pressure sensitivity is discussed on p. 342.

The camera aerea Weberiana is enclosed in a capsule in the genera *Rhinogobio* and *Saurogobio* (Regan, 1911). The whole swim bladder has a double wall. The inner sheet is thin and rather elastic (especially in the anterior chamber), it is homologous with the fused endoderm and splanchnopleura (Chardon and Vandewalle, 1989), and its outer layer contains blood vessels, smooth muscle fibres and autonomic nerve fibres. The outer sheet or tunica externa is the somatopleura; its essential constituent is ichthyocol crystals embedded in fibres so that it is not elastic, but deformable and able to come back to its initial shape by slow viscous retraction when stretched. The camera aerea Weberiana is deeply notched on the mid-dorsal line by an anterior slit on the edges of which the transformatores attach. In Otophysi, the swim bladder has an excess internal pressure (Alexander, 1966).

In response to pressure changes or sound pressure waves, the volume of the inner bubble varies within narrow limits (Alexander, 1966; Popper, 1974; Fay and Popper, 1974; Astafeva and Vaitulevich, 1974; Vaitulevich, 1977). The non-elastic tunica externa (Fig. 11.7) follows the movement due to the dorsal slit, the width of which in turn varies such that the pressure changes are transformed into movements of the transformatores (Chranilov, 1927; Alexander, 1962). In the case of hydrostatic long-lasting pressure changes, the transformatores return to their mean position through viscous movement in the tunica interna, so that the Weberian apparatus is not affected

(Alexander, 1966). As the most elastic part of the inner sheet is anterolateral, the deformation is greater there and its amplitude depends on the total volume of the swim bladder.

The directly observed deformation of the inner bubble in the carp, *Cyprinus carpio* (Vaitulevich, 1979; Altman *et al.*, 1984) is maximal at the resonance frequency, which would be exactly proportional to its diameter if it were spherical. Peculiarities of shape and differences in elasticity explain some of the discrepancy between the calculated resonance frequency (assuming the bubble is ellipsoidal and its wall is homogeneous) and the observed one; Altman *et al.* (1984) even observed several centres of resonance on the surface of the swim bladder, and better responses for a given frequency (500 Hz) next to the calculated resonance frequency and its first harmonics. In the goldfish, the response of the swim bladder decreases for frequencies beyond 900–1000 Hz (Clarke *et al.*, 1978). The sound frequencies giving the best responses of the swim bladder also correspond to the peak of sensitivity of the audiograms obtained by behavioural methods (Popper *et al.*, 1973).

The role of the swim bladder as a pressure receptor was demonstrated in *Phoxinus laevis* by Qutob (1962), who observed, however, that the behavioural reactions of the fish (for example, active descent after pressure decrease) remained unchanged after bilateral extirpation of the tripus. The reaction is very probably evoked through a nervous pathway starting from proprioceptive nerve endings of the inner sheet of the bladder, described by Evans (1925) in *Rutilus rutilus* and Terio (1948) in *Carassius auratus*. Nevertheless, 'yawning' (spitting gas bubbles) responses to slow pressure changes, seem to be mediated through the Weberian ossicles (Guyénot, 1909; Dijkgraaf, 1950).

Harden Jones and Marshal (1953) give a good account of the numerous roles of the swim bladder.

Acoustic performances of the Weberian apparatus *sensu lato*

Acoustic performances are measured either by behavioural or psychophysical methods (Hawkins, 1981) or by neurophysiological ones. Behavioural studies are reliable in the goldfish (Popper *et al.*, 1973). Many publications deal with acoustical nervous pathways and mechanisms in cyprinids, especially in the goldfish (e.g. Enger, 1969; Altman and Astafeva, 1976; Fay 1982; Fay and Ream, 1986; Kuno, 1983; Furukawa and Matsuura, 1978; Furukawa, 1985), and with acoustical performances (e.g. Fay and Passow, 1982). The conclusions drawn from behavioural observations of goldfish may often be extended cautiously to other Otophysi, but not to the other teleosts. Major discrepancies between results and subsequent controversies result from inadequate or inaccurate experimental conditions, including differences in far- or near-field conditions, sound pressure, or particle displacement waves (Popper *et al.*, 1973; Hawkins, 1981).

Audiograms presenting auditory sound intensity thresholds. v. frequencies and the limits of the auditory spectrum, usually for sound pressure waves, show a broader spectrum and much lower auditory thresholds in Otophysi (among which differences are maybe due to experimental procedures) than in most other teleosts (Jacobs and Tavolga, 1968; Lowenstein, 1971; Popper and Fay, 1973; Tavolga and Wodinsky, 1963; Hawkins, 1981). In the goldfish the threshold is lower than -40 dB for 500–1000 Hz; this allows them to hear biological noises easily (Tavolga, 1971).

As suggested by Popper and Fay (1973), cyprinids have numerous acoustic capabilities, like many other teleosts (Hawkins, 1986). They seem able to localize sounds (Schuijf *et al.*, 1977; Fay and Olsho, 1979; Konagaya, 1980; Aoki, 1987) and they can discriminate frequencies (Wohlfahrt, 1939). According to Popper and Fay (1973), the frequency discrimination thresholds of *Carassius auratus* and *Phoxinus laevis* vary from less than 5 Hz around a basal frequency of 50 Hz, up to 50 Hz or more around 1000 Hz. Although they lack a structure like the cochlea of the amniotes, they seem to use temporal discrimination, and to be better at reception of amplitude modulation than of frequency modulation (Fay and Passow, 1982), without any important dependence on intensity (Coombs and Fay, 1985). Sound intensity variations can also be detected with a limen of *c.* 0.13 dB for a continuous tone; the threshold is lower for pure tones than for noise; noise intensity decrements are more poorly detected than increments (Fay, 1985). Discrimination is also possible between noise and pure tones, but with some masking effect, which is strongest when the noise band has the same centre frequency as the test tone (Enger, 1973).

11.3   EQUILIBRATION FUNCTION OF THE LABYRINTHS

So far, the labyrinths have been considered as a merely acoustic apparatus. However, they also contribute to static and dynamic equilibration by reflexes restoring balance, involving eyes, head, fins and trunk, or by dynamic responses such as angular and linear accelerations (Grassé, 1958). As the labyrinths functions in hearing in addition to equilibration, and as experiments are difficult for anatomical reasons, it is difficult to demonstrate acoustic or equilibrative areas unambiguously (Lowenstein, 1971). Extirpation of parts of the labyrinths of cyprinids played a decisive role in demonstrating that the utriculus alone was able to control "the whole range of postural responses to positional changes" (Manning, 1924; Lowenstein, 1932, 1971; von Frisch and Stetter, 1932). Experiments on blind, unilaterally labyrinthectomized (extirpation of the utricular otolith) goldfish made weightless during a parabolic flight of an airplane imply that the 'spinning reflex' is controlled by the contralateral utricular macula (Wetzig, 1987).

11.4 LATERAL LINE SYSTEM

Structural aspects

The cyprinid lateral line system consists, in accordance with the nomenclature of Devillers (1958), of typical sensory canals, pitlines and solitary sensory pits. Pit-lines and solitary sensory pit neuromasts are individually invaginated in the skin, while the neuromasts of the sensory canals are located on incomplete transverse septa, such that the cupula partially occludes the lumen. Any liquid movement in the canal results in shearing displacements of the cupula and therefore of the cilia of the macular cells (Flock, 1971). The canals open to the exterior by pores or canaliculi of variable length, the number of which seem to be equal to the number of neuromasts. In the closely related cobitids, the isolated neuromasts are exactly like those in the canals; they are regularly disposed in relation to the canals (Guarnieri and Cavicchioli, 1968). According to Lekander (1949), pit lines are incompletely developed canals; he argues from ontogenetical observations that in cyprinids the rostral commissure and the antorbital, nasal and anterior mandibular lines are present in the form of pit lines. Isolated neuromasts originating from the principal lines form secondary lines parallel to the principal ones, or extra pit-lines: the vertical and horizontal lines of the cheek, the lateral supraorbital line, and the symphyseal line. The lateral line system of cyprinids is characterized by the abundance of pit-lines. Isolated neuromasts originating from the principal lines form tively to primitive actinopterygians, Jollie, 1969) by the replacement of most anterior canals by pit-lines.

The plan of the canals and their connections in the cyprinids is typically teleostean: a supraorbital, and infraorbital, a preopercular, a mandibular and temporal canals, a supratemporal commissure and the lateral line *sensu stricto* (Fig. 11.8). The supratemporal commissure is sometimes considered a secondary feature in teleosts; it is frequent on Otophysi and especially in cyprinids (Daget, 1964; Devillers, 1958; Hensel, 1978). In cyprinids, the supraorbital canal is always separated anteriorly from the infraorbital one, but posterior connections are reported by Hensel (1976, 1978) and Gosline (1974) as variable inter- and intraspecifically and even between left and right sides of an individual. Gosline (1974, referring to Lekander, 1949) points out that connections appear progressively and late during growth, and that adults of smaller species present the same connections as younger fish of larger species. On the basis of the connection between infra- and supraorbital canals in adults of species of reasonable size (> 10 cm), Gosline (1974) proposes a systematical division of the Old World Cyprinidae. Hensel (1976) proposes a classification of the European species based on the connections of the supraorbital and temporal canals. The very conservative relations between cephalic canals and dermal bones (Lekander, 1949) are shown in Fig. 11.8. The differences in the lateral line pattern often concern sections where the canals run through gaps between bones (Hensel, 1978).

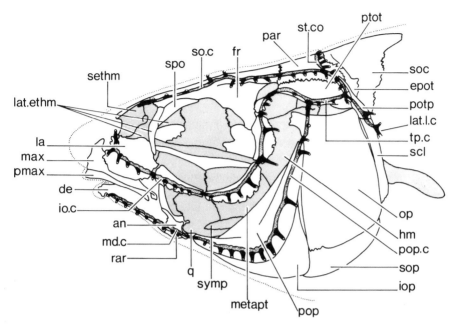

Fig. 11.8 Cephalic lateral lines canals of *Vimba vimba* (slightly modified after Hensel, 1976). Abbreviations, p. 347.

Functional aspects

Aspects of the lateral line system seem to be associated with the way of life. Species dwelling in the upper water layers possess more canaliculi and therefore more neuromasts on the lower part of the head, "in the direction of the most probable danger" (Hensel, 1976).

Location of moving prey and obstacle avoidance by the lateral line sense has been demonstrated in some teleosts (Schwartz, 1971; Bleckmann, 1986) and is probably also possible in some cyprinids. Moreover, the two blind hypogeal cyprinids from Africa, *Caecobarbus geertsi* and *Phreatichthys andruzzi* (Poll, 1957), cannot but rely on hearing, lateral line and maybe taste-bud senses in their locomotion and feeding behaviour, and in the case of *Caecobarbus* (Thines, 1969), in their agonistic interactions as well. In *Caecobarbus* the cephalic canal system is particularly well developed, but in the microphthalm *Eilichthys* from the artesian wells of Somalia, the lateral line is described as "indistinct" (Poll, 1957).

The lateral line system of fishes seems to perform multiple roles. Sand (1981) considers three main functions. (1) Sensitivity to local water movements (demonstrated by Hofer, 1908, and Dijkraaf, 1963) allows the detection of water currents and pressure localization of obstacles, and seems to explain how blind fishes avoid obstacles. (2) Sensitivity to surface waves by the cephalic canals, which display greatest sensitivity to waves travelling parallel to the longitudinal axis of the fish and having a frequency below 15 Hz (optimum at 7 Hz), allows detection of floating prey by fish swimming 2 cm under the water surface (Schwartz, 1970). (3) Sensitivity to low-frequency sounds; this has been argued from recordings from branches of the lateral line nerves, whereas results of behavioural observations are contradictory and do not withstand a rigorous discussion (Sand, 1981).

The most convincing experiments on a possible sensitivity to low-frequency vibrations are those of Sand (1981) on the roach, *Rutilus rutilus*. In an immobilized fish, the trunk lateral line can localize a vibrating item bringing about water movement, with an optimal sensitivity at 30 Hz, for water displacements parallel to the canal. But when the fish can move freely it only responds to very close and strong wave sources. Such response may be elicited through auditory sensitivity to sound pressure waves as well as through lateral line sensitivity, so the lateral line's role in localizing vibration sources remains uncertain. It is also improbable that volume changes of the swim bladder are mechanically registered by the trunk lateral line and transduced by its neuromasts, because the level of the necessary sound pressure is much higher than the sensitivity threshold of the auditory part of the labyrinth. Discrimination between the roles of the labyrinths and lateral line will probably become possible through a pharmacological method of selective blocking of the mechanosensitivity of the lateral line by cobalt cations observed by Karlsen and Sand (1987) on *Rutilus rutilus*. Blaxter *et al.*'s (1981) observations on clupeids suggest a possible sensitivity of the cephalic lateral line to low-frequency sounds, while Partridge (1980, 1981) showed that reciprocal orientation of schooling minnows, *Phoxinus phoxinus*, depends on the integrity of the trunk lateral line.

11.5 CONCLUDING REMARKS

The cyprinids share with the other Otophysi a generalized lateral line system and an extremely efficient hearing apparatus. But at the same time, they possess many other remarkable anatomical devices related to feeding: an edentate and swivelling protrusile mouth (Vandewalle, 1978), which is associated with specialized pharyngeal jaws (Sibbing, 1982) and a palatal organ (Dorier and Bellon, 1952) and a well-developed gustatory system, such that none of these specializations can be considered *a priori* as more important in explaining the success of the group. More ecological and ethological studies in the field would certainly help to clarify the problem.

ACKNOWLEDGEMENTS

The authors gratefully acknowledge Mrs O. Gilson for carefully typing the manuscript and Mrs P. Golinvaux for preparing most of the illustrations.

ABBREVIATIONS

aff	afferent synapse	max	maxillary
amp	ampulla	mb	membrane
amp. hor. c	ampulla of the horizontal canal	md. c	mandibular canal
		metapt	metapterygoid
an	angular	m.o	medulla oblongata
ant.c	anterior canal		
ast	asteriscus	ncr	neurocranium
		nucl	nucleus
br	brain		
		o	opercle
crus	crus communis	op	opercular
cut	cuticle	os. susp	os suspensor
		oth	otolith
de	dentary		
		par	parietal
eff	efferent synapse	pmax	premaxillary
epot	epiotic	p.n	papilla neglecta
		pop	preopercular
fr	frontal	pop.c	preopercular canal
		post.c	posterior canal
g	gill	potp	posttemporal
		ptot	pterotic
h. cell	hair cell		
hm	hyomandibular	q	quadrate
hor. c	horizontal canal		
		rar	retroarticular
intc	intercalarium	rfas	Randfasern
io. c	infraorbital canal		
iop	interopercular	sac	saccule
		sag	sagitta
kcil	kinocil	sc	scaphium
		scl	supracleithrum
la	lachrymal	s.e	sinus endolymphaticus
lag	lagena	sens. epith	sensory epithelium
lap	lapillus	sethm	supraethmoid
lat. ethm	lateral ethmoid	s.i.p	sinus impar perilymphaticus
lat. l. c	lateral line canal		
lat. pr. v1	lateral process of the first vertebra	so.c	supraorbital canal
		soc	supraoccipital
lat. pr. v2	lateral process of the second vertebra	sop	subopercular
		spo	supraopercular
lat. pr. v4	lateral process of the fourth vertebra	stcil	stereocilia
		st. co	supratemporal commissure
lig	interossicular ligament between the scaphium and the intercalarium and between the intercalarium and the tripus	sup. cell	supporting cell

sw	swim bladder	tun. int	tunica interna
symp	sympleric	utr	utricle
tp.c	temporal canal	v3	third vertebra
tr	tripus	v4	fourth vertebra
t.t	transformator tripodis	VIII	otic nerve
tun. ext	tunica externa		

REFERENCES

Alexander, R. McN. (1959) The physical properties of the swimbladder in intact Cypriniformes. *J. exp. Biol.*, **36**, 315–32.

Alexander, R. McN. (1962) The structure of the Weberian apparatus in the Cyprini. *Proc. zool. Soc. Lond.*, **139**, 451–73.

Alexander, R. McN. (1966) Physical aspects of swimbladder function. *Biol. Rev.*, **41**, 141–70.

Altman, J. A. and Astafeva, S. N. (1976) Electrical responses of the acoustico-lateral area of the medulla to acoustic stimulation in *Cyprinus carpio*. *J. evol. Biochem. Physiol.*, **12**, 189–91.

Altman, J. A., Butusov, M. M., Vaitulevich, S. F. and Sokolov, A. V. (1984) Responses of the swimbladder of the carp to sound stimulation. *Hear. Res.*, **14**, 145–54.

Aoki, I. (1987) Control of orientation response by auditory discriminative stimuli in the carp. *Nippon Suisan Gakkai-shi*, **53**, 1933–41.

Astafeva, S. N. and Vaitulevich, S. F. (1974) The role of the swimbladder in the acoustic function of the carp *Cyprinus carpio*. *Zh. evol. Biokhim. Fiziol.*, **10**, 420–23.

Blaxter, J. H. S. Denton, E. J. and Geray, J. A. B. (1981) Acousticolateralis system in clupeid fishes, in *Hearing and Sound Communication in Fishes* (eds W. N. Tavolga, A. N. Popper and R. R. Fay), Springer-Verlag, New York, pp. 39–56.

Bleckmann, H. (1986) Role of the lateral line in fish behaviour, in *The Behaviour of Teleost Fishes* (ed. T. J. Pitcher), Croom Helm, London and Sydney, pp. 114–51.

Chardon, M. (1968) Anatomie comparée de l'appareil de Weber et des structures connexes chez les Siluriformes. *Annls Mus. R. Afr. cent. Tervuren*, **169**, 277 pp.

Chardon, M. and Vandewalle, P. (1989) About identification of swimbladder sheets in Ostariophysi, in *Progress in Zoology*, vol. 35 (eds H. Splechtna and H. Hilgers), Gustav Fischer Verlag, Stuttgart, pp. 264–8.

Chranilov, N. S. (1927) Beiträge zur kenntnis des Weber'schen Apparates des Ostariophysi. I. Vergleichenden-anatomische Übersicht des Knochenelemente der Weber'schen Apparate bei Cypriniformes. *Zool. Jb. Anat.*, **49**, 501–97.

Clarke, N., Popper, A. N. and Mann, J. (1978) Laser-light-scattering investigations of the teleost swimbladder response to acoustic stimuli. *Biophys. J.*, **15**, 307–18.

Coombs, S. and Fay, R. K. (1985) Adaptation effects on amplitude modulation detection: behavioral and neurophysiological assessments in the goldfish auditory system. *Hear. Res.*, **19**, 57–71.

Daget, J. (1964) Le crâne des Téléostéens. *Mém. Mus. Hist. nat. Paris.*, Sér. A, **31**, 167–340.

De Burlet, H. M. (1929) Zur vergleichende Anatomie und Physiologie des perilymphat-ischen Raumes. *Acta Oto-lar. Stockh.*, **13**, 153–87.

De Burlet, H. M. (1934) Die innere Ohrsphäre, in *Handbuch der vergleichenden Anatomie*, Vol. 2 (eds L. Bolk, E. Gopper, E. Kallius and W. Lubosch), Urban and Schwarzenberg, Berlin, pp. 1293–380.

Devillers, C. (1958) Le crâne des Poissons, in *Traité de Zoologie*, vol. 13 (ed. P. P. Grassé), Masson et Cie, Paris, pp. 551–687.

Dijkgraaf, S. (1950) Uber die Auslösung des Gasspuckreflexes bei Fischen. *Experientia,* **6**, 188–90.

Dijkgraaf, S. (1963) The function and significance of the lateral line organs. *Biol. Rev.,* **38**, 51–105.

Dixit, R. K. and Bisht, J. S. (1972) The endoskeleton of a hill-stream teleost, *Schizothorax richardsonni* (Gray and Hard). Part II. The vertebral column, girdles and fins. *Z. wiss. Zool.,* **185** (1/2), 55–68.

Dorier, A. and Bellon, G. (1952) Sur l'organe palatin des Cyprinidae. *Trav. Lab. Hydrob. Piscic. Grenoble,* **44**, 47–60.

Enger, P. S. (1969) Reception of sound and vibrations by the fish ear. *Acta physiol. scand.,* Suppl. **330**, 50.

Enger, P. S. (1973) Masking of auditory responses in the medulla oblongata of goldfish. *J. exp. Biol.,* **59**, 415–24.

Evans, H. M. (1925) A contribution to the anatomy and physiology of the air-bladder and Weberian ossicles in Cyprinidae. *Proc. R. Soc.* **B**, **97**, 545–76.

Fay, R. R. (1981) Coding in acoustic information in the 8th nerve, in *Hearing and Sound Communication in Fishes* (eds W. N. Tavolga, A. N. Popper and R. R. Fay), Springer-Verlag, NY, 189–222.

Fay, R. R. (1982) Neural mechanisms of auditory temporal discrimination by the goldfish. *J. comp. Physiol.,* **147**, 201–16.

Fay, R. R. (1985) Sound intensity processing by the goldfish. *J. acoust. Soc. Am,* **78**, 1296–309.

Fay, R. R. and Olsho, L. W. (1979) Discharge patterns of lagenar and saccular neurons of the goldfish eighth nerve: displacement sensitivity and directional characteristics. *Comp. Biochem. Physiol.,* **62A**, 377–86.

Fay, R. R. and Passow, B. (1982) Temporal discrimination in the goldfish *Carassius auratus. J. acoust. Soc. Am.,* **72**, 753–60.

Fay, R. R. and Popper, A. N. (1974) Acoustic stimulation of the ear of the goldfish (*Carassius auratus*). *J. exp. Biol.,* **61**, 243–60.

Fay, R. R. and Ream, T. J. (1986) Acoustic response and tuning in saccular nerve fibers of the goldfish (*Carassius auratus*). *J. acoust. Soc. Am.,* **79**, 1883–95.

Fink, S. and Fink, W. (1981) Interrelationships of the Ostariophysan fishes (Teleostei). *Zool. J. Linn. Soc.,* **72**, 297–353.

Flock, A. (1971) Sensory transduction in hair cell, in *Handbook of Sensory Physiology,* 1. Principles of receptor physiology (ed. W. R. Loewenstein), Springer-Verlag, Berlin, pp. 396–441.

Frisch, K. von and Stetter, H. (1932) Untersuchungen über den Sitz des Gehörsinnes bei der Elritze. *Z. vergl. Physiol.,* **17**, 686–801.

Furukawa, T. (1985) Slow depolarizing response from supporting cells in the goldfish saccule. *J. Physiol. Lond.,* **366**, 107–17.

Furukawa, T. and Ishii, Y. (1967) Neurophysiological studies on hearing in goldfish. *J. Neurophysiol.,* **30**, 1337–403.

Furukawa, T. and Matsuura, S. (1978) Adaptative rundown of excitatory postsynaptic potentials at synapses between hair cells and 8th nerve fibres in the goldfish. *J. Physiol. Land.,* **276**, 193–209.

Gayet, M. and Chardon, M. (1987) Possible otophysic connections in some fossil and living ostariophysan fishes. *Proc. Vth Congr. europ. Ichthyol.,* Stockholm, 1985, pp. 1337–1403.

Gosline, W. A. (1974) Certain lateral line canals of the head in cyprinid fishes with particular reference to the derivation of north American forms. *Jap. J. Ichthyol.,* **21**, 9–15.

Grassé, P. P. (1958) L'oreille et ses annexes, in *Traité de Zoologie,* vol. 13 (ed. P. P. Grassé), Masson, Paris, pp. 1063–98.

Guarnieri, P. and Cavicchioli, G. (1968) Ulteriori osservazioni sopra la struttura degli organi di senso cutanei nei Cobitidi italiani. *Archo zool. ital.*, **53**, 19–32.

Guyénot, E. (1909) Les fonctions de la vessie natatoire des Poissons. *Bull. scient. Fr. Belg.*, **43**, 203–96.

Harden Jones, F. R. and Marshall, N. B. (1953) The structure and functions of the teleostean swimbladder. *Biol. Rev.*, **28**, 16–83.

Hawkins, A. D. (1981) The hearing abilities of fish, in *Hearing and Sound Communication in Fishes* (eds W. N. Tavolga, A. N. Popper and R. R. Fay), Springer Verlag, NY, pp. 109–38.

Hawkins, A. D. (1986) Underwater sound and fish behaviour, in *The Behaviour of Teleost Fishes* (ed. T. J. Pitcher), Croom Helm, London and Sydney, pp. 114–51.

Hensel, K. (1976) The lateral-line canal system configuration in some Cyprinids. *Revue. Trav. Inst. Pêches marit.*, **40**, 601.

Hensel, K. (1978) Morphology of lateral-line canal system of the genera *Abramis, Blicca* and *Vimba* with regard to their ecology and systematic position. *Acta. Univ. Carol. (Biol.)*, 1975–76, **12**, 105–49.

Hofer, B. (1908) Studien über die Hautsinnesorgane der Fishes, *Ber. Biol. Versuchstation München*, **1**, 115–64.

Howes, G. (1979) Notes on the anatomy of *Macrochirichthys macrochirus* (Valenciennes), 1844, with comments on the Cultrinae (Pisces, Cyprinidae). *Bull. Br. Mus. nat. Hist. (Zool)*, **36**, 147–200.

Jacobs, D. W. and Tavolga, W. N. (1968) Acoustic frequency discrimination in the goldfish. *Anim. Behav.*, **16**, 67–71.

Jollie, M. (1969) Sensory canals of the snout of Actinopterygian fishes. *Trans Ill. St. Acad. Sci.*, **62**, 61–9.

Karlsen, H. E. and Sand. O. (1987) Selective and reversible blocking of the lateral line in freshwater fish. *J. exp. Biol.*, **133**, 249–62.

Konagaya, T. (1980) The sound field of lake Biwa and the effects of the constructing sound on the behavior of the fish. *Bull. Jap. Soc. scient. Fish.*, **46**, 129–32.

Kuno, M. (1983) Adaptative changes in firing rates in goldfish auditory fibers as related to changes in mean amplitude of excitatory postsynaptic potentials. *J. Neurophysiol. (Bethesda)* **50**, 573–81.

Kulshrestha, S. K. (1977) Development of the Weberian apparatus in Indian major carp *Labeo rohita* (Ham.). *Anat. Anz.*, **141**, 433–44.

Lekander, B. (1949) The sensory line system and the canal bones in the head of some Ostariophysi. *Acta zool., Stockh.*, **30**, 1–131.

Lowenstein, O. (1932) Experimentelle Untersuchungen über den Gleichgewichtssinn der Elritze (*Phoxinus laevis* L.) *Z. vergl. Physiol.*, **17**, 806–54.

Lowenstein, O. (1971). The labyrinth, in *Fish Physiology*, vol. 5 (eds W. S. Hoar and D. J. Randall), Academic Press, NY, pp. 207–40.

Mahy, G. (1975) Ostéologie comparée et phylogénie des poissons Cyprinoïdes. 1. Ostéologie crânienne du Goujon à fines écailles, *Chorosomus neogaens* (Cope). *Naturaliste can.*, **102**, 1–31.

Manning, F. B. (1924) Hearing in the goldfish in relation to the structure of its ear. *J. exp. Zool.*, **41**, 5–20.

Matveiev, B. (1929) Die Entwicklung des vorderen Wirbel und des Weber'schen Apparates bei Cyprinidae. *Zool. Jb. Anat.*, **51**, 463–534.

Nakajima, Y. and Wang, D. W. (1974) Morphology of afferent and efferent synapses in the hearing organ of the goldfish. *J. comp. Neurol.*, **156**, 403–16.

Partridge, B. L. (1980) The effect of school size on the structure and dynamics of minnow schools. *Anim. Behav.*, **28**, 68–77.

Partridge, B. L. (1981) Lateral line function and the internal dynamics of fish schools, in *Hearing and Sound Communication in Fishes* (eds W. N. Tavolga, A. N. Popper and R. R. Fay), Springer Verlag, NY, pp. 515–21.

Platt, C. (1977) Hair cell distribution and orientation in goldfish otolith organs. *J. comp. Neurol.*, **172**, 283–98.

Platt, C. and Popper, A. N. (1981) Fine structure and function of the ear, in *Hearing and Sound Communication in Fishes* (eds W. N. Tavolga, A. N. Popper and R. R. Fay), Springer-Verlag, NY, pp. 3–36.

Poll, M. (1957) Les genres de poissons d'eau douce de l'Afrique. *Publication de la Direction de l'Agriculture, des Forêts et de l'Elevage*, Bruxelles, 191 pp.

Popper, A. N. (1974) The response of the swimbladder of the goldfish (*Carassius auratus*) to acoustic stimuli. *J. exp. Biol.*, **60**, 295–304.

Popper, A. N. and Coombs, S. (1982) The morphology and evolution of the ear in Actinopterygian Fishes. *Am. Zool.*, **22**, 311–28.

Popper, A. N. and Fay, R. R. (1973) Sound detection and processing by teleost fishes: a critical review. *J. acoust. Soc. Am.*, **53**, 1515–29.

Popper, A. N. and Platt, C. (1983) Sensory surface of the saccule and lagena in the ears of Ostariophysan fishes. *J. Morph.*, **176**, 121–9.

Popper, A. N., Chan, A. T. H. and Clarke, N. L. (1973) An evaluation of methods for behavioral investigations of teleost audition. *Behav. Res, Methods Instrum.*, **5**, 470–72.

Qutob, Z. (1962) The swimbladder of fishes as a pressure receptor. *Archs néerl, Zool.*, **15**, 1–67.

Radermaker, F., Surlemont, C., Sanna, P., Chardon, M., and Vandewalle, P. (1989) Ontogeny of the Weberian apparatus of *Clarias gariepinus* (Pisces, Siluriformes), *Can. J. Zool.*, **67**, 2090–7.

Ramaswami, L. S. (1955a) Skeleton of cyprinoid fishes in relation to phylogenetic studies. VI. The skull and Weberian apparatus of the subfamily Gobioninae (Cyprinidae). *Acta Zool., Stockh.*, **36**, 127–58.

Ramawsami, L. S. (1955b) Skeleton of Cyprinoid fishes in relation to phylogenetic studies. VII. The skull and Weberian apparatus of Cyprininae (Cyprinidae). *Acta Zool., Stockh.*, **36**, 199–242.

Regan, C. T. (1911) The classification of the Teleostean fishes of the order Ostariophysi, *Ann. mag. nat. Hist.*, 8th Ser., **10**, 553–77.

Retzius, G. (1881) Das Gehörorgan der Wirbeltiere: morphologisch–histologische Studien. *Das Gehörorgan der Fische und Amphibien*, vol. 1 (eds Samson and Wallin), Stockholm, 221 pp.

Sagemehl, M. (1885) Das Cranium der Characiniden nebst allgemeinen Bemerkungen über die mit einem Weber's schen Apparat versehenen Physostomenfamilien. *Morph. Jb.*, **11**, 1–119.

Sand, O. (1981) The lateral line and sound reception, in *Hearing and Sound Communication in Fishes* (eds W. N. Tavolga, A. N. Popper and R. R. Fay), Springer-Verlag, NY, pp. 459–78.

Schnakenbeck, W. (1955) *Handbuch der Zoologie*. **6.** *Erste Klasse der Vertebrate, Pisces* (eds J. G. Helmcke and H. Von Lengerken), De Gruyter and Co, Berlin, pp. 549–904.

Schuijf, A., Visser, C., Villers, A. and Buwalda, R. (1977) Acoustic localization in an ostariophysan fish. *Experientia*, **33**, 1062–3.

Schwartz, E. (1970) Ferntastsinneorgane von Oberflächenfischen. *Z. Morph. Tiere*, **67**, 40–57.

Schwartz, E. (1971) Die Ortung von Wasserwellen durch Oberflächenfische. *Z. vergl. Physiol.*, **74**, 64–80.

Sibbing, F. A. (1982) Pharyngeal mastication and food transport in the carp (*Cyprinus carpio* L.): a cineradiographic and electromyographic study. *J. Morph.*, **172**, 223–58.

Tavolga, W. N. (1971) Sound production and detection, in *Fish Physiology*, vol. 5 (eds W. S. Hoar and D. J. Randall), Academic Press, NY, pp. 135–205.

Tavolga, W. N. and Wodinsky, J. (1963) Auditory capacities in fishes: pure tone thresholds in nine species of marine teleosts. *Bull. Am. Mus. nat. Hist.*, **126**, 177–240.

Terio, B. (1948) Le espansioni nervose della vescica natatoria del ciprinide dorato (*Carassiaus auratus*). *Rc. Acad. Sci. fis. mat.*, *Napoli*, **14**, 17.

Thines, G. (1969) *L'Évolution Régressive des Poissons Cavernicoles et Abyssaux*. Masson, Paris, 394 pp.

Vaitulevich, S. F. (1977) Some acoustic properties of the swimbladder of the carp *Cyprinus carpio*. *Zh. evol. Biokhim. Fiziol.*, **13**, 198–202.

Vaitulevich, S. F. (1979) Characteristics of the wall of the swimbladder in the carp *Cyprinus carpio* during sonic stimulation. *J. evol. Biochem. Physiol.*, **15**, 165–9.

Van Bergeijk, W. A. (1967) The evolution of vertebrate hearing, in *Contributions to Sensory Physiology*, vol. 2 (ed. W. Neff), Academic Press, NY, pp. 1–49.

Vandewalle, P. (1974) On the anatomy of the head region in *Gobio gobio* (L.) (Pisces, Cyprinidae). 1. The Weberian apparatus and connected structures. *Forma Functio*, **7**, 47–54.

Vandewalle, P. (1978) Analyse des mouvements potentiels de la région céphalique du goujon. *Gobio gobio* (L.) (Poissons, Cyprinidae). *Cybium*, **3**, 15–33.

Vandewalle, P., Victor, D., Sanna, P. and Surlemont, C. (1989) The Weberian apparatus of a 18.5 mm fry of *Barbus* (L.), in *Progress in Zoology*, vol. 35 (eds H. Splechtna and H. Hilgers), Gustav Fisher Verlag, Stuttgart, pp. 363–6.

Watson, J. M. (1939) The development of the Weberian ossicles and anterior vertebrae in the goldfish. *Proc. R. Soc.* **B**, **127**, 452–72.

Weber, E. H. (1820) De aure et auditu hominis et animalium. Part I. De aure animalium aquatilium. Leipzig.

Wetzig, J. (1987) Rotation speed of labyrinthectomized fish during short-duration weightlessness. *Aviat. space environ. Med.*, **A252–A261**.

Wilson, H. V. and Mattocks, J. E. (1897) The lateral sensory anlage in the salmon. *Anat. Anz.*, **13**, 658–660.

Wohlfahrt, T. A. (1932) Anatomische Untersuchungen über das Labyrinth der Elritze (*Phoxinus laevis* L.). *Z. vergl. Physiol.*, **17**, 659–88.

Wohlfahrt, T. A. (1939) Untersuchungen über das Tonunterscheidungvermögen der Elritze (*Phoxinus laevis* Agass). *Z. vergl. Physiol.*, **26**, 570–604.

Chapter twelve

Diets and feeding behaviour

E. H. R. R. Lammens and W. Hoogenboezem

12.1 INTRODUCTION

Cyprinids comprise a wide variety of specialists and generalists feeding on all trophic levels. Detailed knowledge is available about the common European cyprinids from running and stagnant fresh water. Most feed on the secondary producers: zooplankton, macrocrustaceans, larvae, pupae and adults of insects, oligochaetes, bryozoans, snails, and mussels. Some also consume primary (macrophytes and phytoplankton) or tertiary producers (fish), but only very few use these as main food. When discussing the diets of cyprinids it is important to know both the type and availability of food organisms. Not only is their digestibility important, but more than this, how they are detected and handled by the different species (see also Chapter 13). Some are eaten by all species, but only during particular ontogenetic stages of the fish and only when the density and size of the food are sufficient. Therefore the diet must be related to the size of the fish and to availability (density, size distribution, visibility etc.) of food. This will be the main emphasis in this chapter, while the relationship with competition is described in Chapter 18. The following section gives a brief résumé of the variation in diets and habitats of the most abundant European cyprinids, together with some information regarding interspecific differences in foraging efficiency. The third and fourth sections deal with pelagic and benthic feeding modes, with emphasis on zooplankton and chironomids as food organisms and using bream, *Abramis brama*, white bream, *Blicca bjoerkna*, and roach, *Rutilus rutilus*, as model fishes. The method of feeding, differences in efficiency and the importance of the gill-raker system are described, followed by a section on switching in feeding modes and food organisms in relation to these major feeding modes. The chapter ends with a summary of major characteristics of cyprinid diets and feeding behaviours, as deduced from our studies of European species, and their likely application to other genera.

12.2 DIETS

None of the cyprinids is strictly monophagous, but many may feed on only one type of food organism, depending on availability. Some species can eat plants or plant remains, whereas others are specialized in pelagic feeding on zooplankton or fishes, and another group is more specialized in benthivorous feeding. Here we describe the diets and habitats of these three major groups. Within these groups, only the most common European cyprinids are mentioned because these are best studied: knowledge of non-European cyprinids is too fragmentary for valid comparison.

Herbivores

Rudd, *Scardinius erythrophthalmus*, roach, dace, *Leuciscus leuciscus*, and nase, *Chondrostoma nasus*, sometimes feed predominantly on macrophytes or filamentous algae (Prejs and Jackowska, 1978; Persson, 1983; Mann, 1973, 1974; Hellawell, 1971, 1972). They are, however, able to live exclusively on animal food as well, particularly zooplankton, snails and mussels (Lammens *et al.*, 1987; Ponton and Gerdeaux, 1988; Prejs, 1973, 1976; Rask, 1989; Hartley, 1947). Rudd lives almost exclusively in stagnant overgrown water, feeding on vegetation and zooplankton or on adult insects near the surface (Prejs, 1976; Hartley, 1947; Kennedy and Fitzmaurice, 1974; Johansson, 1987). Its superior mouth is suited to surface feeding, whereas its pharyngeal teeth are ideal for utilization of vegetation (Chapter 13). In contrast, the very adaptable roach occurs in both stagnant and running water and can live in open and overgrown areas. Roach feeds more efficiently on zooplankton than rudd but less efficiently than bleak *Alburnus alburnus*, bream and white bream (Johansson, 1987; Wanzenbock, 1989; Vockner and Schiemer, 1989; Lammens *et al.*, 1987; Winfield *et al.*, 1983). It is probably one of the most efficient mollusc feeders among European cyprinids (Prejs, 1976; Rask, 1989). Dace and nase occur predominantly in running waters, but also in connected lakes. They eat the same sort of food as roach, but no feeding experiments have been done with these fishes. Nase is more benthic than dace and feeds more on filamentous algae than macrophytes (Willer, 1924; Hartley, 1947). Ide, *Idus idus*, and chub, *Leuciscus cephalus*, feed also on macrophytes (Brabrand, 1985; Cala, 1970; Hellawell, 1971) but have even broader diets as they tap all trophic levels up to small fish (Boikova, 1986; Granado-Lorencio and Garcia-Novo, 1986; Willer, 1924). Both fishes prefer running water, but live very well in connected lakes, in particular in the littoral zone (Brabrand, 1985; Cala, 1970; Boikova, 1986; Hartley, 1947).

Pelagic feeders

There are a few specialized pelagic feeders, such as *Leucaspius delineatus* (Granado-Lorencio and Garcia-Novo, 1986; Boikova, 1986; Hartley, 1947), bleak (Wanzenbock, 1989; Vollestad, 1985; Rask, 1989; Vockner and Schiemer, 1989), *Pelecus cultratus* (Herzig and Winkler, 1983; Adamicka, 1984) and the asp, *Aspius aspius* (Granado-Lorencio and Garcia-Novo, 1986; Boikova, 1986). They eat zooplankton and surface insects, and fish in the case of large *P. cultratus* and asp. *Leucaspius* inhabits stagnant overgrown water (Willer, 1924; Hartley, 1947). The bleak lives in somewhat more open areas than *Leucaspius* and in both stagnant and running waters (Vollestad, 1985; Vockner and Schiemer, 1989). *Pelecus* lives only in the open-water zone of stagnant and running water; this is comparable to the distribution of the asp (Herzig and Winkler, 1983; Adamicka, 1984; Boikova, 1986; Granado-Lorencio and Garcia-Novo, 1986). *Pelecus* and the asp are restricted to the eastern part of Europe.

Benthic feeders

A relatively large group is represented by the benthic feeders, such as carp, *Cyprinus carpio* (Fanget, 1972; Fitzmaurice, 1983; Moyle, 1984), barb, *Barbus barbus* (Granado-Lorencio and Garcia-Novo, 1986), gudgeon, *Gobio gobio* (Kennedy and Fitzmaurice, 1972; Willer, 1924), bream (Laskar, 1948; Kennedy and Fitzmaurice, 1968; Lammens *et al.*, 1987), tench, *Tinca tinca* (Kennedy and Fitzmaurice, 1970), white bream (Lammens, 1984; Brabrand, 1984; Rask, 1989) and crucian carp, *Carassius carassius* (Prejs, 1976; Holopainen and Hyvarinen, 1985). In particular bream, white bream, carp and barb are specialized for feeding on dipteran larvae in the sediments or organisms associated with the sediments (Laskar, 1948; Brabrand, 1984; Lammens, 1984; Tatrai, 1980; Granado-Lorencio and Garcia-Novo, 1986; Fanget, 1972; Loffler, 1984). Molluscs and seeds are often additional food for carp, tench and white bream (Kennedy and Fitzmaurice, 1970; Fitzmaurice, 1983; Crivelli, 1981; Hartley, 1947; Willer, 1924). Zooplankton is also eaten efficiently by carp (Uribe-Zamora, 1975; Sibbing, 1988), crucian carp (Prejs, 1976), and bream (Lammens *et al.*, 1987) and by the other cyprinids when they are young (Hartley, 1947). Only barb and gudgeon prefer running water (Willer, 1924; Hartley, 1947), whereas crucian carp and tench are usually restricted to overgrown areas (Prejs, 1976; Kennedy and Fitzmaurice, 1970). In this respect white bream and carp are facultative, but bream prefers the open-water zone (Hartley, 1947; Laskar, 1948; Willer, 1924).

12.3 PELAGIC FEEDING BEHAVIOUR

General aspects

Cyprinids start feeding on plankton shortly after hatching (van Densen, 1985; Jelonek, 1986; Hammer, 1985). Prey are detected visually and taken one by one. These fishes are gape limited (Zaret, 1980) and particle size is strongly related to mouth size. With increasing size of the fish the prey choice changes, and gradually larger plankton can be swallowed (macrophagy). When the fish becomes large in relation to the plankton (microphagy), special adaptations for the retention of small organisms in the pharyngeal cavity are developed. In all groups of larger planktivorous fishes, a distinct filter apparatus has been observed (e.g. Zander, 1906). Other fishes remain macrophagous with increasing length and develop into herbivores, molluscivores, insectivores or piscivores.

Feeding modes and selectivity

Pelagic plankton is usually diverse in both species composition and size distribution. Studies on the diet of planktivorous fish showed that selectivity is more a rule than an exception (Lazarro, 1987). Food selectivity is initially determined by the feeding mode, namely particulate feeding, pump filter feeding and tow-net filter feeding (Janssen, 1976 a, b; McComas and Drenner, 1982; Gibson and Ezzi, 1985; Lammens, 1985; Chapter 13). The size of fish, mesh size of the branchial sieve, and the size, density, visibility and evasive behaviour of prey determine the selectivity of each feeding mode (Jacobs, 1978; Drenner *et al.*, 1978; Zaret and Kerfoot, 1975; Winfield *et al.* 1983; Wright and O'Brien, 1984; Hessen, 1985). The selectivity is probably also determined by the profitabilities of the different options. It is assumed that natural selection favours optimal foraging (Pyke, 1984). The switching of feeding modes (Crowder, 1985; Gibson and Ezzi, 1985; Holanov and Tash, 1978) and changing selectivity within a feeding mode (Werner and Hall, 1974; Galis and de Jong, 1988) gives some evidence for optimal foraging.

Within the cyprinids, probably all the following feeding modes are used, although most species use only one or two.

Particulate feeding

The fish detects the prey individually, approaches it and attacks it by means of fast, directed suction (for effects of these movement patterns of water and prey see Chapter 13). Janssen (1976a, 1978) distinguishes two other special forms of particulate feeding, darting and gulping.

Most small zooplanktivorous cyprinids (< 15 cm) are mainly particulate feeders. Particulate feeding, particularly darting, is a distinctly size-selective feeding mode, whereas gulping is much less size-selective because several size classes of zooplankton are sucked in simultaneously (Janssen, 1976a; Hoogenboezem, unpubl.).

Darting. The fish begins sucking when swimming towards the prey, thereby minimizing pushing water forwards and preventing evasive action. Although darting has not yet been described for cyprinids, it is likely that the active bleak and *Pelecus* use this foraging technique, because these fishes are efficient copepod feeders comparable with smelt and most percids (Ivlev, 1961;

Herzig and Winkler, 1983; Wanzenbock, 1989). Compared to percids, most cyprinids are much less selective in their first year (Densen, 1985; Bohl, 1982) and do not seem to be efficient particulate feeders. But Winfield *et al.* (1983) showed that in comparison with roach, particulate-feeding 0+beam is more efficient at catching copepods. Probably the protrusible upper jaw of bream creates a much stronger suction force (Alexander, 1966; Osse, 1985) than in roach. Particulate-feeding cyprinids probably use a technique different from that of percids.

Gulping. This is more or less an intermediate between particulate feeding and pump filter feeding (see also Chapter 13). While the fish swims slowly it takes a series of snaps directed more or less towards local areas of higher plankton densities. These series alternate with short pauses. To enclose the maximal volume of water in each snap, the mouth protrudes distinctly during gulping (Janssen, 1976a; Sibbing, 1988). Most *Abramis*-like species and carp use this feeding mode (pers. obs.). The distinction between gulping and pump filter feeding is somewhat arbitrary, and the transition is very gradual in a gradient from light to dark.

Pump filter feeding
A slowly swimming, or stationary, fish taking a long series of suctions is pump filter feeding (Uribe-Zamora, 1975; Drenner *et al.*, 1982; Holanov and Tash, 1978; Lammens, 1985). The fish is not visually orientated, but uses the very numerous taste-buds in the pharyngeal cavity (Chapter 13) to detect prey while swallowing. This feeding mode is used particularly by bream and carp in very turbid lakes and at night. Most benthivorous fish mentioned in Section 12.2 can feed in this way (Lammens *et al.*, 1987).

Tow-net filter feeding
This method involves swimming quickly with the mouth agape and opercula abducted, engulfing a cylinder of water containing the food particles (Janssen, 1976a; Rosen and Hales, 1981; Gibson and Ezzi, 1985). No records of this feeding behaviour have been published for cyprinid species, although *Alburnus alburnus* and *Pelecus cultratus* probably employ this feeding mode under favourable conditions, because they have herring-like gill raker systems. The selectivity of this strategy depends mainly on the mesh size of the branchial sieve and on the evasive abilities of the zooplankters (Janssen, 1976a; Gibson, 1988). Pump filter feeders seem to cause more water disturbance, and therefore allow more evasive zooplankters to escape, than do tow-net filter feeders (Janssen, 1976b).

Fish size and feeding modes
Most cyprinids start to feed a few days after hatching, when they have become 7–8 mm long. Rotifers, nauplii and algae are the main food types (Jelonek,

1986; Mark *et al.*, 1987). In the first weeks the fish rapidly switch to larger organisms (van Densen, 1985). In their first year, on reaching a length of *c.* 5 cm, they can eat all zooplankters, although copepods cannot be taken efficiently by all species, because of their fast escape behaviour. Bream is more efficient in feeding on copepods than roach (Winfield *et al.*, 1983). Most cyprinids can continue feeding on zooplankton until they are *c.* 15 cm long, and they can eat the large daphnids and *Leptodora* throughout life. With increasing fish size the proportions of fish and zooplankton change, in particular when the fish are no longer gape limited (> 5 cm). Then the density and size distribution of the zooplankton and the retention properties of the branchial sieve become important parameters in selection. Within one species the size selection changes in relation to fish size and food species (Lammens *et al.*, 1987). These differences can be explained by the feeding strategy, which is linked to the size of the fish and the mesh sizes of the branchial sieve (Fig. 12.1). A small fish having only a small buccal cavity is unable to process enough water to feed efficiently by means of gulping, pump filter feeding or tow-net filter feeding. For small fishes, particulate feeding is the most efficient feeding mode at natural zooplankton densities. Even at low zooplankton densities these particulate feeders forage intensively, whereas the larger filter-feeding fishes start foraging at much higher densities (Fig. 12.2).

The branchial sieve

In cyprinids the branchial sieve is composed of branchial arches with outer and inner rows of gill rakers. The form and spatial composition is species specific (Zander, 1906). The fifth arch forms the pharyngeal jaw (Sibbing, 1988). Very specialized filters with an epibranchial organ are found in silver carp, *Hypophthalmichthys molitrix* (Chapter 13). Generally the outer rakers of the first arch are longer than those on the other arches. Compared with clupeoids or coregonids, the cyprinids usually have short rakers (Zander, 1906); only *Pelecus cultratus* and *Alburnus alburnus* have comparably long rakers.

The feeding mode is closely related to the structure of this branchial sieve (Magnuson and Heitz, 1971; Matthes, 1963). Gill raker systems of bream, tench, carp, crucian carp, roach, white bream, rudd and ide are compared in Fig. 12.3. The first four fish have the highest preference for cladocerans, which is not surprising in view of the narrow spacings in their gill rakers (Table 12.1). Most studies on the branchial sieve have shown that particles smaller or larger than expected from the inter-raker distances are retained (Seghers, 1975; Kliewer, 1970; Wright *et al.*, 1983). Therefore retention probably is not the simple sieving process suggested by the gaps between gill rakers (Zander, 1906; Matthes, 1963; Lammens, 1984). Hoogenboezem *et al.* (1990), using X-ray cinematography to analyse the interarch distances, showed that sieving by retention between the arches is very unlikely. In the course of one gulping movement, the distance between the arches does not

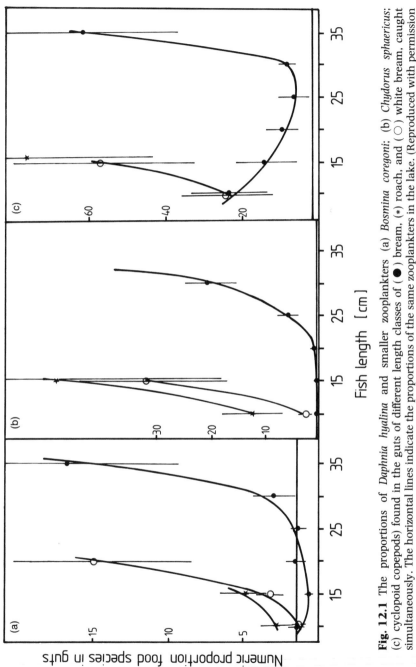

Fig. 12.1 The proportions of *Daphnia hyalina* and smaller zooplankters (a) *Bosmina coregoni*; (c) cyclopoid copepods) found in the guts of different length classes of (●) bream, (*) roach, and (○) white bream, caught simultaneously. The horizontal lines indicate the proportions of the same zooplankters in the lake. (Reproduced with permission from Lammens *et al.*, 1987).

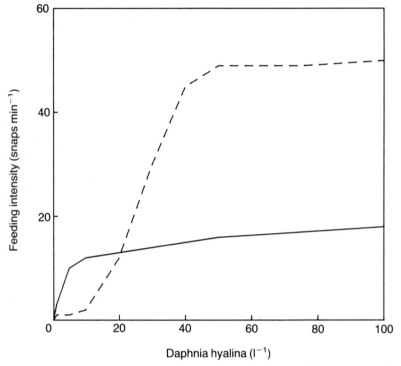

Fig. 12.2 Schematic feeding intensity of small (< 10 cm; solid curve) and large (> 30 cm; broken curve) bream in relation to density of *Daphnia hyalina*.

remain constant, and it is also different for the three successive slits (Fig. 12.4). Thus the mesh width of the branchial sieve is heterogeneous in time and place; a homogeneous filter is necessary for size-selective retention of particles (Boyd, 1976). If the branchial system of bream really acted as a sieve all the particles would disappear between the first and second arch. Apparently the mechanism of retention is not realized between the slits of the gill arches. Therefore another filter mechanism is proposed for bream.

Food particles in the branchial sieve of bream are found in the transverse channels formed between successive rakers of each gill arch. Larger cladocerans are retained in these channels; species considerably smaller than the channel diameter are probably captured by action of the movable gill rakers. Only the rakers of the outer rows are provided with muscles and fit into the transverse channels of the opposing gill arch. By lateral depression these movable rakers reduce the channel diameter when the fish is foraging on small planktonic organisms (Hoogenboezem *et al.*, 1990).

Fig. 12.3 Gill-raker systems of eight cyprinids. (a) Bream; (b) tench; (c) carp; (d) crucian carp; (e) roach; (f) white bream; (g) rudd; (h) ide. The pharyngeal teeth are visible in the lower part of the gill-raker system as modified gill arches.

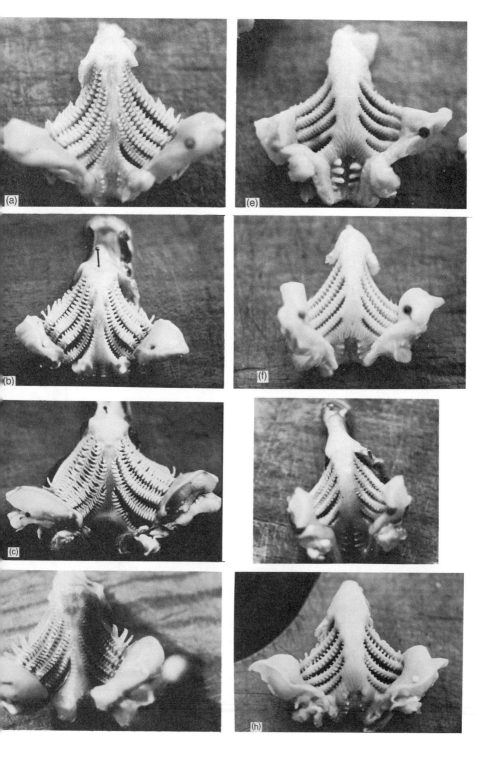

(a)

(b)

(c)

(e)

(f)

(h)

Table 12.1 Diets of the most common European cyprinids*

	Macrophytes	Detritus/ Algae	Molluscs	Macrocrust	Microcrust	Dipteran larvae	Dipteran adults	Fish
Roach *Rutilus rutilus*	**	***	***	*	*	*		*
Rudd. *Scardinius Erythrophthalmus*	***	*	+	*	*		**	
Dace, *Leuciscus leuciscus*	*	**	*	*	**	*	*	
Nase, *Chondrostoma nasus*	***	***	+	*	*	**		
Chub, *Leuciscus cephalus*	**	**	**	*	*	*	**	**
Ide, *Idus idus*	**	***	**	*	*	*	**	**
Sun bleak, *Leucaspius delineatus*					***		**	
Bleak, *Alburnus alburnus*		+			***		***	
Sabre carp, *Pelecus cultratus*				*	***		**	**
Asp, *Aspius aspius*				**	*		**	***
Bream, *Abramis brama*	+	+	+	+	**	***		
White bream, *Blicca bjoerkna*	+	*	**	**	*	***	*	*
Tench, *Tina tinca*	+	*	***	**	**	**		
Crucian carp, *Carassius carassius*	+	*	+	*	***	*		
Gudgeon, *Gobio gobio*		*		**	**			
Barb, *Barbus barbus*	+	*	*		*	***		*
Carp, *Cyprinus carpio*	*	**	**	**	**	***		*

*Frequency of occurrence: +, incidental, *, regular;**, common;**, preferred or very high.

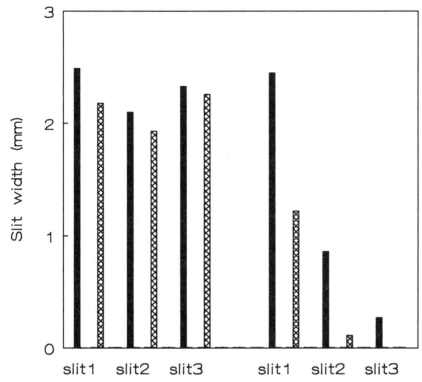

Fig. 12.4 Maximal (black columns) and minimal distances between gill arches of one bream (38.3 cm) during respiration (six columns at left) and feeding on daphnids (*c.* 1 mm) (five columns at right).

12.4 BENTHIC FEEDING BEHAVIOUR

General aspects

One of the most important benthic food resources are the larval chironomids, which can live in the sediment from several weeks to several months (Beattie, 1982; Winkel, 1987; Wilda, 1984; Lundbeck, 1926). Depending on size, species, and the nature of the sediment, these larvae dwell from a few millimetres to several centimetres deep in the sediments (Winkel, 1987). Therefore fish feeding on them require a specialized digging and sieving mechanism to separate them from the sediments (Matthes, 1963; Fryer, 1957; Robotham, 1982; Hyslop, 1982; Lammens *et al.*, 1987). Sibbing *et al.* (1986; see also Chapter 13) suggest that also the palatal organ plays an important role in separating food from non-food particles. All benthivorous fishes mentioned in Table 12.1 probably possess these sorting functions.

Fig. 12.5 Bream feeding on chironomids in sand substratum in a tray. Note the bottom particles, which are sucked in and expelled in clouds behind the opercula.

Cyprinids suck in the sediment particles together with the organisms and separate the organisms in the pharyngeal slit. Sediment particles pass the sieve and are visible as clouds behind the opercula (Fig. 12.5), whereas food organisms are retained. Substratum particles too large to pass the basket are spat out. Key factors determining the efficiency of feeding are the size composition of the sediment particles, the horizontal and vertical distribution of the chironomids, the density and size composition of the chironomids, the fish species and its size.

The influence of sediment characteristics

Bream, white bream and roach show similar responses to particle size of the sediments, although feeding responses are quite different (Fig. 12.6). Feeding efficiency shows an optimum which is different for species and length classes; this optimum is related to the handling time of the sand grains in the mouth cavity. Large sand grains cannot pass the gill rakers and have to be spat out, thus increasing the handling time. Small sand grains are probably eliminated through the small channels in the branchial sieve (p. 358). The size of these channels determines the maximum size of the sediment particles to pass the sieve, a relationship which differs between size classes and species. The very

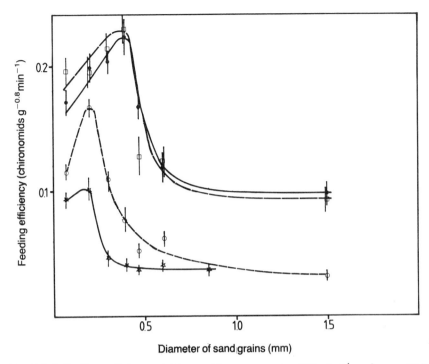

Fig. 12.6 Feeding efficiency (chironomids consumed $g^{-0.8} min^{-1}$, where $g^{-0.8}$ represents metabolic weight, indicating energy demands) in relation to the composition of the sandy substratum. ● Large bream (400–540 g); ○, small bream (50–60 g); □, white bream (160–210 g); ☆, roach (90–140 g) (reproduced with permission from Lammens *et al.*, 1987).

small particles can easily pass the gill rakers, but it probably takes more energy to take a mouthful of this sediment because of its stronger cohesiveness (at least if sediment particles are sand grains). The segregating function of the palatal organ is described in Chapter 13.

Small bream are less efficient than large bream, but also less efficient than white bream of comparable size. Mesh size of the branchial basket in small bream probably obstructs the easy passage of sediment particles. Only when chironomids are too small to be retained by large bream or white bream is the feeding efficiency of small bream higher. Roach has the lowest feeding efficiency, probably due to the poor protrusion of the upper jaw and a poorly developed branchial sieve (Fig. 12.3(e)). Feeding experiments with young roach (Diehl, 1988) also showed its low feeding efficiency compared with bream. The low preference of roach for chironomid larvae in comparison with bream and white bream further corroborates the observed differences in feeding efficiency (Adamek *et al.*, 1985; Lammens *et al.*, 1987).

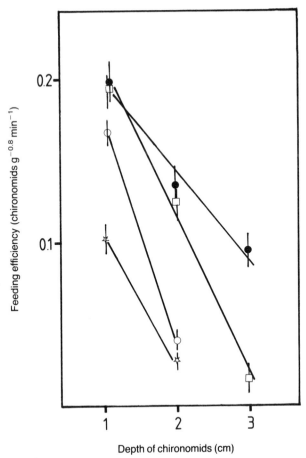

Fig. 12.7 Feeding efficiency (chironomids consumed $g^{-0.8}\,min^{-1}$) in relation to the depth of the chironomids in the substratum. Symbols as in Fig. 12.6. (reproduced with permission from Lammens *et al.*, 1987).

The influence of buried, patchily distributed prey

The capture rates of small and large benthivorous fish in a fine-grained substratum are similar when the chironomids occur less than 1 cm deep; at greater depths the differences increase (Fig. 12.7). Small bream and roach almost give up foraging at 2 cm depth, but white bream at 3 cm depth (see also Brabrand, 1984). Large bream and particularly large carp can 'dig' very deep and reach the largest chironomids (Suietov, 1939). In large bream, suction force and filter mesh size are suitable for feeding most efficiently in the deepest layers. Comparisons of gut contents of white bream, bream and carp feeding on chironomids in the same environment show segregation in chironomid size

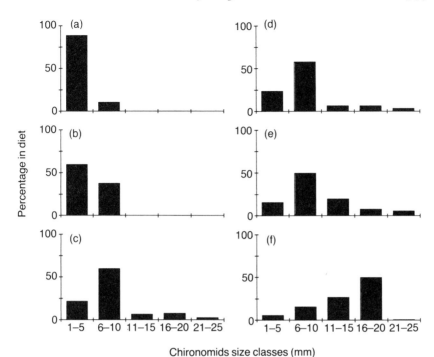

Fig. 12.8 Size composition of chironomids in the guts of different size classes of bream, white bream, and carp. The fishes were caught simultaneously (methods, Lammens, 1984). (a) 10–15 cm bream; (b) 20–25 cm bream; (c) 35–40 cm bream; (d) 10–15 cm white bream; (e) 20–25 cm white bream; (f) 50–60 cm carp.

(Fig. 12.8). Here both the retention and digging capacities are involved in feeding selectivity. Small bream (Fig. 12.8(a)) do not forage deep enough to reach the large chironomids, whereas the large carp (Fig. 12.8(f)) can hardly retain the small chironomids and have to dig deep. Large bream and white bream are intermediate in both respects. Depending on hour and time of the year, the depth of the chironomids may differ and change the feeding conditions for the different size classes and species (Winkel, 1987).

Because the chironomids are not homogeneously distributed, but are clumped vertically and horizontally (Beattie, 1982), random foraging is not efficient for the fish, which must therefore monitor the environment. There are no indications that bream, white bream, or roach can detect the chironomids other than by just taking mouthfuls (Matthes, 1963; Fryer, 1977; Robotham, 1982). Sibbing and Uribe (1985) found very high densities of taste-buds on the pharyngeal sieve and palatal organ in carp. When bream is offered sediments with varying densities of chironomids, it takes mouthfuls even in an empty substratum, and the number of chironomids per mouthful increases linearly with the density in the substratum (Fig. 12.9). So the only way for bream to

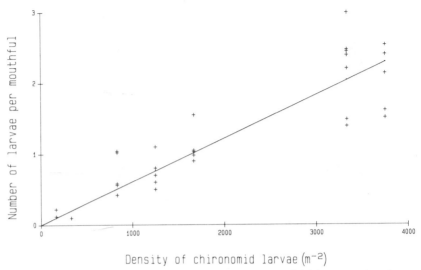

Fig. 12.9 The number of chironomids ingested per mouthful by 30–35 cm bream in relation to the density of chironomids. Each point represents the average of *c.* 25 mouthfuls (methods, Lammens *et al.*, 1987).

monitor the environment is taking 'samples' to know the profitability of the patches. In an unknown heterogeneous environment, bream forages in all places and intensifies foraging in the most rewarding patches: the profitability of a patch is determined by density (Fig. 12.9), substratum (Fig. 12.6), and depth of chironomids (Fig. 12.7). The fish does not, however, stop monitoring the other places. During foraging the profitability changes, and at same point the fish switches to the other patches (Fig. 12.10). In this case, at both high and low chironomid concentrations, three trays with different particle sizes were simultaneously available.

12.5   SWITCHING BETWEEN PELAGIC AND BENTHIC FEEDING

The availability of food organisms is not constant, but related to local, seasonal and diurnal changes. In particular, zooplankton and chironomids show these periodicities (Willer, 1924; Lundbeck, 1926; Beattie, 1982; Winkel, 1987; Beattie *et al.*, 1979; Gliwicz, 1967) and therefore they force the fish to adapt its feeding mode and to switch from one organism to another (Lammens *et al.*, 1985; Townsend *et al.*, 1986; Werner and Hall, 1979) in order to increase foraging profitability (Pyke, 1984). For each species and each ontogenetic stage this switch is related to the specific feeding efficiency for particular organisms. This section will discuss these switches in relation to seasonal, diurnal and local changes in food availability.

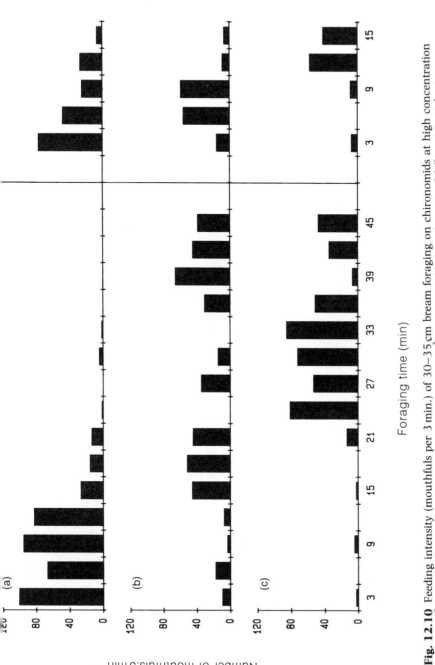

Fig. 12.10 Feeding intensity (mouthfuls per 3 min.) of 30–35 cm bream foraging on chironomids at high concentration (4000 m^{-2}, series at left) and at low concentration (1000 m^{-2}, series at right) in sediments of different particle sizes. (a) Particles 0.2–0.4 mm diameter; (b) 0.6–0.8 mm; (c) 1.7–2.4 mm. For methods see Lammens et al. (1987).

Number of mouthfuls.3 min^{-1}

Foraging time (min)

Switching in feeding mode and habitat

Fishes may shift their diet and feeding modes from day to day when the availability of food changes. The food resources in most natural waters vary continuously and fish have to cope with a variable environment by shifting from pelagic to benthic feeding, from particulate to filter feeding, or by migrating to other habitats.

Among food organisms, zooplankton is one of the most variable components because its availability varies seasonally and it is easily overexploited by a successful recruitment of young-of-the-year fish (Densen and Vijverberg, 1982; Cryer *et al.*, 1986; Lammens *et al.*, 1985). Zooplankton usually reaches a maximum in spring and most fishes profit from this situation to recover from spawning. In particular, fish > 20 cm take advantage of this spring peak because only in this period can they efficiently catch zooplankton by filter feeding (Lammens, 1985). Even for the smaller particulate feeders it is much more profitable to switch to filter feeding in this situation (Crowder, 1985; Gibson and Ezzi, 1985). Hoogenboezem (unpubl.) showed that small bream (*c.* 10 cm fork length) foraged as particulate feeders, positively selecting large (> 1 mm) cladocerans at densities < 100 l^{-1}, but started gulping at very high zooplankton densities (> 500 l^{-1}). Feeding experiments showed that bream of *c.* 20 cm could adjust the selectivity in relation to the availability of prey sizes (Hoogenboezem, unpubl.). When the density of zooplankton > 1 mm was high, the fish selected only them, but if it was relatively low, the fish switched to a wider range of zooplanktons > 0.5 mm length. The ability to do this points to an adjustable branchial sieve with differing energy constraints.

Although the total amount of zooplankton and chironomids hardly changes during 24 h, their availability to fishes does change because of visibility and the behaviour of the prey. In clear water, zooplankton migrate, causing periods of active feeding by bream during dusk and dawn (Kogan, 1970; Schulz and Berg, 1987) or only at night (Bohl, 1980). The fish may respond not only to prey, but to predators as well. The feeding periodicity in turbid lakes is quite different for young fish because as particulate feeders they have enough light only during daytime (Diehl, 1988). Some of them may switch to filter feeding during the night (Holanov and Tash, 1978; Gibson and Ezzi, 1985). In Tjeukemeer, only bream > 20 cm continue feeding on zooplankton at night and show the lowest feeding intensity during the day. Similar bream hardly feed during the night (Lammens, 1983). Similarly, feeding on chironomid larvae is maximal at night, because no light is needed (see also Diehl, 1988) and probably because chironomids are then higher in the sediments in response to changing oxygen tensions.

When the zooplankton density or size distribution drops below some level, only the smaller length classes of fish continue particulate feeding, but larger fishes switch to a more profitable food source. For roach and all the herbivores in Table 12.1, vegetation or molluscs and even detritus will be an alternative.

The benthivores will switch to chironomids, *Tubifex* or benthic cladocerans. With increasing food depletion detritus becomes a very large part of the diet (Chapter 19). Roach seems to utilize detritus relatively well because of its special enzyme system (Prejs, 1977), although it is unknown whether other species can do this. The more specialized pelagic feeders such as bleak and *Pelecus* will only switch from zooplankton in extreme conditions such as in periods when insects pupate and come to the surface.

12.6   CONCLUDING REMARKS AND IMPLICATIONS FOR NON-EUROPEAN CYPRINIDS

European cyprinids show a wide variety of diets and feeding modes and have specialized representatives as zooplanktivores, herbivores, piscivores and benthivores. Most European cyprinids are zooplanktivores from the larval period up to a length of 5–10 cm. Only a few species are specialized as zooplanktivores during a large part of their lives. Some species can live as herbivores, others as benthivores. Several, however, such as roach, white bream, bream and carp can feed in different modes and switch easily between these modes. While the roach is considered one of the most successful generalists, most cyprinids use more than one feeding mode and can feed on both pelagic and benthic prey. The branchio-spinal system is well developed and has an important function in feeding on relatively small organisms, which are filtered from the water or sieved from the substratum. The fifth gill arch, modified into pharyngeal teeth, is crucial in mollusc feeding and herbivory. The feeding mode employed ranges from strict particulate feeding to strict filter feeding, and this gradient in feeding modes is found both in pelagic and in benthic feeders.

From our studies on cyprinids and an extensive literature review, we conclude that the feeding of European cyprinids includes all diets and feeding modes and probably does not differ essentially from cyprinid feeding on the other continents. The feeding modes are not exclusive to cyprinids, as many of them are also found in clupeids (Janssen, 1976a; Holanov and Tash, 1978; Drenner *et al.*, 1982; Gibson and Ezzi, 1985), cichlids (Fryer and Iles, 1972; Galis and de Jong, 1988), and coregonids (Ponton and Gerdeaux, 1988; Svardson, 1979; Bergstrand, 1982). The cyprinids from Asia seem to have the greatest variety in feeding specialists with both small and large species (Grzimek *et al.*, 1970), whereas the cyprinids in North America have the smallest variety apart from South America and Australia, where cyprinids are poorly represented and are mainly small species (Grzimek *et al.*, 1970). Cyprinids in Africa are also relatively small, but more varied in feeding specialists (Matthes, 1963). These are evolutionary aspects and a good comparison between the continents would be very fruitful for a better understanding of the variety of the cyprinids.

ACKNOWLEDGEMENTS

We want to thank Ramesh Gulati, Ferdinand Sibbing, Onno van Tongeren, Koos Vijverberg and an anonymous reviewer for their critical comments on the manuscript.

REFERENCES

Adamek, Z., Jirasek, J., Pravda, D., Sukop, I., Hetesa, J., Provazek, R. and Skrabanek, A. (1985) The food biology and biological value of roach (*Rutilus rutilus* L.) in the Musovska reservoir. *Zivoc. Vyr. (Sb. čsl. Akad. zeměd. Věd.*, Rada **E**), **30**, 901–10.

Adamicka, P. (1984) On the construction of the Pontic cyprinid *Pelecus cultratus* (L.). *Arch. Hydrobiol.*, **101**, 9–19.

Alexander. R. Mc. N. (1966) The functions and mechanisms of the protrusible upper jaws in two species of cyprinid fish. *J. Zool., Lond.*, **149**, 288–96.

Beattie, D. M. (1982) Distribution and larval production of chironomid populations in Tjeukemeer. *Hydrobiologia*, **95**, 287–306.

Beattie, D. M., Golterman, H. L. and Vijverberg, J. (1979) An introduction to the limnology of the Friesian lakes. *Hydrobiologia*, **58**, 49–64.

Bergstrand, E. (1982) The diet of four sympatric whitefish species in Lake Parkijaure. *Rep. Inst. Freshwat. Res. Drottningholm*, **60**, 5–14.

Bohl, E. (1980) Diel pattern of pelagic distribution and feeding in planktivorous fish. *Oecologia*, **44**, 368–75.

Bohl, E. (1982) Food supply and prey selection in planktivorous cyprinidae. *Oecologia*, **53**, 134–8.

Boikova, O. S. (1986) Feeding of fish in Lake Glubokoe. *Hydrobiologia*, **141**, 95–111.

Boyd, C. M. (1976) Selection of particle sizes by filter-feeding copepods: a plea for reason. *Limnol. Oceanogr.*, **21**, 175–80.

Brabrand, A. (1984) Microhabitat segregation between bream (*Abramis brama* (L)) and white beam (*Blicca bjoerkna* (L)) in a mesotrophic lake, SE Norway. *Pol. Arch. Hydrobiol.*, **31**, 99–108.

Brabrand, A. (1985) Food of roach (*Rutilus rutilus*) and ide (*Leuciscus idus*): significance of diet shift for interspecific competition in omnivorous fishes, *Oecologia*, **66**, 461–7.

Cala, P. (1970) On the ecology of the ide *Idus idus* L. in the river Kavlingean, south Sweden. *Rep. Inst. Freshwat. Res. Drottningholm*, **50**, 45–99.

Crivelli, A. J. (1981) The biology of the common carp, *Cyprinus carpio* L. in the Camargue, southern France. *J. Fish Biol.*, **18**, 271–90.

Crowder, L. B. (1985) Optimal foraging and feeding mode shifts in fishes. *Envron. Biol. Fishes*, **12**, 57–62.

Cryer, M., Peirson, G. and Townsend, C. R. (1986) Reciprocal interactions between roach, *Rutilus rutilus*, and zooplankton in a small lake: prey dynamics and fish growth and recruitment. *Limnol. Oceanogr.*, **31**, 1022–38.

Densen, W. L. T. van (1985) Feeding behaviour of major 0+ fish species in a shallow, eutrophic lake (Tjeukemeer, The Netherlands). *Z. angew. Ichtyol.*, **2**, 49–70.

Densen, W. L. T. can and Vijverberg, J. (1982) The relations between 0+ fish density zooplankton size and the vulverability of pikeperch, *Stizostedion lucioperca*, to angling in the Frisian lakes. *Hydrobiologia*, **95**, 321–36.

Diehl, S. (1988) Foraging efficiency of three freshwater fishes: effects of structural complexity and light. *Oikos*, **53**, 207–14.

Drenner, R. W., O'Brien, W. J. and Mummert, J. R. (1982) Filter-feeding rates of gizzard shad. *Trans. Am. Fish. Soc.*, **111**, 210–15.

Drenner, R. W., Strickler, J. R. and O'Brien, W. J. (1978) Capture probability: the role of zooplankter escape in the selective feeding of planktivorous fish. *J. Fish. Res. Bd Can.*, **35**, 1370–73.

Fanget, R. (1972) Contribution à l'écologie des etangs piscicoles de la Dombes: sur le régime alimentaire de la carpe à miroir (*Cyprinus carpio* L.), doctoral thesis, University of Lyon.

Fitzmaurice, P. (1983) Carp (*Cyprinius carpio* L.) in Ireland. *Irish Fish. Invest.*, Ser. A., **23**, 5–10.

Fryer, G. (1957) The tropic interrelationships and ecology of some littoral communities of Lake Nyasa with especial reference to the fishes, and a discussion of the evolution of a group of rock-frequenting cichlidae. *Proc. Zool. Soc. Lond.*, **130**, 11–279.

Fryer, G. and Iles, T. D. (1972) *Cichlid Fishes of the Great Lakes of Africa*, Oliver and Boyd, Edinburgh.

Galis, F. and Jong, P. W. de (1988) Optimal foraging and ontogeny; food selection by *Haplochromis piceatus. Oecologia*, **75**, 175–84.

Gibson, R. N. (1988) Development, morphometry and particle retention capability of the gill rakers in the herring, *Clupea harengus* L. *J. Fish Biol.*, **32**, 949–62.

Gibson, R. N. and Ezzi, I. A. (1985) Effect of particle concentration of filter- and particular-feeding in the herring *Clupea harengus. Mar. Biol.*, **88**, 109–16.

Gliwicz, Z. M. (1967) Zooplankton and temperature–oxygen condition of two alpine lakes of Tatra Mts. *Pol. Arch. Hydrobiol.*, **14**, 53–72.

Grando–Lorencio, C. and Gracia–Novo, F. (1986) Feeding habits of the fish community in a eutrophic reservoir in Spain. *Ekol. pol.*, **34**, 95–110.

Grzimek, B., Ladiges, W., Portman, A. and Thenius, E. (1970) *Grzimek Tierleben, Fische I. Enzyclopodie des Tierreiches*, Kinder Verlag, Zurich.

Hammer, C. (1985) Feeding behaviour of roach (*Rutilus rutilus*) larvae and the fry of perch (*Perca fluviatilis*) in Lake Lankau. *Arch. Hydrobiol.*, **103**, 61–74.

Hartley, P. H. T. (1947) The natural history of some British freshwater fishes. *Proc. zool. Soc. Lond.*, **117**, 129–206.

Hellawell, J. M. (1971) The autecology of the club, *Squalius cephalus* L. of the river Lugg and Afon Llynfi. III. Diet and feeding habits. *Freshwat. Biol.*, **1**, 369–87.

Hellawell, J. M. (1972) The growth, reproduction and food of the roach *Rutilus rutilus* L. of the river Lugg, Herefordshire *J. Fish Biol.*, **4**, 469–86.

Herzig, A. and Winkler, H. (1983) Beiträge zur Biologie des Sichlings, *Pelecus cultratus* L. *Öst. Fisch.*, **36**, 113–28.

Hessen, D. O. (1985) Selective zooplankton predation by pre-adult roach (*Rutilus rutilus*): the size-selective hypothesis versus the visibility-selective hypothesis. *Hydrobiologia*, **124**, 73–9.

Holanov, S. H. and Tash, J. C. (1978) Particulate and filter feeding in threadfin shad, *Dorosoma petenense*, at different light intensities. *J. Fish. Biol.*, **13**, 619–25.

Holopainen, I. J. and Hyvarinen, H. (1985) Ecology and physiology of crucian carp (*Carassius carassius* (L.)) in small Finnish ponds with anoxic conditions in winter. *Verh. Internat. Verein. Limnol.*, **22**, 2566–70.

Hoongenboezem, W., Sibbing, F. A., Osse, J. W. M., Boogaart, J. G. M. van den, Lammens, E. H. R. R. and Terlouw, A. (1990) Measuring gill-arch movements in filter-feeding bream (*Abramis brama*, Cyprinidae). *J. Fish Biol.*, **36**, 47–59.

Hyslop, E. J. (1982) The feeding habits of 0+ stone loach, *Noemacheilus barbatulus* (L.), and bullhead, *Cottus gobio* L. *J. Fish. Biol.*, **21**, 187–96.

Ivlev, V. S. (1961) *Experimental Ecology of the Feeding of Fishes*, Yale Univ. Press, New Haven, 302 pp.

Jacobs, J. (1978) Influence of prey size, light intensity, and alternative prey on the selectivity of plankton feeding fish. *Verh. Internat. Verein. Limnol.*, **20**, 2461–6.

Janssen, J. (1976a) Feeding modes and prey size selection in the alewife (*Alosa pseudoharengus*). *J. Fish. Res. Bd Can.*, **33**, 1972–5.

Janssen, J. (1976b) Selectivity of an artificial filter feeder and suction feeders on calanoid copepods. *Am. Midl. Nat.*, **95**, 491–3.

Janssen, J. (1978) Feeding-behavior repertoire of the alewife, *Alosa pseudoharengus*, and the ciscoes *Coregonus hoyi* and *C. artedii*. *J. Fish. Res. Bd. Can.*, **35** 249–53.

Jelonek, M (1986) Food of juvenile stages of rudd (*Scardinius erythrophtalmus* L.), roach (*Rutilus rutilus* L.), and perch (*Perca fluviatilis* L.) in the heated waters of the Rybnik dam reservoir (Southern Poland). *Acta hydrobiol., Kraków*, **28**, 451–61.

Johansson, L. (1987) Experimental evidence for interactive habitat segregation between roach (*Rutilus rutilus*) and rudd (*Scardinius erythrophthalmus*) in a shallow eutrophic lake. *Oecologia*, **73**, 21–7.

Kennedy, M. and Fitzmaurice, P. (1968) The biology of the bream, *Abramis brama* L. in Irish waters. *Proc. R. Ir. Acad.*, **B**, **67**(5), 95–157.

Kennedy, M and Fitzmaurice, P. (1970) The biology of the tench, *Tinca tinca* L. in Irish waters. *Proc. R. Ir. Acad.*, **B**, **69**(3), 31–82.

Kennedy, M. and Fitzmaurice, P. (1972) Some aspects of the biology of the gudgeon *Gobio gobio* L. in Irish waters. *J. Fish Biol.*, **4**, 425–40.

Kennedy, M. and Fitzmaurice, P. (1974) The biology of the rudd, *Scardinius erythrophthalmus* L. in Irish waters. *Proc. R. Ir. Acad.*, **B**, **74**, 245–305.

Kliewer, E. V. (1970) Gill-raker variation and the diet in lake whitefish *Coregonus clupeaformis* in Northern Manitoba, in *Biology of Coregonid Fishes* (eds C. C. Lindsey and C. S. Woods), Univ. of Manitoba Press, Winnipeg pp. 147–65.

Kogan, A. V. (1970) Age-related and seasonal changes in the daily feeding rhythm of the Tsimlyansk Reservoir bream. *J. Ichthyol.*, **10**, 557–61.

Lammens, E. H. R. R. (1983) *Progress report 1981*. Limnological Institute of the Royal Netherlands Academy of Arts and Sciences, pp. 58–9.

Lammens, E. H. R. R. (1984) A comparison between the feeding of white bream (*Blicca bjoerkna*) and bream (*Abramis brama*). *Verh. Internat. Verein. Limnol.*, **22**, 886–90.

Lammens, E. H. R. R. (1985) A test of a model for planktivorous filter feeding by bream *Abramis brama*. *Environ. Biol. Fishes*, **13**, 288–96.

Lammens, E. H. R. R., Geursen, J. and MacGillavry, P. J. (1987) Diet shifts, feeding efficiency and coexistence of bream *Abramis brama*, roach *Rutilus rutilus* and white bream *Blicca boerkna* in hypertrophic lakes. *Prov. V. Cong. Eur. Ichthyol.*, 153–62.

Lammens, E. H. R. R., Nie, H. W. de, Vijverberg, J. and Densen, W. L. T. van (1985) Resource partitioning and niche shifts of bream (*Abramis brama*) and eel (*Anguilla anguilla*) mediated by predation of smelt (*Osmerus eperlanus*) on *Daphnia hyalina*. *Can. J. Fish. aquat. Sci.*, **42**, 1342–51.

Laskar, K. (1948) Ernahrung des Brassens in eutrophen Seen. *Arch. Hydrobiol.*, **42**, 1–165.

Lazzaro, X. (1987) A review of planktivorous fishes: their evolution, feeding behaviours, selectivities, and impacts. *Hydrobiologia*, **146**, 97–167.

Loffler, H. (1984) Zur Okologie des Brachsen (*Abramis brama* (L.)) im Bodensee. *Schweiz. Z. Hydrol.*, **46**, 147–62.

Lundbeck, J. (1926) Die Bodentierwelt norddeutscher Seen. *Arch. Hydrobiol.*, Suppl. **7**, 1–473.

McComas, S. R. and Drenner, R. W. (1982) Species replacement in a reservoir fish community: silverside feeding mechanics and competition. *Can. J. Fish. aquat. Sci.*, **39**, 815–21.

Magnuson, J. J. and Heitz, J. G. (1971) Gill raker apparatus and food selectivity among mackerels, tunas, and dolphins. *Fish. Bull. Nat. Mar. Fish. Serv.*, **69**, 361–70.

Mann, R. H. K. (1973) Observations on the age, growth, reproduction and food of the roach *Rutilus rutilus* L. in two rivers in Southern England. *J. Fish Biol.*, **5**, 707–36.

Mann, R. H. K. (1974) Observations on the age, growth, reproduction and food of the dace *Leuciscus leuciscus* L. in two rivers in Southern England. *J. Fish Biol.*, **6**, 237–53.

Mark, W., Hofer, R. and Wieser, W. (1987) Diet spectra and resource partitioning in the larvae and juveniles of three species and six cohorts of cyprinids from a subalpine lake. *Oecologia*, **71**, 388–96.

Matthes, H. (1963) A comparative study of the feeding mechanism of some African Cyprinidae (Pisces, Cypriniformes). *Bijdr. Dierk.*, **33**, 1–35.

Moyle, P. B. (1984) America's carp. *Nat. Hist. N.Y.*, **84**(9), 43–50.

Osse, J. W. M. (1985) Jaw protrusion, an optimization of the feeding apparatus of teleosts?. *Acta Biotheor.*, **34**, 219–32.

Persson, L (1983) Food consumption and the significance of detritus and algae to intraspecific competition in roach *Rutilus rutilus* in a shallow eutrophic lake. *Oikos*, **41**, 118–25.

Ponton, D. and Gerdeaux, D. (1988) Quelques aspects de l'alimentation de deux poissons planctonophages du lac leman: le corégone (*Coregonus schinzii palea* Cuv. et Val.) et le gardon (*Rutilus rutilus* (L.)) *Bull. fr. pêche Piscic.*, **308**, 11–23.

Prejs, A. (1973) Feeding of introduced and aurochthonous non-predatory fish, in *Experimentally Increased Fish Stock in the Pond Type Lake Warniak* (ed. E. Pieczinski) *Ekol. pol.*, **21**, 464–505.

Prejs, A. (1976) Fishes and their feeding habits, in *Selected Problems in Lake Littoral Ecology* (ed. E. Pieczinski), Warsaw Univ. Press, Warsaw, pp. 155–71.

Prejs, A. (1977) Relationships between food and cellulase activity in freshwater fishes. *J. Fish Biol.*, **11**, 447–52.

Prejs, A. and Jackowska, H. (1978) Lake macrophytes as the food for roach (*Rutilus rutilus*) and rudd (*Scardinius erythrophthalmus*) I. Species composition and dominance relations in the lake and food. *Ekol. pol.*, **26**, 429–38.

Pyke, G. H. (1984) Optimal foraging theory: a critical review. *A. Rev. Ecol. Syst.*, **15**, 523–75.

Rask, M. (1989) The diet of roach and some other cyprinids in the northern Baltic sea. *Aqua Fenn.*, **19**, 19–27.

Robotham, P. W. J. (1982) An analysis of a specialized feeding mechanism of the spined loach, *Cobitis taenia* (L.), and a description of the related structures. *J. Fish. Biol.*, **20**, 173–81.

Rosen, R. A. and Hales, D. C. (1981) Feeding of paddlefish, *Polyodon spathula. Copeia*, **2** 441–55.

Schulz, U. and Berg, R. (1987) The migration of ultrasonic-tagged bream, *Abramis brama* (L), in Lake Constance (Bodensee-Untersee). *J. Fish Biol.*, **31**, 409–14.

Seghers, B. H. (1975) Role of gill-rakers in the size-selective predation by lake whitefish, *Coregonus clupeaformis* (Mitchill). *Verh. Internat. Verein. Limnol.*, **19**, 2401–5.

Sibbing, F. A. (1988) Specializations and limitations in the utilization of food resources by the carp, *Cyprinus carpio*: a study of oral food processing. *Environ. Biol. Fishes*, **22**, 161–78.

Sibbing, F. A. and Uribe, R. (1985) Regional specializations in the oro-pharyngeal wall and food processing in the carp (*Cyprinus carpio* L.). *Neth. J. Zool.*, **35**, 377–422.

Sibbing, F. A., Osse, J. W. M. and Terlouw, A. (1986) Food handling in the carp (*Cyprinus carpio*): its movement patterns, mechanisms and limitations. *J. Zool., Lond.*, **210** 161–203.

Suietov, S. V. (1939) A contribution to the knowledge of fish productivity in water bodies. Communication 8. The role of silt mass in the use of natural food by fish. (In Russian). *Trudy̆ limnol. Sta. Kosine*, **22**, 241–9.

Svardson, G. (1979) Speciation of Scandinavian *Coregonus*. *Rep. Inst. Freshwat. Res.*, *Drottningholm*, **57**, 1–95.

Tatrai, I. (1980) About feeding conditions of bream, (*Abramis brama* L.) in Lake Balaton. *Hydrobiologia*, **3**, 81–6.

Townsend, C. R., Winfield, I. J., Peirson, G. and Cryer, M. (1986) The response of young roach *Rutilus rutilus* to seasonal changes in abundance of microcrustacean prey: a field demonstration of switching. *Oikos*, **46**, 372–8.

Uribe-Zamora, M. (1975) Selection des proies par le filtre branchial de la carp miroir, *Cyprinus carpio* L., thesis, Lyon (127 pp.)

Vockner, F. H. W. and Schiemer, F. (1990) Spatial distribution and feeding ecology of bleak (*Alburnus alburnus* L.) and roach (*Rutilus rutilus* L.) in an eutrophic lake (Wallersee, Austria). *Holarctic Ecol.* (in press).

Vollestad, L. A. (1985) Resource partitioning of roach *Rutilus rutilus* and bleak *Alburnus alburnus* in two eutrophic lakes in SE Norway. *Holarctic Ecol.* **8**, 88–92.

Wanzenbock, J. (1989) Prey detection in cyprinids during early development. *Can. J. Fish. aquat. Sci.*, **46**, 995–1001.

Werner, E. E. and Hall, D. J. (1974) Optimal foraging and the size selection of prey by the bluegill sunfish (*Lepomis macrochirus*). *Ecology*, **55**, 1042–52.

Werner, E. E. and Hall, D. J. (1979) Foraging efficiency and habitat switching in competing sunfishes. *Ecology*, **60**, 256–64.

Wilda, T. J. (1984) The production of genera of chironomidae (Diptera) in lake Norman, a North Carolina reservoir. *Hydrobiologia*, **108**, 145–52.

Willer, A. (1924) *Die Nahrungstiere der Fische*. Handbuch der Binnenfischerei Mitteleuropas I, Schweizerbart'sche, Stuttgart, 1–145.

Winfield, I. J., Peirson, G., Cryer, M. and Townsend, C. R. (1983) The behavioural basis of prey selection by underyearling bream (*Abramis brama* (L.)) and roach (*Rutilus rutilus* (L.)). *Freshwat. Biol.* **13**, 139–49.

Winkel, E. H. ten (1987) Chironomid larvae and their foodweb relations in the littoral zone of lake Maarseveen, PhD thesis, University of Amsterdam. (145 pp.)

Wright, D. I. and O'Brien, W. J. (1984) The development and field test of a tactical model of the planktivorous feeding of white crappie (*Pomoxis annularis*). *Ecol. Monogr.* **54**, 65–98.

Wright, D. I., O'Brien, W. J. and Luecke, C. (1983) A new estimate of zooplankton retention by gill rakers and its ecological significance. *Trans. Am. Fish. Soc.*, **112**, 638–46.

Zander, E. (1906) Das Kiemenfilter der Teleosta. Eine morphophysiologische Studie. *Z. wiss. Zool.*, **84**, 619–713.

Zaret, T. M. (1980) *Predation and Freshwater Communities*, Yale Univ. Press, New Haven, 187 pp.

Zaret, T. M. and Kerfoot, W. C. (1975) Fish predation on *Bosmina longirostris*, body-size selection versus visibility selection. *Ecology*, **56**, 232–7.

Chapter thirteen

Food capture and oral processing

F. A. Sibbing

13.1 INTRODUCTION

The diversity of food resources available to fish is larger than for any other group of vertebrates (Nikolsky, 1963). Its wide variety in size, shape, location, movement, physical and chemical properties leads one to expect specializations in architecture, functioning and food-handling behaviour of fish species in order to optimize feeding on specific food types while unavoidably limiting the use of others. Fish–food interactions largely depend how efficient each fish is at foraging on particular food items; efficiency is ultimately determined by the food's abundance, size, escape ability and other characteristics (Chapter 12), as well as by the feeding apparatus, how it functions and its versatility.

Holling (1966) divided predation into search, detection, pursuit, capture, retention and digestion. In cyprinids, food handling involves an additional series of internal feeding actions (Sibbing *et al.*, 1986) as part of a more generalized feeding sequence: (1) search, (2) detection, (3) pursuit, (4) intake, (5) taste selection, (6) size selection, (7) transport, (8) mastication, (9) deglutition (swallowing) and (10) digestion. Depending on the type of food, some of these actions may dominate whereas others may play a minor role. For example, in obligate planktivorous fish, search, detection and pursuit are of less importance, whereas these are major components in predatory feeding. In bottom-feeding cyprinids, selecting between food and non-food particles is crucial. This chapter focuses on food intake and internal processing in cyprinids; search, detection and pursuit are mentioned only occasionally.

Feeding success and growth are determined by differing efficiencies of foraging on particular items, rather than by major differences in physiological conversion (Paloheimo and Dickie, 1966). Feeding efficiency is usually taken as the ratio between energy gain and cost per unit of time (Werner and Hall, 1974), and should be conceived of as the product of the efficiencies for each separate part of the feeding process (Hoogenboezem *et al.*, 1990). Energetic costs of feeding are particularly hard to quantify and in practice energy gain merely refers to caloric values of food (Cummins and Wuycheck, 1971). Drost and van den Boogaart (1986) calculated that the energetic costs of particulate intake in 6 mm carp larvae (search not included) are less than 1% of the prey's energy content if prey size approximates to the maximal size that these larvae can handle. On the contrary, it is well known that many herbivorous fish spend much energy and time in feeding, but excrete most of the cellulose-encapsulated cell contents undigested in their faeces (Prowse, 1964). Handling times are usually appropriate for comparing overall feeding efficiencies (Werner, 1974; Paszkowski *et al.*, 1989).

The questions considered in the following sections are:

1. Which mechanisms are involved in intake and internal processing of food by cyprinid fish?
2. Which structures are critical and what is their adaptive value in feeding?
3. Do cyprinid fish adjust their feeding mechanisms to particular food types?
4. What structural and functional features characterize cyprinid feeding compared to other teleosts?
5. What are the consequences of the integrated complex of structural, functional and behavioural chatacters for the differential utilization of aquatic food resources by cyprinids?
6. What are the keys to the success of this largest family of freshwater teleosts?

A vast number of merely descriptive papers show the diversity of cyprinid feeding structures. The most complete studies, integrating structure and function, are those of Curry (1939), Al-Hussaini (1949), Girgis (1952), Matthes (1963) and Veragina (1969). Experimental work on cyprinid feeding mechanisms is extremely rare (Alexander 1969, 1970; Sibbing, 1982, 1988; Sibbing *et al.*, 1986; Hoogenboezem *et al.*, 1990, 1991), mostly owing to taking feeding structures for granted (Werner and Mittelbach, 1981: 814) and to the difficulty of making such observations and measurements within living fish. The development of X-ray and high-speed cinematography, electromyography and electronic transducers allowed substantial progress in this field, and is the reason why much of the experimental work used for this chapter originates from our Wageningen laboratory.

13.2   GENERAL PLAN OF THE CYPRINID FEEDING APPARATUS

Different parts of the headgut (Fig. 13.1) perform their own particular movements during feeding (Sibbing *et al.*, 1986). This even requires a distinction between oral and buccal cavity. Transport of water and food items in teleosts generally proceeds by suction, achieved by an accurate timing of changes in volume in the oral, buccal, pharyngeal and opercular cavities and

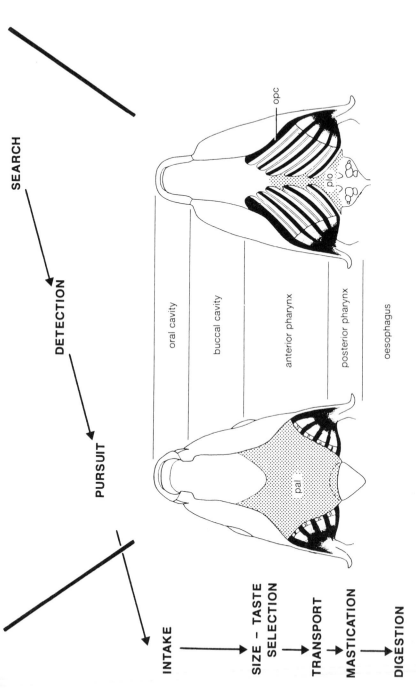

Fig. 13.1 Nomenclature of the cyprinid headgut. The particular role of each area in feeding is indicated. Stippling, palatal organ (pal) in the roof of the mouth, and postlingual organ (plo) in the floor, between the gill arches; black, opercular cavity (opc.) The narrow posteriar pharynx serves as the chewing cavity, with a chewing pad in its roof and pharyngeal teeth in its floor (after Sibbing et al., 1986).

by adjusting the opening of the oral and opercular valves (Lauder, 1980; Muller *et al.*, 1982). Such movements serve respiration (Ballintijn, 1969; Vandewalle, 1979) or feeding (Alexander, 1969; Sibbing *et al.*, 1986). The walls of these cavities are supported by the visceral skeleton (Fig. 13.2), composed of seven paired arches (Harrington, 1955). Its elements articulate in a complicated way, forming mechanical couplings (cf. Ballintijn, 1969, for carp) which permit a wide range of movements: merely in feeding, Sibbing *et al.* (1986) distinguished ten distinct movement patterns (Fig. 13.10). Numerous head muscles and ligaments interconnect parts of the visceral skeleton, making it a highly flexible basket-like structure, or attach them to the skull and pectoral girdle (Takahasi, 1925; Matthes, 1963; Ballintijn, 1969; Sibbing, 1982). A detailed account on the bony elements of the cyprinid skull is given by Ramaswami (1955).

The unique character set shared by cyprinids and catastomids includes (Roberts, 1973): (1) a protrusile mouth, specialized as in advanced teleosts (Acanthopterygii), (2) toothless jaws, (3) toothless palatine, (4) enlarged fifth ceratobranchials (the pharyngeal jaws), (5) no upper branchial elements opposing the pharyngeal jaws, (6) basioccipital skull processes (supporting the chewing pad) uniting below the dorsal aorta, and (7) exceptionally deep subtemporal fossae (accommodating the levator muscles of the pharyngeal jaws). In addition, (8) cyprinids have palatal and postlingual organs, whereas (9) a stomach is lacking. These features highly influence food capture and processing (Section 13.9).

13.3   FOOD CAPTURE

Mechanisms and applications

Four major mechanisms serve food intake: (1) **fast suction**, employed by predaceous fish capturing large and evasive prey, (2) **slow suction**, used by the majority of fish feeding on smaller food items, (3) **overswimming** as seen in obligate planktivorous fish, (4) **biting** and **scraping** (Table 13.1). Intermediate modes of food capture, however, may well be found. The main energetic costs for food capture are (1) accelerating the water containing the food, or (2) accelerating the foraging fish, (3) adding impulse to the water in front of the fish by suction, and (4) adding impulse to the fish and the water at the back of its body by swimming. The relative contributions of these mechanisms to food capture vary among teleosts, and therefore so do the energetic costs.

Fast suction
The key to capturing large evasive prey is a high acceleration towards the oral gape. The large volume sucked decreases their escape abilities, but also increases the energetic costs considerably. In predaceous teleosts, high accelerations of large water volumes are achieved by a combination of (1)

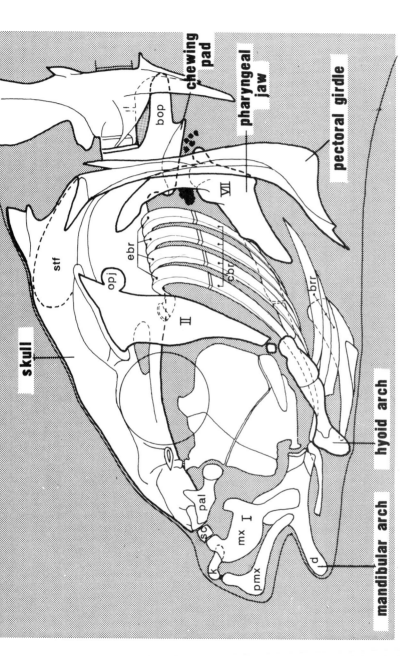

Fig. 13.2 Head skeleton of carp (gill covers and circumorbitalia removed). Only left-side elements are depicted. Seven arches compose the visceral skeleton: (1) mandibular arch (I) bearing the toothless jaws. (2) hyoid arch (II) playing a central role in suction. (3–6) gill arches, and (7) the pharyngeal jaw (VII) derived from the last gill arch (after Sibbing, 1982). Abbreviations: bop. basioccipital process: brr, branchiostegal rays; cbr, ceratobranchials: d. dentary; ebr. epibranchials; k, kinethmoid; mx, maxillary; opj, opercular joint; pal, palatine; pmx, premaxillary; sc, submaxillary cartilage; stf, subtemporal fossa. Black objects under chewing pad represent food particles.

Table 13.1 Methods of food intake, their effects on water and food, and appropriate food types. Biting and scraping are omitted

	Fast suction			Slow suction		Overswimming
	Volume sucking	Velocity sucking	Particulate feeding	Gulping	Pump filter feeding	
Size selection	Visually Single item	Visually Single item	Visually Single particle	Branchial sieve Patches of particles	Branchial sieve Many particles	Branchial sieve Many particles
Movement pattern	Huge and fast expansion + show swimming	Moderate expansion + fast swimming	Moderate expansion + swimming in darting	Small expansion	Slow rhythmic-moderate expansions + slow swimming	Prolonged swimming with open mouth
Frequency	Single event	Single event	Single event	Up to 3 per second	1–2 per second	1 per minute
Volume taken	Large	Large	Moderate	Small	Large	Large
–Acceleration	High	High	Moderate	Low	Low	Minimal
–Impulse water in front of fish (suction)	Large	Moderate	Moderate	Small	Moderate	–
–Impulse body and water behind the fish (swimming)	Small	Large	Small or zero	–	Small or zero	Moderate

Directed capture	Highly	Highly	Highly	Little	–	–
Food type	Large, evasive (predators)	Large, evasive (predators)	Moderate size, evasive (facultative feeders)	Small, non-evasive (Facultative filter feeders)	Small, non-evasive (filter feeders)	Small, evasive (filter feeders)
Foraging area	Benthic–littoral	Open water	Benthic–littoral–open water	Benthic–littoral–open water	Benthic–littoral–open water	Open water
Cyprinid examples	?	*Aspius, Barilius*	*Cyprinus carpio, Abramis brama Blicca bjoerkna, Rutilus rutilus* and most other slowly sucking cyprinids		*Hypophthalmichthys molitrix H. nobilis*	?

dynamic suction, by rapidly expanding voluminous orobuccal, pharyngeal and opercular cavities, and (2) **forward motion**, by suction, protrusion of the upper jaw, or swimming (Muller and Osse, 1984). A proper balance between swimming, and suction with closed opercular valves is required to avoid pushing the prey away (Muller and Osse, 1984; van Leeuwen, 1984). **Volume suckers**, e.g. the flounder *Platichthys flesus*, use only slow swimming but accelerate their prey from confined areas by strong and fast expansion of the head while keeping the opercular valves closed. A large impulse is added to the water. Flounder creates prey velocities of $0.7\,\mathrm{ms}^{-1}$ within $0.035\,\mathrm{s}$ (van Leeuwen and Muller, 1984), **Velocity suckers**, e.g. *Salmo*, are open-water forms which accelerate by fast swimming and open their opercular valves early to pass the engulfed water through the opercular slits. The water in front of the fish meanwhile gains moderate impulse by suction. Prey velocities of $1.9\,\mathrm{m\,s}^{-1}$ with respect to the oral gape are reached within $0.057\,\mathrm{s}$. Piscivorous cyprinid fish (e.g. *Aspius aspius, Ptychocheilus, Barilius, Opsariichthys* and *Elopichtys*) probably employ such fast suction. Experimental data on their prey-capture techniques are still lacking.

Slow suction
Slow suction is characterized by moderate to low accelerations of the food, smaller impulse added to the water, and low swimming velocities, so its energetic costs are lower than for fast suction. Slow suction most effectively serves intake of smaller, less evasive food items and is common among cyprinids. At least three types of food capture by slow suction occur (cf. Janssen 1976, 1978): (1) particulate feeding, (2) gulping and (3) pump filter feeding (Table 13.1). They differ in mode of size selection (visually v. branchial sieve), number of particles taken and general movement pattern. By comparing the movement patterns in detail, their widely different effects on water and food, and the estimated energetic costs, it can be argued that these parameters in particular are key factors in switching feeding modes (Chapter 12) when foraging on a particular type of food from a particular area.

Detailed analyses of food capture in *Cyprinus carpio* (Sibbing *et al.*, 1986) show that during **particulate feeding**, carp protrude the upper jaw, rendering the oral cavity tube-like and aiming their circular gape towards the particle (Fig. 13.3(a)). By fully expanding the head, the fish sucks the particle with velocities up to $0.6\,\mathrm{m\,s}^{-1}$ within about $0.1\,\mathrm{s}$ onto its pharyngeal slit (Fig. 13.6, Frame 18). Prey acceleration and the impulse added to the water are moderate compared to fast suction. Heavy, sticky and less accessible particles (e.g. in the substratum, crevices or macrophytes) can be sucked from distances of up to one head length of the fish. Except in darting towards the prey (Chapter 12), swimming plays a minor role.

During **gulping** (Fig. 13.3(b)), carp give only little acceleration and impulse to water and prey, owing to the small expansion of the orobuccal cavity and the early opening of the opercular valves. Particles do not reach the

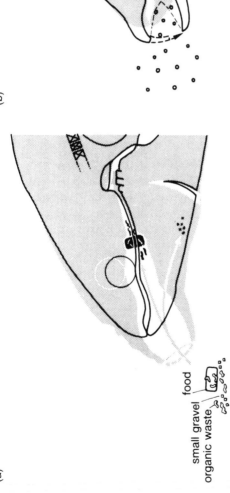

(a)

(b)

Fig. 13.3 (a) Particulate intake. Full compression (outlined image) is followed by overall expansion of the head and protrusion (stippled image), causing a highly directed flow at moderate acceleration. Food and light organic waste are trapped in the narrow pharyngeal slit, whereas dense particles sink into the branchial slit. Finally the mouth is closed by the lower jaw (broken arrow). (b) Gulping proceeds mainly by oral depression (outlined image), producing less-directed suction (even through the open jaw angles, broken outline) of a small volume at low acceleration. Because of the small impulse, water and particles do not reach the pharyngeal cavity. They are secondarily enclosed by protrusion of the upper jaw (arrow). Oral compression (stippled image) pumps particles through the pharyngeal slit onto the branchial sieve (reproduced with permission from Sibbing *et al.*, 1986).

pharyngeal cavity. As protrusion and forward swimming are absent, water and food are slowly sucked from a wider area, even through the open jaw angles. Late protrusion encloses the maximal volume of water and particles prior to oral compression, which would otherwise expel them again. Gulping proceeds at higher frequency than particulate intake and is effective in less selective grazing on patches of buoyant particles making negligible escape movements. It is more efficient in continuous foraging on suspensions since the water is little accelerated. Because of the higher energetic costs for particulate intake, gulping seems to be the best solution for efficient filter feeding, given the particulate feeding apparatus of carp (Sibbing *et al.*, 1986, Sibbing, 1988). Particulate intake and gulping are probably employed by most generalists among cyprinids (also observed in bream, *Abramis brama*). Contrary to Lazzaro (1987), these are evidently separate modes of food capture.

Pump filter feeding resembles intensive ventilation and transports large volumes of suspension with small acceleration but moderate impulse (pers. obs. on the phytoplanktivorous silver carp, *Hypophthalmichthys molitrix*, and the zooplanktivorous bighead, *H. nobilis*). Its frequency in these cyprinids is low, about $1.2\,\mathrm{s}^{-1}$, while swimming slowly or remaining stationary. Many prey items are taken up simultaneously; the capture is non-visual, non-directed and non-size selective (review, Lazzaro, 1987).

Overswimming

Overswimmers (tow-net filter feeders *sensu* Lazzaro, 1987) merely move around with the mouth fully agape without rhythmic expansion of the head. No impulse is added to the water in front of the fish, and prey accelerations are very small or zero. Well-known examples are planktivorous fish like the adult paddlefish, *Polyodon spathula*, the herring, *Clupea harengus*, and the menhaden, *Brevoortia tyrannus*. No overswimmers are reported among cyprinids; perhaps this lack is related to the fluctuating abundance of plankton in temperate fresh waters.

Biting and scraping

Suction or swimming generally play a minor role in initial food capture by biting and scraping. The jaws are variously manipulated to take the food. The cyprinids' lack of oral teeth may be advantageous in bottom feeding (Section 13.9) but evidently limit their abilities (1) for grasping and holding large elusive prey (this might be one reason why few piscivores are found among cyprinids) and (2) for biting pieces from attached or simply too-large food. Even the grass carp, *Ctenopharyngodon idella*, which is specialized to feed on aquatic and littoral weeds (Hickling, 1966; Cross, 1969), is hardly able to take large tough species (e.g. *Carex pseudocyperus* and *Potamogeton lucens*). They tear pieces from vascular plants by gripping them between their cornified oral jaws and pharyngeal teeth and by violently moving the body laterally (Cross, 1969), shaking their heads much as predaceous mammals do.

Chondrostoma nasus, Garra and *Varicorhinus* scrape algae from rocks with their horny-edged, shovel-shaped lower jaw (Verigina, 1969; Matthes, 1963). Owing to the lack of oral teeth, parasites feeding on scales, fins and other body parts of fish (cichlids, Barel, 1983) are not expected among cyprinids. Specializations for biting and scraping involve a wide spectrum of structural (jaws, lips) and behavioural adaptations in response to the specific size, shape, position and texture of the particular food type (oral specializations in *Labeo*, Matthes, 1963).

Adaptive trends in oral jaws

Gape size

Prey size cannot be predicted from maximal gape size. Adult fish often feed on prey considerably smaller than their maximal gape, avoiding extreme handling times. Werner (1974) demonstrated that bluegills, *Lepomis macrochirus*, feed most efficiently (handling time/unit return) on prey $0.59 \times$ their maximal gape, regardless of fish size. Burko (1975) made similar observations on three spine sticklebacks, *Gasterosteus aculeatus*, and stated that prey larger than $0.8 \times$ the maximum gape increased handling times from less than 1 min. to as long as 6–7 min. In carp the diameter of the chewing cavity (4% SL) limits the utilization of hard items, even though they easily pass the oral gape (7% SL in large fish; Sibbing, 1988). Also microphagous fish do not necessarily have small gapes. In the phytoplanktivorous silver carp, *Hypophthalmichthys molitrix*, and the zooplanktivorous bighead, *H. nobilis*, large gapes increase the volume of suspension that can be ingested during pump filter feeding, and the same applies to overswimming filter feeders.

In young and small fish the gape limits the maximal prey size during foraging ('gape-limited predators', Zaret, 1980). Compared to body length, gape in young fish is still relatively large (in 10 cm carp about 9% SL). Their absolute gape generally increases rapidly during growth, but in negative allometry, and appears not to remain a limiting factor.

The position of the mouth may range from upwardly directed in surface feeders, e.g. bleak, *Alburnus alburnus*, and *Pelecus cultratus*, to downwardly directed in bottom feeders, e.g. bream, *Abramis brama*, gudgeon, *Gobio gobio*, and barb, *Barbus barbus*. Species have thus specialized on prey from particular locations, and thereby reduce their abilities to feed in other areas.

Protrusion

Protrusion is the forward shift to the anterior part of the upper jaw (premaxilla) resulting from the movement of its posterior part (maxilla), which is excluded from the oral gape (Fig. 13.2). Protrusion is of general occurrence in advanced teleosts (e.g. percomorph fishes), but among the lower teleosts it has uniquely and independently evolved in cyprinids (Gosline, 1971; Motta, 1984).

The protrusion mechanism in cyprinids was first explained by Alexander

(1966) recording jaw movements in orfe, *Idus idus*, and gudgeon by multi-flash photography. The small kinethmoid or rostral bone (Fig. 13.2) plays a central role by transmitting the ventrad pull on the maxillary bone by complex ligaments to the premaxillae, thereby pushing it forward (Alexander, 1966; Ballintijn *et al.*, 1972). During this movement the lower tips of the upper jaw slide forward and produce the rounded suction tube characteristic of e.g. carp and bream. Protrusion is effected by a complex set of adductor mandibulae muscles. Different timings of their contraction can modify protrusion is amplitude and direction (carp, Ballintijn *et al.*, 1972). Sibbing *et al.* (1986) showed four different applications of protrusion in carp.

Among the functions of upper-jaw protrusion discussed by Motta (1984), van Leeuwen and Muller (1984), Sibbing *et al.* (1986), Osse (1985) and Lazzaro (1987), the following have adaptive value in cyprinid feeding: (1) moving only the mouth suddenly towards elusive prey, thus increasing the velocity of attack at low energetic costs, reducing the volume of water to be sucked; (2) forming an oral tube directing suction to a small area; the higher local accelerations enable particulate-feeding fish to take dense (e.g. seeds), sticky (e.g. molluscs), buried (e.g. chironomid larvae), or more distant prey and allows foraging in otherwise inaccessible or confined locations (e.g. from crevices); (3) enclosing water and food prior to buccal compression in gulping; (4) increasing the versatility in food capture of predators by adjusting the amount and direction of protrusion to changing prey position; (5) closed protrusion (p. 391; Fig. 13.4(d) and (e)) expands the orobuccal cavity, thus resuspending particles during purification of food in bottom feeders; (6) closed protrusion washes particles back from the branchial sieve for repositioning and recollection (p. 395); (7) protrusion often closes the expanding oral cavity during mastication to prevent escape of particles; and (8) ventrad protrusion allows bottom-feeding fish to maintain a horizontal position, facilitating more rapid escape from predators and reducing the energy needed for keeping their position in fast-flowing streams. Cyprinids probably employ protrusion in many other ways, e.g. for scraping algae off rocks (*Labeo cylindricus*, Fryer, 1959), moving the protruded premaxillae posteriorly. It is hypothesized that development of upper jaw protrusion in cyprinids especially enhanced their ability to feed on small benthic or subbenthic food resources, even when these are mixed with organic debris, and to feed between littoral vegetation. Carp penetrate up to 12 cm into a slity bottom (Suietov, 1939).

Grasping large prey imposes different demands on both upper and lower jaws, such as transmitting and resisting high forces. Such jaw constructions need a firm abutment and generally lack the flexibility characteristic of protrusile jaws or show no protrusibility at all. Large-mouthed cyprinids such as the piscivorous *Aspius aspius*, *Elopichthys* and *Ptychocheilus* and the macrophytophagous grass carp, *Ctenopharyngodon idella*, show little protrusion. In these fishes the lower jaw system plays a more prominent role, powered by large adductor mandibulae muscles. Protrusion is also absent in pump filter feeders (*Hypophthalmichthys molitrix* and *H. nobilis*); it would limit the gape, through which large volumes of water must be passed, and aiming plays no role in feeding.

13.4   INTERNAL SELECTION OF FOOD

Food selection is a feature basic to trophic radiation in fish. Usually selection occurs externally during search and capture (Chapter 12). Many planktivorous and most bottom-feeding cyprinids, however, heavily rely on internal mechanisms for selection on palatability and size. How is internal selection achieved and which are the determining factors?

Although selection on taste and size both proceed in the same pharyngeal area (Sibbing *et al.*, 1986; Sibbing, 1988) their mechanisms are very different and should be discussed separately, even though they may well be involved concurrently during benthic feeding (Chapter 12).

Taste selection

Following intake, particles are caught in the horizontal slit (Figs. 13.4(a), 13.6 (frame 18)) between the pharyngeal roof (palatal organ) and the pharyngeal floor (postlingual organ and branchial arches). Taste-buds occur all over the internal lining but their density peaks in this pharyngeal slit area, up to mean values of $820 \, mm^{-2}$ in carp (Sibbing and Uribe, 1985). In carp, *Cyprinus carpio*, taste selection is performed here by different mechanisms (Sibbing *et al.*, 1986) related to size, palatability and mixture with non-food: (1) **spitting**, (2) **rinsing**, and (3) **selective retention**. As no other experimental studies are available, this section is mainly based on evidence in carp, but in view of similar structures in species like bream, roach, rudd and white bream, it may apply to most cyprinids.

Spitting

Spitting is a reversed suction action of the orobuccal cavity, completed by forceful opercular compression. It is a crude mode of selection used to eject large unpalatable particles (e.g. water mites), spiny objects or heavily mudded mouthfuls during substratum probing. It is also used to disperse unmanageable large lumps of food into patches before reintake (Sibbing *et al.*, 1986).

Rinsing

Large food items trapped in the anterior, wider part of the pharyngeal slit are cleaned by intensive pumping, very similar to intensive ventilation. Waste particles are flushed through the branchial slits, while the food item remains clamped within the pharyngeal slit (Fig. 13.6).

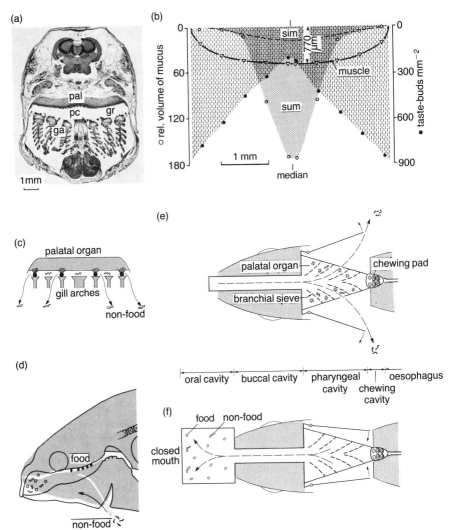

Fig. 13.4 Structures and mechanisms for selective retention. (a) Transverse section (7 μm) through the pharynx region of carp. Note the muscular palatal organ (pal), the perforated branchial floor, and the slit-shaped pharyngeal cavity (pc). ga, gill arch; gr, gill raker. (b) Transverse distribution in the posterior part of the palatal organ of (●) taste-buds, (○) mucines, and (▽) muscle layer. Pecked line separates the volume of sialomucines (sim) and sulfomucines (sum). Note the inverse amounts of taste-buds and sulfomucines, the former serving selection laterally, the latter serving aggregation and transport medially. Short vertical lines at top and bottom denote medians. (c) The mechanism of selective retention. Taste-buds sensing food particles trigger local bulgings of the muscular palatal surface, which clamp the food (●) against the branchial floor. Waste is flushed through the branchial and opercular slits. (d) to (f) Closed protrusion resuspends food–non-food mixtures in the oral cavity. Alternating selective retention (during oral compression: e and stippled image in (d)) and resuspension (by closed protrusion: f and outlined image in (d)) gradually sort the food from the non-food. ((a) and (b) reproduced with permission from Sibbing and Uribe, 1985; (d) reproduced with permission from Sibbing *et al.*, 1986; (c), (e), and (f) reproduced with permission from Sibbing, 1987.)

Selective retention from food–non-food mixtures

Bottom and substratum feeders in particular take up with their food varied amounts of inorganic sediment and organic debris. Swallowing mouthfuls of these materials would decrease the efficiency of food digestion. Most dense particles such as larger sand grains and gravel will readily sink into the large first branchical slits. Less dense and fine particles tend to follow the flow into the pharyngeal slit. Expulsion of debris is highly effective in carp (Wunder, 1936; Uribe-Zamora, 1975). The latter author found only 3% waste was retained with the food. How do cyprinids achieve such good segregation of food and non-food?

Following intake, the mixture is transported into the pharyngeal slit. I hypothesize that selective retention proceeds by momentary, very local bulgings in the palatal organ surface. These clamp the edible particles between the pharyngeal roof and floor while small waste is flushed through the branchial slits (Fig. 13.4(c) to (e)). The slit-shaped pharynx thereby guarantees close contact between roof and floor and provides a large processing surface. This hypothesis is based on observations of small waste expelled through the opercular slits, the peculiar muscle fibre arrangement in the palatal organ (Sibbing and Uribe, 1985), and the concentration of taste-buds (up to $820\,mm^{-2}$) upon the latter which is higher than reported for any other fish (Campos, 1969). Evidence for the 'local bulging hypothesis' was gained from (1) electrical stimulation which produces local bulgings of the palatal organ: (2) chemical stimulation with hydrolysed yeast cells during endoscopy – this evoked amazing brief projections on the palatal organ surface, like fingers pushed into an inflated balloon; and (3) electromyograms of the palatal organ during processing of food–non-food mixtures – these show that the palatal organ rapidly changes its activity in time as well as in place (Sibbing *et al.*, 1986).

In addition, in cyprinids (e.g. goldfish, *Carassius auratus*) the topography of the pharyngeal surface is depicted very accurately on the surface of the large vagal lobe which controls the processes in the pharynx (Morita and Finger, 1985; Finger, 1988). Roof and floor are mapped on the same surface. The peculiar laminar cytoarchitecture of this centre in the hindbrain shows highly organized vertical connections between sensory and motor neurones of each separate spot in the pharynx. Neurones of opposed pharyngeal roof and floor loci are interconnected. This provides the anatomical substrate required for such very local reflexes in opposed pharyngeal roof and floor areas. Vagal lobes of other, especially benthic-feeding, cyprinids show a similar architecture (Kotrschal and Junger, 1988). It is otherwise found in only a few benthic non-cyprinids (Morita and Finger, 1985).

Repetitive back-washing of the food–non-food mixture by **closed protrusion** of the upper jaws plays a crucial role in purification by resuspending the mixture from the pharynx back into the oral cavity (Fig. 13.4(d) to (f)). Oral resuspension and selective retention during oral compression repetitively alternate, creating a back-and-forth flow through the pharyngeal slit and leading to a gradually increasing purification of the engulfed mixture.

Mucus

What role does mucus play in selection? Matthes (1963) supposes that cyprinids eject all non-food particles by spitting, and retain food particles by entangling them in mucus. This, however, cannot explain the effective separation between fine food and non-food particles. Moreover, food processing between intake and mastication in carp-like species is dominated by closed protrusion and not by spitting. Robotham (1982) presumed buccal mucus to play a major role in retention of detritus in the spiny loach, *Cobitis taenia*. Mucus-producing cells certainly abound in the oropharyngeal lining (Fig. 13.4(b)) and different types of mucus even occur in different areas of carp (sialomucines and sulfomucines, Sibbing and Uribe, 1985) and other species thus far studied (bream, white bream, roach, rudd, grass carp, asp, unpubl.). Sialomucine-producing cells have low densities and peak at the site where food is trapped between pharyngeal roof and floor. The hypotheses are that these sialomucines mainly serve (1) protection of the tissues at areas of high mechanical stresses, (2) lubrication in manipulation and transport, and (3) minimizing the boundary layer along the orobuccal walls, thus reducing friction in water transport (Rosen and Cornford, 1971). Sulfomucine-producing cells occur in the posterior parts of the palatal and postlingual organ (Sibbing and Uribe, 1985). They produce large volumes of mucus increasing sharply towards the pharyngeal teeth. This type of mucus has a higher viscosity (Hunt, 1970) and will especially serve aggregation of particles into boluses during their re-collection from the branchial sieve, during transport and mastication (Sibbing and Uribe, 1985). The conflict between aggregation and resuspension explains the absence of these cells in the orobuccal cavity.

The vomero-palatine organ, a non-muscular plicated (folded) system in the buccal roof of e.g. *Labeo lineatus*, might act to mix tiny food particles (e.g. diatoms) thoroughly with mucus, forming clusters before passing them to the branchial sieve (Matthes, 1963). Thus their retention probabilities would be increased. Closed protrusions could wash the tiny particles between its mucous lamellae. Sulfomucines would serve such a hypothesized function.

Further research on the properties, distribution and the release kinetics of mucus in the oropharyngeal lining of fish may provide clues to their role in the successive actions during food processing. Still other specialized mechanisms for food manipulation are expected in cyprinids, in view of the complexity of their oral morphology.

Size selection

Most filter-feeding fish select food size with their branchial sieve once the particles have been slowly engulfed. These gulpers, pump filterers and overswimmers mainly capture the smaller and less evasive particles.

Which structures are responsible for internal size selection in cyprinids? In most teleosts, filtering is achieved by (1) the gill rakers of the branchial arches, developed in some specialized planktivorous fish into (2) epibranchial organs, and by (3) pharyngeal teeth (e.g. in catastomids, Eastman, 1977). This subsection focuses on the branchial sieve and epibranchial organs, since cyprinid pharyngeal teeth are not involved in filtration.

Branchial sieve

Number, length, width and shape of gill rakers are tremendously varied among teleosts (Zander, 1906). Kazansky (1964), Verigina (1969) and Matthes (1963) related such features to food types for cyprinids. The biserial-symmetric type of branchial sieve is most common in cyprinids. In such branchial sieves, gill rakers of similar shape form series on the anterior and posterior inner side of each gill arch (Zander, 1906; Fig. 12.3).

The mesh of such branchial sieves is generally conceived to be the gap between successive gill rakers of a particular arch (King and McLeod, 1976). Secondary profiles on the gill rakers, like those in carp (Sibbing and Uribe, 1985), may further decrease the mesh width (Zander, 1906). The retention performances of fish for particular size classes of particles have been related to the retention probabilities of their branchial filters, determined from the cumulative frequency distribution of their interraker gaps (Nelson, 1979; Wright *et al.*, 1983). Experimental tests, however, failed to demonstrate such a relation. Insight into the actual mechanisms of filtering is completely lacking. For example, which structural and movement features determine functional parameters such as (1) mesh width, (2) band width and sharpness for size selectivity, (3) capacity ($l\,min^{-1}$), (4) adjustability and (5) cleaning?

Rubenstein and Koehl (1977) distinguish five filter mechanisms: sieving, direct interception, inertial impact, gravitational deposition and motile particle deposition. Small pores, irregular flow paths and sticky surfaces generally increase the chance that particles will be retained. In branchial filters, varied combinations of sieving, direct interception and motile particle deposition are probably involved, given the mucous covering of the branchial arches and the motility of some zooplankters. Inertial impact and gravitational deposition will play a minor role because of the low velocities of flow and the specific gravity of planktonic particles, which is comparable to that of water. Experimental research of filtering mechanisms should focus on such aspects.

Does the intra-arch gill raker gap really represent the actual mesh width in the biserial-symmetrical type of branchial filter of cyprinids? Most probably it does not. Fig. 13.5 shows the adjacent parts of two branchial arches with their rakers. In this interdigitation model (unpublished), the mesh size is not the gap between subsequent rakers on the same arch, but is conceived of as the distance between two interdigitating opposing arches. This interarch distance is most probably modulated actively during feeding. The actual mesh width $M = D\sin\alpha$ is a function of the interarch distance D and the top angle (α) of the raker. This two-dimensional model assumes interdigitation and a close fit

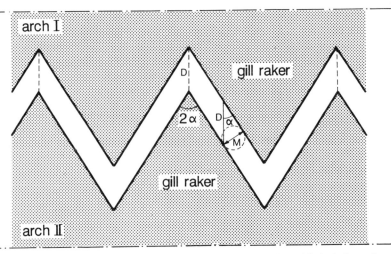

Fig. 13.5 Interdigitation model of the branchial sieve. Mesh width (M) depends on the distance (D) between adjacent gill arches and the top angle of individual rakers (α).

between opposing rakers, which often occur. Adjusting the interarch distance might well explain observations that bream only starts selecting smaller particles once most larger ones have been ingested (Chapter 12).

Research in our laboratory (Hoogenboezem *et al.*, 1990, 1991; Chapter 12) using X-ray cinematography to record gill arch movements in foraging bream, *Abramis brama*, gave first evidence that interarch distances change during respiration and feeding on cladocerans (Fig. 12.4). Gill arch movements during filtering are much larger than during respiration, whereas minimum interarch distances are sharply decreased compared to respiration. Both data suggest a role of gill arch movements in particle retention. However, interarch slit widths differ between successive arches, and the interdigitation model produces an inhomogeneous filter in bream. Structural analysis showed marked differences between rakers of the lateral and medial row of each arch; a new mechanism for retention, based on movable front rakers, is proposed (Hoogenboezem *et al.*, 1991; Chapter 12). Other features also may influence the flow and particle retention in the filtration process, such as deformation of the palatal organ opposing the gill arches and the cleaning frequency of the filter, affecting the slit widths through clogging by particles. In conclusion, it is most doubtful that one could ever predict the retention abilities of cyprinid fish merely from structural parameters of their branchial sieve.

Gill rakers may well serve other functions, e.g. (1) retention of objects which, in bottom feeding, might damage the delicate gill filaments (Zander, 1906), (2) improving grip on larger items during manipulation and transport (e.g. in macrophagous, herbivorous and piscivorous fish), and (3) increasing the area for taste selection in close co-ordination with the palatal organ.

Indeed, gill rakers in cyprinids and other teleosts are densely packed with taste-buds (Iwai, 1964; Campos, 1969; Sibbing and Uribe, 1985). These functions will impose different demands on gill raker structure and functioning, and make explanations of their adaptive value in filtering even more complex.

How are small particles, trapped in the branchial sieve, manoeuvred into the oesophagus? This appears one of the many unsolved problems in plankton filtering. Electromyograms and movement analyses of carp during feeding on zooplankton (Sibbing *et al.*, 1986) suggest that food particles retained in the branchial sieve are gathered by a reversed flow of water through closed protrusion. After this gathering, orobuccal compression moves the particles into the slit between the palatal and postlingual organ, where they will be aggregated and enveloped in mucus for transport towards the chewing cavity and oesophagus.

Epibranchial organs

Silver carp, *Hypophthalmichthys molitrix*, larger than 8 cm are specialized phytoplanktivores. They actively select particles of $11–21\,\mu$m, whereas particles up to 6 μm are equally distributed in guts and environment (Adamek and Spittler, 1984). In silver carp the ceratobranchials extend far forward, thus increasing the surface of the branchial sieve to enormous size. Exceptionally long gill rakers of adjacent arches together form high ridges which closely fit into folds formed by the opposing palatal organ. The rows of gill rakers within each hemibranch are interconnected into a fine lamellar network (Suslowska and Urbanowicz, 1983). The interlamellar slits which should represent the actual mesh width range from 12 to 26 μm (Hampl *et al.*, 1983).

In most cyprinids the branchial sieve ends where the epibranchials meet the palatal organ. In silver carp, however, both the inner (pharyngeal) cavity and the outer (opercular) cavity extend as four double (afferent and efferent) canals between each of the five arches, coil into the palatal organ, and terminate blind. These cochleate tubes lying against the base of the skull together form the supra- or epibranchial organs. Only the blind ends of the afferent channels lack gill rakers but produce much mucus which should serve clustering of food particles into boluses (Verigin, 1957).

What selective value in filter feeding would epibranchial organs have? The main role attributed to this organ is sucking particles retained from the branchial sieve and aggregating them into boluses (Suslowska and Urbanowicz, 1983). It thus represents a further specialization separating the filtering and collecting part of the branchial sieve, preventing clogging of the fine filter and reducing its resistance to water flow during respiration and feeding. Compression of the epibranchial organ could effect a backflow of boluses into the oropharyngeal cavity, which in the absence of protrusile jaws serves gathering as does closed protrusion in the cyprinids. Protrusile jaws closing the jaw angles would limit the oral gape, through which large volumes of water must be passed, and would thus conflict with pump filter feeding. A

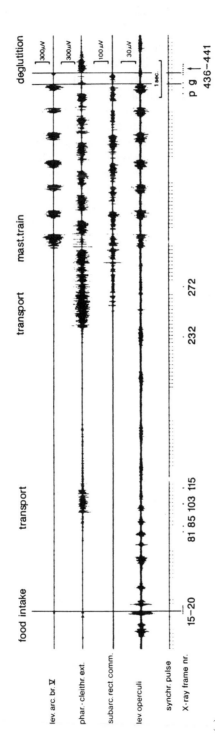

Fig. 13.6 (a) Electromyographic (EMG) record of the feeding process depicted in (b) to (d) (numbers refer to the X-ray frames). Abbreviations; lev. arc. br. V, levator arcus branchialis V; phar, cleithr. ext., pharyngo-cleithralis externus; subarc. rect. comm., subarcualis rectus communis; lev. operculi, levator operculi muscle. (b) to (d) X-ray cine recording of successive feeding actions in the carp (26 frames s^{-1}). Black bars are measuring markers. (b) Feeding starts with rapid intake (60 cm s^{-1}) of the radio-opaque (BaSO$_4$-impregnated) food by suction. Note the expanding buccopharynx (frames 15–20). (c) Later, the food is transported more slowly by muscular peristalsis·through the anterior pharynx to the rostal margin of the chewing pad (frames 81–115), and finally into the expanding posterior pharynx, between teeth and chewing pad (frames 232–72). (d) After the last grinding cycle (frames 422–30) the masticatory train is completed by deglutition (frames 436–41; arrows). The remainder of the pellet stays at the rostral margin of the chewing pad, waiting for another crushing action. (Reproduced with permission from Sibbing, 1982.)

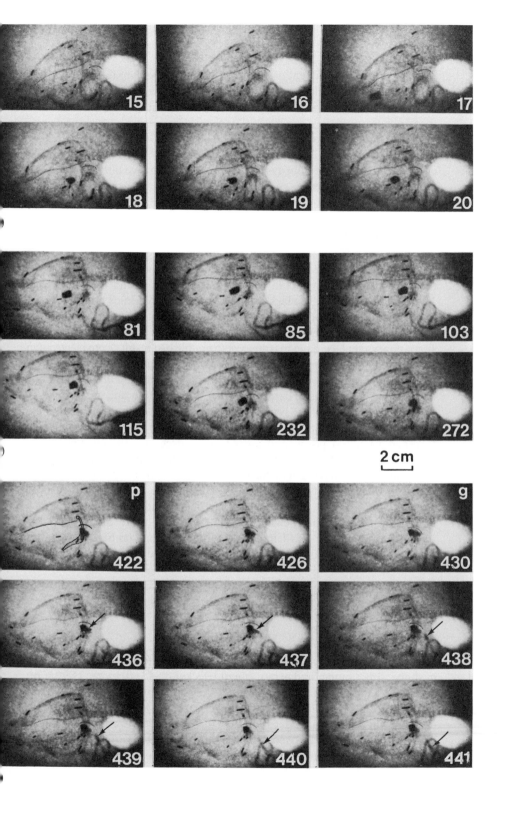

2 cm

similarly built epibranchial organ is found in the zooplanktivorous bighead, *Hypophthalmichthys nobilis*, which also lacks protrusile jaws, combined with an extensive and (less) fine filter and a pump filter feeding mode of food intake (pers. obs.).

Epibranchial organs of different types occur among a variety of teleosts (reviews, Nelson, 1967; Bertmar and Stromberg, 1969). Except in characids, epibranchial organs are always associated with extensive filters composed of long and fine gill rakers.

13.5   FOOD TRANSPORT TOWARDS THE CHEWING CAVITY

In most teleosts, food transport after capture proceeds by movements of toothed branchial elements in the oropharyngeal roof and floor (e.g. Liem, 1973; Lauder, 1983). The lack of such elements in cyprinids imposes serious limitations on transport of large and struggling prey (e.g. macrophytes and fish). Whereas in piscivorous cyprinids, e.g. *Aspius aspius*, the interdigitating sharp pharyngeal teeth aid in transport (unpublished results from electromyography and X-ray cinematography), flattened crushing and grinding teeth, e.g. in *Cyprinus carpio*, are ineffective for transport (Sibbing, 1982). Electromyograms and X-ray films in carp show that after selection and gathering, food boluses are propelled by repetitive peristaltic waves in the palatal and postlingual organ (Sibbing *et al.*, 1986). These opposed muscular pads together act like a piston and push food boluses into the chewing cavity (Fig. 13.6c). The latter is expanded by extreme depression and abduction of the pharyngeal jaws making way for the food. Although this process cannot be observed from the exterior of the fish, it should be included in measuring handling times of food. In carp, particles larger than about 4% of the standard length cannot enter the chewing cavity, even though they are easily sucked into the mouth (about 7% SL in diameter). Thus feeding on hard food items is chewing-cavity-limited rather than oral-gape-limited.

13.6   MASTICATION AND DEGLUTITION

Mastication

Pharyngeal jaws in cyprinids bear up to three rows of teeth. They are so varied in shape, size, number and arrangement (Heckel, 1843; Heincke, 1892; Chu, 1935; Rutte, 1962; Matthes, 1963) that they are commonly used as keys for species identification (Fig. 13.7). This wide variation is generally accepted as reflecting their role in adaptive radiation and trophic segregation. In primitive teleosts, internal teeth transport the prey (Gosline, 1973), but in cyprinids as well as in several groups of more advanced acanthopterygian teleosts (e.g.

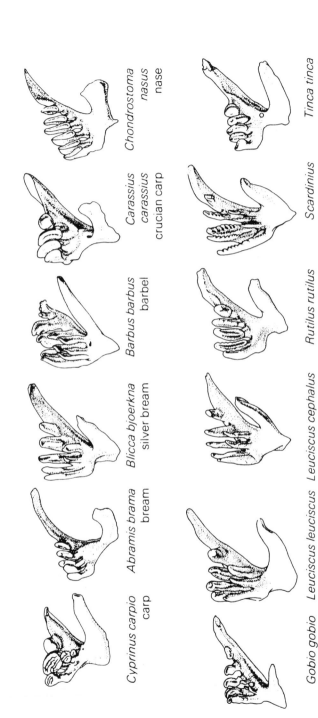

Fig. 13.7 Right pharyngeal jaws of 12 European cyprinid species. Their size, firmness and spatial architecture are varied. Note also the differences in number, arrangement and structure of the teeth. Left and right pharyngeal jaws often interdigitate (not in carp) and oppose a cornified chewing pad in the base of the skull (after Wheeler, 1978).

Cyprinus carpio
carp

Abramis brama
bream

Blicca bjoerkna
silver bream

Barbus barbus
barbel

Carassius carassius
crucian carp

Chondrostoma nasus
nase

Gobio gobio
gudgeon

Leuciscus leuciscus
dace

Leuciscus cephalus
chub

Rutilus rutilus
roach

Scardinius erythrophthalmus
rudd

Tinca tinca
tench

cichlids, labrids, embiotocids, odacids and scarids, Liem and Greenwood, 1981) they are specialized for mastication. Especially in cyprinid fish, which lack oral teeth, a stomach and cellulases (Chapter 14), high demands are imposed on pharyngeal mastication. This certainly applies to herbivorous cyprinids, which need to release at least part of the nutrients contained within cellulose walls.

How are the pharyngeal jaws related to the type of food, what deformation and consequent stresses (compression, tension or shear) do they generate in the food, and how large should these stresses be for fracture? Food items differ widely in size, shape and mechanical texture and demand specific stresses for efficient diminution (conceived of as the creation of new surface area exposed for digestion per unit of energy and time; Sibbing, 1982, 1991). Comparisons of pharyngeal tooth structure and specialized diets suggest general interrelations, e.g. sharp conical teeth in piscivores pierce prey whereas molluscivores have stout blunt teeth for crushing shells (Rutte, 1962; Matthes, 1963). Further relations between pharyngeal tooth design and diets remain, however, mostly unclear. Special features of teeth imposed by specific food items also do not exclude the use of other available resources (Sibbing, 1988). Carp, for example, feed inefficiently on small fish or soft macrophytes (Fischer, 1968) in the absence of more appropriate food.

Natural food types are of heterogeneous composition which makes their mechanical properties difficult to define. In addition, insight into how such materials propagate cracks and breaks is almost lacking. These topics urgently need further investigation. For present purposes, masticatory operations (crushing, splitting, piercing, grinding, cutting, lacerating and shearing) will be used (Fig. 13.8), defined by the dimensions of opposing occlusal surfaces and their direction of movement (Sibbing, 1991). Food types are subdivided into four generally accepted classes of texture: (1) hard–brittle (e.g. seeds, nuts, carrot, bone, some insects), (2) turgid (ripe juicy fruits, many insect larvae), (3) soft–tough (animal soft tissues, some insects), (4) tough–fibrous (grass, fruit skin) (Lucas and Luke, 1984; Sibbing, 1991). These categories are based on differences in deformability, strength, toughness and notch-sensitivity of food items. Hard–brittle materials are most effectively crushed and split (macrodiminution) and finally ground (microdiminution). Turgid items require crushing and subsequent grinding. Cutting and shearing are most effective in mastication of soft–tough food. Tough–fibrous materials are most effectively disrupted by cutting, lacerating and shearing. Not only the diversified occlusal profiles of pharyngeal teeth, but also movements between opposing teeth and relative to the chewing pad, determine the type of masticatory operation and its effectiveness in fracturing a certain food type.

X-ray cinematography combined with electromyography revealed structural and functional features critical for pharyngeal mastication in carp, *Cyprinus carpio*, feeding on such diverse items as commercial pellets, barley and earthworms (Sibbing, 1982). Seven principal observations were made. (1) The

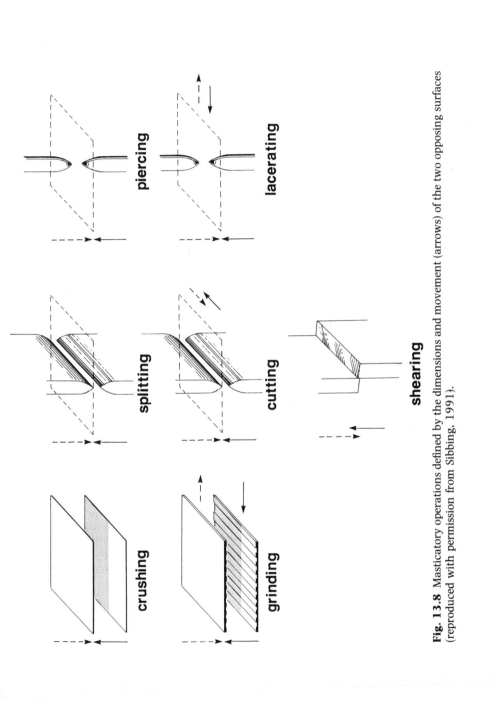

Fig. 13.8 Masticatory operations defined by the dimensions and movement (arrows) of the two opposing surfaces (reproduced with permission from Sibbing, 1991).

carp's chewing apparatus has little ability to cut, shear and lacerate (Sibbing, 1982: Fig. 19) but its architecture and functioning permit distinct crushing and grinding cycles, employed according to the type of food. (2) Very strong, brittle and stiff materials are thoroughly fractured (e.g. shelled molluscs, seeds) whereas tough, soft and fibrous items are only flattened. (3) The heterodont dentition meets different demands during processing. The anterior crushing teeth break large particles into pieces (macrodiminution), which are subsequently ground by the posterior molariform teeth (microdiminution; Fig. 13.6d). (4) Most pharyngeal jaw muscles mainly direct and stabilize the pharyngeal jaw movements. Epaxial body muscles lift the skull and thereby the levator muscles of the pharyngeal jaw, thus transmitting high forces to the teeth during crushing and grinding (Fig. 13.9). (5) Hypaxial body muscles retract the pharyngeal jaws by their connection to the pectoral girdle and thus indirectly power the teeth in grinding. (6) The chewing pad, previously assumed to be motionless, moves with the skull in a direction opposite to the teeth, thus intensifying grinding. (7) The efficiency of food handling appears largely determined by the time spent on mastication. Mastication consumes

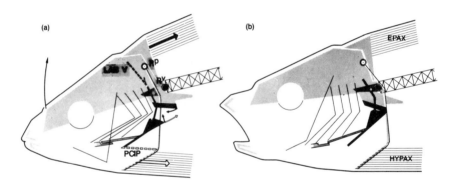

Fig. 13.9 The masticatory mechanism of carp. Body muscles provide the power in crushing and grinding (indirect masticatory muscles). (a) Epaxial muscles (EPAX) rotate the skull dorsad around R^v, and thereby lift the pharyngeal jaws and teeth to the chewing pad through the interposed tendinous levator muscles (LAB V). The chewing pad moves mainly rostrad (black centre of rotation, black arrows). Hypaxial muscles (HYPAX) retract the pectoral girdle around R^p. Their forces are transmitted to pharyngeal jaws and teeth by another set of tendinous muscles (PCIP) and are added in grinding. The ligament between skull and pectoral girdle obstructs pharyngeal jaw retraction dorsally, acts as a fulcrum, and effects rotation by the PCIP with the pharyngeal jaws as long levers (open centres of rotation, open arrows). (b) As a combined result, teeth and chewing pad move in parallel, but in opposite directions, and wedge the food under high pressure. Grinding movements are small but powerful. The extensive movements of the pharyngeal jaw lever are permitted by simultaneous expansion of the buccopharynx and a slide coupling in the branchial floor. Direct masticatory muscles that suspend the pharyngeal jaws in muscular slings, and steer and stabilize these movements, are omitted in this scheme (after Sibbing, 1982).

by far majority of handling time, up to 95% for a barley grain, fed in aquaculture, which may take several minutes (Sibbing, 1982).

The contribution of body muscles to pharyngeal mastication will effect huge masticatory pressures but these cannot easily be measured, although crushing of dried grains of corn can even be heard outside the experimental tank! Rupturing cellulose walls is, however, barely possible for carp as the contact area between teeth, food and chewing pad is large, producing few local stress concentrations. Somewhat similar pharyngeal teeth (Fig. 13.7) occur in crucian carp, *Carassius carassius*, and tench, *Tinca tinca*, which both feed, like carp, on insect larvae, molluscs and larger crustaceans.

Grass carp, *Ctenopharyngodon idella*, however, can cut and lacerate leaves and stems of soft weeds into fragments of about 3 mm². These dimensions match the spacing of their pharyngeal teeth (Hickling, 1966). Only at the edges of these fragments are cells washed out from between disconnected fibres. The large local stresses required are applied by serrated cutting edges of the pharyngeal tooth crowns which also characterize the facultatively herbivorous rudd, *Scardinius erythrophthalmus* (Fig. 13.7). In both grass carp and rudd, pharyngeal teeth from both jaws interdigitate against the chewing pad, leaving deep transverse furrows in its surface during the lacerating action when opposing teeth move apart (unpubl. X-ray data). Contrary to the carp, such lacerating is also expected in many other cyprinids with interdigitating upward-hooked crowns (e.g. benthic-feeding *Abramis brama*, *Barbus barbus*, *Gobio gobio*, and *Leuciscus leuciscus*).

In piscivorous *Aspius aspius* the pharyngeal jaws are slender, elongated and retain much of their original transport function. The gentle pressure on the chewing pad is also reflected by its soft horny nature. The long slender teeth have sharp, slightly hooked crowns which pierce the exposed side of the fish and subsequently move the prey towards the oesophagus, meanwhile lacerating it (Sibbing and Rijken, unpubl.).

Thus, not only do carp, grass carp and asp differ greatly in the shape of their pharyngeal teeth, but also in the direction in which high forces are applied: perpendicular to (carp), transverse across (grass carp) and backward across the chewing pad (asp). Obligate planktivorous fish, e.g. the zooplanktivorous bighead, *Hypophthalmichthys nobilis*, have spatulate flat pharyngeal tooth crowns closely set together, providing a large surface area to squeeze small zooplankters. The phytoplanktivorous silver carp, *H. molitrix*, has closely similar crowns with additional minute ridges (Sibbing, 1991) which probably rupture the algal walls by grinding across the chewing pad. The latter shows distinct wearing facets. Silver carp had crushed sculptured envelopes of *Ceratium hirundinella* among its intestinal contents as well as empty diatom frustules. Filamentous bluegreen algae, however, were not affected by mechanical or chemical processing (Kajak *et al.*, 1977), as in most other fish (Prowse, 1964), emphasizing the special difficulties in food processing by herbivorous fish. Cyprinid fish include a particularly large proportion of herbivores. The heterodont pharyngeal dentition of roach, *Rutilus rutilus* (Fig. 13.7) enables it to crush, split, cut and lacerate (Sibbing, 1991) the extremely wide range of plant and animal food types in its diet (Prejs, 1984; Chapter 12).

Pharyngeal teeth in cyprinids often have their crowns so heavily worn that hooks disappear. They are continuously replaced by new crowns, which develop in the pharyngeal mucosa, in a specific order and frequency (Geyer, 1937; Evans and Deubler, 1955; Schwartz and Dutcher, 1962). Vasnecov (1939) compared developmental changes in pharyngeal tooth generations for cyprinids in a phylogenetic context. Comparison with dietary shifts could further assess the critical role that dentition plays in food processing.

Deglutition

Deglutition or swallowing in carp starts with compression of the chewing cavity. Successive peristaltic waves of contraction through its muscular wall transport the food boluses into the oesophagus (Fig. 13.6d). Bulging of the palatal and postlingual organs closes the entrance of the chewing cavity and thus directs the food towards the oesophagus. Movements of the pharyngeal jaws support this action.

13.7 ADJUSTING FOOD HANDLING TO THE TYPE OF FOOD

Carp display ten distinct movement patterns of the head elements (Fig. 13.10), each serving a particular role in feeding (Sibbing *et al.*, 1986) and stereotyped by its characteristic kinematic profile and associated muscle activities. Food processing in carp can be optimized according to the type and condition of food at three different levels: sequence regulation, switching, and modulation. **Sequence regulation** (cf. Table II in Sibbing *et al.*, 1986) is the regulation of the succession and repetition frequency of the stereotyped patterns over the full time course of a feeding sequence. For example, mastication of hard objects (e.g. molluscs and seeds) requires repetitive crushing strokes prior to grinding, whereas selective retention, alternating with closed protrusion, dominates purification of heavily mudded food. Both require considerable handling times. **Switching** is choosing between different patterns serving a similar functional demand, e.g. the particulate intake of large particles versus the gulping of suspensions. **Modulation** is the momentary adjustment of each single pattern to instantaneous changes in position and reactions of the food. Modulation is exemplified by adjustment of the direction and degree of protrusion of the upper jaw.

Adjusting feeding to the type of food and integrating its component actions into an efficient feeding sequence require a wide range of information from external, internal and proprioceptive sensors as well as a powerful central

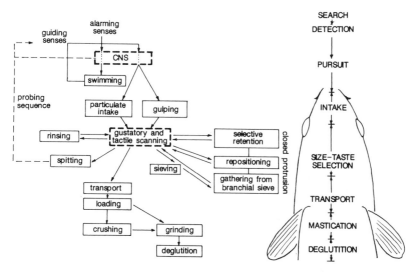

Fig. 13.10 Interrelationships between the distinct components of food handling in carp. Their site of action in the fish is indicated at the right. These stereotyped patterns are variously integrated into effective feeding sequences, adjusted to the type of food (Sibbing *et al.*, 1986). Probing refers to repetitive intake and spitting of bottom material, meanwhile evaluating its profitability (after Sibbing *et al.*, 1986).

processing system. For example, which stimuli during mastication trigger the transition from mechanical to chemical processing? How is the combined action of taste and size selection integrated? Apart from the central and peripheral circuits underlying selective retention (p. 391), little or nothing is known about such aspects. Brain patterns in cyprinids reflect in a broad sense the relative importance of different senses (large facial lobes correspond to 'skintasters', large vagal lobes to 'mouth tasters'; Evans, 1952; Kotrschal and Junger, 1988), but choice experiments should test their role in feeding.

13.8 VERSATILITY IN FOOD HANDLING AND FEEDING GUILDS

According to Liem's definition (1984), specialists are those teleosts that have evolved morphological and functional mechanisms (1) to collect prey that cannot be collected by the basic teleostean slow suction mechanism, or (2) to process food mechanically, before swallowing, or (3) to digest plant materials after swallowing. Specialization in cyprinids may, however, also occur in less apparent internal feeding actions including taste and size selection and transport, thus producing a vast array of unique feeding designs.

Do fish with specialized feeding structures necessarily have a narrow diet? Although this seems true for overswimming planktivorous and fast-sucking piscivorous fish, it certainly does not hold for most species with slow-sucking feeding on intermediate-sized particles. In ambush- and pursuit-hunting piscivorous cichlids, specialization leads to a narrowing of the feeding repertoire (number of neuromuscular programs for switching feeding modes) (Liem, 1984). In non-piscivorous cichlids, structural specialization is often accompanied by a wide feeding repertoire, becoming simultaneously specialists on some and jacks-of-all-trades on other food types. Extreme structural specializations, e.g. in fast-sucking piscivorous and overswimming planktivorous species, are incompatible with demands imposed by other food types. Slow-sucking cyprinids can combine specific demands for one food type with abilities to feed on others. Within this context gulping seems to be a compromise feeding mode, allowing filter feeding given the particulate feeding apparatus of cyprinids.

Categorizing cyprinids into feeding guilds such as carnivory, herbivory and omnivory denies their versatility and opportunism in foraging (Motta, 1988). Morphological characteristics associated with feeding appear to be related more to the way fish capture and process their food than to categories of food (van Oijen *et al.*, 1981; Barel, 1983; Motta, 1988; this chapter). Therefore, a much better approach would be to classify cyprinids according to their type of food capture (Table 13.1) and processing. The architecture of fish can only be used for such classification if relations between structural and functional demands are thoroughly known. Within such types, e.g. particulate feeders, different categories of food can be taken, e.g. zooplankters, molluscs, plant seeds and chironomid larvae in carp. Relations between feeding structures and diets are further concealed for three reasons. (1) Trophic specializations start from ancestral forms and are bound to modifications of this common structural plan. Because of this phylogenetic inertia, specializations generally will not be optimal (Liem and Wake, 1985). Because cyprinids have radiated repetitively from new geographical areas, this may be a major limiting factor. (2) Diet data are mostly varied since time (diurnal and seasonal) and actual feeding location (horizontal and vertical) strongly influence the abundance of different food resources (Chapter 12). (3) When appropriate food types are abundant, a high feeding rate on suboptimal food types may well be more profitable than maximizing energetic efficiency at the expense of time.

Future research on cyprinid feeding should focus more on (1) specializations and limitations in foraging, imposed by sensory systems and body shape (Webb, 1982); (2) analysis of hydrodynamic and mechanical principles basic to the subsequent processes in food handling, to explain the adaptive value of diversified structures and mechanisms employed in cyprinid feeding and to allow their efficiencies in the exploitation of food resources to be predicted (Sibbing, 1988); (3) behavioural studies, preferably quantifying comparative feeding efficiencies on different food types to provide measures for selective value of feeding systems, and analysing versatility in feeding; and (4) ecological research on the role of different feeding techniques and their consequences for the hierarchy of foraging species in particular habitats. It is emphasized that such a multidisciplinary approach combining functional morphology, ethology and ecology is needed to gain insight into the trophic segregation of cyprinid species and their interactions through differential utilization of aquatic food resources.

13.9 FEEDING AND THE SUCCESS OF CYPRINID FISH

How could such a complex biological design as the cyprinid feeding apparatus have evolved, and what implications has it for cyprinid trophic ecology? According to Gosline (1973), the cypriniform ancestor had reduced oral dentition, a small mouth and bottom-feeding habits. It gave rise to the catfishes on one hand and the characin–cyprinid groups on the other. Following Gosline (1973), Sibbing *et al.* (1986) used structural and functional data to reconstruct a possible scheme for the evolution of the cyprinid feeding apparatus. I hypothesize that increased exploitation of littoral bottom deposits imposed increased demands for simple chemosensory functions on lips and jaws (e.g. barbels), vision being less effective for bottom inspection in such habitats. Consumption of hard invertebrate and vegetable items promoted the development of the pharyngeal jaw apparatus while releasing the oral jaws from their biting function. This allowed the oral jaws to develop their unique protrusion kinetics optimizing sucking and penetrating bottom deposits. As a result of these changing demands on the jaws, oral teeth because further reduced and the ability to grasp larger and elusive prey was lost. The posterior position of the pharyngeal jaw apparatus does not interfere with suction and respiratory functions of the branchial basket. In addition, the posterior skull area can accommodate huge levator muscles of the pharyngeal jaws, special retractor muscles unique to lower teleosts (Holstvoogd, 1965) develop from the oesophageal sphincter, and even epaxial and hypaxial body muscles are incorporated to power the masticatory system. The resultant high masticatory pressures are absorbed by cornification of the epithelium into a chewing pad fixed in the base of the skull. At the same time these high pressures led to the reduction of the delicate upper branchial elements in this area and a consequent loss of their function in transporting large struggling prey. For small particles, transport is taken over by the increased size of muscles in the pharyngeal lining (palatal and postlingual organs) propelling food by peristaltic waves towards the chewing cavity and the oesophagus. These muscular organs largely fill the pharyngeal cavity, giving it a slit-like shape, and together with high densities of taste-buds they form an appropriate mechanism for such subtle actions as selecting food from non-food, supported by closed protrusion. The tasting area gradually moved from the external skin into the oral cavity, accompanied by associated changes in brain architecture (p. 391).

Even if such a scheme were incorrect, it would provide logical framework for understanding the interrelations among the set of characters unique to cyprinids (p. 380). It would almost exclude efficient piscivores from the cyprinids, as oral teeth for seizing, retaining and transporting large prey are absent and the small volume of the pharyngeal cavity would contribute little to fast suction. The rare cyprinid piscivores would then be secondarily derived from the early cyprinid stock. Compared to (e.g.) percids, they predate smaller fish.

Sensory lips and barbels, protrusile jaws, slow suction, internal selection by the palatal organ, and the powerful pharyngeal mastication apparatus are the keys which enable cyprinid fish to exploit (sub)benthic organisms mixed with bottom debris, including hard, strong and fibrous food items such as molluscs, seeds and plants, most successfully.

REFERENCES

Adamek, Z. and Spittler, P. (1984) Particle size selection in the food of silvercarp, *Hypophthalmichthys molitrix. Folia zoologica, Brno,* **33**, 363–70.

Alexander, R. McN. (1966) The functions and mechanisms of the protrusible upper jaws of two species of cyprinid fish. *J. Zool., Lond.,* **149**, 288–96.

Alexander, R. McN. (1969) Mechanics of the feeding action of a cyprinid fish. *J. Zool., Lond.,* **159**, 1–15.

Alexander, R. McN. (1970) Mechanics of the feeding action of various teleost fishes. *J. Zool., Lond.,* **162**, 145–56.

Al-Hussaini, A. H. (1949) On the functional morphology of the alimentary tract of some fish in relation to differences in their feeding habits: anatomy and histology. *Q. J. microsc. Sci.,* **90**, 109–39.

Ballintijn, C. M. (1969) Functional anatomy and movement coordination of the respiratory pump of the carp (*Cyprinus carpio* L.). *J. exp. Biol.,* **50**, 547–67.

Ballintijn, C. M., van den Burg, A. and Egberink, B. P. (1972) An electromyographic study of the adductor mandibulae complex of a free-swimming carp (*Cyprinus carpio* L.) during feeding. *J. exp. Biol.,* **57**, 261–83.

Barel, C. D. N. (1983) Towards a constructional morphology of cichlid fishes (Teleostei, Perciformes). *Neth. J. Zool.,* **33**, 357–424.

Bertmar, G. and Stromberg, C. (1969) The feeding mechanisms in plankton eaters. I. The epibranchial organ in whitefish. *Mar. Biol.,* **3**, 107–9.

Burko, T. (1975) Size-selective predation by the threespined stickleback, MSc thesis, University of British Columbia, Vancouver.

Campos, H. (1969) Die Geschmacksknospen in Vorderdarm von Süsswasserfischen, Zahl, Verteilung und Entwicklung. *Z. wiss. Zool.,* **179**, 253–99.

Chu, Y. T. (1935) Comparative studies on the scales and on the pharyngeals and their teeth in Chinese cyprinids, with particular reference to taxonomy and evolution. *Biol. Bull. St. John's Univ., Shanghai,* **2**, 1–225.

Cross, C. G. (1969) Aquatic weed control using grass carp. *J. Fish Biol.,* **1**, 27–30.

Cummins, K. W. and Wuycheck, J. C. (1971) Caloric equivalents for investigations in ecological energetics. *Verh. int. Verein. theor. angew. Limnol.,* **18**, 1–158.

Curry, E. (1939) The histology of the digestive tube of the carp (*Cyprinus carpio communis*). *J. Morph.,* **65**, 53–78.

Drost, M. R. and van den Boogaart, J. G. M. (1986) The energetics of feeding strikes in larval carp (*Cyprinus carpio*). *J. Fish Biol.,* **29**, 371–9.

Eastman, J. T. (1977) The pharyngeal bones and teeth of catastomid fishes. *Am. Midl. Nat.*, **97**, 68–88.

Evans, H. E. (1952) The correlation of brain pattern and feeding habits in four species of of cyprinid fishes. *J. comp. Neurol.*, **97**, 133–42.

Evans, H. E. and Deubler, E. E. jun. (1955) Pharyngeal tooth replacement in *Semotilus atromaculatus* and *Clinostomus elongatus*, two species of cyprinid fishes. *Copeia*, **1**, 31–41.

Finger, T. E. (1988) Sensorimotor mapping in oropharyngeal reflexes in goldfish, *Carassius auratus*. *Brain Behav. Evol.*, **31**, 17–24.

Fischer, Z. (1968) Food selection in grass carp (*Ctenopharyngodon idella* Val.) under experimental conditions. *Polskie Arch. Hydrobiol.*, **15**, 1–8.

Fryer, G. (1959) The trophic interrelationships and ecology of some littoral communities of Lake Nyasa with special reference to the fishes, and a discussion of the evolution of a group of rock-frequenting Cichlidae. *Proc. Zool. Soc. Lond.*, **132**, 153–281.

Geyer, E. (1937) Der Zeitliche Ablauf der Bezahnung und des Zahnwechsels bei *Cyprinus carpio* L., unter besonderer Berucksichtigung des einsömmrigen Karpfens. *Morph. Jb.*, **80**, 280–354.

Girgis, S. (1952) The bucco-pharyngeal feeding mechanism in an herbivorous bottom-feeding cyprinoid, *Labeo horie* (Cuvier). *J. Morph.*, **90**, 281–315.

Gosline, W. A. (1971) *Functional Morphology and Classification of Teleostean Fishes*, Univ. Press of Hawaii, Honolulu, 208 pp.

Gosline, W. A. (1973) Considerations regarding the phylogeny of cypriniform fishes, with special reference to structures associated with feeding. *Copeia*, **1973**, 761–76.

Hampl, A., Jirasek, J. and Sirotek, D. (1983) Growth morphology of the filtering apparatus of silvercarp (*Hypophthalmichthys molitrix*). II. Microscopic anatomy. *Aquaculture*, **31**, 153–8.

Harrington, R. W. (1955) The osteocranium of the American cyprinid fish, *Notropsis bifrenatus*, with an annotated synonymy of teleost skull bones. *Copeia*, **1955**(4), 267–90.

Heckel, J. J. (1843) *Abbildungen und Beschreibungen der Fische Syriens nebst einer neuen Classification und Characteristik sämmtlicher Gattungen der Cyprinen*, E. Schweizerbart'sche Verlagshandlung, Stuttgart, 53 pp.

Heincke, F. (1892) Variabilität und Bastardbildung bei Cyprinoiden, in *Festschrift zum siebenzigsten Geburtstage Rudolf Leuckarts*, Wilhelm Engelmann, Leipzig, pp. 65–73.

Hickling, C. F. (1966) On the feeding process in the White Amur, *Ctenopharyngodon idella*. *J. Zool., Lond.*, **148**, 408–19.

Holling, C. S. (1966) The functional response of invertebrate predators to prey density. *Mem. Ent. Soc. Can.*, **48**, 1–86.

Holstvoogd, C. (1965) The pharyngeal bones and muscles in Teleostei, a taxonomic study. *Proc. K. ned. Acad. Wet.*, **68C**, 209–18.

Hoogenboezem, W., Sibbing, F. A., Osse, J. W. M., van den Boogaart, J. G. M., Lammens, E. H. R. R. and Terlouw, A. (1990) X-ray measurements of gill-arch movements in filter-feeding bream, *Abramis brama* (Cyprinidae), *J. Fish Biol.*, **36**, 47–58.

Hoogenboezem, W., van den Boogaart, J. G. M., Sibbing, F. A., Lammens, E. H. R. R., Terlouw, A. and Osse, J. W. M. (1991) A new model of particle retention and branchial sieve adjustment in filter-feeding bream (*Abramis brama* (L.), Cyprinidae). *Can. J. Fisheries Aquat. Sci.*, **48**, (in press).

Hunt, S. (1970) *Polysaccharide–protein Complexes in Invertebrates*, Academic Press, New York.

Iwai, T. (1964) A comparative study of the taste buds in gill rakers and gill arches of teleostean fishes. *Bull Misaki mar. biol. Inst.*, **7**, 19–34.

Janssen, J. (1976) Feeding modes and prey size selection in the alewife (*Alosa pseudoharengus*). *J. Fish. Res. Bd Can.*, **33**, 1972–5.

Janssen, J. (1978) Feeding behaviour repertoire of the alewife (*Alosa pseudoharengus*), and the ciscoes *Coregonus hoyi* and *C. artedii*. *J. Fish. Res. Bd Can.*, **35**, 249–53.

Kajak, Z., Spodniewska, I. and Wisniewski, R. J. (1977) Studies on food selectivity of silver carp, *Hypophthalmichthys molitrix* (Val.). *Ekol. pol.*, **25**, 227–39.

Kazansky, V. I. (1964) Species differences in the structure of the gill apparatus in Cyprinidae. *Vop. Ikhtiol.*, **4**, 45–60.

King, D. P. F. and McLeod, P. R. (1976) Comparison of the food and filtering mechanism of pilchard, *Sardinops ocellata*, and anchovy, *Engraulis capensis*, of South West Africa, 1971–1972. Sea Fisheries Branch Inv. Rpt. no. 111, 29 pp.

Kotrschal, K. and Junger, H. (1988) Patterns of brain morphology in mid-European Cyprinidae (Pisces, Teleostei): a quantitative histological study. *J. Hirnforsch.*, **29**, 341–52.

Lauder, G. V. (1980) Hydrodynamics of prey capture by teleost fishes, in *Biofluid Mechanics*, Vol. 2 (ed. D. Schneck), Plenum Press, N Y, pp. 161–81.

Lauder, G. V. (1983) Functional design and evolution of the pharyngeal jaw apparatus in euteleostean fishes. *Zool. J. Linn. Soc.*, **77**, 1–38.

Lazzaro, X. (1987) A review of planktivorous fishes: their evolution, feeding behaviours, selectivities, and impacts. *Hydrobiologia*, **146**, 97–167.

Leeuwen, J. L. van (1984) A quantitative study of flow in prey capture by rainbow trout, *Salmo gairdneri*, with general consideration of the actinopterygian feeding mechanism. *Trans. zool. Soc. Lond.*, **37**, 171–227.

Leeuwen, J. L. van and Muller, M. (1984) Optimum sucking techniques for predatory fish. *Trans. zool. Soc. Lond.*, **37**, 137–69.

Liem, K. F. (1973) Evolutionary strategies and morphological innovations: cichlid pharyngeal jaws. *Syst. Zool.*, **22**, 425–41.

Liem, K. F. (1984) Functional versatility, speciation and niche overlap: are fishes different? in *Trophic Interactions Within Aquatic Ecosystems* (eds D. G. Meyers and J. R. Strickler), Am. Ass. Adv. Science, Washington DC, pp. 269–305.

Liem, K. F. and Greenwood, P. H. (1981) A functional approach to the phylogeny of the pharyngognath teleosts. *Am. Zool.*, **21**, 83–101.

Liem, K. F. and Wake, D. B. (1985) Morphology: current approaches and concepts, in *Functional Vertebrate Morphology* (eds M. Hildebrand, D. M. Bramble, K. F. Liem and D. B. Wake), Harvard Univ. Press, London, pp. 366–77.

Lucas, P. W. and Luke, D. A. (1984) Chewing it over: basic principles in food breakdown, in *Food Acquisition and Processing in Primates* (eds D. J. Chivers, B. A. Wood and A. Bilsborough), Plenum Press, NY, pp. 283–301.

Matthes, H. (1963) A comparative study of the feeding mechanisms of some African Cyprinidae (Pisces, Cypriniformes). *Bijdr. Dierk.*, **33**, 3–35.

Morita, Y. and Finger, T. E. (1985) Topographic and laminar organization of the vagal gustatory system in the goldfish (*Carassius auratus*). *J. comp. Neurol.*, **238**, 187–201.

Motta, P. J. (1984) Mechanics and functions of jaw protrusion in teleost fishes: a review. *Copeia*, **1984**, 1–18.

Motta, P. J. (1988) Functional morphology of the feeding apparatus of ten species of Pacific butterflyfishes (Perciformes, Chaetodontidae): an ecomorphological approach. *Environ. Biol. Fishes*, **22**, 39–67.

Muller, M. and Osse, J. W. M. (1984) Hydrodynamics of suction feeding in fish. *Trans. Zool. Soc. Lond.*, **37**, 51–135.

Muller, M., Osse, J. W. M. and Verhagen, J. H. G. (1982) A quantitative hydrodynamical model of suction feeding in fish. *J. theor. Biol.*, **95**, 49–79.

Nelson, D. W. (1979) The mechanisms of filter feeding in three teleosts: *Engraulis mordax, Sardinops caerulea and Rastrelliger kanagurta*. Univ. Washington, Seattle, Zool./Fish. 575, 4 Dec. 1979, 17 pp.

Nelson, G. J. (1967) Epibranchial organs in lower teleostean fishes. *J. Zool., Lond.*, **153**, 71–89.

Nikolsky, G. V. (1963) *The Ecology of Fishes*, Academic Press, London, 352 pp.

Oijen, M. J. P. van, Witte, F. and Witte-Maas, E. L. M. (1981) An introduction to ecological and taxonomic investigations on the haplochromine cichlids from the Mwanza Gulf of Lake Victoria. *Neth. J. Zool.*, **31**, 149–74.

Osse, J. W. M. (1985) Jaw protrusion, an optimization of the feeding apparatus of teleosts? *Acta Biotheor.*, **34**, 219–32.

Paloheimo, J. E. and Dickie, L. M. (1966) Food and growth of fishes. III. Relations among food, body size and growth efficiency. *J. Fish. Res. Bd Can.*, **23**, 1209–48.

Paszkowski, C. A., Tonn, W. M. and Holopainen, I. J. (1989) An experimental study of body size and food size relations in crucian carp, *Carassius carassius*. *Environ. Biol. Fishes*, **24**, 275–86.

Prejs, A. (1984) Herbivory by temperate freshwater fishes and its consequences. *Environ. Biol. Fishes*, **10**, 281–96.

Prowse, G. A. (1964) Some limnological problems in tropical fish ponds. *Verh. Internat. Verein. Limnol.*, **15**, 480–4.

Ramaswami, L. S. (1955) Skeleton of cyprinoid fishes in relation to phylogenetic studies: 7. The skull and Weberian apparatus of Cyprininae (Cyprinidae). *Acta Zool.*, **36**, 199–242.

Roberts, T. R. (1973) Interrelationships of Ostariophysans, in *Interrelationships of Fishes* (eds P. H. Greenwood, R. S. Miles, and C. Patterson), Academic Press, London, pp. 373–96.

Robotham, P. W. J. (1982) An analysis of a specialized feeding mechanism of the spined loach, *Cobitis taenia* (L.), and a description of the related structures. *J. Fish Biol.*, **20**, 173–81.

Rosen, M. W. and Cornford, N. E. (1971) Fluid friction of fish slimes. *Nature, Lond.*, **234**, 49–51.

Rubenstein, D. I. and Koehl, M. A. R. (1977) The mechanisms of filter feeding: some theoretical considerations. *Am. Nat.*, **111**, 981–4.

Rutte, E. (1962) Schlundzähne von Süsswasserfischen. *Palaeontographica Abt. A*, **120**, 165–212.

Schwartz, F. J. and Dutcher, B. W. (1962) Tooth replacement and food of the cyprinid *Notropis cerasinus* from the Roanoke River, Virginia. *Am. Midl. Nat.*, **68**, 369–75.

Sibbing, F. A. (1982) Pharyngeal mastication and food transport in the carp (*Cyprinus carpio* L.): a cineradiographic and electromyographic study. *J. Morph.*, **172**, 223–58.

Sibbing, F. A. (1987) The role of taste in the feeding mechanism of the carp (Cyprinidae). *Ann. N. Y. Acad. Sci.* **510**, 612–15.

Sibbing, F. A. (1988) Specializations and limitations in the utilization of food resources by the carp, *Cyprinus carpio*: a study of oral food processing. *Environ. Biol. Fishes*, **22**, 161–78.

Sibbing, F. A. (1991) Food processing by mastication in fish, in *Food Texture and Feeding* (eds J. Nelson and J. F. V. Vincent), *Symp. Soc. exp. Biol.*, **43**, (in press).

Sibbing, F. A. and Uribe, R. (1985) Regional specializations of the oropharyngeal wall and food processing in the carp (*Cyprinus carpio* L.). *Neth. J. Zool.*, **35**, 377–422.

Sibbing, F. A., Osse, J. W. M. and Terlouw, A. (1986) Food handling in the carp (*Cyprinus carpio* L.), its movement patterns, mechanisms and limitations. *J. Zool., Lond. (A)*, **210**, 161–203.

Suietov, S. V. (1939) Contribution to the fish productivity of fresh waters. VIII. The thickness of bottom deposits and its role in the utilization of natural food by fishes. *Proc. Kossino Limnol. Stat.*, **22**, 241–9.

Suslowska, W. and Urbanowicz, K. (1983) Specific skull structure features and the filter and suprabranchial apparatus of the silvercarp *Hypophthalmichthys molitrix* (Val.). *Zool. Polon.* **30**, 71–95.

Takahasi, N. (1925) On the homology of the cranial muscles of the cypriniform fishes. *J. Morphol.*, **40**, 1–109.

Uribe-Zamora, M. (1975) Selection des proies par le filtre branchial de la carpe miroir (*Cyprinus carpio* L.), PhD thesis, Univ. of Lyon.

Vandewalle, P. (1979) Etude cinematographique et electromyographique des mouvements respiratoires chez trois cyprins, *Gobio gobio* (L.), *Barbus barbus* (L.) et *Leuciscus leuciscus* (L.). *Cybium*, 3e série, **6**, 3–28.

Vasnecov, V. (1939) Evolution of pharyngeal teeth in Cyprinidae, in *À la Memoire de A.N. Sewertzoff*, Acad. Sci. USSR, Moscow, pp. 439–91.

Verigin, B. V. (1957) Structure of gill apparatus and of supragill organ of silvercarp. *Zool. Zh.*, **36**, 595–602.

Verigina, I. A. (1969) Ecological and morphological peculiarities of the alimentary system in some carps, in *Ichthyology. Progress in Science. Zoology* (ed. L. P. Poznanin), Amerilled Publ., New Delhi, pp. 88–117.

Webb, P. W. (1982) Locomotor patterns in the evolution of actinopterygian fishes. *Am. Zool.*, **22**, 329–42.

Werner, E. E. (1974) The fish size, prey size, handling time relation in several sunfishes and some implications. *J. Fish. Res. Bd Can.*, **31**, 1531–6.

Werner, E. E. and Hall, D. J. (1974) Optimal foraging and the size selection of prey by the bluegill sunfish (*Lepomis macrochirus*). *Ecology*, **55**, 1042–52.

Werner, E. E. and Mittelbach, G. G. (1981) Optimal foraging: field test of diet choice and habitat switching. *Amer. Zool.*, **21**, 813–29.

Wheeler, A. (1978) *Key to the Fishes of Northern Europe*, Frederick Warne Publ., London.

Wright, D. J., O'Brien, W. J. and Luecke, C. (1983) A new estimate of zooplankton retention by gill rakers and its ecological significance. *Trans. Am. Fish. Soc.*, **112**, 638–46.

Wunder, W. (1936) Physiologie der Süsswasserfische. *Handb. Binnenfisch. Mitteleur.*, **26**, 1–340.

Zander, E. (1906) Das Kiemenfilter der Teleosteer. *Z. wiss. Zool.*, **84**, 619–713.

Zaret, T. M. (1980) *Predation and Freshwater Communities*, Yale University Press, London, 187 pp.

Chapter fourteen

Digestion

R. Hofer

Dedicated to Professor Dr Wolfgang Wieser on the occasion of his 65th birthday

14.1 INTRODUCTION

In temperate and tropical Eurasian fresh waters, cyprinid species are the most abundant fish, inhabiting several niches and eating a variety of foods, including plants. Despite the diversity of cyprinid feeding habits, from piscivory to herbivory, their intestinal tract varies only in length and is comparatively simple. The first one-third of the intestine, the intestinal bulb, is the main site of digestion and absorption, which can be divided into two main steps. (1) After being mechanically processed by pharyngeal teeth, the components of the diet are hydrolysed into smaller molecules. The enzymes for this phase of gross digestion are secreted by the pancreatic tissue into the lumen of the intestinal bulb. (2) The hydrolysis of fragments of proteins, carbohydrates and lipids is continued on the mucosal surface and, after absorption, in the mucosal cells (peptides, saccharides) or in hepatocytes (monoglycerides).

This chapter does not cover the whole field of digestion but concentrates on ecological aspects.

14.2 CHEMICAL PROCESSING OF PROTEINS

The most remarkable feature of the digestive system of cyprinids (and of some other teleost families, i.e. Cyprinodontidae, Labridae, Blennidae, and Gobiidae) is the lack of a true stomach. In consequence, cyprinids have dispensed with the secretion of hydrochloric acid and of pepsin (pepsinogen), a proteolytic enzyme which requires an acid environment for its activation and activity. In other specialized teleosts, e.g. cichlids, high concentrations of hydrochloric acid (pH 1.5–2.0) effect the denaturation and subsequent lysis of bacterial and plant cells (Moriarty, 1973; Bowen, 1976), thus significantly increasing the ultilization of plant, algal and detrital matter (Buddington, 1979; Mironova, 1974; Bowen, 1979; Moriarty and Moriarty, 1973). Although lacking a stomach, many cyprinids, particularly in tropical and subtropical regions, successfully eat various types of plant material. In fact, no significant differences can be found between species with and those without stomachs, e.g. trout, *Salmo sp.*, and carp, *Cyprinus carpio*, can both digest easily-degradable proteins (Ash, 1985). This raises the question of the importance of the stomach for digestion.

In the presence of hydrochloric acid, peptic hydrolysis results in a partial degradation of proteins to smaller peptides but not to free amino acids (Grabner and Hofer, 1985, 1989). The peptides can be attacked more easily by trypsin and chymotrypsin, thus speeding up intestinal hydrolysis (Hofer *et al.*, 1982a; Grabner and Hofer, 1985). Acid digestion is important for species in which the main portion of the intestinal mucosal surface consists of pyloric caeca (Buddington and Diamond, 1987). However, the processes in the stomach have no effect on the subsequent intestinal digestion except for a significant shift from soluble polypeptides to di- and oligopeptides (Grabner and Hofer, 1989).

The stomach also plays an important role as a storage organ, particularly for carnivorous species which swallow large food items. The lack of this storage capacity in cyprinids is partly made up for by an extension of the foregut, the intestinal bulb, where most of the important digestive processes take place.

The digestive juice secreted by the exocrine pancreatic tissue into the intestinal bulb contains enzymes for processing proteins, carbohydrates and lipids, as well as bicarbonates. The ingested native proteins are first of all attacked by trypsin and chymotrypsin. These two endopeptidases are secreted by the pancreas as inactive zymogens which must be activated by trypsin itself or by enteropeptidase, located in the brush border membrane (Nilsson and Fänge, 1969). The pH optimum for trypsin and chymotrypsin activity in cyprinids ranges from 7.9 to 9.0 with different substrates (Al-Hussaini, 1949; Jany, 1976; Bitterlich, 1985a), although the pH values of the intestinal contents are sometimes outside this range, particularly in the case of animal diets (pH 6.3–9.2: Hofer, 1982; Hofer *et al.*, 1982a; Bitterlich, 1985a).

The products of this endopeptidase activity range from soluble polypeptides to free amino acids. Peptides are further processed by exopeptidases (carboxypeptidases secreted by the pancreas and aminopeptidases bound to the brush border membrane) and by mucosal dipeptidases (Di Costanzo *et al.*, 1983).

Most of the digested protein is observed as free amino acids and dipeptides. In mammals, transport of small peptides plays an important role in the absorption of amino acids (Gardner, 1984; Alpers, 1987). The different transport mechanisms for different classes of amino acids and for peptides appear to facilitate simultaneous transport across the intestinal epithelium (Matthews, 1975). So far, however, few such investigations have been made on fish (review, Ash, 1985).

Some fish, particularly cyprinids, can absorb native proteins in the intestine (Gauthier and Landis, 1972; Noaillac-Depeyre and Gas, 1973, 1976; Stroband and van der Veen, 1981). This process is largely restricted to a section of the intestine located at 70–95% of the total length (Gauthier and Landis, 1972; Stroband *et al.*, 1979). Under the light microscope the mucosal cells of this section are seen to contain large numbers of vacuoles and pinocytotic vesicles. To a much smaller extent, intact proteins are also absorbed in the proximal sections of the intestine (Rombout *et al.*, 1985). The absorption of native proteins has only been demonstrated for horseradish peroxidase and ferritin, proteins which can be identified histochemically. However, there is no convincing evidence for the absorption of dietary proteins and none at all regarding its quantitative aspects. Moreover, the length of time for which horseradish peroxidase is stored in intracellular vesicles (up to 15 d after administration, Watanabe, 1982) indicates a slow rate of intracellular degradation. Although this mechanism has also been found in gastric species (Bergot, 1976; Noaillac-Depeyre and Gas, 1979; Stroband and Kroon, 1981), it seems to be better developed in stomachless fish (Stroband and van der Veen, 1981; Watanabe, 1982). This can be confirmed in the course of the ontogenetic development of gastric species, in which the pinocytotic area becomes smaller as the gastric glands develop (Watanabe and Sawada, 1985). In contrast to the slow intracellular degradation mentioned above, Ash (1985) found significant activities of horseradish peroxidase in the blood plasma of carp, but not in rainbow trout, within minutes of its being ingested. Hence, the absorption of whole protein is often interpreted as a mechanism compensating for the lack of stomach digestion (Gauthier and Landis, 1972; Noaillac-Depeyre and Gas, 1976; Watanabe, 1981). It may be that this mechanism contributes to the absorption of soluble dietary polypeptides which, at least *in vitro*, accumulate in the absence of gastric predigestion (Grabner and Hofer, 1985, 1989).

Moreover, the affinity of cyprinid trypsins for a synthetic substrate (benzoyl-arginine-p-nitroanilide) is considerably higher than that of the trypsins of trout and perch, *Perca fluviatilis* (Hofer *et al.*, 1975). This higher affinity might be interpreted as a compensation for the lack of gastric digestion, or as facilitating the utilization of foods low in protein.

14.3 PROCESSING OF PLANT DIETS

Animals capable of eating plants are exposed to far less competition than carnivorous species, since plants dominate the biomass. Herbivorous cyprinids are found mainly in tropical and subtropical waters where plants are available throughout the year and where the temperature is high. Cyprinids feeding on macrophytes can only digest the contents of broken cells, because the cell walls are resistant to the digestive enzymes of fish and because cellulolytic activity of symbionts is negligible. Although limited hydrolysis of cellulose has been detected in several cyprinids, the low activities originated from ingested food items (mainly detritus or zooplankton; Prejs and Blaszczyk, 1977; Niederholzer and Hofer, 1979). Furthermore, the substrate employed in these experiments was soluble carboxymethylcellulose and not the more resistant native cellulose.

The simple digestive tract of cyprinids does not offer a favourable environment to the symbiotic microorganisms found in the intestinal contents of other fish (Trust *et al.*, 1979; Bitterlich and Schaber, 1986; Lesel *et al.*, 1986). Only in *Labeo dussumieri*, a tropical Asian cyprinid with an extremely long intestine (17 × body length), does the mucosa form distinct concavities (Girgis, 1952; Sinha, 1983) which, theoretically, may serve as niches for symbiotic microorganisms, and only in two non-cyprinid fish (*Acanthurus nigrophuscus* and *Kyphosus* sp.) has a symbiotic microflora been demonstrated in the gut (Fishelson *et al.*, 1985; Rimmer and Wiebe, 1987).

Specific enzymes for other resistant polysaccharides, like chitin or laminarin (a component of algal cell walls), have been found in the digestive tract of cyprinids and non-cyprinid fish (Piavaux, 1977; Peres, 1979). Little is known about the quantitative utilization of the polysaccharides *in vivo*. However, it can be assumed that their partial hydrolysis is of little nutritional value but may help in exposing the digestible intracellular contents of food items.

In the absence of effective chemical processing of plant cell walls, herbivorous cyprinids depend upon mechanical breakdown by pharyngeal teeth. Although the structure and movement of the teeth would be expected to be adapted to the mechanical properties of the preferred diet in specialized fish (Chapter 13; Sibbing, 1982), this kind of mechanical treatment is not always effective. Even with fragile water plants such as *Ceratophyllum* sp. (Hofer and Schiemer, 1983), only 18–38% of the organic matter of macrophyte diets can be assimilated (Fischer and Lyakhnovich, 1973; Hofer and Schiemer, 1983; Hofer *et al.*, 1985). In the phytoplanktivorous silver carp, *Hypophthalmichthys molitrix*, the morphology of the pharyngeal teeth indicates a mechanical processing of unicellular algae. These cells can be ground between the flattened teeth and the dorsal chewing pad. Most of the algal cells, however, leave the digestive tract more or less intact (Bitterlich, 1985b).

Elongation of the intestinal tract, a common adaptation to vegetable diets, is also found in cyprinids. Whereas the length of the intestine of macro-herbivorous species is only about 2.5 BL (body lengths), it attains 6 BL in phytoplanktivorous cyprinids. Exceptionally long intestines (*c.* 17 BL) can be found in *Labeo* sp. (Matthes, 1963; Hofer and Schiemer, 1981). The elongation of the cyprinid intestine (except that of Labeo sp.) seems to be accompanied by a reduction of the mucosal structure (Hofer, 1988) (Fig. 14.1). Thus, the intestinal elongation is not necessarily accompanied by an increase of the total

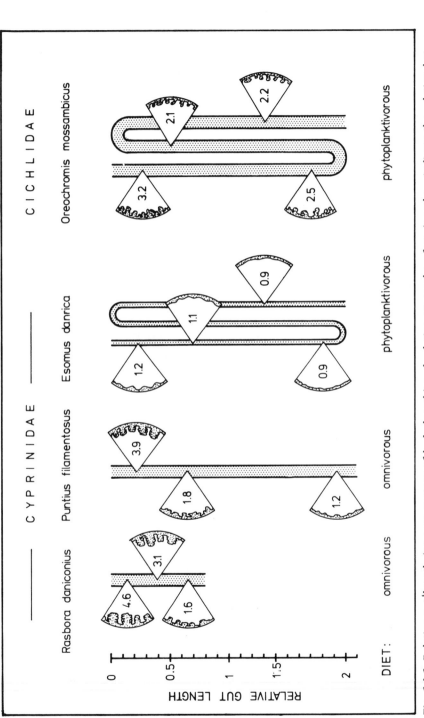

Fig. 14.1 Relative gut length (as a percentage of body length) and relative mucosal surface (numbers indicate the relation between serosal and mucosal circumferences of cross sections) of omnivorous and phytoplanktivorous cyprinids and of a phytoplanktivorous cichlid.

mucosal surface. The intestinal elongation in macroherbivorous cyprinids results in a proportional increase in gut passage time, thus promoting digestive processes and probably to a lesser extent microbial degradation of the more resistant diet. According to the few results available on species of other families, gut passage time during continuous feeding and at a temperature of about 28 °C ranges between 1.3 and 2.2 h per unit body length (Maltzahn, 1957; Moriarty and Moriarty, 1973; Hofer and Newrkla, 1983; Hofer and Schiemer, 1983; Lassuy, 1984). After cessation of feeding, intestinal evacuation takes considerably longer (about 1.5–2 ×) than during continuous feeding (Hofer *et al.*, 1982b). However, the gut passage time of phytoplanktivorous cyprinids (*Amblypharyngodon melettinus* and *Esomus danrica*) does not follow the same pattern. According to less-well-substantiated observations, the low storage capacity of their intestines (only about 2% of body weight instead of up to 5–10% in macroherbivorous species, Hofer and Schiemer, 1983; Hofer, 1988), combined with a poorly digestible diet (Bitterlich, 1985b), force them to accelerate their gut passage (Hofer, 1988).

Many cyprinid species accept a large variety of foodstuffs including plant and detrital material (Chapter 12). In a few species (*Leuciscus cephalus*, *Rasbora daniconius*) the natural diet even ranges from fish to plants (Gyurko and Nagy, 1965; Hofer and Schiemer, 1981). In many omnivorous cyprinids, e.g. *Rutilus rutilus*, the intestinal length does not differ from that of carnivorous species. This shows that even species with less conspicuous features of herbivory can meet their basic energy demands on a purely plant diet. Over longer periods, however, the poor quality of plant proteins leads to a metabolic deficiency (Hofer *et al.*, 1985). On the other hand, a natural plant diet inevitably includes small animals which may furnish the essential amino acids.

The positive correlation between the amount of protein or starch in the diet of fish and the activity of the specific enzymes in the digestive tract is well documented (Fish, 1960; Nagase, 1964; Mukhopadhyay, 1977; Kawai and Ikeda, 1972; Hofer and Schiemer, 1981), although this correlation may be the result of different degrees of dilution of the digestive juices (Hofer, 1982). In fact, with a plant diet (of low protein content) the specific proteolytic activity of the digestive juice is lower, but the daily production of proteolytic enzymes is even higher, than with an animal diet (Hofer, 1982; Hofer and Schiemer, 1981). The large amount of ingested plant material not only dilutes the digestive juice but also accelerates passage through the gut (Hofer *et al.*, 1982b), so that a higher enzyme production is required. This is confirmed by the size and number of zymogen granula in the pancreas: in carnivorous specimens of *Rutilus rutilus*, zymogen granula are few but large, whereas in herbivorous specimens the granula are small but significantly more numerous, indicating a higher turnover (Abd-Elgawad, 1983). This increased enzyme production in herbivorous cyprinids and the modest benefit derived from a plant diet make an economic handling of the digestive enzymes indispensible. Although proteases and amylase are resistant to autolysis *in vitro*, the activity of the digestive enzymes may decrease *in vivo* within the last third of the digestive tract to only about 2–3% of the activity in the foregut (Hofer, 1982). This phenomenon, observed also in mammals (Beynon and Kay, 1976; Diamond, 1978), has been frequently discussed (Nagase, 1964; Kawai and Ikeda, 1972; Mukhopadhyay, 1977; Hofer and Schiemer, 1981), but so far little is known about the mechanism involved. It may be related to the absorption of native proteins in distal sections of the digestive tract. In *Rutilus rutilus* both processes are located at the same site of the intestine. On the other hand, in *Oreochromis mossambicus*, a cichlid with a long intestine, tryptic activity is reduced to a low level before the intestinal contents reach the vacuolated zone of protein absorption (unpubl.).

As a rule, the longer the intestine the greater the 'enzyme reabsorption' and, as a consequence, the longer is the distal section of the gut in which enzyme activity is low (Hofer and Schiemer, 1981). Whereas the adults of non-specialized omnivorous cyprinids such as *Rutilus rutilus* may lose only small amounts of digestive enzymes in the faeces (Hofer, 1982), there is less enzyme reabsorption in their predominantly carnivorous larval and juvenile stages (Hofer and Nasir Uddin, 1985; Köck and Hofer, 1989).

Since readily digestible polysaccharides (starch, glycogen) are only present to any significant degree in plants, the activity of amylase is more specifically adapted to the diet of a given species than other enzymes. Therefore it is not surprising that in cyprinids, which generally tend to omnivory, and particularly in carp, amylase activity is higher than in carnivorous families of fish (Vonk, 1927, 1941; Hofer *et al.*, 1982a).

Reduction of the activity of digestive enzymes by inhibitors, although playing a minor role in wild fish, has become important in aquaculture, particularly since expensive fish meal is increasingly being replaced by cheaper plant proteins. Seeds of several plants contain not only high amounts of proteins, carbohydrates or lipids, but also high concentrations of protease inhibitors (soyabean inhibitor for trypsin-like enzymes in several beans) or amylase inhibitors (in wheat and some other grains), which may reduce digestion and assimilation of the food (Block and Mitchell, 1946; Grabner and Hofer, 1985; Hofer and Sturmbauer, 1985). These inhibitors are easily destroyed by extrusion during feed manufacture.

On the other hand, the presence of inhibitors does not necessarily lead to a drastic reduction in digestion. Under simulated natural conditions *in vitro*, carp amylase activity is inhibited to 10–50% of the original value by amylase inhibitors from wheat (Hofer and Sturmbauer, 1985). *In vivo*, however, carp compensates for the action of amylase inhibitors by increasing the rate of secretion of pancreatic amylase (Sturmbauer and Hofer, 1986). Thus, carp feeding on native wheat have to synthesize about four times as much enzyme as those fed on extruded wheat.

14.4 DIGESTIVE PROCESSES IN CYPRINID LARVAE

Hatching cyprinids are more or less incomplete organisms, as the differenti-ation of organs continues during the postembryonic period (Stroband and Dabrowski, 1979; Tanaka, 1971), particularly the digestive tract (Dabrowski, 1984; Govoni *et al.*, 1986). On the other hand, during the period when growth rates may reach more than 30% d^{-1}, (Bryant and Matty, 1980), digestive processes are of exceptional importance. Exogenous feeding starts even before the yolk sac is completely absorbed. At this stage the larval intestine is short, forming a straight tube measuring about 50% of the body length (Stroband and Dabrowski, 1979). This short intestine can only cope with easily digestible animal diets, mainly zooplankton (Hammer, 1985; Mark *et al.*, 1987). The intestine grows slowly during the larval and fry period (Stroband and Dabrowski, 1979; Hofer and Nasir Uddin, 1985). Since the gut passage time is positively correlated with the relative intestinal length (Hofer and Nasir Uddin, 1985), the time available for digestive and absorptive processes is gradually extended until finally the fish is able to switch to the adult, species-specific diet.

The activity of digestive enzymes is low in the first period of feeding but increases during larval development (Stroband and Dabrowski, 1979; Lauff and Hofer, 1984). The digestive enzymes of living zooplankton – the natural diet of cyprinid larvae – survive in the predator's digestive tube and accelerate its digestive processes. In roach larvae, ingested zooplankton contribute about 25% of the total tryptic activity of the intestinal contents (Lauff and Hofer, 1984). This exogenous contribution to digestion may lead to a reduction in endogenous enzyme production, which could be important because the 'reabsorption of digestive enzymes' in the hindgut is less efficient in larvae than in adults (Hofer and Nasir Uddin, 1985; Köck and Hofer, 1989). In roach larvae fed on zooplankton, the relative tryptic activity of the faeces amounts to about 30% of that of the foregut, whereas in adults it is reduced to as little as 2–5%. However, artificial diets, which lead to low growth and high mortality rates, not only give rise to a significantly higher tryptic activity of the intestinal contents but also, after two weeks of feeding, to the disappearance of the gradient between fore- and hindgut. The resulting loss of considerable amounts of digestive enzymes via the faeces may lead to a negative balance of body proteins. On the other hand, the low efficiency of enzyme reabsorption in the hindgut means that digestion goes on in a longer stretch of gut and may thus enable the larvae to compensate for the short intestine (50% or less of that of the adults) and the proportional reduction in gut passage time. Tryptic activity of adult cyprinids is pronounced in the first and second third of the intestine but is more or less negligible in the last third, where most of the enzymes have already disappeared (Hofer and Schiemer, 1981; Hofer, 1982). In larvae, however, particularly those feeding on less suitable artificial diets, the hydrolytic processes continue into the hindgut.

In cyprinids the morphological and physiological differentiation of the intestinal tract is a continuous process of development, with none of the drastic changes seen in other families of fish, in which stomach or pyloric caeca form and a recognizable 'metamorphosis' takes place (Mähr *et al.*, 1983; Hofer, 1987; Forstner *et al.*, 1983).

ACKNOWLEDGEMENTS

I am grateful to Mrs Joy Wieser for correcting the manuscript.

REFERENCES

Abd-Elgawad, A. M. (1983) Morphometric changes which are induced in the exocrine pancreas of *Rutilus rutilus* L. by different feeding habits, thesis, Univ. Innsbruck (Austria). (134 pp.)

Al-Hussaini, A. H. (1949) On the functional morphology of the alimentary tract of some fish in relation to differences in their feeding habits. I. Anatomy and histology. *Q. J. microsc. Sci.*, **90**, 109–39.

Alpers, D. H. (1987) Digestion and absorption of carbohydrates and proteins, in: *Physiology of the Gastrointestinal Tract*, 2nd edn (ed. L. R. Johnson), Raven Press, NY, pp. 1469–87.

Ash, R. (1985) Protein digestion and absorption, in *Nutrition and Feeding in Fish* (eds C. B. Cowey, A. M. Mackie and J. G. Bell), Academic Press, London, pp. 69–93.

Bergot, P. (1976) Determination par le rouge de ruthenium d'invaginations profondes de la membrane plasmique apicale des enterocytes dans l'intestine posterieur chez la truite arc-enciel. *Annls Biol. anim. Biochim. Biophys.*, **16**, 37–42.

Beynon, R. and Kay, I. (1976) Enteropancreatic circulation of digestive enzymes. *Nature, Lond.*, **260**, 78–9.

Bitterlich, G. (1985a) Digestive enzyme pattern of two stomachless filter feeders, silver carp, *Hypophthalmychthys molitrix* Val., and bighead carp, *Aristichthys nobilis* Rich. *J. Fish Biol.*, **27**, 103–12.

Bitterlich, G. (1985b) The nutrition of stomachless phytoplanktivorous fish in comparison with *Tilapia*. *Hydrobiologia*, **121**, 173–9.

Bitterlich, G. and Schaber, E. (1986) Bacteria – food or food competitors of silver carp, *Hypophthalmichthys molitrix* Val.? *J. Fish Biol.*, **29**, 605–12.

Block, R. J. and Mitchell, H. H. (1946) The effect of heat on protein quality and on its correlation with protein structure. *Nutr. Abstr. Rev.*, **16**, 268–9.

Bowen, S. H. (1976) Mechanism for digestion of detrital bacteria by the cichlid fish *Sarotherodon mossambicus* (Peters). *Nature, Lond.*, **260**, 137–8.

Bowen, S. H. (1979) A nutritional constraint in detrivory by fishes: the stunted population of *Sarotherodon mossambicus* in Lake Sibaya, South Africa. *Ecol. Monogr.* **49**, 17–31.

Bryant, P. L. and Matty, A. J. (1980) Optimisation of *Artemia* feeding rate for carp larvae (*Cyprinus carpio* L.). *Aquaculture*, **21**, 203–12.

Buddington, R. K. (1979) Digestion of an aquatic macrophyte by *Tilapia zilii* (Gervais). *J. Fish Biol.*, **15**, 449–55.

Buddington, R. K. and Diamond, J. M. (1987) Pyloric ceca of fish: a "new" absorptive organ. *Am. J. Physiol.* **252** (*Gastrointest. Liver Physiol.* **15**), G65–G76.

Dabrowski, K. (1984) The feeding of fish larvae: "present state of the art" and perspectives. *Reprod. Nutr. Develop.*, **24**, 807–33.

Diamond, J. M. (1978) Reabsorption of digestive enzymes: playing with poison. *Nature Lond.*, **271**, 111–12.

Di Costanzo, G., Florentz, A., Leray, C. and Nonnotte, L. (1983) Structural and functional organization of the brush border membrane in the rainbow trout intestine. *Mol. Physiol.* **4**, 111–23.

Fischer, Z. and Lyakhnovich, V. P. (1973) Biology and bioenergetics of grass carp (*Ctenopharyngodon idella* Val.). *Pol. Arch. Hydrobiol.*, **20**, 521–57.

Fish, G. R. (1960) The comparative activity of some digestive enzymes in the alimentary canal of *Tilapia* and perch. *Hydrobiology*, **15**, 161–79.

Fishelson, L., Montgomery, W. L. and Myrberg, A. A. (1985) A unique symbiosis in the gut of a tropical herbivorous surgeon-fish (Acanthuridae: Teleostei) from the Red Sea. *Science*, **229** (4708), 49–51.

Forstner, H., Hinterleitner, S., Mähr, K. and Wieser, W. (1983) Towards a better definition of "metamorphosis" in *Coregonus* sp.: biochemical, histological, and physiological data. *Can. J. Fish. aquat. Sci.*, **40**, 1224–32.

Gardner, M. G. (1984) Intestinal assimilation of intact peptides and proteins from the diet – a neglected field? *Biol. Rev.*, **59**, 289–331.

Gauthier, G. F. and Landis, S. (1972) The relationship of ultrastructural and cytochemical features of absorptive activity in the goldfish intestine. *Anat. Rec.*, **172**, 675–702.

Girgis, S. (1952) On the anatomy and histology of the alimentary tract of a herbivorous bottom feeding cyprinoid fish, *Labeo horie* (Curvier). *J. Morph.*, **90**, 317–62.

Govoni, J. J. Boehlert, G. M. and Watanabe, Y. (1986) The physiology of digestion in fish larvae. *Environ. Biol. Fishes*, **16**, 57–77.

Grabner, M. and Hofer, R. (1985) The digestibility of the proteins of broad bean (*Vicia faba*) and soya bean (*Glycine max*) under *in-vitro* conditions simulating the alimentary tract of rainbow trout (*Salmo gairdneri*) and carp (*Cyprinus carpio*). *Aquaculture*, **48**, 111–22.

Grabner, M. and Hofer, R. (1989) Stomach digestion and its effect upon protein hydrolysis in the intestine of rainbow trout (*Salmo gairdneri* Richardson). *Comp. Biochem. Physiol.*, **92A**, 81–3.

Gyurko, S. and Nagy, Z. (1965) Ernährungsdynamik des Döbels (*Leuciscus cephalus* L.) im Fluβ Muresch. *Arch. Hydrobiol.* (Supp.), **32**, 47–64.

Hammer, C. (1985) Feeding behaviour of roach (*Rutilus rutilus*) larvae and the fry of perch (*Perca fluviatilis*) in Lake Lankai. *Arch. Hydrobiol.*, **103**, 61–74.

Hofer, R. (1982) Protein digestion and proteolytic activity in the digestive tract of an omnivorous cyprinid. *Comp. Biochem. Physiol.*, **72A**, 55–63.

Hofer, R. (1987) Verdauungsstrategien bei Fischen. *Biol. Unserer Zeit*, **17**, 84—9.

Hofer, R. (1988) Morphological adaptations of the digestive tract of tropical cyprinids and cichlids to diet. *J. Fish. Biol.*, **33**, 399–408.

Hofer, R. and Nasir Uddin, A. (1985) Digestive processes during the development of the roach (*Rutilus rutilus* L.). *J. Fish Biol.*, **26**, 53–9.

Hofer, R. and Newrkla, P. (1983) Determination of gut passage time in Tilapia-fry (*Oreochromis mossambicus*) under laboratory and field conditions. *Proc. Int. Symp. Tilapia in Aquaculture, Israel*, 8–13 May 1983, Tel Aviv Univ., pp. 323–7.

Hofer, R. and Schiemer, F. (1981) Proteolytic activity in the digestive tract of several species of fish with different feeding habits. *Oecologia*, **48**, 342–5.

Hofer, R. and Schiemer, F. (1983) Feeding ecology, assimilation efficiencies and energetics of two herbivorous fish: *Sarotherodon (Tilapia) mossambicus* (Peters) and *Puntius filamentosus* (Cuv. et Val.), in *Limnology of Parakrama Samudra – Sri Lanka: A Case Study of an Anicient Man-made Lake in the Tropics. Developments in Hydrobiology* (ed. F. Schiemer) Dr W. Junk. The Hague, pp. 155–64.

Hofer, R. and Sturmbauer, C. (1985) Inhibition of trout and carp α-amylase by wheat. *Aquaculture*, **48**, 277–83.

Hofer, R., Dall Via, G., Troppmair, J. and Giussani, G. (1982a)˙Differences in digestive enzymes between cyprinids and non-cyprinid fish. *Memorie Ist. ital. Idrobiol.*, **40**, 201–8.

Hofer, R., Forster, H. and Rettenwander, R. (1982b) Duration of gut passage and its dependence on temperature and food consumption in roach (*Rutilus rutilus*). Laboratory and field experiments. *J. Fish Biol.*, **20**, 289–99.

Hofer, R., Krewedel, G. and Koch, F. (1985) An energy budget for an omnivorous cyprinid: *Rutilus rutilus* (L). *Hydrobiologia*, **122**, 53–9.

Hofer, R., Ladurner, H., Gattringer, A. and Wieser, W. (1975) Relationship between the temperature preferenda of fishes, amphibians and reptiles, and the substrate affinities of their trypsins. *J. comp. Physiol.*, **99**, 345–55.

Jany, K. D. (1976) Studies on the digestive enzymes of the stomachless bonefish *Carassius auratus gibelio* (Bloch): endopeptidases. *Comp. Biochem. Physiol.*, **53B**, 31–8.

Kawai, S. and Ikeda, S. (1972) Studies on digestive enzymes of fishes – II. Effect of dietary changes on the activities of digestive enzymes in carp intestine. *Bull. Jap. Soc. scient. Fish.*, **38**, 265–70.

Köck, G. and Hofer, R. (1989) The effect of natural and artificial diets upon tryptic activities in roach and whitefish larvae. *Pol. Arch. Hydrobiol.*, **36**, 443–453.

Lassuy, D. R. (1984) Diet, intestinal morphology, and nitrogen assimilation efficiency in the damselfish, *Stegastes lividus* in Guam. *Environ. Biol. Fishes*, **10**, 183–93.

Lauff, M. and Hofer, R. (1984) Proteolytic enzymes in fish development and the importance of dietary enzymes. *Aquaculture*, **37**, 335–46.

Lesel, R., Fromageot, C. and Lesel, M. (1986) Cellulose digestibility in grass carp, *Ctenopharyngodon idella* and in goldfish, *Carassius auratus*. *Aquaculture*, **54**, 11–17.

Mähr, K., Grabner, M., Hofer, R. and Moser, H. (1983) Histological and physiological development of the stomach in *Coregonus* sp. *Arch. Hydrobiol.*, **98**, 344–53.

Maltzahn, S. *cited by* Barrington, E. J. W. (1957) The alimentary canal and digestion, in *The Physiology of Fishes*. Vol. I (ed. M. E. Brown) Academic Press, NY, pp. 109–61.

Mark, W., Hofer, R. and Wieser, W. (1987) Diet spectra and resource partitioning in the larvae and juveniles of three species and six cohorts of cyprinids from a subalpine lake. *Oecologia*. **71**, 388–96.

Matthes, H. (1963) A comparative study on the feeding mechanisms of some African cyprinids. *Bijdr. Dierk.*, **33**, 3–35.

Matthews, D. M. (1975) Intestinal absorption of peptides. *Physiol. Rev.*, **55**, 537–608.

Mironova, N. N. (1974) *cited by* Fischer, Z. (1979) Selected problems of fish bioenergetics. *Proc. World Symp. Finfish Nutr. Fishfeed Technol. Hamb.*, 20–23 June 1978: **1**, 17–44.

Moriarty, D. J. W. (1973). The physiology of digestion of blue green algae in the cichlid fish, *Tilapia nilotica*. *J. Zool., Lond.*, **171**, 25–39.

Moriarty, D. J. W. and Moriarty, C. M. (1973) The assimilation of carbon from phytoplankton by two herbivorous fishes: *Tilapia nilotica* and *Haplochromis nigripinnis*. *J. Zool., Lond.*, **171**, 41–55.

Mukhopadhyay, P. K. (1977) Studies on the enzymatic activities related to varied pattern of diets in the airbreathing catfish, *Clarias batrachus*, L. *Hydrobiologia*, **52**, 235–7.

Nagase, G. (1964) Contribution to the physiology of digestion in *Tilapia mossambica* Peters: digestive enzymes and the effects of diet on their activity. *Z. vergl. Physiol.*, **49**, 270–84.

Niederholzer, R. and Hofer, R. (1979) The adaptation of digestive enzymes to temperature, season and diet in roach *Rutilus rutilus* L. and rudd *Scardinius erythrophthalmus* L.: cellulase. *J. Fish Biol.*, **15**, 411–16.

Nilsson, A. and Fänge, R. (1969) Digestive proteases in the holocephalian fish *Chimaera monstrosa* L. *Comp. Biochem. Physiol.*, **31**, 147–65.

Noaillac-Depeyre, J. and Gas, N. (1973) Absorption of protein macromolecules by the enterocytes of the carp (*Cyprinus carpio* L.). *Z. Zellforsch.*, **146**, 525–41.

Noaillac-Depeyre, J. and Gas, N. (1976) Electron microscopic study on gut epithelium of the tench (*Tinca tinca* L.) with respect to its absorptive functions. *Tissue Cell*, **8**, 511–30.

Noaillac-Depeyre, J. and Gas, N. (1979) Structure and function of the intestinal epithelial cells in the perch (*Perca fluviatilis*). *Anat. Rec.*, **195**, 621–40.

Peres, G. (1979) Les proteases – l'amylase, les enzymes chitinolytiques – les laminarinases, in *Nutrition des Poissons* (ed. M. Fontaine) Editions du Centre National de la Recherches Scientifique, Actes du Colloque CNERNA, Paris, pp. 55–67.

Piavaux, A. (1977) Distribution and localization of the digestive laminarinases in animals. *Biochem. Syst. Ecol.*, **5**, 231–9.

Prejs, A. and Blaszczyk, M. (1977) Relationship between food and cellulase activity in freshwater fishes. *J. Fish. Biol.*, **11**, 447–52.

Rimmer, D. W. and Wiebe, W. J. (1987) Fermentative microbial digestion in herbivorous fish. *J. Fish. Biol.*, **31**, 229–36.

Rombout, J. H. W. M., Lamers, C. H. J., Helfrich, M. H., Dekker, A. and Taverne-Thiele, J. J. (1985) Uptake and transport of intact macromolecules in the intestinal epithelium of carp (*Cyprinus carpio* L.) and the possible immunological implications. *Cell. Tissue Res.*, **239**, 519–30.

Sibbing, F. A. (1982) Pharyngeal mastication and food transport in *Cyprinus carpio* (L): a cineradiographic and electromyographic study. *J. Morph.*, **172**, 223–58.

Sinha, G. M. (1983) Scanning electron microscopic study of the intestinal mucosa of an Indian freshwater adult major carp, *Labeo rohita* (Hamilton). *Z. mikrosk.-anat. Forsch.*, **97**, 979–92.

Stroband, H. W. J. and Dabrowski, K. R. (1979) Morphological and physiological aspects of the digestive system and feeding in fresh-water fish larvae, in *Nutrition des Poissons* (ed. M. Fontaine) Editions du Centre National de la Recherches Scientifique, Actes du Colloque CNERNA, Paris, pp. 355–74.

Stroband, H. W. J. and Kroon, A. G. (1981) The development of the stomach in *Clarias lazera* and the intestinal absorption of protein macromolecules. *Cell. Tissue Res.*, **215**, 397–415.

Stroband, H. W. J. and van der Veen, F. H. (1981) The localization of protein absorption during the transport of food along the intestine of the grasscarp, *Ctenopharyngodon idella* (Val.). *J. exp. Zool.*, **218**, 149–56.

Stroband, H. W. J., van der Meer, H. and Timmermans, C. P. M. (1979) Regional functional differentiation in the gut of the grasscarp, *Ctenopharyngodon idella* (Val.) *Histochemistry*, **64**, 235–49.

Sturmbauer, C. and Hofer, R. (1986) Compensation for amylase inhibitors in the intestine of the carp (*Cyprinus carpio*). *Aquaculture*, **52**, 31–3.

Tanaka, M. (1971) Studies on the structure and function of the digestive system in teleost larvae. III: Development of the digestive system during postlarvae stage. *Jap. J. Ichthyol.*, **18**, 164–74.

Trust, T. J., Bull, L. M., Currie, B. R. and Buckle, J. T. (1979) Obligate anaerobic bacteria in the gastrointestinal microflora of the grass carp (*Ctenopharyngodon idella*), goldfish (*Carassius auratus*) and rainbow trout (*Salmo gairdneri*). *J. Fish. Res. Bd Can.*, **36**, 1174–9.

Vonk, H. J. (1927) Die Verdauung bei Fischen. *Z. vergl. Physiol.*, **5**, 445–546.

Vonk, H. J. (1941) Die Verdauung bei den niederen Vertebraten. *Adv. Enzymol.*, **1**, 371–417.

Watanabe, Y. (1981) Ingestion of horseradish peroxidase by the intestinal cells in larve or juveniles of some teleosts. *Bull. Jap. Soc. Scient. Fish.*, **47**, 1299–307.

Watanabe, Y. (1982) Intracellular digestion of horseradish peroxidase by the intestinal cells of teleost larvae and juveniles. *Bull. Jap. Soc. Scient. Fish.*, **48**, 37–42.

Watanabe, Y. and Sawada, N. (1985) Larval development of digestive organs and intestinal absorptive functions in the freshwater goby *Chaenogobius annularis*. *Bull. Tohoku Reg. Fish. Res. Lab.*, **47**, 1–10.

Chapter fifteen

Physiological energetics and ecophysiology

W. Wieser

15.1 PHYSIOLOGICAL ENERGETICS

I shall consider the energetics of swimming in fish and the influence of biological factors on energy turnover. A brief look at the arrangement and structure of fish musculature will be helpful.

The structure and functions of the muscles used in swimming

Muscle accounts for 40–60% of the total body mass of fish, more than in any other group of vertebrates. A characteristic feature of the swimming muscles of fish is the uniform arrangement of the fibres along the body and the distinct spatial separation of fibres serving different functions. The internal organs are surrounded by a compact mass of muscle consisting mainly of muscle fibres capable of fast contraction. This muscle is practically colourless owing to its poor blood supply and the absence of myoglobin in the cells. The metabolic energy required for the fast contraction of these 'white fibres' comes chiefly from glycolysis and – in extreme situations – from the breakdown of creatine phosphate. Such fibres are rich in both glycogen and creatine phosphate but contain only small numbers of mitochondria.

Distal to this muscle tissue a thin, wedge-shaped strand of oxidative muscle fibres runs along the lateral line and gradually fans out posteriorly to form a thin sheet covering almost the entire white musculature in the tail region. These fibres are rich in myoglobin and surrounded by capillaries, and are therefore called 'red' fibres. They deliver the mechanical energy for slow, routine swimming. A number of transitional fibre forms can also be recognized. Between the red and the white zones there is usually a layer of intermediate ('pink') fibres. In many species, thin fibres are found among the thick 'white' fibres of the central muscle mass: it is uncertain whether they represent early stages in the development of the 'white' fibres or are of an altogether different type.

Despite such modifications of the basic structure it appears that, in principle, all fish species have solved the problem of moving in a dense medium in the same way. The white fibres, constituting up to 90% of the total swimming musculature, are used for the rapid manoeuvres involved in hunting and flight. They are abundant because the metabolic energy required by the muscle increases with the square or even the cube of the speed of swimming. For the considerably slower sustained swimming the peripheral red muscle fibres (usually little more than 10% of the muscle mass) come into action. In the transition from one form of swimming to the other the white fibres are switched on or off. In other words they represent a different 'gear' in the locomotory mechanism. By directly recording muscle potentials in the carp, *Cyprinus carpio*, Johnston *et al.* (1977) found for example that the red fibres are switched on at a swimming speed of 0.3–0.5 body lengths (BL) per second, the pink fibres at 1.1–1.5, and the white fibres at $2-2.5\,BL\,s^{-1}$. The general rule seems to be that in cyprinids the white muscle fibres are brought into action at moderate swimming speeds but in salmonids not until almost maximum speeds are attained (Jones, 1983).

The maximum velocities of contraction (V_{max}) of the two types of fibre are finely adapted to their different roles. In carp, V_{max} of the red fibres is about 4.6 muscle lengths per second, that of the white fibres about 12.9, although during the characteristic swimming movements both types of fibre contract at the same relative velocity, i.e. about one-third of V_{max} (Rome *et al.*, 1988). This is the velocity at which the power of a contracting muscle fibre is at its maximum (Hill, 1950). The fact that even at maximum swimming velocity the white fibres contract at only one-third of V_{max} is due to their helical trajectories within the muscle segments. At any given body curvature the shortening of the white fibres is only about 25% of that of the red fibres (Alexander, 1969).

Although, basically, this functional scheme applies to all cyprinid species, within such a large family as the Cyprinidae many modifications are encountered. In a most interesting study Bainbridge (1963) compared the hydrodynamics and swimming efficiency of three cyprinid species differing in body form. In the more or less streamlined dace, *Leuciscus leuciscus*, the propulsive waves of contraction characteristic of swimming fish travel along the body evenly and with a relatively small amplitude until, near the tail, amplitude and velocity increase sharply and attain a maximum at the tip of the caudal fin. In the plumper goldfish, *Carassius auratus*, and especially in the hump-backed bream, *Abramis brama*, the amplitude and velocity of the propulsive wave increase steadily from nose to tail, i.e. the anterior portion of the body swings more strongly and even the head performs transverse pendular movements to compensate for the angular moments produced by the caudal fin. Owing to the greater involvement of their bodies in swimming, bream and goldfish lose considerably more energy as heat of friction than dace, in which the larger part of the muscular force is concentrated in the caudal fin and is thus directly transformed into forward thrust. Under otherwise identical conditions, the energy costs of swimming can be expected to be higher for the bream and goldfish than for the dace. The higher the velocity and the larger the fish, the more pronounced this difference becomes.

Levels of swimming activity

The average swimming activity of a fish over the course of a day is termed routine activity. This consists of regular and irregular fluctuations in the level of activity, both of which are correlated with more or less pronounced fluctuations in energy turnover. The most important regular fluctuations are the diurnal periods, as for the day-active roach, *Rutilus rutilus*, (Fig. 15.1(a)). The lowest activity level in a long-term series of measurements gives an approximate measure of the standard rate of metabolism (Brett, 1964), an exact definition of which requires the simultaneous determination of activity and energy turnover (usually measured as oxygen consumption). This is relatively easy to achieve by allowing the fish to swim against currents of known velocities in a flow-through respirometer. The rate of oxygen consumption ($\dot{M}O_2$) is then a power function of the swimming speed (V), the exponent being somewhere between 2 and 3 depending on the size of the fish. Extrapolation of this function to $V = 0$ gives the standard rate of metabolism. This kind of calculation is of course not feasible for spontaneous swimming. When the oxygen consumption and normal swimming activity of roach were recorded simultaneously (Forstner and Wieser, 1990), however, the energy costs of spontaneous linear movements of different velocities were smaller than the deviation from the mean value of the energy turnover, i.e. in this range the rate of energy dissipation is independent of the level of activity and thus conforms with Brett's definition of the standard metabolic rate (Fig. 15.1(b)). The roach and other pelagic cyprinids swim in this economic manner mainly at night, whereas in daytime the swimming pattern consists of irregular movements, such as starting, stopping, turning, or accelerating; in this range the intensity of activity is quite clearly correlated with the rate of oxygen consumption (Fig. 15.1(b)). In general, it can be said that the standard level of activity is raised by a factor of 2–3 in a routinely swimming

---

Fig. 15.1 Routine activity and oxygen consumption in groups of young roach, *Rutilus rutilus*, as measured in long-term ($\geqslant 66$ h) experiments in a flow-through respirometer coupled to activity monitor (reproduced with permission from Forstner and Wieser, 1990). (a) Periodic fluctuations of ($\blacklozenge$) routine activity and ($\bigcirc$) oxygen consumption at 20 °C under a photoperiod of 11L/13D (bar above x-axis). (b) The metabolic cost of routine activity at 15 °C. The data of seven independent experiments are shown, each symbol representing the average 1 h recording of oxygen consumption and spontaneous swimming activity. (c) Regression lines characterizing 13 long-term experiments at three temperatures (heavy lines, 8 °C; thin lines, 15 °C; dashed lines, 20 °C). Ranges of 'low-cost' activity (horizontal lines) are distinguished from ranges of 'high cost' activity (ascending lines). For explanation see text, p. 428.

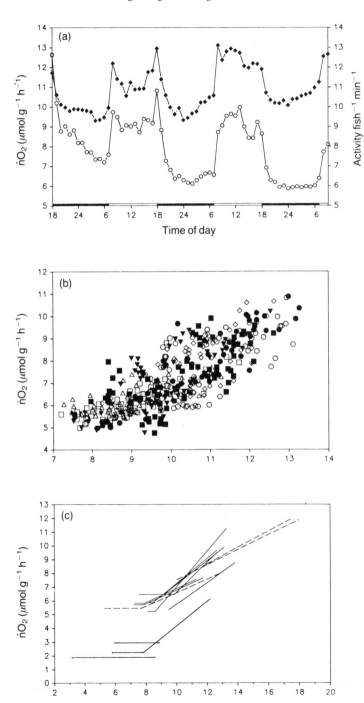

fish. Kausch (1968) found fluctuations in the MO_2 and activity of young carp amounting to 3–4 times the measured minimum values.

The energy spectrum of fish can be extended upwards by defining a maximal swimming speed against which a particular fish can swim for a characteristic length of time (usually 1 h). The difference between the rate of oxygen consumption at this critical swimming velocity and the standard rate is known as the **maximal aerobic scope for activity** of the fish.

If $\dot{M}O_2$ is plotted against swimming velocity the resulting curve can usually be described by a function of the type

$$y = a + b x^c \qquad (15.1)$$

where y is weight-specific $\dot{M}O_2$ (μmol g^{-1} h^{-1}), x swimming velocity (cm s^{-1}) and a, b, c are constants. The constant, a, corresponds to the energy turnover at $x = 0$ and the term bx^c expresses the net cost of swimming. If a tangent is drawn to the exponential function of the equation (15.1), then its slope represents the minimal gross cost of transport (μ mol O_2 g^{-1} cm^{-1}). The net cost of swimming differs very little in adult fish employing the same mode of swimming (for cyprinids and other pelagic freshwater fish, according to Breder (1926), the subcarangiform mode). A list of data (Fry, 1971) revealed very similar values for the goldfish and the rainbow trout, *Oncorhynchus mykiss*, although the latter species would be expected to be the more efficient swimmer. The gross transport costs, however, since they include all energy-consuming functions, vary quite considerably, not only between species but also from one individual to another. The carp, for example, consumes far more energy than most other freshwater fish at comparable swimming velocities (Beamish, 1978), and the $\dot{M}O_2$ of goldfish swimming at one and the same velocity may vary by factor of 2 (Smit 1965).

Larval swimming is very different from that of adults. The minute larvae of cyprinids employ a nearly anguilliform mode, in which a large part of the body performs undulating movements, consuming far more energy than the subcarangiform or carangiform movements of the adults. This was confirmed in a comprehensive study (Kaufmann, 1990), which showed that the gross transport costs of larval Danube bleak, *Chalcalburnus chalcoides*, and roach exceed by a factor of 4–5 the values obtained by extrapolating adult costs into the juvenile weight range.

But even for the same swimming velocity and the same size, the $\dot{M}O_2$ values of cyprinid larvae differ interspecifically. *Pseudorasbora parva*, for example, an eastern species that has immigrated into Central Europe since about 1980, is a much less efficient swimmer than the roach (Kaufmann, 1990).

Energy turnover and body size

Body size is an important variable influencing the animal's energy turnover. In swimming animals, however, the decisive parameter is not the body weight but the (correlated) body length, as contained in the definition of the Reynolds number, $(VL)/\sqrt{}$ (where V = swimming speed, L = hydrodynamically relevant body length, $\sqrt{}$ = kinematic viscosity of water). Nevertheless, for convenience and comparison, in most studies the metabolic power of swimming fish is referred to body weight, according to the following allometric relationship

$$y = a\,x^{b} \qquad (15.2)$$

where y is the energy turnover, x the body weight, and a and b are constants. If the energy turnover of different species is to be compared, then the effect of size on energy turnover has to be taken into consideration. The measure of this effect is the exponent b in Equation 15.2. Winberg (1961) collected all $\dot{M}O_2$ values then known for cyprinids and found that the resulting mass relationship can be described by the function

$$y = 275\,x^{0.80} \qquad (15.3a)$$

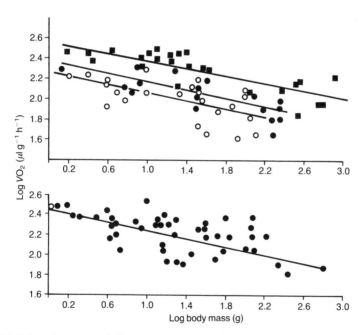

Fig. 15.2 Log–log plots of the intra- and interspecific relationship between mass-specific rate of oxygen consumption (y) and body weight (x) in cyprinids. (a) Data from Winberg (1961): ■, carp, *Cyprinus carpio* (upper line, $y = 2.55 - 0.18\,x$); ●, tench, *Tinca tinca* (middle line, $y = 2.36 - 0.20\,x$); ○, goldfish, *Carassius auratus* (lower line, $y = 2.24 - 0.19\,x$). (b) Data for many species (●) from Winberg (1961) and average of several measurements of young roach, *Rutilus rutilus* (○), from Forstner and Wieser (1990). Regression, $y = 2.44 - 0.206\,x$. All cyprinids were at 20 °C.

(y in $\mu l\, O_2\, h^{-1}$, x in g). The mass-specification $\dot{M}O_2$ then follows from the function

$$y = 275\, x^{-0.20} \qquad (15.3b)$$

and in logarithmic form

$$\log y = 2.44 - 0.20 \log x \qquad (15.3c)$$

Similar relations also appear to hold for intraspecific comparisons, i.e. for the mass-specific rate of metabolism within a species, at least for body weights above about 1 g. According to Winberg (1961), the mass exponent for the routine rate of metabolism is almost the same for carp., goldfish and tench, *Tinca tinca* (b $= -0.20$ to -0.18; Fig. 15.2(a)). On the other hand, there are quite clear species differences in intensity of metabolism, expressed by the coefficient a in Equation 15.2. Under otherwise identical conditions, carp seems to require significantly more oxygen than goldfish and tench. The question as to whether such differences are the result of molecular, cell-biological, physiological or ethological characteristics is one of the major questions in ecophysiological research.

15.2 ECOPHYSIOLOGY I: LIFE UNDER CONDITIONS OF OXYGEN DEFICIENCY

All species of freshwater fish are to some degree adapted to oxygen deficiency in their environment, and a few species have even proved to be masters of the art of survival under these conditions. The mechanisms by which animals adapt to lack of oxygen fall into two categories: (1) better use of the available oxygen through aerobic metabolism, and (2) switchover to anaerobic metabolism.

Adaptation of aerobic energy metabolism

Even if the oxygen content of its environment is lowered, a fish can still meet its energy requirements by aerobic means, either by a reduction of energy turnover or by improved extraction of oxygen from the medium. The second alternative again presents two options: either enhanced ventilation (achieved, for example, by raising the opercular pumping frequency) or improved perfusion (via, for example an increase in the haemoglobin content of the blood and hence in its oxygen capacity). The relationship between oxygen consumption and ambient oxygen concentration is often represented as if two quite different strategies were being employed, one by the 'conformers' and another by the 'regulators'. In conformers, $\dot{M}O_2$ and pO_2 are proportional to one make much sense, because it is at high temperatures that O_2 deficiency critical pO_2 value (P_c), below which the $\dot{M}O_2$ of the regulator also drops rapidly. However, a dichotomous classification of this nature grossly underestimates the flexibility of the adaptive strategies, a flexibility that results from the interplay of many factors. Moreover, the inter- and intra-individual variability of the relationship between $\dot{M}O_2$ and pO_2 may be so large as to prohibit the formulation of simple generalizations (Hughes *et al.*, 1983).

According to a frequently encountered statement, the critical pO_2 increases with water temperature. From an adaptationist's point of view this does not make much sense, because it is at high temperatures that O_2 deficiency becomes most serious in natural environments. A thorough reinvestigation of the relationship between standard rate of metabolism and pO_2 in the carp revealed that the P_c remains reasonably constant over a wide range of temperatures: 1.45 kPa at 5 °C, 2.7 kPa from 10 to 25 °C, and 3.4 kPa at 32 °C (Ott *et al.*, 1980).

Adaptation of ventilation frequency, of oxygen capacity, and of rate of perfusion have been demonstrated in cyprinids. In tench for example, oxygen deficiency (hypoxia) in combination with an excess of carbon dioxide (hypercapnia), which is the natural situation, led to swelling of the erythrocytes (thus facilitating diffusion of oxygen into these cells) and to a reduction in their guanosine triphosphate (GTP) content (Jensen and Weber, 1985). GTP is the most important modulator of the oxygen affinity of haemoglobin (Hb) in fish. The lower the GTP/Hb ratio in the blood cells and the greater the oxygen binding capacity of the Hb, the more oxygen can be taken up by the respiratory pigment even if the pO_2 is low.

Yet another adaptive mechanism has been observed (Johnston and Bernard, 1984) following the adaptation of goldfish to lowered pO_2 values. After 6 weeks at 1.5 kPa O_2, the mitochondrial density in the aerobic red muscles had increased by 67%. This means an increased utilization of the oxygen circulating in the blood and a consequent reduction in venous pO_2. Like increased ventilation frequency, this mechanism maintains a steep oxygen-concentration gradient between water and blood.

After even longer periods of adaptation the respiratory surface itself might increase: a population of roach from warm, eutrophic (and thus oxygen-deficient) waters possessed a significantly greater number of gill lamellae than a population from a cold, oligotrophic lake (Palzenberger, 1986).

Anaerobiosis

Anoxia, the complete absence of oxygen, rarely occurs in the natural environment of fish. His studies on *Cyprinus carassius* in an exceptional environment, ice-covered waters, led Blazka (1958) to the discovery of anoxia tolerance in fish. A temporary decrease in the oxygen content of water to very low levels, however, is a frequently observed event; as a consequence of the ever-increasing occurrence of eutrophication it has now become a much-discussed ecological problem.

Some fish can extract oxygen from water even when the pO_2 is greatly reduced; in this respect cyprinids are among the best-adapted vertebrates. Goldfish, for example, can maintain at least a partially aerobic metabolism at room temperature and 0.4 kPa of oxygen (= 3 mm Hg), the silver carp, *Hypophthalmichthys molitrix*, even at 0.3 kPa, for several days. This tolerance of hypoxia implies the ability to deploy anaerobic energy production in an economical way, and so explains why the most anoxia-resistant species are found among the cyprinids. Since all metabolic processes proceed more slowly at low temperatures, the anoxia resistance of fish is greatest under such conditions, and is the reason why species like the crucian carp, *Carassius carassius*, are able to overwinter under the ice in the complete absence of oxygen (Holopainen *et al.*, 1986). Van den Thillart and van Waarde (1985) summarized the data concerning anoxia tolerance of cyprinids (Table 15.1).

In vertebrates, the ability to survive periods of anoxia is almost invariably combined with the ability to store large quantities of lactate in the tissues. Most cyprinids obey this rule, even if the amounts of lactate accumulating in their tissues under hypoxic to anoxic conditions rarely exceed the typical upper limit for vertebrates, i.e. about $20 \mu mol g^{-1}$. Three species, however, employ a metabolic pathway unknown in any other vertebrate that enables them to survive long periods of hypoxia. The strategy consists of the production of ethanol as an end-product of glycolysis, a variant form of fermentation observed only in invertebrates (chironomid larvae, endoparasites) until it was discovered in the two species of *Carassius* (goldfish and crucian carp) (Shoubridge and Hochachka, 1981) and in the bitterling, *Rhodeus amarus* (Wissing and Zebe, 1988). The significance of this metabolic pathway is that instead of an accumulation of an aggressive acid in the tissues, a harmless alcohol is excreted into the medium, thus avoiding the acid poisoning of tissues

Table 15.1   Anoxia tolerance of three species of cyprinid*

Species	Temperature (°C)	Mean survival time (h)	(d)
Carassius auratus	4	144–192	
	5	45	
	10	65	
	20	22	
C. carassius	2		140
	5		60–100
	18	3–33	
Cyprinus carpio	15	5	
	25	0.8	

*Source: Van den Thillart and van Waarde (1985).

caused by prolonged anaerobiosis. Ethanol is produced in the muscles of the three cyprinid species by reduction of acetaldehyde. This reaction is coupled with the production of lactic acid, because the NADH required for the reduction of acetaldehyde is provided by the reoxidation of lactate to pyruvate. The production of acetaldehyde from pyruvate in the mitochondria gives rise to CO_2, which, like ethanol, is excreted into the water. Thus neither end-product of this, for vertebrates, extremely unusual metabolic pathway places any burden upon the fish, and their production can be regarded as an adaptation to life without oxygen, the trade-off being that the energy content of ethanol is lost to the environment.

It has also been shown (Crawshaw *et al.*, 1989) that the formation of ethanol in the tissues of the goldfish may affect its behaviour. If the concentration of ethanol in certain regions of the brain exceeds a critical value the fish tends to prefer lower temperatures. The result of this change of behaviour is a reduction in the metabolic rate, thus increasing the survival time under anoxia.

However, the list of peculiarities in the anaerobic metabolism of the two *Carassius* species is not yet exhausted. More CO_2 is delivered to the medium than can be explained by the conversion of lactate into ethanol (van den Thillart and van Waarde, 1985). The most likely explanation for the additional CO_2 production is that even under anoxic conditions, the Krebs cycle in fish muscle continues to function slowly, and that the reducing equivalents thus produced are oxidized by unidentified electron acceptors. Candidates for this role are the fatty acids, in which chain elongation and saturation of double bonds could act as electron-consuming reactions. If, so, it would confirm the claim made by the Czech biologist P. Blazka, the pioneer of anaerobic studies on fish, that fatty acids are produced by goldfish during anaerobiosis (Blazka, 1958).

15.3 ECOPHYSIOLOGY II: TEMPERATURE RELATIONSHIPS

Range of tolerance and preferred temperature

Water temperature affects the course of the living processes in fish in fundamental and diverse ways. If we consider the population as being the smallest ecological unit, then for each population in a body of water there is a specific temperature range within which the life of its members usually proceeds. Immediately above and below this **range of tolerance** are **ranges of resistance**, in which the fish survive for a certain time but are unable to complete a full life cycle. Above and below the ranges of resistance are **lethal temperatures.** Subranges within the range of tolerance correspond to the individual optima for the various life processes. The temperature ranges for embryonic development and for growth are invariably narrower than those for routine activities.

Depending on the extent of their range of tolerance we can distinguish between **eurythermic** and **stenothermic** species, and according to whether the latter are mainly found in cold or in warm water they are termed cold- or warm-stenothermic. But even among the eurythermic species, some prefer the upper temperature range and some the lower. Eurythermic species mainly found in the middle temperature range, like the majority of European cyprinids, have been termed **mesothermic** (Elliot, 1981). The optimal temperature range of embryonic development permits a further differentiation of European eurythermic and mesothermic cyprinid species (Fig. 15.3). In this early phase of life the dace is clearly more resistant to cold than the other species studied by Herzig and Winkler (1985, 1986), whereas the tench belongs to the warm-eurythermic group to which carp, crucian carp, goldfish, grass carp, *Ctenopharyngodon idella*, and silver carp also belong. An important term in this connection is the **preferred temperature**, which is the temperature range chosen by a fish if offered a choice. The usual experimental

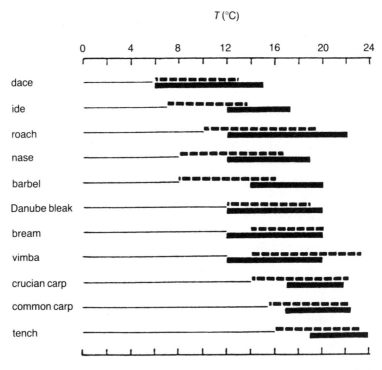

Fig. 15.3 Range of environmental temperature during the spawning period (dashed lines), and experimentally determined range of optimal temperature for embryonic development (solid lines) in several cyprinid species (after Herzig and Winkler, 1985). Scientific names may be found in the text with the exceptions of the ide, *Leuciscus idus*, nase, *Chondrostoma nasus*, barbel *Barbus barbus*, and vimba, *Vimba elongata*.

procedure is to expose the fish to a vertical or a horizontal temperature gradient, or to offer it the possibility of swimming from a central chamber into peripheral chambers held at different temperatures (Fry, 1971; McCauley, 1977). In the first approximation, the preferred temperature can be expected to lie somewhere in the middle of the range of tolerance observed in the wild. Nevertheless, all such experiments are meaningless if one fails to take into consideration the powers of adaptation of the animals and the flexibility of their temperature responses.

Resistance adaptation

The position and the width of the range of temperature tolerance of a species can be influenced by a variety of external and internal factors, the most important of which is the pretreatment, or acclimation, temperature. In most fish species the limits of the range of tolerance vary according to the acclimation temperature. Changes in the upper range of tolerance have been much more thoroughly investigated than those in the lower range. With increasing temperature of acclimation (AT) the resistance of the fish to high temperatures increases up to a maximal value that marks the genetically determined limit of the **reaction norm** of the species. This form of adaptation was called **resistance adaptation** by Precht (1968). The eurythermic cyprinid species in particular, such as roach, carp, Danube bleak (Al-Habib, 1981), gibel (or Prussian) carp, *Carassius auratus gibelio* (Krebs, 1975), and goldfish (Fig. 15.4(a)), possess a remarkable flexibility in this respect. For the goldfish, Cossins *et al.* (1977) demonstrated that the critical temperatures for the onset of behavioural responses preceding heat coma and heat death are from 5 to 6 °C lower in fish acclimated to 5 °C than in fish acclimated to 25 °C.

The more stenothermic salmonides, however, seem to be less adaptable (Fry *et al.*, 1946; Elliot, 1981). Since the preferred temperature of a population is closely connected with its range of tolerance, it is not surprising that it, too, may be influenced by the acclimation temperature. This was first demonstrated by Zahn (1964), in the bitterling (Fig. 15.4(b)). It has since been shown that salmonids and cyprinids behave quite differently: according to Stauffer *et al.* (1984), the preferred temperature of the rainbow trout can hardly be altered at all by acclimation, whereas the preferred temperatures of the North American cyprinids, *Notropis hudsonius* and *Pimephales notatus*, are closely dependent on acclimation temperature. On the other hand, an extensive study (Cherry *et al.*, 1975) revealed that probably all fish species can modify their preferred temperature, but that this trait is more strongly developed in the eurythermic species than in stenotherms.

The term 'final preferendum' was introduced by Fry (1947) to denote the preferred temperature that a population or species gradually assumes after a sufficient length of time, regardless of the temperature conditions to which it has previously been exposed. The implication is, therefore, that this tempera-

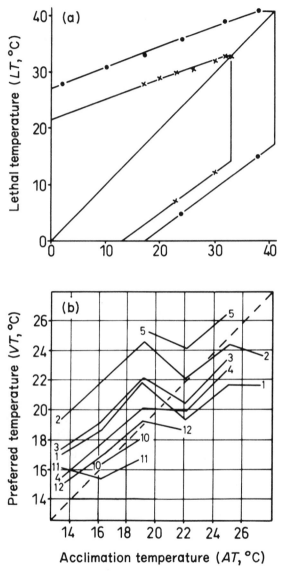

Fig. 15.4 (a) Upper and lower lethal temperature of goldfish (●) and roach (x) as functions of acclimation temperature (after Fry, 1971). Diagonal line, $LT = AT$. (b) Preferred temperature as a function of acclimation temperature and season in the bitterling, *Rhodeus amarus*. Numbers near the individual lines indicate months of the year (after Zahn, 1964). Diagonal line, $VT = AT$.

ture is a genetically determined part of the reaction norm of the population or species. However, this may be too rigid a way of thinking: it does not, for example, allow for the possibility that fluctuations of genetically determined set points may also be part of the reaction norm of a species. Zahn (1964) showed that in the bitterling, although the form of the relationship between preferred temperature and acclimation temperature remained reasonably constant throughout the year, the absolute value of the preferred temperature varied very considerably according to season, the maximum in February being about 6 °C higher than the minimum in December. Cherry *et al.* (1975) also reported a close connection between preferred temperature and time of year in 13 fish species including six American cyprinids, and Reynolds *et al.* (1978) described a daily rhythm in the preferred temperature of goldfish. The ability to vary the preferred temperature is unquestionably a more important characteristic from the ecological point of view than a hypothetical final preferendum.

Resistance adaptations usually require several days or even weeks for their completion; this implies extensive readjustment and reorganization of metabolic processes and cellular structures (Fry and Hochachka, 1970; Wieser, 1973). For the goldfish, Cossins *et al.* (1977) showed that the molecular composition of cell membranes and hence their properties (especially of the membranes of the nerve endings and the synaptosomes) are altered by acclimation at 5 °C. The degree of saturation of the fatty acids in the membranes decreases, causing an increase in membrane fluidity. Defects in membrane function might explain the kind of cold shock experienced by non-acclimatized roach at 4 °C (Wieser *et al.*, 1986).

The genetic component in the programme of temperature adaptations is revealed by species differences, to the extent to which it is possible to exclude or take into account all modifying factors (Cherry *et al.*, 1975). In rarer cases the genetic component in a temperature relationship can be demonstrated by breeding or crossing. Bettoli *et al.* (1985) reported that the F_1 hybrid resulting from crossing two warm-eurythermic species, the grass carp and the silver carp, had significantly higher preferred and upper lethal temperatures (28.2 and 39.7–40.9 °C) than either parent species (*C. idella*, 25.3 and 38.2–40.2 °C; *H. molitrix*, 25.4 and 38–39.6 °C after adaptation at 23 °C).

Temperature relationships of physiological functions

The most immediate effect that a change in ambient temperature exerts on living organisms is a change in the rate of material turnover, characterized by the Q_{10} value or by the energy of activation of the reaction in question. Furthermore, through the mediation of receptors and humoral mechanisms the environmental temperature also exerts a signal effect by triggering, blocking or generally modifying specific reactions. As an example, cooling the spinal cord of carp and crucian carp leads to an immediate slowing of the heart rate, which points to the existence of temperature-sensitive receptors in the central nervous system (Iriki *et al.*, 1976).

Swimming and oxygen consumption

Mode and speed of swimming are in many ways influenced by water temperature. Generally speaking, the locomotor activity of fish appears to be at a minimum at the preferred temperature of the species (Reynolds and Casterlin, 1979), which logically results in a maximization of the length of time spent in this temperature range. This has also been demonstrated experimentally in the goldfish, which exhibited the least swimming activity at its preferred temperature of 28 °C (Jones, 1983). In roach, two forms of spontaneous swimming have been recognized, 'low cost' and 'high cost'; at 8 °C swimming is mainly of the former type, at 20 °C mainly of the high cost type, whereas at 15 °C it is fairly equally divided between the two (Forstner and Wieser, 1990; Fig. 15.1 (c)). It would thus appear that water temperature can influence the swimming style of fish by a direct effect on the motor centres.

The **critical swimming speed** of a fish increases up to a characteristic temperature above which it usually decreases again (Brett, 1964). This, together with the fact that the standard metabolic rate varies with a smaller temperature coefficient than the active metabolic rate, results in the aerobic scope (p. 430) of the fish being at its greatest in the perferred temperature range (Fry, 1971). The increase in temperature dependence of $\dot{M}O_2$ with locomotor activity is probably connected with the exponential relationship between energy turnover and speed of swimming, which has been demonstrated for, among others, the silver carp (von Oertzen, 1985) and the roach. When fish are subjected to a change of temperature, the first reactions can be regarded as stress responses (Elliot, 1981). When these have subsided, either a stable relationship between temperature and metabolism is established or further changes take place, which Precht (1968) termed **capacity adaptation**. Adaptations of this kind can be thought of as general compensatory processes providing long-term stabilization of metabolism and behaviour. At the same time, these stabilizing processes may be masked by other metabolic changes elicited by a direct effect of temperature signals, the most important example being the regulatory effect of temperature on the reproductive cycle of a population. For example, when roach from a cold-oligotrophic lake were exposed to a temperature sinus ranging from 4 to 20 °C over the course of the year, the temperature interval between 14 and 16 °C played a special role in that the $\dot{M}O_2$ rose strikingly over this interval ($Q_{10} = 8.2$; Fig. 15.5). This is roughly the temperature range at which this population, taken from the Seefelder See near Innsbruck, usually spawns between the end of May and beginning of June. It thus appears that even in a group of roach kept under laboratory conditions, the signalling effect of a specific temperature regime remains intact. A very similar effect was described by Roberts (1961) for the crucian carp. In Table 15.2 and Fig. 15.5 the temperature relationships of roach acclimated to seasonal temperature changes are summarized and compared with those of other roach taken from the same lake but whose standard and routine oxygen consumption were measured after only 1–2

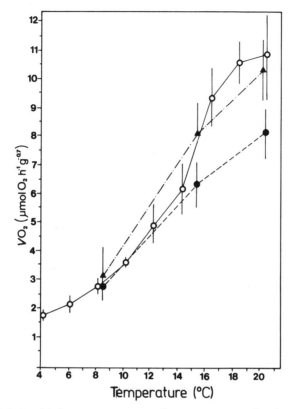

Fig. 15.5 Relationship between mean rate of oxygen consumption (vertical lines are standard deviations) and experimental temperature in roach. ●, Standard rate, ▲, routine rate, both rates after 1–2 d of acclimation to 8, 15, and 20 °C (after Forstner and Wieser, 1990); ○, standard rate after slow, long-term acclimation to a temperature sinus ranging from 4 to 20 °C over the course of the year (after Koch, 1984).

days' acclimation. The following conclusions can be drawn:

1. In the lower temperature range (below about 16 °C) energy turnover shows a much greater dependence on temperature than in the upper temperature range;
2. Routine $\dot{M}O_2$ in the lower temperature range is more strongly dependent upon temperature than standard $\dot{M}O_2$;
3. Independently of the direct effect of temperature on the energy turnover of the animal, a specific temperature interval may induce developmental and growth processes, which in turn have an indirect effect on the level of energy turnover.

Table 15.2 Effect of temperature on the oxygen consumption (in $\mu\,\mathrm{mol\,g^{-1}h^{-1}}$) of two groups of roach from the Seefelder See in the Austrian Tyrol[*]

| AT (°C) | Long-term acclimation[†] | | Short-term acclimation[‡] | | | |
| | | | Standard | | Routine | |
	$\dot{M}O_2$	Q_{10}	$\dot{M}O_2$	Q_{10}	$\dot{M}O_2$	Q_{10}
4	1.7					
6	2.1	2.9				
8	2.7	3.5	2.4		2.7	
10	3.5	3.7				
12	4.8	4.8				
14	6.1	3.3				
15			5.6	3.3	7.2	4.0
16	9.3	8.2				
18	10.5	1.8				
20	10.8	1.1	7.2	1.7	9.2	1.6

[*] Sources: Koch (1984), Forstner and Wieser (1990).
[†] Group acclimated to seasonal temperature pattern, values are for routine activity.
[‡] Group measured after only 1–2 d of acclimation; values are for standard and routine activity.

Digestive activity

The rate at which foodstuffs become available to the cells is an important factor in the animal's energy budget. A key role here is played by the digestive enzymes, which can adapt to the prevailing ecological situation and food supply in a variety of ways. In poikilotherms three characteristics are involved: (1) temperature dependence (expressed by the Q_{10} value; (2) substrate affinity (expressed by the K_m value, the Michaelis constant); every type of digestive enzyme can be represented in one and the same organism by several isoenzymes with different K_m values; (3) capacity, expressed by the quantity of enzyme in the intestinal fluid.

The above characteristics determine the rate at which food is digested in the alimentary canal. They can, however, vary between species, and such genetically determined differences are an expression of evolutionary strategies. For example, the amylases of roach and rudd, *Scardinius erythrophthalmus*, from the same lake differ in their temperature relationships as well as in seasonal aspects (Hofer, 1987). In a series of cyprinid species (bitterling, tench, goldfish, carp) the K_m value of trypsin increased from 0.41 to $0.84 \times 10^{-4}\,\mathrm{M}$ as the preferred temperature increased from 20 to 28 °C (Hofer et al., 1975).

Although the role of this correlation is not yet understood, perhaps the increasing rate of hydrolysis resulting from a rise in temperature is counterbalanced by a concurrent decrease in substrate affinity, thus stabilizing the rate at which protein is digested.

Capacity adaptation

The temperature relationship of a physiological activity is evidently dependent upon the temperature of acclimation; this implies that time of year is an important ecophysiological factor in poikilotherms. In many poikilothermic species the turnover rates of metabolic processes are higher following acclimation to low temperatures. Such processes therefore depend less upon temperature after acclimation than they do after brief fluctuations. This phenomenon illustrates the characteristic tendency of poikilotherms to maintain metabolic stability in the face of fluctuating environmental temperatures. The extent to which the metabolism of a species is temperature compensated can be quantified by acclimatizing two groups of a population to different temperatures and measuring a physiological function (such as oxygen consumption) at the acclimation temperatures. If the turnover rates are equal, the function is said to exhibit perfect temperature compensation. Two general conclusions are relevant to our considerations:

1. Temperature-compensated and -noncompensated processes can proceed concurrently in the same individual (Hazel and Prosser, 1974);
2. Of the freshwater fish so far investigated, the cyprinids exhibit particularly well-developed powers of temperature compensation. This may be connected with the eury- or mesothermic habits of most species (Guderley and Blier, 1988), but almost all such experiments have dealt with only the most typically eurythermic cyprinids, i.e. goldfish, crucian carp and common carp.

The rest of this section summarizes the most important physiological functions for which the phenomena of capacity adaptation and temperature compensation have been investigated.

Swimming speed
Carp adapted to a temperature of 10 °C exhibit a considerably higher critical swimming speed at low temperatures than those adapted to 28 °C (Heap and Goldspink, 1986). At higher experimental temperatures, however, the warm-adapted animals are superior in this respect, which indicates that an analysis of the temperature relationships of poikilothermic animals should not only take into account compensatory functions, but controlling and directing functions as well (Wieser, 1973).

Muscle functions
In cold-acclimated carp and goldfish the isometric force (in $N m^{-2}$), the maximal speed of contraction ($L s^{-1}$) and the maximal total capacity ($W kg^{-1}$) of the swimming muscles are much higher than in warm-acclimatized animals (Johnston et al., 1985). The cyprinids are the only family of fish in which this property has been demonstrated. Also, the enzyme responsible for the speed of

muscular contraction, myofibrillar ATPase, shows a pronounced temperature compensation in roach, carp, goldfish, crucian carp and tench, but not in the eel, *Anguilla anguilla*, salmonids and representatives of other fish families (Penney and Goldspink, 1981; Heap *et al.*, 1985; Guderley and Blier, 1988). The observation that the adaptive properties of the myofibrillar ATPase disappear if the regulatory proteins of the contractile apparatus, troponin and tropomyosin, are removed (Johnston, 1979) suggests that these proteins play an important role in the temperature adaptation of the ATPase.

Circulation and capillarization

Acclimation to low temperatures is also connected with visible morphological changes in the blood supply. The increase in red muscle fibres and in their capillarization seen in the goldfish (Johnston and Lucking, 1978: Sidell, 1980) is a strategy that is apparently not available to cold-stenotherms such as *Coregonus* spp. (Guderley and Blier, 1988). An increase in mass and an enhanced blood flow in the red musculature imply a rise in the minute volume of the heart. It has in fact been shown that the cardiac mass of the carp is greater in cold-acclimated animals (Goolish, 1987).

Energy metabolism

In carp, goldfish, crucian carp, and gibel carp, the activity of a series of enzymes involved in energy metabolism has proved to be temperature compensated. It is conspicuous that mainly (perhaps even exclusively) enzymes connected with aerobic energy metabolism, such as citrate synthetase, cytochrome oxidase, succinate dehydrogenase and enzymes involved in the β-oxidation of fatty acids, exhibit this compensatory behaviour, whereas the acclimation temperature appears to have no effect whatever on the key enzymes of anaerobic metabolism, such as phosphofructokinase and lactate dehydrogenase (Johnson *et al.*, 1985). The increased activity of the respiratory chain enzymes is also reflected in a proportional increase in mitochondrial density. Johnston and Maitland (1980), for example, report decreases from 25% to 14%, 20% to 11%, and 4% to 1% of fibre volume in red, pink, and white muscle fibres respectively, when comparing cold-acclimated (2 °C) with warm-acclimated (28 °C) crucian carp.

If the activity of the enzymes of anaerobic metabolism should prove not to be temperature compensated, this would agree with the observation that the rate of energy turnover in short anaerobic sprints of swimming is largely independent of water temperature (Brett, 1964).

The compensatory activities so far considered imply an elevation of material turnover and an acceleration of physiological processes at low environmental temperatures. In an open system in steady state such adaptive processes ought to be perceptible at many levels of molecular and cellular organization. In the typically warm-eurythermic cyprinids, membrane fluidity (Cossins *et al.*,

1977; Wodtke *et al.*, 1986), rate of ion transport (Gibson *et al.*, 1985), and rate of protein synthesis are elevated following acclimation to low temperatures. On the other hand, the more stenothermic rainbow trout seemingly cannot make these metabolic adjustments (Loughna and Goldspink, 1985).

In summarizing, it can be said of this aspect of temperature relationships that nearly all studies on temperature adaptations in behaviour and metabolism of cyprinids have so far been carried out on the warm-eurythermic species, common carp, crucian carp and goldfish. An expansion of such studies to include other ecological types within this family is much needed. In the roach, for example, temperature compensation of oxygen consumption could not be demonstrated (Koch, 1984; Forstner and Wieser, 1990) although the activity of its myofibrillar ATPase is quite clearly temperature compensated (p. 444).

15.4   ECOPHYSIOLOGY III: PERIODICITY

Almost every aspect of the behaviour and metabolism of fish is associated with the diurnal and annual periodicity of the environment. Nevertheless, the form taken by this periodicity depends not only on ecological conditions but also on the habits of the species. Periodicity in living processes is determined by exogenous zeitgebers as well as by endogenous cellular oscillators.

Diurnal periodicity

The diurnal periodicity of a fish species is intimately connected with nutrition. Siegmund (1969) recorded the spontaneous activity of rudd and tench under natural light conditions and showed that rudd is light-active whereas tench is dark- or twilight-active. This confirms Wunder's (1925) opinion that the tench must be a twilight-active species on account of its poorly developed eyes. The rudd is an omnivorous species with a preference for 'anflug' (plankton and plant matter), whereas the tench, a deposit feeder, spends the day resting on the bottom with its fins outspread. The periodic alternation of rest and activity is reflected in the animals' oxygen consumption. Activity maxima after sunrise and before sundown have been demonstrated in roach, bream (Alabaster and Robertson, 1961) and goldfish (Reynolds *et al.*, 1978), corresponding to the times at which plankton maxima occur in their natural environment. The most important zeitgeber is probably the change in light intensity, although concurrent fluctuations in temperature and pO_2 might also be of importance in setting the phase of the activity period (Alabaster and Robertson, 1961).

Flexibility in the temporal structure of activity is suggested by experiments in which different fish species were offered chironomid larvae in patches of vegetation (Diehl, 1988): roach and bream continued their activity even in the dark, whereas perch, *Perca fluviatilis*, did not. Perhaps rest and activity should not be regarded in all fish species as being completely different forms of behaviour. Closer scrutiny of the activity cycle reveals that it is made up of short-term bursts of activity, whose so-called 'ultradian' rhythmicity is maintained not only under natural light/dark conditions but also in continuous darkness. Such a pattern of behaviour, the finer structure of which was studied by Kavaliers (1981) in an American cyprinid, *Couesius plumbeus*, might be a mechanism for adjusting locomotor activity to unpredictable changes in the environment.

Annual periodicity

All biological functions of fish originating in boreal waters are adapted to the seasonal changes in ecological factors. On the one hand the organism must adapt to the sometimes extreme conditions prevailing in winters; on the other hand the processes involved in body growth, maturation of the gonads, and embryonic development have to be adjusted to a spectrum of ecological conditions (particularly to the food supply) prevailing in spring and summer. The demands made upon the organism in these two different situations are closely linked. In all European cyprinids, metabolism begins to switch to synthetic processes in summer: energy reserves are accumulated for the winter and gonads develop to the extent that spawning can take place in spring, sometimes immediately after ice break. Hence June and July are marked by a drastic switchover in the metabolism of the fish fauna of boreal–temperate waters; in the roach and other cyprinids the new gonads begin to develop in July (Hellawell, 1972; Koch, 1984; Fig. 15.6(a)). At the same time the size of the liver and the glycogen content of liver and muscle increase, e.g. in the tench (Demael-Suard and Peres, 1964) and in a population of crucian carp from Finland (Hyvärinen *et al.*, 1985; Fig. 15.6(c)). The large stores of glycogen, together with a reduction in metabolic activity, allow these fish to survive the winter on the bottom of ice-covered waters under almost totally anoxic conditions (Holopainen *et al.*, 1986). The increase in anabolic processes in summer is also reflected in an increased activity of the digestive enzymes. In the intestine of roach and rudd from cold-oligotrophic Tyrolean lakes, protease activity roughly parallels the progress of gonadal development (Hofer, 1979a; Fig. 15.6(b)). Amylase activity in the roach is additionally characterized by a compensatory mechanism: although the relationship between activity and temperature remains unaltered, the amount of amylase secreted into the intestine rises drastically from about September (Hofer, 1979b).

What determines the seasonal course of such processes is not known. As in other animals and in other cases, the answer is probably a combination of temperature dependence, photoperiod, and endogenous timing programmes (Wieser, 1973). The temperature interval 14–16 °C provokes a disproportionately large increase (Fig. 15.5) in the oxygen consumption of roach from Tyrolean lakes – and this at a constant photoperiod. Conversely, the same

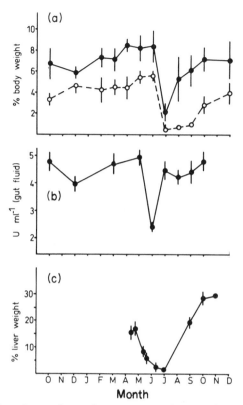

Fig. 15.6 Examples of annual periodicity in cyprinids. (a) Relative weight of gonads (●, ovaries; ○, testes) of roach (reproduced with permission from Koch, 1984). (b) Protease activity from the gut of roach and rudd (reproduced with permission from Hofer, 1979a). (c) Relative glycogen content of liver in crucian carp (reproduced with permission from Hyvärinen *et al.*, 1985).

roach kept at constant temperature and photoperiod exhibit reactions that can only be interpreted as being the expression of an internal clock (Koch, 1984). Long-day conditions elicit a rise in oxygen consumption in the crucian carp (Roberts, 1961).

Parallel to the seasonal changes in metabolism, the behaviour of cyprinid species also exhibits marked seasonal dependence, e.g. the locomotor activity of roach decreases in inverse proportion to the progress of gonadal maturation (Koch and Wieser, 1983). In tench and rudd, maintained at a constant temperature, swimming activity increased between April and June, and decreased from July onwards (Siegmund, 1969). The cost of gonadal development, beginning in July, is therefore partly met by a reduction in locomotor activity.

15.5   ION REGULATION AND WATER BALANCE

In all bony fish, whether they live in the sea or in fresh water, the osmotic concentration of the body fluids is roughly 280 mosmol l^{-1}. Obviously the problems of ion regulation and water balance differ very considerably in these two ecological groups. Whereas the osmotic concentration of seawater is about 1 osmol l^{-1}, that of fresh water is at most a few mosmol l^{-1}. Accordingly, the excess ions taken up by saltwater fish from food and water have to be actively eliminated into the environment, and conversely, freshwater fish have to make good the passive loss of ions by active uptake from the medium; the gills and kidneys are mainly responsible for these processes. In marine teleosts the monovalent ions Na$^+$, K$^+$ and Cl$^-$ are excreted via the gills, and the bivalent ions Ca^{2+}, Mg^{2+} and SO^{2-} leave the body either in the rectal fluid or, if they have reached the blood, via the kidneys. Water diffusing from the body is replaced by drinking. In freshwater fish, the gills effect the active transport of mono- and bivalent ions from the medium into the blood. At the same time, by active reabsorption of ions the kidneys produce a very dilute urine, thus eliminating from the body the water that has entered via the gills and other permeable epithelia. The different routes and directions of flow of ions and water lead to very dissimilar transepithelial potential differences between blood and water. In saltwater fish the interior of the body is 10–25 mV positive with respect to the surrounding medium; this difference facilitates the export of cations. The interior of freshwater fish, on the other hand, is 30–40 mV (sometimes less) negative with respect to the surroundings, which favours the import of cations.

We would expect such different forms of adaptation to the milieu to be achieved in very different ways, i.e. that saltwater and freshwater fish must possess quite specific and distinctive mechanisms for maintaining their ion and water balance. Nevertheless, many fish species can migrate from fresh water to salt water and back again. In a manner of speaking, they are able to reverse the polarity of their ion regulation: this implies a highly dynamic and flexible mechanism capable of adapting at short notice to environmental conditions.

Although many cyprinids are restricted to fresh water, others – mainly those living in large rivers – get as far as the estuaries and thus enter brackish water, e.g. many Danube fish species, such as the predatory sichling, *Pelecus cultratus*, and the asp, *Aspius aspius*. However, most cyprinid species would probably be able to live in brackish water after appropriate acclimation. For the roach (Müller, 1974), gibel carp (Hentschel, 1978), grass carp (Kilambi and Zdinak, 1980), and silver carp (Zabka, 1983; von Oertzen, 1985), the upper limit of tolerance appears to be a salt concentration of 1.2–1.5% (360–450 mosmol l^{-1}). The mean oxygen consumption of the silver carp is at a minimum at a salt concentration of 0.3% (= 90 mosmol l^{-1}) (von Oertzen, 1985), implying that the energy costs of osmoregulation are minimal at this concentration. Accordingly, common carp, silver carp, and grass carp show high growth rates in oligosaline water, a fact that can be exploited for aquaculture (Chervinski, 1977; Schildhauer, 1981, 1983).

The two organs most prominently involved in ion regulation of fish are the gills and the kidneys.

Gills

The gills receive their blood supply from two branches of the circulatory system. Firstly, an afferent artery carries blood to each gill filament, the blood then flows through the gill lamellae and leaves the filament again via an efferent artery. Secondly, a central sinus running the length of each filament collects the blood and passes it on to the heart. In this way, a change in the composition of the blood at the level of the gills can exert a feedback effect on the heart. In the exchange of ions between water and blood, which proceeds via the epithelium of the gill lamellae and gill filaments, two types of cells are involved: the respiratory cells of the lamellar epithelium, and the chloride cells (Keys and Willmer, 1932) situated at the base of the gill lamellae and in the epithelium of the gill filaments (Laurent and Dunel, 1978).

It is usually (but not universally) assumed that the chloride cells, which are packed with mitochondria and glycogen, are mainly responsible for active ion transport. The two quantitatively most important ions, Na^+ and Cl^-, are exchanged for NH_4 and H^+ on the one hand, and HCO_3 on the other. Thus the gills play an important role in maintaining the acid-base balance and in the excretion of ammonia, two vegetative functions that in higher vertebrates are performed by the kidneys (de Renzis, 1978, cited in Payan *et al.*, 1984). Ca^{2+} appears to enter the blood exclusively across the chloride cells of the gill filaments, with the help of a calmodulin-dependent transport system (Perry and Flik, 1988).

More energy is expended by marine fish on the active transport of ions from the blood into the medium than by freshwater fish on transport in the opposite direction. This conclusion is based on the fact that the activity of the Na^+/K^+ – ATPase, which is responsible for transport of Na^+ and Cl^-, is much higher in the gills of marine fish than in those of freshwater species (Epstein *et al.*, 1967; de Renzis and Bornancin, 1984), which again seems to result from the greater permeability to ions of the epithelia of saltwater fish compared with those of freshwater fish. However, extremely soft waters have not yet been looked into. Values of 0.018 and 0.009 mequ l^{-1}, respectively, have been found for the concentrations of Na^+ and Cl^- in some high mountain lakes. The gill lamellae of fish inhabiting such lakes seem to contain many more chloride cells than the same organs of the catadromic, anadromic and eurytopic species so far used in the majority of experiments.

Kidney

The nephron of the fish kidney is made up of the following sections (Hickman and Trump, 1969); glomerulus, neck, proximal segment i, proximal segment ii, intermediate segment, distal segment, collecting duct.

In the cyprinid kidney all these segments are as a rule well developed; only in a few species is the intermediate segment lacking. As Jaffee (1956) showed in the goldfish, the reabsorption of filtered organic plasma components takes place in the first segment of the proximal tubule. However, the most outstanding characteristic of the kidney of freshwater fish is that renal tubules absorb up to 99% of Na^+ and Cl^-. This process is performed chiefly by the 'renal chloride cells', which are localized in the distal segment and closely resemble the typical chloride cells of the gills (Komuro and Yamamoto, 1975). In some freshwater fish it is thought that the urinary bladder is additionally involved in the active reabsorption of Na^+ and Cl^- (Loretz and Bern, 1981). Owing to the orientation of the osmotic gradients, very little water is reabsorbed by the kidneys of freshwater fish – often only 5% or even less – so that superfluous body water is returned to the medium in the form of an extremely dilute urine. This is assisted by the almost complete impermeability of the distal segment of the tubule and the collecting duct. With respect to urine production, cyprinids appear to be some of the most efficient of all freshwater fish. Carp and goldfish, for example, produce between 8 and 15 ml urine $kg^{-1} h^{-1}$ at their preferred temperature, whereas the corresponding values for salmonids are only $1.6–4.7 \, ml \, kg^{-1} h^{-1}$ (Hickman and Trump, 1969).

15.6   CONCLUDING REMARKS

I should like to stress once more that by restricting their observations to only a few eurytopic species, zoologists have hardly begun to uncover the full range of ecophysiological plasticity and flexibility in this heterogeneous family of freshwater fish.

ACKNOWLEDGEMENTS

The original work reported, and the writing of this chapter, have been supported by the Fonds zur Förderung der wissenschaftlichen Forschung in Österreich, project no. S-35/04. I am most grateful to my wife, Joy Wieser, for translating this article into English.

REFERENCES

Alabaster, J. S. and Robertson, K. R (1961) The effect of diurnal changes in temperature, dissolved oxygen and illumination on the behaviour of roach (*Rutilus rutilus* L.), bream (*Abramis brama* L.) and perch (*Perca fluviatilis* L.) *Anim. Behav.*, **9**, 187–92.

Alexander, R. McN. (1969) The orientation of muscle fibres in the myomeres of fishes. *J. mar. biol. Ass. U.K.*, **49**, 263–90.

Al-Habib, O. A. M. (1981) Acclimation to temperature and death at changing lethal temperatures in the freshwater fish *Chalcalburnus chalcoides*. *J. therm. Biol.*, **6**, 365–71.

Bainbridge, R. (1963) Çaudal fin and body movement in the propulsion of some fish. *J. exp. Biol.*, **40**, 23–56.

Beamish, F. W. H. (1978) Swimming capacity, in *Fish Physiology*, Vol. 7 (eds W. S. Hoar and D. J. Randall), Academic Press, NY, pp. 101–87.

Bettoli, P. W., Neill, W. H. and Kelsch, S. W. (1985) Temperature preference and heat resistance of grass carp, *Ctenopharyngodon idella* (Valenciennes), bighead carp, *Hypophthalmichthys nobilis* (Gray), and their F_1 hybrid. *J. Fish Biol.*, **27**, 239–47.

Blazka, P. (1958) The anaerobic metabolism of fish. *Physiol. Zool.*, **31**, 117–28.

Breder, C. M. (1926) The locomotion of fishes. *Zoologica (N.Y.)*, **4**, 159–297.

Brett, J. R. (1964) The respiratory metabolism and swimming performance of young sockeye salmon. *J. Fish. Res. Bd Can.*, **21**, 1183–226.

Cherry, D. S., Dickson, K. L. and Cairns, J. jun., (1975) Temperature selected and avoided by fish at various acclimation temperatures. *J. Fish Res. Bd Can.*, **32**, 485–91.

Chervinski, J. (1977) Note on the adaptability of silver carp – *Hypophthalmichthys molitirix* (Val.) and grass carp – *Ctenopharyngodon idella* (Val.) to various saline concentrations. *Aquaculture*, **11**, 179–82.

Cossins, A. R., Friedlander, M. J. and Prosser, C. L. (1977) Correlations between behavioral temperature adaptations of goldfish and the viscosity and fatty acid composition of their synaptic membranes. *J. comp. Physiol.*, **120**, 109–21.

Crawshaw, D. I., Wollmuth, L. P. and O'Connor, C. S. (1989) Intracranial ethanol and ambient anoxia elicit selection of cooler water by goldfish. *Am. J. Physiol.* **256**, R133–R137.

Demael-Suard, A. and Peres, G. (1964) Les variations des reserves en glycogène de la tanche (*Tinca tinca* L.) au cours de l'année. *J. Physiol., Paris*, **56**, 356–65.

de Renzis, G. and Bornancin, M. (1984) Ion transport and gill ATPase, in *Fish Physiology*, Vol. 10B (eds W. S. Hoar and D. J. Randall), Academic Press, NY, pp. 65–104.

Diehl, S. (1988) Foraging efficiency of three freshwater fishes. Effects of structural complexity and light. *Oikos*, **53**, 207–14.

Elliott, J. M. (1981) Some aspects of thermal stress on freshwater teleosts, in *Stress and Fish* (ed. A. D. Pickering), Academic Press, London and New York, pp. 209–45.

Epstein, F. H., Katz, A. I. and Pickford, G. (1967) Sodium and potassium activated adenosine triphosphatase of gills. *Science*, **156**, 1245–7.

Forstner, H. and Wieser, W. (1990) Patterns of routine swimming and metabolic rate in juvenile cyprinids at three temperatures: analysis with a respirometer-activity-monitoring system. *J. comp. Physiol.*, **160**, 71–6.

Fry, F. E. J. (1947) Effects of the environment on animal activity. *Publs. Ont. Fish. Res. Lab.*, **68**, 1–68.

Fry, F. E. J. (1971) The effects of environmental factors on the physiology of fish, in *Fish Physiology*, Vol. 6 (eds W. S. Hoar and D. J. Randall), Academic Press, NY, pp. 1–98.

Fry, F. E. J. and Hochachka, P. W. (1970) Fish, in *Comparative Physiology of Thermoregulation*, *Vol. 1. Invertebrates and Non-mammalian Vertebrates* (ed. G. C. Whitton), Academic Press, London and New York, pp. 79–134.

Fry, F. E. J., Hart, J. S. and Walker, K. F. (1946) Lethal temperature relations for a sample of young speckled trout, *Salvelinus fontinalis* (Univ. Toronto Stud. Biol. Ser. 54), *Publs Ont. Fish. Res. Lab.*, **66**, 9–35.

Gibson, J. S., Ellory, J. C. and Cossins, A. R. (1985) Temperature acclimation of intestinal sodium transport in the carp (*Cyprinus carpio* L.). *J. exp. Biol.*, **114**, 355–64.

Goolish, E. M. (1987) Cold-acclimation increases the ventricle size of carp. *Cyprinus carpio. J. therm. Biol.*, **12**, 203–5.

Guderley, H. and Blier, P. (1988) Thermal acclimation in fish: conservative and labile properties of swimming muscle. *Can. J. Zool.*, **66**, 1105–15.

Hazel, J. R. and Prosser, C. L. (1974) Molecular mechanisms of temperature compensation in poikilotherms. *Physiol. Rev.*, **54**, 620–77.

Heap, S. P. and Goldspink, G. (1986) Alterations to the swimming performance of carp, *Cyprinus carpio*, as a result of temperature acclimation. *J. Fish Biol.*, **29**, 747–53.

Heap, S. P., Watt, P. W. and Goldspink, G. (1985) Consequences of thermal change on the myofibrillar ATPase of five freshwater teleosts. *J. Fish Biol.*, **26**, 733–8.

Hellawell, J. M. (1972) The growth, reproduction and food of the roach, *Rutilus rutilus* L., of the river Lugg, Herefordshire. *J. Fish Biol.*, **4**, 469–86.

Hentschel, H. (1978) The kidney of the Prussian Carp, *Carassius auratus gibelio* (Cyprinidae). III. Glycogen-rich cells in the distal segment of nephronic tubule. *Tissue Cell*, **10**, 319–30.

Herzig, A. and Winkler, H. (1985) Der Einfluß der Temperatur auf die embryonale Entwicklung der Cypriniden. *Öst. Fisch.*, **38**, 182–96.

Herzig, A. and Winkler, H. (1986) The influence of temperature on the embryonic development of three cyprinid fishes, *Abramis brama, Chalcalburnus mento* and *Vimba vimba. J. Fish Biol.*, **28**, 171–81.

Hickman, C. P. and Trump, B. F. (1969) The kidney, in *Fish Physiology*, Vol. 1 (eds W. S. Hoar and D. J. Randall), Academic Press, NY pp. 91–239.

Hill, A. V. (1950) The dimensions of animals and their muscular dynamics. *Sci. Prog., Lond.*, **38**, 209–30.

Hofer, R. (1979b) The adaptation of digestive enzymes to temperature, season and diet in roach, *Rutilus rutilus* L. and rudd, *Scardinius erythrophthalmus*; proteases. *J. Fish Biol.*, **15**, 373–9.

Hofer, R. (1979b) The adaptation of digestive enzymes to temperature, season and diet in roach, *Rutilus rutilus* L. and rudd, *Scardinius erythrophthalmus* L.: amylase. *J. Fish Biol.*, **14**, 564–72.

Hofer, R. (1987) Verdauungsstrategien bei Fischen. *Biol. i. u. Zeit.*, **17**, Jg., 84–9.

Hofer, R., Ladurner, H., Gattringer, A and Wieser, W. (1975) Relationship between the temperature preferenda of fishes, amphibians and reptiles, and the substrate affinities of their trypsins. *J. comp. Physiol.*, **99**, 345–55.

Holopainen, I. J., Hyvärinen, H. and Piironen, J. (1986) Anaerobic wintering of crucian carp (*Carassius carassius* L.) – II. Metabolic products. *Comp. Biochem. Physiol.*, **83A**, 239–42.

Hughes, G. M., Albers, C., Muster, D. and Götz, K. H. (1983) Respiration of the carp, *Cyprinus carpio* L., at 10 and 20 °C and the effects of hypoxia. *J. Fish Biol.*, **22**, 613–28.

Hyvärinen, H., Holopainen, I. J. and Piironen J. (1985) Anaerobic wintering of crucian carp (*Carassius carassius* L.) – I. Annual dynamics of glycogen reserves in nature. *Comp. Biochem. Physiol.*, **82A**, 797–803.

Iriki, M., Seiko, M., Nagai, M. and Tsuchiya, K. (1976) Effects of thermal stimulation to the spinal cord on heart rate in cyprinid fishes. *Comp. Biochem. Physiol.*, **53A**, 61–3.

Jaffee, O. C. (1956) Some morphological aspects of protein absorption in isolated renal tubules of the goldfish. *Anat. Rec.*, **125**, 495–508.

Jensen, F. B. and Weber, R. E. (1985) Kinetics of the acclimational response of tench to combined hypoxia and hypercapnia. I. Respiratory responses. *J. comp. Physiol.* **B**, **156**, 1997–203.

Johnston, I. A. (1979) Calcium regulatory proteins and temperature acclimation of actomyosin ATPase from a eurythermal teleost (*Carassius auratus* L.) *J. comp. Physiol.*, **129B**, 163–7.

Johnston, I. A. and Bernard, L. M. (1984) Quantitative study of capillary supply to the skeletal muscles of crucian carp, *Carassius carassius* L.: effects of hypoxic acclimation. *Physiol. Zool.*, **57**, 9–18.

Johnston, I. A. and Lucking, M. (1978) Temperature induced variation in the distribution of different types of muscle fibre in the goldfish (*Carassius auratus*). *J. comp. Physiol.*, **124B**, 111–16.

Johnston, I. A. and Maitland, B. (1980) Temperature acclimation in crucian carp, *Carassius carassius* L., morphometric analyses of muscle fibre ultrastructure. *J. Fish Biol.*, **17**, 113–25.

Johnston, I. A., Davison, W. and Goldspink, G. (1977) Energy metabolism of carp swimming muscles. *J. comp. Physiol.*, **114B**, 203–16.

Johnston, I. A., Sidell, B. D. and Driedzic, W. R. (1985) Force–velocity characteristics and metabolism of carp muscle fibres following temperature acclimation. *J. exp. Biol.*, **119**, 239–49.

Jones, D. R. (1983) Anaerobic exercise in teleost fish. *Can. J. Zool.*, **60**, 1131–4.

Kaufmann, R. (1990) Respiratory cost of swimming in larval and juvenile cyprinids. I. Power–performance relations during early life. *J. exp. Biol.*, **150**, 343–66.

Kausch, H. (1968) Der Einfluß der Spontanaktivität auf die Stoffwechselrate junger Karpfen (*Cyprinus carpio* L.) im Hunger und bei Fütterung. *Arch. Hydrobiol.*, **33** (Supp.), 263–330.

Kavaliers, M. (1981) Seasonal changes in the short-term activity and ultradian rhythms of a cyprinid fish, the lake chub, *Couesius plumbeus. Can. J. Zool.*, **59**, 486–92.

Keys, A. B. and Willmer, E. N. (1932) Chloride secreting cells in the gills of fishes with special reference to the common eel. *J. Physiol. Lond.*, **76**, 368–78.

Kilambi, R. V. and Zdinak, A. (1980) The effects of acclimation on the salinity tolerance of grass carp, *Ctenopharyngodon idella* (Cuv. and Val.). *J. Fish Biol.*, **16**, 171–5.

Koch, F. (1984) Der Einfluß von Temperatur, Jahreszeit und Schwarmgröße auf den Sauerstoffverbrauch von Rotaugen, *Rutilus rutilus* L. Dissertation, Univ. Innsbruck, 112 pp.

Koch, F. and Wieser, W. (1983) Partitioning of energy in fish: can reduction of swimming activity compensate for the cost of reproduction? *J. exp. Biol.*, **107**, 141–6.

Komuro, T. and Yamamoto, T. (1975) The renal chloride cell of the fresh-water catfish, with special reference to the tubular membrane system. *Cell Tissue Res.*, **160**, 263–71.

Krebs, F. (1975) Der Einfluß der Sauerstoffspannung auf die Temperaturadaptation des Giebels (*Carassius auratus gibelio* Bloch). *Arch. Hydrobiol.*, **76**, 89–131.

Laurent, P. and Dunel, S. (1978) Relations anatomiques des ionocytes (cellules à chlorure) avec le compartiment veineux branchial: défiinition de deux types d'épithelium de la branchie des Poissons. *C.r. hebd. Séanc. Acad. Sci., Paris*, **286**, 1447–50.

Loretz, C. A. and Bern, H. A. (1981) Ion transport by the urinary bladder of the gobiid teleost. *Am. J. Physiol.*, **239**, R414–R422.

Loughna, P. T. and Goldspink, G. (1985) Muscle protein synthesis during temperature acclimation in a eurythermal (*Cyprinus carpio*) and a stenothermal (*Salmo gairdneri*) species of teleost. *J. exp. Biol.*, **118**, 267–76.

McCauley, R. W. (1977) Laboratory methods for determining temperature preference. *J. Fish. Res. Bd Can.*, **34**, 749–52.

Müller, R. (1974) Die Beziehungen zwischen Kohlehydratstoffwechsel und der Regulation des Osmomineralhaushaltes bei *Leuciscus rutilus* L. *Zool. Jb. Physiol.*, **78**, 85–107.

Oertzen, J.-A. von (1985) Resistance and capacity adaptation of juvenile silver carp.

Hypophthalmichthys molitrix (Val.), to temperature and salinity. *Aquaculture*, **44**, 321–32.

Ott, M. E., Heisler, N. and Ultsch, G. R. (1980) A re-evaluation of the relationship between temperature and the critical oxygen tension in freshwater fishes. *Comp. Biochem. Physiol.*, **67A**, 337–40.

Palzenberger, M. (1986) "Etwas über Fischohren". Gasaustausch über Fischkiemen (Teleosteer) mit besonderer Berücksichtigung der respiratorischen Oberfläche. Diplomarbeit (thesis), Univ. Salzburg, 126 pp.

Payan, P., Girard, J. P. and Mayer-Gostan, N. (1984) Branchial ion movement in teleosts: the role of respiratory and chloride cells, in *Fish Physiology*, vol. 10B (eds W. S Hoar and D. J. Randall), pp. 39–64.

Penney, R. K. and Goldspink, G. (1981) Short term temperature acclimation in myofibrillar ATPase of a stenotherm *Salmo gairdneri* Richardson and an eurytherm *Carassius auratus*. *J. Fish Biol.*, **18**, 715–21.

Perry, S. F. and Flik, G. (1988) Characterization of branchial transepithelial calcium fluxes in freshwater trout, *Salmo gairdneri*. *Am. J. Physiol.*, **254**, R491–R498.

Precht, H. (1968) Der Einfluß "normaler" Temperaturen auf Lebensprozesse bei wechselwarmen Tieren unter Ausschluß der Wachstums- und Entwicklungsprozesse. *Helgolander wiss. Meeresunters.*, **18**, 487–548.

Reynolds, W. W. and Casterlin, M. E. (1979) Effect of temperature on locomotor activity in the goldfish (*Carassius auratus*) and the bluegill (*Lepomis macrochirus*): presence of an 'activity well' in the region of the final preferendum. *Hydrobiologia*, **65**, 3–5.

Reynolds, W. W., Casterlin, M. E., Matthey, J. K., Millington, S. T. and Ostrowski, A. C. (1978) Diel patterns of preferred temperature and locomotor activity in the goldfish. *Comp. Biochem. Physiol.*, **59A**, 225–7.

Roberts, J. L. (1961) The influence of photoperiod upon thermal acclimation by the crucian carp, *Carassius carassius* L. *Zool. Anz.*, **24** (Supp.), 73–8.

Rome, L. C., Funke, R. P., Alexander, R. McN., Lutz, G., Aldridge, H., Scott, F., and Freadman, M. (1988) Why animals have different muscle fibre types. *Nature, Lond.*, **355**, 824–7.

Schildhauer, B. (1981) Zur Salzgehaltsverträglichkeit des Silberkarpfens (*Hypophthalmichthys molitrix* Valentin). *Fischereiforsch. wiss. Schriftenreihe*, **19**, 35–9.

Schildhauer, B. (1983) Untersuchungen der Salzgehaltsverträglichkeit juveniler Karpfen (*Cyprinus carpio* L.) und Marmorkarpfenhybriden (*Aristichthys nobilis* Rich. × *Hypophthalmichthys molitrix* Val.). *Fischereiforsch. wiss. Schriftenreihe*, **21**, 24–30.

Shoubridge, E. A. and Hochachka, P. W. (1981) The origin and significance of metabolic carbon dioxide production in the anoxic goldfish. *Mol. Physiol.* **1**, 315–38.

Sidell, B. D. (1980) Response of goldfish *Carassius auratus* muscle to acclimation temperature alterations in biochemistry and proportions of different fiber types. *Physiol. Zool.*, **53**, 98–107.

Siegmund, R. (1969) Lokomotorische Aktivität und Ruheverhalten bei einheimischen Süßwasserfischen (Pisces; Percidae, Cyprinidae). *Biol. Zbl.*, **88**, 295–312.

Smit, H. (1965) Some experiments on the oxygen consumption of goldfish (*Carassius auratus* L.) in relation to swimming speed. *Can. J. Zool.*, **43**, 623–33.

Stauffer, J. R., Melisky, E. L. and Hocutt, C. H. (1984) Interrelationship among preferred, avoided, and lethal temperatures of 3 fish species. *Arch. Hydrobiol.*, **100**, 159–69.

Van den Thillart, G. and van Waarde, A. (1985) Teleosts in hypoxia: aspects of anaerobic metabolism. *Mol. Physiol.*, **8**, 383–409.

Wieser, W. (1973) Temperature relations of ectotherms. A speculative review, in *Effects of Temperature on Ectothermic Organisms* (ed. W. Wieser). Springer Verlag, Heidelberg. pp. 1–24.

Wieser, W., Koch, F., Drexel, E. and Platzer, U. (1986) "Stress" reactions in teleosts: effects of temperature and activity on anaerobic energy production in roach (*Rutilus rutilus* L.), *Comp. Biochem, Physiol.*, **83A**, 41–5.

Winberg, G. G. (1961) New information on metabolic rate in fishes, *Fish. Res. Bd Can. Transl. Ser.*, no. 362, 38pp.

Wissing, J. and Zebe, E. (1988) The anaerobic metabolism of the bitterling *Rhodeus amarus* (Cyprinidae, Teleostei). *Comp. Biochem. Physiol.*, **89B**, 299–303.

Wodtke, E., Teichert, T. and König, A. (1986) Control of membrane fluidity in carp upon cold stress, in *Living in the Cold: Physiological and Biochemical Adaptations* (eds H. C. Heller *et al.*), Elsevier, pp. 35–42.

Wunder, W. (1925) Physiologische und vergleichend anatomische Untersuchungen an der Knochenfischnetzhaut. *Z. vergl. Physiol.*, **3**, 1–61.

Zabka, H. (1986) Der Einfluß abrupter Salinitätsänderungen auf die Schwimmaktivität des Silberkarpfens, *Hypophthalmichthys molitrix* (Val.), (Pisces, Cyprinidae). *Zool. Jb. Physiol.*, **87**, 317–24.

Zahn, M. (1964) Jahreszeitliche Veräderungen der Vorzugstemperaturen von Scholle (*Pleuronectes platessa* Linne) und Bitterling (*Rhodeus sericeus* Pallas). *Verh. Dtsch. Zoolog. Ges. München*, 1983, Akad. Verlag, Leipzig, pp. 562–80.

Chapter sixteen

Growth and production

R. H. K. Mann

16.1   INTRODUCTION

The family Cyprinidae is the most successful group of freshwater teleosts; representatives occur in most freshwater habitats in all the major continents, although their presence in Australasia results from introductions by Man. The family's ubiquity stems in part from the wide range in growth rate and ultimate size shown by different species, often in the same river or lake. This feature, allied to the range of reproductive requirements (Chapter 17), means that most freshwater habitats are suitable for at least one species, and many habitats support several. In addition, there is frequently marked intraspecific variability in growth rate between different life history types (Fig. 16.1) and between sexes. This variation may reflect genetic adaptations to particular local environments, but the evidence from fish transfers (e.g. Mann and Steinmetz, 1985) suggests that individuals within a population show wide phenotypic plasticity. This plasticity confers the potential for a rapid response to changes in environmental conditions in an individual fish's growth rate and development to sexual maturity. Indeed, the sensitive response of fish growth to manipulations of population density and of the nutrient status of the environment underlies much of fish culture practice.

In this chapter, I examine the principal factors that determine growth rates and production levels in cyprinid fishes, particularly in natural populations. Both abiotic and biotic features of the environment are involved, although current thought is that the maximum potential growth rate, ultimate size and longevity of each species is under genetic control (review, Beverton, 1987). In addition, I describe the consequences of growth plasticity in relation to the onset of sexual maturity and to the level of recruitment of individual cohorts. However, it should be remembered that most of these relationships are not peculiar to the Cyprinidae. The majority of examples are for European species, with which I am most familiar. In fact, many of the relationships described are relevant also to tropical cyprinids, although the difficulty of ageing in these

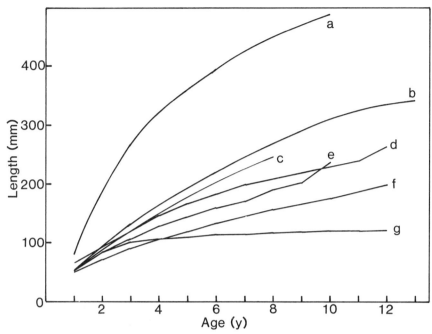

Fig. 16.1 Growth in length (mm) in seven *Rutilus rutilus* populations: a, Klicava reservoir (Pivnicka, 1982); b, River Frome (Mann, 1973); c, Pilica River (Penczak *et al.*,1979); d, River Exe (Cowx, 1988); e, Tjeukemeer (Goldspink, 1979); f, Lake Volvi (Papageorgiou, 1979); g, Grey Mist Mere (Linfield, 1980).

species (Weatherley and Gill, 1987) must decrease the reliability of such extrapolations.

Growth is essentially a bioenergetic process, the elements of which are common to all teleosts. Details are not repeated here, but there are many excellent reviews (e.g. Weatherley, 1972; Gerking, 1978; Weatherley and Gill, 1987; Wootton, 1990).

Most of the chapter deals with quantitative changes in weight and the consequences of these changes. However, Beamish *et al.* (1975) have warned that over-emphasis of quantitative changes in fish size may distract attention from important qualitative changes in body tissue that might affect subsequent growth and survival rates, and reproductive output. For example, Meili (1987) observed an increase in the water content of *Rutilus rutilus* in late summer when the condition factor C (p. 458) was increasing. As increased water content is often associated with starvation, it is evident that a simple measure of gross changes in weight may be misleading.

For this chapter, the following symbols will be used:

L = Length of fish (fork length, FL, unless stated otherwise)
W = Weight of fish

G = Instantaneous growth rate $(\ln W_2 - \ln W_1)/(t_2 - t_1)$, where W_1 and W_2 are fish weights at times t_1 and t_2

C = Condition factor $100\,W/L^3$

B = Biomass (total weight of a population or age group)

$\bar{B}$ = Mean biomass of a population or age group, calculated either as (1) $\bar{B} = (B_1 + B_2/2$, where B_1 and B_2 are the biomasses at times t_1 and t_2, or as (2) $\bar{B} = B_1 (\exp(G - Z) - 1)/(G - Z)$ (Chapman, 1968).

P = Production (as defined by Ivlev, 1966) = BG, with values here given as $\text{kg ha}^{-1}\text{y}^{-1}$

Z = Instantaneous mortality rate $(\ln N_1 - \ln N_2)/(t_2 - t_1)$, where N_1 and N_2 are numers of fish at times t_1 and t_2

GSI = Gonadosomatic index = gonad weight/total weight.

16.2 GROWTH

Growth – general

Studies of cyprinids in north temperate waters have shown that asymptotic growth curves can be used to describe the year-to-year growth patterns of many populations. Although the von Bertalanffy (1957) model has gained the widest acceptance for fisheries studies, other growth models have been used (Gompertz, logistic, exponential; reviews, Weatherley, 1972; Weatherley and Gill, 1987). Figure 16.2 illustrates the characteristic relationships between length and age, weight and age, and weight and length. A Ford–Walford plot (Ford, 1933; Walford, 1946) (Fig. 16.2(d)) is used to determine the coefficients (L_∞, K, t_0) of the von Bertalanffy model:

$$L_t = L_\infty[1 - \exp(-K(t - t_0))] \tag{16.1}$$

where L_∞ is the asymptotic length, L_t is the length at age t years, K is a constant that describes the rate of change in length and has units y^{-1}, t_0 is the hypothetical time at which length is zero.

These asymptotic growth models only describe growth rates based on year-to-year progression in size. Within-season growth changes in the Cyprinidae are most noticeable among 0+ fish, especially during the first two or three months of life. Thus, Tong (1986), following Vasnetsov (1953), described the morphology of eight developmental steps of the roach, *Rutilus rutilus*, and noted that changes in weight fitted a logistic model:

$$W = W_{max}/(1 + \exp(a - bt)) \tag{16.2}$$

where W_{max} is the weight at 1 y. Moreover, several studies have shown that the relationship between length and weight alters during the metamorphosis from larval to juvenile stage. Rheinberger *et al.* (1987) suggested that this transformation occurred in the Cyprinidae at a length of 15–16 mm, and that

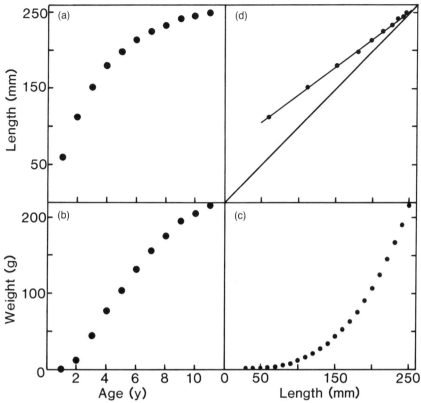

Fig. 16.2 (a) to (c) Relationships among age, length and weight of dace, *Leuciscus leuciscus*, in the River Frome, southern England (author, unpublished data) (d) Ford–Walford plot (horizontal axis, length at age *t*; vertical axis, length at age *t* + 1; diagonal, line of equality). Intersection of growth trajectory with diagonal gives estimate of L_∞. Slope of growth trajectory is k, where K (von Bertalamffy) = $-\log_e$ k.

the age (days) at which the change took place depended on the initial size of the hatching embryo. For example, they observed that chub *Leuciscus cephalus*, which has a large embryo, metamorphosed after fewer days than *R. rutilus*, which has a small embryo.

In temperate zones, growth seasonality is a function of water temperature, daylength and food availability, and is reflected in a rapid increase in length and weight in the summer and virtually no increase during the winter months (Fig. 16.3). Seasonal changes in weight are more complex; they are strongly influenced by the development of the gonads and the accumulation of storage products, each of which has a major influence on the gross condition factor (C). An excellent review of the dynamics of these processes is provided by Weatherley and Gill (1987). In the tropics, seasonal growth is more usually a

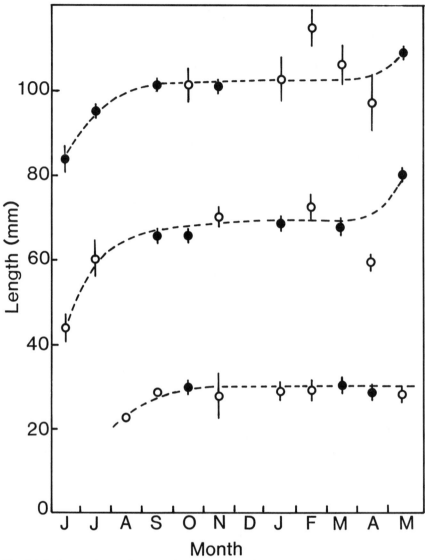

Fig. 16.3 Seasonal growth curves (with 95% confidence intervals) for bleak, *Alburnus alburnus*, from the River Stour, southern England (author, unpublished data); ○, < 30 fish; ●, 30 or more fish; top, 2 group; middle, 1 group; bottom, 0 group.

consequence of wet and dry periods, with most growth occurring during the former (Welcomme, 1985; Moreau, 1987).

Data for seasonal growth curves are often obtained from regular sampling throughout the year and the construction of a series of length-frequency histograms. But in many Cyprinidae, only the youngest age groups can be

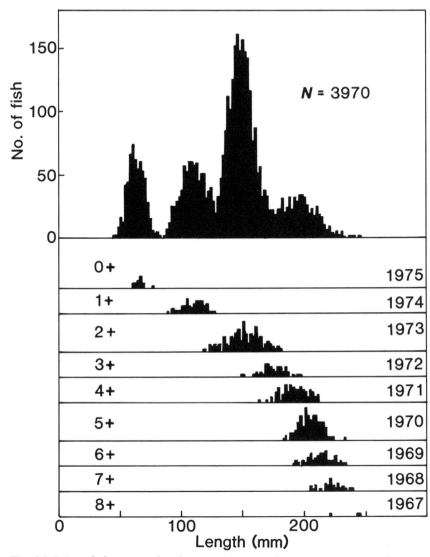

Fig. 16.4 Length-frequency distribution of *Leuciscus leuciscus* captured in the River Frome, southern England, from November 1975 to April 1976 ($N = 3970$), and length distributions of subsamples aged by scale examination (age classes at left, year classes at right) (author, unpublished data).

readily identified from length-distribution data. In the example for dace (Fig. 16.4) the first three age groups are evident but there is considerable overlap in the lengths of subsequent age groups. Thus, a fish of 200 mm FL could belong to one of at least four age groups. Separation of these overlapping cohorts requires the age and length of individual fish to be determined, as in the subsamples shown in Fig. 16.4. However, in species that have an extended spawning and hatching season, cohort identification solely from size can be difficult, even in the first year of life. This is exemplified by the minnow, *Phoxinus phoxinus*, in English chalk streams, where spawning occurs from May to August (Mills, 1987).

In the Cyprinidae, scales are the most frequently used structure for determining age; Bagenal (1973) discusses many of the technical problems. Opercular bones are sometimes advantageous for ageing older fish (> 12 y) because the annuli are more widely spaced on the edge of these bones than on scales from the same fish (Mann, 1976; Penczak *et al.*, 1979). In contrast to marine studies, otoliths have been used rarely in freshwater investigations, but Mills and Eloranta (1985) and Mills (1988) found them useful to age *P. phoxinus* in slow -growing fish in a Finnish Lapland stream, where individuals up to 13 y old were found, and in fast-growing fish from a English chalk stream.

Although scales are the most commonly used structure (several scales can be taken from one fish, which need not be killed), the first annulus can be difficult to identify, especially in slow growing fish. Mann and Steinmetz (1985) describe the problem in relation to rudd, *Scardinius erythrophthalmus*, and the same problem has been encountered in the River Stour. southern England, in chub, *Leuciscus cephalus* (Mann 1976) and bleak, *Alburnus alburnus* (author, unpubl.). In the bleak, scales were not formed on fish less than 25 mm FL. Therefore, as the mean length at 1y was only 29 mm (range *c.* 20–42 mm), many one-year-old bleak had no scales or only had scales consisting of two or three circuli. Thus, the first annulus on scales from older bleak was often difficult to see, or was not present. Correct age determinations were made only by reference to length-frequency distributions, which showed clear modes for the first three age groups, and by adding one year to the number of annuli seen on the scales.

Effect of water temperature on growth

Environmental temperature has a profound influence on the growth of fish through its impact upon rates of digestion and assimilation (Backiel, 1971, 1979; Webb, 1978). Swimming activity is also affected and this can determine the frequency of encounter with prey (Jezierska, 1979). Thus, in summer, fish feed more frequently and digest their food more rapidly than in winter. Although maintenance costs are greater at higher temperatures, there is also a greater difference between the level of food intake and its non-growth utilization; hence, growth rates are higher in summer than in winter.

Studies in temperate waters have indicated lower temperature thresholds for cyprinid growth in the range 12–15 °C (Mann, 1973, 1976, 1980; Pivnicka, 1982; Mills and Mann, 1985; Müller and Meng, 1986). However, fish inhabiting more northerly latitudes can acclimate to lower temperatures, e.g. *P. phoxinus* in the River Utsjoki, Finland, continues to grow at water temperatures down to 7 °C (Mills, 1988). In contrast, the same species in southern England ceased to grow in length when the water temperature was less than 12 °C (Mills, 1987). These two populations also demonstrate the inverse relationship between growth rate and longevity that occurs in many fish species (Leveque, 1978). Indirect evidence for this relationship was identified by Moreau *et al.* (1985) from 42 cyprinid populations in French rivers; a correlation coefficient of 0.939 was found for the relationship between the von Bertalanffy coefficients L_∞ and K:

$$L_\infty = 10.371/K^{0.744} \tag{16.3}$$

This equation shows that a large ultimate size (L_∞) is associated with a slow growth rate (K) and, thereby, a longer life-span.

Some evidence for a general change in cyprinid growth rates with latitude (hence environmental temperature) was claimed by Pivnicka (1983), based upon a review of growth studies in a range of European and Scandinavian reservoirs and lakes. The results are not completely convincing because of the range of population densities encountered. Nevertheless, Pivnicka concluded

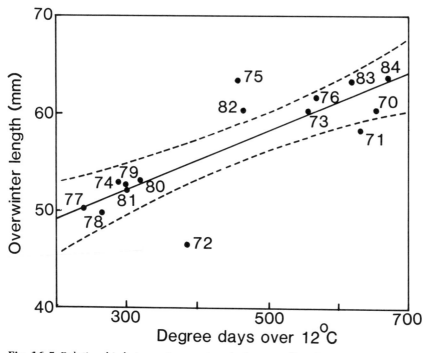

Fig. 16.5 Relationship between temperature in the year of hatching (*T*) and the mean overwinter length (*L*) of 0 group *Leuciscus leuciscus* in the River Frome from 1970 to 1984. Solid curve (with 95% confidence intervals) represents the fit to the linear model: $L = 43.2 + 0.0299T$ (redrawn from Mills and Mann, 1985, by permission of *Journal of Fish Biology*).

that *L. cephalus* and *S. erythrophthalmus* growth rates were controlled more by temperature than by density, with the converse being true for *R. rutilus* and *Abramis brama*.

Many studies have demonstrated a close correlation between the growth of 0 group cyprinids and water temperature (Kempe, 1962; Cragg-Hine and Jones, 1969; Mann, 1973, 1976, 1980; Broughton and Jones, 1978; Pivnicka, 1983; Mills and Mann, 1985; Kubecka *et al.*, 1985; Ponton and Gerdaux, 1987; Wieser *et al.*, 1988). Figure 16.5 shows the form of a typical correlation, from which it is clear that only part of the variance in growth of *L. leuciscus* in their first year of life is attributable to temperature (Mills and Mann, 1985). Müller and Meng (1986) found that the growth of older *R. rutilus* in Lake Sarnen (Sarnen See), Switzerland was more closely correlated with temperature than was that of 0 group roach. They emphasized that complex processes determined the numbers of progeny that survive the egg and larval periods, and hence determine the strength of the year class. These processes include oogenesis, pre- and post-larval production, food availability, and predation, all of which are themselves temperature-dependent. Year-to-year variations in growth are a common phenomenon also in older Cyprinidae; each curve in Fig. 16.6 represents the growth in a particular year, assuming that the environmental conditions in that year remained constant throughout the life span of the dace. In parallel with Pivnicka's studies (1983). Müller and Meng (1986) observed that the effects of population density can confound those of temperature in Lake Sarnen, where local high densities of 0 and 1 group *R. rutilus* in the littoral zone can cause a reduction in growth when food resources are limited. In contrast, the older age groups were more dispersed in the lake and could eat both pelagic and benthic food.

Wieser *et al.* (1988) compared the growth rates of larval and juvenile *R. rutilus. L. cephalus* and *A. alburnus* in warmwater and coldwater lakes in Austria. They found that 0 group fish in the warmer habitats grew rapidly (up to 20% d^{-1}) for the first 1–2 months, but then the rate decreased slowly. This supported the work on *R. rutilus* by Tong (1986), who found that initial 0 group growth fitted a logistic curve under constant temperature and *ad libitum* feeding conditions. After *c.* 60 d (Wieser *et al.*, 1988) the growth rate decreased towards the winter, when growth virtually ceased. Conversely, in the coldwater lakes, growth was initially slow but then increased up to 30% d^{-1} as the larval and juvenile fish improved their ability to catch zooplankton and no longer relied on phytoplankton. From their temperature-controlled tank experiments, Wieser *et al.* extrapolated the observed growth in the lakes to a common temperature of 20 °C and so were able to minimize the effect of temperature on growth. Thus any residual differences could be attributed to factors other than temperature.

Experimental studies on temperature–growth relationships (e.g. Müller and Meng, 1986; Wieser *et al.*, 1988) have usually used stable temperature regimes. However, under natural conditions, fish experience fluctuating

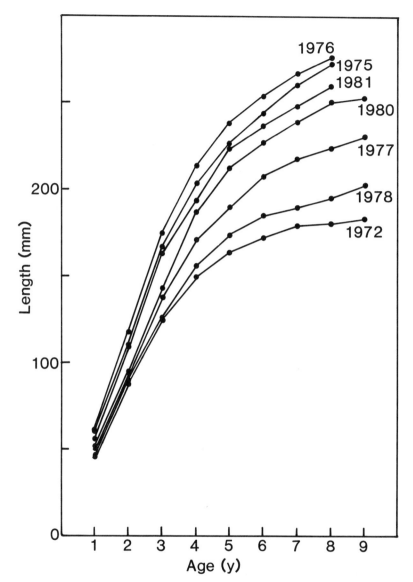

Fig. 16.6 Composite growth curves for 7 different years for *Leuciscus leuciscus* in the River Frome, based on back-calculated length increments over 14 y; each curve represents the growth of all age groups in the year specified.

temperatures, either through diel changes in water temperature, or through their own diel movements (e.g. vertical migrations in lakes). Growth rates of *Cyprinus carpio, Carassius auratus* and the hybrid *Hypophthalmichthys molitrix* × *Aristichthys nobilis* are higher under fluctuating temperatures than at a stable temperature, whether the latter is the mean, minimum or maximum of the range (Konstantinov and Zdanovich, 1986). These authors noted also that, under fluctuating temperatures, qualitative changes in fish tissue occurred, namely a decrease in the water content and the proportion of dry defatted tissue and an increase in the lipid content, the haemoglobin content and the erythrocyte count.

Substantial knowledge of fish growth:temperature correlates comes from studies of the effects of heated effluents, especially those from electricity generating stations (Alabaster, 1964; Brown, 1973). Wilkonska (1979) observed local increases in the growth of juvenile *R. rutilus. Blicca bjoerkna, S. erythrophthalmus* and *L. cephalus*, as a result of heated effluents, in the River Vistula, Poland, in addition to natural variations in growth rates between years. She also noted that the effect of heated effluents was even more evident in still-water habitats; in a series of Polish lakes, an 8 °C rise increased the growth period of four species of cyprinid by 2–4 months (Wilkonska and Zuromska, 1977). In a review, Backiel (1979) postulated that heated effluents could have a direct effect on growth rate by increasing the environmental temperature, and an indirect effect by extending the growth season for 0 group fish by inducing an earlier spawning and hatching, and delaying the effect of the colder months of late autumn.

Elevated temperatures appear to have an inconsistent effect on the production of invertebrate food organisms (Leszczynski, 1976; Soszka and Soszka, 1976). In one lake a deterioration in the benthic invertebrate community was noted following a 7 °C rise in water temperature, but the numbers of predatory Chironomidae larvae increased. In other waters, higher temperatures resulted in increased zooplankton production. But in all the waters studied, higher temperatures led to faster fish growth rates.

Effect of population density on growth

Density-dependent growth in the Cyprinidae is most often associated with food availability, although under crowded conditions, some species produce growth inhibitors. Thus, Pfuderer and Francis (1972) discovered that crowded goldfish, *Carassius auratus*, and carp, *Cyprinus carpio*, liberated a hormone that inhibited growth and production and depressed the heart rate. Very high densities may result in decreased food consumption rates because of low oxygen levels in the water. For example, Shireman *et al.* (1977) recorded decrease in the growth rate of *Ctenopharyngodon idella* at very high densities if the oxygen level was less than $4 \, \mathrm{mg} \, l^{-1}$, even when the fish were fed to satiation. These phenomena were observed for fish kept artificially in tanks or small ponds and it is debatable whether similar effects occur naturally. A study by Cowx (1988) on natural populations of *R. rutilus* and *L. leuciscus* in the River Exe, south-west England, found that the fastest rates of growth occurred in sections of the river where each species was most abundant, namely *R. rutilus* in the slow-flowing lower reaches and *L. leuciscus* in the faster-flowing middle reaches.

Backiel and Le Cren (1978) suggested that many species of cyprinids (and other schooling species) occur in dense populations with growth rates much lower than the potential for the species. They proposed that, in unmanaged fisheries, many species move towards an equilibrium state of a dense slow-growing population, which is a problem faced by many operators of still-water fisheries in which the aim is to produce high numbers of large fish. In apparent contrast to these negative aspects of high fish density, Pitcher *et al.*, (1982) recorded the advantages of schooling behaviour in *Carassius auratus*, namely that large shoals of fish found patchily distributed food more quickly than did small shoals. However, there are no data to show whether, or when, such improved foraging efficiency is translated into changes in growth rate.

Mills (1982) kept 0 group *L. leuciscus* for 20–30 weeks in fine-mesh cages in a river backwater. Both growth rate and mortality rate varied with the initial stocking density, and a change from fine mesh to a coarser mesh (9 meshes cm^{-1} to 5 meshes cm^{-1}) resulted in faster growth. However, growth at the lowest density was lower than occurred naturally in the river, presumably because the caged fish had a less abundant supply of appropriate food organisms. Previously, Jacobsen (1979) had found no density-dependent relationship for caged 1 group *Phoxinus phoxinus* because, according to Mills (1982), his stocking densities of $0.33–1.0\,1^{-1}$ were too low (Mills used densities up to $7.23\,1^{-1}$) and the duration of the experiment (2 months) was too short. Smith *et al.* (1978) found that *Pimephales promelas* in North America grew faster in tanks when given extra food, although at very high fish densities growth remained the same regardless of food abundance. This 'tolerance density' has been referred to earlier (Shireman *et al.*, 1977). Data of similar quality from natural populations are few, but Cazemier (1975) recorded that *A. brama* grew to 0.2, 0.5 or 1.0 kg by age 9 y in habitats where the densities of chironomid larvae (their main prey) were < 5, 5–20 and $> 20\,g\,m^{-2}$, respectively. Similarly, the increased nutrient content of the Mušov reservoir, Czechoslovakia, following inundation of the lower River Dyje, augmented the amount of available food to individual white bream, *Blicca bjoerkna*, because growth rate (G) and condition (C) increased in the years immediately after flooding (Libosvarsky, 1987).

Data from aquaculture provide strong evidence of density-dependent growth in cyprinids. Walter (1934) demonstrated this phenomenon in 3-year-old *Cyprinus carpio* (see the excellent review by Backiel and Le Cren, 1978). More recently, Hulata *et al.* (1982) noted, also with *C. carpio*, that initial growth after hatching was affected by severe crowding because the amount of food available to an individual fish was decreased. The results of such cage experiments must be interpreted carefully because often the feeding regimes and population densities are much higher than occur naturally (Weatherley and Gill, 1987).

Pivnicka (1982) suggested that in new reservoirs, where the balance between fish species is initially in a state of flux, the growth:abundance relationship is often more pronounced than in established water bodies. However, differences between species were observed in his 14 y study of fish in the Klicava reservoir in Czechoslovakia. For *R. rutilus* and *L. cephalus*, linear regression lines could be drawn of log mean weight per individual fish on log number of fish, with population density accounting for 62% of the variances in mean individual weight of roach, and 38% of that for chub. However, for the rudd, *Scardinius erythrophthalmus*, no density-dependent effect on growth could be demonstrated, and Pivnicka suggested that this was because rudd densities were always very low.

Alterations to growth rates as a result of changes in fish abundance have been recorded by many other workers (Frank, 1961; Zawisza, 1961; Kempe, 1962; Kennedy and Fitzmaurice, 1969; Aldoori, 1971; Burrough and Kennedy, 1979; Linfield, 1980), although the causes of the changes in population density were varied. Thus, Kennedy and Fitzmaurice (1969) observed increases in the widths of the growth zones on the scales of *S. erythrophthalmus* following a reduction in their number in a lake through rotenone poisoning. Aldoori (1971) described the increase in growth rate of *R. rutilus* after their transfer to a new reservoir. A more complex example comes from Burrough and Kennedy (1979), who correlated changes in the growth rate of *R. rutilus* over several years with changes in their abundance; the presence of the very abundant 1972 year class caused growth rates to decrease, but low numbers after 1976, following a high mortality through heavy infestation by the cestode *Ligula intestinalis*, coincided with an increased growth rate. The effect of strong year classes was observed also by Linfield (1980), who recorded a reduction in growth rate of *R. rutilus* in a small lake. Grey Mist Mere (Cheshire), following a succession of good recruitment years and artificial stocking. This situation was reversed following an abandonment of stocking and a sequence of poor recruitment years.

High recruitment of 0 group *R. rutilus* depressed the growth of older fish in the same year because all size groups ate mainly Cladocera (Townsend and Perrow, 1989). In this population in Alderfen Broad (Norfolk) *R. rutilus* became sexually mature at 2 and 3 y of age and there were few older fish. Hence, the mature fish were closer in size to the 0 group fish than is usual in most *R. rutilus* populations.

Changes in the trophic state of aquatic habitats that make more food available per individual fish do not always result in increased growth rates, as was noted by Müller and Meng (1986) for *R. rutilus* in Lake Sarnen, Switzerland. However, this may have been because natural year-to-year variations in growth in response to temperature changes masked the more subtle modulations resulting from variations in lake productivity. The level at which nutrient enrichment (eutrophication) of a water body becomes unacceptable is not always clear. Initial enrichment can lead through the food chain to higher growth rates of fish, but excess eutrophication may result in pollution, and hence in decreased oxygenation. An example of the potential impact of such pollution is described by Zalewski and Penczak (1978), who recorded very low growth rates of cyprinid fish in organically polluted waters in Poland, compared with growth rates in similar but unpolluted lakes and streams. Reference was made earlier (p. 466) (Shireman *et al.*, 1977) to the effect of low levels of oxygen on fish growth rates even when food supplies are not restricted.

Growth rate and year class strength (YCS)

It is widely recognized that many cyprinid populations are dominated by a few year classes (Fig. 16.7), rather than showing the decrease in numbers of fish in successive age groups that is evident in most populations of Salmonidae. The production of dominant year classes is often synchronous in different species and habitats, which points strongly to climatic conditions as the cause. Mills and Mann (1985) showed that strong year classes of *L. leuciscus* originated in years when the growth of the newly hatched fish was above average, and that there was a strong correlation between water temperature in the year of hatching and the resulting YCS (Fig. 16.8). Other factors were also important, but much of the variance in YCS could be attributed to temperature. A common explanation (though not as yet demonstrated unequivocally) is that, because 0 group cyprinids grow faster in warm summers than in cool summers, they pass more rapidly through the stage when they are vulnerable to predation by such aquatic invertebrates as Odonata nymphs and Coleoptera larvae. Certainly an ability to minimize the periods of high vulnerability to predation confers a distinct adaptive advantage to an individual fish (review, Williams, 1966). Whether or not predators are more abundant, or feed more often, at higher water temperatures are questions that have yet to be answered. However, laboratory studies (Mills and Mann, 1985) have shown that Odonata and Hemiptera nymphs eat more smaller (= younger) and fewer larger larvae of *L. leuciscus*.

In addition to such intraspecific differences in growth and survival, interspecific differences can occur within a particular assemblage. Genetic differences between species will play a major role in setting rates of growth, but the sequence of strong and weak year classes within a particular assemblage may show different chronologies according to species. This is because two species may not spawn and hatch at the same time: e.g. *L. leuciscus* in the River Frome spawn and hatch in April/May, whereas *R. rutilus* in the same river do not spawn and hatch until one month later (Mann, 1973, 1974). Thus the early lives of the two species are separated in time, and are subject to different

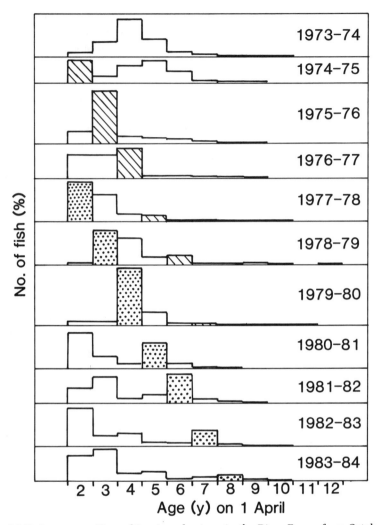

Fig. 16.7 Age composition of *Leuciscus leuciscus* in the River Frome from October to April, inclusive, in 11 consecutive years (top histogram, 1973–74; bottom, 1983–84). Hatching, 1973 years class; stipple, 1976 year class. Values on y-axis set at 20% intervals (redrawn from Mills and Mann, 1985, by permission of *Journal of Fish Biology*).

ranges of climatic and environmental conditions year by year. As a result, the year-to-year changes in the relative growth rate (hence YCS) of the two species do not always coincide.

Growth rate, sexual dimorphism, age at first maturity

Among the teleost fishes, males are frequently smaller than females; the Cyprinidae are no exception to this general rule. In 32 populations recorded in

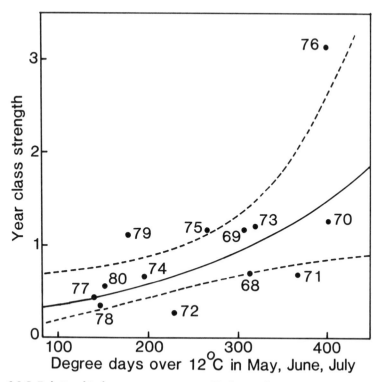

Fig. 16.8 Relationship between temperature (T, degree days $> 12\,°C$) in May, June and July in the year of hatching (1968–80) and the subsequent year class strength of *Leuciscus leuciscus* in the River Frome. Solid curve (with 95% confidence intervals) represents the fit to the exponential mode: ln YCS $= -1.48 + 0.0046T$ (redrawn from Mills and Mann, 1985, by permission of *Journal of Fish Biology*).

the literature, females grew faster than males in 19, no differences were observed in nine, and males grew faster in four. In the first category (females > males), the females mostly become sexually mature 1 y later than the males, i.e. they have, on average, one extra year of only somatic growth. However, once the females are sexually mature, natural selection favours those with fast growth rates because, in any one population, larger fish are more fecund than smaller fish of the same species (egg number/fish length). Of course, inter population differences can occur, for example *Gobio gobio* in the River Jarama, Spain laid more and larger eggs than *G. gobio* in the nearby Pinilla reservoir (Lobon-Cervia and Torres, 1983/84). A similar selection process is not necessary for male Cyprinidae as even small individuals produce enough sperm to fertilize the eggs of many females. However, in two populations of *G. gobio*, males grew marginally faster than females but, unusually, a greater percentage (89 and 74%) of females were mature at age 2 y than males (63 and 64%, respectively) (Mann, 1980).

Table 16.1 Significant differences between mean lengths of immature and mature dace, *Leuciscus leuciscus*, and gudgeon, *Gobio gobio*

Species	Sex	Age (y)	Mean fork length (mm) Immature	Mean fork length (mm) Mature	P*	Author
Dace	Female	3	143.4	160.1	< 0.001	Mann (1974)
	Male	3	149.8	158.7	< 0.001	Mann (1974)
Gudgeon	Female	2	87.1	92.9	< 0.05	Mann (1980)
	Male	2	88.7	96.6	< 0.001	Mann (1980)

* Significance of difference between means.

In some cyprinid and non-cyprinid species, the fast-growing fish of a particular cohort often attain sexual maturity at an earlier age than those that grow slowly (Table 16.1). A complex example is that of *P. phoxinus* in the River Frome (Mills, 1987); fish that hatched early in the year (May/June) and reached 30 mm by their first winter, spawned late (July/August) in the following summer. Their progeny were too small to spawn in the following year, but did so early (May/June) in the next year.

It is important to realize that the links between growth, sexual development, sexual size dimorphism and survival are features that identify the life-history tactics of particular species or populations. Examination of growth aspects alone can lead to a lack of understanding of the environmental factors that determine growth rates and of the way that natural selection has channelled growth rate potentials in particular directions.

Effects of hybridization on growth

There are numerous records of hybridization between cyprinid species (Wheeler, 1976; Wheeler and Easton, 1978; Swinney and Coles, 1982; Cowx, 1983; Fahy *et al.*, 1988), but few studies have compared the growth of parents and hybrids. Fahy *et al.*, (1988) found that *R. rutilus* × *A. brama* progeny grew at a rate intermediate to that of the two parents. They speculated that the hybrids were the F_1 generation and that if these were back-crossed with parents, then more intermediate forms would be produced. Cowx (1983) found similar growth rates between the same hybrids and the parental *A. brama* population over their first 6 y of life, but thereafter, hybrid growth was intermediate between the slower-growing *R. rutilus* and the faster-growing *A. brama*. Many hybrids exhibit heterosis (hybrid vigour), with the hybrids having superior traits to those of either parent. However, it appears from the limited evidence available that heterosis does not occur in the Cyprinidae.

Table 16.2 Ranges of biomass (B) and production (P) estimates for Cyprinidae in European waters*

Species	B ($kg\,ha^{-1}$)	[N†]	P ($kg\,ha^{-1}\,y^{-2}$)	[N†]
Abramis brama	0.06 –160.	6	0.02 – 46.8	6
Alburnoides bipunctatus	0.002– 0.32	4	0.002– 0.66	4
Alburnus alburnus	0.398–477	4	0.5 –528	2
Aspius aspius	0.37 – 2.73	2	0.06 – 1.54	3
Barbus barbus	0.81 – 92.6	4	0.63 – 12.93	3
Barbus bocagei	62.08 –145.23	2	15.52 – 37.75	2
Barbus callensis	2.31	1	4.27	1
Barbus cyclolepis	20.5	1	50.8	1
Blicca bjoerkna	0.03 – 0.12	3	0.01 – 0.10	3
Carassius carassius	0.13	1	0.04	1
Chondrostoma nasus	0.06 – 83.1	2	0.05 – 15.78	3
Chondrostoma polylepis	35.82 – 88.68	2	22.10 – 74.23	2
Cyprinus carpio	12.0	1	5.20 – 8.4	3
Gobio gobio	0.03 –149	9	0.03 –117	9
Leucaspius delineatus	0.09	1	2.25	1
Leuciscus cephalus	0.23 – 31.20	10	0.10 – 23.0	11
Leuciscus idus	0.002	1	0.002	1
Leuciscus leuciscus	1.62 – 32.6	5	0.76 – 26.0	6
Phoxinus phoxinus	0.01 – 70	7	0.02 – 39.0	7
Rutilus arcasii	0.68 – 1.42	2	1.40 – 3.24	6
Rutilus rutilus	0.48 –251.3	6	0.34 –178	8
Scardinius erythrophthalmus	4.3	1	2.7	1
Tinca tinca	0.94 – 2.0	2	0.18 – 1.0	2

*Sources: Backiel (1970, 1971) Biro (1983), Goldspink (1979), Hickley and Bailey (1982), Holcik (1972), Lind et al. (1973), Lobon-Cervia et al. (1986) Mann (1965, 1971), Mann and Penczak (1984), Mathews (1971), Mills and Eloranta (1985), Penczak (1981), Penczak and Molinski (1984), Penczak and Tatrai (1985), Penczak et al. (1982, 1985, 1986), Philippart (1977, 1981), Pivnicka (1982), White and Williams (1978) Wolny and Grygierek (1972).
† Number of estimates.

16.3 PRODUCTION

Production (*P*) is used here in Ivlev's (1966) sense to signify the formation of somatic and gonad tissue by a fish population within a specified time period (usually 1 y) and includes material formed by fish that die or migrate from the area studied before the end of the time period. Production is therefore a rate and, as a synthesis of the instantaneous rates of growth and mortality, it constitutes a valuable summary of a population's response to environmental conditions. The methods of computation have been fully described by Chapman (1968) annd Weatherley (1972); for symbols see p. 458.

Compared with the many production estimates of salmonid populations, few data are available for the Cyprinidae (Mann and Penczak, 1986). Several estimates of cyprinid production were obtained incidentally to, and less accurately than in, more intensive investigations of salmonid species (*Salmo, Salvelinus, Oncorhynchus* spp.). However, estimates are available from several rivers and lakes, mostly in Europe and North America (Tables 16.2 to 16.4).

In most studies of fish production, the accuracy of the estimates depends greatly upon the precision of the population density estimates (Mann and Penczak, 1986). For the Cyprinidae, this precision is difficult to achieve for the very small 0 group fish and many of the values given in Tables 16.2 to 16.4 do not include this age group. This omission can have a major effect on the production estimate (Mathews 1971; Table 16.5).

Table 16.3 Range of biomass (*B*) and production (*P*) estimates for North American Cyprinidae*

Species	B [(kg ha^{-1})]	N[†]	P [(kg ha^{-1} y^{-1})]	N[†]
Campastoma anomalum			0.89 – 1.36	2
Clinostomus funduloides			1.13	1
Notropis cornutus	6.33– 33.69	5	2.98 – 42.36	6
Notemigonus crysoleucas	0.03– 37.7	3	0.061– 23.3	4
Phoxinus oreas			<0.01	1
Pimephales notatus	2.29– 16.49	5	3.85 – 28.02	6
Pimephales promelas	1.51– 7.47	2	1.77 – 7.47	2
Rhinichthys atratulus	5.87	1	3.58 – 8.23	2
Rhinichthys cataractae	9.91	1	3.48 – 12.83	1
Semotilus atromaculatus	0.18–116.81	6	0.24 –174.79	10
Semotilus margarita	1.31	1	1.25	1

* Sources: Chadwick (1976), Cooper *et al.* (1971), Freeman *et al.* (1988), Halyk and Balon (1983), Lotrich (1973), Mahon and Balon (1977), Mahon *et al.* (1979), Neves and Pardue (1983), Penczak *et al.* (1984), Portt *et al.* (1986).
† Numbers of estimates.

Table 16.4 Range of biomass (B) and production (P) estimates for non-European and non-North American species*

Species	B $[(kg\,ha^{-1})]$	$N^{\dagger}$	P $[(kg\,ha^{-1}\,y^{-1})]$	$N^{\dagger}$
Barbus callensis	2.32	1	4.27	1
Cyclocheilichthys apogon	5.94	1	9.00	1
Hampala macolepidota	9.64	1	14.96	1
Lobocheilus bo	3.16	1	3.49	1
Nematobramis everetti	0.82– 2.51	4	1.23– 3.41	4
Osteocheilus kahajenensis	2.89– 5.07	3	3.56– 6.60	3
Paracrossocheilus acerus	0.46	1	0.59	1
Parculiosoma dusonensis	2.89– 2.96	2	3.63– 3.99	2
Puntius collingwoodi	0.24– 0.50	2	0.31– 0.32	2
Rasbora bankanensis	0.74	1	0.62	1
Rasbora sumatrana	1.36–35.68	3	3.10–66.64	3

*Source: *B. callensis*, North Algeria (Penczak and Molinski, 1984); all other species from Borneo (Watson and Balon, 1984).
† Numbers of estimates.

Table 16.5 Contribution of 0 group and older fish to the annual production of cyprinid fish in the River Thames*

Species	Production ($g\,m^{-2}\,y^{-1}$)			% 0 group contribution (%)
	0 group	> 0 group	Total	
Alburnus alburnus	24.40	28.40	52.80	46.2
rutilus rutilus	8.20	9.60	17.80	46.1
Leuciscus leuciscus	1.16	1.44	2.60	44.6
Gobio gobio	3.70	8.00	11.70	31.6

*Source: Mathews (1971).

Some of the estimates in Tables 16.2 to 16.4 refer to statistical populations (Mann and Penczak, 1986), i.e. those derived from studies of short sections of a stream when the population is distributed unevenly over a much larger area. Some studies sample the population much more reliably than others. For example, in the Pilica River, central Poland, production estimates for a 2.5 ha section of the main river (Mann and Penczak, 1984) omitted many of the younger age groups of *A. brama. L. cephalus. L. leuciscus, R. rutilus* and other cyprinids, because these inhabited the various backwaters and side-channels.

The importance of taking a holistic view of the life history of a species was emphasized by Halyk and Balon (1983), who estimated fish production in a series of pools adjacent to Irvine Creek, Ontario. Some were permanently connected to the river, whereas others had a shorter period of stream connection. The authors emphasized the importance of river floodplain habitats in maintaining the abundance and species richness of the Cyprinidae and other families. They noted that such species are relatively easy to observe and that they can be a useful indicator of environmental changes.

Another type of problem that can be encountered with shoaling Cyprinidae is described by Mann (1971) for *P. phoxinus* in a small softwater stream in southern England. The study area was a *c.* 100 m long segment into and from which a shoal moved freely. Thus, in the sequence of monthly samples, the shoal could be present, partly present or absent, so the (usually relatively smooth) curve of fish number against time became an extremely erratic line of peaks and troughs.

Ideally, for estimates of fish production the fate of individual cohorts needs to be followed through the year, but many of the estimates given in Tables 16.2 to 16.4 are derived from single samples. Growth estimates are often based on back-calculated length (hence weight) increments, although Halyk and Balon (1983) have shown that this can lead to an underestimate of annual production (as much as 63% in one example for *Notropis cornutus*).

Within-species variation in growth rate (i.e. between populations) (p. 462), combined with marked variations in population density, can result in appreciable differences between habitats in the annual production of a species. For example, published estimates for eight populations of *R. rutilus* range from 0.34 to 178 kg ha^{-1} y^{-1}.

As gonad products form up to 30% of the total weight of female Cyprinidae (e.g. *L. leuciscus*, Mann and Mills, 1985), they can account for a high proportion of the annual production of some populations. For *R. rutilus* and *A. alburnus*, Mann (1965) estimated that male and female gonad products together represented 19% and 7%, respectively, of each species' annual production. Note also that the contribution of gonad products in terms of weight is likely to be less than their true contribution because the energy content of gonad material is higher than that of somatic tissue (review, Le Cren, 1962). Unfortunately, this aspect of cyprinid production has attracted little attention.

Several authors (e.g. Le Cren, 1962) have encouraged the use of fish production estimates as a stepping-stone to increased understanding of the patterns of energy flow in aquatic ecosystems. Few workers, however, have proceeded in this direction with cyprinid species, although notable exceptions are Mann (1965) and Backiel (1971). The latter examined the growth and production of various fish piscivores in the River Vistula (Wisła), including *Aspius aspius* and *L. cephalus*, in relation to their food consumption rates and their exploitation by commercial fishermen. Further studies along similar lines would greatly advance our understanding of cyprinid population dynamics. The success of the Cyprinidae can be attributed to the flexible response of their growth and other parameters to environmental conditions. Growth is a measure of seasonal and/or annual increments of gonad and somatic tissue whereas production summarizes the population biomass level and the rates of growth and mortality into a single value. The role of biotic and abiotic features of the environment in setting the levels of growth and production is discussed in this chapter, but a complete knowledge of cyprinid population dynamics must involve the topics considered in other chapters in this book, especially reproduction and life history (Chapter 17). Only through such integrated studies will it be possible to achieve rational policies to manage commercial and sport fisheries and to protect populations of rare species and communities.

ACKNOWLEDGEMENTS

The author acknowledges gratefully the late Dr C. A. Mills for his critical comments on an early draft of the chapter. The work was funded by the Natural Environment Research Council.

REFERENCES

Alabaster, J. S. (1964) The effect of heated effluents on fish. *Proc. Int. Conf. Wat. Pollution Res., London.* Pergamon Press, Oxford and London, pp. 261–91.

Aldoori, T. Y. (1971) Food and growth of roach (*Rutilus rutilus* L.) in two different environments. *Proc. 5th Br. Coarse Fish. Conf., Liverpool.* 72–5.

Backiel, T. (1970) Production and food consumption in the population of *Aspius aspius* (L.) of the Vistula River. *Polskie Archwm Hydrobiol.,* **17**, 249–58.

Backiel, T. (1971) Production and food consumption of predatory fish in the Vistula River. *J. Fish Biol.,* **3**, 369–405.

Backiel, T. (1979) Feeding of fish and their feeding grounds, in *Biology of Fish as a Test for Heated Effluents* (eds L. Horoszewicz and T. Backiel), *Pol. ecol. Stud.,* **5**, 72–9.

Backiel, T. and Le Cren, E. D. (1978) Some density relationships for fish population parameters, in *Ecology of Freshwater Fish Production* (ed. S. D. Gerking), Blackwell, Oxford, pp. 279–302.

Bagenal, T. B. (1973) *Ageing of Fish,* Unwin Bros., London.

Beamish, F. W. H., Niimi, A. J. and Lett, P. F. K. P. (1975) Bioenergetics of teleost fishes: environmental influences, in *Comparative Physiology: Functional Aspects of Standard Materials* (eds L. Bolis, H. P. Maddrell and K. Schmidt-Nielsen), North Holland Publ. Co., Amsterdam, pp. 187–209.

Bertalanffy, L. von (1957) Quantitative laws in metabolism and growth. *Q. Rev. Biol.,* **32**, 217–31.

Beverton, R. J. H. (1987) Longevity in fish; some ecological and evolutionary perspectives, in *Ageing Processes in Animals* (eds A. D. Woodhead, M. Witten and K. Thompson), Blackwell, Oxford, pp. 165–201.

Biro, P. (1983) On the dynamics of fish populations in Lake Balaton. *Roczn. Nauk. roln.,* H **100**, 55–64.

Broughton, N. M. and Jones, N. V. (1978) An investigation into the growth of O-group roach (*Rutilus rutilus* L.) with special reference to temperature. *J. Fish Biol.*, **12**, 345–57.

Brown, D. J. A. (1973) The effect of power station cooling water discharges on the growth of coarse fish fry. *Proc. 6th Br. Coarse Fish Conf., Liverpool*, 191–202.

Burrough, R. J. and Kennedy C. R. (1979) The occurrence and natural alleviation of stunting in a population of roach, *Rutilus rutilus* (L.). *Fish Biol.*, **15**, 93–109.

Cazemier, W. G. (1975) Onderzoek naar de oorzaken van groeiverschillen bij brasem (*Abramis brama* L.). *Viss. Niews*, **28**, 197–207.

Chadwick, E. M. P. (1976) Ecological fish production in a small Precambrian shield lake. *Env. Biol. Fishes.*, **1**, 13–60.

Chapman, D. W. (1968) Production, in *Methods for Assessment of Fish Production in Fresh Waters* (ed. W. E. Ricker), Blackwell, Oxford and Edinburgh, pp. 182–96.

Cooper, E. L., Wagner, C. C. and Krantz. G. E. (1971) Bluegills dominate production in a mixed population of fishes. *Ecology.* **52**, 280–90.

Cowx, I. G. (1983) The biology of bream, *Abramis brama* (L), and its natural hybrid with roach, *Rutilus rutilus* (L), in the River Exe. *J. Fish Biol.*, **22**, 631–46.

Cowx, I. G. (1988) Distribution and variation in growth of roach. *Rutilus rutilus* (L.), and dace, *Leuciscus leuciscus* (L.), in a river catchment in south-west England. *J. Fish. Biol.*, **33**, 59–72.

Cragg-Hine, D. and Jones, J. W. (1969) The growth of dace *Leuciscus leuciscus* (L.), roach *Rutilus rutilus* (L.) and chub *Squalius cephalus* (L.) in Willow Brook, Northamptonshire. *J. Fish Biol.*, **1**, 59–82.

Fahy, E., Martin, S. and Mulrooney, M. (1988) Interactions of roach and bream in an Irish reservoir. *Arch. Hydrobiol.*, **114**, 291–309.

Ford, E. (1933) An account of the herring investigations conducted at Plymouth during the years from 1924–1933. *J. mar. biol. Ass. U.K.*, **19**, 305–84.

Frank, S. (1961) A contribution to the growth of roach, rudd and white bream in some waters of Czechoslovakia and Poland. *Věst. čsl. Spol. zool.*, **26**, 65–74.

Freeman, M. C., Crawford, M. K., Barrett, J. C., Facey, D. E., Flood, M. G., Hill, J., Stouder, D. J. and Grossman, G. D. (1988) Fish assemblage stability in a southern Appalachian stream. *Can. J. Fish. aquat. sci.*, **45**, 1949–58.

Gerking, S. D. (ed.) (1978) *The Ecology of Freshwater Fish Production*, Blackwell, Oxford and Edinburgh.

Goldspink, C. R. (1979) The population density, growth rate and production of roach *Rutilus rutilus* (L.) in Tjeukemeer. The Netherlands. *J. Fish Biol.*, **15**, 473–98.

Halyk, L. C. and Balon, E. K. (1983) Structure and ecological production of the fish taxocene of a small floodplain system. *Can. J. Zool.*, **61**, 2446–64.

Hickley, P. and Bailey, R. G. (1982) Observations on the growth and production of chub *Leuciscus cephalus* and dace *Leuciscus leuciscus* in a small lowland river in southeast England. *Freshwat. Biol.*, **12**, 167–78.

Holcik, J. (1972) Abundance, ichthyomass and production of fish populations in three types of water-bodies in Czechoslovakia (man-made lake, trout lake, arm of Danube River), in *Productivity Problems of Freshwaters* (eds Z. Kajak and A. Hillbricht-Ilkowska), IBP, UNESCO, Pol. Sci. Publ., Warsaw, pp. 843–55.

Hulata, G., Moav, R. and Wohlfarth, G. (1982) Effects of crowding and availability of food on growth rates of fry in the European and Chinese races of the common carp. *J. Fish Biol.*, **20**, 323–7.

Ivlev, V. S. (1966) The biological productivity of waters. *J. Fish Res. Bd Can.* **23**, 1727–59.

Jacobsen, O. J. (1979) On density-dependent growth in a cyprinid. *Phoxinus phoxinus* L.. *Folia biol., Kraków*, **27**, 225–9.

Jezierska, B. (1979) Fish metabolism, in *Biology of Fish as a Test for Heated Effluents* (eds L. Horoszewicz and T. Backiel), *Pol. ecol. Stud.*, **5**, 43–51.

Kempe, O, (1962) The growth of roach (*Leuciscus rutilus* L.) in some Swedish Lakes. *Rep. Inst. Freshwat. Res. Drottningholm*, **44**, 42–104.

Kennedy, M. and Fitzmaurice, P. (1969) Factors affecting the growth of coarse fish. *Proc. 4th Brit. Coarse Fish Conf., Liverpool*, 42–9.

Konstantinov, A. S. and Zdanovich, V. V. (1986) Peculiarities of fish growth in relation to temperature fluctuation. *J. Ichthyol.*, **26**, 65–74.

Kubecka, J., Svatora, M. and Vrba, J. (1985) The growth of the fry of rudd (*Scardinius erythrophthalmus*) in Klicava reservoir. *Sb. čsl. Akad. zeměd. Ved. ser. E.*, **30**, 911–18.

Le Cren, E. D. (1962) Reproduction and recruitment in freshwater fish, in *The Exploitation of Natural Animal Populations* (eds E. D. Le Cren and M. W. Holdgate), Blackwell, Oxford, pp. 283–96.

Leszczynski, L. (1976) The influence of preheated waters on the bottom fauna of lakes in the vicinity of Konin. III. An effort to explain the causes and results of changes in the bottom fauna, *Roczn. Nauk. roln.*, H**97**, 49–68.

Leveque, C. (1978) Estimation du rapport P/B à partir de la longevité des espèces. *Verh. int. Verein. Limnol.*, **20**, 2122–6.

Libosvarsky, J. (1987) Impact of a newly built reservoir on silver bream, *Blicca bjoerkna*. *Zool. Listy*. **36**, 359–70.

Lind, E., Hytinkoski, P., Keranen, M. and Kukko, O (1973) Spawning and population structure of the roach, *Rutilus rutilus* (L.) in Lake Kintajarvi, N. E. Finland. *Ichthyol. Fenn. Borealis*, **1**, 1–30.

Linfield, R. S. J. (1980) Ecological changes in a lake fishery and their effects on a stunted roach *Rutilus rutilus* population. *J. Fish Biol.*, **16**, 123–44.

Lobon-Cervia, J. and Torres, S. (1983/84) On the growth and reproduction of two populations of gudgeon (*Gobio gobio* L.) in central Spain. *Acta Hydrobiol.*, **25/26**, 101–15.

Lobon-Cervia, J., Sostoa, A. de and Montanes, C. (1986) Fish production and its relation with the community structure in an aquifer-fed stream of Old Castile (Spain). *Polskie Archwm Hydrobiol.*, **33**, 333–43.

Lotrich, V. A. (1973) Growth, production, and community composition of fishes inhabiting a first-, second-, and a third-order stream of eastern Kentucky. *Ecol. Monoqr.*, **43**, 377–97.

Mahon, R. and Balon, E. K. (1977) Ecological fish production in Long Pond, a lakeshore lagoon on Long Point, Lake Erie. *Env. Biol. Fishes.*, **2**, 261–84.

Mahon, R., Balon, E. K. and Noakes, D. L. G. (1979) Distribution, community structure and production of fishes in the upper Speed River, Ontario: a preimpoundment study, *Env. Biol. Fishes*, **4**, 219–44.

Mann, K. H. (1965) Energy transformations by a population of fish in the River Thames. *J. Anim. Ecol.*, **34**, 253–75.

Mann, R. H. K. (1971) The populations, growth and production of fish in four small streams in southern England. *J. Anim. Ecol.*, **40**, 155–90.

Mann, R. H. K. (1973) Observations on the age, growth, reproduction and food of the roach *Rutilus rutilus* (L.) in two rivers in southern England. *J. Fish Biol.*, **5**, 707–36.

Mann, R. H. K. (1974) Observations on the age, growth, reproduction and food of the dace *Leuciscus leuciscus* (L.) in two rivers in southern England. *J. Fish Biol.*, **6**, 237–53.

Mann, R. H. K. (1976) Observations on the age, growth, reproduction and food of the chub *Squalius cephalus* (L.) in the River Stour, Dorset. *J. Fish Biol.*, **8**, 265–88.

Mann, R. H. K. (1980) The growth and reproductive strategy of the gudgeon *Gobio gobio* (L.) in two hard-water rivers in southern England. *J. Fish Biol.*, **17**, 163–76.

Mann, R. H. K. and Mills, C. A. (1985) Variations in the sizes of gonads, eggs and larvae of the dace. *Leuciscus leuciscus*. *Env. Biol. Fishes*, **13**, 277–87.

Mann, R. H. K. and Penczak, T. (1984) The efficiency of a new electro-fishing technique in determining fish numbers in a large river in central Poland. *J. Fish Biol.*, **24**, 173–85.

Mann, R. H. K. and Penczak, T. (1986) Fish production in rivers: a review. *Polskie Archwm Hydrobiol.*, **33**, 233–47.

Mann, R. H. K. and Steinmetz, B. (1985) On the accuracy of age determination using scales from rudd *Scardinius erythrophthalmus* (L.) of known age. *J. Fish Biol.*, **27**, 621–8.

Mathews, C. P. (1971) Contribution of young fish to total production of fish in the River Thames at Reading. *J. Fish Biol.*, **3**, 157–80.

Meili, M. (1987) Seasonal growth patterns in a population of roach (*Rutilus rutilus*) after spawning. *Proc. 5th Congr. europ. Ichthyol., Stockholm (1985)*, 163–7.

Mills, C. A. (1982) Factors affecting the survival of dace, *Leuciscus leuciscus* (L.) in the early post-hatching period. *J. Fish Biol.*, **20**, 645–55.

Mills, C. A. (1987) The life history of the minnow *Phoxinus phoxinus* (L.) in a productive stream. *Freshwat. Biol.*, **17**, 53–67.

Mills, C. A. (1988) The effect of extreme northerly climatic conditions on the life history of the minnow. *Phoxinus phoxinus* (L.). *J. Fish Biol.*, **33**, 545–61.

Mills, C. A. and Eloranta, A. (1985)s The biology of *Phoxinus phoxinus* (L) and other littoral zone fishes in Lake Konnevesi, central Finland. *Annls zool. fenn.*, **22**, 1–12.

Mills, C. A. and Mann, R. H. K. (1985) Environmentally-induced fluctuations in year-class strength and their implications for management. *J. Fish Biol.*, **27** (Supp. A), 209–26.

Moreau, J. (1987) Mathematical and biological expression of growth in fishes: recent trends and further developments, in *The Age and Growth of Fish* (eds R. C. Sommerfelt and G. E. Hall), Iowa State Univ. Press., Iowa, pp. 81–113.

Moreau, J., Belaud,A, Dauba, F. and Nelva, A. (1985) A model for rapid growth evaluation in fishes: the case of the Cyprinids of some large French rivers. *Hydrobiologia*, **120**, 225–7.

Müller, R. and Meng, H. J. (1986) Factors governing the growth rate of roach *Rutilus rutilus* (L.) in pre-Alpine Lake Sarnen. *Schweiz. Z. Hydrol.*, **48**, 135–44.

Neves, R. J. and Pardue, G. B. (1983) Abundance and production of fishes in a small Appalachian stream. *Trans. Am. Fish. Soc.*, **112**, 21–6.

Papageorgiou, N. K. (1979) The length weight relationship, age, growth and reproduction of the roach *Rutilus rutilus* (L.) in Lake Volvi. *J. Fish. Biol.*, **14**, 529–38.

Penczak, T. (1981) Ecological fish production in two small lowland rivers in Poland. *Oecologia*, **48**, 107–11.

Penczak, T. and Molinski, M. (1984) Fish production in Oued Sebaou, a seasonal river in North Algeria. *J. Fish Biol.*, **25**, 723–32.

Penczak, T. and Tatrai, I. (1985) Contribution of bream. *Abramis brama* (L.) to the nutrient dynamics of Lake Balaton. *Hydrobiologia*, **126**, 59–64.

Penczak, T., Jankov, J., Dikov, T. J. and Zalewski, M. (1985) Fish production in the Mesta River, Rila Mountain, Samokov, Bulgaria. *Fish. Res. (Amsterdam)*, **3**, 201–21.

Penczak, T., Lobon–Cervia, J., O'Hara, K. and Jakubowski, H. (1986) Production and food consumption by fish populations in the Pilawa and Dobrzyca Rivers, North Poland. *Polskie Archwm Hydrobiol.*, **33**, 345–72.

Penczak, T., Lorenc, E., Lorenc, J. and Zdziennicka, M. (1979) The ecology of roach, *Rutilus rutilus* (L.), in the barbel region of the polluted Pilica River V. Estimation of the age and growth according to the opercular bones. *Ekol. pol.*, **27**, 135–54.

Penczak, T., Mahon, R. and Balon, E. K. (1984) The effect of impoundment on the upstream and downstream taxocenes (Speed River, Ontario, Canada). *Arch. Hydrobiol.*, **99**, 200–207.

Penczak, T., Suszycka, E. and Molinski, M. (1982) Production, consumption and energy transformations by fish populations in two small lowland rivers in Poland. *Hydrobiologia*, **108**, 135–44.

Pfuderer, P. and Francis, A. A. (1972) Isolation of a new heart rate depressing pheromone from the water of crowded fish. *Fedn Proc. Fedn Am. Socs exp. Biol.*, **31**, 486.

Philippart, J.C. (1979) Contribution à l'étude de l'écosystème ⟨⟨Rivière de la zone à barbeau supérieure ⟩⟩: densilé, biomass et production des populations de poissons de l'Ourthe, in *Productivité biologique en Belgique* (eds P. Duvigneaud and P. Kestemont). Duculot, Gembloux, pp. 551–67.

Philippart, J. C. (1981) Ecologie d'une population de vandoises, *Leuciscus leuciscus* (L.), dans la rivière Ourthe (bassin de la Meuse, belgique). *Annls Limnol.*, **17**, 41–62.

Pitcher, T. J., Magurran, A. E. and Winfield, I. J. (1982) Fish in larger shoals find food faster. *Behav. Ecol. Sociobiol.*, **10**, 149–51.

Pivnicka, K. (1982) Long-termed studies of fish populations in the Klicava reservoir. *Acta Sci. nat. Acad. Sci. Bohemoslov., Brno*, **16**, 1–46.

Pivnicka, K. (1983) Growth capacity of some fish species in different environmental conditions. *Věst. čsl. Spol. zool.*, **47**, 272–87.

Ponton, D. and Gerdaux, D. (1987) La population de gardons (*Rutilus rutilus* (L.)) du lac Leman en 1983–85: Structure en age, determinisme du recruitment, analyse de la croissance. *Bull. fr. Pêche Piscic.*, **305**, 43–53.

Portt, C. B., Balon, E. K. and Noakes, D. L. G. (1986) Biomass and production of fishes in natural and channelized streams. *Can. J. Fish. aquat. Sci.*, **43**, 1926–34.

Rheinberger, V., Hofer, R. and Wieser, W. (1987) Growth and habitat separation in eight cohorts of three species of cyprinids in subalpine lakes. *Env. Biol. Fishes*, **18**, 209–17.

Shireman, J. V., Colle, D. E. and Rottmann, R. W. (1977) Intensive culture of grass carp. *Ctenopharyngdon idella*, in circular tanks. *J. Fish Biol.*, **11**, 267–72.

Smith, H. T., Schreck, C. B. and Maughan, O. (1978) Effect of population density and feeding rate on the fathead minnow (*Pimephales promelas*). *J. Fish Biol.*, **12**, 449–55.

Soszka, H. and Soszka, G. L. (1976) Reakja biocenoz na podgrazewanie wody (Biocenosis reaction in heated water). *Wiad. ekol.*, **22**, 117–35.

Swinney, G. N. and Coles, T. F. (1982) Description of two hybrids involving silver bream, *Blicca bjoerkna* (L.), from British waters. *J. Fish Biol.*, **20**, 121–9.

Tong, H. Y. (1986) A qualitative and quantitative description of the early growth of roach, *Rutilus rutilus*, in the laboratory. *Env. Biol. Fishes*, **15**, 293–300.

Townsend, C. R. and Perrow, M. R. (1989) Eutrophication may produce population cycles in roach, *Rutilus rutilus* (L.), by contrasting mechanisms. *J. Fish Biol.*, **34**, 161–4.

Vasnetsov, V. V. (1953) 'Etaps' in the development of bony fishes, in *Otcherky po Obshtchin Voprosam Ikhtiologii* (ed. E. N. Pavlovsky), AN SSSR Press, Moscow, pp. 207–17.

Walford, L. A. (1946) A new graphic method of describing the growth of animals. *Biol. Bull. mar. biol. Lab., Woods Hole*, **90**, 141–7.

Walter, E. (1934) Grundlagen der allgemeinen fischereilichen Produktionslehre, einschliessen ihrer Anwendung auf die Futterung. *Handb. Binnenfisch. Mitteleur.*, **4**, 481–662.

Watson, D. W. and Balon, E. K. (1984) Structure and production of fish communities in tropical rain forest streams. *Can. J. Zool.*, **62**, 927–40.

Weatherley, A. H. (1972) *Growth and Ecology of Fish Populations*, Academic Press, London and New York.

Weatherley, A. H. and Gill, H. S. (1987) *The Biology of Fish Growth*, Academic Press, London and New York.

Webb, P. W. (1978) Partitioning of energy into metabolism and growth, in *Ecology of Freshwater Fish Production* (ed. S. D. Gerking), Blackwell, Oxford and London, pp. 184–214.

Welcomme, R. L. (1985) River fisheries. *FAO Fish. Biol. tech. Pap.*, **262**, 1–330.

Wheeler, A. (1976) On the populations of roach (*Rutilus rutilus*), rudd (*Scardinius erythrophthalmus*), and their hybrid in Esthwaite Water, with notes on the distinctions between them. *J. Fish Biol.*, **9**, 391–400.

Wheeler, A. and Easton, K. (1978) Hybrids of chub and roach (*Leuciscus cephalus* and *Rutilus rutilus*) in English rivers. *J. Fish Biol.*, **12**, 167–71.

White, R. W. G. and Williams, W. P. (1978) Studies of the ecology of fish populations in the Rye Meads sewage effluent lagoons. *J. Fish Biol.*, **13**, 379–400.

Wieser, W., Forstner, H., Schiemer, F. and Mark, W. (1988) Growth rates and growth efficiencies in larvae and juveniles of *Rutilus rutilus* and other cyprinid species: effects of temperature and food in the laboratory and in the field. *Can. J. Fish. aquat. Sci.*, **45**, 943–50.

Wilkonska, H. (1979) Growth of fish in heated environments, in *Biology of Fish as a Test for Heated Effluents* (eds L. Horoszewicz and T. Backiel), *Pol. ecol. Stud.*, **5**, 80–85.

Wilkonska, H. and Zuromska, H. (1977) Growth of fry in the heated Konin lakes complex. *Roczn. Nauk roln.*, H **97**, 91–111.

Williams, G. C. (1966) *Adaptive and Natural Selection. A Critique of Some Current Evolutionary Thought*, Princeton Univ. Press, Princeton, NJ.

Wolny, P. and Grygierek, E. (1972) Intensification of fish pond production, in *Productivity Problems of Freshwaters* (eds Z. Kajak and A. Hillbricht–Ilkowska), IBP, UNESCO, Pol. Sci. Publ., Warsaw, pp. 563–71.

Wootton, R. J. (1990) *Ecology of Teleost Fishes*, Chapman and Hall, London.

Zalewski, M. and Penczak, T. (1978) The effect of anthropogenous changes in the environment on the growth of roach *Rutilus rutilus* (L.). *Wiad. ekol.*, **24**, 367–76.

Zawisza, J. (1961) The growth of fishes in lakes of Wegorzewo district. *Roczn. Nauk roln.*, B **77**, 731–48.

Chapter seventeen

Reproduction and life history

C. A. Mills*

17.1 INTRODUCTION

This chapter aims to cover the key areas of cyprinid reproduction and life history, and in particular to highlight areas (such as the timing of reproduction and the survival of eggs and larvae) where the need for more information is greatest. In most topics covered there are many suitable examples from northern latitudes and especially from those parts of Europe where cyprinids dominate the fish fauna. The literature shows that cyprinid species exhibit a wide range of life histories and reproductive styles. This variation can be both inter- and intraspecific and occurs both within and between habitats. The within-habitat variability, together with the paucity of detailed information from some areas, particularly sub tropics and tropics, limits the scope for exploration of broad geographical trends, and highlights the need for the emphasis of future research to be less skewed towards the northern latitudes.

17.2 PHYSIOLOGY OF REPRODUCTION

Studies on the reproductive physiology of cyprinids have concentrated on a single species, the common carp, *Cyprinus carpio*. This interest has been stimulated by the desire to understand and control the reproductive processes in a species used extensively in aquaculture from the cooler temperate regions to the tropics. The remaining studies generally focus on applied aspects of reproduction in other species of importance in aquaculture such as the Chinese carps and the Indian major carps, or on cyprinids commonly used in experimental studies. The principal examples of the latter are the goldfish, *Carassius auratus*, and the zebra fish, *Brachydanio rerio*. This section does not provide a comprehensive review of physiological mechanisms because several

---

*Deceased.

excellent reviews are available elsewhere. Rather more space is devoted here to the overall relationship between environmental stimuli and the timing of reproduction.

Put at its simplest, the timing of the endogenous reproductive cycle is synchronized by environmental stimuli, especially changes in temperature and photoperiod. This external information is transmitted to the brain via the nervous system. The hypothalamus, which forms part of the central nervous system, in turn regulates the anterior pituitary gland. This gland controls gonadal development via the endocrine system. *Aquaculture of Cyprinids* (Billard and Marcel, 1986) provides a valuable source of references on the endocrinology of reproduction in carp and some other cyprinids. It contains an especially useful review on ovulation and spermiation (Weil *et al.*, 1986). A review devoted solely to carp (Horvath, 1985) covers the physical and environmental requirements for maturation, together with a detailed description of the histology of the carp ovary at differing stages of development. Billard and Marcel (1986) and Jhingran and Pullin (1985) are sources of information on the Indian and Chinese carps. For the zebra fish there is a comprehensive, though now rather dated, review by Laale (1977).

In strongly seasonal environments, the regulatory process will be of enormous adaptive significance in synchronizing the eggs and larvae with the seasonal conditions most suitable for their survival. Both temperature and photoperiod are important in controlling the reproductive cycle in many cyprinids (de Vlaming, 1974), but it is often difficult to judge their relative importance because these and other cues tend to covary. The roach, *Rutilus rutilus*, seems to display no obvious relationship between the timing of spawning and the temperature regime, either within or between populations (Diamond, 1985; and Vollestad and L'Abée-Lund, 1987). Advancing the photoperiod at twice the normal rate from late November onwards resulted in synchronous spawning of roach in early February. This was when the accelerated photoperiod equalled that of mid May, the start of the natural spawning season. Control fish did not spawn; neither did fish that were not exposed to a prior period of low temperature and short photoperiod (Worthington *et al.*, 1982). In this and probably in other temperate species, photoperiod may be the principal environmental factor co-ordinating the reproductive cycle. However, the onset and duration of spawning of the roach and other species do show modest year-to-year variation (Diamond, 1985; Vollestad and L'Abée-Lund, 1987), so other environmental stimuli must have a complementary role. There are some species for which there is a clear lower temperature limit below which spawning will not occur. A review of ten populations of the tench, *Tinca tinca*, found that they all had minimum spawning temperatures of between 18 and 20 °C. Subsequent falls in temperature resulted in the interruption of spawning and the reabsorption of maturing eggs in the gonads (atresia). Otherwise cycles of egg maturation and spawning continued periodically until mid August, when all remaining mature eggs were reabsorbed, irrespective of temperature or feeding conditions. This reabsorption was probably controlled by the decline in daylength and occurred earlier in more southerly populations (Horoszewicz *et al.*, 1981). Populations of the widely distributed European minnow, *Phoxinus phoxinus*, showed a clear trend towards later spawning in more northerly populations (Mills, 1988). This could be either a direct temperature effect or an adaptation to set the reproductive cycle to different photoperiods. Studies on this species under controlled conditions did find that changes in photoperiod stimulated vitellogenesis. However, Scott (1979) suggests that in the normal environment it is changes in temperature that initiate the behavioural responses which expose the fish to the stimulatory effect of photoperiod. It is clear that much painstaking experimental work will be necessary before there is a comprehensive understanding of these processes and their relative importance for cyprinid species. Particular attention must be paid to experimental design, because the effects of temperature, photoperiod and social interaction are so often confounded in physiological studies of maturation.

In tropical regions, where the thermal regime is relatively stable and photoperiod variation is low, it is still possible that there are sufficient small but reliable changes to provide adequate timing cues. Good evidence of this is lacking, and under these conditions some cyprinids show no obvious seasonality in spawning, whilst in others, control of spawning depends on other cues (such as flow changes) related to seasonal rainfall patterns (Section 17.7).

17.3 SPAWNING

Earlier work on the secondary sexual characteristics of the cyprinids, the behaviours associated with spawning, spawning sites, and spawning seasons, especially of North American species, is reviewed on pages 173–234 of Breder and Rosen's (1966) *Modes of Reproduction in Fishes*. This section gives a much briefer and more general account, and indicates some later studies in this area.

Pre-spawning migrations

With their limited ability to resist current, larval cyprinids will tend to be displaced downstream, and in fast-flowing water with insufficient refuge areas there will be a serious danger that a large proportion may either starve or be flushed out into saline conditions. In addition there are cyprinids whose spawning requirements (in terms of suitable macrophytes or spawning gravel) may be met better in flowing waters, although associated lakes provide the principal feeding grounds. Consequently, many reports of migrations say that they are associated with spawning or that most often they are made upstream.

However, there have been few thorough studies in this field and many reports are anecdotal or peripheral comments in studies devoted primarily to other aspects of cyprinid biology. Species reported migrating upstream shortly before spawning include the European minnow 'leaping a small weir like tiny salmon', dace, *Leuciscus leuciscus*, roach, bream, *Abramis brama*, barbel, *Barbus barbus*, nase, *Chondrostoma nasus*, and chub, *Leuciscus cephalus*. Whilst many of these migrations will extend over a few kilometres or less, there are distinct semi-migratory forms of several species, including roach and bream, which have summer feeding grounds in the Black, Caspian, Aral and Azov seas but which may migrate hundreds of kilometres up inflowing rivers to spawn.

There is also evidence from several common species that the spawning shoals migrate each year to utilize the same spawning sites even though there may exist other similar sites which are not used. This is true of dace in the River Frome, a small productive stream in southern England, and of roach in a variety of habitats (review, Diamond, 1985). The implication that homing may be involved is borne out by tagging studies on bream and roach. For example, a 10 km section of a large (100 m wide) Irish river contained four separate feeding shoals of bream, each with a distinct home range. Each year these shoals migrated to a single mixed spawning site. Following spawning, the adult fish dispersed into the feeding shoals and returned to their respective feeding areas (Whelan, 1983). Roach living in Lake Arungen (Norway) spawn both within the lake and in five inflowing streams. A detailed tagging study showed that the fish migrating into the tributaries to spawn exhibited considerable repeat homing (83.5–92.0%). Furthermore, the roach spawning in different tributaries intermingled freely in the lake during summer feeding and must have been able to actively select the home tributary for subsequent spawnings (L'Abée-Lund and Vollestad, 1985).

The upstream spawning migrations of many cyprinid populations have been disrupted by dams and other modifications to natural watercourses. It is most important to determine the extent of upstream movements (both pre-spawning and generally) and to ensure that the adult fish remain free to migrate upstream to spawn. A corollary is that care must also be taken to safeguard the drifting larvae (Section 17.6).

Choice of spawning sites

Several schemes have been devised to group fishes according to their choice of spawning site and the degree of any post-spawning care. These are reviewed by Balon (1975a), who also provides the most satisfactory set of groups or guilds. Most European cyprinid species do not guard their eggs and are open substratum spawners. Further grouping rests on the type of substratum over which the adhesive eggs are scattered. The **lithophils** (such as the dace, the chub and many members of the large genus *Barbus*) deposit eggs on the rock or gravel bottoms of rivers. This tends to limit the distribution of these species, though some species such as the minnow are also common in those lakes where there is access to suitable spawning sites. **Psammophils** (such as the gudgeon, *Gobio gobio*) scatter their eggs on sand or near the roots of plants where the bottom is sandy, again principally in flowing water. **Phytophils**, which include widespread species like carp and tench, *Tinca tinca*, spawn on aquatic or flooded terrestrial vegetation. These spawning sites are more likely to suffer oxygen depletion and the larvae tend to leave the eggs before the free-swimming stage and attach to vegetation with the cement glands on their heads. The Asian cyprinids, silver carp, *Hypophthalmichthys molitrix*, grass carp, *Ctenopharyngodon idella*, and bighead carp, *Aristichthys nobilis*, are **pelagophils**. They spawn in rivers where the turbulence and flow conditions ensure the suspension of the semi-pelagic eggs.

However, some of the most widely distributed species have very flexible spawning requirements, as shown by a more detailed look at a widely studied species such as the roach. There are several reports of spawning in beds of *Phragmites communis* in lakes (reviews, Mills, 1981a; Gillet, 1985) and in the Baltic, although some Baltic roach also migrate into rivers to spawn. Water depth at these sites ranged from less than 15 cm to between 100 and 150 cm. Roach have also been described spawning on a gravel substratum at a depth of 20–100 cm in a reservoir, and there are Soviet reports of *R. rutilus heckeli* spawning at depths of 3–4 m and occasionally down to 9 m providing that weed was present. In flowing waters, roach are reported spawning in various situations: on a rocky substratum in a fast-flowing river (Penaz and Prokes, 1972); close to the surface amongst beds of the aquatic moss *Fontinalis antipyretica* growing adjacent to a fast current (Mills, 1981a); amongst terrestrial vegetation overhanging into another fast-flowing river (Vollestad and L'Abée-Lund, 1987), and in beds of *Elodea canadensis* and filamentous algae in a canal, again close to the surface (Diamond, 1985). These adaptable species such as roach and bream are termed **phyto-lithophils.**

A good example of a European species with a more specialist spawning mode is the bitterling, *Rhodeus amarus*. Along with several related species, this fish is a **brood hider** which deposits its eggs into the excurrent syphon of freshwater mussels (Breder and Rosen, 1966). *Leucaspius delineatus* provides a rare example of a European cyprinid that belongs to the second major grouping, the **egg guarders**. The female spawns its eggs in a ribbon over aquatic macrophytes and the male fans and guards them.

The spawning habits of the North American cyprinid species are considerably more diverse. Amongst those species that do not guard their eggs there are nest builders as well as a wide range of open substratum spawning types. Indeed species from the genus *Notropis* alone can be found which fall into all of the principal open substratum spawning groups. The other notable contrast with the European species is the abundance of species that also guard their eggs.

Spawning behaviour

Studies on the spawning behaviour of cyprinids tend to fall into two categories, field observations and aquarium observations. Many of the former are available, including a series on the common European open substratum spawners. Two basic patterns emerge from field studies: species where males defend territories, and those where they do not. The best-documented example of the former behaviour type is the bream, where large males with the white spawning tubercles characteristic of many male cyprinids in spawning condition occupied territories along shallow shoreline areas. The size of the territories range from 1 m² amongst emergent vegetation to 5 m² along more open shoreline (Svardson, 1948; Fabricius, 1951). The males circled the territories, occasionally rushing aggressively at any neighbouring male that happened to trespass, although no true fighting or lateral displays were observed. Smaller males were chased off into deeper water and one (invariably the original territory holder) returned. Schools of bream, presumably females and non-territory-holding males, moved jerkily in the adjacent deeper water. When a female moved into the territory, the male tried to swim under her from behind and to drive her into thick vegetation where the spawning took place. In contrast, species such as roach and rudd showed no male territory holding. Male roach moved in irregular circles within large shoals which were ranged alongside marginal vegetation. There was occasional chasing and nipping between males, possibly when one was mistaken for a female. Females entered the male belt from deeper water and followed an erratic, zigzag path at the surface of the water and amongst vegetation. They were accompanied by several males, of which one or two appeared to adhere to the female laterally; males also butted the female on her anterior sides. During egg release the females swam slowly with a rapid tailbeat, possibly to disperse the eggs, whilst the flanking males trembled and released milt (Svardson, 1951; Diamond, 1985).

However, in an interesting book, Balon (1985) contrasts a general statement that amongst open substratum group spawners "there is little specialised courtship; males chase, push and butt the female and each other. Gamete release is probably synchronised by tactile and chemical signalling" with his detailed aquarium observations of pair spawning by roach. These showed a considerably more complex series of behaviours than those described in the field, though the basic pattern was similar. There is a general problem here: some elements which are fully displayed in aquaria may be truncated, at least some of the time, under natural conditions as a result of group activity. However, it is inevitable that some details of behaviour will be missed under field conditions, where vigorous spawning activity often severely restricts visibility, and it is a pity that most studies only adopt one of these approaches.

17.4   EGG AND LARVAL DEVELOPMENT

Descriptions of egg and larval development of the cyprinids, particularly of the common European species, are widespread in the literature; e.g. see Tong (1982) for references to the roach, Laale (1977) for the zebra fish, and Penaz and Prokes (1978) for the gudgeon, *Gobio gobio*, and other species. Most make little attempt to relate the developmental processes to specific ecological requirements. There has also been a parallel, though not always complementary, interest in developing a suitable terminology to describe these events (review, Balon, 1971), the lack of which tends to complicate comparisons between or even within species. The most satisfactory scheme, especially since the replacement of the original complex terms with their English equivalents, divides the life of a fish, from fertilization to death, into five periods: embryonic, larval, juvenile, adult and senile (Balon, 1975b, 1985). The first two periods and their subdivision into a series of phases are of interest here:

1. The **embryonic period** commences at fertilization and is characterized by exclusively endogenous nutrition;
   (a) The **cleavage phase** encompasses development within the egg membrane from fertilization to the start of organogenesis;
   (b) The **embryonic phase** lasts from the start of organ formation to the end of hatching;
   (c) The **free embryo phase** extends from hatching to the start of exogenous feeding;
2. The **larval period** commences with exogenous feeding and lasts until the axial skeleton is ossified and the embryonic median finfold is differentiated or no longer apparent;
   (a) The **finfold phase** encompasses the transition to exogenous feeding and the start of the differentiation of the fins;
   (b) The **finformed phase** then lasts to the end of the larval period.

Balon describes development through each phase as a series of steps; a step occurs where a series of developmental processes are completed synchronously. For example in the Danubian cyprinid *Abramis ballerus*, the completion of a broad finfold, a posterior part of the swim bladder, and cement glands, combined with a change from photophobia to phototaxis, enable the larvae to leave the bottom, swim up to the surface and attach themselves to plants. Then whilst they hang on the plants, above the anoxic bottom and camouflaged from predators, a subsequent series of developments prepares the larvae for the next step, the onset of exogenous feeding (Balon, 1985).

Whilst development as a whole will be dependent upon the genetic instructions inherited from the parents, it will be tempered by a variety of other influences. Up to the start of exogenous feeding, important factors will be the biochemical resources supplied by the female parent, the temperature and the oxygen levels. In roach the fat content of the eggs was higher following years of favourable feeding conditions, though egg weight showed little between-year variation. Although smaller, younger roach tended to lay lighter eggs (see also Section 17.7), their fat content was particularly high following years of good growth (Table 17.1). However, the possible developmental consequences of these changes remain a matter for speculation. In carp, eggs from females of medium ages had the highest levels of cysteine, tryptophan, and histidine, whilst the leucine and isoleucine concentrations continued to increase with age. Most importantly Vladimirov (cited in Zukinskii and Kim, 1980) established a direct dependence between the degree of fertilization of carp eggs and survival of larvae, and an inverse dependence of the percentage of deformed larvae on the total content of these and other amino acids in the eggs.

The importance of temperature in development is twofold: development will only proceed successfully within a certain temperature range; and within this range, temperature greatly influences the speed of development. The temperature range seems to be adapted to the spawning season of the species. The dace, *Leuciscus leuciscus*, is an early spawner (March/April) and the percentage of eggs hatching fell sharply above 15 °C (Mills, 1980), whereas eggs of the later-spawning *A. ballerus* developed normally from 6 to 20 °C. Even a short exposure to 6 °C killed eggs of the white bream, *Blicca bjoerkna*, which spawns later still. In both these breams the start of cleavage and the start of embryo formation were the most sensitive stages (Volodin, 1960). Both dace (Mills, 1980) and roach (Diamond, 1985), and presumably other cyprinid species, show a negative exponential relationship between temperature (T) and the duration of developmental stages (D) of the form: $\log D = a + bT$. The much shorter incubation times cited for summer-spawning species are due, at least in part, to differences in water temperature. At 15 °C dace eggs took 14.4 d from fertilization to 50% hatching, roach took 10.2 d to hatch, and minnows 14–17 d to reach the free-swimming stage. At 7 °C this time lengthened to 30 d for roach and to 44 d for dace. A further complication in any discussion of hatching time is the variable nature of the boundary (the release from the egg membranes) between the embryonic and free larval phases. Dace larvae hatch with a straight body, considerable melanophore development and a cigar-shaped or only slightly pear-shaped yolk sac. Some other species, particularly those with cement glands for attachment to plants, tend to hatch at an earlier stage in the developmental process. This tendency can vary considerably, within as well as between species, depending on the environmental conditions. Roach from Deep Lake hatched at a length of 4.5–5.0 mm with large pear-shaped yolk sacs, heads bent downwards and little pigmentation. However, in Rybinsk reservoir (USSR), cold weather delayed hatching until the larvae were 5.5–6.0 mm long and at a similar stage of development to the dace larvae. Where eggs occurred in clumps, there were clear indications that lack of oxygen retarded development, with the embryos on the periphery developing fastest and those in the middle the slowest (Lange, 1960).

Table 17.1 The relative fecundity and size, weight and fat content of eggs from roach, *Rutilus rutilus*, of different length classes, following a year of good feeding conditions (1970) and a year of poor feeding conditions (1973)*

		Body length (mm)							
	Year	12–14	14–16	16–18	18–20	20–22	22–24	24–26
Relative fecundity	1971	157	143	163	177	172	170	160
(eggs g^{-1} fish wt)	1974	122	131	134	116	122	154	–
Egg diameter (mm)	1971	1.13	1.18	1.18	1.28	1.34	1.38	1.42
	1974	1.24	1.29	1.33	1.34	1.38	1.29	–
Egg weight (fresh, mg)	1971	0.67	0.76	0.79	0.91	1.04	1.12	1.21
	1974	0.64	0.99	0.88	0.95	0.91	0.95	–
Egg fat content (% wet wt)	1971	7.38	7.09	8.97	5.72	6.12	5.33	5.46
	1974	2.55	2.05	1.96	2.96	2.43	2.58	–

*Source: Kuznetsov and Khalitov (1978).

In natural populations there tends to be a transient decline in the growth rates of at least some species at the interface of the embryonic and larval periods (Kuznetsov, 1972). Once exogenous feeding has commenced, the influence of the yolk sac food supply on development will decline, and the length of the subsequent developmental phases will be dependent upon temperature and upon the availability and quality of the food organisms. Protracted development stages will generally be indicative of unsatisfactory conditions (Lange, 1960) and may leave the larvae vulnerable to high rates of mortality (Section 17.6).

17.5   ECOLOGY OF EGGS

The survival of naturally spawned eggs is perhaps the single most neglected area of the ecology of the cyprinid fishes. However, there have been a number of studies in the Mazurian Lake District of Poland. Quantitative studies on bream, ide (*Leuciscus idus*), roach, rudd, and tench spawning sites found that virtually all eggs were successfully fertilized (98–100%) but thereafter egg survival was extremely variable (Pliszka, 1953). The ide is considered to be a lithophilous river spawner, but in Lake Harsz the eggs were densely scattered on plants and also on the bottom itself. Where there was little water movement, mortality was 99–100%, though where the water was more disturbed by wind, up to 15% of eggs were alive. Bream eggs were well scattered on submerged vegetation, most densely at 60–70 cm below the surface in water 1–1.8 m deep. Between 60 and 90% of the eggs hatched, though up to 60% of eggs on parts of plants close to the lake bottom were dead. There was no evidence of predation on the eggs during their 3 d incubation period. Tench and rudd also had brief incubation periods on submerged plants, and shortly before hatching around 90% of the eggs were alive. Most roach eggs were attached to plants close to, or even just above, the water surface. Successive surveys from spawning in late April to the end of the 12 d incubation period recorded between 96 and 99% live eggs. However occasional dense masses on the lake floor contained only 30–70% live eggs. Some roach eggs were found empty with round punctures, probably indicating predation by invertebrates.

Estimating the proportion of live eggs at one point in time cannot give an accurate estimate of egg survival from spawning to hatching, as predation or death and decay may remove all trace of eggs from the spawning site. In a more detailed study of roach spawning sites in three Mazurian lakes over several years, overall survival up to the larval stage rarely exceeded 5% (Zuromska, 1967 a,b). Occasional large-scale mortalities were caused by low dissolved oxygen concentrations or by heavy wave action, but most losses of eggs and newly hatched, inactive larvae were ascribed to invertebrate predation. Though not evident in this study, fish, especially eels, also predate the eggs of roach and other cyprinids, including dace and bleak, *Alburnus alburnus* (Mills, 1981 a,b; Diamond and Brown, 1984).

River-spawned eggs face additional hazards from the effects of current. However, dace eggs shed at the upstream edge of gravel riffles almost all successfully adhered to the substratum within a few metres of the point of release (Mills, 1981c). The proportion of eggs drifting off the site during the 30 d incubation period was low, even under spate conditions. Over the site there was a close correlation between the percentage of eggs surviving and substratum composition, with poor survival in areas of high silt and low gravel content. Laboratory studies and field estimates indicated that whilst the macroinvertebrates present on the site could scavenge large numbers of dead eggs, they were not important predators of live eggs. Dead eggs were rapidly attacked by a fungus and became unrecognizable within a few days. The number of live eggs declined steadily from the end of spawning (Fig. 17.1), and overall egg survival from spawning to hatching was estimated at between 9 and 22% over the 30 d incubation period (Mills, 1981 b,c). Little detailed information is available for pelagophils but Verigin *et al.* (1978) examined the

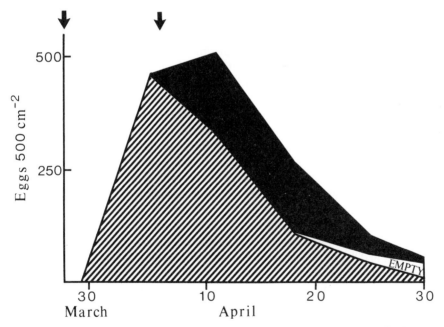

Fig. 17.1 Changes in the mean numbers of live eggs (hatched polygon), dead eggs (dark polygon), and empty egg shells (white polygon) in 500 cm² samples taken on a gravel spawning site of dace, *Leuciscus leuciscus*, in the River Frome, England. Catches of female dace in the area showed a rapid rise in the proportion of spent females (left arrow, 4.4%; right arrow, 91.3%) coinciding with the initial rise in egg numbers (reproduced with permission from Mills 1981b).

drifting eggs of three introduced phytophagous species, namely silver, grass and bighead carp. On average, 35% of the eggs in the Syr-Dar'ya River were dead, and in addition 2–3% of the living embryos were deformed.

17.6   ECOLOGY OF LARVAE

An essential prerequisite to the study of larval cyprinids is a key to their identification. Mooij (1989) lists several partial keys for European larvae and there are others by Pekar (1965) and Spindler (1988). Fuiman *et al.* (1983) provide a key for 62 North American species. A second prerequisite, particularly for quantitative work, is a suitable sampling technique (reviews, Bagenal and Braum, 1968; Treasurer, 1978). Despite the variety of traps, nets and pumps that are available, the aggregated distribution and difficulty of marking the fragile larvae tend to limit the scope of most studies. Therefore there are numerous studies on feeding, on growth and, in the laboratory, on growth and survival under a variety of controlled conditions, but few quantitative accounts of larval survival.

The feeding studies include many on roach (see Tong, 1982), bream and other species, particularly in Eastern Europe; Lohnisky, 1970, provides a substantial list of these references. Given the small size of most cyprinid larvae on hatching (< 10 mm), it is not surprising that phytoplankton and rotifers are the dominant food types in the guts of first-feeding cyprinids. For example, first-feeding roach larvae (mean length 7 mm) from the littoral zone of a small lake fed exclusively on green and bluegreen algae. As in most studies the diet broadened rapidly as fish size increased, and at a mean size of 12 mm the diet included a wide variety of rotifers and zooplankton (Hammar, 1985). Dace larvae are rather larger at first feeding (mean length 9.5 mm), and in the margins of a small river principally contained rotifers and the diatoms on which the rotifers themselves had fed. Other prey taxa included a few copepod nauplii and the small cladoceran *Chydorus sphaericus* (Mills, 1985). Three weeks later adult copepods and cladocerans formed the two most important components of the diet, followed by rotifers, desmids, chironomids and oligochaetes. There were significant differences in diet composition between larvae from different sites along the river margin and at different times of day. The volume of the stomach contents was lowest at night; studies on diel feeding in larval roach also found that feeding either ceased or nearly ceased during darkness (Grigorash, 1961; Lightfoot, 1976). A weakness of most feeding studies on larval cyprinids is that no attempt is made to analyse the relationship between the available food organisms in the environment and those ingested, or indeed to assess the impact on prey communities. Hewitt and George (1987) do, however, make an indirect attempt to do this for larvel roach feeding on the rotifer *Keratella cochliaris* in a small lake (English Lake District). Thus there is little information on interspecific competition for food at the larval stage, though for juveniles, this information is widely available from both laboratory and field studies (e.g. Winfield and Townsend, 1988).

The potential for competition will be reduced by a combination of the short duration of the larval stage and the differences in hatching times of different species. Thus Dolinskiy (1984) found that in reservoirs the dominant species occupying shallow-water macrophyte communities switched from the larvae of the early-spawning cyprinids white bream, roach, bitterling and rudd to the later-spawning bleak and verkhova, *Leucaspius delineatus*. The marginal vegetation is essential to larval fishes: zooplankton densities were one or two orders of magnitude higher than in the open water, and it provided shelter from some predators and, in rivers, from current. In a small Kentucky stream (7–40 m wide), Floyd *et al.* (1984) examined the chronology of appearance and habitat use of larvae of 28 species, including 11 cyprinids which occupied all the habitats surveyed where flow was low. On average, larvae of each cyprinid were collected over a six-week period, partly because at least some of the species were fractional spawners with a long breeding period. It would be surprising if at least some competition did not occur, though there is no direct evidence for the existence of competitive juvenile bottlenecks (Chapter 19) amongst the cyprinids.

Maximum sustainable swimming speed of fish is a function of length, and given their small size, current will be a dominant factor in the ecology of larval cyprinids. For instance, newly hatched dace larvae can swim only at about two body lengths per second (*c.* 17 mm s^{-1}) and were washed passively downstream from the spawning sites into marginal areas where current speed was low (< 20 mm s^{-1}). During the summer this represented only 2–3% of the surface area of the River Frome sites investigated by Mann and Mills (1986). Experimental studies demonstrated that 50% of 7.5 mm roach larvae could hold station against a current of 69 mm s^{-1}; larvae in the River Hull chose to hold station amongst macrophytes where current was less than 20 mm s^{-1}. Larval cyprinids will not be able to maintain their position over most of the surface area of most rivers, and the availability of refuge areas of low flow will delimit the available habitat. The practice of cutting weeds to reduce hydraulic resistance and increase current velocity may have detrimental effects on both eggs and larvae (Broughton *et al.*, 1977; Mills, 1981c). Some 2 d after batching, grass carp larvae moved from the swift currents required for egg incubation to quiet nursery areas for feeding, though it is unclear to what extent this is the result of specific larval behaviour. Where the distance from the spawning site to suitable nursery areas is too great the larvae may starve. Sites having all the requirements for the species are rare, and thus few self-sustaining populations have arisen despite widespread stocking of juveniles and adults for weed control (Zimpfer *et al.*, 1987). A further threat to drifting larvae or small juveniles is posed by the proliferation of fish farms and power plants, through which a high proportion of the total flow may be diverted. Few are likely to pass through these installations unscathed.

In eastern England there is concern over the poor spawning success of cyprinids in rivers where factors such as recreational boat traffic and nutrient enrichment have led to a general loss of macrophytes (Linfield, 1985). This problem is being tackled by introducing mature broodstock of phytophilous spawners to a holding pool well in advance of spawning, and then allowing them access to a specially prepared spawning pond via a sluice. The brood fish are returned to the holding pond after spawning and the young stages are allowed to develop in the protected environment of the spawning pond. At the end of their first season's growth they are released into the river system via a sluice and connecting channel.

To say that cyprinids suffer high rates of mortality at the larval stage but that this mortality varies between species, between environments, and between years would incite few to disagree. On the other hand, the detection of actual rates and the demonstration of causal mechanisms in the field is rarely attempted, let alone achieved. At best it may be possible to work backwards by calculating the strengths of particular year classes and relating these to environmental variables. High temperatures in the months after hatching increase both growth and survival in species such as the dace (Mills and Mann, 1985). There has long been discussion of the concept of 'critical periods' in the early life history of fish, including substantial reviews by Vladimirov (1975) and by Li and Mathias (1987). The latter authors argue that "the deepest, sharpest and fastest physiological and ecological changes during the development of the larvae are produced with the shift from endogenous nutrition to exogenous" and at this time the larvae are particularly sensitive to environmental factors, particularly food supply (Section 17.3). Thus mortality may be greatest at the start of exogenous feeding. For cyprinids there are experimental studies which support this hypothesis, e.g. a study of roach larvae by Cerny (1975), and others like the study of barbel and nase by Penaz (1971) which do not. Dace larvae, stocked into a river backwater in mesh cages that allowed access to drifting plankton, started feeding between 2 and 4 d after hatching. This was long before the exhaustion of endogenous food supplies; starved larvae could survive about 20 d at typical river temperatures. It was after about this long time that heavy mortalities occurred in those cages stocked at very high densities (6–12 larvae l^{-1}). This suggests that a critical period was generated by starvation soon after the exhaustion of the endogenous food reserves. At lower stocking densities, there was no evidence of a critical period in the sense of a sharp increase in mortality. Survival was up to 46% over 20 weeks and 43% over 31 weeks, even though growth was slower than that of free-living fish (Mills, 1982), Free-living roach and dace have death rates an order of magnitude higher than those of the lowest-density (0.044 larvae l^{-1}) caged larvae over the first 10–12 weeks post-hatching (Table 17.2; Mills, 1982).

The pattern of early mortality is probably one facet of the overall adaptation of cyprinids to their environment, alongside those such as egg size and

Table 17.2 Mortality rates of free-living and caged cyprinids in the first few weeks of life

Species	Habitat	Weeks after hatching	Mean instantaneous death rate (week^{-1})	Year of hatching	Source
(a) Free-living					
Roach	small lake	*c.* 0–12	0.197	1972	Bagenal, 1974
		c. 12–24	0.369	1972	
Roach	large river	*c.* 0–12	0.400	1967	Mathews, 1971
		c. 12–24	0.087	1967	
Roach	large river	0–12	0.480	1968	Mathews, 1971
Dace	large river	0–12	0.434	1968	
(b) Caged					
Dace	low initial density*	0–10	0.031	1978	Mills, 1982
		10–20	0.046	1978	
Dace	High initial density[†]	0–10	0.300	1977	Mills, 1982
		10–20	0.321	1977	

* 0.044–0.22 fish l^{-1} (11 cages).
[†] 0.72–7.23 fish l^{-1} (8 cages).

reproductive effort that are discussed in Section 17.7. Neither competition for food nor inherent genetic defects seem likely to be the major causes of mortality. Therefore, in warm years when larval survival (measured in terms of subsequent year class strength) is high, the rapid growth of the larvae enhances their ability to survive (assuming that vulnerability is an inverse function of size). Predation will normally be the principal cause of mortality. Just such an explanation has been advanced for the decline of the Colorado squawfish, *Ptychocheilus lucius*, where water-development programmes have led to falls in water temperature and poor 0-group growth and survival (Kaeding and Osmundson, 1988).

17.7 REPRODUCTIVE STRATEGIES

The reproductive strategy of a species will be the summation of a suite of adaptive traits that enables individual fish to leave the maximum number of offspring. These traits will encompass size and age at first reproduction, size- and age-specific fecundity schedules, reproductive effort, and the manner and timing of spawning. However, the reproductive strategy will also be strongly related to the development of other adaptive traits such as physiology and body size. The optimal reproductive effort will be derived from a trade-off between present reproductive effort and future expected reproductive output. The latter will be a function of post-breeding survival, growth and fecundity. Though there have been few conclusive experimental demonstrations of the cost of reproduction (Reznick, 1985), it is likely that the earlier and the greater the degree to which energy resources are diverted from maintenance and somatic growth, the lower will be the parent's survival to future spawnings. It has been argued that this trade-off will be conditioned by the balance between pre- and post-maturity rates of mortality, and by the predictability of the causes of mortality, and that selection will favour lower fecundity and greater longevity with increased variation in spawning success (Mann and Mills, 1979). Within the constraints of the optimal effort there will be a further necessary trade-off between the production of more eggs to offset high larval mortality and production of larger eggs to increase the fitness of individual larvae.

In reviewing the reproductive strategies of selected cyprinid species within this context it is necessary to focus attention at a series of levels: within populations, between populations, and between species. It is also important to recognize that though it is generally impossible to disentangle the effects of proximate (direct environmental) and ultimate (genetic) influences, the former will obviously predominate at the population level. However, the tactical responses of the individual fish within populations to changes in environmental conditions will themselves have an underlying adaptive component.

The reduction in the fat content of roach, *Rutilus rutilus*, eggs following a year of poor feeding was accompanied by a sharp decline in relative fecundity, but both egg size and egg weight showed little change (Table 17.1). Mann and Mills (1985) investigated between-years variation in the reproductive effort of the dace, *Leuciscus leuciscus*, population of the River Frome in southern England. In this small productive river, female dace mature at between 2 and 5 (mostly 3–4) years of age and then shed a single batch of eggs each year up to their maximum age of 10 or 11 y. There was no evidence to suggest that any fish had a 'rest' year, nor was follicular regression (atresia) of the ovaries ever observed. The spawning season lasted for 2–3 weeks each April, and as only a single batch of eggs was produced, the weight of the gonads a few days before spawning was used as an approximate measure of reproductive effort. Over six of the seven years surveyed, there was an inverse between-years relationship between egg size and egg number, with gonad size remaining constant. Fewer, larger eggs were spawned when the previous summer had been warm. The exception was in 1977 when, following an unusually warm summer when somatic growth was the highest recorded, both fecundity and egg size were low, resulting in a substantial decline in reproductive effort. There were also significant within-year trends. The relative weight of the ovaries increased by a factor of two with increasing fish length (Fig. 17.2(a)). Fecundity, however,

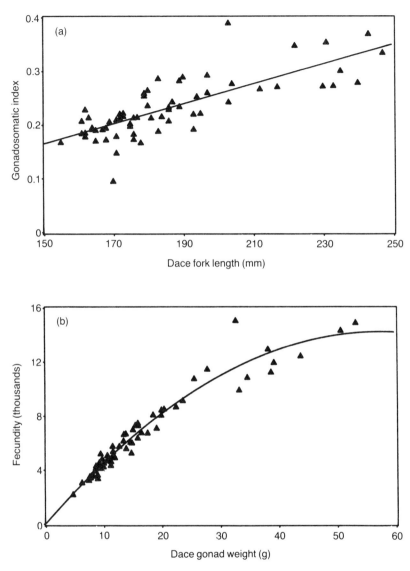

Fig. 17.2 (a) Relationship between gonadosomatic index (*GSI*) and fork length (*L*) for individual dace caught in March 1980 in the River Frome, England (redrawn from Mann and Mills, 1985). The line denotes the fit ($r^2 = 0.60$) of the linear regression: $GSI = -0.114 + 0.00186L$. (b) Relationship between fecundity (*F*) and gonad weight (*GW*) for the same sample of dace. The line denotes the fit ($r^2 = 0.947$) of the quadratic regression: $F = 0.080 + 0.494GW - 0.0043\,GW^2$.

did not show a proportionate increase (Fig. 17.2(b)) because larger gonads (hence larger fish) also contained larger eggs; there was no increase in the proportion of connective tissue. The Russian roach population showed the same trends with increasing fish length (Table 17.1). Overall the between-years variations in egg size in the dace population were small in relation to the within-year variations. For example, for a 200 mm (fork length) female, the mean egg volume ranged from 1.65 mm^{-3} in 1977 to 1.99 mm^{-3} in 1976. In contrast, in 1978 (a typical year), egg size ranged from 1.35 mm^{-3} in a 170 mm dace to 2.15 mm^{-3} in a large 230 mm female. Egg size, egg and larval dry weight, and the length of the female were all positively correlated with each other. Thus larger (and older) female dace produce larger and possibly fitter larvae. However, the cost of increasing reproductive effort with size (and age) may be reflected in the steady rise in mortality rate with age (Mann and Mills, 1986). Philippart (1981a) summarizes the demography of several dace populations. The fecundities of a 200 mm female all fall within the between-years variation of R. Frome dace, i.e. between 5973 eggs (1977) and 8714 eggs (1975), with the sole exception of the slow-growing river Thames population (3800 eggs). In most populations, females matured at 3–4 y of age and 160 mm or more in length, with a few fish (usually females) reaching 10 y or more and a maximum size of 240–80 mm. Slow growth in the Thames resulted in low reproductive effort and in reduced adult size rather than increased age at maturity (Williams, 1967). A common feature of dace populations is great between-years variability in the success of reproduction (Mills and Mann, 1985).

This suite of reproductive traits – relatively late maturity but with the potential to spawn in successive years; increasing reproductive effort and mortality with age; a short spawning season and highly variable reproductive success from year to year – are typical of many of the larger temperate cyprinids. Well-documented examples include the nase, *Chondrostoma nasus* (Philippart, 1981b) and the chub, *Leuciscus cephalus* (Hellawell, 1971; Mann, 1976). In both species, individuals can live over 20 y and approach 500 mm length, with sexual maturity at age 5–7 y and highly variable recruitment. There is some evidence that the oldest individuals may only reproduce in alternate years. However, there are other long-lived and large species which have the capacity to ripen successive batches of eggs within a season (**fractional spawning**). The tench, *Tinca tinca*, produced three to four batches under pond conditions at intervals of 14 d at temperatures of 19–25 °C, with the female gonad accounting for 10–15% of total body weight (Horoszewicz *et al.*, 1981; Epler *et al.*, 1981). The common carp, *Cyprinus carpio*, is particularly interesting. Though in temperate conditions it spawns a single batch per year, it may spawn in one uninterrupted session or spawning may be spread over several days but drawing on portions of a single batch of matured eggs (Horvath, 1985). This 'repeat spawning within days' is quite distinct from fractional spawning, as the carp requires some 3–3.5 months at 20–22 °C between two ovulations. In temperate climates any possible second spawning is suppressed until the following year by low temperature. However, in the warmer parts of the carp's range it is a true fractional spawner, producing two or even three batches of eggs each year. Reproductive effort may be relatively low, with the female gonads forming around 10% of body weight at maturity (Horvath, 1986).

A second group of smaller-sized temperate species (such as the gudgeon, *Gobio gobio*, and the bleak, *Alburnus alburnus*) mature sooner, generally at age 2–3 y, and then shed several batches of eggs each year (fractional spawning) up to a maximum age of 5–8 y (Mackay and Mann, 1969; Mann, 1980). As found in other species e.g. the dace (Mann, 1974), the earlier-maturing fish were significantly larger than immature fish of the same age; at age 2 y, mature male gudgeon in the Frome averaged 105 mm, immature fish averaged 84 mm.

A well-studied species at the other extreme of temperate cyprinid life histories is the European minnow, *Phoxinus phoxinus*. The short-lived R. Frome population contains two spawning age groups and the largest fish caught was only 78 mm long (Mills, 1987). Spawning lasts from April to August, but early in the season the spawners are two-year-old fish with lengths of 50 mm and over. During May the remaining two-year-olds, now generally at least 55 mm long, commence spawning. From June onwards two-year-olds begin to disappear and are replaced in the spawning shoals by one-year-old fish which mature at a length of approximately 49–50 mm (Fig. 17.3). Of this population, 50% matured as one-year-olds. These were mostly fish that had reached a length of 30 mm before their first winter and were presumably fish that had been spawned early in the previous spawning season; few of them survived to spawn again as two-year-olds. Though few individual minnows participated in more than one spawning season, their reproductive effort was extremely high and accompanied by a loss in somatic condition amongst two-year-olds as they ripened successive batches of eggs. At spawning the female gonads accounted for 15–25% (mean = 20%) of total body weight, and given the distended appearance of ripe female minnows, the mass of eggs spawned may be constrained by the physical space available. This constraint is overcome by ripening up to seven successive batches of eggs, which summed would exceed the total mass of individual females. This is far in excess of the longer-lived cyprinids in the Frome and neighbouring rivers; in only 12% of roach and 15% of chub did the weight of the single batch of eggs spawned exceed 15% of total body weight. The gudgeon was again intermediate, with 32% of the gonads exceeding 15% of body weight and two to three annual spawnings (Mann, 1980).

The minnow is an extremely widespread cyprinid with a range that encompasses almost the whole of Europe, including Arctic fresh waters, and also extends into northern Asia. Therefore it also provides a good opportunity to examine life history variation between populations in contrasting environ-

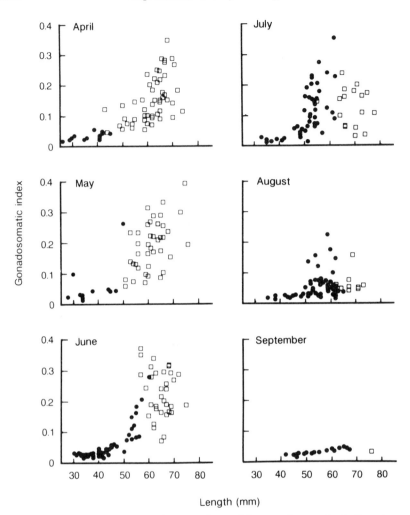

Fig. 17.3 Changes in the distribution of monthly gonadosomatic indices (gonad weight/(fork length)³) and fish lengths for two age groups of female minnows, *Phoxinus phoxinus*, in the River Frome, England. ●, one-year-olds; □, two-year-olds (reproduced with permission from Mills, 1987).

ments. In the River Utsjoki in Finnish Lapland, maturity was strongly size-dependent and delayed until the fish reached 48–50 mm at 5,6 or even 7 y of age, with a maximum age of 13 y at a length of only 75 mm. Individual females ripened two to three batches of eggs over the 4–5 week spawning season. The maximum estimated egg production over the season for a 65 mm female was 824 compared with 3172 for a Frome fish. However, at a second Arctic site in eastern Lapland, growth rates were higher and maturity earlier, yet clutch size was greatly reduced with a seasonal fecundity estimate of 314 eggs for a

65 mm female. There were only small differences in size of eggs or larvae between the populations (Mills, 1988).

Viewed on a wider geographical scale it is evident that, particularly in warm regions, the majority of cyprinid species are small and short-lived with a high reproductive effort. Good examples can be found in a series of experiments with species from the North American genera *Notropis* and *Pimephales*. Pairs of fathead minnow, *P. promelas*, in experimental enclosures spawned 16–26 clutches of eggs over 3 months; individual females (57–67 mm total length) averaged between 391 and 480 eggs per spawning. There was no decline in egg output as the spawning season progressed. Two months after spawning ended, all the fish were still alive and most had gained weight (Gale and Buynak, 1982). Pairs of satinfin shiners, *N. analostanus* (53–81 mm TL), spawned 11 times at a mean interval of 7.6 d. In this species egg size declined during the spawning season (Gale and Buynak, 1978). The absence of mortality or signs of physiological stress in these experiments might be related to an abundant food supply. In the wild the longnose shiner, *N. longirostris*, spawned from March to October in the south-eastern United States. Emaciated specimens were encountered during spawning, and Heins and Clemmer (1976) concluded that almost all mature fish died by the end of spawning. As in *Phoxinus phoxinus*, no correlation was found between fish length and egg size.

A similar situation is found in other warm areas, with 43(82%) of the 52 *Barbus* spp. in southern Africa attaining maximum fork lengths of less than 150 mm (Cambray and Bruton, 1985). Six *Barbus* spp. studied in Sri Lanka had maximum total lengths of between 42 and 101 mm and a short life span (de Silva *et al.*, 1985). Interestingly, whilst three of the species spawned throughout the year, the others spawned seasonally, with extremely high *GSI* values coinciding with the seasonal peaks in precipitation. It is argued (e.g. Cambray and Bruton, 1985) that early maturity and multiple spawning is an adaptation to enable recolonization of unstable environments where adult mortality may be high. The example is given of catches of *B. paludinosus* (sexual maturity reached at 50 mm TL within a year), which fell from 2800 to $7 \, t \, y^{-1}$ as Lake Chilwa (Malaŵi) dried up but reached 1460 t within 2 y of its refilling. It is also argued that a long reproductive life will be a selective advantage when larval survival is highly variable in relation to adult survival and an individual can only ensure it leaves progeny by spawning over successive years, as in the large temperate cyprinids (Stearns, 1976; Mann *et al.*, 1984). There is also some evidence to suggest that when one such species was reduced to a single breeding cohort by high adult mortality rates, this reduction in itself generated marked cyclical variations in spawning success (Townsend and Perrow, 1989). However, neither of these propositions has any universal validity. Minnows and large cyprinids persist sympatrically over wide areas; repeated spawnings over a long season may at least partly address the same goal as repeated spawnings in successive years.

It has also been suggested that as multiple spawning within years can result in a much higher annual reproductive effort, strategies of early and continuous reproduction should be considered the base line condition (Burt *et al.*, 1988). This condition would be associated with less seasonal environments, smaller body sizes and smaller relative ovary sizes (Burt *et al.*, 1988), presumably at the cost of a short life span. At least some species from tropical environments can spawn continuously. In addition to the *Barbus* spp. mentioned above, the small Asian species *B. rerio* spawned batches of 23–60 eggs with an average frequency of only 1.9 d over a long period (3 months) although the frequency declined slightly in older fish (Eaton and Farley, 1974). The relationship between multiple spawning and body size seems a good general rule, but as demonstrated above, the final proposition concerning ovary size is not generally true. At least in temperate conditions, it is the small multiple spawners that have the greatest relative gonad sizes. However it is interesting to pursue the hypothesis that the life history of a species such as the European minnow is closest to a 'base line'. This requires an explanation of why most other sympatric cyprinids have evolved towards larger body size. The minnow is largely restricted to lake and river margins and to very shallow riffle areas. Large size may confer a competitive advantage in occupying deeper, faster and more habitats. It will certainly enable some individuals to become much less vulnerable to piscivorous fish which tend to be strongly size-limited. The trend towards delayed maturity, single spawning and low reproductive effort can thus be seen as a necessary consequence of selection for greater body size. However, it is evident that there is no single optimum level of reproductive effort within a habitat, and a key test of any general theory of cyprinid life histories should be its ability to explain how cyprinid species with a wide range of strategies are able to persist sympatrically over such wide geographical areas.

REFERENCES

Bagenal, T. B. (1974) A buoyant net designed to catch freshwater fish larvae quantitatively. *Freshwat. Biol.*, **4**, 107–9.

Bagenal, T. B. and Braum, E. (1968) Eggs and early life history, in *Methods of Assessment of Fish Production in Fresh Waters (IBP Handbook No. 3)* (ed. T. B. Bagenal), Blackwells, Oxford, pp. 165–201.

Balon, E. K. (1971) The intervals of early fish development and their terminology. *Věst. čsl. Spol. zool.*, **35**, 1–8.

Balon, E. K. (1975a) Reproductive guilds of fishes: a proposal and definition. *J. Fish. Res. Bd Can.*, **32**, 821–64.

Balon, E. K. (1975b) Terminology of intervals in fish development. *J. Fish. Res. Bd Can.*, **32**, 1664–70.

Balon, E. K. (1985) *Early Life Histories of Fishes*, Dr. W. Junk, Dordrecht, 280 pp.

Billard, R. and Marcel, J. (1986) *Aquaculture of Cyprinids*, Institut National de la Recherche Agronomique, Paris, 502 pp.

Breder, C. M., jun. and Rosen, D. E. (1966) *Modes of Reproduction in Fish*, Natural History Press, NY, 941 pp.

Broughton, N. M., Jones, N. V. and Lightfoot, G. W. (1977) The growth of 0-group roach in some Humberside waters. *Proc. 8th Br. Coarse Fish Conf.*, University of Liverpool, 53–60.

Burt, A., Kramer, D. L., Nakatsuru, K. and Spry, C. (1988) The tempo of reproduction in *Hyphessobrycon pulchripinnis* (Characidae), with a discussion on the biology of 'multiple spawning' in fishes. *Env. Biol. Fishes*, **22**, 15–27.

Cambray, J. A. and Bruton, M. N. (1985) Age and growth of a colonising minnow, *Barbus anoplus*, in a man-made lake in South Africa. *Env. Biol. Fishes*, **12**, 131–41.

Cerny, K. (1975) Mortality of the early developmental stages of the roach – *Rutilus rutilus* (Linnaeus, 1758). *Věst. čsl. Spol. zool.*, **39**, 81–93.

Diamond, M. (1985) Some observations of spawning by roach, *Rutilus rutilus* L., and bream, *Abramis brama* L., and their implications for management. *Aquacult. Fish. Mgmt*, **16**, 359–67.

Diamond, M. and Brown, A. F. (1984) Predation by the eel, *Anguilla anguilla* on the eggs and spawning population of the roach, *Rutilus rutilus*. *Fish. Manage.*, **15**, 71–3.

Dolinskiy, V. L. (1984) Fish fry in beds of aerial–aquatic weeds. *Hydrobiol. J.*, **19**, 86–91.

Eaton, R. C. and Farley, R. D. (1974) Spawning cycle and egg production in the zebrafish, *Brachydanio rerio*, in the laboratory. *Copeia*, **1974**, 195–204.

Epler, P., Bieniarz, K. and Horoszewicz, L. (1981) Effect of different thermal regimes on reproductive cycles of tench *Tinca tinca* (L.). Part III. Histological characteristics of ovaries. *Pol. Arch. Hydrobiol.*, **28**, 197–205.

Fabricius, E. (1951) The topography of the spawning bottom as a factor influencing the size of the territory of some species of fish. *Rep. Inst. Freshwat. Res. Drottningholm*, **29**, 102–7.

Floyd, K. B., Hoyt, R. D. and Timbrook, S. (1984) Chronology of appearance and habitat partitioning by stream larval fishes. *Trans. Am. Fish. Soc.*, **113**, 217–23.

Fuiman, L. A., Conner, J. V., Lathrop, B. F., Buynak, G. L., Snyder, D. E. and Loos, J. J. (1983) State of the art of identification for cyprinid larvae from eastern North America. *Trans. Am. Fish. Soc.*, **112**, 319–32.

Gale, W. F. and Buynak, G. L. (1978) Spawning frequency and fecundity of satinfin shiner (*Notropis analostanus*) – a fractional, crevice spawner. *Trans. Am. Fish. Soc.*, **107**, 460–63.

Gale, W. F. and Buynak, G. L. (1982) Fecundity and spawning frequency of the fathead minnow – a fractional spawner. *Trans. Am. Fish. Soc.*, **111**, 35–40.

Gillet, C. (1985) Le déroulement de la fraie des principaux poissons lacustres, in *Gestion Piscicole des Lacs et Retenues Artificielles* (eds D. Gerdeaux and R. Billard), INRA, Paris, pp. 167–85.

Grigorash, V. A. (1961) Data regarding the feeding habits of larvae of the roach at the stage of mixed feeding. *Trudy Soveshch. ikhtiol. Kom.*, **13**, 348–52. (Available as Ministry of Fisheries and Food Translation. Lowestoft. England. New Series 16.)

Hammar, C. (1985) Feeding behaviour of roach (*Rutilus rutilus*) larvae and the fry of perch (*Perca fluviatilis*) in Lake Lankau. *Arch. Hydrobiol.*, **103**, 61–74.

Heins, D. C. and Clemmer, G. H. (1976) The reproductive biology, age and growth of the North American cyprinid, *Notropis longirostris* (Hay). *J. Fish Biol.*, **8**, 365–79.

Hellawell, J. M. (1971) The autecology of the chub, *Squalius cephalus* (L.), of the River Lugg and the Afon Llynfi. *Freshwat. Biol.*, **1**, 135–48.

Hewitt, D. P. and George, D. G. (1987) The population dynamics of *Keratella cochlearis* in a hypereutrophic tarn and the possible impact of predation by young roach. *Hydrobiologia*, **147**, 221–7.

Horoszewicz, L., Bieniarz, K. and Epler, P. (1981) Effect of different thermal regimes on reproductive cycles of tench *Tinca tinca* (L.). Part IV. Duration and temperature of spawnings. *Pol. Arch. Hydrobiol.*, **28**, 207–16.

Horvath, L. (1985) Egg development in the common carp, in *Recent advances in Aquaculture*, (eds J. F. Muir and R. J. Roberts), Vol. 2, Croom Helm, London, pp. 31–77.

Horvath, L. (1986) Carp oogenesis and the environment, in *Aquaculture of Cyprinids* (eds R. Billard and J. Marcel), Institut National de la Recherche Agronomique, Paris, pp. 109–17.

Jhingran, V. G. and Pullin, R. S. V. (1985) *A Hatchery Manual For the Common, Chinese and Major Carps*, Asian Development Bank, Manila, 191 pp.

Kaeding, L. R. and Osmundson, D. B. (1988) Interaction of slow growth and increased early-life mortality: an hypothesis on the decline of Colorado squawfish in the upstream regions of its historic range. *Env. Biol. Fishes*, **22**, 287–98.

Kuznetsov, V. A. (1972) The growth pattern of the larvae and young of some freshwater fish at different stages of development. *J. Ichthyol.* **12**, 433–42.

Kuznetsov, V. A. and Khalitov, N. K. (1978) Alterations in the fecundity and egg quality of the roach, *Rutilus rutilus* in connection with different feeding conditions. *J. Ichthyol.*, **18**, 63–70.

Laale, H. W. (1977) The biology and use of the zebrafish, *Brachydanio rerio* in fisheries research. A literature review *J. Fish Biol.*, **10**, 121–73.

L'Abée-Lund, J. H. and Vollestad, L. A. (1985) Homing precision of roach *Rutilus rutilus* in Lake Årungen, Norway. *Env. Biol. Fishes*, **13**, 235–9.

Lange, N. O. (1960) Development stages of the roach in varying ecological conditions. *Trudy Inst. Morph. Zhivot.*, **28**, 5–40. (Available as British Library translation RTS 10348.)

Lightfoot, G. W. (1976) A study of young roach (*Rutilus rutilus* L.) in the River Hull, doctoral dissertation, University of Hull, England.

Li, S. and Mathias, J. (1987) The critical period of high mortality of larval fish – a discussion based on current research. *Chin. J, Oceanol. Limnol.*, **5**, 81–96.

Linfield, R. S. J. (1985) The effect of habitat modification on freshwater fisheries in lowland areas of eastern England, in *Habitat Modification and Freshwater Fishes* (ed. J. S. Alabaster), Butterworths, London, pp. 223–35.

Lohnisky, K. (1970) Methods and main results of a study on the food of larvae and juvenile fishes. *Vertebrat. zpravy*, 89–102.

Mackay, I. and Mann, K. H. (1969) Fecundity of two cyprinid fishes in the River Thames, Reading, England. *J. Fish. Res. Bd Can.*, **26**, 2795–805.

Mann, R. H. K. (1974) Observations on the age, growth, reproduction and food of the dace, *Leuciscus leuciscus* (L.) in two rivers in Southern England. *J. Fish Biol.*, **6**, 237–53.

Mann, R. H. K. (1976) Observations on the age, growth, reproduction and food of the chub *Squalius cephalus* (L.) in the River Stour, Dorset. *J. Fish Biol.*, **8**, 265–88.

Mann, R. H. K. (1980) The growth and reproductive strategy of the gudgeon, *Gobio gobio* (L.), in two hard-water rivers in southern England. *J. Fish Biol.*, **17**, 163–76.

Mann, R. H. K. and Mills, C. A. (1979) Demographic aspects of fish fecundity. *Symp. zool. Soc. Lond.*, **44**, 161–77.

Mann, R. H. K. and Mills, C. A. (1985) Variations in the sizes of gonads, eggs and larvae of the dace, *Leuciscus leuciscus*. *Env. Biol. Fish.*, **13**, 277–87.

Mann, R. H. K. and Mills, C. A. (1986) Biological and climatic influence on the dace *Leuciscus leuciscus* in a southern chalk stream. *Rep. Freshwat. biol. Assoc.*, **54**, 123–36.

Mann, R. H. K., Mills, C. A. and Crisp, D. T. (1984) Geographical variation in the life-history tactics of some species of freshwater fish, in *Fish Reproduction: Strategies and Tactics* (eds G. W. Potts and R. J. Wootton), Academic Press, London, pp. 171–86.

Mathews, C. P. (1971) Contribution of young fish to total production of fish in the river Thames near Reading. *J. Fish Biol.*, **3**, 157–80.

Mills, C. A. (1980) Spawning and rearing eggs of the dace *Leuciscus leuciscus* (L.). *Fish. Manage.*, **11**, 67–72.

Mills, C. A. (1981a) The spawning of roach, *Rutilus rutilus* (L.) in a chalk stream. *Fish. Manage.*, **10**, 49–54.

Mills, C. A. (1981b) Egg population dynamics of naturally spawning dace, *Leuciscus leuciscus* (L.). *Env. Biol. Fishes*, **6**, 151–8.

Mills, C. A. (1981c) The attachment of dace, *Leuciscus leuciscus* L., eggs to the spawning substratum and the influence of changes in water current on their survival. *J. Fish Biol.*, **19**, 129–34.

Mills, C. A. (1982) Factors affecting the survival of dace, *Leuciscus leuciscus* (L.), in the early post-hatching period. *J. Fish. Biol.*, **20**, 645–55.

Mills, C. A. (1985) Sources of variation in the feeding of larval dace *Leuciscus leuciscus* in an English River. *Trans. Am. Fish. Soc.*, **114**, 519–24.

Mills, C. A. (1987) The life history of the minnow *Phoxinus phoxinus* (L.) in a productive stream. *Freshwat. Biol.*, **17**, 53–67.

Mills, C. A. (1988) The effect of extreme northerly climatic conditions on the life history of the minnow, *Phoxinus phoxinus* (L.). *J. Fish Biol.*, **33**, 545–61.

Mills, C. A. and Mann, R. H. K. (1985) Environmentally induced fluctuations in year class strength and their implications for management. *J. Fish Biol.*, **27** (Supp. A), 209–26.

Mooij, W. M. (1989) A key to the identification of larval bream, *Abramis brama*, white bream, *Blicca bjoerkna*, and roach, *Rutilus rutilus*. *J. Fish Biol.*, **34**, 111–18.

Pekar, C. (1965) Distinguishing the fry of cyprinidae from the Lipno Valley Reservoir. *Bul. Vyz. Ustav Ryb. Hydrobiol., Vodnany.*, **5**, 171–214. (Available as British Library translation RTS 12021.)

Penaz, M. (1971) Differences in mortality rate and development in feeding and starving larvae of *Chondrostoma nasus* and *Barbus barbus* (Pisces). *Zool. Listy*, **20**, 85–94.

Penaz, M. and Prokes, M. (1972) Das Laichen der Plötze, *Rutilus rutilus* (Linnaeus, 1758), im strömenden Abschnitt des Oslava–Flusses. *Zool. Listy*, **21**, 383–8.

Penaz, M. and Prokes, M. (1978) Reproduction and early development of the gudgeon, *Gobio gobio*. I. Spawning and development. *Folia Zool. (Brn.)*, **27**, 257–67.

Philippart, J. A. (1981a) Écologie d'une population de vandoises, *Leuciscus leuciscus* (L.) dans la rivière Ourthe (bassin de la Meuse, Belgique). *Annls Limnol.*, **17**, 41–62.

Philippart, J. A. (1981b) Démographie du hotu *Chondrostoma nasus* (Linné) (Teleostei: Cyprinidae) dans L'Ourthe (bassin de la Meuse, Belgique). *Annales. Soc. r. zool. Belg.*, **110**, 119–219.

Pliszka, F. (1953) The effect of spawning conditions in lakes on young fish populations. *Pol. Arch. Hydrobiol.*, **14**, 165–88.

Reznick, D. (1985) Costs of reproduction: an evaluation of the empirical evidence. *Oikos*, **44**, 257–67.

Scott, D. B. C. (1979) Environmental timing and the control of reproduction in teleost fish. *Symp. zool. Soc. Lond.*, **44**, 105–32.

Silva, S. S. de, Schut, J. and Kortmulder, K. (1985) Reproductive biology of six *Barbus* species indigenous to Sri Lanka. *Env. Biol. Fishes*, **12**, 201–18.

Spindler, T. (1988) The identification of Central European cyprinid larvae (Teleostei, Cyprinidae). *Öst. Fisch.*, **41**, 75–9.

Stearns, S. C. (1976) Life history tactics: a review of the ideas. *Q. Rev. Biol.*, **51**, 3–47.

Svardson, G. (1948) Note on spawning habits of *Leuciscus erythrophthalmus* (L.),

Abramis brama (L.) and *Esox lucius* L. *Rep. Inst. Freshwat. Res. Drottningholm*, **29**, 102–7.

Svardson, G. (1951) Spawning behaviour of *Leuciscus rutilus* (Linne). *Rep. Inst. Freshwat. Res. Drottningholm*, **33**, 199–203.

Tong, H. Y. (1982) A qualitative and quantitative description of the early growth of roach, *Rutilus rutilus*, in the laboratory. *Env. Biol. Fishes*, **15**, 293–300.

Townsend, C. R. and Perrow, M. R. (1989) Eutrophication may produce population cycles in roach, *Rutilus rutilus* (L.), by two contrasting mechanisms. *J. Fish Biol.*, **34**, 161–4.

Treasurer, J. W. (1978) Sampling larval and juvenile fish populations in freshwater. *Fish. Manage.*, **9**, 6–17.

Verigin, B. V., Makeyeva, A. P. and Zaki Mokhamed, M. I. (1978) Natural spawning of the silver carp, *Hypophthalmichthys molitrix*, the bighead carp, *Aristichthys nobilis*, and the grass carp, *Ctenopharyngodon idella*, in the Syr-Dar'ya River. *J. Ichthyol.*, **18**, 143–6.

Vladimirov, V. I. (1975) Critical periods in the development of fishes. *J. Ichthyol.*, **15**, 851–68.

Vlaming, V. L. de, (1974) Environmental and endocrine control of teleost reproduction, in *Control of Sex in Fishes* (ed. C. B. Schrek), Virginia Polytechnic and State University, Blacksburg, pp. 18–83.

Vollestad, L. A. and L'Abée–Lund, J. H. (1987) Reproductive biology of stream-spawning roach, *Rutilus rutilus*. *Env. Biol. Fishes*, **18**, 219–27.

Volodin, V. M. (1960) Effect of temperature on the embryonic development of the pike (*Esox lucius* L.), the blue bream (*Abramis ballerus* L.) and the white bream (*Blicca bjoerkna* L.). *Trudy̆ Inst. Biol. Vodokhrau.*, **3**, 231–7. (Available in translation from the Office of Technical Services, US Department of Commerce, Washington as IPST Cat. No. 941.)

Weil, C., Fostier, A. and Billard, R. (1986) Induced spawning (ovulation and spermiation) in carp and related species, in *Aquaculture of Cyprinids* (eds R. Billard and J. Marcel), Institut National de la Recherche Agronomique, Paris, pp. 119–37.

Whelan, K. F. (1983) Migratory patterns of bream *Abramis brama* L. shoals in the River Suck system. *Ir. Fish. Invest., Ser. A.*, **23**, 11–15.

Williams, W. P. (1967) The growth and mortality of four species of fish in the River Thames at Reading. *J. Anim. Ecol.*, **36**, 695–720.

Winfield, I. J. and Townsend, C. R. (1988) Factors affecting prey selection by young roach *Rutilus rutilus*: insights provided by parallel studies in the laboratory and field. *Env. Biol. Fishes*, **21**, 279–92.

Worthington, A. D., MacFarlane, N. A. A. and Easton, K. W. (1982) Controlled reproduction in the roach (*Rutilus rutilus*) in *Proc. Int. Symp. Reprod. Physiol. Fish* (eds C. J. J. Richter and H. J. H. Goos), Centre for Agricultural Publishing and Document-ation, Wageningen, pp. 220–23.

Zukinskii, V. N. and Kim, E. D. (1980) Characteristics of age-related variability in the composition of amino acids and lipids in mature and overripe eggs of the Azov roach, *Rutilus rutilus heckeli*, and the bream, *Abramis brama*. *J. Ichthyol.*, **20**, 121–31.

Zimpfer, P. S., Bryan, C. F. and Pennington, C. H. (1987) Factors associated with the dynamics of grass carp larvae in the lower Mississippi River valley. *Am. Fish. Soc. Symp.*, (ed. R. D. Hoyt), vol. 2, Am. Fish. Soc., Bethesda, pp. 102–8.

Zuromska, H. (1967a) Mortality estimation of roach (*Rutilus rutilus* L.) eggs and larvae on lacustrine spawning grounds. *Roczn. Nauk Roln.*, **90**, 539–56.

Zuromska, H. (1967b) Some causes of mortality of roach (*Rutilus rutilus* L.) eggs and larvae on lake spawning grounds. *Roczn. Nauk Roln.*, **90**, 557–79.

Chapter eighteen

Social behaviour, homing and migration

R. J. F. Smith

Small transposable fishes, in constant motion: often this is our first impression of cyprinid behaviour. It seems impossible to distinguish individuals or to pick out discrete behavioural acts. This impression is partially correct, for good reason, but it also obscures the behavioural complexity that is present. Many cyprinids are shoaling prey fish. Their confusing motion and standardized appearance are important elements in their defence against predators. Their continuous swimming lacks the breaks that punctuate the activity of the sticklebacks and cichlids so beloved by ethologists. However, the problems to be solved in survival and reproduction are no less difficult for cyprinids, and their solutions have much to tell us about the evolution of social groups and the individual benefits of co-operation with others.

18.1 THE SENSORY BASIS OF SOCIAL COMMUNICATION

Social communication depends on the production of signals and their detection by senses. Social interaction may be limited by the communication channel in use. Visual signals are fast but can be ineffective at night or in murky water. Chemical signals (pheromones) can be used when vision is blocked, and allow precision in identifying individuals and locations, but they travel slowly. Sound is fast and not dependent upon water clarity. Touch and the lateral line sense are short-range senses, not suitable for such functions as luring mates from a distance, but appropriate in agonistic and mating encounters.

Cyprinid fishes have good vision, including colour vision, and use visual displays. Bright nuptial coloration is common and has given rise to a variety of colourful common names, such as redside shiners, *Richardsonius balteatus*, bluenose shiners, *Notropis welaka*, and rosyface shiners, *Notropis rubellus*. These colours are commonly associated with conspicuous displays. Breeding tubercles are often conspicuous and may serve in visual displays as well as providing tactile stimuli (p. 511). Visual displays, such as lateral displays, are important in breeding and non-breeding contexts. Schooling, the quintessential cyprinid social behaviour, is based on an interaction of visual and lateral line information (Pitcher, 1979).

The use of pheromones in cyprinid social communication is well established. Perhaps because chemical stimuli are less obvious to human observers, there are probably more experimental tests of pheromonal information transmission than there are of visual transmission. The alarm pheromone (schreckstoff) of the European minnow, *Phoxinus phoxinus*, was among the first fish pheromones to be examined experimentally (von Frisch, 1941). A report of individual recognition through chemical signals, and transmission of predator identification information by the association of alarm pheromone with predator odour, soon followed (Göz, 1941).

Aggregation pheromones occur, for example, in European minnows (Wrede, 1932), rudd, *Scardinius erythrophthalmus* (Keenleyside, 1955), zebra danios, *Brachydanio rerio* (Algranati and Perlmutter, 1981), goldfish, *Carassius auratus* (Le Martret and Saglio, 1982), and roach, *Rutilus rutilus* (Hemmings, 1966). 'Crowding factors', inhibiting reproduction or growth, occur in whitecloud mountain fish, *Tanichthys albonubes* (Rose, 1959), and zebra danios (Yu and Perlmutter, 1970) and may be widespread. Reproductive priming pheromones released by male zebra danios induce ovulation in females (Chen and Martinich, 1975). Ovulated female goldfish (Partridge *et al.*, 1976) and zebra danios (van den Hurk *et al.*, 1982) release chemicals that attract males and induce courtship. In fathead minnows, *Pimephales promelas* (Cole and Smith, 1987b) and goldfish (Sorennsen *et al.*, 1986), release of such attractants can be induced by prostaglandins. Sex pheromones in goldfish have been the subject of intensive study (Stacey, 1987).

Cypriniform fishes have excellent hearing, so sound communication would seem to be a logical channel for social interaction. Cyprinids, however, provide remarkably few examples of sound production. This may reflect lack of study. Sound production during social interaction has been reported in four species in the subgenus *Cyprinella* of the genus *Notropis* (Delco, 1960; Stout, 1975). Male satinfin shiners. *Notropis analostanus*, produce knocks during male–male interactions, and knocks and purrs when courting females (Stout, 1975). *N. lutrensis* and *N. venustus* prefer to approach conspecific sounds when offered a choice (Delco, 1960). Möderlieschen, *Leucaspius delineatus*, prcduce sounds (of unknown function) during the day, but not at night (Protasov *et al.*, 1972). Gudgeon, *Gobio gobio*, emit creaks during agonistic encounters and when disturbed by conspecifics (Ladich, 1988). Sound production has also been reported in goldfish (Guidarelli and Antonini, 1972).

Touch and lateral line senses are undoubtedly stimulated by tail beating, butting, and biting, common elements in cyprinid agonistic behaviour, and by the various pressing behaviours and nuptial embraces that occur during spawning (e.g. fathead minnows, McMillan and Smith, 1974). The tubercles present during the breeding season in many species (Collette, 1977) are morphological features that enhance the tactile effect of butting, or of mating embraces.

18.2 THE FORMATION OF SOCIAL GROUPS

Shoaling and schooling

Fish schooling has attracted interest and study for many years (Keenleyside, 1955), but until recently it has proven remarkably refractory to functional analysis. One problem has been the lack of sufficiently fine distinctions among the various types of social groups in fish. The formation of groups can provide many benefits to animals (e.g. Pulliam and Caraco, 1984). A single species may form several different types of group with different characteristics and functions. In fishes, all groups were traditionally called schools. This use of a single term for different functional categories of grouping often obscured important distinctions. Pitcher (1979, 1983, 1986) has attempted to correct this situation by using **shoal** to refer to any group of fish formed by social attraction. The term **school** is then restricted to "synchronized and polarized swimming groups" (Pitcher, 1986: 295). This convention is gaining acceptance (e.g. Godin, 1986; Morgan, 1988).

Emphasis on the importance of individual selection in evolution has given new impetus to study of the evolution of social groups, including shoals. Many interesting problems in the evolution of shoaling fish were formerly obscured by the assumption that shoaling benefited the majority. Now, there is increased effort to understand the apparent conflict between the seemingly cooperative and mutually dependent nature of fish shoals and the idea that such social groups have evolved through benefits to individuals. Cyprinids have frequently been used as experimental subjects in these efforts, providing a substantial body of information on the nature of cyprinid shoals (e.g. Pitcher, 1986; Magurran and Pitcher, 1987).

Pitcher (1986) reviews the costs and benefits of shoaling. Predators and food, he suggests, are the important factors. Shoaling European minnows and goldfish, for example, find food more quickly in groups (Section 18.4) and may be less vulnerable to predation (Section 18.3). Other postulated benefits of shoaling or schooling, such as hydrodynamic advantages, are less well supported by the available evidence. Abrahams and Colgan (1985, 1987), however, provide evidence that hydrodynamic benefits should not be ignored. Small groups of blackchin shiners, *Notropis heterodon*, adopt a one-layer schooling pattern, which may be more hydrodynamically efficient, when there is no predator present. On detecting a predator, they switch to a potentially less efficient, multi-layer pattern that allows each fish a greater field of vision.

Social attraction may develop early in cyprinids. European minnows showed some shoaling and schooling within 3 d of emergence from the spawning gravel, the earliest stage examined (Magurran, 1986). Shoaling increased with time to become the most frequent behaviour after 3 weeks. Schooling became predominant after 4 weeks in undisturbed fish. Simulated predation, a net chase, led to higher levels and earlier expression both of shoaling and of schooling.

The **elective group size** (Pitcher *et al.*, 1983, 1986b) is the group size that occurs when fish are able to assort themselves into groups without interference from an experimenter. It may reflect the balance of benefits and liabilities of group formation (Pitcher, 1986). European minnows, for example, show a higher mean elective group size in the presence of a predator (Pitcher *et al.*, 1983; Magurran and Pitcher, 1987). Similarly, European minnows from regions that lack pike, *Esox lucius*, have a smaller mean elective group size than minnows from regions with pike (Magurran and Pitcher, 1987). Smaller European minnows and dace, *Leuciscus leuciscus*, are more likely to leave the group and forage alone than are large fish (Pitcher *et al.*, 1983). The smaller fish tend to lose food to larger fish in agonistic encounters, lowering the benefits the smaller fish derive from staying in a group. This tips the balance toward lone, or size-segregated, foraging.

Optimum group size is the 'best' group size for an individual. It may differ from the elective group size, and individuals in the same group might differ in their optimal group sizes. There is debate on theoretical grounds regarding whether an optimal group size can ever be stable (e.g. Sibly, 1983 v. Giraldeau and Gillis, 1985). Fish may tend to join shoals until there is no net benefit, rather than maintain shoals of optimum size (Pitcher, 1986). The options may be to stay with an oversized shoal, or to leave. Fish in an oversized shoal might try to recruit an optimal number of companions to leave together. This could appear as individuals or small groups breaking away from the main group and leaving or returning on the basis of the number in the breakaway group. Alternatively, fish might try to exclude new arrivals (Pitcher, 1986: 330).

The traditional view has been that shoals or schools lacked leaders or dominance hierarchies and were thus without internal social distinctions. Most fish shoals that have been examined lack specific leaders, but there may be more subtle, yet important, sources of social structure. These individual variations may be particularly difficult to discern because selection has favoured uniform appearance in animals that depend on groups for predator confusion. There is evidence from non-cyprinid schools for position preferences (salmon, Healey and Prieston, 1973; mackerel, Pitcher *et al.*, 1982b). Pitcher (1986) mentions unpublished studies by Muscialwicz and Cullen that found consistent 'initiators' and 'followers' in shoals of zebra danios. Similar effects occur in bream, *Abramis brama* (Pitcher, 1979).

An interesting possibility is that related individuals might associate in shoals, allowing kin-selection benefits to accrue to individuals that assisted shoalmates through warning signals, predator defence, or food location. Such kin association has been found in a wide variety of animals. Consistent position preferences in a shoal could allow related fish to stay together, even in a shoal or school that contained a portion of unrelated fish. Salmon, non-cyprinids, can recognize siblings by smell (Quinn and Busack, 1985). Ferguson and Noakes (1981) reported non-random genetic relationships in shoals of common shiners. *Notropis cornutus*. However, Dowling and Moore (1986) did not find population subdivision in the same species, although they did not examine individual shoals. Even in the absence of specific recognition mechanisms, siblings may tend to school together through the effects of proximity. A single spawn of eggs will tend to hatch at the same time and place. If the fish start to associate in shoals almost immediately, as found by Magurran (1986), then proximity in time and space could lead to siblings being in the same shoal as one another. The subject of kin association in cyprinids, and fish in general, deserves much more research (Smith, 1977; Magurran and Pitcher, 1987).

Territoriality

Territoriality, the defence of an area, is probably the most common, or at least the most conspicuous, non-shoaling pattern in cyprinids. The defence of spawning sites from conspecifics occurs in many cyprinids that provide parental care for the eggs (Section 18.5). Some spawning territories may be very complex, including hierarchies of nest-building males and 'satellites', as occur in fallfish, *Semotilus corporalis* (p. 521) (Ross, 1983). Non-reproductive territoriality, associated with the defence of foraging areas, may occur in cyprinids.

Solitary life

Some individual cyprinids select an elective group size of one in laboratory studies (e.g. Magurran, 1986; Magurran and Pitcher, 1987). This is usually considered as simply one extreme in a continuum of shoal sizes, but it is conceivable that some species or individuals spend considerable portions of their life in a solitary, non-territorial state. Perhaps large adult fish such as carp display such behaviour.

18.3 SOCIAL ASPECTS OF PREDATOR–PREY INTERACTIONS

Interaction with predators is a normal day-to-day activity for many cyprinids. Pitcher (1980) calculated that shoals of roach in the River Nene (England) were seldom more than 2 m from pike. The first event in an interaction occurs when a predator is detected. Important elements at this stage may be the recognition of a predator and the distinction between active hunting and non-hunting behaviour. European minnows respond to realistic model pike with more skitters (potential warning signals) than they perform for less realistic models (Magurran and Girling, 1986), and show slower habituation and less foraging when exposed to realistic models.

Information about the presence of a threat is transmitted through cyprinid shoals. Schutz (1956) demonstrated the visual transmission of **alarm responses** between adjacent tanks of European minnows. This information exchange may be facilitated by specific behaviour patterns, such as the 'skittering' performed by European minnows (e.g. Magurran and Pitcher, 1987). Minnows suddenly accelerate 1–5 body lengths, then turn back into the school. Skitters may be Mauthner-neurone-driven startle responses (Pfeiffer *et al.*, 1986). Individuals that skitter change their location in the school and may thus make it more difficult for a predator to fixate on them. Groups may also skitter in synchrony, leading to sudden positional changes by the whole school. Although the primary function of skittering may be as an antipredator response, its occurrence when a predator is detected (Pitcher and Turner, 1986; Magurran and Pitcher, 1987) may also allow it to serve as an alarm signal (Pitcher, 1986). The distribution of skittering and similar behaviour among the Cyprinidae is not yet clear.

Early in an encounter with a predator, European minnows congregate into a compact school and begin to perform **inspection visits** (e.g. Pitcher *et al.*, 1986a). The inspecting minnows, either alone or in groups, approach to within 4–6 body lengths of the predator, pause for about 1 s then return to the school. Solitary minnows that have inspected a live pike move to the centre of the school on their return in 83% of cases (Magurran and Pitcher, 1987). Inspections probably allow the inspector to judge whether or not another fish is a predator and whether or not it is hunting. Schoolmates may be able to read the behaviour of the returning inspectors and act accordingly, including learning to identify dangerous predators. Magurran and Girling (1986) found that minnows returned to foraging after inspections of unrealistic model pike but switched to evasive behaviour after inspecting realistic models. Inspectors might also detect kairomones, chemical stimuli from the predator (Brown *et al.*, 1970).

Once a predator attacks, several co-ordinated group activities may occur, such a 'flash expansion' and 'fast avoidance' (Magurran and Pitcher, 1987). These patterns probably reduce the predator's success rate, but there is some risk of fish becoming separated from the shoal or being vulnerable in areas of confusion where fish are rejoining the school. In some cases, minnows that become separated hide in weeds or the substratum rather than rejoin the group. Hiding becomes a more attractive option if the alternative is joining a small shoal (Magurran and Pitcher, 1987).

The importance of predation in moulding these behaviour patterns is illustrated by differences between minnows from 'provenances' (geographic areas) that differ in predators (Magurran and Pitcher, 1987; Levesley and Magurran, 1988). Populations that co-occur with pike showed better co-ordination of their social anti-predator behaviour, and stronger responses to stimuli associated with predation, such as alarm substance.

The capture or injury of a cypriniform fish will release the alarm pheromone (alarm substance, schreckstoff) that is contained in fragile, epidermal club cells called alarm substance cells (ASCs) (reviews: Pfeiffer, 1982; Smith, 1977, 1982, 1986a). **Alarm substance** is released only by damage, and is detected by olfaction (Pfeiffer *et al.*, 1984). Detection of alarm substance usually elicits a **fright reaction**, behavioural and physiological responses that may reduce the receiver's vulnerability to predation. Fright reactions vary from species to species, but frequently include physiological stress responses (Malyukina *et al.*, 1982; Rehnberg *et al.*, 1987), tighter schooling (Waldman, 1982), changes in depth preference (Waldman, 1982), and initial rapid dashing and turning (Pfeiffer *et al.*, 1986; Rehnberg *et al.*, 1987) followed by a period of reduced activity (Rehnberg *et al.*, 1987; Lawrence and Smith, 1989), often associated with hiding. Basically, the response resembles the response to detection of a predator (Levesley and Magurran, 1988). Once the alarm substance has been detected, the fright reaction may spread through the shoal by visual transmission (Schutz, 1956; Verheijen, 1956), much more rapidly and completely than could occur by chemical transmission.

Exposure to alarm substance may have long-lasting effects on behaviour. Von Frisch (1941) found that European minnows avoided a feeding station for days after detecting alarm substance. The alarm substance probably acts as an unconditioned stimulus allowing cyprinids to associate locations or predator characteristics with danger. Göz (1941) exposed naïve European minnows to pike odour and found that they did not perform a fright reaction. Pairing pike odour with alarm substance 'trained' the minnows to respond with a fright reaction when pike odour was presented alone. Zebra danios respond to the formerly neutral odour of morpholine with a fright reaction after morpholine has been paired with alarm pheromone, and they pass this association on to naïve companions (Suboski, 1988). European minnows from the River Frome (Dorset, England), where pike are present, showed stronger response to pike models and alarm substance together than they did to either stimulus by itself (Levesley and Magurran, 1988).

The question arises, do true alarm displays occur in the cyprinid fishes? A **display** is an act or feature that has been modified in evolution to enhance its communication function. Have skitters or the production of alarm pheromone been selected for an alarm signal function? The alternative is that skitters and club cells have evolved because they benefit the individual that performs or possesses them, without influence from other individuals that respond. (The response of the receivers could evolve without regard to the primary function of the action or secretion.)

Skitters and dashes, bouts of rapid swimming, may reduce the performer's chance of getting caught. Skittering, for example, may make it harder for a predator to fixate on the performer. Club cells (ASCs) and their contents may have some unknown function in the epidermis (Smith, 1977, 1982, 1986a): possibilities include production of predator-deterrent compounds (Williams, 1964) or anti-pathogenic compounds (Smith, 1977). To test the predator-deterrence hypothesis, Bernstein and Smith (1983) presented rainbow trout, *Oncorhynchus mykiss*, with fathead minnows that had ASCs or hormone-treated individuals that lacked ASCs (Section 18.5). The trout did not prefer one type over the other. The widespread use of cyprinids as bait fish also argues against the deterrance hypothesis. Club cells closely resembling cyprinid ASCs occur in some non-cypriniform species that lack a fright reaction to conspecific skin extract. An example is the polypteriform reedfish, *Erpetoichthys calabaricus*. Zebra danios do not show a fright reaction to the contents of reedfish club cells (Hugie and Smith, 1987), indicating that the alarm pheromone is not a universal component of club cells.

Several mechanisms have been proposed by which a sender might benefit from sending alarm signals (review, Caro, 1986). Benefits to kin could be favoured, even if the sender did not survive. The possibility of kin association in cyprinids is discussed in Section 18.2. Direct benefits are available if the sender survives to reap them. The issue of sender survival may not be very important for skittering or dashing, but it is for alarm substance, which requires physical contact for release. Common sense suggests that survival after alarm substance release will be rare. However, in one aggregation of fathead minnows, 16% had injury marks from bird attacks. The injuries would have been sufficient to release alarm substance, and their bearers survived for more than a year in captivity (Smith and Lemly, 1986). Non-cyprinid coregonid fish in northern Canada can show healed scars on 40% of individuals (Reist *et al.*, 1987). These results indicate that escape from damaging encounters with predators may be fairly common. Benefits to surviving senders could include reduced predator success, leading to less hunting in the prey's region or for the prey species (Trivers, 1971), improved defensive behaviour by the group (e.g. McCullough, 1969), or retention of group members (Smith, 1986b). Charnov and Krebs (1975) suggested that alarm signallers might benefit if predators were diverted to warned conspecifics.

Predator defence in cyprinids obviously involves social interaction at several levels, from shoal formation to co-ordination of activities, and potential alarm signalling. The balance between social organization and individual benefit is worth considerably more research. There may, for example, be important differences in benefit in different regions of a shoal. As well, research has been concentrated on very few species; more should be examined.

18.4 SOCIAL ASPECTS OF FORAGING AND FEEDING

Cyprinids in shoals find food more quickly and are less vulnerable to predators than lone fish (reviews: Pitcher, 1986; Magurran and Pitcher, 1987). Reduced vulnerability interacts with foraging because fish that are less vulnerable can forage longer, forage in more dangerous areas, and devote more attention to finding food. Fish sometimes defend food resources from conspecifics, but in cyprinids the facilitating effect of shoal formation on feeding has been studied more often than food competition. Social influences on cyprinid feeding have been studied experimentally in the laboratory using only a few shoaling species. The field situation remains unexplored.

Captive juvenile goldfish and European minnows locate food faster as shoal size increases from two fish to 20 (Pitcher *et al.*, 1982a). Both species also tend to spend longer on artificial food patches, and make more visits to the food patches and fewer visits to cover, when they are in larger shoals (Magurran and Pitcher, 1983). The lower vulnerability of fish in larger shoals allows these increases in foraging.

Shoal members may benefit by **foraging area copying** (FAC), foraging close to fish that are feeding. Pitcher and House (1987) demonstrated that goldfish choose to feed close to feeding conspecifics rather than non-feeding conspecifics. This FAC response only occurred in goldfish that were receiving intermediate food levels. Fish fed at high levels, and those with no feeding site in the test tank, did not remain close to the stimulus group. These goldfish were able to integrate three factors: (1) their own feeding levels, (2) the presence or absence of conspecifics, and (3) whether the stimulus fish were feeding or not. Pitcher and House (1987) suggest that the goldfish were following rules of thumb in their decision making, rather than behaving exactly as predicted by either optimal foraging theory or the ideal free distribution. Such rules could include: 'if food levels are high, stay where you are', 'if food is low, join feeding conspecifics', and 'if food is absent, search elsewhere'.

As well as FAC, there may be more-specific responses to feeding behaviour by other fish. For example, the head-down behaviour of bottom-feeding goldfish or minnows can serve as a specific stimulus that attracts other fish (Magurran, 1984), or a well-motivated fish that knows the location of food may be followed. Pitcher and Magurran (1983) transferred 'informed' goldfish to groups of 'uninformed' fish. In groups of five fish, the whole group quickly found a food location that was initially known only to the informed individual.

The benefits of foraging near others may be counterbalanced in part by increased intraspecific competition. Goldfish in groups reduce their handling time for food pellets as shoal size increases from two to 15 (Street *et al.*, 1984). Increased competition may force them to gulp their food in order to get their share; on the other hand, the reduced need for vigilance may allow them to devote more energy to food handling. Street *et al.* (1984) were unable to distinguish these alternatives. Small European minnows, foraging in mixed shoals of large and small individuals, were displaced from feeding sites by larger fish (Pitcher *et al.*, 1986b). This may be one factor favouring size assortment in shoals.

The presence of live predators, models of predators, or other stimuli associated with predation may bring out specific attributes of the relation between feeding, group formation and vulnerability. Magurran *et al.* (1985) pulled a model pike toward shoals of European minnows feeding on an artificial food patch. Larger shoals reduced their feeding sooner than smaller shoals, and started responding to the predator with skitters and investigative approaches, but continued to feed. The smaller shoals seemed to discover the predator later and then to react more strongly by ceasing their feeding behaviour altogether. One interpretation is that the predator-detection benefits of the larger shoal allowed earlier detection, followed by warnings (skitters) and information gathering (inspection approaches). Their prepared state and the safety of the larger shoal then allowed the goldfish to remain on the patch longer.

In a field study, spottail shiners, *Notropis hudsonius*, in shoals of two or more, did not flee from a predator model as soon as lone fish (Seghers, 1981). This could be interpreted as later detection of the predator by the shoal, or as reduced timidity; Seghers' observations did not distinguish these possibilities. At his site, 12% of the minnows were alone, making single fish the most frequent group size. Shoals may interfere with the visual field during plankton feeding and thus reduce foraging efficiency.

Morgan (1988) exposed bluntnose minnows, *Pimephales notatus*, to live largemouth bass, *Micropterus salmoides*, separated from the minnows by a transparent, perforated barrier. She used six shoal sizes and three hunger levels to examine the relationships between hunger, shoal size, and predator threat. The feeding latency (time to start feeding) was shorter for larger shoal sizes and in hungrier fish, but lengthened when the predator was present. The number of bites per minute was higher in larger shoals and hungry fish, but declined in the presence of the predator. Again, shoaling seems to facilitate feeding. The possible presence of alarm pheromone was an uncontrolled variable in this experiment. Just before the experiments, Morgan (1988) fed the bass either a guppy, which would not release alarm pheromone, or a minnow, which would. The perforated barrier would have allowed the alarm pheromone to reach the experimental minnows. Although Rehnberg and Smith (1988), working with zebra danios, *Brachydanio rerio* found that shoal sizes of one to 12 fish responded to alarm pheromone similarly, pheromone might have been present in some of Morgan's minnow trials and not in others.

In summary, shoaling cyprinids are able to benefit, in their feeding, by gaining information about food location and by taking advantage of the protective shoal to forage more effectively when predators are present. In general the benefits increase with increasing shoal size – at least within the range of shoal sizes tested, usually a maximum of 20 fish. There is some evidence of species differences, e.g. goldfish shoals of 12 and 20 spent the same time on food patches but minnow shoals of 20 fish were on the patches significantly longer than shoals of 12 (Magurran and Pitcher, 1983). Most of the research has been on two species, goldfish *Carassius auratus*, and European minnows, *Phoxinus phoxinus*; other cyprinids may differ, as indicated by Seghers' (1981) work on spottail shiners. For example, the role of agonistic behaviour in the acquisition and defence of food may be much more important in other species than in the two species most studied.

18.5 REPRODUCTION AND PARENTAL CARE

Social interactions are involved in reproduction at three stages. First, a breeding social structure is established: some species congregate in a suitable habitat; in other species, males defend territories around spawning sites. Second comes courtship and mating, including mate choice, fertilization of eggs and their placement where they can survive. Third, parental care, in some cyprinids, is a social interaction between an adult and the developing embryos. Defending the eggs from conspecific egg predators is often an important element in parental care.

There is substantial variety in cyprinid reproduction (Breder and Rosen, 1966: 173–235). However, certain breeding or parental systems found in other teleosts seem to be absent. These include monogamy or long-term pair bonding (Barlow, 1984), female parental care (Blumer, 1982), mouthbrooding or brood carrying, socially controlled sex reversal or functional hermaphroditism, and internal development of the young. Care of young after hatching is very rare.

Most accounts of cyprinid spawning describe fairly brief clasps or pressing together with release of eggs into vegetation or gravel (Breder and Rosen, 1966). In some species a single male and female pair briefly within a larger group. In others, larger groups may spawn together. The eggs are usually left to develop without parental care. While these mating systems have seldom been studied rigorously, it would be a mistake to assume that the behavioural interactions involved are simple or unimportant. The choice of mates and specific spawning locations, such as vegetation of suitable density, and the timing and spatial co-ordination of gamete release may be of critical importance in the survival of progeny. Mating behaviour is often an amalgam of chemical, tactile and visual communication (Section 18.1).

The fathead minnow
Species with complex mating systems and parental care have received more experimental study. The fathead minnow, *Pimephales promelas*, of North America falls into this category. Males set up territories around suitable spawning sites (McMillan and Smith, 1974; Unger, 1983; Ming and Noakes, 1984). Preferred sites always include a solid, horizontal under-surface to which the eggs will eventually be attached. In response to rising androgen levels, males develop sharp breeding tubercles on the snout and pectoral fins,

and a spongy, mucus-secreting dorsal pad (Smith, 1974; Smith and Murphy, 1974; Smith, 1978). The rostral tubercles are used in agonistic encounters and in defending the nest from egg predators (including conspecific females). The pectoral tubercles grip the female during the spawning embrace. The dorsal pad is initially rubbed vigorously against the spawning surface; this cleans the site and deposits a layer of mucus on the surface (Smith and Murphy, 1974).

The male also develops visually striking dark and light vertical bands. At this time, the alarm substance cells disappear from the epidermis in males, not females, eliminating release of alarm pheromone during the abrasive surface-cleaning behaviour (Smith, 1973, 1976a). Males still respond to alarm pheromone (Smith, 1976b). Breeding males release phermones that attract females, irrespective of the female's readiness to spawn (Cole and Smith, in prep.). The male also performs distinctive courting and leading behaviour (Cole and Smith, 1987a). Males are attracted to the odour of eggs (Sargent, 1988) and rubbed surfaces (J. Czerneda, unpubl.), and tend to set up their territories close to each other.

Females, when ready to spawn, leave their shoal and approach the territorial males, presumably responding to both chemical and visual stimuli. Some individual female fathead minnows persist in entering territories despite attacks by the male. Their persistence leading to successful spawning (McMillan and Smith, 1974). Other females, and perhaps the same female in other situations, can be lured by courtship (Cole and Smith, 1987a) and site quality (Unger and Sargent, 1988; Sargent, 1988). Females prefer to spawn with males that already have eggs (Unger and Sargent, 1988), probably because egg survival and paternal care both increase with clutch size (Sargent, 1988). Clutches below a minimum size (determined in part by predation rate) have virtually no chance of survival (Sargent, 1988). In threespine stick-lebacks, *Gasterosteus aculeatus*, this type of situation leads to egg stealing (Rohwer, 1978), but fathead eggs cannot be reattached after removal from the spawning surface (Gale and Buynak, 1982). Instead, males usurp the nests, and clutches, of established males and provide 'allopaternal' care for the eggs (Unger and Sargent, 1988). In this way they can start their spawning cycle with enough eggs to lure females.

Males may practice 'deceit' (Unger, 1983). Lone territorial males lose body weight as their breeding cycle progresses, owing to lack of feeding opportunities and high activity levels. Territorial males in groups retain the body weight and robust appearance of new territory holders. They do this by adjusting their hydromineral balance to retain more water, while losing dry weight. This presumably makes them appear to be more formidable opponents.

Once a female enters a male's territory, he still must distinguish, perhaps by pheromones (Cole and Smith, 1987b), between female egg predators and ovulated females ready for spawning. The pair then co-ordinate their behaviour so as to stick eggs to the ceiling and fertilize them simultaneously

(McMillan and Smith, 1974), a feat requiring considerable co-ordination. The male then cares for the eggs by rubbing them with the dorsal pad, defending them, and removing dead eggs. Without this care, egg survival is virtually nil. At hatching the male's vigorous rubbing assists the young in breaking free of the egg membrane, but no further post-hatching care is provided.

Other species

The fathead minnow has been used as an example because it is relatively well studied. There are many other cyprinid species, with mating systems at least as complex, that await detailed study. Consider, for example, the nest-building cyprinids, and their associated brood parasites, of North America (Lachner and Jenkins, 1971). Creek chub, *Semotilus atromaculatus*, fallfish, *S. corporalis*, and several species of *Nocomis*, among others, dig pits in river gravel, spawn with females, then carry gravel back and cover the eggs, forming large ridges of pebbles and boulders (e.g. 1.2 m wide by 0.6 m high in fallfish, Reed, 1971). The nests and associated spawning opportunities are vigorously defended from conspecific males (Ross, 1977), but several other species of cyprinids spawn over the boulder nests, parasitizing the builder's parental care.

In fallfish, fewer than 10% of males build nests. Others are satellite males that attempt to fertilize eggs as the builder spawns with a female (Ross, 1983). Fallfish males do not clasp the female, thus, Ross suggests, providing opportunity for sneak fertilization. Creek chub clasp while spawning and there are fewer satellite males. The satellites court females at the nest, when the owner is away, rather than attempt sneak fertilizing with a spawning pair (Ross, 1977).

Some species, such as the common shiner, *Notropis cornutus*, are facultative nest diggers, preferring to spawn over the nests of other species (Breder and Rosen, 1966) but capable of digging their own nest pits. Cutlips minnows, *Exoglossum maxillingua*, continue to protect the mound while the hatched young remain among the stones for about 6 d (Van Duzer, 1939), one of the few examples of post-hatching care in cyprinids. Several of these species show seasonal loss of alarm substance cells, in one sex or both, and many have other modifications of the skin (Smith, 1976a), including sometimes-spectacular breeding tubercles (Collette, 1977). Despite the research potential of this group, North American researchers have travelled to the tropics to watch cichlids while nest-building cyprinids spawned within their home campus.

18.6 MIGRATION AND HOMING

Reviews of fish migration (McKeown, 1984; McCleave *et al.*, 1984; Smith, 1985) contain few references to cyprinid migration. This reflects a real imbalance in the study of migration and homing. Migration allows a fish to utilize more than one type of habitat during its life cycle. One area may be best for early growth of young fish, another for overwintering, and a third habitat for spawning and survival of embryos. Homing allows a fish to return to a general area that has proven suitable, or a displaced fish may home to a specific site where it has invested in territory defence, egg care, or acquisition of local knowledge.

Migratory cyprinids may be particularly vulnerable to habitat alteration. Strong economic pressures favour the damming and diversion of rivers. Even populations of highly valued salmon and trout may be sacrificed in the face of these pressures. When fish ladders are provided for migrant fish they are usually designed for the larger and more economically valuable species. If cyprinids are able to use fishways designed for salmon, for example, it is normally just a fortunate accident.

Sensory capabilities related to migration and homing

In the early phases of the study of the home-stream odour hypothesis of salmon migration, the bluntnose minnow, *Pimephales notatus*, was used to study the ability of fishes to distinguish the odour of different natural waters (Walker and Hasler, 1949). In response to positive reinforcement with food and negative reinforcement with electric shock, the minnows could readily be trained to distinguish such odours. They retained the conditioned responses for at least 15 weeks, the longest period tested. This convinced Hasler that fishes possessed the discriminatory ability required by the home-stream odour hypothesis (Smith, 1985). The role that this ability might play in the life of the minnows was not examined.

Some common shiner populations migrate upstream in the spring and, in an optomotor apparatus, the fish showed positive rheotaxis (upstream movement) when subjected to spring photoperiod (12L:12D) and warm water (20 °C). Short-term increases of 5 °C induced immediate increases in positive rheotaxis (Dodson and Young, 1977). The upstream migration itself was not described.

Goldfish have become a standard test species in sensory physiology. They can respond to the plane of polarization of light (e.g. Waterman and Hashimoto, 1974). Becker (1974) found some evidence of magnetic orientation in goldfish. Walker and Bitterman (1986), however, could not condition goldfish to respond to magnetic field intensity. These abilities may be useful in orientation, and hence in migration and homing.

Migratory behaviour and homing

Few studies specifically describe and analyse migratory behaviour in cyprinids. More commonly, a few words or lines in a paper on some other subject state that migration occurs in the species. For example, migration is mentioned for 20% of the cyprinids listed in Scott and Crossman's (1973) survey of Canadian freshwater fishes. Most of the remaining 80% have simply not been examined for migration. Similarly, Nikol'skii (1961) mentions that some cyprinids migrate over 1000 km (e.g. *Rutilus frisii*), and he frequently mentions migration in species descriptions of European and Asian cyprinids. Such brief reports of migration are too numerous and general to review here. They do indicate that migration is important in cyprinid biology.

Lindsey and Northcote (1963) conducted one of the few detailed studies of cyprinid migration. Redside shiners *Richardsonius balteatus* spawn in streams and move between streams and lakes in central British Columbia. The upstream migration of adults into the spawning stream began in the spring when daily maximum stream temperature reached 10 °C. The number of migrating adults was correlated with increasing temperature rather than with water flow. Adults tended to migrate upstream during daylight whereas fry tended to move downstream to the lake at night. This association of upstream migration with daylight and downstream migration with darkness or poor visibility is common in fish (Smith, 1985). Marked redside shiners that were recovered in successive years tended to return to spawn in the same stream each year. It was not known whether they were returning to their natal stream.

Roach in Lake Årungen, Norway, make two separate migrations, feeding and reproductive (L'Abée–Lund and Vøllestad, 1985, 1987). A reproductive migration up Vollebeken, one of five tributaries of the lake, occurs primarily in May and early June. The newly emerged young drift downstream into the lake. The second migration, possibly in response to higher levels of prey or fewer predators in the stream, occurs in late June and July. Recovery of marked fish indicates a strong tendency to return to the same stream on subsequent migrations.

Another cyprinid, the Colorado squawfish, *Ptychocheilus lucius*, returns to the same spawning area more than once (Tyus, 1985). These large fish (to 45 kg) can carry a radio tag. Tyus tracked tagged individuals as they migrated from the home ranges that they occupied outside the breeding season to a breeding area in the Yampa River. Some individuals made round trips of about 400 km. Individuals converged at the spawning areas from both upstream and downstream, and fish tagged in earlier years returned to the same spawning site. It is not known whether these fish were returning to the stream where they had hatched, but imprinting on home spawning areas is possible (Tyus, 1985).

Fish that have invested in territorial defence, parental care, or acquiring local knowledge may benefit by being able to return to their home area after accidental displacement. These fish need not be migratory; they might never voluntarily leave their home range. Gudgeon, *Gobio gobio*, are able to return after such displacement (Stott *et al.*, 1963). Kennedy and Pitcher (1975), using aquaria divided into two sections, found that European minnows returned to a preferred home area after displacement.

These examples indicate that cyprinids are capable of long-distance migrations and of accurate homing. These requirements and abilities must be taken into account in any attempt to maintain suitable environments for cyprinids. In particular, the blockage and diversion of natural streams and rivers may interfere with required migrations. On the positive side, the presence of migratory and homing abilities in fish that are often small and amenable to experimental manipulation in captivity provides an opportunity to study these phenomena experimentally in a way that would be very difficult with larger fish.

18.7   CONCLUSIONS

Study of cyprinid behaviour has produced a mosaic. We have detailed knowledge of some species and some aspects of behaviour, but glaring omissions (and opportunities) as well. Pheromones are receiving attention but, in a group with excellent hearing, sound communication is little studied. The role of tubercles in visual and tactile communication deserves study. The functions and mechanisms of shoaling and schooling remain an enduring problem, but new theoretical emphasis on the individual is clarifying the interrelationships between foraging, defensive behaviour and the formation of social groups. Alarm signalling and kin selection are promising areas for research. The breeding behaviour of cyprinids can provide new insights into the evolution of sexual selection and parental care, by contrasting communal breeding strategies, territorial systems and brood parasitism within one group. Migration and homing are insufficiently studied, but important in cyprinids. Dams and stream 'improvement' may make migration the most vulnerable stage in the life cycle.

REFERENCES

Abrahams, M. V. and Colgan, P. W. (1985) Risk of predation, hydrodynamic efficiency and their influence on school structure. *Env. Biol. Fishes*, **13**, 195–202.

Abrahams, M. V. and Colgan, P. W. (1987) Fish schools and their hydrodynamic function: a reanalysis. *Env. Biol. Fishes*, **20**, 79–80.

Algranati, F. D. and Perlmutter, A. (1981) Attraction of zebrafish, *Brachydanio rerio*, to isolated and partially purified chromatographic fractions. *Env. Biol. Fishes*, **6**, 31–8.

Barlow, G. W. (1984) Patterns of monogamy among teleost fishes. *Arch. FischWiss.*, **35**, 75–123.

Becker, G. (1974) Einflus des Magnetfelds auf das Richtungsverhalten von Goldfischen. *Naturwissenschaften*, **61**, 220–21.

Bernstein, J. W. and Smith, R. J. F. (1983) Alarm substance cells in fathead minnows do not affect the feeding preference of rainbow trout. *Env. Biol. Fishes*, **9**, 307–11.

Blumer, L. S. (1982) A bibliography and categorization of bony fishes exhibiting parental care. *Zool. J. Linn. Soc.*, **76**, 1–22.

Breder, C. M. and Rosen, D. E. (1966) *Modes of Reproduction in Fishes*, Natural History Press, Garden City, NJ.

Brown, W. L., Eisner, T. and Whittaker, R. H. (1970) Allomones and kairomones: transpecific chemical messages. *Bioscience*, **20**, 21–2.

Caro, T. M. (1986) The functions of stotting: a review of the hypotheses. *Anim. Behav.*, **34**, 649–62.

Charnov, E. L. and Krebs, J. R. (1975) The evolution of alarm calls: altruism or manipulation? *Am. Nat.*, **109**, 107–12.

Chen, L. C. and Martinich, R. L. (1975) Pheromonal stimulation and metabolite inhibition of ovulation in the zebrafish, *Brachydanio rerio. NMFS Fish. Bull.*, **73**, 889–94.

Cole, K. S. and Smith, R. J. F. (1987a) Male courting behaviour in the fathead minnow, *Pimephales promelas. Env. Biol. Fishes*, **18**, 235–9.

Cole, K. S. and Smith, R. J. F. (1987b) Release of chemicals by prostaglandin-treated female fathead minnows, *Pimephales promelas*, that stimulate male courtship. *Horm. Behav.*, **21**, 440–56.

Collette, B. B. (1977) Epidermal breeding tubercles and bony contact organs in fishes. *Symp. zool. Soc. Lond.*, **39**, 225–68.

Delco, E. A. (1960) Sound discrimination by males of two cyprinid fishes. *Tex. J. Sci.*, **12**, 48–54.

Dodson, J. J. and Young, J. C. (1977) Temperature and photoperiod regulation of rheotropic behaviour in prespawning common shiners, *Notropis cornutus* (Mitchell). *J. Fish. Res. Bd. Can.*, **34**, 341–6.

Dowling, T. E. and Moore, W. S. (1986) Absence of population subdivision in the common shiner, *Notropis cornutus. Env. Biol. Fishes*, **15**, 151–5.

Ferguson, M. M. and Noakes, D. L. G. (1981) Social grouping and genetic variation in common shiners, *Notropis cornutus* (Pisces, Cyprinidae). *Env. Biol. Fishes*, **6**, 357–60.

Frisch, K. von (1941) Über einen Schreckstoff der Fischhaut und seine biologische Bedeutung. *Z. vergl. Physiol.*, **29**, 46–145.

Gale, W. F. and Buynak, G. L. (1982) Fecundity and spawning frequency of the fathead minnow – a fractional spawner. *Trans. Am. Fish. Soc.*, **111**, 35–40.

Giraldeau, L.-A. and Gillis, D. (1985) Optimal group size can be stable: a reply to Sibly. *Anim. Behav.*, **33**, 666–7.

Godin, J.-G. J. (1986) Antipredator function of shoaling in teleost fishes: a selective review. *Naturaliste can.*, **113**, 241–50.

Göz, H. (1941) Über den art und individualgeruch bei fischen. *Z. vergl. Physiol.*, **29**, 1–45.

Guidarelli, G. and Antonini, A. (1972) Ricerche sull'émissione di suoni da parte des *Carassius auratus* L. *Riv. Idrobiol.*, **11** (1), 1–9.

Healey, M. C. and Prieston, R. (1973) The interrelationships among individuals in a fish school. *Tech. Rep. Fish. Res. Bd Can.*, **389**, 1–15.

Hemmings, C. C. (1966) Olfaction and vision in fish schooling. *J. exp. Biol.*, **45**, 449–64.

Hugie, D. M. and Smith, R. J. F. (1987) Epidermal club cells are not linked with an alarm response in reedfish, *Erpetoichthys* (= *Calamoichthys*) *calabaricus. Can. J. Zool.*, **65**, 2057–61.

Hurk, R. van den, Hart, L. A.'t, Lambert, J. G. D. and Oordt, P. G. W. J. van (1982) On the regulation of sexual behaviour of male zebrafish, *Brachydanio rerio. Gen. comp. Endocrinol.*, **46**, 403.

Keenleyside, M. H. A. (1955) Some aspects of the schooling behaviour of fish. *Behaviour*, **8**, 183–248.

Kennedy, G. J. A. and Pitcher, T. J. (1975) Experiments on homing in shoals of the European minnow *Phoxinus phoxinus* (L.). *Trans. Am. Fish. Soc.*, **104**, 454–7.

L'Abée-Lund, J. H. and Vøllestad, I. A. (1985) Homing precision of the roach *Rutilus rutilus* in Lake Årungen, Norway. *Env. Biol. Fishes*, **13**, 235–9.

L'Abée-Lund, J. H. and Vøllestad, L. A. (1987) Feeding migration of roach *Rutilus rutilus* (L.) in Lake Årungen, Norway. *J. Fish Biol.*, **30**, 349–55.

Lachner, E. A. and Jenkins, R. E. (1971) Systematics, distribution, and evolution of the chub genus *Nocomis* Girard (Pisces, Cyprinidae) of the Eastern United States, with descriptions of new species. *Smithsonian Contr. Zool.*, **85**, 1–97.

Ladich, F. (1988) Sound production by the gudgeon, *Gobio gobio* L., a common European freshwater fish (Cyprinidae, Teleostei). *J. Fish Biol.*, **32**, 707–15.

Lawrence, B. J. and Smith, R. J. F. (1989) The behavioral response of solitary fathead minnows, *Pimephales promelas*, to alarm substance. *J. Chem. Ecol.*, **15**, 209–19.

Le Martret, M.-A. and Saglio, P. (1982) Communication intraspecifique d'origine phéromonale chez le carassin doré immature, *Carassius auratus* L. *Biol. Behav.*, **7**, 41–5.

Levesley, P. B. and Magurran, A. E. (1988) Population differences in the reaction of minnows to alarm substance. *J. Fish. Biol.*, **32**, 699–706.

Lindsey, C. C. and Northcote, T.G. (1963) Life history of redside shiners, *Richardsonius balteatus*, with particular reference to movements in and out of Sixteen Mile Lake streams. *J. Fish. Res. Bd Can.*, **20**, 1001–30.

McCleave, J. D., Arnold, G. P., Dodson, J. J. and Neill, W. H. (eds) (1984) *Mechanisms of Migration in Fishes*, Plenum Press, NY.

McCullough, D. R. (1969) The tule elk: its history, behaviour, and ecology. *Univ. Calif. Publs. Zool.*, **8**, 1–209.

McKeown, B. A. (1984) *Fish Migration*, Croom Helm, London.

McMillan, V. E. and Smith, R. J. F. (1974) Agonistic and reproductive behaviour of the fathead minnow (*Pimephales promelas* Rafinesque). *Z. Tierpsychol.*, **34**, 25–58.

Magurran, A. E. (1984) Gregarious goldfish. *New Scient.*, **103**, 32–3.

Magurran, A. E. (1986) The development of shoaling behaviour in the European minnow, *Phoxinus phoxinus*. *J. Fish Biol.*, **29**, (Supp. A), 159–69.

Magurran, A. E. and Girling, S. L. (1986) Predator recognition and response habituation in shoaling minnows. *Anim. Behav.*, **34**, 510–18.

Magurran, A. E. and Pitcher, T. J. (1983) Foraging, timidity and shoal size in minnows and goldfish. *Behav. Ecol. Sociobiol.*, **12**, 147–52.

Magurran, A. E. and Pitcher, T. J. (1987) Provenance, shoal size and sociobiology of predator evasion behaviour in minnow shoals. *Proc. R. Soc. Lond.*, **229B**, 439–65.

Magurran, A. E., Oulton, W. J. and Pitcher, T. J. (1985) Vigilant behaviour and shoal size in minnows. *Z. Tierpsychol.*, **67**, 167–78.

Malyukina, G. A., Martem'yanov, V. I. and Flerova, G. I. (1982) Alarm pheromone as a stress factor for fish. *J. Ichthyol.*, **22**, 147–50.

Ming, F. W. and Noakes, D. L. G. (1984) Spawning site selection and competition in minnows (*Pimephales promelas*) (Pisces, Cyprinidae). *Biol. Behav.*, **9**, 227–34.

Morgan, M. J. (1988) The influence of hunger, shoal size and predator presence on foraging in bluntnose minnows. *Anim. Behav.*, **36**, 1317–22.

Nikol'skii, G. V. (1961) *Special Ichthyology*, publ. for National Science Foundation, Washington, DC by Israel Program for Scientific Translations, Jerusalem.

Partridge, B. L., Liley, N. R. and Stacey, N. E. (1976) The role of pheromones in the sexual behaviour of the goldfish. *Anim. Behav.*, **24**, 291–9.

Pfeiffer, W. (1982) Chemical signals in communication, in *Chemoreception in Fishes* (ed. T. J. Hara), Elsevier, Amsterdam, pp. 306–26.

Pfeiffer, W., Denoix, M., Wehr, R., Gnass, D., Zachert, I. and Breisch, M. (1986) Videotechnische Verhaltensanalyse der Schreckreaction von Ostariophysen (Pisces) und die Bedeutung des "Mauthner Reflexes" *Zool. Jb. Abt. Physiol.*, **90**, 115–65.

Pfeiffer, W., Mangold-Wernado, U. and Neusteuer, P. (1984) Identification of the nerve bundle in the tractus olfactorius of the tench, *Tinca tinca* L., which conducts the nervous excitation elicited by the alarm substance. *Experientia*, **40**, 219–20.

Pitcher, T. J. (1979) Sensory information and the organization of behaviour in a shoaling cyprinid fish. *Anim. Behav.*, **27**, 126–49.

Pitcher, T. J. (1980) Some ecological consequences of fish school volumes. *Freshwat. Biol.*, **10**, 539–44.

Pitcher, T. J. (1983) Heuristic definitions of shoaling behaviour. *Anim. Behav.*, **31**, 611–13.

Pitcher, T. J. (1986) Functions of shoaling behaviour in teleosts, in *The Behaviour of Teleost Fishes* (ed. T. J. Pitcher), Croom Helm, London, pp. 294–337.

Pitcher, T. J. and House, A. C. (1987) Foraging rules for group feeders: area copying depends upon food density in shoaling goldfish. *Ethology*, **76**, 161–7.

Pitcher, T. J. and Magurran, A. E. (1983) Shoal size, patch profitability and information exchange in foraging goldfish. *Anim. Behav.*, **31**, 546–55.

Pitcher, T. J. and Turner, J. R. (1986) Danger at dawn: experimental support for the twilight hypothesis in shoaling minnows. *J. Fish Biol.*, **29**, (supp. A), 59–70.

Pitcher, T. J., Green, D. and Magurran, A. E. (1986a) Dicing with death: predator inspection behaviour in minnow shoals. *J. Fish. Biol.*, **28**, 439–48.

Pitcher, T. J., Magurran, A. E. and Allan, J. R. (1983) Shifts of behaviour with shoal size in cyprinids. *Proc. Br. Freshwat. Fish. Conf.* **3**, 220–8.

Pitcher, T. J., Magurran, A. E. and Allan, J. R. (1986b) Size-segregative behaviour in minnow shoals. *J. Fish Biol.*, **29**, (Supp. A), 83–95.

Pitcher, T. J., Magurran, A. E. and Winfield, I. J. (1982a) Fish in larger shoals find food faster. *Behav. Ecol. Sociobiol.*, **10**, 149–51.

Pitcher, T. J., Wyche, C. J. and Magurran, A. E. (1982b) Evidence for position preference in schooling mackerel. *Anim. Behav.*, **30**, 932–4.

Protasov, V. R., Neproshin, A. Yu., Gusar, A. G. and Kupriynanov, V. S. (1972) The sounds emitted by the anchovy (*Engraulis encrasicholus* (L.)) in a light field. *J. Ichthyol.*, **12**, 357–61.

Pulliam, H. R. and Caraco, T. (1984) Living in groups: is there an optimum groups size? in *Behavioural Ecology: an Evolutionary Approach* (eds J. R. Krebs and N. B. Davies), Blackwell, Oxford, pp. 122–47.

Quinn, T. P. and Busack, C. A. (1985) Chemosensory recognition of siblings in juvenile coho salmon, *Oncorhynchus kisutch. Anim. Behav.*, **33**, 51–6.

Reed, R. J. (1971) Biology of the fallfish, *Semotilus corporalis* (Pisces: Cyprinidae). *Trans. Am. Fish Soc.*, **100**, 717–25.

Rehnberg, B. G. and Smith, R. J. F. (1988) The influence of alarm substance and shoal size on the behaviour of zebra danios, *Brachydanio rerio* (Cyprinidae). *J. Fish. Biol.*, **33**, 155–63.

Rehnberg, B. G., Smith, R. J. F. and Sloley, B. D. (1987) The reaction of pearl dace (Pisces, Cyprinidae) to alarm substance: time-course of behavior, brain amines, and stress physiology. *Can. J. Zool.*, **65**, 2916–21.

Reist, J. D., Bodaly, R. A., Fudge, R. J. P., Cash, K. J. and Stevens, T. V. (1987) External scarring of whitefish, *Coregonus nasus* and *C. clupeaformis* complex, from the western Northwest Territories, Canada. *Can. J. Zool.*, **65**, 1230–34.

Rohwer, S. (1978) Parent cannibalism of offspring and egg raiding as a courtship strategy, *Am. Nat.*, **112**, 429–40.

Rose, S. M. (1959) Failure of survival of slowly growing members of a population. *Science*, **129**, 1026.

Ross, M. R. (1977) Aggression as a social mechanism in the creek chub. *Semotilus atromaculatus. Copeia*, **1977**, 393–7.

Ross, M. R. (1983) The frequency of nest construction and satellite male behavior in the fallfish minnow. *Env. Biol. Fishes*, **9**, 65–70.

Sargent, R. C. (1988) Paternal care and egg survival both increase with clutch size in the fathead minnow. *Pimephales promelas*. *Behav. Ecol. Sociobiol.*, **23**, 33–7.

Schutz, F. (1956) Vergleichende Untersuchungen über die Schreckreaktion bei Fischen und deren Verbreitung. *Z. vergl. Physiol.*, **38**, 84–135.

Scott, W. F. and Crossman, E. J. (1973) Freshwater fishes of Canada. *Bull. Fish. Res. Bd Can.*, no. 184, 966 pp.

Seghers, B. H. (1981) Facultative schooling behaviour in the spottail Shiner (*Notropis hudsonius*): possible costs and benefits. *Env. Biol. Fishes*, **6**, 21–4.

Sibly, R. M. (1983) Optimal group size is unstable. *Anim. Behav.*, **31**, 947–8.

Smith, R. J. F. (1973) Testosterone eliminates alarm substance in male fathead minnows. *Can. J. Zool.*, **51**, 875–6.

Smith, R. J. F. (1974) Effects of 17 α-methyltestosterone on the dorsal pad and tubercles of fathead minnows (*Pimephales promelas*). *Can. J. Zool.*, **52**, 1031–8.

Smith, R. J. F. (1976a) Seasonal loss of alarm substance cells in North American cyprinoid fishes and its relation to abrasive spawning behaviour. *Can. J. Zool.*, **54**, 1172–82.

Smith, R. J. F. (1976b) Male fathead minnows (*Pimephales promelas* Rafinesque) retain their fright reaction to alarm substance during the breeding season. *Can. J. A. Zool.*, **54**, 2230–1.

Smith, R. J. F. (1977) Chemical communication as adaptation: alarm substance of fish in *Chemical Signals in Vertebrates* (eds D. Müller-Schwarze and M. M. Mozell), Plenum, NY, pp. 303–20.

Smith, R. J. F. (1978) Seasonal changes in the histology of the gonads and dorsal skin of the fathead minnow, *Pimephales promelas*. *Can. J. Zool.*, **56**, 2103–9.

Smith, R. J. F. (1982) The adaptive significance of the alarm substance–fright reaction system, in *Chemoreception in Fishes* (ed. T. J. Hara), Elsevier, Amsterdam, pp. 327–42.

Smith, R. J. F. (1985) *The Control of Fish Migration*, Springer-Verlag, Berlin.

Smith, R. J. F. (1986a) The evolution of chemical alarm signals in fishes, in *Chemical Signals in Vertebrates, Vol 4* (eds D. Duvall, D. Müller-Schwarze and R. M. Silverstein), Plenum, NY, pp. 99–115.

Smith, R. J. F. (1986b) Evolution of alarm signals – role of benefits of retaining group members or territorial neighbors. *Am. Nat.*, **128**, 604–10.

Smith, R. J. F. and Lemly, A. D. (1986) Survival of fathead minnows after injury by predators and its possible role in the evolution of alarm signals. *Env. Biol. Fishes*, **15**, 147–9.

Smith, R. J. F. and Murphy, B. D. (1974) Functional morphology of the dorsal pad in fathead minnows (*Pimephales promelas*). *Trans. Am. Fish. Soc.*, **103**, 65–72.

Sorennsen, P. W., Stacey, N. E. and Naidu, P. (1986) Release of spawning pheromone(s) by naturally ovulated and prostaglandin-injected, nonovulated female goldfish, in *Chemical Signals in Vertebrates*, Vol. 4 (eds D. Duvall, D. Müller-Schwarze and R. M. Silverstein), Plenum, NY, pp. 149–54.

Stacey, N. E. (1987) Roles of hormones and pheromones in fish reproductive behavior, in *Psychobiology of Reproductive Behavior* (ed. D. Crews), Prentice-Hall, Englewood Cliffs, NJ, pp. 28–60.

Stott, B., Elsdon, J. W. V. and Johnston, J. A. A. (1963) Homing behaviour in gudgeon (*Gobio gobio* (L.)). *Anim. Behav.*, **11**, 93–6.

Stout, J. F. (1975) Sound communication during the reproductive behavior of *Notropis analostanus* (Pisces, Cyprinidae). *Am. Midl. Nat.*, **94**, 296–325.

Street, N. E., Magurran, A. E. and Pitcher, T. J. (1984) The effects of increasing shoal size on handling time in goldfish, *Carassius auratus* L. *J. Fish Biol.*, **25**, 561–6.

Suboski, M. D. (1988) Acquisttition and social communication of stimulus recognition by fish. *Behav. Process.*, **16**, 213–44.

Trivers, R. L. (1971) The evolution of reciprocal altruism. *Q. Rev. Biol.*, **46**, 35–57.

Tyus, H. M. (1985) Homing behaviour noted for Colorado squawfish. *Copeia*, **1985**, 213–15.

Unger, L. M. (1983) Nest defense by deceit in the fathead minnow, *Pimephales promelas*. *Behav. Ecol Sociobiol.*, **13**, 125–30.

Unger, L. M. and Sargent, R. C. (1988) Allopaternal care in the fathead minnow, *Pimephales promelas*: females prefer males with eggs. *Behav. Ecol. Sociobiol.*, **23**, 27–32.

Van Duzer, E. M. (1939) Observations on the breeding habits of the cutlips minnow (*Exoglossum maxillingua*). *Copeia*, **1939**, 69–75.

Verheijen, F. J. (1956) Transmission of a flight reaction amongst a school of fish and the underlying sensory mechanisms. *Experientia*, **12**, 202–4.

Waldman, B. (1982) Quantitative and developmental analysis of the alarm reaction in the zebra danio, *Brachydanio rerio*. *Copeia*, **1982**, 1–9.

Walker, M. M. and Bitterman, M. E. (1986) Attempts to train goldfish to respond to magnetic field stimuli. *Naturwissenschaften*, **73**, 12–16.

Walker, T. J. and Hasler, A. D. (1949) Detection and discrimination of odors of aquatic plants by the bluntnose minnow (*Hyborhynchus notatus*, Raf.). *Physiol. Zool.*, **22**, 45–63.

Waterman, T. H. and Hashimoto, H. (1974) E-vector discrimination by goldfish optic tectum. *J. comp. Physiol.*, **95A**, 1–12.

Williams, G. C. (1964) Measurement of consociation among fishes and comments on the evolution of schooling. *Publs Mich. St. Univ. Mus. biol. Ser.*, **2**, 349–84.

Wrede, W. L. (1932) Versuch über den Artduft der Elritzen. *Z. vergl. Physiol.*, **17**, 510–19.

Yu, M.-L. and Perlmutter, A. (1970) Growth inhibiting factors in the zebrafish (*Brachydanio rerio*). *Growth*, **34**, 153–75.

Chapter nineteen

Interspecific interactions

L. Persson

19.1 INTRODUCTION

The literature dealing with interactions among cyprinids and between cyprinids and other groups of fishes is enormous, so it would be impossible to cover all species here. Instead, I have chosen to focus on a smaller number of mainly European species with the aim of advancing some general patterns concerning interactions between cyprinids and other fish species. Indeed, in many parts my treatment will only deal with the interactions between roach, *Rutilus rutilus*, and perch, *Perca fluviatilis*, because these two species are the most thoroughly studied, and the interactions between them reflect at least to some extent the general pattern of interactions between cyprinids and other groups. Furthermore, although field studies and laboratory experiments exist for other cyprinids, conclusive field experimental evidence is extremely rare. Because cyprinids achieve their greatest levels of dominance in lakes, especially productive ones, the focus of this chapter will be on lake systems.

The chapter begins with a general description of the abundance relationships between cyprinids and other families under different environmental conditions (general productivity). Thereafter a mechanistic basis for the competitive abilities of different cyprinids, related to their physiological and behavioural capacities, is advanced. From this basis, I explore field experimental evidence for interactions between species. Throughout this review, emphasis will be put on the implications of size structure for interactions among fish species.

19.2 A GENERAL DESCRIPTION OF LAKE FISH COMMUNITY STRUCTURE AND SUCCESSION

As is evident from previous chapters, cyprinids form a family very successful in both their regional and local abundance. Furthermore, during the last 20 y it has become apparent that the abundance of cyprinids as a group is closely

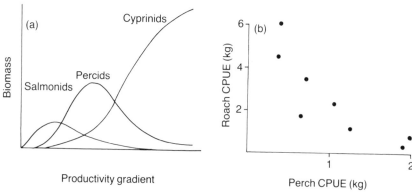

Fig. 19.1 (a) Schematic view of community succession along the productivity gradient. (b) Relationship between roach and perch biomass. CPUE (catch per unit effort) is the catch per survey net and 24 h in kg and dots represent different lakes (based on data in Persson 1983c).

correlated with the productivity of the system that they inhabit. A major reason why this relationship became recognized is the man-induced eutrophication of many lakes that has caused big changes in their fish communities. Basically, the change in the fish community along the productivity gradient involves a transition from communities dominated by salmonids (i.e. the families Salmonidae and Coregonidae) in very low productivity systems, through a situation where percids dominate in moderately productive systems, to highly productive systems dominated by cyprinids (Nümann, 1972; Hartmann and Nümann, 1977; Kitchell *et al.*, 1977; Leach *et al.*, 1977; Persson, 1983c; Johansson and Persson, 1986) (Fig. 19.1(a)). Although not experimentally demonstrated, the decrease in salmonids can be attributed to the disappearance of an oxygenated low-temperature habitat, the hypolimnion. In agreement with this hypothesis, Hartmann and Nümann (1977) showed that the decrease in salmonids in Lake Constance, West Germany, was correlated with a decrease in oxygen saturation in the hypolimnion from 82% in the period 1925–36 to 29% in 1952–75. The importance of the hypolimnion as a competitive refuge for salmonids is suggested by their lower temperature optima for growth compared to other groups such as percids and cyprinids (Elliott, 1976; Brett *et al.*, 1969; Lessmark, 1983). In addition to being a competitive refuge for salmonids, the hypolimnion may also offer a spatial refuge from predators inhabiting warmer waters.

Cyprinids increase monotonically with the productivity of the system, but it is only with the progression to highly productive conditions that they will become the numerically dominating group at the expense of percids (Svärdson, 1976; Kitchell *et al.*, 1977; Leach *et al.*, 1977; Persson, 1983c; Johansson and Persson, 1986). This succession pattern has been observed both when comparing the fish communities in systems of different productivity and when studying productivity changes within systems over time (Johansson and

Persson, 1986). For example, Svärdson (1976) and Persson (1983c) compared data on abundance relationships of different lakes, while Holcik (1977) and Burrough *et al.* (1979) observed changes with a system over several years. It is worth pointing out that the decrease in percids in highly productive systems is related to the decrease in perch, while the two other common European percids, ruffe, *Gymnocephalus cernuus*, and zander, *Stizostedion lucioperca*, increase with productivity (Rundberg, 1977; Leach *et al.*, 1977). Similarly, certain cyprinid species such as rudd, *Scardinius erythrophthalmus*, decrease in abundance with increasing productivity (Burrough *et al.*, 1979; Winfield, 1986). Furthermore, bream, *Abramis brama*, seems to replace roach as the most abundant cyprinid species in very productive systems (Bíró and Garádi, 1974; Lammens *et al.*, 1987). Viewed as a group, however, cyprinids will increase at the expense of percids.

The change from a percid-dominated to a cyprinid-dominated community is reflected in the abundance relationship between roach and perch (Fig. 19.1(b)). Although a negative relationship between roach and perch density has been shown in several studies (Sumari, 1971; Svärdson, 1976; Persson, 1983c; Lessmark, 1983), it is only recently that experimental verifications of a competitive effect of roach on perch have been given (Persson, 1986, 1987 b,c; Persson and Greenberg, 1990). Recent studies also suggest that the interaction between roach and perch shifts from a mainly predatory to a mainly competitive one along the productivity gradient (Persson *et al.*, 1988; Persson, 1988).

19.3   MECHANISTIC BASES OF SPECIES INTERACTIONS INVOLVING CYPRINIDS

Omnivory

A number of factors influence the success of cyprinids in interactions with species of many other families. One major factor is undoubtedly the capacity of cyprinid species to eat non-animal (plant, algal and detrital) food items. The ability of cyprinids to digest plant and algal material is connected to an evolutionary reduction of the stomach, including the lack of pepsin and acid-secreting cells (Kapoor *et al.*, 1975; Chapters 12 and 14). This capacity is important because plant material can serve as a competitive dietary refuge for cyprinids in relation to other species (Persson, 1983b). When animal food becomes scarce, cyprinids can shift to feeding on plant material and thereby buffer variation in animal food availability. The maximum biomass of cyprinids sustained within a lake is, as a consequence, also expected to increase. The proportion of detritus or algae in the diet of cyprinids can be quite high: for roach an average as high as 80% of the total diet has been found (Niederholzer and Hofer, 1980; Persson, 1983b; Brabrand, 1985; Persson and Greenberg, 1990). In lakes in the temperate region of Europe, the proportion

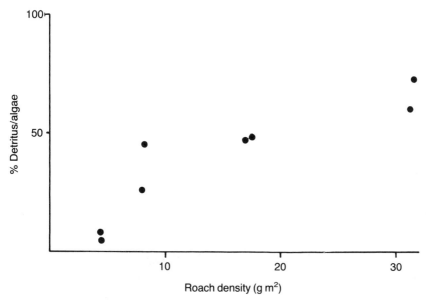

Fig. 19.2 Relationship between proportion of plant material in the diet and roach density (data from Persson and Greenberg, 1990).

of non-animal food used by cyprinids varies seasonally (Niederholzer and Hofer, 1980; Persson, 1983b). Different interpretations of this observation have been made; Niederhofer and Holzer (1980) suggested that the increased utilization of non-animal food items was a result of an increased availability of these resources, while Persson (1983b) suggested that the increased utilization was a response to an increased resource limitation with respect to animal prey items (see also Brabrand, 1985, and, for an American cyprinid, Grimm, 1988). Recent experimental studies have supported the latter hypothesis, because an increase in roach density (i.e. increased resource limitation) has resulted in an increased proportional use of plant material (Fig. 19.2) (Johansson, 1987; Persson and Greenberg, 1990).

Cyprinids may differ in diet in relation to their functional morphology, e.g. rudd feeds primarily on macrophytes, while roach feeds primarily on algae and detritus (Prejs, 1984). The type of plant resources eaten may also depend on what is available. For example, in systems dominated by submersed macrophytes, roach feed primarily on these higher plants (Brabrand, 1985), while in systems with sparse submersed vegetation, roach feed primarily on algae and detritus (Persson, 1983b).

The degree to which cyprinids can utilize non-animal food items varies and depends on the quality of the resources utilized (Chapters 12, 13 and 14). One circumstance that has been suggested to have positive effects on the competitive ability of roach in highly productive systems is the abundant presence therein of bluegreen algae (Persson, 1983 b,c; Johansson and

Persson, 1986). Two experimental studies have shown that the degree to which roach can utilize bluegreen algae is much higher than that for other algae and plant materials (Sorokin, 1968; Lessmark, 1983). Lessmark (1983) demonstrated that the specific growth rate of roach feeding on filamentous algae was not significantly different from that of a starving fish, while significant positive growth was present when the fish were fed the bluegreen alga *Aphanizomenon*. Similarly, Sorokin (1968) showed that the assimilation efficiency of roach feeding on *Aphanizomenon* was as high as 62%, while that on a green alga was only 14%. Interestingly, in this study the degree by which bream could assimilate bluegreen algae was very low (1%), indicating that the availability of this resource may have a substantial effect on the interaction between roach and other cyprinids.

Zooplanktivory

The capacity of cyprinids to feed on non-animal material is thus one factor that greatly contributes to the outcome of their interactions with other species. A second factor of importance is the capacity of cyprinids as zooplankton feeders. Zooplanktivory and different feeding modes have been treated in Chapter 12, and will be considered here mainly with respect to foraging efficiencies of different cyprinids and perch. The most extensive experimental studies on zooplankton feeding in cyprinids have been carried out on roach, and to a smaller extent on rudd, bream and white bream, *Blicca bjoerkna* (Winfield, 1986; Johansson, 1987; Persson, 1987 b,c; Andersson, 1984; Lammens *et al.*, 1987). The efficiency of roach as a zooplankton feeder, especially in relation to perch, has been experimentally documented at different spatial and temporal levels, from laboratory experiments, to enclosure experiments in lakes, to whole-lake experiments (Persson, 1986, 1987 b,c; Johansson and Persson, 1986; Johansson, 1987). Laboratory experiments have shown that the capture rate of roach fed pelagic prey (cladocerans and cyclopoid copepods) is considerably higher than that of perch (Fig. 19.3). The handling time of roach when feeding on *Daphnia* is only half of that of perch and only one-third of that for cyclopoid copepods (Persson, 1987c). The difference in foraging efficiency between roach and perch can be related to differences in handling time and in swimming speed; roach swimming speed when foraging is approximately 15 times higher than that of perch (47 versus 3 cm s^{-1}) (Johansson and Persson, 1986). Field experiments have demonstrated that roach depress zooplankton abundance to very low levels (Andersson, 1984; Persson, 1987c). In enclosure experiments, zooplankton densities were highest in enclosures containing perch alone, whereas enclosures containing roach only or both roach and perch had equally low zooplankton levels (Persson, 1987c). The addition of perch to roach enclosures thus did not result in any further decrease in zooplankton densities when compared with enclosures containing only roach.

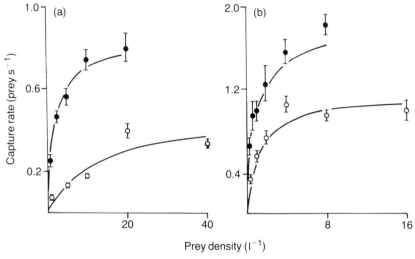

Fig. 19.3 Capture rate of perch ($\bigcirc$) and roach ($\bullet$) in relation to density of two pelagic prey: (a) *Cyclops*, (b) *Daphnia*. Points are means $\pm$ 1SE and the data have been fitted to Holling Type II functional response curves (data from Persson, 1988).

Among cyprinids, rudd is a less efficient zooplankton feeder than roach in open water, which may potentially affect the abundance relationship between these species among lakes and also their habitat distributions within lakes (Winfield, 1986; Johansson, 1987). The relative foraging efficiencies of these species are moreover dependent on the structural complexity of the system.

Structural complexity and light conditions

A third factor affecting interactions between cyprinids and percids, and also interactions among different cyprinid species, is the structural complexity of the environment. The structural complexity in the form of submersed vegetation and light conditions is correlated with the productivity of the system, such that the primary production in highly productive systems is in most cases dominated by phytoplankton, resulting in uniformly poor light conditions over most of the water column and a scarcity or total lack of submersed vegetation (Phillips *et al.*, 1978; Wetzel, 1979; Sand-Jensen, 1979; Lodge *et al.*, 1988). It can therefore be suggested that observed species abundance patterns along the productivity gradient also depend on the structural complexity of the system *per se*. Laboratory experiments have shown that perch is a more efficient forager than cyprinids (bream and roach) on both pelagic (*Daphnia*) and benthic prey (chironomids) in structurally complex environments, while the opposite applies, at least for pelagic prey, in environments lacking structure (Fig. 19.4(a)) (Winfield, 1986: Diehl, 1988). In particular, the foraging efficiency of bream decreases markedly with

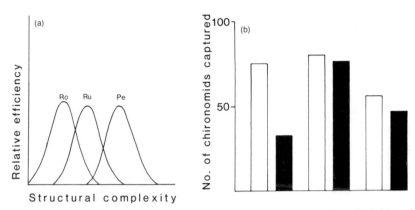

Fig. 19.4 (a) Schematic view of the relative foraging capacity of roach (left), rudd (centre) and perch (right) on pelagic prey in relation to structural complexity (based on Winfield, 1986). (b) Numbers of chironomids captured during an experimental trial by perch (left), bream (centre) and roach (right) in daylight (open columns) and under darkness (black columns) (modified from Diehl, 1988).

increasing vegetation complexity (Diehl, 1988). Laboratory studies on habitat selection also showed that bream selected the most simple environment (no vegetation), while perch was uniformly common in three tested environments of increasing macrophyte structure (Diehl, 1988). The relevance of these laboratory results to natural conditions is supported by the distributions of these species between lakes and between habitats within the same lake (Winfield, 1986; Diehl, 1988). Within cyprinids, laboratory experiments suggest that low structural complexity favours roach and bream relative to cyprinid species such as rudd, a contention which is supported by the distribution of these species among and within lakes (Fig. 19.4(a)) (Burrough *et al.*, 1979; Winfield, 1986).

Previous studies have suggested that the animal food resources attached to littoral submersed vegetation, on which perch is a more efficient forager than roach, should be of prime importance for the interactions between these species (Johansson and Persson, 1986; Persson, 1987c, 1988). In addition, these studies suggest that a habitat's structural complexity *per se* induced by submersed vegetation may affect the species interactions. Thus the hypothesis may be advanced that perch is competitively favoured against cyprinids by submerged vegetation. Supporting evidence comes from species abundance patterns in a minority of highly productive systems where the primary production is dominated by submersed macrophytes. These lakes deviate from the normal pattern in that, in spite of high productivity, perch can be numerically more common than bream and roach. However, cyprinid species exploiting macrophyte-related resources not used by perch (e.g. tench, *Tinca tinca*, feeding on snails) may increase in abundance with increasing submerged macrophyte cover.

The decreased light level generally associated with increased primary production is also a factor that will favour cyprinids against perch. Townsend and Risebrow (1982) showed that underyearling bream were capable of capturing *Daphnia* at very low light levels, and Diehl (1988) showed that the capture rate of roach and bream feeding on benthic prey in darkness was as high as that under daylight. In contrast, the capture rate of perch decreased substantially (Fig. 19.4(b)). One explanation for this pattern may be related to the presence of the Weberian apparatus in cyprinids (Chapter 11). The importance of light conditions for the interactions between perch and cyprinids is also indicated by the fact that ruffe and zander, percids adapted to feed under poor light conditions, show an increase in abundance with system productivity (Ali *et al.*, 1977; Disler and Smirnov, 1977; Bergman 1987, 1988).

19.4   THE INFLUENCE OF ONTOGENETIC NICHE SHIFTS ON SPECIES INTERACTIONS INVOLVING CYPRINIDS

A fundamental feature of fish is their potential to grow during most of their life. While increasing in size, they undergo size-specific changes in niche, generally involving an increase in the mean size of prey eaten. Considering foraging efficiency alone, these ontogenetic niche shifts can be related to morphological changes and increasing energetic costs: the former result from an increased capacity to capture larger prey and a loss in the ability to capture and retain smaller prey, while the latter relate to the necessity to switch to increasingly larger prey to compensate for increased energetic demands resulting from increasing body size (Kerr, 1971; Mittelbach, 1981; Persson, 1987a). Ontogenetic niche shifts are as ubiquitous among cyprinids as among other fish species. The consequences of such niche shifts in cyprinids to their population dynamics are, however, less explored. In many species, cyprinid ontogenetic niche shifts involve a move from feeding as carnivores (generally zooplankton feeding) to feeding on non-animal food items (plants, detritus and algae) (Prejs, 1984; Johansson and Persson, 1986). Hofer and Wieser (1987) suggested that a basic pattern of ontogenetic niche shifts could be discerned for the very young stages of several European cyprinids, from phytoplankton feeding to feeding on rotifers, then switching to larger crustaceans. The shift to non-animal food items appears to be related to increasing resource limitation with increasing body size and, under conditions of less resource limitation, roach may shift to feeding on prey such as gastropods (Kempe, 1962; Persson, 1983b). Some species such as bream seem to avoid this size-related increase in resource limitation by shifting feeding technique from particulate feeding to filter feeding (Lammens, 1985). Lammens also suggests that bream continue to feed on zooplankton to very large sizes (see also Andersson *et al.*, 1975; Lammens *et al.*, 1987), although contradictory evidence does exist (Tatrai,

1980; Löffler, 1984). Ontogenetic changes with increasing size also generally involve changes in activity patterns. Bohl (1980) showed that juvenile cyprinids have their highest feeding activity during the night, whereas this is not so far larger size classes of cyprinid species (Persson, 1983b). This difference in activity pattern can be related to the higher predation risk for juveniles compared to larger fish (Werner and Gilliam, 1984).

19.5 THE ROLES OF COMPETITION AND PREDATION IN SPECIES INTERACTIONS INVOLVING CYPRINIDS

General principles

Since individual growth rates in fish are indeterminate and dependent on resource supply, resource competition will directly affect ontogenetic niche shifts by depressing growth rates. In most species, however, competition and predation interact, and ontogenetic niche shifts in fishes therefore often result from both competitive and predatory processes (Larkin, 1956; Werner and Gilliam, 1984; Werner, 1986; Mittelbach and Chesson, 1987). An illustrative example of how competitive interactions may interact with predation is competition-induced reduction in growth rate, which will prolong the time the fish is susceptible to gape-limited predators (Tonn *et al.*, 1986). The relative strengths of competitive and predatory interactions may also change ontogenetically, such that while competitive interactions prevail between certain size (age) classes, predatory interactions are dominant between others. The conceptualization of the complex interplay between predation and competition into a general and theoretical framework, developed by Werner and Gilliam (1984) and Werner (1986), has focused on two major aspects: first, effects of mixed competition–predation on ontogenetic niche shifts predicted by a certain growth rate–mortality rate trade-off (Werner and Gilliam, 1984; Werner, 1986), and second, and perhaps less explored, the effects of interspecific competition at the juvenile stage, potentially resulting in juvenile competitive bottlenecks. A **juvenile competitive bottleneck** can be defined as the situation where juvenile interspecific competition results in profound effects on population dynamics or population size structure (Johansson and Persson, 1986; Persson, 1988). Species that undergo large ontogenetic shifts in prey size may commonly exhibit juvenile competitive bottlenecks, since natural selection operates on morphologies and other traits to cope with a broad spectrum of resources (Werner and Gilliam, 1984). As a consequence, trade-offs in foraging efficiency are likely to cause juveniles of such species to be less efficient when feeding on small prey than are the young of other species undergoing less dramatic ontogenetic shifts in resource use (Werner and Hall, 1979; Werner, 1986; Persson and Greenberg, 1990). Experimental

Species

Planktivore   **Piscivore**

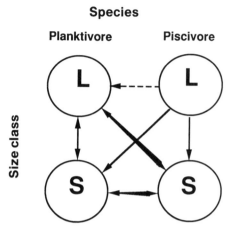

Fig. 19.5 Size-specific (S, small; L, large) interactions between a planktivorous fish species (left) and a fish species undergoing substantial niche shifts leading to piscivory if becoming large (right). Thickness of arrows indicates strength of negative effects and broken arrow indicates a weak interaction (redrawn from Persson, 1988).

demonstrations of such trade-offs have been documented in at least two cases, the roach–perch and bluegill sunfish, *Lepomis macrochirus* – largemouth bass, *Micropterus salmoides*, interactions, both involving situations where the larger species becomes piscivorous when adult (Werner, 1977; Persson, 1987c). The resulting asymmetry in the competitive and predatory interactions between such a species pair may be summarized graphically (Fig. 19.5). As a consequence of its competitive superiority for smaller prey types, the smaller species may limit the recruitment to piscivorous classes of individuals of the larger species. On the other hand, predation by piscivorous classes of the larger species may depress the population size of the smaller species, counteracting the limitations set by the interspecifically-induced juvenile bottleneck.

Relatively few cyprinids become piscivorous when large (e.g. ide, *Leuciscus idus*, asp, *Aspius aspius*, white bream), hence a cyprinid species will generally be the species causing a juvenile competitive bottleneck in the recruitment of juveniles to piscivorous classes in piscivorous species. To illustrate this type of mixed predation–competition interaction, I will use the roach–perch interaction. While the asymmetry in the competitive relationship between perch and roach is a result of several factors, the asymmetry with respect to predator–prey interactions is more simple. Large perch are predators on both roach and perch, whereas roach extremely rarely consume fish. Perch are gape-limited predators and they prey largely on small immature fish (Popova and Sytina, 1977; Willemsen, 1977), so large roach are not very susceptible to perch predation. Because the roach–perch abundance pattern along the productivity gradient largely reflects the abundance pattern between cyprinids and percids in general, the relationship between these two species can be suggested to have implications beyond that at the population level.

Productive systems

Resource use with respect to food and habitat has been studied for several European cyprinids. Brabrand (1985) studied the feeding relationships between ide and roach and showed a separation between the species with respect to both food and habitat. The resource partitioning between the similar species bream and white bream has also been documented; these species differ, among other features, in their ability to penetrate the sediment (Brabrand, 1984; Lammens *et al.*, 1987). When studying the feeding relationships of larvae and juveniles of three cyprinid species (roach, rudd and chub, *Leuciscus cephalus*), Mark *et al.* (1987) found that the food overlap was of the same magnitude between representatives of different species or different cohorts, and between members of schools belonging to the same cohort.

Despite the number of field studies on feeding and habitat relationships in European cyprinids, experimental evidence for competitive (or predatory) interactions between cyprinids is extremely scarce. In enclosure experiments in a highly productive lake, Johansson (1987) demonstrated the presence of competition between roach and rudd, both in the open-water and vegetation areas of the lake. Johansson also suggested that competion might be responsible for the observed habitat separation between these species, in which rudd is largely confined to the shore vegetation area.

In contrast to cyprinids, perch is a strict carnivore and possesses a well-developed stomach with acid- and pepsin-secreting cells (Fish, 1960), and potentially undergoes three major ontogenetic shifts in diet: as young they feed on zooplankton, thereafter they switch to macroinvertebrates, and as adults they potentially become piscivorous. The macroinvertebrate feeding phase has been proposed as the competitive bottleneck in perch populations; juveniles that switch to this feeding stage early and at small sizes show retarded growth, and very few ever turn to piscivory. Perch populations of this type are consequently dominated by small non-piscivorous individuals. In contrast, in populations where perch shift to feeding on macroinvertebrates at a late stage, this feeding phase is relatively transitory and a shift to piscivory occurs early (Persson, 1986; Johansson and Persson, 1986). These perch populations are consequently dominated by large piscivorous perch.

The length of the zooplanktivorous stage in perch is negatively correlated with the density of cyprinids such as roach. In lakes with no or very few roach, yearlings of perch may feed almost exclusively on zooplankton (Gumaá, 1978; Craig, 1978; Nyberg, 1979), and zooplankton may form an important portion of the diet of even large perch (Thorpe, 1977). In contrast, in highly productive lakes dominated by cyprinids, yearlings of perch switch to macroinvertebrates at a small size and young age (Persson, 1983a, 1986). The impact of roach prolonging the time needed for perch to reach piscivorous size might be a result of two factors: (1) the advantage in feeding efficiency on zooplankton of roach over perch, resulting in a direct negative effect on zooplankton-feeding perch, and (2) an indirect negative effect on macroinvertebrate-feeding perch by producing an early switch from zooplankton- to macroinvertebrate-feeding in juvenile perch.

A whole-lake experiment carried out in a highly productive lake supports the above hypotheses. After a reduction in the population size of roach by more than 70%, zooplankton abundance increased by an average of four times (Persson, 1986). Consequently, young-of-the-year (0+) perch continued to feed on zooplankton for both a longer time and to a larger size than before the roach removal, resulting in increased individual growth rates and population size. The change in resource use of 0+ perch resulted in an increase in the growth rate of larger (older) macroinvertebrate-feeding perch, and as a consequence they started to shift to piscivory earlier than before the removal experiment. Density dependence in growth rate of roach was also observed; roach growth rate increased after the reduction in population size. The same strong density-dependent effects of roach on zooplankton density and on both 0+ and 1+ perch growth rates were found in enclosure experiments in the pelagic habitat of the lakes, and in a pond experiment (Fig. 19.6) (Persson, 1987a; Persson and Greenberg, 1990).

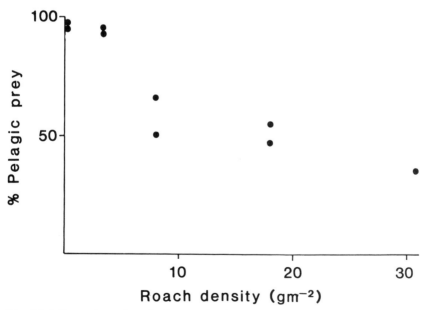

Fig. 19.6 Percentage of zooplankton in the diet of juvenile perch in relation to roach density (data from Persson and Greenberg, 1990).

These experiments support the hypothesis that roach in highly productive systems reduce zooplankton densities, induce an early diet shift in 0+ perch, and therefore increase size-class competition in perch for macroinvertebrates. This increased size-class competition results in a decreased individual growth rate in perch, and few individuals can be expected to enter the piscivorous stage. These experiments thus give a mechanistic explanation for the domination of perch populations by small non-piscivorous individuals in highly productive lakes where cyprinids are numerically dominant. The rarity with which perch enter the piscivorous stage in these systems is also influenced by the fact that decreased individual growth rates will prolong the time period that they are susceptible to predation by coexisting piscivorous such as northern pike, *Esox lucius*, and zander. Hence, although competition is the cause of the slow individual growth rates, predation may act as an important mortality agent, preventing slow-growing perch individuals from living long enough to reach piscivorous size.

Less productive systems

The abundance relationship between cyprinids and percids, specifically between roach and perch, is dependent on the productivity of the system. In less productive systems, perch are more common than roach (Svärdson, 1976; Persson, 1983c), an observation which can be related to factors acting to decrease the competitive advantage of roach (Johansson and Persson, 1986). With decreasing productivity, the importance of the littoral relative to the pelagic increases (Wetzel, 1979; Sand-Jensen, 1979; Lodge *et al.*, 1988), and the phytoplankton community shifts from one dominated by bluegreens to a community dominated by other algae which are less nutritious to roach. The increase of the littoral habitat increases the abundance of submerged macrophytes and their attached macroinvertebrates, on which perch have a higher foraging efficiency than roach (Persson, 1988). An increase in the structural complexity *per se*, as a result of increased abundance of submerged macrophytes, will favour perch over cyprinids such as roach (Winfield, 1986; Diehl, 1988).

The competitive impact of perch on roach is also expected to be low in unproductive systems. The foraging rate of roach on littoral prey seems independent of prey density (Persson, 1987c) and, although bluegreens are less common in unproductive systems, plant material still offers a competitive refuge for roach. Enclosure experiments in the littoral of a highly productive system also failed to demonstrate any competitive effect of perch on roach (Persson, 1987b). One simple explanation for the observed abundance relationship between roach and perch in low-productivity systems could be that only weak interactions occur between the species. According to this hypothesis, the abundances of the two species are merely set by the availabilty of different resources. However, the change in the abundance relationship between roach and perch along the productivity gradient also involves a change in the size distribution of the populations, such that the median size of both perch and roach increases with decreasing productivity (Persson, 1983a; Persson *et al.*, 1988). Therefore, an alternative hypothesis can be advanced, that the interaction between roach and perch changes from a mainly competitive interaction in highly productive systems to a mainly predatory interaction, with perch predation limiting roach density, in low-productivity systems. Support for this hypothesis already exists in the positive correlation between the median size of roach and the proportion of piscivorous perch (Fig. 19.7) (Persson *et al.*, 1988). The evidence for piscivorous perch affecting roach density in low-productivity systems is only suggestive and the shift in abundance relationship may also involve indirect effects. One potential example of this is that along the productivity gradient, changes may occur in

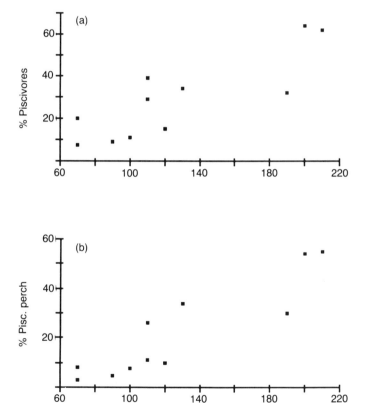

Fig 19.7 Median size of roach in relation to the percentage of piscivores of total fish biomass, (a) All piscivores included, (b) piscivores others than perch excluded. Data points represent different lakes (modified from Persson *et al.*, 1988).

abundance of alternative forage fish for perch, forage fish that at the same time are interacting with roach.

The change in the proportion of piscivorous perch along the productivity gradient is expected to have major effects on processes at the ecosystem level, because the change in biomass of total piscivores largely reflects changes in biomass of piscivorous perch (Fig. 19.8). Perch can thus be viewed as a potentially keystone species (*senu* Paine, 1966), and understanding the dynamics of perch populations will probably clarify general aquatic ecosystem processes. In very-low-productivity systems, lower than those considered here, the proportion of piscivorous perch is low and increases with productivity to a maximum at a moderately low productivity (Fig. 19.8). This part of the data suggests that the biomass of piscivores (fourth trophic level) increases with primary productivity, which is partly in accord with the hypothesis of Oksanen *et al.* (1981; see also Fretwell, 1977) predicting an increase in food chain length with productivity. However, the decrease in proportional piscivore biomass in highly productive systems is in conflict with these predictions. The most probable explanation for this is that the model ignores the possibility that the same individual may shift trophic level ontogenetically, a common feature in aquatic ecosystems (Mittelbach *et al.*, 1988). The importance of including size structure when studying processes at the ecosystem level was considered by Riemann *et al.* (1986; see also Persson *et al.*, 1988). Riemann *et al.* (1986)

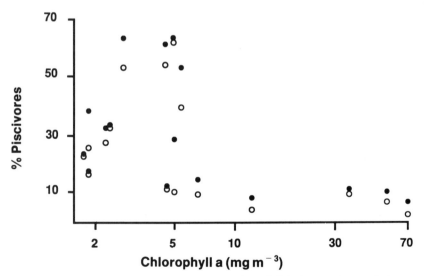

Fig. 19.8 Piscivore biomass (as percentage of total fish biomass) in relation to phytoplankton biomass. ●, total piscivores; ○, piscivorous perch only; see also Fig. 19.7 (data from Persson *et al.*, 1988).

did, for example, show that the change in proportion of piscivorous perch along the productivity gradient had profound effects on the production and biomass of other components of the ecosystem such as zooplankton, phytoplankton and bacteria (see also Chapter 20).

19.6 SPECIES INTERACTIONS AND THE SIZE STRUCTURE OF CYPRINID POPULATIONS

The mechanisms behind the dynamics leading to different size structures of cyprinid populations are far from understood. However, it is evident that the relative strength of competitive versus predatory interactions is of major importance. When competition is intense, cyprinid populations tend towards a smaller mean individual size as a result of low individual growth rates (Persson, 1983b). In contrast, when predation can be expected to be intense (i.e. when piscivores form a large proportion of total fish biomass), the median size of cyprinids is large (Fig. 19.7) (Persson *et al.* 1988). The different size structures are related to the productivity of the system, supporting the hypothesis of a change in dominating asymmetry along the productivity gradient. The ability of European cyprinids to respond to increased predation pressure by gape-limited predators by increasing their median size might be one explanation for their success compared to their generally smaller North American relatives, which may be driven extinct by predators (Tonn *et al.*, in press). Size structure and predation intensity may also be of importance for the abundance relationship between the two common European cyprinid species, bream and roach. In many very productive lakes, bream is more abundant than roach (Bíró and Garádi, 1974; Lammens *et al.*, 1986, 1987) for reasons which are not well understood (but see Chapter 12 and Lammens *et al.*, 1986, 1987). Roach is a more efficient zooplanktivore than bream, a contention suggested by the observation that Dutch lakes numerically dominated by roach support smaller zooplankton species and lower zooplankton biomasses overall than lakes numerically dominated by bream (Lammens *et al.*, 1986). Roach can also utilize bluegreen algae to a larger extent than can bream (Sorokin, 1968). On the other hand, bream is a more efficient forager on benthic chironomids, and large bream have, in contrast to large roach, the potential to continue to feed on zooplankton with an increase in size, by shifting from particulate to filter feeding (Lammens, 1985; Lammens *et al.*, 1986). Although experimental demonstrations are lacking, the abundance relationship between these two species may thus be a simple consequence of the relative abundances of different resource types.

However, the interaction between bream and roach is probably more complex, owing to the presence of piscivorous zander in many highly productive lakes, and dependent on the relative development of the shore vegetation (Lammens *et al.*, 1986). Perhaps the interactions between roach and bream are mediated through this piscivore, and the presence of the shore vegetation as a predation refuge affects this interaction. Although supporting field evidence is scarce and experimental evidence absent, the following scenario may be advanced. The presence of vegetation will allow a high recruitment of cyprinids, leading to increased resource limitation in juvenile fishes. As roach is a very efficient zooplanktivore, the species will depress zooplankton density to low levels, disfavouring both bream and zooplankton-feeding juvenile zander, causing a juvenile bottleneck in the recruitment of piscivorous zander. In competition for resources with juvenile roach in vegetational predatory refuges, juvenile bream is also disfavoured by the local structural complexity (Diehl, 1988). Consequently, if submerged vegetation is present, juvenile bream and roach will possibly prefer the vegetation habitat to avoid piscivorous zander, in which case roach will be additionally favoured. In contrast, when the shore vegetation is poorly developed, juvenile fish such as roach and bream will be more susceptible to predation, and the recruitment of zander to piscivorous stages should therefore increase. Increased predation pressure from piscivores is also expected to reduce predation pressure on zooplankton, facilitating the recruitment of zooplanktivorous zander to piscivorous stages. Furthermore, bream is less susceptible to gape-limited zander predation, because of both its body form and its higher potential growth rate compared with roach (Goldspink, 1979). It is therefore possible that a positive relationship exists between bream and zander abundance, despite this piscivore preying on juvenile bream, because meanwhile such predation releases bream from competition with roach. To conclude, it is important to point out that this suggested predator-mediated interaction is dependent on the presence of size-structure in both the predator population, related to a potential juvenile bottleneck, and in the prey populations, related to a size refuge.

19.7   CONCLUDING REMARKS AND IMPLICATIONS FOR NON-EUROPEAN CYPRINIDS

The treatment of interspecific interactions in this chapter has admittedly been biased towards European cyprinids. This partly relates to the fact that cyprinids play a very important role in the fish fauna of European lakes, and are as a result the most thoroughly studied group. In particular, the productivity-related succession of the fish fauna from a dominance of percids to a dominance of cyprinids has been well developed for European conditions, while, for example, North American studies have focused more on the shift from salmonids to percids (Colby *et al.*, 1972). The difference in focus between North American and European studies may also arise because centrarchids, naturally lacking in European systems, constitute an important component of the fish fauna in many North American lakes (Wermer and Hall, 1988).

Despite this divergence there are also similarities. For example, a figure similar to Fig. 19.1 with respect to the productivity-related succession of the fish fauna has been suggested for the Great Lakes area, with the exception that centrarchids also increase monotonically with productivity, as do cyprinids (Oglesby *et al.*, 1987).

ACKNOWLEDGEMENTS

I thank Sebastian Diehl and Ian J. Winfield for valuable comments on a previous draft of this chapter. Financial support for my research reported herein has been received from the Swedish Natural Science Research Council, the Swedish National Environmental Protection Board, The Fisheries Board of Sweden and the Swedish Council for Forestry and Agricultural Research.

REFERENCES

Ali, M. A., Ryder, R. A. and Anctil, M. (1977) Photoreceptors and visual pigments as related to behavioural responses and preferred habitats of perches (*Perca* spp.) and pikeperches (*Stizostedion* spp.). *J. Fish. Res. Bd Can.*, **34**, 1475–80.

Andersson, G. (1984). The role of fish in lake ecosystems – and in limnology, in *Interaksjoner mellan trofiske nivåer i ferskvann* (eds S. Bosheim and M. Nicholls), Nordisk limnologisymposium, University of Oslo, 1984, pp. 189–97.

Andersson, G., Bergren, H. and Hamrin, S. (1975) Lake Trummen restoration project. III. Zooplankton, macrobenthos and fish. *Verh. Internat. Verein. Limnol.*, **19**, 1097–106.

Bergman, E. (1987) Temperature-dependent differences in foraging ability of two percids: perch (*Perca fluviatilis*) and ruffe (*Gymnocephalus cernuum*). *Env. Biol. Fishes*, **19**, 45–54.

Bergman, E. (1988) Foraging abilities and niche breadths of two percids, *Perca fluviatilis* and *Gymnocephalus cernuum* under different environmental conditions. *J. Anim. Ecol.*, **57**, 434–53.

Bíró, P. and Garádi, P. (1974) Investigations on the growth and population structure of bream (*Abramis brama* L.) at different areas of Lake Balaton. The assessment of mortality and production. *Annal. Biol. Tihany*, **41**, 153–79.

Bohl, E. (1980) Diel pattern of pelagic distribution and feeding in planktivorous fish. *Oecologia*, **44**, 368–75.

Brabrand, Å. (1984) Microhabitat segregation between bream (*Abramis brama* (L.)) and white bream (*Blicca bjoerkna* (L.)) in a mesotrophic lake, SE Norway. *Pol. Arch. Hydrobiol.*, **31**, 99–108.

Brabrand, Å. (1985) Food of roach (*Rutilus rutilus*) and ide (*Leuciscus idus*): significance of diet shift for interspecific competition in omnivorous fishes. *Oecologia*, **66**, 461–7.

Brett, J. R., Shelbourn, J. E. and Shoop, C. T. (1969) Growth rate and body composition of fingerling sockeye salmon, *Oncorhynchus nerka*, in relation to temperature and ration size. *J. Fish. Res. Bd Can.*, **26**, 2263–94.

Burrough, R. J., Bregazzi, P. R. and Kennedy, C. R. (1979) Interspecific dominance amongst three spcies of coarse fish in Slapton Ley, Devon. *J. Fish Biol.*, **15**, 535–44.

Colby, P. J., Spangler, G. R., Hurley, D. A. and McCombie, A. M. (1972) Effects of eutrophication on salmonid communities in oligotrophic lakes. *J. Fish. Res. Bd Can.*, **29**, 1602–12.

Craig, J. F. (1978) A study of the food and feeding of perch, *Perca fluviatilis* L. in Windermere. *Freshwat. Biol.*, **8**, 59–68.

Diehl, S. (1968) Foraging efficiency of three freshwater fish: effects of structural complexity and light. *Oikos*, **53**, 207–14.

Disler, N. N. and Smirnov, S. A. (1977) Sensory organs of the lateral-line canal system in two percids and their importance in behaviour. *J. Fish. Res. Bd Can.*, **34**, 1492–503.

Elliott, J. M. (1976) The growth rate of brown trout (*Salmo trutta*) fed on reduced rations. *J. Anim. Ecol.*, **44**, 823–42.

Fish, G. R. (1960) The comparative activity of some digestive enzymes in the alimentary canal of Tilapia and Perch. *Hydrobiologia*, **15**, 161–78.

Fretwell, S. D. (1977) The regulation of plant communities by the food chains exploiting them. *Perspect. Biol. Med.*, **20**, 169–85.

Goldspink, C. R. (1979) The population density, growth rate and production of roach *Rutilus rutilus* (L.) in Tjeukemmer, The Netherlands. *J. Fish. Biol.*, **15**, 473–98.

Grimm, N. B. (1988) Feeding dynamics, nitrogen budgets, and ecosystem role of a desert stream omnivore, *Agosia chrysogaster* (Pisces: Cyprinidae). *Env. Biol. Fishes*, **21**, 143–52.

Gumaá, S. A. (1978) The food and feeding habits of young perch, *Perca fluviatilis*, in Windermere. *Freshwat. Biol.*, **8**, 177–87.

Hartmann, J. and Nümann, W. (1977) Percids of Lake Constance, a lake undergoing eutrophication. *J. Fish. Res. Bd Can.*, **34**, 1670–7.

Hofer, W. M. R. and Wieser, W. (1987) Diet spectra and resource partitioning in the larvae and juveniles of three species and six cohorts of cyprinids from a subalpine lake. *Oecologia*, **71**, 388–96.

Holcik, J. (1977) Changes in the fish community of Klicava reservoir with particular reference to Eurasian perch (*Perch fluviatilis*), 1957–1972. *J. Fish. Res. Bd Can.*, **34**, 1734–47.

Johansson. L. (1987) Experimental evidence for interactive habitat segregation between roach (*Rutilus rutilus*) and rudd (*Scardinius erythrophthalmus*). *Oecologia*, **73**, 21–7.

Johansson, L. and Persson, L. (1986) The fish community of temperate, eutrophic lakes, in *Carbon Dynamics of Eutrophic, Temperate Lakes: The Structure and Functions of the Pelagic Environment* (eds. B. Riemann and M. Søndergaard), Elsevier, Amsterdam, pp. 237–66.

Kapoor, B. G., Smit, H. and Verighina, I. A. (1975) The alimentary canal and digestion in teleosts, in *Advances in Marine Biology*, Vol. 13 (eds F. Russell and C. M. Younge), Academic Press, London, pp. 109–239.

Kempe, O. (1962) The growth of roach (*Leuciscus rutilus* L.) in some Swedish lakes. *Rep. Inst. Freshwat. Res. Drottningholm*, **44**, 42–104.

Kerr, S. R. (1971) Analysis of laboratory experiments on growth efficiency of fishes. *J. Fish. Res. Bd Can.*, **28**, 801–8.

Kitchell, J. F., Johnson, M. G., Minns, C. K., Loftus, K. H., Greig, L. and Olver, C. H. (1977) Percid habitat: the river analogy. *J. Fish. Res. Bd Can.*, **34**, 1959–63.

Lammens, E. H. R. R. (1985) A test of a model for planktivorous filter feeding by bream, *Abramis brama*. *Env. Biol. Fishes*, **13**, 289–96.

Lammens, E. H. R. R. Densen, W. L. T van and Vijverberg, J. (1986) The role of predation in the community structure of fish and zooplankton in Dutch hypertrophic lakes, a comparative study, in *Interactions between fishes and the structure of fish communities in Dutch shallow, eutrophic lakes*, E. H. R. R. Lammens, PhD thesis, University of Wageningen, pp. 82–98.

Lammens, E. H. R. R., Geursen, J. and McGillavry, P. J. (1987) Diet shifts, feeding efficiency and coexistence of bream *Abramis brama*, roach *Rutilus rutilus* and white bream *Blicca bjoerkna* in eutrophicated lakes. *Proc. V Congr. Europ. Ichthyol., Stockholm, 1985*, 153–62.

Larkin, P. A. (1956) Interspecific competition and population control in freshwater fish. *J. Fish. Res. Bd Can.*, **13**, 327–40.

Leach, J. H., Johnson, M. G., Kelso, J. R. M., Hartmann, J., Nümann, W. and Entz, B. (1977) Responses of percid fishes and their habitats to eutrophication. *J. Fish. Res. Bd Can.*, **34**, 1964–71.

Lessmark, O. (1983) Competition between perch (*Perca fluviatilis*) and roach (*Rutilus rutilus*) in South Swedish lakes, unpubl. PhD thesis, University of Lund, 172 pp.

Lodge, D. M., Barko, J. W., Strayer, D., Melack, J. M., Mittelbach, G. G., Howarth, R. W., Menge, B. and Titus, J. E. (1988) Spatial heterogeneity and habitat interactions in lake communities, in *Complex Interactions in Lake Communities* (ed. S. C. Carpenter), Springer Verlag, NY etc., pp. 183–208.

Löffler, H. (1984) Zur Ökologie des Brachsen (*Abramis brama* (L.)) im Bodensee. *Schweiz. Z. Hydrobiol.*, **46**, 147–62.

Mark, W., Hofer, R. and Wieser, W. (1987) Diet spectra and resource partitioning in the larvae and juveniles of three species and six cohorts of cyprinids from a subalpine lake. *Oecologia*, **71**, 388–96.

Mittelbach, G. G. (1981) Foraging efficiency and body size: a study of optimal diet and habitat use by bluegills. *Ecology*, **62**, 1370–86.

Mittelbach, G. G. and Chesson, P. L. (1987) Predation risk: indirect effects on fish populations, in *Predation: Direct and Indirect Impacts on Aquatic Communities* (eds W. C. Kerfoot and A. Sih), University Press of New England, Hannover and London, pp. 315–32.

Mittelbach, G. G., Osenberg, C. W. and Leibold, M. A. (1988) Trophic relations and ontogenetic niche shifts in aquatic systems, in *Size-structured Populations – Ecology and Evolution* (eds B. Ebenman and L. Persson), Springer Verlag, Berlin, etc., pp. 218–35.

Niederholzer, R. and Hofer, R. (1980) The feeding of roach (*Rutilus rutilus* L.) and rudd (*Scardinius erythrophthalmus* L.) 1. Studies on natural populations. *Ekol. pol.*, **28**, 45–59.

Nümann, W. (1972) The Bodensee: effects of exploitation and eutrophication on the salmonid community. *J. Fish. Res. Bd Can.*, **29**, 833–47.

Nyberg, P. (1979) Production and food consumption of perch, *Perca fluviatilis* L., in two Swedish forest lakes. *Rep. Inst. Freshwat. Res. Drottningholm*, **58**, 140–57.

Oglesby, R. T., Leach, J. H. and Forney. J. (1987) Potential *Stizostedion* yield as a function of chlorophyll concentration with special reference to Lake Erie. *Can. J. Fish. Aquat. Sci.*, **44**, 166–70.

Oksanen, L., Fretwell, S. D., Arruda, J. and Niemelä. P. (1981) Exploitation ecosystems in gradients of primary productivity. *Am. Nat.*, **118**, 240–61.

Paine. R. T. (1966) Food web complexity and species diversity. *Am. Nat.*, **100**, 65–76.

Persson, L. (1983a) Food consumption and competition between age classes in a perch *Perca fluviatilis* population in a shallow eutrophic lake. *Oikos*, **40**, 197–207.

Persson, L. (1983b) Food consumption and the significance of detritus and algae to intraspecific competition in roach *Rutilus rutilus* in a shallow eutrophic lake. *Oikos*, **41**, 118–25.

Persson, L. (1983c) Effects of intra- and interspecific competition on dynamics and size structure of a perch *Perca fluviatilis* and a roach *Rutilus rutilus* population. *Oikos*, **41**, 126–32.

Persson, L. (1986) Effects of reduced interspecific competition on resource utilization in perch (*Perca fluviatilis*). *Ecology*, **67**, 355–64.

Persson L. (1987a) The effects of resource availability and distribution on size class interactions in perch *Perca fluviatilis*. *Oikos*, 148–60.

Persson, L. (1987b) Competition-induced diet shift in young-of-the-year perch (*Perca fluviatilis*): an experimental test of resource limitation. *Env. Biol. Fishes*, **19**, 235–9.

Persson, L. (1987c) Effects of habitat and season on competitive interactions between roach (*Rutilus rutilus*) and perch (*Perca fluviatilis*). *Oecologia*, **73**, 170–7.

Persson, L. (1988) Asymmetries in competitive and predatory interactions in fish populations, in *Size-structured Populations – Ecology and Evolution* (eds B. Ebenman and L. Persson), Springer Verlag, Berlin etc., pp. 203–18.

Persson, L. and Greenberg, L. A. (1990) Competitive juvenile bottlenecks: the perch (*Perca fluviatilis*)–roach (*Rutilus rutilus*) interaction. *Ecology*, **71**, 44–56.

Persson, L., Andersson, G., Hamrin, S. F. and Johansson, L. (1988) Predator regulation and primary productivity along the productivity gradient of temperate lake ecosystems, in *Complex Interactions in Lake Communities* (ed. S. C. Carpenter), Springer Verlag, NY etc., pp. 45–65.

Phillips, G. L., Eminson, D. and Moss, B. (1978) A mechanism to account for macrophyte decline in progressively eutrophicated freshwater. *Aquat. Bot.*, **4**, 103–26.

Popava, O. A. and Sytina, L. A. (1977) Food and feeding relations of Eurasian perch (*Perca fluviatilis*) and pikeperch (*Stizostedion lucioperca*) in various waters of the USSR. *J. Fish. Res. Bd Can.*, **34**, 1559–70.

Prejs, A. (1984) Herbivory by temperate freshwater fishes and its consequences. *Env. Biol. Fishes*, **10**, 281–96.

Riemann B., Søndergaard, M., Persson, L. and Johansson, L. (1986) Carbon metabolism and community regulation in eutrophic, temperate lakes, in *Carbon Dynamics of Eutrophic Temperate Lakes: The Structure and Functions of the Pelagic Environment* (eds B. Riemann and M. Søndergaard), Elsevier, Amsterdam, pp. 267–80.

Rundberg, H. (1977) Trends in harvest of pike perch (*Stizostedion lucioperca*), Eurasian perch (*Perca fluviatilis*), and nothern pike (*Esox lucius*) and associated environmental changes in lakes Mälaren and Hjälmaren, 1914–1974. *J. Fish Res. Bd Can.*, **34**, 1720–4.

Sand-Jensen, K. (1979) Balancen mellan autotrofe komponenter i tempererade søer med forskellig næringsbelastning. (The balance between autotrophic components in temperate lakes with different nutrient loading.) *Vatten*, 2/80, 104–15 (In Danish with Englih summary).

Sorokin, J. I. (1968) The use of ^{14}C in the study of nutrition of aquatic animals. *Mitt. int. Verein. theor. angew. Limnol.*, **16**.

Sumari, O. (1971) Structure of perch populations in some ponds in Finland. *Annls. zool. fenni.* **8**, 406–21.

Svärdson, G. (1976) Interspecific population dominance in fish communities. *Rep. Inst. Freshwat. Res. Drottningholm.* **56**, 144–71.

Tatrai, I. (1980) About feeding conditions of bream, (*Abramis brama* L.) in Lake Balaton. *Dev. Hydrobiol.*, 81–6.

Thorpe, J. E. (1977) Daily ration of adult perch, *Perca fluviatilis* L., in Loch Leven, Scotland. *J. Fish Biol.*, **11**, 55–68.

Tonn, W. M., Magnuson, J. J. Rask, M. and Toivonen, J. Intercontinental comparison of small-lake fish assemblages: the balance between local and regional processes. *Am. Nat.* (in press).

Tonn, W. M., Paszkowski, C. A. and Moermond, T. C. (1986) Competition in *Umbra–Perca* fish assemblages: experimental and field evidence. *Oecologia*, **69**, 126–33.

Townsend, S. R. and Risebrow, A. J. (1982) The influence of light level on the functional response of a zooplanktivorous fish. *Oecologia*, **53**, 293–5.

Werner, E. E. (1977) Species packing and niche complementarity in three sunfishes. *Am. Nat.*, **111**, 553–78.

Werner, E. E. (1986) Species interactions in freshwater fish communities, in *Community Ecology* (eds J. Diamond and T. Case), Harper and Row, NY, pp. 344–58.

Werner, E. E. and Gilliam, J. (1984) The ontogenetic niche and species interactions in size-structured populations. *A. Rev. Ecol. Syst.*, **15**, 393–425.

Werner, E. E. and Hall, D. J. (1979) foraging efficiency and habitat switching in competing sunfishes. *Ecology*, **60**, 256–64.

Werner. E. E. and Hall, D. J. (1988) Ontogenetic habitat shifts in the bluegill sunfish (*Lepomis macrochirus*). The foraging rate–predation risk tradeoff. *Ecology*, **69**, 1352–66.

Wetzel, R. G. (1979) The role of the littoral zone and detritus in lake metabolism. *Arch. Hydrobiol. Beih. Ergebn. Limnol.*, **13**, 145–61.

Willemsen, J. (1977) Population dynamics of percids in Lake Ijssel and some smaller lakes in The Netherlands. *J. Fish. Res. Bd Can.*, **34**, 1710–19.

Winfield, I. J (1986) The influence of simulated aquatic macrophytes on the zooplankton consumption rate of juvenile roach, *Rutilus rutilus*, rudd, *Scardinius erythrophthalmus*, and perch, *Perch fluviatilis*. *J. Fish Biol.*, **29**, (Supp. A), 37–48.

Chapter twenty

The role of cyprinids in ecosystems

I. J. Winfield and C. R. Townsend

20.1   INTRODUCTION

The study of fresh waters from an ecosystem perspective has a long history, but it is only recently that fishes have become truly incorporated within the scope of limnology (Andersson, 1984). This development has greatly increased our understanding of the functioning of freshwater ecosystems, demonstrating amongst many other things the crucial role that fish play in determining zooplankton community structure and abundance. More recently, field-based studies have been complemented by experimental laboratory investigations of the foraging behaviour of fishes, foreshadowed by the work of Ivlev (1961), resulting in a discipline in which field observations, experimental manipulations and theoretical models have been profitably integrated. This chapter reviews our knowledge of the roles of cyprinids in ecosystems, focusing on their interactions with the rest of the biota.

20.2   INTERACTIONS WITH PLANTS

The nature of cyprinid–plant interactions

Although there are considerable problems associated with the efficient utilization of plant material as food, a few cyprinids feed extensively on algae or higher plants. In addition, higher plants may interact with cyprinids through their provision of physical structure.

Algae

Phytoplankton
In addition to the problem of the digestion-resistance of phytoplankton cells, a phytoplankton-based diet requires specializations to cope with their small

size which makes capture very difficult. As a result, very few cyprinids are obligate phytoplanktivores.

Phytoplanktivorous cichlids, which possess a distinct stomach with low pH, can achieve an assimilation efficiency of 70–80% for phytoplankton (Moriarty, 1973), but values reported for the truly phytoplanktivorous cyprinids are significantly lower. Miura and Wang (1985) found that 35% of chlorophyll *a* remains after passage through the intestine of silver carp, *Hypophthalmichthys molitrix*, while for bighead carp, *Aristichthys nobilis*, which feeds on larger cells, the figure is 50%. After passage through the gut of fish feeding on *Anabaena spiroides* and *Microcystis aeruginosa*, the algae showed 22% of the maximum gross production per unit of chlorophyll *a* of those before passage in silver carp and 103% in bighead carp. An enhancement of algal growth following passage through the guts of grazers has been observed elsewhere, for example in *Sphaerocystis schroeteri* being grazed by *Daphnia magna* (Porter, 1976), and may be due to nutrient uptake during passage. This effect could explain the observations of Opuszynski (1979) and Milstein *et al.* (1985 a, b) that experimental stocking of fish ponds with silver carp results in increases in primary productivity, and a reduction in herbivorous zooplankton. In another experiment, Milstein *et al.* (1988) have shown a differential effect of silver carp on plankton community composition: a decrease in netplankton (phyto- and zooplankton) and an increase in the minute nannoplankton which passes through the filter apparatus of the fish.

Facultative phytoplanktivores such as roach, *Rutilus rutilus*, and bleak, *Alburnus alburnus*, feed on phytoplankton, or their newly-deposited aggregations, only seasonally in the absence of alternative food (Persson, 1983; Vollestad, 1985). Consequently they are less likely to affect these prey populations directly, although this food source may be important in their own competitive relationships (Chapter 19).

Periphyton

While its utilization probably involves assimilation problems similar to those of phytoplankton, more cyprinids and other fish seem able to use periphyton as at least an occasional food source. For example, filamentous algae (*Spirogyra* sp.) dominated the midsummer diet of three cyprinids (*Pachychilon pictum*, *Leuciscus cephalus* and *Rutilus rubilio*) in Skadar Lake (Skadarsko Jezero), Yugoslavia (Kitchell *et al.*, 1978), although no investigation was made of the consequent effect on periphyton populations.

The minnow *Campostoma anomalum* is widespread and abundant in streams in parts of the United States, where it forages almost exclusively on diatoms and filamentous algae. Power and Matthews (1983) found that stream pools containing *Campostoma* had only small populations of attached algae, while pools devoid of this cyprinid showed luxuriant growth (principally *Spirogyra* sp. and *Rhizoclonium* sp.). Experimental manipulations (Power *et al.*, 1985) confirmed that this relationship was causal. The same studies revealed that the distributions of *Campostoma* themselves were strongly influenced by piscivorous bass (*Micropterus salmoides* and *M. punctualatus*), although piscivorous birds may also have had some influence (Power, 1987). Thus the effects of this cyprinid on its prey populations are strongly influenced by its own predators.

Power and Matthews (1983) concluded that *Campostoma* is an important factor contributing to pool-to-pool variation in periphyton in small streams of the central and eastern United States. Furthermore, Power (1984) has also shown that in a stream in Central America, where the Cyprinidae are geographically absent, armoured catfish of the family Loricariidae have a similar impact on attached algae. Perhaps similar interactions involving cyprinids occur in European streams, and perhaps lakes, although no investigations have yet been carried out.

Higher plants

Grazing effects

In the context of macrophyte-consuming fishes, the grass carp or white amur, *Ctenopharyngodon idella*, is undoubtedly one of the most studied cyprinids. However, with few exceptions this work has concentrated on the use of the species in weed control (Europe, Fowler, 1985; North America, Terrell and Terrell, 1975). Although grass carp can consume their own weight in macrophytes per day, and excrete large amounts of phosphorus and nitrogen while doing so (Stanley, 1974), no studies have addressed their effects on nutrient dynamics in their natural habitat (but under the unnatural conditions of fish ponds they have produced algal blooms – Prowse, 1969). The impact of grass carp on its prey populations is not necessarily negative: ingested seeds of *Najas marina* and *Ruppia maritima* survived digestion, showing increased germination rates (Agami and Waisel, 1988). Grass carp may thus play a role in the natural distribution of some macrophytes.

The common carp, *Cyprinus carpio*, has also received considerable attention, mainly as a result of impacts on macrophytes following its introduction to new habitats outside Europe. In experiments in southern France, Crivelli (1983) found that, although they fed mainly on benthic animals, carp destroyed plant beds. The mechanism of this interaction was primarily physical disturbance, and the damage was proportional to individual size, a relationship which explains why effects are most dramatic in larger-growing introduced populations. Introductions of carp to Australia have greatest impact on shallow-rooted and soft-leaved vegetation such as *Potomageton* spp. (Fletcher *et al.*, 1985).

Direct grazing is the primary mechanism in interactions between higher plants and truly herbivorous fishes. While many littoral-zone species of European lakes may consume some plant material during their lives it is only the cyprinids roach, rudd, *Scardinius erythrophthalmus*, and ide, *Leuciscus idus*, that eat significant amounts (Prejs, 1984). In eutrophic Polish lakes, Prejs and Jackowska (1978) found that macrophytes accounted for 35–90% by weight of the diet of adult roach, and 85–99% of the diet of adult rudd. Higher plants are also important in the diets of roach and rudd in several Tyrolean lakes in Austria (Niederholzer and Hofer, 1980), and in the diets of roach and ide in a mesotrophic Norwegian lake (Brabrand, 1985). Conservative estimates of the annual consumption of plants by roach and rudd in Lake Mikolajskie amounted to *c.* 1800 kg of submerged macrophytes and *c.* 3809 kg of filamentous algae per hectare of littoral zone, and *c.* 1237 kg of macrophytes in Lake Warniak (Prejs, 1984). Hofer and Niederholzer (1980) consider that only the contents of plant cells which have been mechanically broken can be digested, and thus large amounts of plant material must be consumed, much of which is returned to the environment in a degraded form. We shall return to the nutrient-mobilizing effects of such grazing activities (p. 565).

We know of only one study that has attempted to show by experiment that cyprinid grazing pressure can influence macrophyte populations. Using pond compartments, Hansson *et al.* (1987) subjected *Anacharis canadensis* to zero, low and high grazing pressures from rudd. In the zero and low grazing pressure treatments, macrophyte biomass increased significantly, but when rudd were stocked at a level similar to natural densities of cyprinids in eutrophic waters, no increase was observed (Fig. 20.1). Under these experimental conditions, a common European herbivorous cyprinid was able to affect the abundance of a higher plant, and thus may be an important factor in determining population abundance in the wild.

Structural effects
Resource partitioning by habitat is a common feature of community organization in freshwater fishes (Werner, 1984), and one important way in which habitats differ is in the nature and degree of the physical structure they contain. In lacustrine habitats, such structure is typically provided by higher plants, and several studies have shown that this can offer refuge to the prey of a variety of cyprinids. Examples include young fish (roach and rudd, Winfield, 1986; dace, *Leuciscus leuciscus*, Scott, 1987) eating zooplankton, and older fish feeding on snails, corixids and chironomid larvae (carp and goldfish, *Carassius auratus*, Covich and Knezevic, 1978; roach, Oscarson, 1987; bream, *Abramis brama*, Diehl, 1988). These interactions are discussed in greater detail in Chapter 19.

In addition, higher plants may have the beneficial effect of providing cyprinids with a refuge from the attentions of their own predators. Peirson *et al.* (1985) found the attack efficiencies of pike, *Esox lucius*, feeding on roach to be significantly reduced in the presence of dense artificial submerged macrophytes, although this effect was not observed when rudd were the prey.

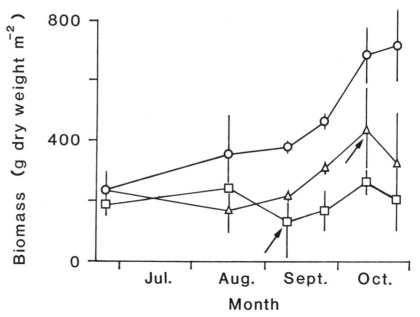

Fig. 20.1 Biomass development of the higher plant *Anacharis canadensis* (means ± 1S.D.) in experimental ponds in Sweden stocked with zero (○), low (△) and high (□) densities of herbivorous rudd, *Scardinius erythrophthalmus*. Arrows indicate the first appearance of epiphytic algae in the low and high rudd treatments, but note that epiphytes never developed in the absence of fish (p. 555) (after Hansson *et al.*, 1987).

Hart and Hamrin (1988) also found rudd to remain vulnerable to pike under varied conditions of structure, even when it was high enough to impair the performances of largemouth bass, *Macropterus salmoides*, in similar experiments with non-cyprinid prey (Savino and Stein, 1982; Anderson, 1984). The influence of the structural effects of higher plants on the efficiency of pike feeding on cyprinids and other species is thus fundamentally different from that involving a chasing predator such as the largemouth bass.

20.3   INTERACTIONS WITH INVERTEBRATES

The nature of cyprinid–invertebrate interactions

Herbivorous and piscivorous cyprinids are relatively rare; the vast majority of species feed extensively on invertebrates. This is most marked during the first few weeks or months of life when, owing to size and morphological constraints, many cyprinids pass through a common zooplanktivorous stage (Chapter 12).

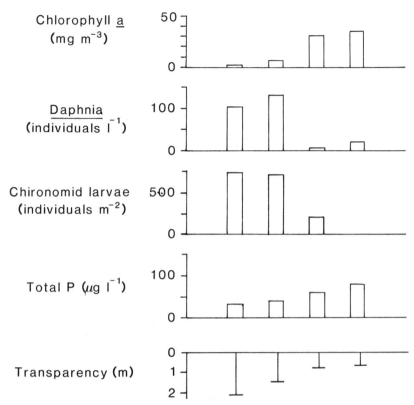

Fig. 20.2 The effects of the cyprinids roach and bream, and the non-cyprinid perch, on phytoplankton (chlorophyll *a*, p. 564), zooplankton (*Daphnia*, p. 558), macroinvertebrates (chironomid larvae, p. 559), nutrients (total phosphorus, p. 564), and an abiotic parameter (transparency, p. 564), revealed by enclosure experiments in the eutrophic Lake Trummen, Sweden (after Andersson, 1984). Columns, from left: no fish; perch, *Perca fluviatilus*; roach, *Rutilus rutilus*; bream, *Abramis brama*.

Zooplankton

One of the first demonstrations of the effect of fish on zooplankton populations was performed by Hrbacek *et al.* (1961). Predation pressure from the cyprinids *Rhodeus sericeus*, *Leucaspius delineatus* and *Gobio gobio* selectively removed larger cladocerans such as *Daphnia hyalina*. Many subsequent studies have documented this relationship in a wide variety of water bodies, and have done much to elucidate the mechanisms involved.

By the experimental manipulation of a lake in the United States, Elser and Carpenter (1988) were able to show that predation pressure from the cyprinids redbelly dace, *Phoxinus eos*, and finescale dace, *P. neogaeus*, and the non-cyprinid central mudminnow, *Umbra limi*, strongly influenced the zoo-

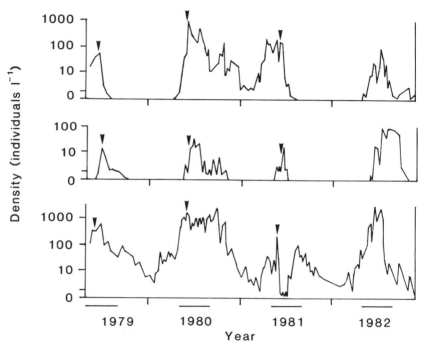

Fig. 20.3 Densities of the three principal species of planktonic Cladocera from May 1979 to November 1982 in Alderfen Broad, England. Mean body size decreases amongst these species in the order (top) *Daphnia hyalina*, (middle) *Ceriodaphnia quadrangula*, and (bottom) *Bosmina longirostris*. Arrowheads indicate when each species became a significant component of the diet of underyearling roach; horizontal lines represent the summer months (May to August inclusive) (after Cryer *et al.*, 1986).

plankton community. The removal of these 'minnows' resulted in an increase in large-bodied cladocerans such as *Daphnia pulex* and *Holopedium gibberum*. Similarly, cladoceran populations were depressed in experimental ponds stocked with fathead minnows, *Pimephales promelas*, and brook sticklebacks, *Culaea inconstans* (Spencer and King, 1984). In Europe, experimental enclosure work in the eutrophic Lake Trummen in southern Sweden (Andersson *et al.*, 1978; Andersson, 1984) revealed that roach and bream depressed *Daphnia* populations to a greater degree than the non-cyprinid perch, *Perca fluviatilis* (Fig. 20.2). A further example of the influences of cyprinids comes from Alderfen Broad, a small eutrophic lake in England where the dominant zooplanktivore is young roach. Cryer *et al.* (1986) and Townsend (1988) followed population changes in predator and prey over a period of several years and found that during summers of high roach recruitment, the larger planktonic cladocerans (*Daphnia hyalina* and *Ceriodaphina quadrangula*) decreased in mean body size and were driven almost to extinction (Fig. 20.3). Furthermore, the sequence of decline of cladocerans observed when underyearling roach were abundant, with the large species declining before the smaller, could be linked to the timing of their first appearance in the diet of underyearling roach (Fig. 20.3). Enclosure experiments confirmed that population densities and mean lengths of cladocerans are reduced in the presence of young roach. Roach can also influence the dynamics of such small-bodied cladocerans as *Bosmina longirostris* (Stenson, 1976; Henrikson *et al.*, 1980; Hessen and Nilssen, 1986), an ability which may be shared by other, as yet unstudied, cyprinids.

In contrast to the numerous investigations demonstrating the effects of cyprinids on cladocerans, their direct influences on copepod populations have been less frequently reported. This is due in part to the greater powers of escape shown by the Copepoda which are extremely important in determining their selectivity by fish (Chapter 12). However, Winfield and Townsend (1983) found that the cyclopoid copepod *Cyclops vicinus* loses some of its escape ability when it develops egg sacs, thus making it more susceptible in the laboratory to predation by roach and bream. To our knowledge, no field studies of this cyprinid–copepod interaction have been carried out, but predation pressure from threespine sticklebacks, *Gasterosteus aculeatus*, may influence the distribution of ovigerous individuals of the calanoid copepod *Eurytemora hirundoides* (Vuorinen *et al.*, 1983).

Macroinvertebrates

Studies of the effects of fish on macroinvertebrate populations are at an early stage and most have been carried out in North America or have addressed fish species other than cyprinids. In a study of the effects of *Lepomis* sunfishes, Mittelbach (1988) showed that this predation is typically strongly size-selective, and thus produces a very complex effect as important large macroinvertebrate predators may be removed, thus reducing their own predation pressure within the macroinvertebrate community. In a European lake study, Henrikson (1988) was able to implicate another member of the Perciformes, the perch, in the intra-pond distribution of larvae of an odonate dragonfly, *Leucorrhina dubia*. Thus non-cyprinid fish species have considerable effects on macroinvertebrates, ranging from influences on the behaviour of individuals through to the abundance and composition of entire communities.

The few studies of cyprinids in this context suggest that they have similar influences. In a small oligotrophic lake in Sweden, predation pressure by introduced roach affected the abundance and distribution of three species of corixids (Oscarson, 1987), while in the laboratory the presence of chub, *Leuciscus cephalus*, inhibits feeding behaviour of the larval odonate *Ischnura elegans*, and probably decreases growth rate and survival (Heads, 1986). In the enclosure experiments of Andersson *et al.* (1978), roach and bream depressed the densities of oligochaetes (Tubificidae) and chironomids (mainly *Chironomus plumosus and Tanypus* sp.). Furthermore (Fig. 20.2), like their effect on zooplankton, their influence was more marked than that of perch (Andersson, 1984). Adult bream also depress benthic populations of large larval chironomids (*Polypedilum nubeculosum, Einfeldia carbonaria* and *Chironomus plumosus*) under certain conditions in a eutrophic lake, Tjeuke Meer, in The Netherlands (Lammens *et al.*, 1985).

Although much remains to be learnt of an extremely complex interaction, the effect of cyprinids on macroinvertebrates seems likely to be considerable and must be one of the priorities of future research.

20.4   INTERACTIONS WITH VERTEBRATES

The nature of cyprinid–vertebrate interactions

As vertebrates are larger than the invertebrate animals previously considered, and are much more similar to cyprinids themselves, interactions with them involve more than just predation. In these instances, cyprinids may also act as competitors or even prey.

Cyprinids as predators

Piscivory is relatively rare in the Cyprinidae, particularly in the North American and European species which have been most widely investigated (Chapter 12), and so their interactions with prey fish populations have been little studied. One exception is the chubs (*Leuciscus* in Europe and *Semotilus* in North America), which as adults can be abundant piscivores in temperate streams. While the European chub remains relatively unstudied in this context, the creek chub, *Semotilus atromaculatus*, of North America has been the subject of several investigations.

In an experimental study, adult creek chub influenced the distribution of conspecific juveniles and adult blacknose dace, *Rhinichthys atratulus*, another common cyprinid of headwater streams in eastern North America (Fraser and Cerri, 1982). However, the chub only restricted the distribution of their prey during the night, because during daylight the chub retired into refuges (Fraser, 1983). Cerri (1983) studied the mechanisms of the *Semotilus–Rhinichthys* interaction and showed that fewer prey were captured under bright light, because chub stayed in refuges and the dace schooled, and more in the dark, when the chub became more active and the dace were unable to school (schooling is an important defence of cyprinids generally, Chapter 18). At the intermediate stage of twilight, predation rates were higher than during the day because of the increased activity of chub, but the dace were still able to school and so offered at least some defence.

Thus the activities of piscivorous creek chub influence the distribution of their prey, although in contrast to the more extensive effects of centrarchid basses in streams (p. 554) and ponds (Werner *et al.*, 1983), this effect only occurs during the night. The susceptibility of cyprinids themselves to predation will be addressed later (p. 562).

Cyprinids as competitors

Given the abilities of cyprinids to depress prey populations, it is not surprising that exploitative competition is a major way in which they interact with other fishes, and that they are often competitively dominant, particularly in eutrophic lakes. This large and important aspect of their interactions is dealt with in detail elsewhere (Chapter 19) and will not be considered further here.

However, cyprinids may also compete with waterfowl. Eriksson (1979) found that the distribution among oligotrophic Swedish lakes of fledged goldeneye, *Bucephala clangula*, a benthivorous diving duck, was negatively correlated with the abundance of fish, mainly roach and the non-cyprinid perch. Mallard, *Anas platyrhynchos*, an omnivorous dabbling duck, also suffered from the negative effects of fish, including the cyprinids roach and rudd (Pehrsson, 1984); again, experiments showed that competition for food was the mechanism responsible. In more eutrophic conditions in England, roach and bream adversely affected feeding conditions for mallard ducklings in enclosure experiments (Hill *et al.*, 1987), while in North America, breeding mallards were rare in ponds stocked with fathead minnows and brook sticklebacks (Spencer and King, 1984), although in this case indirect interactions rather than direct competition for food was thought to be the mechanism responsible (p. 565).

Two studies have implied that cyprinids may also influence long-term trends in waterfowl populations. Since 1970, the numbers of waterfowl, including tufted duck, *Aythya fuligula*, on lakes in southern Sweden have declined significantly and Andersson (1981) has suggested that a synchronous increase in the abundance of cyprinids, principally roach and bream, is at least partly responsible. Andersson suggests that in addition to direct competition for macroinvertebrates with benthivorous waterfowl, the cyprinids may also exert an adverse influence on herbivorous ducks by indirectly reducing the abundance of higher plants and promoting eutrophication (Section 20.5). A more recent study by Winfield *et al.*, (1989) has documented a 'natural experiment' addressing potential competitive interactions between roach and tufted duck in the eutrophic Lough Neagh in Northern Ireland. In the early 1970s, the roach was introduced to this lake and their dramatic population increase was accompanied by an obvious decline in the numbers of overwintering tufted duck. Furthermore, a subsequent decline in the roach population, due to extensive infestation by the tapeworm *Ligula intestinalis*, has been accompanied by a recovery in the numbers of tufted ducks to the levels seen before the roach arrived. As Lough Neagh had already been eutrophic for many years before these changes were observed, and higher plants have always been scarce due to high turbidity and exposure conditions, it is clear that of Andersson's three mechanisms, only direct competition for macroinvertebrates could have produced the observed changes.

Cyprinids as prey

The Cyprinidae are widespread, abundant, and often very productive (Chapter 16). Furthermore, in contrast to many other fishes, they typically possess few morphological defences such as armour, spines, or toxins, and their relatively small adult size means that they often cannot find a refuge in size from the attentions of predators. Many species, such as *Campostoma* in the streams studied by Power *et al.*, are thus "soft, thin fish that remained vulnerable... throughout their lives" (Power, 1987). Although the Cyprinidae have developed protective shoaling to a high degree (Chapter 18), and so are not completely defenceless, they would appear to be more liable to predation than many other fishes. In conjunction with their high productivity, one might therefore expect them to form a major part of the diet of many piscivores.

In North America, the larger centrarchids such as bass, *Micropterus* spp, are widespread piscivores, and cyprinids are indeed important components of their diet (Kramer and Smith, 1962). Moreover, they are usually the preferred prey. Lewis *et al.* (1961) found that largemouth bass consumed golden shiners, *Notemigonus crysoleucas*, more readily than a range of centrarchid and ictalurid species, while Webb (1986) found that largemouth bass preyed on fathead minnow more efficiently than on other largemouth bass, bluegill sunfish, *Lepomis macrochirus*, or tiger musky, *Esox masquinongy* × *E. lucius* hybrids. The *Esox* genus is another very important group of freshwater piscivores in North America and, in contrast to the basses, is also widespread in Europe. Like largemouth bass, these predators generally prefer cyprinids over centrarchids and other species with morphological defenses; for example Coble (1973) showed that pike selected carp and fathead minnows over green sunfish *Lepomis cyanellus*, and bluegill sunfish, and Moody *et al.* (1983) found that tiger musky required four times as many strikes and longer pursuit times to capture bluegill sunfish than fathead minnows. Similar results were obtained by Wahl and Stein (1988), investigating the efficiency of three esocids [muskellunge (*Esox muskellunge*) pike and tiger musky] feeding on fathead minnows, gizzard shad, *Dorosoma cepedianum*, and bluegill sunfish; they concluded that all three esocids found the minnows and shad easier to catch than the bluegills.

In Europe, Peirson *et al.* (1985) found that the cyprinids roach and rudd were more susceptible than perch to predation by pike, particularly when moderate to high densities of artificial macrophytes were present. Not surprisingly, cyprinids are important in the diet of pike in both lakes, e.g. Slapton Ley in England (Bregazzi and Kennedy, 1980), and rivers, e.g. the

Rivers Frome and Stour in England (Mann, 1976). Mann reported that small cyprinids in the 30–80 mm size range dominated the diet of pike even as large as 700 mm fork length (*c.* 2.7 kg). Growth rates of pike in both rivers were comparable to the highest recorded elsewhere, which was attributed at least in part to the large populations of cyprinid prey fish.

Cyprinids are not only important as the prey of piscivorous fishes, they also contribute to the diet of piscivorous birds including herons, *Ardea* spp., and grebes, *Podiceps* spp. (Cramp and Simmons, 1977), kingfishers, *Alcedo* spp. (Cramp, 1985), and gulls, *Larus* spp. (Cramp and Simmons, 1983). While cyprinids are able to form and employ complex shoaling defences against predators such as basses or esocids, this strategy may be of less use against surprise attacks from birds, and post-capture escape is also unlikely (Recher and Recher, 1968). The only reliable way of escaping predation by birds may be to avoid the areas in which they forage, and will have considerable costs in terms of reduced feeding opportunities. The arrival, increase, and subsequent decrease of roach in Lough Neagh (p. 561) was accompanied by an increase and decrease in the numbers of piscivorous great crested grebes, *Podiceps cristatus*, overwintering on the lough (Winfield *et al.*, 1989). The spread of roach in other parts of Ireland has been accompanied by increases in the overwintering numbers and distribution of another piscivorous bird, the cormorant, *Phalacrocorax carbo* (Macdonald, 1987), demonstrating again the value of cyprinids as prey for avian piscivores.

Cyprinids thus form an important part of the diet of a variety of piscivores and are subject to considerable predation pressure, perhaps more so than other fishes such as sunfishes, *Lepomis* spp., or perches, *Perca* spp. Furthermore, many species of cyprinids are unlikely to find a refuge in size from their predators, in contrast to bluegill sunfish (Werner *et al.*, 1983). Given the great importance that predation pressure has for the foraging behaviour of bluegills (review, Mittelbach and Chesson, 1987), it is likely to have an at least equally considerable effect on the temporal and spatial patterns of foraging in many cyprinids, as indeed it does in the creek chub (p. 560).

20.5 INDIRECT INTERACTIONS

The nature of cyprinid-induced indirect interactions

The previous sections have considered the direct ways, including foraging, competition and predation, in which cyprinids interact with other components of their ecosystems. However, recent research suggests that indirect interactions are a common facet of cyprinid ecology. In broad terms, these interactions can be divided into those that operate through the zooplankton, and those that work through increasing the availability of nutrients to primary producers.

Indirect interactions through the zooplankton

The enclosure experiments of Andersson *et al.* (1978) (p. 558) also demonstrate several indirect effects. The observed increase in large Cladocera in the fish-free enclosure was accompanied by a reduction in chlorophyll *a* concentration, while this parameter increased in the enclosure stocked with roach and bream (Fig. 20.2). The composition of the phytoplankton also changed, with *Microcystis* becoming dominant in the fish enclosure, while in the absence of fish the phytoplankton was a more mixed community of cryptomonads, small bluegreens, and diatoms. In addition, other factors including pH, total phosphorus, total nitogen, and transparency were all relatively higher in the enclosure stocked with roach and bream. As with the direct effects on zooplankton and macroinvertebrates (p. 558), further experiments (Andersson, 1984) showed that these indirect effects were stronger for the cyprinids roach and bream than for perch (Fig. 20.2). Similar effects on zooplankton, phytoplankton, transparency and pH were obtained using bream alone in enclosures in the eutrophic Lake Balaton in Hungary (Tatrai *et al.*, 1985). In both studies, indirect effects on the phytoplankton constituted the main mechanism involved, although increased release of nutrients from the sediments may also have been a contributing factor. Using small enclosures in the eutrophic Lake Gjersjoen in Norway, Hessen and Nilssen (1986) found that young roach depressed the populations of advanced stages of crustaceans including *Daphnia* spp. and *Bosmina longirostris*, which in turn caused increases in the biomass of small and medium-sized algae, and increases in bacterial biomass and the amounts of sedimenting organic matter. This latter effect is particularly important as it represents a diversion of primary production from the grazer food chain to the detritus food chain.

Henrikson *et al.* (1980) followed changes in various characteristics of an oligotrophic forest lake in Sweden after its fish community (mainly roach) had been removed by rotenone. The zooplankton, previously dominated by small herbivorous cladocerans (e.g. *Bosmina longirostris*), became dominated by larger herbivorous copepods (e.g. *Eudiaptomus gracilis* G.O. Sars), while the phytoplankton increased in density and changed in species composition. Limnetic primary production decreased by 90% after fish reduction, and pH, total phosphorus, and total nitrogen all declined. Although changes in invertebrate zooplanktivores and fish-induced changes in nutrient availability were involved to some degree, Henrikson *et al.* (1980) concluded that the planktivore–zooplankton–phytoplankton chain was the main mechanism responsible. In European waters at least, the indirect effects of zooplanktivorous cyprinids on phytoplankton and abiotic factors such as pH and nutrient concentrations occur in both eutrophic and oligotrophic systems.

Investigations of the indirect effects of cyprinids in North American lakes are fewer in number, due in large part to the justified focus of research on the more abundant percids and centrarchids (examples, Kerfoot and Sih, 1987).

However, a notable exception is the whole-lake study by Elser and Carpenter (1988) of the removal of redbelly dace, finescale dace, and central mud-minnow (557). The observed increase in herbivorous zooplankton, when fish were removed, produced changes in the phytoplankton, including a decline in dinoflagellates and small flagellated chlorophytes, and an increase in *Mallomonas caudata* and *Oocystis lacustris*. *Cryptomonas orata* maintained the same absolute biomass, but increased in relative importance in the sparser phytoplankton community until it became the dominant species. Experimental ponds with fathead minnows and the non-cyprinid brook sticklebacks (Spencer and King, 1984 – p. 558) developed dense bluegreen algal blooms (primarily *Anabaenopsis elenkinii* and *Microcystis* sp.) in the absence of significant grazing populations of *Daphnia pulex* and *Ceriodaphnia* sp., and had few higher plants. In contrast, in the absence of minnows and sticklebacks, abundant Cladocera resulted in a sparse phytoplankton community dominated by pennate diatoms, small green algae, and flagellates. In turn, this development facilitated dense growths of *Elodea canadensis*, *Potamogeton* spp., and *Cladophora* sp., which themselves attracted waterfowl (mallards) and mammals (muskrats, *Ondatra zibethica*). Thus, the zooplanktivore-induced alteration of the dominant plant type had profound and widespread effects on the ecology of the ponds.

Indirect interactions through increased nutrient availability

Cyprinids not only have 'beneficial' indirect effects on phytoplankton through the removal of grazing zooplankton, but may also increase their productivity by increasing the availability of nutrients. Such effects have been observed in a series of studies investigating the role of bream in the nutrient budgets of the eutrophic Lake Balaton in Hungary, where it is the most abundant fish. Enclosure experiments (Tatrai and Istvanovics, 1986) demonstrated that dense populations of benthivorous bream increase phytoplankton productivity, and thus may enhance the eutrophication process. Subsequent laboratory experiments (Tatrai, 1987) measured the rates of release of total nitrogen and ammonia by bream which, when combined with their population density in Lake Balaton, suggested that bream excretion provided about one-fifth of the annual nitrogen loading of the lake. Similarly, bream, roach, and the non-cyprinid perch excreted significant amounts of phosphorus and nitrogen, as soluble molybdate-reactive phosphorus and ammonia respectively, in the eutrophic Lake Gjersjoen in Norway (Brabrand *et al.*, 1986). Furthermore, during the summer the waste products of roach alone constituted approximately 30% of the total phosphorus supply to the epilimnion. In addition to zooplanktivorous and benthivorous cyprinids, herbivorous species can also enhance algal growth by releasing nutrients in their faeces (Prejs, 1984). Independent support for this view was produced by the experimental study of Hansson *et al.* (1987) (p. 555 Fig. 20.1), which showed that grazing on a higher plant by rudd released phosphorus into the water column, promoting the growth of epiphytic algae (mainly *Spirogyra* sp.).

The ability of cyprinids to enhance algal growth by increasing nutrient availability has also been observed in ecosystems outside Europe. Lamarra (1975) was able to show experimentally that the digestive activities of carp in a North American lake increased the availability of total phosphorus and in a study of the ecosystem role of omnivorous longfin dace, *Agosia chrysogaster*, in a desert stream in the United States, Grimm (1988) found that 3–6% of the nitrogen stored in the ecosystem was in the biomass of this abundant cyprinid, and ammonia excretion by this fish represented 5–10% of the nitrogen uptake by algae in this nitrogen-limited stream. We consider it likely that many further examples of this nutrient-releasing role of cyprinid defecation will be discovered.

Finally, cyprinids can increase the availability of nutrients by mere physical means through disturbance of bottom sediments while foraging for benthic macroinvertebrates. Such an effect by benthivorous bream was considered by Lammens (1988) to be an important factor in complex trophic interactions observed in a hypereutrophic lake, Tjeuke Meer, while in another lake in The Netherlands, Ten Winkel and Davids (1985) calculated that during the course of a year, 300–400% of the lake bottom was disturbed, or 'bioturbated' by foraging bream. Again, further work in this area of indirect interactions should prove enlightening.

20.6 CLOSING REMARKS

The preceding sections have shown that cyprinids have a variety of significant direct effects on other biotic components of their ecosystems, including algae, higher plants, zooplankton, macroinvertebrates, and vertebrates. Furthermore, through such agencies they may also influence species with which they have no direct interactions, such as phytoplankton, and even abiotic parameters such as nutrient levels and pH. Cyprinids are an integral part of freshwater ecosystems (Andersson *et al.*, 1988; Persson *et al.*, 1988) and their effects must be taken into account by researchers studying all aspects of limnology.

The magnitudes of the direct and indirect effects of cyprinids on their ecosystems are such that they have important consequences for applied ecology. The embryonic science of biomanipulation (Chapter 13 of Cooke *et al.*, 1986) holds considerable potential as a powerful tool to combat the widespread problem of eutrophication, although much research remains to be done (Benndorf, 1988). Cyprinids, with their demonstrated impacts on herbivorous cladocerans but high susceptibility to predation, seem to be ideal candidates for use in such measures, and are currently the subject of interest in eutrophic European waters (e.g. Richter, 1986). because of their profound influences on aspects as diverse as water quality and waterfowl, the management of cyprinid populations should not be the exclusive domain of fishery managers. On the general question of cyprinid introductions and management, we would do well to remember the observation made long ago by Cahn (1929) that "the introduced carp is capable of changing the entire [fish] community composition, bringing about a change as marked as that produced by civilized man on the original vegetation.".

REFERENCES

Agami, M. and Waisel, Y. (1988) The role of fish in distribution and germination of seeds of the submerged macrophytes *Najas marina* L. and *Ruppia maritima* L. *Oecologia*, **76**, 83–8.

Anderson, O. (1984) Optimal foraging by largemouth bass in structured environments. *Ecology*, **65**, 851–61.

Andersson, G. (1981) Fiskars inverkan på sjöfågel och fågelsjör. (Influence of fish on waterfowl and lakes. In Swedish with English summary.) *Anser*, **20**, 21–34.

Andersson, G. (1984) The role of fish in lake ecosystems – and in limnology, in *Interaksjoner mellom trofiske nivaer i ferskvann* (eds B. Bosheim and M. Nicholls), Nordisk Limnolog Symposium, Oslo, pp. 189–97.

Andersson, G., Berggren, H., Cronberg, G. and Gelin, C. (1978) Effects of planktivorous and benthivorous fish on organisms and water chemistry in eutrophic lakes. *Hydrobiologia*, **59**, 9–15.

Andersson, G., Graneli, W. and Stenson, J. (1988) The influence of animals on phosphorus cycling in lake ecosystems. *Hydrobiologia*, **170**, 267–84.

Benndorf, J. (1988) Objectives and unsolved problems in ecotechnology and bio-manipulation: a preface. *Limnologica*, **19**, 5–8.

Brabrand, A. (1985) Food of roach (*Rutilus rutilus*) and ide (*Leuciscus idus*): significance of diet shift for interspecific competition in omnivorous fishes. *Oecologia*, **66**, 461–7.

Brabrand, A., Faafeng, B. and Nilssen, J. P. M. (1986) Juvenile roach and invertebrate predators: delaying the recovery phase of eutrophic lakes by suppression of efficient filter-feeders. *J. Fish Biol.*, **29**, 99–106.

Bregazzi, P. R. and Kennedy, C. R. (1980) The biology of pike, *Esox lucius* L., in a southern eutrophic lake. *J. Fish Biol.*, **17**, 91–112.

Cahn, A. H. (1929) The effect of carp on a small lake: the carp as a dominant. *Ecology*, **10**, 271–4.

Cerri, R. D. (1983) The effect of light intensity on predator and prey behaviour in cyprinid fish. *Anim. Behav.*, **31**, 736–42.

Coble, D. W. (1973) Influence of appearance of prey and satiation of predator on food selection by northern pike (*Esox lucius*). *J. Fish. Res. Bd Can.*, **30**, 317–20.

Cooke, G. D., Welch, E. B., Peterson, S. A. and Newroth, P. R. (1986) *Lake and Reservoir Restoration*, Butterworth, Stoneham.

Covich, A. P. and Knezevic, B. (1978) Size-selective predation by fish on thin-shelled gastropods (*Lymnaea*): the significance of floating vegetation (*Trapa*) as a physical refuge. *Verh. Internat. Verein. Limnol.*, **20**, 2172–7.

Cramp, S. (1985) *Handbook of the Birds of Europe, the Middle East, and North Africa: the Birds of the Western Palearctic.* Vol. II, Oxford University Press, Oxford.

Cramp, S. and Simmons, K. E. L. (1977) *Handbook of the Birds of Europe, the Middle East, and North Africa: the Birds of the Western Palearctic*. Vol. I, Oxford University Press, Oxford.

Cramp, S. and Simmons, K. E. L. (1983) *Handbook of the Birds of Europe, the Middle East, and North Africa: the Birds of the Western Palearctic*. Vol. III, Oxford University Press, Oxford.

Crivelli, A. J. (1983) The destruction of aquatic vegetation by carp. *Hydrobiologia*, **106**, 37–41.

Cryer, M., Peirson, G. and Townsend, C. R. (1986) Reciprocal interactions between roach, *Rutilus rutilus*, and zooplankton in a small lake: prey dynamics and fish growth and recruitment. *Limnol. Oceanogr.*, **31**, 1022–38.

Diehl, S. (1988) Foraging efficiency of three freshwater fishes: effects of structural complexity and light. *Oikos*, **53**, 207–14.

Elser, J. J. and Carpenter, S. R. (1988) Predation-driven dynamics of zooplankton and phytoplankton communities in a whole-lake experiment. *Oecologia*, **76**, 148–54.

Eriksson, M. O. G. (1979) Competition between freshwater fish and goldeneyes *Bucephala clangula* (L.) for common prey. *Oecologia*, **41**, 99–107.

Fletcher, A. R., Morison, A. K. and Hume, D. J. (1985) Effects of carp, *Cyprinus carpio* L., on communities of aquatic vegetation and turbidity of waterbodies in the Lower Goulburn River Basin. *Aust. J. mar. Freshwat. Res.*, **36**, 311–27.

Fowler, M. C. (1985) The results of introducing grass carp, *Ctenopharyngodon idella* Val. into small lakes. *Aquacult. Fish. Manage.*, **16**, 189–201.

Fraser, D. F. (1983) An experimental investigation of refuging behaviour in a minnow. *Can. J. Zool.*, **61**, 666–72.

Fraser, D. F. and Cerri, R. D. (1982) Experimental evaluation of predator–prey relationships in a patchy environment: consequences for habitat use patterns in minnows. *Ecology*, **63**, 307–13.

Grimm, N. B. (1988) Feeding dynamics, nitrogen budgets, and ecosystem role of a desert stream omnivore *Agosia chrysogaster* (Pisces: Cyprinidae). *Environ. Biol. Fishes*, **21**, 143–52.

Hansson, L.-A., Johansson, L. and Persson, L. (1987) Effects of fish grazing on nutrient release and succession of primary producers. *Limnol. Oceanogr.*, **32**, 723–9.

Hart, P. and Hamrin, S. F. (1988) Pike as a selective predator. Effects of prey size, availability, cover and pike jaw dimensions. *Oikos*, **51**, 220–26.

Heads, P.A. (1986) The costs of reduced feeding rate due to predator avoidance: potential effects on growth and fitness in *Ischnura elegans* larvae (Odonata: Zygoptera). *Ecol. Entomol.*, **11**, 369–77.

Henrikson, B.-I. (1988) The absence of antipredator behaviour in the larvae of *Leucorrhinia dubia* (Odonata) and the consequences for their distribution. *Oikos*, **51**, 179–83.

Henrikson, L., Nyman, H. G., Oscarson, H. G. and Stenson, J. A. E. (1980) Trophic changes, without changes in the external nutrient loading. *Hydrobiologia*, **68**, 257–63.

Hessen, D. O. and Nilssen, J. P. (1986) From phytoplankton to detritus and bacteria: effects of short-term nutrient and fish perturbations in a eutrophic lake. *Arch. Hydrobiol.*, **105**, 273–84.

Hill, D., Wright, R. and Street, M. (1987) Survival of mallard ducklings *Anas platyrhynchos* and competition with fish for invertebrates on a flooded gravel quarry in England. *Ibis*, **129**, 159–67.

Hofer, R. and Niederholzer, R. (1980) The feeding of roach (*Rutilus rutilus* L.) and rudd (*Scardinius erythrophthalmus* L.) II. Feeding experiments in the laboratory. *Ekol. pol.*, **28**, 61–70.

Hrbacek, J., Dvorakova, M.,Korinek, V. and Prochazkova, L. (1961) Demonstration of the effect of the fish stock on the species composition of zooplankton and the intensity of metabolism of the whole plankton association. *Verh. Internat. Verein. Limnol.*, **14**, 192–5.

Ivlev, V. S. (1961) *Experimental Ecology of the Feeding of Fishes*, Yale University Press, New Haven, Conu.

Kerfoot, W. C. and Sih, A. (eds) (1987) *Predation: Direct and Indirect Impacts on Aquatic Communities*, University Press of New England, Hanover, NH.

Kitchell, J. F., Stein, R. A. and Knezivic, B. (1978) Utilization of filamentous algae by fishes in Skadar Lake, Yugoslavia. *Verh. Internat. Verein. Limnol.*, **20**, 2159–65.

Kramer, R. H. and Smith, L. L. (1962) Formation of year classes in largemouth bass. *Trans. Am. Fish. Soc.*, **91**, 29–41.

Lamarra, V. A. (1975) Digestive activities of carp as a major contributor to the nutrient loading of lakes. *Verh. Internat. Verein. Limnol.*, **19**, 2461–8.

Lammens, E. H. R. R. (1988) Trophic interactions in the hypertrophic Lake Tjeukemeer: top–down and bottom–up effects in relation to hydrology, predation and bioturbation during the period 1974–1985. *Limnologica*, **19**, 81–5.

Lammens, E. H. R. R., De Nie, H. W., Vijverberg, J. and Van Densen, W. L. T. (1985) Resource partitioning and niche shifts of bream (*Abramis brama*) and eel (*Anguilla anguilla*) mediated by predation of smelt (*Osmerus eperlanus*) on *Daphnia hyalina*. *Can. J. Fish. aquat. Sci.*, **42**, 1342–51.

Lewis, W. M., Gunning, G. E., Lyles, E. and Bridges, W. L. (1961) Food choice of largemouth bass as a function of availability and vulnerability of food items. *Trans. Am. Fish. Soc.*, **90**, 277–80.

Macdonald, R. A. (1987) The breeding population and distribution of the cormorant in Ireland. *Ir. Birds*, **3**, 405–16.

Mann, R. H. K. (1976) Observations on the age, growth, reproduction and food of the pike *Esox lucius* (L.) in two rivers in southern England. *J. Fish Biol.*, **8**, 179–97.

Milstein, A., Hepher, B. and Teltsch, B. (1985a) Principal component analysis of interactions between fish species and the ecological conditions in fish ponds: I. Phytoplankton. *Aquacult. Fish. Manage.*, **16**, 305–17.

Milstein, A., Hepher, B. and Teltsch, B. (1985b) Principal component analysis of interactions between fish species and the ecological conditions in fish ponds: II. Zooplankton. *Aquacult. Fish. Manage.*, **16**, 319–30.

Milstein, A., Hepher, B. and Teltsch, B. (1988) The effect of fish species combination in fish ponds on plankton composition. *Aquacult. Fish Manage.*, **19**, 127–37.

Mittelbach, G. G. (1988) Competition among refuging sunfishes and effects of fish density on littoral zone invertebrates. *Ecology*, **69**, 614–23.

Mittelbach, G. G. and Chesson, P. L. (1987) Predation risk: indirect effects on fish populations, in *Predation: Direct and Indirect Impacts on Aquatic Communities* (eds W. C. Kerfoot and A. Sih), University Press of New England, Hanover, NH, pp. 315–32.

Miura, T. and Wang, J. (1985) Chlorophyll *a* found in feces of phytoplanktivorous cyprinids and its photosynthetic activity. *Verh. Internat. Verein. Limnol.*, **22**, 2636–42.

Moody, R. C., Helland, J. M. and Stein, R. A. (1983) Escape tactics used by bluegills and fathead minnows to avoid predation by tiger muskellunge. *Environ. Biol. Fishes*, **8**, 61–5.

Moriarty, D. J. W. (1973) The physiology of digestion of bluegreen algae in the cichlid fish, *Tilapia nilotica*. *J. Zool., Lond.*, **171**, 25–39.

Niederholzer, R. and Hofer, R. (1980) The feeding of roach (*Rutilus rutilus* L.) and rudd (*Scardinius erythrophthalmus* L.). I. Studies on natural populations. *Ekol. pol.*, **28**, 45–59.

Opuszynski, K. (1979) Silver carp, *Hypophthalmichthys molitrix* (Val.), in carp ponds, 3. Influence on ecosystem. *Ekol. pol.*, **27**, 117–33.

Oscarson, H. G. (1987) Habitat segregation in a water boatman (Corixidae) assemblage – the role of predation. *Oikos*, **49**, 133–40.

Pehrsson, P. (1984) Relationships of food to spatial and temporal breeding strategies of mallard in Sweden. *J. Wildlife Mgmt*, **48**, 322–39.

Peirson, G., Cryer, M., Winfield, I. J. and Townsend, C. R. (1985) The impact of reduced nutrient loading on the fish community of a small isolated lake, Alderfen Broad. *Proc. 4th Brit. Freshwat. Fish. Conf. Univ. Liverpool*, 167–75.

Persson, L. (1983) Food consumption and the significance of detritus and algae to intraspecific competition in roach *Rutilus rutilus* in a shallow eutrophic lake. *Oikos*, **41**, 118–25.

Persson, L., Andersson, G., Hamrin, S. F. and Johansson, L. (1988) Predator regulation and primary production along the productivity gradient of temperate lake ecosystems, in *Complex Interactions in Lake Communities* (ed. S. D. Carpenter), Springer-Verlag, NY, pp. 45–65.

Porter, K. G. (1976) Enhancement of algal growth and productivity by grazing zooplankton. *Science*, **192**, 1332–4.

Power, M. E. (1984) Depth distribution of armored catfish: predator-induced resource avoidance? *Ecology*, **65**, 523–8.

Power, M. E. (1987) Predator avoidance by grazing fishes in temperate and tropical streams: the importance of stream depth and prey size, in *Predation: Direct and Indirect Impacts on Aquatic Communities* (eds W. C. Kerfoot and A. Sih), University Press of New England, Hanover, NH, pp. 333–51.

Power, M. E. and Matthews, W. J. (1983) Algae-grazing minnows (*Compostoma anomalum*), piscivorous bass (*Micropterus* spp.) and the distribution of attached algae in a small prairie-margin stream. *Oecologia*, **60**, 328–32.

Power, M. E., Matthews, W. J. and Stewart, A. J. (1985) Grazing minnows, piscivorous bass, and stream algae: dynamics of a strong interaction. *Ecology*, **66**, 1448–56.

Prejs, A. (1984) Herbivory by temperate freshwater fishes and its consequences. *Environ. Biol. Fishes*, **10**, 281–96.

Prejs, A. and Jackowska, H. (1978) Lake macrophytes as the food of roach (*Rutilus rutilus* L.) and rudd (*Scardinius erythrophthalmus* L.) I. Species composition and dominance relations in the lake and food. *Ekol. pol.*, **26**, 429–38.

Prowse, G. (1969) The role of cultured pond fish in the control of eutrophication in lakes and dams. *Verh. Internat. Verein. Limnol.*, **17**, 714–18.

Recher, H. F. and Recher, J. A. (1968) Comments on the escape of prey from avian predators. *Ecology*, **49**, 560–2.

Richter, A. F. (1986) Biomanipulation and its feasibility for water quality management in shallow eutrophic water bodies in The Netherlands. *Hydrobiol. Bull.*, **20**, 165–72.

Savino, J. F. and Stein, R. A. (1982) Predator–prey interaction between largemouth bass and bluegills as influenced by simulated, submersed vegetation. *Trans. Am. Fish. Soc.*, **111**, 255–66.

Scott, A. (1987) Prey selection by juvenile cyprinids from running water. *Freshwat. Biol.*, **17**, 129–42.

Spencer, C. N. and King, D. L. (1984) Role of fish in regulation of plant and animal communities in eutrophic ponds. *Can. J. Fish. aquat. Sci.*, **41**, 1851–5.

Stanley, J. G. (1974) Nitrogen and phosphorus balance of grass carp *Ctenopharyngodon idella*, fed elodea, *Egeria densa. Trans. Am. Fish. Soc.*, **103**, 587–92.

Stenson, J. A. E. (1976) Significance of predator influence on composition of *Bosmina* spp. populations. *Limnol. Oceanogr.*, **21**, 814–22.

Tatrai, I. (1987) The role of fish and benthos in the nitrogen budget of Lake Balaton, Hungary. *Arch. Hydrobiol.*, **110**, 291–302.

Tatrai, I. and Istvanovics, V. (1986) The role of fish in the regulation of nutrient cycling in Lake Balaton, Hungary. *Freshwat. Biol.*, **16**, 417–24.

Tatrai, I., Toth, L. G. and Ponyi, J. E. (1985) Effects of bream (*Abramis brama* L.) on the lower trophic level and on the water quality in Lake Balaton. *Arch. Hydrobiol.*, **105**, 205–17.

Ten Winkel, E. H. and Davids, C. (1985) Bioturbation by cyprinid fish affecting the food availability for predatory water mites. *Oecologia*, **67**, 218–19.

Terrell, J. W. and Terrell, T. T. (1975) Macrophyte control and food habits of the grass carp in Georgia ponds. *Verh. Internat. Verein. Limnol.*, **19**, 2515–20.

Townsend, C.R. (1988) Fish, fleas and phytoplankton. *New Scient.*, **118**, 67–70.

Vollestad, L. A. (1985) Resource partitioning of roach *Rutilus rutilus* and bleak *Alburnus alburnus* in two eutrophic lakes in SE Norway. *Holarctic Ecol.*, **8**, 88–92.

Vuorinen, I., Rajasilta, M. and Salo, J. (1983) Selective predation and habitat shift in a copepod species – support for the predation hypothesis. *Oecologia*, **59**, 62–4.

Wahl, D. H. and Stein, R. A. (1988) Selective predation by three esocids: the role of prey behaviour and morphology. *Trans. Am. Fish. Soc.*, **117**, 142–51.

Webb, P. W. (1986) Effect of body form and response threshold on the vulnerability of four species of teleost prey attacked by largemouth bass (*Micropterus salmoides*). *Can. J. Fish. aquat. Sci.*, **43**, 763–71.

Werner, E. E. (1984) The mechanisms of species interactions and community organization in fish, in *Ecological Communities: Conceptual Issues and the Evidence* (eds. D. R. Strong, D. Simberloff, L. G. Abele and A. B. Thistle), Princeton University Press, Princeton, NJ, pp. 360–82.

Werner, E. E., Gilliam, J. F., Hall, D. J. and Mittelbach, G. G. (1983) An experimental test of the effects of predation risk on habitat use in fish. *Ecology*, **64**, 1540–8.

Winfield, D. K., Davidson, R. D. and Winfield, I. J. (1989) Long-term trends (1965–1988) in the numbers of waterfowl overwintering on Lough Neagh and Lough Beg, Northern Ireland. *Ir. Birds*, **4**, 19–42.

Winfield, I. J. (1986) The influence of simulated aquatic macrophytes on the zooplankton consumption rate of juvenile roach, *Rutilus rutilus*, rudd, *Scardinius erythrophthalmus*, and perch, *Perca fluviatilis*. *J. Fish. Biol.*, **29** (Supp. A), 37–48.

Winfield, I. J. and Townsend, C. R. (1983) The cost of copepod reproduction: increased susceptibility to fish predation. *Oecologia*, **60**, 406–11.

Chapter twenty one

Fisheries

M. Bnińska

21.1 INTRODUCTION

Cyprinids are basically freshwater fishes: about 99% of total world catches of these species originate from inland waters. Moreover, cyprinids are more common in Europe than anywhere else: 55–70% of overall cyprinid catches in the world are obtained in Europe and the USSR (mostly the European part) (FAO, 1987). Hence, this chapter is devoted to cyprinid fishery and management in fresh waters of the temperate zone, particularly Europe.

Lakes and dam reservoirs

The relationships among cyprinid species, and with other fishes, and their size-frequency distributions in lakes and dam reservoirs are basically determined by two major factors: trophic status of the aquatic ecosystem, and the fishery management (especially exploitation and stocking). The first is of primary significance.

It has been known for some time that quantitative and qualitative relationships between particular fish groups change with increasing lake trophy (Colby *et al.*, 1972; Leach *et al.*, 1977; Hartmann, 1978). Studies on some 1000 Polish lakes led to a model of changes in the fish stocks parallel to progressing lake trophy (Bnińska, 1985a, 1988, in prep.; Leopold *et al.*, 1986, 1987). In general terms, in temperate lakes increasing lake trophy is coupled with an increasing percentage of cyprinids in the fish stock and gradual elimination of other fish groups. Figure 21.1 depicts a typical picture of changing relations between cyprinids and other fishes for two Polish lakes. The effects of trophic changes from oligo- to α-mesotrophy and from β-mesotrophy to eutrophy are quite obvious. There is no doubt that, apart from a few exceptions, cyprinids already dominate the fish stocks in lakes of the temperate zone, and that this domination will continue to increase. The same can be observed in dam reservoirs (Mastyński, 1985), two basic factors make them

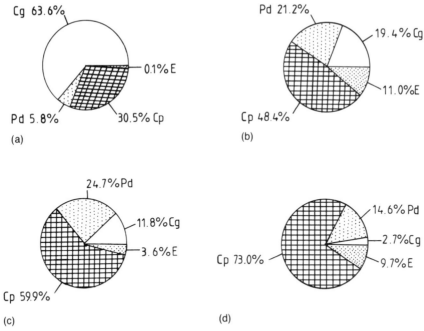

Fig. 21.1 Changes in lake fish stocks (% by weight of total commercial catch) induced by eutrophication. Based on commercial fish catch from two Polish lakes. (a) Oligotrophic Lake Bobecino (508.3 ha), 1960–64; (b) a-mesotrophic Lake Bobecino, 1980–84; (c) b-mesotrophic Lake Mamry (2711.0 ha), 1953–57; (d) eutrophic Lake Mamry, 1980–84. Cg, Coregonids (Coregonidae); Cp, cyprinids (Cyprinidae); E, eel, *Anguilla anguilla* L.; Pd, predators.

even more susceptible to the eutrophication process than natural lakes, namely (1) man-made reservoirs have less developed self-regulatory eco-system mechanisms than natural waters, and (2) European rivers are generally highly polluted (Welcomme, 1985). Most dam reservoirs constitute specific sedimentation 'tanks', accumulating nutrients and pollutants brought in by the rivers, and are therefore more prone to eutrophication. Consequently, cyprinids predominate in most dam reservoirs and may represent up to 100% of the fish fauna, especially in lowland reservoirs (Mastyński, 1985).

However, development of cyprinids with increasing lake or reservoir trophy is not as simple as it seems on first inspection. Eutrophication induces a gradual degradation of the aquatic ecosystems, and as a result, cyprinids considered more valuable from an economic point of view (e.g. tench. *Tinca tinca* L., in lakes) as well as those characterized by higher environmental quality requirements tend to disappear, being replaced by less valuable and less demanding ones. In reality, the cyprinid community in highly eutrophic lakes and reservoirs is usually composed of only a few species, of which roach, *Rutilus rutilus* L., bream, *Abramis brama* L., and white bream, *Blicca bjoerkna* L.,

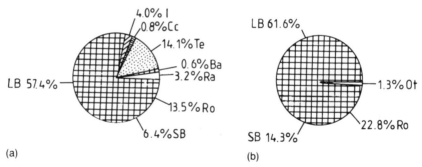

Fig. 21.2 Changes in reservoir fish stocks induced by eutrophication. Based on commercial fish catch from Zegrze Dam Reservoir (2500 ha). (a) 1965–69; (b) 1977–81. Ba, Barbel, *Barbus barbus* L.; Cc, crucian carp, *Carassius carassius* L.; I, ide, *Leuciscus idus* L.; LB, large bream, *Abramis brama* L.; Ot, other; Ra, rapfen, *Aspius aspius* L.; Ro, roach, *Rutilus rutilus* L.; SB, Small bream and white bream, *Blicca bjoerkna* L.; Te, tench, *Tinca tinca* L.

tend to be most abundant. In addition, the rate of fish growth decreases so that small roach (< 200 g), small bream (< 500 g) and white bream increase in abundance, while large specimens disappear. This is exemplified by the total fish catch from Zegrze Dam Reservoir on the Vistula (Wisła) River, Poland, (Fig. 21.2) and cyprinid catch composition in Lake Białe Augustowskie, North-east Poland (Fig. 21.3).

    This general picture can be modified by fishery management.

Rivers

Scientists around the world have not yet agreed whether rivers are subject to eutrophication (Welcomme, 1985). However, it is generally accepted that the

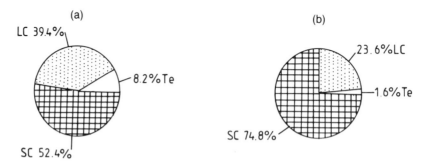

Fig. 21.3 Changes in the cyprinid community induced by eutrophication. Based on commercial catches of cyprinids from Lake Białe Augustowskie (479.0 ha). (a) Eutrophic (8.18 kg ha^{-1}), 1958–62; (b) strongly eutrophic (27.49 kg ha^{-1}), 1974–78. LC, Large cyprinids (large bream and large roach); SC, small cyprinids (small bream, small roach and white bream); Te, tench.

succession of physical and chemical conditions in rivers from the head waters to the mouth may be regarded as a natural eutrophication process (Welcomme, 1985). Consequently, the distribution of living organisms in rivers, including fish, is characterized by specific zonations, although the pattern has been clearly defined only for the north temperate zone (Welcomme, 1985). Fortunately, this zone is the most important with respect to cyprinids. The composition of fish communities in particular zones of European rivers is presented in Fig. 21.4, based on an annual catch by more than 1000 anglers fishing in the San River (Poland). Fast-water cyprinids appear in the fish community as early as the grayling zone. The general pattern is consistent with that in lakes and reservoirs: cyprinids dominate in the most eutrophic bream zone, bream and especially roach being most abundant. Also, as in lakes and dam reservoirs, this pattern may be changed by fishery management.

21.2 ECONOMIC, ECOLOGICAL AND SOCIAL SIGNIFICANCE OF CYPRINIDS

Commercial catches of cyprinids world-wide amounted to 798 550 tonnes in 1985 (inland waters), of which 377 000 t, i.e. 47.2%, originated from natural waters (lakes, rivers, dam reservoirs) and 52.8% from aquaculture (mostly carp, *Cyprinus carpio* L., and crucian carp, *Carassius carassius* L.: FAO, 1987; Billard and Marcel, 1986). Cyprinid catches from natural waters tended to increase (299 069 t in 1979), especially for *Abramis* and *Rutilus* species (from 65 428 t in 1979 to 84 411 t in 1985), largely because of water eutrophication. As far as commercial catches are concerned, cyprinids are of direct economic significance only in Europe and the USSR, where they represent 42% of total fish landings from natural inland waters (fish culture excluded). In other continents, commercial landings of these fishes are negligible (FAO, 1987). Apart from the USSR, cyprinids are exploited commercially by a few countries in Central, East and South Europe: Poland, Czechoslovakia, Germany, Hungary, Romania, Bulgaria, Jugoslavia, The Netherlands, and to some extent also by Sweden, Finland, Denmark, Switzerland and Turkey (FAO, 1987).

However, commercial landings do not illustrate the real importance of cyprinids. These fishes are in addition extensively exploited by anglers all over Europe and are thus of considerable social importance. For instance, cyprinids represent the basic component of anglers' catches in rivers of the United Kingdom (Cowx, 1988). Furthermore, in many cases (all countries of Central and East Europe) anglers' catches are consumed and thus become of economic significance as well, being an additional source of fish in human diet. For instance in Poland, where all inland waters are exploited commercially, anglers' catches from these waters have been estimated as of the same

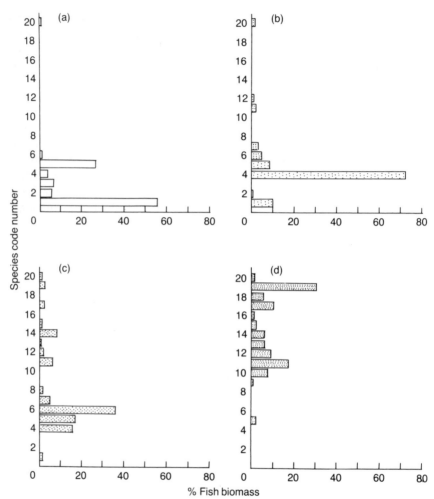

Fig. 21.4 Fish community structures (% of biomass) in particular zones of a river: (a) trout zone, (b) grayling zone; (c) barbel zone; (d) bream zone. Based on anglers' catches from the San River, Poland. Species codes: 1, brown trout, *Salmo trutta* m. *fario* L.; 2, rainbow trout, *Oncorhynchus mykiss* Rich; 3, brook trout, *Salvelinus fontinalis* Mitch.; 4, grayling, *Thymallus thymallus* L.; 5, chub, *Leuciscus cephalus* L.; 6, barbel, *Barbus barbus* L.; 7, undermouth, *Chondrostoma nasus* L.; 8, vimba, *Vimba vimba* L.; 9, ide, *Leuciscus idus* L.; 10, wels, *Silurus glanis* L. + *Ictalurus nebulosus* Le Seur; 11, pike, *Esox lucius* L.; 12, perch, *Perca fluviatilis* L.; 13, pikeperch, *Stizostedion lucioperca* L.; 14, common carp, *Cyprinus carpio* L.; 15, crucian carp, *Carassius carassius* L.; 16, tench, *Tinca tinca* L.; 17, bream *Abramis brama* L.; 18, white bream, *Blicca bjoerkna* L.; 19, roach, *Rutilus rutilus* L.; 20, other.

magnitude as commercial catches (Bnińska, 1985b), and the same is true of Czechoslovakia, the USSR, Hungary and other countries.

The ecological role of cyprinids is very complex. In general terms mention should be made of three factors. (1) The trophy of most inland waters tends to increase. Cyprinids can eat the resulting growing food resources which cannot be used by other fishes that require higher environmental quality. (2) Production of cyprinids in natural waters can be very high and tends to increase with progressing eutrophication. Removal of these fishes (as fish catch) will automatically withdraw nutrients responsible for eutrophication, and thereby contribute to its control. Cases are known (e.g. Lake Piekiełko in Poland: Leopold and Bnińska, 1987) where with proper management over $500\,kg\,ha^{-1}$ can be obtained from natural waters in the form of a cyprinid catch. (3) Proper management of cyprinid communities in natural waters may contribute to total fish stock biomanipulation and maintenance of its balance.

The domination of most fish stocks by cyprinids in natural European inland waters, together with the continuous increase of cyprinid densities, make the economic, ecological, and social significance of these fishes very complex. Consequently, the precise determination of their importance in general terms is almost impossible. For analytical purposes it is advisable to divide this group into subgroups with a reservation that the division lines cannot be clearly defined, as follows:

1. Species important and unimportant from an economic or social point of view (professional and sport fisheries), although not necessarily from an ecological point of view;
2. Calm- and fast-water cyprinids. The first are usually present in lakes, the latter in rivers, although this is not so clear in dam reservoirs, estuaries etc.;
3. Species able and unable to reproduce in existing natural conditions. Water eutrophication and degradation affect natural reproduction of fish, including some cyprinids. In addition, a number of cyprinids produced in the natural waters of Europe are not able to reproduce there (e.g. carp and grass carp, *Ctenopharyngodon idella* (Val.));
4. Species susceptible and resistant to unfavourable changes in the aquatic environments.

In analysing the significance of cyprinids in economic, productive, ecological and social aspects, some distinction should also be made between 'positive' and 'negative' significance, which might depend on the adopted view or the management objective. Fishes of positive productive (economic) significance may be of negative ecological importance, which might change with time, conditions and so on. In view of this, in discussing cyprinid fisheries and management in natural inland waters, only a general outline can be given.

21.3   BASIC PRINCIPLES OF CYPRINID FISHERIES AND MANAGEMENT

Fundamental aspects

Inland fishery and management is an art as well as a science. Like the management of any other fish community, cyprinid management should conform to certain basic principles and rules, which are valid irrespective of the management objective and subject, and should always be borne in mind.

First, fisheries comprise complex human and intersectorial activities and are often aimed at serving more than one objective, which may be complementary or contradictory; multiple objectives are not necessarily compatible. Accordingly, legal frameworks are essential if the objectives for management are to be achieved, especially when there is competition among commercial fishermen and between commercial and recreational fisheries, or competition from other water and land users.

Second, since the conditions within which fisheries are conducted are highly dynamic, objectives which may be appropriate at one time may not be appropriate at another. Periodic evaluation of the validity of objectives, as well as of the management measures used is a necessity.

Third, the formulation of management decisions should be made on the basis of the most reliable data and research on the biological, environmental, economic and social aspects of fisheries. Fishery resources are defined as renewable, but they are subject to overexploitation, depletion, and the influence of environmental factors. Owing to the need for understanding the natural fluctuations and changes of fish stocks, and the relationships between these changes and environmental factors, the focus of management should be shifted toward entire ecosystems, and management measures should be adapted to a given situation. Management should take into account the need to protect aquatic habitats from the effects of pollution and other forms of environmental degradation. Ideally, management policy and measures should be determined for each water body separately.

Finally, in view of the above, reliable and timely data and statistics are needed for proper fishery management.

It is usually accepted that modern, rational and proper fishery management, irrespective of the specific objectives, should ensure maximal possible fish production (quantitatively and qualitatively) at optimal economic effectiveness (profitability) which, at the same time, would not lead to degradation of the fish stocks or of the aquatic environment, while ensuring continuity of production (sustained fisheries).

Objectives

Traditionally, inland fisheries are divided into professional (commercial) and recreational (sport) operations, and so, too, are the objectives of management.

A given water body can, however, be used by either a professional fishery or a recreational fishery, or by both. The two types of fishery management may have a variety of objectives, and the cyprinid fishery is no exception. These can be generalized as follows.

Economic objectives. Economic objectives are achieved through commercial catch, recreational catch, or both. Profit is the manager's main objective. This can be achieved in three ways.

First, by a relatively lower catch of the most valuable fish species (one or more) or of larger individuals of higher financial value. In natural aquatic ecosystems, these fishes are less abundant (in terms of numbers or biomass) than less-valuable or smaller fishes, so their catch will always be lower, although of high financial value. Commercial fishing for selected species or paid fishing grounds for recreational fishing exemplify this type of fishery. However, it should be underlined that management aimed at obtaining a catch only of selected species requires considerable knowledge. This type of fishery in natural waters tends to deplete stocks of the exploited species and to disturb the balance of the overall fish community, so that alleviating and counteracting measures are necessary to prevent the collapse of the fishery.

Second, by a relatively higher catch of less-valuable fish species (one or more) or of smaller individuals. Lower unit value (in financial terms) of the catch is compensated by its high level. The same reservations as above apply also to this type of fishery.

Third, by optimal catches (with respect to level) of all fish species present in the catchable stock.

Social objectives. Social objectives fulfil the needs and preferences of the public. These objectives pertain almost exclusively to recreational fisheries and relate to the species sought by anglers. In general terms, the management of cyprinid communities should enhance either sport species (caught with active methods such as spinning) or still fishing, depending on the situation.

It is obvious that in some cases the economic and social objectives of management may be contradictory.

Ecological objectives. Ecological objectives arise when maintenance of an ecosystem in balance and in an unchanged state is of utmost importance, irrespective of the economic efficiency of fishery management or of social feelings. Fishery management of this type should be conducted when the value of the ecosystem is higher than its possible fishery value, e.g. in nature reserves, reservoirs of drinking water, model ecosystems, gene banks, etc.

Principal management measures

Irrespective of the management objective and of the type of aquatic environment, the fishery manager has at his disposal three basic management measures: protection, exploitation and stocking (Bnińska, 1988; Bnińska and Leopold, 1988; Leopold, 1988). Character, aims, and especially intensity of

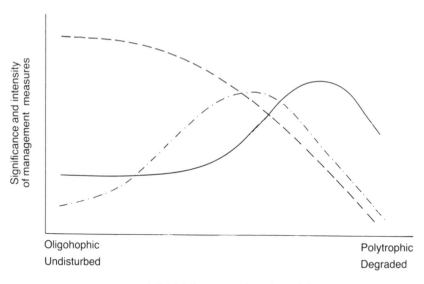

Lake trophy, ecosystem degradation

Fig. 21.5 General model illustrating the importance and intensity of particular management measures in relation to trophic status, pollution and degradation of aquatic ecosystems. Solid curve, exploitation; dashed curve, protection; Morse curve, stocking.

these measures change, depending upon the trophic status of an aquatic environment, its degradation, pollution etc. (Fig. 21.5).

Protection

In water bodies of relatively low trophy and in undisturbed ecosystems, all protective measures (e.g. closed seasons during fish reproduction, protection of spawning grounds, legal sizes) are very important. These ecosystems have good self-regulatory mechanisms which the fishery management should sustain and enhance irrespective of its other objectives. As trophy of the system increases and degradation progresses, protective measures become less and less important (Fig. 21.5). They are of no practical value in highly trophic, disturbed or strongly polluted environments, in which self-regulatory mechanisms are almost non-existent and natural fish reproduction is impaired or totally impossible (especially with respect to the most valuable species).

Exploitation

In general terms, there are four basic objectives of exploitation: fish catches, regulation of the fish stock, acquisition of spawners for artificial reproduction, and acquisition of information on the fish stocks and on the state of the ecosystem. The last objective is possible because advantage may be taken of the form of the relationship between catch and effort, as well as catch trends, in assessing the density of the exploited fish community as well as the adjustments or changes taking place in this community and possible under- or overfishing.

In well-balanced, undisturbed ecosystems of relatively low trophy, the fishing effort should be more or less evenly distributed over the entire fish community to maintain its balance. For protective purposes, no fishing should take place during fish reproduction (except to acquire spawners for artificial spawning), and legal fish sizes should be strictly observed. Increasing trophy calls for increasing fishing effort (Fig. 21.5), but also the exploitation should become more and more a regulatory measure: overdeveloping species should be exploited using higher fishing effort, while the disappearing ones should be subjected to lower effort. Fishing effort with respect to the latter species may be increased only if their stocks are enhanced by artificial stocking. No legal sizes need to be observed for overdeveloping species in highly eutrophic waters or disturbed ecosystems. Small roach, small bream and white bream should be intensively exploited in highly eutrophic and polytrophic waters, because their excessive densities degrade the fish stocks and disturb their balance.

Stocking

The importance and intensity of artificial stocking increases with increasing trophy or water pollution and environmental degradation (Fig 21.5). It is now generally accepted that in European inland waters, this measure is essential for sustaining the fish stocks, especially of the most important species (EIFAC, 1984; Bnińska, 1985c, 1988; Leopold and Bnińska, 1987; Bnińska and Leopold, 1988; Leopold, 1988), and that its importance will grow with time. Although natural reproduction is impaired in highly eutrophic waters, conditions for fish growth are still good owing to abundant food resources, hence the importance of stocking. Stocking is of no use, and gives no results, only in cases of extreme polytrophy or complete ecosystem degradation. This measure can also be used to enhance the stocks of selected species, and to change the fish stock composition, e.g. to substitute a desired species for an unwanted one.

Basic principles specific to lakes and dam reservoirs

Management of cyprinid communities in lakes and dam reservoirs, whether by professional or recreational fishery, may: (1) constitute an integral part of the management of an entire fish stock in the aquatic environment, in which case species of higher value (cyprinids and non-cyprinids) are usually enhanced, while those of lower value are limited; (2) be directed at enhancing the cyprinid community or its individual species; or (3) be directed at just the opposite.

In each case, the trophic status of the aquatic environment should be taken into account, especially changes in the fish stocks induced by eutrophication. Each of these aims is achieved by proper application of exploitation and stocking, according to the outlined general rules with specific solutions adapted to the given situation.

Exploitation

Cyprinids are caught with practically all types of fishing gear. Anglers fishing for cyprinids in lakes and dam reservoirs usually use still-fishing methods (rods), since cyprinids in these waters are almost entirely represented by calm-water fishes. As regards professional fisheries, seines, gill and trammel nets, and a variety of trap nets are used in temperate zone lakes and reservoirs. Selectivity of these gears differs considerably, depending on the environment, species, and fishing period. However, some general rules have been worked out on the basis of data from the literature (Welcomme, 1975), taking into account (1) catches obtained with a given fishing gear and the percentage of individual cyprinid species in these catches, and (2) catches of a given cyprinid species and the percentage share (in fishing effort) of the individual fishing gears used to obtain these catches.

Tench is most successfully caught with fyke nets (types I and II, Welcomme, 1975). Its percentage in seine catches is usually small, but since these nets are very effective, they may contribute considerably to the overall catch of this fish.

Crucian carp and common carp are also caught essentially by seines on the same principle as tench. In lakes stocked with carp, this gear is of utmost importance.

Bream is most successfully caught with so-called bream gill nets (mesh size 60–90 mm) but also with seines (especially in winter, under ice), fyke nets II, trammel nets, and combined pound nets. Small bream is readily caught with seines and combined pound nets.

White bream are caught mostly by seines on the same principle as bream.

Roach is most effectively caught with so-called perch–roach gill nets (mesh size 30–45 mm), but also with seines (especially in autumn), combined pound nets, fyke nets II and trammel nets. Seines, gill nets and combined pound nets provide most roach catches.

In general, seines are the most important gear, especially when used to regulate the fish stock. They are highly effective and the catch requires relatively little labour.

The fishing method, gear etc. should be selected according to specific situations as these are highly variable. For instance, when enhancing one species it may be necessary to limit another, as when bream in lakes is substituted with whitefish, *Coregonus lavaretus*. Recreational fishing is usually very selective and the manager should prevent disturbances of the stock balance by exploiting the underexploited fishes. There is such a variety of situations that it is impossible to discuss them even briefly. The fishery manager should be sufficiently well qualified and knowledgeable to be able to decide what should be done, how and when.

Stocking

In broad terms the aims of artificial stocking may be:

1. To change species composition of the fish stock in terms of quantitative relations between the species;
2. To introduce new species into the fish fauna;
3. To enhance production (catch) of a given species (one or more);
4. To sustain production (catch) of a given species (one or more) at a given level when, owing to environmental factors, it would otherwise decrease;
5. To slow the rate with which a given species (one or more) would otherwise disappear;
6. To strengthen the spawning population of a given species (one or more) so as to improve natural reproductive potential;
7. To improve environmental quality by better use of its productive potential (food resources) and by withdrawing (at least partly) some nutrients, thereby slowing down the eutrophication process.

These objectives overlap and in a majority of cases multiple purposes are fulfilled.

Stocking of non-cyprinid fishes into lakes and dam reservoirs is quite popular in European countries that conduct fishery management in inland waters. Stocking with eel, *Anguilla anguilla*, and coregonids is very popular and is generally accepted as being highly effective (EIFAC, 1984). It should be underlined that stocking affects the entire fish community, so even when non-cyprinids are stocked this is noticeable in the cyprinid community. For example, whitefish may well replace bream in eutrophic lakes (Hus, 1988). Lake Białe Augustowskie (Poland) is regularly stocked with coregonids (whitefish and vendace, *Coregonous albula* L.). As a result, their percentage in the fish catch increased from 0.1 to 13.3% over 21 y (Fig. 21.6), whereas the cyprinid catch composition (Fig. 21.3) reveals that the lake is very strongly eutrophic. Without stocking, coregonids would certainly have disappeared from the lake by now, whereas cyprinids would represent more than 75% of the fish catch.

Stocking of cyprinid fishes into lakes and dam reservoirs is quite popular in Central and East Europe. Tench, crucian carp and common carp are most frequently stocked, usually as fry or yearlings, but phytophagous Chinese carps are also introduced (grass carp, silver carp, *Hypophthalmichthys molitrix* (Val.), bighead carp, *Aristichthys nobilis* (Rich.)). Studies conducted on about 1000 Polish lakes showed that stockings with cyprinids are usually quite effective (Bnińska, 1985c; Leopold and Bnińska, 1987; Bnińska and Leopold, 1988). Also, the relationship between stocking and catch is usually curvilinear, yielding certain minimum and maximum stocking rates which are effective in a given lake or reservoir. Lower or higher stocking rates are ineffective. The maximum corresponds to the capacity of a given environment

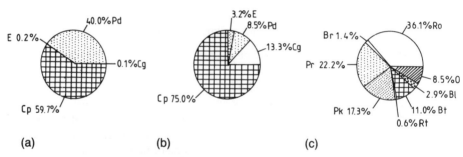

Fig. 21.6 Changes induced in fish stock composition by artificial stocking. Results of coregonid stocking in a strongly eutrophic lake and of trout stocking into the bream zone of a river. (a) Lake Białe Augustowskie, 1958–62 (13.69 kg ha⁻¹); (b) Lake Białe Augustowskie, 1974–78 (36.67 kg ha⁻¹); (c) River Brda. Bl, Bleak, *Alburnus alburnus* L.; Br, bream, Bt, brown trout; Cg, coregonids *Coregonus albula* L. + C. lavaretus L; Cp, cyprinids; E, eel; Ot, other; Pd, predators; Pk, pike; Pr, perch; Ro, roach; Rt, rainbow trout.

in the ecological sense. The minima and maxima are different for individual water bodies and individual fish species, and this implies that, ideally, the most appropriate stocking rates should be established for each lake separately, based on existing and comparative data. When no such data are available, trial-and-error is the only suitable method, because no valid general rules have been established (Leopold and Bnińska, 1987; Bnińska and Leopold, 1988).

An example of the effects of stocking crucian and common carp into a lake, and of the relationship between stocking and catch, is presented in Fig. 21.7. To determine this relationship curvilinear regression (least-squares parabola) of catch on stocking was used.

Stocking intensity should increase with increasing trophy (Fig. 21.5). Moreover, stocking should be applied fairly regularly to be most effective, although irregular stocking may also be effective (Fig. 21.8). In the two lakes it was possible neither to establish the character of the relationship between stocking and catch, nor to determine the optimal stocking doses; nevertheless, the dependence of catch on stocking is evident (Fig. 21.8): stocking resulted in an increased catch in subsequent years. The effects of stocking are to be expected after a time lag, the length of which depends on the age of the fish stocked (the younger the fish used, the later it appears in the catch).

Stocking is of utmost importance in lake and reservoir management, and in view of eutrophication and degradation of waters its significance will increase. However, proper application of stocking is a real art, requiring much knowledge and experience. Several factors determine the effects, apart from the quality of the ecosystem, quality of the stocking material, and stocking rates, such as time of stocking, place and method of fish release, water temperature, and weather conditions, and no detailed rules and procedures can be given.

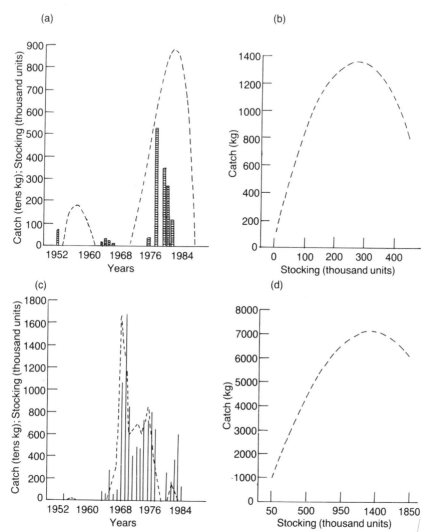

Fig. 21.7 The effects of stocking crucian carp and common carp into a lake (Lake Gil Maly, Poland) and the relationships between stocking and catch. (a) Crucian carp, catch (broken curve) and stocking (columns); (b) crucian carp, regression of catch on stocking ($r = 0.65$, $P = 0.001$); (c) common carp, catch (broken curve) and stocking (columns); (d) common carp, regression of catch on stocking ($r = 0.56$, $P = 0.001$).

Nevertheless, a few general points should be remembered:

1. Stocking must be adapted to the trophic status of the environment.
2. This measure should be applied regularly to be most effective.
3. Bream, roach and white bream should not be stocked into highly trophic (polytrophic) lakes and reservoirs.

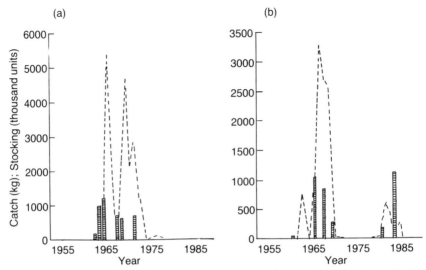

Fig. 21.8 The effects of stocking common carp into Polish lakes. (a) Lake Braniki; (b) Lake Kinkajny. Broken curve, catch; columns, stocking.

4. Phytophagous cyprinids (Chinese carps) should not be stocked into natural ecosystems of good quality (undisturbed, well balanced), because these species tend to disturb the balance of fish stocks in European lakes (Barthelmes, 1984; Wegleńska *et al.*, in press). In contrast, they can usefully be stocked into highly polytrophic and degraded lakes and reservoirs, as well as into small, closed (no outflow) eutrophic lakes.
5. Stocking of common carp into eutrophic and highly eutrophic lakes and reservoirs is usually very effective, and may result in high production (catch) at relatively low cost (much lower than in pond culture, Leopold, 1986). This fish is very attractive, both for professional fisheries and anglers.
6. Data and statistics are essential for establishing the effectiveness of stocking, as well as for determining the most effective stocking rates in a given situation, with stocking treated as an input and catch as an output. When these are lacking, trial-and-error methods must be used.

Basic principles specific to rivers

The general principles of fishery management in rivers do not differ fundamentally from those given for lakes, although there are some differences. Rivers in most European countries are used essentially for sport fishing, and therefore the manager should take into account anglers' needs and preferences. Management of cyprinids is restricted to three river zones in which cyprinids occur, but mostly to the river-mouth sectors.

Exploitation

Anglers fishing for cyprinids usually apply still-fishing methods in the barbel and bream zones, and active methods in the grayling zone in which fast-water cyprinids occur. Fishing gear used by professional fisheries is the same as in lakes and reservoirs, but the use of tow nets (seines) is limited by water flow, whereas trap nets and electrofishing are more popular.

The principles of proper exploitation are similar to those for lakes, although pollution is more important in rivers than in lakes, whereas trophic state is less so. Pollution induces considerable changes in riverine fish stocks (Welcomme, 1985), so the regulatory function of exploitation is very important.

Stocking

Cyprinids have seldom been stocked into rivers, which in contrast are widely stocked with salmonids. However, in view of increasing river pollution and other negative human impacts (such as river regulation and damming), it may be expected that cyprinids will eventually need also to be stocked into flowing waters. Attempts at stocking barbel, *Barbus barbus* L. (e.g. United Kingdom, Poland), rapfen, *Aspius aspius* L., chub, *Leuciscus cephalus* L., and ide, *Leuciscus idus* L., fry (Poland) into rivers have already been made where spawning grounds of these fishes have been destroyed, and further efforts are under way.

It should also be pointed out that stocking of non-cyprinid fishes may change the composition of the fish community in typical cyprinid zones (barbel and bream). For instance, brown trout, *Salmo trutta* m. *fario* L., and rainbow trout, *Oncorhyuchus mykiss* Rich., have been stocked for a number of years into the bream zone of the Brda River in Poland, and so now represent more than 11% of total anglers' catch from this zone (Fig. 21.6). Trout is stocked into several lowland rivers in Poland (North Poland, mostly), with fairly good results.

21.4   CURRENT STATUS AND PROSPECTS OF CYPRINID FISHERIES AND MANAGEMENT

Cyprinids are usually considered to be of low value, so perception of cyprinid fisheries and management is usually far from satisfactory. At the same time, this group of fishes tends to be more and more abundant in European inland waters, while other, more valuable fishes disappear. Moreover, individual growth of fishes, including cyprinids, is inhibited in highly trophic conditions, so that stocks become dominated by stunted specimens, particularly when there is no proper fishery management. All this implies an urgent need to pay more attention to cyprinid fishes, and that their proper management will soon become a necessity. Prospective objectives of this management can be formulated as follows.

Cyprinid management should be recognized as an important element of aquatic ecosystem protection and control. The significance of this management should be regarded as much higher than the fishery value alone. Research on the specific roles of cyprinid fishes in the aquatic ecosystems should be intensified. There is an urgent need to define precisely those specific circumstances in which individual species of cyprinids should be enhanced, limited or replaced by other fishes.

Cyprinid fishes should become more widely exploited by commercial fisheries. Large specimens can be eaten, while smaller individuals may be processed, e.g. as fish meal, and used for other purposes, e.g. in trout feeds. Cyprinid fishes, especially larger specimens, are very tasty. Successful promotion of their consumption is a matter of overcoming reservations and traditions through proper information and advertising.

REFERENCES

Barthelmes, D. (1984) Heavy silver carp (*Hypophthalmichthys molitrix* (Val.)) stocking in lakes and its influence on indigenous fish stocks. *EIFAC tech. Pap.*, **42**, Supp. vol. 2, 313–24. (*see entry* EIFAC, 1984)

Billard, R. and Marcel, J. (eds) (1986) *Aquaculture of cyprinids*, INRA, Paris, 502 pp.

Bnińska, M. (1985a) The effect of recreational uses upon aquatic ecosystems and fish resources, in *Habitat Modification and Freshwater Fisheries* (ed. J. S. Alabaster), FAO and Butterworth, London, pp. 223–35.

Bnińska, M. (1985b) Wydajności rybackie rzek i jezior Polski. (Fish catches and landings from Polish rivers and lakes). *Gospodarka Rybna*, (7/8), 3–5 (in Polish).

Bnińska, M. (1985c) The possibilities of improving catchable fish stocks in lakes undergoing eutrophication. *J. Fish Biol.*, **27** (Supp. 1), 253–61.

Bnińska, M. (1988) Methods used to determine fish community structures and the resulting needs for the fishery management. Symposium on management schemes for inland fisheries, held in Goteborg, Sweden, 31 May – 3 June 1988 in conjunction with the 15th session of EIFAC: 11 pp. (mimeo)

Bnińska, M. and Leopold, M. (1988) Analyses of lake fishery management for the decision-making process. Symposium on management schemes for inland fisheries, held in Goteborg, Sweden, 31 May – 3 June 1988 in conjunction with the 15th session of EIFAC: 9 pp. (mimeo)

Colby, P. J., Spangler, G. R., Hurley, D. A. and McCombie, A. M. (1972) Effects of eutrophication on salmonid communities in lakes. *J. Fish. Res. Bd Can.*, **29**, 975–83.

Cowx, I. G. (1988) Application of creel census data for the management of fish stocks in large rivers in the United Kingdom. Symposium on management schemes for inland fisheries, held in Goteborg, Sweden, 31 May – 3 June 1988 in conjunction with the 15th session of EIFAC: 15 pp. (mimeo)

European Inland Fisheries Advisory Commission (EIFAC) (1984) Documents presented at the symposium on stock enhancement in the management of freshwater fisheries, Budapest, Hungary, 31 May – 3 June 1982 in conjunction with the 12th session of EIFAC. *EIFAC tech. Pap.*, **42**, Supp., Vol. 1 (1–281) and Vol. 2 (283–554).

FAO (1987) *Yearbook of Fishery Statistics: 1985 Catches and Landings* (FAO Fish. Ser., Vol. 60), FAO, Rome, 461 pp.

Hartmann, J. (1978) Fischereiliche Veranderungen in Kulturbedingt eutrophierenden seen. *Schweiz. Z. Hydrol.*, **39**, 243–54.

Hus, M. (1988) Zwiazki rekreacji i rybactwa na przykĺadzie jezior Augustowskich (Relationships between recreation and fisheries as exemplified by lakes in Augustów area), doctorate dissertation, IRS, Olsztyn (Inland Fisheries Institute, Olsztyn, Poland). (200 pp. mimeo, in Polish)

Leach, J. H., Johnson, M. G., Kelso, J. R. M., Hartmann, J., Nümann, W. and Entz, B. (1977) Responses of percid fishes and their habitats to eutrophication. *J. Fish. Res. Bd. Can.*, **34**, 1964–71.

Leopold, M. (ed.) (1986) Stan i perspektywy rybactwa śródladowego w Polsce (Status and prospects of freshwater fisheries in Poland). Expertise for the Ministry of Agriculture, IRS, Olsztyn (Inland Fisheries Institute, Olsztyn, Poland), 44 pp. (mimeo, in Polish)

Leopold, M. (1988) General outline and basic premises of the management schemes for lake fisheries in Poland. Symposium on management schemes for inland fisheries, held in Goteborg, Sweden, 31 May – 3 June 1988 in conjunction with the 15th session of EIFAC: 8 pp. (mimeo)

Leopold, M. and Bnińska, M. (1987) Methods used in Poland for estimating the effectiveness of stocking practices. EIFAC Workshop on methods of determining the effectiveness of stocking practices, held in Olsztyn, Poland, 5–11 October 1987: 28 pp. (mimeo)

Leopold, M., Bnińska, M. and Nowak, W. (1986) Commercial fish catches as an index of lake eutrophiation. *Arch. Hydrobiol.*, **106**, 513–24.

Leopold, M., Bnińska, M., Woĺos, A., Szlażyǹska, K. and Gogola, H. (1987) Ocena stanu troficzności wybranych jezior woj. sĺupskiego na podstawie analiz wieloletnich odĺowów (Determination of the trophic status of selected lakes in Sĺupsk District on the basis of long-term catch statistics). Expertise for the District Authorities, IRS, Olsztyn (Inland Fisheries Institute, Olsztyn, Poland), 298 pp. (mimeo, in Polish)

Mastyński, J. (1985) Gospodarka rybacka i mozliwości produkcyj ne wybranych zbiorników zaporoaych Polski (Fishery management and productivity of selected dam reservoirs in Poland). *Roczniki Akademii Rolniczej w Poznaniu, Rozprawy Naukowe*, **146**, 91 pp. (in Polish)

Wegleńska, T, Zdanowski, B., Ejsmont–Karabim, J., Karabin, A. and Koriycka, A. (in press) Effect of changing fish stock on the biocenosis of the pond-type Lake Warniak. *Ekol. pol.*

Welcomme, R. L. (ed.) (1975) Symposium on the methodology for the survey, monitoring and appraisal of fishery resources in lakes and large rivers. *EIFAC tech. Pap.* **23**, Supp. 1: 747 pp.

Welcomme, R. L. (1985) River fisheries. *FAO Fish. Tech. Pap.*, **262**, 330 pp.

Chapter twenty two

Aquaculture

H. R. Lin and R. E. Peter

22.1 INTRODUCTION

Aquaculture, the rearing of aquatic organisms under controlled or semi-controlled conditions, has expanded rapidly world-wide over the past two to three decades. The discipline includes the culture of both freshwater and marine organisms, and freshwater fish species include both cool-water and warm-water species. Cool-water species are best cultured in the 12–25 °C range, while warm-water species have temperature optima in the vicinity of 25–30°C. Among the former, various species of the family Salmonidae are widely cultured in suitable environments. The latter group includes the most important freshwater species, the cyprinid fishes, which are cultured around the world, and recently reached a total annual production of 1.8 million tonnes (Billard and Marcel, 1986).

Cyprinids have many advantages for fish culture. Species in this family have colonized a very wide variety of biotopes, possess the ability to withstand a wide range of temperatures and oxygen levels (e.g. common carp, *Cyprinus carpio*, are especially tolerant of low dissolved oxygen concentrations and can respire anaerobically over short periods), feed at all levels of the trophic chain (phytoplankton, macro- and microzooplankton, benthos, macrophytes and fish), and display varied modes of reproduction. Cyprinids are naturally found in very diverse habitats (e.g. streams, rivers, lakes, ponds) and can therefore be raised in a variety of culture conditions. Cyprinids have a wide geographic distribution, thanks in part to human intervention, and are now found and cultured on most continents.

This chapter summarizes the state of knowledge in the main fields of cyprinid aquaculture: culture systems, nutrition, growth, reproduction, raising of larvae, selection for stocking, and genetics. The common carp, the Chinese major carps (grass carp, *Ctenopharyngodon idella*; bighead carp, *Aristichthys nobilis*; silver carp, *Hypophthalmichthys molitrix*; black carp, *Mylopharyngodon piceus*; crucian carp, *Carassius carassius*) and the Indian major carps (rohu, *Labeo rohita*; catla, *Catla catla*; mrigal, *Cirrhinus mrigala*) are the species considered in detail.

22.2 CULTURE SYSTEMS

The vast majority of cyprinids reared under aquaculture are raised in ponds, although other culture systems, such as raceways, cages, circular tanks, closed systems, rivers, lakes and canals, are employed in specialized instances.

Ponds

Fish culture ponds range in size from a fraction of a hectare to several hectares. In general, small ponds are used for spawning, fry rearing and fingerling production. Small ponds are also most commonly employed for research because of the relative ease and economy with which replicated experiments can be conducted. Large ponds are utilized for market-size fish production. Ponds larger than 100 ha are difficult to manage and do not appear to be in favour for commercial production.

Typical ponds are rectangular or square, and have well controlled levee and bottom slopes. Sufficient water is available to fill than within a reasonable period of time and to maintain the desired level, commonly 1–1.5 m. Drains may be constructed utilizing gate valves, which employ boards to control water levels. Pond levees should be wide enough to mow, and each pond should have at least one side with the levee wide enough to support vehicles used during stocking, feeding and harvesting.

The production capabilities of ponds will vary, depending upon the species, stocking densities and management. The degree of culture intensity ranges from highly extensive (low stocking densities with no supplemental feeding or fertilization) to relatively highly intensive (high-density stocking, fertilization, provision of complete diets, mechanical aeration, exchange of water, etc.). Traditional carp culture in Europe is mostly extensive, usually with no feeding or fertilization; production averages about 300 kg ha^{-1}. However, in some countries such as Poland, pond culture of carp leads to production levels of around 500 kg ha^{-1}. The addition of grain as supplemental feed increases production to levels of 1000–1200 kg ha^{-1} and experiments in which pelleted feed was provided led to further increases in production to 4000 kg ha^{-1}, while the use of continuous aeration doubled the latter production figure (McGeachin, 1986). The culture of tench, *Tinca tinca*, has been developed in Hungary as fish farmers become increasingly aware that polyculture has advantages over monospecies production. Although tench grows more slowly than carp, it is considered to be more resistant to disease and crowding. Because tench utilize approximately the same natural food resources as common carp, the yield of carp decreases if the tench population is too high;

therefore, tench production should not exceed 10% of the weight of the entire stock in normal carp ponds. The production of 2-year-old tench stocked together with common carp and silver carp in polyculture ponds is $1087 \, kg \, ha^{-1}$ (Von Lukowicz *et al.*, 1986). Intensive carp culture is practised in China, and some other Asian countries, as well as Israel. Among them, the polyculture system of pond fish culture in China is probably the most successful, the highest unit area production being more than $7500 \, kg \, ha^{-1}$, and the average unit area production $2500 \, kg \, ha^{-1}$ (Lin, 1982). Because of the high productivity of the polycultural system of freshwater fish in China, it will be described in detail.

Fish polyculture in China
Polyculture has a long history in China. It is believed that towards the end of the Tang Dynasty (about 1000 y ago), mixed culture of the four major Chinese carps (grass carp, silver carp, bighead, and black carp) was already productively developed. Since then, polyculture as an important principle and widespread technique has been applied more and more in fish culture in China. Monoculture is used only for fry and fingerlings up to about 3 cm long (Lin, 1982).

The major advantage of polyculture is to use fully the space and food available in the pond, as well as to maximize the beneficial interactions between compatible species with different feeding habits and ecology. Polyculture systems have evolved accordingly, with methods of stocking the same pond with various species that eat different types of food and dwell at different depths (Freshwater Fishculture Experimental Committee, 1973).

Species cultured. According to their habitats, species cultured can be divided into surface, mid-water, and bottom fishes. Surface-layer dwellers include plankton feeders such as silver carp and bighead; mid-water species consist of herbivores like grass carp, bream, *Parabramis pekinensis*, and round head bream (*Megalobrama amblycephala*); bottom-living fish comprise black carp feeding on gastropods and bivalves, common carp and crucian carp feeding on benthic burrowers, bottom dwellers and benthic algae. With these different species in ponds, all food resources at different depths will be fully utilized.

The interactions of stocked fishes are complex: some are beneficial and should be promoted, whereas those that are competitive and mutually exclusive should be avoided.

Although herbivorous, grass carp cannot digest whole plant cells because they lack cellulase. Their excreta therefore contain many intact and undigested plant cells. Because the grass carp is a frequent feeder, the amount of food it ingests is voluminous. As a result, water in ponds soon becomes very eutrophic and thus unfavourable to the grass carp. Eutrophic water promotes the proliferation of plankton, food for silver carp and bighead. If the pond is mix-cultured with these species, the fertility of the water will be reduced, rendering it suitable for grass carp. Such an interaction fully utilizes the food (plant material given to grass carp), promotes yield, and reduces cost. Furthermore, phytoplankton are the primary producers in the food chain; since silver carp are phytoplankton feeders, they have the shortest food chain, and so can more efficiently utilize the nutrient available and reduce more effectively the fertility of the water. Therefore, the grass carp and silver carp should be cultured together, as illustrated in the Chinese proverb, one grass carp supports three silver carps.

As plankton feeders throughout life, silver carp and bighead are indispensable for polyculture. They are also less competitive with other adult fishes, less susceptible to disease, and grow rapidly. Silver carp and bighead are basically competitive in their diet since both are plankton feeders. Also, silver carp feed more actively than bighead. Thus, when these two species are cultured together, they are never stocked in equal numbers; the number of silver carp is usually the smaller, in a ratio of 1:3–5.

Black carp are often cultured together with silver carp and bighead. Excreta of black carp also increase the fertility of water. Growth rate and yield of silver carp and bighead in black carp ponds are similar to those in grass carp ponds.

Common carp interact with silver carp and bighead in the same way as black carp, without competing for food. Though the growth rate of common carp is lower than those of black carp and grass carp, it is still acceptable. Fry of common carp are easily obtained and are highly adaptable, making them the ideal principal species to be cultured. If they are to be mix-cultured with grass carp or black carp, their number should be small so that the feeding of the latter will not be affected.

The diet of crucian carp is similar to that of common carp, but more varied because crucian carp can ingest small quantities of larger plankton. Crucian carp are suitable for polyculture if stocked in small numbers, and are the best species for ponds with low nutrient content and high acidity which are unsuitable for most species.

Mud carp, *Cirrhinus molitorella*, feed on decomposing grasses and manure. They do not compete with other species for food, and their ability to ingest detritus is greater than that of common carp. Therefore they should be mix-cultured with other species, especially if grass carp is the principal species. In central and northern China, where mud carp are not available, silvery chub, *Xenocypris* sp., which resemble mud carp in their mode of life and feeding habits, are used in polyculture in their stead.

Choice of species. In the polyculture system there generally are one or two principal species with large populations in the ponds, and four or five, or as many as seven or eight, compatible species cultured with them. The choice of principal species to be reared depends largely on three criteria:

1. Availability of fish fry and fingerlings: in China, most fish farms produce their own fry and fingerlings. Thus, in places where the availability of

fingerlings of grass carp, black carp, bighead, or silver carp is sufficient, it will be best to have these fishes as the principal species. In southern China where fingerlings of mud carp abound, they too can be reared as a principal species.

2. Availability of feed: because of the high rates of stocking, very heavy fertilization and feeding are used in all polycultural ponds. Therefore, to minimize the cost and to avoid transporting food over long distances, the principal species to be cultured should be determined by the type of food available locally.

3. Fertility of pond: the water quality and the composition of natural foods are closely related to pond fertility. Generally, silver carp or bighead should be the principal species for fertile water, grass carp for less fertile water, black carp and common carp for deep ponds, and crucian carp for waste pools.

The choice of compatible species will also be influenced by these three criteria, but it depends mainly on the interaction with the principal species.

The relative proportions of surface, mid-water, and bottom fish vary greatly, according to locality and fertility of the ponds. Practical experience indicates that in some places, with silver carp and bighead as the compatible species, their number can at most be only about 50% of the total mid-water and bottom fishes. If the ratio is increased, the excreta of the latter cannot fertilize the water sufficiently to favour growth of silver carp and bighead, so the pond must be fertilized artificially or additional food must be given.

Management. The rearing of fry to marketable size may take 1 or 2 y depending on the geographic conditions and the species. In southern China, where the growth period is long and temperature higher, marketable size can be achieved in 1 y. In the basin of the Yangtze River and other northern districts, the rearing period is normally 2 y.

Fish farmers always start to harvest the marketable fishes in October and continue until December. Ponds are cleared in winter and stocking is complete again in early February. This practice is advantageous because air and water temperatures are low during the winter and the fish are less active, so less physical damage is likely to be inflicted during harvesting and stocking; moreover, fish stocked earlier will start to feed earlier and the growing period will be prolonged.

In general, high stocking density is necessary for high yield. For instance, from a stocking density of 600–750 grass carp and 6000–7500 mud carp per hectare and some other compatible species, one fish farm in Guangdong Province obtained a yield of less than $2250 \, kg \, ha^{-1}$ in 1964. When the stocking density was 1050–1200 grass carp and 15 000 mud carp ha^{-1} in 1969, and the two species were mix-cultured with other species, more feeding, and better management, the yield was increased to more than $4500 \, kg \, ha^{-1}$. However, there are two limiting factors affecting stocking density: living space and dissolved oxygen. If the stocking density exceeds a reasonable limit, the yield will be reduced and the fish will be stunted and unmarketable.

Stocking density should be determined by pond condition, species cultured, availability of fry and fingerlings, managerial procedures, and production planning. It appears that a stocking density of 10 500–21 000 ha^{-1} is most suitable for ponds with depths of 1.0–2.0 m.

The main purpose of fertilization is to enrich the water and thereby promote the proliferation of plankton and benthos. For newly constructed ponds and ponds with low fertility, about 2500–4000 kg manure ha^{-1} is generally applied in winter after the ponds are drained and cleaned. Pig manure is often used, and in many places pigs are penned on pond banks. If human sewage is used, it should be decomposed fully. A pond with a large proportion of silver carp or bighead requires continuous replenishment of nutrients, hence supplementary fertilization should be frequent but in small quantities. Excess fertilization will adversely affect the fish, because it can easily lead to hypoxia due to decomposition of organic matter. If after a few applications of fertilizer the water becomes too fertile, treatment must be temporarily stopped and the pond must be diluted with fresh water. In addition, part of the fertile pond water may be allowed to drain into paddy fields which fresh water from the paddy field is drawn into the pond.

For high-density ponds, feeding is more important than fertilization. The quality and quantity of food, together with the way it is administered (fixed location and fixed time of feeding), greatly influence fish production. The application of food should depend on the type of fish cultured, the stage of fish development, the season, weather, water temperature, water quality, etc. Furthermore, food must be palatable to the fish, economical, and in adequate supply.

There are two types of polyculture practised in China, namely multiple harvesting and restocking, and multigrade polyculture.

Multiple harvesting and restocking polyculture is a traditional method whereby fish of different species of various sizes are reared in the same pond from fingerling to marketable size; depending on the growth of fish and time of year, selective harvesting is used to remove the larger individuals during the rearing period. The pond is then restocked with small fish to replace the ones removed and thus maintain an optimal stocking density. With this method, a total stocking density of about 15 000 ha^{-1} is common. The combination of species varies from place to place. For example, in the basin of the Yangtze, where black carp is the principal species, the composition is about 42% block carp, with 24% grass carp, 12–13% silver carp, 7–8% bighead, 7–8% round head bream, 3–4% common carp, and 3–4% crucian carp. Harvesting and restocking is carried out two to four times during summer and autumn; all fishes are removed in winter after the pond is drained completely.

In multigrade polyculture, fish are reared in a series of ponds from fry to marketable size, with fish sorted into different ponds according to size. As in multiple harvesting and restocking, such a method provides enough living space and food for the fish to grow because their density can be adjusted according to their size and to the productive capacity of the pond. Subsequently the technique also takes advantage of the maximum growth potential of the fish, and the yield increases.

Multigrade polyculture is generally divided into four to six grades. The number of grades varies with different species, stocking density, marketable size, etc.

Fish polyculture in other countries

About half of the common carp produced in Japan are reared intensively in ponds. There are two types of carp culture, namely farm (or irrigation) pond culture and running-water pond culture (Suzuki, 1986). Ponds are heavily stocked, fish are intensively fed with both pelleted feed and silkworm pupae several times a day, and each irrigation pond is provided with aeration pumps. Production ranges from 0.4 to $1.6 \, \mathrm{kg \, m^{-2}}$ for farm pond culture, and $100–200 \, \mathrm{kg \, m^{-2}}$ for running-water pond culture.

In India, traditional polyculture of major Indian carps, catla, rohu, mrigal and calbasu, *Labeo calbasu*, has been replaced by composite fish culture, a system in which these indigenous species are cultured together with common carp, Chinese silver carp and grass carp, each species occupying a distinct ecological niche in the pond (Jhingran, 1986). As with polyculture in China, the basic advantage of composite fish culture is that when compatible fishes of different feeding habits are stocked together, they obtain their requirements without harming each other, and each species may have a beneficial influence on growth and production of the other. This culture system, together with manuring and fertilization, supplementary feeding and pond aeration, resulted in high fish production in ponds in India. After a decade of applied research, composite fish culture makes it possible to obtain an average yield of $5 \, \mathrm{t \, ha^{-1}}$ in Indian freshwater ponds (Opuszynski, 1986).

Nowadays, Israeli fish culture is based on an intensive polyculture system, generally consisting of a mixture of common carp, silver carp, tilapia, *Tilapia aurea*, and mullet, *Mugil cephalus*, and produces about $8–10 \, \mathrm{t \, ha^{-1}}$ (Opuszynski, 1986). During the growing season, fish ponds are fertilized twice a weak with poultry manure and chemical fertilizers, pelleted feeds or grains are provided, and mechanical aeration is used. Stocking densities for common carp at some high-yield ponds ranges from 2500 to 6500 fish $\mathrm{ha^{-1}}$, and may account for 32–59% of total production (McGeachin, 1986).

Cages

In floating cage culture, fish are reared in streams, canals, reservoirs, lakes, or the intake or discharge channels of power plants. Cages are constructed of rigid frames over which welded wire fibre or nylon netting is stretched and secured. Cages may be provided with flotation materials, or may be tied to a floating platform. Because there is free circulation through each cage, water quality within cages is generally good. Recently, carp production by this method has increased more than that by the other methods in some countries, because of its various advantages, such as high productivity per unit area and ease of management and harvesting. For example, in 1982 about 42% of cultured carp in Japan were produced by this system, compared with only 21.8% in 1973 (Suzuki, 1986). The cages range in area from 25 to 100 m², are constructed to float to a depth of 1.5–2.5 m, and are held in position by poles driven into the bottom of the lake; pelleted feed with high protein content is provided several times daily from an automatic feeding machine. Production averages are equivalent to 431 t ha⁻¹ (McGeachin, 1986).

Raceways

Raceways are culture chambers in which water is introduced at a relatively rapid rate so that the water within each unit is replaced at intervals of from a few minutes to a few hours. Because of the rapid turnover rate, the fish are constantly exposed to new water of high quality; thus it is possible to stock very high densities of fish in small volumes. Raceways may be linear or circular. Linear raceways are constructed of concrete, while circular raceways may be of concrete, fibreglass or metal. Circular raceways normally have centre drains and are rarely over 10 m in diameter, whereas linear raceways have different lengths. The stocking capacity of a raceway will depend upon the flow rate, the species under culture, and the quality of the incoming water. In Japan, 14–17% of carp production is produced in raceways, where the water flow ranges from 91 to 455 l s⁻¹ and the carp are fed pelleted diets containing silkworm pupae; the production from this system is equivalent to 2203 t ha⁻¹ (McGeachin, 1986).

Rivers, lakes and canals

In China, not only are ponds used for fish culture, but also large water bodies such as lakes, reservoirs, canals, small rivers and their tributaries have been developed into extensive fish culture facilities. The inlets and outlets of lakes and reservoirs have been blocked off with nets, predators controlled, and carp stocked and supplementally fed. There is an increasingly widespread practice of stocking a mixture of carps and other species in lakes and reservoirs. Fingerlings are obtained from hatcheries and fingerling rearing farms, which are co-ordinated with fish culture of lakes and reservoirs. In these cases, even without feeding or fertilization, the annual yield is about 150–375 kg ha⁻¹. In small lakes and reservoirs, where feeding and fertilization are carried out, the yield is much higher, e.g. for a reservoir in

Zhejiang Province, the annual yield is $870\,kg\,ha^{-1}$. Because the growth of stocked fishes mainly depends on natural food occurring in lakes and reservoirs, stocking densities should be based on the natural food resources in the water and the abundance of the different foods for different fish. For instance, lakes and reservoirs initially undertaking fish culture can be stocked with 40–60% grass carp, black carp and common carp, and 60 or 40% silver carp and bighead; for lakes and reservoirs where fish culture has taken place for several years, fewer grass carp, black carp and common carp should be stocked because of the decline in food items for these species (Lin, 1982).

22.3   NUTRITION AND GROWTH

Nutritional requirements

Most cyprinids lack stomachs and consume small quantities of food, so evacuate more frequently than fish having a stomach; however, the nutritional requirements of cyprinids differ little from those of carnivorous fish. Each group of the basic components, whether organic or inorganic in origin, is important in the nutrition of fish and must be provided in its ration.

The protein content of fish cultured in ponds varies from 15 to 20%. Althouh the optimum protein content in carp diet was estimated to be 35%, in a diet containing 18% lipid it was possible to reduce protein level to 29% without any decrease in weight gain (Dabrowski *et al.*, 1986). Proteins play an important role in fish nutrition. They cannot be replaced, either by fat or by carbohydrates. In the assessment of the nutritional value of proteins, the amino acid composition is also important. More than 20 amino acids have been identified in animals and plants; some are non-essential and others essential. The former are synthesized in the animal, while the latter are not and must be obtained from the food. There is a special group of semi-essential amino acids, in the presence of which the non-essential ones are consumed more efficiently. Fish proteins comprise the total complex of essential amino acids, but their individual quantity varies in different species. By using test diets it was determined that the same 10 amino acids as those for most animals are indispensable for carp growth. Quantitative requirements of amino acids can be established, based on the growth response of fish fed the test diet for 6 weeks. Ogino (1980) proposed that amino acid requirements can be estimated from data on amino acid composition of the whole body and daily body protein deposition. If a diet containing 35% protein with 80% absorbability is fed at a level of 3% biomass daily, it can be assumed that the fish deposits 0.58 g of protein per 100 g of body weight daily. However, the deposition rate does not account for metabolic pathways of amino acids that do not lead to protein synthesis. In addition, absorbability of individual amino acids differs greatly, depending on the protein source and time after feeding (Dabrowski, 1986).

Fats are formed from carbohydrates in the food, constitute an important source of energy, and serve as solvents for certain biologically active substances, in particular vitamins. Fat reserves in the body of fish constitute a most unstable component, varying according to season, age, and conditions of feeding and rearing. Under satisfactory rearing conditions and supply of natural food and artificial feeds, the fat content increases with advancing age. On the basis of fat content and intensity of fat accumulation, it is possible to determine the biological condition of fish. The quantity and quality of fat formation is particularly important in the process of rearing stock material. The quality of the fat is assessed on the basis of fatty acid composition; the most important are myristic, palmitic, arachidonic, oleic, linoleic and linolenic acids. However, not all the fatty acids essential for fish can be synthesized. In particular, carp need linoleic and linolenic acids, essential fatty acids (EFAs) that can only be obtained from the food. Based on the difference in growth rate caused by feeding diets containing various fatty acids to carp of 0.5 g for 6 weeks, Takeuchi and Watanabe (1977) concluded that a mixture of 1% 18:2n-6 and 1% 18:3n-3 could satisfy EFA requirements, and were superior to either fatty acid fed separately. In addition, highly unsaturated fatty acids such as 20:5n-3 and 22:6n-3 were assimilated more efficiently than linoleic and linolenic acids.

The carbohydrate metabolism of carp is associated with fat accumulation. When carbohydrates are increased in the ration, the body fat content increases. When fingerlings are being raised and prepared to live through the winter, the practice is to increase the supply of carbohydrates to augment fat deposition, a factor related to winter hardiness. However, an excess of carbohydrates in the ration is harmful to the protein content of the body, particularly in growing fish.

It is believed that fish require the same vitamins as homoiothermal animals. A deficiency in vitamins in carp feeds does not cause such severe physiological dislocations as in homiotherms, but it does result in retarded growth, reduced resistance to diseases, convulsions, muscular atrophy, exudation, and exophthalmos. Artificial feeds containing vitamin requirements of carp, according to the findings of a number of experiments, are as follows; B_2, 0.11–0.33 mg; B_6, 0.15 mg; nicotinic acid, 0.55 mg; pantothenic acid, 1.0–1.4 mg; vitamin A,100–500 units per kg body weight of fish. Carp also need vitamins C, D and E. Carp assimilate feed containing vitamins A, B, C, D and E better, their growth rates increase, and the food coefficient (food conversion to fish tissue) decreases considerably. In general, fish obtain all the essential vitamins from natural foods, although the composition is quite variable in the food spectrum of carp. When the possibility of obtaining vitamins from natural foods decreases considerably or is almost excluded (e.g. during culture in cages or enclosures), the addition of vitamins under highly dense stocking is especially important.

Minerals are essential for bone formation, normal metabolism and other vital functions. A deficiency in minerals disrupts mineral metabolism, leads to diseased conditions, and even increases mortality; minerals must be included in a balanced carp diet. Essential requirements of dietary Zn, Mn, Cu, Mg, and Cr have been established in carp (Satoh *et al.*, 1983). The extent of accumulation of trace elements by fish varies seasonally and is determined by intensity of feeding and physiological activity. The growth and development of fish depend not only on the presence of minerals, but also on the ratio of mineral substances in natural food, feeds, and pond water. Quantitative requirements of minerals have to be considered in connection with the level of particular minerals in the water; e.g. the dietary Ca requirement of carp appears to be nil if the water contains Ca at a level of 14–20 P.P.M. (Ogino and Takeda, 1976).

Food and feeding habits

The natural food of cyprinids can be classified into three groups: (1) main food, or the natural food which the fish prefers under favourable conditions and on which it thrives best, (2) occasional food, or the natural food that is well liked and consumed as and when available, and (3) emergency food, which is ingested when the preferred food items are not available and on which the fish is just able to survive. For instance, certain planktonic crustaceans and rotifers form the main food of the fry (15–20 mm) of most cyprinids, and phytoplankton form the emergency food.

Feeding habits of adult fishes may vary according to the amount and type of food present. The food spectrum of fishes varies seasonally, depending on availability.

The food and feeding habits of fingerling and adult cyprinids differ markedly from those of their fry. In general, adult fishes can be classified as herbivores, carnivores, or omnivores. Most are omnivorous, and some are hervibores (such as grass carp). In addition, plankton- and detritus-feeding species can be put into a separate class, including silver carp, bighead, catla, and mud carp, which consume phyto- and zoo-plankton, decayed microvegetation and detritus. Cyprinids can also be classified according to the trophic niche they occupy: (1) plankton-eating surface feeders, such as catla, silver carp, and bighead, (2) mid-water feeders, such as grass carp and rohu, and (3) bottom feeders, such as black carp, mud carp, mrigal, and calbasu.

The composition of pelleted diets suited to their nutritional requirements has been widely researched and applied. Optimum feeding rates for carp vary, depending on fish size and age, water temperature, relative amount of natural food available, and the quality of the feed. Feeding rates for pond culture are generally 2–4% of body weight daily. Carp are fed either once in the morning, or continuously with demand or automatic feeders.

Growth and growth hormone

The rate of body growth exhibits a seasonal cycle in several cyprinid species, including common carp (Kawamoto *et al.*, 1957) and goldfish (Marchant *et al.*, 1986). These species are found in temperate climatic zones and have a decreased growth rate in the winter and an increased growth rate in the summer. A number of variables, including food availability, reproductive activities, temperature and photoperiod, probably contribute to seasonal changes in growth rate. In general, growth rates increase with increasing water temperature until an optimum temperature is reached, above which growth rates decrease (Brett, 1979). Environmental temperature influences several processes related to body growth, including metabolic expenditure, food intake and conversion rates. The influence of photoperiod on body growth in fish is not clear, as experiments have often yielded conflicting results (Brett, 1979). Studies on goldfish, *Carassius auratus* (Marchant and Peter, 1985) have shown that changes in growth rates are more closely related to tempera-ture changes, although a modifying influence of photoperiod on the growth response to temperature cannot be ruled out. Further studies (Marchant *et al.*, 1986) indicated that there are at least three influences on growth rate in the goldfish. First, warm water temperature causes an increase in growth rate at all times of the year, irrespective of photoperiod. Second, photoperiodic conditions can modify the growth response to temperature. Third, the photo-period modification of growth is itself modified by the time of year during which the experiment is conducted, indicating that the previous environ-mental history of the experimental fish is important, or that a circannual rhythm in growth is present which can only be partially modified by environ-mental manipulations.

The relationship between growth hormone (GH) and body growth in fish has been investigated (Marchant *et al.*, 1986). In goldfish, serum GH levels can be correlated to the rates of body growth, and both growth and serum GH levels can be influenced by environmental variables. For instance, seasonal changes in serum GH levels appear to be correlated with seasonal changes in daylength; also, serum GH levels are usually elevated at warmer temperatures. These results indicate that increased levels of serium GH do have a stimulatory influence on body growth in goldfish. Further studies on the influence of environment on GH and growth, the neural regulation of GH secretion, the mechanism of action of GH, and interactions with other hormones are of interest to aquaculturists. It is probable that use of environ-mental manipulations, as well as manipulation of hypothalamic neuroendo-crine mechanisms regulating GH secretion, will be fruitful methods of stimulating increased blood levels of GH, and consequently, increased body growth rates in cultured fishes.

22.4 INDUCING BREEDING

Reproductive cycles and environmental cues

Most cyprinid fishes are seasonal breeders, but a few breed continuously. Among the seasonal breeders, there is variation in the time of year when breeding occurs. Fishes integrate their physiological function with environmental cycles, and the endogenous periodicities of physiological processes are responsible in part for seasonal reproduction. In addition, certain environmental factors that act as cues for the approaching favourable season for reproduction impinge on the sensory organs, and through them affect the central nervous system, the hypothalamus and pituitary, and finally the gonads. It is through such environmental factors that the endogenous rhythm is brought into phase for the precise breeding time. Photoperiod, temperature and seasonal rainfall are important environmental factors in regulating reproductive cycles in fishes.

In the common carp, the reproductive cycle is dependent more on temperature than on photoperiod. In southern China, common carp usually breeds in January and February when water temperature reaches 18 °C. In India, common carp shows two main peaks of breeding activity in a year, once during spring and again in autumn when optimal thermal conditions prevail (Sundararaj, 1981). In Israel, the carp normally breeds in April and May. Maintenance of carp at a warm temperature (23 °C) accelerates ovarian recrudescence and spawning (Gupta, 1975). In France, common carp spawns in the summer. Pituitary concentration of gonadotropin is low in winter and increase in spring at the time of gonadal recrudescence and in the spawning season (Billard and Breton, 1978).

Chinese carps have been reared in temperate and tropical climes, where they attain sexual maturity 1–2 y earlier in tropical than in temperate waters. Warm temperatures and long photoperiod coupled with good diet are responsible for accelerated growth and gonadal maturation. In natural waters, Chinese carps spawn only once a year, but under cultivation they can spawn several times a year. This change of reproductive cycle is induced by changes of environmental conditions. If intensified feeding is given to the post-spawn breeders when water temperature is above 20 °C, they will reach maturity again after 40–50 d.

The Indian major carps show gonadal recrudescence from March to June at a time when both photoperiod and temperature are increasing; it is surmised that these two factors are involved in initiating gonadal recrudescence. Spawning in the Indian major carps is stimulated by environmental factors that prevail during the rains or the monsoon season. Rains bring about increase water levels and velocity of flow, flooding of shallow areas, dilution of certain ions and concentration of others, changes in smell and taste of water, as well as changes in biotic parameters such as growth of algae and other green vegetation. Specific combinations of some or all of these factors may be perceived through sensory organs and conveyed to the hypothalamus, which then activates the pituitary to produce gonadotropin to induce maturation, ovulation and spawning (Sundararaj, 1981).

Traditional methods of induced breeding

The traditional methods of induced spawning for cyprinids are based on injection of either crude extract of common carp pituitary glands (CPE), that is hypophysation, or partially purified human chorionic gonadotropin (HCG), with the addition, in a few species, of [D-Ala^6, Pro^{9}NEt]-luteinizing hormone-releasing hormone (LHRH-A). Two injections are required; the first injection consists of a low dosage, and the second, given about 6 h later, a large dosage. The first injection serves as a primer for the second, resolving dosage (Levani-Zermonsky and Yaron, 1986). When natural fertilization is adopted, five to ten females can be induced to spawn in each spawning pond. The sex ratio (females to males) is usually 1:2 or 2:3. Ovulation and spawning generally occurs about 8 h after the second injection, giving a total of about 14 h from start to finish for the whole process (Table 22.1). After spawning, brooders should be captured with a large-meshed net and then the fertilized eggs are collected with a finemeshed net which is set at the outlet of the spawning pond. A circular incubation course is commonly used in production, but incubation jars and incubation net-cases, etc. are also used.

The use of CPE and HCG to induce ovulation and spawning of cyprinids, although generally successful, has several drawbacks. For example, to induce ovulation and spawning of 100 grass carp brooders with CPE would require collecting 8000–10 000 common carp pituitary glands. CPE and HCG is highly variable in potency and has a very short storage life, and some species do not respond to HCG. In addition, resistance to HCG develops in some species, particularly silver carp and bighead; although it has been suggested that this lack of responsiveness is due to development of an immune response (Fujien–Kiangsu–Chekiang–Shanghai Cooperative Group, 1977), antibodies to HCG could not be detected in silver carp resistant to HCG (Van Der Kraak *et al.*, 1988).

Contrary to earlier claims of successful induction of ovulation and spawning of Chinese carp by a single, or two injections of LHRH-A (Cooperative Team for Hormonal Application in Pisciculture, 1977; Fish Reproduction Physiology Research Group, and Peptide Hormone Group, 1978; Fujien–Kiangsu–Chekiang–Shanghai Cooperative Group, 1977), controlled experiments with LHRH-A injections induced only relatively low and variable rates of ovulation in common carp, silver carp, mud carp, grass carp, bighead carp and bream (Lin *et al.*, 1986, 1987, 1988). Currently, LHRH-A is not used alone to induce ovulation and spawning in the traditional methods, although it may be used to supplement treatments with CPE or HCG (Peter *et al.*, 1988).

Recent advances in the understanding of the neuroendocrine regulation of gonadotropin (GtH) secretion in teleost fishes have led to an explanation of

Table 22.1 Traditional methods of induced spawning of cultured carp in China*

Species	Water temp. (°C)	First injection†	Interval (h)	Second injection†	Time to ovulation (or spawning) following last injection (h)
Common carp *Cyprinus carpio*	20–30	CPE(2–4 kg⁻¹) HCG(800–1000 IU kg⁻¹)	— 	— 	14–12 14–12
Silver carp *Hypophthalmichthys molitrix*	20–30	CPE(2–4 kg⁻¹) HCG(100–200 IU kg⁻¹) HCG(100–200 IU kg⁻¹)	5–6 5–6 5–6	CPE(10–20 kg⁻¹) HCG(700–1000 IU kg⁻¹) HCG(400 IU) + LHRH-A(10 µg kg⁻¹)	8–6 8–6 8–6
Mud carp *Cirrhinus molitorella*	22–28	CPE(2–4 kg⁻¹) CPE(2 per fish) + LHRH-A(100 µg kg⁻¹)	4–5 4–5	CPE(16–30 kg⁻¹) CPE(10–16 kg⁻¹) + LHRH-A (100 µg kg⁻¹)	6–4 6–4
Bream *Parabramis pekinensis*	22–30	CPE(2–4 kg⁻¹) CPE(2 per fish) + LHRH-A(10 µg kg⁻¹)	5–6 5–6	CPE(12–24 kg⁻¹) CPE(6–10 kg⁻¹) + LHRH-A(50 µg kg⁻¹)	10–8 10–8
Grass carp *Ctenopharyngodon idella*	18–30	CPE(1–2 kg⁻¹) CPE(1 kg⁻¹) LHRH-A(10 µg per fish)	5–6 5–6 5–6	CPE(6–12 kg⁻¹) CPE(4–10 kg⁻¹) + LHRH-A(10 µg kg⁻¹) CPE(2–4 kg⁻¹) + LHRH-A(10 µg kg⁻¹)	8–6 8–6 8–6
Bighead carp *Aristichthys nobilis*	20–30	CPE(2–4 kg⁻¹) HCG(100–200 IU kg⁻¹) HCG(100–200 IU kg⁻¹)	5–6 5–6 5–6	CPE(10–20 kg⁻¹) HCG(700–1000 IU kg⁻¹) HCG(400 IU kg⁻¹) + LHRH-A (10 µk kg⁻¹)	8–6 8–6 8–6
Black carp *Mylopharyngodon piceus*	20–30	CPE(2–4 kg⁻¹) CPE(2 kg⁻¹) + LHRH-A(100 µg kg⁻¹)	6–8 4–5	CPE(16–30 kg⁻¹) CPE(10–16 kg⁻¹) + LHRH-A (100 µg kg⁻¹)	10–8 10–8

* Information gathered from a number of fish hatcheries in Guangdong Province, P. R. China.
† CPE, carp pituitary extract; HCG, human chorionic gonadotropin: LHRH-A. [D-Ala⁶. Pro⁹ NEt]-luteinizing hormone-releasing hormone

why injection of LHRH-A alone has not been widely adopted by Chinese fish farmers to induce ovulation and spawning of cyprinids, and to the development of a new, highly efficient and effective technique for induced ovulation and spawning of cultured fish.

Neuroendocrine regulation of gonadotropin secretion

Gonadotropin (GtH) secretion in teleosts is regulated by a dual neurohormonal system, with GtH release stimulated by a gonadotropin-releasing hormone (GnRH) and inhibited by dopamine, which functions as a gonadotropin release-inhibitory factor (GRIF) by acting directly at the level of the pituitary to modulate the actions of GnRH as well as by modulating the spontaneous release of GtH (Fig. 22.1) (Peter *et al.*, 1986). However, the inhibitory actions of dopamine on GtH secretion can vary in potency between different species. For example, in goldfish and common carp, the dopamine inhibition is very strong, the superactive mammalian GnRH agonist [D-Ala^6, Pro^9-NEt]-LHRH (LHRH-A) and salmon GnRH agonist [D-Arg^6, Trp^7, Leu^8, Pro^{9}NEt]-LHRH (sGnRH-A) stimulate only a modest increase in serum GtH and are ineffective in inducing ovulation (Peter *et al.*, 1985, 1986, 1987c; Sokolowska *et al.*, 1985; Lin *et al.*, 1987). Administration of the dopamine receptor antagonst pimozide (PIM) or domperidone (DOM) greatly potentiates the action of LHRH-A and sGnRH-A on GtH release, and combined injections of PIM or DOM and LHRH-A or sGnRH-A are highly effective in inducing ovulation and spawning in these species (Lin *et al.*, 1988; Peter *et al.*, 1988). In the bream, injection of a high dosage of LHRH-A or sGnRH-A alone is effective in stimulating GtH release and ovulation; however, the combination of pimozide with LHRH-A results in potentiation of the GtH response and shortening of the response time from injection to ovulation (Lin *et al.*, 1986).

The most potent analogue of salmon GnRH (sGnRH), in terms of stimulating GtH release, is sGnRH-A (Peter *et al.*, 1985, 1987a). sGnRH-A, in combination with pimozide or domperidone, is more potent than LHRH-A in inducing ovulation in goldfish and common carp. In order to minimize dosages of analogue for induced ovulation of cultured brood fish, sGnRH-A appears to be highly advantageous.

As indicated in Fig. 22.1, a number of drugs can block the inhibitory actions of dopamine on GtH release (Peter *et al.*, 1986, 1987 a,b). Reserpine, a drug that depletes all catecholamines, is highly effective in potentiating the actions of LHRH-A (Lin *et al.*, 1986); however, this drug can have severe side-effects and is not recommended for applied use. Domperidone and pimozide are the most effective dopamine antagonists in the goldfish (Omeljaniak *et al.*, 1987). Notably, domperidone does not cross the blood-brain barrier in the goldfish (Omeljaniak *et al.*, 1987), thereby minimizing the possible side-effects by central actions of drugs such as pimozide and reserpine. Domperidone was more potent than pimozide in potentiating the actions of LHRH-A in common

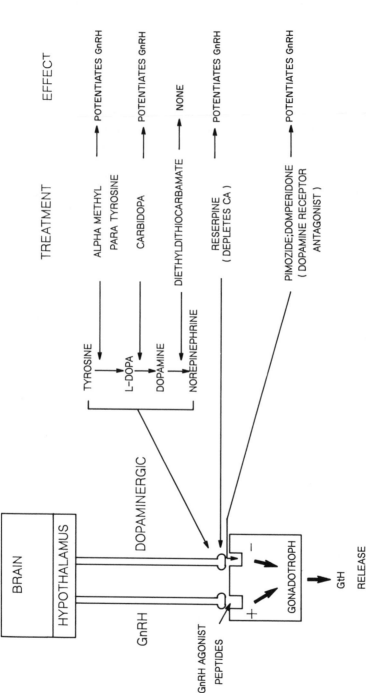

Fig. 22.1 Model of the neuroendocrine regulation of gonadotropin (GtH) release in teleosts (reproduced with permission from Peter *et al.*, 1987b). Gonadotropin-releasing hormone (GnRH) and dopaminergic neurons from the brain innervate the pituitary gland and its gonadotroph cells. GnRH stimulates (+) and dopamine inhibits (−) GtH release. GnRH agonist peptides injected into the fish act on the GnRH receptors on the gonadotroph cells. Catecholamine (CA) synthesis occurs in the terminals of the dopaminergic neurons. Various drug treatments (e.g., injection of alpha methyl para tyrosine, carbidopa, diethyldithiocarbamate, reserpine, pimozide, domperidone) have different actions on CA synthesis or at the receptor level, and if the drug blocks the actions of dopamine on the gonadotroph cells by any of these actions, the actions of GnRH peptides are potentiated.

carp (Lin *et al.*, 1988). To minimize drug dosages and to limit the potential side-effects, domperidone is the most desirable dopamine blocker for use in induced ovulation and spawning of cultured fish.

The Linpe method of induced ovulation and spawning

The combination of a GnRH analogue (LHRH-A or sGnRH-A) and a dopamine antagonist (domperidone) for induced ovulation and spawning of cultured fish is called the Linpe method. On the basis of experimental work and field trials (Lin *et al.*, 1986, 1987, 1988; Peter *et al.*, 1987b), Table 22.2 summarizes the latest information available on effective dosages of domperidone and sGnRH-A and LHRH-A for the Chinese carp. The effectiveness of the Linpe method has been judged against several criteria (Peter *et al.*, 1987b, 1988): a high rate of ovulation occurs consistently from one group of brooders to another within each species, ovulations are complete rather than partial, the time from injection to ovulation is short and predictable, the ovulated eggs are fertile and viable, and induction of ovulation by this technique does not affect subsequent reproductive cycles by the same brood fish (Peter *et al.*, 1988). Experiments and field trials at fish farms on each species of cultured carp were highly successful in meeting these criteria. The main advantages of the Linpe method compared to the traditional methods include lower cost of the synthetic drugs, long drug stability, high predictability of the time from injection to ovulation,

Table 22.2 Linpe method of induced ovulation and spawning of cultured carp in China

Species	Water temp. (°C)	Domperi-done (mg kg^{-1})	+	LHRH-A (μg kg^{-1})	sGnRH-A (μg kg^{-1})	Time from injection to ovulation (or spawning) (h)
Common carp	20–25	5	+	10	—	16–14
		1	+	—	10	16–14
Silver carp	20–30	5	+	20	—	12–8
		5	+	—	10	12–8
Mud carp	22–28	5	+	10	—	6
Bream	22–30	3	+	10	—	10–8
Grass carp	18–30	5	+	10	—	12–8
Bighead carp	20–30	5	+	50	—	12–8
Black carp	20–30	3	+	10,	—	
			plus, 6 h later,			
		7	+	15	—	6–8

decreased stress on broodstock because only a single injection is needed, and lack of any side-effects on subsequent reproductive cycles.

The Linpe method has been commercialized by Syndel Laboratories, Inc., Vancouver, BC, Canada, under the trade name Ovaprim. The Ovaprim spawning kit is specially formulated for use with carp, salmonids and other freshwater cultured fish. The Ovaprim kit has been successfully used in a number of species (including Chinese carps and Indian carps) as the preferred method for induced ovulation and spawning of cultured freshwater fish.

22.5   REARING LARVAE

The larval stage in fish generally includes the period from hatching until the adult form is assumed at a clear change or metamorphosis (Blaxter, 1969). In cyprinids, the most obvious signs at this stage are the laying down of scales and other pigmentation and the appearance of haemoglobin in the circulation, as well as the development of the swim bladder and lateral line. Newly hatched fish are sometimes called yolk-sac larvae until the yolk is absorbed, then larvae until the completion of adult form. The term fry is commonly use by carp culturists in reference to the late larval stage from yolk-sac larvae (3–4 d after hatching) to 25–30 mm in total length.

Larval development

The early morphological descriptions of the eggs and larvae of cultured Chinese carp were made by Chung *et al.* (1965) on the basis of samples obtained during artificial propagation in Guangdong Province, southern China. Detailed descriptions of early embryonic and larval development of some Chinese carps were also provided by Tsuchiya (1967).

Since the developmental characteristics of the larvae (or fry) of the Chinese cultured carp are basically similar, the important features may be summarized as follows.

1. Newly hatched fry: total length 4.8–5.9 mm; body transparent; abdomen filled with pear-shaped yolk; blood light yellow. The larvae possess a developing form of the brain, notochord, optic organ, auditory organ, olfactory organ, anus, intestine and gill slits. They depend on the yolk for nutrition. The fry cannot swim, but wave their tails vigorously to rise towards the water surface once every few minutes and then sink slowly to the bottom, lying on their back.
2. First day after hatching: total length 5.5–6.8 mm; yellowish-brown pigments appear in eyes; pectoral fins appear; gill slits become conspicuous; fin folds well developed; mouth slit ventrally positioned; yolk sac shrinks gradually.

3. Second day after hatching: total length 7.5–8.0 mm; swim bladder begins to form, but is not yet filled; yolk sac becomes narrow and elongated; lower jaw now able to move; mouth moves to anterior position; pectoral fins are slightly larger, but have no bony rays; the larvae begin swimming horizontally.

4. Third day after hatching: total length 8.2–8.5 mm; swim bladder filled with gas; intestine completed in tube form, slightly bent at the portion beneath the swim bladder; mouth anterior; gill rakers conical; yolk sac almost totally absorbed; many colour pigments appear on body surface; the fry begin to feed on small zooplankton, such as rotifers and nauplii of Cladocera and copepods.

5. Fourth day after hatching: total length 8.7–9.4 mm; dorsal fin membrane upheaved, but without bony rays; bony rays appear in caudal fin; posterior end of notochord slightly bent upwards; thorn-like pharyngeal teeth appear; yolk sac completely absorbed; feeding habit unchanged.

6. Seventh day after hatching: total length 12–13.5 mm; caudal fin begins to fork; bony rays appear in dorsal and anal fins; ventral fins just begin to grow; swim bladder divides into two chambers, anterior chamber small and round, posterior chamber oval; gill rakers increase in number; first coil appears at anterior portion of intestine; principal foods are Cladocera, copepods and rotifers.

7. Tenth day after hatching: total length about 18 mm; all fins except ventrals are more developed; caudal fin rays begin segmentation; the fry swim actively; feeding habit similar to that of the previous days.

8. Thirteenth day after hatching: total length about 24 mm; all fins are developed and appear like those of the adult; gill rakers are well developed; scales begin to appear; intestine conspicuously elongated; feeding habits begin to change to adult.

9. Seventeeth day after hatching: total length about 27–30 mm. The juvenile fish (or fingerlings) are similar to adults in both external appearance and internal structure.

The above observations on larval development were made at water temperatures of 28–29 °C. The developmental rate is largely related to the water temperature. When the water temperature is high, the development process is fast, and vice versa.

Stocking and feeding of larvae

In order to avoid competition among larvae, monoculture is performed from 3–4 d after hatching to 25–30 mm body length, because the feeding habits of the Chinese cultured carps are almost identical. If feeding is sufficient, it takes about 15–25 d to nurse the larvae to completion of development.

The larvae can be reared on live foods or artificial feed, or a mixture of both, and using various stocking and feeding systems.

Extensive larval culture

Extensive larval carp culture employs fertilizer to induce phytoplankton and zooplankton blooms. This system offers a wide variety of live food types and sizes, so acceptable food materials are always available for the larvae as they grow and change their food requirements. For example, in southern China, extensive larval culture includes the following procedures (Chung *et al.*, 1965).

1. Pond cleaning: earth ponds with excessive silt and decayed food deposited on the bottom must be cleaned before stocking, because these sediments decompose rapidly at high water temperatures, producing poisonous materials such as organic acids, hydrogen sulphide and methane.
2. Manure application: a combination of different kinds of herbaceous plants, compost, and inorganic manure integrated with an organic form, are applied into ponds to propagate plankton. Generally, manure is put into ponds 15–20 d before the release of larvae, so that the decomposed materials can spread out in the water and produce large numbers of phytoplankton, protozoa, rotifers, cladocerans and copepods.
3. Eradiction of predators: predator eradication is the most important procedure in raising the survival rates of larvae, because manure heaps in the pond attract some insects or aquatic insects and frogs to lay eggs or to live in the heaps.
4. Stocking: stocking density is closely related to larval survival growth rates. If the density is too high, the larvae will grow slowly and have a low survival rate. The stocking density is generally based on the larvae species and quality, pond area, depth of water and season. In general, for Chinese carp, 2.4–3.3 million larvae per hectare are used.
5. Culture management: the key task in culture management is the control of water fertility, which influences the quantity of plankton and the prevention of water deterioration.

Artificial foods

The use of artificial foods, prepared from either synthetic or naturally occurring components, for larval rearing of carp has received more attention in recent years.

For instance, the usual practice for the rearing of larvae from hatching to the post-larvae stage in Japan (Tsuchiya, 1967) was to use the net-cage system and feed with synthetic foods. The net cage is placed in an ordinary large rearing pond and tied to bamboo or wooden stakes. The mesh size is determined and adjusted according to the growth of the larvae. In the initial stocking (3–4 d after hatching), the mesh size should be at least 30 mesh per inch (12 mesh per cm) to prevent escape. As the fry grow, larger mesh sizes, which also permit the free passage of water, must be adopted. Each cage should preferably be supplemented with a water spray system or an aeration system to prevent oxygen deficiency. The initial feeding may consist of zooplankton such as *Daphnia* or rotifers. Since these materials may not be easily available, other foods can be substituted, such as egg-yolk (boiled or half boiled), liver, powdered milk, yeast, soybean milk, fish meal, codfish roe, fermented soybean, roasted wheat meal, *Daphnia* (frozen or dried), or synthetic fish food. Following experiments, boiled egg-yolk and liver have become the most commonly used items. The synthetic food is applied by sprayer on the pond water. The tiny food particles disperse slowly in the water and are eaten by the fish over a number of hours, thus reducing the chance of water pollution, and can be rationed accurately. With the spraying method, the daily ration of egg-yolk may be one unit (i.e. one egg-yolk) per 10 000 larvae. The daily ration of liver is estimated to weigh 3–5 g per 10 000 larvae. As the fry grow, the ration is gradually increased; the amount of both egg-yolk and liver is increased by 10% every day or every second day.

It is now possible to rear common carp larvae on artificial diets only. For example, a batch of 12 000 larvae of common carp was reared exclusively on artificial food for 43 d (21 d on a diet of mainly liver and yeast, and then commercial trout starter feed); survival rate was 71–87%, and total food conversion ratio was 0.62 (6.08 kg of food produced a final total weight of 9.88 kg of fish). These results indicate that it is possible to rear carp larvae without zooplankton (Charlon *et al.*, 1986). Food particle availability and the preservation of water quality are important limiting factors in the interaction between larvae, their food and the rearing medium. Food distribution, water renewal, waste elimination and tank cleaning therefore require further attention (Bergot, 1986).

The currently successful artificial diets for carp larval rearing contain variable amounts of single cell proteins, although the effects of the contribution of nucleic acids during early growth are not yet well understand (Kaushik, 1986).

22.6   SELECTION AND GENETICS

The purposes of selection

In improving the qualities of cultured fish by selection, use is made of their variation in many morphological, physiological and biochemical features. Because much of this variation is hereditary, selection will be effective. The level of genetic variation in fish populations is very high, as can be deduced from studies on protein polymorphism (Kirpichnikov, 1981). Therefore, genetic manipulation and selection are equally necessary in the domestication and creation of new fish breeds for aquaculture.

The main purpose of selection of fully domesticated carp species in aquaculture is that of increasing the productivity of the existing and newly developed breeds. Such an increase may be achieved primarily by raising the growth rate and survival. The growth rate depends upon the quantity of food consumed and the assimilation efficiency. Correspondingly, two main trends in selection can be adopted: selection for more complete consumption of the living or artificial food, e.g. an increase in feeding activity; and selection for better food assimilation, e.g. a decrease in the food coefficient (Kirpichnikov, 1966; Steffens, 1975; Merla, 1979). In both cases, the success of genetic selection will markedly depend on the resistance of the fish to unfavourable environmental factors, in particular to high or low temperatures, decreased oxygen content, low pH, the presence of waste materials, and the accumulation of metabolic end products (Kirpichnikov, 1971; Swarts *et al.*, 1978) or to various invasive and infectious diseases, particularly to widespread global viral or bacterial diseases, as well as to the local endemic ones that are difficult to treat or to prevent by ordinary means (Kirpichnikov, 1966, 1971; Kirpichnikov *et al.*, 1972, 1976, 1979; Gjedrem and Aulstad, 1974).

Improvement of reproductive characteristics is very important for the further development of fish breeding in aquaculture. The aim of selection may vary greatly, depending on the species and the conditions of cultivation. For example, delayed sexual maturation is advantageous for the common carp; a shift in the maturation time, accompanied by a more effective response to hypophysation, is essential for the selection of grass carp, silver carp and bighead in some areas (Konradt, 1973).

Successful selection requires vast, well-planned and frequently long selective programmes. It is particularly difficult to obtain changes in the characters associated with reproduction. The heritability of such characters is usually low since they are determined to a large extent by well-balanced, stable, polymorphic genetic systems established by natural selection which operates permanently (Kirpichnikov, 1981).

Mass selection

Mass selection is used to control the subsequent reproduction of individuals having the best phenotypes. The features used in such selection can be quite different and generally depend on specific purposes. The characters used in selecting cultured carp may include increased body weight or body size, good exterior indices, the absence of any defects, resistance to unfavourable environmental effects and diseases, and certain improved physiological or biochemical characteristics. During mass selection, the genotype of the selected or the discarded individual remains unknown, because mass selection only applies to the phenotype and is therefore always associated with greater risk of error (Kirpichnikov, 1981).

Mass selection in Europe and Israel selected the largest Israeli mirror carp individuals, with the highest ratio of height to length; the response to selecting the largest individuals was tested in a bidirectional selection experiment conducted over five consecutive generations (Moav and Wohlfarth, 1976). Comparison of the up-select lines (mass selected for faster growth rate) with the random control showed a negative response for two generations, followed by a positive response for two generations. Both up-select and their control lines showed slower growth than that of a standard crossbred control. Down selection (mass selection for slower growth rate) generated a response during the first three generations, equivalent to a realized heritability of 0.3, but thereafter the down lines ceased to respond to further selection. These results were obtained when the selection lines and their controls were tested in ponds. When samples of the same lines were tested in cages, up selection showed a continued response, and during the last three generations, growth of the up-select lines exceeded that of the crossbred control. The applied conclusion from these tests is that selection of the larger individuals is not an effective method for improving the growth rate of carp in ponds (Wohlfarth, 1986). However, beginning from about the fifteenth century, selection of the common carp in Europe was achieved predominantly by mass selection, and until recently mass selection was the main technique used in cultured fish breeding. Although success has not been very pronounced because selection techniques were primitive and many rules for performing selection work were violated, mass selection will continue to play a role, particularly with regard to characters with a relatively high heritability, and it can be very useful when combined with other forms of selection (Kirpichnikov, 1981).

Selection for relatives

In contrast to mass selection, selection for relatives does, to a large extent, involve selection for genotypes; the positive characteristics of individuals chosen for subsequent reproduction are determined from an analysis of their close relatives. Two forms of such selection are used in fish breeding: family selection, and evaluation of parents by testing progeny.

In family selection, several families or offspring from different pairs or small parental groups are cultivated under standardized conditions. After the quality of these families is evaluated, the best family is taken for further reproduction. A family is evaluated on the basis of the mean values calculated for it. The 'nest', including one female and two males, is frequently used instead of parental pairs in breeding the common carp; less frequently, the families are the progeny of several individuals. Family selection when correctly conducted can be highly effectively (Kirpichnikov, 1981).

Progeny testing can be conducted using different techniques. The simplest method involves comparison of the offspring obtained from different pairs or nests of parents; the evaluation refers not to individual parents but to their combinations. For example, common carp breeders frequently use simplified diallele crosses. Males or females are separately crossed with one or more individuals. The mating of each of the males tested with the same two females provides a sufficiently reliable evaluation of the breeding value of these males (Kirpichnikov, 1981).

In family selection, the best of the most productive and resistant families is retained for subsequent reproduction, whereas progeny testing yields parents providing the best offspring. The testing of parents requires one or even two years, so the interval between generations is increased. A slowing of the selection rate is highly undesirable, and therefore family selection is to be preferred in fish breeding.

Crossbreeding

Inbreeding has been shown to interfere with the growth of cultivated carp. For example, in the common carp one inbreeding generation after the crossing of sibs retards growth by 10–20% and is accompanied by decreased viability and a marked increase in the number of malformations (Moav and Wohlfarth, 1968; Wahlfarth and Moav, 1971). Even moderate inbreeding leads to reduced growth in the common carp (Kirpichnikov, 1969). Although inbreeding is in general harmful, it can also be useful in fish selection. This usefulness stems primarily from the stabilization of selection traits due to increased homozygosity and the augmented expression of several of them. It is applicable in the creation of commercial hybrids possessing heterosis i.e. they are superior to their parents in a number of traits, as a consequence of crosses of individuals from different inbred strains. For example, in Hungary inbred strains have been developed aimed at the rearing of a commercial 'double' interstrain hybrid of the common carp (Bakos, 1979). This very difficult work is incomplete, but several hybrid combinations have been tested and proved to be highly productive.

Crossbreeding between unrelated individuals increases the genetic component of their variation and thereby facilites selection. It is important, before beginning selection with any fish species, to choose the most suitable breeding system for establishing the desired characteristics of the breed and maintaining sufficient heterogeneity. Only with this approach can one guarantee further improvement of the productive traits of the broodstock. One of the simplest approaches involves the separation of the selected group into two, three or even more subgroups. Each is reproduced separately under conditions of moderate inbreeding with artificial selection in each generation (Kirpichnikov, 1960; Golovinskaya, 1962). Individuals from different subgroups are periodically crossed with one another. Meanwhile, the crosses are also used in commercial fish production because it is advantageous to cultivate hybrids of the first generation commercially if they possess heterosis. For example, crossbreeding between different genetic groups of the European carp resulted in heterosis of growth rate (Moav and Wohlfarth, 1968; Lobchenko, 1972; Moav *et al.*, 1975a; Bakos, 1979; Smisek, 1979). Heterosis has also been demonstrated in crosses between Chinese and European carp

(Moav *et al.*, 1975b; Tapiador *et al.*, 1977; Wohlfarth *et al.*, 1983) and between Japanese and European carp (Suzuki, 1979; Suzuki and Yamaguchi, 1980; Shimma *et al.*, 1983).

The more promising hybrid cyprinids are:

1. Interbred hybrids of the carp, *Cyprinus carpio*. Good results are obtained in crosses between the Ropsha and the Ukrainian carps (Kuzema and Tomilenko, 1962; Kuzema *et al.*, 1968; Kirpichnikov *et al.*, 1971; Tomilenko *et al.*, 1978; Alexeenko, 1979), the scaled and framed Ukrainian carps (Kuzema, 1953), two stocks of the Para carp (Boborova, 1978), and three stocks of the Krasnodar carp (Kirpichnikov *et al.*, 1979). To increase the productivity of the Chinese carp it is recommended that European carp should be crossed with the Chinese big-belly carp (Moav *et al.*, 1975; Wohlfarth *et al.*, 1975; Moav, 1979). Heterosis manifested in better survival and productivity has been noted after crosses of Hungarian and Polish carps, as well as Chinese mirror carp of the scatter-scaled type and Hsingkuo red carp (The Editorial Board of *Acta Hydrobiologica* Sinica, 1977). A similar phenomenon has been reported after crosses of the Japanese Yamato carp with the European mirror carp (Suzuki, 1979);
2. Hybrids of the silver carp of Amur and Chinese origin (Poljarush, 1979). Heterosis manifested in the improved survival rate and increased growth rate (11%) has been observed for the larvae of such hybrids;
3. Hybrids of the domestic carp and the Amur wild carp, *Cyprinus carpio haematopterus*, are widely used in the Ukraine (Tomilenko *et al.*, 1977);
4. Intergeneric hybrids of the common and crucian carp (Nikoljukin, 1952). These infertile hybrids fortuitously combine several useful traits of the parents and can be used for water bodies poorly suited to the cultivation of the common carp;
5. Intergeneric hybrids of the silver carp and the bighead (Grechkovskaja *et al.*, 1979);
6. Intergeneric hybrids of the Indian carps *Catla catla* and *Labeo rohita* (Chaudhuri, 1971); rohu–catla, rohu–mrigal, catla–mrigal, catla–calbasu (Kowtal, 1986), showing better growth rate than one of the parents.

The search for fish hybrids possessing heterosis is now being conducted in many countries, especially in the USSR, the USA, China and India. The high fertility of external fertilization characteristic of many fish species facilitates the production of first-generation hybrids in quantities sufficient for large commercial farms. One of the main obstacles in selection with hybrids of distantly-related species is the partial or complete infertility characteristic of some hybrid forms. It is not easy to restore the fertility of hybrids. The highly complex work on the development of fertile hybrids of the common and crucian carp which was initiated in the Ukraine (USSR) more than 40 y ago is of outstanding theoretical and practical importance in this respect (Kuzema and Tomilenko, 1965). However, some fish hybrids are fertile and this frequently creates a risk of contamination of broodstocks of the initial forms. Therefore, it is now necessary to develop methods of breeding infertile or unisexual commercial hybrids.

Gynogenesis in selection

The significance of gynogenesis for raising selection responses has already been considered. Gynogenesis has been induced in a number of cyprinids by inseminating eggs with irradiated sperm and restoring the diploid number of chromosomes through thermal or pressure shocks (Cherfas, 1975, 1981; Nagy et al., 1978, 1979; Nagy and Csanyi, 1982, 1984; Gervai et al., 1980; Stanley, 1976; John et al., 1984, 1986).

The main advantage of gynogenesis stems from the opportunity to construct highly homozygous inbred lines which can then be used to develop heterotic hybrids. Crossbreeds between gynogenetically produced parents are claimed to show a higher degree of heterosis than crossbreeds between the same lines, but from 'normally' produced parents, and this is applied commercially in Hungary (Bakos, 1982).

Polyploidy is induced by similar shock techniques using normally fertilized eggs. Direct inducement of triploidy has been achieved in three cyprinids: common carp (Gervai et al., 1980), *Rhodeus ocellatus* (Ueno and Arimoto, 1982), and grass carp (Cassani and Caston, 1985). The major aim of inducing polyploidy is the production of sterile triploids. Their potential application in aquaculture is the prevention of uncontrolled reproduction, i.e. it may allow populations in production ponds to be controlled. Sterility may also result in an improvement in meat quality and behavioural traits (Wohlfarth, 1986).

22.7   CONCLUDING REMARKS

The Chinese carps have been widely distributed for aquaculture around the world. A challenge for researchers is to adapt local cyprinids species for aquaculture in various regions, to lessen the probability of imported species displacing native species in the wild.

Polyculture plays an important role in the highly productive carp culture in China. The balance of species in polyculture is based on successful tradition. However, transfer of polyculture of other countries has not always been successful, owing to a lack of understanding of the food chain. The development of polyculture using new species would require additional research, but give the productivity per unit cost, such research could be of importance to developing countries.

Basic nutritional needs of cultured carps are reasonably well understood. Where the cultured fish consume natural foods, as in polyculture ponds, nutritive values may occasionally vary. When artificial diets are fed, nutritive value of the food can be controlled. As more fish species are brought into intensive aquaculture, the task of understanding nutritive requirements and construction of new diets will become bigger. Also, the possibilities of accelerating growth rates through manipulation of growth hormone levels or by stimulating greater food intake are open for research.

While induced ovulation and spawning of carps can be accomplished by the traditional methods of hypophysation or injection of HCG, more effective and efficient means are now possible through the use sGnRH-A and dopamine antagonists (Linpe method), now available as a commercial spawning kit. Although the Linpe method has been tested on a wide range of species, research needs to be done on new species being adapted to aquaculture. The manipulation of cyprinid reproductive cycles so that spawners are available at several times of the year remains a problem. Understanding more about larval nutrition, to enable successful development of aquaculture in new locations or in different seasons, also requires additional research.

Finally, the development and maintenance of special strains of carps requires particular attention. Selection for certain traits could increase the efficiency of aquaculture, and would be a very worthwhile endeavour.

ACKNOWLEDGEMENTS

This work was supported in part by grants from the International Development Research Centre of Canada.

REFERENCES

Alexeenko, A. A. (1979) Physiological traits of Ropsha-Ukrainian hybrid carps and its parental forms, in *Selection of Pond Fishes*, Kolos, Moscow, pp. 61–6 (in Russian with English abstract).

Bakos, J. (1979) Cross breeding Hungarian races of common carp to develop more productive hybrid, in *Advances in Aquaculture* (eds T. V. R. Pillay and W. A. Dill), Fishing News Books Ltd, Farnham, England, pp. 633–5.

Bakos, J. (1982) Ergebnisse der zuchtungsforschung bei karpfen in der Ungarishen Volksrepublik. *Fortschritte der Fischerei-Wissenschaft*, **1**, 99–102.

Bergot, P. (1986) Elevage larvaire de la carpe commune (*Cyprinus carpio* L.): Alimentation artificielle, in *Aquaculture of Cyprinids* (eds R. Billard and J. Marcel), INRA, Paris, pp. 227–34.

Billard, R. and Breton, B. (1978) Rhythms of reproduction in teleost fish, in *Rhythmic Activity of Fishes* (ed. J. E. Thorpe), Academic Press, London, pp. 31–53.

Billard, R. and Marcel, J. (1986) Preface, in *Aquaculture of Cyprinids* (eds R. Billard and J. Marcel), INRA, Paris, pp. 7–8.

Blaxter, J. H. S. (1969) Development of eggs and larvae, in *Fish Physiology*, Vol. 3 (eds W. S. Hoar and D. J. Randall), Academic Press, NY, pp. 177–252.

Bobrova, J. (1978) Organization and basic results of breeding work with common carp in Para Fish farm, in *Genetics and Selection of Fishes*, All-Union Res. Inst. Pond Fish, Moscow, pp. 99–111 (in Russian with English abstract).

Brett, J. R. (1979) Environmental factors and growth, in *Fish Physiology*, Vol. 8 (eds W. S. Hoar, D. J. Randall and J. R. Brett), Academic Press, NY, pp. 599–675.

Cassani, J. R. and Caston, W. E. (1985) Induced triploidy in grass carp, *Ctenopharyngodon idella* Val. *Aquaculture*, **46**, 37–44.

Charlon, N., Durante, H., Escaffre, A. M. and Bergot, P. (1986) Artificial feeding of carp (*Cyprinus carpio*) larvae, in *Aquaculture of Cyprinids* (eds. Billard and J. Marcel), INRA, Paris, p. 235.

Chaudhuri, H. (1971) Fish hybridization in Asia with special refrence to India. *Ref. FAO/UNDP(TA), (2926), Rome*, 151–9.

Cherfas, N. B. (1975) Investigations of radiation-induced gynogenesis in the carp (*Cyprinus carpio* L.). I. Experiments on obtaining the diploid gynogenetic progeny in mass quantities. *Genetika (Moscow)*, **11**, 78–86 (in Russian with English abstract).

Cherfas, N. B. (1981) Gynogenesis in fishes, in *Genetic Bases of Fish Selection* (ed. V. S. Kirpichnikov), Springer-Verlag, Berlin, pp. 255–73.

Chung, L., Lee, Y. K., Chang, S. T., Liu, C. C., and Chen, F. C. (1965) *The Biology and Artificial Propagation of Farm Fishes*, Science Publishing Association, Beijing, 242 pp.

Cooperative Team for Hormonal Application in Pisciculture (1977) A new effective ovulating agent for fish reproduction. *Sci Sinica*, **20**, 469–74.

Dabrowski, K. (1986) Protein digestion and amino acid absorption along the intestine of stomachless fish, common carp (*Cyprinus carpio* L.), *in vivo* study. *Reprod. Nutr. Develop.*, **26**, 755–66.

Dabrowski, K. Murai, T. and Becker, K. (1986) Physiological and nutritional aspects of intensive feeding of carp, in *Aquaculture of Cyprinids* (eds. R. Billard and J. Marcel), INRA, Paris, pp. 55–70.

Fish Reproduction Physiology Research Group and Peptide Hormone Group (1978) Radioimmunoassay on serum gonadotropin of carp (*Cyprinus carpio*). *Acta Biochem. Biophys. Sinica*, **10**, 399–407.

Freshwater Fishculture Experimental Committee (1973) *Study of Cultivation and Biology of Fishes in Chinese Freshwater*, 2nd edn, Academic Press, Beijing, 598 pp. (English translation).

Fujien-Kiangsu-Chekiang-Shanghai Cooperative Group for Actificial Reproduction of Freshwater Fishes (1977) A further investigation on the stimulatory effect of a synthetic analogue of hypothalamic luteinizing hormone releasing hormone (LRH-A) on spawning in domestic fishes. *Acta Biochem. Biophys. Sinica*, **9**, 15–24.

Gervai, J., Peter, S., Nagy, A., Horvath, L. and Csanyi, V. (1980) Induced triploidy in carp, *Cyprinus carpio* L. *J. Fish Biol.*, **17**, 667–71.

Gjedrem, T. and Aulstad, D. (1974) Selection experiments with salmon. I. Difference in resistance to vibro disease of salmon parr (*Salmo salar*). *Aquaculture*, **3**, 51–9.

Golorinskaya, K. A. (1962) Selective breeding in pond fish industry. *Ryborodstro Rybolorstro*, **3**, 7–10 (in Russian).

Grechkovskaja, A. P., Turanov, V. F. and Puljaeva, V. I. (1979) Backcrossings of the hybrids between silver carp and bighead, in *Materials of All-Union Scientific Conference on Development and Intensification of Fisheries in Inland Water of North Caucasus*, Rostor-Don., pp. 58–61 (in Russian).

Gupta, S. (1975) The development of carp gonads in warm water aquaria. *J. Fish Biol.*, **7**, 775–82.

Jhingran, V. G. (1986) Aquaculture of Indian major carps, in *Aquaculture of Cyprinids* (eds R. Billard and J. Marcel), INRA, Paris, pp. 335–46.

John, G., Reddy, R. V. G. K. and Gupta, S. D. (1984) Artificial gynogenesis in two Indian major carp, *Labeo rohita* (Ham.) and *Calta calta* (Ham.). *Aquaculture*, **42**, 161–8.

John, G., Reddy, R. V. G. K. and Jana, R. K. (1986) Artificial gynogenesis in the Indian carp, *Cirrhinus mrigala* (Ham.), in *Aquaculture of Cyprinids* (eds R. Billard and J. Marcel), INRA, Paris, p. 209.

Kaushik, S. J. (1986) Some aspects of larval nutritional physiology in carp, in *Aquaculture of Cyprinids* (eds R. Billard and J. Marcel), INRA, Paris, pp. 216–26.

Kawamoto, N. Y., Inouye, Y. and Nakanishi, S. (1957) Studies on the effects by pond areas and the densities of fish in water upon the growth rate of carp (*Cyprinus carpio* L.) *Rep. Fac. Fish. prefect. Univ. Mie*, **2**, 437–47.

Kirpichnikov, V. S. (1960) Organization of carp selective breeding. *Nauchna-Tech. Bull VNIORKH*, **11**, 38–40 (in Russian).

Kirpichnikov, V. S. (1966) Goals and methods of common carp selection. *Investija Gosud. nauchno-issled. Inst. Ozern Rech. Rybn. Khos. (GOSNIORKH)*, **61**, 7–28 (in Russian with English abstract).

Kirpichnikov, V. S. (1969) The present state of fish genetics, in *Genetics, Selection and Hybridization of Fishes*, Naka, Moscow, pp. 9–29 (in Russian).

Kirpichnikov, V. S. (1971) Methods of fish selection. 1. Aims of selection and methods of artificial selection. 2. Crossing, modern genetic methods of selection. *Rep. FAO/UNDP (TA) (2926)*, Rome, 202–16, 217–27.

Kirpichnikov, V. S. (1981) *Genetic Bases of Fish Selection*, Springer-Verlag, Berlin, pp. 274–8.

Kirpichnikov, V. S. and Faktorovitsch, K. A. (1972) The increase of the common carp resistance to dropsy by selection. II. The course of selection and the evaluation of the selected stocks. *Genetika (Moscow)*, **8**, 44–54 (in Russian with English abstract).

Kirpichnikov, V. S., Factorovich, K. A. Babushkin, J. and Ninburg, E. A. (1971) Selection of common carp for resistance to dropsy. *Izvestija Gosud. nauchna-issled. Inst. Ozern. Rechn. Rybn. Khos. (GosNIORKh)*, **74**, 140–53 (in Russian).

Kirpichnikov, V. S., Ilijasov, J., Shart, L. A. and Faktorovich, K. A. (1979) Selection of common carp (*Cyprinus carpio*) for resistance to dropsy, in *Advances in Aquaculture*, Fish News Books Ltd, Farnham, pp. 628–33.

Kirpichnikov, V. S. and Shart, L. A. (1976) Acceleration in the succession of common carp generations in the course of selective breeding of carp in southern regions of the USSR. *TrVNIIPRKH*, **23**, 55–63 (in Russian with English abstract).

Konradt, A. G. (1971) Problems of phytophagous fish selective breeding. *Izvestija Gosud. naucha-issled. Inst. Ozern. Rechn. Rybn. Khos. (GosNIORKh)*, 8512–9 (in Russian with English abstract).

Kowtal, G. V. (1986) Current status of hybridization amongst cultivated carps in India, in *Aquaculture of Cyprinids* (eds R. Billard and J. Marcel), INRA, Paris, p. 209.

Kuzema, A. I. (1953) Ukrainian breeds of the carps, in *Proc. Conf. Pond Fish Breeding*, Moscow, pp. 65–70 (in Russian).

Kuzema, A. I. and Tomilenko, V. G. (1962) Reserves for the increase of pond fish productivity. *Nauk. Pracy. Ukrain Inst. Rybn. Cosp.*, **14**, 71–84 (in Russian).

Kuzema, A. I. and Tomilenko, V. G. (1965) Development of new greeds of the commont breeds carp using the method of distant hybridization, *Rybn. Khoz. (Kiev)*, 213–7 (in Russian).

Kuzema, A. I. Kucherenko, A. P. and Tomilenko, V. G. (1968) Economic efficiency of rearing of Ropsha-Ukrainian hybrid common carp. *Ryb. Khoz.*, **6**, 68–74 (in Russian).

Levani-Zermonsky, B. and Yaron, Z. (1986) Changes in gonadotropin and ovarian steroids associated with oocyte maturation during spawning induction in the carp. *Gen. comp. Endocrinol.*, **62**, 89–98.

Lin, H. R. (1982) Polycultural systems of freshwater fish in China. *Can. J. Fish. aquat. Sci.*, **39**, 143–50.

Lin, H. R., Liang, J. Y., Van Der Kraak, G. and Peter, R. E. (1987) Stimulation of gonadotropin secretion and ovulation in common carp by an analogue of salmon GnRH and domperidone, in *Proc. First Congr. Asia Oceanic Soc. Comp. Endocrinol.* (eds E. Ohnishi, Y. Nagahama and H. Ishizaki), Nagoya University Corporation, Nagoya, Japan, pp. 155–6.

Lin, H. R. Van Der Kraak, G., Liang, J. Y., Peng, C., Li, G. Y., Lu, L. Z., Zhou, X. J., Chang, M. L. and Peter, R. E. (1986) The effects of LHRH analogue and drugs which block the effects of dopamine on gonadotropin secretion and ovulation in fish cultured in China, in *Aquaculture of Cyprinids* (eds R. Billard and J. Marcel), INRA, Paris, pp. 139–50.

Lin, H. R., Van der Kraak, G., Zhou, X. J. Liang, J. Y., Peter, R. E., Rivier, J. E. and Vale, W. W. (1988) Effects of (D-Arg⁶, Trp⁷, Leu⁸, Pro⁹ NEt)-LHRH (sGnRH-A) and (D-Ala⁶, Pro⁹NEt)-LHRH(LHRH-A), in combination with pimozide or domperidone, on gonadotropin release and ovulation in the Chinese loach and common carp. *Gen. comp. Endocrinol.*, **69** (1), 31–40.

Lobchenko, V. V. (1972) Crossing of mongrel Moldavian carp with Ukrainian and Kursk carp and with Eastern carp, in *Genetics, Selection and Hybridization of Fish* (ed. B. I. Cherfas), NTIS, US Dept Commerce, Springfield, VA pp. 245–6.

Lukowicz, M. von, Tamas, G. and Horvath, L. (1986) Aquaculture of tench, in *Aquaculture of Cyprinids* (eds R. Billard and J. Marcel), INRA, Paris, pp. 357–67.

McGeachin, R. B. (1986) Carp and buffalo, in *Culture of Nonsalmonid Freshwater Fishes* (ed. R. R. Stickney), CRC Press, Boca Raton, Florida, pp. 47–54.

Marchant, T. A. and Peter, R. E. (1985) Seasonal variations in body growth rates and circulating levels of growth hormone in the goldfish, *Carassius auratus. J. exp. Zool.*, **237**, 231–9.

Marchant, T. A., Cook, A. F. and Peter, R. E. (1986) The relationship between circulating growth hormone levels and somatic growth in a teleost species, *Carassius auratus* L., *Aquaculture of Cyprinids* (eds R. Billard and J. Marcel), INRA, Paris, pp. 43–54.

Merla, G. (1979) Grundlagen der Fischzuchtung, in *Industriemassige Fischproduktion,* Dtsch. Landwirtsch Verlag, Berlin, pp. 219–34.

Moav, R. (1979) Genetic improvement in aquaculture industry, in *Advances in Aquaculture*, Fish News Books, Farnham, pp. 610–22.

Moav, R. and Wohlfarth, G. (1968) Genetic improvement of yield in carp. *FAO Fish Rep. (44), Rome*, **4**, 12–29.

Moav, R. and Wohlfarth, G. (1976) Two-way selection for growth rate in the common carp (*Cyprinus carpio* L.). *Genetics NN*, **82**, 83–101.

Moav, R., Finkel, A. and Wohlfarth, G. (1975a) Variability of intermuscular bones, vertebrae, ribs, dorsal fin rays and skeletal disorder in the common carp. *Theoret. appl. Genet.*, **46**, 33–43.

Moav, R., Hulata, G. and Wohlfarth, G. (1975b) Genetic difference between the Chinese and European races of the common carp. I. Analysis of genotype–environment interactions. *Heredity Lond.*, **34**, 323–40.

Nagy, A. and Csanyi, V. (1982) Changes of genetic parameters in successive gynogenetic generations and some circulations for carp gynogenesis. *Theoret. appl. Genet.*, **63**, 105–10.

Nagy, A. and Csanyi, V. (1984) A new breeding system using gynogenesis and sex-reversal for fast inbreeding in carp. *Theoret. appl. Genet.*, **67**, 485–90.

Nagy, A. Rajki, K., Bakos, J. and Csanyi, V. (1979) Genetic analysis in carp (*Cyprinus carpio*) using gynogenesis. *Heredity, Lond.*, **43**, 35–40.

Nagy, A., Rajki, K., Horvath, L. and Csanyi, V. (1978) Investigation on carp (*Cyprinus carpio*) gynogenesis. *J. Fish Biol.*, **13**, 215–24.

Nikoljukin, N. I. (1952) Interspecies hybridization in fishes. *Gosud. Oblast. Izdatelstuo.*, Saratov, 10–38 (in Russian).

Ogino, C. (1980) Protein requirements of carp and rainbow trout. *Bull. Jap. Soc. Scient. Fish.*, **46**, 385–8.

Ogino, C. and Takeda, H. (1976) Mineral requirements in fish. III. Calcium and phosphorus requirements in carp. *Bull. Jap. Soc. Scient. Fish.*, **42**, 793–9.

Omeljaniuk, R. J., Shih, S. H. and Peter, R. E. (1987) *In vivo* evaluation of dopamine receptor-mediated inhibition of gonadotropin secretion from the pituitary of the goldfish, *Carassius auratus. J. Endocrinol.*, **114**, 449–58.

Opuszynski, K. (1986) Polyculture in carp ponds, in *Aquaculture of Cyprinids* (eds R. Billard and J. Marcel), INRA, Paris, pp. 269–81.

Peter, R. E., Chang, J. P., Nahorniak, C. S., Omeljaniuk, R. J., Sokolowska, M., Shih, S. H. and Billard, R. (1986) Interactions of catecholamines and GnRH in regulation of gonadotropin secretion in teleost fish. *Recent Prog. Horm. Res.*, **42**, 513–48.

Peter, R. E., Habibi, H. R., Marchant, T. A. and Nahorniak, C. S. (1987a) Vertebrate gonadotropin-releasing hormones: phylogeny and structure–function relationships. *Ann. NY Acad. Sci.*, **519**, 299–309.

Peter, R. E., Lin, H. R. and Van Der Kraak, G. (1987b) Drug/hormone induced breeding of Chinese teleosts, in *Proc. Third Int. Symp. reprod. Physiol. Fish* (eds D. R. Idler, L. W. Crim and J. M. Walsh), Memorial University of Newfoundland, St Johns, Canada, pp. 120–23.

Peter, R. E., Lin, H. R. and Van Der Kraak, G. (1988) Induced ovulation and spawning of cultured freshwater fish in China: advances in application of GnRH analogues and dopamine antagonists. *Aquaculture*, **74**, 1–10.

Peter, R. E., Nahorniak, C. S. Sokolowska, M., Chang, J. P., Rivier, J. E., Vale, W. W., King, J. A. and Millar, R. P. (1985) Structure–activity relationships of mammalian, chicken and salmon gonadotropin releasing hormones *in vivo* in goldfish. *Gen. Comp. Endocrinol.*, **58**, 231–42.

Peter, R. E., Sokolowska, M. Nahorniak, C. S. Rivier, J. E. and Vale, W. W. (1987c) Comparison of (D-Arg[6], Trp[7], Leu[8], Pro[9] NEt) luteinizing hormone-releasing hormone (sGnRH-A), and (D-Ala[6], Pro[9] NEt) luteinizing hormone-releasing hormone (LHRH-A), in combination with pimozide, in stimulating gonadotropin release and ovulation in the goldfish *Carassius auratus. Can. J. Zool.*, **65**, 987–91.

Satoh, S., Yamamoto, H., Takeuchi, T. and Watanabe, T. (1983) Effects on growth and mineral composition of carp of deletion of trace elements or magnesium from fish meal diet. *Bull. Jap. Soc. Scient. Fish.*, **49**, 431–5.

Shimma, Y., Suzuki, R. and Yamaguchi, M. (1983) Growth performance and body composition of F[1] hybrids between Yamoto and mirror carp reared with four kinds of practical diets. *Bull. National Res. Inst. Aquaculture* (Tamaki, Japan), **4**, 1–8.

Smisek, J. (1979) Hybridization of carp of the Vodnany and Hungarian lines. *Bull. Vurh. Vodnany*, **15**, 3–12 (in Czeck, with English abstract).

Sokolowska, M., Peter, R. E. and Nahorniak, C. S. (1985) The effects of different doses of pimozide and (D-Ala[6], Pro[9]-*N*-ethylamide)-LHRH (LHRH-A) on gonadotropin release and ovulation in female goldfish. *Can. J. Zool.*, **63**, 1252–6.

Stanley, J. G. (1976) Female homogamety in grass carp (*Ctenopharyngodon idella*) determined by artificial gynogenesis. *J. Fish. Res. Bd. Can.*, **33**, 1372–4.

Steffens, W. (1975) *Der Karfen* Cyprinus carpio, 4. Aufl. A. Ziemsen Verlag, Wittenberg Lutherstadt, pp. 1–35.

Sundararaj, B. I. (1981) *Reproductive Physiology of Teleost Fishes*. Aquaculture Development and Coordination Programme. ADCP/REP/81/16, p. 4.

Suzuki, R. (1979) The culture of common carp in Japan, in *Advances in Aquaculture* (eds T. V. R. Pillay and W. A. Dill), Fishing News Books Ltd, Farnham, England, pp. 161–6.

Suzuki, R. (1986) Intensive carp rearing in Japan, in *Aquaculture of Cyprinids* (eds R. Billard and J. Marcel), INRA, Paris, pp. 327–33.

Suzuki, R. and Yamaguchi, M. (1980) Improvement of quality in the common carp by crossbreeding. *Bull. Jap. Soc. Scient. Fish.*, **46**, 1427–34.

Swarts, F. A., Dunson, W. A. and Wright, J. E. (1978) Genetic and environmental factors involved in increased resistance of brook trout to sulfuric acid solutions and nine acid polluted waters. *Trans. Am. Fish. Soc.*, **107**, 651–77.

Takeuchi, T. and Watanabe, R. (1977) Requirement of carp for essential fatty acids. *Bull. Jap. Soc. Scient. Fish.*, **43**, 541–51.

Tapiador, D. D., Hendenson, H. F., Delmondo, M. N. and Tsuitsui, H. (1977) Freshwater fisheries and aquaculture in China. *F. A. O. Fish Biol. Tech. Pap.*, **168**.

The Editorial Board of *Acta Hydrobiologica Sinica* (1977) The introduction of an intervarietal hybrid carp, *Cyprinus carpio*, as a new object in freshwater fish culture. *Acta Hydrobiologica Sinica*, **6** (2), 147–8.

Tomilenko, V. G., Alexeenko, A. A. Panchenko, S. M., Olenetz, U. I. and Drok, V. M. (1977) Winter resistance of the different common carp hybrids. *Rybn. Khos.*, **2**, 17–19 (in Russian).

Tomilenko, V. G., Panchenko, S. M. and Zheltov, Y. (1978) Common carp breeding. *Urozhay. Kiev, Ukrain*, 32–4 (in Russian).

Tsuchiya, M. (1967) *Grass Carp and Silver Carp: Production of Fry*, Midori Shobo Book Company, Tokyo, 89 pp.

Ueno, K, and Arimoto, B. (1982) Induction of triploids in *Rhodeus ocellatus ocellatus* by cold shock treatment of fertilized eggs. *Experimentia*, **38**, 544–6.

Van Der Kraak, G., Pankhurst, N. W., Peter, R. E. and Lin, H. R. (1989) The antigenicity of human chorionic gonadotropin in silver carp (*Hypophthalmichthys molitrix*) and goldfish (Carassius auratus). *Aquaculture*, **78**, 81–6.

Wohlfarth, G. (1986) Selective breeding of the common carp, in *Aquaculture of Cyprinids* (eds R. Billard and J. Marcel), INRA, Paris, pp. 195–208.

Wohlfarth, G. and Moav, R. (1971) *Genetic investigations and breeding methods of carp in Israel*. Rep. FAO/UNDP (TA) (2926): 160–85.

Wohlfarth, G., Moav, R. and Hulata, G. (1975) Genetic differences between the Chinese and European races of the common carp. II. Multi character variation – a response to the diverse methods of fish cultivation in Europe and China. *Heredity* **34**, 341–50.

Wohlfarth, G., Moav, R. and Hulata, G. (1983) A genotype environment interaction for growth rate in the common carp, growing in intensively manured ponds. *Aquaculture*, **33**, 187–95.

Author index

Abd-Elgawad, A. M. 418
Abrahams, M. V. 511
Accame Muratori, R. 98–100
Adair, B. M. 277
Adam, H. 296, 299, 314, 319, 321
Adamek, Z. 365, 395
Adamicka, P. 355
Adams, C. G. 27
Agami, M. 554
Aguade, M. 112
Ahlquist, J. E. 104, 107–8
Akai, Y. 13
Alabaster, J. S. 445, 466
Al-Absy, A. 8
Alberch, P. 321
Albers, C. 433
Aldoori, T. Y. 468
Aldridge, H. 427
Aleev, Y. G. 141
Alexander, R. McN. 337, 341–2,
   357, 378, 380, 387–8, 427
Alexeenko, A. A. 615
Alfred, E. R. 168
Algranati, F. D. 510
Al-Habib, O. A. M. 437
Al-Hussaini, A. H. 378, 414
Ali, M. A. 296, 299, 537
Alikunhi, K. H. 148
Allan, J. R. 512, 517
Allendorf, F. W. 85, 104
Allum, M. O. 74

Almaca, C. 129, 214, 219, 221
Almeida Toledo, L. M. 102–3
Alpers, D. H. 414
Altman, J. A. 341–2
Amato, D. 108
Ambak, M. A. 168, 173, 179, 182,
   189
Amemiya, C. T. 95, 98, 101–4,
   106–7
Amthauer, R. 108
Anctil, M. 537
Anderson, J. R. 264, 267
Anderson, O. 556
Andersson, G. 532, 534, 537,
   543–4, 552, 557–61, 564, 566
Andrews, S. M. 37
Angerer, R. C. 105
Anker, G. C. 294, 299
Annandale, N. 134, 168
Antonini, A. 510
Aoki, I. 343
Aoyagi, S. 108
Aquadro, C. F. 112
Arai, R. 9, 11, 13, 17–18, 95–7, 100,
   130, 169
Araya, A. 108
Archie, J. W. 59–60, 62, 78
Ariens Kappers, C. U. 285
Arimoto, B. 616
Arnheim, 112
Arnold, G. P. 521

Arnold, J. 104, 108
Arrignon, J. 221, 232
Arruda, J. 544
Arthington, A. H. 267–8, 280
Asano, N. 100
Ash, R. 414–5
Astafeva, S. N. 341–2
Atema, J. 285, 303, 305, 310, 314, 317
Atkin, N. B. 92, 99–100, 106
Aubenton, F. d' 168, 187
Aulstad, D. 612
Avise, J. C. 85, 89–91, 93–4, 98, 104, 107–8, 111
Axelrod, H. R. 149, 224
Ayala, F. J. 85, 89, 91, 94, 107
Azada, M. A. 187

Baatrup, E. 314, 317
Babushkin, J. 612, 615
Bachmann, K. 106–7
Bachrach, W. 62
Backhouse, G. N. 267, 275, 279
Backiel, T. 148, 462, 466–7, 473, 476
Bagenal, T. B. 462, 494, 497
Bailey, J. 149
Bailey, R. G. 473
Bailey, R. M. 11, 74
Bainbridge, R. 427
Baker, A. J. 70, 251
Bakos, J. 614, 616
Ball, R. M. 104, 108
Ballantyne, P. K. 72
Ballintijn, C. M. 380, 388
Balon, E. K. 24, 144, 147, 226, 474–6, 486, 488–9
Banarescu, P. 9, 14–17, 19, 22, 25, 27, 43, 45, 99, 134–6, 139–40, 166–7, 169, 171, 178, 183, 242
Banister, K. E. 8, 12, 146, 214, 217, 222–3
Barat, A. 97–8, 100–1
Barbour, C. D. 240, 245
Bardach, J. E. 303, 310
Barel, C. D. N. 229, 387, 406
Barlow, G. W. 519
Barlow, J. A. 98
Barnett, J. C. 474
Baron, G. 288

Barthelmes, D. 586
Batchelor, B. C. 164, 185
Bauchot, M. L. 285
Bauchot, R. 285
Baumann, L. R. 296, 299
Baumgartner, J. V. 62
Beadle, L. C. 211–2, 222
Beamish, F. W. H. 430, 457
Beattie, D. M. 363, 367–8
Beaufort, L. F. de 15, 26, 164, 168, 178, 182
Beck, M. L. 92
Beckenbach, A. T. 108
Becker, G. 522
Becker, G. C. 256
Becker, K. 598
Beckwitt, R. 108
Begg, G. 227
Behnke, R. J. 72
Beiles, A. 112
Belaud, A. 463
Bell, M. A. 62
Bell-Cross, G. 222
Bellon, G. 346
Bender, F. 162
Benndorf, J. 566
Bennett, M. D. 107
Ben-Tuvia, A. 148
Bentzen, P. 108
Berg, L. S. 7, 12–13, 17, 19–20, 23, 25–7, 133, 167, 173
Berg, R. 370
Berg, W. J. 104, 108
Bergeijk, W. A. van 332, 336
Berggren, H. 537, 558–9, 564
Berggren, W. A. 35, 47
Bergman, E. 537
Bergot, P. 415, 611
Bergstrand, E. 371
Berlocher, S. H. 94
Bermingham, E. 104, 108
Bern, H. A. 450
Bernard, L. M. 433
Bernardi, G. 105
Bernacsek, G. M. 227
Bernhardt, R. 300
Bernstein, J. W. 516
Berrebi, P. 92–3

Bertalanffy, L. von 458
Bertmar, G. 398
Bertollo, L. A. C. 102–3
Berven, K. A. 92
Bettoli, P. W. 439
Beverton, R. J. H. 456
Beynon, R. 419
Bieniarz, K. 485, 500
Biggers, C. L. 92
Bigorne, R. 218–19
Billard, R. 484, 575, 590, 602, 605
Biro, P. 473, 532, 545
Birt 108
Bishi, J. S. 341
Bishop, J. E. 173, 189
Bitterlich, G. 414, 416, 418
Bitterman, M. E. 522
Blache, J. 187
Blackith, R. A. 55
Bland, M. M. 112
Blaszczyk, M. 416
Blaxter, J. H. S. 294, 296, 317, 346, 608
Blazka, P. 433, 435
Bleckmann, H. 317–18, 345
Bleeker, P. 8, 12–13, 168–70, 172–3
Blier, P. 443–4
Block, R. J. 419
Blumer, L. S. 519
Blyth, E. 168
Bninska, M. 572, 577, 579, 581, 583–4
Boborova, J. 615
Bock, W. J. 322
Bodaly, R. A. 516
Boehlert, G. W. 296, 420
Bogachev, V. V. 43
Bogdanowicz, S. D. 104
Bogutskaya, N. G. 8, 18
Bohl, E. 357, 370, 538
Boikova, O. S. 354–5
Bonaparte, C. L. 8–10, 12–13, 170
Bond, C. E. 242, 248
Boogaart, J. G. M. van de 358, 360, 378, 394
Bookstein, F. L. 55–61, 67, 70–74, 77–8
Bornancin, M. 449
Bortone, S. A. 246

Boulding, E. G. 61
Boulenger, G. A. 214, 219
Bowen, S. H. 413–14
Bowmaker, A. P. 222–3
Boycott, B. B. 297, 301
Boyd, C. M. 360
Brabrand, A. 354–5, 366, 532–3, 540, 555, 565
Braford, M. R. 285
Brandstatter, R. 285, 287, 291, 293–4, 296, 299, 319, 321
Braum, E. 494
Breder, C. M. 141, 144, 188, 250, 253, 430, 485, 487, 519, 521
Breed, C. S. 28
Bregazzi, P. R. 532, 536, 562
Breisch, M. 514–15
Bresnick, G. I. 250–51
Breton, B. 602
Brett, J. R. 428, 440, 444, 531, 601
Brewer 89
Bridges, W. L. 562
Briggs, J. C. 27, 45, 139, 214, 221
Brittan, M. R. 144, 186
Britten, R. J. 105
Broin, F. de 39
Broughton, N. M. 464, 495
Brown, A. F. 493
Brown, B. 112
Brown, D. J. A. 466
Brown, E. E. 147
Brown, G. G. 108
Brown, W. L. 514
Brown, W. M. 91, 104, 108, 110–12
Brown, S. 112
Brumley, A. R. 264, 267
Bruton, M. N. 221–2, 224–5, 228, 232–3, 503
Bruun, A. F. 146
Bry, R. W. de 111
Bryan, C. F. 495
Bryant, P. L. 420
Buchanan (Hamilton), F. 186
Buckle, J. T. 416
Buddington, R. K. 414
Buhl, E. H. 301
Bull, L. M. 416
Bunni, M. K. 8, 12, 146

Bunt, S. M. 300
Burg, A. van den 388
Burgess, G. H. 246
Burgess, W. E. 149, 224
Burian, R. 321
Burkhardt, T. 38
Burko, T. 387
Burlet, H. M. de 336-7
Burnet, A. M. R. 279
Burr, B. M. 74, 94
Burrough, R. J. 468, 532, 536
Burt, A. 504
Burton, F. 112
Busack, C. A. 513
Bush, G. L. 83
Butasov, M. M. 341-2
Buth, D. G. 84-5, 90-91, 93-4, 97, 110, 245
Buwalda, R. 343
Buynak, G. L. 494, 503, 520

Cabrera, Ll. 38
Caccone, A. G. 108
Cadwallader, P. L. 267, 269-70, 276, 278-9
Cadwalladr, D. R. 229, 233
Cahn, A. H. 567
Cairns, J. 437, 439
Cala, P. 354
Cambray, J. A. 223-5, 228, 233, 503
Campbell, J. 321
Campos, H. 391, 395
Cann, R. L. 104
Cao, W. 138
Cao, W. -X. 167, 177
Capanna, E. 95, 97-100
Caprio, C. 305
Caprio, J. 303, 308, 310
Caraco, T. 511
Carbonnel, J. P. 166
Carl, G. C. 7
Carlander, K. D. 250
Caro, T. M. 516
Carpenter, S. R. 557, 565
Carr, S. M. 104
Carr, W. E. S. 303
Cash, K. J. 516
Cashner, R. C. 94

Cassani, J. R. 616
Casterlin, M. E. 439-40, 445
Caston, W. E. 616
Cataudella, S. 95, 98-100
Cattaneo-Berrebi, G. 92
Cavalier-Smith 107
Cavallo, O. 39
Cavender, T. M. 35, 41-2, 46, 72, 76, 140, 242
Cavicchiolo, G. 344
Cazemier, W. G. 467
Cerminaro, R. T. 102
Cerny, K. 496
Cerri, R. D. 560
Chadwick, E. N. P. 474
Chambers, K. L. 107
Chan, A. T. H. 342
Chan, K. 112
Chanda, T. 97-8, 100-1
Chang, H. W. 167
Chang, J. P. 605
Chang, M. L. 603, 605, 607
Chang, M. -M. 28, 45
Chang, S. T. 608, 610
Chang, S. -Y. 167
Chang, Y. -L. 133
Chang, Y. P. 605
Chaodumrong, P. 178
Chapman, D. W. 458, 474
Chardon, M. 317, 336, 340-1
Charlon, N. 611
Charnov, E. L. 516
Chaudhuri, H. 615
Chen, F. C. 608, 610
Chen, J. -X. 167
Chen, L. C. 510
Chen, X. 35, 130, 138, 140
Chen, X. -L. 9, 17
Chen, X. -Y. 18, 169, 171
Chen, Y. 13, 24, 28, 138, 146, 167
Chen, Y. -Y. 167, 177
Cheng, C. C. 45
Cheng, P. -S. 167
Cherfas, N. B. 99, 616
Chernoff, B. 55-61, 67, 70-8
Cherry, D. S. 437, 439
Chervinski, J. 449
Chesson, P. L. 538, 563

Cheverud, J. M. 62
Chevey, P. 168, 178
Chiarelli, B. 98
Chin, P. K. 168, 173, 178, 189
Chmielewski, M. A. 70
Chow, C. -C. 28, 45
Chow, M. M. 45
Chranilov, N. S. 337, 339–41
Christian, L. 92, 99–100
Chu, X. 146
Chu, X. -L. 179, 182
Chu, Y. T. 8, 28, 398
Chu, Y. -T. 167, 169
Chung, L. 608, 610
Chyung, M. K. 167
Clarke, M. A. 222–3
Clarke, N. L. 342
Clayton, J. W. 89
Clegg, M. T. 105
Clemens, W. A. 7
Clemmer, G. H. 503
Coad, B. W. 25, 91, 133, 150
Coble, D. W. 562
Coburn, M. M. 35, 41, 101, 103, 106,
    245, 251, 261
Coche, A. G. 148
Cockerham, C. C. 108
Coelho, M. M. 93
Coen, E. 112
Colby, P. J. 546, 572
Cole, K. S. 510, 520
Coles, T. F. 472
Colgan, P. W. 72, 511
Collares-Perreira, M. J. 6, 92–3
Colle, D. E. 467, 469
Collette, B. B. 145, 511, 521
Comer, M. 112
Conner, J. V. 494
Cook, A. F. 600–1
Cooke, G. D. 566
Coombs, S. 317–18, 334, 336, 343
Cooper, E. L. 474
Cooperative Team for Hormonal
    Application in Pisciculture 603
Cornford, N. E. 392
Cortadas, J. 105
Corti, M. 97
Cossins, A. R. 437, 439, 444

Courtenay, W. R. 233, 256
Couturier, J. 105
Couvering, J. A. H. van 43–44, 221
Covich, A. P. 555
Cowx, I. G. 457, 467, 472, 575
Cox, M. 317
Crabtree, C. B. 93
Cracraft, J. C. 107–8
Cragg-Hine, D. 464
Craig, J. F. 540
Cramp, S. 563
Cranbrook, The Earl of 26
Crass, R. S. 224, 226
Crawford, M. K. 474
Crawshaw, D. I. 435
Crisp, D. T. 503
Crivelli, A. J. 92, 355, 554
Croizat, L. 19
Cronberg, G. 558–9, 564
Crosby, E. C. 285
Cross, C. G. 386
Cross, F. B. 41
Crossman, E. J. 522
Crowder, L. B. 356, 370
Cryer, M. 354, 356–8, 368, 370,
    555, 558, 562
Csanyi, V. 616
Cucchi, C. 98
Cummins, K. W. 188, 378
Cuny, G. 105
Currie, B. R. 416
Curry, E. 378
Cushing, C. E. 188
Cuvier, G. 8
Czelusniak, J. 112
Czerneda, J. 520

Dabrowski, K. R. 420, 598
Daget, J. 213, 215, 222, 230, 344
Dai, D. -Y. 133
Dallas, J. 112
Dall Via, G. 414, 419
Danil'chenko, P. G. 43, 45
Danzmann, R. G. 92
Darlington, P. J. 45
Das, N. K. 133
Das, K. N. 168
Datta, A. K. 168

Dauba, F. 463
Davenport, D. E. 310
David, A. 133, 168
Davids, C. 566
Davidson, E. H. 105
Davidson, R. D. 561, 563
Davidson, W. S. 108
Davies, B. R. 227, 232
Davis, R. E. 285, 287
Davis, S. K. 112
Davison, W. 427
Dawley, R. M. 92, 109
Day, F. E. 167–8, 186
Deal, F. H. 98
Deese, S. F. 112
Dekker, A. 415
Delco, E. A. 510
Delmastro, G. B. 133
Delmondo, M. N. 615
Demael-Suard, A. 446
Demski, L. S. 308
Denoix, M. 514–15
Densen, W. L. T. van 355, 357–8,
    368, 370, 545, 560
Densmore, L. D. 108
Denton, E. J. 317, 346
Deraniyagala, P. E. P. 168
Deubler, E. E. 404
Devillers, C. 344
Diamond, J. M. 414, 419
Diamond, M. 484, 486–8, 490, 493
Dickie, L. M. 377
Dickinson, T. A. 62, 69–70
Dickson, K. L. 437, 439
Diehl, S. 365, 370, 445, 535–7,
    542, 546, 555
Dijkgraaf, S. 342, 346
Dill, W. A. 148
Dimmick, W. W. 94, 261
Disler, N. N. 537
Dixit, R. K. 341
Dizon, A. E. 104, 108
Dodson, J. J. 521–2
Dolinskiy, V. L. 495
Donnelly, B. G. 223, 233
Dorier, A. 346
Dorit, R. 229
Douglas, M. E. 76

Doves, G. A. 112
Doving, K. B. 305, 314, 317
Dowling, J. E. 297
Dowling, T. E. 85, 91–3, 104,
    108–12, 513
Down, N. E. 92
Dratewka-Kos, E. 85
Drenner, R. W. 356–7, 371
Drexel, E. 439
Driedzic, W. R. 443–4
Drok, V. M. 615
Drost, M. R. 378
Dubois-Dauphin, M. 305
Dumitrescu, M. 17
Du Mont, H. J. 222
Dunel, S. 449
Dunson, W. A. 611
Dupont, F. 92
Dupree, H. K. 92
Durand, J-R. 222
Durante, H. 611
Dutcher, B. W. 404
Dutrillaux, B. 105
Duzer, E. M. van 521
Dvorakova, M. 557
Dybowski, B. 13, 15

Easter, S. S. 296, 299–301
Eastman, C. R. 41
Eastman, J. T. 46, 393
Easton, K. 472
Easton, K. W. 484
Eaton, R. C. 504
Eccles, D. H. 233
Echteler, S. 285
Economidis, P. S. 8
Edgell, M. H. 112
Editorial Board of Acta Hydrobiologika
    Sinica 615
Edwards, D. J. 278
Edwards, R. J. 74
Egberink, B. P. 388
Ehrlich, R. 60
EIFAC 581, 583
Eisner, T. 514
Ejsmont-Karabin, J. 586
Elder, R. L. 55–61, 67, 70–4, 77–8
El-Fiky, N. 319

Elliott, J. M. 436–7, 440, 531
Ellison, J. R. 98
Ellory, J. C. 444
Eloranta, A. 462, 473
Elsdon, J. W. V. 523
Elser, J. J. 557, 565
Elvira, B. 20
Embury, J. E. 112
Eminson, D. 535
Emmens, C. W. 224
Endler, J. A. 76
Engel, W. 89, 105
Enger, P. S. 341–3
Engstrom, K. 296
Entz, B. 531–2, 572
Epis, R. C. 42
Epler, P. 485, 500
Epstein, F. H. 449
Eriksson, M. O. G. 561
Erk'arkan, F. 133
Ernst, W. G. 36
Escaffre, A. M. 611
Estabrook, G. F. 97
Evans, H. E. 285, 404–5
Evans, H. M. 342
Evans, M. H. 285, 287
Evans, W. A. 228
Evermann, B. W. 250
Evernden, J. F. 41
Ezzi, I.A. 356–7, 370–1

Faafeng, B. 565
Fabricius, E. 488
Facey, D. E. 474
Fahrmeier, L. 290
Fahy, E. 472
Faktorovich, K. A. 612, 615
Fang, P. W. 167
Fang, S. -M. 167
Fange, R. 414
Fanget, R. 355
FAO 224, 227, 575
Farley, R. D. 504
Farris, S. D. 94
Faust, J. 89
Fay, R. R. 303, 332, 341–3
Felley, J. D. 56, 58, 73–4
Felsenstein, J. 94

Ferguson, H. W. 277
Ferguson, M. M. 93, 513
Fernald, R. D. 296, 299
Ferrantelli, O. 98
Ferris, S. D. 84, 93, 104, 108
Ferson, S. 60
Filipski, J. 105
Fily, M. 168, 187
Finger, T. E. 285, 290, 301, 303, 305,
    310, 314, 317, 391
Fink, W. L. 2, 11, 28, 35, 62–3, 97,
    334, 341
Fink, S. V. 2, 11, 28, 35, 97, 334, 341
Finkel, A. 614
Fischer, Z. 400, 416
Fish, G. R. 279, 418, 540
Fishelson, L. 416
Fisheries Research Institute, Guangxi
    Zhuang Self-Governed Territory 133
Fishery Bureau of the Uighur
    Autonomous Region 133
Fish Reproduction Physiology
    Research Group, and Peptide
    Hormone Group 603
Fitch, W. M. 108
Fitzmaurice, P. 354–5, 468
Flavel, R. B. 112
Flerova, G. I. 515
Fletcher, A. R. 264, 267, 273–7, 554
Flik, G. 449
Flock, A. 332, 344
Flood, M. G. 474
Florentz, A. 414
Floyd, K. B. 495
Flynn, J. J. 35, 47
Folmar, L. 85
Fontaine, H. 166
Ford, E. 458
Foresti, F. 102–3
Forney, J. 547
Forstner, H. 418, 421, 428, 431,
    440–2, 445, 464
Fostier, A. 484
Fowler, H. W. 8, 12–13, 168, 172, 184
Fowler, M. C. 554
Francis, A. A. 466
Frank, S. 468
Frankel, J. S. 92

Fraser, D. F. 560
Freadman, M. 427
Freeman, N. C. 474
Freifelder, D. 105
Freshwater Fishculture Experimental
  Committee 592
Fretwell, S. D. 544
Friedlander, M. J. 437, 439, 444
Frisch, K. von 294, 308
Fristch, E. F. 104
Fristrom, J. W. 105
Fromageot, C. 416
Fry, F. E. J. 7, 430, 437, 439–40
Fryer, G. 229, 233, 363, 367, 371, 388
Fudge, R. J. P. 516
Fujien-Kiangsu-Chekiang-Shanghai
  Cooperative Group 603
Fujio, Y. 85, 90
Fulman, L. A. 494
Funke, R. P. 427
Fuog, E. 112
Furnier, G. R. 112
Furse, M. T. 226, 228, 231
Furtado, J. I. 189
Furukawa, T. 332, 342

Gaigher, I. G. 224, 230, 233
Galau, G. A. 105
Gale, W. F. 503, 520
Galetti, P. M. 102–3
Galis, F. 356, 371
Ganesan, T. M. 178
Garadi, P. 532, 545
Garcia-Novo, F. 354–5
Gardiner, B. G. 37
Gardner, M. G. 414
Garrett, G. P. 74
Gas, N. 415
Gattringer, A. 415, 442
Gatz, A. J. 73
Gaudant, J. 28, 37–40
Gaur, R. 178
Gauthier, G. F. 415
Gayet, M. 28, 40, 341
Geiger, W. 285, 293, 308
Geisler, R. 177
Gelin, C. 558–9, 564
Gensler, P. 294

George, D. G. 494
George, M. 104, 108
George, W. 178
Gentry, J. B. 89
Geray, J. A. B. 346
Gerdeaux, D. 354, 371, 464
Gerking, S. D. 457
Gervai, J. 616
Gery, J. 214
Getchell, M. L. 308
Getchell, T. V. 308
Geursen, J. 354–5, 357–9, 363,
  365–6, 368–9, 532, 534, 537,
  540, 545
Geyer, E. 404
Gharrett, A. J. 105, 108
Gibbs, R. H. 76
Gibson, A. R. 70
Gibson, J. S. 444
Gibson, R. N. 356–7, 370–71
Giddings, L. V. 109
Gilbert, C. R. 11, 26, 74–5, 110,
  245–6, 261
Gill, H. S. 457–9, 468
Gillett, C. 487
Gilliam, J. 538, 561, 563
Gillis, D. 512
Gilmartin, A. J. 65
Giraldeau, L. A. 512
Girard, C. 13, 15, 170
Girard, J. P. 449
Girgis, S. 378, 416
Girling, S. L. 514
Giussani, G. 414, 419
Gjedrem, T. 612
Gliwicz, Z. M. 368
Gnass, D. 514–15
Goddard, K. A. 92, 109
Godin, J. G. J. 293, 319, 511
Gogola, H. 572
Goin, C. J. 106–7
Goin, O. B. 106–7
Gold, J. R. 95, 98, 101–8
Goldschmid, A. 284, 291, 296, 299,
  303, 309–13, 314, 316, 319, 321
Goldspink, C. R. 457, 473, 546
Goldspink, G. 427, 443–5
Golovinskaya, K. A. 614

Golterman, H. L. 368
Gomahr, A. 291, 303, 309–10, 314, 316
Goodall, D. W. 127
Goodfellow, W. L. 85
Goodman, M. 112
Goodwin, B. 321
Goossens, J. 187
Goolish, E. M. 444
Gosline, W. A. 8–9, 17, 130, 169, 242, 344, 387, 398, 407
Gosse, J. 213, 215
Gotz, K. H. 433
Govoni, J. J. 420
Goz, H. 510, 515
Grabner, M. 414–15, 419, 421
Granado-Lorencio, C. 354
Granado-Lorencio, F. 355
Grande, L. 42, 46
Graneli, W. 566
Grasse, P. P. 334, 336–7, 343
Graves, J. E. 104, 108
Gray, J. A. B. 317
Grechkovskaja, A. P. 615
Green, D. 514
Green, J. M. 108
Greenberg, L. A. 532–3, 538, 541
Greenwood, P. H. 43, 45, 141, 211, 215, 219, 221–2, 225–6, 229, 400
Gregory, W. K. 9
Greig, L. 531
Grigorash, V. A. 494
Grimm, N. B. 533, 566
Grossman, G. D. 474
Grygierek, E. 473
Grzimek, B. 141, 371
Guarnieri, P. 344
Guderley, H. 443–4
Gui, J. 98
Guidarelli, G. 510
Guma'a, S. A. 540
Gunning, G. E. 562
Gunther, A. 8, 13, 45, 172, 178
Gupta, S. D. 602, 616
Gusar, A. G. 510
Guthrie, D. M. 294, 296, 303
Guttman, T. 105

Guyenot, E. 342
Gyllensten, U. 104
Gyurko, S. 418

Habibi, H. R. 605
Hairston, N. G. 296, 299
Hales, D. C. 357
Hall, D. J. 356, 368, 377, 538, 546, 561, 563
Halyk, L. C. 474, 476
Hamele, A. 290
Hamilton, F. 167, 173, 186
Hamilton, M. J. 97
Hammer, C. 355, 420, 494
Hampl, A. 395
Hamrin, S. F. 532, 537, 543–5, 556, 566·
Hanchet, S. 276
Hanham, A. 105, 108
Hansson, L. -A. 555–6, 565
Hanzawa, N. 109
Hara, T. J. 305, 308
Hardenbol, J. 47
Harden Jones, F. R. 342
Hardies, S. C. 112
Harrington, R. W. 380
Harrison, T. A. 308
Hart, G. 65
Hart, J. S. 437
Hart, L. A.'t 510
Hart, P. 556
Hartl, D. L. 105
Hartley, P. H. T. 354–5
Hartley, S. E. 105
Hartmann, J. 531–2, 572
Haschmeyer, A. E. V. 105
Hasegawa, Y. 44
Hashimoto, H. 522
Hasler, A. D. 254, 522
Hautt, C. H. 26
Hawkins, A. D. 317, 342–3
Hazel, J. R. 443
Heads, P. A. 559
Healey, M. C. 512
Healy-Williams, N. 60
Heap, S. P. 443–4
Heckel, J. J. 173, 398
Heckman, C. W. 177

Heincke, F. 398
Heins, D. C. 250–1, 255, 503
Heisler, N. 433
Heitz, J. G. 358
Helfrich, C. H. J. 415
Helland, J. M. 562
Hellawell, J. M. 354, 446, 500
Helm, W. R. 273
Helm-Bychowski, K. 104
Hemmings, C. C. 510
Hendenson, H. F. 615
Hendrickson, D. A. 242, 248
Henrikson, B. -I. 559
Henrikson, L. 559, 564
Hensel, K. 8, 344–5
Hensley, D. A. 256
Hentschel, H. 448
Hepher, B. 553
Herre, A. W. C. T. 7
Herrick, C. J. 285, 303
Herzenstein, S. M. 167
Herzig, A. 355, 357, 436
Hessen, D. O. 356, 559, 564
HEST 230
Hetesa, J. 365
Hewitt, D. P. 494
Hickley, P. 473
Hickling, C. F. 386, 403
Hickman, C. P. 449–50
Hidaka, I. 310
Higuchi, R. G. 104
Hill, A. 112
Hill, A. V. 427
Hill, D. 561
Hill, J. 474
Hillis, D. M. 104, 111–12
Hine, P. M. 278
Hinegardner, R. 97, 106
Hinterleitner, S. 319, 421
Hitchcock, P. F. 296, 299, 301
Ho, C. -W. 167
Hochachka, P. W. 434, 439
Hocutt, C. H. 26, 85, 241, 244,
    246–7, 437
Hoeh, W. R. 109
Hofer, B. 346
Hofer, R. 358, 414–6, 418–21,

442, 446–7, 458, 532–3, 537,
    540, 555
Hohenauer, C. 296, 299, 319
Holanov, S. H. 356–7, 370–1
Holcik, J. 473, 532
Holl, A. 314
Holley, A. 305
Holling, C. S. 377
Holopainen, I. J. 355, 378, 434, 446–7
Holstvoogd, C. 407
Hoogenboezem, W. 358, 360, 378, 394
Hopkirk, J. D. 27
Hopson, A. J. 215
Hopson, J. 215
Hora, S. L. 19, 27, 44, 142, 168
Horne, M. T. 105
Horoszewicz, L. 485, 500
Horvath, L. 148, 484, 500–1, 592,
    616
Hosoya, K. 13, 25, 136, 169, 171
Housby, T. 148
House, A. C. 517
Howard, J. 317
Howarth, R. W. 535, 542
Howell, W. M. 101
Howes, G. J. 5–6, 8–10, 12–16, 18, 20,
    22, 24–27, 35, 43, 97, 130,
    134–5, 137–40, 169–73, 214,
    218–19, 223, 232, 242, 244, 341
Hoyt, R. D. 495
Hrbacek, 557
Huang, H. -J. 147
Huang, H. -M. 133
Hubbs, C. L. 57, 74, 242, 250
Huber, G. C. 285
Huber, R. 285, 294, 308, 313
Hudson, A. P. 105
Hudspeth, A. J. 317
Hughes, G. M. 433
Hughes, N. 229
Hughie, D. M. 516
Hulata, G. 467, 615
Hume, D. J. 267, 273–7, 554
Humphries, J. M. 55–61, 67, 70–4,
    77–8
Hunt, G. S. 273
Hunt, S. 392

Hunter, J. R. 254
Huntingford, F. A. 293
Hurk, R. van den 510
Hurley, D. A. 546, 572
Hus, M. 583
Hussakof, L. 46
Hutchinson, C. A. 112
Hyslop, E. J. 363
Hytinkoski, P. 473
Hyvarinen, H. 355, 434, 446–7

Ichthyology Laboratory, Hupei
   Institute of Hydrobiology 133
Ihssen, P. E. 102
Ikeda, S. 418–19
Iles, T. D. 229, 371
Ilijasov, J. 612, 615
Imaki, A. 168
Inger, R. F. 168, 173, 178, 189
Ingersol, R. V. 36
Inoue, M. 44
Inouye, Y. 600
Institute of Zoology, Academia Sinica
   133
Iriki, M. 439
Ishii, Y. 332
Islam, M. N. 187
Istanovics, V. 565
Ito, H. 300–1
IUBNC 84
IUCN 146, 230
Ivlev, V. S. 356, 474, 552
Iwai, T. 395

Jackowska, H. 354–5
Jackson, P. B. N. 222–9
Jacobs, D. W. 343
Jacobs, J. 356
Jacobsen, O. J. 467
Jaffee, D. C. 450
Jakubowski, M. 308, 318
James, G. T. 41
Jana, R. K. 616
Janssen, J. 317–8, 356–7, 371,
   384
Jany, K. D. 414
Jayaram, K. C. 8, 133, 136, 139, 168

Jeffreys, A. J. 112
Jelonek, M. 355, 357
Jenkins, R. E. 75, 246, 521
Jennings, D. P. 148
Jensen, F. B. 433
Jensen, R. J. 245
Jezierska, B. 462
Jhaveri, V. G. 150
Jhingran, V. G. 147–8, 187, 484, 596
Jin, X. 144, 149
Jirasek, J. 365, 395
Job, T. J. 133, 168
Johansson, L. 354, 531–4,
   536–8, 540, 542–5, 555–6,
   565–6
John, G. 616
Johnsen, P. 168
Johnson, D. S. 173, 177, 179
Johnson, M. G. 531–2, 572
Johnson, W. E. 89
Johnston, I. A. 427, 433, 443–4
Johnston, J. A. A. 523
Johnston, J. S. 108
Jolicouer, P. 70, 288
Jollie, M. 344
Jones, D. R. 427, 440
Jones, J. W. 464
Jones, N. V. 464, 495
Jong, P. W. de 356, 371
Jordan, D. S. 13, 250
Joswiak, G. R. 84, 92–3, 97, 109
Jourdan, F. 305
Jubb, R. A. 214, 221–4, 232
Junger, H. 285, 287, 290–1, 296,
   299–301, 319, 321, 391, 405

Kaeding, L. R. 497
Kafuku, T. 169
Kaiser, E. W. 146
Kajak, Z. 403
Kajishima, T. 98
Kalat, M. 95, 101
Kalk, M. 226, 228
Kalmijn, A. J. 317
Kamil, A. C. 321
Kang, Y. S. 106
Kao, S. -T. 167

Kao, T. L. 299
Kapoor, B. G. 532
Karabin, J. 586
Karaman, M. S. 170
Karim, M. R. 187
Karel, W. J. 98, 102, 105–6
Karlsen, H. E. 346
Katz, A. I. 449
Kaufmann, R. 430
Kaufmann, S. 321
Kausch, H. 430
Kaushik, S. J. 611
Kavaliers, M. 446
Kawai, S. 418–19
Kawamoto, A. 168
Kawamoto, N. Y. 600
Kawanabe, H. 229
Kawashima, Y. 99
Kay, I. 419
Kazansky, V. I. 393
Keenleyside, M. H. A. 510–11
Kelsch, S. W. 439
Kelso, J. R. M. 531–2, 572
Kempe, O. 464, 468, 537
Kenchington, T. J. 67
Kennedy, C. R. 468, 532, 536, 562
Kennedy, G. J. A. 523
Kennedy, M. 354–5, 468, 473
Kennett, J. P. 58
Kent, D. V. 35, 47
Keranen, M. 473
Kerfoot, W. C. 356, 564
Kerr, S. R. 537
Kessler, L. G. 108
Kessler, K. T. 167
Keys, A. B. 449
Khalitov, N. K. 491
Khan, H. A. 148
Khanna, S. S. 285
Khuda-Bukhsh, A. R. 97-101
Kilambi, R. V. 448
Kim, E. D. 490
Kimura, S. 44
King, D. L. 558, 561, 565
King, D. P. F. 393
King, D. R. 273
King, J. A. 605
Kinnamon, J. C. 308

Kirk, R. G. 231
Kirpichnikov, V. S. 611–15
Kish, P. E. 299
Kishida, R. 301
Kitchell, J. F. 531, 553
Kitoh, J. 308, 310
Kitto, G. B. 83
Kiyohara, S. 308, 310
Kleerekoper, H. 294
Klein, J. 99, 106
Kleynhans, C. J. 224
Kliewer, E. V. 358
Knezevic, B. 553, 555
Kobayashi, H. 99
Koch, F. 416, 418, 439, 441, 445–7
Kock, G. 419–20
Kock, J. H. 296
Koehl, M. A. R. 393
Kogan, A. V. 370
Kok, H. M. 222
Komuro, T. 450
Konagaya, T. 343
Konig, A. 444
Konishi, J. 310
Konradt, A. G. 612
Konstantinov, A. S. 466
Koop, B. F. 109, 112
Korinek, V. 557
Koriyaka, A. 586
Kornfield, I. 104
Kortmulder, K. 503
Kotrschal, K. 284–5, 287,
    290–1, 293–4, 296, 299–301,
    303, 305, 309–10, 314, 316–17,
    319, 321, 391, 405
Kosarev, A. 150
Koster, W. J. 75
Kotlia, B. S. 178
Kottelat, M. 6–7, 14, 168
Kowtal, G. V. 615
Kraak, G. van der 603, 605–7
Kramer, D. L. 504
Kramer, R. H. 562
Krantz, G. E. 474
Krauskopf, M. 108
Krautgartner, W. -D. 305, 317
Krebs, F. 437
Krebs, J. R. 516

Kreitman, M. 104, 112
Krempf, A. 178
Krewedel, G. 416, 418
Krone, W. 89
Kroon, A. G. 415
Krupp, F. 8, 25, 129, 133, 143, 217, 222
Kryzanovskii, S. G. 9, 16
Kryzanowsky, S. G. 170
Kubecka, J. 464
Kubicz, A. 85
Kucherenko, A. P. 615
Kukko, O. 473
Kulshrestha, S. K. 338
Kund, M. 342
Kupriynanov, V. S. 510
Kuru, M. 133
Kuzema, A. I. 615
Kuznetsov, V. A. 491–2

Laale, H. W. 484, 489
L'Abee-Lund, J. H. 484, 486–7, 523
Lachner, E. A. 253, 521
Ladich, F. 510
Ladiges, W. 133, 284, 371
Ladurner, H. 415, 442
Lagler, K. F. 57, 163, 168
Lagler, K. L. 242
Lake, J. S. 264
Lamarra, V. A. 566
Lamb, T. 104, 108
Lambert, J. 215
Lambert, J. G. D. 510
Lamers, C. H. J. 415
Lammens, E. H. R. R. 354–60, 363,
    365–70, 378, 394, 532, 534,
    537, 540, 545, 560, 566
Lande, R. 321
Landis, S. 415
Lane, E. B. 314
Lange, N. O. 490, 492
Langley, C. H. 112
Lansman, R. A. 104, 108
Larkin, P. A. 538
Larson, A. 97
Laskar, K. 355
Lassuy, D. R. 418
Lathrop, B. F. 494
Latif, A. F. A. 228

Laube, G. 39
Lauder, G. V. 97, 380, 398
Lauff, M. 420
Laurent, P. 449
Lauric-Ahlberg, C. C. 112
Lawrence, B. J. 515
Lawson, R. 93
Lazarro, X. 356, 386, 388
Leach, C. H. 531
Leach. J. H. 532, 547, 572
Leary, R. F. 104
Lebedev, V. D. 43
Le Cren, E. D. 467, 476
Lee, D. S. 26
Lee, Y. K. 608, 610
Leeden, F. van der 127
Leeuwen, J. L. 384, 388
Legendre, L. 180
Legendre, P. 180
Leggett, W. C. 108
Le Grande, W. H. 97
Leibold, M. A. 544
Leipoldt, M. 105
Leith, W. 24
Lekander, B. 332, 344
Lelek, A. 146
Le Martret, M. A. 510
Lemasson, J. 168
Lemly, A. D. 516
Leon, G. 108
Leopold, M. 572, 577, 579, 581,
    583–4, 586
Leray, C. 414
Lesel, R. 416
Lessmark, O. 531–2, 534
Lestrel, P. E. 60
Leszczynski, L. 466
Lett, P. F. K. P. 457
Levani-Zermonsky, B. 603
Leveque, C. 214–15, 218–19, 232,
    463
Levesley, P. B. 514–15
Lewis, D. S. C. 223, 227–8, 230
Lewis, J. L. 62
Lewis, W. D. 62
Lewis, W. M. 185, 562
Li, G. Y. 603, 605, 607
Li, K. 95–98, 100–1

Li, K. T. 296, 299
Li, S. 20, 496
Li, S. -S. 167, 185
Li, S. -Z. 167
Li, W. -H. 111
Li, Y. 95–8, 100–1
Liang, J. Y. 603, 605, 607
Libosvarsky, J. 467
Liem, K. F. 97, 398, 400, 405–6
Lightfoot, G. W. 494–495
Liley, N. R. 510
Lin, H. R. 592, 598, 603, 605–7
Lin, R. 35, 130, 138, 140
Lin, R. -D. 9, 17–18
Lind, E. 473
Lindsey, C. C. 6–7, 523
Linfield, R. S. J. 457, 468, 496
Liu, C. C. 608, 610
Liu, H. T. 45
Liu, W. 95, 98, 100–1, 106
Liu, X. 28
Llewellyn, L. C. 267
Lobchenko, V. V. 614
Lobon-Cervia, J. 471, 473
Lodge, D. M. 535, 542
Loffler, H. 355, 538
Loftus, K. H. 531
Lohberger, K. 167
Lohnisky, K. 494
Loos, J. J. 494
Lopes, S. 227
Lorenc, E. 457, 462
Lorenc, J. 457, 462
Loretz, C. A. 450
Lotrich, V. A. 474
Loughna, P. T. 445
Lowe-McConnell, R. H. 2, 139, 177,
    186, 212, 221, 229
Lowenstein, O. 343
Lu, L. Z. 603, 605, 607
Lucas, P. W. 400
Lucking, M. 444
Luecke, C. 358, 393
Luiten, P. G. M. 310
Luke, D. A. 400
Lukowicz, M. von 592
Lundbeck, J. 363, 368
Lutz, G. 427

Lyakhnovich, V. P. 416
Lyles, E. 562
Lythgoe, J. N. 294

Ma, D. P. 105–6
Ma, K. -C. 167
Macaya, G. 105
MacCrimmon, H. R. 273
Macdonald, J. A. 317, 319
Macdonald, R. A. 563
Macfarlane, N. A. A. 484
MacGillavry, P. J. 354–5, 357–9,
    363, 365–6, 368–9, 532, 534,
    537, 540, 545
Mackay, I. 501
Macy, A. 296
Magee, S. M. 85
Magnuson, J. J. 358, 545
Magurran, A. E. 319, 467, 511–18
Mahdi, N. 141
Mahnert, V. 214
Mahon, R. 474
Mahr, K. 421
Mahy, G. 336, 338
Mai, D. Y. 168
Maitland, B. 444
Maitland, P. S. 133, 287
Majumdar, N. 168
Makeyeva, A. P. 493
Maltzahn, S. 418
Malyukina, G. A. 515
Mangold-Wernado, U. 515
Maniatis, T. 104
Mann, J. 342
Mann, K. H. 473, 476, 501
Mann, R. H. K. 354, 456–7, 462,
    464, 469–6, 495–6, 498–501,
    503, 563
Manna, G. K. 98
Manning, F. B. 343
Marcel, J. 484, 575, 590
Marchant, T. A. 600–1, 605
Mark, W. 296, 299, 319, 358, 420,
    464, 540
Marks, W. B. 301
Marlier, G. 224
Marotte, L. R. 296
Marsh, E. 74

Marshall, B. E. 227
Marshall, N. B. 342
Martem'yanov, V. I. 515
Martin, S. 472
Martinich, R. L. 510
Marui, T. 310
Masai, H. 310
Mastynski, J. 572–3
Mathews, C. P. 473–5, 497
Mathias, J. 496
Matis, J. H. 294
Matsuura, S. 342
Matthes, H. 169, 217, 225, 358,
    363, 367, 371, 378, 380, 387,
    392–3, 398, 400, 416
Matthews, D. M. 414
Matthews, W. J. 75–77, 553–4
Matthey, J. K. 439, 445
Mattocks, J. E. 332
Matty, A. J. 420
Matveiev, B. 338
Maughan, O. 467
Mayden, R. L. 41, 77, 83, 85, 90-91,
    94, 101, 103, 106–7, 245–6,
    250, 253–5, 261
Mayer-Gostan, N. 449
Mayfield, J. E. 105
Maynard Smith, J. 321
Mayr, B. 95, 101
Mazin, A .L. 107
McAllister, D. E. 91, 129
McCann, J. A. 256
McCauley, J. F. 28
McCauley, R. W. 437
McCleave, J. D. 521
McComas, S. R. 356
McCombie, A. M. 546, 572
McCormick, C. A. 285
McCullough, D. R. 516
McDowall, R. M. 268–70, 276–9
McGeachin, R. B. 591, 596–7
McGlade, J. M. 61
McIntyre, J. D. 105, 108
McKay, R. J. 264, 267–8, 277, 280
McKeown, B. A. 521
McLeod, P. R. 393
McMillan, V. E. 510, 519–21
M'Clelland, J. M. 167, 173

Meagher, S. 110
Mednick, A. S. 300
Medrano, L. 105
Meer, H. van der 415
Meer, H. J. van der 294, 299
Meili, M. 457
Melack, J. M. 535, 542
Melisky, E. L. 437
Meng, H. J. 462, 464, 468
Meng, Q. -W. 169
Menge, B. 535, 542
Menon, A. G. K. 44, 139, 168, 217
Menzel, B. W. 92
Merla, G. 612
Merrick, J. R. 264, 267
Meunier-Rotival, M. 105
Meyer, D. L. 299, 301
Miles, R. S. 37
Millar, R. P. 605
Miller, D. L. 72
Miller, R. J. 285
Miller, R. R. 41, 74–5, 240, 242,
    245, 248, 250
Millington, S. T. 439, 445
Mills, C. A. 462–4, 467, 469–3,
    476, 485, 487, 490, 493–503
Millstein, A. 553
Milton, D. A. 267–8
Min, M. S. 91
Minckley, W. L. 85, 242, 248, 251, 255
Ming, F. W. 519
Minns, C. K. 531
Minshall, G. W. 188
Mir, S. 8
Mironova, N. N. 414
Mirza, M. R. 133, 168
Misra, R. K. 67
Mitchell, A. H. G. 24, 28
Mitchell, C. P. 279
Mitchell, D. S. 279–80
Mitchell, H. H. 419
Mitchum, R. M. 47
Mittelbach, G. G. 378, 535, 537–8,
    542, 544, 559, 561, 563
Miura, T. 553
Miyamoto, M. M. 112
Mizuno, T. 189
Moav, R. 467, 613–15

Moeed, A. 70
Moermond, T. C. 538
Mohsin, A. K. M. 168, 173, 179, 182, 189
Molengraaff, G. A. F. 163, 178, 182
Molinski, M. 473, 475
Montanes, C. 473
Montgomery, J. C. 317, 319
Montgomery, W. L. 416
Moodie, G. E. E. 5
Moody, R. C. 562
Mooij, W. M. 494
Moor, I. J. de 221, 232
Moore, E. 278
Moore, W. S. 85, 91–3, 110, 513
Moreau, J. 460, 463
Moreira-Filho, O. 102–3
Moreau, J. 221, 232
Morgan, M. J. 511, 518
Morgan, P. R. 226, 228, 231
Morgan, R. P. 85
Mori, I. 108
Mori, S. 189
Mori, T. 19, 25, 133
Moriarty, C. M. 414, 418
Moriarty, D. J. W. 413–4, 418, 553
Morison, A. K. 264, 267, 273–7, 280, 554
Morita, Y. 310, 391
Moritz, C. 104, 108, 111
Moriwaki, K. 112
Morris, D. J. 74
Morrison, D. F. 70
Moser, H. 421
Moss, B. 535
Motta, P. J. 387–8, 406
Mourer-Chauvire, C. 39
Moyer, S. P. 105–6
Moyle, P. B. 250–1, 255, 355
Mukerji, D. D. 168
Mukhopadhyay, P. K. 418–19
Mulder, P. F. S. 233
Muller, H. 299
Muller, M. 380, 384, 388
Muller, R. 448, 462, 464, 468
Mulley, J. C. 264, 267, 273
Mulrooney, M. 472

Mummert, J. R. 357, 371
Murai, T. 598
Muramoto, J. 92, 99–100, 106
Murakami, T. 300–1
Murphy, B. D. 520
Muster, D. 433
Myberg, A. A. 416
Myers, G. S. 7, 183–4

Nagai, M. 439
Nagase, G. 418–19
Nagoshi, M. 229
Nagy, A. 616
Nagy, Z. 418
Nahorniak, C. S. 605
Naidu, P. 510
Nakajima, T. 44, 139, 177
Nakajima, Y. 332–3
Nakanishi, S. 600
Nakatsuru, K. 504
Nalbant, T. T. 136, 166–7, 169, 171
Narayan, R. K. J. 107
Nasir Uddin, A. 419–20
Naylor, E. 149
Neff, N. A. 72
Nei, M. 90–91, 108, 111
Neigel, J. E. 104, 108, 111
Neill, W. H. 439, 521
Nelson, D. W. 393
Nelson, G. J. 398
Nelson, J. S. 130
Nelva, A. 463
Neproshin, A. Y. 510
Neusteur, P. 515
Neumeyer, C. 294
Neves, R. J. 474
Nevo, E. 112
Newrkla, P. 418
Newroth, P. R. 566
Nguyen, V. T. 168
Ni, I. -H. 67
Ni, Y. 144, 149
Nie, H. W. de 368, 370, 560
Niederholzer, R. 416, 532–3, 555
Niemela, P. 544
Nieuwenhuys, R. 285, 287
Niimi, A. J. 457

Nikoljukin, N. I. 615
Nikolsky, G. V. 9–10, 14, 141, 167, 170, 377, 523
Nikolyukin, N. I. 12
Nilssen, J. P. 559, 564
Nilssen, J. P. M. 565
Nilsson, A. 414
Ninborg, E. A. 612, 615
Noaillac-Depeyre, J. 415
Noakes, D. L. G. 226, 293, 319, 474, 513, 519
Nonnote, L. 414
Norman, J. R. 141, 217
Northcote, T. G. 523
Northcutt, R. G. 284–5, 287, 299, 301, 322
Northmore, D. P. M. 290, 303
Nowak, W. 572
Numachi, K. 109
Numann, W. 531–2, 572
Nurmi, K. 62, 65
Nyberg, P. 540
Nyman, H. G. 559, 564

Obrhelova, N. 38–40
O'Brien, W. J. 356–8, 371, 393
Ochiai, A. 180
O'Connor, C. S. 435
O'Dell, M. 112
Oellerman, L. K. 99–1, 232
Oertzen, J. A. von 440, 448
Ogino, C. 598, 600
Oglesby, R. T. 547
Ohno, S. 92–93, 99–100, 106
Oijen, M. J. P. van 406
Ojima, Y. 95, 97–103
Okada, Y. 7, 167
Oksanen, L. 544
Olenetz, V. I. 615
Olmo, E. 105
Olofsson, B. 105
Olsen, G. J. 112
Olsho, L. W. 343
Olver, C. H. 531
Omeljaniuk, R. J. 605
Oordt, P. G. W. J. van 510
Op't Hof, J. 89

Opuszynski, K. 553, 596
Oscarson, H. G. 555, 559, 564
Osenberg, C. W. 544
Osmundsen, D. B. 497
Osse, J. W. 5, 357–58, 360, 363, 377–80, 384–6, 388–91, 394–5, 398, 404–5, 407
Ostrokowski, A. C. 439, 445
Ott, M. E. 433
Otten, E. 294, 296, 299
Oulton, W. J. 518
Owen, J. G. 70

Pace, N. R. 112
Page, L. M. 254
Paicheler, J. C. 39
Paine, R. T. 544
Paisley, T. 148
Paloheimo, J. E. 377
Palumbi, S. R. 104
Palzenberger, M. 287, 291, 310–13, 433
Panchenko, S. M. 615
Pankakoski, E. 62, 65
Pankhurst, N. W. 603
Papageorgiou, N. K. 457
Parcefall, J. 285
Pardue, G. B. 474
Park, E. H. 100, 106
Parker, W. H. 62, 69
Partridge, B. L. 346, 510
Passow, B. 342–3
Paszkowski, C. A. 378, 538
Patra, R. W. R. 187
Patterson, C. 27, 37, 40, 45, 140
Paugy, D. 214–15, 232
Paugy, G. 227
Payan, P. 449
Payne, A. I. 233
Pearce, F. 150
Pehrsson, O. 561
Peirson, G. 354, 356–8, 368, 370, 555, 558, 562
Peichi, L. 301
Pekar, C. 494
Penaz, M. 100, 487, 489, 496
Penczak, T. 457, 462, 469, 473–5

Peng, C. 603, 605, 607
Penney, R. K. 444
Pennington, C. H. 495
Perera, J. 150
Peres, G. 416, 446
Perlmutter, A. 510
Perrow, M. R. 468, 503
Perry, S. F. 449
Persson, L. 354, 531–45, 553,
  555–6, 565–6
Peter, R. E. 320, 600–1, 603, 605–7
Peter, S. 616
Peters, R. C. 305, 310, 314, 317
Peterson, S. A. 566
Petruska, J. 108
Pfeiffer, W. 514–5
Pfuderer, P. 466
Pharr, R. B. 60
Philipp, D. P. 85
Philippart, J. A. 500
Philippart, J. C. 473
Phillips, G. L. 535
Phillips, R. B. 102
Phillips, S. 112
Piatel, R. 285
Piavaux, A. 416
Pickford, G. 449
Pienaar, U. de V. 225–6
Piironen, J. 434, 446–7
Pillai, R. S. 168
Pimentel, R. A. 78
Pitcher, T. J. 317, 467, 510–14,
  516–18, 523
Pivec, L. 105
Pivnicka, K. 457, 462–4, 468, 473
Platt, C. 332–3, 336, 338
Platzer, U. 439
Pletscher, S. 108
Pliszka, F. 492
Pohla, H. 310–13
Poljarush, 615
Poll, M. 214–15, 217, 222, 345
Pollard, D. A. 267
Polling, L. 223
Pomerol, C. 35, 37
Ponton, D. 354, 371, 464
Ponyi, J. E. 564
Popova, O. A. 539

Popper, A. N. 303, 317, 332–4,
  336, 341–3
Popta, C. M. L. 168
Porter, K. G. 553
Portman, A. 371
Portt, C. B. 474
Poss, S. G. 57, 67, 70–1, 78
Pouwels, E. 285, 287
Powell, G. L. 74, 108
Power, M. E. 553–4, 562
Powers, M. K. 296
Prager, E. M. 97, 104
Prashad, B. 168
Pravda, D. 365
Precht, H. 437, 440
Prejs, A. 354–5, 371, 404, 416,
  533, 537, 555, 565
Prentice, H. C. 61–62
Price, H. J. 106–7
Prieston, R. 512
Prochazkova, L. 557
Prokes, M. 100, 487, 489
Pronek, N. 149, 224
Prosser, C. L. 89, 437, 439, 443–4
Protasov, V. R. 510
Prothero, D. R. 35, 41, 47
Provazek, R. 365
Prowse, G. 554
Prowse, G. A. 378, 403
Puljaeva, V. I. 615
Pullan, S. 269–70, 276–7
Pulliam, H. R. 511
Pullin, R. S. V. 148, 484
Pyke, G. H. 356, 368

Quinn, T. P. 513
Quinn, T. W. 104, 112
Qumsiyeh, M. B. 97
Qutob, Z. 342

Rab, P. 95, 100-101
Rabito, F. G. 251, 255
Radermaker, F. 336
Raffin-Peyloz, R. 10
Rafinesque-Schmaltz, C. S. 170
Rage, J. C. 39
Ragland, C. J. 106–7
Ragunathan, M. B. 168

Rahman, A. K. A. 168
Rahman, K. U. M. S. 187
Raicu, P. 99
Rainboth, W. J. 84, 95, 97, 99, 168, 180
Rajasilta, M. 559
Rajki, K. 616
Rakocinski, C. F. 92
Ramaswami, L. S. 13, 169, 334, 337, 341, 380
Rask, M. 354–5, 545
Rasmussen, D.L. 41
Raup, D. 321
Raymond, P. A. 296, 299
Raymond Johns, P. 296, 299
Read, D. W. 60
Ream, T. J. 342
Recher, H. F. 563
Recher, J. A. 563
Reddy, R. V.G. K. 616
Reeb, C. A. 104, 108
Reed, R. J. 521
Regan, C. T. 9–10, 15, 341
Rehnberg, B. G. 515, 518
Reid, G. McG. 4–5, 12, 26, 43, 45, 139, 169, 172, 183–4, 214, 217, 223, 225
Reist, J. D. 55, 516
Renduan, L. 14
Renzis, G. de 449
Rettenwander, R. 418
Retzius, G. 336
Reuter, T. 296
Reutter, K. 305, 308, 314
Reyment, R. A. 55–6
Reynolds, J. D. 233
Reynolds, L. F. 275–6, 279
Reynolds, W. W. 439–40, 445
Reznick, D. 498
Rheinberger, V. 458
Ribbink, A. J. V. L. 229
Richardson, L. R. 108
Richmond, M. C. 92
Richter, A. F. 566
Ridet, J. M. 285
Riemann, B. 544
Riggins, R. 78
Rijken 403
Rimmer, D. W. 416

Risch, L. 217
Risebrow, A. J. 537
Rishi, K. K. 98
Rivier, J. E. 603, 605, 607
Robel, R. J. 273
Roberts, J. L. 440, 447
Roberts, T. R. 6, 26, 142, 145, 168–9, 171, 173, 186, 211–12, 221, 380
Roberts, W. M. 317
Robertson, K. R. 445
Robins, C. R. 233
Robotham, P. W. J. 363, 367, 392
Rodier, F. 105
Rogers, J. S. 90, 94
Rogers, P. H. 317
Rohlf, F. J. 59–60, 62, 64–5, 70, 330
Rohwer, S. 520
Rombout, J. H. W. M. 415
Rome, L. C. 427
Romer, A. S. 35
Root, A. 5
Root, J. 5
Rose, S. M. 510
Rosen, D. 97, 106
Rosen, D. E. 45, 141, 144, 188, 250, 253, 485, 487, 519, 521
Rosen, M. W. 392
Rosen, R. A. 357
Ross, M. R. 72, 521
Rottmann, R. W. 466–7, 469
Rousset, C. 37
Rowe, D. K. 279
Roxburgh, I. 279
Rubenstein, D. I. 393
Rundberg, H. 532
Rutte, E. 34, 38–9, 398, 400
Ruvolo, M. 108
Ryder, R. A. 537

Sachlan, M. 189
Sackler, M. L. 89
Sage, R. D. 104
Sagemehl, M. 337
Saglio, P. 510
Sahni, A. 178
Saidel, W. M. 317
Saitou, N. 108

Salinas, J. 105
Salle, R. de 108, 109, 112
Salo, J. 559
Sambrook, J. 104
Sand, O. 332, 345–6
Sand-Jensen, K. 535, 542
Sandy, J. M. 296
Sanna, P. 336, 338
Sargent, R. C. 520
Sarig, S. 148
Satoh, S. 600
Sattaur, O. 150
Saunders, M. 45, 178
Saunders, N. C. 104, 108
Sauvage, H. E. 168
Savino, J. F. 556
Sawada, N. 415
Sawada, Y. 19
Schaber, E. 416
Schaber, G. G. 28
Schaefer, S. A. 76
Schiemer, F. 284, 299, 354–5, 416, 418–20, 464
Schildhauer, B. 449
Schindel, D. E. 56
Schliesing, L. J. 106–7
Schlitter, D. A. 97
Schmida, G. E. 264, 267
Schmidt, J. T. 301
Schmidtke, J. 105
Schnakenbeck, W. 294, 334, 339
Schnitzlein, H. N. 285
Scholtissek, C. 149
Schreck, C. B. 467
Schuijf, A. 317, 343
Schulte, E. 314
Schultz, R. J. 92, 100, 109
Schulz, U. 370
Schut, J. 503
Schutz, F. 514–15
Schmid, M. 101
Schmidt, G. W. 177
Schtylko, B. A. 43
Schwanzel-Fukuda, M. 308
Schwartz, E. 345–6
Schwartz, F. J. 8, 404
Scmitt, E. 105
Scott, A. 555

Scott, D. B. C. 485
Scott, F. 427
Scott, J. W. 308
Scott, W. F. 522
Sedell, J. R. 188
Seghers, B. H. 358, 518–19
Seiko, M. 439
Selander, R. K. 89
Sen, T. K. 168
Sharma, O. P. 98
Sharp, P. 112
Shart, L .A. 612, 615
Shea, B. T. 70
Shearer, K. D. 264, 267, 273
Shelbourn, J. E. 531
Sheldon, F. H. 104, 107–8
Shih, S. H. 605
Shimma, Y. 615
Shiratani, T. 310
Shireman, J. V. 148, 278, 466–7, 469
Shoop, C. T. 531
Shoubridge, E. A. 434
Shrestha, J. 168
Shuter, B. J. 107
Shutov, V. A. 8
Sibbing, F. A. 5, 310, 321, 346, 355, 357–8, 360, 363, 367, 377–80, 384–95, 397–8, 400–7, 416
Sibley, C. G. 104, 107–8
Sibly, R. M. 512
Sidell, B. D. 443–4
Siebert, D. J. 46
Siegmund, R. 445, 447
Sih, A. 564
Silva, E. B. da 102
Silva, S. S. de 133, 503
Silver, W. L. 305, 314, 317
Simmons, K. E. L. 563
Simon, R. C. 105, 108
Simpson, G. G. 322
Singh, H. R. 285
Singh, K. P. 133
Sinha, G. M. 416
Sinis, A. I. 8
Sirotek, D. 395
Skelton, P. H. 18, 217, 223–4, 230, 232
Skrabanek, A. 365

Slade, N. A. 111
Slatkin, M. 85
Slightom, J. L. 112
Sloley, B. D. 515
Smirnov, S. A. 537
Smisek, J. 614
Smit, H. 430, 532
Smith, C. R. 148
Smith, G. R. 34, 41, 55–61, 67,
   70–4, 77–8, 91, 97, 110–11
Smith, H. M. 7, 26, 168, 173, 186,
   188–9
Smith, H. T. 467
Smith, J. J. 89
Smith, L. L. 562
Smith, M. H. 89, 105, 108
Smith, M. L. 41–2, 56, 240, 248
Smith, P. J. 85, 90, 277
Smith, R. J. F. 308, 510, 513,
   515–16, 518–21, 523
Smith, T. F. 108
Smouse, P. E. 111
Sneath, P. H. A. 94, 180–81
Snyder, D. E. 494
Snyder, L. A. 105
Sokal, R. R. 64, 70, 94, 180–81, 330
Sokolov, A. V. 341–2
Sokolowska, M. 605
Sola, L. 95, 98–100
Sondergaard, M. 544
Song, S. -L. 167
Song, Z. 95, 98, 100–101, 106
Sontirat, S. 168
Sookvibul, S. 177
Sorennsen, P. W. 510
Soriano, P. 105
Sorokin, J. I. 534, 545
Sostoa, A. de 473
Soszka, G. L. 466
Soszka, H. 466
Soule, M. E. 65
Spangler, G. R. 546, 572
Spencer, C. N. 558, 561, 565
Spindler, T. 494
Spittler, P. 395
Spodniewska, I. 403
Springer, A. D. 300
Spry, C. 504

Srikantia, S. V. 178
Srivastava, G. J. 133, 168
Ssentongo, G. W. 230
Stacey, N. E. 510
Staines, M. 296
Stanley, J. G. 554, 616
Stasiak, R. H. 92, 109
Stauffer, J. R. 85, 246, 437
Stearns, S. C. 503
Steenderen, G. W. van 310, 314, 317
Steffens, W. 612
Stein, D. W. 94
Stein, R. A. 553, 556, 562
Steinmetz, B. 456, 462
Stenson, J. A. E. 559, 564, 566
Sterba, G. 141–2
Stetter, H. 334, 336–7, 343
Stevens, T. V. 516
Stewart, A. J. 553
Stewart, D. J. 215, 222, 226
Stewart, F. H. 143, 167
Stewart, J. D. 41
Stoneking, M. 104
Stott, B. 523
Stouder, D. J. 474
Stout, J. F. 510
Strachan, T. 112
Strand, M. R. 102
Strauss, R. E. 55–62, 69–74, 77–8
Strayer, D. 535, 542
Street, M. 561
Street, N. E. 517
Strickler, J. R. 356
Stroband, H. W. J. 415, 420
Strobeck, C. 112
Stromberg, C. 398
Sturmbauer, C. 419
Styron, J. T. 75
Stuart, C. T. 233
Su, T. 45
Subla, B. A. 5
Suboski, M. D. 515
Suietov, S. V. 366, 388
Sukop, I. 365
Sumari, O. 532
Sundararaj, B. I. 602
Sunder, S. 5
Surlemont, C. 336, 338

Suslowska, W. 395
Suszycka, E. 473
Suvatti, N. C. 168
Suzuki, A. 168
Suzuki, H. 112
Suzuki, R. 596–7, 615
Svardson, G. 371, 488, 531–2, 542
Svatora, M. 464
Swarts, F. A. 611
Swift, C. C. 246
Swinney, G. N. 472
Swofford, D. L. 94
Sykes, W. H. 169
Sytchevskaya, E. K. 43–4, 46, 177
Sytina, L. A. 539
Szarski, H. 107
Szlazynska, K. 572

Tai, T. -Y. 167
Taisescu, E. 99
Takahasi, N. 380
Takai, A. 95, 98, 101–3
Takeda, H. 600
Takeuchi, N. 99
Takeuchi, T. 599–600
Taki, Y. 5, 7, 24, 168, 173, 179, 182, 189
Tamas, G. 148
Tan, J. -H. 167
Tanaka, M. 420
Tapiador, D. D. 615
Tash, J. C. 356–7, 370–1
Tatrai, I. 355, 473, 537, 564–5
Taverne-Thiele, J. J. 415
Tavolga, W. N. 303, 343
Taylor, J. N. 256
Taylor, W. D. 107
Tchang, T. L. 8, 167
Teichert, T. 444
Teltsch, B. 553
Templeton, A. R. 108–9, 111
Terio, B. 342
Terlouw, A. 5, 358, 360, 363, 377–80, 384–6, 388–91, 394–5, 398, 404–5, 407
Terrell, J. W. 554
Terrell, T. T. 554
Teugels, G. G. 26, 219, 232–3

Thamas, G. 592
Thenius, E. 371
Thien, S. L. 112
Thiery, J. P. 105
Thillart, G. van den 434–5
Thines, G. 345
Thomas, J. E. 107
Thomas, T. L. 105–6
Thomas, W. K. 108
Thompson, D'A. W. 55
Thompson, K. W. 74
Thompson, S. 47
Thorpe, J. E. 540
Thrienen, C. W. 273
Thys van den Audenaerde, D. F. E. 213, 215, 217
Tijia, H. D. 164, 182
Tilak, R. 168
Tilzey, R.D.J. 264, 267
Timbrook, S. 495
Timmermans, C. P. M. 415
Timms, A. M. 294
Tint Hlaing, U. 168
Tissot, B. N. 58, 67, 69–71
Titus, J. E. 535, 542
Toivonen, J. 545
Toledo, S. A. 102–3
Tomasson, T. 223–5, 228
Tomilenko, V. G. 615
Tong, H. Y. 458, 464, 489, 494
Tonn, W. M. 378, 538, 545
Torres, S. 471
Toth, L. G. 564
Townsend, C. R. 354, 356–8, 368, 370, 468, 495, 503, 537, 555, 558–9, 562
Travers, R. A. 7
Treasurer, J. W. 494
Tretiak, D. N. 89
Trewavas, E. 146, 229
Trick, M. 112
Tripathi, N. K. 98
Trivers, R. L. 516
Troppmair, J. 414, 419
Trump, B. F. 449–50
Trust, T. J. 416
Tsai, C. -F. 187
Tsao, W. S. 167

Tsuchiya, K. 439
Tsuchiya, M. 608, 610
Tsuitsui, H. 615
Turanov, V. F. 615
Turdakov, F. A. 133
Turner, J. R. 514
Tweddle, D. 222–4, 227–8,
  230–1, 233
Tyus, H.M. 523

Uchihashi, K. 285
Ueda, T. 95, 98, 100
Ueno, K. 616
Ultsch, G. R. 433
Unger, L. M. 519–20
Urbanowicz, K. 395
Uribe, R. 310, 367, 389–93, 395
Uribe-Zamora, M. 355, 357, 391
Utter, F. 85
Uyeno, T. 28, 34, 41, 44, 97, 178

Vaas, K. F. 173, 189
Vail, P. R. 47
Vaillant, L. L. 168
Vaisanen, R. A. 62, 65
Vaitulevich, S. F. 341–2
Vale, W. W. 603, 605, 607
Valenciennes, A. 173
Vandermeer, J. H. 74
Vanderpuye, J. 228
Vandewalle, P. 317, 334, 336–9,
  341, 346, 380
Vanegas, H. 299, 303
Vannote, R. L. 188
Vasnecsov, V. 404
Vasnetzov, V. V. 167, 458
Vawter, L. 108
Veen, F. H. van der 415
Venkateswarlu, T. 168
Vergnaud-Grazzini, C. 39
Verhagen, J. H. G. 380
Verheijen, F. J. 515
Verighina, I. A. 532
Verigin, B. V. 395, 493
Verigina, I. A. 378, 387, 393
Verwijst, T. 61–2
Victor, D. 338
Vijverberg, J. 368, 370, 545, 560

Villers, A. 343
Vinciguerra, D. 168
Visser, C. 343
Vitek, A. 105
Vladimirov, V. I. 496
Vlaming, V. L. de 484
Vockner, F. H. W. 354–5
Vogt, D. 133, 284
Voliva, C. 112
Vollestad, L. A. 355, 484, 486–7,
  523, 553
Volodin, V. M. 490
Volz, W. 168
Vonk, H. J. 419
Voropaev, G. 150
Vrba, J. 464
Vrijenhoek, R. 104
Vuorinen, I. 559

Waarde, A. van 434–5
Wagner, C. C. 474
Wagner, H. J. 296, 299
Wahl, D. H. 562
Waisal, Y. 554
Wake, D. B. 406
Waldman, B. 515
Walford, L. A. 458
Walker, K. F. 437
Walker, M. M. 522
Walker, T. J. 522
Wallace, A. R. 163, 178
Walls, G. L. 296
Walls, J. G. 149
Walter, E. 467
Wang, D. W. 332–3
Wang, J. 553
Wang, X. -T. 167
Wang, Y. 130
Wangdus, C. 178
Wanink, J. H. 230
Wanzenbock, J. 299, 354–5, 357
Wartzok, D. 301
Watanabe, R. 599
Watanabe, T. 600
Watanabe, Y. 415, 420
Waterman, T. H. 294, 522
Watrous, L. E. 95
Watson, D. W. 475

Watson, J. M. 338
Watt, P. W. 444
Weatherley, A. H. 264, 279, 457–9, 468, 474
Weaver, S. 112
Webb, J. F. 317–18
Webb, P. W. 406, 462, 562
Weber, E. H. 336
Weber, M. 15, 26, 163, 168, 178, 182
Weber, R. E. 433
Weglenska, T. 586
Wehr, R. 514–15
Weil, E. 484
Weiler, W. 38
Weinberg, P. H. 62
Weir, B. S. 108
Weitzman, S. H. 39
Welch, E. B. 566
Welcomme, R. L. 158, 460, 573–5, 582, 587
Werner, E. E. 284, 296, 319, 356, 368, 377–8, 387, 538–9, 546, 555, 561, 563
Wetterer, J. K. 296, 299
Wetzel, R. G. 535, 542
Wetzig, J. 343
Wharton, J. C. F. 274
Wheeler, A. 133, 141, 399, 472
Wheeler, A. C. 7
Wheeler, Q. D. 97
Whelan, K. F. 486
White, B. N. 104, 112
White, E. I. 37
White, R. J. 61–2
White, R. W. G. 473
Whitear, M. 305, 308, 314
Whitehead, P. J. P. 233
Whitlock, C. W. 98
Whitmore, T. C. 158, 162
Whitt, G. S. 84, 89, 93
Whittaker, R. H. 514
Wie, K. -Y. 58
Wiebe, W. J. 416
Wieser, W. 296, 299, 319, 358, 415, 420–1, 428, 431, 439–43, 445–7, 458, 464, 537, 540
Wilcox, R. S. 318
Wilda, T. J. 363

Wiley, E. O. 26, 241, 244, 247
Wiley, M. L. 145
Wilkonska, H. 466
Willemsen, J. 539
Willer, A. 354–5, 368
Williams, G. C. 469, 516
Williams, S. M. 112
Williams, W. P. 473, 500
Willmer, E. N. 449
Willoughby, N. G. 223
Wilson, A. C. 97, 104, 108
Wilson, F. R. 89
Wilson, H. V. 332
Wilson, M. V. H. 42, 46, 48, 72
Wilson, V. 112
Win, K. 168
Winberg, G. G. 431–2
Winfield, D. K. 561, 563
Winfield, I. J. 354, 356–8, 368, 467, 495, 517, 532, 534–6, 542, 555, 559, 561–3
Winkel, E. H. ten 363, 367–8, 566
Winkelmann, E. 301
Winkelmann, L. 301
Winkler, H. 355, 357, 436
Wiraatmadja, G. 189
Wisniewski, R. J. 403
Wissing, J. 434
Withler, R. E. 108
Witt, H. de 168
Witte, F. 229, 406
Witte-Maas, E. L. M. 406
Wodinsky, J. 343
Wodtke, E. 444
Woese, C. R. 112
Wohlfahrt, T. A. 334–6, 343
Wohlfarth, G. 467, 613–16
Wolf, U. 89
Wolfe, J. A. 46
Wollmuth, L. P. 435
Wolny, P. 473
Wolos, A. 572
Wolpert, L. 321
Womac, W. D. 98
Wood, G. L. 142
Woodman, D. A. 245–6, 261
Woods, T. D. 93
Wootton, R. J. 457

Workman, D. R. 164, 166
Worthington, A. D. 484
Wrede, W. L. 510
Wright, D. E. 356
Wright, D. I. 358
Wright, D. J. 393
Wright, J. E. 611
Wright, J. W. 108
Wright, R. 561
Wright, S. 85
Wu, C. -Z. 167
Wu, H. 130, 144, 147, 149, 150
Wu, H. W. 8, 167
Wu, L. 167
Wu, Y. 12, 24, 138
Wu, Y. -F. 167, 177
Wullimann, M. F. 299, 301
Wunder, W. 294, 391, 445
Wuycheck, J. C. 378
Wyche, C. J. 512

Xie, X. 98
Xie, Y. -H. 167
Xinjiang Institute of Biology, Soil and
  Desert, Academia Sinica 133
Xu, P. 112
Xu, R. 166
Xu, T. -Q. 167

Yakovlev, V. N. 43
Yamaguchi, M. 615
Yamamoto, H. 600
Yamamoto, T. 98, 450
Yamaoka, K. 229
Yamashita, S. 308, 310
Yang, G. 147
Yang, S. Y. 89, 91, 94
Yaron, Z. 603
Yazdani, G. M. 168
Yerger, R. W. 246
Yonekawa, H. 109

Young, C. C. 45
Young, J. C. 522
Younker, J. L. 60
Yu, M. L. 510
Yu, X. 95–8, 100–1
Yue, P. 35, 130, 138, 140, 147
Yue, P. -Q. 9, 17–18

Zabka, H. 448
Zachert, I. 514–15
Zahn, M. 437–8
Zaki Mohamed, M. I. 493
Zalewski, M. 469
Zan, R. 95, 98, 100–1, 106
Zander, E. 356, 358, 393–4
Zaret, T. M. 355–6, 387
Zaunreiter, M. 296, 298–9, 319, 321
Zawisza, J. 148, 468
Zdanovich, V. V. 466
Zdanowski, B. 586
Zdinak, A. 448
Zdziennicka, M. 457, 462
Zebe, E. 434
Zerial, M. 105
Zerr, R. W. 74
Zhang, M. 45
Zhen, P. -S. 133
Zhou, J. 45
Zhou, M. 95–8, 100–1
Zhou, T. 95–8, 100–1
Zhou, X. J. 603, 605, 607
Zhu, S. Q. 138, 167, 177
Zhukanskii, V. N. 490
Zimmerman, E. G. 92
Zimmerman, M. 107
Zimpfer, P. S. 495
Zippel, H. P. 305
Zoch, P. K. 95, 98, 101, 103–4
Zottermann, Y. 310
Zugmayer, E. 167
Zuromska, H. 466, 492
Zygmuntowicz, R. 85

Taxonomic index

Abbottina 13, 194
  A. rivularis 144
Abramidinae 8, 13, 15, 142, 242
Abramidini 13
Abramiformes 13
Abraminae 14, 17, 20–21
Abramis 7, 14, 20, 37, 43, 48, 134,
  138, 141, 242, 291, 575
  A. ballerus (blue bream) 287, 295,
  305, 310–11, 316, 318, 489–90
  A. brama (bronze bream, common
  bream) 141, 143, 147–8,
  286–7, 291–3, 301, 303,
  310–12, 318, 320–1, 341,
  353–5, 357–71, 383, 386–9,
  392, 394, 399, 403, 427, 445,
  464, 467, 472–3, 475, 486–8,
  492, 512, 532, 534–7, 540,
  545–6, 555, 557–61, 564–6,
  573–6, 581–3, 585
  A. sapa 287, 295
Acanthalburnus 15, 134
Acanthobrama 20, 134, 194
  A. centisquama 142
  A. terraesanctae (lavnun) 148
Acanthogobio 136, 194
Acanthorhodeus 13, 137, 145, 185,
  193
  A. asmussii 142
  A. diegnani 136
Acanthorutilus 14, 135
  A. handlirschi 146

Acapoeta 213
Acheilognathinae 12–13, 23, 27, 35,
  48, 96–7, 134, 136–7, 158,
  170, 173–4, 193
Acheilognathus 13, 137, 193
  A. asmussii 142
  A. lanceolata 44
Acrocheilus (chiselmouth) 5, 243, 246,
  255
  A. alutaceus 71
Acrossocheilus 138, 142, 144, 199
Agosia 246
  A. chrysogaster (longfin dace) 566
Albulichthys 198
Alburniformes 15
Alburninae 12, 15, 17–18, 21–2, 27,
  96, 158, 170, 174, 195
Alburnoides 15, 22, 43, 134, 140
  A. bipunctatus (schneider) 287, 473
Alburnus 15, 18, 22, 39, 43, 48, 134
  A. alburnus (European bleak) 92,
  142–3, 149, 287, 293, 301,
  305, 311–12, 315–16, 354–8,
  362, 371, 387, 460, 462, 464,
  473, 475–6, 493, 495, 501,
  553, 584
  A. chalcoides 341
Algansea 243, 245–6
Amblypharyngodon 136, 172, 190, 196
  A. melettinus 418
Amblyrhynchichthys 190, 198
Amphilus natalensis 231

Anabarilius 137, 185
Anaecypris 6, 14, 134
Ancherythroculter 15, 195
Aphyocypris 137, 196
Aristichthys 8, 14, 148
  A. (= *Hypophthalmichthys*) *nobilis*
    (bighead carp) 92, 144–5,
    147–8, 256, 466, 487, 494,
    553, 583, 590, 592–5, 598,
    600, 603–4, 607, 612, 615
Asp, *see Aspius aspius*
Aspidoparia 16, 136, 196
Aspiini 14, 17, 20-21, 27, 137,
    170–1, 174, 195
Aspiolucius 14, 20, 134
Aspiopsis 14, 20, 135
Aspiorhynchus 135, 200
Aspiurnus 43
Aspius 14, 20, 39, 43, 48, 134, 383
  A. *aspius* (asp) 144, 287, 295–6,
    303, 305–6, 311, 319, 321,
    355, 362, 384, 388, 392, 398,
    403, 448, 473, 476, 539, 574
Atrilinea 137, 172, 197
Aulopyge 12, 24, 134, 142
Aztecula 243, 246

Balantocheilus 25, 190, 198
Bangana 173, 190, 201
Barb
  blind cave, *see Caecobarbus geertsi*
  European, *see Barbus barbus*
  rosy, *see Puntius conchonius*
Barbel
  Damascus, *see Capoeta damascina*
  European, *see Barbus barbus*
  large-scaled, *see Barbus canis*
  long-headed, *see Barbus longiceps*
  Mediterranean, *see Barbus*
    meridionalis
Barbichthys 12, 201
Barbinae 7, 12, 17–18, 23, 35, 43,
    48, 135, 138–9, 171,
    216–17, 223–5
Barbodes 7, 190–1, 199
Barboides 213, 215
  B. *gracilis* 217
Barbopsis 7–8, 213, 215, 217

Barbs 5, 100, 138, 142, 185, 189, 268
  African large 184
Barbus 3, 8–10, 12–13, 18, 23, 26,
    39–40, 45, 92–3, 130,
    134–5, 138, 142, 172, 198,
    213–15, 222–6, 231–2,
    280, 486, 503–4
  B. (South African yellowfish) 100
  B. *altianalis* 225
  B. *aphya* 172
  B. *andrewi* 214, 223
  B. *aeneus* 225, 228
  B. *anoplus* 223–5, 228
  B. *barbus* (barbel, European barb)
    100, 144, 270, 287, 291–2,
    321, 341, 355, 362, 387, 399,
    403, 436, 473, 486, 496, 574, 576
  B. *bocaquei* 473
  B. *brachycephalus* 143
  B. *calidus* 224
  B. *callensis* 143, 473, 475
  B. *canis* (large-scaled barbel) 148
  B. *choloensis* 231
  B. *erubescens* 224
  B. *esocinus* 141
  B. *eurystomus* 223–4, 226
  B. *eutaenia* 231
  B. *fasciolatus* 224
  B. *hospes* 225
  B. *intermedius* 184, 214
  B. *jacksoni* 215–16
  B. *johnstonii* 223, 226
  B. *kimberleyensis* 216, 224–5
  B. *litamba* 214, 223-224, 226
  B. *longiceps* (long-headed
    barbel) 148
  B. *luteus* 142
  B. *macrolepis* 216, 223
  B. *marequensis* 223, 225
  B. *mattozi* 214, 216, 223
  B. *megacephalus* 45, 178
  B. *meridionalis* (Mediterranean
    barbel) 100
  B. *multilineatus* 224
  B. *orientalis* 43
  B. *pallidus* 223
  B. *paludinosus* 222, 226, 228, 503
  B. *plebius* 100

Barbus (Contd.)
  B. poechii 215
  B. profundus 226
  B. radiatus 215, 222
  B. schoutedeni 216
  B. serra 214, 223
  B. srilankensis 146
  B. trachypterus 225
  B. treurensis 224
  B. trevelyani 224
  B. trimaculatus 215, 222
  B. viviparus 223
Barilinae 6, 15–16, 35, 43, 48, 139,
  214–15, 218–20, 224–8
Barilius 5, 9, 16, 25, 137, 173, 196,
  218, 383–4
  B. bola (Indian trout) 148
  B. mesopotamicus 135
Belica, *see Leucaspius delineatus*
Belligobio 194
Bengala 16, 196
Bitterling, *see Rhodeus*
Biwia 13, 136
Bleak
  Danube, *see Chalcalburnus chalcoides*
  European, *see Alburnus alburnus*
Blicca 37, 43, 48, 134
  B. bjoerkna (silver bream, white
    bream) 37, 287, 291, 311–12,
    353–5, 358–9, 361–2,
    364–7, 371, 383, 389, 392,
    399, 466–7, 473, 490, 495,
    534, 539–40, 573–4, 576,
    581–2, 585
  B. croydonensis 40, 48
Blind cave fish, *see Caecobarbus geertsi*
Brachydanio 16, 136, 196
  B. rerio (zebra danio) 149,
    483–4, 504, 510, 512, 515, 518
Bream
  common, *see Abramis brama*
  blue, *see Abramis ballerus*
  bronze, *see Abramis brama*
  roundhead, *see Megalobrama
    amblycephala*
  silver, *see Blicca bjoerkna*
  white, *see Blicca bjoerkna*

Caecobarbus 7, 213, 215, 217
  C. geertsi (blind cave barb) 230,
    285, 345
Caecocypris 3, 7, 135
  C. basimi 146
Calbasu, *see Labeo calbasu*
Campostoma 94, 243, 246, 250–2,
    254–6, 562
  C. anomalum (stoneroller) 74, 92,
    102, 251, 474, 553–4
  C. oligolepis 92
Candida 196
Capoeta 5, 8, 12, 23, 134–5, 138,
    144, 146, 280
  C. damascina (Damascus barbel) 148
  C. trutta 171
Capoetabrama 134
Carassioides 197
Carassius 7, 12, 17, 24, 39–40, 43,
    45, 48, 95, 134, 141–2, 197, 435
  C. auratus (goldfish) 92–3, 95,
    98–100, 138, 142, 149, 221,
    256, 265–71, 276–8, 280,
    284, 287, 291, 294–6,
    299–300, 305, 332–4,
    336–8, 342–3, 391, 427,
    430–34, 436–7, 439–440,
    442–5, 448, 450, 466–7,
    483, 510–11, 517–19, 522,
    555, 600–1, 605
  C. carassius (crucian carp) 99, 135,
    141, 143, 146, 266, 268, 287,
    291–2, 296, 299–301, 310,
    312, 318, 321, 355, 358,
    361–2, 399, 403, 433–4,
    436, 439–40, 443–7, 473,
    574–6, 582–5, 590,
    592–5, 615
Carp
  bighead, *see Aristichthys*
    (= *Hypophthalmichthys*) *nobilis*
  black, *see Mylopharyngodon piceus*
  common, *see Cyprinus carpio*
  crucian, *see Carassius carassius*
  grass, *see Ctenopharyngodon idella*
  koi, *see Cyprinus carpio*
  mrigal, *see Cirrhinus mrigala*

mud, *see Cirrhinus molitorella*
silver, *see Hypophthalmichthys molitrix*
Carps 5, 24, 138, 143, 146–8, 187
Catla 12, 136, 172–3
    C. catla 148, 591, 596, 600, 615
Catlacarpio 136, 172, 190, 197
    C. siamensis 141, 186
Catlae 172
Cephalokompsus 199
Chagunius 199
Chalcalburnus 3, 8, 15, 22, 134
    C. chalcalburnus 293
    C. chalcoides (Danube bleak, shemaya) 143, 287, 295, 430, 437
Chanodichthys 15, 173, 195
Chanoides 37
Chekhon, *see Pelecus cultratus*
Chela 6, 15-16, 190, 196
Chelaethiops 16, 213, 215, 219
    C. elongatus 220
Cheline group 15–16
Chiselmouth, *see Acrocheilus*
Chondrostoma 14, 20, 43, 48, 134, 138, 144
    C. nasus (nase) 147, 287, 295, 307, 315–16, 354, 362, 387, 399, 436, 473, 486, 496, 500, 576
    C. polylepis 473
Chondrostomini 13, 170, 172, 174, 194
Chorosomus neogaeus 338
Chuanchia 12, 135, 200
Chub
    European, *see Leuciscus cephalus*
    creek, *see Semotilus atromaculatus*
Cirrhina 25
Cirrhinus 12, 136, 201
    C. molitorella (mud carp) 593–4, 600, 603-604, 607
    C. mrigala (mrigal, mrigal carp) 148, 187, 591, 596, 600, 615
Clinostomus 243, 246, 252–3
    C. funduloides 474
Clypeobarbus 214–15
    C. schoutedeni 216
Colorado squawfish, *see Ptychocheilus lucius*

Coptostomabarbus 213, 215, 217
    C. bellcrossi 216
Coreius 3, 13, 137, 193
Coreoleuciscus 13
Cosmochilus 191, 198
Couesius (Lake chub) 14, 22, 243–4, 246, 252
Crossocheilus 25, 136, 138, 201
Ctenopharyngodon 5, 12, 25, 45, 138, 145, 197
    C. idella (grass carp) 92, 143, 144–9, 221, 256, 269–70, 272, 278–9, 287, 386, 388, 392, 403, 436, 439, 448, 466, 487, 494–5, 554, 577, 583, 590, 592–6, 598, 600, 603–4, 607, 612, 616,
Culter 15, 22, 190, 195
Cultrinae 6, 12, 14–15, 18, 21–2, 27, 35, 96–7, 134, 136–8, 142, 158, 170–1, 174, 195
Cultrops 22
Cycloheilichthys 190–91, 198
    C. apogon 475
Cypraea caputserpentis 69
Cyprinella 103, 243, 245–6, 250–6, 510
    C. lepida 105
    C. lutrensis 76–7, 92, 105–6, 255
    C. venusta 105
Cyprininae 10–12, 16–18, 23–7, 35, 40, 45, 48, 96, 99, 134–6, 138, 158, 170–2, 174, 197, 214–17
Cyprinion 5, 13, 135–6, 171, 200
    C. watsoni 143
Cyprinion-Onychostoma 24
Cyprinodon 57
Cyprinus 3–4, 10, 12, 24, 39, 43, 45, 95, 130, 134, 138, 142, 185, 197–8
    C. carpio (common carp) 44, 85, 92–3, 95, 99, 141–2, 146–8, 221, 232, 256, 266–76, 280, 286–7, 291–3, 295, 301, 303, 305–6, 310, 320–1, 342,

Cyprinus (*Contd.*)
   355, 357–8, 361–2,
   366–7, 371, 378, 380–1,
   383–4, 386–93, 395,
   397–400, 402–6, 414–15,
   419, 427, 430–4, 436–7,
   439, 442–5, 448, 450,
   466–7, 473, 483–4, 487,
   490, 500–1, 513, 554, 562,
   566–7, 575–7, 582–5,
   590–6, 600, 602–5, 607,
   611–6
   C. dero 173

Dace
   American, *see Rhinichthys atratulus*
   blacknose, *see Rhinichthys atratulus*
   European, *see Leuciscus leuciscus*
   finescale, *see Phoxinus neogaeus*
   Japanese, *see Tribolodon hakonensis*
   Kendall Warm Springs, *see*
      Rhinichthys osculus
   longfin, *see Agosia chrysogaster*
   pearl, *see Semotilus atromaculatus*
   redbelly, *see Phoxinus eos*
Dangila 190, 201
Danio 6, 16, 190, 196
Danionella 142, 197
   D. translucida 141, 186
Danioninae 9, 15, 96, 137, 158, 170,
   172, 174, 189, 196
Danios 142
Dionda 243, 246, 250–2, 254–5
Diptychus 3, 12, 135, 139, 177, 200
Discherodontus 199
Discognathus 341
Discogobio 185, 201
Distoechodon 14, 20, 194

Ellichthys 345
Ellopostoma 10
Elopichthyini 13
Elopichthys 4–6, 14, 195, 384, 388
   E. bambusa 141, 144–5
Engraulicypris 16, 213, 215, 218
   E. sardella (usipa) 219–20,
      226–8, 230
Enteromius 214–15

Eocyprinus 45
   E. sumatranus 45, 178
Eocypris 45
Eodiptychus 44, 177
Epalzeorhynchos 190, 201
Eremichthys 243, 246, 248, 255
Ericymba 243, 246, 253
Erimonax 243, 245–6, 252
Erimystax 243, 245–6
Erythroculter 3, 15, 137, 173
   E. erythropterus (star gazer) 144
Esomus 10, 16, 187, 190, 197
   E. danrica 142, 147, 417–18
Eupsallasella 14, 134, 137
   E. percnura 135
Evarra 243, 246
Exoglossum 243, 246, 254
   E. maxillingua 521
Extrarius 243, 245–6, 252–3

Fallfish, *see Semotilus corporalis*
Filirasbora rubripinna 172
Folifer 199

Garra 3–4, 7–8, 12, 25–6, 44, 130,
   135–6, 138–9, 141, 144,
   146, 190, 201, 213, 217, 225, 387
   G. barreimiae 146
   G. dembeensis 218
   G. dunsirei 146
   G. johnstonii 225
   G. lamta 98
   G. tibanica 143, 217
Garrae 5, 7, 12, 170, 174, 201
Genghis 14
Gibelion 13, 172–3, 201
   G. catla 187
Gila 3, 6–7, 243–6, 248, 252–3, 255
   G. cypha 73
   G. elegans 73
   G. robusta 73
Gnathopogon 13, 172, 193
   G. javanicus 172
Gobio 7, 10, 13, 25, 39, 43, 48, 134,
   136, 141–2, 194
   G. gobio (gudgeon) 11, 135, 143,
      147, 287, 292, 334, 355, 362,
      387–8, 399, 403, 471–3,

475, 487, 489, 501, 510, 523, 557
Gobiobotia 13, 137, 145, 194
Gobiocypris 137, 197
Gobioninae 7, 10, 12–13, 18, 25, 27,
   35, 48, 96, 134, 136, 158,
   170–1, 173–4, 193–4
Goldfish, *see Carassius auratus*
Gudgeon, *see Gobio gobio*
Gymnocypris 12, 135, 139, 177, 200
Gymnodiptychus 135, 200
Gyrinocheilus 341

Hainania 195
Hampala 189, 191, 199
   H. macrolepidota 189, 475
Hemibarbus 13, 43, 194
   H. barbus 44
Hemiculter 15, 22, 145, 195
Hemiculterella 15, 22, 137, 185,
   195
Hemigarra 135
Hemigrammocapoeta 135
Hemigrammocypris 137
Hemitremia 243, 246, 252
Heniorhynchus 190, 201
Herzensteinia 135, 200
Hesperoleucus 243, 246, 254
Horadandia 136, 197
Hybognathus 243, 246, 251, 253, 255
Hybopsis 243, 245–6, 251–2
   H. imeldae 242
   H. moralesi 242
Hydrophlox 254
Hypophthalmichthyinae 13, 97
Hypophthalmichthys 3, 5, 8, 14, 20,
   44, 137, 148, 172, 194
   H. molitrix (silver carp) 143,
   145–8, 221, 256, 269–70,
   272, 279, 287, 293, 358, 383,
   386–9, 395, 398, 403, 416,
   434, 436, 439, 448, 466, 487,
   494, 553, 583, 590, 592–6,
   598, 600, 603–4, 607, 612, 615
   H. (= *Aristichthys*) *nobilis* (bighead
   carp) 92, 144–5, 147–8,
   256, 466, 487, 494, 553, 583,
   590, 592–5, 598, 600,
   603–4, 607, 612, 615

Hypselobarbus 199

Iberocypris 134
Ide, *see Leuciscus* (= *Idus*) *idus*
Idus (= *Leuciscus*) *idus* (ide, orfe) 135,
   256, 287, 305, 341, 354, 358,
   361–2, 388, 436, 473, 492,
   539–40, 555, 574, 576
Indian trout, *see Barilius bola*
Inlecypris 16, 185, 197
Iotichthys 243, 246, 248
Iranocypris 7, 135
   I. typhlops 146
Ischikauia 15, 137

Kantaka 200

Labeo (freshwater shark) 3–5, 12,
   25–6, 43, 130, 136, 138, 142,
   144, 190, 201, 213–14, 217,
   224–5, 228–9, 387, 416
   L. altivelis 225, 227, 229
   L. annectens 218
   L. calbasu (calbasu) 187, 596, 600,
   615
   L. capensis 224, 228
   L. chrysophekadion (black shark) 336
   L. congoro 227
   L. coubie 217–18, 225
   L. cylindricus 225–6, 388
   L. dussemieri 416
   L. fisheri 146
   L. forskahlii 217, 225
   L. gregorii 217
   L. lineatus 392
   L. longipinnis 218
   L. macrostoma 217
   L. mesops 225, 228–9
   L. niloticus 217, 228
   L. rohita (rohu) 148, 187, 591,
   596, 600, 615
   L. seeberi 218
   L. umbratus 217, 223, 228
   L. victorianus 225, 229
Labeobarbus 12
Labeoinae 4, 12, 24–5, 35, 43, 45,
   48, 139, 170, 172, 174, 177,
   201, 217, 224–5, 227–8

Ladigesocypris 134
Ladislavia 13, 136
Lagowskiella 14, 137, 195
  L. *czekanowskii* 135
  L. *lagowskii* 135, 142
Laichowcypris 198
Lavinia 243–4, 246, 251, 253,
  255
  L. *exilicauda* 251
Lavnun, *see Acanthobrama*
  terraesanctae
Lebias furcatus 39
Lepidomeda 243, 246, 248
Lepidopygopsis 135–6, 200
Leptobarbus 172, 189–91, 197
  L. *hoevenii* 147, 172
Leptocypris 16, 213, 215, 218–19
  L. *niloticus* 220
Leucalburnus 15, 134
Leucaspius 14, 134
  L. *delineatus* (belica) 144, 149,
    287, 310, 312, 318, 354–5,
    362, 473, 487, 495, 510, 557
Leuciscinae 8–10, 12–13, 15, 17,
    19–22, 26–7, 35, 37–40, 42–3,
    45, 48, 96–7, 134, 136, 138,
    158, 170, 174, 194–5,
    214–15, 219, 221, 242
Leuciscus 8, 14, 37, 39, 43, 45, 48,
    134, 137, 139, 141, 560
  L. *antunesi* 38
  L. *cephalus* (European chub) 287,
    301, 316, 341, 354, 362, 399,
    418, 459, 462, 464, 466, 468,
    473, 475–6, 486, 500, 540,
    553, 559–60, 576
  L. *etilus* 39
  L. (= *Idus*) *idus* (ide, orfe) 135, 256,
    287, 305, 341, 354, 358,
    361–2, 388, 436, 473, 492,
    539–40, 555, 574, 576
  L. *leuciscus* (European dace) 135,
    287, 354, 362, 399, 403, 427,
    436, 459, 461, 463–5, 467,
    469–73, 476, 486, 490, 493,
    495–500, 512, 555
  L. *primigenius* 38
  L. *socoloriensis* 38

Lissocheilichthys wenchowensis 144
Lobocheilus 189–90, 201
  L. *bo* 475
Longiculter 15, 195
Luciobrama 4, 6, 14, 195
Luciocyprinus 14, 171–2, 185, 200
Luciosoma 10, 16, 190, 196
  L. *setigerum* 11
Luxilus 243, 245–6, 250–2, 254,
  256
  L. *albeolus* 110
  L. *cerasinus* 92, 109–10
  L. *chrysocephalus* 92, 109–10
  L. *cornutus* 91–2, 109–10
  L. *pilsbryi* 94
  L. *zonatus* 91
Lythrurus 243, 245–6, 250,
  252–4, 256
  L. *roseipinnis* 94, 250–1

Macrhybopsis 243, 245–6, 253
Macrochirichthys 4, 6, 15–16, 18,
  191, 196
  M. *macrochirus* 341
Mahseer, *see Tor*
Mandibularca 5, 7, 190
Margariscus 243, 246, 252, 254, 256
Marinka, *see Schizothorax*
  pseudaksaiensis
Meda 243, 246, 248
Megalobrama 15, 137, 195
  M. *amblycephala* (roundhead
    bream) 592, 595
Mekongina 190, 201
Mesobola 16, 213, 215, 219
  M. *bredoi* 219
  M. *brevianalis* 219–20, 225–6
  M. *moeruensis* 219
  M. *spinifer* 219
Mesocyprinus 185, 197
Mesogobio 13
Microphysogobio 13, 137, 145, 194
Microrasbora 185, 197
Minnow
  bluntnose, *see Pimephales notatus*
  European, *see Phoxinus phoxinus*
  fathead, *see Pimephales promelas*
  White Cloud Mountain, *see*

Tanichthys albonubes
Moapa 243, 246, 248
Moroco 91
Mpasa, *see Opsaridium microlepis*
Mrigal, *see Cirrhinus mrigala*
Mylocheilus 7, 41, 243, 246, 253, 256
Mylopharodon 243–4, 246
 M. conocephalus 255
Mylopharyngodon 12, 25, 138, 197
 M. piceus (black carp) 144–5,
  147–8, 590, 592–5, 598,
  600, 604, 607
Mystacoleucus 13, 190, 198

Nase, *see Chondrostoma nasus*
Naziritor 198
Ndaga, *see Rastrineobola argentea*
Nematabramis 10, 16, 190, 197
 N. alestes 11
 N. everetti 475
Neobola 16, 213, 215, 219
 N. bottegoi 220
Neobolines 16, 43, 218, 224–6
Neolissochilus 198
Neorohita 201
Nicholsicypris 197
Nocomis 102, 243, 246, 250,
  252–4, 256, 521
 N. leptocephalus 253
 N. micropogon 253
Notemigonus 18, 35, 42, 48,
  140–1, 242–4, 246, 253–4
 N. crysoleucas (golden shiner) 250,
  256, 474, 562
Notropis 2–3, 90, 243, 245–6, 250,
  252–4, 256, 285, 294, 487,
  503, 510
 N. analostanus 503, 510
 N. atherinoides 74
 N. buchanani 251
 N. cahabae 248
 N. cardinalis 77
 N. chihuahua 252
 N. cornutus (common shiner) 74,
  474, 476, 513, 521–2
 N. heterodon 511
 N. hubbsi 253
 N. hudsonius 437, 518–19

N. longirostris 503
N. lutrensis 510
N. mekistocholas 248
N. orca 74-5
N. pilsbryi 77
N. rubellus 509
N. rupestre 248
N. saladonis 250
N. sallei 74
N. semperasper 252
N. simus 74–5
N. spilopterus 76
N. tropicus 250
N. venustus 510
N. welaka 509
N. zonatus 77
Novumbra oregonensis 41

Ochetobius 3, 14, 137, 171, 195
Omuls 7
Onychostoma 13, 24–5, 138, 171,
  191,199
Opsaridium 16, 213, 218, 226
 O. microcephalus (sanjika) 226–8
 O. microlepis (mpasa) 224, 226–8
 O. moorii 224
 O. ubangense 220, 226–7
 O. zambezense 227
Opsariichthys 3, 9, 16, 25, 137, 196,
  384
 O. tau 341
 O. uncirostris 95
Opsarius 173, 190–1, 196
Opsopoeodus 243, 245–6, 254
Oregonichthys 243, 245–6
Oreichthys 190
Oreininae 12, 99, 170–1, 173–4
  177, 200
Oreinus 25, 135, 200
Oreodaimon 13
Oreoleuciscus 7, 14, 20, 135
Orfe, *see Leuciscus* (= *Idus*) *idus*
Orthodon 14, 243, 246, 253, 255–6
Ospatulus 190
Osteobrama 3, 15, 136, 169–70,
  174, 198

Osteocheilus 12, 25
　O. kahajenensis 475
Osteochilichthys 200
Osteochilus 45, 138, 190, 201
　O. fossilis 45, 178
　O. liniensis 45
Oxygaster 15–16, 18, 191, 196
Oxygastrini 170, 174, 196
Oxygymnocypris 135, 200

Pachychilon 134
　P. pictum 553
Palaeocarassius 40, 48
Palaeoleuciscus 38, 40
　P. etilus 39
　P. primigenius 38
　P. socoloriensis 38
Palaeorutilus papyraceus 38
Palaeotinca 40, 44, 48, 177
　P. egerians 38
Parabarbus 44, 48, 177
Parabramis 15, 137, 195
　P. pekinensis 592, 603–5, 607
Paracanthobrama 194
Paracheilognathus 13, 193
Parachela 16, 190–1, 196
Paracrossocheilus 201
　P. acerus 475
　P. dusonensis 475
Paralaubuca 15, 22, 137, 191, 195
Paraphoxinus 14
Pararhodeus 14, 137, 193
Parasilorhynchus 136, 201
Parasinolabeo 201
Parazacco 196
Parluciosoma 16, 172
Pectinocypris 6, 197
Pelecus 3, 7, 15, 137, 145
　P. cultratus (chekhon) 134, 143,
　　149, 286–7, 292–3, 295,
　　301, 305–6, 310, 312, 318,
　　320, 340, 355–8, 362, 371,
　　387, 448
Percocypris 185, 199
　P. compressiformis 185
Phenacobius 243, 246, 252–3
　P. mirabilis 102

Phoxinellus 14, 26, 134
Phoxinini 14, 17, 20, 22, 35, 42, 48
Phoxinus 2–3, 14, 17–18, 20, 22, 27,
　　134, 136–7, 139–40, 143,
　　145, 240, 244, 246, 252–4, 270
　P. eos (redbelly dace) 92, 109, 557,
　　565
　P. laevis 334–5, 337, 342–3
　P. neogaeus (finescale dace) 92,
　　109, 557, 565
　P. oreas 474
　P. phoxinus (European minnow)
　　135, 143, 145, 147, 149, 287,
　　312, 316, 346, 462, 467,
　　472–3, 476, 485–7,
　　501–4, 510–5, 517–19, 523
Phreatichthys 7, 213, 215, 217
　P. andruzzi 345
Pimephales 7, 103, 244, 250–6, 503
　P. notatus (bluntnose minnow)
　　437, 474, 518, 522
　P. promelas (fathead minnow) 74,
　　256, 467, 474, 503, 510, 516,
　　519–21, 558, 561–2, 565
Placocheilus 201
Plagiognathops 14, 20, 194
Plagopterus (woundfin) 6, 244, 246
Platygobio (Flathead chub) 244–6, 256
Platypharodon 135, 200
Plesioschizothorax macrocephalus 139
Pogonichthi 13
Pogonichthys 14, 20, 27, 244, 246
Poropuntii 170–4, 199
Poropuntius 136, 138, 185, 190, 199
Probarbus 12, 189–91, 198
Procypris 198
Prolabeo 213, 215
　P. batesi 217
Prolabeops 213, 215
　P. cameroonensis 217
Pseudaspius 14
Pseudobarbus 13, 100, 213, 215,
　　217, 223
　P. quathlambae 216
Pseudobrama 20
Pseudogobio 13, 194
Pseudohemiculter 195
Pseudolaubuca 15, 22, 195

Pseudoperilampus 13, 193
Pseudophoxinus 134, 213, 215, 219
  P. callensis 221
Pseudopungtungia 13
Pseudorasbora 16, 25, 45, 193
  P. parva 144, 430
Pteronotropis 103, 244–6, 252, 256
  P. euryzonus 248
  P. welaka 253
Ptychidio 138, 201
  P. jordani 142
Ptychobarbus 200
Ptychocheilus 4, 6, 244, 246, 250,
  253, 255–6, 384, 388
  P. grandis 251
  P. lucius (Colorado squawfish) 6,
  250–1, 497, 523
Pungtungia 13, 136
Puntioplites 191, 198
Puntius 13, 15, 18, 44–5, 130, 136,
  138, 172, 178, 187, 189–91,
  199, 280
  P. binotatus 62–3
  P. bussyi 45, 178
  P. collingwoodi 475
  P. conchonius (rosy barb) 265,
  267–8
  P. filamentosus 417
  P. sophore 145

Raiamas 16, 26, 189, 191, 196, 213,
  218
  R. senegalensis 220
Rasbora 6, 10, 16, 45, 130,
  136–7, 142, 172, 186,
  190–1, 197
  R. antiqua 45, 178
  R. bankanensis 475
  R. daniconia 145
  R. daniconius (slender rasbora)
  417–8
  R. maculata (spotted rasbora) 186
  R. mohri 45, 178
  R. sumatrana 475
  R. urophthalma (miniature rasbora)
  186
  R. vaterifloris (fire rasbora) 146
Rasbora

fire, *see Rasbora vaterifloris*
  miniature, *see Rasbora urophthalma*
  slender, *see Rasbora daniconius*
  spotted, *see Rasbora maculata*
Rasborichthys 172, 197
Rasborinae 10, 12, 15–18, 23, 25–7,
  35, 136–7
Rasborinus 195
Rastrineobola 16, 213, 215
  R. argentea (ndaga) 219–20, 226,
  228–30
Rectoris 138, 201
Relictus 244, 246, 248, 250
Rhinichthys 244–6, 248, 251–2, 254
  R. atratulus (American dace,
  blacknose dace) 75, 474, 560
  R. cataractae 72, 474
  R. chrysogaster 251
  R. osculus (Kendall Warm Springs
  dace) 72, 109
Rhinogobio 3, 13, 137, 194, 341
Rhodeina 13
Rhodeus (bitterling) 13, 23, 39, 137, 193
  R. amarus 434, 438–9, 442,
  487, 495
  R. ocellatus 616
  R. sericeus 134, 142, 144, 256,
  287, 310, 312, 557
Rhotee 15
Rhynchocypris 14, 137, 195
Richardsonius 244, 246, 252, 254
  R. balteatus 71–2, 509, 523
Roach, *see Rutilus rutilus*
Rohtee 136, 169, 198
  R. belangeri 171
Rohteichthys 199
Rohu, *see Labeo rohita*
Rudd, *see Scardinius erythrophthalmus*
Rutilus 7–8, 14, 17, 20, 43–4, 48,
  134, 138, 141, 194, 575
  R. alburnoides 92
  R. antiquus 38
  R. arcasii 473
  R. frisii 143, 523
  R. pachecoi 38
  R. pachecri 39
  R. rubilio 92, 553
  R. rutilus (roach) 135, 143, 147,

Rutilus (Contd.)
  149, 265–8, 279, 286–7,
  291, 293–5, 297–8, 301,
  303–7, 311–12, 316, 318,
  320, 332, 342, 346, 353–4,
  357–9, 361–2, 364–7,
  370–1, 383, 389, 392, 399,
  404, 418–20, 428, 430–1,
  433, 437, 439–42, 444–8,
  457–9, 464, 466–9,
  472–3, 475–6, 484,
  486–98, 500, 510, 513, 523,
  530–7, 539–46, 553, 555,
  557–9, 561–5, 573–6,
  581–2, 584–5

Salmostoma 16, 136, 145, 196
Sanagia 213, 215
  S. velifera 216–7
Sanjika, *see Opsaridium microcephalus*
Sarcocheilichthyini 170–1, 174, 193
Sarcocheilichthys 13, 145, 193
Sarcochilichthyna 170
Saurogobio 13, 137, 145, 194, 341
Sawbwa 185, 199
  S. resplendens 134, 142
Scaphiodon 171
Scaphiodonichthys 13, 24, 171, 191, 200
Scaphognathops 5, 7, 171, 190, 199
Scardinius 8, 39, 43, 48, 134
  S. erythrophthalmus (rudd) 98,
    144, 256, 270, 272, 278, 280,
    287, 316, 354, 358, 361–2,
    389, 392, 399, 403, 442,
    445–7, 462, 464, 466, 468,
    473, 488, 492, 495, 510,
    532–6, 540, 555–6,
    561–2, 566
Schizocypris 12, 135, 171, 177, 201
  S. ladigesi 171
Schizopyge 135
Schizopygopsis 135, 200
  S. stoliczkae 143
Schizothoracinae 5, 7, 12, 18, 24, 35,
    135–6, 138, 142, 167
Schizothorax 12, 44, 100–1, 130,

    135, 139, 141, 143–4, 177,
    185, 200
  S. pseudaksaienesis (marinka) 144
  S. richardsonii 341
Schneider, *see Alburnoides bipunctatus*
Securicula 16, 136, 196
Semilabeo 138, 201
Semiplotini 170–1, 174, 200
Semiplotus 5, 13, 24, 135–6, 201
Semotilus 41, 244, 246, 251–4,
    256, 560
  S. atromaculatus (creek chub) 102,
    474, 521, 560, 563
  S. corporalis (fallfish) 513, 521
  S. lumbee 248
  S. margarita (pearl dace) 474
Serrodens 39
Shark
  black, *see Labeo chrysphekadion*
  freshwater, *see Labeo*
Shemaya, *see Chalcalburnus chalcoides*
Shiner
  common, *see Notropis cornutus*
  golden, *see Notemigonus crysoleucus*
Sikukia 190, 199
Sinibrama 15, 195
Sinilabeo 138
Sinocrossocheilus 201
Sinocyclocheilus 134, 138, 172, 185, 200
Smiliogastrinae 171
South African yellowfish, *see Barbus*
Spinibarbus 100, 185, 198
Spinophoxinellus 14
Spratellicypris 190
Squalidus 13, 194
Squaliobarbinae 12, 25, 170, 172,
    174, 197
Squaliobarbus 5, 12, 25, 138, 197
Squalius 134
Star gazer, *see Erythroculter erythropterus*
Stoneroller, *see Campostoma anomalum*
Stypodon 244
Systomini 99, 170, 174, 189, 198, 199

Tanakia 13, 137

Tanichthys 137, 197
 T. albonubes (White Cloud
  Mountain minnow) 510
Tarsichthys macrurus 38
Telestes 134
Tench, *see Tinca tinca*
Tetrostichodon 200
Thrissocypris 3, 6, 16, 197
Thynnichthys 45, 172, 190, 198
 T. amblyostoma 45, 178
 T. thynnoides 189
Tiaroga 246
Tinca 3, 10, 16–17, 39, 43, 48, 134
 T. furcata 39
 T. tinca (tench) 135, 144, 147,
  149, 221, 256, 265–71, 279,
  287, 292, 295–6, 318, 321,
  341, 355, 358, 361–2, 399,
  403, 431–3, 442, 444–5,
  447, 473, 484, 487, 492, 500,
  536, 573–4, 576, 582–3, 591
Tincini 35, 40, 48
Tor (mahseer) 13, 100, 142, 148,
  183, 186, 189, 191, 198
 T. mosal 186
 T. putitora 141, 186
 T. tor 141
Tores 170, 174, 198
Torini 170
Toxabramis 195
Tribolodon 7, 14, 44, 143, 244
 T. brandti 145
 T. hakonensis (Japanese dace) 39, 109
Tropidophoxinellus 14
Tylognathus 12, 173
 T. klatti 146

Typhlobarbus 185, 201
 T. nudiventris 146
Typhlogarra 7, 12, 135
 T. widowsoni 146

Usipa, *see Engraulicypris sardella*

Varhostichthys 37, 40
 V. brevis 38
Varicorhinus 5, 12, 213, 217,
  224–6, 387
 V. nelspruitensis 216, 231
Vimba 134
 V. elongata 436
 V. vimba (vimba) 287, 291, 312,
  345, 576
Vimba, *see Vimba vimba*

Woundfin, *see Plagopterus*

Xenobarbus 213, 215, 217
Xenocypridinae 13, 20, 97, 138, 172
Xenocyprioides 137, 194
Xenocypris 14, 20, 137, 144, 185,
  194, 593
 X. macrolepis 145

Yaoshanicus 197
Yuriria 244–6

Zacco 16, 25, 137, 196
 Z. platypus 95–6
 Z. temminkii 44
Zaissanotinca 177
Zebra danio, *see Brachydanio rerio*

Subject index

Absorption 415
Acoustico-lateralis system 332–46
Activity periodicity 445–7
Africa 211–12
Age at first maturity 470–2
Ageing 462
Alarm
  displays 515–16
  substance 308, 515
  response 514
Algae
  as prey 354, 357, 532–4
  promotion of 565
Alimentary canal, see intestinal tract
Allozymes 83–94
Anaerobiosis 433–5
Angling, see fisheries
Anoxia tolerance 433–5
Anti-predator behaviour 514–15
Aquaculture 590–617
  cages 596–7
  canals 597–8
  crossbreeding 614–16
  development of 616–17
  diets 598–600, 609–11
  feeding behaviour 600
  genetics 611–16
  global production 590
  growth 600–1
  gynogenesis 616
  inducing breeding 601–8
  lakes 597–8
  larvae rearing 608–11

mass selection 612–13
polyculture 592–6
polyploidy 616
ponds 591–6
raceways 597
reproductive cycle 601–2
reservoirs 597–8
rivers 597–8
selection 611–16
stocking 594–8, 609–10
suitability of cyprinids 590
systems 591–8
Asia, see Eurasia
Auditory apparatus 334–43
Australia 264–6

Barbel morphotypes 10–12
Behaviour, see anti-predator
    behaviour; feeding behaviour;
    homing; migration
Benthivory 355, 363–8
Bering land-bridge 48
Biogeography 19–28
  Africa 221–3
  Australia 266–8
  East Asia 136–8, 167
  Eurasia 129–30
  Europe 134
  High Asia 135, 167
  New Zealand 268–70
  North America 241–2, 246–50
  Siberia 135
  South Asia 136, 167–8

South East Asia 156–8, 168,
173–7, 178–85
South West Asia 134–5
Western Mongolia 135–6
Biomanipulation 566, 577
Bioturbation 566
Body form, see morphological
diversity; morphometrics
Body size
and effects on macrophytes 554
and energetics 430–2
North America 250
and niche shifts 537–8
and reproductive strategies 504
South East Asia 186
and vulnerability 562
Branchial sieve 358–60, 393–5
Brain 285–94
acoustico-lateralis areas 291
and ecology 285, 301, 303, 321–2
growth 293–4
structure 285–7, 291–3
types 291–3, 320–1
variability 287–91
Breeding, see reproduction;
spawning

Cave dwelling 7–8, 146, 185
Capacity adaptation 443–5
Capillarization 444
Chemosenses 303–17
Chromosomal banding
C-banding 95
Nucleolus organizer regions (NORs)
101–4
G- and R- banding 105
Chromosomes, see karyotypes
Circulation 444
Clustering techniques 94
Common chemical sense 305
Communication 509–11
Community structure 530–2, see
also interspecific interactions
Competition, see also interspecific
interactions
bottlenecks 538–40
and hatching time 495
interspecific 495, 538–45

intraspecific 468
in larvae 495
and shoaling 517
with waterfowl 561–2
Conservation, see also endangered or
threatened species
Africa 230–3
Australasia 276–80
Eurasia 150
Courtship 488
Critical period 496

Defences 562–3
Detritivory 532–3
Diets 354–5, see also feeding behaviour
Africa 224–225
in aquaculture 598–600, 609–11
Eurasia 143–4
of larvae 494
North America 255
South East Asia 188–91
Digestion 413–21
of artificial diets 420
of cellulose 415–16
in larvae 420–1
ontogenetic development 420
of plants 415–19
of polysaccharides 416
of proteins 413–15
Digestive activity 442
Diversity, see morphological diversity
DNA, see also gene
DNA-DNA hybridization 107–8
mitochondrial 104–12
nuclear 112
Dispersal 48–49, see also fossils

Ecophysiology 426–50
Ecosystem, role in 273–4, 476–7,
552–67, 588
Eggs
development 489–92
ecology 492–4
and oxygen deficiency 492
survival 492–3
quality 490
Elective group size 512

Endangered or threatened species
146, 230–2, 240, *see also*
conservation
Endemism
Africa 26, 218–19, 223
East Asia 130, 134, 136–8
Europe 134
High Asia 20, 135
North America 26, 242, 246–8
Siberia 20, 135
South Asia 136
South East Asia 7, 25, 157, 162,
183–5
South West Asia 135
Energetics, *see* physiological energetics
Environment, *see* habitat
Enzymes 413–21
activity 418
inhibitors 419
production 418
reabsorption 419
Epibranchial organs 395–8
Escape response, *see* anti-predator
behaviour
Evolution, *see* fossils
Eurasia 127–50
East Asia 129
Europe 127
High Asia 129
Siberia 129
South Asia 129
South East Asia 156–201
South West Asia 127
Western Mongolia 129, 135–6
Europe, *see* Eurasia
Eurythermy 436
Eutrophication
and community structure 530–2
and fisheries 572–4
promotion of 561–2, 565
Eye, *see* vision
Exogenous feeding, start of 494
Extinctions 47, 240

Fecundity, *see also* reproductive
strategies
North America 251
Feeding adaptations 4–7

Africa 224–5
Eurasia 143–4
fossils 41, 48
North America 255
South East Asia 188–91
Feeding apparatus 378–80
Feeding behaviour
in aquaculture 600
benthic 355, 363–8
biting and scraping 386–7
and cyprinid evolution 407–8
deglutition 404
digging 364–8, 388, 566
efficiency 377–8, 534–5
exogenous feeding, start of 420
fast suction 380–4
filter-feeding 370
and fish size 357–8
gulping 384–6
internal selection of prey 389–98
mastication 398–404
modes 356–8
mucus, role of 392
ontogenetic shifts 357–8
oral processing 377–408
overswimming 386
particulate feeding 356–7, 384
pelagic 354–63
periodicity 370
and predator detection 518
prey availability 370–1
prey capture 377–408
prey detection 317, 345, 367
prey transport 398
pump filter 357, 386, 388–9
rinsing 389
selective retention 391–2
selectivity 356–7, 392–8
slow suction 384–6
and social groups 516–19
specialisation 405–7
spitting 389
and success of cyprinids 407–8
and swimming speed 534
switching 368–71, 404–5
taste selection 389–92
tow-net filter 357, 386
versatility 405–7

Fertilization, *see* eggs
Filter apparatus 356–7
Fin, *see* morphological diversity
Fisheries 572–88, *see also*
    aquaculture; human uses
  Africa 228–30
  Australasia 275–6, 279
  current status 587–8
  Eurasia 147–9
  and eutrophication 572–4
  exploitation 580–1, 582, 587
  global catch 575
  importance 575–7
  lakes 572–4
  management 578–88
  North America 255–6
  promotion of 588
  prospects 587–8
  protection 580
  reservoirs 572–4
  rivers 574–5
  stocking 581, 583–6, 587
Food, *see* diets; feeding behaviour
Foraging, *see* feeding behaviour
Foraging area copying (FAC) 517
Fossils 28
  Africa 43–4, 221–3
  Asian-Oriental 44–5
  and climatic change 46–8
  Eurasia 138–41
  Europe 37–40
  India 44
  North America 40–3, 241–2
  Siberia 43
  South East Asia 163–6, 177–8
Fright substance, *see* alarm, substance

Gastric evacuation, *see* intestinal tract
Gene, *see also* DNA
  duplication 92–3
  silencing 92–3
Genetics
  in aquaculture 611–16
  and temperature adaptation 439
Genotype, *see* DNA; gene
Gill
  arch 393–5
  rakers 358–60, 393–5, *see also*

branchial sieve
Gills 449
Gonads, *see* reproduction
Group
  elective size 512
  optimum size 512–3
Growth 456–72
  and age at first maturity 470–2
  in aquaculture 600–1
  Ford-Walford plot 458
  hormone 600–1
  and hybridization 472
  and intraspecific competition 468
  in larvae 458–9, 464
  and longevity 463
  of optic tract 301
  and photoperiod 600–1
  and population density 466–9
  seasonality 459–62
  of sensory system 319
  and sexual dimorphism 470–2
  and temperature 462–6, 600–1
  and vision 296–9
  von Bertalanffy curve 458
  and year-class strength 469–70
Gut, *see* intestinal tract
Gynogenesis 99–100

Habitat 7–8, 35
  Africa 225–6
  Eurasia 130–4, 143
  multivariate analysis of 73–4
  South East Asia 179
  selection 535–7, 554
Hatching, *see* eggs
Head-elevating mechanism 6, 35
Hearing, *see* sensory systems
Herbivory 354, 415–9
Heterosis 472
Higher plants, *see* macrophytes
Homing 486, 521–4
Hormones 603–8
Human uses 278–9, *see also* fisheries
  Eurasia 147–9
  North America 255–6
Hybridization 8, 12, 17, 91–2, 99,
  101, 277
  in aquaculture 614–16

Hybridization (Contd.)
  DNA-DNA 107–8
  and growth 472
  mitochondrial DNA 109–10
  multivariate analysis of 71–3
Hydrodynamics, *see* swimming
Hypoxia tolerance 433–5

Ideal free distribution 517
Insects, as prey 355
Inspection visit 514
Interactions
  with abiotic factors 273–4
  with algae 552–4
  indirect 563–6
  interspecific, *see* interspecific
    interactions
  with invertebrates 556–60
  with macroinvertebrates 559–60
  with macrophytes 273–4, 554–6
  with periphyton 553–4
  with phytoplankton 552–3
  with plants 552–6
  with vertebrates 560–3
  with zooplankton 557–9
Interspecific interactions 275–6,
    530–7
  competition 275–6, 530–7
  in less productive systems 542–5
  and light 535–47
  and macrophytes 535–6
  mechanistic bases 532–7
  and ontogenetic niche shifts 537–8
  and population size structure 545–6
  predation 545–8
  in productive systems 540–2
  and structural complexity 535–7,
    545–6
  and zooplanktivory 540–2
Intestinal tract 413
  elongation 416–18
  evacuation rates 418–19
  pH 414
Introductions 561, 567, 583–6
  Africa 221, 229–30, 232
  Australasia 264–80
  East Asia 25

North America 240, 256
South East Asia 25
Ion regulation 448–50
Isozymes 83–94
Iteroparity 500

Jaws
  gape size 387
  pharyngeal 398–404, 407
  protrusion 384, 387–9, 391–2,
    407

Karyotypes 17–18, 95–104
Kidneys 449–50
Kin-selection 512–13

Labyrinths 334–6, 343
Larvae
  artificial diets 610–11
  development 489–92, 608–9
  diets 494
  digestion in 420–1
  ecology 494–7
  feeding in aquaculture 609–11
  feeding periodicity 494
  growth 458–9, 464
  identification 494
  interspecific competition 495
  mortality 496–7
  predation of 497
  rearing 608–11
  sampling 494
  stocking in aquaculture 609–10
  swimming 430
  vision 296, 299
  and water currents 495
  zooplankton, effect on 494
Lateral line 317–19, 344–6
  functional aspects 345–6
  pit-lines 344
  structural aspects 344
  and taxonomy 344
Learning 515
Legends 146–7
Life history 483–503
Light
  and interspecific interactions 535–7

and vision, *see* vision
Locomotion, *see* swimming
Longevity
  Eurasia 142
  and growth 463
  North America 250

Macroinvertebrates, as prey 536
Macrophytes
  as a habitat 540
  indirect effects on 565
  and interspecific interactions 535–6
  as prey 354, 386–7, 414,
    415–19, 532–4
  as structural complexity 535–6,
    555–6, 562
Mastication 402–3
Mating, *see* reproduction
Maturity, *see* reproduction
Mesothermy 436
Metabolism
  anaerobic 433–5
  adaptation of aerobic 432–3
  and capacity adaptation 444–5
  rate of 428, 430–2
Migration 143, 521–4
  Africa 223–4
  South East Asia 186–8
Molluscs, as prey 355
Morphological diversity 2–7
  Africa 214–9
  Eurasia 141–2
  North America 250
  South East Asia 186
Morphometrics 55–79
  canonical correlation (CCA) 67, 70–1
  canonical variates (CVA) 67
  discriminant functions (DFA) 67
  multivariate 65, 67
  multivariate analysis of variance
    (MANOVA) 70
  principal components analysis
    (PCA) 67–70
  sheared principal components
    analysis (S-PCA) 70, 76
Mortality, *see* life history; population;
  reproductive strategies

Mouth, *see* jaws
Movement, *see* homing; migration
Muscles 426–8, 443–4

Nauplii, as prey 357
Nest building 253–5, 521
Neuromasts 317–18, 332–3, 344
New Zealand 268
Niche, *see* diets; habitat; interspecific
  interactions
North America 240–2
Nursery areas 495
Nutrient release 555, 564, 565–6
Nutrition, in aquaculture 598–600

Olfaction 303, 305–8
Olfactory organ 305, 308
Omnivory 532–4
Ontogenetic shift 296, 319, 356
  and digestion 420
  and feeding behaviour 357–8
  and interspecific interactions 537–8
Opercular bones 462
Optic tract 299–301
Optimal foraging theory 356,
  377–8, 517
Optimal group size 512–13
Oropharyngeal sorting 310
Osmoregulation 448–50
Otoliths 336, 462
Oxygen
  consumption 428–30, 433
  response to deficiency of 432–5

Palatal organ 310, 391
Parental care 519–21
Periodicity 445–7
  annual 446–7
  diurnal 445–6
Pharyngeal
  jaws 398–404, 407
  teeth 34–5, 398–404, 416
Pharynx 391
Phenotype, *see* morphological diversity
Phenotypic plasticity 226
Pheromones 510, *see also* alarm,
  substance

Photoperiod
  and growth 600–1
  and reproduction 484–5
Physiological energetics 426–50
Physiology 426–50, *see also*
    ecophysiology; physiological
    energetics
  of reproduction 483–5
Phytoplanktivory 395, 416, 552–3
Piscivory 355, 386, 388, 408, 560–1
Planktivory, *see* phytoplanktivory;
    zooplanktivory
Plants, *see* algae; macrophytes
Polyploidy 99–101
Population
  bottlenecks 538–40, 545–6
  density estimates 474–5
  genetics 108–9
  size structure 545–6
Predation, *see also* interspecific
    interactions
  and habitat selection 554
  size selective 392–8, 558–9
  and year-class strength 469
Predator detection 514, 518
Pressure, response to 341–3
Prey, *see* diets; feeding behaviour
Production 456–8, 474–7

Recruitment, *see* reproduction
Refuge, *see* macrophytes, as structural
    complexity
Reproduction
  Africa 223–4, 228–9
  and aquaculture 601–2
  courtship 488
  cost of 498
  Eurasia 144–6
  North America 250–5
  parental care 519–21
  physiology 483–5
  South East Asia 186–8
  strategies 497–504
  timing 484–5
Reproductive
  effort 503
  strategies 497–504

Resource partitioning, *see* interspecific
    interactions; feeding behaviour
Respiration, *see* ecophysiology
Retina 294–9
Rhythm, *see* periodicity
Rotifera, as prey 357

Scales 462
Schooling 511–13, 560, *see also*
    shoaling
Schreckstoff, *see* alarm substance
Sensory systems 284–322, 332–46
  and communication 509–11
  and homing 522
  and migration 522
Sexual dimorphism 7, 16, 252–3,
    470–2
Shoaling 511–13, 517, *see also*
    schooling
Signals 509–11
Size selective predation 392–8,
    558–9
Social behaviour 509–19
  communication 509–511
  anti-predator 513–16
  feeding 516–19
  formation 511–13
Solitary chemosensory cells 305,
    314–17
Solitary life 513
Sound, response to 341–3, 346
Spawning 485–8, *see also*
    reproduction
  and aquaculture 601–8
  behaviour 488
  fractional 500
  guilds 486–7
  induction by the Linpe method
    607–8
  induction by traditional methods
    603–5
  migration 485–6, 523
  multiple 503
  site selection 486–7
  site territoriality 513, 519–21
  tubercles 519–520
Stenothermy 436

Stock, *see* population
Stocking
    in aquaculture 594–8, 609–10
    in fisheries 581, 583–6, 587
Stomach, lack of 413–14
Structural complexity, and
        interspecific interactions
        535–7, 545–6
Stunting 468
Sundaland 158, 161, 164
Survivorship, *see* life history;
    reproductive strategies
Swallowing, *see* deglutition
Swim bladder 7, 13, 74, 341–2
Swimming
    activity levels 428–30
    and capacity adaptation 443
    energetics 427–8
    in larvae 430
    muscles 426–8
    oxygen consumption 440–1
    speed 534

Taste 291, 305, 308–14, 389
Tectum opticum 301–3
Teeth, pharyngeal 34–5, 398–404, 416
Temperature
    acclimatization 437–9
    capacity adaptation 443–5
    compensation 443
    and development 490
    and digestive activity 442
    and ecophysiology 435–45
    genetic component of adaptations 439
    and growth 462–6, 600–1

and oxygen consumption 433
preferred range 435–7
and reproduction 484–5
resistance adaptation 437–9
tolerance range 7, 143, 435–7
and year-class strength 469–70, 496
Territory 488, 513, 519–21
Threatened or endangered species
        146, 230–2, 240, *see also*
        conservation
Trophic groups, *see* benthivory;
        detritivory, diets, herbivory,
        piscivory, phytoplanktivory,
        zooplanktivory
Truss network, the 60–1, 76

Vision 294–303

Water balance 448–50
Wallace's Line 178
Weberian ossicles 336–41
Weed, *see* macrophytes

Year-class strength
    and growth 469–70
    and predation 469
    and temperature 469–70, 496

Zooplanktivory 355–63, 370–1,
        420, 534–35, 540–2, 564
Zooplankton
    effects on 541–2, 564
    as prey 355–63, 370–1, 420,
        534–5, 540–2